Handbook of
the Life Course

Handbooks of Sociology and Social Research

Series Editor:
Howard B. Kaplan, *Texas A&M University, College Station, Texas*

HANDBOOK OF DRUG ABUSE PREVENTION
Theory, Science, and Practice
Edited by Zili Sloboda and William J. Bukoski

HANDBOOK OF THE LIFE COURSE
Edited by Jeyaln T. Mortimer and Michael J. Shanahan

HANDBOOK OF SOCIAL PSYCHOLOGY
Edited by John Delamater

HANDBOOK OF SOCIOLOGICAL THEORY
Edited by Jonathan H. Turner

HANDBOOK OF THE SOCIOLOGY OF EDUCATION
Edited by Maureen T. Hallinan

HANDBOOK OF THE SOCIOLOGY OF GENDER
Edited by Janet Saltzman Chafetz

HANDBOOK OF THE SOCIOLOGY OF MENTAL HEALTH
Edited by Carol S. Aneshensel and Jo C. Phelan

HANDBOOK OF THE SOCIOLOGY OF THE MILTARY
Edited by Giuseppe Caforio

A Continuation Order Plan is available for this series. A continuation order will bring delivery of each new volume immediately upon publication. Volumes are billed only upon actual shipment. For further information please contact the publisher.

Handbook of
the Life Course

Edited by

Jeylan T. Mortimer

University of Minnesota
Minneapolis, Minnesota

Michael J. Shanahan

University of North Carolina
Chapel Hill, North Carolina

Kluwer Academic / Plenum Publishers
New York   Boston   Dordrecht   London   Moscow

Library of Congress Cataloging-in-Publication Data

Handbook of the life course / [edited by] Jeylan T. Mortimer, Michael J. Shanahan
    p. cm. – (Handbooks of sociology and social research)
    Includes bibliographical references and index
    ISBN 0-306-47498-0
    1. Life cycle, Human—Social aspects. 2. Developmental psychology. I. Mortimer, Jeylan
T., 1943- II. Shanahan, Michael J. III. Series.

HQ799.95 .H36 2003
305.2—dc21   2002042769

ISBN: 0-306-47498-0

© 2003 Kluwer Academic/Plenum Publishers, New York
233 Spring Street, New York, New York 10013

http://www.wkap.nl

10 9 8 7 6 5 4 3 2 1

A C.I.P. Catalogue record for this book is available form the Library of Congress

Copyright © 2003 by Kluwer Academic Publishers

To Glen and Karen Elder,
who have inspired and supported generations of
life course scholars

Contributors

Karl L. Alexander, Department of Sociology, Johns Hopkins University, Baltimore, Maryland 21218-2685

Elbert P. Almazan, Department of Sociology, Indiana University, Bloomington, Indiana 47405

Duane F. Alwin, Department of Sociology and Population Research Institute, Pennsylvania State University, University Park, Pennsylvania 16802

Vern L. Bengtson, Department of Sociology, University of Southern California, Los Angeles, California 90089-2539

Avshalom Caspi, Social, Genetic and Developmental Psychiatry Research Centre, London, SE5 8AF United Kingdom

Bertram J. Cohler, Committee on Human Development, University of Chicago, Chicago, Illinois 60637

Robert Crosnoe, Department of Sociology, University of Texas at Austin, Texas 87112-1088

Dale Dannefer, Margaret Warner Graduate School of Education and Human Development, University of Rochester, Rochester, New York 14627

Glen H. Elder, Jr., Department of Sociology, University of North Carolina at Chapel Hill, Chapel Hill, North Carolina 27516-3997

Scott R. Eliason, Department of Sociology, University of Minnesota, Minneapolis, Minnesota 55455

Doris R. Entwisle, Department of Sociology, Johns Hopkins University, Baltimore, Maryland 21218-2685

Michael D. Finch, Center for Health Care Policy and Evaluation, UnitedHealth Group, Minnetonka, Minnesota 55343

Jennifer R. Frytak, Economic Outcomes Research, Ingenix Pharmaceutical Services, Eden Prairie, Minnesota 55344

Frank Furstenberg, Department of Sociology, University of Pennsylvania, Philadelphia, Pennsylvania 19104-6299

Viktor Gecas, Departments of Sociology and Rural Sociology, Washington State University, Pullman, Washington 99164-4020

Linda K. George, Duke University, Durham, North Carolina 27708

Norval D. Glenn, Department of Sociology, University of Texas, Austin, Texas 78712-1088

Frances K. Goldscheider, Department of Sociology, Brown University, Providence, Rhode Island 02912

Charles N. Halaby, Department of Sociology, University of Wisconsin, Madison, Wisconsin 53706

Carolyn R. Harley, Economic Outcomes Research, Ingenix Pharmaceutical Services, Eden Prairie, Minnesota 55344

Walter R. Heinz, University of Bremen, D-28334 Bremen, Germany

Scott M. Hofer, Pennsylvania State University, University Park, Pennsylvania 16802-6504

Dennis P. Hogan, Department of Sociology, Brown University, Providence, Rhode Island 02912

Andrew Hostetler, Committee on Human Development, University of Chicago, Chicago, Illinois 60637

Guillermina Jasso, Department of Sociology, New York University, New York, New York 10003

Monica Kirkpatrick Johnson, Department of Sociology, Washington State University, Pullman, Washington 99164-4020

Takehiko Kariya, University of Tokyo, Tokyo, Japan

Alan C. Kerckhoff, Department of Sociology, Duke University, Durham, North Carolina 27708-0088[†]

John H. Laub, University of Maryland, College Park, Maryland 20742-8235

Lutz Leisering, Department of Sociology, University of Bielefeld, D-33501 Bielefeld, Germany

Ross Macmillan, Department of Sociology, University of Minnesota, Minneapolis, Minnesota 55455

Jennifer L. Maggs, Family Studies and Human Development, University of Arizona, Tucson, Arizona 85721

Michael Massoglia, Department of Sociology, University of Minnesota, Minneapolis, Minnesota 55455

Ryan J. McCammon, University of Michigan Survey Research Center, Ann Arbor, Michigan 48109-1382

Jane D. McLeod, Department of Sociology, Indiana University, Bloomington, Indiana 47405

[†]Deceased.

Phyllis Moen, Department of Sociology, University of Minnesota, Minneapolis, Minnesota 55455

Jeylan T. Mortimer, Department of Sociology, University of Minnesota, Minneapolis, Minnesota 55455

Margaret Mueller, Department of Sociology, University of North Carolina at Chapel Hill, Chapel Hill, North Carolina 27599-3210

Patrick M. O'Malley, Institute for Social Research, University of Michigan, Ann Arbor, Michigan 48104-2321

Angela M. O'Rand, Department of Sociology, Duke University, Durham, North Carolina 27708-0088

Sabrina Oesterle, University of North Carolina-Chapel Hill, Chapel Hill, North Carolina 27516

Linda Steffel Olson, Department of Sociology, Johns Hopkins University, Baltimore, Maryland 21218-2685

Aaron M. Pallas, Teachers College, Columbia University, New York, New York 10027

Norella M. Putney, Department of Sociology, University of Southern California, Los Angeles, California 90089-2539

Brent W. Roberts, Department of Psychology, University of Illinois at Urbana-Champaign, Champaign, Illinois 61820

Richard W. Robins, University of California, Davis, California 95616

James E. Rosenbaum, Department of Education and Social Policy, Northwestern University, Evanston, Illinois 60208-2610

Robert J. Sampson, Department of Sociology, Harvard University, Cambridge, Massachusetts 02138

John E. Schulenberg, Institute for Social Research, University of Michigan, Ann Arbor, Michigan 48104-2321

Richard A. Settersten Jr., Department of Sociology, Case Western Reserve University, Cleveland, Ohio 44106-7124

Lilly Shanahan, Pennsylvania State University, University Park, Pennsylvania 16802–6504

Michael J. Shanahan, Department of Sociology, University of North Carolina, Chapel Hill, North Carolina 27599-3210

Jeremy Staff, Department of Sociology, University of Minnesota, Minneapolis, Minnesota 55455

Irving Tallman, Department of Sociology, Washington State University, Pullman, Washington, 99164-4020

Kali H. Trzesniewski, University of California, Davis, California 95616

Christopher Uggen, Department of Sociology, University of Minnesota, Minneapolis, Minnesota 55455

Peter Uhlenberg, Department of Sociology, University of North Carolina at Chapel Hill, Chapel Hill, North Carolina 27599-3210

Ansgar Weymann, University of Bremen Graduate School of Social Sciences, D-28359 Bremen, Germany

Lawrence L. Wu, Department of Sociology, University of Wisconsin, Madison, Wisconsin 53706

Preface

THE IMPETUS FOR THIS HANDBOOK

The development of the life course as a field of study parallels in some respects another prominent subfield of sociology, social psychology. In his now-classic assessment, House (1977) observed that social psychology's highly general and abstract concepts are well suited to elucidate a broad range of phenomena. As a result, however, social psychological theorizing and research had tended to "dissipate" across several academic disciplines and many applied areas of research. These circumstances presented a challenge to social psychologists in their efforts to maintain a core identity and to evaluate the development of their field.

A similar situation may be said to characterize the contemporary literature surrounding the life course. As a concept, the life course refers to the age-graded, socially-embedded sequence of roles that connect the phases of life. As a paradigm, the life course refers to an imaginative framework comprised of a set of interrelated presuppositions, concepts, and methods that are used to study these age-graded, socially embedded roles. In this relatively new subfield of the social sciences, a common core of generalized concepts and premises is now taking hold and giving definite form to the life course paradigm. As with social psychology, the generalized nature of this paradigm has led to its diffusion across diverse problem areas. Indeed, the utility of the life course for the study of a wide range of temporally structured phenomena is clearly demonstrated by the contributions to this volume from leading specialists in their subfields.

Further paralleling the circumstances of social psychology, academic infrastructures are not conducive to the recognition and development of life course studies as a field. Academic specializations, departments, professional societies, and scholarly journals all tend to promote a focus on single age groups or particular life phases (e.g., adolescence or old age). This emphasis is not in accord with the life course paradigm's central premise—that no period of life can be understood in isolation from people's prior experiences, as well as their aspirations for the future. Thus, whereas the life course has proven highly useful in the study of lives, it likewise tends toward the "organizationally challenged."

In this context, a handbook becomes especially important because it provides, in one place, an overview of key theoretical perspectives, concepts, and methodological approaches that, while applied to diverse phenomena, are united in their general approach to the study of lives across age phases. Consideration of the life course in this more unified manner heightens sensitivity to the ways that theoretical insights and methods can be fruitfully applied to multiple life phases and the transitions between them. As a result, the similarities, parallels, and linkages between phases of life are revealed and new conceptualizations and hypotheses are suggested. The purpose of this handbook is thus to survey the wide terrain of life course studies with dual emphases on theory and empirical research; in doing so, the handbook allows us to take stock of probative concepts and methods and to identify promising avenues for future research.

THE ORGANIZATION OF THIS
HANDBOOK: OVERVIEW

We begin with an essay by Elder, Johnson, and Crosnoe. In his diverse empirical studies—encompassing children growing up during the Great Depression, men encountering World War II, and youth negotiating adolescence during the Farm Crisis of the 1980s—Elder made and continues to make seminal contributions to the founding and development of life course studies. In Chapter 1, the authors examine the historical emergence of the life course paradigm, the many rich streams of thought that this paradigm synthesizes, and the substantial progress that has been made. Elder and his colleagues' principles of life course analysis, synthesized in this initial chapter, will continue to guide future generations of life course scholars.

The chapters then proceed from the consideration of macro- to micro-level phenomena, paralleling the multilevel and multifaceted features and determinants of the life course in modern and post-modern societies. Whereas the parts of the *Handbook* proceed from the macro—encompassing social change and changes in age-graded institutions and the organization of age-graded roles—to the micro—focusing on the regulatory influences of social institutions and people's responses to these forces—this division of scholarship is based on prominent themes in the authors' contributions and does not capture the full richness of their work. Although we found the macro–micro continuum to be the most useful organizing principle, most studies of the life course reflect a more holistic perspective. Investigators consider in tandem the connections among social change, the changing nature of age-graded institutions, the organization of age-graded roles, and how the life course is experienced by individuals and groups. These actors are not only imbued with regulatory forces of the social order, but also active agents who respond to them.

Part II of the *Handbook* focuses on variability in the life course across historical and cross-national settings. The chapters in this section share a common concern for how the organization of lives varies across societies defined by history and geography. Part III addresses the normative age-grading of the life course, which is thought to reflect the demands and opportunities of societal structures. This focal point reflects a primary interest in the social psychology of social norms, with emphasis on how norms gain or lose their force with broader social change. Part IV considers how the life course reflects societal institutions. That is, how do enduring, purposive patterns of social organizations and relationships shape the age-graded phases of life and their interconnections? This overarching question is addressed through studies of the family, schools, the workplace, governments, and the connections among these institutions.

There is now widespread appreciation that people are not passive recipients of the social order, as reflected in many contributions throughout this volume. Part V considers how the life course is constructed by motivation and diverse processes that serve to unify experiences from childhood into old age and, in some instances, promote discontinuities. The chapters focus on individual-level processes, unlike the collective and group-level processes suggested by the contributions to Parts II, III, and IV. Part VI addresses methodological advances and different disciplinary perspectives that are well suited to the study of the life course. All of the contributors urge further sophistication in research, whether through the use of more refined methods or the development of more inclusive conceptual models through interdisciplinary collaborations.

Finally, we have invited senior scholars to reflect on the future of the life course as a multilevel phenomenon and as a field of academic inquiry. Studies of the life course are fundamentally about social change and the biography, and these contributors consider the ways in which the life course and its study are changing. The contributions to this final section make abundantly clear that while much has been accomplished in the science of the life course, the inevitable and often unpredictable nature of social change calls for increasingly complex models of how lives are organized through time.

Part II. Historical and Cross-National Variability. In Chapter 2, Alwin and McCammon provide an overview of research on generations, focusing on how age groups both reflect social forces and are social forces in their own right, producing historical change through time. In doing so, they provide fresh insights about the long-standing sociological interest in the generational basis for social stability and change. Their assessment of the historical use and controversy over the term "generation" also does much to clarify terminological confusion. In Chapter 3, Kariya and Rosenbaum develop a model of stratified incentives to explain differences between American and Japanese students, and among Japanese students through historical time. They provide evidence that different structural arrangements linking schools and work can lead to different incentives for achievement. In the case of Japan, educational reforms altered the incentive structure to the (unintentional) disadvantage of the lower socioeconomic strata. Historical shifts, and their implications for the life course, are addressed in many other selections throughout the volume, especially the chapters by Settersten (on age grading), Putney and Bengtson (with respect to the family), Heinz and Moen (regarding work), and Leisering and Weymann (assessing change in state regulation). Furthermore, essays examining the future of the life course, placed at the end of this volume, reflect the ubiquity of historical variation in the life courses of successive cohorts.

Part III: Normative Structuring. Part III of the *Handbook* considers the normative age grading of the life course. In Chapter 4, Settersten examines both formal and informal age structuring and historical change in the age differentiation of societies through time. Of central interest in his essay are long-term controversies over the existence and content of age norms and their consequences—both objective and subjective—for persons who manifest "untimely" behavior as modern societies become increasingly "de-chronologized."

Part IV: Movement through the Life Course. Part IV of the *Handbook* examines the institutional structuring of lives, which is at the core of life course analysis in sociology. Institutional contexts define both the normative pathways of social roles, including key transitions, and the psychological, behavioral, and health-related trajectories of persons as they move through them. Tallman (Chapter 5), Uhlenberg and Mueller (Chapter 6), and Putney and Bengtson (Chapter 7) assess institutional structuring in the context of the family. Pallas (Chapter 8) addresses educational pathways and their consequences, and Heinz (Chapter 9) examines the changing institution of work. Leisering (Chapter 10) notes the many ways that governmental institutions structure the life courses of the citizenry, and attempt to assuage life course risks.

Because lives are structured as persons move within, across, and through institutional settings, the character of the *inter*institutional linkages between them are exceedingly important.

Entwisle, Alexander, and Olson (Chapter 11) examine the process of entry to school, a key transition in a child's life between family and education. Kerckhoff (Chapter 12) highlights the variability of the school-to-work transition across industrial societies. Moen (Chapter 13) notes that the exit from work occurs relatively early in contemporary societies when compared to prior historical periods. In fact, she proclaims the emergence of a new "midcourse" life stage, perhaps representing the most recent addition to the long-term historical differentiation of the life course.

Whereas institutions may be considered key contexts for the unfolding of lives, persons often diverge from institutional pathways or from patterns that would be predicted from their social locations or prior trajectories. Elder's life course principle of "life long openness" is recognized by Sampson and Laub (Chapter 14) and Uggen and Massoglia (Chapter 15), who assess processes of desistance from crime. Furthermore, Jasso (Chapter 16) considers immigration as a major turning point in the life course. Many of the analyses in Part IV bear in direct and important ways on policy issues surrounding how families, workplaces, and schools can be coordinated, as well as the possible roles that the state may play in this coordination.

Part V. Life Course Construction.   Life course pathways, trajectories, and transitions manifest much variability in pluralistic, contemporary societies. Despite this variability across persons, and increasing individualization of the life course (Shanahan, 2000), continuity is often found to be the predominant feature of individual psychological and behavioral trajectories, including those describing substance use (Schulenberg, Maggs, and O'Malley, Chapter 19) and socioeconomic attainment (Mortimer, Staff, and Oesterle, Chapter 20) from adolescence to adulthood. Understanding the social and psychological processes that underly this stability is a central objective of life course analysis (McLeod and Almazan, Chapter 18; also Alwin and McCammon Chapter 2), implicating the self (Gecas, Chapter 17) as well as the operations of key social structures (see Entwisle, Alexander, and Olson, Chapter 11; Kariya and Rosenbaum, Chapter 3). Turning points, involving alterations of long-term trajectories, also occur, as demonstrated by Sampson and Laub and Uggen and Massoglia.

Part VI. Methods and Interdisciplinary Approaches.   As scholars pursue these complex themes, increasingly sophisticated methods, statistics, and conceptual models will be needed. Glenn (Chapter 21) presents an accessible overview of the age–period–cohort identification problem, arguing that their unique effects cannot be estimated with precision. Rather, side-information that illuminates developmental and historical processes must be used. Wu (Chapter 22) comprehensively reviews event-history models, which have long played an important role in life course research. As he notes, these models are becoming increasingly sophisticated and new developments will undoubtedly create opportunities to address previously unexplored research questions.

Halaby (Chapter 23) considers recent developments in the analysis of panel data, arguing forcefully for more attention to modeling strategies when using data with repeated measures. His examples illustrate that model specification is a substantive issue, and as models become increasingly complex, care must be exercised to insure that the estimated model is based on reasonable assumptions about the nature of the variables and the processes by which they are interrelated. Macmillan and Eliason (Chapter 24) provide an overview of latent class models. They maintain that these models offer new and exciting opportunities to identify multi-faceted pathways and trajectories in the life course, illustrating their argument with a fascinating model of the transition to adulthood. Finally, Cohler and Hostetler (Chapter 25) discuss the use of narrative methods to discern the meanings that social changes have for individuals. They illustrate their sophisticated treatment with a study of American gay men who have negotiated the challenges and opportunities of the late 20th century. While the

Handbook only touches the surface of the rich array of extant quantitative, and especially, qualitative methods that elucidate the life course, the availability of authors and limitations of space precluded more widespread coverage.

Several contributions explore the relevance of "neighboring disciplines" for interdisciplinary research. Roberts, Robins, Caspi, and Trzesniewski (Chapter 26) consider recent advances in personality psychology and their connections to life course issues. Life course sociologists have a long-standing interest in such concerns, especially since Caspi and Elder's pathbreaking research on personality across the life course. Their chapter focuses on how dimensions of personality and attributes of the life course may be reciprocally interrelated and exhibit elements of both continuity and discontinuity. Shanahan, Hofer, and Shanahan (Chapter 27) consider the possible intersections between life course research and biological models of behavior. There is much excitement in the media and scientific forums about continuing advances in the biological sciences. They identify points of integration between biological models and the life course at a conceptual level, but also urge avoiding "the twin dangers of destructive cynicism and gullible expectations." Finally, Frytak, Harley, and Finch (Chapter 28) promote the integration of social models of human health and life course thinking. The authors argue that human health, and especially, inequality in health-related resources and outcomes, cannot be fully understood without reference to prior experience and dynamic patterns of social and human capital formation.

Part VII. The Future of the Life Course.   At the beginning of the 21st century, there is no indication that radical social changes, and their impacts on human lives, will abate. Indeed, although every generation claims as much, many of the contributors believe that ongoing structural forces point to the acceleration of change at the turn of the millennium: the globalization of economic, political, organizational, technological, and cultural facets of life; the intermixing of peoples through travel, migration, and ever more rapid and convenient communications; and the on-going development of new technologies (Anderson, 2002). Changes that are already in process, coupled with those on the horizon, will likely alter all the phenomena with which this book deals (the anthology edited by Mortimer and Larson, 2002, addresses institutional changes affecting adolescence and the transition to adulthood).

Prominent sociologists of the life course, including Dale Dannefer, Frank Furstenberg, Linda George, Dennis Hogan and Francis Goldscheider, Angela O'Rand, and Ansgar Weymann, consider future developments and prospects (Chapters 29–34). While these scholars address a wide range of issues and developments in life course studies, they all note the challenges to our field posed by high levels of differentiation and inequality in life course options and outcomes. Dale Dannefer urges life course researchers to move beyond the confines of Western modern societies, extending our conceptual apparatus and empirical studies to the impoverished life courses of most inhabitants of developing societies across the world. Frank Furstenberg highlights the social class differentiation in contemporary American lives and life chances, encompassing family, educational, and work trajectories. Linda George notes the difficulties of explanation, particularly in distinguishing social selection from social causation, in a context of high levels of heterogeneity and the exercise of individual agency. Dennis Hogan and Francis Goldscheider relate how the growing integration of life course and population studies have contributed to the theoretical and methodological development of demography. They feature lifetime benefits and costs of economic behaviors in contemporary research on families and welfare. Angela O'Rand considers the movement from retirement pensions to individually managed accounts as increasing individual risk and jeopardizing economic well-being in old age. Ansgar Weymann emphasizes that governmental regulation has traditionally sought to minimize these and other major life course risks. He asks whether the role of government in making the life course more predictable will diminish in the contemporary era of increasing globalization, superseded in at least some respects by emergent cross-societal regulatory institutions.

The richly diverse conceptual, methodological, and empirical contents of these chapters indicate the current vitality of the life course paradigm and its present applications. This volume offers a wealth of theory, concepts, and methods that will further illuminate the nexus of historical, institutional, interpersonal, and subjective processes within which the multiple contours of human lives unfold.

In closing, we express our appreciation to the many people who have contributed to this project since its inception. We thank Howard Kaplan, the *Handbooks of sociology and social research* Series Editor, whose vision and persuasive powers convinced us three years ago to embark on this initiative. Eliot Werner, then Executive Editor of the Behavioral and Social Sciences Division, gave us further support and guidance as the project got underway. Teresa Krauss, Editor for Archaeology and Sociology, provided enthusiastic encouragement in the final phases of the work.

Each of the authors of these thirty-four chapters deserves our heartfelt thanks for their efforts in synthesizing the considerable literatures on their topics and for formulating their theoretical and methodological insights and/or empirical work in a manner suitable for a volume of this kind. Their expertise and enthusiastic cooperation has made this project a source of great fulfillment.

The Life Course Center at the University of Minnesota has provided much appreciated institutional support. Holly Schoonover, Principal Secretary of the Center, has been an invaluable resource to the project in all its phases. She has conducted innumerable correspondences with the authors and our contacts at Kluwer Academic/Plenum, has kept our records and files exceedingly well organized, and has spent many hours working on the various formatting and related tasks. Her extraordinary attention to detail has undoubtedly contributed to the quality of the volume.

We are both fortunate to have supportive and helpful spouses. We thank Jeffrey Broadbent and Lilly Shanahan, both of whom possess an uncommon combination of intelligence, warmth, and good humor.

Finally, we express our gratitude to Glen and Karen Elder, on behalf of the generations of scholars of the life course who have been so aptly guided and supported by them. In recognition of their life works, this volume is dedicated to them.

JEYLAN T. MORTIMER
MICHAEL J. SHANAHAN

REFERENCES

Anderson, R. E. (2002). Youth and information technology. In J. R. Mortimer & R. W. Larson (Eds.), *The changing experience of adolescence: Societal trends and the transition to adulthood* (pp. 175–207). New York: Cambridge University Press.

House, J. S. (1977). The three faces of social psychology. *Sociometry, 40*, 161–177.

Mortimer, J. T., & Larson, R. W. (2002). *The changing experience of adolescence: Societal trends and the transition to adulthood.* New York: Cambridge University Press.

Shanahan, M. J. (2000). Pathways to adulthod in changing societies: Variability and mechanisms in life course perspective. *Annual Review of Sociology, 26*, 667–692.

Contents

[†]Deceased.

PART I

THE LIFE COURSE
PERSPECTIVE

CHAPTER 1

The Emergence and Development of Life Course Theory

GLEN H. ELDER Jr.
MONICA KIRKPATRICK JOHNSON
ROBERT CROSNOE

Today, the life course perspective is perhaps the pre-eminent theoretical orientation in the study of lives, but this has not always been the case. The life histories and future trajectories of individuals and groups were largely neglected by early sociological research. In the pioneering study, *The Polish Peasant in Europe and America (1918–1920)*, W. I. Thomas (with Florian Znaniecki) first made use of such histories and trajectories and argued strongly that they be investigated more fully by sociologists. By the mid-1920s, Thomas was emphasizing the vital need for a "longitudinal approach to life history" using life record data (Volkart, 1951, p. 593). He advocated that studies investigate "many types of individuals with regard to their experiences and various past periods of life in different situations" and follow "groups of individuals into the future, getting a continuous record of experiences as they occur." Though this advice went unheeded for decades, Thomas's early recommendations anticipated study of the life course and longitudinal research that has become such a central part of modern sociology and other disciplines.

As late as the 1950s, C. Wright Mills lacked an appropriate research base when he proposed a field of life course study in the behavioral sciences, a field which was intended to encompass, in his words, "the study of biography, of history, and of the problems of their

GLEN H. ELDER, JR. • Department of Sociology, University of North Carolina at Chapel Hill, Chapel Hill, North Carolina 27516-3997. MONICA KIRKPATRICK JOHNSON • Department of Sociology, Washington State University, Pullman, Washington 99164-4020. ROBERT CROSNOE • Department of Sociology, University of Texas at Austin, Austin, Texas 87112-1088.

Handbook of the Life Course, edited by Jeylan T. Mortimer and Michael J. Shanahan. Kluwer Academic/Plenum Publishers, New York, 2003.

intersection within social structure" (1959, p. 149). Quite simply, the social pathways of human lives, particularly in their historical time and place, were not a common subject of study at this time. Consequently, social scientists knew little about how people lived their lives from childhood to old age, even less about how their life pathways influenced the course of development and aging, and still less about the importance of historical and geographic contexts. Considering this, one should not be surprised that, during this period, the scholarly literature contained no reference to the concept of the life course and graduate programs offered no seminars on life course topics.

Disruptive societal events, such as the Great Depression and World War II, and the pre-war lack of financial support for the social and behavioral sciences all contributed to this neglect of life histories and trajectories. Not until the 1960s were Thomas's recommendations acted upon, after a convergence of influences necessitated the understanding of how people lived their lives in changing times and across various contexts. At the onset of the 21st century, however, such life pathways are widely recognized within the social and behavioral sciences as the life course. The study of the life course crosses disciplinary boundaries (e.g., sociology, psychology, history), fields (e.g., aging, human development, family demography), and cultural borders (e.g., North America, Europe, Asia).

The purpose of this introductory chapter is to trace the evolution of life course study from its inauspicious beginning to its contemporary prominence. We begin with the "contextual challenge," in which the rise of the life course movement clearly has its origins. This challenge represents the confluence of major social and intellectual changes during the 20th century, beginning with the maturation of pioneering longitudinal studies and the recognition that knowledge about adolescent and adult development could not be extrapolated from child-based models. We also cover the articulation and refinement of theoretical models, such as the life cycle and career, and review basic life course concepts, such as age-based trajectories and transitions. We close by describing, discussing, and illustrating five paradigmatic principles that collectively define the primary analytic and conceptual themes of life course studies. This discussion should provide a context for the life course studies that are presented in this volume.

Before moving on, we should pause to explain two important details that are embedded in our discussion. First, we view the life course as a *theoretical orientation*, one with particular relevance to scholarship on human development and aging, and we use the term "theory" with this particular meaning. According to Merton (1968), theoretical orientations establish a common field of inquiry by providing a framework for descriptive and explanatory research. Such a framework covers the identification and formulation of research problems, rationales for variable selection, and strategies for research design and data analysis. Drawing on this definition of a theoretical orientation, we view the life course as consisting of age-graded patterns that are embedded in social institutions and history. This view is grounded in a contextualist perspective and emphasizes the implications of social pathways in historical time and place for human development and aging.

Second, the life course is often used interchangeably with other terms, such as life span, life history, and life cycle. All three terms are part of life course vocabulary, but we argue that none is synonymous with the life course. For example, life span, as in life-span sociology or psychology, specifies the temporal scope of inquiry and specialization. Thus, a life-span study is one that extends across a substantial portion of life, particularly one that links behavior in two or more life stages. This scope moves beyond age-specific studies on childhood or early adulthood. Life history, on the other hand, typically indicates the chronology of activities or events across the life course (e.g., residence, household composition, family events) and is often drawn from age-event matrices or retrospective life calendars, which record the year and month at which a transition occurs in each domain and are well-suited for event history analysis (Brückner & Mayer, 1998; Mayer & Tuma, 1990). Lastly, life cycle has been used to describe a sequence of events in life, but in population studies it refers to the reproductive process from one generation to the next. All populations have a life cycle, but only some people have children.

THE CONTEXTUAL CHALLENGE

Unlike today, the study of human lives was once exceedingly rare in sociology and psychology, especially in relation to socio-historical context (Elder, 1998). During the 1950s, sociological theory and research had stagnated to a certain degree. Sociological activities rarely dug deep into the complexities of life and too often, in the words of Robert Nisbet (1969), existed in the "timeless realm of the abstract". This perspective was encouraged by the rapid diffusion of social surveys, which covered a wide breadth of topics with little depth, and the pursuit of grand theory, as embodied by Talcott Parsons. Yet, this period was soon replaced by a virtual explosion of inquiry that explored the continuity and change of human lives in relation to interpersonal, structural, and historical forces (Elder & Johnson, 2001).

How could a vigorous era of research arise from such seemingly infertile ground? The answer to this question lies in five major trends of the 20th century: (1) the maturation of early child development samples; (2) the rapidity of social change; (3) changes in the composition of the U.S. and other populations; (4) the changing age structure of society; and 5) the revolutionary growth of longitudinal research over the last three decades. These trends refer to developments in North America and particularly in the United States, though some (such as the pace of social change, rate of aging in society, and the growth of the longitudinal studies) also apply to Europe (Heinz & Krüger, 2001).

Pioneering psychologists of the early 20th century launched key longitudinal studies of young people. Prominent examples include the Oakland Growth Study of children born in 1920–21 (Jones, Bayley, MacFarlane, & Honzik, 1971), the Berkeley Guidance Study of children born in 1928–29 (MacFarlane, 1938), and the Stanford-Terman study of gifted children born in 1900–1920 (Terman & Oden, 1959). Typically, such studies were designed to follow the developmental patterns of children and were not meant to extend past childhood. Nevertheless, many were extended into the adult years and beyond, collecting information on education, work, marriage, and parenthood. This wealth of data prompted a new way of thinking about human lives and development—studying life trajectories across multiple stages of life, recognizing that developmental processes extend past childhood, exploring issues of behavioral continuity and change (Elder, 1994). In other words, these early studies, originally modest in scope, lay the groundwork for longitudinal study of life history advocated by Thomas.

The young people in these early studies experienced the enormous social change that swept through the 20th century—the Great Depression, two World Wars, the Cold War, Vietnam, the Civil Rights Movement, the Women's Movement, periodic prosperity and economic downturns. These unforeseen events had profound influences on life trajectories, both individual and age cohort. The early longitudinal studies were not designed with such sweeping changes in mind. For example, Jean MacFarlane's carefully formulated randomized experimental design for the Berkeley study was destroyed by the pressing needs of the study families in the Great Depression (Elder, 1998); families in the control and experimental groups sought guidance and support from the research staff.

The men in Terman's study who fought in World War II wrote about their war experiences in the margins of surveys that neglected to ask them about such experiences. They were puzzled by the study's indifference to the war, an indifference noted many years later by Robert Sears, a distinguished psychologist at Stanford (personal communication, 1989). Yet, such events, and the new circumstances they ushered in, could not be ignored for long. New interest evolved in the ways that individual lives are linked to social change. Research that grew out of such interest, largely centered on the study of cohort and period effects, advanced sociological understanding of temporality and historical time (Ryder, 1965). This new sociological activity mirrored the emergence, in the 1960s, of social history (Thernstrom, 1964), a field of study that sought to understand the lives and times of ordinary people.

Related to social change is the changing demography of the American population over the last century. As the "first new nation" (Lipset, 1963), the United States served as a crucible for the study of diversity. The mixture of various immigrant groups within the general population gave greater visibility to the importance of social and cultural ecologies. The racial and ethnic diversity of the United States, growing with time (Portes & Rumbaut, 1996; U.S. Bureau of the Census, 1999), mirrors other forms of diversity that are entrenched in American society: socioeconomic, gender, urban versus rural. The salience of such diversity on a social level emphasized the need to understand diversity on an individual level—how the trajectories of individual lives differ across social groups (Elder, 1998). Such questions are now a common part of sociological inquiry on the social context of human lives.

One key aspect of the changing American demography concerns the age structure of society, which has undergone a major transformation in recent decades due to increasing longevity and declining fertility and mortality (Uhlenberg and Kirby, 1998). Rapid growth of the oldest segment of society—the aging of the United States—assigned greater significance to problems of the aged (Elder, 2000). Efforts to study such problems led to increasing interest in the relation of earlier phases of life to later phases, from childhood to adulthood, and the power of larger social forces to shape the lifelong developmental trajectories of individuals (Elder & Johnson, 2001). One of the more fruitful areas of aging research, including developmental psychology and social demography, involves the concept of social clocks, or normative timetables, which refer to the expectations for appropriate times and ages of important life transitions. This line of research, pioneered by Bernice Neugarten in the 1950s (Neugarten & Datan, 1973), helped to demonstrate the enormous diversity of people's lives and also how social norms give meaning to, and even direct, individual trajectories.

The final push towards a more complex treatment of human lives came from the longitudinal research projects that began in the 1960s. Examples include the National Longitudinal Surveys (see Pavalko & Smith, 1999), the National Longitudinal Study of Mature Women (see Moen, Dempster-McClain, & Williams, 1992), the Panel Study of Income Dynamics (see Duncan & Morgan, 1985), the British national longitudinal studies (1946, 1958, 1970) and the 1958 Swedish cohort studied by David Magnusson (Magnusson, 1988). In many ways, such projects launched the long-term study of human lives in life-span psychology and life course sociology (Elder, 1998) by allowing the examination of life trajectories across multiple stages of life and by creating the need for new theoretical and methodological models for studying life-long development (Cairns, Elder, & Costello, 1996; Young, Savola, & Phelps, 1991).

One key innovation has been the use of both prospective and retrospective data collection, which allows the creation of detailed life histories (Giele & Elder, 1998). This innovation goes hand in hand with statistical innovations, such as event history analysis (Mayer & Tuma, 1990). Such changes in empirical procedures, statistical techniques, and interpretive approaches are at the heart of life course research. Though life-course development in the United States has been quantitative to a large extent, a distinctive emphasis in European studies centers on individual biographies and in-depth interviews (Heinz & Krüger, 2001).

The five factors, which encompass changes in history, social demography, and scientific inquiry, converged to generate interest in life course research. The contextual study of lives advanced from near invisibility to a thriving area of sociological research, and particularly of developmental and sociological social psychology. Collectively across disciplines, this work entails multiple levels, from the macro structures and social institutions of society to the micro experience of individuals, and draws upon both quantitative and qualitative data in a mixed method approach.

RESPONSES TO THE CHALLENGE

Out of these developments came greater recognition that lives are influenced by an ever-changing historical and biographical context. Yet a variety of conceptual and methodological tools were still needed in order to study life patterns and their dynamics in time. The life course as a theoretical orientation came from this desire to understand social pathways, their developmental effects, and their relation to personal and social-historical conditions.

Early models of social pathways generally centered on a single role sequence like that of a life cycle (Elder, 1978; Hareven, 1978). Children mature, marry, and have children who then grow up and start a family as the cycle continues into another generation. The writings of Paul Glick (1946) and Reuben Hill (1970) on the family cycle exemplify this approach. They described a set of ordered stages in adult family life from courtship and engagement to marital dissolution through a spouse's death. Of course, this concept was limited in that not everyone participated in familial reproduction and by its narrow application to family life.

The concept of "career" was another way of linking roles across the life course. These careers are based on role histories in education, work, or family. Though readily applicable to multiple domains of life, these models most often focused on a single domain, oversimplifying to a great extent the lives of people who were in reality dealing with multiple roles simultaneously. Moreover, much like the family cycle, the concept of career did not locate individuals in historical context or identify their temporal location within the life span. In other words, the available models of social pathways lacked mechanisms connecting lives with biographical and historical time, and the changes in social life that spanned this time.

With a renewed consciousness that linked individual lives to social change, a number of historically based studies emerged (Modell, 1989). Bringing in history provided a necessary contextual understanding. As historian E. P. Thompson once put it, "The discipline of history is above all a discipline of context" (cited by Goldthorpe, 1991, p. 212). Hareven's (1982) study of families in the textile mill community of Manchester explores the implications of industrial change for workers and their families. Growing rapidly at the turn of the century, the Amoskeag Mill was at one time the largest mill in the world. After its peak of prosperity during World War I, the industry declined, eventually collapsing in the 1930s. The mill's shutdown in 1936 left an entire labor force stranded. Hareven's focus on successive worker cohorts during the declining economic conditions of the 1920s and 1930s relates changing historical circumstance to individual lives.

Another excellent example of this type of sociohistoric research is Barker's (Barker & Schoggen, 1973; Barker & Wright 1955; see also Modell & Elder, 2002) examination of the changing developmental contexts of children in rural Kansas in the 1950s and 1960s. His study explores the implications of age-specialization in behavior settings, which limits children's observation of grown-up behavior. Barker observed a decline in the proportion of child and adolescent public activities that involved prominent roles for children upon whom all participants depended. This accompanied an increasing concentration of their activity within the formal institution of education.

Within schools, the number and variety of behavior settings (and, by far, formal classes most prominent among these) increased, as newer, larger schools came into being. Yet Barker viewed children's involvement in community settings *not* intentionally organized around children (e.g., shops, offices, churches), in contrast to schools, as having unique implications for development. For in proximity to those who enacted the chief roles in public behavior settings to which young people were admitted, grown-up behavior could be observed, modeled, and if adults entrusted kids with active roles, informally apprenticed.

In pursuit of models of the life course that would reflect historical and biographical context, a number of useful concepts have been developed. Each provides a way of thinking about how lives are socially organized. *Social pathways* are the trajectories of education and work, family and residences that are followed by individuals and groups through society. These pathways are shaped by historical forces and are often structured by social institutions. Individuals generally work out their own life course and trajectories in relation to institutionalized pathways and normative patterns. They are subject to change, both from the impact of the broader contexts in which they are embedded and from the impact of the aggregation of lives that follow these pathways. Large-scale social forces can alter these pathways through planned interventions (e.g., funding for tertiary education) and unplanned changes (e.g., economic cycles and war). Individuals choose the paths they follow, yet choices are always constrained by the opportunities structured by social institutions and culture.

Trajectories, or sequences of roles and experiences, are themselves made up of *transitions*, or changes in state or role. Examples of transitions include leaving the parental home, becoming a parent, or retiring. The time between transitions is known as a *duration*. Long durations enhance behavioral stability through acquired obligations and vested interests.

Transitions often involve changes in status or identity, both personally and socially, and thus open up opportunities for behavioral change. For instance, Wellman et al. (1997) found that the nature and composition of friendship networks change dramatically when young adults marry. Transitions early in life may also have lifelong implications for trajectories, by shaping later events, experiences, and transitions. Adolescent child-bearing (Furstenberg, Brooks-Gunn, & Morgan, 1987) and military service (Sampson & Laub, 1996), are two well-documented examples of transition experiences with lifetime consequences.

Turning points involve a substantial change in the direction of one's life, whether subjective or objective. A turning point may involve returning to school during midlife, for example. Turning points at work were perceived by respondents in the Cornell Couples and Careers Study to be quite common, with over half reporting such an experience in the prior three years (Wethington, Pixley, & Kavey, 2003). Most of these turning points specifically involve work issues, including job changes and job insecurity, rather than family transitions that might be thought to alter the direction of one's work life.

These concepts reflect the temporal nature of lives, conveying movement through historical and biographical time. Age and its varied connections to time became a primary vehicle for understanding the changing contexts of lives.

AGE, TIMING, AND THE LIFE COURSE

Time operates at both a sociohistorical and personal level. In early studies, time entered through the concept of *generation* and the succession of generations in the life cycle.

Membership in a generation linked individuals to the lives of older and younger family members. Generation-based models viewed individual lives in terms of the reproductive life cycle and intergenerational processes of socialization. Ultimately, however, the concept proved inadequate. It suffered from the same basic limitation as the family cycle—a loose connection to historical time. One only needs to consider the wide age-range of men and women having their first child to see potential disparity between age and generational status.

Locating people in cohorts by birth year provides more precise historical placement. Cohorts, in effect, link age and historical time. Historical changes often have different implications for people of different ages—that is, for people who differ in life stage (Ryder, 1965). People of different ages bring different experiences and resources to situations and consequently adapt in different ways to new conditions. When historical change differentiates the lives of successive birth cohorts, it generates a *cohort effect*. Older and younger children, for example, were differentially vulnerable to the economic stresses of the Great Depression (Elder, 1974, 1999). History also takes the form of a *period effect* when the impact of social change is relatively uniform across successive birth cohorts. Both period and cohort effects constitute evidence of historical influences.

An example of these multiple effects is provided by Robinson and Jackson (2001) in their analysis of social change in interpersonal trust from 1972 to 1998. Social scientists have posed the question of whether trust has declined in America, owing to events of the past 30 years, such as Watergate. Using annual national surveys (the General Social Survey), the authors attempt to estimate age, period and cohort effects. They find an aging effect in which trust is lowest among the youngest respondents, increases up to middle age, and then levels off. They also find evidence of a decline in levels of trust for American cohorts born after 1940, perhaps representing a non-linear cohort effect. Alternatively, this pattern could represent an age-specific period effect, as social factors began to decrease trust in the 1980s among young and middle-aged adults. It should be noted that the estimation of age-period-cohort effects is always provisional since age, period and year are confounded.

Much effort to understand historical influence on lives has been devoted to examining variations in age-related change across successive birth cohorts (e.g., Nesselroade & Baltes, 1974). Alternatively, measuring the exposure of people to changing environments even within a cohort has advantages (e.g., Elder & Pellerin, 1998). Members of a birth cohort are not uniformly exposed to change, suggesting that cohort subgroups should be identified in terms of similar exposure. Cohort membership is often only a proxy for exposure to historical change. The historical experience of people in a specific birth cohort may vary significantly.

Variation can occur at both macro- and micro-levels. One macro-level example of within cohort variations concerns geography, from a longitudinal study that is following 12th grade students (1983–1985) from fifteen regions of the former Soviet Union up to 1999 and beyond (Titma & Tuma, 1995). Called "Paths of a Generation", the study assessed the life expectations, achievements and backgrounds of these young people before the Soviet Union disintegrated circa 1990, and then traced their lives into a period of extraordinary change and instability. One region retained the command economy of the old Soviet Union (Belarus), while others adopted a market economy (e.g., Estonia) or returned to a more primitive rural exchange system (e.g., Tajikistan).

The socioeconomic lives of men and women resembled the changes of their respective regions of the old Soviet Union. The Estonian cohort is most prosperous, whereas downward trajectories are common among other youth, such as those from Belarus. Despite such regional differences in the Titma and Tuma (1995) study, and profound social instability, the future of this generation to date was written in large part by their personal accomplishments, self-assessments, and goals when they were first contacted in high school, which were more consequential than family background.

A micro-level example of within cohort variation concerns individual roles and personal attributes. Consider children who grew up in hard times during the Great Depression (Elder, 1974, 1999). Girls were drawn into domestic responsibilities with their mothers and sometimes *instead* of their employed mothers, while the greater autonomy of boys was coupled with earning opportunities in the larger community. The greater family involvement of girls exposed them to more family tensions and conflicts than boys. These different roles were coupled with corresponding pathways into the adult years, as involved girls became more family-centered women. Employed boys became more attached to their work role and career as adults.

In addition to the link between age and historical time, age as a social construction also differentiates the life course. The social meanings of age can structure the life course through age expectations, and informal sanctions, social timetables, and generalized age grades (such as childhood or adolescence) (Neugarten, 1996; Settersten & Hagestad, 1996a, 1996b). A normative concept of social time specifies an appropriate age for transitions such as entry into school, marriage, and retirement, leading to relatively "early" and "late" transitions.

Explanations of life events that are based on these normative beliefs are common in the research literature, yet we still have little empirical knowledge of such norms and how they are experienced. How are age expectations constructed, maintained, and learned by others? Moreover, little is known about variability in age expectations and sanctions across social class and racial/ethnic groups. Yet, empirical findings are beginning to cumulate on variations in the age boundaries of particular phases of the life course, such as the transition to adulthood (Shanahan, 2000).

Thus, age represents not only a point in the life span and a historical marker (Ryder, 1965) but also a subjective understanding about the temporal nature of life. With the recognition that social and personal meanings are attached to age came greater attention to the timing of transitions and the duration of states in the life course. The timing of entry into first grade, for example, can place children on different trajectories of success and failure (Alexander & Entwisle, 1988). Duration refers to the span of time between successive changes in state. Length of exposure to environmental conditions may have developmental consequences, as when persistently poor children have increasing rates of antisocial behavior compared to other children (McLeod & Shanahan, 1996). Duration is also linked to embeddedness in the social environment. The greater the duration of a status or social role, the more occupants are committed by others to remain in place (Becker, 1961). Examples include the duration of residence. Long durations, therefore, increase the likelihood of behavioral continuity over the life course.

PARADIGMATIC PRINCIPLES IN
LIFE COURSE THEORY

The life course paradigm that emerged from the complex interplay of forces described previously is best viewed as a theoretical orientation that guides research on human lives within context. As such, it aids scientists in the formulation of empirical questions, conceptual development, and research design. The life course provides a framework for studying phenomena at the nexus of social pathways, developmental trajectories, and social change. Five general principles, derived from research in the social and behavioral sciences, provide guidance for such pursuits. This foundation is described in some detail after we present and discuss each principle.

1. *The Principle of Life-Span Development: Human development and aging are lifelong processes*

Understanding developmental processes is advanced by taking a long-term perspective. Development does not end at age 18. Adults can and do experience fundamental changes— biological, psychological, social—that are developmentally meaningful. Substantial changes occur, for example, in work orientations during the early adult years (Johnson, 2001b). For instance, adult women receive benefits, in both mental and physical health, from social integration and multiple role activity across the life course, and these benefits may increase in the later years (Moen et al., 1992). Indeed, patterns of late-life adaptation and aging are generally linked to the formative years of life course development.

By studying lives over substantial periods of time we increase the potential interplay of social change with individual development. Though longitudinal studies are often long-term projects, very few provide the necessary data on contextual changes over time, including changes in residences and socioeconomic conditions. The availability of geo-codes with coordinates that locate households on a map for users of large data sets now enables an increasing number of studies to assess environmental changes and their impact on individual lives. Greater opportunities exist to collect data on lives and their changing environments, including relationships, workplaces, schools, and communities.

2. *The Principle of Agency: Individuals construct their own life course through the choices and actions they take within the opportunities and constraints of history and social circumstance*

Children, adolescents, and adults are not passively acted upon by social influence and structural constraints. Instead, they make choices and compromises based on the alternatives that they perceive before them. For example, workers' values influence work experiences, including the rewards and characteristics of jobs like pay, autonomy and service to others (Johnson, 2001a; Mortimer & Lorence, 1979). Inner-city families provide another example of this phenomenon. These families live in difficult circumstances and often struggle with poverty and crime, but many parents actively manage their children's environments to minimize their risks, by joining churches and signing children up for youth programs (Furstenberg et al., 1999). Parents' involvement in their children's schooling is structured to some extent by their resources and the school's openness to their participation, but also reflects their assessments of whether their children need their involvement (Crosnoe, 2001).

The planning and choice-making of individuals, within the particular limitations of their world, can have important consequences for future trajectories. Clausen (1993) has argued, for example, that adolescents' "planful competence" furthers their educational and occupational attainments. By their self-confidence, intellectual investment, and dependability, which together define planfulness, adolescents can "better prepare themselves for adult roles and will select, and be selected for, opportunities that give them a head start" (Clausen, 1993, p. 21).

But planfulness and its behavioral expression depend on context and its constraints. In the older cohort of California men in the Lewis Terman sample (born 1900–1911) for example, most men had completed college before 1930 and consequently, entered a labor market that soon became stagnant in the financial crisis of the 1930s. Their dismal chances in the labor market led them back to school, acquiring advanced degrees (Shanahan & Elder, 2002; Shanahan, Miech, & Elder, 1998). By contrast, the younger men (born 1911–1920) were engaged in finishing secondary school and college through most of the 1930s, a time span that was long enough for them to acquire attractive jobs as the economy improved through wartime orders. The teenage planfulness of the younger men predicted a relatively stable and successful life course—in advanced education, in maintaining their marriages, in civic involvement, and in life satisfaction. However, teenage planfulness in the older cohort revealed very little about their future lives.

3. *The Principle of Time and Place: The life course of individuals is embedded and shaped by the historical times and places they experience over their lifetime*
Individuals and birth cohorts are influenced by historical context and place. As Gieryn (2000) observes, a place possesses three essential features: geographic location; a material form or culture of one kind or another; and investment with meaning and value. The Chinese Cultural Revolution was a political movement in such a place, extending as it did from 1966 to 1976. A number of Chinese youth had their life trajectories drastically altered by this revolution. "Sent down", separated from their families and communities, forced into manual labor, a good many of these young people were changed by their experiences at the time. In this way they were set apart from young Chinese of adjacent birth cohorts and those of similar age who were not sent down to the country side (cf. Zhou & Hou, 1999).

The same historical event or change may differ in substance and meaning across different regions or nations. World War II provides relevant examples of this point. The immediate postwar years were deprivational in many parts of Europe, unlike the prosperity of the United States, and war experiences entailed widespread suffering among veterans and civilians. Using a retrospective life history method, Mayer (1988) found that German men, born between 1915 and 1925, were almost universally involved in the armed forces. These men lost as many as nine years of their occupational careers in the war, and many of the 75% that survived the war could not find employment afterward. The cohort of 1931 also suffered widespread hardship in the war that disrupted their families and schooling. The devastated economy made stable employment illusory for many. Even the economic boom of the 1950s and 1960s did not fully compensate this younger cohort for its war-related losses in occupational advancement.

4. *The Principle of Timing: The developmental antecedents and consequences of life transitions, events, and behavioral patterns vary according to their timing in a person's life*
The same events or experiences may affect individuals in different ways depending on when they occur in the life course (George, 1993). The very meaning of the event can change at different developmental stages (Wheaton, 1990). For example, Harley and Mortimer (2000) find that very early transitions to adult statuses, like leaving the parental home at a relatively young age, entering marriage or a cohabiting relationship, and becoming a parent, have detrimental effects on mental health. Moreover, the young people in their panel study who became parents early and who experienced a "pile up" of transitions (multiple transitions in the same year) experienced poorer mental health, compared to young people who experienced a "pile up" without early parenthood. These differential experiences in the transition to adulthood explain the emergence of a socioeconomic gradient in mental health in early adulthood through cumulative advantages and disadvantages.

The social and developmental implications of life course timing help to explain why two birth cohorts from the 1920s were affected so differently by life in the Great Depression (Elder, 1974, 1999). Born at the beginning of the 1920s, the Oakland Growth Study children were not as susceptible to the effects of family hardship and disruption as their younger counterparts in the Berkeley Guidance Study (birth dates in the late 1920s). The Oakland children were also too young to be exposed to the harsh labor conditions of a depressed economy. If we think in terms of a developmental match between these children and their environment, the best fit applies to the Oakland Study members. The particular timing of prosperity, depression, and war, placed the two birth cohorts on different developmental pathways.

A similar perspective applies to the time at which men and women have entered the military service. An early transition to the service, before the establishment of families and careers, has the potential to minimize life disruptions, and even enhance life chances through early skill training and leadership experience, the formation of life goals, and post-service education through the GI Bill. From this perspective, early entry provides the best fit between the recruit and his or her social world, notwithstanding the risk of combat and injuries or death. Consistent with this account, the Berkeley boys from hard-pressed families tended to rise above the disadvantage of their childhoods by entering the service at relatively young age (Elder, 1974, 1999). Later entry resulted in more life disruptions and fewer benefits. Sampson and Laub (1996) also obtained such results in their longitudinal study of low-income youth from Boston who entered World War II.

5. *The Principle of Linked Lives: Lives are lived interdependently and socio-historical influences are expressed through this network of shared relationships*

Often, individuals are affected by larger social changes through the impact that such changes have on their interpersonal contexts within more micro-level settings. The Iowa farm crisis illustrates this principle (Conger & Elder, 1994). Economic hardship affected child development in negative ways largely because it increased the depressed feelings of parents. A second part of this study (Elder & Conger, 2000) revealed the positive developmental influence of joint activities and shared responsibilities among youth with their families.

The initiation of new relationships can shape lives as well, by fostering "turning points" that lead to a change in behavior or by fostering behavioral continuity. Sampson and Laub (1993), for example, found that marriage and employment helped turn troubled young men toward more conventional lives by providing a network of individuals to reinforce conventional behavior. Not surprisingly, Simons and his colleagues (2001) found that the effects of these social networks depend on whether the activities of the individuals involved were conventional or anti-social. Because friend and mate selection tends to follow the homophily principle, the crucial factor for youth with delinquent histories is managing to circumvent this tendency and form relationships with more conventional individuals.

Because lives are lived interdependently, transitions in one person's life often entail transitions for other people as well. In a study of African American families, Burton and Bengtson (1985) found that a daughter's early transition to motherhood, and therefore her own mother's early transition to grandparenthood had repercussions for their roles, responsibilities and social identities. The new mothers still thought of themselves as children and expected their mothers to help care for their child. This expectation seldom materialized because the new grandmothers felt too young for the grandmother role. Women who have their own children early in life frequently also enter the grandparent role at an early age, generating feelings of being "older" than their agemates (Neugarten & Datan, 1973).

These five principles steer research away from age-specific studies and towards the recognition of individual choice and decision-making. They promote awareness of larger social contexts and history and of the timing of events and role change. They also enhance the understanding that human lives cannot be adequately represented when removed from relationships with significant others. Allowing these principles to guide inquiry promotes the holistic understanding of lives over time and across changing social contexts.

The basis of the life course principles, and the ideas underlying them, emerged over a period of decades. Examples of life-span thinking before 1900 provide an orientation to the first principle, that human development and aging are life long processes. In a sense, it represents a definitional premise of the theoretical orientation's scope—that the temporal span of study extends from birth to death and draws upon research on development and aging across the life span (see Featherman, 1981). To our knowledge, the other principles first appeared in a paper by Elder (1994), which was based on his Cooley-Mead Award presentation at the American Sociological Association (1993), in Miami, Florida. In preparing for this event, Elder surveyed studies of the life course and some key premises of the research. Thus, the principle of human agency depicts the role of the individual as an active force in constructing his or her life course through the choices and actions taken. With this point in mind, it is not surprising that the principle has characterized life history work dating back to the 19th century (Thomas & Znaniecki, 1918–1920).

The multiple meanings of age in theory brought time and temporality to life course thinking and study, especially during the 1960s (Neugarten, 1996). Age and time also helped to place individuals and cohorts in their social and historical contexts (Riley, Jonson, & Foner, 1972). The principle of linked lives refers to the social embeddedness of lives and has its origins in role theoretical accounts of life histories and lives that date back to the 19th century (Thomas & Znaniecki, 1918–1920). This principle represents an early theoretical approach to individual lives, as seen in applications of the life cycle concept or model.

The fifth principle on historical time and place derives much of its richness from the emergence of social history and from such early studies as *Children of the Great Depression* (Elder, 1974, 1999). When times change, lives change. *Children of the Great Depression* illustrates and documents all five principles. Most of the principles also address issues of contextualism by placing people in context.

CONCLUDING THOUGHTS

At the dawn of the 20th century, social research was uninformed by a concept of the life course. By the end of the century, however, life course theory had truly come of age. It has been used and adapted to research needs by sociologists, psychologists, and historians, among others, who are interested in a variety of research questions. Psychologist Anne Colby notes the "tremendous impact on social science that the life course approach has had in the past three decades" (1998, p. xiii), concluding that "the establishment of this approach, which is widely shared internationally as well as across disciplines, is one of the most important achievements of social science in the second half of the 20th century" (p. x). This slow, yet dramatic, change of events has its origins in the improvement of research and data collection as well as changes in history, population, and geography.

Developments of this kind have drawn upon theories of social relations (e.g., role theory and the concepts of life cycle and generations), aging research, and developmental psychology. In turn, these areas have been enriched by the life course approach. For example, contemporary research on social relations, manifested in the study of social networks, social capital, and attachment, has often failed to locate people in time and place, but it has become more common in these areas to explore historical *and* ecological context, such as differences between the inner-city and rural communities.

Finally, life span developmental psychology has begun to incorporate the importance of social context and individual variation while adding a sociological understanding of individual development and aging (see Heckhausen, 1999). New thinking about the meaning of aging has provided a correction to aging research by focusing on the link between age and time. Birth year locates people in historical context and age places them in a particular stage of life, while age also indicates the timing of lives and documents whether an event or transition occurs relatively early or late.

What are the most promising frontiers in studies of the life course? In this flourishing field, a number of frontiers could be noted. Consider, for example, the challenge of crossing levels of analysis and the many important unknowns that remain. Multiple levels of the life course provide research opportunities for investigating their interplay over time. Structured or institutionalized pathways establish a context in which people make choices, plans, and initiatives regarding their lives—they construct their lives within the constraints of established pathways in a culture, organization, or community. Social change may alter routine pathways and the life trajectories of individuals, thereby changing in some manner their developmental course. Thus drastic income loss in the 1930s changed the daily pattern of family life and the life experience of children (Elder, 1974, 1999). Later on, mobilization for war changed or delayed future options.

Each level can be thought of as a defining point of entry for study. Some sociological research centers on the macroscopic level of social institutions and population aggregates (Mayer, 2001). Other studies focus on the individual life course and its trajectory over time. A third type of study investigates the behavioral development of the individual and pays no attention to its contextual environment. The study of multiple levels of the life course requires interdisciplinary research, including contributions from psychology, anthropology, history, economics and biology.

Theories and methods have centered largely on specific levels thereby increasing the challenge in bridging levels, from the macro to the micro level. To date, the growth of multilevel studies (see Furstenberg et al., 1999) has given fresh visibility to cross-level research, as in studies of neighborhood and school effects, but it has made little contribution to an understanding of lives. These studies typically provide only a skeletal view of the life course.

Individual development and aging generally occur in a changing world that can be indexed with an age-graded life course. Techniques for analysis (hierarchical linear and latent growth models) provide a way to investigate such contextual effects over time, but our purview should extend to the interacting contexts themselves in which people live their lives. Children, for example, live in neighborhoods, particular communities, and attend certain schools. They are members of distinctive families and friendship groups. In a short-term longitudinal study of early adolescents, Cook and his associates (2002) found that the multiple contexts of their lives (schools, neighborhoods, peers, and families) had independent and additive influences on adolescent success (see also, Call & Mortimer, 2001). Cumulative disadvantages or advantages tend to maximize the contextual influences. We need lifelong studies of the young adult and late-life adult that also assess their multiple contexts, including those of family, workplace, and community or neighborhood.

Lastly, the growth of longitudinal studies among advanced societies, in particular, offers an opportunity for studies of the life course that take seriously the principle of historical time and place. The very same birth cohort is certain to have varied historical and cultural experiences in different societies. Strategic comparative studies of the life course are needed to reveal the trajectory of life patterns in societies that differ in political regime, welfare state policies, and the centralization of government. Blossfeld and Dröbnic (2002) provide an example of such work in their anthology of studies that focus on the careers of couples in contemporary societies. However, such research seldom crosses levels of analysis by investigating the developmental and aging effects of life patterns.

At this time, the life course is primarily viewed as an age-graded sequence of socially defined roles and events that are enacted over historical time and place. This view comes with the understanding that changes in the life course of individuals have consequences for development and that historical change may alter the life course and developmental trajectories by recasting established pathways. By drawing on life course theory, contemporary researchers can situate the processes by which social change influences and alters the developmental paths of young and old. The five paradigmatic principles discussed in this introduction (development and aging as lifelong processes, human agency, lives in historical time and place, social timing, and interdependent lives) provide the most concise, yet inclusive, conceptual map of life course theory. This map enables studies of the life course to build upon a wider network of cross-disciplinary scholarship that emphasizes the role of time, context, and process.

In this chapter we describe the "life course" of life course theory and life course research that is currently in the middle of a vibrant adulthood. The following handbook chapters show the vitality that characterizes this field of scholarship today.

ACKNOWLEDGMENTS: We acknowledge support by the National Institute of Mental Health (MH 00567, MH 57549), research support from the MacArthur Foundation Research Network on Successful Adolescent Development Among Youth in High-Risk Settings, a grant from the National Institute of Child Health and Human Development to the Carolina Population Center at the University of North Carolina at Chapel Hill (PO1-HD31921A), a National Research Service Award from the National Institute on Aging (2 T32-AG00155-12A1) and a Spencer Foundation Senior Scholar Award to Elder.

REFERENCES

Alexander, K. L., & Entwisle, D. R. (1988). Achievement in the first two years of school: Patterns and processes. *Monographs of the Society for Research in Child Development, 53*(2, Serial No. 218). Chicago: University of Chicago Press.

Barker, R. G., & Schoggen, P. (1973). *Qualities of community life.* San Francisco: Jossey-Bass, Behavioral Science Series.

Barker, R. G., & Wright, H. F. (1955). *Midwest and its children: The psychological ecology of an American town.* Evanston, IL: Row, Peterson.

Becker, H. S. (1961). Notes on the concept of commitment. *American Journal of Sociology, 66*, 32–40.

Blossfeld, H-P., & Dröbnic, S. (Eds.). (2001). *Careers of couples in contemporary societies: From male breadwinner to dual earner families.* New York: Oxford University Press.

Brückner, E., & Mayer, K. U. (1998). Collecting life history data: Experiences from the German Life History Study. In J. Z. Giele & G. H. Elder, Jr. (Eds.), *Methods of life course research: Qualitative and quantitative approaches* (pp. 152–181). Thousand Oaks, CA: Sage.

Burton, L. M., & Bengtson, V. L. (1985). Black grandmothers: Issues of timing and continuity of roles. In V. L. Bengston & J. F. Robertson (Eds.), *Grandparenthood* (pp. 61–77). Beverly Hills, CA: Sage.

Cairns, R. B., Elder, G. H., Jr., & Costello, E. J. (1996). *Developmental science.* New York: Cambridge University Press.

Call, K. T., & Mortimer, J. T. (2001). *Arenas of comfort in adolescence: A study of adjustment in context.* Mahwah, NJ: Lawrence Erlbaum.

Clausen, J. A. (1993). *American lives: Looking back at the children of the Great Depression.* New York: Free Press.

Colby, A. (1998). Foreword: Crafting life course studies. In J. Z. Giele & G. H. Elder, Jr. (Eds.), *Methods of life course research: Qualitative and quantitative approaches.* Thousand Oaks, CA: Sage.

Conger, R. D., & Elder, G. H., Jr. (1994). *Families in troubled times: Adapting to change in rural America.* Hawthorne, NY: Aldine de Gruyter.

Cook, T. D., Herman, M. R., Phillips, M., & Settersten, R. A., Jr. (2002). Some ways in which neighborhoods, nuclear families, friendship groups and schools jointly affect changes in early adolescent development. *Child Development, 73*, 1283–1309.

Crosnoe, R. (2001). Trends in academic orientation and parental involvement in education over the course of high school. *Sociology of Education, 74*, 210–230.

Duncan, G. J., & Morgan, J. N. (1985). The Panel Study of Income Dynamics. In G. H. Elder, Jr. (Ed.), *Life course dynamics: Trajectories and transitions, 1968–1980* (pp. 50–71). Ithaca, NY: Cornell.

Elder, G. H., Jr. (1999). *Children of the Great Depression: Social change in life experience, 25th anniversary edition.* Boulder, CO: Westview Press.

Elder, G. H., Jr. (1978). Family history and the life course. In T. K. Hareven (Ed.), *Transitions* (pp. 17–64). New York: Academic Press.

Elder, G. H., Jr. (1994). Time, human agency, and social change: Perspectives on the life course. *Social Psychology Quarterly, 57,* 4–15.

Elder, G. H., Jr. (1998). Life course and human development. In W. Damon (Ed.), *Handbook of child psychology* (pp. 939–991). New York: Wiley.

Elder, G. H., Jr. (2000). The life course. In E. F. Borgatta & R. J. V. Montgomery (Eds.), *Encyclopedia of sociology* (2nd ed., Vol. 3, pp. 1614–1622). New York: Macmillan.

Elder, G. H., Jr., & Conger, R. D. (2000). *Children of the land: Adversity and success in rural America.* Chicago: University of Chicago Press.

Elder, G. H., Jr., & Johnson, M. K. (2001). The life course and human development: Challenges, lessons, and new directions. In R. A. Settersten (Ed.), *Invitation to the life course: Toward new understandings of later life.* Amityville, NY: Baywood.

Elder, G. H., Jr., & Pellerin, L. A. (1998). Linking history and human lives. In J. Z. Giele, & G. H. Elder, Jr. (Eds.), *Methods of life course research: Quantitative and qualitative approaches* (pp. 264–294). Thousand Oaks, CA: Sage.

Featherman, D. L. (1983). The life-span perspective in social science research. In P. B. Baltes & O. G. Brim, Jr. (Eds.), *Life-span development and behavior* (Vol. 5, pp. 1–57). New York: Academic.

Furstenberg, F., Cook, T., Eccles, J., Elder, G. H., Jr., & Sameroff, A. (1999). *Managing to make it: Urban families and adolescent success.* Chicago: University of Chicago Press.

Furstenberg, F. F., Jr., Brooks-Gunn, J., & Morgan, S. P. (1987). *Adolescent mothers in later life.* New York: Cambridge University Press.

George, L. K. (1993). Sociological perspectives on life transitions. *Annual Review of Sociology, 19,* 353–373.

Giele, J. A., & Elder, G. H., Jr. (Eds.) (1998). *Methods of life course research: Qualitative and quantitative approaches.* Thousand Oaks, CA: Sage.

Gieryn, T. F. (2000). A space for place in sociology. *Annual Review of Sociology, 26,* 463–496.

Gieryn, T. F. (2001). *If identity was geography.* Society for the Study of Human Development, Ann Arbor, MI: University of Michigan.

Glick, P. C. (1947). The family cycle. *American Sociological Review, 12,* 164–174.

Goldthorpe, J. H. (1991). The uses of history in sociology: Reflections on some recent tendencies. *British Journal of Sociology, 42(2),* 211–229.

Hareven, T. K. (1978). *Transitions: The family and the life course in historical perspective.* New York: Academic Press.

Hareven, T. K. (1982). *Family time and industrial time.* New York: Cambridge University Press.

Harley, C., & Mortimer, J. T. (2000). *Social status and mental health in young adulthood: The mediating role of the transition to adulthood.* Paper presented at the Biennial Meeting of the Society for Research on Adolescence, Chicago, March 30–April 2.

Heckhausen, J. (1999). *Developmental regulation in adulthood: Age-normative and sociostructural constraints as adaptive challenges.* New York: Cambridge University Press.

Heinz, W. R., & Krüger, H. (2001) Life course: Innovations and challenges for social research. *Current Sociology, 49(2),* 29–45.

Hill, R. (1970). *Family development in three generations.* Cambridge, MA: Schenkman.

Johnson, M. K. (2001a). Change in job values during the transition to adulthood. *Work and Occupations, 28,* 315–345.

Johnson, M. K. (2001b). Job values in the young adult transition: Stability and change with age. *Social Psychology Quarterly, 64,* 297–317.

Jones, M. C., Bayley, N., MacFarlane, J. W., & Honzik, M. H. (1971). The course of human development: Selected papers from the longitudinal studies, Institute of Human Development, University of California, Berkeley. Waltham, MA: Xerox College Publishers.

Lipset, S. M. (1963). *The first new nation. The United States in historical and comparative perspective.* New York: Basic Books.

MacFarlane, J. W. (1938). Studies in child guidance, I: Methodology of data collection and organization. *Monographs of the Society for Research in Child Development, 3*(6, Serial No. 19).

Magnusson, D. (1988). Individual development from an interactional perspective: A longitudinal study. In D. Magnusson (Ed.), *Paths Through Life* (Vol. 1). Hillsdale, NJ: Erlbaum.

Mayer, K. U., (2001). The sociology of the life course and life span psychology—diverging or converging pathways. Society for the Study of Human Development, Ann Arbor, MI: University of Michigan.

Mayer, K. U. (1988). German survivors of World War II: The impact on the life course of the collective experience of birth cohorts. In M. R. Riley (in association with Bettina J. Huber & Beth B. Hess) (Eds.), *Social change and the life course, Volume 1: Social structures and human lives* (pp. 229–246). Newbury Park, CA: Sage. American Sociological Association's Presidential Series.

Mayer, K. U., & Tuma, N. B. (1990). *Event history analysis in life course research.* Madison: University of Wisconsin Press.

McLeod, D., & Shanahan, M. J. (1996). Trajectories of poverty and children's mental health. *Journal of Health and Social Behavior, 37,* 207–220.

Merton, R. K. (1968). *Social theory and social structure.* New York: Free Press.

Mills, C. W. (1959). *The sociological imagination.* New York: Oxford University Press.

Modell, J. (1989). *Into one's own: From youth to adulthood in the United States 1920–1975.* Berkeley: University of California Press.

Modell, J., & Elder, G. H. (2002). Children develop in history: So what's new? In W. W. Hartup & R. A. Weinberg (Eds.), *Child psychology in retrospect and prospect: In celebration of the 75th anniversary of the Institute of Child Development* (pp. 173–205).

Moen, P., Dempster-McClain, D., & Williams, R. W., Jr. (1992). Successful aging: A life-course perspective on women's multiple roles and health. *American Journal of Sociology, 97,* 1612–1638.

Mortimer, J. T., & Lorence, J. (1979). Work experience and occupational value socialization: A longitudinal study. *American Journal of Sociology, 84,* 1361–1385.

Nesselroade, J. R., & Baltes, P. B. (1974). Adolescent personality development and historical change: 1970–1972. *Monographs of the Society for Research in Child Development, 30 (1, Serial No. 154).*

Neugarten, B. L., & Datan, N. (1973). Sociological perspectives on the life cycle. In P. B. Baltes & K. W. Schaie (Eds.), *Life-span developmental psychology: Personality and socialization* (pp. 53–69). New York: Academic Press.

Neugarten, B. L. (Ed.) (1996). *The meanings of age: Selected papers of Bernice L Neugarten.* Chicago: University of Chicago Press.

Nisbet, R. A. (1969). *Social change and history.* New York: Oxford University Press.

Pavalko, E. K., & Smith, B. (1999). The rhythm of work: Health effects of women's work dynamics. *Social Forces, 77,* 1141–1162.

Portes, A., & Rumbaut, R. G. (1996). *Immigrant America: A portrait, second edition.* Berkeley: University of California Press.

Riley, M. W., Johnson, M. E., & Foner, A. (Eds.) (1972). *Aging and society, Volume 3: A sociology of age stratification.* New York: Russell Sage.

Robinson, R. V., & Jackson, E. F. (2001). Is trust in others declining in America? An age-period-cohort analysis. *Social Science Research, 30,* 117–145.

Ryder, N. B. (1965). The cohort as a concept in the study of social change. *American Sociological Review, 30,* 843–861.

Sampson, R. J., & Laub, J. H. (1993). *Crime in the making: Pathways and turning points through life.* Cambridge, MA: Harvard University Press.

Sampson, R. J., & Laub, J. H. (1996). Socioeconomic achievement in the life course of disadvantaged men: Military service as a turning point circa 1940–1965. *American Sociological Review, 61(3),* 347–367.

Settersten, R. A., & Hagestad, G. O. (1996a). What's the latest? Cultural age deadlines for family transitions. *Gerontologist, 36(2),* 178–188.

Settersten, R. A., & Hagestad, G. O. (1996b). What's the latest? Cultural age deadlines for educational and work transitions. *Gerontologist, 36(5),* 602–613.

Shanahan, M. J. (2000). Pathways to adulthood in changing societies: Variability and mechanisms in life course perspective. *Annual Review of Sociology, 26,* 667–692.

Shanahan, M. J., & Elder, G. H. Jr. (2002). History, human agency, and the life course. In L. Crockett (Ed.), *Agency motivation, and the life course* (pp. 143–185). Lincoln: University of Nebraska Press.

Shanahan, M. J., R. A. Miech, & Elder, G. H. Jr. (1998). Changing pathways to attainment in men's lives: Historical patterns of school, work, and social class. *Social Forces, 77(1),* 231–256.

Terman, L. M., & Oden, M. H. (1959). *Genetic studies of genius, Volume 5: The gifted group at mid-life: Thirty-five years of follow-up of the superior child.* Stanford, CA: Stanford University Press.

Thernstrom, S. (1964). *Poverty and progress: Social mobility in a Nineteenth Century city.* Cambridge, MA: Harvard University Press.

Thomas, W. I., & Znaniecki, F. (1918–20). *The Polish peasant in Europe and America* (Vols. 1&2). Boston: Badger.

Titma, M., & Tuma, N. (1995). *Paths of a generation: A comparative longitudinal study of young adults in the former Soviet Union.* Center for Social Research in Eastern Europe, Tallinn, Estonia. Stanford, CA: Stanford University Press.

U.S. Bureau of the Census. (1999). *Statistical abstract of the United States.* Washington, DC: Author.

Uhlenberg, P., & Kirby, J. B. (1998). Grandparenthood over time: Historical and demographic trends. In M. E. Szinovacz (Ed.), *Handbook on grandparenthood* (pp. 23–39). Westport, CT: Greenwood Press.

Volkart, E. H. (1951). *Social behavior and personality: Contributions of W. I. Thomas to theory and social research.* New York: Social Science Research Council.

Wellman, B., Wong, R. Y., Tindall, D., & Nazer, N. (1997). A decade of network change: Turnover, persistence, and stability in personal communities. *Social Networks, 19,* 27–50.

Wethington, E., Pixley, J., & Kavey, A. (2003). Turning points in work careers. In P. Moen (Ed.), *It's about time: Couples' career strains, strategies, and successes.* Ithaca, NY: Cornell University Press.

Wheaton, B. (1990). Life transitions, role histories, and mental health. *American Sociological Review, 55(2),* 209–223.

Young, H. C., Savola, K. L., & Phelps, E. (1991). *Inventory of longitudinal studies in the social sciences.* Newbury Park, CA: Sage.

Zhou, X., & Hou, L. (1999). Children of the Cultural Revolution: The state and the life course in the People's Republic of China. *American Sociological Review, 64,* 12–36.

PART II

HISTORICAL AND CROSS-NATIONAL VARIABILITY IN THE LIFE COURSE

CHAPTER 2

Generations, Cohorts, and Social Change

Duane F. Alwin
Ryan J. McCammon

The transformations that occur via a *succession of cohorts* cannot, for basic demographic reasons, be equated to the product of a *procession of "generations."* ... this brute fact is a profound key to the understanding of social continuity and social change. Indeed, a characteristically human type of society might well be impossible were the demography of the species structured differently. (Otis Dudley Duncan, 1966, p. 59)

INTRODUCTION

Social philosophers from Auguste Comte to David Hume considered the fundamental linkage between the biological succession of generations and change in the nature of society. As early as 1835, the statistician Adolphe Quetelet wrote about the importance of taking *year of birth* into account when examining human development (see Becker, 1992, p. 19). In the 1920s, the German sociologist Karl Mannheim wrote a highly cited treatise entitled "The Problem of Generations," arguing that having shared the same formative experiences contributes to a unique world view or frame of reference that can be a powerful force in people's lives. In Mannheim's words (1952, p. 298): "Even if the rest of one's life consisted of one long process of negation and destruction of the natural world view acquired in youth, the determining

Duane F. Alwin • Department of Sociology and Population Research Institute, Pennsylvania State University, University Park, Pennsylvania 16802.   Ryan J. McCammon • University of Michigan Survey Research Center, Ann Arbor, Michigan 48109-1382.
Handbook of the Life Course, edited by Jeylan T. Mortimer and Michael J. Shanahan. Kluwer Academic/Plenum Publishers, New York, 2003.

influence of these early impressions would still be predominant." Similarly, the Spanish sociologist José Ortega y Gasset wrote that generation "is the most important conception in history" (1933, p. 15) arguing that each generation has a special mission even if it goes unachieved (see Kertzer, 1983, p. 128).

In the modern era of social science, a similar sort of generational reasoning has been widely employed in empirical studies aimed at documenting how societies change. For example, in the 1950s Samuel Stouffer found that popular support for the toleration of Communists, atheists, and socialists followed generational lines, with more recent generations being significantly more tolerant than their elders. He argued that this was due in part to their higher levels of education, which fostered openness to "freedom of speech" and the exchange of ideas (Stouffer, 1955). In the 1970s, Ronald Inglehart found that post-World War II generations in Western Europe sought freedom and self-expression, in contrast to the pre-War generations' concern for economic security and political order (Inglehart, 1977, 1986, 1990). He argued from a Maslowian "hierarchy of needs" perspective that more recent generations had the luxury of economic prosperity that could not be taken for granted by their elders who had to focus on a more basic set of needs in an earlier time. More recently, Robert Putnam (2000) argued in his popular book *Bowling Alone* that civic engagement has declined, not because individual Americans have become less civic-minded, but mostly because earlier-born, engaged Americans have died off and been replaced by younger, more alienated ones, who are by and large less tied to traditional institutions, such as the church, the lodge, the bridge club, and the bowling league.

According to this theoretical perspective, how people think about the social world around them may depend as much on what was happening in the world *at the time they were growing up* as it does on what is happening in the present. The reference to this as a "generational" phenomenon is probably derived from the presumption that historically based influences shaped the development of all or most people growing up at a particular time and that there is nearly always a shared cultural identity that sets them apart from the parental generation. The idea of distinctive generations is, however, a complex one whose existence and effects are not easily documented. One of the persistent questions in research on social change upon which we focus considerable attention in this chapter is whether the unique formative experiences of different generations become distinctively imprinted on their world views making them distinct in their orientations and identities; or whatever the nature of their formative experiences, do people nevertheless adapt to change, remaining evanescent in their dispositions, identities, and beliefs throughout their lives? Unique historical events that happen during youth are no doubt powerful. Certainly, some eras and social movements (e.g., the Women's movement, or the Civil Rights Era) or the emergence of some new ideologies (e.g., Roosevelt's New Deal of the 1930s, or the environmental movement of the 1970s) provide distinctive experiences for youth during particular times. As Norman Ryder put it "the potential for change is concentrated in the cohorts of young adults who are old enough to participate directly in the movements impelled by change, but not old enough to have become committed to an occupation, a residence, a family of procreation or a way of life" (Ryder, 1965, p. 848).

In this chapter we focus not only on the potential of the concept of *generations* to reveal how societies change, but also on some of the major problems with trying to make sense of the social world in this way. In order to do so we first distinguish the concept from other related concepts, and in our next section (Section II) we review the multiple meanings of the concept of generation. We focus on how it is different from and related to other concepts used in the analysis of social change. Following this initial effort to reduce what we consider to be a prevalent terminological confusion in the area, we examine in detail the two major ways in which the concept of *generation* is employed in contemporary social science: first referring to *a position in the natural line of descent* within families (Section III) and second the *historical timing of birth* (Sections IV and V). Given the prominence of theories of *cohort replacement* (as distinct from generational replacement) in the study of social change, we review the essential assumptions made by the theoretical framework and discuss some of the difficulties involved in employing the theory in life course research (Section VI). We examine the evidence for the theory and discuss several empirical examples from recent research to illustrate the prospects and pitfalls of the proposed conceptual apparatus. We end the essay with a brief consideration of a third meaning of the term *generation* (based on the theories of Mannheim and Ortega y Gasset) which is distinct from the others, but which has the unrealized potential to help understand the origins of social change. This concept of *generation* (referred to in what follows with a capital "G" or *Generations*), while related to other uses of the term, is quite distinct, referring to historical phenomena that are not as easily located and quantified as are cohorts and cohort effects. Still, we argue that such phenomena may have as much, if not more, potential for understanding the origins and nature of social change. Generations, in this sense may be more a matter of quality than of degree, and their temporal boundaries may not be as easily identified as is sometimes assumed. We conclude the essay with a summary of the territory covered, along with a call for more research on generations that will improve their usefulness as a tool in the study of life course processes.

GENERATIONS AND COHORTS—SOME DEFINITIONS

One of the first difficulties we encounter in studying the phenomenon of generations is with the term "generation" itself. This is because the concept of *generation* has more than one legitimate meaning and this multiplicity of meanings can produce confusion. It is first and foremost a kinship term, referring to relationships between individuals who have a common ancestor. As a term denoting kinship relations, a generation consists of a single stage or degree in the natural line of descent. Thus, within a given family, generations are very clearly defined, and while *generational replacement* is more or less a biological inevitability *within families* (assuming continuous life cycle processes), the replacement of generations in this sense does not correspond in any neat manner to the historical process at the macrosocial level because of individual differences in fertility (i.e., parents do not all replace themselves at the same rate) and the fact that the temporal gap between generations is variable across families.

The term *generation* is also frequently used, as we ourselves have used it in the introductory paragraphs, to refer to the people born at about the same time and who therefore experience historical events at the same times in their lives. This meaning of the term was popularized by Mannheim's classic treatise on "generations" in which he used the term to refer to the unique influences of historical location on the development of the shared meaning of events and experiences of youth. As we discuss below, many sociologists understandably confuse this meaning of the concept of "generation" with the concept of "cohort", since they share a historical referent. We hope our discussion will reduce the confusion rather than add to it.

The fact that there are at least two accepted meanings of the concept of generation has been a source of confusion, and various authors have tried to resolve the seeming incompatibility of these meanings. Indeed, some have argued that Mannheim, Ortega y Gasset and their followers have usurped what may be thought of as principally a kinship term to inappropriately refer to groups of people who share a distinctive culture and/or a self-conscious identity by virtue of their having experienced the same historical events at the same time in their lives, setting them apart from their parents and grandparents (see Kertzer, 1983).

Because of this potential confusion of meanings, and in an apparent effort to be more precise, some sociologists prefer the term *birth cohort* for what many others refer to as generations in the historical sense of the term (see Ryder, 1965). In general a *cohort* is a group of people who have shared some critical experience during the same interval of time. For example, people who enter college in a given year are referred to as an "entering cohort" and those who graduate in the same year would be called a "graduating cohort". Or, those persons marrying in a given year are called a "marriage cohort". In each case, there is an event or experience in common that defines the cohort. When sociologists talk about *generations* in the sense of a group of people who share the same historical time frame during their youth, they are often implicitly using "year of birth" as the event that defines the cohort. Thus, the term "cohort" is often used as shorthand for "birth cohort", which refers to all persons born in the same year. This is the way in which we use the term in this chapter. Defined in this way, knowing a person's *cohort* membership may be thought to index the unique historical period in which a group's common experiences are embedded, but as we shall argue, this does not necessarily make a "cohort" (or a set of cohorts) a "generation".

Members of a birth cohort share a social history, that is, historical events and the opportunities and constraints posed by society at a given time. Further, members of a birth cohort share the experience of the life cycle at the same time, that is, they experience childhood, reach adolescence, grow into early adulthood, and mature into midlife and old age at the same time. And finally, members of a birth cohort share the experience of the cohort itself, that is, the distinctive aspects of the cohort, for example, its size or its level of education, are something unique to the cohort. The sharing of experiences by members of the same cohort, as we shall see, does not necessarily define a "generation" in the sense of Mannheim and Ortega y Gasset.

Given the above definitions, a *cohort effect* refers to a distinctive formative experience which members of a birth cohort (or set of birth cohorts) share that lasts—and marks them— throughout their lives. For example, people who grew up during the Great Depression of the 1930s have different ideas about money than those who grew up in more prosperous times (Elder, 1974). Or, the women who were the first to have exercised their political enfranchisement after the 19th Amendment was passed in the early part of this century may have taken voting more seriously throughout their lives and reported higher rates of voter turnout (Firebaugh & Chen, 1995).

Birth cohorts are also affected by their own characteristics, and another example of a cohort effect involves the phenomenon of cohort size. For example, in a path-breaking series of studies, Easterlin (1987) argues that the numerically large set of birth cohorts making up the Baby Boom are at a significant socioeconomic disadvantage relative to that of their predecessors, simply because of its size. The number of persons born in a particular year, thus, has far-reaching consequences, given its effects on competition for jobs and the strain it produces on the opportunity structure. Easterlin (1987) argues that relative cohort size affects, not only the economic well-being of cohort members, but many features of the family and individual functioning, including fertility rates. Individuals in large cohorts will be less likely to marry, more likely to put off having children, mothers will be more likely to work outside the home, and as young adults they will be more likely to experience psychological stress and feelings of alienation. For a review of the current status of research on the "Easterlin effect", see Pampel (1993).

Cohort effects, as described above, refer to the impact of historical events and processes on individual lives. As Modell (1989) notes, however, we need not limit our conception of cohort effects to this sort of one-way relationship between history and the individual. He argues for "a sociohistorical approach to the life course" that focuses as well on "the way those altered individual experiences *aggregated* to constitute a new *context* for others living through these changes" (Modell, 1989, p. 22). The reactions of some cohorts to their historical experiences often become normative patterns that, once rationalized by society, influence the lives of later cohorts. In this sense cohort effects can be thought of as both direct and indirect. He uses the example of dating patterns among youth in American society to illustrate this point, and his analysis shows that adolescent dating, an invention of the 1920s (invented mainly by adolescent women), became a normative pattern among adolescents of the 1950s and 1960s, one which he argues actually constrained the choices that young women could make (Modell, 1989).

It is often correctly suggested that the term generation should *not* be used when we mean birth cohort (Ryder, 1965; Kertzer, 1983). From the foregoing we can see that generations in the kinship sense of the term are nested within families and individual family members are nested within generations. We also know that as part of the historical process individuals are simultaneously nested within cohorts. Differences between generations within families do not easily translate into differences among cohorts and vice versa, and there is no identity between generations and cohorts in this sense. This is because members of a given generation are likely to be members of several different cohorts, because of individual differences in fertility within generations, and because of the variability in the historical distance between generations within families.

With respect to laying claim on the concept of generation, we do not see the importance of phrasing the terminological issue as a competition among historical theorists on the one hand and life course analysts on the other (Kertzer, 1983). We agree that neither meaning of the concept of "generation" should be confused with the ideas of "cohort" and cohort effects. However, despite the potential confusion in terminology, it seems to us plausible to tolerate all meanings (given above) for generation, using it both in its genealogical sense of a stage in a line of descent when appropriate, but we would also allow the term (in the historical sense) when the focus is on *groups of people who share a distinctive culture and/or a self-conscious identity by virtue of their having experienced the same historical events* at roughly the same time in their lives [we will henceforth capitalize the word whenever we use it in this second way, i.e., as Generation]. In this sense the concept of "Generation", found in the work of Mannheim and Ortega y Gasset, is not intended to be the same thing as "cohort", and when one appreciates the meaning of the concept as used in their writings it will become obvious that the concept of Generation implies much more than simply cohort differences. The latter may be suggestive of Generational differences, but although cohort differentiation may be thought to be a necessary condition for Generational differences, they by themselves may not be sufficient for saying that Generations truly exist in the sense of having a distinctive culture and shared identity.

In other words, cohort effects do not automatically imply the existence of Generations. According to White (1991), cohorts only become "actors" when they cohere enough around historical events, in both their own and others' eyes, to be called "Generations". In this sense, we would distinguish between cohorts and Generations, in that the former refers simply to the effects attributable to having been placed by one's birth in a particular historical period, whereas a Generation is (in White's words) a "joint interpretive construction which insists upon and builds among tangible cohorts in defining a style recognized from outside and from within" (p. 31). Through such mechanisms "cohort effects" are given life through these interpretive and behavioral aspects. The point here is that there is an "identity" component to

Generations, made explicit in the work of Mannheim (1952) and Ortega y Gasset (1933) that may be difficult to pin down when simply studying cohort differences and their tendencies to persevere. The existence of cohort effects and the existence of Generations are two different albeit related questions. We return to this issue later in the chapter.

INTERGENERATIONAL DIFFERENCES

In virtually all societies, each generation experiences life differently. Each has its "unique themes and problems [regularly facing] situations vastly different from those that confronted their parents" (Clausen, 1986, p. 7). The parental generation is often responsible for mediating the influences of social change on their children, and the role of the elder generations in promoting adaptation to social change is sometimes acknowledged (Inkeles, 1958). As we observed in the earlier discussion, assuming the continuity of reproduction, generational replacement (not to be confused with cohort replacement) is a virtual biological inevitability within families (although some family lines do die out). While it is important to study the relationship between generations, both with regard to the socialization of children (Alwin, 1996c), as well as intergenerational relationships across the life span (Riley & Riley, 1996), conceptualization of generational influences in this sense may be less useful for studying social change. As we pointed out earlier, this stems from the fact that the distance between generations is variable within families and therefore generational differences (in this kinship sense) do not translate in any neat manner into cohort effects (Duncan, 1966; Ryder, 1965).

To use the terminology developed in this essay (see below), generational differences in this sense contain the influences of two independent factors, age effects and cohort effects, and under normal circumstances it is difficult to identify the extent to which either may be operating. Studies of intergenerational differences are nonetheless interesting because they can tell us about family influences and the relationships between generations, and in this section we review some of these possibilities. The simplest and probably the most common type of intergenerational research design is one in which a sample of persons is interviewed about themselves and one or both of their parents. There is, for example, a long tradition in research on social mobility that gathers intergenerational data on occupational attainments by asking a sample of men and women about their own and their father's socioeconomic attainments, and then using the comparisons across generations to say something about social stratification (see, e.g., Biblarz, Bengtson, & Bucur, 1996; Blau & Duncan, 1967; Duncan, 1966, 1968; Featherman & Hauser, 1978). This literature has painstakingly pointed out that *while the generation of children in such analyses represents sets of birth cohorts, the generation of parents do not*, due to individual differences in fertility (see Blau & Duncan, 1967, pp. 82–91). It would therefore be inappropriate and misleading to draw inferences about social change from such intergenerational data, as if they represented differences in cohorts.

The reverse error can also be made, that is, making inferences about generational differences from differences between cohorts. A 1993 article in the *Harvard Educational Review* argued that "today's high-school-educated males earn less than their fathers did" on the basis of differences among cohorts in a cross-sectional survey (Murnane & Levy, 1993). While the authors provide some interesting intercohort comparisons of earnings differentials, their article did not contain any information about intergenerational change in incomes within families.

Other research designs actually collect data from more than one generation. Jennings and Neimi's (1981) classic study of a nationally representative sample of high-school seniors and their parents charted the development of political views among young adults in relation to their parents through the 1960s and early 1970s. Bengtson's (1975) study of the "generation gap" in attitudes and values between generations was based on tracking members of subsequent generations down family lineages and interviewing three generations (see Glass, Bengtson, & Dunham, 1986). Bengtson and Roberts (1991) studied intergenerational solidarity using extensive reinterviews of many of the same sample members. Similarly, Rossi and Rossi (1990) use a three-generation data set to study intergenerational relations, focusing (among other things) on normative obligations to kin. They find that such normative beliefs are structured according to the degree of relatedness, not by type of relative within levels of relatedness—that is, obligations to parents and children were roughly equal, but greater than obligations to grandparents and grandchildren, which were greater than felt obligations to aunts and uncles and nieces and nephews. One advantage of multigenerational research is that the data represent related individuals rather than separate and unrelated birth cohorts, and for purposes of assessing similarities and differences within families controlling for a range of family-related factors, this approach has considerable merit. For example, in the General Social Survey, cross-sectional samples of individuals are interviewed and (among other things) report information about their parents; taken by themselves, however, the data on parents do not necessarily generalize to any easily identifiable group in society (see, e.g., Blau & Duncan, 1967, pp. 82–84). These methodological problems do not always stop the creative analyst (Bengtson & Cutler, 1976; Rossi & Rossi, 1990, pp. 92–101).

MECHANISMS OF SOCIAL CHANGE

Popular theories of social change rest on the idea that culture, social norms, and social behavior change through two main mechanisms: (1) through changes undergone by individuals (due to aging or period effects), and (2) through the succession of cohorts (Ryder, 1965; Firebaugh, 1992; Glenn, this volume). Several things connected to the lives of individuals have a bearing on how society changes, and thus, there is a linkage between individuals and social change—society changes (paradoxically) both because individuals change and because they remain stable or unchanged after an early period of socialization. Demographers refer to this set of mechanisms as the *Age–Period–Cohort model* of social change because these mechanisms summarize the influences of aging, time period, and cohort membership on social change (see Mason & Fienberg, 1985). [It is unnecessary for present purposes to introduce either notion of generation discussed above, as this is simply a statistical framework that aims to account for variation.] These influences, discussed here, can be visualized with respect to Figure 2-1, which depicts the intersection of biographical and historical time in the lives of four hypothetical cohorts.

Changes to individuals, occurring in biographical time (see Figure 2-1), that influence social change are normally thought to happen because of factors associated with two different phenomena. The first of these is *aging*. Simply put, people change as they get older due to some combination of biological, psychological and social mechanisms. Aging is usually identified with differences among individuals that are linked to their getting older, becoming more mature as a function of having lived more of life, or because of physical or cognitive decline and impairment. For example, the population may be becoming more conservative as a function of the dual facts that people become more conservative as they age and that the population on average is getting older (see Alwin, 1998a). The second source of individual change comes about through people's responses to historical events and processes—called *period effects*—occurring in historical time (see Figure 2-1). When the entire society gets caught up in and is affected by a set

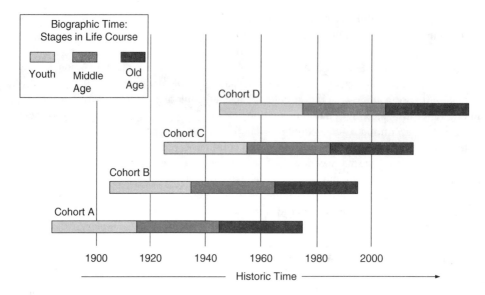

FIGURE 2-1. **Intersection of biographic and historic time.**

of historical events, such as a war, an economic depression, or a social movement, the wide-spread changes that occur are called period effects. The Civil Rights movement, for example, may have changed ideas about race for all Americans, not just those birth cohorts growing up in the 1960s (if it affected primarily the young it would be called a cohort effect—see below). Similarly, not only were the youngest cohorts of women and men affected by the Feminist movement of the 1960s and 1970s, the movement may have influenced the views of almost everyone living in the society during that time to some extent. There is a fine line between what should be considered a "cohort" versus a "period" effect, but it usually comes down to *who* is affected by the events in question. In some cases it is impossible for most members of society to remain unaffected by some changes—such as changes in the economy or the influence of computers on society. Or, to take an example of more recent history, the September 11, 2001 terrorist attacks on the World Trade Center in New York and the Pentagon in Washington, DC have had profound effects on *all* members of American society, regardless of year of birth.

The third source of change in society is *cohort succession*, which is the gradual replace-ment of earlier born cohorts by later ones. This results not from individual change, as is the case with aging and period effects, but from individual stability. When the effects of histori-cal events tied to particular eras mainly affect the young, the result is potentially a cohort effect. Recall, we earlier defined a *cohort effect* as a distinctive formative experience that members of a birth cohort (or set of birth cohorts) share that *persists throughout their lives.** For example, as noted earlier, it is sometimes suggested that civic engagement has declined in America overall, even though individual Americans have not necessarily become less civic-minded (Putnam, 2000). This may be because older, more publicly engaged citizens are dying off and being replaced by younger, more alienated Americans who are less tied to institutions such as a church, lodge, political party, or bowling league. Or, if those cohorts who reached

---

*We eschew the commonly used term "age cohorts" which conflates the two elements "aging" and "cohort" into one, elements that refer to distinct sources of social change.

economic independence during the Great Depression are seen to be particularly thrifty, this implies that the experience of growing up under privation permanently changed this set of cohorts' economic style of life due to their formative years. As these members of society die off, they may leave behind a somewhat less frugal set of cohorts.

Now that we have defined the nature of age, period, and cohort effects, how do these factors combine to shape social change, and how can their influences be studied using empirical data? The age-period-cohort model recognizes that these are all important causal factors. Unfortunately the individual parts of this model—namely the effects of aging, cohorts, and time periods—are not easy to understand in isolation from one another, and there are serious problems with uniquely identifying their separate effects. It is thus sometimes difficult to place any one interpretation on observed data. Generally speaking, it is often necessary to concede that social change could be due to the operation of all three of these factors at once without knowing which is more powerful.

The best research designs for the study of aging are longitudinal studies of the same people over time, otherwise known as panel designs (Alwin & Scott, 1996; Duncan & Kalton, 1987; Halaby, this volume). Panel data are necessary to ascertain information on gross rates of constancy and change and ultimately to assess levels of human stability, and it may be possible to gain some insight into the extent of aging effects by analyzing the extent of change in individual differences in panel designs. Often such designs control for cohort differences, but while it is possible to study how individuals change using such designs, it is usually more difficult to understand why they change as they do. Specifically, as noted above, change happening to individuals may be due to aging and/or period, and it is often difficult to sort out which explains the change. By contrast the best designs for studying cohort effects are repeated cross-sectional surveys, which do not study the same people but the same cohorts over time (Campbell, Abolafia, & Maddox, 1985). Such survey designs can study the same cohorts over time, and while less useful for studying how individuals change, they can provide estimates of net change and of cohort replacement as we discuss further below. There are many potential pitfalls that await the age-period-cohort analyst, and many precautions must be taken to guard against potential fallacies and errors of inference in repeated cross-section designs (Mason & Fienberg, 1985; see also Glenn in this volume). The cohort sequential design—one that combines features of the cross-sectional and panel designs—follows repeated cohorts over time (see Schaie, 1996, pp. 30–32). To the extent sampled cohorts are representative of society (or relevant subgroups), such a design can yield information on both gross and net change.

THE IDENTIFICATION OF
COHORT EFFECTS

If we were to look at a cross-section of adults in American society, it would be easy to confuse cohort differences with the possibility that they might instead reflect differences due to experience or maturity (i.e., aging). Earlier-born cohorts not only grew up in a different era, they are now also older and more experienced. By contrast, cohorts born more recently are younger and have less experience. So, if one is looking at a phenomenon that is influenced both by the amount of experience one has as well as the particular slice of history in which one participated when growing up, the results of empirical analyses can be quite puzzling. Similarly, if one is studying the changes in a single cohort (or set of cohorts) over time, effects that might otherwise be attributable to aging are confounded with period effects, and disentangling the two sets of influences can be exceedingly difficult.

To illustrate the seriousness of the problem, we assume from the above discussion that variables representing the three main sets of factors can be thought of as affecting the mean levels of variables: aging (A), chronological time or period (P), and birth cohort (C). These are conceptual categories of variables representing rich and complex sets of influences that operate primarily through (1) processes of aging and life cycle changes, (2) those effects due to the distinctiveness of the time of measurement or historical period, and (3) processes influencing specific cohorts. The problem is, however, that within a given survey, A (age) and C (cohort) are perfectly correlated. And in a series of repeated cross-sections, within cohorts, A (age) and C (cohort) are perfectly correlated (Mason & Fienberg, 1985). Because Age = Time − Birth Date (A = P − C), it is rarely possible to separate the influences of "aging", "cohorts", and "time periods" using cross-sectional data in any purely exploratory fashion. One needs to be able to impose a strong set of assumptions about the nature of one or more of these three sources of variation—aging, cohorts, and periods—in order to identify these separate influences unequivocally. By turning to supplementary types of data, what Converse (1976) and others have called "side information", assumptions about the nature of certain historical, aging, or cohort processes, it may be possible to simplify the problem. If one can make strong theoretical assumptions about the nature of certain influences, for example setting either cohort, aging, or period effects to zero, it is possible to creatively interpret survey data. Short of such strong assumptions, it is usually not possible to cleanly disentangle these processes empirically from such data alone.

An example of the ambiguity of the evaluation and interpretation of social change with respect to age, period, and cohort influences involves the case of self-reports of attendance at religious services (see Alwin & McCammon, 2002). Data collected to assess these trends from the General Social Survey (GSS) asked random samples of the American public to report how often they attended religious services over the past year (data not shown here). Such data point to major cohort differences in observance of weekly services. Those born in the years from 1915 to 1930—sometimes called the "greatest generation"—as well as those born earlier report typical attendance at church services about 25 weeks per year, or about half the time on average. By contrast, people born after World War II attended church substantially less often—those born from 1963 to 1980 report attending services an average of less than 15 weeks per year. These changes may be due to an overall decline in attendance levels among churchgoers, or to the expansion of the group that does not attend church at all, or both (see Hout & Fischer, 2002).

If one were to place a cohort replacement interpretation on these figures, one might argue that as the older cohorts of church attenders die off and are replaced by much more secularly oriented and less participatory cohorts, society as a whole will become decidedly less observant of church services. This type of conclusion would fit well the kinds of interpretations made by Putnam (2000) and others decrying the state of modern life as one devoid of communal ties. But perhaps there are no such cohort effects at all, once other factors are taken into account. For example, these results might be explained, fully or partly, by aging and life cycle factors. Typically, after a youthful period of church avoidance, people may participate more in religious activities. One common explanation for these patterns is that levels of religious participation reflect the effects of aging or the life cycle rather than cohort influences, and that the higher levels of involvement among the cohorts born earlier has as much to do with their age as it does their cohort membership (Hout & Greeley, 1987).

Of course, although it is not always foolproof, one of the most important strategies for the analysis of aging, period, and cohort effects is to plot the data by cohort (or cohort categories) over time, examining the empirical regularities directly. Moreover, it is often very important to take other factors into account in such analyses. For the example of church attendance it is important to examine the data separately for denominational groups because members of the Roman Catholic faith account for virtually all the decline in church attendance in American society from the early1970s through the 1990s (data not shown). Catholics attended some 35 weeks per year in the early 1970s and some 30 years later had declined to nearly 22 weeks per year. These patterns were due, as most religious scholars agree, to the profound differences between Vatican policy on the reproductive rights of women and the views of many lay Catholics (see Greeley, 1989; Hout & Greeley, 1987). By contrast, the level of church attendance among Protestants has not changed significantly over this period, remaining relatively stable at around 24 weeks per year.

Consequently, it should be clear that life course factors interact with other variables (in this case religious denomination), and it is important that the analysis of cohort effects take such factors into account. The question can be raised in this example about the extent to which cohort replacement has a role in the Catholic and Protestant trends. Are the more recently born, less active Catholics replacing the more active Catholics who had died, and is this also true among Protestants? Overall, there appear to be clear cohort trends revealing declining church service attendance in the most recent cohorts (i.e., a cohort effect). Among Catholics there appears to also be a decline in church attendance among all cohort categories, which we can probably attribute at least in part to period factors. Such period factors would not be operating among Protestants given their origin in the institutional policies of the Catholic Church. In fact, among Protestants the cohort trends appear to be accompanied by positive within cohort changes for most of the cohort groups suggesting either a life cycle effect favoring increased church attendance or a period effect in a direction opposite that operating among Catholics. Given the lack of net change in church attendance over this period among Protestants, it is conceivable that the declining cohort trend is balanced by a positive within-cohort trend over the period covered here. Unfortunately, from such analyses it may be not clear whether the within-cohort differences result from unique effects of historical factors on different cohorts, or whether they reflect the age composition of the cohort categories, or to some combination of both. This is an example, however, where cohort analysis would appear to be fruitless without considering additional variables.

There are some cases in which the exploratory analysis of the data can quite clearly demonstrate the nature of the influences of age, period, and cohort. An example of this from recent analyses involves data concerning *trust in government* from the National Election Studies (NES) (Alwin, 2002a). The NES surveys included the question: "How much of the time do you think you can trust the government in Washington to do what is right—just about always, most of the time, or only some of the time?" These results fairly convincingly show that the amount of trust one has in the government at any point in time has mostly to do with the government at a particular point in time and not to characteristics of the individual, such as when they were born. All cohorts follow virtually the same pattern, moving from very high levels of support in the 1950s to rather low levels in the 1990s. In other words, it does not appear to be the case that either cohort differences or the experiences of aging contribute in any detectable way to variation in trust in the government and that period factors largely explain the patterns over time. One would need to postulate a rather complicated combination of aging and cohort effects to contradict this rather simple explanation of the results in this case (see Alwin, 2002a).

Generally speaking the contribution of age, period, and cohort factors to variation in individuals' scores on such questions is far from clear and their confounding in longitudinal designs creates several challenges in isolating the effects of any set of influences. For example, when political scientists find that younger voters are much less likely to identify with either major political party, this could be due to the fact that more recent cohorts are turned off by partisan politics, or to the fact that the intensity of party loyalty is a function of aging and the experience that comes with it, *or both* (see Converse, 1976). As we have suggested, due to the confounding of aging, period, and cohort influences in any series of replicate surveys, it is rarely possible to separate the effects of aging, cohorts, and time period by simply analyzing the linear additive effects of age, birth year, and time of survey. Without the ability to make some assumptions, which is often lacking, there is no straightforward solution to the identification problem. However, one can decompose trend data reflecting social change into two orthogonal components: the between-cohort versus within-cohort part of the trend (see Firebaugh, 1989). The between-cohort component can be interpreted in terms of cohort replacement if one is willing to assume that the age compositional differences between the cohorts are not actually producing the effect. The within-cohort component, as mentioned above, can be interpreted either in terms of aging or life cycle effects, or in terms of historic or period effects. Again, if one assumes that the effects of aging do not operate on the means but on the stability of individual differences, then this component is likely to represent period effects (see Alwin, 1996a). The problems with doing this are discussed in greater detail by Firebaugh (1989) and Rodgers (1990).

SOCIAL CHANGE AS COHORT REPLACEMENT

As we already noted, popular theories of social change rest on the idea that change occurs through the succession of cohorts. The theory of "cohort replacement", as we refer to it here, makes several critical assumptions, which we explore in greater detail in this section: (1) the *impressionable youth* assumption—that youth is an impressionable period of the life course in which individuals are maximally open to the socialization influences of the social environment; (2) the *individual persistence* assumption—people acquire their world views (values, beliefs, and attitudes) during these impressionable years and largely maintain those views over most of their lives; (3) the *cohort effects* assumption—unique cohort experiences are formed, due to the distinctive influence of historical events and experiences, such that there are clear differences across birth cohorts in typical beliefs and attitudes; and (4) the assumption of *social change*—as a consequence of the above processes society changes gradually in the direction of the more recent cohorts.

An alternative view would argue that the theory exaggerates the potential for the lasting effects of early socialization experiences, that individuals' views are not particularly stable over their lives, that members of particular cohorts or generations do not differ uniformly in their social experiences and their identities, and that social change results as much from aggregate changes within society, indeed within cohorts, via shifts in individual lives or to macrolevel historical (or period) effects, than it does from generational replacement.

So, which perspective is most likely to be true? Is there any evidence for these components of the cohort replacement theory of social change? Given the way we have formulated the theory in the above paragraphs, the answer would seem to lie in the truth of the four major assumptions that go into the cohort replacement argument and the kinds of evidence that exist for them. In the remainder of the chapter we summarize what is known about each of these elements of the theory.

The Impressionable Years

How open are young people to change, relative to other times in their lives? Developmental psychologists have argued that youth, at least in Western culture, does appear to represent a time of susceptibility to change. In the words of Erik Erikson (1988: 21) "to enter history, each generation of youth must find an identity consonant with its own childhood and consonant with an ideological promise in the perceptible historical process." During youth the tables are turned, continues Erikson: "No longer is it merely for the old to teach the young the meaning of life ... it is the young who, by their responses and actions, tell the old whether life as represented by the old and presented to the young has meaning; and it is the young who carry in them the power to confirm those who confirm them and, joining the issues, to renew and to regenerate, or to reform and to rebel."

Thus, youth is a stage that represents an intersection of life history with social history, and developmentally, it is a time when individuals confirm their own identities within a historical context. It is also the case that developmental trajectories and stages of the life cycle for children interact in significant ways with historical period. For example, Elder (1980) develops an interesting argument regarding the linkage between social changes and the life-cycle definition of adolescence, which has a more general applicability to the issues being addressed here. He suggests that in a society characterized by a lengthy youthful stage in which the individual experiences a great deal of independence and a period of flexibility and openness to change, it may be reasonable to theorize about the lifelong impact of youthful socialization experiences (see Alwin, 1994; Alwin, Cohen, & Newcomb, 1991).

On the other hand, in a society characterized by a rather abrupt transition from childhood to adulthood, with fewer choices open to the individual, there may not be such a youthful stage during which the individual is preoccupied with the pursuit of identity and autonomy (Kett, 1977; Shanahan, 2000). Elder's (1980; Elder, Caspi, & Burton, 1988) argument illustrates the great value of recent theorizing with respect to the consideration of the interaction of social change and life-span development, and his recent collaborative project on the implications of a changing society for children's growth and development is a landmark accomplishment (Elder, Modell, & Parke, 1993). From an historical perspective the life course period of youth can be quite malleable. Modell (1989, p. 26) argues that the transformation in the transition to adulthood in American society over the 20th century "underlines much of the enlarged *salience* of the youthful life course ... [reinforcing the view that] ... the way one grows up is closely related to what one becomes."

One of the classic studies in sociology that illustrates these points was carried out in the 1930s and 1940s by Theodore Newcomb at Bennington College, then a newly formed women's college in southwestern Vermont. The young women who attended Bennington at that time came primarily from conservative backgrounds. By contrast, the faculty members were notably *progressive* in their economic and political views. Newcomb observed that the longer the young women stayed at Bennington, the more their political and economic views changed in the direction of the more liberal faculty. He concluded that young adulthood is constituted in terms of an openness to identity formation and change and that the individual's immediate environment plays a powerful role in shaping their views (Newcomb, 1943). His theoretical insights into the processes by which responses to social change are shaped by the individual's immediate environment have since become incorporated into social psychological perspectives on human development. It is now commonplace to assume that an individual's reference groups mediate and interpret the influences of social and political events (see Alwin, Cohen, & Newcomb, 1991).

There is also some indirect evidence to support the conclusion that youth is a particularly impressionable time when people's experiences are highly salient. When older adults are asked in laboratory settings to provide autobiographical memories from their lives without restrictions to the content or time period, they show a preponderance of memories for events that occurred during their adolescence and early adulthood (Rubin, 1999). In addition, when people are asked in surveys to report the most important event or change in the past half-century, there is often a heightened tendency to report things that occurred when they were young, say 10–30 years old (Schuman & Scott, 1989; Scott & Zac, 1993). Thus, there is some tangible support for the idea that youth is a particularly impressionable period, insofar as memories of youthful experiences often seem to be the most salient.

The Stability of Individual Differences over the Life Span

Youth does appear, then, to be an impressionable period in the life course, where there is considerably more openness to change compared to other stages in life. Indeed, many hold that not only is youth an impressionable period, but that these early experiences are the most powerful in terms of their lasting influences on human tendencies. Some would even put the period of "openness" much earlier. Sears (1981) recounts the story told about the Jesuits, who believed that they could control a person's thinking for life if they were able to control their education up to the age of 7 years. Such a view is echoed in the words of Bertrand Russell in his book *Education*, published in 1926, quoted by Frank Musgrove in the following:

> education of character "ought to be nearly complete by the age of six." Courage was an important virtue, but there was nothing that schools could do about this—it had already been done in the home and "One generation of fearless women could transform the world..." (Musgrove, 1977, p. 215)

Another picture of human development is frequently drawn that establishes some aspects of the individual's personality to be established somewhat later in life, not until age 30 or 35 years, but then set "like plaster" throughout the remainder of the life span (James, 1950/1890, p. 121). This has become the preferred metaphor for personality researchers who believe that measured dispositions for behavior are highly stable in adult life (Costa & McRae, 1994).

How stable are individuals over their lives, subsequent to early periods of socialization? Or, put another way, how stable are differences among individuals over time? The relationship between aging and human stability is not very well understood, although we have been learning more. The stability patterns of individual differences are capable of following any number of different trajectories. Alwin (1994, 1995) described six different phenotypic models of human stability—(a) the persistence model, (b) the lifelong-openness model, (c) the increasing persistence model, (d) the impressionable-years model, (e) the midlife-stability model, and (f) the decreasing persistence model. These are shown in Figure 2-2 in which each depiction of the magnitude of stability is charted with respect to age in adulthood. What is depicted is the expected level of *molar stability* in a particular segment of the life span under a particular stability regime. These quantities reflect degrees of stability in individual differences as expressed in the rate of change in a particular attribute for an age-homogenous cohort over a specified interval of time (see Alwin, 1994, pp. 139–140). For convenience we are here using a set of 8-year periods to gauge hypothetical levels of *molar stability* across life-span intervals of equal length.

In Model A, which is referred to as the *persistence model*, a uniformly high level of stability is depicted over each segment of the adult life cycle. In this first model the expected magnitude, on a scale ranging from 0 to 1, over each such 8-year period depicts a high level of stability that is uniform with respect to age. Traits for which such patterns are observed would seemingly represent a very high level of stability in individual differences across the entire adult life span. For many human characteristics, such as cognitive and intellectual abilities, various

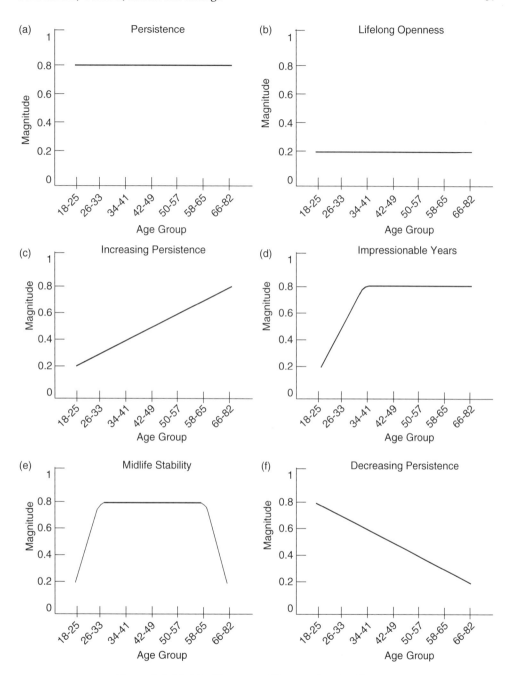

FIGURE 2-2. Models of human stability over the adult life span.

aspects of identities, and some personality traits, there is a strong empirical basis for assuming high levels of stability after adolescence and early adulthood (Alwin, 1994, pp. 159–164). One such domain with high levels of stability of individual differences is intellectual ability. There is a great deal of evidence that individual differences in cognitive test scores grow in stability in adolescence and are quite stable over even rather lengthy periods of the life span

(Alwin, McCammon, & Wray, 2000; Arbuckle, Gold, & Andres, 1986; Hertzog & Schaie, 1986; Kohn & Schooler, 1978; Nesslreoade & Baltes, 1974). Another such domain with high levels of stability of individual differences is personality traits, where research suggests that personality traits increase in relative stability in adolescence (Nesselroade & Baltes, 1974) and grow to high levels of stability in adulthood, with little increase in stability over most of the adult life span (Costa & McRae, 1980, 1994; Costa, McRae, & Arenberg, 1980, 1983).

Citing the lack of evidence for high degrees of stability after early adulthood in many other aspects of individual functioning, Gergen (1980) proposed a model for stability that calls attention to the inherent potential for adjustment and adaptation to changes in the social environment. The depiction of stability in Model B—here referred to as the *lifelong openness model*—represents a developmental pattern that is consistent with a view of life as full of adaptation and change. In Gergen's (1980) words, in this model "existing (developmental) patterns appear potentially evanescent, the unstable result of the particular juxtaposition of contemporary historical events. For any individual the life course seems fundamentally open-ended. Even with full knowledge of the individual's past experience, one can render little more than a probabilistic account of the broad contours of future development" (Gergen, 1980, pp. 34–35). The depiction of stability in Model B similarly reveals a great degree of uniformity in stability with respect to age, but at a much lower magnitude. In this model there is considerable individual flexibility and change during young adulthood, but the degree of change is just as likely in all segments of the life span as it is in young adulthood. The interpretation of patterns of stability in terms of lifelong openness does not always require such a low magnitude of stability, and many use this phrase to describe patterns of stability that are much higher (e.g., Jennings & Niemi, 1981). Writing about the stability of personality (see above), Ardelt (2000) argues that the prevailing view of high degrees of stability in personality is an exaggeration, and that the *lifelong openness* model is a more accurate response to the question: Can personality change? (Heatherton & Weinberger, 1994).

For some human attributes neither of these models is thought to fit the developmental pattern. In the quote given above from James (1950/1890), suggesting that personality or "character" is not fully established until early adulthood and that influence from the environment persists through early adulthood, another model of stability is indicated. Figure 2-2 depicts two models (Models D and E) that portray high levels of change in young adulthood, but with a growth in stability reaching a high level thereafter and leveling off through midlife. In Model D— *the impressionable years model*—stability remains relatively high throughout the remainder of the life span (Sears, 1981, 1983). This model represents what we take to be the most prominent view of the relationship between individual development and macrosocial change. The *impressionable years* model suggests that through late childhood and early adolescence, human characteristics are still quite malleable, with many experiencing increases in strength through early adult socialization, but with the potential for dramatic change still possible in late adolescence or early adulthood. However, once this period of early sorting and sifting is over, differences in individual characteristics are highly persistent throughout the life span. In Model E— *the midlife stability model*—by contrast, stability levels similarly reach a high level through midlife, but return to "youthful" levels in old age. During midlife people have a range of commitments—to a job, a marriage, a place of residence, to a set of organizational memberships— but when they move into old age they often find themselves in an altered set of social arrangements, due to retirement, death or change in their spouse, a changing residential location, and changing organizational commitments. These changes in social network ties may parallel the instability of relationships in youth and may consequently alter their beliefs, attitudes or values (see Alwin, Cohen, & Newcomb, 1991).

Two additional models of age-graded human stability depicted in Figure 2-2 portray processes of more or less linear (or at least monotonic) increases or decreases in human stability over time. The *aging stability* or *increasing persistence* model (see Model C in Figure 2-2) is critically different from the preceding two models, in that it posits continued changes over time in the level of stability. A final model (Model F) reverses the process of change by positing a process of *aging-instability* or *decreasing persistence*, a loosening up of behavioral tendencies over time.

The model *increasing persistence model* is quite common in many discussions of age and stability (e.g., Glenn, 1980; Lorence & Mortimer, 1985; Mortimer, Finch, & Murayama, 1988; Mortimer et al., 1982). Writing specifically about attitudes, Sears (1981), for example, suggested that with time an "affective mass" is developed in the attitude structure, making "change progressively more difficult with age" (pp. 186–187). Although we describe such a model as linear, it need not be so. Sears and his colleagues (Sears & Weber, 1988) suggest that political socialization may actually proceed in "fits and starts," reflecting a more jagged or steplike, relationship with time, but the net relationship between age and stability would be monotonically increasing. In a recent study of a nationally representative panel of youth, for example, Johnson (2001) found evidence of growing stability in job values during the transition to adulthood.

With regard to central beliefs or identities—such as "Who am I?" and "What do I most value?"—people are highly stable after a period of early socialization and the *impressionable years* model is probably the most applicable. For example, following their collegiate experiences the Bennington women just described were highly stable in their basic political identities over more than 50 years in their lives. Using data from Newcombs's 1960s follow-up study of the original Bennington women studied in the 1930s (Newcomb, Koenig, Flacks, & Warwick, 1967), and our 1984 follow up of the same group (Alwin, Cohen, & Newcomb, 1991), we found that political identities that had developed in young adulthood had gained considerable strength and continued with a rather high degree of persistence into old age. Similar results are reported by Sears and Funk (1990) in a longitudinal study of the political attitudes and identities held by a large sample of Americans originally recruited as children in the Terman Gifted Children Study. They studied two aspects of the self—political party identification and political ideology—measured at four times between 1940 and 1977. They found a high degree of stability in these dimensions across the 37-year period of the studies. Similarly, other studies of political identities using synthetic cohorts report a consistent set of findings, namely that stabilities in political identities are lowest in young adulthood and grow in magnitude to a very high level in midlife and remain relatively high throughout the life span (Alwin, Cohen, & Newcomb, 1991; Alwin & Krosnick, 1991).

Researchers find much less stability as they move away from studying those more cognitively central beliefs and dispositions toward those attitudes and opinions that lie on the surface of cognitive structure. Individuals change their beliefs and attitudes, often in response to major social movements and events. Substantial changes in beliefs and attitudes about sex-roles, for example, have been witnessed within cohorts over the past two decades in response to the women's movement and political events surrounding it. The same was true of changes in racial attitudes in response to the Civil Rights movement and its aftermath. Thus, while there may be unique influences occurring during people's youth that leave an indelible mark on their characteristic modes of thought and experience, this may not necessarily be true for more superficial expressions of those orientations which we find in their attitudes and opinions. Work on the life-span stability of beliefs, attitudes, and subjective self-assessments, suggests that such dimensions tend to follow the *midlife stability* pattern (Alwin & Krosnick, 1991; Krosnick & Alwin, 1989; Alwin, 2001).

Evidence for Cohort Replacement in Social Change

Are there cohort differences in people's basic beliefs and orientations that are attributable to the unique exposure to historical events? Major events like wars, depressions, technological change, and so forth, which affect everyone in the population are probably *not* going to be recognizable as cohort effects because they tend to affect everyone, not just the young. As noted earlier, we reserve the term "period effects" for the effects of change agents that have a more pervasive effect on society as a whole. Of course, if these events primarily affect the young, then we will presumably be able to detect their impact, and if the residues of their effects persist, we have the making of a cohort effect. There are some aspects of wars that only affect the young, since they are the ones that have to fight them, and certainly the economic orientations of young people growing up during periods of prosperity may be quite different than those of their elders. The point is that cohort effects stemming from historical events may be relatively difficult to isolate in the face of period influences, despite the presence of apparent effects on the most recent cohorts. The main problem confronting the cohort analyst, however, is that cohort is almost inextricably confounded with age in the kinds of data social scientists use to examine such matters (Campbell, Abolafia, & Maddox, 1985).

Despite these difficulties, cohort replacement has been offered as an explanation for social changes across a wide range of beliefs, attitudes, and behaviors, including the realms of politics, religion, family, race, gender, morality, and test scores, to name just a few. There is hardly any social phenomenon that has not been subject to the kind of generational theorizing that is the focus of this chapter, and the concept of "cohort" is arguably one of the most popular explanatory devices used in contemporary social research. Research and scholarship over the past few decades has debated the evidence for cohort replacement effects on a number of different topics, including church attendance (Alwin & McCammon, 2003; Chaves, 1989; Firebaugh & Harley, 1991; Greeley, 1989; Hout & Greeley, 1987), religious orientations (Roof, 1999), belief in an afterlife (Greeley & Hout, 1999), beliefs about abortion (Scott, 1998), sex role beliefs and attitudes (Alwin, 2002b; Alwin, Scott, & Braun, 1996; Alwin, 2002b; Brewster & Padavic, 2000; Mason & Lu, 1988; Neve, 1992, 1995; Scott, Alwin, & Braun, 1996), child-rearing values (Alwin, 1989, 1996c), co-residence beliefs (Alwin, 1996b), job satisfaction (Firebaugh & Harley, 1995), racial beliefs and prejudice (Firebaugh & Davis, 1988; Schuman et al., 1997), electoral behavior (Firebaugh & Chen, 1995), political partisanship (Alwin, 1992, 1998a, 1998b; Converse, 1976), post-materialism values (Inglehart, 1977, 1986, 1990), intergenerational obligations (Bengtson & Cutler, 1976; Rossi & Rossi, 1990), political tolerance (Davis, 1975; Stouffer, 1955), vocabulary knowledge (Alwin, 1991; Alwin & McCammon, 1999, 2001), mass media consumption (Glenn, 1994), heritability of some behaviors (Shanahan, Hofer, & Shanahan, this volume), autobiographical memories (Schuman & Scott, 1989; Schuman & Rieger, 1992; Schuman, Rieger, & Gaidys, 1994; Scott & Zac, 1993), and a range of family and demographic phenomena (Cherlin, 1992; Lesthaeghe, 1996; Modell, 1989). Despite the apparent extensiveness of this list, we are confident that this bibliographic reconnaissance merely skims the surface of the existing research terrain dealing with cohort replacement effects.

The most extensive effort to date to identify the presence of cohort effects and their impact on social change via cohort replacement is seen in the work of James Davis, the progenitor of the GSS (Davis, 1992, 1996). Analyzing social change primarily in terms of the liberal/conservative dimension underlying social attitudes, Davis has found a general trend in the liberal direction across cohorts—a broad shift he calls the "great 'liberal' shift since World War II". The aggregate shift, he argues, hides the dynamics of the cohort replacement phenomenon, because within cohorts Davis finds a "conservative trend between the early and late 1970s and a liberal 'rebound' in the 1980s". The cohort succession results in Davis's analysis point in the direction of a cumulative liberal cohort replacement contribution to the aggregate shift, and these patterns are largely consistent with results from the studies cited above on topics such as abortion, sex roles, racial attitudes, and the like.

As noted above, a major difficulty with any interpretation that lends support to the evidence for cohort replacement effects is that such results are almost always subject to alternative explanations. This stems from the complexity introduced by the age-period-cohort confounding mentioned above, owing to the fact that the interpretation of data potentially containing age, period, and cohort effects, must assume away at least one of these three influences to arrive at a conclusion (see the chapter by Glenn in this volume). In many instances, for example, the effects of aging on attitudes and beliefs are assumed to be nonexistent (or at least ignored). In this case the cohort replacement effects apparent cross-sectionally can more readily be interpreted as due to cohort effects (rather than age composition effects) and any intracohort trends then can be interpreted as period effects (see Alwin & Scott, 1996). Or, to take another example, if one is able to assume that period effects do not exist, then any observed intracohort shifts can be seen as due solely to aging, and given this, the cross-sectional data can then be rendered in such a way as to isolate cohort effects (see Alwin & McCammon, 1999, 2001). The point here is that while we may believe that there is a preponderance of evidence in support of cohort replacement effects, such interpretations usually come at the expense of some type of (usually unstated) assumption regarding the nature of age and/or period effects.

EVIDENCE FOR GENERATIONAL IDENTITIES

Earlier, we defined Generations as groups of people sharing a distinctive culture or identity by virtue of having experienced the same historical events at *approximately* the same time in their lives. As such, Generations are distinct historical phenomena, which do not map neatly to birth cohort, or even to a fixed number of birth cohorts. Unlike cohort, Generations do not enjoy a fixed metric that easily lends itself to statistical analysis. Rather, the distinction between Generations is a matter of quality, not degree, and the temporal location of their boundaries cannot be easily identified, particularly without the context of a set of particular analytic questions. Rosow (1978) suggests that incisive historical events may distinguish Generations, but that when such events "are soft and indistinct, (Generations) ... may be clearest at their centers, but blurred and fuzzy at the edges. They may remain so as long as transitional events are still gathering force, but a new (Generation) ... has not yet blossomed" (p. 69). Similarly, Mannheim (1952) suggests that distinctive Generations may fail to materialize for long periods of time should economic and social conditions remain stable, such that "largely static ... communities like the peasantry display no such phenomenon as new generation units sharply set off from their predecessors ... the tempo of change is so gradual that new generations evolve ... without any visible break" (Mannheim, 1952, p. 309).

Further complicating the study of Generations is the fact that they are not monolithic, homogenous groupings of all members of a set of birth cohorts, but instead are divided into what Mannheim called "generational units", the division of a Generation by social position and level of involvement in the events of the day. How these subgroupings are identified and understood is again contingent on the substantive questions at hand, as Generations do not exist in a vacuum, operating in the same way at all times for all members. Rather, like all good sociological variables, Generational experiences differ by social position and the corresponding differential experience of events based on those contexts. The Civil Rights movement in the United States was largely carried out by the youth of the era, and there are clear Generational identities associated with the movement, but the content of this identity obviously varies along geographic and racial dimensions. Similarly, the Vietnam War was a defining experience for the so-called Baby Boom generation, but the imprint of the war on identity for a conscientious objector who fled the country was vastly different than for his shared cohort counterpart that experienced the war as a soldier in Hanoi (Hagan, 2001). Both may have Generational identities linked to the war, but those identities are far from uniform. In contrast to cohorts, which have extremely broad coverage and precise boundaries, but lack specific explanations for the phenomena to which they are related, Generations lack specific boundaries and are meaningful in their distinctiveness largely as subpopulations, but offer the potential of being used as powerful explanations in and of themselves for distinctive patterns of attitudes, beliefs, and behaviors.

Given these distinctions between Generations and cohorts, what then is the basis of their interrelatedness, and how do we get from one to the other? White (1992), argues that, "Cohort can turn into (G)eneration only if there is some previous (G)eneration, and then only as previous (G)enerations—and the concerns they wrap around—are moved out of the way" (p. 32). Thus, Generations are frequently formed through identification with and participation in youth-based social movements that cohere around a particular event or the conditions left to them by a previous generation. While this seems a compelling enough mechanism for the formation of Generations, there is also the potential for Generational units to influence their cohort contemporaries in ways that may manifest themselves as cohort effects, or more importantly as period effects. The effects of the Civil Rights activists of the early 1960s on their contemporaries and the country as a whole provide an excellent example of this (see McAdam, 1988). Another example of this is when cohort experiences produce Generational units that lead to revolutions. The origins of the political events in the late 1950s in Cuba, for example, that embodied the formation of Castro's Revolutionary Generation and the fall of Batista's dictatorship can be seen in the youthful experiences of Castro and his contemporaries who grew up during a period of relative political democracy and economic stability (Zeitlin, 1967). At the same time, the social movement that formed the Revolutionary Government in 1959 and established several political changes, including the nationalization of industry and the declaration of a "socialist" regime, clearly had consequences that dramatically shaped the experiences of multiple sets of later cohorts.

In the end, we must concede that modern social science has done a better job of documenting, if not explaining, cohort replacement effects on social change than it has in articulating the historical moments that bring definition to Generational units in the sense of Mannheim, and in providing a meaningful set of methodological tools for understanding and demonstrating their importance.

CONCLUSIONS

Social scientists have long recognized the potential value of theories postulating the *succession of generations*, or what others call *cohort turnover*, in understanding the nature of social change. In this chapter we have reviewed the basic concepts that underlie this theory and have attempted to add some clarity to the discussion of the interpretive meaning of the concepts of *generations* and *cohorts*. In contrast to Kertzer (1983) we do not see the importance of phrasing the terminological distinction between generations and cohort as a zero-sum competition among historical theorists on the one hand and life course analysts on the other. The concept of generation is first and foremost a kinship term referring to discrete stages in the natural line of descent from a common ancestor, and we agree that this concept should not be confused either theoretically or operationally with the idea of cohort, which is normally used to refer to when one is born in historical time. Many have noted that the concept of generation as kinship location does not correspond in any neat manner to the historical process at the macro-social level because individuals differ in their rates of reproduction and because the temporal gap between generations is variable across families. At the same time we have argued that there is also room for more than one meaning of the term "generation", and the concept of Generation as used by Mannheim, Ortega y Gasset and their followers to refer to groups of people who share a distinctive culture and/or a self-conscious identity by virtue of their having experienced the same historical events at the same time is, sociologically speaking, of great importance. This notion of Generation is very different from the idea of cohort (recall that when used in this manner in the current essay we capitalize Generation). While cohort may be related to Generation in that they both refer to the location of individuals in historical time, this commonality does not make them equivalent. In using the concept of Generation in reference to social change and the historical process Mannheim and Ortega y Gasset were referring to much more than cohort effects. There may clearly be cohort effects in the absence of any subjective attachment to a social movement or an identification of the self with a particular era. We do not diminish the usefulness of the concept of cohort as a tool for understanding social change by insisting that it differs from Generation. Nor do we necessarily extol the concept of Generation by arguing, with Mannheim and Ortega y Gasset, that it involves much more than cohort effects. The value of either concept depends on the empirical evidence to support it.

This has meant that when we refer to cohort replacement as a mechanism of social change we mean something very different from generational replacement or Generational replacement. In the course of this discussion we have limited ourselves primarily to a consideration of the utility of a cohort replacement model of social change and have considered several elements of this model and the evidence that exists in support of them. While many of the pieces of this theoretical model seem to accord with the empirical world, there are many instances wherein the data are less clear-cut. We find some support for the idea that social change occurs at least in part through cohort replacement and that society changes in the direction of more recent cohorts. The analyst describing society at any given time will take cohort differences into account in coming up with an aggregate representation of society. However, cohorts differ in their size, and those largest cohorts will dominate the snapshot. But, if there are no major differences among cohorts (as in the example of *trust in government*), the cohort composition of society will hardly be of any consequence.

Where there are cohort differences that persist, however, we can expect that these will be reflected in social change. For example, by its sheer size alone the Baby Boom cohorts and their tendency toward liberal positions on a range of political and social issues would seem to be having major impacts on trends in political beliefs and behavior well into the next century, as a function of cohort replacement. But even here, with the passage of time the Baby Boom cohorts may not be all that distinctive (Alwin, 1998b). Whatever differences that may have formerly existed may not persist over time, due to the influences of historical factors and the potential effects of aging. In other words, some of the recent shifts toward political conservatism in American society may not be due to cohort differences and cohort replacement, but rather may be due to individual change or aging. This seems to be the case in the example showing that the Baby Boomers may be growing more conservative with age. This argues in favor of the alternative view: that members of particular cohorts or generations do not necessarily differ uniformly in their social experiences, that individuals are not particularly stable over their lives, and that social change results as much from aggregate changes within society, indeed within cohorts, via shifts in individual lives due either to aging or macrolevel historical (or period) effects.

Before we leave it at that, however, we should recognize that these matters are often more complex than they appear, and there is much more that can be said. As we argued above, it may be that the effects of age, cohort, and period factors may operate in countervailing ways. So yes, there may be cohort differences in social beliefs and attitudes that contribute to cohort replacement, but the within-cohort shifts are often just as great, and in some cases cancel out change due to cohort turnover. On balance, while there is relatively clear evidence for some contribution of cohort replacement to social change, the source of the underlying cohort effects is not always clear, and in many cases there is much more change that occurs within cohorts. Thus, while we find some support for the cohort replacement model of social change in some instances, there is also plenty of support for alternative views.

For all the attention in recent years to the historical influences on the life course, we find it surprising that most all of this work can be characterized by a unidirectional relationship between the individual and society. Traditionally in social psychology, it has often been assumed that there was a unidirectional pattern to socialization, with influences moving from the environment to the individual. Sociohistorical events and processes are often conceptualized within models of the life course in this way, as unidirectional influences on the lives of individuals (e.g., see Modell's [1989] commentary on Elder, 1975). This traditional framework legitimizes the study of cohort effects and cohort replacement, as embodying the historical influences on people at particular points in their life cycles. On the other hand, many now accept Bronfenbrenner's (1979) argument about reciprocal influences between the individual and his or her environment. Theories of socialization and the life course cannot ignore the ways in which individuals influence their environments—their societies—and are not simply passive recipients of culture (Alwin, 1995).

However desirable it might be to trace the reverse relationship, the impact of the individual on society, it is not all that straightforward. To do so students of the life course must step out of the unidirectional "box" that characterizes the majority of research on the life course and embrace the concept of *agency* as conceptualized in contemporary sociological theories (see Sewell, 1992). A move in this direction will perhaps bring them to the concept of Generations (in the sense of Mannheim) as an embodiment of cohorts as agents of social change. Rather than rejecting the idea of Generations because it does not map neatly to the concept of birth cohort or sets of birth cohorts or because it does not easily lend itself to statistical analysis, students of the life course can benefit from further research on Generations, as groups of people sharing a distinctive culture or identity who compete with others for dominance. We noted above that modern social science has done a better job of studying and documenting cohort replacement effects than it has of articulating and understanding the nature of Generation effects in the sense of Mannheim. Perhaps future life course research on cohorts and Generations will do a better job of demonstrating the importance of both cohort and Generational influences on society than has heretofore been the case.

ACKNOWLEDGMENTS: This research was supported in part by grant funds provided to the senior author from the National Institute on Aging (R01-AG04743-09). The authors wish to acknowledge the research assistance of David Klingel, Timothy Manning and Pauline Mitchell, and the valuable comments of Jeylan Mortimer and Michael Shanahan.

REFERENCES

Alwin, D. F. (1990). Cohort replacement and parental socialization values. *Journal of Marriage and the Family, 52,* 347–360.

Alwin, D. F. (1991). Family of origin and cohort differences in verbal ability. *American Sociological Review, 56,* 625–638.

Alwin, D. F. (1992). Aging, cohorts, and social change: An examination of the generational replacement model of social change. In H. A. Becker (Ed.), *Dynamics of cohort and generations research.* Amsterdam: Thesis.

Alwin, D. F. (1994). Aging, personality, and social change: The stability of individual differences over the adult life span. In D. L. Featherman, R. M. Lerner, & M. Perlmutter (Eds.), *Life-Span development and behavior,* vol. 12 (pp. 135–185). Hillsdale, NJ: Lawrence Erlbaum.

Alwin, D. F. (1995). Taking time seriously: Studying social change, social structure, and human lives. In P. Moen, G. H. Elder, Jr., & K. Lüscher (Eds.), *Examining lives in context: Perspectives on the ecology of human development* (pp. 211–262). Washington, DC: American Psychological Association.

Alwin, D. F. (1996a). Aging, social change and conservatism: The link between historical and biographical time in the study of political identities. In M. A. Hardy (Ed.), *Studying aging and social change: Conceptual and methodological issues* (pp. 164–190). Thousand Oaks, CA: SAGE Publications.

Alwin, D. F. (1996b). Co-Residence beliefs in American society—1973–1991. *Journal of Marriage and Family, 58,* 393–403.

Alwin, D. F. (1996c). Parental socialization in historical perspective. In C. Ryff & M. M. Seltzer (Eds.), *The parental experience at midlife* (pp. 105–167). Chicago: University of Chicago Press.

Alwin, D. F. (1998a). Aging, cohorts, and political change. Paper presented at the 93rd Annual Meeting of the American Sociological Association. San Francisco, CA. August.

Alwin, D. F. (1998b). The political impact of the baby boom: Are there persistent generational differences in political beliefs and behavior? *Generations, 22,* 46–54.

Alwin, D. F. (2001). Aging and the stability of social beliefs, attitudes and identities. Unpublished paper, Institute for Social Research, University of Michigan.

Alwin, D. F. (2002a). Generations X, Y and Z: Are they changing America? *Contexts, 1,* 42–51.

Alwin, D. F. (2002b). Social change in beliefs about sex roles: Cohort replacement versus intracohort change. Institute for Social Research, University of Michigan. Unpublished paper.

Alwin, D. F., Cohen, R. L., & Newcomb, T. M. (1991). *Political attitudes over the life span: The Bennington women after fifty years.* Madison: University of Wisconsin Press.

Alwin, D. F., & Krosnick, J. A. (1991). Aging, cohorts and stability of socio-political orientations over the life-span. *American Journal of Sociology, 97,* 169–195.

Alwin, D. F., & McCammon, R. J. (1999). Aging versus cohort interpretations of intercohort differences in GSS vocabulary scores. *American Sociological Review, 64,* 272–286.

Alwin, D. F., & McCammon, R. J. (2001). Aging, cohorts and verbal ability. *Journal of Gerontology: Social Sciences, 56B,* S151–S161.

Alwin, D. F., & McCammon, R. J. (2003). Aging, cohorts and religious participation. Manuscript in progress.

Alwin, D. F., McCammon, R. J., & Wray, L. A. (2000). Selection or socialization? The link between occupational position and intellectual functioning in adulthood. Paper presented at the annual meetings of the American Sociological Association, Washington, DC. August.

Alwin, D. F., & Scott, J. (1996). Attitude change: Its measurement and interpretation using longitudinal surveys. In B. Taylor & K. Thomson (Eds.), *Understanding change in social attitudes* (pp. 75–106). Brookfield, VT: Dartmouth.

Alwin, D. F., Scott, J., & Braun, M. (1996). *Sex-role attitude change in the United States: National trends and cross-national comparisons.* Paper presented at the biannual meetings of the Research Committee on Social Stratification of the International Sociological Association. Ann Arbor, MI. August.

Arbuckle, T. Y., Gold, D., & Andres. D. (1986). Cognitive functioning of older people in relation to social and personality variables. *Psychology and Aging, 1,* 55–62.

Ardelt, M. (2000). Still stable after all these years? Personality stability theory revisited. *Social Psychology Quarterly, 63,* 392–405.

Becker, H. A. (1992). *Dynamics of cohort and generations research*. Amsterdam: Thesis.

Bengtson, V. L. (1975). Generation and family effects in value socialization. *American Sociological Review, 40*, 358–371.

Bengtson, V. L., & Cutler. N. E. (1976). Generations and intergenerational relations: Perspectives on age groups and social change. In R. H. Binstock & E. Shanas (Eds.), *Handbook on aging and the social sciences* (pp. 130–159). New York: Van Nostrand Reinhold.

Bengtson, V. L., & Roberts, R. E. L. (1991). Intergenerational solidarity in aging families: An example of formal theory construction. *Journal of Marriage and the Family, 52*, 856–870.

Biblarz, T. J., Bengtson, V. L., & Bucur, A. (1996). Social mobility across three generations. *Journal of Marriage and the Family, 58*, 188–200.

Blau, P., & Duncan, O. D. (1967). *The American occupational structure*. New York: John Wiley.

Brewster, K. L., & Padavic, I. (2000). Change in gender-ideology, 1977–1996: The contributions of intracohort change and population turnover. *Journal of Marriage and the Family, 62*, 477–487.

Bronfenbrenner, U. (1979). *The ecology of human development*. Cambridge: Harvard University Press.

Campbell, R. T., Abolafia, J., & Maddox, G. (1985). Life-course analysis in social gerontology: Using replicated social surveys to study cohort differences. In A. S. Rossi (Ed.), *Gender and the life course* (pp. 301–318). New York: Aldine.

Chaves, M. (1989). Secularization and religious revival: Evidence from U.S. church attendance rates, 1972–1986. *Journal for the Scientific Study of Religion, 28*, 464–477.

Cherlin, A. J. (1992). *Marriage, divorce, remarriage*. Cambridge: Harvard University Press.

Clausen, J. A. (1986). *The life course: A sociological perspective*. Englewood Cliffs, NJ: Prentice-Hall.

Converse. (1976). *The dynamics of party support: Cohort analyzing party identification*. Beverly Hills, CA: Sage.

Costa, P. T., Jr., & McCrae, R. R. (1980). Still stable after all these years: Personality as a key to some issues in adulthood and old age. In P. B. Baltes & O. G. Brim, Jr. (Eds.). *Life-span development and behavior*, vol. 3 (pp. 65–102). New York: Academic Press.

Costa, P. T., Jr., & McCrae, R. R. (1994). Set like plaster? Evidence for the stability of adult personality. In T. F. Heatherton & J. L. Weinberger (Eds.), *Can personality change?* (pp. 21–40). Washington, DC: American Psychological Association.

Costa, P. T., Jr., McCrae, R. R., & Arenberg, D. (1980). Enduring dispositions in adult males. *Journal of Personality and Social Psychology, 38*, 793–800.

Costa, P. T., Jr., McCrae, R. R., & Arenberg, D. (1983). Recent longitudinal research on personality and aging. In K. W. Schaie (Ed.), *Longitudinal studies of adult psychological development* (pp. 222–263). New York: Guilford.

Davis, J. A. (1975). Communism, conformity, cohorts, and categories: American tolerance in 1954 and 1972–73. *American Journal of Sociology, 81*, 491–513.

Davis, J. A. (1992). Changeable weather in a cooling climate atop the liberal plateau: Conversion and replacement in forty-two general social survey items, 1972–1989. *Public Opinion Quarterly, 56*, 261–306.

Davis, J. A. (1996). Patterns of attitude change in the USA: 1972–1994. In B. Taylor & K. Thomson (Eds.), *Understanding change in social attitudes* (pp. 151–183). Brookfield, VT: Dartmouth.

Duncan, G. J., & Kalton, G. (1987). Issues of design and analysis of surveys across time. *International Statistical Review, 55*, 7–117.

Duncan, O. D. (1966). Methodological issues in the analysis of social mobility. In N. J. Smelser & S. M. Lipset (Eds.), *Social structure and mobility in economic development* (pp. 51–97). Chicago: Aldine Publishing Company.

Duncan, O. D. (1968). Social stratification and mobility: Problems in the measurement of trend. In E. B. Sheldon & W. E. Moore (Eds.), *Indicators of social change: Concepts and measurements* (pp. 675–719). New York: Russell Sage Foundation.

Easterlin, R. A. (1987). *Birth and fortune: The impact of numbers on personal welfare*. Chicago: University of Chicago Press.

Elder, G. H., Jr. (1974). *Children of the great depression*. Chicago: University of Chicago Press.

Elder, G. H., Jr. (1980). Adolescence in historical perspective. In J. Adelson (Ed.), *Handbook of adolescent psychology*. New York: John Wiley & Sons.

Elder, G. H., Jr., Caspi, A., & Burton, L. M. (1988). Adolescent transitions in developmental perspective: Sociological and historical insights. In M. Gunnar (Ed.), *Minnesota symposium on child psychology* (pp. 151–179). Hillsdale, NJ: Lawrence Erlbaum Associates.

Elder, G. H., Jr., Modell, J., & Parke, R. D. (Eds.) (1993). *Children in time and place*. Cambridge: Cambridge University Press.

Erikson, E. H.(1988). Youth: fidelity and diversity. *Daedalus, 117*, 1–24.

Featherman, D. L., & Hauser, R. M. (1978). *Opportunity and change*. New York: Academic Press.

Firebaugh, G. (1989). Methods for estimating cohort replacement effects. In C. C. Clogg (Ed.), *Sociological methodology 1989* (pp. 243–262). Oxford: Basil Blackwell.

Firebaugh, G. (1992). Where does social change come from? Estimating the relative contributions of individual change and population turnover. *Population Research and Policy Review, 11*, 1–20.

Firebaugh, G., & Chen, K. (1995). Vote turnout of nineteenth amendment women: The enduring effect of disenfranchisement. *American Journal of Sociology, 100*, 972–996.

Firebaugh, G., & Davis, K. E. (1988). Trends in anti-black prejudice, 1972–1984: Region and cohort effects. *American Journal of Sociology, 94*, 251–272.

Firebaugh, G., & Harley, B. (1991). Trends in U.S. church attendance: Secularization and revival, or merely lifecycle effects? *Journal for the Scientific Study of Religion, 30*, 487–500.

Firebaugh, G., & Harley, B. (1995). Trends in job satisfaction in the United States by race, gender, and type of occupation. *Research in the Sociology of Work, 5*, 87–104.

Gergen, K. J. (1980). The emerging crisis in life-span developmental theory. In P. B. Baltes & O. G. Brim, Jr. (Eds.), *Life-span development and behavior* (pp. 32–65). New York: Academic Press.

Glass, J., Bengtson, V. L., & Dunham, C. C. (1986). Attitude similarity in three-generation families: Socialization, status inheritance or reciprocal influence? *American Sociological Review, 51*, 685–698.

Glenn, N. D. (1980). Values, attitudes, and beliefs. In O. G. Brim, Jr., & J. Kagan (Eds.), *Constancy and change in human development* (pp. 596–640). Cambridge: Harvard University Press.

Glenn, N. D. (1994). Television watching, newspaper reading, and cohort differences in verbal ability. *Sociology of Education, 67*, 216–230.

Greeley, A. M. (1989). *Religious change in America*. Cambridge: Harvard University Press.

Greeley, A. M. & Hout, M. (1999). Americans' increasing belief in life after death: Religious competition and acculturation. *American Sociological Review, 64*, 813–835.

Hagen, J. (2001). *Northern passage: American Vietnam war resisters in Canada*. Cambridge: Harvard University Press.

Heatherton, T. F., & Weinberger, J. L. (Eds.). (1994). *Can personality change?* Washington, DC: American Psychological Association.

Hertzog, C., & Schaie, K. W. (1986). Stability and change in adult intelligence I. Analysis of longitudinal covariance structures. *Psychology and Aging, 1*, 159–171.

Hout, M., & Fischer, C. (2002). Americans with "no religion": Why their numbers are growing. *American Sociological Review, 67*, 165–190.

Hout, M., & Greeley, A. (1987). The center doesn't hold. *American Sociological Review, 52*, 325–345.

Inglehart, R. (1977). *The silent revolution: Changing values and political styles among western publics*. Princeton: Princeton University Press.

Inglehart, R. (1986). Intergenerational changes in politics and culture: The shift from materialist to postmaterialist value priorities. In R. G. Braungart & M. M. Braungart (Eds.), *Research in political sociology* (pp. 81–105). Greenwich, CT: JAI Press.

Inglehart, R. (1990). *Culture shift in advanced industrial society*. Princeton: Princeton University Press.

Inkeles, A. (1955). Social change and social character: The role of parental mediation. *Journal of Social Issues, 11*, 12–23.

Jennings, M. K., & Niemi, R. G. (1981). *Generations and politics: A panel study of young adults and their parents*. Princeton: Princeton University Press.

Johnson, M. K. (2001). Job values in the young adult transition: Change and stability with age. *Social Psychology Quarterly, 64*, 297–317.

Kertzer, D. I. (1983). Generation as a sociological problem. In R. H. Turner & J. F. Short, Jr. (Eds.), *Annual review of sociology* (pp. 125–149). Palo Alto, CA: Annual Reviews Inc.

Kett, J. F. (1977). *Rites of passage: Adolescence in America, 1790 to the present*. New York: Basic Books.

Kohn, M. L., & Schooler, C. (1978). The reciprocal effects of the substantive complexity of work and intellectual flexibility: A longitudinal assessment. *American Journal of Sociology, 84*, 24–52.

Krosnick, J. A., & Alwin, D. F. (1989). Aging and susceptibility to attitude change. *Journal of Personality and Social Psychology, 57*, 416–425.

Lesthaeghe, R. (1996). The second demographic transition in western countries: An interpretation. In K. O. Mason & Jensen, A-M. (Eds.), *Gender and family change in industrialized countries* (pp. 18–62). Oxford: Clarendon Press.

Lorence, J., & Mortimer, Jeylan T. (1985). Job involvement through the life course: A panel study of three age groups. *American Sociological Review, 50*, 618–638.

Mannheim, K. (1952). The problem of generations. In P. Kecskemeti (Ed.), *Essays in the sociology of knowledge* (pp. 276–322). Boston: Routledge & Kegan Paul. (Original work published in 1927.)

Mason, K. O. & Lu, Y-H. (1988). Attitudes toward women's familial roles: Changes in the United States 1977–1985. *Gender and Society, 2,* 39–57.

Mason, W. M., & Fienberg, S. E. (1985). *Cohort analysis in social research: Beyond the identification problem.* New York: Springer-Verlag.

McAdam, D. (1988). *Freedom summer.* New York: Oxford University Press.

Modell, J. (1989). *Into one's own.* Berkeley: University of California Press.

Mortimer, J. T., Finch, M. D., & Kumka, D. (1982). Persistence and change in development: The multidimensional self-concept. In P. B. Baltes & O. G. Brim, Jr. (Eds.), *Life-span development and behavior* (vol. 4, pp. 263–313) New York: Academic Press.

Mortimer, J. T., Finch, M. D., & Kumka, D. (1985). Work experience and job satisfaction: Variation by age and gender. In J. T. Mortimer & K. M. Borman (Eds.), *Work experience and psychological development through the life span.* Boulder, CO: Westview Press.

Murnane, R. J., & Levy, F. (1993). Why today's high-school-educated males earn less than their fathers did: The problem and an assessment of responses. *Harvard Educational Review, 63,* 1–19.

Musgrove, F. (1977). *Margins of the mind.* London: Methuen & Co. Ltd.

Nesselroade, J. R., & Baltes, P. B. (1974). Adolescent personality development and historical change, 1970–1972. *Monographs of the Society for Research in Child Development, 39*(1, Serial No. 54).

Neve, R. (1992). Developments in the attitudes towards women's emancipation in the Netherlands from 1970 to 1985: A cohort analysis. In H. A. Becker (Ed.), *Dynamics of cohort and generations research* (pp. 621–640). Amsterdam: Thesis.

Neve, R. (1995). Changes in attitudes toward women's emancipation in the Netherlands over two decades: Unraveling a trend. *Social Science Research, 24,* 167–187.

Newcomb, T. M. (1943). *Personality and social change: Attitude formation in a student community.* New York: Dryden Press.

Newcomb, T. M., Koenig, K. E., Flacks, R., & Warwick, D. P. (1967). *Persistence and change: Bennington College and its students after 25 years.* New York: John Wiley & Sons.

Ortega y Gasset, J. (1933). *The modern theme.* New York: Norton.

Pampel, F. C. (1993). Relative cohort size and fertility: The socio-political context of the Easterlin effect. *American Sociological Review, 58,* 496–514.

Putnam, R. D. (2000). *Bowling alone: The collapse and revival of American community.* New York: Simon & Schuster.

Riley, M. W. (1973). Aging and cohort succession: Interpretations and misinterpretations. *Public Opinion Quarterly, 37,* 774–787.

Riley, M. W., & Riley, J. W., Jr. (1996). Generational relations: A future perspective. In T. Hareven (Ed.), *Aging and generational relations: Life course and cross-cultural perspectives* (pp. 283–291). New York: Aldine de Gruyter.

Rodgers, W. L. (1990). Interpreting the components of time trends. In C. C. Clogg (Ed.), *Sociological methodology 1990.* Oxford: Basil Blackwell.

Roof, W. C. (1999). *Spiritual marketplace: Baby boomers and the remaking of American religion.* Princeton: Princeton University Press.

Roscow, I. (1978). What is a cohort and why? *Human Development, 21,* 65–75.

Rossi, A. S., & Rossi, P. H. (1990). *Of human bonding: Parent–child relations across the life course.* New York: Aldine de Gruyter.

Rubin, D. C. (1999). Autobiographical memory and aging: Distributions of memories across the life-span and their implications for survey research. In N. Schwarz, D. Park, B. Knäuper, & S. Sudman (Eds.), *Cognition, aging, and self-reports* (pp. 163–183). Washington, DC: Taylor & Francis.

Ryder, N. B. (1965). The cohort as a concept in the study of social change. *American Sociological Review, 30,* 843–861.

Schaie, K. W. (1996). *Intellectual development in adulthood: The Seattle longitudinal study.* New York: Cambridge University Press.

Schuman, H., & Rieger, C. (1992). Historical analogies, generational effects, and attitudes towards war. *American Sociological Review, 57,* 315–326.

Schuman, H., Reiger, C., & Gaidys, V. (1994). Collective memories in the United States and Lithuania. In N. Schwarz & S. Sudman (Eds.), *Autobiographical memory and the validity of retrospective reports.* New York: Springer-Verlag.

Schuman, H., & Scott, J. (1989). Generations and collective memories. *American Sociological Review, 54,* 359–381.

Schuman, H., Steeh, C., Bobo, L., & Krysan, M. (1997). *Racial attitudes in America: Trends and interpretations.* Cambridge: Harvard University Press.

Scott, J. (1998). Generational changes in attitudes to abortion: A cross-national comparison. *European Sociological Review, 14*, 177–190.

Scott, J., & Zac, L. (1993). Collective memories in the United States and Britain. *Public Opinion Quarterly, 57*, 315–331.

Scott, J., Alwin, D. F., & Braun, M. (1996). Generational changes in gender role attitudes: Britain in cross national perspective. *Sociology, 30*, 471–492.

Sears, D. O. (1981). Life-stage effects on attitude change, especially among the elderly. In S. B. Kiesler, J. N. Morgan, & V. K. Oppenheimer (Eds.), *Aging: Social change*. New York: Academic Press.

Sears, D. O. (1983). On the persistence of early political predispositions: The roles of attitude object and life stage. *Review of Personality and Social Psychology, 4*, 79–116.

Sears, D. O., & Funk, C.L. (1990). The persistence and crystallization of political attitudes over the life-span: The Terman gifted children panel. Unpublished manuscript, University of California, Los Angeles.

Sears, D. O., & Weber, J. P. (1988). Presidential campaigns as agents of preadult political socialization. Paper presented at the 11th annual meetings of the International Society of Political Psychology. Meadowlands, NJ. July.

Sewell, W. H., Jr. (1992). A theory of structure: Duality, agency, and transformation. *American Journal of Sociology, 98*, 1–29.

Shanahan, M. J. (2000). Adolescence. In E. F. Borgatta & Montgomery, R. J. V. (Eds.), *Encyclopedia of sociology* (2nd ed., pp. 1–18). New York: Macmillan Reference USA.

Stouffer, S. A. (1955). *Communism, conformity, and civil liberties*. Garden City, NY: Doubleday.

White, H. (1992). Succession and generations: Looking back on chains of opportunity. In H. A. Becker (Ed.), *Dynamics of cohort and generations research* (pp. 31–51). Amsterdam: Thesis.

Zeitlin, M. (1967). *Revolutionary politics and the Cuban working class*. Princeton: Princeton University Press.

CHAPTER 3

Stratified Incentives and Life Course Behaviors

TAKEHIKO KARIYA

JAMES E. ROSENBAUM

INTRODUCTION

Psychologists have observed that American adolescents often have difficulty committing themselves to efforts either in school or in other activities (Erikson, 1963; Keniston, 1970). While Erikson and Keniston recognize that this lack of commitment arises due to psychological, interpersonal, cultural, economic, and social factors, psychologists usually focus on intrapsychic processes. For instance, a textbook identifies "identity disorder" as one source of low achievement in late adolescence, recommends psychotherapeutic techniques to address the internal disorder, and does not even consider the possible influence of external social context on these behaviors (Mandel & Marcus, 1988, p. 299). Another psychologist says that adolescents lack "career maturity," which makes them unwilling to work hard in school for the sake of their future careers (Crites, 1976). Psychologists are not the only ones to make such inferences. In the 1980s, labor economists sometimes explained youths' job turnover by saying that some youth are unstable and immature (Osterman, 1980). Practitioners often make such inferences. In interviews in the 1990s, we have heard high school teachers and counselors say that adolescents are "present oriented," cannot defer gratification, and will not work hard in school for future benefits. One guidance counselor reported, "these kids cannot plan beyond next Saturday night's date." In many of these accounts, the problem is inside students, and it comes from the adolescent life stage. These interpretations rarely mention social context.

TAKEHIKO KARIYA • University of Tokyo, Tokyo, Japan.   JAMES E. ROSENBAUM • Department of Education and Social Policy, Northwestern University, Evanston, Illinois 60208-2610.
Handbook of the Life Course, edited by Jeylan T. Mortimer and Michael J. Shanahan. Kluwer Academic/Plenum Publishers, New York, 2003.

Lifespan theorists are divided about the influence of social context in the life course. Dannefer (1992) identified four ways that social context has been conceptualized in life course research.

1. *Functionally unimportant.*   Some theorists have proposed models in which social context is largely irrelevant. For example, although Levinson et al. (1978) pay lip service to the important influence of social context, they describe stages and sequences of adult development that are universal across cultures and historical periods. They even assert that age timetables exist which do not vary across different contexts. As a result, context is in effect irrelevant and adult development stages are "not subject to environmental shaping except at the pathological extremes" (Dannefer, 1992, p. 86).

2. *Powerful, but random.*   Other theorists suggest that social context has large influences, but its effects are random. For instance, Baltes contends that the life course is affected by non-normative influences, "determinants that, although significant in their effect on individual life histories, are not general. They do not occur for everyone nor do they necessarily occur in easily discernible and invariant sequences or patterns" (Baltes, 1983, p. 95). In this formulation, "non-normative influences include migration, career changes, unemployment, divorce, and 'unexpected' changes in health" (Dannefer, 1992, p. 87). When psychologists view individuals in a therapeutic session or in a university laboratory, the influence of context may seem random. Although psychologists may view these events as unexplained by their models, Dannefer (1992, p. 87) suggests that they are not "inexplicable in their origins when viewed from other perspectives, such as sociology or epidemiology."

3. *Organized, but static.*   Bronfenbrenner (1979) provides extensive discussion of contextual influences on development at the micro-, meso-, macro-, and exo-systems levels. He stresses the importance of looking at settings and environments, which may be damaging to the child under certain conditions. He emphasizes the interaction of levels, the ways that interpersonal supports affect individuals' coping with new organizations. Bronfenbrenner (1979) and Magnusson and Allen (1983) have provided descriptive topologies of various aspects of social context, but they tend to miss the dynamic aspects, and they do not explain the process of change of direction or trend. Generalities can be inferred based on observations, but they have an ad hoc character, without suggesting an underlying mechanism. Prediction is possible based on prior observations of existing trends, but the behavioral consequences of policies that represent radical changes are not included in these analyses.

4. *Systematically organized and dynamic.*   In this view, context is viewed as "not only a powerful organizer of individual developmental patterns, but also as consisting of processes that are themselves organized: self-generating and self-perpetuating in systematic ways" (Dannefer, 1992, p. 91). Some prior work has incorporated this perspective. "Within the systems conception, context shifts from the status of a static independent variable to a structured, interactive set of relations. Human development, then, is not just influenced by environment but is caught in these extended networks of relations, which systematically provide messages about what developmental outcomes are to be valued, and which supply specific, and sometimes limited, resources for development to individuals" (Dannefer, 1992, p. 91).

This fourth level poses a difficult challenge. While empirical analyses can describe the correspondence between social policy and observable behaviors, it is difficult to discern underlying social processes and mechanisms which create the correspondence. Moreover, under most circumstances, the researcher is observing social processes that are not changing or are changing very slowly, so the cause of behavioral change is difficult to attribute to specific social actions.

Indeed, at a more basic level, it is even difficult to comprehend the distinctive qualities of social policies and individual behaviors in a single context. The impact of social policies is best seen in comparative perspective. "International comparisons challenge our assumptions about what is universal, natural, and inevitable. Looking at another country's customs and institutions puts our own in a new light, extending our vision of what is possible and desirable" (Hamilton, 1986).

Although the study of American adolescents comes in the context of American society, a different society might show different patterns. In addition, there is a great deal of stratification within societies, and adolescents at different strata may face different circumstances and respond differently. Moreover, if society radically changed over a relatively short time span, then adolescent behaviors within that society might also change in ways observable to research.

DO ADOLESCENT EFFORTS CHANGE
WHEN SOCIAL CONTEXT CHANGES
THEIR INCENTIVES?

This chapter seeks to understand the determinants of adolescents' school efforts by examining the recent reforms of the social context in Japan. During the period under study, Japanese society underwent dramatic reforms in a relatively short period of time, radically changing students' incentives for school effort. This study focuses on the ways these reforms affected students' incentives, the ways that students' school efforts changed over this time period, and the differential pattern of changes for different groups of students.

In addition, like Dannefer's fourth model, we argue that these adolescent behaviors could arise from properties of social context. We find that the above-noted problem of adolescent underachievement is largely absent in pre-reform Japan, but it appears after a change of social context created by drastic reforms.

We present a new model. The stratified-incentive model contends that societal institutions create patterns of incentives that affect adolescents' behaviors, and different positions in a school social hierarchy offer different incentives to the individuals in these different positions. Many commonly observed properties of the adolescent life stage could be explained as the result of the incentives offered by societal institutions like colleges and the labor market. Differences in adolescents' behaviors could be explained by the incentive structure of the institutions for which they are being prepared, and may not be due to individual attributes (Rosenbaum, 1991).

Specifically, we contend that youths with different levels of school achievement are directed to different societal goals (colleges or jobs), and the college and job structure of society defines the incentives for high school youth. While adolescents appear to differ in internal motivation, youth who face contexts which offer high incentives will see reasons to exert effort, they will have many experiences of exerting effort, and they may develop more capacity to exert effort. In contrast, youth who face low incentives will exert little effort and have little reason to develop motivational capacity.

Moreover, these various college and job goals can pose high or low incentives, depending on social context, and social policies that change the social context can also change the incentives for these goals. Unlike United States, pre-reform Japan created a context where all students had strong incentives for effort to attain their goals. More recently, Japan's reforms created a situation more like that in the United States, such that those who aspire to selective colleges faced high incentives, and others faced low incentives. We shall examine whether and how students' efforts changed over the period when these contextual changes were occurring.

This model leads to three hypotheses. First, if a society offers a different pattern of incentives than the United States, adolescents in that society will exhibit quite different behaviors. Second, if different positions of a school social hierarchy offer different incentives, students in those positions will behave differently. Third, if a society changes the incentives for a group of adolescents, then adolescent behaviors will change accordingly.

Japan is a good place to study these hypotheses. First, in the late 1970s, Japan offered a different pattern of incentives than the United States (Rosenbaum & Kariya, 1991). Like youth in the United States, university-bound students in Japan had strong incentives for increasing their school achievement. However, unlike work-bound youth in the United States, who get no benefit in the labor market for improved academic achievement, Japanese work-bound students got clear benefits from improved academic achievement.

However, the Japanese social structure changed very rapidly over the past two decades. In the earlier period, Japan presented strong incentives for all youth, in marked contrast with the American pattern where stong incentives were offered only by selective colleges. In the later period, Japan quickly shifted to the American pattern of stratified incentives.

This feature of the Japanese situation is particularly important for our study of the life course model. In less than two decades, Japan self-consciously initiated extensive choice-based reforms. As we shall show, while Japan initially presented a unified incentive structure (strong incentives to all adolescents), its new institutional arrangements offered stratified incentives, with a radically different level of incentives offered to students depending on their prior high school achievement. Did this radical change from unified to stratified incentives affect adolescent behavior, or did these changes fail to have any systematic impact?

This chapter begins by describing the theoretical importance of effort. Then we describe pre- and post-reform policies and practices, and the way Japan shifted from offering all ado-lescents similar incentives to only offering high incentives to youth in a position to compete for top universities. We then present empirical analyses which show the effects of these reforms on adolescents' behaviors. Comparing youths' behaviors in 1979 and 1997, we find dramatic declines in the academic efforts of most students, but little decline for top students. The reforms reduce the incentives for effort for most students, but not for students aspiring to top universities (the ones actually affected by "exam hell" who were the initial reason for the reforms).

The reforms create stratified incentives, where the top students still have strong incentives and they still work hard, while others have weak incentives and work much less or not at all. The result was a dramatic change in their behaviors. The reforms thus created another form of inequality: students responded quite differently, depending on the rank of their school and the incentives it offered.

As a result, adolescent achievement and underachievement, which are commonly considered "life stage" phenomena, change in ways that are related to the incentives created by the social context and its reforms. This chapter deals with important questions regarding the interrelations of culture, history, social institutions, and human agency. Cross-cultural and historical data allow us to examine differences in adolescents' strategies of attainment as they encounter different opportunities and incentives, which are variable across time and amenable to intervention. In so doing, we seek to contribute to a large body of research that examines the structure of educational systems and their impact on young people in various nations (Hallinan, 2000; Shavit & Mueller, 1998). This chapter identifies key features of educational systems that influence students' actions.

BACKGROUND

How can society engage large portions of youth in productive activities, and do social policies affect the amount and distribution of youths' efforts? To persist into a new generation, society must engage youths' efforts toward societal goals (Durkheim, 1912), and the disengagement of large portions of youth is a real threat to society and to youths' own prospects, especially for low-achieving or low-SES youths.

This study examines the stratification of individuals' school efforts. While status attainment models incorporate social psychological factors, they often ignore students' efforts (Heyns, 1978; Jencks et al., 1979; Sewell, 1971; however, see Jencks et al., 1979). While aspirations are assumed to increase effort (Sewell & Hauser, 1975; Rosenfeld & Hearn, 1982; Velez, 1985), many youth with high aspirations exert little effort (Rosenbaum, 1998; 2001; Steinberg, 1996; Stevenson & Stigler, 1992). Ethnographic researchers have noted social influences on youths' efforts at pursuing societal goals, particularly for working-class (Willis, 1977) and minority youths (Fordham & Ogbu, 1986). Merton (1957) and Stinchcombe (1965) propose a more institutional approach, suggesting that rebellion occurs if youth, who desire society's goals, believe that society's means will not help them gain those goals.

Is there a society where low-achieving students do not become disengaged from schools? Is there a society where, contrary to Willis's findings, manual workers' children continue to exert effort in school through their high school years? Moreover, if such a society exists, what institutional conditions make that happen? Can we identify conditions which, when altered, lead to observable changes in youths' efforts? How does the distribution of efforts change and which kinds of youth experience the most change? As we shall see, Japan provides a pertinent case.

JAPANESE UNIFIED
INCENTIVE MERITOCRACY

Japan has a penchant for taking Western ideas more seriously than the West, and doing them more thoroughly. This is a study of Japan's initial implementation of the meritocratic ideal and subsequent implementation of choice-based ideals. Both ideals are very salient in British and American norms (cf. Halsey, 1977; Jencks & Phillips, 1998; Young, 1958). We rarely get to see our intellectual ideals so thoroughly implemented as Japan did, especially ideals as demanding as meritocracy and choice.

Moreover, because Japan later implemented American-style "choice" reforms to soften its meritocracy, the results of Japan's reforms point to possible causal influences. Similar reforms were implemented in the United States over the course of 80 years, so it is hard to identify their effects, but, in Japan, it took less than ten years to implement these reforms. This study of Japan may give us a better understanding of American practices and their potential effects.

Until 1987, Japan was very meritocratic. A single merit criterion, academic achievement, based on the national curriculum and measured on objective exams, was the only factor used for admitting youth to different ranks of public high schools or colleges. Unlike the American situation where nearly all high school seniors aspired to college (Rosenbaum, 1998; Schneider & Stevenson, 1999), Japanese youth often planned to take jobs after high school. Unlike the American situation where many ambitious young people do not see what actions they can take to improve their future careers (Schneider & Stevenson, 1999), Japanese youth know that school effort is an effective activity regardless of their career goals.

This meritocracy provided conditions for motivating a large portion of youth. Japanese college-bound students had strong incentives for school achievement. University admission was based solely on examinations testing achievement on the school curriculum (not aptitude or any other factor). Moreover, even non-college youth had strong incentives for school achievement. In Japan, high schools have relationships with employers, and they strongly influence job hiring (Rosenbaum & Kariya, 1989, 1991). High schools nominate students for jobs based solely on students' academic achievement, and employers generally hire nominated students. Thus, even for low-achieving students, small increases in achievement lead to better jobs.

In this period, most Japanese students exerted considerable effort in high school, vastly more effort than their counterparts in the United States. Indeed, manual workers' children did much more homework than the average American student. While many observers have attributed these behaviors to Japanese culture (Rohlen, 1983; Okano, 1993), we will show that Japanese institutional arrangements are a potential explanation (Ishida, 1993; LeTendre, 1996). Institutional arrangements provide clear attainable incentives to students at every portion of the achievement distribution to increase their school achievement, both for college-bound and work-bound youth. While the effects of these incentives cannot be proven in the early era, we show how youths' efforts changed when these incentives were weakened by reforms, and, in the process, provide an explanation for recent research findings (Brinton, 1998, 2000).

Japan's system was uncompromisingly dedicated to this one dimension, which made it ruthlessly severe but also unwaveringly fair. Japan has a very stratified school structure. While American high schools stratify students in different tracks in the same school based upon multiple criteria, Japanese high schools are ranked in about four or five different levels in a school district, which are totally determined by students' academic achievement on an achievement test taken in ninth grade.

Similarly, achievement is the only determinant in university admissions. Thus, rich students from expensive private high schools frequently score below the best working-class students from public schools, and poor-achieving rich students do not attend the top Japanese universities, but high-achieving low-income students do. Social background correlates with college admissions and jobs, but the SES influence is mediated by academic achievement, as we shall see later. Even fame does not override insufficient achievement—a very popular baseball star with fairly high test scores was not admitted when he applied to one of the best private universities.*

Not only did Japan's meritocracy create clear incentives, but it also told students that their efforts determine their success. Success was under their own control. Young (1958) notes the risk that meritocracy can become an inherited IQ aristocracy where children quickly become resigned to their inherited limitations. Japan avoids this pitfall with strong beliefs that people do not differ in ability and that ability is not a major influence on achievement. In Japan, effort is nearly everything—the main determinant of achievement. Thus, better colleges and jobs are equally available to all who strive for them; it is widely believed that effort, not ability, determines who is selected. Students regularly take practice tests, and, if their scores fall short of what is required for their academic plans, teachers, parents, and students believe that insufficient effort is the cause, and students are told they must work harder (Kariya & Rosenbaum, 1987). While American children quickly get the message that they

---

*The strongest effects of SES came through Japan's private high schools, but our sample studies only public schools.

should give up because they lack the ability to do well enough, Japanese children are told that everyone has the ability, and low achievement only indicates that more effort is required (Stevenson and Stigler, 1992).

Japan's meritocratic system was ideally suited to encourage school effort of a large portion of youth. In 1980, a year after our initial data collection, 43% of American 17-year-olds did no homework on an average school night (NAEP, 1985), but only 22% of our Japanese students did no homework. While 67% of American 17-year-olds devoted less than one hour a night to homework (NAEP, 1985), only 43.1% of our Japanese 17-year-olds did so. Indeed, the average student in our sample spent 97 min a night on homework in 1979. Moreover, Americans would do much worse in weekly comparisons, for while the daily homework time for Americans is multiplied by 5 school days a week, Japan's is multiplied by 6 school days a week.

The result was high achievement. In the 1980s, Japan had among the highest-achieving youth in the world. While American youth trailed near the bottom of developed nations on tests of math and science, Japan was at or near the top in most comparisons for most age groups (Lynn, 1988, ch. 2; Stevenson & Stigler, 1992). This was true for 18-year-olds (where Japan had a higher percent of the cohort enrolled in school than every nation except the United States), and for 13-year-olds (Lynn, 1988, p. 7). Indeed, in national comparisons of all math "majors" (students whose curriculum emphasizes math), non-math majors, top 4% of math "majors," and top 3% of non-math "majors," Japanese 18-year-olds were at or near the top (Husen, 1967 cited in Lynn, 1988, p. 7).

JAPAN'S CHOICE-BASED REFORMS

Although Japan's meritocracy was widely accepted in the four decades after World War II, its disadvantages became increasingly apparent. Newspaper stories and governmental policy papers frequently noted three problems in their meritocratic system—pressures, narrowness, and inequality.

The high pressures were one of the most obvious behavioral costs. Newspapers reported stories of 10-year-old children taking the subway home from after-school schools (juku) after dark and stressed adolescents getting little sleep because they worked long hours every night on homework. Such stories were repeated in government reports and legislative deliberations. The years before students took college entrance exams were called "exam hell," and students' lack of sleep and mental distress were frequently mentioned by policymakers.

Moreover, these pressures were believed to narrow students' experiences, to prevent them from developing social, personal, and other skills, and to reduce their creativity. "Creativity," while never defined, was viewed as suffering from a single-minded pursuit of schoolwork and the one-dimensional focus on academics.

Finally, these one-dimensional pressures were believed to increase inequalities among students. To the democratic sensibilities of post-war Japan, the one-dimensional hierarchy based on test scores was disturbing. Since tests were the sole basis for placing students into different levels of high schools and universities, tests made inequalities more salient and thus were disturbing. In addition, tests were blamed for accentuating inequalities by forcing students to be ranked on achievement in general, rather than considering each on his or her own areas of strength.

"Choice" was believed to be the solution to these problems. Youths' pressures, narrow focus, lack of creativity, and inequalities were diagnosed as having been caused by the lack of choice in

Japan's system. It was believed that Japan's selection system could be repaired by a few minor reforms to increase student choice, without altering its essential meritocratic character.

Reforms were proposed and quickly implemented. To Americans used to seeing school reform done at the local or state level in a slow and cumbersome process, seeing massive school reform implemented in Japan's centralized educational system is a wonder to behold. Three kinds of choice-based reforms were quickly implemented to increase students' latitude of choice about how to spend their time and what skill areas to stress.

1. *Instruction responsive to students' interests.* To give students more choice about their learning, teachers were directed to make instruction more responsive to students' interests. While instruction in 1979 was nearly entirely focused on textbooks and lectures, a 1996 survey of elementary school teachers found strong emphasis on including students' experience (64%), students' presentations (57%), letting students do research (45%), and group activity (44%), and low emphasis on textbooks (14%), and lectures (1%) (Benesse Educational Research Center 1999).

2. *Reduced demands on students.* To give students more choice about their activities and areas of skill, teachers were directed to reduce their demands on students, to slow the pace of instruction, and to give less homework. Moreover, in the highly centralized educational system in Japan, other steps were easily taken. In the mid-1990s, the Ministry of Education decreased the number of school days, deleting two Saturdays every month (attendance had formerly included all Saturdays). The Ministry of Education, which determined the curriculum in every school in the nation, reduced the number of required subjects in the curriculum, so the number of credits for a diploma declined from 85 to 80 after 1981. The national curriculum also reduced the number of topics covered in subjects. Thus, in 1979, virtually all high school students took physics, geology, political economy, and geography, but by 1997, less than 60% of students took these courses (Arai, 2000). Consistent with this, colleges were directed to reduce entrance requirements. Even the top universities in the nation, which formerly required students to pass entrance exams in 7 subjects in 1979, now only required 5 subjects or less. Other colleges had lower requirements, which they reduced further.

3. *Multiple criteria.* To increase students' choices about their areas of skills, colleges were directed to decide admissions on multiple criteria, so that low achievement in one area could be offset by high achievement in another. In addition, besides academic achievement, college should consider school recommendations, which would allow colleges to recognize other kinds of achievement and personal qualities. Teachers' comments about personality, and participation and leadership in activities became criteria. College essays could also offset somewhat deficient academic achievement. Students could choose whether to emphasize hobbies, artistic endeavors, or personal charm to counterbalance mediocre grades, and, in many colleges, they could avoid math exams if they found that a difficult area.

4. *Making college an option for more students.* Besides reducing requirements, colleges also were urged to provide programs for new kinds of students who previously would have been excluded. New programs were initiated to allow the admission of students from vocational and other low-ranking high schools. The new variety of programs was accompanied by increased number of slots. The Ministry of Education, which controls the number of admissions slots in every university in the nation (including most private universities which receive national funds), drastically increased the number of slots, from 377,468 in 1975, to 607,575 in 1990, to 711,345 in 1997. In the decade since 1990, when the number of young people was declining in Japan, when there was a 15% decline in the number of high school graduates (from 1,767,000 to 1,504,000), an increased portion of all Japanese young people

could attend college. Thus, acceptance rates to 4-year colleges dramatically increased from 55.5% to 77.9%, while the 2-year college's rate increased from 86.0% to 96.7%. College became an option for many more students.

These reforms dramatically reduced college-bound students' incentives for school achievement. The multiple criteria for college admissions meant that if one had difficulty achieving in one or several academic areas (say math or science), one no longer had to exert effort in that area, because it was no longer a barrier to college. In addition, the large increases in college attendance (as the number of young people was declining), dramatically increased acceptance rates. Teachers' responsiveness to students' interests and reduced demands made school easier and reduced the need for effort on unpleasant assignments.

In turn, these reforms also reduced the incentives for "work-bound students". First, two of the reforms transformed some students who formerly would have been "work-bound" into college-bound students. The multiple criteria for college admissions and increasing the availability of college meant that some former "work-bound" students (formerly excluded from considering college) could now attend college. Second, the other two reforms (instruction responsive to students' interests and reduced demands) reduced the need for effort on unpleasant assignments for all students, regardless of plans. Third, changes in the job world led to reduced incentives for work-bound students. After the college admissions reforms, only the lowest achieving high school graduates sought jobs right after high school. In response, employers reported (to high school placement staff) that high school graduates could no longer handle white-collar jobs, and they raised the credential requirements for white-collar jobs. They no longer hired high school graduates for these jobs, but instead recruited college graduates for these jobs. The jobs available to high school graduates became more homogeneously undemanding, and they offered few incentives (Tsutsui & Miki, 2001).

While Americans often view Japanese youth as "workaholics", genetically or culturally driven to overwork from an early age (or at birth), Stinchcombe's model suggests the possibility that the impetus for Japanese hard work was in the social structure and its strong incentives. If reforms weakened these incentives, Stinchcombe's model would suggest that students' behaviors might change. Other studies have noted the factors encouraging student effort in Japan's high schools of the earlier period (Rohlen, 1983), and recent research has noted students' poor motivation in the lowest rank high schools in the recent era (Brinton, 1998). However, the present study is distinctive in having systematic survey data on a large number of comparable students from the same broad range of high schools studied in two periods, so this study can conduct comparable analyses which help elucidate the changes that have occurred.

The reformers hoped that these reforms would lead to many desirable outcomes. They hoped that multiple criteria would encourage top students to reduce their excessively narrow focus on the pursuit of academic achievement and to broaden to other activities. At the same time, they hoped the reforms would encourage lower achieving students to work harder in school since they could gain recognition from areas in which they were stronger and more interested. Moreover, if reforms reduced the intense pressures on top students so they stopped spending absurdly long hours on homework, they would become more like other students, and social and achievement inequalities might decline.

The reformers' expectations can be stated succinctly.

1. Reforms will reduce excessive amounts of homework time while raising the efforts of the least engaged students. Thus, there will be increased equality of effort among all students.

2. Reforms will free more students to engage in extracurricular activities, so students' participation in activities will increase and be more widespread among all students.
3. Reforms will free students for involvement in creative activities so their involvement in creative activities will be more widespread.

However, we must note the possibility that these reforms may operate somewhat differently than intended. Responsiveness to students' interests, reduced demands, multiple criteria, and greater availability of colleges might give students the impression that the same valuable goal is now more easily attained. There is now less incentive for special efforts, and some students might get the impression that now they can simply coast into college without much effort. College might be thought to promise the same rewards, at much less cost of effort.

DATA AND PLAN OF ANALYSIS

To examine these issues, we shall use three sources of data. First, we shall examine the Japanese High School and Beyond survey. This national longitudinal survey of high school seniors in 1980 allows us to an examine whether SES affects college attendance independent of merit and whether homework time influences college attendance independent of SES. Then we shall turn to a survey of Japanese students which was first conducted in 1979 and then replicated in 1997. These two surveys allow us to examine changes in the patterns of homework over this 18-year period, during which the Japanese reforms took place.

HOMEWORK TIME IS A MAJOR INFLUENCE
ON COLLEGE ATTENDANCE

To Americans, homework time is an unusual focus for research. American research has focused on achievement outcomes, and even thoughtful studies of social psychological factors do not consider homework time (Kerckhoff, 1974). Although we didn't have test scores, in the context of Japan, homework time is a reasonable second choice. Indeed, homework time might even be a first choice. Japanese people believe that achievement is almost totally a consequence of effort. A teacher, parent, or student looks at a high or low achievement outcome and says it indicates the individual's level of effort. Ability is almost never considered, except in extreme cases, for example, after a student has tried very hard and repeatedly gotten a low score. But this is believed to be unusual.

Homework time is probably not a perfect indicator of effort. Individuals may vary in their efforts during school, but it is hard to measure such efforts concretely, and efforts during school probably correlate strongly with homework time. Homework time has the virtue of referring to an objective behavior which can be precisely measured. Students may misperceive or misreport their homework time, but on a paper and pencil survey, there is little reason to expect intentional distortion.

Before turning to the main focus of this study, we examine our initial premise—to what extent is the college admissions process meritocratic and influenced by homework time? For this question, we examine the Japanese High School and Beyond survey. This national longitudinal survey of high school seniors in 1980 ($n = 1716$) was designed to resemble its American counterpart, and it is described in a previous article (Rosenbaum & Kariya, 1991). We examined whether SES affects college attendance independent of merit factors and whether homework time influences college attendance. (Since virtually all students who enter 4-year colleges succeed in graduating, this is also an analysis of BA degree attainment.) We run logistic regressions on whether students enter 4-year colleges or not, examining the influence of family SES and school factors.

Using logistic analyses to explain which students attended 4-year colleges (vs. those who did not), we find that fathers' occupational status (a scale similar to Blau & Duncan, 1967) and gender have significant influences on college attendance, although fathers' and mothers' education do not (Table 3-1, Model 1). We next consider the influence of two merit variables: high school grades and ranks. High schools are ranked in an explicit formal hierarchy, and objective codes of schools' ranks were added to the students' file. Since students are admitted to high schools based solely on achievement test scores, students' school ranks are an indicator of their prior achievement.* When added to the regression (Models 2 and 3), grades and high school ranks have strong significant influences. Moreover, in the last stage (Model 4), the effects of high school grades and ranks seem to be mediated in part by a third merit factor, homework time, and these three merit variables mediate some of the effect of fathers' occupation, bringing it to insignificance. Apparently, Japanese educational attainment is meritocratic—the effects of fathers' occupational status on college attendance are totally mediated by the merit factors that indicate students' attainments and efforts. These results in the Japanese HSB sharply contrast with the large significant SES effects on college attainment in comparable regressions on the American HSB data (Rosenbaum, 1998, 2001).

Just as important for this paper, we find that homework time is a major influence on attainment. While high-school rank has the strongest influence on college attendance, homework time also has a major influence, just slightly smaller than high-school rank. Indeed, it is remarkable that its influence is independent of the effect of grades. Apparently, students who do more homework are indeed more likely to pass college entrance exams, net of their high-school grades. Just as Japan's popular culture assumes, students' homework efforts have strong signficant impact on whether they attend four-year colleges.

Homework time is the behavior that Japanese people believe is the first and most important cause of achievement, and it may be more highly valued than achievement. The present analyses seem to support that assumption. In a system where college admissions is determined by achievement exams, homework time is a stronger influence on college attendance than grades or SES. Thus, the variable we are studying, homework time, is an outcome of primary importance in Japan, perhaps the most important outcome.

THE JAPANESE SURVEY IN 1979 AND 1997

The JHSB of 1980 was not repeated in later years, but we do have a large survey that permits study of change. In 1979, Professor Matsubara (1981) directed a survey of 2625 students in three prefectures. That survey asked students about their school efforts and other activities. A number of researchers who had worked on that study, conducted a new study of the same schools in 1997 with a comparable sampling design. This pair of studies separated by an 18-year period provide measures of pre-reform and post-reform periods.

---

*These exam-based school-placement policies were designed to prevent SES influences in distorting merit selection. While Rohlen (1983) has noted an association between SES and high-school rank, he did not examine whether it was mediated by any merit factors. Our own analyses (available from authors) indicate that most or all of that association is mediated by achievement—junior high grades.

TABLE 3-1. Logistic Regression Analysis for Chance to Enter 4 Year University Upon High School Graduation ($n = 1716$)

Variable	Model 1 (Chi-Square = 95.291***, df. = 4)			Model 2 (Chi-Square = 83.677***, df. = 5)			Model 3 (Chi-Square = 32.252***, df. = 6)			Model 4 (Chi-Square = 39.436***, df. = 7)		
	B	S.E.	R	B	S.E.	R	B	S.E.	R	B	S.E.	R
Father's education	-0.001	0.021	0.000	-0.024	0.022	0.000	-0.020	0.022	0.000	-0.018	0.022	0.000
Mother's education	0.030	0.028	0.000	0.011	0.029	0.000	0.011	0.029	0.000	0.004	0.030	0.000
Father's occupation	0.018	0.005**	0.063	0.013	0.006*	0.041	0.011	0.006*	0.031	0.009	0.006	0.015
Male	0.836	0.105***	0.165	0.383	0.117**	0.063	0.392	0.119**	0.065	0.375	0.119**	0.062
HS rank				0.763	0.086***	0.187	0.793	0.087***	0.196	0.633	0.091***	0.150
Grades							0.200	0.036***	0.118	0.135	0.038***	0.073
Study hours										0.005	0.001***	0.132
Constant	-2.264	0.321***		-3.788	0.376***		-4.768	0.423***		-4.565	0.430***	

In 1979, three prefectures were selected for the survey. The present paper focuses on the two prefectures that had experienced very little change in student composition over the following two decades, and in particular, they had not experienced much student outflow to private schools. These prefectures had good public high schools and a clear hierarchy among schools (which creates a form of tracking between schools). Over the last two decades, these two prefectures have had almost no change in their school district and tracking policies (including admissions criteria for each rank). Since changes in tracking policies in Japanese public high schools have led to departures of some of the most motivated students to private schools and changes in the student body composition in public schools (Kariya & Rosenbaum, 1999), it was important to select prefectures where such changes had not occured over this 18-year span. In addition, these prefectures had few good private schools to draw away good students. Moreover, there were no other kinds of changes in the economy or social attributes in these prefectures that might raise concerns about the comparability of the kinds of students in the two time periods. While our 1997 sample includes more children whose fathers were from professional and service occupations, and fewer from self-employed, clerical, and manual occupations, these changes are in line with national changes in adult male employment.*

While the Japanese discussion of "exam hell" views it as an aggregate problem in high schools generally, our analyses examine it in more detail, with special focus on if they are manifest in the different ranks of high schools. Our analyses give special focus to the main form of tracking in Japan. Japan has no tracking before high school, but at the end of ninth grade, all students take achievement tests, and they are admitted to high schools based on their achievement test scores. Thus, high schools are ranked within school districts, and most districts have four or more ranks.

This study draws its sample from 5 high schools in one prefecture and 6 high schools in the other. Following the customary research practice of grouping high schools into four ranks, we sample at least one school in each rank from each prefecture.

---

*Unlike the JHSB which is a national sample, we cannot claim that these two prefectures are representative. While it is possible that the schools in these prefectures are unrepresentative of the nation's schools, the data on our students are similar to the results in the JHSB national survey. For instance, on our dependent variable, homework minutes per night, while the high school juniors in the top-rank high schools in our sample spent 151 min a night, the national JHSB seniors spent 173 min. Similar differences are evident for the second and fourth ranks of high schools—Rank 2: 125 in our sample vs. 142 min in JHSB; Rank4: 30 vs. 42 (the difference is in the opposite direction, but equally small in Rank 3: 107 vs. 84). These results indicating 17–22 min increases in the top two ranks are to be expected, since seniors probably spend more time on homework than juniors because of university exams. Although we cannot be certain about the generalizability of our results to other prefectures, this comparison suggests that our sample of juniors does not seem very different than the JHSB national sample of seniors in homework time.

Despite these analyses, the absence of elite private schools in these prefectures might make us expect that the schools in our sample include more high-achieving students than the nation's other public schools, particularly public schools in major cities like Tokyo and Kyoto. If so, then our sample might show somewhat higher effort than in Japan as a whole. That would make our findings of declining student effort even more surprising. Of course, studying public high schools in Tokyo or Kyoto in 1979 and 1997 would make a bad comparison, because the most motivated students left the public schools over this period (Kariya and Rosenbaum, 1999).

We cannot estimate response rate. Surveys were administered on one day, so absent students on that day are not represented in the 1979 and 1997 surveys. However, this is less of a problem since Japan has better attendance than the United States. While 27.9% of U.S. students report never being absent in senior year, 57.1% of Japanese students were never absent. On the other side of the spectrum, while 20.1% of U.S. students were absent 5 or more days, only 8.0% of Japanese students were (unpublished analyses, JSHB and US-HSB). Moreover, since attendance rates have decreased in Japan over this 18-year period, our 1997 analyses of homework time underrepresent the lowest-effort students. In light of the findings reported later, this indicates that the changes we note are probably underestimates of the real declines in effort.

While ranks are defined in terms of achievement scores on admissions exams, the qualitative implications of ranks can be seen in terms of their outcomes. At the time of our first data collection in 1979, graduates of top high schools tended to be admitted at top and middle national universities, graduates of second-rank schools tended to be admitted to other national universities, graduates of third-rank schools tended to be admitted to private universities, graduates of fourth-rank (vocational) schools tended to take jobs and a few attended vocational post-secondary schools. There is no gender difference in the top-rank schools in either period: 27.5% of males are in top-rank HS, while 26.9% of females are. In 1997, these percentages are 27.1% and 27.3% correspondingly.*

Obviously, causality cannot be inferred with certainty. Many other changes occurred over this period. However, it is our judgement that the reforms were the major influences on the outcomes being measured, and no other factor had such clear potential influences. Regardless, these analyses indicate whether the outcomes the reforms sought were happening.

THE PRE-REFORM "EXAM HELL" ERA

To understand the meaning of homework time, it should be considered in the context of the number of discretionary hours in a student's day. A national survey of Japanese students found that in an average day, high school students typically spend 8 hr in school, 1.5 hr going to school, 2.5 hr in meals, chores, and personal care, and 7 hr sleeping (NHK, 1991). This leaves 5 hr in the day for everything else, so our findings about students' reported homework time can be judged in the context of roughly 5 hr of discretionary time.

In the earlier era, the Japanese system elicited widespread effort. As noted, while 43% of American 17-year-olds did no homework on an average school night, only 22% of Japanese students did. Moreover, even in lower ranked high schools, where students had lower achievement, large portions of students did substantial amounts of homework. While 67% of Americans did one hour or less homework a night, only 27% of students in Japan's third-ranked high schools made such low efforts, and much smaller proportions did so in the first- and second-ranked schools (Figure 3-1). Only in Japan's lowest rank high schools do we see similar levels of low effort as are typical in the average American school. Given Japan's 6-day week and longer school year, the national differences in total homework hours in a year are actually far greater than these daily reports suggest. Clearly, the Japanese system managed to motivate a large portion of youth in three of the four levels of schools.

Indeed, our analyses of 1979 indicate that policymakers had some reason for concern about overwork (Figure 3-1, square data points). In the highest rank general high schools, where students strived for entrance at the highest rank universities, 12.4% of students work over 4 hr a day on homework, and another 23.9% work 3–4 hr a day. Four hours of homework leaves little time for recreation and may sometimes cut into sleep. In the year before the university exams, students have a common saying, "Four is a pass, and five is a fail" which means that students who get 5-hr sleep a night will not pass the exams. While our findings do

---

*While we lack data on test scores, junior high grades correlate highly with the examination scores of students applying for high schools. Our data on junior high grades confirm the distinctions among high schools with the differences between the first- and third-school ranks and the third- and fourth-school ranks being larger than the standard deviations within schools. The second-rank schools fell evenly between first- and third-ranks, but not quite a standard deviation separated them.

not necessarily indicate that students have this extreme shortage of sleep, we find that some students are spending a great deal of time on homework. This is a serious burden that prompted policymakers to make the reforms.

However, even in the top high schools, "exam hell" is not universal. Less than 37% of students work over 3 hr a night. Indeed, 5.4% do no homework at night, and another 8.6% do less than an hour a night or none.

Moreover, the pressure is much lower at lower rank high schools. In the second-rank general high schools, where students are all college-bound, but few will gain entrance to top-rank universities, only 6% of students work over 4 hr a day on homework, and another 15.7%

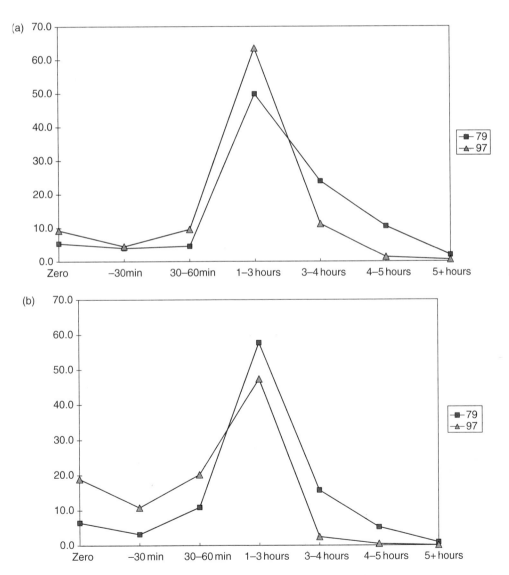

FIGURE 3-1. (a) Homework time of rank-1 students; (b) Homework time of rank-2 students; (c) Homework time rank-3 students; (d) Homework time of rank-4 students.

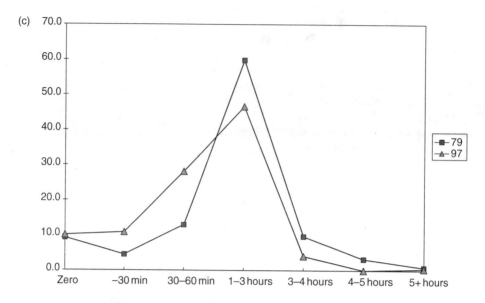

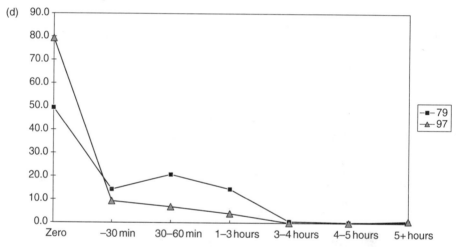

FIGURE 3-1. Continued

work 3–4 hr a day. Thus less than 22% of students in these schools are under "exam hell" pressures. Moreover, 6.5% do no homework at night, and another 14.2% do less than an hour a night. In these college-bound high schools, fewer students face "exam-hell" pressures than do less than an hour a night. The pattern is very similar in third-rank high schools.

Turning to fourth-rank high schools, we find that less than 1% students work over 4 hr a day, less than 1% work 3–4 hr, while 50% do no homework a night, and another 35% do less than an hour a night. This distribution looks nothing like the exam-hell fears expressed by policymakers.

Thus, even at the outset, as the policymakers were concerned about highly pressured students caught in an exam-hell of frantic activity and sleepless nights, many students did not appear to be under much pressure, and only at the top-rank general high schools were sub-stantial numbers under such pressure. If one considers over 4 hr as too much pressure, only

5.5% of our sample is experiencing an "exam hell" (only 16.8% of our sample if 3 hr is the criterion).

AFTER THE REFORMS

What happened after the reforms? Did these reforms lead to fewer pressured students? Judging from students' homework time, the reforms had their desired effects. However, they also had some unanticipated effects as well.

Almost 20 years later, in 1997, analyses indicate that policymakers accomplished some of what they wanted (Figure 3-1, triangle data points). In the highest-rank high schools, the proportion of students working 4 or more hours a day on homework declined, from 12.4% to 1.8%, and those working over 3 hr a day declined from 36.3% to 13.0%. The most pressured students had not vanished, but there were fewer of them. Also as the reformers hoped, the proportion doing a moderate amount of homework (1–3 hr) increased a great deal, from 49.9% to 63.5%.

However, the reforms also had effects at the other end of the scale—the least pressured students also felt less pressure. The proportion of students doing no homework a night increased by 72% (from 5.4 to 9.3%), and those doing less than an hour a night increased by 67% (from 14.0% to 23.4%).

Moreover, the reforms had stronger effects at lower-rank high schools. In the second-rank general high schools, the proportion of students working over 3 hr a day on homework plunged from 21.7% to 2.8%, so that few students in these schools are under high pressures. On the other end of the scale, the proportion doing no homework nearly tripled (from 6.5% to 18.9%), and those doing less than an hour a night more than doubled (from 20.7% to 49.8%, including those who did no homework). The proportion doing a moderate amount (1–3 hr) declined precipitously (from 57.7% to 47.4%). Thus, while the small number of highly pressured students in these schools declined, the big shift was from doing moderate to little homework.

In third-rank high schools, the proportion of students working over 3 hours a day on homework plunged (13.6% to 4.4%), and, on the other end of the scale, those doing an hour or less a night soared from 26.5% to 48.8%. The proportion doing a moderate amount (1–3 hr) declined substantially (from 59.8% to 46.6%), so there was a major shift from doing moderate to little homework.

Turning to fourth-rank high schools, we find that the reform had no impact on highly pressured students in these schools for there were almost none to start with. Indeed, only 14.5% did a moderate amount of homework, so, while this group declined to only 3.9% after the reform, it didn't affect many individuals. However, the reform had very large effects on students who were under little pressure. The proportion doing no homework dramatically increased from 49.4% to 79.3% at the same time that there was a pronounced decline in the numbers who did 1–60 min a night. In 1979, some students in these schools worked hard, and in some vocational programs in technical fields they learned calculus. Today, vocational students do not learn calculus, and few do any homework

Thus, the reforms accomplished their goal of reducing "exam hell", but they also had unanticipated consequences on other students too. The concern about overworked students seems to apply mostly to students in top-rank high schools, and the reforms succeeded in reducing the incidence of overworked students in these schools, although overwork was not entirely eliminated. In the other schools, there were few highly pressured students, but there were big shifts from moderate to low levels of homework, and, in the lowest rank, big shifts from doing little homework to doing none. The goal of reducing pressure on the most pressured students affected some pressured students. However, the same reform had substantial effects in reducing the efforts of less pressured students. The reformers somehow had not anticipated that the reforms would affect these students.

INEQUALITY OF HOMEWORK TIME

Moreover, the reforms had another effect—an increase in inequality. As noted, one of the goals of the reforms was to reduce inequality, and the decreased academic pressure and multiple criteria were expected to reduce the narrow one-dimensional hierarchy. Unfortunately, in a nation that believes that effort is the key influence on achievement, we find that the reforms increased inequality.*

While declining in all high-school levels, homework time decreased relatively more in the middle-level schools, especially the second level. Students in top-rank high schools worked more than students in second-rank schools by 26 min in 1979 and by 48 min in 1997 (Table 3-2a). The difference is even larger when considered as a proportion of total time. Students in second-rank high schools worked 82.6% of the hours of top-rank students in 1979, but only 62.0% in 1997. Of course, the lowest level (rank-4 schools) had already begun with a low level of homework in 1979 (only 29.5 min).

TABLE 3-2a. **Means of Homework Minutes per Night by High-School Rank**

	Mean	S.D.	n	Amount change	Percent change
Rank 1					
1979	151.05	78.01	373	−25.33	−16.8%
1997	125.72	71.20	375		
Rank 2					
1979	124.78	72.27	248	−46.77	−37.5%
1997	78.01	62.68	249		
Rank 3					
1979	106.81	69.15	249	−24.46	−22.9%
1997	82.35	61.94	249		
Rank 4					
1979	29.52	45.46	498	−18.25	−61.8%
1997	11.27	37.01	487		

*For simplicity, the previous graphs recoded homework time to a limited number of categories to make the graphs easier to read, collapsing 1–2 hr and 2–3 hr (these were the items to which students responded). All categories were used for computing means. Students reporting more than 30 and up to 60 min are assigned 45 min, and those reporting more than 1 hr and up to 2 hr are assigned 1.5 hr, 2–3 hr as 2.5, etc. Since homework time should include time in after-school schools (juku), all homework time variables add 1 hour per night for students who said they attended juku. The present analyses compute means averaging these values. However, the juku adjustment added new data points to the 1997 homework scale which were not present in 1979, when juku attendance was rare. Some individuals have 3.25 hr in 1997, but none do in 1979. We use such values in computing their means, but, since nonequivalent scales could affect regression results, the regression results (reported later) collapse some categories of homework time so both years had the same number of categories. Thus, individuals with 3.25 hr of homework are coded as 3.5, included in the 3–4 hr range. We experimented with various other sets of recodes, and, while coefficients changed, our conclusions were not altered.

TABLE 3-2b. **Means of TV Minutes per Night by High-School Rank**

	Mean	S.D.	*n*	Amount change	Percent change
Rank 1					
1979	92.57	88.22	375	12.13	13.1%
1997	104.70	111.57	375		
Rank 2					
1979	100.19	114.35	250	24.06	24.0%
1997	124.25	117.03	250		
Rank 3					
1979	97.36	79.90	250	50.74	52.1%
1997	148.09	160.51	250		
Rank 4					
1979	142.88	83.27	500	28.88	20.2%
1997	171.76	142.43	500		

While the reforms led to more moderate levels of homework for the top-rank high schools, some students in these schools maintained high levels of homework. In other high schools, large numbers of students did nearly no homework. To the extent that homework hours leads to academic achievement and the development of work habits, the reforms are decreasing education for a large proportion of students, particularly outside the top-rank high schools. As a result, the reforms may be increasing inequalities among students.

SOCIAL CLASS DIFFERENCES

Having noted increased inequalities among students, we may wonder if they are related to social class effects. The survey asked students to code their fathers' occupations in one of 9 different occupational categories, among which we identified 4 status levels: (1) professionals and managers, (2) clerical, (3) skilled (manual, sales, self-employed), and (4) unskilled (transportation, service). (Farmers are not discussed because of too few cases in 1997.)

Analyzing homework time, we find that 1979 homework time increases with increasing SES—(1) prof/mgr, 116–119 min, (2) clerical, 107 min, (3) skilled (manual, sales, self-employed), 86–89 min, (4) unskilled (transport, service) 66–73 min (Table 3-3a). However, there is a fairly small span from top to second and third occupational levels. The two largest occupations, which represent second- and third-level occupations, clerical and manual children, do 90% and 72% as much homework as professionals' children.

By 1997, homework declines for all groups of students, but students from prof/mgr families reduced their homework less than those from lower status occupational origins. While managers' and professsionals' children's homework time declined by 22% and 27%, clerical, manual, and self-employed children's homework time dropped even more (by 41%, 52%, 40%). By 1997, the two largest groups, clerical and manual children have increased their discrepancy in homework time from 90% and 72% of professionals' children down to 72% and 48%. The reforms have given all children more freedom of choice, and students' choices have exacerbated social class differences.*

---

*Sales, service, and transport dropped 30% or less between 1979 and 1997, but they already started at very low levels.

TABLE 3-3a. Means of Homework Minutes per Night by Fathers' Occupations

	1979			1997				
	Mean (min.)	S.D.	Cases	Mean (min.)	S.D.	Cases	Amount Change	Percent Change
Occ. Status 1								
Professional	119.47	89.59	171	87.36	81.00	227	−32.12	−26.9%
Managerial	115.76	79.91	230	90.93	70.37	242	−24.83	−21.5%
Occ. Status 2								
Clerical	106.55	82.52	203	63.05	63.33	172	−43.50	−40.8%
Occ. Status 3								
Sales	89.20	78.98	75	61.83	73.99	90	−27.37	−30.7%
Self-employed	86.67	79.06	153	52.01	70.16	92	−34.66	−40.0%
Manual	86.59	81.94	229	41.70	63.18	182	−44.89	−51.8%
Occ. Status 4								
Transportation	66.11	71.31	113	61.73	81.59	78	−4.38	−6.6%
Service	73.46	73.47	39	41.70	63.18	182	−31.76	−43.2%
Farmers	56.41	68.95	96	76.36	107.01	11	19.96	35.4%

TABLE 3-3b. Means of TV Minutes per Night by Fathers' Occupations

	1979			1997				
	Mean (min.)	S.D.	Cases	Mean (min.)	S.D.	Cases	Amount Change	Percent Change
Occ. Status 1								
Professional	95.60	112.81	172	121.94	101.16	229	26.34	27.6%
Managerial	101.42	84.32	232	122.75	129.82	242	21.33	21.0%
Occ. Status 2								
Clerical	108.29	106.69	206	136.94	118.03	172	28.64	26.5%
Occ. Status 3								
Sales	112.00	70.41	75	123.30	78.77	91	11.30	10.1%
Self-employed	107.55	66.39	153	157.14	151.82	95	49.59	46.1%
Manual	117.31	68.20	229	159.91	171.07	184	42.60	36.3%
Occ. Status 4								
Transportation	139.76	133.41	114	153.34	124.49	79	13.58	9.7%
Service	127.31	77.93	39	133.97	85.86	58	6.66	5.2%
Farmers	138.59	80.81	96	222.23	252.05	13	83.64	60.3%

While Herrnstein and Murray (1994) worry about increasing ability inequalities in society, these findings indicate another risk—increasing effort inequalities—which are even more serious in a society that values hard work and strong achievement.

PARTICIPATION IN EXTRACURRICULAR ACTIVITIES

What about the second concern—did 1979 school pressures for homework prevent students from engaging in other activities? Did the reforms succeed in getting students to turn their efforts to other activities that would build other skills or creativity?

Reformers were concerned that the one-dimensional meritocratic emphasis on grades was preventing students from spending time on other activities. The 1979 patterns in the top-rank high schools support that concern. For students in top-rank high schools, the number of minutes in the day was perhaps the factor limiting activities in 1979. Students who did extracurricular activities spent 30–50 min fewer on homework than nonparticipants. In a system where college admission was based solely on academic performance, their lower homework time may have caused an academic disadvantage.

However, students in the second-rank high schools did not show this same pattern in 1979: participation in extracurricular activities did not reduce their homework time, indeed, participants had higher homework time than nonparticipants. Similarly, the reformers' assumption that activities forced students to sacrifice necessary homework time does not seem to be fully suppported in the third- and fourth-rank schools. Thus one of the premises for the reforms was not supported in 1979, before the reforms began.

As the reformers had hoped, after the reforms, participation in extracurricular activities greatly increased in top-rank high schools. In these schools, the portion of nonparticipants dropped from 15.3% to 5.9% of students surveyed (table available from authors). However, in second-rank general high schools, participation rates changed very little (nonparticipation declined from 14.9% to 13.3%), and participation declined in the two lower ranks. In third-rank high schools, nonparticipants increased from 14.2% to 21.7% and in fourth-rank high schools, nonparticipants almost doubled (from 9.6% to 16.9%). The assumption that relieving homework pressures would increase participation in activities worked in top-rank high schools, but not in the others. In the lower two ranks, students given a freer choice opted out of participation.

Not only did the reforms allow a higher percentage of students in the top two ranks of high schools to engage in activities in 1997, but they also allowed them to do so without sacrificing homework time. Indeed, participants spent more time on homework than nonparticipants by a small margin. With the lower levels of homework required, participation could fit into students' lives. However, for the two lower-rank high schools, nonparticipants spent the same or less time on homework in 1979, and after the reforms, nonparticipants spent even less time on homework than participants. As reformers planned, reforms made more time for students in the top two ranks of high school to be in activities, and they could do so at little cost to their homework time. But for students in the two lower ranks of high schools, the reforms offered a freedom to avoid school activities and homework, and many students chose to avoid both.

MORE TIME FOR UNCREATIVE ACTIVITIES?—TV WATCHING

Did the reforms allow time for other creative activities, as the reformers hoped? Although we lack measures of other creative activities, we have measures of an activity that many consider uncreative—TV watching. TV was extensively available in both time periods. Nearly all Japanese homes had TV sets in 1979, and there were several channels in most areas of the country, so there were ample opportunities for TV watching in the earlier era. Indeed, the availability of TV in our sample is evident in the finding that only a small number of students spent no time watching TV in 1979, and these individuals were mostly in the higher occupation families that could most afford TVs. Thus, the changes that occur over this period are probably not due to the physical availability of TV sets.

Students were asked how much time they spent watching TV on an average day. All groups show increases, but the gain is much less in the top-rank high schools than in the other three ranks (see Table 3-2b). Inspecting the distributions of students spending different amounts of time watching TV, the distributions are virtually identical in 1979 and 1997 for students in the top-ranked schools (figure available from authors). Although students in second- and third-rank high schools show no change in the incidence of TV watching at the lower and upper extremes (watching less than 30 min a day or more than 5 hr), students in mid-rank schools show a large increase in the percentage watching 3–5 hr a day, while those watching one hour or less a day declined. While high-dosage TV watching (5 or more hours) remained infrequent (less than 3%) in second- and third-rank schools, it doubled for students in fourth-rank schools (from 5% to 10%).

Thus the reforms freed students' time for activities other than schoolwork, but this seems to have led to an increase in lengthy TV watching. The reforms were often described as "student-centered," "democratic", and following the American lead of respecting youths' own free choices, but unfortunately they led to a phenomenon well-known in the US—massive TV watching.

Moreover, while the reforms were intended to promote equality, they led to inequality in students' TV watching. Students in top-rank high schools devoted less time to TV and increased less over the 18-year span than other students (Table 3-2b). Their distribution of TV watching changed relatively little over the 18-year period. However, TV watching drastically increased in the lower-rank high schools, with especially great increases in the numbers spending over 3 hr a day in front of the TV.

SOCIAL BACKGROUND AND TV TIME

How are these changes distributed among occupational groups? We find that 1979 TV time generally increases with decreasing SES—(1) prof/mgr, 96–101 min, (2) clerical, 108 min, (3) skilled (manual, sales, self-employed), 117, 112, 108 min, (4) unskilled (transport, service) 140, 127 min (Table 3-3b). However, there is a fairly small span from top to second and third occupational levels—the two largest occupations, which represent second- and third-level occupations, clerical and manual children, do only 7% and 16% more TV time than managers' children.

By 1997, TV time has increased for all groups of students, but students from prof/mgr families increased their TV time less than lower status occupations. While managers' and professionals' children increased their TV time by 26 and 21 min, manual and self-employed increased their higher TV time even more (by 43 and 50 min a day). In the earlier period, manual workers' children spent 16% more time watching TV than managers' children, but that increases to 30% more by 1997. The reforms have given all children more freedom of choice, and students' choices may have exacerbated some social class differences.*

MULTIVARIATE ANALYSIS OF
HOMEWORK TIME

We have noted multiple factors associated with students' homework time and TV time: raw changes over the 18 years, differences by high-school rank and fathers' occupation. In addition,

---

*Not all class differences were increased. Unlike their big declines in homework time, children of clerical, sales, service, and transport workers increased TV time only a little (by only 28, 11, and 7 min), so their TV time stayed close to the level of managers' children, even though their homework time did not. Transport workers' children increased their TV time by only 14 min; however, their TV watching was already at a high level in 1979. Farmers' children show a dramatic increase, but this is based on only 13 cases.

we might expect gender differences and possibly effects of mothers' education. We can analyze the net effects of all these factors by modelling them with multiple regression analyses.

Fathers' occupations were coded by prestige score, using an occupational code developed by the Japanese Social Stratification and Mobility Survey similar to that of prestige scores (Blau & Duncan, 1965). Mothers' education was coded into four categories, gender is dichotomous, and dummies were created for the top three school ranks, with the fourth excluded (fathers' education was not included because it was never a significant influence; mothers' and fathers' education are highly correlated: 0.555 in 1979 and 0.519 in 1997). As noted above, some categories of 1997 homework time were collapsed to make the same number of categories as in 1979.

Homework time was regressed on fathers' occupation, mothers' education, gender, and high-school rank dummies in 1979 and 1997 (Table 3-4). In the earlier year, high-school ranks were strongly related to homework time, but fathers' occupation, mothers' education, and gender had no significant effects. Eighteen years later, the effects of the first rank were nearly as large as previously, but the effects of the second rank had declined.

While gender and mothers' education had no influence pre-reform, the efforts of females and youths with more educated mothers become significant after the reform. Social class differences (from mothers' education) were absent in the earlier period, but they are strong and significant after the reforms.

Moreover, these changes were statistically significant. In an analysis pooling data from both years, and using interaction terms for all variables by the later year, we find that all students showed a significant decline in effort, and males, students in second-rank schools, and students with less educated mothers showed additional significant declines (table available from authors). The reform's success in decreasing school pressures for effort let students choose how much homework to do, and their choices were related to their mothers' education and gender.*

TABLE 3-4. Regression Analysis for Homework Minutes per Night in 1979 and 1997

	1979 (Adj R^2 = .372, F = 124.882***, n = 1255)		1997 Adj R^2 = .435, F = 142.466***, n = 1102)	
	B	Beta	B	Beta
Father's Occupation	0.259	0.029	0.235	0.031
Mother's Education	−1.134	−0.028	3.836	0.092***
Male	−4.045	−0.024	−7.281	−0.050**
Rank1	116.876	0.659***	108.601	0.683***
Rank2	91.613	0.441***	65.482	0.352***
Rank3	75.531	0.368***	74.912	0.392***
Constant	37.387	**	−42.266	**

*p < .05; **p < 0.01; ***p < .001

*We also ran regression analysis to examine the various influences on TV time (tables omitted for brevity). In 1979, neither fathers' occupation nor mothers' education had significant effect on TV time, but by 1997 mothers' education had become significant. Moreover, the pattern of high-school ranks changes. Over this 18-year period, the top-rank students increase their TV time less than students in rank-4 schools, while rank-3 students become increasingly like rank-4 students in their TV time. It is also noteworthy that females have come close to catching up with males in TV time. Thus, youth with more highly educated mothers spend less time watching TV, and top-rank high schools have increasingly strong effects in decreasing TV time. Estimating the coefficients in an interaction model like the preceding one on homework time finds that the mothers' education effect, though significant in 1997, is not quite significantly different from that of 1979.

CONCLUSION

Contrary to American stereotype, Japanese youth are not "workaholics," genetically or cul-turally driven to overwork. In a competition for laziness, the Japanese can keep up with Americans given the right conditions. Japan's meritocracy did not provide those conditions, but its American-style reforms did. These results indicate that the impetus for Japanese youths' hard work was the strong incentive system. After reforms decreased those incentives, youths' efforts dramatically declined.

These results have important implications for our understanding of the adolescent life stage. Within the United States, adolescents' low school efforts are so prevalent that they seem to be a feature of the adolescent life stage. However, such low efforts were not an attribute of adolescent behavior in pre-reform Japan. They only came to be prevalent after Japan imple-mented its school reforms. These behaviors are not a feature of the life stage; they arose only with dramatic changes in the social context.

Even Japanese policymakers may have misjudged Japanese youth. As intended, reforms reduced the intense pressures on top students, reducing 'exam hell' and the number of stu-dents spending over 3 hr a day on homework. But the policies had similar or greater impact throughout the system, also reducing the efforts of students who were not overworking. The reforms led to severe decreases in students' homework time, even for students in the lowest-rank high schools, where zero homework became the overwhelming norm. Thus, reforms which intended to decrease overwork actually had some success in achieving that goal, but they had additional unintended effects of decreasing low levels of homework even lower.

In addition, reducing the overwork by top students did not reduce inequalities among students. Instead, the reforms actually increased inequalities of efforts across different high schools. In particular, the reforms increased the gap between the students in top-rank schools and all others. In second-rank high schools, where many students had formerly worked almost as hard as students in top-rank high schools, the number of such students drastically declined after the reforms. After the reforms, students in top-rank schools stood out even more, as stu-dents in second-rank schools came to resemble students in third-rank schools.

At the same time as the advantage of the top students was increasing, the lowest groups were falling more. Reformers hoped that multidimensional criteria would motivate students with lower achievement in one field (say, math) to devote time to other areas where they had interests or strengths (say, literature). Nonetheless, the reforms were accompanied by strong decreases in homework in lower-rank high schools, and most students in the lowest-rank schools decreased their low efforts down to none at all.

Moreover, there were large declines in effort by students from low-SES families, partic-ularly manual workers. While school efforts declined a little for high-SES students, efforts declined much more for other students. Even after controls for school rank, mothers' educa-tion has a much stronger influence on students' efforts after the reform, both for males and females. Lessening the school pressures for homework leaves the choice about homework time on students and their parents, and family socioeconomic background becomes a more important influence. Given the chance to devote their efforts to any activities, low-SES students and students in the lower-rank high schools also dramatically increased their TV time.

Japanese policymakers cite stories about individual students indicating the reforms' suc-cesses and failures. The reduced pressures on top students are commonly discussed. While pol-icymakers are quick to take credit for their successes, they blame the problems on other causes. When some students do little homework, this is blamed on American influences, pop culture, or increased affluence. While these interpretations cannot be ruled out, American pop culture has been a strong influence for many decades, and affluence does not explain why high SES students work harder than low-SES students or why this SES difference has increased over time.

But policymakers do not seem aware of how many students or which students are affected by the reforms' failures. The most serious shortcoming of policymakers is a failure to examine how reforms have altered incentives for different groups of students. The reforms have led to lower efforts by many more students than reformers have recognized (publicly, at least). Moreover, the reforms' impact on middle- and lower-rank schools and on middle- and lower SES students is not noted by policymakers, and perhaps not realized by them.

Obviously, these reforms were not the only changes happening over this time period. The weakening Japanese economy in the 1990s may have pushed more students into college, just as the reforms were increasing the availability of college. However, even in 1997, the labor market demand for high school graduates continued to exceed the supply, because so few graduates did not attend college. The weak economy hurt the demand for college-educated youth much more than for high school graduates. The weak economy may have contributed to employers' decision not to hire high school graduates into white-collar jobs, which reduced work-bound students' incentives, but the school reforms also probably contributed, since the high schools reported that employers no longer believed high school graduates could handle white-collar jobs, and employers would likely prefer cheap high school graduates if they could handle the jobs. While the weak economy may have had some impact, it seems likely that the reforms had the biggest impact on students' declining incentives.

While the effects of the specific reforms cannot be separated, all the reforms are mutually reinforcing, pushing incentives in similar directions. Japan implemented reforms to increase responsiveness to students' interests, reduce demands, introduce multiple criteria, and provide greater availability of colleges. All the reforms sought to reduce pressure, by reducing the incentives for achievement. By reducing the levels of school effort to get three kinds of payoffs—high school graduation, teachers' recommendations, and college entrance requirements—the reforms reduced incentives for school effort. Moreover, the only incentives that remained undiminished were admissions to the top-rank universities, so only the students aspiring to these universities, the top students in the top high schools, remained relatively unaffected by the reforms. The reforms lowered incentives for all other students. What is especially disappointing was that they had their greatest impact on the students who would be most hurt by decreased efforts and participation.

Magic tricks occur while everyone is looking most intently—but at the wrong place. The same may be true for the perverse consequences of reforms. In terms of their goals, the reforms were very successful—the most pressured students experienced declines in pressure and lower numbers showed high levels of homework time. However, as reforms successfully reduced school pressures, inequalities in student effort and participation loomed even larger, and were even more strongly influenced by social class background. In the pre-reform era, strong school ranks and strong teacher and school pressures for effort reduced inequalities in student effort and reduced social class influences. Weakening these universalistic influences left effort up to students' choices, but not surprisingly, not all students make the same choices, and students' choices are highly influenced by their upbringing. SES had increasing influence on students' efforts.

These results suggest a tradeoff between freedom and equality. When high schools reduce their uniformly high demands and leave students' efforts up to individuals' choices, inequalities emerge and become more pronounced, particularly differences arising from family influences. When given the freedom to choose, students whose families encourage school efforts continue striving in school, while students from other families strive less and devote more time to TV. Inequalities in student social class more strongly influenced their efforts, and, presumably what they learned in school.

In retrospect, we can better appreciate the positive qualities of Japan's old meritocracy. While the old system demanded high effort from all students, it reduced social class differences in students' effort. While the old system created intense pressures on the most motivated students, it stimulated students from less advantaged families to exert some effort, which they otherwise would not have done (and which they stopped when the reforms decreased the pressures). These relatively high efforts (with manual workers' children doing 1.5 hours of homework a night, more than that of 67% of American 17-year-olds at that time) may account for the high academic competencies and personal work habits that made Japanese youth the best in the world in national comparisons. The reforms reduced the seemingly oppressive demands by schools, but in the process, they allowed social class influences to have increasing influence as students made different choices about their homework efforts and TV time. Schools cannot reduce social class influences by making low demands, unless they actively suppress the efforts of the more motivated students. Schools can only reduce social class influences by demanding high effort from all.

Japanese youths' efforts declined sharply over these two decades, and these reforms are the probable cause. There is a sad irony to these outcomes, which Durkheim (1912) would have anticipated. In its effort to free youth from school pressures, Japan may have subjected youth more strongly to their family circumstances, which are associated with social class. Ironically, while one-dimensional meritocracies make inequalities more salient, they also make the rules perfectly clear to all, just the kind of articulation that Stinchcombe (1965) said would encourage youths' school efforts. Perhaps as a consequence, this articulated meritocracy reduced the actual behavioral inequalities among youth. As Japan moved away from a one-dimensional meritocracy, youth's behavior became more unequal.

ACKNOWLEDGMENTS: Support for this work was provided by the Spencer Foundation and the Institute for Policy Research at Northwestern University. Of course, the opinions expressed here are solely those of the authors.

REFERENCES

Arai, Katsuhiro (Ed.) (2000). *What High School Students Learn in School? (Kouokusei ha Nani wo Manande Kuruka)*, National Center for College Entrance Examinations.

Baltes, P. B. (1983). "Life-span developmental psychology." In *Developmental psychology*, R. Lerner (ed.). Hillsdale, NJ: Lawrence Erlbaum, pp. 79–111.

Benesse Educational Research Center (1999). *The Second Report on Basic Survey of Teaching* (Dai 2 kai Gakushuu Shido Kihon Chousa Houkokusho).

Blau, P., & Duncan, O. D. (1967). *The American Occupational Structure*. New York: Wiley.

Brinton, Mary (1998 December). "From high school to work in Japan: Lessons for the United States?" *Social Service Review, 72*(4), 442–451.

Brinton, Mary (2000). "Social capital in the Japanese youth labor market." *Policy Sciences, 33*, 289–306.

Bronfenbrenner, U. (1979). *The ecology of human development*. Cambridge, MA: Harvard University Press.

Chubb, John E., & Moe, Terry M. (1990). *Politics, Markets, and America's Schools*. Washington, DC: Brookings.

Crites, John O. (1976). "A comprehensive model of career adjustment in early adulthood." *Journal of Vocational Behavior, 9*, 105–118.

Dannefer, Dale (1992). "On the conceptualization of context in developmental discourse," pp. 84–110. In *Lifespan development and behavior*, vol. 2, David Featherman, Richard Lerman, Marion Perlmutter (Eds.). Hillsdale, NJ: Lawrence Erlbaum.

Durkheim, Emile 1912 (1964). *The division of labor in society*. New York: Free Press

Erikson, E. H. (1963). *Childhood and society*. (2nd ed.). New York: Norton.

Fordham, S., & Ogbu, J. U. (1986). Black students' school success. *Urban Review, 18*, 176–206.

Hallinan, Maureen (Ed.) (2000). *Handbook of the sociology of education*. New York: Plenum.

Halsey, A. H. (1977). "Towards meritocracy? The case of Britain. In *Power and ideology in education* (Eds.), Jerome Karabel and A. H. Halsey (pp. 173–185). New York: Oxford University Press.

Hamilton, Stephen F. (1986). School and work in the lives of German adolescents. *Journal of Early Adolescence, 2*(2), 99–110.

Herrnstein, Richard J. & Murray, C. (1994). *The bell curve*. New York: Free Press.

Heyns, Barbara (1978). *Summer learning and the effects of schooling*. New York: Academic Press.

Husen, T. (1967). *International study of achievement in mathematics: A comparison of twelve countries*. New York: Wiley.

Ishida, Hiroshi (1993). *Social mobility in contemporary Japan*. Stanford: Stanford University Press.

Jencks, Christopher, et al. (1972). *Inequality*. New York: Basic

Jencks, Christopher, & Phillips, Meredith (1998). *The Black-White test score gap*. Washington, DC: Brookings

Kariya, Takehiko (forthcoming). Koudo Ryuudouka Shakai (A high mobility society: social mobility and education in Postwar Japan). In Naoi Masaru and Hidenori Fujita (Eds.), *Kaiso* (Social stratification), vol. 13, Kouza Shakaigaku (Series of lectures of sociology), University of Tokyo Press.

Kariya, T., & Rosenbaum, J. (1987). Self-selection in Japanese junior high schools: A longitudinal study of students' educational plans. *Sociology of Education, 60*(3), 168–180.

Kariya, T., & Rosenbaum, J. (1999). Bright flight: unintended consequences of de-tracking policy. *American Journal of Education, 107*(3), 210–230.

Keniston, Kenneth (1970). Youth: a new stage of life. *American Scholar, 39*, 631–641.

Kerckhoff, Alan C. (1974). *Ambition and attainment*. Washington, DC: ASA Monographs.

Lee, Valerie E., Chow-How, Todd K., Berham, David K. Geverdt Douglas, & Smerdon, Becky A. (1989). Sector differences in high school course taking. *Sociology of Education 71*(4), 314–335.

LeTendre, Gerald (1996). Constructed aspirations. *Sociology of Education 69*, 193–216.

Levinson, D. J. et al. (1978). *The seasons of a man's life*. New York: Knopf.

Lynn, Richard (1988). *Educational achievement in Japan: Lessons for the West*. Armonk, New York: M. E. Sharpe.

Magnusson, D., & Allen, U. L. (1983). *Human development*. New York: Academic Press

Mandel, H. P., & Markus, S. I. (1988). *The psychology of underachievement*. New York: John Wiley & Sons.

Matsubara, Haruo et al. (1981). *Kokosei no Seitobunka to Gakkou Keiei* (High school students' subculture and school organization), Tokyo Daigaku Kyouikugakubu Kiyou (vol. 20, pp. 21–57).

Merton, Robert (1957). Social structure and anomie. In *Social theory and social structure* (pp. 131–160). New York: Free Press.

Meyer, John (1977). The effects of education as an institution. *American Journal of Sociology, 83*, 55–77

Meyer, John, & Rowan, Brian (1977). Institutional organizations: Formal structure as myth and ceremony. *American Journal of Sociology, 83,* 341–363.

NAEP (National Assessment of Educational Progress). (1985). *The reading report card*. Princeton, N.J.: Educational Testing Service.

NHK Hoso Bunka Kenkyujo (1991). *Kokumin Seikatu Jikan Chosa* (A survey report of people's time spent for life). Nihon Hoso Shuppan Kyoukai.

Okano, Kaori (1993). *School to work transition in Japan*. Philadelphia: Multilingual Mattters.

Osterman, Paul (1980). *Getting started: The youth labor market*. Cambridge, MA: MIT Press.

Rohlen, Thomas (1983). *Japan's high schools*. Berkeley: University of California.

Rosenbaum, J. (1991). Are adolescent problems caused by school or society? *Journal of Research on Adolescence, 1*(3), 301–322.

Rosenbaum, J. (1998). College for All: Do Students understand what college demands? *Social Psychology of Education 2*(1), 55–80.

Rosenbaum, James E. (2001). *Beyond college for all*. New York: Russell Sage Foundation Press.

Rosenbaum, J., & Kariya, T. (1989). From high school to work: Market and institutional mechanisms in Japan. *American Journal of Sociology, 94*(6), 1334–1365.

Rosenbaum, J., & Kariya, T. (1991). Do school achievements affect the early jobs of high school graduates?—Results from the High School and Beyond Surveys in the United States and Japan. *Sociology of Education, 64*(2), 78–95.

Rosenfeld, Rachel, & Hearn, James (1982). Sex differences in the significance of economic resources for choosing and attending a college. In P. Perun (Ed.), *Undergraduate woman*. Lexington, MA.: Lexington.

Shavit, Yossi, & Muller, Walter (1998). *From school to work*, Oxford: Clarendon Press.

Schneider, Barbara, & Stevenson, David (1999). *The ambitious generation*. New Haven: Yale University Press.

Sewell, W. H. (1971). Inequality of opportunity for higher education. *American Sociological Review. 34*: 793–809.

Sewell, W. H., & Hauser, Robert M. (1975). *Education, occupation, and earnings*. New York: Academic Press.

Sewell, W., & Shah, V. P. (1967). Socioeconomic status, intelligence, and the attainment of higher education. *Sociology of Education, 40*, 1–23.

Sorensen, A. (1979). Schools and the distribution of educational opportunities. *Research in the Sociology of Education and Socialization, 8*, 3–26.

Steinberg, L. (1997). *Beyond the classroom*. New York: Simon & Schuster.

Stevenson, H. W., & Stigler, J. W. (1992). *The learning gap*. New York: Touchstone.

Stinchcombe, Arthur L. (1965). *Rebellion in a high school*. Chicago: Quadrangle.

Tsutsui, Miki (2001). Changes in the labor market for high school graduates and the employment strategies of small- and medium-sized companies." *Kyouiku Shakaigaku Kenkyuu, 69*, 5–21.

Velez, William (1985). Finishing college: The effects of college type. *Sociology of Education 58*, 191–200.

Willis, P. (1977). *Learning to labor*. New York: Columbia University Press.

Young, M. (1958). *The rise of the meritocracy*. London: Penguin.

PART III

NORMATIVE STRUCTURING OF THE LIFE COURSE

CHAPTER 4

Age Structuring and the Rhythm of the Life Course*

RICHARD A. SETTERSTEN Jr.

Age is important from the perspectives of societies, groups, and individuals. For societies, the meanings and uses of age are often formal. For example, age underlies the organization of family, educational, work, and leisure institutions and organizations. Many laws and policies structure rights, responsibilities, and entitlements on the basis of age, whether through explicit age-related rules or implicit judgments about the nature of particular life periods. At the same time, members of a society, or large subgroups of the population, may share informal ideas about the changes that occur between birth and death, and how these changes are significant. For example, age may be tied to common notions about appropriate behavior or the proper timing and progression of experiences and roles.

For individuals and small groups, the meanings and uses of age are often informal. Individuals use age-related ideas to organize their lives, the lives of others, and their general expectations about the life course. Age enters into and shapes everyday social interactions, often in subtle ways, affecting the expectations and evaluations of individuals involved in those exchanges. Age is also often linked to personality attributes and behavioral dispositions, conceptions of the self, and processes of self-regulation, coping, and goal setting.

These meanings and uses of age—ranging from formal to informal, and from macro to micro—are instances of "age structuring", to use Kertzer's (1989) phrase. This chapter begins

*This chapter is dedicated to Bernice L. Neugarten (1916–2001): pioneer, mentor, and friend. "Though lost to sight, to memory dear Thou ever wilt remain" (*Song*, George Linley, 1798–1865). This chapter undoubtedly carries her imprint, along with that of Gunhild Hagestad, with whom I have shared an active conversation, now 15 years strong, about age and age norms. I am indebted to them both.

RICHARD A. SETTERSTEN JR. • Department of Sociology, Case Western Reserve University, Cleveland, Ohio 44106-7124.

Handbook of the Life Course, edited by Jeylan T. Mortimer and Michael J. Shanahan. Kluwer Academic/Plenum Publishers, New York, 2003.

by considering some of the formal institutional and societal-level issues related to age structuring in various life spheres, and historical shifts in these forms of age structuring. The bulk of the chapter then explores some of the informal and social-psychological issues related to age norms and expectations. It closes with a discussion of unresolved issues and new directions for scholarship in these areas.

FORMAL AGE STRUCTURING
IN LIFE SPHERES

In most Western societies, the life course is at least partially age-differentiated, with social roles and activities allocated on the basis of age or life period. Indeed, the modern life course is often viewed as rigidly structured into three separate periods related to work: an early segment devoted to *education and training* for work; a middle segment devoted to *continuous work activity*; and a final segment devoted to *leisure and retirement*. This structure is convenient because it creates "orderliness" in the entry to, and exit from, roles and activities; at the same time, it is "ageist" because it restricts opportunities for various roles and activities to specific periods of life (Riley, Kahn, & Foner, 1994). This structure is also reinforced through many social policies (for illustrations, see Settersten, 2003).

The degree of age structuring, and the *relative* degree of formal and informal age structuring, may vary by life sphere. For example, age structuring in the spheres of education and work may be especially strong because age and time often formally calibrate movement through these institutions. These more public spheres are heavily regulated by social policies. Primary and secondary educational institutions are strictly age-graded; educational programs require the completion of a specific number of credit hours; courses must be tackled at a specific pace and in a specific sequence; time limits are set for obtaining degrees. Similarly, work institutions often structure promotion opportunities and retirement benefits around age and seniority; organizations operate on specific schedules and shifts; hours are clocked; production is timed; deadlines are set; sick, personal, and holiday time is monitored and negotiated. Experiences in these settings march to the clock, and age is wound up in the clocks that time them.

There is evidence, however, that age structuring in the spheres of work and education is coming undone. Modernization and rapid technological change have prompted the need for adults to update their skills and knowledge, particularly with the erosion of "lifetime" models of employment (Henretta, 2003). (In lifetime models of employment, employers and employees invest in long-term partnerships and there is a strong emphasis on promotion from within organizations.) Individuals may now be forced to alternate between periods of schooling and periods of short-term employment. As a result, individuals may no longer consider age as relevant in these spheres if the possibility of stable work life appears uncertain, especially for young adults in their formative years of occupational training and experience. At the other end of life, the transition to retirement, once a transition from full-time work to full-time leisure, is also loosening, as evidenced by a wide array of contemporary work patterns through midlife and into old age (O'Rand & Henretta, 1999). While the gap between men's and women's educational and occupational attainment has been closing in recent decades, women's experiences in these spheres continue to be heavily conditioned by family roles and responsibilities, resulting in highly variable work trajectories (Moen, 2001).

The sphere of family, on the other hand, may not be as age-structured as the spheres of education and work. Family forms and trajectories seem especially complex and diverse

(Mason, Skolnick, & Sugarman, 1998), and the experience of time in the family is more contingent and less predictable than it is in other spheres (Daly, 1996). The family is also considered relatively private and not as legitimately controlled by the state, though many aspects of family life clearly are subject to regulation and intervention (Moen & Forest, 1999; Settersten, 2003). At the same time, families are clearly age-differentiated, especially because generational position defines an individual's place in the extended family matrix and shapes identities, roles, and responsibilities. Yet families also seem naturally age-integrated in that individuals of a wide variety of ages and cohorts are joined together and family-related roles and activities extend across life, despite the fact that specific roles and activities shift as individuals move up the family matrix over time.

Demographic change in the past century has also dramatically changed the look and feel of contemporary families (Hagestad, 2003). Increases in longevity and decreases in fertility have created "taller and skinnier" family structures in which more generations are alive at once, fewer members exist within each generation, and the age gap between generations is much larger. Children now come to know grandparents, great-grandparents, and even great-great-grandparents; and the lives of parents, spouses, siblings, and children overlap for long periods of time. These new securities also mean that patterns of illness and death among family members have become more predictable. We count on significant periods of joint survival with family members precisely because disease, disability, and death are generally confined to late life. These shifts bring the possibility that family relationships may become more significant now and in the future. At the same time, the new securities of lifetime, and of joint survival for many decades, may lead individuals to invest less in family ties during particular periods under the assumption that family ties can later be renewed. Of course, dramatic decreases in mortality, morbidity, and fertility have also altered spheres outside the family, though life course scholarship is only now beginning to explore these transformations.

HISTORICAL CHANGES IN FORMAL AGE STRUCTURING

Important historical changes in Western societies have occurred in the structure and content of the education–work–leisure tripartition. The boundaries between the three "boxes" have shifted. The trend toward early retirement at the upper end of work life, coupled with an extension of schooling at the lower end of work life, has made the period of gainful work shorter. Early retirement, coupled with increased longevity, has also lengthened the period of retirement. In addition, life experiences within these boxes have changed rapidly over the past century. Institutions and organizations often fail to keep pace with these changes, creating what Riley, Kahn, and Foner (1994) call "structural lag". The problem of structural lag is so strong, these authors argue, that societies are unable to provide "meaningful opportunities" for people of all ages in the spheres of education, work, family, and leisure. This problem is taken to be a by-product of the heavily age-differentiated life course common to most Western societies. As a result, there is growing interest in how to build age-integrated social settings in which people of a wide variety of ages interact and hold productive roles (see a recent collection of papers edited by Uhlenberg and Riley, 2000).

Three emerging scholarly and policy debates address historical shifts in age structuring: these surround the chronologization, institutionalization, and standardization of lives (for a complete discussion, see Settersten, 1999). The thesis of *chronologization*, to use Kohli's (1986) term, asserts that age and time are (or have become) salient dimensions of life. Here, an important turning point occurred in the early part of the 20th century (Chudacoff, 1989; Graff, 1995). Organizations became more bureaucratic. Revolutionary advances took place in science, industry, and communication. Significant shifts occurred in immigration and urbanization. Concerns about efficiency and productivity grew. These and other large-scale developments prompted greater emphases on age and time. *Institutionalization* refers to the ways in which the life course is structured by organizations, institutions, and the state. European scholarship especially has emphasized the ways in which modern nation-states shape the life course via structural arrangements and the allocation of resources. As individuals have been freed from traditional forms of informal social control, the state began to regulate individuals formally and in far-reaching ways, thereby institutionalizing lives (Kohli, 1999; Mayer, 1997). With this shift, age and lifetime became central dimensions of concern for the state. While institutionalization occurs through state regulation and intervention, it also occurs through the structuring of pathways through educational institutions and work organizations. The effects of institutionalization presumably trickle down to the minds of individuals as they set and strive for developmental goals, thereby serving to create and constrain options, and to organize and link life experiences over time (Kohli & Mayer, 1986). *Standardization* refers to the regularity of life patterns and is a direct result of chronologization and institutionalization. When chronologization and institutionalization are high, the standardization of the life course should also be high.

At the same time, there is evidence that lives are (or have become) *de-chronologized, de-institutionalized,* and *de-standardized.** New opportunities exist for individuals to move between or simultaneously pursue educational, work, and leisure experiences throughout life (rather than restrict them to the first, second, and third ages of life, respectively), and to better meet family demands and responsibilities by adjusting commitments in other spheres. This evidence suggests that the life course is becoming flexibly organized and experienced (for an extended discussion, see Settersten, 1999). For example, shifts in mortality, morbidity, and fertility have brought longer and healthier lives and reduced the period of active child rearing for most couples. Multiple pathways exist into and through retirement. Employers no longer invest in their employees as they once did, and individuals no longer work for a single organization for most of their careers. Educational programs for adults have grown, as has adult enrollment in higher education.

These and other indicators reveal that life course patterns that were once relatively standard are now crumbling. These shifts have led to significant worry, especially in Europe, that current structural arrangements, which are based on outdated models of life, may put at risk those individuals whose lives no longer follow older models (Beck, 2000; Heinz, 1996; Levy, 1996). Trends toward the individualization of the life course clearly bring new freedoms for the pursuit of personal goals, but they also bring new responsibilities and risks. The experimental nature of "do-it-yourself" biographies makes them prone to "biological slippage and collapse" (Beck, 2000). When individuals choose courses that are not widely shared by others and not reinforced by organizations, institutions, and social policies, individuals may lose important sources of informal and formal support along the way. In this scenario, personal failures, in particular, become no one's fault but one's own.

---

*It is important to note that evidence need not relate exclusively to *either* the chronologization, institutionalization, and standardization theses *or* the de-chronologization, de-institutionalization, and de-standardization theses. Indeed, evidence for both sides may co-exist and even be compatible. For example, while the timing of many life course transitions became more uniform over the course of the 20th century, their sequencing simultaneously became more diverse. This is especially true of transitions typically associated with entry into adulthood (Shanahan, 2000).

For each of these debates, systematic evidence is critically needed to evaluate how life course patterns have shifted in different spheres for successive cohorts of men and women, for subgroups of men and women (especially by race and social class), and across cultures. This and the prior section have explored age structuring in different life spheres at formal institutional and societal levels, and how these patterns have shifted historically. The next section explores age structuring at an informal, social-psychological level by turning attention to age norms and expectations.

INFORMAL AGE STRUCTURING: NORMS AND EXPECTATIONS*

What Are Age "Norms"? Definitions and Theoretical Starting Points

Life course scholarship often begins with the assumption that lives are socially structured, and that age becomes most interesting as a social phenomenon. The life course is conceptualized as a sequence of age-linked transitions, times when social roles change, when new rights, duties, and resources are encountered, and when identities are in flux. As members of groups, we share notions about what Neugarten (1969) called the "normal, expectable life cycle," ideas about the seasons of life and the markers within and between them.

Some age-related expectations are based on formal laws and policies. For example, age-based laws determine when one can vote, drink, marry, have consensual sex, serve the military, be prosecuted, and retire. Other expectations are based on statistical patterns, observed frequencies that reflect general patterns of human development and aging. For example, parents are quick to plot their children's height, weight, intelligence, and other characteristics relative to "normal" curves, and women expect to encounter menopause around age 50. Still other expectations are not closely linked to laws or statistical patterns, but may nonetheless be part of informal and shared ideas about the timing of transitions, such as when schooling or childbearing are to be finished or when children are to have left home. We relate easily to the notion that transitions can come "on time" or "off time," and that untimely transitions often catch us off guard and bring limited support from similarly aged peers.

Age-linked expectations about the life course clearly exist. But of what are they made? The answer, in part, depends on the vantage point from which we approach them. *Demographers* have used the terms "age norm" and "age-normative" to refer to statistical regularity in the actual timing of transitions in the population or for subgroups of the population. If we observe regularity in transition patterns, at least four possible explanations exist. (These explanations need not be mutually exclusive.) First, regularity in the timing of transitions may reflect universal patterns of human growth and maturation found across societies and historical times (though developmental scientists now assume that most of human development is instead

---

*Several related bodies of research are important to note, though they are outside the purview of this chapter. Life course research will benefit from renewed attention to each of these traditions (for a discussion, see Settersten, 1999). One body of research addresses *subjective age identification*. This research examines how old a person feels, into which age group an individual categorizes her or himself, or how old one would most like to be. A second body of research examines *age-related images and stereotypes*. This research explores commonplace images associated with people of different ages, especially with respect to their personality traits and characteristics. A third but small body of research explores *life phases*. This literature examines how individuals in a society divide the span of life into distinct categories, and the age boundaries and markers that are used to define categories and designate movement from one phase to another.

variable and contingent, not universal). Second, it may reflect shared ideas about the optimal timing of experiences. Third, it may reflect structural conditions that create different types of opportunities and constraints for different age groups. Fourth, it may reflect informal social norms that govern experiences. Research on the demography of life course transitions generally assumes that regularity in behavior reflects, and is driven by, informal social norms. (In contrast, the second explanation is emphasized in psychological approaches, and the third and fourth explanations in sociological approaches, as discussed below.) This assumption is problematic, as Marini (1984) also noted in her classic critique of scholarship on age norms, not only because behavior that is statistically regular need not be socially "normative," but because empirical research has not actually measured social norms (a point which will also be elaborated below).

Psychologists have used the terms "age norm" and "age-normative" in conjunction with investigations of the optimal ages ("best," "ideal," or "preferred" ages) at which to experience various transitions. The implicit assumption underlying most psychological theory and research on age norms is that these optimal ages equip individuals with a "mental map" of the life course (Hagestad & Neugarten, 1985). This map lends individuals a sense of what lies ahead, and gives them a chance to prepare for those experiences. The focus of psychological approaches to age norms is therefore on individuals, and on how these mental maps, as frames of reference for orienting behavior, fulfill important needs for predictability and order.

Sociologists have a theoretical interest in how age is central to social organization and the maintenance of social order. The essence of sociological theorizing about age norms is tied to social prescriptions and proscriptions governing the timing of transitions (for a recent multi-disciplinary discussion of social norms, see Hechter & Opp, 2001; for further sociological discussion, see Horne, 2001). It is from this perspective that I will later evaluate empirical evidence. For sociologists, informal social norms are defined by three components. First, they are *prescriptions for*, or *proscriptions against*, engaging in certain behaviors and taking on certain roles. Second, there is *consensus* about these rules. And third, these rules are enforced through various mechanisms of *social control*, particularly positive sanctions to keep people "on track," and negative sanctions to bring "back into line" those individuals who stray from these tracks. If an age-normative system is operating, individuals should be aware of the sanctions and consequences for violating norms, and be sensitive to social approval and disapproval. These sanctions may be informal (e.g., interpersonal sanctions in the form of persuasion, encouragement, reinforcement, ridicule, gossip, ostracism) or formal (e.g., political, legal, or economic sanctions). For example, when people deviate from a norm, their behavior is not only evaluated negatively by others, but it is often taken to reflect something problematic about their personalities or abilities (e.g., Krueger, Heckhausen, & Hundertmark, 1995).

Psychologists and sociologists alike assume that norms are "internalized" through socialization processes that incorporate "collective-cultural" meanings into individual consciousness, meanings which become so ingrained that they seem part of nature itself (Dannefer, 1996; see also Settersten, 2002; Valsiner & Lawrence, 1997). The psychological viewpoint ends once norms are internalized as frames of reference and "brought to life" as individuals do their part. But individuals will not always do their part, and it is here that sociological perspectives continue. For sociologists, deviations from norms become problematic when they jeopardize social order and functioning. Norms become a way to "construct appropriate individuals", to use Meyer's (1986) phrase. When *informal* norms are strong, individuals regulate themselves and others, and the need for *formal* regulation is low. Yet the strong ethos of individualism typical of modern societies may lead individuals to regulate themselves and others only loosely, if at all—which, in turn, may prompt the need for greater *formal* regulation, bringing us full-circle to the institutional and societal concerns that opened the chapter.

Earlier Evidence on Optimal Age Norms

Neugarten, Moore, and Lowe (1965) conducted the classic study of informal age norms in the late 1950s. The larger project on which their study was based—the Kansas City Study of Adult Life—not only had a profound impact on what was then a "young" field of gerontology, but also on its evolution in the decades since (Hendricks, 1994). Neugarten's landmark study utilized two specific instruments: "Timetables for Men and Women" and the "Age Norm Checklist". The 11-item "Timetables for Men and Women" instrument asked respondents for the "best age" for accomplishing a variety of major life transitions (e.g., "What do you think is the best age for a man to marry?" "What do you think is the best age for most people to leave home?"). For these items, respondents provided a specific age or age band. To address the issue of consensus, Neugarten and her colleagues examined the proportion of individuals who cited an age (or ages) within a small band that "produced the most accurate reflection of the consensus that existed in the data" (pp. 712–713). Depending on the breadth of responses given for any particular item, the age band they used to calculate consensus was widely variable, ranging anywhere from 2 to 15 years.

The issue of sanctions was addressed in a separate "Age Norm Checklist," which tapped feelings about minor lifestyle behaviors. The 48-item checklist asked whether respondents "approve of, feel favorable" or "disapprove of, feel unfavorable" about a variety of behaviors at three specific ages that the investigators deemed inappropriate, marginal, or appropriate (e.g., "A woman who wears bikini on the beach—when she's 45; when she's 30; when she's 18" or "A man who buys himself a red sports car—when he's 60; when he's 45; when he's 25").

Negarten's study supported the notion that a set of age expectations underlie adult life, and that men and women are aware of the social clocks that operate in their lives and of their own timing in relation to them. They demonstrated a high degree of consensus about the age-linked life transitions in the "timetables" instrument, and about the age-appropriate or inappropriate lifestyle behaviors in the "age norm checklist".

Two subsequent studies are direct replications of Neugarten's study: Passuth and Maines' (1981) Chicago study, and Plath and Ikeda's (1975) Japanese study. One other study is a partial replication of Neugarten's study and addresses age timetables for a wide range of transitions and in a broad sample: Zepelin, Sills, and Heath's (1987) study of white- and blue-collar men and women in Michigan, California, and Florida.* Taken together, these subsequent studies supported Neugarten's contentions and demonstrated a rather remarkable consensus on timetables for major life transitions, in particular. Relative to Neugarten's original study, however, data from these later studies suggest that individuals not only advocate later ages for most transitions, but a wider range of ages. Nonetheless, the average values cited for transitions generally reveal an age-based sequence of transitions comparable to that found in Neguarten's study.

Recent Evidence on Prescriptive-Proscriptive Age Norms

The studies noted above measured optimal ages for accomplishing life transitions, not age norms in a prescriptive-proscriptive sense. While these studies addressed the issue of consensus,

---

*Several other studies continue the tradition begun by Neugarten, Moore, and Lowe (1965). These include Fallo-Mitchell and Ryff (1982), Gee (1990), Peterson (1996), Rook, Catalano, and Dooley (1989), Roscoe and Peterson (1989), and Veevers, Gee, and Wister (1996). Because these studies have restricted samples or address a limited range of experiences, they are not discussed here.

they largely ignored the issue of whether social sanctions and other consequences exist for violating age-related expectations. The lack of attention to sanctions is troublesome because it is reasonable that consensus can exist without sanctions. To further complicate matters, it is conceivable that individuals can be "punished" without being sanctioned. Being off time can be inconvenient and uncomfortable—and even come with costs for the individual—but these penalties need not result from social sanctioning. Some phenomena may also be statistically regular but inherently cannot be approached on prescriptive or proscriptive terms. For example, this is the case with menopause, widowhood, and the death of parents. These transitions become predictable at certain points in life, but individuals who experience these transitions early or late are not likely to be negatively sanctioned by others.

The age-normative framework has been widely accepted in life course scholarship, despite the many limitations noted above and a paucity of research on the topic. How relevant are these assumptions in today's world? Is there consensus about informal age timetables, and does such consensus, even when it exists, constitute informal cultural "norms"? In response to these questions, let me highlight some recent research with Gunhild Hagestad.

Because prior research on age norms focused on convenient or restricted samples, Hagestad and I studied a random representative sample of 319 adults 18 and older in the Chicago metropolitan area (for further information on the sample and methods, see Settersten & Hagestad, 1996b). The interviews explored individuals' thinking about "age deadlines" for family, educational, and work transitions.* Past research on age norms had been plagued by a host of problems, not the least of which was the ambiguity of items meant to tap "norms" (e.g., items eliciting fuzzy bands of "best" ages for "people" to accomplish various transitions). In an effort to improve the precision of measurement, we not only asked about men and women separately, but clearly targeted inquiry at upper age boundaries. We also developed items that would address the three critical components of norms noted earlier: (a) prescriptive or proscriptive rules that are (b) supported by consensus and (c) enforced through social sanctions.

The structure of the interview schedule emerged directly out of this framework. Respondents were first asked to identify the age deadline for each transition (e.g., "By what age should a man retire?"). Respondents who mentioned a specific deadline were asked to discuss why men or women should meet it (e.g., "Why should a man retire by that age?") and the potential consequences for those who do not (e.g., "Does anything happen to him if he doesn't retire by that age? Are there any consequences that come to mind?"). Respondents' ideas were probed with a series of open-ended questions, the responses to which were noted verbatim and later coded. Three categories of response are central to the findings highlighted below: "interpersonal sanctions" (which tapped social pressures to adhere to deadlines and negative social repercussions for violating deadlines); "development" (which covered concerns about self and personality, as well as physical development and health); and "sequencing" (which captured concerns about the order of multiple transitions). Examples of responses for these and the remaining six categories can be found in Settersten and Hagestad (1996b).

The upper panel of Table 4-1 presents descriptive information on the *family transitions*—leaving home, returning home, marrying, entering parenthood, completing

---

*Several age expectations related to health and death were also explored: expecting the death of one's spouse, the death of one's parents, and one's own failing health. These transitions are not discussed here. For basic findings, see Settersten (1997).

TABLE 4-1. Perceived Age Deadlines for Life Course Transitions

	About Men's Lives (n = 161)				About Women's Lives (n = 158)			
	% Perceiving a deadline	Average Age deadline (SD)	% Mode (age)	% 6-year band	% Perceiving a deadline	Average Age deadline (SD)	% Mode (age)	% 6-year band
Family transitions								
Leave home	77.6	21.70 (2.6)	20.9 (21)	72.3 (20–25)	69.0	21.90 (3.3)	18.9 (18)	83.4 (18–23)
Return home	38.5	27.16 (5.2)	26.7 (30)	53.3 (25–30)	23.4	28.20 (5.7)	32.0 (25)	56.0 (25–30)
Marry	85.1	27.89 (4.3)	25.8 (25)	74.2 (25–30)	82.3	25.93 (3.9)	35.2 (25)	67.2 (25–30)
Enter Parenthood	75.2	29.88 (4.4)	22.7 (30)	60.8 (25–30)	78.5	28.84 (5.2)	28.4 (30)	66.6 (25–30)
Complete childbearing	70.2	44.19 (7.3)	34.7 (40)	51.1 (40–45)	86.1	39.08 (4.8)	37.4 (40)	72.1 (35–40)
Enter Grandparenthood	75.2	52.30 (7.2)	27.6 (50)	43.6 (50–55)	70.9	50.96 (7.2)	31.5 (50)	52.0 (50–55)
Educational/work transitions								
Exit full-time schooling	63.4	26.37 (4.5)	15.5 (25)	60.8 (25–30)	48.1	25.51 (3.4)	31.1 (25)	72.2 (21–26)
Enter full-time work	77.6	22.79 (3.3)	26.7 (22)	67.4 (20–25)	75.3	21.66 (2.6)	19.4 (18, 21)	75.3 (18–23)
Settle on career/job	79.5	28.96 (4.8)	41.4 (30)	69.3 (25–30)	69.6	28.92 (4.7)	31.5 (30)	61.9 (25–30)
Peak of work career	82.0	41.69 (7.8)	21.1 (40)	43.1 (35–40)	67.7	39.80 (8.4)	18.4 (40)	37.8 (40–45)
Reach Retirement	54.7	61.31 (5.7)	29.6 (65)	62.9 (60–65)	46.8	59.32 (6.7)	20.0 (65)	53.8 (60–65)

Source: Settersten and Hagestad, 1996a, 1996b.

childbearing, and entering grandparenthood.* For each transition, information is provided on the percentage of respondents who perceived an age deadline, the average age deadline and standard deviation, the modal age, and the percentage of responses that fell within a 6-year age band (as a measure of the concentration of the distribution).†

The majority of respondents perceived age deadlines for most of these transitions. The only family transition for which age limits were not often cited was for a return to a parental home. Family support of this type was not viewed as something that should be limited by age. Instead, a move home would depend on the needs and circumstances of the child. Deadlines for leaving home and age limits on returning home were cited more often for men than women, whereas deadlines for entering parenthood and, especially, completing childbearing were cited more often for women than men. The latter findings are clearly tied to the fact that women's biological clocks impose significant constraints on their reproduction, despite the fact that recent advances in reproductive technologies bring the potential to extend these possibilities.

While the distributions exhibited significant range, they were also fairly concentrated around modal values. About half or more of the deadlines for each family transition clustered within a six-year span. The range of deadlines was smaller, and the distributions more concentrated, for women's lives than men's. Again, this was linked to the fact that women have pressing biological clocks for several family transitions.

The bottom panel of Table 4-1 presents parallel information on the *educational and work transitions*—exiting full-time schooling, entering full-time work, settling on a career/job area, reaching the peak of the work trajectory, and entering retirement.‡ For men's lives, the majority of respondents cited deadlines for all five transitions, though the proportions were low for exiting full-time schooling and entering retirement. For women's lives, exiting full-time schooling and entering retirement were not even viewed by the majority as being age-dependent. Across the board, deadlines were cited more often for men than women. The distributions for most transitions were also fairly clustered around modal values, with the exception of reaching the peak of the work trajectory, which had an especially large range and was the least concentrated distribution for men and women alike. These data are consistent with Kohli's (1994) suggestion that once individuals enter the workforce, there are no normative transitions until retirement—though our findings suggest that even entering the workforce and retirement may not be truly normative (i.e., culturally prescribed and socially regulated). Nonetheless, there may be enough regularity in work trajectories to speak of the organization of the life course *through* work, particularly at the firm level and as part of the education–work–leisure tripartition (Kohli, 1994).

Two trends emerge when these spheres are compared. First, deadlines are generally mentioned more often in relation to family transitions than to educational and work transitions, and for both men and women. This supports the hypothesis that a greater degree of *informal*

---

*Two family-related items address age *proscriptions* rather than prescriptions: Returning home (the age after which a man or woman should not be allowed to return to his or her parents' home) and completing childbearing (the age after which a man or woman should no longer have a child). For a more complete discussion of the family transitions as a set, see Settersten and Hagestad (1996b). For an in-depth look at leaving and returning home, see Settersten (1998b). For similar Canadian data, see Veevers, Gee, and Wister (1996).

†To determine the 6-year band, we took the modal value and that set of values on either side of the mode that maximized the degree of concentration within 6 years. This band served as a crude anchor with which to compare distributions.

‡For a more complete discussion of the educational and work transitions as a set, and of how they compare to the family transitions, see Settersten and Hagestad (1996a). For an in-depth look at the transition to retirement, see Settersten (1998a).

age structuring may exist in spheres for which the degree of *formal* age structuring is not likely as strong. Second, deadlines are generally perceived more often for men than women, regardless of sphere (with the exception of childbearing). This supports the hypothesis that men's lives are (or are perceived as) more rigidly structured by age, while women's lives are (or are perceived as) more fluid, unpredictable, and discontinuous.

In analyses not shown here, non-whites, non-professionals, and those with lower educational levels cited age deadlines more often than their counterparts. These trends may be understood in terms of prevalent perceptions—and realities—of limited opportunities for minorities, the underclass, and the working class, and the fact that advantage or disadvantage cumulate over time, heightening the importance of age and early experiences. Members of these same subgroups also gave earlier deadlines than their counterparts. These trends support the notion that clocks of many types—especially those related to social roles and physical health—may tick faster for members of these groups, what Burton, Allison, and Obeidallah (1995) describe as an "accelerated life course." The pace of these timetables may be especially pronounced in adolescence, as young people from these groups often move quickly into adult roles and responsibilities and face (or feel themselves to have) foreclosed futures (Geronimus, 1996).

Also in analyses not shown here, the central dimensions underlying individuals' thinking about the importance of age deadlines overwhelmingly related to concerns about individual growth and potential, and then to concerns about the place of particular transitions within a larger sequence. This was true of both the sphere of family and the sphere of education and work. At the same time, consequences were seldom perceived for men or women who miss deadlines. Late timing of transitions was generally viewed as being acceptable, accompanied by little social tension, and without major consequences for the individual or significant others.

These findings seem paradoxical. On the one hand, individuals are able to cite deadlines for many transitions and discuss the developmental gains associated with meeting those deadlines. On the other hand, they do not automatically associate an *inability* to achieve deadlines with significant developmental losses. Developmental benefits and losses are not simply viewed as two sides of the same coin. Individuals' visions of the life course are complex, diverse, and flexible. Above all, they find it imperative to "live a life of their own," to paraphrase Beck (2000). Timetables that are self-constructed and self-imposed prevail over general cultural timetables. What is crucial to individuals' thinking, however, is that when personal timetables mesh with cultural timetables, the process of navigating life is easier—and when life is easier to navigate, development comes more easily. Crafting a life of one's own, especially when it goes against the grain, is viewed as a difficult enterprise. But this need not mean that one's development is compromised in the process. To the contrary, developmental gains may even be greater, especially over the long run, when individuals must rely on themselves and even endure hardships as they go about composing their lives as they wish. Individuals approach age deadlines as flexible developmental markers that guide the life course, not as widely shared and firmly enforced age norms that dictate it, as scholars once assumed.

The tremendous emphasis on individual growth and potential in our interviews is in line with what Meyer (1986) calls the dominant "cultural theory of the individual" in the United States. This "theory" emphasizes self-esteem and an internal locus of control, and takes life to be a continuous journey and discovery of personhood. The high degree of "psychologizing" reflects the rapid and deep penetration of psychology into most aspects of American life, evident in popular television talk shows, self-help books, magazines, and newspaper advice columns. The ever-present language of "therapeutic culture" (Karp, 1996) has risen conjointly with the ideology of individualism. While these forces emphasize self-esteem and an internal locus of control, they have, paradoxically, also produced an "age of melancholy" character-ized by the erosion of significant social attachments and unprecedented levels of alienation, depression, and mental "dis-ease" (Karp, 1996).

The opening sections of this chapter focused on institutional and societal-level processes, while this section has focused on individual-level processes. Both sets of processes are simulta-neously at work and clearly influence each other. For example, formal laws and policies may reflect, create, or be reshaped by patterns of behavior. As noted earlier, laws and policies are often explicitly based on age or implicitly based on judgments about the nature of particular periods of life. Consider the shifting boundary of retirement discussed earlier. Organizational policies and practices have often encouraged individuals to retire early or take "bridge jobs," while Social Security and Medicare rules have reinforced age 65 as the appropriate age for retirement. In the case of Social Security, however, later age-eligibility thresholds are now being phased in. In addition, longstanding earnings penalties to Social Security recipients were also recently lifted. These changes not only bring to an end a policy that has, since the time of the Depression, devalued and discouraged the work of older adults. They are interventions meant to actively redirect the course of behavioral patterns, which in turn will undoubtedly affect informal age-related expectations about work and retirement. (Questions about social policy and the life course are addressed elsewhere in this volume. For additional discussion, see Settersten, 2003.)

UNRESOLVED ISSUES AND NEW DIRECTIONS FOR SCHOLARSHIP

The biggest challenges confronting this area of study are to clarify what is meant by "age norms," explicate the levels at and units with which age norms are studied, and specify their form and content. Do age-related expectations constitute "norms" or are they simply "cognitive maps"? As Modell (1997, p. 286) also asks, "do age norms dispose or do they just propose, or do they perhaps dispose for others but only propose for oneself? Or are they instead hopes, or mere verbal nods to a set of rules thrown off by the activities of the state and institutions, well-known but hollow?" If age-related expectations are really norms, we must approach them as prescriptive and proscriptive phenomena, demonstrate consensus, and find evidence of sanctions for departures from these rules. This is tricky theoretically and empirically because norms and sanctions cannot really be separated: Identifying an age norm requires observing a sanction, so age norms cannot be studied independently of their enforcement mechanism (Lawrence, 1996).

In contrast, if we take age-related expectations to be cognitive maps, we must approach them differently. From this standpoint, we need not care whether they are truly normative (i.e., "oughts" backed by consensus and sanctions). We need only recognize that these expec-tations help guide and evaluate our behavior and that of others. Life course scholarship also generally assumes that age expectations are clear. In reality, however, individuals are often unaware of these expectations, either because the expectations are unclear or because they are part of the taken-for-granted world (Lawrence, 1996). For this reason, age expectations are especially challenging to study. It is difficult to get people to discuss things they take for granted, and because age is so commonplace, it may produce indifference or be invisible. Worse still, when people are asked direct questions about the taken-for-granted, they may feel "ridicule, discomfort, embarrassment, or even hostility" (Lawrence, 1996, p. 210). To study these phenomena effectively, we must use methods that make conscious information that is difficult to access. Innovative methods, such as those developed as part of Project A.G.E. (Keith et al., 1994), help us do so.

Another definitional problem relates to the fact that norms are necessarily group-level phenomena. Whose norms are they, and how clearly defined are the parameters of the group? In addition, how do individuals, as members of many groups, manage multiple, and even conflicting, norms? These questions relate to how broadly or specifically norms operate, and whether they operate at varying strengths for different types of experiences. For example, "national" norms may exist for "highly institutionalized" age-linked transitions, such as the transition into school or retirement (Dannefer, 1996). Other norms may operate locally, such as work-related norms, which may vary by occupation and organizational context (Lashbrook, 1996; Lawrence, 1996), or childbearing norms, which may vary across families or across ethnic communities (Burton, 1996; Geronimus, 1996). These examples also beg a larger question: Where do norms have their greatest strength and create their greatest meaning? Action at the "meso" level—in the central settings of everyday life—seems especially important to understand, especially that which occurs in families, peer and friendship groups, school settings, work organizations, and neighborhoods. It is in these settings that the meanings and uses of age are directly encountered and experienced, and in which age norms, if they exist, will be clearest and strongest. Little research to date has been aimed at understanding the form and content of age expectations in these settings.

Life maps in individuals' minds often cover whole sequences or pathways. But empirically, research has focused on separate transitions, sometimes piled on top of each other to create synthetic pathways. This type of inquiry misses important questions about how multiple transitions are *sequenced* and even *interdependent* (e.g., timing of school completion often conditions the timing of marriage, which in turn often conditions the timing of parenthood). It also misses important questions about the *distance* between multiple transitions (e.g., the spacing of subsequent children in relation to the timing of the first birth), the *density* of transitions (e.g., the number of children born to an individual within a particular period of time), and the *duration* of transitions (e.g., the time spent in a relationship before marriage, and the time spent in a marriage before the birth of a first child).

Much remains to be learned about the repercussions of "timely" and "untimely" behavior. The effects of timing likely depend on the degree to which it constrains or promotes later opportunities, whether it accelerates or delays subsequent experiences, and how well it fits within, or gives shape to, a trajectory or set of trajectories. Sociologists, in particular, assume that negative consequences result for individuals who deviate from norms, and that positive rewards come to those who conform to norms. Neither of these propositions has been well explored. For example, we know little about how adherence or non-adherence to norms might have positive or negative effects on opportunities in education, work, family, or leisure, or on the physical and psychological development of individuals. It is entirely possible that being on time may not bring the advantages, and being off time the disadvantages, that earlier work on age norms has assumed. Indeed, being off time may even carry positive effects. For example, managers who are viewed by their superiors as being ahead of schedule are given higher performance evaluations; those who are behind schedule are penalized with lower evaluations (Lawrence, 1996). Consider, too, a 12-year-old who attends college and a 20-year-old who receives an Academy Award nomination (Lawrence, 1996). In these cases, the individual receives high status because these accomplishments come early. (Of course, the larger cultural context conditions such evaluations. In the United States, early achievements are especially likely to be rewarded.) Another possible positive effect of being "off time" is that individuals who might otherwise be dealing with multiple role transitions are able to avoid that strain by hastening or delaying one or more of these transitions.

Much remains to be learned about how age-related expectations matter in developmental decision-making: in shaping the types of goals individuals set at different points in life, the strategies and resources individuals use to pursue them, and the conditions under which they engage or disengage goals, especially in the face of age-based opportunities and constraints. The "life-span theory of control" and corresponding OPS (optimization in primary and secondary control) models developed by Heckhausen and her colleagues are particularly fruitful areas for future scholarship in this area (e.g., Heckhausen, 1997, 2000; Schulz & Heckhausen, 1999). These authors suggest that individuals, as they grow older, express an awareness of a reduced potential for growth in themselves and control over their environments. In response, individuals narrow their goals to those that are most age-appropriate. They select fewer goals aimed at achieving developmental gains and more goals aimed at minimizing developmental losses. And they compensate for losses in primary control (altering the external world to fit one's needs and desires) by more often relying on secondary control strategies (which instead target internal processes and therefore free up resources for more limited attempts to establish primary control). (For empirical illustrations related to intimate relationships, childbearing, and health and financial stress, see, respectively, Wrosch & Heckhausen [1999], Heckhausen, Wrosch, & Fleeson [2001], and Wrosch, Heckhausen, & Lachman [2000].) These ideas are also in line with the work of Brandtstädter (e.g., 1998), who suggests that individuals naturally shift from "assimilative" to "accommodative" coping strategies as they age.

Similarly, it is important to examine how individuals regulate their development in the face of "non-normative" demands (Wrosch & Freund, 2001).* When developmental demands are non-normative, individuals must play more active roles to compensate for the lack of structure, such as when historical events or periods of social change disturb existing norms, or as life experiences become de-standardized (see also Beck, 2000; Heinz, 2002). As Heinz (2002) argues, "doing biography" in post-traditional societies means relying less on institutionalized criteria, conventionalized behaviors, and organizational routines, and relying more on self-initiated sequences. Multiple options exist for family and other social relationships, and for navigating the spheres of education and work. These now seem more weakly defined by cultural age norms than in the past—though the degree to which biographies have been freed from norms related to participation in social roles and institutions, and have become less dependent on social class and gender inequalities, remain open empirical questions.

Finally, several specific types of timetables must be explored: "general timetables," "specialized timetables," "personal timetables," and "interdependent timetables" (Nydegger, 1986; Settersten, 1999). *General timetables* are widely shared timetables for major transitions that most individuals experience. In contrast, *specialized timetables* exist for specific populations or for specific kinds of experiences. For example, there is a critical need to systematically document and explain variability in age expectations and in actual behavioral patterns across divisions such as cohort, sex, race, and social class. We also have much to learn about "deep structure" cultural differences in understandings and experiences of age and the life course, and how these have shifted historically (Fry, 2003).

Personal timetables are those timetables that are "not shared and not normative" (Nydegger, 1986, p. 145). Little is known about personal timetables, and the degree to which they mesh with specialized or generalized timetables. Perhaps the most complicated type of

---

*"Non-normative" experiences are understood to be those experiences that (1) are not generally expected by individuals (such as divorce or the death of a child) and only loosely coupled with age, if at all; or (2) occur much earlier or later than expected (such as when the death of a spouse happens in early adulthood, or when the birth of a child occurs during adolescence or midlife).

personal timetable is the *interdependent timetable*. The lives of individuals are intimately woven together, and little is known about how the timetables of intimates fit together or are jointly negotiated, and the consequences of good or bad fits. Several recent papers begin to reveal the importance of interdependent timetables. Hagestad's (1996) "personal ethnography" of illness examines how an unexpected illness for an individual causes "ripple effects" throughout familial and social networks. Similarly, Cohler, Pickett, and Cook (1996) describe how schizophrenic adults and their families live "outside of time" as their lives are disrupted by episodes of hospitalization, discharge, and re-hospitalization. Tobin (1996), too, shows how parents of mentally retarded children become "perpetual parents," faced with the responsibility of actively caring for their children all their lives, even into advanced old age.

In closing, it is interesting to note that two major principles in developmental science—one stressing the "normative," and one stressing "heterogeneity"—are at odds with one another (Dannefer, 1996). Too great an emphasis on the normative brings the risk of neglecting diversity, but too great an emphasis on diversity brings the risk of overlooking important shared experiences within and between groups. As Dannefer (2003 and in this volume) notes, many of our descriptions and explanations of life course patterns are irrelevant to the everyday reality of many groups of individuals worldwide. (Dannefer provides interesting illustrations related to the lives of child laborers in Pakistan, gang members in New York and Los Angeles, and Amazonian Shamans.) What, then, can we expect of life course scholarship if it does not reflect the range of actual patterns globally?

Over 25 years ago, Neugarten and Hagestad (1976) asked whether age had become more or less significant for individuals, groups, and societies. Their question had no simple answers, for in some ways age had become more important, and in other ways age had become less important. "It is the mark of a complex society," they remarked, "that both pictures [may be] true. It is also a reasonable prediction that in the decades that lie ahead, the pictures are likely to become neither more stable nor more coherent" (p. 51). Their prediction has come true, for now, decades later, the pictures seem more complicated than ever before.

REFERENCES

Beck, U. (2000). Living your own life in a runaway world: Individualisation, globalisation, and politics. In W. Hutton & A. Giddens (Eds.), *Global capitalism* (pp. 164–174). New York: The New Press.

Brandtstädter, J. (1998). Action perspectives on human development. In R. M. Lerner (Ed.), *Handbook of child psychology: Vol. 1. Theoretical models of human development* (5th ed., pp. 807–863). New York: John Wiley & Sons.

Burton, L. (1996). Age norms, the timing of family role transitions, and intergenerational caregiving among aging African-American women. *The Gerontologist, 36*(2), 199–208.

Burton, L., Allison, K., & Obeidallah, D. (1995). Social context and adolescence: Perspectives on development among inner-city African-American teens. In L. Crockett & A. Crouter (Eds.), *Pathways through adolescence* (pp. 119–138). Mahwah, NJ: Lawrence Erlbaum.

Byrd, M., & Bruess, T. (1992). Perceptions of sociological and psychological age norms by young, middle-aged, and elderly New Zealanders. *International Journal of Aging and Human Development, 34*(2), 145–163.

Chudacoff, H. P. (1989). *How old are you? Age consciousness in American culture*. Princeton, NJ: Princeton University Press.

Cohler, B., Pickett, S. A., & Cook, J. A. (1996). Life course and persistent psychiatric illness: Social timing, cohort, and intervention. In V. Bengtson (Ed.), *Adulthood and aging: Research on continuities and discontinuities* (pp. 69–95). New York: Springer Publishing Company.

Daly, K. J. (1996). *Families and time: Keeping pace in a hurried culture*. Thousand Oaks, CA: Sage.

Dannefer, D. (1996). The social organization of diversity, and the normative organization of age. *The Gerontologist, 36*(2), 174–177.

Dannefer, D. (2003). Whose life course is it, anyway? Diversity and "linked lives" in global perspective. In R. A. Settersten, Jr. (Ed.), *Invitation to the life course: Toward new understandings of later life* (pp. 259–268). Amityville, NY: Baywood Publishing Company.

Fallo-Mitchell, L., & Ryff, C. D. (1982). Preferred timing of female life events: Cohort differences. *Research on Aging, 4*, 249–267.

Fry, C. L. (2003). The life course as a cultural construct. In R. A. Settersten, Jr. (Ed.). *Invitation to the life course: Toward new understandings of later life* (pp. 269–294). Amityville, NY: Baywood.

Gee, E. M. (1990). Preferred timing of women's life events: A Canadian study. *International Journal of Aging and Human Development, 31*(4), 279–294.

Geronimus, A. (1996). What teen mothers know. *Human Nature, 7(4)*, 323–352.

Graff, H. (1995). *Conflicting paths: Growing up in America*. Cambridge, MA: Harvard University Press.

Hagestad, G. O. (1996). On-time, off-time, out of time? Reflections on continuity and discontinuity from an illness process. In V. Bengtson (Ed.), *Adulthood and aging: Research on continuities and discontinuities* (pp. 204–222). New York: Springer Publishing Company.

Hagestad G. O. (2003). Interdependent lives and relationships in changing times: A life-course view of families and aging. In R. A. Settersten, Jr. (Ed.), *Invitation to the life course: Toward new understandings of later life* (pp. 135–159). Amityville, NY: Baywood Publishing Company.

Hagestad, G. O., & Neugarten, B. L. (1985). Age and the life course. In E. Shanas & R. Binstock (Eds.), *Handbook of aging and the social sciences* (2nd ed., pp. 36–61). New York: Van Nostrand and Reinhold Company.

Hechter, M., & Opp, K.-D. (Eds.). (2001). *Social norms*. New York: Russell Sage Foundation.

Heckhausen, J. (1997). Developmental regulation across adulthood: Primary and secondary control of age-related challenges. *Developmental Psychology, 33(1)*, 176–187.

Heckhausen, J. (2000). Developmental regulation across the life span: An action-phase model of engagement and disengagement with developmental goals. In J. Heckhausen (Ed.), *Motivational psychology of human development: Developing motivation and motivating development* (pp. 213–231). New York: Elsevier Science.

Heckhausen, J., Wrosch, C., & Fleeson, W. (2001). Developmental regulation before and after a developmental deadline: The sample case of the "biological clock" for childbearing. *Psychology and Aging, 16*(3), 400–413.

Heinz, W. R. (1996). Status passages as micro-macro linkages in life-course research. In A. Weymann and W.R. Heinz (Eds.), *Society and biography* (pp. 51–65). Weinheim: Deutscher Studien Verlag.

Heinz, W. R. (2002). Self-socialization and post-traditional society. In R. A. Settersten & T. Owens (Eds.), *Advances in life-course research: New frontiers in socialization* (pp. 41–64). London: Elsevier Science.

Hendricks, J. (1994). Revisiting the Kansas City Study of Adult Life: Roots of the disengagement model in social gerontology. *The Gerontologist, 34*(6), 753–755.

Henretta, J. (2003). The life-course perspective on work and retirement. In R. A. Settersten, Jr. (Ed.), *Invitation to the life course: Toward new understandings of later life* (pp. 85–105). Amityville, NY: Baywood.

Horne, C. (2001). Sociological perspectives on the emergence of social norms. In M. Hechter & K.-D. Opp (Eds.), *Social norms* (pp. 3–34). New York: Russell Sage Foundation.

Karp, D. A. (1996). *Speaking of sadness: Depression, disconnection, and the meanings of illness*. New York: Oxford University Press.

Keith, J., Fry, C. L., Glascock, A. P., Ikels, C., Dickerson-Putnam, J., Harpending, H. C., & Draper, P. (1994). *The aging experience: Diversity and commonality across cultures*. Newbury Park, CA: Sage.

Kertzer, D. I. (1989). Age structuring in comparative and historical perspective. In D. I. Kertzer & K. Warner Schaie (Eds.), *Age structuring in comparative and historical perspective* (pp. 3–21). Hillsdale, New Jersey: Lawrence Erlbaum Associates.

Kohli, M. (1986). The world we forgot: A historical review of the life course. In V. Marshall (Ed.), *Later life* (pp. 271–303). Beverly Hills, CA: Sage.

Kohli, M. (1994). Work and retirement: A comparative perspective. In M. W. Riley, R. L. Kahn, & A. Foner (Eds.), *Age and structural lag* (pp. 80–106). New York: John Wiley & Sons.

Kohli, M. (1999). Private and public transfers between generations: Linking the family and the state. *European Societies, 1*, 81–104.

Kohli, M., & Meyer, J. W. (1986). Social structure and the social construction of life stages. *Human Development, 29*, 145–149.

Krueger, J., Heckhausen, J., & Hundertmark, J. (1995). Perceiving middle-aged adults: Effects of stereotype-congruent and incongruent information. *Journal of Gerontology: Psychological Sciences, 50*, P82–P93.

Lashbrook, J. (1996). Promotional timetables: An exploratory investigation of age norms for promotional expectations and their association with job well-being. *The Gerontologist, 36*(2), 189–198.

Lawrence, B. S. (1996). Organizational age norms: Why is it so important to know one when you see one? *The Gerontologist, 36*, 209–220.

Levy, R. (1996). Toward a theory of life-course institutionalization. In A. Weymann and W.R. Heinz (Eds.), *Society and biography* (pp. 83–108). Weinheim: Deutscher Studien Verlag.

Marini, M. M. (1984). Age and sequencing norms in the transition to adulthood. *Social Forces, 63*, 229–243.

Mason, M., Skolnick, A., & Sugarman, S. D. (1998). *All our families: New policies for a new century*. New York: Oxford University Press.

Mayer, K. U. (1997). Life courses in the welfare state. In W.R. Heinz (Ed.), *Theoretical advances in life-course research* (2nd ed., pp. 146–158). Weinheim: Deutscher Studien Verlag.

Meyer, J. W. (1986). Myths of socialization and personality. In T. C. Heller, M. Sosna, & D. E. Wellberg (Eds.), *Reconstructing individualism: Autonomy, individuality, and the self in Western thought* (pp. 209–221). Stanford, CA: Stanford University Press.

Modell, J. (1997). What do life-course norms mean? *Human Development, 40*, 282–286.

Moen, P. (2001). The gendered life course. In R. Binstock & L. George (Eds.), *Handbook of aging and the social sciences* (pp. 179–190). San Diego, CA: Academic Press.

Moen, P., & Forest, K. B. (1999). Strengthening families: Policy issues for the 21st Century. In M. Sussman, S. Steinmetz, & G. Peterson (Eds.), *Handbook of marriage and the family* (pp. 633–664). New York: Plenum Press.

Neugarten, B. L. (1969). Continuities and discontinuities of psychological issues into adult life. *Human Development, 12*, 121–130.

Neugarten, B. L., & Hagestad, G. O. (1976). Age and the life course. In R. Binstock & E. Shanas (Eds.), *Handbook of aging and the social sciences* (pp. 35–55). New York: Van Nostrand Reinhold Company.

Neugarten, B. L., Moore, J. W., & Lowe, J. C. (1965). Age norms, age constraints, and adult socialization. *American Journal of Sociology, 70*, 710–717.

Nydegger, C. N. (1986). Age and life-course transitions. In C. L. Fry & J. Keith (Eds.), *New methods for old age research: Strategies for studying diversity* (pp. 131–161). South Hadley, MA: Bergin and Garvey.

O'Rand, A. M., & Henretta, J. (1999). *Age and inequality: Diverse pathways through later life*. Boulder, CO: Westview Press.

Passuth, P. M., & Maines, D. R. (1981). *Transformations in age norms and age constraints: Evidence bearing on the age-irrelevancy hypothesis*. Paper presented at the meeting of the World Congress of Gerontology, Hamburg, Germany.

Peterson, C. C. (1996). The ticking of the social clock: Adults' beliefs about the timing of transition events. *International Journal of Aging and Human Development, 42*(3), 189–203.

Plath, D. W., & Ikeda, K. (1975). After coming of age: Adult awareness of age norms. In T. R. Williams (Ed.), *Socialization and communication in primary groups*. Mouton: The Hague.

Riley, M. W., Kahn, R. L., & Foner, A. (Eds.). (1994). *Age and structural lag: Society's failure to provide meaningful opportunities in work, family, and leisure*. New York: John Wiley & Sons.

Rook, K. S., Catalano, R., & Dooley, D. (1989). The timing of major life events: Effects of departing from the social clock. *American Journal of Community Psychology, 17*(2), 233–258.

Roscoe, B., & Peterson, K. L. (1989). Age-appropriate behaviors: A comparison of three generations of females. *Adolescence, 24*(93), 167–178.

Schulz, R., & Heckhausen, J. (1999). Aging, culture, and control: Setting a new research agenda. *Journal of Gerontology: Psychological Sciences and Social Sciences, 54B*(3), 139–145.

Settersten, R. A., Jr. (1997). The salience of age in the life course. *Human Development, 40*(5), 257–281.

Settersten, R. A., Jr. (1998a). Time, age, and the transition to retirement: New evidence on life-course flexibility? *International Journal of Aging and Human Development, 47*(3), 177–203.

Settersten, R. A., Jr. (1998b). A time to leave home and a time never to return? Age constraints around the living arrangements of young adults. *Social Forces, 76*(4), 1373–1400.

Settersten, R. A., Jr. (1999). *Lives in time and place: The problems and promises of developmental science*. Amityville, NY: Baywood.

Settersten, R. A., Jr. (2002). Socialization and the life course: New frontiers in theory and research. In R. A. Settersten, Jr. & Owens, T. (Eds.), *Advances in life course research: New frontiers in socialization* (pp. 13–40). London: Elsevier Science.

Settersten, R. A., Jr. (2003). Rethinking social policy: Lessons of a life-course perspective. In R. A. Settersten, Jr. (Ed.), *Invitation to the life course: Toward new understandings of later life* (pp. 191–222). Amityville, NY: Baywood.

Settersten, R. A., Jr., & Hagestad, G. O. (1996a). What's the latest? II. Cultural age deadlines for educational and work transitions. *The Gerontologist, 36*(5), 602–613.

Settersten, R. A., Jr., & Hagestad, G. O. (1996b). What's the latest?: Cultural age deadlines for family transitions. *The Gerontologist, 36*(2), 178–188.

Shanahan, M. J. (2000). Pathways to adulthood in changing societies: Variability and mechanisms in life course perspective. *Annual Review of Sociology, 26*, 967–692.

Tobin, S. (1996). A non-normative old age contrast: Elderly parents caring for offspring with mental retardation. In V. Bengtson (Ed.), *Adulthood and aging: Research on continuities and discontinuities* (pp. 124–142). New York: Springer.

Uhlenberg, P., & Riley, M. W. (Eds.)(2000). Essays on age integration. *The Gerontologist, 40*(3), 261–307.

Valsiner, J., & Lawrence, J. A. (1997). Human development in culture across the life span. In J. W. Berry, P. R. Dasen, & T. S. Saraswathi (Eds.), *Handbook of cross-cultural psychology: Vol. 2. Basic processes and human development* (pp. 69–106). Boston, MA: Allyn & Bacon.

Veevers, J. E., Gee, E. M., & Wister, A. V. (1996). Homeleaving age norms: Conflict or consensus? *International Journal of Aging and Human Development, 43* (4), 227–295.

Wrosch, C., & Freund, A. (2001). Self-regulation of normative and non-normative developmental challenges. *Human Development, 44*(5), 264–283.

Wrosch, C., & Heckhausen, J. (1999). Control processes before and after passing a developmental deadline: Activation and deactivation of intimate relationship goals. *Journal of Personality and Social Psychology, 77*(2), 415–427.

Wrosch, C., Heckhausen, J., & Lachman, M. E. (2000). Primary and secondary control strategies for managing health and financial stress across adulthood. *Psychology and Aging, 15*(3), 387–399.

Zepelin, H., Sills, R. A., & Heath, M. W. (1986–87). Is age becoming irrelevant? An exploratory study of perceived age norms. *International Journal of Aging and Human Development, 24*, 241–246.

PART IV

MOVEMENT THROUGH THE LIFE COURSE

A. Institutional Structuring of Life Course Trajectories

CHAPTER 5

Parental Identification, Couple Commitment, and Problem Solving among Newlyweds

IRVING TALLMAN

INTRODUCTION

The rapidity of the social and economic changes that characterized industrial and post-industrialized societies in the last century was accompanied by corresponding changes in family structure and relationships. The transitions from rural to urban-industrial and from an industrial to the current post-industrial information based society have all been associated with fundamental alterations in family composition, values, and goals.* By the late 1960s the "baby boom" generation, seeking greater social equality and personal freedom, tended to put off marriage for longer periods and were more likely to live together prior to marriage (Cherlin, 1992; Lindsey, 1990). Between the 1960s and 1970s the divorce rate doubled, the number of children born out of wedlock rose dramatically, and there was a proliferation of single female-headed households (Cherlin, 1992).

---

*See Modell and Hareven (1973) and Hareven (1978; 1982), for depictions of the transition from rural to industrial societies. Elder (1974) and Komarovsky (1940) for discussions of the impacts of the great depression on family life, Elder (1974), Elder and Rockwell (1978), Cherlin (1992) for data relevant to changes in family life in the post depression, World War II years. See also Cherlin (1992) for a discussion of post "baby boom" era changes in family structures.

IRVING TALLMAN • Department of Sociology, Washington State University, Pullman, Washington 99164-4020.
Handbook of the Life Course, edited by Jeylan T. Mortimer and Michael J. Shanahan. Kluwer Academic/Plenum Publishers, New York, 2003.

Perhaps the most profound change in Western societies in the past three decades has been that married women with or without children are now an integral part of the employed working population (Bielby, 1992). Some scholars have attributed the rise in the divorce rate directly to the dislocations in family life produced by this phenomenon (see Cherlin, 1992 for a discussion of these issues). Although the ultimate effects on family structure and relationships is still not clear, it is apparent that as women seek and obtain greater opportunities in education and the work place, their roles as wives and mothers are inevitably modified or altered.

In this first decade of the 21st century there is no evidence that these rates or processes of change will diminish or crystalize. Thus the alterations in family structures and values experienced during the life cycle of the baby boomer generation do not portend greater stability or predictability over the life cycle of the next generation. The rapidity of the social and economic changes has left young people entering marriage with uncertain priorities and conflicting expectations. They are provided with few if any standards about how to balance their obligations to jobs/careers, spouse, marriage, and children as well as how to plan for their futures.

We remain a society in flux. It is reasonable to expect that the current generation of families will continue to be challenged by social, economic, cultural, and personal conditions that were not faced by their parents. Now as in the past century the rapidity of social changes has placed great demands on the adaptive capacity of individuals and families alike. The effects of changing social conditions on family structure and relationships as well as the ways families have adapted to such changes have been well documented by social historians and life course scholars (see as examples key studies by Laslett, 1971; Hareven, 1982; and Elder, 1974). However, the question of the specific characteristics and behaviors used by families to make effective adaptations has not been thoroughly investigated. One approach to addressing this question derives from the assumption that families whose members have the requisite problem-solving skills will make the most effective adaptations. Given this assumption, the fundamental questions that I will address in this chapter are what are the attributes that enable families to be effective problem solvers? And what are the conditions that foster or hinder couples from obtaining these attributes?

A basic premise underlying the theory and the research to be discussed below is that the course of action an individual selects in a given situation is based on prior experiences in similar situations. Moreover, every action an individual takes is accompanied by an expectation of how others in the environment will respond to that action (Donahoe & Palmer, 1994). The extensive body of research by Elder and his colleagues is exemplar of this principle. They have repeatedly demonstrated that people's inabilities (and by implication abilities) to adapt to changing conditions over the life span are effected, in large part, by their prior histories in their families of origin (see Caspi & Elder, 1988; Elder, 1974, 1981; Elder & Rockwell, 1978).

My effort to account for the development of problem-solving skills in family behavior therefore starts by considering the impact of family of origin experiences on the behaviors of the key family subgroup, the marital partners. Although there is clear evidence that childhood experiences affect adult behaviors in family relationships and that adults who have had positive relationships with their parents as children tend to have positive marital relationships, there remains some question as to how pervasive these influences are on couple problem-solving over the course of a marriage (cf., Tallman, Rotolo, & Gray, 2001). Marriages involve the coming together of two people with different family experiences and, consequently, different learned behavioral patterns and expectations. To function effectively couples need to resolve these inevitable differences. In the process they may be called upon to alter or modify patterns of behavior and orientations learned in their formative years. Such a process could involve weakening parental influence over offsprings' marital behaviors over the course of time.

It is this process through which individual partners come together to resolve key problems that is the focal point of the investigation to be described in this chapter. In subsequent pages I develop and test a model that incorporates both individual and couple level behaviors. Beginning with parent-offspring relationships the model stipulates a set of individual experiences, orientations, and dispositional states, which are hypothesized to influence the partners' readiness and effectiveness in working jointly to resolve their marital problems. The model is tested with couples who were observed over the first two years of their marriage. It is during these first years that couples establish interaction trajectories effecting the long-term quality and stability of their marital relationship (Huston et al., 2001; Huston & Houts, 1998; Karney, Bradbury, & Johnson, 1999; Veroff, Douvan, & Hatchett, 1995). The research reported below is based on the premise that these long-term outcomes can be attributed to the couple's success or failure in confronting and resolving their key interpersonal problems during these critical years.

I begin by first defining problem solving and the problem-solving process as they are viewed in this investigation. These definitions and distinctions serve to specify the scope conditions of the present study. I then present the theoretical and empirical basis for developing a model that stipulates key experiences hypothesized to contribute to effective marital problem solving. The remainder of the chapter is devoted to a discussion of the test of the model, an evaluation of its findings, and an exploration of its implications for understanding the adaptive capacities of couples to deal with the vicissitudes of a society in flux.

Marital Problems, Marital Disagreements, and Marital Conflicts

A marital problem is defined here as a situation that occurs when one or both partners believe(s) that the current state of their marital relationship is not as it should be and that rectifying the situation requires some individual or collective behavioral changes. It is important to note that externally induced problems such as economic distress or the illness of a spouse is not considered here as a marital problem *unless* the condition can be directly attributed to the deliberate actions of a spouse, and these actions affect the marital relationship (cf., Tallman, 1988; Tallman et al., 1993).

Disagreements take place when the partners express different views as to how the problem might be resolved or even whether a resolution is necessary. When managed appropriately, disagreements can be considered as an initial step in problem resolution (Gottman, 1993; Vuchinich, 1999).* Disagreements often arouse feelings of anger, fear, frustration, and resentment eliciting fight or flight responses on the part of one or both spouses. When such emotional reactions and behaviors color the couple's interactions over an extended period of time, the couple can be described as involved in "marital conflict". The more extended the marital conflict, the more difficult it will be to solve the underlying problem (Vuchinich, 1999: 185–193). In brief, I propose that the process of solving marital problems begins with couple disagreements and whether these disagreements are confronted determines whether they dissipate or escalate into serious marital conflict.

---

*Gottman and Vuchinich refer to such behaviors as "conflicts" rather than disagreements, I prefer to reserve the term conflict for serious and prolonged confrontations characterized by hostile interactions.

Problem Solving

It will be helpful to draw a distinction between coping and problem-solving behaviors. Coping refers to mechanisms people use to avoid experiencing a stressful situation. Problem solving pertains to taking actions designed to remove the source of the problem (Tallman, 1988; Tallman et al., 1993). Most marital problems are dealt with through coping mechanisms such as avoidance, humor, denial or by comparing one's plight with other married couples that "could be worse". The focus here is on the less common, but in my view, more crucial, problem-solving behavior. Problem solving, as compared to coping, is potentially the more profitable behavioral choice because it offers the possibility of eliminating the source of the problem. Problem solving is also the more precarious alternative because it increases the chances that strong negative emotions will emerge accompanied by harsh accusations and counter accusations. Although it is frequently the case that couples who ignore or are not aware of potentially troubling issues may never have to confront them because they dissipate over time (Vuchinich, 1999: 188–189), the failure to perceive some situations as problems can contribute to their growing seriousness and thereby increase the difficulty of their eventual resolution (Noller & Feeney, 1998: 14–15).

The Problem-Solving Process

Virtually all marital problems are interpersonal problems that are initiated by disagreements between the partners. The problem-solving process starts when the partners acknowledge that they disagree about an issue. This shared acknowledgment involves the identification of some event or incident that pertains to perceived troubling, inappropriate or damaging behavior on the part of one or both partners and the recognition that they differ in their allocation of responsibility, their ideas as to how the problem should be resolved or both. This state of affairs inevitably involves the arousal of strong emotions. How these emotions are expressed is critical in the eventual resolution of the problem. There is a remarkable degree of consensus among investigators indicating that negative affect is a key component in impeding effective problem solving and increasing the rate and intensity of marital conflict (Forgatch, 1989; Gottman, 1979, 1994; Gottman & Krokoff, 1989; Huston & Charost, 1994; Jacobson, Follette, & McDonald, 1982 to name just a few). As in most conflagrations, it takes two to make a fight. Conflicts develop only if angry or accusatory expressions incite responses in kind, or even more damaging, withdrawals into bitter silences. When these types of exchanges are carried on for extended periods of time they contribute to a growing sense of futility and the belief that the couples' problems are intractable (Huston and Vangelisti, 1991).

Conditions Influencing the Control of Negative Affect

If conflict is to be avoided and problem solving is to take place when disagreements arise, at least one of the partners must act in a way that avoids or derails the potential for reciprocal patterns of emotionally negative and accusatory expressions. If one partner "A" voices his or her concerns through angry criticisms, complaints or derogatory and demeaning statements aimed at damaging partner "B" 's character and stature, the key to resolving the conflict rests on the behavior of B. If he or she responds by a counterattack or withdrawal the problem will more likely escalate into another round of negative exchanges or degenerate into mutual withdrawal in which one or both partners silently keep or intensify their negative image of the other (Gottman, 1979). However, if B does not respond to A's attacks in kind but rather reacts with positive or neutral affect while offering alternative modes of action, the chances that the problem will dissipate or be resolved are greatly improved (Rusbult et al., 1991; Tallman et al., 2001). If extended marital conflicts and their contribution to persistent and debilitating marital problems are to be reduced, we would want fewer persons ready to take accusatory or aggressive stances and more persons willing to be accommodating and even make conciliatory initiatives (cf., Lawler, Ford, & Large, 1999). The question is what are the conditions that contribute to the former behaviors and which lead to the latter? The remainder of the chapter is devoted to my effort to answer this question.

DEVELOPING AN EXPLANATORY MODEL

Family Background

There is a considerable body of research indicating that marital problems tend to be transmitted from one generation to the next. Most of the research focuses on the transfer of problematic behaviors from parents to offspring (Amato, 1996; Belsky & Pensky, 1988, Caspi & Elder, 1988; Tallman et al., 1999). Parents who because of personal, interpersonal, social or economic conditions are ineffective in dealing with their family problems are also likely to be ineffective in their child-rearing practices (Patterson, 1982; Simons et al., 1994). Erratic, neglecting, coercive, inconsistent or harsh parenting behaviors increase the likelihood that children when they reach adulthood will develop similar orientations and behaviors in their intimate relationships (Caspi & Elder, 1988; Gottman & Katz, 1989; Simons, Whitbeck, & Wu, 1994; Whitbeck, et al., 1992). Thus persons with unhappy childhood experiences are more likely to be tentative, wary, and defensive in their own intimate relationships; behaviors that do not facilitate effective problem solving.

Linking Childhood Experiences, Individual Orientations, and Couple Relationships

Much of the research discussed above emphasizes the impact of family experiences on individuals. But the experiences of one individual may not be sufficient to predict the course of a marital relationship. Several recent studies demonstrate the obvious but sometimes overlooked fact that marital relationships are a product of dyadic, rather than individual behaviors (Rusbult et al., 1998; Tallman et al., 1999, 2001). If childhood experiences influence the course of marital relationships, then the backgrounds of *both* partners should be necessary to account for how marital relationships develop.

Even if the family influences on the personalities and predispositions of both partners are considered, it remains necessary to explore how this mix may be modified in a new emerging marital relationship. Not only does the intensity and immediacy of this new intimate relationship exert a powerful independent effect on the two partners, they are likely to be faced with problems that differ from and were unanticipated by their parents. The changing opportunity structure, especially for women, the cultural and ethnic variability that characterizes life in the post-industrialized world, combined with high rates of geographical and social mobility, make it likely that the backgrounds and histories of persons getting married in the past few decades will be dissimilar on a number of key dimensions. Given these conditions it seems inevitable, in an era when romantic love is the prime criterion for the decision to marry, that many of the expectations partners bring into their marriage will not be realized. The question is, what aspects of the emerging relationship make it possible for some couples to overcome these unmet expectations while others succumb to disappointments and either dissolve the relationship or grow increasingly disenchanted with one another? Part of the answer I suggest is in how they deal with their disagreements.

The Relevance of Commitments

Since disagreements tend to arouse feelings of annoyance and resentment in most people, why do some give vent to these feelings more readily than others?* Some spouses are simply intent on winning the argument. Some may be so fearful of retaliation from their partner that they refuse to express their disagreement. Such persons are likely to engage in silent withdrawal from exchanges. Other spouses may care more about their partner's feelings or about the well-being of their marital relationship than they do about protecting themselves or seeking release for their frustration. Such orientations are key elements of marital commitment (Leik, Owens, & Tallman, 1999; Lydon, 1999; Rusbult, 1980). It seems reasonable to expect that spouses with strong commitments to the marriage will be likely not only to control their use of negative expressions, but to persist in seeking appropriate resolutions to the disagreements with which they are confronted. In brief, there should be a positive relationship between marital commitment and marital problem solving.

Forming and Maintaining Commitments

Interpersonal commitments have been generally viewed as a developing and changing process rather than a single decision (Lawler and Yoon, 1993; Leik et al., 1999; Rusbult, 1983). The process begins with the partners' attraction for one another (Levinger, 1976, 1999). Attraction is considered here as the total of the partners' positive assessments of their spouse's attributes and traits. It is these assessments that initially draw people together. The degree to which partners feel attracted to one another creates an incentive to do things with and for each other; that is, exchange goods and services. If these exchanges are mutually satisfying there is a desire to continue the process. Repeated exchanges foster increasingly strong emotional ties and stronger feelings of pleasure and satisfaction with the relationship (Lawler & Yoon, 1993; Lawler et al., 1995; Lawler & Yoon, 1996). The result is that the partners grow dependent on one another for more and more goods and services, not the least of which are love, admiration, and affection. With growing dependence there is an increasing desire for a continuing relationship as well as a growing sense of vulnerability if the relationship were to be severed (cf., Tallman, Gray, & Leik, 1991). Commitment assures the former and protects against the latter.

However, principally because of growing dependence and vulnerability, partners may be reluctant to make strong commitments if they do not trust their spouses' good intentions and shared commitment to the relationship (Hsiao, 1998; Kollock, 1994). A spouse's trust in

---

*I do not consider here cases of biochemical malfunctioning that affect impulse control.

his or her partner represents some confidence that the partner's future behaviors will continue to be a source of satisfaction (Hsiao, 1998). At the couple level, it represents faith in the partners' mutual attachments and involvement in the relationship (Holmes, 1991). Trust derives from two sources, one is the spouse's experiences prior to the relationship, generally in his or her family of origin, the other is the evolving experiences and exchanges with his or her partner (Boon & Holmes, 1991; Tallman et al., 1999).

Much of the commitment process discussed so far focuses on the individual benefits to the spouses, but commitment requires a shift in focus from the assessment of individual benefits to a concern for the strength and well-being of the relationship (cf., Lawler & Yoon, 1993; Leik & Leik, 1977; Leik et al., 1999; Scanzoni, 1979). The final component of commitment therefore consists of a willingness to expend personal "costs" for the sake of the relationship. "Costs" refer to the investments, difficulties, painful events, disappointments, and rewards forgone that partners are willing to endure. To the extent that couples share the same readiness to bear costs, they can be considered to share a similar level of commitment.

This linkage between attraction, satisfaction, mutual trust, and the willingness to assume costs is important not only in the formation of commitment but in maintaining commitment throughout the course of the marriage.

Parent–Child Relationships and Marital Commitment

Most students of developmental processes seem to agree that childhood interactions with parents or parent surrogates provide people with their first experiences in intimate loving relationships (Gopnik et al., 1999). The ebb and flow of parent–child interactions give children their earliest evidences of the pleasures and the dangers associated with close relationships. I am not aware of research linking adult–parent relationships with adult marital functioning. It seems reasonable, however, to surmise that other things being equal, positive parent–child relationships are likely to be carried forward when the child reaches adulthood. If this is true, then, based on the previously described parent–child research, it should follow that identification with and respect for parents should influence adults' dispositional sets toward their partners. The important implication that derives from prior research is that a bridge is established between generations. Thus, people who come from stable family backgrounds should be more likely to feel closer to and more admiring of their parents than those who come from conflicted households. Such people should also be more inclined to view their marriage partner's traits and behaviors in the best possible light; whereas persons with less affirming conceptions of their parents may enter marital relationships with more ambivalent feelings, both about themselves and their partners.* Thus from the beginning of the marriage onward the potential for strong commitments should be greater for persons who experience positive relationships with their parents.

In sum, I propose that persons' abilities to resolve their marital problems are initially learned in their families of origin. Moreover, the quality of their relationships with their parents affects their readiness to view their spouses' attributes and behaviors in a positive light, thereby enabling them to experience ardent feelings of attraction. The more likely partners are to be strongly attracted to their spouse, the greater the probability that their interactions will be experienced as satisfying. The more satisfying the interactions, the more frequently they will occur. This growing cycle of positive perceptions and satisfying interactions on the part

---

*See Huston et al. (2001) for evidence that many couples enter marriage with strong conceptions of their partner's inadequacies. Our data also show that some couples express serious couple disagreements and conflict from the first days of their marriage.

of both spouses increases their reliance on one another and their trust in each other's benevolence. Coexisting with this mutual belief that the partner is trustworthy is an emphasis on fostering the well-being of the relationship even at some personal cost to the individual partner. Finally, this commitment process is expected to contribute to effectively solving problems primarily because it emphasizes the collective well-being of the marriage relationship over personal benefits to the individual. Consequently strongly committed spouses would be more likely than those who were less committed to restrain their impulses to strike out or strike back when they have disagreements with their partners.

THE MODEL

The above discussion provides the basis for deriving a six-factor model designed to link spouses' experiences in their families of origin with their appraisal of their partner's attributes, their satisfaction in the marital relationship, and the processes through which they become a cohesive group capable of effective problem solving. Figure 5-1 provides a depiction of this hypothesized set of relationships.

   The model depicts the separate experiences of husbands and wives which contribute to their joining together in collective endeavors such as solving their interpersonal problems. The key constructs in the model can be interpreted as latent factors, each of which is defined by specific measured indicators. Formulating the model in this way makes it possible to use structural equation modeling as a mode of analysis. This allows for testing the sequential process predicted by the model. The exogenous factor is "Parents' Marital Status" which is used as a surrogate for parental marital conflict in the husbands' or wives' families of origin. As indicated earlier, parents' marital relationships affect parent–child relationships and these childhood experiences can be carried into adulthood affecting adult offsprings' relationships with their parents. Thus the path between factors 1 and 2 represents the hypothesis that respondents from stable family backgrounds will be more likely to identify with their parents and hold them in higher respect than those whose parents divorced. The hypothesis that persons who are positively identified with their parents should be more inclined to consider their

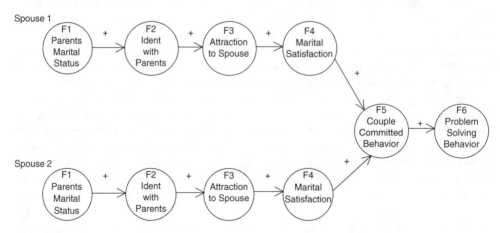

FIGURE 5-1. Model depicting hypothesized sequence of family influences, disposition toward partners, and behaviors affecting couple problem solving.

partners as highly attractive people is reflected in the path between factors 2 and 3; the path between factors 3 and 4 predicts a positive relationship between attraction and marital satisfaction; and the path between factors 4 and 5 links marital satisfaction to the couples' mutual committed behaviors. Finally, the committed behaviors represented by factor 5 are linked to effective couple problem solving as indicated by the control of hostile emotional outbursts in problematic situations.

Factors 1 to 4 all reflect personal experiences. Although factors 3 and 4 pertain to couple commitment, they represent the individual benefits contributing to the desire to make a commitment or the perceived benefits resulting from the commitment. Factor 5 is comprised of indicators of reciprocal attachments such as mutual trust (cf., Holmes, 1991) and the readiness to expend personal costs for the well-being of the relationship. Since factor 6 pertains to interactions it can only be measured at the couple level. The model is intended to account for couple behaviors beginning in the first few weeks or months of marriage and extending over the next two years.

SAMPLE, DESIGN, AND MEASURES

Design

The data used to test the model come from a longitudinal five-year, three wave study of newly wed couples. The sample was drawn during 1991 and 1992 from marriage registration records in two mid-sized cities in the State of Washington. Couples who had not been previously married, were over the age of 18, and did not have children were eligible for sample selection.

The first wave of data collection began in the spring of 1992 and the final wave was completed by the summer of 1995. An attempt was made to conduct the initial interview as close to the date of the marriage as possible. The interviews ranged from 2 to 219 days after the wedding, the median was 50 days. The second wave was administered approximately one year later and the third the following year. In each of the 3 waves husbands and wives were interviewed separately in their homes for approximately 90 minutes. Approximately 4 to 8 weeks following the interviews an appointment was made for couples to participate in videotaped interactions preceded by a brief interview. During this interview they were asked to complete a checklist indicating their major disagreements and the importance they placed on these disagreements. A facilitator, usually an interviewer who had previously met the couple, reviewed the checklist with them pointing out their major areas of disagreements. After a brief discussion the facilitator asked the couple to attempt to resolve one or more of the disagreements they indicated were most important. The facilitator then left the room indicating he or she would return in 15 minutes. Couples were aware that their discussion would be videotaped. These videotaped interactions provided the data for our measures of couple problem solving.

Sample

Two hundred and seventy-eight couples completed all of the data collection procedures for wave 1. This sample approximates the national data for newly married couples in 1992. The mean age at marriage for husbands was 26 and for wives it was 24 (U.S. Bureau of the Census, March, 1998).

Almost all husbands (92%) and wives (84%) were employed. Nineteen percent of the husbands and 25% of the wives were involved in some kind of educational or technical training program, indicating that some proportion of the husbands and wives worked and attended school simultaneously. The median and modal couple income was between $25,000 to $35,000 per year. The median and modal educational category was "some college" for both husbands and wives. This again is similar to the national average of men and women marrying for the first time (Vital Statistics, 1987). The sample consisted of 89% whites, 3% blacks, and 9% other minorities. This distribution underestimates the size of blacks and other minorities in the country but it reflects the racial distribution in the state of Washington in 1992 (World Almanac, 1992).

The attrition rate between years 1 and 2 was 15%. An additional 4.2% did not participate in the third wave of data collection. In addition, 13 couples were separated or divorced after year 1 and were eliminated from the study. Another 16 couples were dropped after year 2 for the same reason. The couples that left the study because their marriages had dissolved had significantly lower income, occupational status, and educational attainment than the rest of the sample. The analysis in this study was restricted to only those couples that participated in all three waves of interviews and videotaped interactions (n = 198 couples). Clearly those who left the study comprised couples that were either at risk for, or had experienced, greater marital conflict. This is likely to limit the range of scores on measures of marital interaction, trust and conflict laden interactions. Thus the loss of the most "at risk" couples provides a more stringent test of the model than I would have preferred.

Measures

Parents' *marital status*, the indicator of factor 1 in the model, was measured by responses to the question "What was your biological or adoptive parents' marital situation before you reached the age of 18?" Twenty-four percent of the husbands (52) and 27% of the wives (54) came from divorced families.

Latent factor 2, "Identification With Parents" reflects four indicators. Respondents were asked whom they felt closest to while growing up. For the purposes of this study I created dummy variables which coded husbands' and wives' closeness to either parent as 1 and closeness to "others" as 0. The second measured variable was based on responses to the question, "Which person (on a list of 15 options including biological parents, siblings, step parents, grandparents, and so forth) do you feel you are most like in your actions, attitudes, and values?" Again I created dummy variables for husbands and wives employing the same criteria used for the responses to the closeness questions, that is, similarity to either parent was coded 1 and similarity to "others" was 0.

Two scales assessing respondents' mothers' and fathers' character traits (measured separately for husbands and wives) were also included as indicators of latent factor 2. The scales each consisted of 13 adjectives representing parents' characteristics such as "strong", "moral", "generous", "trustworthy", and so forth.*

All of the indicators contributing to latent factors 1 and 2 were measured only during the first wave of data collection. The remaining variables, which form factors 3 through 6, were measured over all three waves of the study. Factor 3, the "Attraction" factor, represents the level of the spouse's appeal for the respondent. Two scales contribute to this factor. One is Zick Rubin's (1973) "Liking Scale". This scale reflects the respondent's respect and admiration for

---

*Exploratory factor analyses indicated that the 13 adjectives formed a single dimension on each of the scales.

his or her spouse as exemplified by such items as "I have great confidence in (spouse's) good judgment" and "I think that (spouse) is one of those people who quickly wins respect". In the second indicator contributing to factor 3 respondents were asked to rate their spouses on a scale of 0 to 100 on their intelligence, physical appearance, likeableness, friendliness, and understanding.

Factor 4 pertains to the respondent's satisfaction in the marriage. Two Likert style scales contribute to this factor. One asked respondents "How happy are you with your marriage at this time?" Responses were indicated on a five-point scale ranging from "very happy" to "not at all happy". The second scale asked respondents "How close do you feel toward your spouse today?" and responses ranged from "very close" to "not at all close". The fifth factor is labeled "committed behavior" because it focuses directly on the participant's involvement and investment in the marriage. It is formed by two different scales. The first is the Larzelere's and Huston's (1980) Dyadic Trust Scale. The scale consists of 8 items designed to estimate the respondent's sense of his or her spouse's benevolence and honesty in the marital relationship as evidenced by such statements as "My partner is primarily interested in his or her own welfare" and, " My partner is perfectly honest and truthful with me". The second measure is based on the "costs" a respondent believes he or she is willing to forgo for the sake of the relationship. Participants were provided with the following stem sentence "I would break up my marriage if"; they were then given a list of 10 options ranging from "My spouse and I were constantly bored with one another" to "My spouse continually yelled, screamed, insulted and hit me" and were asked to indicate on a four-point scale the extent to which they agreed with each option. Factor five represents the merging of the husbands' and wives' individual orientations into a combined level of commitment. Accordingly the two scales provide four indicators of the commitment factor, reflecting both husbands' and wives' "trust" and "cost" scores.

Factor 6 represents the degree to which couples use contemptuous and destructive statements when engaged in problem-solving activities. In the preliminary interview prior to engaging in their videotaped interactions, each partner filled out a separate checklist of 14 areas of possible disagreements and were asked to indicate on a scale ranging from 0 to 100 the extent to which they and their spouses disagree about each area. They were also asked to include any other areas of disagreement not covered by the checklist. Couples rarely added new items. The facilitator reviewed each partner's checklist pointing out shared areas as well as differences between the partners as to what they considered major disagreements. Couples were then asked to resolve one or more of these disagreements during their videotaped inter- actions. Although the problems couples sought to work on were not predetermined, virtually all couples focused on one or more of the following issues: "money", "who does what around the house", "communication", and "the time we spend together".

The videotapes were coded by trained judges who followed a written transcript while viewing a video monitor. The transcript was used primarily to assist the judges in clarifying words used by the partners in their verbal exchanges. The codes emphasized both verbal and non-verbal aspects of communication. Although both speaking and listening behaviors were coded, the analysis in this report is restricted to the speaking codes. Speaking behavior was assessed by taking into account voice intonation, facial expressions, and body language in the verbalizations of words and phrases. The coding system was based on a slightly revised version of John Gottman's Rapid Couple Interaction System "RCISS" (see Krokoff, Gottman, & Hass, 1989). In this method speaking and listening sequences are coded by "turns". A turn is the period of time in which one partner speaks and the other is listening. It lasts until the speaker stops talking or is interrupted. The emphasis is on the dynamic flow in the give and take that characterize couple interactions. Judges received 5–6 weeks' training in the coding system using videotapes of pre-study couples. Virtually all tapes were double coded. Inter-coder reliability using Cohen's "kappa" ranged from .71 to .85. When coder differences occurred, the eventual code was determined by mutual agreement.

The specific codes used in this study include statements that are judged to be hurtful, demeaning, and seek to embarrass or humiliate the partner. They also include statements that escalate negative affect in the interchange by raising one's voice or increasing the level of anger extant in the exchanges. These codes fall under the category of "contemptuous state-ments". An indication of the predictive validity of this category of codes is its ability to dif-ferentiate the couples in the sample that divorced over the course of the study from the rest of the sample. Significant differences were found over all 3 waves between these two groups.* Thus, couple problem solving in this study is represented by the restraint in the use of contemptuous statements in the midst of resolving disagreements.

FINDINGS

The sequential pattern depicted in Figure 5-1 posits a set of individual experiences that facilitates the emergence of couple commitment; commitment, in turn, is associated with effective couple problem solving. The model was tested using the *EQS 6 for Windows* statistical package. The nor-mal theory maximum likelihood method was used to estimate the goodness of fit between the theoretical and data models. Tests were conducted separately for husbands and wives.

Figures 5-2a and 5-2b present the findings for wave 1 data. It should be remembered that these data were collected within the first few weeks and months of the marriage. Since neither partner had been previously married, the findings reflect the partners' orientations and behav-ioral patterns at a time when they were in the initial throes of negotiating essential marital roles and key aspects of their relationship. It is a time when each partner might be confronted with different expectations challenging his or her previously learned behavioral patterns.

As indicated in Figure 5-2a,b the theoretical model fits the wave 1 data well for both husbands and wives. Not only were all of the paths between latent factors significant but each of the measured variables was significantly related to its specific latent factor. Thus it appears that, at least in the earliest stages of the marriage, the presence or absence of marital conflict in the family of origin is significantly associated with the respondents' identification with and respect for their parents regardless of the gender of the respondent. The significant linkage between factors 2 and 3 provides the bridge between the partners' relationship with their parents and their marital relationship. These data support the hypothesis that respon-dents' positive identification with and admiration for their parents is associated with positive assessments of their marriage partners. Moreover this linkage holds for both husbands and wives, although it should be noted that the standardized path coefficient between factors 2 and 3 is considerably stronger for husbands than wives. The significant paths between factors 3, 4, 5, and 6 support the general premise that high levels of commitment to the relationship, as defined in this study, are associated with the lower use of contemptuous statements by cou-ples as they seek to resolve their disagreements.

---

*Logistic regression analysis testing whether the "contemptuous statements" predicts divorce during the course of the study yielded the following results: for wave 1 coefficient = 0.08, odds ratio = 1.09, $z = 4.057$, $p < .000$; for wave 2 coefficient = 0.07, odds ratio = 1.08, $z = 3.239$, $p < 0.002$; for wave 3 coefficient = 0.08, odds ratio = 1.08, $z = 2.860$, $p < .005$.

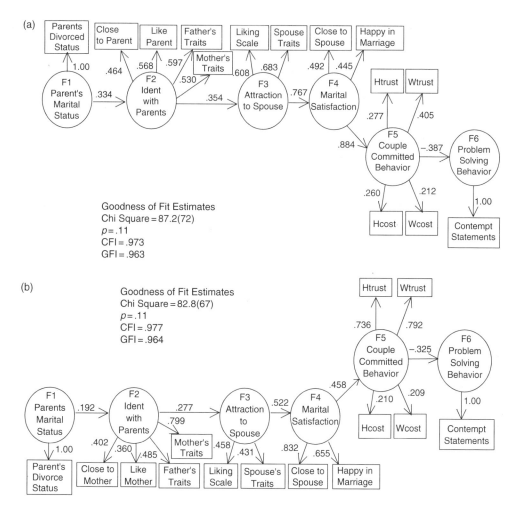

FIGURE 5-2. (a) Husband's wave 1 Measurement Model indicating goodness of fit with theoretical model, as well as strength of relationships between factors and between factors and measured variables. All reported standardized coefficients are significant at $p < .05$. (b) Wive's wave 1 Measurement Model indicating goodness of fit with theoretical model, as well as strength of relationships between factors and between factors and measured variables. All reported standardized coefficients are significant at $p < .05$.

Wave 2 and wave 3 data yielded similar results to those reported for wave 1 with the important exception that the path between the identification with parents factor (F2) and the attraction to spouse factor (F3) was no longer significant for either husbands or wives.* This lack of significance did not influence the overall "goodness of fit" of the models;† nor did it

---

*The standardized coefficients for these paths were very low. For husbands they were: 0.06 and −0.101 for wave 2 and 3 respectively. For wives they were 0.004 for wave 2 and 0.027 for wave 3. Figures and complete data for waves 2 and 3 are not presented to conserve space.

†The goodness of fit estimates are as follows: for wave 2: Husbands' Chi Square = 73.3 (62) p = 0.16, CFI = .998; Wives' Chi Square = 71.6(67) p = 0.32 CFI = .998; for Wave 3: Husbands' Chi Square = 79.2(62) p = 0.07, CFI = 0.997. Wives' Chi Square = 86.4 (68) p = 0.07, CFI = 0.996.

alter the significant relationship between the paths representing the hypothesized commitment process and its effect on minimizing contemptuous statements.

Given this finding, I explored whether "Parents' Marital Status" (F1) might have a direct influence on any of the commitment factors without the mediating influence of the "Identification with Parents" Factor. I also explored whether significant paths or adequate fits could be obtained by linking the "identification with parents" factor to "marital satisfaction" (F4), "committed behavior" (F5), or directly to the problem solving factor (F6). None of these analyses yielded significant findings. It appears that after a year of marriage parental influences on the factors pertaining to the marital relationship are greatly reduced. These data, along with other recent findings (Tallman et al., 1999) suggest that as couples increasingly rely on their exchanges and interactions for personal and collective benefits, their assessment of their partners depends more on the results of those exchanges and less on parental or other outside influences.

The other result from the wave 2 and wave 3 models worth noting is the extremely high standardized path coefficients between factors 3, 4, and 5. This finding suggests that the factors hypothesized to form a commitment process are so closely related that they seem to represent a single construct. I tested this notion by doing a confirmatory factor analysis in which all of the measured indicators for the 3 factors representing the commitment process in this model could be combined to form a single factor. I included measures of both husbands and wives for this single test. The results strongly supported that conclusion (Chi Square = 17.8 (14) $p = 0.22$ CFI = 0.994, GFI = 0.989). I have used the model depicted in Figure 5-1 in this report however, because the theory tested here considers commitment as a process involving a series of choices and evaluations rather than a single decision, behavior, or orientation. The data demonstrate rather clearly that, for all three waves, the hypothesized process of commitment is linked to couples' restraint in the use of contemptuous statements as they go about resolving their most serious disagreements.

SUMMARY AND CONCLUSION

The vast majority of the couples who participated in this study can be considered as part of the vanguard of the post baby-boomer generation. This generation, like their parents before them, is confronted with changing social structural conditions that require novel and unanticipated behavioral adaptations. One important aspect of these structural changes is the growing relevance of women's labor force participation for the economies of the United States and other industrial societies. The increased opportunities for women in the educational and occupational spheres has produced serious challenges to traditional norms governing gender relationships both in the work place and the family. Although the established norms appear to many as anachronistic, no new agreed upon set of behavioral standards has been integrated into our social fabric.

Under these conditions of ambiguity and uncertainty, marital disagreements are inevitable. How and when couples confront and deal with these disagreements have profound implications for the long-term satisfaction and stability of the marital relationship. Dealing with these disagreements is particularly important during the transition from singlehood to marriage. It is during this period that the marriage partners are faced with the task of merging their individual goals and desires with the need to forge and maintain a viable and mutually satisfying marital unit. There is a consistent body of evidence suggesting that the effectiveness with which couples deal with their problems during the first two years of marriage influences the long-term stability of the union. In this chapter I have attempted to identify some key elements and conditions that contribute to couples' abilities to resolve their problems during these early years of marriage.

The study reported above is limited to an investigation of marital partners' efforts to resolve rather than cope with their interpersonal problems. Such efforts begin with the couples' mutual acknowledgment about the nature of their disagreements. Disagreements, tend to arouse feelings of disappointment and at least some frustration on the part of the partners. Spouses' abilities or willingness to exercise control over the expression of these emotions, while working at resolving their differences, has been shown to be an essential component of effective problem solving in marital relationships. The model developed and tested for this study was designed to account for the antecedent conditions that contributed to spouses' abilities to practice such control.

The model depicted in Figure 5-1 sought to account for two primary influences, one emanating from respondents' experiences with their parents and the other pertaining to dispositions affecting the partners' commitment to the relationship. The essential underlying premise was that the more committed the partners were to the relationship, the less likely they would be to use hostile and accusatory speech when confronting their disagreements.

The model was tested with longitudinal data from a sample of 198 just married couples that had no children and had not been previously married. Three waves of data were collected over a two-year period. The first interviews and observations occurred within the first month or two of the marriage; two subsequent sets of interviews and observations were repeated at yearly intervals. Structural equation modeling techniques were used to determine the extent to which the theoretical model fit the data. The entire 6-factor model was supported for wave 1 data but the path from the factor representing respondents' identification with the parents (F2) and the attraction factor (F3) was not significant with waves 2 and 3 data. Given these findings I sought to modify the model by exploring whether significant paths could be found for either parent's marital status (F1) or the identification factor (F2) with any of the 3 commitment factors in waves 2 and 3. No significant paths were found.

This lack of association between the "Identification with Parents" factor and the factors leading to marital commitment in waves 2 and 3 suggests a tendency for couples to separate themselves from parental influences early in the marriage. Even within wave 1 data, these associations were weaker, albeit significant, than the linkages between the other factors in the model. This was especially true for wives; whose path coefficients between "parental identification" and "attraction to spouse" were considerably lower than those of husbands. The finding is at least suggestive that the women in this sample evidenced a distancing from traditional family ties that is greater than that experienced by their husbands. It also suggests that in this era of rapid social change the parental experiences and knowledge are perceived as less relevant than might have been the case in earlier eras.

Unlike the indicators of parental influence, the sequence of factors representing the commitment process—"attraction", "satisfaction", "committed behavior"—maintained the same directional pattern over the three waves of data collection. Moreover, the relationship between the "committed behavior" factor (F5) and effective problem-solving behavior, as indicated by restraint in the use of contemptuous statements (F6) was significant for all 3 waves of data collection. In brief, although parental influences on the marital commitment process appear to decline within the first year of marriage, the hypothesized relationship between the commitment process and effective problem-solving behavior is maintained over the entire two years of the study.

Paradoxically there are data, not reported in this chapter, demonstrating that all 6 measured variables contributing to the commitment factors declined in value over the two-year period.* This is not altogether surprising. The factor most often studied in family research is marital satisfaction, and declines in measures of this variable are frequently reported for couples in the early years of marriage (Bradbury, Cohan, & Karney, 1998; Kurdek, 1998). It is likely that, with increased experience, spouses lose some of the romantic halo that colors their perceptions during the first months of marriage. The data reported here suggest however that, even in the light of more realistic assessments of their partners' attributes, the couples that maintain the most positive perceptions of these attributes are more likely to stay committed to the marital relationship and, consequently, are best able to deal effectively with their marital problems (see Kurdek, 1998 for evidence regarding the importance of *rate* of decline as an indicator of marital distress as opposed to absolute differences).

There is another possible explanation for the finding that declining scores in the measures contributing to the commitment factors do not change the overall patterns of findings. The conception of commitment proposed here is based in part on the premise that with each phase of the process couples grow more dependent upon one another. Increased interdependency increases the sense of loss if the marriage were dissolved. Consequently, the desire to resolve marital disagreements should be high and the tendency toward relationship-damaging statements during those disagreements would be curtailed. Thus, as interdependency grows, the stability of the marital relationship should increase even if the factors contributing to commitment do not increase.

The findings pertaining to parental influences are of special interest given the importance placed on early childhood experiences in the developmental literature. A reasonable interpretation of the available data is that modes of relating in intimate relationships that were learned in childhood play a significant role in influencing the early course of such relationships in adulthood. Thus, early experiences in the family of origin should affect an individual's chances of forming and maintaining successful marital relationships. The data reported here and elsewhere, however, raise the possibility that proximate intimate relationships with one's partner can become sufficiently important even in the first few years of marriage to overcome such early childhood influences (Tallman et al., 1999, 2001). This suggests that the assertion that "the first years last forever",[†] which has been extrapolated from brain research and the research of developmental psychologists influenced by attachment theory, has been overdrawn. The brain, despite the massive pruning of synapses that takes place in early childhood, remains a "plastic" instrument capable of adaptations throughout life. It may be more difficult to change or relearn behavioral patterns in adulthood, but as the noted developmental psychologists Alison Gopnik, Andrew Meltzoff, and Patricia Kuhl state, "Even as adults the process of making new connections, pruning old ones, and generating new brain cells continues to go on" (Gopnik et al., 1999: 189; see also Bruer, 1999: 174–180). The data presented in this chapter suggest that a parallel process can take place in developing marital relationships.

*These data and other descriptive statistics of the variables used in this study are available on request.
[†]The phrase is used facetiously by Bruer (1999: 54).

REFERENCES

Amato, P. R. (1996). Explaining the Intergenerational Transmission of Divorce. *Journal of Marriage and the Family,* *58,* 28–655.

Belsky, J., & Pensky, E. (1988). Developmental history, personality, and family relationships: toward an emergent family system. In R. A. Hinde & J. Stevenson-Hinde (Ed.), *Relationships within families: mutual influences* (pp. 193–217). Oxford: Clarendon Press.

Bielby, D. D. (1992). Commitment to work and family. In J. Blake and J. Hagan (Eds.), *Annual Review of Sociology* (vol. 18, pp. 281–302). Palo Alto, CA: Annual Reviews Inc.

Boon, S. D., & Holmes, J. G. (1991). The dynamics of interpersonal trust: Resolving uncertainty in the face of risk. In R. A. Hiwde & J. Groebel (Eds.), *Cooperation and pro-social behavior* (pp. 167–182). New York: Cambridge University Press.

Bradbury, T. N., Cohan, C. L., & Karney, B. R. (1998). Optimizing longitudinal research for understanding and preventing marital dysfunction. In T. N. Bradbury (Ed.), *The developmental course of marital dysfunction* (pp. 279–311). Cambridge, UK: Cambridge University Press.

Bruer, J. T. (1999). *The myth of the first three years.* New York: The Free Press.

Caspi, A., & Elder, G. H., Jr. (1988). Emergent family patterns: the intergeneratonal construction of problem behavior and relationships. In R. A. Hinde & J. Stevenson-Hinde (Eds.), *Relationships within families: mutual influences* (pp. 218–240). Oxford: Clarendon Press.

Cherlin, A. J. (1992). *Marriage, divorce, remarriage* (2nd, revised ed.). Cambridge, MA: Harvard University Press.

Donahue, J. W., & Palmer, D. E. (1994). *Learning and Complex Behavior.* Needham Heights, MA: Allyn & Bacon.

Elder, G. H., Jr. (1974). *Children of the great depression.* Chicago: University of Chicago Press.

Elder, G. H. Jr. (1981). Social history and life experience. In D. Eichorn (Ed.), *Present and past in middle life* (pp. 3–31). New York: Academic Press.

Elder, G. H., Jr., & Rockwell, R. C. (1978). Economic depression and post-war opportunity: a study of life patterns and health. In R. A. Simmons (Ed.), *Research on community and mental health* (pp. 479–504). Greenwich, CT: JAI.

Forgatch, M. S. (1989). Patterns and outcomes in family problem solving: the disrupting effect of negative emotion. *Journal of Marriage and the Family, 51,* 115–124.

Gopnik, A., Metzoff, A. N., & Kuhl, P. K. (1999). *The scientist in the crib.* New York: William Morrow.

Gottman, J. M. (1979). *Marital interaction.* San Francisco: Academic Press.

Gottman, J. M. (1993). The roles of conflict engagement, escalation and avoidance in marital interaction: a longitudinal study of five types of couples. *Journal of Consulting and Clinical Psychology, 61,* 6–15.

Gottman, J. M. (1994). *What predicts divorce: The relationships between marital processes and marital outcomes.* Hillsdale, NJ: Erlbaum.

Gottman, J. M., & Katz, L. F. (1989). Effects of marital discord on young children's peer interaction and health. *Developmental Psychology, 25,* 373–381.

Gottman, J. M., & Krokoff, L. J. (1989). Marital interaction and satisfaction: A longitudinal view. *Journal of Consulting and Clinical Psychology, 57(1),* 47–52.

Hareven, T. K. (1978). Introduction: the historical study of the life course. In T. Hareven (Ed.), *Transitions: The family and the life course in historical perspective* (pp. 1–16). New York: Academic Press.

Hareven, T. K. (1982). *Family time and industrial time.* Cambridge: Cambridge University Press.

Holmes, J. G. (1991). Trust and the appraisal process in close relationships in advances in personal relationships. In W. H. Hones & D. Perlman (Eds.), *Advances in personal relationships: a research manual* (Vol. 2, pp. 57–104). London: Jessica Kinsley.

Hsiao, Y. L. (1998). *Dependence and commitment in marital relationships.* Washington State University, Pullman, WA.

Huston, T. L., Caughlin, J. P., Houts, R. M., Smith, S. E., & George, L. J. (2001). The connubial crucible: Newlywed years as predictors of marital delight, distress, and divorce. *Journal of Personality & Social Psychology, 80(2),* 237–252.

Huston, T. L., & Charost, A. F. (1994). Behavioral buffers on the effect of negtivity on marital satisfaction: a longitudinal study. *Personal Relationships, 1,* 223–239.

Huston, T. L., & Houts, R. M. (1998). The psychological infrastructure of courtship and marriage: the role of personality and compatability in romantic relationships. In T. N. Bradbury (Ed.), *The developmental course of marital dysfunction* (pp. 114–151). Cambridge, UK: Cambridge University Press.

Huston, T. L., & Vangelisti, A. L. (1991). Socioemotional behavior and satisfaction in marital relationships. *Journal of Personality and Social Psychology, 61,* 54–73.

Jacobson, N. S., Follette, W. C., & McDonald, D. W. (1982). Reactivity to positive and negative behavior in distressed and nondistressed married couples. *Journal of Consulting and Clinical Psychology, 50*, 706–714.

Karney, B. R., Bradbury, T. N., & Johnson, M. J. (1999). Deconstructing stability: the distinction between the course of a close relationship and its endpoint. In J. M. Adams & W. H. Jones (Eds.), *Handbook of interpersonal commitment and relationship stability* (pp. 481–499). New York: Plenum.

Kollock , P. (1994). The emergence of exchange structures; an experimental study of uncertainty, commitment, and trust. *American Journal of Sociology, 100*, 313–345.

Komarovsky, M. (1940). *The unemployed man and his family*. New York: Dryden Press.

Krokoff, L. J., Gottman, J. M., & Hass, S. D. (1989). Validation of a global rapid couples interaction scoring system. *Behavioral Assessments, 11*, 65–79.

Kurdek, L. A. (1998). Developmental changes in marital satisfaction: a 6-year prospective longitudinal study of newlywed couples. In T. N. Bradbury (Ed.), *The developmental course of marital dysfunction*. Cambridge, UK: Cambridge University Press.

Larzelere, R. E., & Huston, T. L. (1980). The Dyadic Trust Scale: Toward understanding interpersonal trust in close relationships. *Journal of Marriage and the Family, 42*, 595–604.

Laslett, P. (1971). *The world we lost*. New York: Scribner's.

Lawler, E. J., & Yoon, J. (1993). Power and the emergence of commitment behavior in negotiated exchange. *American Sociological Review, 58*, 456–481.

Lawler, E. J., & Yoon, J. (1996). Commitment in exchange relations: test of a theory of relational cohesion. *American Sociological Review, 61*, 89–108.

Lawler, E. J., Yoon, J., Baker, M. R., & Large, M. D. (1995). Mutual dependence and gift giving in exchange relationships. *Advances in Group Processes, 12*, 271–98.

Lawler, E. J., Ford, R., & Large, M. D. (1999). Unilateral initiatives as a conflict resolution strategy. *Social Psychology, 62*, 240–256.

Leik , R. K., & Leik , S. A. (1977). Transition to commitment. In R. L. Hamblin & J. H. Kunkel (Eds.), *Behavioral theory in sociology* (pp. 299–322). New Brunswick, NJ: Transaction Books.

Leik , R. K., Owens, T. J., & Tallman, I. (1999). Interpersonal commitments: the interplay of social networks and individual identities. In J. M. Adams & W. H. Jones (Eds.), *Handbook of interpersonal commitment and relationship stability* (pp. 239–256). New York: Kluwer Academic/Plenum.

Lindsey, L. L. (1990). *Gender roles: a sociological perspecive*. Englewood Cliffs, NJ: Prentice-Hall.

Lydon, J. (1999). Commitment and adversity: a reciprocal relation. In J. M. Adams & W. H. Jones (Eds.), *Handbook of interpersonal commitment and relationship stability* (pp. 193–219). New York: Kluwer Academic/Plenum Publishers.

Microsoft (1992). *World almanac and book of facts*. Redmond, WA.

Modell, J., & Hareven, T. K. (1973). Urbanization and the malleable household: an examination of boarding and lodging in American families. *Journal of Marriage and the Family, 35*(3), 467–479.

Noller, P., & Feeney, J. A. (1998). Communication in early marriage: reponses to conflict, nonverbal accuracy, and conventional patterns. In T. N. Bradbury (Ed.) (pp. 11–43). Cambridge, UK: Cambridge University Press.

Patterson, G. R. (1982). *Coercive family process*. Eugene, OR: Castalia Publishing Co.

Rubin, Z. (1973). *Liking and loving: An invitation to social psychology*. New York: Holt.

Rusbult, C. E. (1980). Commitment and satisfaction in romantic associations: a test of the investment model. *Journal of Experimental Social Psychology, 16*, 172–186.

Rusbult, C. E. (1983). A longitudinal study of the investment model: the development and deterioration of satisfaction and commitment in heterosexual involvements. *Journal of Personality and Social Psychology, 45*, 101–117.

Rusbult, C. E., Bissonnette, V. L., Arriaga, X. B., & Cox, C. L. (1998). Accommodation processes during the early years of marriage. In T. N. Bradbury (Ed.), *The developmental course of marital disfunction* (pp. 74–113). Cambridge, UK: Cambridge University Press.

Rusbult, C. E., Verette, J., Whitney, G. A., Slovik, L. F., & Lipkus, I. (1991). Accommodation processes in close relationships: theory and preliminary empirical evidence. *Journal of Personality and Social Psychology, 60*, 53–78.

Scanzoni, J. (1979). Social exchange and behavioral interdependence. In T. L. Huston & R. L. Burgess (Eds.), *Social exchange and developing relationships* (pp. 61–98). New York: Academic Press.

Simons, R. L., Whitbeck, L. B., Melby, J. N., & Wu, C.-I. (1994). Economic pressure and harsh parenting. In R. D. Conger & Elder, G. H., Jr. (Eds.), *Families in troubled times: Adapting to change in rural America*. New York: Aldine De Gruyter.

Simons, R. L., Whitbeck, L. B., & Wu, C.-I. (1994). Resilient and vulnerable adolescents. In R. D. Conger & Elder, G. H., Jr. (Eds.), *Families in troubled times: Adapting to change in rural America*. New York: Aldine.

Tallman, I. (1988). Problem solving in families: a revisonist perspective. In D. M. Klein & J. Aldous (Eds.), *Social stress and family development*. New York: Guilford Press.

Tallman, I., Gray, L., Kullberg, V., & Henderson, D. (1999). The intergenerational transition of marital conflict: testing a process model. *Social Psychology Quarterly, 62*, 219–239.

Tallman, I., Gray, L. N., & Leik, R. K. (1991). Decisions, dependency and commitment. In E. J. Lawler, B. Markovsky, C. Ridgeway, & H. A. Walker (Eds.), *Advances in group processes* (Vol. 8, pp. 227–257). Greenwich, CT: JAI Press.

Tallman, I., Leik , R. K., Gray, L. N., & Stafford, M. C. (1993). A theory of problem solving behavior. *Social Psychology Quarterly, 56*, 157–177.

Tallman, I., Rotolo, T., & Gray, L. (2001). Continuity or change? The impact of parent's divorce on newly married couples. *Social Psychology Quarterly, 64*(4), 333–346.

Veroff, J., Douvan, E., & Hatchett, S. (1995). *Marital stability*. Westport, CT: Praeger.

Vital Statistics of the United States (1987). *Marriage and divorce*, v. 3 Hyattsville, MD: National Center for Health Statistics.

Vuchinich, S. (1999). *Problem solving in families*. Thousand Oaks, CA: Sage.

Whitbeck, L. B., Hoyt, D. R., Simons, R. L., Conger, R. D., Elder, G. H., Jr., Lorenz, F. O., & Huck, S. M. (1992). Intergenerational continuity of parental rejection and depressed affect. *Journal of Personality and Social Psychology, 63*, 1036–1045.

CHAPTER 6

Family Context and Individual Well-Being

Patterns and Mechanisms in Life Course Perspective

PETER UHLENBERG

MARGARET MUELLER

INTRODUCTION

The assertion that the family environment experienced by an individual at any point in life has consequences for her/his subsequent life course outcomes is not likely to provoke much disagreement. Nevertheless, there are some important and interesting questions related to linkages between family context and subsequent outcomes. How significant is the family in shaping the life course? What aspects of family have genuinely significant implications for particular outcomes? What are the implications of changing family behavior in one generation for the well-being of those in other generations? These questions have received a good deal of research attention and are the subject of this essay. Before reviewing existing research findings on the role of the family in determining life course outcomes, several preliminary observations on this topic may nevertheless be useful.

PETER UHLENBERG and MARGARET MUELLER • Department of Sociology, University of North Carolina at Chapel Hill, Chapel Hill, North Carolina 27599-3210.
Handbook of the Life Course, edited by Jeylan T. Mortimer and Michael J. Shanahan. Kluwer Academic/Plenum Publishers, New York, 2003.

Preliminary Notes

First, we will not argue that the family has been a major force leading to the institutionalization of the life course in modern society. It has been the institutionalization of formal education, the organization of work, and the development of the welfare state that have encouraged
the division of life into distinct stages based on chronological age (Kohli, 1988; Meyer, 1986).
As several authors (Best, 1980; Riley & Riley, 1994) have pointed out, the ideal of childhood
involving education, adulthood involving work, and old age involving retirement and leisure
became normative over the twentieth century. This socially constructed life course pattern is
now generally considered "natural". The family, as a social institution, has probably not
played a major role in structuring this basic form of the modern life course. However, within
this broad normative life course trajectory, individuals experience diverse outcomes. Some
experience "failure" in education, work, health, and social relationships, some experience
"success", and others fall somewhere in between. In this chapter we focus on the role of
the family in determining how successfully individuals navigate the culturally prescribed life
course. The particular life course outcomes that we examine are discussed below.

Second, one should not discuss consequences of family context for particular life course
outcomes as if those relationships were universal. The significance of any specific family
environment may vary markedly across societies and across time (and even across individuals *within* the same family) (Dannefer, 2001). Consider, for example, the future educational
achievement and marital prospects of a young girl growing up in a family where the only parent is a poor, unmarried mother. In no case may this family context be advantageous, but how
much of a burden it presents for future achievement clearly depends on the society in which
it occurs. In contemporary Pakistan this situation may present overwhelming obstacles, while
in Sweden they may only be moderate and in Jamaica only minor. Our focus in this chapter
is on the effects of family context in contemporary American society. Even with this restriction, however, attention will need to be given to ways in which the effects of a particular family environment may vary across social classes or across racial/ethnic groups. In other words,
the relationship between family context and particular outcomes may be contingent on other
economic, social, cultural, and psychological factors.

Third, the effects of specific family environments on life course outcomes can only be
studied by comparing individuals who experience different family types. For example, one
cannot gain insight into consequences of parental divorce for children by studying only children whose parents have divorced. One cannot understand the effects of childhood poverty by
looking only at lives of children who grow up in poverty. But recognizing the need for comparisons immediately leads to the question of what aspects of "family context" we should
examine. Family environment includes a wide array of factors. Family structure, family
dynamics, and family resources may each have independent, as well as combined, influences.
Theoretical discussions of the family have identified each of these as being potentially significant, and we will review research dealing with each. The multiple dimensions of family
context are discussed more fully below.

Life Course Outcomes

What life course outcomes should receive attention? At any stage of life, one can think of an
almost limitless range of individual outcomes that might be examined. For children, one could
ask what determines whether one chooses blue as a favorite color, whether one prefers to wear

shorts or long pants, and whether one usually takes a bath or a shower. But these are not the questions that receive research attention. Rather, a great deal of research effort has been directed to such things as what determines school performance, "normal development," health, and socioeconomic status. In general, the outcomes that capture attention in social science research (and funding) relate to the *well-being* of individuals. One might argue that "well-being" is a subjective term; that each person has his or her private definition of what this involves. In reality, there is little disagreement regarding what outcomes are important and desirable. We focus on outcomes that are widely agreed upon as indicators of well-being.

One category of outcomes deals with survival and physical health. Determinants of health and longevity have received a great deal of attention and research support in recent years. Among the most interesting findings is that social factors, including family environment, play an important role in determining physical well-being. For example, the lower death rates experienced by married adults compared to unmarried adults is a solidly established research finding (Lillard & Waite, 1995). The challenge confronting social scientists is to explicate the mechanisms that relate an individual's family context to his or her subsequent health.

A second category of well-being relates to emotional and mental health. Do particular family environments contribute to depression or mental illness? Or, more positively, are there aspects of family context that facilitate having a joyful, optimistic, and exuberant attitude toward life? Although there is a tendency for research to focus on social problems and failure to achieve "normal" outcomes, it is no less interesting to ask what conditions lead to especially positive and desirable outcomes.

A third category of outcomes concerns socioeconomic status. Any observer of contemporary American society must be struck by the vast differences in income and wealth between individuals. Related to these differences, there is heterogeneity in levels of educational attainment and occupational status. As has been true throughout history, the family one is born into has implications for the level of economic success and social status that one is likely to enjoy over the entire life course. Further, family context during early adulthood may have implications for later life economic security. How important is the family in comparison to other factors in determining socioeconomic status (SES), and what aspects of family are most important?

The final category of outcomes that we discuss relates to success in social relationships. One aspect deals with establishing stable, positive relationships with other people and maintaining adequate social support networks. Of course the most common means of developing enduring, intimate relationships is through marriage, and we look at this as one outcome. In this case, family context during one phase of the life course is considered as a determinant of family context at a later time. Another aspect of social engagement involves relationships with the larger community—functioning as a responsible citizen versus engaging in anti-social and deviant activities. Again, more attention is given to factors leading to delinquency and criminal behavior than to positive civic engagement, but both are important issues.

Family Contexts

As already indicated, we are interested in how the family context an individual experiences at one point in life is related to subsequent life course outcomes. But "family context" is a complex term, involving several different dimensions. In an essay on family and delinquency, Lawrence Rosen (1985) points to the fundamental difference between research focusing on family "structure" and that focusing on family "function." Because these approaches look at different aspects of the family, they reach different conclusions about the mechanisms through which the family influences children and what efforts are needed to reach more positive outcomes. The "structure" approach might see the advantages of promoting marriage and keeping families together, while the "function" approach might emphasize quality of parent–child relationships and social support for single-parents. There is no reason, of course, to anticipate that one approach is "correct" and the other "incorrect." Three aspects of family context will be included in the discussion that follows: family structure, family interactions, and family resources.

Although "family" is not synonymous with "household," family structure most often refers to household composition. For children, family structure deals with number of siblings and, above all, with parents in the household. Are there two biological parents? A mother only? A stepparent? A parent and her cohabiting partner? One might also ask whether a grandparent or some other adult lives in the family. A great deal of literature from this perspective focuses on the consequences for children of being born out-of-wedlock or of experiencing a single parent family because of parental divorce (McLanahan & Sandefur, 1994). Family structure questions for adults relate to marital status (never married, cohabiting, married, divorced, widowed, re-married), and parental status (childless, children in the home, empty nest). In some cases family structure is viewed as extending beyond the household to include parents or parents-in-law or adult siblings who are living.

An advantage of focusing on family structure is that measuring family structure at a given point in time is more straightforward than measuring other aspects of the family. Consequently, there are a number of large, nationally representative data sets that include good measures of family structure. A major disadvantage, however, is that family structure is in fact fluid rather than static. Unfortunately, social science lacks the theory and measurement tools to effectively capture the complexity of family life (Shanahan, Sulloway, & Hofer, 2001). Most researchers oversimplify family structure by using a static measure of parent's marital status. This approach ends up grouping all single-parent families together, whether the source was divorce, widowhood, or nonmarital childbearing. However, parent's marital status at a single point in time is found to be only slightly predictive of subsequent household composition (Wu & Martinson, 1993). Family structure is dynamic in that as parents divorce and remarry both adults and children move in and out of the household. Often the timing and history of family structure transitions turn out to be the factors that really matter. For example, Ryan (2001) found that among girls who live with a single parent, the greatest risk of experiencing emotional problems occurs when their family structure history entailed multiple transitions or they had always lived with a single mother, rather than experiencing a single divorce or separation.

The second dimension of "family" involves the dynamic quality and character of relationships between family members. For children, much of this topic is covered by research on socialization. Socialization concerns both intended and unintended transmission of attitudes and behavior across generations (Clausen, 1968). What are the effects of differences in parental discipline, teaching, and modeling of behavior? But socialization is not a one-way process. One may also ask how children shape the lives of their parents. (For example, do children teach men and women how to be mothers and fathers? [Bell & Harper, 1977; Clausen, 1968].) Not only relationships between adults and children, but also those among adults in the family may be consequential. The quality of a relationship with a spouse or adult children or adult siblings may have consequences for later life. In general, because family dynamics tend to be "backstage behavior," they are difficult to measure. Therefore, researchers may find it easier to form hypotheses regarding implications of family interaction patterns than to empirically study them. Nevertheless, some interesting and provocative studies dealing with this aspect of family will be reviewed.

Family resources, the third aspect of family context distinguished in this chapter, have two major components. One component refers to economic capital—the family's income, wealth, housing, and other physical resources. A life course perspective anticipates that living in an economically advantaged family context at one phase of life would predict more positive outcomes (health, income, marital stability, etc.) at subsequent periods of life. The other component of resources refers to social capital. Social capital has become a popular term in sociological literature only in recent years, although the basic concept has always been central to sociological theory. Social capital involves the access to benefits that comes through inclusion in social networks. The social capital of a family thus consists of the various networks (kin, friend, political, employment, etc.) that members of the family belong to, and the resources available from others in these networks. The resources involve not only potential financial assistance, but also such things as knowledge, information, influence, and support. However difficult social capital may be to measure, there are theoretical reasons for thinking that this aspect of family context may be very important in shaping life course outcomes.

FAMILY OF ORIGIN AND CHILD OUTCOMES

From the beginning of life, different children experience vastly different childhoods. In the first days after birth, some children die and others survive. By age one, some children are happy, well nourished, and can communicate with words, but others are sullen, sickly, and cannot talk at all. A typical class of first graders contains children with widely ranging academic and social skills, and this diversity among children increases as they move to higher grades (see Entwisle, Alexander, & Olson, this volume). There are, of course, factors other than family context that determine which outcome a particular child will experience. But the type of family into which a child is born, and her family context during early years of life, are among the strongest predictors of how healthy and socially and academically successful she will be during childhood.

One thing a family determines is the economic environment within which a child will develop. Sophisticated analyses of high-quality survey data by a number of researchers reported in *Consequences of Growing Up Poor* (Duncan & Brooks-Gunn, 1997) confirm what may seem obvious—poverty has significantly adverse consequences for children. Compared to non-poor children, those who have lived in poor families are more likely to perform poorly on tests of cognitive ability and academic achievement and to have more health and developmental problems (also see Klerman, 1991; Mayer, 1997). Childhood poverty is directly linked to family structure. Eggebeen and Lichter (1991) estimate that child poverty rates would be only about 60% of the 1988 actual rate if family structure had not changed after 1960. Additionally, they claim that changing family structure accounted for nearly 50% of the increase in child poverty overall between 1980 and 1990, and further widened the black–white economic gap for children.

Plausible linkages between economic resources available from the family and successful childhood outcomes are straightforward. Children in more affluent households receive better nutrition, better quality health care, and have greater access to educational resources both in and out of the home (books, computers, classes). But economic factors do not matter only for the material goods and services they afford the family. Children are more successful when their parents relate to them in a warm and responsive way (Hanson, McLanahan, & Thomson, 1997). A good deal of research has established that low income, as well as significant drops in income, tend to create stress on parents and children that undermines effective socialization.

Economic stress affects children's lives both directly and indirectly. Research by both psychologists and sociologists has established a direct link between economic hardship, parental stress, and ineffective parenting styles. Parents who experience financial stress are more likely to adopt harsh and coercive parenting styles, using anger, violence, and other behaviors that undermine socially integrative parent–child relationships and interactions (Conger et al., 1992; Elder, Caspi, & Downey, 1986; Elder et al., 1992; Sampson & Laub, 1994). Economic stress also may affect children *indirectly* through the toll it takes on their parents' marital relationship. When the parents' relationship is strained, children perceive less involvement and support from their parents, which often results in low self-esteem and subsequent problem behavior (Skinner, Elder, & Conger, 1992; Whitbeck et al., 1991). Ultimately the family systemic nature of psychological maladjustment and poor interpersonal relationships of parents leads to the transmission of problems across generations (Caspi & Elder, 1988).

In addition to family economic status, family structure also is strongly associated with the well-being of children. The infant mortality rate is 1.8 times higher for those born to unmarried mothers than for those born to married mothers (Monthly Vital Statistics Report, v. 46:12). Several literature reviews (Amato, 2000; McLanahan & Sandefur, 1994; Seltzer, 1994) provide abundant research evidence that children in single-parent families, compared to children who live with continuously married parents, tend to score lower on measures of academic success, have more problematic social behavior, and suffer more health problems. Further, those living in stepfamilies do not, on average, experience better outcomes than those in single-parent families (McLanahan, 1997). In other words, children who grow up living with both biological parents are more likely to experience positive outcomes on a wide range of indicators than children in other family structures.

The question of why family structure correlates with childhood success generates a great deal more controversy than the question of why family income does (see McLeod & Almazan, this volume). As divorce and out of wedlock births increased rapidly after the 1960s, some social scientists emphasized that these trends reflected the increasing freedom in choice of lifestyles that adults were experiencing, and they minimized any possible negative consequences these trends might have for children. They argued that the association between single-parent families and problems for children was simply a consequence of the vastly higher rates of poverty for children without fathers present in the household. Although clearly differential poverty by family structure is a factor, few researchers now deny the important role that family structure plays. To argue that what matters is economics rather than family structure is misleading. If one finds that the coefficient for family structure is reduced when family income is entered into an equation predicting adverse child outcomes, it does not follow that absence of a parent is unimportant. As long as father absence is a cause of lower family income, family structure does matter. Equally important, economic factors account for only about half of the disadvantages associated with growing up without two parents. Researchers now recognize that children often suffer from the emotionally stressful experience of having their parents divorce, and that not living with a father often leads to disadvantages by reducing parental supervision and access to social capital (Booth & Amato, 2001; McLanahan & Sandefur, 1994; Seltzer, 1994).

Scholarly interest in fatherhood and the influence of fathers on children's well-being grew rapidly in the decade of the 1990s (Marsiglio et al., 2000). The important contribution that fathers make through economic support of the family has long been recognized, but three other aspects have only recently received serious attention. First is the finding that children had fewer behavior problems and were more responsive when their fathers were involved with them and helped supervise them. Positive outcomes are associated with such paternal behaviors as spending time with children, supervising and disciplining children's behavior, and providing emotional support (Parke & Buriel, 1998). Of course not all fathers in two-parent families actively engage in their children's lives, and some fathers who are not living with their children manage to remain highly involved in their lives. Nevertheless, intact families are conducive to fathers playing a greater direct role in their children's lives.

A second way in which a father may have a positive effect on his child's outcomes is through being supportive of the child's mother. Providing emotional support to a mother and backing up her authority have been found to be important. The quality of interactions between the parents is related to behavior of the child both within the family and outside of the family (Amato, 1998; Cherlin, 1998; Parke & Buriel, 1998). In other words, fathers can play an important role in shaping the family dynamics that in turn influence child development.

A third, and increasingly recognized, way in which fathers potentially influence child outcomes is through contributing social capital. James Coleman was the first to explicitly articulate the importance of social capital for "the creation of human capital in the next generation" (Coleman, 1988). Sociologists have recently noted the special potential fathers may have to create social capital for children. Fathers can foster positive outcomes for their children when they connect them to their own social networks that provide access to information and resources. Given the importance of social capital, one might think that single fathers would have an advantage over single mothers in promoting positive outcomes in their children. However, research has shown that fathers do no better than mothers in raising their children outside of intact home environments (Harris & Ryan, 2000; McLanahan & Sandefur, 1994).

Several caveats in the research on family structure are important to note. First is a question regarding the assumption of unidirectionality. For example, it is possible that an over-aggressive child, combined with financial stress in the home, may actually *lead* parents to divorce. In some cases it is possible that negative child and adolescent outcomes associated with certain family structures may be due to other factors related to both the child's behavior and parental divorce, such as financial stress (Sampson & Laub, 1994) or a conflictual home environment (Cherlin, Chase-Lansdale, & McRae, 1998). Second, measures of family structure variables are often problematic. Family structure is not static—families move in and out of categories and this fluidity of family life is not well-captured by most models (Downey, Ainsworth-Darnell, & Dufler, 1998). Additionally, by focusing on family structure alone, the larger *context* in which these families are situated is obscured (Edwards, 1987). This is particularly important when trying to use explanatory models based on white middle-class norms to understand influences among non-white urban youth (Zimmerman, Salem, & Maton, 1995). Third, the negative relationship between non-intact biological families and disadvantage for children may be affected by the prevalence of disapproval of alternative family forms in the society. If so, one might anticipate change in the future as alternative families (e.g., single professional women with adopted children, homosexual couples with adopted children) become increasingly common and tolerated. Finally, what matters may not be family structure per se but the *amount* of contact and *quality* of the parent–child relationship. Regardless of family structure, both time spent with parents and perceived emotional support from parents are associated with a number of psychosocial outcomes such as anxiety, depression and psychological well-being (Ge et al., 1994; Zimmerman, Salem, & Maton, 1995). Fathers in intact families may have a positive impact even when they do not spend more quality time with their children than absent fathers. Beyond his mere presence, a father who lives with his child tends to have a level of commitment and involvement in that child's life that is effectual in development (Bianchi, 2000).

ADOLESCENCE AND YOUNG ADULTHOOD

Although a fixed chronological age (18 or 21) is often used as a legal definition of when adulthood begins, there seems to be a good deal of ambiguity regarding when young people complete the transition from adolescence to adulthood. Numerous markers may be used to signal the transition to adulthood, including leaving school, entering the labor force, leaving the parental home, and perhaps forming a second family (Shanahan, 2000). However, given the decreasing "chronologization" and increasing "individualization" of the life course in contemporary America (Modell, 1989), there is little uniformity in the timing and sequencing of these various events. There is no standard trajectory that leads from adolescence to adulthood in contemporary American society (Rindfuss, Swicegood, & Rosenfeld, 1987). Thus, rather than separating these phases of life, we combine our discussion of adolescence and adulthood into one section centering on the transition between the two life stages. This approach is consistent with the recognition of the life course as both a social and developmental process (Cairns, Elder, & Costello, 1996; Hogan & Astone, 1986).

Not only is the transition from adolescence to adulthood ambiguous, but also it is the most pivotal turning point in the life course. This "transition" involves *multiple* transitions in such areas as education, work, and family, and outcomes in each of these areas have important consequences for future options (Hogan & Astone, 1986). The complex combination of events and the decisions one makes during the transition to adulthood have the potential to determine much of the subsequent course of one's life. With this perspective, we address several questions in the following section. In general we want to understand the role one's family of origin plays in these processes. Specifically, what aspects of family life foster "successful" or "unsuccessful" adolescent outcomes? How does one's family influence how he or she navigates the various transitions to adulthood? How critical are these transitions for the subsequent adult life a person lives?

We do not intend, of course, to argue that there is an optimal pathway from adolescence to adulthood that everyone should follow. We simply recognize that in contemporary American society, most people value a life course trajectory that includes completing one's education, obtaining suitable work, entering into a stable and satisfying relationship, and enjoying good health. Alternatively, most would agree that "unsuccessful" outcomes in adolescence and young adulthood include such things as poor health, delinquency, dropping out of high school, unemployment, and teen pregnancy. Using this popular perspective on indicators of an ideal early life course helps to organize the voluminous literature on family influences on adolescent and young adult outcomes.

Health and Emotional Well-Being

An obvious aspect of "health" in adolescence and young adulthood deals with general physical health. The family's location in the social structure is known to have strong direct and indirect effects on general health of people at all phases of life, including adolescence. Mechanisms through which social status affects health include knowledge about diet and exercise, access to medical care, quality of health insurance, preventative measures, etc. (Krieger, Williams, & Moss, 1997). But two other aspects of "health" are especially salient for young people—emotional well-being and health behaviors.

EMOTIONAL WELL-BEING.   High levels of parental involvement are associated with such indicators of adolescent emotional well-being as self-esteem and life satisfaction (Furstenberg, Morgan, & Allison, 1987; Wenk et al., 1994). There is a great deal of documentation on the relationship between parental divorce and children's self-control, aggressive behavior, and delinquency. Father absence, or a negative father relationship, often results in lower self-esteem (Zimmerman, Salem, & Maton, 1995) and in male children's difficulty in forming peer relationships (Edwards, 1987). On the positive side, perceptions of parental warmth and support can moderate the impact of stressful life events on depressive symptoms in adolescence (Ge et al., 1994).

HEALTH BEHAVIORS.   Adolescent health behaviors are shaped, to a large extent, by the family environment they have experienced. Children are directly and indirectly affected by such parental health behaviors as smoking, nutrition habits, and routine care. Even before birth, a mother's behaviors, such as smoking and drinking, may compromise fetal in utero development and result in low birth weight and respiratory illness. Throughout childhood and adolescence, poor nutrition and quality of life further compromise development and are associated with later adult health risks. At the same time, children who are sickly tend to do poorly in school and have lower levels of educational attainment. Lower education is often related to less secure employment, and unsteady work lives are directly associated with poor health and reduced life expectancy (Mutchler et al., 1997; Verbrugge, 1983). Further, there are specific health behaviors of parents that are directly correlated with the health behaviors of their adolescent children, such as exercise, smoking, drinking, and diet (Wickrama et al., 1999). Also, early family experiences, such as divorce, attachment to parents, father's absence, and general home atmosphere are related to levels of drug and alcohol addiction (Nurco & Lerner, 1996; Zimmerman, Salem, & Maton, 1995).

Health patterns in adolescence often cumulate and become even more visible in adulthood. In a comprehensive essay on health inequalities over the life course, Wadsworth (1997) illustrates the complex interlacing of influences that lead to the striking relationship between childhood family environment and adult health: "It may be concluded that social factors probably operate in a cumulative fashion. ...(V)ulnerability to physical ill health in childhood and later adult life is associated with poor parental socioeconomic circumstances and low levels of parental education and concern, and consequent lower levels of educational attainment with chances of lower occupational status, greater vulnerability to unemployment, risk of more adverse health related behaviour in adulthood, and poorer health" (p. 863).

Relationships with Others

DELINQUENCY.   The relative influence of family versus peers on adolescent behavior is a hotly debated topic (Harris, 1998; Harris, Furstenberg, & Marmer, 1998). Parents may have more influence on long-term issues such as family formation plans while peers prevail over short-range behaviors in adolescence such as daily tastes and preferences. Generally, the influence of friends on these behaviors peaks in adolescence and declines through the transition to adulthood (Crosnoe, 2000). A strong family context often protects against negative peer influences, but when parent–child relationships are weak, adolescents and young adults are highly susceptible to the influences of their peers (Berndt, 1996; Warr, 1993).

Three aspects of family life are closely associated with adolescent delinquency. First, when parent–child attachment is absent, the child often fails to internalize a set of socially accepted norms and values (Sokol-Katz, Dunham, & Zimmerman, 1997; Paschall, Ennett, & Flewelling, 1996). Second, the structural disadvantages associated with poor and single-parent families often lead to poor parenting practices. A lack of parental supervision and formal social controls in these situations results in ineffective inhibition of impulsive and antisocial behaviors (Sampson & Laub, 1994). Finally, disruptions in the family and transitions in family structure interfere with the socialization processes, resulting in poor decision-making and coping strategies in adolescents that may persist throughout the life course (Coughlin & Vuchinich, 1996; Paschall et al., 1996).

No matter what the measure, children living in families with their two biological parents are far less likely, on average, to exhibit delinquent behaviors in adolescence than children in other environments (Coughlin & Vuchinich, 1996). Studies rarely report a direct effect, but rather find that family structure, particularly father absence in single-mother households, has an *indirect* influence on delinquency. Mechanisms that link father absence and delinquency are parental attachment (Amato & Rivera, 1999; Sokol-Katz et al., 1997) and parental supervision (Sampson & Laub, 1994). Also, there is evidence that the psychological effects of experiencing divorce produce unhealthy externalizing behaviors in boys, such as drinking and aggressive behavior, and internalizing behaviors in girls, such as depression and low self-esteem (Chase-Lansdale & Hetherington, 1990). In his chapter in this volume, Uggen discusses how family formation in adulthood can serve as a protective factor for adult trajectories of criminality and deviance.

MARRIAGE AND BIVORCE.   The intergenerational transmission of divorce, sometimes referred to as the "legacy of divorce", has been well documented (Cherlin, 1992; Wallerstein, Lewis, & Blakeslee, 2000). Figure 6-1 suggests ways in which parental divorce may increase the risk of offspring divorce.

We will comment briefly on the linkages between parental divorce and offspring divorce. Age at marriage is the strongest predictor of marital dissolution, and women who experience childhood divorce are more likely to marry early (Amato, 1996; Feng, Giarrusso, Bengtson, & Frye, 1999). Children of divorced parents tend to have lower incomes and levels of education

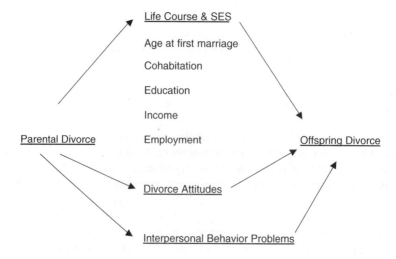

FIGURE 6-1. **Ways in which parental divorce may increase the risk of offspring divorce.**

in general, which are risk factors for subsequent divorce (Bumpass, Martin, & Sweet, 1991; Feng et al., 1999). The risk of divorce is especially high when there is both an early marriage and when both partners have limited education and compromised prospects for economic stability (Mueller & Pope, 1977).

Cohabitation as a linking mechanism between parental divorce and offspring divorce raises interesting questions. A number of studies have established both that coming from a divorced family increases the likelihood of cohabitation, and that couples that cohabit before marrying are more likely to divorce than couples that did not cohabit (Axinn & Thornton, 1992; Manning & Smock, 1995). There is disagreement, however, over whether or not cohabitation actually has a causal influence on divorce. Clearly couples that select to cohabit often have characteristics associated with greater probability of divorce (coming from divorced families, being less committed to permanence of marriage, having low religious commitment). But does self-selection fully account for the relationship between cohabitation and divorce? Or, does the cohabitation experience have a feedback effect, signaling to the couple a lack of commitment to marriage and increasing acceptance of divorce and setting up expectations for gender equity that may change with marriage and children, thereby increasing the likelihood of actual divorce once the couple transitions to marriage? Probably cohabitation does change the way individuals view marriage and divorce in ways that lead to more frequent divorce (Axinn & Thornton, 1992).

Aside from sociodemographic factors, certain social-psychological variables are also important to consider. Experiencing conflict in the home may lead to problems with intimacy and trust which ultimately strains marital relations and may result in subsequent divorce (Amato, 1996; Tallman, Gray, Kullberg, & Henderson, 1999; Tallman, this volume). The findings are mixed for divorce attitudes. Some research suggests that adult children of divorced families are more pessimistic about marriage and less negative about divorce while other research finds no evidence for a link between parental divorce and attitudes about divorce (Amato, 1996).

PARENTING.   Fertility behaviors, and ultimately family size, are shaped by the intergenerational transmission of norms, values, and preferences (Anderton, Tsuya, Bean, & Mineau, 1987). Whether an individual chooses to have children and the timing of parenthood are both significantly influenced by family context. A great deal of attention has been given to adolescent pregnancies. Although the rate of teen pregnancy in the United States declined in the 1990s, it is still far higher than any other industrialized nation. Family environments characterized by single parents, lack of parental supervision, poor parent–child communication, and economically deprived households, are strong risk factors for teenage pregnancy and childbearing (Moore & Sugland, 1999; Forste & Heaton, 1988). Subsequently, teen childbearing is linked to lower educational attainment, limited employment prospects, and lower incomes in adulthood. However, teen childbearing may not really be the primary cause of these poor adult outcomes. A good deal of evidence suggests that the predisposing conditions of poverty and low school achievement are the fundamental causes of low economic achievement in adulthood. The originating situations of teenage mothers is often so bleak that they are already on a trajectory that is likely to leave them in a state of relative disadvantage in later life, regardless of whether they have a child in adolescence (Geronimus & Korenman, 1993; Luker, 1991). When youth perceive little opportunity and lack bridges to social networks outside their impoverished community that control access to a larger set of resources and opportunities, they often are not motivated to avoid early childbearing (Fernandez Kelly, 1994). However, when girls perceive that they have good employment opportunities, they are less

likely to have a child in their teens. Because lives are linked, teenage childbearing has consequences for the children as well as the parents. Children born to teenage parents are at greater
risk of low birth weight, poor cognitive functioning, behavioral problems, and poor school
performance (Moore & Sugland, 1999).

Regardless of age at first birth, parenting practices are in part a function of childhood
experiences. Parents may transmit their parenting orientations, including their goals for their
children, directly to the next generation. For example, significant relationships are found
between parents' parenting practices and adult children's parenting practices (Simons,
Beaman, Conger, & Chao, 1992, 1993). Maternal attitudes about marriage and parenting
influence children's, particularly daughters', union formation behavior above and beyond the
children's own attitudes (Axinn & Thornton, 1992; Starrels & Holm, 2000). Socialization
within the family is also in large part nonverbal and *indirect*, through experience and observation. Children often observe and experience the consequences of their own, as well as their
parents' behaviors, learning what is and is not appropriate behavior. Simons et al. (1992) find
no association between parents' beliefs about parenting and adolescents' beliefs once parental
behavior is taken into account, indicating that parents convey their parenting beliefs to their
children *indirectly* through parenting practices.

DOMESTIC VIOLENCE.   Some effects of growing up in a home with domestic violence are
not manifest until the child reaches adulthood. Witnessing violence against a parent (usually
the mother) and actually experiencing physical abuse as a child are both influential factors in
understanding violent relationships in later life. As one would expect, witnessing marital violence as a child is related to attitudes toward women and attitudes about violence in adulthood, while the experience of physical abuse is directly related to men's adult violent
behavior (Alexander, Moore, & Alexander, 1991; Kalmuss, 1984). However, one should
remember that even among adults who experienced child abuse, most do not continue the pattern and abuse their own children as adults.

Educational Achievement

In his 1966 report on *Equality of Educational Opportunity*, James Coleman concluded that
family background matters more for school achievement than any school-level factor.
Although family resources and school resources interact, children in *any* school tend to fare
better when they come from strong family backgrounds as opposed to weak ones. Christopher
Jencks' subsequent research on inequality and education supported Coleman's conclusions
that family background has the largest influence on school achievement, and that on their
own, educational reforms have only a marginal effect on inequality (Jencks et al., 1972; see
also Hofferth, Boisjoly, & Duncan, 1998).

What is it about family background that matters for adolescent school achievement? As
with many outcomes, family structure, family income, and parents' educational attainment are
all related to adolescent school achievement. Children from disadvantaged and single-parent
or step families are consistently more likely to drop out of high school than are other children
(Astone & McLanahan, 1991; Hofferth, Boisjoly, & Duncan, 1998; Lichter, Cornwell, &
Eggebeen, 1993).

Intact and higher-income families not only have more time and resources to invest in
children, but they also are more likely to be embedded in social networks that facilitate the
development of human capital in their children. Social capital *outside* of the family, such as

that generated when the family is embedded in social relationships with other families and community institutions, is crucial for understanding the relationship between family social context and adolescent development (Furstenberg & Hughes, 1995; Hofferth, Boisjoly, & Duncan, 1998). Besides having lower incomes and mothers who are over-extended, children in divorced families tend to move much more frequently than do children in intact families. Migration results in changing schools and leaving neighborhoods, which effectively dissolves the social capital available from community ties. The negative effects of migration are even more pronounced in families with uninvolved fathers (Hagan, MacMillan, & Wheaton, 1996; Hao & Bonstead-Bruns, 1998).

Community-based sources of social capital, such as neighborhood organizations and schools, potentially augment parents' efforts to both support and monitor kids. But all neighborhoods are not created equal. Being deeply embedded in poor neighborhoods may actually inhibit adolescent development (Fernandez Kelly, 1994). In studies of how families manage risk and opportunity in disadvantaged neighborhoods, Furstenberg and his colleagues demonstrate that parents who effectively link their children to wider social networks and organizations *outside of* the immediate residential neighborhood foster successful development in their adolescent youth (Furstenberg et al., 1999). Community ties are also transmitted across the generations with parental community involvement associated with feelings of community connectedness and involvement in adolescent offspring (Fletcher & Shaw, 2000).

Many of the same family factors that predict whether or not a child will graduate from high school also are relevant for attending college. Family SES, parental divorce, mother's and father's education, and embeddedness in social networks all contribute to the probability that a high school graduate will attend college.

Education is one outcome for which *mother's* status is particularly important, at times having substantial effects that are independent of the influence of fathers. In terms of gender effects, mothers who hold more egalitarian roles in their families and mothers with higher educational and occupational status tend to have daughters who fare better in school (Updegraff, McHale, & Crouter, 1996). But the positive relationship between mother's educational attainment and child's achievement holds for both sons and daughters and the relationship may actually be stronger than the effect of family structure alone (Garasky, 1995; Kalmijn, 1994).

Parents' attitudes toward school and their expectations for the child also matter. Attitudes and expectations are likely a function of the parent's own educational attainment and family context, particularly economic stress. In a study of inner-city black youth, Reynolds and Sukhdeep (1994) find that school achievement can be explained by differences in *attitudes* and educational *expectations* rather than specific behaviors. Parents with high expectations are likely to set high educational standards for and convey the value of doing well in school to their children. Again, context matters, and parent expectations may have the greatest influence on the school achievement for youth in low-income families.

One additional family variable influencing school achievement that has been given considerable attention is family size, or number of siblings. Judith Blake's 1989 study on *Family Size and Achievement* analyzed several data sets and consistently found a significant negative relationship between family size and educational performance. Other researchers have replicated her results with the conclusion that parents with fewer children produce "higher quality" children (Downey, 1995; Powell & Steelman, 1993). However, longitudinal research using repeated measures shows no decrease in intellectual development of older siblings as younger siblings enter the family and family size increases over time (Guo & VanWey, 1999). Thus other time-invariant family factors, such as home environment or genetic heritage, may explain the relationship between family size and children's intellectual development.

Work and Status Attainment

Blau and Duncan's (1967) classic work on status attainment, and the subsequent Wisconsin Model (Sewell, Hauser, & Alwin, 1975), state that one's educational and occupational attainment are primarily a function of the father's educational and occupational statuses. Ultimately, family factors influence the status attainment of children through educational attainment. Blau and Duncan (1967) concluded that, "the family into which a man is born exerts a significant influence on his occupational life, ascribing a status to him at birth that influences his chances for achieving any other status later in his career" (p. 295). However, given the growing diversity and rapid social change in recent years, especially the dramatic gains in female labor force participation, the classic status attainment model may no longer be adequate. In particular, are there other family factors that matter for adult work life?

One line of research has focused on parental attitudes and has found strong relationships between parents' and children's attitudes toward employment. Mother's attitudes about maternal employment are found to have a particularly strong effect on daughter's attitudes, and these effects continue well into adulthood (Moen, Erickson, & Dempster-McClain, 1997; Sandberg et al., 1987; Starrels, 1992). In adulthood, this intergenerational relationship also holds for mother's employment experiences and daughter's own life experiences. We also see high levels of attitude similarity on maternal employment between parents and children over time (Moen et al., 1997). Mother's attitudes about work, marriage, and childbearing have especially strong relationships with daughter's attitudes toward maternal employment (Steele & Barling, 1996). The unanswered question remains whether parent–child attitude similarities persist because of effective socialization processes, or because adult children often end up at the same socioeconomic status position as their parents, which leads to them having similar life experiences (Starrels, 1992). Similarity with their parents is least among children who go away to college, suggesting that family socialization is quite strong and more than education, living away from home provides a hiatus from the home environment that allows daughters to change their attitudes about maternal employment (Goldscheider & Waite, 1991).

A process of cumulative advantage and disadvantage over the life course becomes evident as we track individuals through adulthood. Attitudes about school influence school performance, which determines whether or not an individual graduates high school and attends college. In turn, these educational experiences have long-term consequences for adult work trajectories and opportunity for "success" in life. The earlier work on the status attainment model, which claims that much of the variance in adult status attainment can be explained by father's occupational status and educational attainment, misses much that sets a child on a particular course. Some of the other relevant family factors are family structure, race, religion, social capital, and gender. Regardless of which variables are used to predict status attainment, the predominant mediator continues to be educational attainment (Powell & Parcel, 1997).

There are many subtle ways in which parents transmit advantages or disadvantages to their children. Parental resources influence adult children's "employability" through the cultivation of skills, self-esteem, aspirations, attitudes toward work, and school performance (Caspi, Wright, Moffitt, & Silva, 1998; Ryu & Mortimer, 1996). The more time parents spend with their children working on projects together enhances their problem-solving behaviors and the way they approach dilemmas. Parents who are successful in their own careers and transmit positive attitudes about work to their children may encourage high work aspirations. Both mothers and fathers play important roles in the transmission of work attitudes and occupational attainment (Biblarz, Raftery, & Bucur, 1997; Steele & Barling, 1996).

If childhood family context influences adult work status, it may also influence the risk of becoming welfare-dependent in adulthood. Most of the research on welfare has looked at the relationship between family poverty and childhood outcomes (Duncan & Brooks-Gunn, 1997). Public discourse has assumed a strong intergenerational transmission of welfare dependence but empirical evidence offers mixed support. Only one fifth of children in "heavily dependent" homes, that is, homes in which AFDC income was reported for all three years of the study period, grow up to be heavily dependent on welfare as adults. While the majority of women who grew up in homes high on welfare receipt are not heavily dependent on welfare as adults, about 40% of these women *are* moderately to highly dependent on welfare later in life, meaning they receive AFDC income during at least one of the three subsequent study years (Duncan, Hill, & Hoffman, 1988). Cultural theories have posited that counter-productive attitudes and values of parents are passed onto their children and that these attitudes persist into adulthood. A structural view, however, looks at how these children end up confronting the same kinds of structural barriers to getting jobs, such as discrimination and lack of opportunity in their neighborhoods, that their parents faced.

LATER LIFE

A great deal of research has demonstrated that family context, past and current, continues to affect the well-being of persons in their later years of life. The risks of experiencing a wide range of adverse outcomes (death, health problems, poverty, depression, institutionalization) vary by marital and fertility history. For married persons, retirement experiences are partially shaped by the spouse's behavior (see Moen, this volume). Experiencing widowhood can profoundly alter the life course of the surviving spouse. Relationships with adult children are affected by past family experiences and by marital transitions in either generation. In other words, family context tends to be an important factor influencing the life course in old age.

Mortality

Lillard and Panis (1996) clearly are correct when they write, "One of the most robust findings in demographic research is that married individuals' mortality rates are lower than those of their unmarried counterparts" (p. 313). Not only has this finding been replicated by numerous studies in the United States, but also with data from a wide range of other countries (Hu & Goldman, 1990). Most of the early research on this subject was based on cross-sectional analyses, often using information from death certificates to examine marital status differentials. More recently, however, advances have been made by examining data from longitudinal studies (Kotler & Wingard, 1989; Lillard & Waite, 1995; Rogers, 1995; Schaefer, Queensbury, & Wi, 1995). These studies find the same basic relationships, but in addition allow analyses that control for baseline information. Using longitudinal data, interest has shifted from establishing that married people experience lower mortality rates (no one questions this), to explaining why this relationship exists. Several possible mechanisms linking marital status and mortality have been suggested.

One possibility is the selection explanation, which argues that unmarried individuals who are at greater risk of dying are less likely to marry or remarry. If the higher mortality of unmarried persons is simply a consequence of selectivity into marriage of healthier, more robust individuals, then marriage is not a cause of the differential mortality. As far back as

1858, researchers were suggesting that because those in poor physical or mental health were at a disadvantage in the mate selection process, a disproportionate number of unmarried persons would have a short life expectancy (Goldman, 1993). In addition, others have noted that those who are poor or who live high-risk lifestyles might both be less prone to marry and more likely to experience higher death rates (Pienta, Hayward, & Jenkins, 2000). An interesting empirical examination of the "selectivity" hypothesis was based on a study of nearly 2000 men who attended Amherst College in the nineteenth century. Using a measure of health status in early adulthood, Murray found that selectivity into marriage did account for some of the lower mortality experienced by those who married. However, he also found that marriage had an independent effect on lowering mortality risk (Murray, 2000). Because a number of studies have found that controlling for premarital factors does not eliminate the survival advantage of married compared to unmarried persons, there is general agreement among researchers that marriage provides some protection against premature death.

There are several ways in which family context may play a role in health and survival outcomes for individuals in later life. First, living with a spouse (especially for men) appears to reduce the likelihood of engaging in risk taking behaviors such as excessive drinking, substance abuse, and reckless driving (Ross, Mirowsky, & Goldsteen, 1990; Umberson, 1987). On the positive side, being married encourages a healthier lifestyle (better diet, more regular sleep patterns, wearing seat belts, regular doctor visits) (Waite & Gallagher, 2000). The health and survival advantages of living a healthier lifestyle should accumulate over the life course, so those who have maintained stable marriages should be most advantaged in old age. This is the result that Lillard and Waite (1995) found for both men and women (also see Pienta, Hayward, & Jenkins, 2000).

A second possible reason why living with a spouse might reduce risk of death is that marriage facilitates social integration (Kobrin & Hendershot, 1977; Sherbourne & Hays, 1990). The important role that social support plays in preventing illness and in facilitating recovery is well established (Berkman & Syme, 1979; Thoits, 1995). A spouse not only may provide support, but also may link one to the support of a larger kinship network. A third contribution of marriage to lower mortality rates comes from the economic advantages enjoyed by married persons. Research clearly finds both that there is a positive relationship between socioeconomic status and health (Feinstein, 1993) and that married people tend to enjoy higher standards of living than unmarried (Uhlenberg, 1996). The study by Lillard and Waite (1995) concludes that marriage improves the life chances of women primarily through improving their economic position, but other factors associated with marriage are more important for men.

Institutionalization

When older people suffer disabilities that leave them dependent upon others for care, family structure is a strong predictor of whether they will receive care at home or will be institutionalized. Studies have repeatedly found that living alone increases the risk that an older person will be admitted to a nursing home at some future time (Newman & Struyk, 1990; Steinbach, 1992). Further, older people living in the community with disabilities are much less likely to become institutionalized if they have either a spouse or an adult child who functions as their caregiver (Pearlman & Crown, 1992). Freedman (1996) reports that after controlling for health, age, sex, and income, married persons are only about half as likely as unmarried to be admitted to a nursing home. Further, she found that having a daughter or a living sibling reduces the chances that an older person will enter a nursing home by about one-fourth.

Why does having a family structure that includes a spouse and/or a daughter lead to a lower risk of being institutionalized? The most straightforward explanation is that these family members provide the care that enables the older person to remain at home. The importance of informal caregiving in meeting the needs of disabled older people is widely recognized, and without this it is estimated that the demand for nursing home care would be much greater than it now is. The National Academy on Aging reports that among older people with long-term care needs, half who lack family caregivers are in nursing homes, compared to 7% of those with family caregivers (1997). But two other potentially important reasons why older people with supportive family members are frequently able to avoid institutionalization also have been suggested (Freedman, 1996). One is the assistance that kin may provide in obtaining home and community-based services that enable a dependent older person to remain living at home. The other way in which a spouse and other kin may help an older person avoid institutionalization is by the positive effect they have on her health. The better health of those who are married (Pienta et al., 2000) and those who have adequate social support networks (Bosworth & Schaie, 1997; House, Landis, & Umberson, 1988) suggests that being embedded in a family may reduce the likelihood of becoming disabled and requiring regular care from others.

Older people not only receive care from family members, but also they provide care (see Bengtson, this volume). Older parents often care for their adult children who are developmentally disabled or who suffer from chronic mental illness (Freedman, Krauss, & Seltzer, 1997; Smith, Tobin, & Fullmer, 1995). And a great deal of attention has been given to grandparents who care for their grandchildren, either as surrogate parents or as regular child care providers (Fuller-Thomson & Minkler, 2001; Pruchno, 1999). Most attention has been given to the burden that these types of caregiving place upon older people, but research also finds that caregiving often brings positive things into their lives (Pruchno, 1999). There is satisfaction from meeting needs of someone you care about, and this can provide purpose in life.

Intergenerational Relationships

Intergenerational relationships potentially contribute to the well-being of people in later life. Not only can children and grandchildren bring social and emotional support, but also they can provide much of the assistance required by dependent older people (Horowitz, 1985; Stone, Cafferata, & Sangl, 1987). But how much support an older person receives from children and grandchildren depends upon past family experiences. At a most basic level, the existence of intergenerational relationships depends upon prior childbearing. Older people without children do not have parent–child or grandparent–grandchild relationships. Further, those who have several children receive more intergenerational support than those who have only one child (Uhlenberg & Cooney, 1990). Beyond that, several other aspects of family behavior are relevant for intergenerational relationships.

The quality of parent–child relationships in later life is affected by the marital history of both the parent and the child. Older men who are divorced tend to have much poorer quality relationships with their adult children than those who are still married to their child's mother (Cooney & Uhlenberg, 1990; Seltzer, 1994). The divorced fathers have less contact with their children (Cooney & Uhlenberg, 1990; Webster & Herzog, 1995), have more strained relationships (Silverstein & Bengtson, 1997; Umberson, 1992), and are less likely to receive assistance (Furstenberg, Hoffman, & Sherestha, 1995; White, 1992). The negative effect of parental divorce is smaller for the child–mother relationship than the child–father relationship, but nevertheless is significant (Aquilino, 1994). A child's divorce also may have negative consequences for the quality of intergenerational relationships (Hagestad, 1988; Kaufman & Uhlenberg, 1998). However, some survey data suggest that divorced daughters have more contact with their parents than their married counterparts (Spitze et al., 1994).

The structure and dynamics of the family system shape the quality and type of relationships that a person in later life has with grandchildren. First, the number of grandchildren in the kin network affects the relationship. The more grandchildren there are in the family, the less involvement a grandparent is likely to have with any particular grandchild (Elder & Conger, 2000; Uhlenberg & Hammill, 1998). Second, the quality of the grandparent–parent relationship has a significant effect on the amount of contact and the type of relationship between grandparent and grandchild (Cherlin & Furstenberg, 1986, King, Russell, & Elder, 1998; Rossi & Rossi, 1990). The person in the middle generation functions as a gatekeeper, either encouraging or discouraging the relationship between her child and her parent. The better the relationship with the parent, the more likely the adult child is to promote the grandparent–grandchild relationship. Third, the matrilineal tilt of American kinship networks (Hagestad, 1986) results in somewhat greater involvement of maternal than paternal grandparents with their grandchildren (Rossi & Rossi, 1990; Uhlenberg & Hammill, 1998). This is especially evident when divorce occurs in the parent generation. Fourth, divorce in either the grandparent or the parent generation can greatly alter the grandparent–grandchild relationship (Johnson, 1998; Cherlin & Furstenberg, 1986). Divorce in the grandparent generation is associated with decreasing involvement of grandfathers with their grandchildren. Divorce in the parent generation tends to increase involvement of grandparents if their child has custody of the grandchildren, and reduce it otherwise. However, when the grandchild is already an adult at the time of her parent's divorce, the grandchild–grandparent relationship may not be affected (Cooney & Smith, 1996).

CONCLUSIONS

In this essay we chose to look at effects of family context over the entire life course. By taking this broad perspective we were unable to discuss much of the detail that has emerged from recent life course research. But looking at the big picture enables us to appreciate the profound significance of family environment in shaping the lives of individuals. Life course research has firmly established that well-being from birth until death is related to the family context within which one has lived. And family research has been very generative in proposing mechanisms that produce continuities and discontinuities in the life course. Reflecting on this literature, we conclude by suggesting four challenges that face researchers who study linkages between family and individual outcomes.

First, what outcomes should receive attention? Reviewing the existing literature, one discovers that research tends to be driven by a "problems" perspective. What causes health problems and premature death? What is responsible for educational failure and poverty? What leads to delinquency and drug use? What are the causes of teenage pregnancy? What increases the risk of divorce? Future research might give greater attention to family factors that produce positive outcomes. This is not the same question as asking what allows individuals to avoid undesirable outcomes. Among those who are not depressed, some are joyful and exuberant. Among those who are not sick, some have strength and vitality. Among those who graduate from college, some are well educated and interesting. Among those who are not divorced, some experience rewarding and intimate marriage relationships. Among those who are not delinquent drug users, some contribute to the civic life of the community. By more carefully conceptualizing and measuring positive life course outcomes, future researchers could add to our understanding of what would facilitate the development of rich and meaningful lives.

Second, life course research has made an important contribution by calling attention to ways in which the lives of individuals are linked. Research within families finds both that parental behavior affects the lives of children, and having children affects the lives of adults. Siblings are sources of mutual influence across the life course. Behavior of one spouse can have profound implications for the life of the other spouse. In many ways adult children can influence the quality of life of their parents in old age. But the importance of family is not only in the various dyadic relationships. We must give greater attention to the family as a dynamic system to appreciate the full force of family context on individual lives. For example, the quality of the marriage relationship of the parents may affect the well-being of a child. An adolescent becoming a mother may alter the life course of the adolescent's parents. A change in the marital status of an older person may significantly impact the life of an adult child. Thus in multiple ways, an individual's life course may be shaped not only by her own family context, but also the family context of others to whom she is tied. And this web of relationships is dynamic, continuously changing in character over time. Obviously the methodological challenge of how to measure such a complex, time-varying set of family relationships is immense.

Third, the role of family structure versus family resources and family functioning in determining life course outcomes is tricky. A great deal of high-quality research has established that family structure is related to well-being at all phases of life. Most simply, children living with their two biological parents tend to do better than children in alternative families; adults living in non-disrupted marriages tend to do better than those who live in alternative arrangements; older people who are married tend to do better than those who are not married. Some would say that this is evidence that supports a conservative political agenda that privileges two-parent households. Others discount the importance of the link between family structure and well-being, and argue that resources and family functioning are all that really matter. There may be little hope of compromise between these two camps, but some middle position makes sense. Other things being equal, there seem to be real advantages associated with stable marriages, both for adults and children. At the same time, there is no reason to doubt that more positive life outcomes would be facilitated by improving interpersonal relationships in all family types and by increasing resources available to the disadvantaged.

Finally, how important is the family? Research has repeatedly found family context to have significant effects on a wide range of outcomes, such as health, socioeconomic status, attitudes, and interpersonal relationships. However, the variance in models predicting outcomes that is explained by family variables is not overwhelming. Does this mean that the family is less important than is generally assumed? Before reaching that conclusion, two weaknesses of the research literature need to be considered. First, a particular family context could have strong effects, but those effects could differ across individuals. For example, poor parenting may interfere with one child developing effective parenting skills, but may motivate another child to strive to not reproduce the same family environment for his children. Thus a weak association between quality of parenting in two generations might not mean that parenting in one generation does not have a strong effect on parenting in the next generation. A seemingly "null relationship" may need to be explored more carefully to adequately understand how family context influences subsequent behaviors. Second, much of the conceptualization and measurement of family context is crude. The family is often elusive and some of the most salient experiences we have in our families may not be captured by either our measures of the family, or the stochastic models we impose upon the data. Further, family life is fluid—both the structure of a family and interactions within a family change over time. Thus to expect that a snapshot of family context at one point in time would be adequate to explain some outcome at a later time is simplistic. We expect that patterning in the *history* of lived family experiences and the *timing* of family transitional events matter, not simply the state of the family at any given point (Wu, 1996). Thus relating family context at one point in time to specific outcomes at some later time is a gross simplification of the actual process linking family and outcomes.

One must also acknowledge that there may be substantive reasons why research so often finds only modest effects of family on various outcomes. Outside of the family, the independent and combined influences of other *institutions* such as schools, neighborhoods, and religious organizations, as well as other *individuals*, such as peers, nonrelated adults, significant others, and work colleagues, matter. The family is one of many institutions in which the life course is embedded. Taking a life course perspective, one recognizes that many potentially deleterious experiences in the family (e.g., parental divorce and subsequent loss of income) can be countered by later, positive experiences in some other institution. For example, academic success in college no doubt has a much stronger direct relationship to occupational status at mid-life than does stability of parents' marriage during childhood.

Obviously there are other important determinants of outcomes (genetic makeup, luck, non-family networks) than the family. But research over the past several decades has established that the family does play a critical role in shaping the lives of individuals. A fuller understanding of the significance of the family may be gained as family researchers develop better theories and methodology. Existing research makes clear, however, that one has a better understanding of the determinants of life course trajectories if one has information regarding preceding family contexts.

REFERENCES

Alexander, P. C., Moore, S., & Alexander III, E. R. (1991). What is transmitted in the intergenerational transmission of violence? *Journal of Marriage and the Family, 53,* 657–668.

Amato, P. R. (1996). Explaining the intergenerational transmission of divorce. *Journal of Marriage and the Family, 58,* 628–640.

Amato, P. R. (1998). More than money? Men's contributions to their children's lives. In A. Booth & A. C. Crouter (Eds.), *Men in families: When do they get involved? What difference does it make?* (pp. 241–278). Mahwah, NJ: Erlbaum.

Amato, P. R. (2000). The consequences of divorce for adults and children. *Journal of Marriage and the Family, 62,* 1269–1287.

Amato, P. R., & Rivera, F. (1999). Paternal involvement and children's behavior problems. *Journal of Marriage and the Family, 61,* 375–384.

Anderton, D. L., Tsuya, N. O., Bean, L. L., & Mineau, G. (1987). Intergenerational transmission of relative fertility and life course patterns. *Demography, 24,* 467–480.

Aquilino, W. S. (1994). Impact of childhood family disruption on young adults' relationships with parents. *Journal of Marriage and the Family, 56,* 295–313.

Astone, N. M., & McLanahan, S. S. (1991). Family structure, parental practices and high school completion. *American Sociological Review, 56,* 309–320.

Axinn, W., & Thornton, A. (1992). The relationship between cohabitation and divorce: selectivity or causal inference? *Demography, 29,* 357–374.

Bell, R. Q., & Harper, L. V. (1977). *Child effects on adults.* Hillsdale, NJ: Lawrence Erlbaum Associates.

Berkman, L. F., & Syme, S. L. (1979). Social networks, host resistance, and mortality: a nine-year follow-up of Alameda County residents. *American Journal of Epidemiology, 109,* 186–204.

Berndt, T. (1996). Transition in friendship and friends' influence. In J. A. Graber, J. Brooks-Gunn, & A. C. Petersen (Eds.), *Transition through adolescence: Interpersonal domains and contexts* (pp. 57–84). Mahwah, NJ: Lawrence Erlbaum Associates.

Best, F. (1980). *Flexible life scheduling*. New York: Praeger.

Bianchi, S. M. (2000). Maternal employment and time with children: dramatic change or surprising continuity? *Demography, 37*, 401–414.

Biblarz, T. J., Raftery, A. E., & Bucur, A. (1997). Family structure and social mobility. *Social Forces, 75*, 1319–1339.

Blau, P., & Duncan, O. D. (1967). *The American occupational structure*. New York: John Wiley & Sons.

Booth, A., & Amato, P. R. (2001). Parental predivorce relations and offspring postdivorce well-being. *Journal of Marriage and Family, 63*, 197–212.

Bosworth, H. B., & Schaie, K. W. (1997). The relationship of social environment, social networks, and health outcomes in the Seattle Longitudinal Study: two analytic approaches. *Journal of Gerontology: Psychological Sciences, 52B*, P197–P205.

Bumpass, L. L., Martin, T. C., & Sweet, J. A. (1991). The impact of family background and early marital factors on marital disruption. *Journal of Family Issues, 12*(22–42).

Cairns, R. B., Elder, G. H., & Costello, E. J. (1996). *Developmental science*. New York: Cambridge University Press.

Caspi, A., & Elder, G. H. Jr. (1988). The intergenerational construction of problem behaviour and relationships. In R. A. Hinde & J. Stevenson-Hinde (Eds.), *In relationships within families: Mutual influences*. New York: Oxford University Press.

Caspi, A., Wright, B. R. E., Moffitt, T. E., & Silva, P. A. (1998). Early failure in the labor market: childhood and adolescent predictors of unemployment in the transition to adulthood. *American Sociological Review, 63*, 424–451.

Chase-Lansdale, P. L., & Hetherington, M. (1990). The impact of divorce on life-span development: short and longterm effects. In P. B. Baltes, D. L. Featherman, & R. M. Lerner (Eds.), *Life-span development and behavior* (vol. 10). Hillsdale, NJ: Lawrence Erlbaum Associates.

Cherlin, A. J. (1992). *Marriage, divorce, remarriage*. Cambridge, MA: Harvard University Press.

Cherlin, A. J. (1998). On the flexibility of fatherhood. In A. Booth & A. C. Crouter (Eds.), *Men in families: when do they get involved? what difference does it make?* (pp. 41–46). Mahwah, NJ: Erlbaum.

Cherlin, A., Chase-Lansdale, P. L., & McRae, C. (1998). Effects of parental divorce on mental health throughout the life course. *American Sociological Review, 63*, 239–249.

Cherlin, A. J., & Furstenberg, F. F., Jr. (1986). *The new American grandparent: A place in the family*. New York: Basic Books.

Clausen, J. A. (1968). *Socialization and society*. Boston: Little, Brown.

Coleman, J. (1988). Social capital in the creation of human capital. *American Journal of Sociology, 94*, 95–120.

Conger, R. D., Conger, K. J., Elder, G. H. Jr., Lorenz, F. O., Simons, R. L., & Whitbeck, L. B. (1992). A family process model of economic hardship and adjustment of early adolescent boys. *Child Development, 63*, 526–541.

Cooney, T. M., & Smith, L. A. (1996). Young adults' relations with grandparents following recent parental divorce. *Journal of Gerontology: Social Sciences, 51B*, S91–S95.

Cooney, T. M., & Uhlenberg, P. (1990). The role of divorce in men's relationships with their adult children. *Journal of Marriage and the Family, 52*, 677–688.

Coughlin, C., & Vuchinich, S. (1996). Family experience in preadolescence and the development of male delinquency. *Journal of Marriage and the Family, 58*, 491–501.

Crosnoe, R. (2000). Friendships in childhood and adolescence: the life course and new directions. *Social Psychology Quarterly, 63*, 377–391.

Dannefer, D. (2001). Whose life course is it anyway? In R. A. Settersten (Ed.), *Invitation to the life course* (pp. 259–268). Amityville, NY: Baywood.

Downey, D. B. (1995). When bigger is not better: family size, parental resources, and children's educational performance. *American Sociological Review, 60*, 746–759.

Downey, D. B., Ainsworth-Darnell, J. W., & Dufler, M. J. (1998). Sex of parent and children's well-being in single-parent households. *Journal of Marriage and the Family, 60*, 878–893.

Duncan, G. J., & Brooks-Gunn, J. (1997). *Consequences of growing up poor*. New York: Russell Sage Foundation.

Duncan, G. J., Hill, M. S., & Hoffman, S. D. (1988). Welfare dependence within and across generations. *Science, 239*, 467–471.

Edwards, J. N. (1987). Changing family structure and youthful well-being: assessing the future. *Journal of Family Issues, 8*, 355–372.

Eggebeen, D. J., & Lichter, D. T. (1991). Race, family structure, and changing poverty among American children. *American Sociological Review, 56*, 801–817.

Elder, G. H. Jr., Caspi, A., & Downey, G. (1986). Problem behavior and family relationships: life course and inter-generational themes. In A. B. Sorensen, F. E. Weinert, & L. R. Sherrod (Eds.), *Human development and the life course: Multidisciplinary perspectives*. Hillsdale, NJ: Erlbaum.

Elder, G. H. Jr., & Conger, R. D. (2000). *Children of the land: adversity and success in rural America*. Chicago: University of Chicago Press.

Elder, G. H. Jr., Conger, R. D., Foster, E. M., & Ardelt, M. (1992). Families under economic pressure. *Journal of Family Issues, 13*, 5–37.

Feinstein, J. (1993). The relationship between socioeconomic status and health: a review of the literature. *Milbank Quarterly, 71*, 279–322.

Feng, D., Giarrusso, R., Bengtson, V. L., & Frye, N. (1999). Intergenerational transmission of marital quality and marital instability. *Journal of Marriage and the Family, 61*, 451–463.

Fernandez Kelly, M. P. (1994). Towanda's triumph: social and cultural capital in the transition to adulthood in the urban ghetto. *International Journal of Urban and Regional Research, 18*, 88–111.

Fletcher, A. C., & Shaw, R. A. (2000). Sex differences in associations between parental behaviors and characteristics and adolescent social integration. *Social Development, 9*, 133–148.

Forste, R. T., & Heaton, T. B. (1988). Initiation of sexual activity among female adolescents. *Youth and Society, 19*, 250–268.

Freedman, R. I., Krauss, M. W., & Seltzer, M. M. (1997). Aging parents' residential plans for adult children with mental retardation. *Mental Retardation, 35*, 114–123.

Freedman, V. A. (1996). Family structure and the risk of nursing home admission. *Journal of Gerontology: Social Sciences, 51B*, S61–S69.

Fuller-Thomson, E., & Minkler, M. (2001). American grandparents providing extensive child care to their grand-children: prevalence and profile. *The Gerontologist, 41*, 201–209.

Furstenberg Jr., F. F., Cook, T. D., Eccles, J., Elder Jr., G. H., & Sameroff, A. (1999). *Managing to make it: Urban families and adolescent success*. Chicago: University of Chicago Press.

Furstenberg Jr., F. F., Hoffman, S. D., & Sherestha, L. (1995). The effect of divorce on intergenerational transfers: new evidence. *Demography, 32*, 319–333.

Furstenberg Jr., F. F., & Hughes, M. E. (1995). Social capital and successful development among at-risk youth. *Journal of Marriage and the Family, 57*, 580–592.

Furstenberg Jr., F. F., Morgan, S. P., & Allison, P. D. (1987). Paternal participation and children's well-being after marital dissolution. *American Sociological Review, 52*, 695–701.

Garasky, S. (1995). The effects of family structure on educational attainment: do the effects vary by the age of the child? *American Journal of Economics and Sociology, 54*, 89–105.

Ge, X., Lorenz, F. O., Conger, R. D., Elder, G. H. Jr., & Simons, R. L. (1994). Trajectories of stressful life events and depressive symptoms during adolescence. *Developmental Psychology, 30*, 467–483.

Geronimus, A. T., & Korenman, S. (1993). The socioeconomic costs of teenage childbearing: evidence and interpre-tation. *Demography, 30*, 281–290.

Goldman, N. (1993). Marriage selection and mortality patterns: inferences and fallacies. *Demography, 30*, 189–208.

Goldscheider, F. K., & Waite, L. J. (1991). *New families, no families? The transformation of the American home*. Berkeley: University of California Press.

Guo, G., & VanWey, L. K. (1999). Family size and birth order: does either matter? *American Sociological Review, 64*, 169–187.

Hagan, J., Macmillan, R., & Wheaton, B. (1996). New kid in town: social capital and the life course effects of family migration on children. *American Sociological Review, 61*, 368–385.

Hagestad, G. O. (1986). The aging society as a context for family life. *Daedalus, 115*, 119–139.

Hagestad, G. O. (1988). Demographic change and the life course: some emerging trends in the family realm. *Family Relations, 37*, 405–410.

Hanson, T. L., McLanahan, S., & Thomson, E. (1997). Economic resources, parental practices, and children's well-being. In G. J. Duncan & J. Brooks-Gunn (Eds.), *Consequences of growing up poor* (pp. 190–238). New York: Russell Sage Foundation.

Hao, L., & Bonstead-Bruns, M. (1998). Parent–child differences in educational expectations and the academic achievement of immigrant and native students. *Sociology of Education, 71*, 175–198.

Harris, J. R. (1998). *The nurture assumption: why children turn out the way they do*. New York: Free Press.

Harris, K. M., Furstenberg Jr., F. F., & Marmer, J. K. (1998). Paternal involvement with adolescents in intact fami-lies: the influence of fathers over the life course. *Demography, 35*, 201–216.

Harris, K. M., & Ryan, S. (2000). Family processes, neighborhood context, and adolescent risk behavior. Presented at *Annual meeting of the Population Association of America*. Washington, DC.

Hatch, L. R., & Thompson, A. (1992). Family responsibilities and women's retirement. In M. Szinovacz, D. J. Ekerdt, & B. H. Vinick (Eds.), (pp. 99–113). Newbury Park, CA: Sage.

Hofferth, S. L., Boisjoly, J., & Duncan, G. J. (1998). Parents' extrafamilial resources and children's school attainment. *Sociology of Education, 71*, 246–268.

Hogan, D. P., & Astone, N. M. (1986). The transition to adulthood. *Annual Review of Sociology, 12*, 109–130.

Horowitz, A. (1985). Sons and daughters as caregivers to older parents: differences in role performance and consequences. *The Gerontologist, 25*, 612–617.

House, J. S., Landis, H. R., & Umberson, D. (1988). Social relationships and health. *Science, 241*, 540–545.

Hu, Y., & Goldman, N. (1990). Mortality differentials by marital status: an international comparison. *Demography, 27*, 233–50.

Jencks, C., Smith, M., Acland, H., Bane, M. J., Cohen, D., Gintis, H., Heynes, B., & Michelson, S. (1972). *Inequality: a reassessment of the effect of family and schooling in America.* New York: Harper & Row.

Kalmijn, M. (1994). Mother's occupational status and children's schooling. *American Sociological Review, 59*, 257–275.

Kalmuss, D. (1984). The intergenerational transmission of marital aggression. *Journal of Marriage and the Family, 46*, 11–19.

Kaufman, G., & Uhlenberg, P. (1998). Effects of life course transitions on the quality of relationships between adult children and their parents. *Journal of Marriage and the Family, 60*, 924–938.

King, V., Russell, S. T., & Elder, G. H., Jr. (1998). Grandparenting in family systems: an ecological approach. In M. E. Szinovacz (Ed.), *Handbook on grandparenthood* (pp. 53–69). Westport, CN: Greenwood Press.

Klerman, L. V. (1991). The health status of poor children: problems and programs. In A. C. Huston (Ed.), *Children in Poverty: Child Development and Public Policy* (pp. 136–157). Cambridge, MA: Cambridge University Press.

Kobrin, F. E., & Hendershot, G. E. (1977). Do family ties reduce mortality? evidence from the United States, 1966–1968. *Journal of Marriage and the Family, 39*, 737–745.

Kohli, M. L. (1988). Social organization and subjective construction of the life course. In A. B. Sorensen, F. E. Weiner, & L. R. Sherrod (Eds.), *Human development and the life cycle* (pp. 271–292). Hillsdale, NJ: Erlbaum.

Kotler, P., & Wingard, D. L. (1989). The effect of occupational, marital and parental roles on mortality: the Alameda County study. *American Journal of Public Health, 79*, 607–611.

Krieger, N., Williams, D. R., & Moss, N. (1997). Measuring social class in U.S. public health research. *Annual Review of Public Health, 18*, 341–378.

Lichter, D. T., Cornwell, G. T., & Eggebeen, D. J. (1993). Harvesting human capital: family structure and education among rural youth. *Rural Sociology, 58*, 53–75.

Lillard, L. A., & Panis, C. W. A. (1996). Marital status and mortality: the role of health. *Demography, 33*, 313–327.

Lillard, L. A., & Waite, L. J. (1995). Till death do us part: marital disruption and mortality. *American Journal of Sociology, 100*, 1131–56.

Luker, K. (1991). Dubious conceptions: the controversy over teen pregnancy. *The American Prospect, 2*, 73–83.

Manning, W. D., & Smock, P. J. (1995). Why marry? Race and the transition to marriage among cohabiters. *Demography, 32*, 509–520.

Marsiglio, W., Amato, P., Day, R. D., & Lamb, M. E. (2000). Scholarship on fatherhood in the 1990s and beyond. *Journal of Marriage and the Family, 62*, 1173–1191.

Mayer, S. E. (1997). *What money can't buy: Family income and children's life chances.* Cambridge, MA: Harvard University Press.

McLanahan, S. S. (1997). Parent absence or poverty: which matters more? In G. J. Duncan & J. Brooks-Gunn (Eds.), *Consequences of growing up poor* (pp. 35–48). New York: Russell Sage Foundation.

McLanahan, S. S., & Sandefur, G. (1994). *Growing up with a single parent: What hurts, what helps?* Cambridge, MA: Harvard University Press.

Meyer, J. W. (1986). The self and the life course: Institutionalization and its effects. In A. B. Sorensen, F. E. Weinert, & L. R. Sherrod (Eds.), *Human development and the life course: Multidisciplinary perspectives* (pp. 209–221). Hillsdale, NJ: Laurence Erlbaum Associates.

Modell, J. (1989). *Into one's own: From youth to adulthood in the United States, 1920–1975.* Berkeley, CA: University of California Press.

Moen, P., Erickson, M. A., & Dempster-McClain, D. (1997). Their mothers' daughters? The intergenerational transmission of gender attitudes in a world of changing roles. *Journal of Marriage and the Family, 59*, 281–293.

Moore, K. A., & Sugland, B. W. (1999). Piecing together the puzzle of teenage childbearing. *Policy and Practice, 57*, 36–42.

Mueller, C. W., & Pope, H. (1977). Marital instability: A study of its transmission between generations. *Journal of Marriage and the Family, 39*(83–93).

Murray, J. E. (2000). Marital protection and marital selection: evidence from a historical-prospective sample of American men. *Demography, 37*, 511–521.

Mutchler, J. E., Burr, J. A., Pienta, A. M., & Massagli, M. P. (1997). Pathways to labor force exit: work transitions and work instability. *Journal of Gerontology: Social Sciences, 52B* , S4–S12.

National Academy on Aging (1997). *Facts on long-term care*. Washington, DC.

Newman, S., & Struyk, R. (1990). Overwhelming odds: caregiving and the risk of institutionalization. *Journal of Gerontology: Social Sciences, 45*, S173–S183.

Nurco, D. N., & Lerner, M. (1996). Vulnerability to narcotic addiction: family structure and functioning. *Journal of Drug Issues, 26*, 1007–1025.

Parke, R. D., & Buriel, R. (1998). Socialization in the family: ethnic and ecological perspectives. In W. Damon & N. Eisenberg (Eds.), *Handbook of child psychology, vol. 3: Social, emotional, and personality development* (pp. 463–552). New York: Wiley.

Paschall, M. J., Ennett, S. T., & Flewelling, R. L. (1996). Relationships among family characteristics and violent behavior by black and white male adolescents. *Journal of Youth and Adolescence, 25*, 177–197.

Pearlman, D., & Crown, W. H. (1992). Alternative sources of social support and their impacts on institutional risk. *The Gerontologist, 32*, 527–535.

Pienta, A. M., Hayward, M. D., & Jenkins, K. R. (2000). Health consequences of marriage for the retirement years. *Journal of Family Issues, 21*, 559–586.

Powell, B., & Steelman, L. C. (1993). The educational benefit of being spaced out: sibship density and educational progress. *American Sociological Review, 58*, 367–381.

Pruchno, R. (1999). Raising grandchildren: the experiences of black and white grandmothers. *The Gerontologist, 39*, 209–221.

Powell, M. A., & Parcel, T. L. (1997). Effects of family structure on the earnings attainment process: differences by gender. *Journal of Marriage and the Family, 59*, 419–433.

Reynolds, A. J., & Sukhdeep, G. (1994). The role of parental perspectives in the school adjustment of inner-city black children. *Journal of Youth and Adolescence, 23*, 671–694.

Riley, M. W., & Riley, J. W., Jr. (1994). Age integration and the lives of older people. *The Gerontologist, 34*, 110–115.

Rindfuss, R., Swicegood, C., & Rosenfeld, R. (1987). Disorder in the life course: how common and does it matter. *American Sociological Review, 52*, 785–801.

Rogers, R. G. (1995). Marriage, sex, and mortality. *Journal of Marriage and the Family, 57*, 515–526.

Rosen, L. (1985). Family and delinquency: structure or function? *Criminology, 23(3)*, 553–573.

Ross, C. E., Mirowsky, J., & Goldsteen, K. (1990). The impact of the family on health: decade in review. *Journal of Marriage and the Family, 52*, 1059–1078.

Rossi, A. S., & Rossi, P. H. (1990). *Of human bonding: Parent–child relations across the life course*. New York: Aldine de Gruyter.

Ryan, S. (2001). Poverty, social context, and adolescent emotional health. Unpublished Doctoral Dissertation. University of North Carolina at Chapel Hill.

Ryu, S., & Mortimer, J. T. (1996). The 'occupational linkage hypothesis' applied to occupational value formation in adolescence. In Mortimer, J. T., & Finch, M. D. (Eds.). *Adolescents, work, and family: An intergenerational developmental analysis*. Thousand Oaks, CA: Sage.

Sampson, R. J., & Laub, J. H. (1994). Urban poverty and the family context of delinquency: a new look at structure and process in a classic study. *Child Development, 65*, 523–540.

Sandberg, D. E., Ehrardt, A. A., Mellins, C. A., Ince, S. E., & Meyer-Bahlburg, F. L. (1987). The influence of individual and family characteristics upon career aspirations of girls during childhood and adolescence. *Sex Roles, 16*, 649–668.

Schaefer, C., Queensbury, C. P., Jr., & Wi, S. (1995). Mortality following conjugal bereavement and the effects of a shared environment. *American Journal of Epidemiology, 141*, 1142–1152.

Seltzer, J. A. (1994). Consequences of marital dissolution for children. *Annual Review of Sociology, 20*, 235–266.

Sewell, W. H., Hauser, R. M., & Alwin, D. F. (1975). *Education, occupation, and earnings: Achievement in the early career*. New York: Academic Press.

Shanahan, M. J. (2000). Pathways to adulthood in a changing society: variability and mechanisms in life course perspective. *Annual Review of Sociology, 26*, 667–692.

Shanahan, M. J., Sulloway, R., & Hofer, S. M. (2001). Change and constancy in development contexts. *International Journal of Behavioral Development, 24*, 421–427.

Sherbourne, C. D., & Hays, R. D. (1990). Marital status, social support, and health transitions in chronic disease patients. *Journal of Health and Social Behavior, 31*, 328–343.

Silverstein, M., & Bengtson, V. L. (1997). Intergenerational solidarity and the structure of adult child-parent relationships in American families. *American Journal of Sociology, 103*, 429–460.

Simons, R. L., Beaman, J., Conger, R. D., & Chao, W. (1992). Gender differences in the intergenerational transmission of parenting beliefs. *Journal of Marriage and the Family, 54*, 823–836.

Simons, R. L., Beaman, J., Conger, R. D., & Chao, W. (1993). Childhood experience, conceptions of parenting, and attitudes of spouse as determinants of parental behavior. *Journal of Marriage and the Family, 55*, 91–106.

Skinner, M. L., Elder, G. H. Jr., & Conger, R. D. (1992). Linking economic hardship to adolescent aggression. *Journal of Youth and Adolescence, 21*, 259–276.

Smith, G. C., Tobin, S. S., & Fullmer, E. M. (1995). Assisting older families with lifelong disabilities. In G. C. Smith, S. S. Tobin, E. A. Robertson-Tchabo, & P. Power (Eds.). *Strengthening aging families: Diversity in practice and policy*. Thousand Oaks, CA: Sage.

Sokol-Katz, J., Dunham, R., & Zimmerman, R. (1997). Family structure versus parental attachment in controlling adolescent deviant behavior: a social control model. *Adolescence, 32*, 199–215.

Spitze, G., Logan, J. R., Deane, G., & Zeiger, S. (1994). Adult children's divorce and intergenerational relationships. *Journal of Marriage and the Family, 56*, 279–293.

Starrels, M. (1992). Attitude similarity between mothers and children regarding maternal employment. *Journal of Marriage and the Family, 54*, 91–103.

Starrels, M. E., & Holm, K. E. (2000). Adolescents' plans for family formation: is parental socialization important? *Journal of Marriage and the Family, 62*, 416–429.

Steele, J., & Barling, J. (1996). Influence of maternal gender-role beliefs and role satisfaction on daughters' vocational interests. *Sex Roles, 34*, 637–648.

Steinbach, U. (1992). Social networks, institutionalization, and mortality among elderly people in the United States. *Journal of Gerontology: Social Sciences, 47*, S183–S190.

Stone, R., Cafferata, G. L., & Sangl, J. (1987). Caregivers of the frail elderly. *The Gerontologist, 27*, 616–626.

Tallman, I., Gray, L. N., Kullberg, V., & Henderson, D. (1999). The intergenerational transmission of marital conflict: testing a process model. *Social Psychology Quarterly, 62*, 219–239.

Thoits, P. A. (1995). Stress, coping, and social support processes: where are we? what next? *Journal of Health and Social Behavior, 35*, 53–79.

Uhlenberg, P. (1996). Marriage and the elderly. In L. A. Vitt & J. K. Siegenthaler (Eds.), *Encyclopedia of Financial Gerontology* (pp. 330–334). Westport, CN: Greenwood.

Uhlenberg, P., & Cooney, T. M. (1990). Family size and mother-child relations in later life. *The Gerontologist, 30*, 618–625.

Uhlenberg, P., & Hammill, B. G. (1998). Frequency of grandparents contact with grandchildren: six factors that make a difference. *The Gerontologist, 38*, 276–285.

Umberson, D. (1987). Family status and health behaviors: social control as a dimension of social integration. *Journal of Health and Social Behavior, 28*, 306–319.

Umberson, D. (1992). Relationships between adult children and their parents: psychological consequences of both generations. *Journal of Marriage and the Family, 54*, 664–674.

Updegraff, K. A., McHale, S. M., & Crouter, A. C. (1996). Gender roles in marriage: what do they mean for girls' and boys' school achievement? *Journal of Youth and Adolescence, 25*, 73–88.

Verbrugge, L. M. (1983). Multiple roles and physical health of women and men. *Journal of Health and Social Behavior, 24*, 16–30.

Wadsworth, M. E. J. (1997). Health Inequalities in the life course perspective. *Social Science Medicine, 44*, 859–869.

Waite, L. J., & Gallagher, M. (2000). *The case for marriage: Why married people are happier, healthier, and better off financially*. New York: Doubleday.

Wallerstein, J. S., Lewis, J., & Blakeslee, S. (2000). *The unexpected legacy of divorce: A 25 year landmark study*. New York: Hyperion.

Warr, M. (1993). Parents, peers, and delinquency. *Social Forces, 72*(1), 247–264.

Webster, P., & Herzog, A. R. (1995). Effects of parental divorce and memories of family problems on relationships between adult children and their parents. *Journal of Gerontology: Social Sciences, 50B*, S24–S34.

Wenk, D., Hardesty, C. L., Morgan, C. S., & Blair, S. L. (1994). The influence of parental involvement on the well-being of sons and daughters. *Journal of Marriage and the Family, 56*, 229–234.

Whitbeck, L. B., Simons, R. L., Conger, R. D., Lorenz, F. O., Huck, S., & Elder, G. H. Jr. (1991). Family economic hardship, parental support, and adolescent self-esteem. *Social Psychology Quarterly, 54*, 353–363.

White, L. (1992). The effect of parental divorce and remarriage on parental support for adult children. *Journal of Family Issues, 13*, 234–250.

Wickrama, K. A. S., Conger, R. D., Wallace, L. E., & Elder, G. H., Jr. (1999). The intergenerational transmission of health-risk behaviors: adolescent lifestyles and gender moderating effects. *Journal of Health and Social Behavior, 40*, 258–272.

Wu, L. L. (1996). Effects of family instability, income, and income instability on the risk of a premarital birth. *American Sociological Review, 61*, 386–406.

Wu, L. L., & Martinson, B. C. (1993). Family structure and the risk of a premarital birth. *American Sociological Review, 58*, 210–232.

Zimmerman, M. A., Salem, D. A., & Maton, K. I. (1995). Family structure and psychosocial correlates among urban African-American adolescents. *Child Development, 66*, 1598–1613.

CHAPTER 7

Intergenerational Relations in Changing Times

NORELLA M. PUTNEY
VERN L. BENGTSON

Families have changed remarkably over the last century—in age structure and generational composition, in their diversity of forms and functions, in family members' expectations of one another and ways of relating. One consequence of the dramatic increase in longevity has been the growing prevalence of three-, four-, and five-generation families, lengthening the time spent in family roles, such as grandparenthood. At the same time, increases in divorce and remarriage, single-parenthood, and cohabitation have greatly increased the complexity of family configurations and relationships.

Early in the 20th century Burgess (1926) observed that the family had become more specialized in its functions and that the productive and instrumental aspects of family life—characterizing the traditional extended family—had been replaced by more emotional and subjective functions—characterizing the modern nuclear family. Burgess conceptualized this modern "companionship" family as not just a structure or a household, but as a process, an interaction system influenced by each of its members. With the ascendancy of the companionate nuclear family, the importance of grandparents and the extended family necessarily weakened. Burgess thought the three-generation family would persist as a network of relations still significant in the lives of older people, but kinship ties were no longer central and vital (Burgess, 1960). Parsons (1944) also saw less need for the kinship system in the modern era; rather, the nuclear family form was the most functional for industrialized society. It was not

NORELLA M. PUTNEY and VERN L. BENGTSON • Department of Sociology, University of Southern California, Los Angeles, California 90089-2539.

Handbook of the Life Course, edited by Jeylan T. Mortimer and Michael J. Shanahan. Kluwer Academic/Plenum Publishers, New York, 2003.

obvious, however, that such perceptions of the family arose from specific economic and cultural conditions within specific historical contexts. In the past few decades, which have seen rapid social and economic change, the nuclear family form has become less prominent.

Ironically, the complexities of today's family configurations appear not too different from what they were at the beginning of the 20th century, although they clearly depart from the relatively simple and idealized nuclear family form that characterized mid-century America. In recent decades, remarriage and cohabitation following divorce, and childbearing in second and third marriages as well as outside of marriage, have reintroduced a diversity of kinship compositions—half siblings, a variety of step relatives, ex-relatives, fictive kin—similar to families in earlier centuries when remarriage frequently occurred following the death of a young mother or young father (Hareven, 2001). So, in certain ways, families of yesterday have more in common with contemporary families than we often recognize.

As multigenerational family structures and functions have evolved over time, so too have our theoretical approaches and methods for understanding these changes. What we now recognize, as early family sociologists did not, is that changing social, economic, and cultural conditions affect, in essential ways, intergenerational family structures and relationships and the individual lives within those families. The maturation of several longitudinal studies now allows us to examine the dynamics of family life and individual development across different social and historical contexts. This research, guided by insights from the "life course" perspective, is expanding and amplifying our knowledge of the complexities of multigenerational family life.

In this chapter we first discuss how the life course perspective informs the study of intergenerational relations and multigenerational families. Second, we examine a number of demographic and social trends since the 1960s and their consequences for intergenerational relations and individual well-being: population aging and its effects on generational structures and kin resources; marital instability and single parenthood; changes in life cycle boundaries and intergenerational family roles; and women's increased labor force participation and its effects on family kinkeeping. Third, we describe an example of a theoretical and methodological approach used in life course research on multigenerational families. Fourth, we summarize two studies that illustrate the utility of life course precepts applied to intergenerational relations and individual development research. We conclude with suggestions for future research.

APPLICATION OF THE LIFE COURSE MODEL TO MULTIGENERATIONAL FAMILY RESEARCH

Our investigations of the changes and continuities in multigenerational family relations in changing historical contexts draw upon fundamental insights of the life course perspective. Elder (1974) developed the life course framework almost three decades ago, building on observations of Cain (1964) and Neugarten, Moore, and Lowe (1965). The life course framework has itself developed and changed over the years, and in this volume (Chapter 1), Elder summarizes five principles that guide life course research.

Two principles—life span development, and linked lives—are integral to research on multigenerational family processes. The first principle is that *development and aging are lifelong processes*, and that the relationships, events and processes of earlier life stages have consequences for later life relationships, processes, and outcomes. For example, longitudinal research has shown that parental affirmation received in childhood continues to make a significant contribution to self-esteem in adulthood (Roberts & Bengtson, 1996). Research has also shown that socialization occurs not only in childhood but also throughout the adult years, particularly evident in the domain of work (Bengtson, Biblarz, & Roberts, 2002). The second principle concerns the *interdependence of lives over time*, especially in the family, where individuals are linked across generations by bonds of kinship and processes of intergenerational transmission. This principle also includes the impact of larger social changes on interpersonal relations. For example, economic declines can have reverberating effects on the interconnected life paths of family members, as Elder has demonstrated in his examination of effects of the Great Depression and World War II (Elder, 1974, 1986; Elder & Johnson, 2002).

The third principle guiding life course research concerns *agency* in human development and the idea that planfulness and intention can affect life course outcomes. Individuals are active agents in the construction of their lives and make choices within the constraints of social structures and historical conditions. Family life also has agentic aspects, as reflected in negotiation processes. For example, in a qualitative study, Pyke and Bengtson (1996) examined the differences between "individualistic" and "collectivistic" families as choices are made regarding caregiving for dependent elders.

The fourth principle, *the impact of history and place*, has become increasingly important in multigenerational family longitudinal research. Researchers now recognize the necessity of nesting individual lives and family processes in social and historical contexts. While individual development shapes and is shaped by interactions within the immediate context of family relations, these relationships affect and are affected by larger social, economic, and cultural events and conditions. Multilevel modeling techniques now allow researchers to more accurately specify these complexities of family relationships within their environments.

A fifth principle of the life course perspective—*biographical time, family time, and historical time*—emphasizes the importance of transitions and their timing relative to structural and historical contexts. As noted by Elder (Chapter 1), there can be a "best fit" in the timing of individual development and family life stage, and their temporal convergence with structural and historically created opportunities.

The life course perspective points to the fundamental importance of historical conditions and change for understanding individual development and family life. It is therefore important to consider current demographic and social trends, to which we now turn.

DEMOGRAPHIC AND SOCIAL TRENDS: CONSEQUENCES FOR INTERGENERATIONAL RELATIONS

Population Aging

Population aging, which is accelerating around the world, will be a major challenge facing all societies in the 21st century (Bengtson, Kim, Myers, & Eun, 2000). It is more than just a demographic phenomenon—it affects the social, political, economic, and cultural conditions of life for entire societies. The worldwide decline in fertility coupled with significant increases in life expectancy will mean greater numbers and proportions of elders, especially those aged 85 and over. This will strain existing health care and support resources of nations and families. In the United States, for example, the proportion of the population 65 and over was 14% in 2000. It will increase to 20% of the total population by 2030, when the last of the Baby Boom cohorts reach 65 (Bengtson & Putney, 2000).

Population aging in conjunction with later age at marriage and childbearing not only is altering the age-dependency ratios in nations, but also has profound implications for generational dynamics and family well-being. It is changing family structures, bringing about changes in living arrangements between generations (especially in Asian societies) and reducing the numbers of adult children available to care for aging parents and grandparents. Longer lives and women's increased labor force activity are putting pressures on traditional caregiving arrangements. Societies do not approach the problem of population aging in the same ways. Much depends on their unique social and political histories as well as their cultural traditions and economic resources. In Asian societies, evidence suggests that there will be increased state responsibility for providing care to elders as family support resources become more strained. In the United States and other Western nations, by contrast, there appears to be a retrenchment of family support policies because of strains on national budgets. Still, reliance on the family to provide support and care to elders remains central in all societies (Bengtson & Putney, 2000). These macro-societal changes in age distribution have implications for the generational structure of American families.

LONGER YEARS OF SHARED LIVES ACROSS GENERATIONS.   The average life expectancy of Americans increased by almost three decades during the last century, from about 47 years in 1900 to over 77 years in 2000 (U.S. Census, 2001). This increase in longevity coupled with declining fertility (with the exception of the Baby Boom cohort) is reflected in the changing age structure of the American population over the past 100 years. In 1900, the shape of the population age structure was that of a pyramid, with a large base (represented by children under age 5) progressively tapering into a narrow group of those aged 65 and older. By 2030, dramatic declines in the fertility rate and extended life spans will cause the age structure to look more like a rectangle, with similar numbers in each age category (Population Reference Bureau, 1999).

Longer lives and fewer births have changed the age structure of most American families such that their "shape" is more like a beanpole—long and thin, with more family generations alive but with fewer members in each generation (Bengtson, 2001). Uhlenberg (1996) showed how mortality changes over the course of the 20th century have affected generational structures. The chances of a child becoming an orphan (both parents dying before the child reached age 18) were 15% for children born in 1900, compared to less than 1% for children born in 2000. Among children born in 2000, 68% will have four (or more) living grandparents. It is more likely that a 20-year-old alive today has a grandmother still living (91%) than a 20-year-old alive in 1900 had his or her mother living (83%). These statistics suggest that there are now more years of "co-survivorship between generations" than ever before in human history (Bengtson, 1996). One positive effect of this is the increased potential for aging parents and grandparents to provide family continuity and stability across time (Silverstein, Giarrusso, & Bengtson, 1998).

CHANGES IN "KIN RESOURCES" ACROSS GENERATIONS.   One of the major functions of multigenerational families is the provision of care and support to dependent members—in childhood, youth, and old age. Longer lives and the changes in family structure that ensue have important implications for family functions and relationships, because they affect the availability of potential caregivers and the chances of receiving family support. The increased longevity of parents, grandparents, great-grandparents, and other family members represents a resource of kin available for help and support that can be, and frequently is, activated in times of need (Silverstein, Parrott, & Bengtson, 1995). At the same time, as people live longer, they transfer wealth in the form of inheritances much later in life, often at a time when the younger generation is in less need of financial help than would have been the case earlier. In some countries, such as Germany, intergenerational wealth transfers are mandated by law when people are younger (e.g., parents may have to pay their children a monthly sum if they are enrolled in higher education). This means that wealth transfer may take place when the younger generation is most in need, but it also means that the younger generation has lowered expectations of inheritance upon parents' deaths.

There are also other potentially negative consequences of the "longer years of shared lives" across generations. The years of caregiving for dependent elders may be protracted (Bengtson, Rosenthal, & Burton, 1995). Such family demographic changes may also increase the potential for protracted family conflict—what an 84-year-old mother termed a "life-long lousy parent–child relationship" (Bengtson, 2001). Thus, an important research agenda is the examination of the quality of intergenerational relationships to find out why some families get along better than others and to identify the conditions that contribute to greater satisfaction, affection, and less tension in the relationships.

Marital Instability and Single Parenthood

Over the last several decades changing patterns of family formation and dissolution, child-bearing, and other types of kinship arrangements have altered family configurations and dramatically increased the diversity of family forms. In 2000, 53% of the adult population were married compared to 72% in 1970; 11% were separated or divorced in 2000, up from 4.5% in 1970 (U.S. Census, 2001). The 2000 Census demonstrates the continued shift from two-parent to one-parent families. The proportion of family households consisting of married couples with their own children (which can include stepchildren) declined from 40% in 1970 to 24% in 2000 (Bianchi & Casper, 2001), while those consisting of one parent with children increased from 11% in 1970 to 16% in 2000. Approximately half of the first marriages of the Baby Boom cohort will end in divorce (a rate that may be lower for more recent birth cohorts), while about 60% of second marriages end in divorce (Emery, 1999). The number of couples living together outside of marriage has increased substantially since the 1950s but this group still comprises only 5% of U.S. households at any given time. About one-half of couples marrying now have lived together first (Bianchi & Casper, 2001), and among those currently divorced, 16% are cohabiting (Smith, 1998).

Increases in divorce and remarriage, and childbearing outside of marriage are forcing reconsideration of how families and kinship relations are defined. For poor and minority fam-ilies in particular, young women have come to rely less on marriage and husbands and more on other kinship ties for support—mothers who help them in raising their children, grand-parents, siblings, other relatives, and fictive kin. In general, African-Americans are more likely than whites to reside in extended family households with other kin nearby and to report having "fictive kin" (Chatters & Jayakody, 1995). Latinos are also more likely to reside in multigenerational households than whites (Himes, Hogan, & Eggebeen, 1996).

Changes in family configurations brought about by divorce, single parenthood, and remarriage have important implications for individual and family well-being. Duncan and Morgan (1985) found that the economic environment faced by most people is not stable but volatile, and that much of this volatility can be explained by frequent changes in marital status and hence family composition. They found such family composition changes to be far more important for the family's economic status than were changes in the labor force participation and wage rates of the adults in the household or any of the initial characteristics of the adults, such as educational attainment or attitudes. In particular, divorce had devastating effects on the economic status of women and children, while marriage or remarriage had almost equally beneficial effects.

Changes in Life Cycle Boundaries and Intergenerational Family Roles

DELAYED NEST-LEAVING AND THE EXTENSION OF PARENTING.   The life course perspective calls attention to how economic, social, and historical changes over the 20th century have altered the timing of "nest-leaving" for different cohorts of young adults. Economic conditions and occupational opportunities determine in no small way when young adult children leave the parental home and transition to independence. The relatively prosperous 1950s promoted early nest-leaving through marriage (Goldscheider & Goldscheider, 1998), and during that decade age at first marriage reached its lowest point in the century. But when unemployment is high and the labor market is unfavorable, early nest-leaving is impeded. Since the early 1980s, the timing of this life course transition has changed; the boundaries of nest-leaving have been extended outward and have become more fluid. In 2000, 56% of men and 43% of women age 18 to 24 years lived at home with one or both parents (Spain & Casper, 2001). Some adult children don't leave home at all (Crimmins & Ingegneri, 1990). Other young adults find they must return to their parents' home because of economic hardship or when their marriages fail. Adult children may return with their own children, or these grandchildren may come alone, causing grandparents to take on the responsibility of parenting their grandchildren (Minkler & Roe, 1993). Under contemporary economic conditions, adult children benefit from coresidence with parents into their mid-20s, particularly in terms of educational attainment (White & Lacy, 1997).

Less is known about how coresidence affects the quality of the parent–adult child relationship. Do the economic and instrumental benefits of coresidence come at the expense of feelings of closeness and affection between parents and adult children? Are the effects of coresidence different for adult children than for their parents? Aquilino and Supple (1991) found generally high parent satisfaction and positive parent–child interactions in such circumstances, although there were also strains, primarily having to do with expectations about the timing of leaving home. Coresidence can intensify parent–child interactions (Ward & Spitz, 1992). There can also be differences in how parents and adult children perceive their coresidential situation, with parents generally feeling more positive than their adult children. This may have to do with different expectations regarding the achievement of autonomy in young adulthood (White & Rogers, 1997). Coresidence may also reflect the adult child's need and the parents' feelings of obligation, not necessarily feelings of closeness.

Alwin (1996) found that younger cohorts (born after 1940) are more favorable to the idea of intergenerational coresidence than earlier born cohorts, but this may be because parents are helping to support the younger generation. In terms of intergenerational relations, benefits from extended coresidence may take the form of increased individual well-being and strengthened family bonds. In the past, coresidence was generally a strategy for meeting the disability needs of aging parents. Today, coresidence is more likely to meet the needs of adult children—recently referred to as "adultolescents" (Tyre, 2002). By delaying nest-leaving, young adults receive a significant amount of parental support, both tangible and emotional, over a longer period of time. Only when parents reach late life do they receive more help and support from adult children than they provide (Bengtson & Harootyan, 1994; Eggebeen & Hogan, 1990; Rossi & Rossi, 1990).

THE INCREASING IMPORTANCE OF GRANDPARENTS.   Changing demographic and socio-economic conditions suggest that grandparents will play an increasingly important role in multigenerational families (Bengtson, 2001). In a culture enamored with youth, the positive attributes of grandparents and their contributions to family well-being are often inadequately appreciated. In the public imagination, grandparents are still more likely to be associated with declining health, nonproductivity, dependency, and need for caregiving. Empirical evidence suggests quite a different picture, with grandparents providing many unacknowledged functions in contemporary families (Szinovacz, 1998). Often, for example, grandparents are important role models in the socialization of grandchildren (Elder, Rudkin, & Conger, 1994; King & Elder, 1997). They also often provide significant economic resources to younger-generation family members (Bengtson & Harootyan, 1994), and they contribute to cross-generational solidarity and family continuity over time (Silverstein, Giarrusso, & Bengtson, 1998). In situations in which teenage mothers are raising infants, grandparents can represent a bedrock of stability (Burton, 1995). Perhaps the most dramatic contribution is when grand-parents (or great-grandparents) actually raise grandchildren or great-grandchildren. In 2000, over 4.5 million children under age 18 were living in a grandparent-headed household, representing 6.3% of all children. The number of children in grandparent-headed households has increased 30% since 1990 (AARP, 2002).

The contemporary grandparent role has several distinct features which shape, and are reflected in, grandparent–grandchild relationships (Silverstein, Giarrusso, & Bengtson, 1998). These role attributes include (1) normative ambiguity; (2) the fact that grandparent–grandchild relations are mediated by the middle generation, which has crucial implications for the strength or weakness of the grandparent–grandchild relationship when parents divorce, depending on custody arrangements; (3) a far wider array of competing roles enacted by grandparents than in the past; and (4) the normative contradictions that inhere in the questions of noninterference and familial obligation and support. This last dilemma is particularly evident in the situation of the surrogate parenting of grandchildren.

Silverstein and Long's (1998) examination of the patterns of grandparents' association with their adult grandchildren over 23 years found evidence that the grandparent role has indeed changed in recent history. They found that grandparents' affection declined somewhat as grandchildren grew from adolescence into young adulthood, but then increased. The reasons for these changes in the grandparenting role may include greater wealth, earlier retirement, and better health—each of which provides opportunity for alternative social roles. At the same time, emotional closeness and support from grandparents may compensate for or mitigate divorce-related family processes and custodial-parent role-overload that can negatively impact the well-being of both adult children and grandchildren (Silverstein, Giarrusso, & Bengtson, 1998).

Women's Increased Labor Force Participation and the Kinkeeping Role

The principles of the life course perspective are exemplified in several aspects of family kinkeeping: the interconnectedness of family members' lives over time; the duration of the kinkeeping role which may span many years of the incumbent's life; and the volitional quality of kinkeeping—that is, why the kinkeeping role may or may not be chosen and the constraints that impinge on that decision. Because social and economic conditions and changing demography affect the meaning of kinkeeping and the likelihood of its enactment, the kinkeeping role can be said to be shaped by history.

Kinkeeping is what family members "do" in support of one another in the context of promoting family ties and collective well-being (Rosenthal, 1985), and therefore is an important mechanism for maintaining intergenerational bonds. Kinkeeping is also linked to broader economic and normative structures through women's employment decisions and beliefs about family obligations. Kinkeepers act as communication links between family members up and down the family lineage and laterally within the extended family. Some researchers see caregiving to elderly family members as an aspect of the kinkeeping role (Gerstel & Gallagher, 1993). Underlying the activities of kinkeeping are the bonds of affection and norms of obligation that tie one generation to another. Research shows that the bonds of intergenerational solidarity are strong and families often rely on the work of kinkeepers to maintain those bonds (Bengtson et al., 1990). Kinkeeping is usually performed by women (Aronson, 1992; Gerstel & Gallagher, 1993; Rosenthal, 1985; Rossi & Rossi, 1990), with the kinkeeper role often passing from mother to daughter. Traditional gendered expectations about the emotional and caring work in families has meant that women take on these responsibilities. However, women's lives have changed dramatically over the past few decades, and in the future women may not be as available, or willing, to take on the kinkeeping role.

A major reason for this is women's increased participation in the labor force. Seventy-five % of middle-age women—those traditionally responsible for kin work—are now in the work force (Spain & Bianchi, 1996), which puts pressure on the time and energy they have available for kinkeeping activity (Genovese, 1997; Moen, 1992). For economic reasons alone, it is unlikely women's commitment to market work will decline. A second factor pertains to cultural changes and preferences. Noting the marked increase in nonfamily living arrangements among young adults over the past three decades, Goldscheider and Lawton (1998) suggested that women who leave their parents' home for nonfamily living rather than marriage may later value work and privacy more highly than kin work and be less inclined to take on the responsibilities of kinkeeping. Third, women's kinkeeping activities are not always chosen, and may be considered an unwelcome obligation, particularly among younger women (Aronson, 1992). Finally, because of the declining birth rate, a designated family kinkeeper may be less needed in the future to maintain lateral siblings relationships within the extended family, which has traditionally been a major kinkeeping function (Rosenthal, 1985). On the other hand, because of longer life expectancy and the increasing verticalization of multigenerational families (Bengtson et al., 1995), a kinkeeper who keeps family members in touch with one another and takes care of the oldest and youngest generations may be especially needed.

AN EXAMPLE OF A THEORETICAL AND METHODOLOGICAL APPROACH USED IN LIFE COURSE RESEARCH ON MULTIGENERATIONAL FAMILIES

Are intergenerational relationships changing? Have the dramatic social changes of the past four decades weakened family bonds? In what ways do strong intergenerational bonds promote individual family members' well-being over time? Such questions take on new importance as increased life expectancies extend the duration of shared lives and role occupancy in multigenerational families. A major aim of the Longitudinal Study of Generations (LSOG) research program is to investigate the effects of sociohistorical change on the interactions among and aging of successive family generations.

The LSOG, begun in 1971 and now including seven waves of data, is a study of linked members from some 300 three- and four-generation families as they have grown up and grown old during a period of dramatic social and economic change. The study examines long-term relationships between parents and children and between grandparents and grandchildren, how these relationships have changed over time, and the consequences of these changes for the well-being of family members over several generations. An important objective of the LSOG program has been the development of a theory of family solidarity and conflict and elaboration of the dimensions of intergenerational relations as a means of providing a better understanding of the complexities of family life. The research has identified six distinct dimensions of intergenerational solidarity: affection, association, consensus, functional support and exchange, norms of family obligation, and structural opportunities or barriers (Roberts & Bengtson, 1990).

Consistent with a life course approach, the solidarity and conflict model of intergenerational relations was forged on the notion that broad social structures and large social contexts affect family life and relationships. Using nationally representative data and latent class analysis, Silverstein & Bengtson (1997) demonstrated that the dimensions of solidarity and conflict may be arrayed in a variety of configurations, as typologies of parent–adult child relations. Five types of extended families are identified: tight-knit, sociable, intimate-but-distant, obligatory, and detached. Tight-knit and sociable are the most frequently found parent–adult child relationship types, with the other three types in smaller but similar proportions. Such typologies can empirically represent the inherently multidimensional nature and diversity of parent–child relationships as they have responded to changes in the economy and occupational structures, in marriage and divorce, and in childbearing patterns. Moreover, shifts between types over time can be used for examining family processes as parents grow older.

Silverstein and Bengtson (1997) examined differences in the types of relations adult children maintain with their mothers and their fathers. Adult children's relationships with mothers are more likely to be tight-knit, with daughters more likely than sons to have tight-knit relationships with their mothers. About four times as many adult children are detached from their fathers as from their mothers. Divorced fathers have weaker emotional attachments with their adult children than do married fathers or divorced mothers. The odds of having detached relations are about five times greater for divorced fathers than for divorced mothers.

A life course approach to multigenerational family research considers how family relationships change or remain stable across individual lives and families and how these processes are linked to multiple and evolving historical contexts (Bengtson & Allen, 1993). With panel data collected over 30 years that have seen rapid social change, the LSOG now allows us to examine these issues. The study is unique because of its accumulation of parallel longitudinal assessments for multiple generations within the same families in different historical periods. This makes it possible to draw conclusions about the relationship between historical change in family structures and intergenerational influence and socialization outcomes. Another unique feature of the LSOG is that sufficient time has elapsed since 1971, when data were first collected, that the chronological ages at which members of different generations were assessed have begun to overlap. This allows us to utilize a generation-sequential design, comparing sets of parents and children at the same ages across different historical periods. In the next section we discuss two studies that demonstrate the utility of the life course perspective for investigating changes in intergenerational relations and individual development over time. The reader may also wish to refer to the chapter in this volume by Alwin and McCammon, who discuss the "meanings" of different generational labels (such as "Generation X") and the importance of studying generationally defined demographic groups.

TWO STUDIES USING THE LIFE COURSE
APPROACH

Changes in Parental Influence on the Life Course Outcomes of Offspring

Our recent research examines how family relationships serve as conduits by which values, resources, and behaviors are transmitted across multiple generations. Bengtson, Biblarz, and Roberts (2002) used a generation-sequential design and parent–child dyads to investigate intergenerational influences on sons' and daughters' education and occupational aspiration, self-esteem and values (individualism and materialism). The study also examined how transmission processes have been affected by parental divorce and maternal employment. The analytic design is based on two general research questions, one focusing on intergenerational transmission *outcomes*, the other on intergenerational transmission *processes*. The first question is: have the aspirations, values, and self-esteem of Generation X youth (G4s, born between 1966 and 1980) been adversely affected by changing opportunity structures and rising divorce and maternal employment rates over recent decades? The second question is: were Baby Boom parents (G3s) less influential for the development of their Generation X children's aspirations, values, and self-esteem than G2 parents had been for the development of these attributes among Baby Boom youth? Three critical connections between family influences and young adults' outcomes are examined: one grounded in the family's socialization functions, a second based on particular families' access to social resources, and a third stemming from the quality of parent–child emotional bonds in particular families and their effect upon intergenerational transmission processes.

Findings indicate that the patterns of parental *influences* on youths' outcomes are remarkably similar across two generations (young Baby Boomers and Generation X youth) and historical time periods (growing up in the 1960s and the 1990s). This suggests that despite changes in family structure and socioeconomic context, intergenerational influences on youths' educational and occupational aspirations, self-esteem and value orientations are still strong—and haven't changed much since the 1960s. When Generation X youth are compared with their Baby Boom parents when they were in youth 26 years earlier, Generation Xers have higher aspirations and higher self-esteem, and are more collectivistic. Across generations, parental resources strongly affected their children's educational and occupational aspirations, suggesting the continuing importance of learning and modeling processes within families.

We might now ask about the importance of period effects, such as the increases in women's labor force participation and marital disruption since the 1960s. Findings indicate that maternal employment has not affected the aspirations, values, and self-esteem of youth across these two generations in a negative way. Generation Xers whose parents divorced were slightly less advantaged in terms of educational and occupational aspirations and self-esteem than those who came from nondivorced families, but they were nevertheless higher on these measures than were their Baby Boomer parents were at the same age, regardless of family structure. Among Generation Xers, parental divorce affected the influence of mothers' affirmation on their children's self-esteem. It is not that children of divorce feel less close to their mothers than children from two-parent families. Rather, in the context of divorce, closeness to mothers turns out to be a weaker determinant of the self-esteem that children ultimately develop. Consistent with other research (Amato, 1994; Amato & Sobolewski, 2001; Silverstein & Bengtson, 1997), father–child affective bonds were found to be significantly weaker for Generation Xers than they were for Baby Boomers in their youth, a result that can be largely attributed to the increase in parental divorce. Divorced fathers were found to have significantly weaker emotional bonds with their children than mothers, whether divorced or not. Also, parental divorce reduced to almost nil the ability of Baby Boom fathers to influence their Generation X children's aspirations, self-esteem, and collectivist values. Nonetheless, in the context of divorce, fathers do influence the assumption of materialist values in their children. The study found that Generation Xers are becoming more collectivist in their value orientation. This may indicate a possible shift in cultural values among more recently born cohorts.

The Life Paths of Baby Boom Women

Using LSOG panel data and a cohort sequential design, Putney (2002) used a life course perspective to examine changes in women's life paths and the consequences of historical change on mental health outcomes, such as depression and self-esteem. Specific focus was on contrasting the life paths of Baby Boom women with those of women of the Silent Generation (born 1931–1945) who came before them. Four factors relevant to women's life course mental health outcomes were examined: work/family balance, the quality of women's relationships with parents, changing norms of egalitarianism and familism, and changes in marital stability.

Because of their historical circumstances, Baby Boom women seemed more advantaged than earlier-born cohorts of women. Growing up in the prosperous postwar period, they experienced, in early adulthood, favorable economic conditions, expanded opportunities for higher education and professional achievement, and changing gender norms. The question is whether by midlife Baby Boom women were better off in terms of their psychological well-being than earlier-born cohorts of women had been in midlife.

The answer is no. Indeed, findings indicate that Baby Boom women were significantly more depressed and had lower self-esteem in midlife than Silent Generation or Depression Era women at the same life stage. Several factors contributed to Baby Boom women's lower psychological functioning. In contrast to the earlier-born cohorts of women, Baby Boom women experienced greater stress in trying to balance the demands of work and family, and this contributed to their higher depression. As one Baby Boom mother put it, "I feel too much pressure between work and family" (p. 146). Results show that having a close supportive relationship with parents positively affected women's professional achievement and psychological well-being. For Baby Boom women, weak affective bonds with their father in late adolescence contributed significantly to lower self-esteem and higher depression when they were in young adulthood, twenty years later. Conversely, affective closeness with father in youth contributed to positive mental health outcomes in young adulthood. In midlife, the quality of Baby Boom women's relations with their fathers remained a significant predictor of their psychological well-being, with those having weaker emotional bonds with their fathers being significantly more depressed. Parental divorce also seems to be playing a role. Consistent with other research (Amato, 1994; Amato & Sobolewski, 2001; Kaufman & Uhlenberg, 1998; Silverstein & Bengtson, 1997), findings indicate that parental divorce adversely affected the quality of Baby Boom women's relations with their fathers in midlife. (For Generation X women, incidentally, having close affective bonds with their mothers contributed to their higher self-esteem and lower depression in young adulthood.)

Marital dissatisfaction contributed significantly to Baby Boom women's higher levels of depression. In contrast to Silent Generation women, Baby Boom women were not only less satisfied with their marriages in midlife but also felt that their satisfaction had significantly declined from what it had been in young adulthood. The emotional responsiveness of Baby Boom women to being dissatisfied in their marriages seemed more volatile than that of Silent

Generation women. Marital dissatisfaction contributed to midlife Baby Boom women being significantly more depressed than midlife Silent Generation women at a comparable level of dissatisfaction. This suggests that the meaning or expectations of marriage may have shifted, which lends empirical support to observations that marriage has changed in the past few decades (Cherlin, 1999; Giddens, 1991).

Stronger egalitarian views contributed to younger cohorts' professional achievement and psychological well-being. This was especially the case for Baby Boom and Generation X women, but also for Silent Generation women. In the last decade, all female cohorts in the study became slightly more traditional in their gender role views although younger cohorts remained more egalitarian than earlier-born cohorts, suggesting both period and cohort effects. Familism increased among Baby Boom and Generation X women in the past decade, and for these two younger cohorts familism is associated with higher self-esteem.

Reflecting a core principle of the life course perspective, biographical and historical timing appears to have mattered for the mental health outcomes of the Baby Boom and Silent Generation cohorts in midlife. Both cohorts were affected by the rapid social and economic changes of the 1970s and 80s. However, the two cohorts encountered these changes at different stages in the life course. Silent Generation women, having completed their heavy child-rearing responsibilities, did not have to juggle the demands of work and family in the same way as did Baby Boom women. Having generally started their childbearing at a later age, Baby Boom women were then confronted by the dislocations of economic restructuring and other dilemmas they could not anticipate: the intensified demands of work and family and the increasing contingency of employment and marriage.

SUMMARY AND CONCLUSION

A major aim of contemporary research on multigenerational families is to investigate changes in family intergenerational dynamics within the context of changing historical times. This research objective highlights the importance of the life course perspective for guiding family research today. The life course perspective emphasizes the importance of historical events and conditions for understanding people's lives. We discussed a number of demographic and social trends and their implications for families. These trends—population aging, marital instability and single parenthood, changes in life cycle boundaries and family roles, and women's increased labor force participation and its effects on the family kinkeeping—are affecting family structures and dynamics today, with consequences for future intergenerational relations and support.

First, population aging during the last half-century has changed the age structures of societies and families, the living arrangements between generations, family roles in the provision of elder care, and government policies toward the elderly and their families. Greater longevity has meant a growing number of three-, four-, and even five-generation families, and the longer years of joint survivorship are increasing the pool of kin resources and the potential for mutual support and assistance. Second, macrolevel trends in family formation, marital instability, and childbearing have dramatically altered the configurations of families, resulting in an increasing diversity of family forms. A major consequence of divorce or single parenthood is that mother-maintained families and their children are far more likely to live in poverty. Third, the life cycle boundaries of active parenting have been extended out and have become more fluid in the last two decades. Less favorable labor market conditions and the need for additional years of education have meant adult children are remaining "in the nest" longer or are returning to the nest when things don't work out. There is a bright side to this trend, however. Additional years of parent–adult child coresidence mean more intergenerational exchange and support, which tends to promote long-term family attachments. There has also been a dramatic increase in the number of grandparents raising their grandchildren, a reflection of the increasing importance of grandparents for family well-being. Fourth, women's increased commitment to full-time market work may affect family kinkeeping, a role traditionally carried out by women. Changes in gender roles and preferences suggest that younger women may not be as available to do the work of kinkeeping in the future as they have been in the past. This has implications for intergenerational family relationships and for the likelihood that family members will be able to support and care for one another in time of need.

We then discussed a theoretical and methodological approach used in life course research on intergenerational relations, with specific reference to the Longitudinal Study of Generations (LSOG). The theoretical development of a model of family solidarity and conflict and the elaboration of relationship "types" have yielded important understandings with respect to the complexities and contradictions of family relations. With 30 years of panel data collected from multiple generations of families, the LSOG has sufficiently matured to support generation-sequential and cohort-sequential designs for investigating the effects of macrosocial changes on family relationships and individual development. We presented two studies to demonstrate how the life course perspective is being applied in family research.

The Meaning and Function of Families

The study of multigenerational families is concerned with the nature and strength of bonds between older and younger generational kin and the consequences of these bonds for individual well-being, the propensity of members to provide care and support to one another, and the significance of kinship relations and roles for members as they respond to changing socioeconomic, cultural, and historical conditions. Research demonstrates the continuing influence and importance of families for the nurturance and socialization of its youth, for the care and support of elders, and for the long-term well-being of family members. Our life course research of intergenerational relations shows that the family is still fulfilling its basic functions, but in a world very different from that of the 1950s. There is much greater diversity in family forms. Kin resources today may include not only grandparents, great-grandparents, grandchildren, and siblings, but also step relatives, ex-relatives, or fictive kin. We suggest that at the beginning of the 21st century multigenerational families and other kinship systems are taking on greater importance as sources of stability and support.

Future Directions

Future life course research on intergenerational relations should give attention to several issues. First, there is a need to explore how trends in longevity, elder health, the verticalization of the multigenerational family structure, and the aging of Baby Boomers are affecting intergenerational solidarity and support. Second, research should examine whether families who are experiencing changes in structure or roles, through events such as divorce, are adapting by extending and expanding functions across generations. As family forms have diversified, multi- and inter-generational exchange and support over the life course of children must also become an important object of study. Third, the relationships that children and parents have with their grandparents following divorce should be carefully explored. Fourth, we need to confirm whether familism is truly on the rise among young cohorts, and if it is we need to investigate why this is occurring and what it portends for the multigenerational family. Finally, comparative and cross-national research on the effects of historical trends on multi-generational families is needed. Research within single societies often fails to reveal the influence of culture as a social force. Comparing caregiving in Eastern and Western societies, for example, would help us to examine the underlying importance of values. Cultural values prescribe different roles and responsibilities for families and government in caring for the needs of dependent family members, and this in turn has important implications for the kinds of policies that are put in place.

REFERENCES

AARP (2002). *Census 2000 number and percentage change since 1990. Children under 18 living in grandparent-headed households*. Washington, DC: AARP Grandparent Information Center. Retrieved March 2002 from the World Wide Web: http://www.aarp.org/confacts/grandparents/grandfacts.html

Alwin, D. F. (1996). Coresidence beliefs in American society—1973–1991. *Journal of Marriage and the Family, 58,* 393–403.

Amato, P. R. (1994). Father–child relations, mother–child relations, and offspring psychological well-being in early adulthood. *Journal of Marriage and the Family, 56,* 1031–1042.

Amato, P. R., & Sobolewski, J. M. (2001). The effects of divorce and marital discord on adult children's psycholog-ical well-being. *American Sociological Review, 66,* 900–921.

Aquilino, W. S., & Supple, K. R. (1991). Parent–child relations and parent's satisfaction with living arrangements when adult children live at home. *Journal of Marriage and the Family, 53,* 13–27.

Aronson, J. (1992). Women's sense of responsibility for the care of old people: "But who else is going to do it?" *Gender & Society, 6,* 8–29.

Bengtson, V. L. (1996). Continuities and discontinuities in intergenerational relationship over time. In V. L. Bengtson (Ed.), *Adulthood and aging: Research on continuities and discontinuities* (pp. 246–268). New York: Springer.

Bengtson, V. L. (2001). Beyond the nuclear family: The increasing importance of multigenerational relationships in American society. The 1998 Burgess Award Lecture. *Journal of Marriage and Family, 63,* 1–16.

Bengtson, V. L., & Allen, K. R. (1993). The life course perspective applied to families over time. In P. Boss, W. Doherty, R. LaRossa, W. Schumm, & S. Steinmetz (Eds.). *Sourcebook of family theories and methods: A contextual approach* (pp. 469–498). New York: Plenum Press.

Bengtson, V. L., Biblarz, T. J., & Roberts, R. E. L. (2002). *How families still matter: A longitudinal study of youth in two generations*. New York: Cambridge University Press.

Bengtson, V. L., & Harootyan, R. A. (1994). *Intergenerational linkages: Hidden connections in American society*. New York: Springer.

Bengtson, V. L., Kim, K-D, Myers, G. C., & Eun, K-S (Eds.). (2000). *Aging in East and West: Families, states, and the elderly*. New York: Springer.

Bengtson, V. L., & Putney, N. M. (2000). Who will care for the elderly? Consequences of population aging East and West. In K. D. Kim, V. L. Bengtson, G. D. Meyers, & K. S. Eun (Eds.). *Aging in East and West: Families, states, and the elderly* (pp. 263–285). New York: Springer.

Bengtson, V., Rosenthal, C., & Burton, L. (1990). Families and aging: Diversity and heterogeneity. In R. H. Binstock & L. K. George (Eds.), *Handbook of aging and the social sciences* (3rd ed., pp. 263–287). New York: Academic Press.

Bengtson, V. L., Rosenthal, C. J., & Burton, L. M. (1995). Paradoxes of families and aging. In R. H. Binstock & L. K. George (Eds.), *Handbook of aging and the social sciences* (4th ed., pp. 253–282). San Diego: Academic Press.

Bianchi, S. M., & Casper, L. M. (2001) *News Release: American families resilient after 50 years of change*. Washington, DC: Population Reference Bureau.

Burgess, E. W. (1926). The family as a unity of interacting personalities. *The Family, 7,* 3–9.

Burgess, E. W. (Ed.). (1960). *Aging in Western societies: A comparative survey*. Chicago: University of Chicago Press.

Burton, L. M. (1995). Intergenerational patterns of providing care in African-American families with teenage child-bearers: Emergent patterns in an ethnographic study. In V. L. Bengtson, K. W. Schaie, & L. M. Burton (Eds.), *Adult intergenerational relations: Effects of social change* (pp. 79–96). New York: Springer.

Cain, L. D., Jr. (1964). Life course and social structure. In R. E. L. Faris (Ed.), *Handbook of modern sociology* (pp. 272–309). Chicago: Rand McNally.

Chatters, L. M., & Jayakody, R. (1995). Commentary: Intergenerational support within African-American families: Concepts and methods. In V. L. Bengtson, K. W. Schaie, & L. M. Burton (Eds.), *Adult intergenerational relations: Effects of social change* (pp. 97–118). New York: Springer.

Cherlin, A. J. (1999). *Public and private families: An introduction* (2nd ed.). New York: McGraw-Hill.

Crimmins, E. M., & Ingegneri, D. G. (1990). Interaction and living arrangements of older parents and their children: Past trends, present determinants, future implications. *Research on Aging, 12*, 3–35.

Duncan, G. J., & Morgan, J. N. (1985). The Panel Study of Income Dynamics. In G. H. Elder, Jr. (Ed.). *Life course dynamics: Trajectories and transitions, 1968–1980* (pp. 50–71). Ithaca, NY: Cornell University Press.

Eggebeen, D. J., & Hogan, D. P. (1990). Giving between generations in American families. *Human Nature, 1*, 211–232.

Elder, G. H., Jr. (1974). *Children of the great depression: Social change in life experience*. Chicago: University of Chicago Press.

Elder, G. H., Jr. (1986). Military times and turning points in men's lives. *Developmental Psychology, 22*, 233–245.

Elder, G. H., Jr., & Johnson, M. K. (2002). The life course and aging: Challenges, lessons, and new directions. In R. A. Settersten, Jr. (Ed.). *Invitation to the life course: Toward new understandings of later life* (pp. 49–81). Amityville, New York: Baywood.

Elder, G. H., Jr., Rudkin, L., & Conger, R. D. (1994). Intergenerational continuity and change in rural America. In V. L. Bengtson, K. W. Schaie, L. M. Burton (Ed.). *Adulthood intergenerational relations: Effects of societal change* (pp. 30–65). New York: Springer.

Emery, R. E. (1999). *Marriage, divorce and children's adjustment (2nd ed)*. Thousand Oaks, CA: Sage.

Genovese, R. G. (1997). *Americans at midlife*. Westport, CT: Bergin & Garvey.

Gerstel, N., & Gallagher, S. K. (1993). Kinkeeping and distress: Gender, recipients of care, and work-family conflict. *Journal of Marriage and the Family, 55*, 598–607.

Giddens, A. (1991). *Modernity and self-identity: Self and society in the late modern age*. Stanford, CA: Stanford University Press.

Goldscheider, F. K., & Goldscheider, C. (1998). The effects of childhood family structure on leaving and returning home. *Journal of Marriage and the Family 60*, 745–756.

Goldscheider, F. K., & Lawton, L. (1998). Family experiences and the erosion of support for intergenerational coresidence. *Journal of Marriage and the Family, 60*, 623–632.

Hareven, T. K. (2001). Historical perspectives on aging and family relations. In R. H. Binstock & L. K. George (Eds.) *Handbook of aging and the social sciences* (5th ed., pp. 141–155). San Diego, CA: Academic Press.

Himes, C. L., Hogan D. P., & Eggebeen, D. J. (1996). Living arrangements of minority elders. *Journal of Gerontology: Social Sciences, 51B*, S42–S48.

Kaufman, G., & Uhlenberg, P. (1998). Effects of life course transitions on the quality of relationships between adult children and their parents. *Journal of Marriage and the Family, 60*, 924–938.

King V., & Elder. G. H., Jr. (1997). The legacy of grandparenting: Childhood experiences with grandparents and current involvement with grandchildren. *Journal of Marriage and the Family, 59*, 848–859.

Minkler, M., & Roe, J. (1993). *Grandparents as caregivers*. Newbury Park, CA: Sage.

Moen, P. (1992). *Women's two roles: A contemporary dilemma*. New York: Auburn House.

Neugarten, B. L., Moore, J. W., & Lowe, J. C. (1965). Age norms, age constraints, and adult socialization. *American Journal of Sociology, 70*, 710–717.

Parsons, T. (1944). The social structure of the family. In R. N. Anshen (Ed.). *The family: Its function and destiny* (pp. 173–201). New York: Harper.

Population Reference Bureau (1999). *1999 World Population Data Sheet*. Washington, DC: The Bureau.

Putney, N. M. (2002). The life paths of baby boom women: A tale of unexpected consequences. Unpublished doctoral dissertation, University of Southern California, Los Angeles.

Pyke, K. D., & Bengtson, V. L. (1996). Caring more or less: Individualistic and collectivist systems of family eldercare. *Journal of Marriage and the Family, 58*, 1–14.

Roberts, R. E. L., & Bengtson, V. L. (1990). Is intergenerational solidarity a unidimensional construct? A second test of a formal model. *Journal of Gerontology, 45*, S12–S20.

Rosenthal, C. J. (1985). Kinkeeping in the familial division of labor. *Journal of Marriage and the Family, 47*, 965–974.

Rossi, A. S., & Rossi, P. H. (1990). *Of human bonding: Parent–child relations across the life course.* New York: Aldine de Gruyter.

Silverstein, M., & Bengtson, V. L. (1997). Intergenerational solidarity and the structure of adult child–parent relationships in American families. *American Journal of Sociology, 103*, 429–460.

Silverstein, M., Giarrusso, R., & Bengtson, V. L. (1998). Intergenerational solidarity and the grandparent role. In M. Szinovacz (Ed.), *Handbook on grandparenthood* (pp. 144–158). Westport, CT: Greenwood Press.

Silverstein, M., & Long, J. D. (1998). Trajectories of grandparents' perceived solidarity with adult grandchildren: A growth curve analysis over 23 years. *Journal of Marriage and the Family, 60*, 912–923.

Silverstein, M., Parrott, T. M., & Bengtson, V. L. (1995), Factors that predispose middle-aged sons and daughters to provide social support to older parents. *Journal of Marriage and the Family, 57*, 465–475.

Smith, T. W. (1998). *The emerging 21st century American family. GSS Social Change, Report No. 42.* Chicago: National Opinion Research Center, University of Chicago.

Spain, D., & Bianchi, S. M. (1996). *Balancing act: Motherhood, marriage and employment among American women.* New York: Russell Sage Foundation.

Szinovacz, M. (1998). *Handbook on grandparenthood* (pp. 144–158). Westport, CT: Greenwood Press.

Tyre, P. (2002, March 25). Back with mom and dad: Enter the adultolescents. *Newsweek, 139*, 38–40.

Uhlenberg, P. (1996). Mutual attraction: Demography and life-course analysis. *Gerontologist, 36*, 226–229.

U.S. Bureau of the Census. (2001). *America's families and living arrangements: 2000.* Current Population Reports. P20-537. Retrieved December 2001 from the World Wide Web: www.census.gov/population/www/socdemo/hh-fam/p20-537_00.html

U.S. Bureau of the Census. (2001), *Statistical abstract of the United States. No. 98. Expectation of life and expected deaths by race, sex, and age: 1998.* Retrieved March 2002 from the World Wide Web: http://www.gensus.gov/prod/20-02/pubs/01/statabs/vitstat.pdf

Ward, R. A., & Spitze, G. (1992). Consequences of parent–adult child coresidence: A review and research agenda. *Journal of Family Issues, 13*, 553–572.

White, L., & Lacy, N. (1997). The effects of age at home leaving and pathways from home on educational attainment. *Journal of Marriage and the Family, 59*, 982–995.

White, L. K., & Rogers, S. J. (1997). Strong support but uneasy relationships: Coresidence and adult children's relationships with their parents. *Journal of Marriage and the Family, 59*, 62–76.

CHAPTER 8

Educational Transitions, Trajectories, and Pathways

Aaron M. Pallas

Education is a prominent social institution in advanced societies, with primary responsibility for socializing the young to become productive adults. The movement of individuals through the education system is thus a central object of study in sociology, both as a phenomenon to be explained and as a determinant of subsequent outcomes throughout the life course. In this chapter, I examine the study of educational trajectories, including the transitions that punctuate these trajectories, and the well-traveled pathways that shape them. I begin by explaining why educational trajectories have only recently become a central analytic concept in the sociology of education, and discussing the linkages between educational pathways and educational trajectories. Drawing on the sociology of the life course's concern with age, aging, and historical time, I then examine the conceptualization and measurement of educational trajectories, and the analytic models that are used to describe them. Next, I summarize some recent research on educational trajectories in Great Britain and the United States. I conclude by charting some future directions for research on educational pathways and trajectories.

THE ORIGINS OF RESEARCH ON EDUCATIONAL TRAJECTORIES

A central focus of sociology is social stratification, defined as the presence of differentiated, and unequal, statuses associated with the various positions in a social system. Status can be

Aaron M. Pallas • Teachers College, Columbia University, New York, New York 10027.

Handbook of the Life Course, edited by Jeylan T. Mortimer and Michael J. Shanahan. Kluwer Academic/Plenum Publishers, New York, 2003.

ascribed (i.e., assigned at birth by virtue of one's social characteristics), or achieved (i.e., earned through attaining some social position that is not simply awarded at birth). The statuses associated with various levels of educational attainment and with various occupations are typically described as achieved. Through the course of the twentieth century, a great deal of sociological research and theorizing was devoted to understanding the ways in which sons inherited status from their fathers, as well as social mobility, in which sons achieve higher or lower statuses than their fathers.*

Blau and Duncan (1967) fundamentally reconceptualized the study of social mobility in *The American Occupational Structure*. Drawing on methodological developments in quantitative social research, they were less concerned with describing the extent of social mobility in a given society (i.e., the United States) than in quantifying and explaining the linkage between social origins and social destinations. The pattern of social mobility described by mobility matrices, relating fathers' occupational achievements to those of their sons, was the point of departure for the so-called "basic model" linking social origins (e.g., father's educational attainment and occupational status), educational attainment, and social destinations (i.e., the occupational status of a man's first job and his job in 1962).

Blau and Duncan's work is often cited as the clarion call for status attainment research, a tradition of research very prominent in American empirical sociology in the 1960s and 1970s, and nowhere more so than in the sociology of education. Researchers such as William H. Sewell and his colleagues at the University of Wisconsin (see, e.g., Sewell, Haller, & Ohlendorf, 1970; Sewell, Haller, & Portes, 1969), along with others such as Duncan, Featherman, and Duncan (1972), elaborated the relationship between social origins and educational attainment by emphasizing the social psychology of the status attainment process, developing what came to be known as the "Wisconsin model" of status attainment. The initial formulations of the Wisconsin model saw it primarily as a theory of socialization. The model's attention to the linkages among family social status, the influence of significant others, and a youth's own aspirations suggested that the primary mechanism for determining adult status was class-linked socialization, in which working-class youth were surrounded by parents, teachers and peers who had low expectations for their academic performance, and frequently internalized these expectations, leading them to lower academic performance, fewer years of schooling completed, and jobs with lower socioeconomic rewards. In contrast, the model viewed middle-class youth as benefiting from the high expectations that significant others held for them, leading them to strive for scholastic success, and paying off with more years of schooling and well-paying, prestigious jobs. The link between social origins and social destinations was rooted in studies of family and kinship relations.

The status attainment tradition, coupled with the tradition of human capital research in economics, has left little doubt about the effects of educational attainment on socioeconomic outcomes. First, individuals with more education are more likely to participate in the labor force (Bound, Schoenbaum, & Waidmann 1995). Second, the status attainment studies routinely find large effects of education on occupational status (Featherman & Hauser, 1978; Grusky & DiPrete, 1990). Third, individuals who go farther through school earn more than those who obtain less schooling (e.g., Jencks et al., 1979; Murnane, Willett, & Levy, 1995; Sewell & Hauser, 1980), even when controlling for family background and academic ability, each of which might influence both educational attainment and earnings. And finally, even beyond the immediate effects on earnings, educational attainment also is associated with

---

*Much early research only analyzed fathers and sons, and thus presented only a partial picture of the phenomenon of social mobility.

household wealth. Households in which the head is highly educated have greater net worth, looking across a range of assets and debts, than households in which the head is poorly educated (Land & Russell, 1996).

Most status attainment and human capital studies, however, have treated education as fixed at the highest level of schooling an individual has completed. The key advances in the study of educational trajectories did not occur until researchers shifted from kinship models to life course models that explicitly incorporated age, aging, and time as analytic concepts. This is primarily a matter of emphasis; studies of the life course continue to rely on kinship concepts, and social mobility continues to be defined in terms of the intergenerational transmission of social status, which draws attention to kin relations, especially the linkages between fathers and their sons. Glen Elder's (1992) characterization of *The American Occupational Structure* as a life course study helps to illuminate the shift. Blau and Duncan's work addressed *intra*generational mobility processes and careers; drew attention to the timing of life course events in studies of education and mobility; and suggested both cohort and generational differences in the occupational attainment process. Similarly, Featherman and Hauser's (1978) analyses incorporated historical time explicitly into the status attainment model. Many of these ideas have become central to how we think about the relationship between education and social life.

There was, however, a feature of *The American Occupational Structure* that worked against this shift from kinship ties to age and age-grading, and that is the mixed blessing of path analysis. The relatively small number of parameters in Blau and Duncan's "basic model," a consequence of the translation of occupational class categories into the metric of a socioeconomic index of occupational status, was appealing on the grounds of parsimony, and led many researchers following in their footsteps to concentrate their attention on explaining within-population variation in occupational status scores.

This focus directed attention *away* from occupational positions, which were always central to the father-to-son mobility tables used in the 1950s to summarize the amount of social mobility in a society, and *toward* the social status associated with those positions. Variability across the continuum of social status often was analyzed and discussed in ways that decoupled status from the hierarchical structure of positions in the occupational and educational structures. The renewed attention in the 1970s to an individual's position in relation to a structure of positions was a critical turning point in the study of educational trajectories. In the analysis of education, the emphasis on educational attainment, measured in terms of years of schooling, was supplemented by a concern with educational achievement, measured in terms of the acquisition of educational credentials.

The Increasing Role of Structure

A central critique of the Wisconsin model was its failure to account adequately for the context in which decisions about schooling and work are formulated. Kerckhoff (1976) initiated this line of thinking by questioning whether the status attainment model could profitably be viewed as a theory of allocation as well as a theory of socialization. He stressed the possibility that individuals are allocated by the education system and the economy to various social positions on the basis of their social background characteristics.

At approximately the same time, Spilerman (1977) reintroduced the concept of the career—an individual's sequence of jobs held across the socioeconomic life cycle—into the sociological literature. He distinguished careers from career lines, a sequence of jobs common to the experience of many workers (cf., Spenner, Otto, & Call, 1982). Spilerman showed that career lines depend on structural features of the labor market, and thus drew attention to the ways in which opportunity structures shape individual careers. His analysis prompted Kerckhoff (1993, 1996) to extend the concept of career first to the educational career, a concept synonymous with the educational trajectory, and then to a conception that bridges educational and labor force careers.

Just as careers are equated with trajectories, so too do I define pathways as identical to career lines. Pathways are well-traveled sequences of transitions that are shaped by cultural and structural forces (Elder, 1985). Although trajectories and pathways may both be described by a sequence of transitions, analytically they are quite distinct. A trajectory is an attribute of an individual, whereas a pathway is an attribute of a social system. Pathways are of particular interest in their ability to illuminate structures—for example, constraints, incentives, and choice opportunities—that link different social locations within a social system.

Thus, whereas the initial formulations of the status attainment model placed the individual in the foreground and the opportunity structure in the background, more recent theorizing has placed the opportunity structure in the foreground and individual decision-making in the background. Considering both individual agency and social structure, however, provides a more complete accounting of status attainment than focusing on one to the exclusion of the other. In considering the implications of status attainment models for understanding educational trajectories, the key insight is that social background influences educational and occupational transitions, both by structuring the choices that individuals make, and by shaping the structures in which individuals can exercise choice.

All modern educational systems intentionally sort students into differing positions, whether within schools, between schools, or both. Natriello (1994) describes tracking, ability grouping, disability grouping (e.g., special education and compensatory education), age grouping, and interest grouping as the most common within-school stratification mechanisms. These mechanisms can structure educational pathways by opening some doors and closing others. In the United States, for example, there have been countless studies of tracking (i.e., between-class ability grouping) and ability grouping (i.e., grouping students by ability within classrooms), most of which have attempted to determine whether placement in a particular position facilitates or impedes future educational success (Gamoran, 1992; Loveless, 1999; Lucas, 1999; Oakes, 1985). Similarly, retention in grade is associated with a much greater likelihood of dropping out of high school before completion (Anderson, 1994; National Research Council, 1999; Roderick, 1993).

The primary challenge of studies of within-school stratification mechanisms—as is true for the study of educational pathways more generally—is distinguishing selection from influence. Individuals typically are sorted into educational positions on the basis of characteristics that by themselves might determine subsequent educational success or failure. For example, students are often retained in the first grade because they have not yet learned to read. Early reading difficulties predict later difficulties in school. If one were to contrast the later educational performance of children who were promoted with those who were retained in grade, one might conclude that retention *caused* the lower performance observed among retainees. It is not obvious, however, that the kinds of students who are retained in first grade would be any better off if they had been promoted instead (Alexander, Entwisle, & Dauber, 1994).

Although a full exposition of educational pathways is beyond the scope of this chapter, I note here some analytic tools that may prove useful in generating hypotheses about the links between educational pathways and educational trajectories. Drawing on the work of Allmendinger (1989), Gamoran (1989, 1992), Kerckhoff (1995, 2000, 2001), Kilgore (1993),

Müller & Shavit (1998), Sørensen (1970), among others, I identify eight features of educational pathways that can structure educational trajectories.

Scope refers to the extent to which a particular stratified location in the education system shapes a student's entire educational experience. In a wide-scope tracking system, being in the low track might govern placement in all school subjects. Conversely, in a narrow-scope tracking system, a student might be in a low track in English, but a high track in mathematics. *Selectivity* is the extent to which a particular stratified location in the education system consists of students who are homogeneous on one or more characteristics. Such homogeneity may pertain to the ascribed characteristics of sex, race/ethnicity, social class, religion, and native language, or to scholastic achievement. *Specificity* is the extent to which a particular stratified location in the education system dictates access to desirable future options. We can distinguish between educational specificity and vocational or occupational specificity. The former represents the ability of a particular educational position to grant access to a desirable subsequent educational position. The latter pertains to the constraints a particular educational position places on desirable occupations.

Mobility is the extent to which movement into or out of a particular stratified location in the education system is fluid or rare. Lucas and Good (2001) show that there is both downward and upward mobility across tracks in contemporary U.S. high schools. *Curricular differentiation* is the extent to which a particular stratified location in the schooling system exposes a student to a different quality, quantity, and pace of instruction than other students. Oakes (1985) and Page (1991) provide persuasive evidence that students in lower-track classrooms receive uninteresting and dated instructional materials, and are frequently taught by rote.

Electivity is the extent to which a student's own choice or preference determines his or her placement in a particular stratified location in the educational system. The greater a student's opportunity for choice, the more likely that the student's social background will structure his or her educational trajectories. *Stigma* is the extent to which a particular stratified location in the schooling system confers a devalued social identity on a student. Students in special education classes frequently are stigmatized, as are students who are retained in grade. Finally, *institutionalization* is the extent to which there is a widespread and shared public understanding about the meaning of a particular stratified location in the education system. For example, although the college-preparatory track in high school is widely understood to prepare students for the academic rigors of college, there is little shared understanding of the meaning of the general track.

EDUCATIONAL TRANSITIONS AS LIFE COURSE TRANSITIONS

As the sociology of the life course has matured, the study of educational transitions and trajectories has quite sensibly drawn on life course theory. Elder (1992) notes that the sociology of the life course emerged from the twin traditions of sociological research on kinship and on age and time. A kin-based model of the life course focuses on families and the ways societies reproduce themselves across generations. In contrast, an age-based model of the life course emphasizes aging and the ways in which age sorts individuals into positions that have varying levels of rewards.

Current perspectives on the life course blend these two models, and the concept of the social role, a set of behavioral expectations associated with a position in the social structure, is a common denominator. The social roles performed by individuals are a primary source of identity, and are often associated with specific social institutions, such as the family, school, or work. Since most people are connected to multiple social institutions, they typically perform multiple social roles simultaneously, which may be mutually supportive or conflicting.

Until recently, sociologists studied educational trajectories primarily with regard to the transition from adolescence to adulthood. The student role is typically one of dependence, particularly in elementary and secondary school (Pallas, 1993). Since adulthood is characterized by financial and socioemotional independence from the family of origin, leaving school, along with working and forming a family through marriage and parenthood, have been key markers of this transition. But participation in education beyond the age of compulsory schooling is another matter, and sociological theory has not yet caught up to the expanding opportunities for education in the United States that are no longer highly age-graded.

Formal schooling (e.g., participation in credential programs) is increasingly becoming a recurring phase of the life course, and informal schooling is even less contingent on age. As Rubinson (1986) and others have argued, the U.S. educational system is much less stratified than the systems of many other industrialized societies, both in the West and elsewhere. That is, the U.S. system affords many more opportunities for investing in education beyond the age of compulsory schooling. Many postsecondary institutions have identified such "nontraditional" students outside of the 18–24 age range as potential markets for their educational wares. Evidence of the prevalence of nontraditional enrollment in higher education is provided by data from the U.S. Department of Education's Integrated Postsecondary Education Data System (IPEDS) fall enrollment surveys, which show that the proportion of postsecondary students over the age of 25 has risen from 28% in 1970 to 41% in 1998 (U.S. Department of Education, 2001). The greatest increase has been in the older age groups. Approximately one in five postsecondary enrollees is currently over the age of 35.* There are no similar trend data for education taking place outside of institutions of higher education.

A life course perspective implies that educational trajectories ought not be studied in isolation from other social institutions and from the other social roles associated with participation in those institutions, because such roles are intertwined in complex ways. For example, many young people interrupt their schooling, leaving and re-entering the educational system multiple times, and others combine their participation in schooling with other activities, such as working, getting married, or becoming a parent (Kerckhoff, 1990, 1995, 2000, 2001; Marini, 1987; Rindfuss, Swicegood, & Rosenfeld, 1987). In part, this is because educational attainment has increased overall. The prolonged time in school has resulted in more frequent combinations of schooling with work and family roles, as the timing of entry into work and family roles has not changed dramatically. The timing and sequencing of educational transitions, juxtaposed with these other activities, is highly differentiated, varying cross-nationally, temporally, and across individuals in a particular country at a particular time (Kerckhoff, 1995, 2000, 2001; Pallas, 1993). A life course perspective views the role of student as dynamic, reversible and renewable, not as a static attribute of individuals.

From a life course perspective, an individual's age and both work and family roles are likely to influence the dynamics of educational trajectories. For example, employers may not wish to provide work-related education to employees who are seen as too old or too young to benefit substantially from such education. Also, the demands of caring for school-aged children may conflict with a parent's desire to participate in some forms of adult education. These are just two examples of the implications of age and work and family roles for educational

---

*These data do pertain to both part-time and full-time enrollees. The changing age profile of the student population has not been as striking among full-time students as it is among the overall population of postsecondary students.

transitions. Moreover, age and role effects on educational trajectories may differ by gender. For example, mothers are frequently the primary caretakers for their school-aged children. Thus, having school-aged children in the household may be more consequential for the adult education of women than for men. Conversely, the fact that men are the primary breadwinners in many households may result in a greater propensity for work-related education than that of women in the labor force.

DESCRIBING EDUCATIONAL TRAJECTORIES

Life course studies originating in the United States have paid relatively little attention to the challenges of describing educational trajectories. In the United States, an individual's position in the education system is reasonably well described by the number of years of schooling completed. It is certainly convenient to be able to summarize an individual's standing in a single number. But this vertical differentiation of educational statuses is not an adequate representation of the educational systems of a great many countries around the world. Even in the United States, the number of years of schooling completed does not convey precisely the educational credentials an individual has acquired. Fourteen years of schooling can, for example, represent successful completion of a 2-year technical college degree program, or 2 years of liberal arts coursework that falls short of any credential. Other educational systems rely more upon the horizontal differentiation of individuals into differing types of educational institutions, or into differing locations within the same institutions, than upon the number of years of schooling completed.

Only recently has a concerted effort been made to develop a classification system for educational attainment that might facilitate comparisons across countries and time periods. Müller (Braun & Müller, 1997; Müller, 1988; Müller, Lüttinger, König, & Karle, 1989) is credited with developing a system for an ambitious project entitled "Comparative Analysis of Social Mobility in Industrial Nations" (CASMIN). The classification system, known as the CASMIN classification after the project title, is displayed in Table 8-1. It is based on two primary criteria: (1) a hierarchy of educational levels, defined in terms of the length of the educational experience, its cost and quality, and the academic ability required to be successful, and (2) a distinction between "general" and "vocationally-oriented" educational experiences. This latter distinction is based on curricular intent rather than empirical linkages between educational qualifications and specific vocational outcomes. That is, the central distinction is between educational programs that are intended to teach the knowledge and skills needed for specific occupations and those intending to teach general knowledge.

Comparative research inevitably involves tradeoffs between the commonalities and uniquenesses of the cases under consideration. Classification schemes such as the CASMIN classification are intended to balance such tradeoffs. Nevertheless, the same classification that facilitates comparisons *across* countries can seriously distort comparisons *within* countries. This is the thrust of Kerckhoff, Ezell, and Brown's (2002) analysis of the applicability of the CASMIN classification to the United States case. They show that within the United States and other countries, the relationship between educational qualifications and occupational attainment is generally greater if the analyst uses *indigenous* qualifications—that is, qualifications that are recognized locally—than if the association is estimated with classification schemes such as CASMIN developed for comparative purposes. Thus, although the CASMIN classification is useful for some purposes, it presents difficulties when an analyst wishes to study the

TABLE 8-1. The CASMIN Classification of Educational Qualifications

Educational qualification	Description
1a	Inadequately completed elementary education: Completion of less than the compulsory level of schooling with no formal certification
1b	Completed (compulsory) elementary education: Completion of general education that corresponds to the minimum that society views as acceptable
1c	(Compulsory) elementary education *and* basic vocational qualification: Completion of compulsory elementary education plus basic vocational qualifications
2a	Secondary, intermediate vocational qualification or intermediate general qualification *and* vocational qualification: Programs in which general intermediate schooling is joined with vocational training or qualifications
2b	Secondary, intermediate general qualification: Includes general or academically oriented tracks at the intermediate level, but lacks completion of exit exams
2c-gen	Full *general* maturity certificates: Completion of exams at the end of secondary schooling in a general or academic track; usually provides access to tertiary education
2c-voc	Full vocational maturity certificate or general maturity certificate *and* additional vocational qualification
3a	Lower tertiary education: Completion of a vocational or practical program of study at the tertiary level that is generally shorter than higher tertiary education
3b	Higher tertiary education: Completion of a traditional, academically oriented university education

link between educational qualifications and occupational attainment. Kerckhoff et al.'s (2002) proposed revision to the CASMIN scheme yields estimates of the education–occupation association that more closely approximate the estimates stemming from indigenous credentials.

Although this is an important enhancement to the content validity of the CASMIN classification, it does invite closer scrutiny of the notion of indigenous qualifications. For example, Kerckhoff et al. (2002) describe the indigenous credentials of the United States as (1) less than high school; (2) some high school; (3) GED or high school equivalency; (4) high school graduate; (5) vocational, trade, or business school; (6) less than 2 years of college; (7) associate's degree; (8) 2+ years of college, no degree; (9) bachelor's degree; (10) postgraduate attendance, no degree; and (11) postgraduate degree (MA, PhD, MD, etc.). Although these are standard reporting categories in social surveys such as the longitudinal studies sponsored by the National Center for Education Statistics, the claim that these categories represent indigenous qualifications is asserted, rather than demonstrated with evidence. The categories may be indigenous to social scientists, but there is no assurance that these are the categories that populate the cognitive maps of U.S. employers or the general public. I am particularly skeptical about combining bachelor's degrees from highly selective institutions (e.g., the Ivy League) and less selective four-year institutions into the same category.*

Analytic Models for Studying Educational Transitions

The most commonly used analytic model for studying educational transitions draws on the distinctive structure of the U.S. education system. Mare (1980, 1981) conceptualized educational

---

*Kerckhoff et al. (2002) acknowledge that there may be multiple ways to classify a country's indigenous qualifications. They argue, however, that since the categories used by official agencies are stable and familiar, these categories are well-suited for cumulating research knowledge.

attainment as movement through an ordered sequence of educational transitions. For example, an individual who had attained a 4-year college degree had first made the transition from high school entrant to high school graduate; then from high school graduate to college entrant; and finally from college entrant to college graduate. Only those individuals who enter college can ever graduate; thus the probability of graduating from college is conditional on having entered it. Mare argued that educational attainment could be modeled as a set of ordered school continuation probabilities showing the probability of attaining a given level of schooling conditional on having completed the level immediately preceding it. These conditional probabilities could then be modeled as a function of individuals' social backgrounds and birth cohort membership.

Mare estimated this model on data from the 1973 Occupational Changes in a Generation survey. He sought evidence that the effects of social background on making particular educational transitions across successive cohorts were declining, as predicted by theories of modernization. His logistic regression estimates revealed that within cohorts, social background effects on educational transitions decline from earlier to later transitions.

Mare interpreted this decline as an artifact of differential selectivity across transitions. For any given educational transition, there are both measured and unmeasured determinants of the likelihood of a successful outcome. For example, data sets such as OCG are frequently lacking measures of individuals' academic ability and motivation. There is likely to be more variability in academic ability and motivation at earlier transition points than at later points. That is, there will be more variability in academic ability among high school entrants seeking to complete high school than among college graduates seeking to enter graduate school, because the transitions involved in completing college have weeded out many students of lesser ability (and, perhaps, motivation).

Since factors such as academic ability and motivation are correlated with students' social backgrounds, the failure to take account of their effects on educational transitions represents a form of misspecification that can distort the estimated effects of the measured variables included in the model. In subsequent work, Mare (1993) attempted to correct for this specification error by introducing information on brothers, controlling for unmeasured family-specific influences by assuming that all siblings within a family share the same unmeasured family background characteristics and genetic endowments. Although not definitive, these latent-class log-linear analyses suggest that the failure to account for unobserved heterogeneity could dramatically overstate the extent to which family background effects decline over successive transitions.

Cameron and Heckman (1998) critique the Mare (1980) model on several grounds. They demonstrate that the empirical pattern of declining social background effects across successive educational transitions depends on arbitrary assumptions about the nature of the selection bias stemming from unobserved heterogeneity in the data. An ordered discrete-choice model fits the data better, but yields a different pattern of social background effects on schooling transitions.

Beyond this methodological critique, Cameron and Heckman describe the Mare (1980) model as "myopic," in the sense that individuals facing a set of successive educational transitions are presumed to focus only on the next transition, rather than a longer sequence of prospective educational transitions. Their preferred model assumes that individuals choose the ultimate level of schooling that maximizes their net returns to schooling, and that all of the successive transitions are governed by this longer-term view.

Breen and Jonsson (1998) levy a different critique at Mare's (1980) model, pointing out that it assumes a sequence of binary decisions that fails to represent the more differentiated pathways traveled in many European countries. For example, consideration of the choice alternatives of pursuing academic education, pursuing vocational education, and leaving school altogether obliges the analyst to group two of the categories together in contrast with the third. A multinomial logit model allows not only for multiple pathways, but also for an accounting of path dependence—the extent to which the probability of a particular transition depends on which path an individual traveled to reach that decision point. Breen and Jonsson hypothesize that the social background effects on the probability of entering higher education depend on the difficulty of the path traveled to reach that transition point. Estimating the model for a large sample of Swedish men and women, they find stronger social background effects on the probability of a successful transition when the route traveled to that point is the road not usually taken. This analysis promises to allow for more realistic models of educational careers and trajectories.

The Description and Distribution of Educational Trajectories

Although such models of school continuation decisions are very useful, they do not describe the shape of educational trajectories. The most widely recognized account of the shape of educational trajectories has been referred to as the Matthew effect, so coined by Merton (1968) in his account of how the logic of "the rich get richer, and the poor get poorer" applies to the system by which scientists allocate recognition to one another. Dannefer (1987) introduced the Matthew effect explicitly into the literature on aging and the life course. He expressed concern that the study of cohort differences was overshadowing heterogeneity within cohorts that might be due to the interaction of age and social structure, including variations across individuals in their structural positions in one or more stratification systems. By positing that initial inequalities are magnified over the life course, the Matthew effect, which is sometimes referred to as the cumulative dis/advantage hypothesis (O'Rand & Henretta, 1999), offers one account of how intracohort inequality is produced.

An alternative account, termed the "status maintenance" hypothesis, assumes that initial inequalities are carried along as individuals move through the life course, such that the within-cohort inequality present at any particular moment can be mapped onto similar levels of inequality both before and after that moment. A third explanation points to the possibility of a narrowing of the gap in the latter stages of the life course, as upon retirement, individuals are subject to the influence of state institutions that offset the inequalities produced by private markets.* This account is termed the "status leveling or redistribution" hypothesis (O'Rand & Henretta, 1999).

Empirical studies of educational transitions and trajectories are generally consistent with the presence of a Matthew effect in U.S. education. The evidence derives from a series of studies examining returning to school (e.g., Bradburn, Moen, & Dempster-McClain, 1995; Elman & O'Rand, 1998; Felmlee, 1988; Pallas, 2002) and three provocative studies by Kerckhoff and his colleagues (Kerckhoff, 1993; Kerckhoff & Glennie, 1999; Kerckhoff, Haney, & Glennie, 2001). I briefly describe these below.

Felmlee (1988) relied on human capital theory to frame her analysis, hypothesizing that women would view a return to school as a human capital investment that would have a subsequent payoff in the labor market in the form of greater future earnings. If women make the decision to leave work for full-time schooling on the basis of an accounting of the potential

---

*Crystal and Shea (1990) suggest that this shift may actually exacerbate income differences, and thus reflect a cumulative dis/advantage process.

costs and benefits of doing so, she argued, then their personal and job characteristics would influence the likelihood of making the transition from full-time work to full-time schooling. She speculated that because older women would probably not realize as great a return on investing in education as younger women, a woman's age would be an important determinant of the transition rate. And women of greater ability (defined in terms of IQ score) would likely obtain a higher rate of return to educational investment than women of lesser ability. Modeling the rate of change from full-time employment to full-time schooling (with no employment) over a 5-year period, she found substantial support for her predictions.

Felmlee (1988) also examined the potential implications of women's family roles for making the transition from full-time work to full-time schooling. She speculated that investing in education would be more costly for married women than for single, widowed, or divorced women, and that women with more children would be less likely to leave full-time work for full-time schooling. In her analyses, she distinguished between the number of children aged 0–5, and the number of children aged 6 and older. Women with children aged 0–5 were less likely to leave work for school, but the presence of older children did not depress the transition rate. Felmlee interpreted this pattern in terms of the costs of leaving work for schooling. It may be, she suggested, that women's obligations to support their children financially make it impractical to leave work for school, regardless of their husband's income. This might be, at least in part, a selection issue, in that women with young children who are working full-time may be under more family financial pressure than women with older children, whose full-time work may be more discretionary.

One difficulty with Felmlee's study is that the data derive from the National Longitudinal Survey of Labor Market Experience of Young Women, a national sample of women aged 14–24 in 1968. It is hard to conceive of this as a study of education across the life course when the women were aged 19 to 29 at the conclusion of the 5 years of data collection. Moreover, the study is located at a particular historical moment, and thus does not provide any evidence on whether there are cohort differences in patterns of work to school transitions. Bradburn et al.'s (1995) study addresses both of these limitations. These researchers drew on a panel study of 296 white women born between 1905 and 1933 who were initially interviewed in 1956 and followed up 30 years later, in 1986. All of the women in this sample were married and had children at the time of the initial interviews. By exploring subsequent participation in schooling, Bradburn et al. were in effect examining women's return to school following the transition to marriage and motherhood.

Bradburn et al. hypothesized that women with higher initial levels of educational attainment would be more likely to return to school than women with lower initial levels. But they also wondered if there might be a ceiling effect, such that women at the highest levels of education would not have the highest rate of return to school. Their results are generally supportive of their hypotheses, as women who had attended some college or graduated from college were more likely to return to school following first birth. Owing to the small sample, however, the stability (and plausibility) of the estimates for women with less than ninth grade educations or with some post-college is questionable.

Although the findings of these two studies are provocative, it is unclear whether they will generalize to the contemporary context. First, participation in schooling across the life course has expanded dramatically since these earlier studies. When returning to school was a rare (and perhaps non-normative) event, the women who elected to return may have had unusual personal strengths and/or opportunities that enabled them to overcome barriers to participation. Second, these studies of necessity construed educational transitions rather narrowly. Felmlee, for example, studied the specific transition from full-time work to full-time schooling.

Relatively few participants in adult education describe schooling as their primary activity. The range of adult education opportunities has expanded well beyond the scope of activities available in earlier periods.

One recent study makes use of data that pertain to contemporary contexts for studying educational trajectories. Elman and O'Rand (1998) drew on two waves of the National Survey of Families and Households to examine the impact of various work pathways on educational reentry between the ages of 42 and 62. They contrasted three theoretical approaches: status attainment, status maintenance, and cumulative dis/advantage. As I have discussed earlier, the focus of the status attainment approach is the influence of social origins on adult attainments, and the ways in which educational and early occupational experiences mediate those effects. The status maintenance approach emphasizes patterns of stability in achieved status across the life course, and assumes that individuals act to maintain and conserve their status. In contrast, the cumulative dis/advantage approach emphasizes the increasingly divergent trajectories that develop over the life course, in which initial advantages or disadvantages cumulate over time, resulting in greater inequality in opportunity and outcomes.

Elman and O'Rand conceptualize educational transitions and trajectories primarily in terms of retraining to maintain occupational status or enhance occupational mobility in the face of changing labor market conditions. They argue that the status maintenance and cumulative dis/advantage models predict that middle-aged workers with few educational and social resources will be less likely to retrain than those with higher levels of resources. They note, however, that individuals with high resources who have stable jobs may not elect to retrain, because individuals in stable careers have less incentive to change jobs, and hence a weaker motive for retraining. On balance, they hypothesize that non-white and female workers will be less likely to return to school in midlife, mainly because they are likely to have had longer spells of unemployment than white and male workers.

Elman and O'Rand summarize their hypotheses by stating that "those at midlife whose resources do not closely match their work experience are more likely to pursue educational activities at midlife" (Elman & O'Rand, 1998: 480). Obviously, testing these hypotheses requires detailed information on job histories and current job conditions. Although the National Survey of Families and Households has an array of data on work histories, the data on adult participation in education are not as extensive. School attendance of more than two courses or enrollment for more than six weeks is coded as educational reentry, but no data are gathered for individuals who have not completed a high school diploma or its equivalent, who represent a substantial share of the midlife individuals examined in the study. The survey thus is picking up relatively intense participation among those with relatively high levels of initial education.

Elman and O'Rand find that differing work pathways result in differing likelihoods of educational reentry. Those individuals with the most job continuity are the least likely to reenter school, whereas those with disrupted patterns are most likely to return to school in midlife. Regardless of an individual's work pathway, educational attainment and family configurations influence the likelihood of educational reentry. In general, those with college or advanced degrees were more likely to reenter school at midlife than high school graduates.

In my own work (Pallas, 2002), I have sought a Matthew effect that examines a broader array of educational experiences than simply enrollment in programs that lead to educational credentials. Drawing on the Adult Education Component of the 1995 wave of the National Household Education Survey, a nationally representative sample of 19,700 interviews, I analyze the probability of participating in three distinct forms of adult education in 1994: (a) programs leading to a postsecondary educational credential; (b) work-related education that is not embedded in a credential program; and (c) other structured activities or courses, which I refer to as "personal development" courses, since they are not primarily for the instrumental purpose of enhancing one's stock of human capital and/or improving one's labor-market standing. I also analyze the probability of participating in *any* form of adult education (including the relatively rare forms of English as a Second Language classes and adult basic education). For each form of adult education, I estimated a logistic regression model predicting participation as a function of region of the country, sex, race/ethnicity, age, educational attainment, and family configuration. I then added a vector of socioeconomic measures, including household income, home ownership, and labor force position.

Table 8-2 summarizes the evidence reported in this study for a Matthew effect in education. The table entries are the estimated probabilities of participation in various forms of adult education for individuals with differing levels of educational attainment, holding constant other factors. The probabilities for individuals with less than 12 years of schooling are actual participation probabilities, whereas the probabilities for those with other levels of education are estimated based on the logistic regression equations. The probabilities in columns (1) in Table 8-2 show that for each form of adult education, those with the least schooling have the lowest probability of participation, and those with the most schooling have the highest participation probability. For example, respondents with fewer than 12 years of schooling had a 5% probability of participating in work-related education in 1994, whereas those who had attended graduate school had a 32% probability of participating in work-related education. In most cases, the gradient is quite steep, with respondents with a 4-year college degree or more education three to six times more likely to participate in adult education in 1994 than those who have not completed high school. This is as true for participation in personal development classes as it is for participation in postsecondary credential programs and work-related education. I conclude, therefore, that those who are already "rich" by virtue of attending college do get richer. The differences among those who have some college education are, however, generally much smaller than the differences between the college-educated and non-college-educated.

Table 8-2 also examines the extent to which the Matthew effect might be explained by the socioeconomic advantages—household income, home ownership status, employment status, and occupational type—of those who have accumulated more schooling to begin with. That is, I considered whether the total effects of educational attainment on participation in adult education could be accounted for by the association between educational attainment and socioeconomic status, on the one hand, and the association between socioeconomic status and participation in adult education, on the other. Table 8-2 shows that the effects of educational attainment on the probability of work-related education are substantially mediated by socioeconomic success. Comparing column (1), the total effect of educational attainment, and column (2), the effect net of socioeconomic status, it is clear that the probabilities are much less dispersed when socioeconomic success is controlled. The sixfold increase in the probability of participating in work-related education observed when contrasting individuals who had not completed high school with those who had attended graduate school (0.05 vs. 0.32) shrinks to a threefold spread when SES is taken into account (0.05 vs. 0.16). In contrast, educational attainment effects on participation in postsecondary credential programs are not mediated by socioeconomic status, and the effects on participation in personal development courses remain large even when socioeconomic status is controlled. Thus, we still have much to learn about both the personal and structural determinants of participation in adult education.

Deflections and Diverging Pathways

The studies cited above provide brief glimpses of trajectories that play out over the course of individuals' lives. Kerckhoff's (1993) analysis of a British birth cohort through age 23 provides

TABLE 8-2. Probability of Participation in Adult Education by Respondent's Educational Attainment

		Estimated probability of participation in								
	Postsecondary credential programs		Work-related education		Personal development classes		Any form of adult education	
	Total	Net of SES	Total	Net of SES	Total	Net of SES	Total	Net of SES
Rs educational attainment	(1)	(2)	(1)	(2)	(1)	(2)	(1)	(2)
<12 years of schooling	0.02	0.02	0.05	0.05	0.09	0.09	0.18	0.18
12 years of schooling	0.06	0.06	0.11	0.08	0.14	0.14	0.28	0.24
Some college	0.24	0.24	0.17	0.11	0.22	0.20	0.50	0.43
Two-year degree	0.22	0.22	0.23	0.14	0.25	0.22	0.55	0.46
Four-year degree	0.13	0.13	0.28	0.14	0.26	0.22	0.55	0.44
Graduate school	0.23	0.23	0.32	0.16	0.29	0.25	0.63	0.50

Note: Data are derived from Pallas (2002). Estimated probabilities are derived from logistic regression equations predicting participation in particular forms of adult education. Covariates for Equations (1) include region of the country, sex, race/ethnicity, age, and family status. Equation (2) also controls for household income, home ownership, employment status, and type of occupation.

the richest account of educational trajectories, largely because individuals' positions can be measured at multiple points over this time period. He exploited the fact that individuals' positions in the education system and occupational structure can be arrayed hierarchically, such that some positions are valued more highly, and lead to more desirable consequences, than others. Within primary and secondary schools, students may be enrolled in higher or lower ability groups or tracks. Across secondary schools, students may be in elite schools leading to a prestigious university education, or lower-status comprehensive or secondary modern schools leading to less-prestigious educational qualifications. Postsecondary qualifications can include university education, "further education" (i.e., technical colleges), and on-the-job training (including apprenticeships). Within the occupational structure, individuals may obtain more or less prestigious jobs, with more or less favorable firm characteristics.

Converting these varying positions in the social structure into a common metric—percentile rank within the distribution*—Kerckhoff traced the trajectories, or careers, of individuals from infant school to elementary school to secondary school to postsecondary schooling to the labor force. As individuals move through their educational careers, he demonstrated, individuals' trajectories are typically deflected either upward or downward. Those in favorable positions at a given career stage typically move up, whereas those in lesser positions frequently are deflected downward. But if the notion of career is extended from the education system to labor force experience at age 23, the pattern changes. Among men, the cumulative effects of the structure of the education system reverse, such that those in the highest and lowest positions in the postsecondary schooling distribution are deflected toward the middle of the distribution, rather than continuing to disperse. Among women, these cumulative education effects do not increase, but neither do they decrease, as is observed among the men in the sample.

Kerckhoff and Glennie (1999) used a similar method to examine the evidence for a Matthew effect in the United States. They trace the trajectories of a cohort of American tenth-graders over a 12-year period as they move from high school to college and beyond. Net of social background and prior academic performance, a student's location in the education system influences his or her achievement and subsequent educational attainment. Those in higher locations gain more, and those in lower locations gain less, than those in intermediate positions. This contributes to a pattern of cumulative advantage and disadvantage over the educational career, consistent with a Matthew effect. Although the U.S. educational system is often viewed as more open than the British system, the patterns of upward and downward deflections are similar across the two societies.

As more recent data from the British cohort became available, Kerckhoff and his colleagues sharpened the comparison between Great Britain and the United States (Kerckhoff, Haney, & Glennie, 2001). They constructed parallel measures of location in the education system for ages 16, 18, 22 or 23, and 28. Recognizing the "greater orderliness and predictability" of the British system (Kerckhoff et al., 2001: 500), they anticipated finding larger cumulative effects of academic locations in Great Britain than in the United States. Surprisingly, there is more variability in locations by age 28 in the United States than in Great Britain. These larger cumulative deflections in the United States apparently are a function of both structural and normative differences across the two societies. One such difference is that

---

*Kerckhoff arrayed the positions into a hierarchy, and then assigned the individuals in a particular position the percentile of the overall distribution associated with the position. For example, the conversion of a Trieman occupational prestige score into a percentile would be based on the percentile ranking of that score in the distribution of all occupational prestige scores in the sample.

most British students have obtained their highest educational credentials by age 23, whereas many U.S. students obtain postsecondary credentials after age 22.

FUTURE DIRECTIONS IN THE ANALYSIS OF EDUCATIONAL TRAJECTORIES

The universal acknowledgment of a connection between education and social mobility within societies has led researchers to consider several kinds of questions about educational trajectories. Some of these are descriptive: within a society, have educational trajectories and careers changed over time? And, does the shape of these trajectories and careers differ across countries? Others are more analytical: if there *are* variations over time within countries, or variations across countries, what attributes of these countries can explain this variation? (And if there *aren't* variations over time or across countries, why not?) Such studies (e.g., Shavit & Blossfeld, 1993; Shavit & Müller, 1998) treat the country as the unit of analysis, and attempt to correlate political, cultural, and institutional features of a given country to within-country parameters governing the shape of educational trajectories.

There have been great strides over the past 20 years in characterizing the features of national educational systems, the national occupational structure, and mechanisms linking the two together. The most often discussed features of the educational system are its centralization, that is, the extent to which control over schooling is centralized or decentralized; its standardization, which refers to the extent to which the quality of education meets uniform standards within a country; and its stratification or saturation, which refers to the proportion of a cohort that attains a given level of educational attainment within a system. We might also attend to the amount of curricular differentiation within a given level of the system—the sheer variety of educational qualifications that are available in the system, and when in the educational career this differentiation occurs. There may even be societal variation in the purpose of schooling, which can be viewed either as a feature of the education system itself, or treated as a feature of the linkages between education and the occupational structure. These features are often correlated, such that centralized systems are more likely to be standardized, and stratified systems are more likely to have differentiated curricula. Many of these ideas, and their implications for education and social stratification processes, have been developed and explored in the comparative studies reported in Allmendinger (1989), Ishida, Müller, and Ridge (1995), Kerckhoff (1995, 2000, 2001), Maurice, Sellier, and Silvestre (1986), Shavit and Blossfeld (1993), and Shavit and Müller (1998).

These systemic features have implications for the importance of social origins in determining educational trajectories and careers, and also for the transitions from school to work. There has been less attention to identifying the features of particular transitions that can broaden our understanding of how specific transitions can structure subsequent transitions and achievements. It is likely that the literature on within-school stratification will be especially useful in charting these features.

Some Lingering Tensions

I conclude by drawing attention to four tensions confronting scholars seeking to understand the dynamics of educational trajectories and careers. The first is a tension between the economic and non-economic value of education. The human capital tradition arising from neoclassical economic theory has argued that workers are rewarded (in the form of wages and other job benefits) in direct proportion to their contribution to their firm's productivity. In this view, acquiring human capital, in the form of education, experience, and/or training, is the central way for individuals to enhance their economic standing. Hence, education is but a means to a more favorable economic end.

Not all educational transitions, however, can be understood as a means to greater economic success. To be sure, work-related education—particularly education that is required as a condition of employment—is primarily instrumental. A similar argument can be made for participation in credential programs, since most credentials have an economic value in the marketplace, either by granting individuals access to more rewarding jobs, or by enhancing their productivity in their current jobs. Conversely, education for personal development is primarily non-economic, since the value of such education lies within the individual, and not in its exchange value in a market.

With few exceptions (e.g., Antikainen, Houtsonen, Kauppila, & Huotelin, 1996; Edwards, 1993; Luttrell, 1997; Pallas, 2002), studies of educational trajectories have emphasized the decision to acquire education as an instrumental, economic phenomenon. This is an overly narrow view, particularly in the context of the growing importance of the self as an organizing feature of modern life (Meyer, 1986). It may be increasingly important to consider participation in education as an expression of the self, as well as to consider education's economic value.

The second tension, pitting parsimony against complexity, pertains to the challenges of summarizing heterogeneous systems. Having developed some ways of classifying educational systems that are useful, there is a tendency to employ the categories in ways that may mask the variability within a system. For example, it is common to describe a country's education system in terms of standardization and stratification, features that Allmendinger (1989) emphasized in her analyses comparing the educational systems of the United States, Norway, and West Germany. But one of Allmendinger's key insights is that within a country, the amount of standardization and stratification might vary across the primary, secondary, and tertiary levels of the educational system. Her analyses led her to locate Norway differently for primary schooling than secondary schooling. Although both the primary and secondary schooling systems in Norway are stratified, Allmendinger characterized primary schooling in Norway as unstandardized, and secondary schooling as standardized. And although there is little standardization at any level of schooling within the United States, she reported primary and secondary education to be relatively unstratified, and tertiary education to be highly stratified.

I refer to the third tension as the tension between politics and markets. Most research on educational careers treats political boundaries as isomorphic with market boundaries. There is a natural tendency to assume this, particularly in nation-states that have centralized and standardized education systems. But the standardization of the system does not necessarily imply that the arena in which educational qualifications are matched with employers' needs is national. We need to pay more attention to the boundaries of actual markets, as these are defined both by individuals' willingness to consider positions in various geographic locations, and by how employers circumscribe where they look for pools of prospective workers (cf., Breen & Rottman, 1998). Similar dynamics may be at play in matching individuals with educational opportunities.

And the final tension is between macro- and micro-perspectives on educational trajectories and careers. The dividing line between macro- and micro-phenomena is anything but clearcut, but it is fair to say that what is largely missing from the literature is attention to theories of individual action—that is, theories of the educational and occupational choices that individuals make—that could produce the educational transitions and trajectories that have been the subject of this chapter. This is a point that Goldthorpe and Breen have made in a series of papers over the past several years (Breen & Goldthorpe, 1997; Goldthorpe, 1996). They set out to explain why class differentials in educational participation rates persist even in the face of educational expansion. Drawing on rational action theory, Breen and Goldthorpe developed a mathematical model of educational decisions. Although it has long been recognized that some individuals may benefit more from educational investment than others, the model provides new tools for understanding how individuals might incorporate the risk of failure into the rational calculation of costs and benefits that underlies a view of education as an investment in human capital.

What are still lacking are compelling theories of how social origins and institutional arrangements within countries shape individuals' beliefs about what kinds of choices are possible, with what likely costs and benefits, and what likely probability of success. Such theories may help us bridge the macro–micro divide that bedevils so much of the sociological enterprise, by linking subjective experience to large-scale social structures.

REFERENCES

Alexander, K. L., Entwisle, D. R., & Dauber, S. L. (1994). *On the success of failure: A reassessment of the effects of retention in the primary grades*. New York: Cambridge University Press.

Allmendinger, J. (1989). Educational systems and labor market outcomes. *European Sociological Review, 5*, 231–250.

Anderson, D. K. (1994). Paths through secondary education: Race/ethnic and gender differences. Unpublished doctoral dissertation, University of Wisconsin-Madison.

Antikainen, A., Houtsonen, J., Kauppila, J., & Huotelin, H. (1996). *Living in a learning society: Life histories, identities, and education*. London: Falmer.

Blau, P. M., & Duncan, O. D. (1967). *The American occupational structure*. New York: Free Press.

Bound, J., Schoenbaum, M., & Waidmann, T. (1995). Race and education differences in disability status and labor force attachment in the Health and Retirement Survey. *Journal of Human Resources, 30*, S227–S269.

Bradburn, E. M., Moen, P., & Dempster-McClain, D. (1995). Women's return to school following the transition to motherhood. *Social Forces, 73*, 1517–1551.

Braun, M., & Müller, W. (1997). Measurement of education in comparative research. *Comparative Social Research, 16*, 163–201.

Breen, R., & Goldthorpe, J. H. (1997). Explaining educational differentials: Towards a formal rational action theory. *Rationality and Society, 9*, 275–305.

Breen, R., & Jonsson, J. O. (2000). Analyzing educational careers: A multinomial transition model. *American Sociological Review, 65*, 754–772.

Breen, R., & Rottman, D. B. (1998). Is the national state the appropriate geographical unit for class analysis? *Sociology, 32*, 1–21.

Cameron, S., & Heckman, J. J. (1998). Life cycle schooling and dynamic selection bias: Models and evidence for five cohorts of American males. *Journal of Political Economy, 106*, 262–333.

Crystal, S., & Shea, D. G. (1990). Cumulative advantage, cumulative disadvantage, and inequality among elderly people. *The Gerontologist, 30*(4), 437–443.

Dannefer, D. (1987). Aging as intracohort differentiation: Accentuation, the Matthew effect, and the life course. *Sociological Forum, 2*, 211–236.

Duncan, O. D, Featherman, D. L., & Duncan, B. (1972). *Socioeconomic background and achievement*. New York: Seminar Press.

Edwards, R. (1993). *Mature women students: Separating or connecting family and education*. London: Taylor & Francis.

Elder, G. H., Jr. (1985). Perspectives on the life course. In G. H. Elder, Jr. (Ed.), *Life course dynamics: Trajectories and transitions, 1968–1980* (pp. 23–49). Ithaca, NY: Cornell University Press.

Elder, G. H., Jr. (1992). Models of the life course. *Contemporary Sociology, 21*, 632–635.

Elman, C., & O'Rand, A. M. (1998). Midlife work pathways and educational entry. *Research on Aging, 20*, 475–505.

Featherman, D. L., & Hauser, R. M. (1978). *Opportunity and change.* New York: Academic Press.

Felmlee, D. (1988). Returning to school and women's occupational attainment. *Sociology of Education, 61*, 29–41.

Gamoran, A. (1989). Measuring curriculum differentiation. *American Journal of Education, 97*, 129–143.

Gamoran, A. (1992). The variable effects of high school tracking. *American Sociological Review, 57*, 812–828.

Goldthorpe, J. H. (1996). Class analysis and the reorientation of class theory: the case of persisting differentials in educational attainment. *British Journal of Sociology, 47*, 481–505.

Grusky, D. B., & DiPrete, T. A. (1990). Recent trends in the process of stratification. *Demography, 27*, 617–637.

Ishida, H., Müller, W., & Ridge, J. (1995). Class origin, class destination, and education: A cross-national comparison of ten industrial nations. *American Journal of Sociology, 101*, 145–193.

Jencks, C. S., Bartlett, S., Corcoran, M., Crouse, J., Eaglesfield, D., Jackson, G., McClelland, K., Mueser, P., Olneck, M., Schwartz, J., Ward, S., & Williams, J. (1979). *Who gets ahead? The determinants of economic success in America.* New York: Basic.

Kerckhoff, A. C. (1976). The status attainment process: Socialization or allocation? *Social Forces, 55*, 368–381.

Kerckhoff, A. C. (1990). *Getting started: Transition to adulthood in Great Britain.* Boulder, CO: Westview.

Kerckhoff, A. C. (1993). *Diverging pathways: Social structure and career deflections.* New York: Cambridge University Press.

Kerckhoff, A. C. (1995). Institutional arrangements and stratification processes in industrial societies. *Annual Review of Sociology, 15*, 323–347.

Kerckhoff, A. C. (1996). Building conceptual and empirical bridges between studies of educational and labor force careers. In A. C. Kerckhoff (Ed.), *Generating social stratification: Toward a new research agenda* (pp. 37–56). Boulder, CO: Westview.

Kerckhoff, A. C. (2000). Transition from school to work in comparative perspective. In M. T. Hallinan (Ed.), *Handbook of the sociology of education* (pp. 453–474). New York: Kluwer Academic/Plenum.

Kerckhoff, A. C. (2001). Education and social stratification processes in comparative perspective. *Sociology of Education, Extra Issue*, 3–18.

Kerckhoff, A. C., Ezell, E. D., & Brown, J. S. (2002). Toward an improved measure of educational attainment in social stratification research. *Social Science Research, 31*, 1–25.

Kerckhoff, A. C., & Glennie, E. (1999). The Matthew effect in American education. *Research in Sociology of Education and Socialization, 12*, 35–66.

Kerckhoff, A. C., Haney, L. B., & Glennie, E. (2001). System effects on educational achievement: A British–American comparison. *Social Science Research, 30*, 497–528.

Kilgore, S. B. (1993). The organizational context of tracking in schools. *American Sociological Review, 56*, 189–203.

König, W., Lüttinger, P., & Müller, W. (1988). *A comparative analysis of the development and structure of educational systems*, CASMIN Working Paper, No.12. Institut fur Sozialwissenschaften, University of Mannheim.

Land, K. C., & Russell, S. T. (1996). Wealth accumulation across the adult life course: Stability and change in sociodemographic covariate structures of net worth data in the Survey of Income and Program Participation, 1984–1991. *Social Science Research, 25*, 423–462.

Loveless, T. (1999). *The tracking wars: State reform meets school policy.* Washington, DC: Brookings Institution Press.

Lucas, S. R. (1999). *Tracking inequality: Stratification and mobility in American high schools.* New York: Teachers College Press.

Lucas, S. R., & Good, A. D. (2001). Race, class, and tournament mobility. *Sociology of Education, 74*, 139–156.

Luttrell, W. (1997). *Schoolsmart and motherwise: Working class women's identity and schooling.* New York: Routledge.

Mare, R. D. (1980). Social background and school continuation decisions. *Journal of the American Statistical Association, 75*, 295–305.

Mare, R. D. (1981). Change and stability in educational stratification. *American Sociological Review, 46*, 72–87.

Mare, R. D. (1993). Educational stratification on observed and unobserved components of family background. In Y. Shavit & H.-P. Blossfeld (Eds.), *Persistent inequality: Changing educational attainment in thirteen countries* (pp. 351–376). Boulder, CO: Westview.

Marini, M. M. (1987). Measuring the process of role change during the transition to adulthood. *Social Science Research 16*, 1–38.

Maurice, M., Sellier, F., & Silvestre, J.-J. (1986). *Social foundations of industrial power.* Cambridge, MA: MIT Press.

Merton, R. K. (1968). The Matthew effect in science. *Science, 159*, 56–63.

Meyer, J. W. (1986). The self and the life course: Institutionalization and its effects. In A. B. Sørensen, F. E., Weinert, & L. R. Sherrod (Eds.), *Human development and the life course* (pp. 199–216). Hillsdale, NJ: Lawrence Erlbaum.

Müller, W., Lüttinger, P., König, W., & Karle, W. (1989). Class and education in industrial nations. *International Journal of Sociology, 19*, 3–39.

Müller, W., & Shavit, Y. (1998). The institutional embeddedness of the stratification process: A comparative study of qualifications and occupations in thirteen countries. In Y. Shavit & W. Müller (Eds.), *From school to work: A comparative study of educational qualifications and occupational destinations* (pp. 1–48). Oxford, England: Clarendon Press.

Murnane, R. J., Willett, J. B., & Levy, F. (1995). The growing importance of cognitive skills in wage determination. *Review of Economics and Statistics, 77*, 251–266.

National Research Council. (1999). In J. P. Heubert & R. M. Hauser (Eds.), *High stakes: Testing for tracking, promotion, and graduation*. Washington, DC: National Academy Press.

Natriello, G. (1994). Coming together and breaking apart: Unifying and differentiating processes in schools and classrooms. *Research in Sociology of Education and Socialization, 10*, 111–145.

Oakes, J. (1985). *Keeping track: How schools structure inequality*. New Haven, CT: Yale University Press.

O'Rand, A. M., & Henretta, J. C. (1999). *Age and inequality: Diverse pathways through later life*. Boulder, CO: Westview.

Page, R. N. (1991). *Lower-track classrooms: A curricular and cultural perspective*. New York: Teachers College Press.

Pallas, A. M. (1993). Schooling in the course of human lives: The social context of education and the transition to adulthood in industrial society. *Review of Educational Research, 63*, 409–447.

Pallas, A. M. (2002). Educational participation across the life course: Do the rich get richer? In R. A. Settersten, Jr. & T. J. Owens (Eds.), *Advances in life course research: New frontiers in socialization* (pp. 327–354). New York: Elsevier Science.

Rindfuss, R. R., Swicegood, C. G., & Rosenfeld, R. A. (1987). Disorder in the life course: How common and does it matter? *American Sociological Review, 52*, 785–801.

Roderick, M. (1993). *The path to dropping out: Evidence for intervention*. Westport, CT: Auburn House.

Rubinson, R. B. (1986). Class formation, politics, and institutions: Schooling in the United States. *American Journal of Sociology, 92*, 519–548.

Sewell, W. H., Haller, A. O., & Ohlendorf, G. W. (1970). The educational and early occupational status attainment process: Replication and revision. *American Sociological Review, 35*, 1014–1027.

Sewell, W. H., Haller, A. O., & Portes, A. (1969). The educational and early occupational attainment process. *American Sociological Review, 34*, 82–92.

Sewell, W. H., & Hauser, R. M. (1980). The Wisconsin Longitudinal Study of Social and Psychological Factors in Aspirations and Achievements. In A. C. Kerckhoff (Ed.), *Research in sociology of education and socialization*, (Vol. 1, pp. 59–99). Greenwich, CT: JAI Press.

Shavit, Y., & Blossfeld, H.-P. (Eds.). (1993). *Persistent inequality: Changing educational attainment in thirteen countries*. Boulder, CO: Westview.

Shavit, Y., & Müller, W. (Eds.). (1998). *From school to work: A comparative study of educational qualifications and occupational destinations*. Oxford: Clarendon Press.

Sørensen, A. B. (1970). Organizational differentiation of students and educational opportunity. *Sociology of Education, 43*, 355–376.

Spenner, K., Otto, L., & Call, V. (1982). *Career lines and careers*. Lexington, MA: Lexington Books.

Spilerman, S. (1977). Careers, labor market structures, and socioeconomic achievement. *American Journal of Sociology, 83*, 551–593.

U.S. Department of Education. (2001). *Digest of Education Statistics, 2000 Edition*. Washington, DC: U.S. Government Printing Office.

CHAPTER 9

From Work Trajectories to Negotiated Careers

The Contingent Work Life Course

WALTER R. HEINZ

OVERVIEW

In the social sciences work trajectories tend to be studied as careers which link individual participation histories in labor markets, occupations, and firms. Career models conceptualize the process of passing through socially defined pathways, but they neglect the mechanisms that connect these histories to biographical time and processes of social change (see Elder, Johnson, & Crosnoe, this volume). In this chapter, the work life course is regarded as a career, which is embedded in labor markets and organizations, and evolves through the interaction between social institutions and biographical actors. I argue that in post-industrial society there is an increasing emphasis upon personal decisions and responsibility in the shaping of the work life course, and a corresponding decline of normative age-markers for the timing and sequencing of labor market participation.

As a conceptual framework for the selection and presentation of the following themes, Gidden's (1984) structuration theory is used. This theory proposes that there is a reciprocal relationship between social structure and individual agency over the life course. It implies that institutions are contributing to the structuring of social relations across time and space.

The following chapter is organized according to this basic idea. The work life course unfolds in the structural context of labor markets, occupations, and firms. It is constructed by

WALTER R. HEINZ • University of Bremen, D-28334 Bremen, Germany.

Handbook of the Life Course, edited by Jeylan T. Mortimer and Michael J. Shanahan. Kluwer Academic/Plenum Publishers, New York, 2003.

individuals via pathways and careers, which implies agency and socialization. Careers, in turn, are more or less regulated by social institutions, which mediate between labor markets, opportunities, types and sequences of work. Since the structuration of the work life course still differs by gender, the theme of coupled careers is introduced in order to illuminate that careers are not solo passages but are part of linked lives.

The chapter begins with a sketch of the major changes in work and their effects on the life course, with an emphasis on the economic turbulence during the last quarter of the 20th century. A discussion of the impact of labor market segmentation follows in order to clarify how occupations and organizations contribute to the distribution of life chances and the shaping of work histories. This discussion of social structures contextualizes research on the micro-social career processes that combine career experiences and socialization dynamics. Here, institutionalized pathways are contrasted with market-driven arrangements. These contexts condition the reciprocal effects of work conditions, job involvement, and personality over time. The process of self-socialization in flexible careers is described.

Then we look at the effects of institutionalized regulations and resources on employment sequences and discuss the consequences of the destandardization of pathways and contracts on careers. The way the gendered life course is implied in the structuration of coupled careers, on the levels of institutions and negotiations, is discussed next.

Finally, the contours of the contingent work life course, which emerges from negotiated careers, are outlined. Since the institutional approach to the analysis of work careers becomes most convincing with comparative data, examples derive from North America and Europe.

THE CHANGING LANDSCAPE OF WORK

In the last decade of the 20th century, the end of work (Rifkin, 1995), or the erosion of the work-centered life course (Beck, 1999), became a prominent topic in both the social sciences and the public debate. Empirical evidence shows that economic globalization, the decline of manufacturing jobs, the progress of information and communication technology, and waves of company restructuring had complex, partly contradictory effects on work careers (Tilly & Tilly, 1998). On the one side, continuous careers and stable employment are less certain and unemployment is rising because of more volatile and deregulated labor markets; on the other side, there are more employment opportunities for women, and risky options for self-employment and business start-ups. In post-industrial society, paid employment has not ceased to be the cornerstone of the life course; most people still spend their adult lives either working, qualifying themselves, or looking for work.

In industrial society, the work life course followed definite age and gender norms, status transitions, and ensuing role changes; the "normal biography" reflected the relative stability of cultural norms and social structures in the era of mass production. Over the 20th century, economic and political changes transformed the world of work. This century was an "age of extremes" (Hobsbawm, 1994), especially its second half; it was characterized by an ongoing decline of farming, a shift from manufacturing to services, increasing enrollment in post-secondary education, and women's rising participation in the labor market. These social transformations have contributed to the growth of ever larger metropolitan regions; increasing travel time between home, work place, and shopping malls; and finally, to more flexible careers and a destandardized work life course.

The post-World War II years can be divided into a period of economic improvement with full (male) employment in North America and West Europe (around the 1960s)—a "Golden

Age" from the 1950s to the mid-1970s—and the "crisis decades" which marked the last quarter of the 20th century, when economic turbulence led to rising income gaps and growing structural unemployment (Hobsbawm, 1994). In order to understand the social transformations in the second half of the 20th century, which fundamentally restructured the linkage between work and the life course, the following five changes in labor force composition have to be kept in mind:

First, the massive exodus from the land continued and went together with the growth of a capital-intensive agri-business, which has set farmers and land laborers free to migrate into the urban centers (Conger & Elder, 1994). This process, which started with the Industrial Revolution, is still going on in Third World countries. Second, skilled and professional occupations, which required at least secondary, and increasingly, a post-secondary education, became more important. Third, the industrial working classes declined since the 1970s with de-industrialization and the ascendance of information technology and the lean factory. These trends led to rising structural unemployment and to a contraction of simple production jobs, which used to shape the work life course of less educated and less skilled men. Fourth, the growth and internal differentiation of the service sector, from McDonald's-type jobs to public, financial, and social service occupations, required higher-level qualifications. Career and employment opportunities for women were thereby expanded.

Tragic historical events also have had their impact on the work life course: by analyzing results of the German microcensus, Socio-Economic Panel (SOEP) and the Life History Study, Mayer (1988) documents that the employment consequences of World War II differed by birth cohort. For instance, women born between 1929 and 1931, who had to make the transition from education to vocational training right after the war, were cut off from an educational career. Right after the war, women were engaged in maintaining their families and were employed in agriculture and unpaid domestic work; their representation in white-collar work at the time of marriage did not reach its former level until the early 1960s. The work life was also adversely affected for men who entered the labor market for the first time around the end of the war. Mayer (1988) suggests an institutional explanation: because of the strong links between labor market entry pathways and careers in Germany, initial disadvantages could not be compensated, despite the improvement of the economy .The story is different for job-entry cohorts after World War II in the United States (Elder, 1987), where veterans could use the GI-bill, which offered the opportunity to enter college.

The Golden Age, however, transformed the life course of the younger cohorts in North America and Western Europe who entered training and the labor market between the late 1950s and early 1970s. They found entry jobs and apprenticeships easily, embarked on stable careers, and could spend more income on consumer goods than any other cohort in the past: they fully participated in the rise of the "affluent society".

All this changed drastically for the cohorts who entered the labor market for the first time in the 1980s and 1990s, when jobs became scarce and income dropped. Social inequality increased again as the gap between high-and low-income groups got wider, a process which led to intra-cohort differences in life chances and life courses as well. However, in the decades of crisis more and more women entered the labor market, though in different rates in the United States, the Scandinavian countries, and West Germany. The number of employed women has tripled since the 1960s: By 1999, 62% of German women were participating in the labor market, 76% in Sweden, and 63% in the United States (OECD, 2001).

Looking back at the social changes in the second half of the 20th century, in the Golden Age two life course models were shaped: (1) The tripartite model of men's biography: education (youth)—work (adulthood)—retirement (old age); a model that centered on the world of work (Kohli, 1986). (2) the three-phase model of women's biography, focused on family and employment in a normative sequence: education—employment—mother and homemaker—employment (Born, Krüger, & Lorenz-Meyer, 1996).

The period of crisis brought a restructuring of the gendered models into a variety of new flexible arrangements which are less guided by traditional age and gender norms but by changing opportunities and supply/demand in the labor market.

LABOR MARKETS, OCCUPATIONS, AND FIRMS

Life chances are strongly dependent upon the structural context of employment opportunities that constitute social inequality across the life course. Beginning with the timing and status of job entry and ending with the timing of the transition to retirement, biographical options and life course outcomes hinge on material and social resources that can only be provided by participating in the labor market. In advanced industrial and post-industrial service societies, there is no unified labor market. The labor market is instead divided in occupations and firms, which are more or less separated in casual, company-specific, and occupational segments (Doeringer & Piore, 1971; Edwards, 1979). In theory, these segments are closed off from each other; it is difficult to cross their boundaries.

The casual segment consists of unskilled and semiskilled jobs with low income and little employment security. The company-specific or internal segment is characterized by employment careers within a firm that provides on-the-job training, continuing training, and promotion ladders. Large companies and public administration are work organizations that tend to establish internal markets because they must rely on a stable labor force. Occupational labor markets, in turn, depend on specific skill profiles that may be certified by vocational credentials on the intermediate job-level, or by academic titles on the professional and managerial levels.

While the North American labor markets emphasize the casual and internal segments, the German labor market is characterized by a strong occupational segment (Sengenberger, 1987). This segment is linked to an institutionalized transition pathway, the "dual system" of vocational education and training, which provides certified occupational skills. Standardized vocational training improves the match between job requirements and skills of applicants, and thus reduces the transaction costs in placement negotiations and the duration of job-adjustment. The occupational structure is the backbone of labor market dynamics in Germany, where the Vocational Training Act, industrial relations, and labor laws combine in regulating employment transactions and income differentiation. This feature is responsible for the slow, hesitant trend toward increased flexibility in career patterns and for relatively few occupational changes in past generations.

Recent comparative studies (Allmendinger & Hinz, 1998; Heinz, 1999; Shavit & Müller, 1998) relate social stratification and labor market issues to the life course and document that careers do not only depend on labor markets but also on education, training, and social policy. For instance, the United States has a non-stratified, comprehensive school system and no standardized pathways from school to work, while Germany is characterized by a stratified and standardized school and transition-to-employment system. The United Kingdom has a stratified education structure and a weakly regulated arrangement for vocational training. In comparing the United Kingdom, Sweden, and Germany, Allmendinger and Hinz (1998) show that the national structures of education and training provisions correspond to characteristic patterns of work careers, with variable stability and different levels of social integration across the life course. The relative strength of market forces and welfare-state policies contributes to the respective options for combining or alternating between education, training, employment, retraining, and retirement. An active welfare state tends to establish links between the economy, the labor market, and social concerns in order to distribute life chances more equally. In periods of crisis, its social policy institutions launch job-creation and training programs, instead of limited employment schemes (Leisering & Leibfried, 1999).

Labor market participation varies between countries by age and gender. In the United Kingdom the 15- to 20-year-olds show the highest employment rate, mainly in the casual labor market segment, whereas in Germany most of the teenagers are either still in school or in apprenticeship training for the occupational segment. Labor market exits occur relatively early in Germany, where employment rates start to decline by age 55, and just 43% of men and 15% of women older than age 60 are still in the work force. This contrasts with the United Kingdom where more than half of men and 18% of women, and Norway, where almost three-fourths of men and 60% of women in this age group are still employed (EUROSTAT, 2000).

Countries with a highly flexible labor market, like the United Kingdom and the United States, seem to compensate low job or career stability with considerable opportunity for re-employment after episodes of short-term joblessness. In more regulated labor markets, a high level of occupational training and career continuity is maintained, though with the tendency to socially exclude people with inadequate skills. Life course consequences could not differ more dramatically: in the United States low income and non-standard jobs expanded and unemployment declined in the 1990s to 4% and 5%, while in Germany the jobless rate increased to around 10%. The work life courses of women and job-entry and exit cohorts have been more adversely affected in the new federal states (former GDR), which still cope with the consequences of the prior socialist economy and authoritarian state (Diewald, 2000; Weymann, 1999). The individual experiences of discontinuity due to job shifts and unemployment were widespread, due to the transformation into a capitalistic economy with a flexible labor market, which preserved the stratification of skill levels and the allocation mechanisms that characterize an occupation-centered labor market.

These examples show that transitions in the labor market range from pathways that are individually negotiated and mediated by social networks, to administratively regulated patterns of mobility in the framework of institutional guidelines for employment and retirement.

It is important to note in this context that different types of work organizations provide or restrict career opportunities (Hannan, 1988). In contrast to status attainment models, which focus on skills and occupations as sources of career diversity, the institutional view regards work organizations as social systems that mediate between the state of the economy and the shape of individual careers. Independent of workers' characteristics, employment in a young and small firm tends to be less stable than in an older and large firm. This in turn increases job-entrants' risk of job-hopping, which reduces their opportunities to be hired for positions with career prospects because they cannot accumulate enough skills and sufficient organization-based experiences. There is also a reciprocal effect of careers on organizational diversity, for example, good career prospects in large companies and public administration reduce the rate at which young and innovative firms are founded. As the example of Germany with a high proportion of orderly career patterns documents, there are much fewer exits from paid work into self-employment and a slower process of founding start-ups than in England and the United States.

Mobility in the labor market thus neither depends only on the individual's experiences and skills, nor on the economy, but also on the sectoral expansion or decline of job offers or vacancies in companies. According to Sørensen (1983), worker mobility is related to opportunity structures that reflect the rate at which new vacancies occur and their distribution between large and small firms and industrial sectors. For instance, when companies in declining industries are keeping promotion rules based on seniority, this will lead to less recruitment of new employees and to an increasingly experienced work force.

From a life course perspective, these trends indicate possible intercohort or generation effects of job entry and job exit transitions: for instance, does early retirement lead to corresponding job openings that would improve the employment chances of the job-start cohorts? Can employment and welfare policy actively promote or invest in such a transfer of life chances by contributing to a reduction of youth unemployment and maintaining a decent quality of life for early retirees at the same time? As Sackmann (1998) shows, the qualitative properties of transition structures, and the kind of institutionalized linkages between education, employment, and retirement, are making a big difference in the unemployment rates of young and old workers in different countries. In societies like Germany, where companies are at the core of the standardized vocational training system, youth unemployment continues to stay lower than general joblessness, but unemployment among older workers is higher. A well-structured training and job-entry arrangement in which firms tend to invest in order to guarantee a supply of reliable and able employees delays the risk of unemployment at least until the end of vocational education and training. In this chapter, we have seen that the segmented labor market structures the interaction between employers and employees and affects the way in which occupations are linked to career opportunities. Now we will discuss from an agency perspective how individuals contribute to the shape of their work life course.

PATHWAYS, CAREERS, AND SOCIALIZATION

The variability of transition markers is a crucial characteristic of the education-to-work passage in post-industrial societies. In flexible labor markets, occupational expectations at the time of school-leaving tend to be influenced by a mix of school experiences, parental hopes, personal interests, teenage work experiences, and the assessment of regional employment opportunities. Thus, labor market entry is a complicated matching process of personal claims, skills, and job opportunities. As we have argued, economic and cultural change in the second half of the 20th century have contributed to social conditions that promote more individualized passages from education to occupation (see Kerckhoff, this volume) and from employment to retirement. There is greater diversity in transition paths after college (Buchmann, 1989), more career discontinuity after leaving high school (Rindfuss, Swicegood, & Rosenfeld, 1987), and a longer duration of time before full integration into the labor market (Morris, Bernhardt, Handcock, & Scott,1998). The young person's risk-taking behavior should not be considered responsible for these frequent career breaks; instead, such instability is due to sectoral shifts from manufacturing to low-income service jobs and the short-term contract policy of firms; in short, the collapse of the youth labor market. Such a collapse is observed in the UK for low achievers (Bynner, 1999) and for the sub-BA labor market in the USA (Grubb, 1999).

The matching between persons and jobs in the labor market can take place in different ways, either via organized pathways (*the institutional model*) or via informal linkages (*the market model*). The weaker the institutionalization of school-to-work pathways, the more are young women and men required to actively shape their passage to employment. The capacity to shape one's transition presupposes socialization contexts that promote planning (Clausen, 1993) and negotiation skills (Heinz, 2002a, 2002b), as well as access to social capital or social networks (Granovetter, 1995). These transition resources are difficult to accumulate for socially disadvantaged school leavers who need passage-helpers in order to enter the first steps of a career. Moreover, the diversity in contexts of opportunity leads to a variety of transition sequences (the timing and duration of employment episodes), which, in turn, are creating very different socialization experiences (Shanahan, 2000). For example, compared to continental Europe, in the United States there is a much higher involvement in paid jobs among high school students, jobs that tend to be of low quality and pay. These early jobs, however, may improve the gateway to employment for many non-college bound youth because they provide work experience and contacts with firms (Mortimer & Johnson, 1998).

In the market model, a combination of job experience and passage-helpers or mentors is expected to support young people, but not all potential passage-helpers are effective. Analyzing data from the U.S.-study "High School and Beyond", Rosenbaum and associates (1999) found that relatives and school contacts promoted students' placement in jobs that lead to higher income, though with a time lag, 9 years after leaving school. Friends and job-placement agencies were less successful. Blacks and women were more likely than white males to enter the labor market with the help of contacts between teachers and employers; the latter trusted the recommended students because of positive experiences in the past. The young workers who got such support tended to be allocated to entry jobs that offered better career pathways and income in the long run. Thus, links between schools and firms can act as a mediating device for youth who cannot count on other passage-help; these links seem to establish trusting ties, which substitute for formal relationships that are found in transition arrangements with institutionalized pathways.

The occupational attainment process in market arrangements makes it likely that school-leavers lack a clear orientation about work-entry and career pathways and thus will have to modify their career goals in response to the employment opportunities. Indeed, there is substantial instability of occupational expectations among U.S. young adults; as late as age 25, fewer than half actually achieved their aspirations (Rindfuss et al., 1999). The transition history of the high school class of 1972 (National Longitudinal Study) shows furthermore that occupation and gender make a big difference. Craftsmen, who received initial training, were on their chosen career pathway well before age 30, as were those with specific college degrees. Gender also has a powerful effect on career dynamics: when no match was possible between original expectations and occupation, men moved up the status ladder, whereas women moved down or withdrew from the labor force. It is interesting to note that social background characteristics, at least in this longitudinal study, showed little influence on the relationship between early aspirations and actual occupation at age 30. This study illustrates an individualized, unstandardized career entry process that may become characteristic of post-industrial societies.

The lessons from these longitudinal studies are twofold: first, employers' preferences, applicants' work histories, and a limited portfolio of resources create constraints for shaping the career according to aspirations; and second, market-led transition systems require that individuals invest more time in career scouting and negotiation, in order to "sort themselves into jobs for which they have both an interest and an aptitude" (Rindfuss et al., 1999, 255).

The example of Germany, which has an institutionalized transition arrangement for young people who are not college-bound, also shows that there has been growing job-discontinuity in the 1990s despite formal training provisions and occupation-specific certification. A longitudinal study of job-entry (in 1989) and career processes of skilled workers in crafts, manufacturing, and service occupations documented that 60% still were employed in their training occupation (up to 8 years after completing training), whereas 17% returned to school or went to college, and 11% were unemployed or not looking for work. However, only 10% did not work in the occupation they were trained for. This indicates a better match between expectations, occupational training, and career outcome than in the USA. Nevertheless, about 40% were confronted with, or had themselves initiated, a career break. The kind of interruption was influenced by occupation, gender, and the persons' biographical action orientations, like wage worker's-habitus, company-identification, or optimizing-chances (Heinz et al., 1998). Such orientations result from transition experiences and occupational contexts; they promote understanding of how career expectations and decisions are developed in view of changing employment opportunities. Instability, however, does not necessarily lead to a precarious life course because young people with better educational credentials opted for a voluntary turning point when leaving their jobs for post-secondary educational alternatives in order to improve their career prospects.

Such a comparative perspective illustrates that entry into work and career prospects hinge on the linkage between educational and employment institutions. Formal and connected pathways create less variability in the transition and less uncertainty in the work life course, compared to more market-driven and flexible arrangements in the United States or the United Kingdom. Economic turbulence in the wake of globalization and company restructuring in the last decade of the 20th century, however, have also affected the start of the work life in societies with institutionalized transition arrangements by creating more destandardization of the nexus between school, training, and employment.

In view of recent transformations of the work life, it is likely that persons have to cope with more discontinuity in their careers than prior assumptions about the influence of early formative years on personality across the life course would predict.

Longitudinal studies from the 1970s and 1980s (Kohn & Schooler, 1983; Mortimer, 1988; Mortimer & Borman, 1988) showed that there is an association between work experience and personality that can be explained by job selection processes and socialization at work. Work contexts and personality are reciprocally related over time: job conditions affect identity and persons select their own work experiences. The results are consistent in documenting that alienating employment circumstances restrict job involvement and productivity over the work life course, while occupational self-direction (Kohn & Schooler, 1983) or work autonomy (Mortimer, 1988) enhance psychological well-being and job-involvement across the life course. Biographically meaningful job tasks, in combination with social recognition, are intrinsically motivating and increase self-esteem.

Three competing hypotheses describe the relation between socialization and work orientations across the life course. First is the expectation of increasing stability with age, which assumes a strong impact of socialization in pre-adulthood and early employment on work identity and involvement. The second posits flexibility across age, which is an active adjustment or self-socialization in response to changing work conditions. The third emphasizes the duration of employment episodes, that is, the formation of work habits and job-involvement depends on the duration of stable work conditions. When social and economic circumstances provide continuous employment and meaningful job tasks, job-involvement, occupational satisfaction, and work-based identity are likely to stabilize with age. In periods of social transformation, however, self-socialization in the sense of developing self-reflexive strategies for coming to terms with changing job conditions and career breaks becomes a dominant pattern, especially in job-entry cohorts, but also for the older workers who are affected by down-sizing. For those who are confronted with declining durations of employment contracts, job-related motives and work identity will reflect a series of short-term adjustments with limited opportunity for forming biographical meaning (Sennett, 1998). Thus, with the 21st century it becomes more likely that "shifting economic conditions could also influence the relative propensities of workers of different ages to change jobs and thereby alter their work conditions" (Mortimer, 1988, 277).

We still know very little about the reasons and effects of voluntary and involuntary job shifts on the duration of unemployment, and thus need to conduct more longitudinal research to understand cohort and age effects on the relationship between stable and unstable work conditions and socialization. For example, does it still hold that work conditions become more stable with evolving career sequences? How do internal labor markets, occupation, and social policy on the one hand, and education, skill profiles, and gender, on the other, modify this pattern?

It is still unclear which mechanisms account for the reciprocal relationship between occupational contexts, agency, and work socialization for persons who are in different stages of their work lives. If we take into account that there is a loose coupling between social structure and the life course (see Elder, Johnson, & Crosnoe, this volume), then the accentuation principle or the person's work history/biography gains in importance, as does linked lives, for explaining adult career socialization. For job-entry and job-exit transitions, historical conditions (e.g., Great Depression, Golden Age, era of globalization) restructure the links between education and work, family and employment, and work and retirement.

In order to better understand the relationship between career conditions and the pacing of the work life course in increasingly flexible labor markets, self-reflexive learning processes seem to become more important. The conventional socialization approach tends to assume that coping with career demands is based on stable, internalized occupational role expectations and values. In contrast, the concept of "self-socialization" (Heinz, 2002a, 2002b; see also Dannefer, 1999) emphasizes that in post-industrial society the work life course requires a series of involuntary, and sometimes voluntary job moves, which initiate self-reflexive readjustments. The experience of job shifts, unemployment, and career breaks is interpreted in the context of the person's work biography. According to Giddens (1984), the structuration of the work life course implies individual agency and institutional resources, which come into play when decisions are taken between pathways and employment conditions. Thus, the analysis of work careers from the perspective of self-socialization may illuminate the variable ways in which work experiences and the life course are reflexively constructed in the contexts of institutions, social networks, and linked lives. Our longitudinal study of a German job-entry cohort has shown that processes of self-socialization are reflected in different modes of biographical agency in the shaping of early employment careers (Heinz et al., 1998; Heinz, 2002a, 2002b).

The early post-education life course is still an important "sensitive phase", but only one of many phases for the shaping of biographical orientations that direct a person's work involvement and career transitions. The restructuring of work settings and the prevalence of short-term employment will make labor market participation and careers increasingly dependent on the person's capacity to adapt to changing demands on short notice. This will require commitment to a kind of just-in-time flexibility, for instance, by acquiring new skills and knowledge or by changing employer and/or occupation, a commitment that may affect the stability of a person's work biography.

Empirical evidence for the growing frequency of contract negotiations required in fluid labor markets comes from research on part-time jobs in the United States and in Europe (Blossfeld & Hakim, 1997). There is wide variation in the occurrence and distribution of those jobs among countries and between men and women. All kinds of non-standard work, taken together, show the strongest increase in the 1990s in the age groups 15–24 and 55–64, which indicates less predictability of the work life course at the entry and exit transitions than in the middle years of employment (OECD, 2001).

The norm of an uninterrupted work life until retirement age is fundamental for most public pension and social insurance systems. This standard is rapidly becoming flexible in EU welfare states, where the departure from work is occurring earlier and earlier. For example, in Germany, the employment rate in the age group between 55 and 64 dropped from 75% to 43% for men during the decades of crisis (1972–2000). As a result, the duration of the retirement years has become extended and the burden on the public pension fund is increasing. A similar consequence results from the downsizing strategy of companies, which use early retirement packages to set older workers free (Marshall, 1999). These changes in the pathways at job entry and exit transitions of the work life course have introduced career dislocations that require readjustments through self-socialization.

SOCIAL INSTITUTIONS, OPPORTUNITIES, AND CAREERS

As Kohli (1986) has argued, the institutionalization of the life course emerged in the industrial society; it coincided with state politics that introduced obligatory schooling and social retirement insurance. This led to a work-based distinction between childhood/youth, adulthood and old age, thus to a tripartite life course, which consists of the preparation for work, working, and retiring from paid work.

The movement of cohorts, that is people born in the same year or in a certain historical period (the Great Depression or the Golden Age), through life can be conceptualized as an institutionalized allocation process to social roles that define the start of adulthood or the entry into old age. Intriguing cohort comparisons can be made with respect to the timing of transitions into and out of work (Carroll & Mayer, 1986; Sackmann, 1998). There is cross-national evidence that economic and social change has modified both cultural standards and persons' biographical timing, which in turn have led to a more flexible sequencing of male and female work life courses (Marshall, 2001). This research suggests that instead of relying on age as the major indicator of the individual life course, the timing, kind and duration of a person's involvement with labor market institutions is more useful as a focus of career analysis. A career then can be analyzed as a sequence of life events and movements in education, work, and family life, a sequence which is co-constructed by institutional gate-keeping and personal decisions (Heinz, 1996).

Both the contours and contexts of life course transitions and sequences are becoming less defined by age-markers and more by variable timing and duration of participation in the institutional fields of education and employment. Economic and social changes in the last quarter of the 20th century have been affecting these institutions, modifying the rules and resources of the labor market and the social policies of the state in the direction of a more flexible framework and individualized ways of integrating work and the life course (Beck, 1992; Giddens, 1991; Heinz, 2001). Job entries, durations, and exits across the life course became more diversified. The employment-family arrangements of couples, and the relationship between (competing) generations in the labor market for employment opportunities were transformed.

These transformations were mediated by the social institutions of the labor market, education, family, and the welfare system, which contribute to the way individuals shape their working life course (Heinz, 1992; Leisering & Leibfried, 1999; Leisering, Müller, & Schumann, 2001; Mayer & Schöpflin, 1989). They provide guidelines and resources for individuals who are constructing their careers through decisions and self-reflexive actions in the context of inter-related biographies (Born & Krüger, 2001; Elder & O'Rand, 1995; Heinz & Krüger, 2001; Moen, 2001). As the structuration approach (Giddens, 1984) suggests, a systematic analysis of the nexus between work and the life course should take into account the reciprocal effects of work transitions and durations and the timing of participation in the other main institutions of education and the family (see Elder, Johnson, & Crosnoe, this volume). For instance, the presence of children constitutes a restriction of career resources and behavioral constraint for women, which increase the likelihood of interrupting labor market participation; whereas for men, career breaks usually are not linked to fatherhood, but rather to lay-offs or to the decision to return to education.

Macro-social, economic, and political changes in the wake of globalization (see Weymann, this volume) have been affecting the shape of the life course not directly, but via institutional processes, for instance, company restructuring and labor market deregulation. Shifts in the structure of the work life course are, in turn, influenced by the sum of individual decisions concerning the timing of biographical transitions and the selection between social pathways (Hagestad & Dannefer, 2001). For example, the influx of women and mothers into the service industries precipitated a change in employers' hiring practices, as they turned to hiring women to fill full-time and, especially, part-time jobs. This strategy had to be promoted by affirmative action legislation in the USA and equal rights legislation in the European Union. Another example is the rise and prolongation of post-secondary studies, which delay labor market entry, lead to new role configurations of student and worker or student and parent, and create the life stage of young adulthood (Modell, 1989; Shanahan, 2000). A final example is the greater flexibility of the retirement age, which corresponds to company downsizing, pension reform (from public to private insurance), and to a new life style and self-esteem among the elderly (see Moen, this volume).

In flexible labor markets, the individual must assume greater importance as the agent of the timing of transitions, as investor of time in education and paid work, and as the producer of self-constructed pathways through the employment system. However, the extent to which there is individual autonomy in the rational organization of time allocation depends on the institutional fabric of labor market transactions and the welfare politics of the state. The balance of the deregulation of the labor market and welfare state provisions differs between neo-liberal, conservative, and social democratic social policies (see Leisering, this volume), which create a range of new opportunities as well as substantial risks and uncertainty for the work life course (Anisef et al., 2000; Beck, 1992; Sennett, 1998).

Essential for an adequate understanding of the work life course is to investigate the relative impacts of institutional guidance and control, and individual autonomy and capacity, on the selection of pathways into, in and from employment across the life course. In other words, it is important to discern the degree of choice in the timing and sequencing of transitions between jobs, occupations, and firms and the extent to which institutions facilitate or restrict multiple participation in different institutional fields, for example, university and company, family and paid work, retirement and part-time employment. Macro-, meso-, and micro-social analysis is needed to understand the impacts of social change on the coupling of work (re)structuring, labor market participation, and employment careers over the life course (Elder & O'Rand, 1995; Hagestad & Dannefer, 2001).

As the examples of temporary and part-time employment show, non-standard work deviates from the adult (male) norm of full employment, but it is acceptable for youth, mothers, and older workers. In post-industrial society, the gap between the institutionalized models or scripts for gender and age-appropriate timing and sequencing of career moves, and the actual distributions of career moves and employment opportunities, is growing. Cultural modernization and social transformation have made scripts for the "normal" male and female work life course less binding; such scripts are coming out of tune as yardsticks for the proper pacing of participation in the field of work. When we analyze the life course as a sequence of multiple participations in the major institutional sectors of work, education, and family, the loose coupling of cultural norms, sectoral circumstances, and individual participation patterns must be taken into account. This is obvious in the increasing variation in actual male and female work careers, which results from the combined effects of labor market deregulation and individuals' biographical decisions in the context of linked lives. The latter issue will be inspected in more detail below.

According to Levy (1996, p. 92), it is possible that "inconsistencies and frictions between institutional regulations, but also structural influences may interfere with traditional biographical patterns and provoke life course consciousness and innovation." This means that institutions may be shifting responsibility to individuals who are expected to synchronize their life courses in view of declining job tenure, family support, and social benefits. These trends will eventually open more space for a number of coexisting life course patterns that may even cut across the lines of gender segmentation. There is ample evidence, however, of an incomplete or even fragmented institutionalization of women's work participation (Gerson, 1985; Hochschild, 1989; Moen, 1992), and some evidence that men's careers are becoming less institutionally integrated. Because training, employment, and retirement opportunities are still quite differently distributed by gender, skill-level, industry, and location, and given variable access to kindergarten, parental leave, day care, and family-friendly companies, women's careers are structurally more unstable than men's (Hochschild, 1997; Krüger, 2001).

Therefore, the institutional view with its focus on norms, control, and gate-keeping, has to be supplemented first, by the recognition of unequally distributed resources for a proper sequencing of employment careers; and second, by taking into account biographical actors, who attempt to actively shape their living and working circumstances. In post-industrial service societies, continuity and change of work biographies are resulting from time-dependent joint ventures of biographical actors, social networks, and work organizations. Though career lines are more or less embedded in institutional regulations (Carroll & Mayer, 1986; Spilerman, 1977), actual careers are neither assigned nor guaranteed but rather negotiated (Gershuny, 1998; Heinz, 1996; Strauss, 1991). Negotiating a career confronts the biographical actor, as a participant in the labor market, with the problem that work organizations are mainly interested in processing, using, and regulating its members and tend to neglect the variability of employees' role configurations across their work life course. Due to the absence of linkages between social institutions, individuals must structure their biographies by negotiating transitions and participations. Cultural modernization defines individuals as responsible for their biographies and requires them to become less dependent on the family or charitable associations, and to rely increasingly on the labor market and collective systems of security (Leisering & Leibfried, 1999).

At the beginning of the 21st century, it has become obvious that the tripartite model of the institutionalized, work-centered life course has two weak points. First, it does not incorporate the increasing variability of transitions and sequences; in short, it favors the standardized over the flexible (individualized) life course. Second, it reflects the dominance of the labor market institutions and neglects the person's involvement in the institutions of family life.

GENDER AND COUPLED CAREERS

Life course research and women's studies have documented that gender is a cultural and structural feature that shapes transitions and the biographical pacing of work sequences

(Born, Krüger, & Lorenz-Meyer, 1996; Gerson, 1985; Moen, 2001). "Women's lives are typically contingent lives, shaped around the experiences of others: their husbands, children and parents" (Moen 2001, 189). Women's life courses are also shaped more and more by the labor market, as indicated above. At the intersection of work and family, gendered configurations and time allocations put more demands on employed women than on employed men across the life course. Therefore, the conditions and meanings of careers also differ between women and men, for instance, there are gender differences in age markers or deadlines of transitions in the fields of work, family life, and retirement (Settersten, 1997; see also Settersten, this volume). Although there is some convergence in the range of age-related transitions, women are disadvantaged in the accumulation of work-related returns because they tend to allocate more time for care and domestic responsibilities than men.

Research about male and female work histories shows repeatedly that there is a structural imbalance in the social pathways and biographical options at the employment-family intersection; greater responsibility is placed on the shoulders of women as daughters, wives, and mothers (Born, Krüger, & Lorenz-Meyer, 1996; Hochschild, 1989). There is indeed a persistent "structural lag" (Riley & Riley, 1994) or discrepancy between the promise of equal opportunities for women and the social and political provisions for enabling full participation, as comparative studies of part-time work demonstrate (Blossfeld & Hakim, 1997). How does this lag impact women's biographical involvement in work?

Occupational qualifications and labor market histories provide experiences that lead to variations in work identities; they are based on employment, income, career, and autonomy. Work identity develops from a person's employment history and influences personal career dynamics. Because of their strong family commitment, women's multiple responsibilities may very well constrain formation of a career identity. A study by Rosenfeld and Spenner (1988, p. 303) shows with retrospective (1966–1979) employment history data that "women's work identities reflect the constraints of social structure and labor demand." Whereas men employed full-time tend to see their jobs in career terms, women form "employed-income" or "employed-career" identities, work identities that differ according to mobility chains, type of firm, job-tasks, and inter- as well as intra-occupational variations in employment experiences. Lower-level educational resources, non-professional jobs, and family responsibility restrict socialization into a career-identity, and make the formation of an income-related identity more likely. Women with an employment-career identity are more likely to have experienced a continuous work biography, in the context of stability of both employer and occupational segment. In addition to the type of work-identity, there are also career consequences that evolve from the interrelationship of life courses.

As Moen (2001; Moen & Han, 2001) argues, men and women construct the work identity in the context of "linked lives" (Elder, 1998) or "interrelated life courses" (Born & Krüger, 2001; Krüger, 2003). Therefore, the concept of occupational career must be modified to reflect both men's and women's life transitions, "as they negotiate status passages of work and family in tandem" (Moen, 2001, 184; see also Moen, this volume). The example of retirement transitions documents that the person's work history is more influential than experiences in education and family life. Past opportunities and restrictions contribute to an uneven accumulation of experiences, and both material and social resources, which affect individual and in-tandem retirement decisions (O'Rand & Henretta, 1999).

We referred above to occupations and organizations as institutions that contribute to the shaping of the work life course. A retrospective study of women in transition to retirement (Born, Krüger, & Lorenz-Meyer, 1996) sheds light on the importance of the occupation as a social institution that structures the female life course in Germany. Both the level of education and the family event-history were less important for explaining women's careers than their occupation. For instance, when talking about their work histories, the women reported up to 12 interruptions. Sequence analysis demonstrated that these interruptions did not so much depend on domestic demands than on the respective occupation's labor market opportunities.

Women's career histories thus can be driven by their certified skill profiles, as this example shows, which presuppose a more or less occupation-centered life course. In addition to occupational qualification, companies' human resource management can make a difference, as documented in a case study by Hochschild (1997) of dual-earner couples in a family-friendly firm. In her interpretation of the couples' work and career experiences, she suggests that the workplace may be winning over the home, mainly because the former provides more recognition. In a life course perspective, however, this interpretation needs to be verified with cohort and work-history data, because the rewards persons expect from the workplace may very well differ across the life course.

The reorganization of employment conditions in lean companies and the increase of non-standard jobs should have an impact on working couples' role-configurations. While in continental European welfare states women's part-time employment is promoted without radically transforming the traditional male career model of the breadwinner, in the United States there is no institutional support for women's employment, but rather private sector arrangements with various opportunities to combine paid work and family tasks.

Han and Moen (2001) investigated pathways through work and marriage in the USA, based on the fact that in the United States at least half of the workers are dual-earner couples at the end of the 20th century. Assuming that there is a transformation of the traditional man-breadwinner and woman-homemaker division of labor, they analyzed the role configurations and career pathways of two-career couples with U.S. retirees' life history data. The multiple pathways traversed by men and women across their employment trajectory are considered together with their marital trajectory. By applying sequence analysis, they found five types of occupational pathways which were systematically related to the number of career transitions and to the shape of marital trajectories. "High-geared" and "intermittent" types showed much more mobility between companies, though the former changed jobs in order to move upward, while the latter indicated unstable employment sequences. Not unexpectedly, gender differentiated between the career types; men were located in the "orderly" or "high-geared" pathway types. These pathways also had a substantial representation of women. Most women, however, were associated with "delayed-entry" and "intermittent" pathways, and the majority in the "steady part-time" pathway was female. The main finding concerns the persistence of unequal comparative advantages and life chances between men and women at the interface of work and home: working women suffered more marital instability than did men; and wives' employment sequences were highly contingent on their husbands' careers. This research confirms that work sequences contribute to the specific shape of linked lives which are still structured by gender inequality and asymmetry.

It is likely that in societies with a high level of women's culturally supported labor market participation, the spouses' careers will be more independent of each other. Research in socialist countries like the former German Democratic Republic (Kreckel & Schenk, 2001) or China document that there the conventional, gender typed work transitions and sequences do (did) not exist. The job-shifts of wives and husbands between 1949 and 1994 in China, a state-socialist country undergoing waves of politically enforced economic and social changes, indicate career patterns in a life course regime which strongly contrast with gender-specific careers in the North American and EU-countries' market economies (Zhou & Moen, 2001). The hierarchy of the respective work organizations (with the government administration on top) and the wife's and husband's specific work histories determine job-shift patterns across a period of more than 40 years. Again, this study shows how institutional arrangements can facilitate or restrict the multiple participations/role configurations at the interface of family and employment and access to pathways through the working life.

In capitalist market economies, the life course is shaped by linked or interrelated lives embedded in gendered role configurations and institutional arrangements that are documented in individual contracts and unequal career patterns. These macro-social and institutional contexts are reflected in individuals' multiple and interdependent transitions, which influence the timing and duration of employment careers. Therefore, even the individualized career in a flexible labor market is not a solo passage. Instead, social contexts, which create mutual social obligations, options, and obstacles that constitute conditions of career diversity and deviations from the most likely path, influence work histories.

WORK TRAJECTORIES AS NEGOTIATED CAREERS: THE CONTINGENT WORK LIFE COURSE

The concept of "trajectory" stems from rocket technology; here it designates a ballistic curve with a highly predictable slope between firing and hitting the target. As a metaphor for the life course, trajectory applies to continuous careers, which are characteristic of orderly pathways in the internal labor markets of large companies and state bureaucracies of industrial societies. It does not reflect less ordered pathways, especially those of women, and of job-entry and job-exit cohorts in the 1990s, who were confronted with much less employment stability than earlier cohorts. There are also intercohort differences that make for less career continuity for middle aged and older managers who became victims of company downsizing. Therefore, "transitions and sequences" seem to be better suited for describing the "contingent work life course" (Heinz, 2001), because these concepts do not carry the latent meaning of continuity, but make it an empirical issue.

The remodeling of the tripartite life course is an unfinished process; it has created socially legitimate periods of non-work, namely education, family (for women), and retirement which in reality did not become completely separated from the sphere of work. There are students and retirees who are employed in low-income, non-standard jobs and socially disadvantaged youth and worn-out workers who are regarded as not productive and thus get excluded from the labor market and become welfare recipients (Leisering & Leibfried, 1999). Each move into work or out of work, as well as career moves, upward, downward or horizontal/lateral, are transitions that are shaped by work organizations and persons' employment decisions as well (George, 1993; Sackmann & Wingens, 2001). From the institutions' point of view, such transitions occur in an organized framework that links past status with the target status, for instance, by screening of applicants, job interviews, and periodic reviews; while from the person's perspective, transitions mean learning new membership roles and organizational rules.

The prolongation of the job-entry process, the increase of job-shifts, and the rise of early retirement are indicators of a transformation of both the human resource strategies of companies as well as the labor market and social policy of the state. In employment systems that rest on long-term contracts, combined with a strong, usually union-supported element of seniority, companies can reduce layoffs by taking advantage of state programs for early retirement and partly subsidized temporary jobs for young people and mothers.

We have argued that in post-industrial society, social transformations and work biographies are linked through self-socialization and individual career management as well as repair, in the structural context of labor markets and firms, mediated by institutional rules and resources. Employment opportunities and career options are embedded in contested exchange arrangements between employers and employees that contribute to the shape of the work life course. These arrangements involve contracts with different employment durations, career prospects, and varying autonomy and learning chances at the workplace. Contracts are negotiated in a social framework of institutional guidelines and industrial relations, which permit occupation- and company-based, short-term bargaining (*the market model*) or require industry-wide, long-term agreements (*the institutional or corporatist model*). In both circumstances, there is interactive bargaining, which occurs via more or less institutionalized procedures. As Chris and Charles Tilly (1998, 264) emphasize: "The character of work under capitalism has always depended on hard bargaining within stringent institutional limits established by the previous histories of shared understandings and social relations." This notion of interactive bargaining is useful for analyzing the options and restrictions that people are faced with in the process of career negotiations. It points to the variability of contextual forces that supplement the temporal aspects of employment sequences and promote understanding of career stability and instability.

The negotiating power of job applicants and workers depends on their position in vacancy chains, which, in turn, relates to their education, gender, and work history. These employee characteristics are important for school-to-work transitions, status-attainment, and career patterns in post-industrial societies because they are criteria for matching workers and jobs (Erikson & Goldthorpe, 1992; Shavit & Müller, 1998). In the market model, this matching may occur in informal negotiations, which are embedded in social networks (Granovetter, 1995; Tilly & Tilly, 1998) and account for variations in the frequency of transitions and job-durations. In flexible, deregulated labor markets (United States, Canada, United Kingdom), careers negotiated through social networks influence the timing, sequencing, and duration of employment, joblessness, and retirement more strongly than in the European continental welfare states, where career negotiations are embedded in occupational labor markets and industrial relations that are operating in the context of the principle of social partnership or corporatism.

A fundamental transformation of employment standards into a decentralized patchwork of flexible and precarious career patterns is still counterbalanced in the European Union by bargaining agreements concerning contracts, work time arrangements, time accounts, and social policy provisions like unemployment benefits and allowances for retraining. Nonetheless, the temporal destandardization of work sequences and the individualization of employment pathways have increased, especially among recent job entry cohorts.

The various forms of non-standard work constitute new challenges and obstacles for building a work career with some continuity and require that persons develop competence in negotiating contracts on short notice and come to terms with having to alternate between episodes of full- and part-time jobs, under-employment (Livingstone, 1998), unemployment, and retraining.

These challenges will require more frequent negotiations at career turning points, greater involvement in self-socialization across the life course, and, perhaps, lead to more flexible work identities. These processes have been accelerated in the less regulated North American and UK labor markets, where firms have been moving faster away from internal labor market strategies with stable employment to non-standard contracts. In continental European welfare states, there are indications that occupational credentials gain in value in the labor market when combined with work experience, self-presentation, and social contacts.

The preceding sections have intended to show the extent to which the structure and meaning of work and career have changed in the 20th century with respect to labor market entry, employment continuity, retirement, and the reconciling of work and family life. Individual flexibility in the timing, sequencing, and duration of work-related transitions has become characteristic of post-industrial service societies. There is, however, substantial difference among nations with respect to the new lifetime budgets, which results from the degree of labor market regulation and the institutionalization of linkages/pathways among education, training, work, family, and retirement. Economic turbulence and social transformations have brought about change in female and male career sequences, changes that have been more dramatic in market economies than in welfare states. This observation suggests the need to analyze the work life course from both an institutional and biographical perspective. Pathways have become destandardized and employment careers discontinuous, and the ensuing "contingent work life course" (Heinz, 2001) transforms the relationship between social institutions and the life domains of education, work, and family. Such transformations loosen the coupling between social structure and work biographies because they shift the challenge and responsibility for managing one's career, for coordinating transitions and durations, to the individual. Moreover, individual work careers evolve in the context of linked lives; they are tied to multiple, interlocking pathways. Because in post-industrial service society, the social structure of work and the shape of the life course are loosely coupled, careers do not simply result from the sum total of work transitions and employment durations; they rather emerge from negotiations based on qualifications, work experiences, and biographical decisions on the one side, and institutional gate-keeping on the other side.

REFERENCES

Allmendinger, J., & Hinz, T. (1998). Occupational careers under different welfare regimes: West Germany, Great Britain and Sweden. In L. Leisering & R. Walker (Eds.), *The dynamics of modern society: Poverty, policy and welfare* (pp. 63–84). Bristol: The Policy Press.

Anisef, P., Axelrod, P., Baichman-Anisef, E., James, C., & Turrittin, A. (2000). *Opportunity and uncertainty. Life-course experiences of the class of '73*. Toronto/Buffalo/London: University of Toronto Press.

Beck, U. (1992). *Risk society*. Newbury Park, CA: Sage.

Beck, U. (1999). *Schöne neue Arbeitswelt*. Frankfurt a.M./New York: Campus.

Blossfeld, H.-P., & Hakim, C. (Eds.) (1997). *Between equalization and marginalization: Women working part-time in Europe and the United States of America*. New York: Oxford University Press.

Born, C., Krüger, H., & Lorenz-Meyer, D. (1996). *Der unentdeckte Wandel. Annäherung an das Verhältnis von Struktur und Norm im weiblichen Lebenslauf*. Berlin: edition sigma.

Born, C., & Krüger, H. (Eds.) (2001). *Individualisierung und Verflechtung. Geschlecht und Generation im deutschen Lebenslaufregime*. Weinheim/München: Juventa Verlag.

Buchmann, M. (1989). *The script of life in modern society: Entry into adulthood in a changing world*. Chicago: University of Chicago Press.

Bynner, J. (1999). New routes to employment: Integration and exclusion. In W. R. Heinz (Ed.), *From education to work: Cross-national perspectives* (pp. 65–86). Cambridge: Cambridge University Press.

Carroll, G. R., & Mayer, K. U. (1986). Job-shift patterns in the Federal Republic of Germany. The effects of social class, industrial sector, and organizational size. *American Sociological Review, 51*(3), 323–341.

Clausen, J. (1993). *American lives. Looking back at the children of the Great Depression*. Berkeley, CA: University of California Press.

Conger, R. D., & Elder, G. H. (1994). *Families in troubled times. Adapting to change in rural America*. New York: Aldine de Gruyter.

Dannefer, D. (1999). Freedom isn't free: Power, alienation and the consequences of action. In J. Brandtstädter & R. M. Lerner (Eds.), *Action and self-development: Theory and research through the life-span* (pp. 105–131). Thousand Oaks, CA: Sage.

Diewald, M. (2000). Continuities and breaks in occupational careers and subjective control: The case of the East German transformation. In R. Silbereisen & J. Bynner (Eds.), *The effects of adverse and challenging circumstances on life-course trajectories in the new Germany and England* (pp. 239–267). London: Macmillan.

Doeringer, P., & Piore, M. (1971). *Internal labor markets and manpower analysis*. Lexington: D. C. Heath.

Edwards, R. C. (1979). *Contested terrain*. New York: Basic Books.

Elder, G. H., Jr. (1987). War mobilization and the life course: A cohort of World War II veterans. *Sociological Forum, 2*, 449–472.

Elder, G. H., Jr. (1998). Life course and human development. In W. Damon (Ed.), *Handbook of child psychology* (pp. 939–991). New York: Wiley.

Elder, G. H., Jr., & O'Rand, A. M. (1995). Adult lives in a changing society. In K. S. Cook, G. A. Fine, & J. S. House (Eds.), *Sociological perspectives on social psychology* (pp. 452–475). Needham Heights: Allyn & Bacon.

Erikson, R., & Goldthorpe, J. H. (1992). *The constant flux: A study of class mobility in industrial societies*. Oxford: Clarendon Press.

European Commission (1996). *The learning society*. Luxembourg: Author.

George, L. K. (1993). Sociological perspectives on life transitions. *Annual Review of Sociology, 19*, 353–373.

Gershuny, J. (1998). Thinking dynamically: Sociology and narrative data. In L. Leisering & R. Walker (Eds.), *The dynamics of modern society: Poverty, policy and welfare* (pp. 34–58). Bristol: The Policy Press.

Gerson, K. (1985). *Hard choices: How women decide about work, career and motherhood*. Berkeley, CA: University of California Press.

Giddens, A. (1984). *The constitution of society*. Berkeley, CA: University of California Press.

Giddens, A. (1991). *Modernity and self-identity*. Stanford, CA: Stanford University Press.

Granovetter, M. (1995). *Getting a job* (2nd ed.). Chicago: University of Chicago Press.

Grubb, W. N. (1999). The subbaccalaureate labor market in the United States: Challenges for the school-to-work transition. In W. R. Heinz (Ed.), *From education to work. Cross-national perspectives* (pp. 171–193). New York: Cambridge University Press.

Hagestad, G. O., & Dannefer, D. (2001). Concepts and theories of aging. Beyond microfication in social science approaches. In R. H. Binstock & L. K. George (Eds.), *Handbook of aging and the social sciences.* (5th ed., pp. 3–21). New York: Academic Press.

Han, S.-K., & Moen, P. (2001). Coupled careers: Pathways through work and marriage in the United States. In H.-P. Blossfeld & S. Drobnic (Eds.), *Careers of couples in contemporary societies. From male breadwinner to dual earner families* (pp. 201–231). New York: Oxford University Press.

Hannan, M. T. (1988). Social change, organizational diversity, and individual careers. In M. W. Riley (Ed.), *Social structures & human lives* (pp. 161–174). Newbury Park: Sage.

Heinz, W. R. (Ed.). (1992). *Institutions and gatekeeping in the life course*. Weinheim: Deutscher Studien Verlag.

Heinz, W. R. (1996). Status passages as micro-macro linkages in life-course research. In A. Weymann, & W. R. Heinz (Eds.), *Society and biography. Interrelationships between social structure, institutions and the life course* (pp. 51–65). Weinheim: Deutscher Studien Verlag.

Heinz, W. R. (1999). Job-entry patterns in a life-course perspective. In W. R. Heinz (Ed.), *From education to work: Cross-national perspectives* (pp. 214–231). New York: Cambridge University Press.

Heinz, W. R. (2001). Work and the life course: A cosmopolitan-local perspective. In V. W. Marshall, W. R. Heinz, H. Krüger, & A. Verma (Eds.), *Restructuring work and the life course* (pp. 3–22). Toronto: University of Toronto Press.

Heinz, W. R. (2002a). Transition discontinuities and the biographical shaping of early work careers. *Journal of Vocational Behavior 60*, 220–240.

Heinz, W. R. (2002b). Self-socialization and post-traditional society. In R. A Settersten & T. J. Owens (Eds.), *Advances in life-course research: New frontiers in socialization* (pp. 41–64). New York: Elsevier.

Heinz, W. R., Kelle, U., Witzel, A., & Zinn, J. (1998). Vocational training and career development in Germany— Results from a longitudinal study. *International Journal for Behavioral Development, 22*, 77–101.

Heinz, W. R., & Krüger, H. (2001). Life course: Innovations and challenges for social research. *Current Sociology, 49(2)*, 29–45.

Hobsbawm, E. (1994). *Age of extremes. The short twentieth century 1914–1991*. London: Abacus.

Hochschild, A. (1989). *The second shift*. New York: Avon.

Hochschild, A. (1997). *The time bind: When work becomes home and home becomes work*. New York: Metropolitan Books.

Kohli, M. (1986). The world we forget: A historical review of the life course. In V. W. Marshall (Ed.), *Later life: The social psychology of aging* (pp. 271–303). Beverly Hills, CA: Sage.

Kohn, M. L., & Schooler, C., with the collaboration of Miller, J., Miller, K. A., Schoenbach, C., & Schoenberg, R. (1983). *Work and personality: An inquiry into the impact of social stratification*. Norwood: Ablex.

Kreckel, R., & Schenk, S. (2001). Full time or part time? The contradictory integration of the East German female labor force in unified Germany. In V. M. Marshall, W. R. Heinz, H. Krüger, & A. Verma (Eds.), *Restructuring work and the life course* (pp. 159–176). Toronto: University of Toronto Press.

Krüger, H. (2001). Social change in two generations: Employment patterns and their costs for family life. In V. W. Marshall, W. R. Heinz, H. Krüger, & A. Verma (Eds.), *Restructuring work and the life course* (pp. 401–423). Toronto: University of Toronto Press.

Krüger, H. (2003). The life course regime; Ambiguities between interrelatedness and individualization. In W. R. Heinz & V. W. Marshall (Eds.), *Social dynamics of the life course.* New York; Aldine de Gruyter (forthcoming).

Leisering, L., & Leibfried, S. (1999). *Times of poverty in western welfare states.* Cambridge: Cambridge University Press.

Leisering, L., Müller, R., & Schumann, K. F. (Eds.) (2001). *Institutionen und Lebensläufe im Wandel. Institutionelle Regulierungen von Lebensläufen.* Weinheim: Juventa.

Levy, R. (1996). Toward a theory of life-course institutionalization. In A. Weymann & W. R. Heinz (Eds.), *Society and biography. Interrelationships between social structure, institutions and the life course* (pp. 83–108). Weinheim: Deutscher Studien Verlag.

Livingstone, D. W. (1998). *The education-jobs gap.* Boulder, CO: Westview Press.

Marshall, V. W., & Marshall, J. G. (1999). Age and changes in work: Causes and contrasts. *Ageing International 25,* 46–68.

Marshall, H. (2001). *Restructuring work and the life course.* Toronto: University of Toronto Press.

Mayer, K. U. (1988). German survivors of World War II: The impact on the life course of the collective experience of birth cohorts. In M. M. Riley (Ed.), *Social structures & human lives* (pp. 229–246). Newbury Park: Sage.

Mayer, K. U., & Schöpflin, U. (1989). The state and the life course. *Annual Review of Sociology, 15,* 187–209.

Modell, J. (1989). *Into one's own.* Berkeley, CA: University of California Press.

Moen, P. (1992). *Women's two roles: A contemporary dilemma.* Westport, CT: Greenwood.

Moen, P. (2001). The gendered life course. In *Handbook of Aging and the Social Sciences.* (5th ed., pp. 179–196). New York: Academic Press.

Moen, P., & Han, S.-K. (2001). Reframing careers: Work, family, and gender. In V. W. Marshall et al. (Eds.), *Restructuring work and the life course* (pp. 424–445). Toronto: University of Toronto Press.

Morris, M., Bernhardt, A., Handcock, M., & Scott, M. (1998). *The transition to work in the post-industrial labor market.* Presented at Annual Meeting of the American Sociological Association, San Francisco.

Mortimer, J. T. (1988): Work experience and psychological change throughout the life course. In M. W. Riley (Ed.), *Social structures & human lives* (pp. 267–284). Newbury Park: Sage.

Mortimer, J. T. (1995). Social psychology of work. In K. S. Cook, G. A. Fine, & J. S. House (Eds.), *Sociological perspectives on social psychology* (pp. 497–523). Boston: Allyn & Bacon.

Mortimer, J. T., & Borman, K. M. (Eds.) (1988). *Work experience and psychological development through the life span.* Boulder, CO: Westview.

Mortimer, J. T., & Johnson, M. K. (1998). New perspectives on adolescent work and the transition to adulthood. In R. Jessor (Ed.), *New perspectives on adolescent risk behaviors* (pp. 425–496). New York: Cambridge University Press.

OECD (2001). *Employment outlook.* Paris: OECD.

O'Rand, A. M., & Henretta, J. C. (1999). *Age and inequality: Diverse pathways through later life.* Boulder, CO: Westview Press.

Rifkin, J. (1995). *The end of work.* New York: Putnam.

Riley, M. W., & Riley, J. W. (1994). Structural lag: Past and future. In M. W. Riley, R. L. Kahn, & A. Foner (Eds.), *Age and structural lag* (pp. 15–36). New York: Wiley.

Rindfuss, R. R., Swicegood, C. G., & Rosenfeld, R. A. (1987). Disorder in the life course: How common and does it matter? *American Sociological Review, 52,* 785–801.

Rindfuss, R. R., Cooksey, E. C., & Sutterlin, R. L. (1999). Young adult occupational achievement. Early expectations versus behavioral reality. *Work and Occupations, 26*(2), 220–263.

Rosenbaum, J. E., DeLuca, S., Miller, S. R., & Roy, K. (1999). Pathways into work: Short- and long-term effects of personal and institutional ties. *Sociology of Education, 72,* 179–196.

Rosenfeld, R. A., & Spenner, K. I. (1988). Women's work and women's careers: A dynamic analysis of work identity in the early life course. In M. W. Riley (Ed.), *Social structure & human lives* (pp. 285–305). Newbury Park: Sage.

Sackmann, R. (1998). *Konkurrierende Generationen auf dem Arbeitsmarkt.* Opladen/Wiesbaden: Westdeutscher Verlag.

Sackmann, R., & Wingens, M. (Eds.) (2001). *Strukturen des Lebenslaufs. Übergang—Sequenz —Verlauf.* Weinheim: Juventa.

Sengenberger, W. (1987). *Struktur und Funktionsweisen von Arbeitsmärkten.* Frankfurt a.M./New York: Campus.

Sennett, R. (1998). *The corrosion of character. The personal consequences of work in the new capitalism.* New York/London: W. W. Norton & Company.

Settersten, R. A., Jr. (1997). The salience of age in the life course. *Human Development, 40,* 257–281.

Settersten, R. A., Jr. (1999). *Lives in time and place: The problems and promises of developmental science.* Amityville, NY: Baywood Publishing Company.

Shanahan, M. J. (2000). Pathways to adulthood in changing societies: Variability and mechanisms in life-course perspective. *Annual Review of Sociology, 26,* 667–692.

Shavit, Y., & Müller, W. (Eds.). (1998). *From school to work: A comparative study of educational qualifications and occupational destinations.* Oxford/New York: Oxford University Press.

Sørensen, A. B. (1983). Process of allocation to open and closed positions in the social structure. *Zeitschrift für Soziologie, 12,* 103–124.

Spilerman, S. (1977). Careers, labor-market structure, and socioeconomic achievement. *American Journal of Sociology, 83,* 551–593.

Strauss, A. (1991). *Creating sociological awareness. Collective images and symbolic representations.* New Brunswick: Transaction Publishers.

Tilly, C., & Tilly, C. (1998). *Work under capitalism.* Boulder, CO: Westview Press.

Weymann, A. (1999). From education to employment: Occupations and careers in the social transformation of East Germany. In W. R. Heinz (Ed.), *From education to work. Cross-national perspectives* (pp. 87–108). New York: Cambridge University Press.

Zhou, X., & Moen, P. (2001). Job-shift patterns of husbands and wives in urban China. In H.-P. Blossfeld & S. Drobni (Eds.), *Careers of couples in contemporary societies. From male breadwinner to dual earner families* (pp. 332–367). New York: Oxford University Press.

CHAPTER 10

Government and the Life Course

Lutz Leisering

All government policies affect the lives of citizens in some direct or indirect way. Despite the pervasiveness of the influence, relatively little attention has been given to the manner in which government impinges on the individual life course. This article aims to show that exploring the relationship between government and life course provides a seminal perspective both for the study of the life course and for welfare state analysis, especially with regard to cross-national comparison. "A thorough examination of the state and its policies may provide further insights into the ways in which age and the life course are treated in a society" (Settersten, 1999, p. 74).

To examine the relationship between government and life course, both sides need to be specified. First, "life course" refers to *temporal* patterns of life. We only look for government influences on temporal patterns, not on individual lives in general (as analyzed, e.g., by social policy studies). Second, "government" is taken to refer to the overall structure of governmental policies and institutions. Particular policies and programs, like old-age pensions, education, and labor force regulation, are dealt with elsewhere (e.g., see Heinz, Kerckhoff, Moen, and O'Rand, this volume)—this chapter focuses on the *overall impact* and *patterns* of the policies, institutions, and philosophies that make up the state. In this way we can explore if different state traditions, different politico-legal cultures, produce different life course patterns.

Third, we mainly look at measures *intended* to influence the life course. Without this specification we would have to cover virtually any measure taken by any government department, because every policy has at least a latent or indirect bearing on the life course. Since the institutions of the welfare state are at the heart of government's programmatic concern for individual lives, we concentrate on the welfare state. The welfare state is more than a range of social services. The welfare state is a structural component of what T. H. Marshall (1981)

Lutz Leisering • Department of Sociology, University of Bielefeld, D-33501 Bielefeld, Germany.

Handbook of the Life Course, edited by Jeylan T. Mortimer and Michael J. Shanahan. Kluwer Academic/Plenum Publishers, New York, 2003.

termed "democratic welfare capitalism" (see also Esping-Andersen, 1990), even if the balance between the three components of this "hyphenated society" (Marshall) varies between countries. The welfare state is about law, institutions, values, and culture. "The welfare state is the institutional outcome of the assumption by a society of legal and therefore formal and explicit responsibility for the basic well-being of all of its members. Such a state emerges when a society or its decision-making groups become convinced that the welfare of the individual [...] is too important to be left to custom or to informal arrangements and private understandings and is therefore a concern of government" (Girvetz, 1968, p. 512).

The chapter starts by contrasting North American and European traditions of life course research (section one), then goes on to sketch the historical emergence of the interest of governments in individual lives (section two), followed by a general (section three) and more policy-specific (section four) analysis of the influence of contemporary governments on the life course. Section five presents cross-national comparisons. The chapter concludes with an analysis of the current problems (section six) and future prospects (section seven) of "life course policies".

GOVERNMENT AND STATE IN NORTH AMERICAN AND EUROPEAN LIFE COURSE RESEARCH

In North American life course research government figures less than in European research. The emphasis lies on "the primary worlds of family, work, and friends" (Elder, 1991, p. 71) and on particular fields of government. Studies of the overall impact of government are rare (for exceptions see Hirschhorn, 1977; Brim & Phillips, 1988; Settersten, 1999). Government mainly comes in through education and the impact of educational achievement on the work life. Retirement and old-age pensions also figure in life course research, though private and public pension plans are often treated together.

The United States has a comparatively small government—the state's share in Gross Domestic Product (i.e., the percentage of all generated wealth devoted to the public sector), social spending as percent of GDP, and public employment as percent of total employment are worlds apart from most other developed countries. The United States is a "residual welfare state", with a last safety net (welfare) that is weaker and less rights-based than in most other countries (Gough, Bradshaw, Ditch, Eardley, & Whiteford, 1997), with a short duration of entitlement to unemployment benefit and without universal coverage of health insurance. For Americans, the very term "welfare" conjures up the idea of needs-based programs for the poor and weak. The small size of the welfare state reflects an individualistic culture and a preference by most citizens for a smaller role of government in directing their lives than is customary in Europe. There is a strong public spirit in American society with a concern for individual well-being but "public" often does not translate into "state" and legal entitlements. Local community action, voluntary welfare organizations, and private donations and foundations play an important role. Government activities are more designed to secure equal opportunities, for example, through federal, state, and local grants for higher education, than to promote security across the life course or even equality of outcomes (see section five).

Continental Western Europe has a stronger "state tradition" (Dyson, 1980)—that is, a stronger tradition of public law, public administration, and ideas about the essence and the responsibility of the state—that also permeates life course research (for a comparison of the North American and the European research traditions see Marshall & Mueller, 2003; for an

American perspective on European research see Settersten, 1999). There is a stronger emphasis on the role of the "state"—the more substantial term "state" being preferred to the technical term "government"—and of institutions and organizations in general. Even family and work are conceptualized in more structural and institutional terms (see, e.g., Heinz & Krüger, 2001). The life course itself is seen as a social institution, its emergence as the "institutionalization of the life course" (Heinz, 1991; Kohli, 1986; Levy, 1977, 1996; for the USA see mainly Meyer, 1986). In this view, the life course is a new social structure in its own right, an "institutional program" that defines a "normal biography" (Levy, 1977), not just a 'pattern of socially defined, age-graded events and roles" (Elder, 1999, p. 302). As a consequence, the distinction between institutional program ("life course" in the strict sense) and subjective construction of one's own life ("biography") is particularly pronounced in European scholarship. In a broader sense, the life course is conceived as the interface of institutional control (macro) and individual strategies of action (micro) (Heinz, 1991).

While age grading in relation to primary groups is the backbone of North-American life course research, the analysis of "secondary institutions" (Beck, 1992) is at the heart of its European counterpart. However, the American concept of "life course markers" leads beyond age grading and provides a link to more structural European approaches. "Life course markers" are events and transitions in life that are both highly prevalent and highly predictable (George, 1993, 360 f.; Shanahan, 2000). Some events, such as the death of a parent during middle age and widowhood in old age, have become life course markers in the course of the historical increase in life expectancy. Timing of marriage and parenthood is related to attitudes and life-styles. In the second half of the 20th century, the welfare state has emerged as a major creator of life course markers in many countries, by establishing mandatory and universal programs and legal entitlements. Retirement is the most important example.

We may conclude that North American and European approaches to the life course have different emphases that reflect distinct realities. On both continents, life course research has been tailored to its subject matter. Future research should aim to bridge the two traditions to allow mutual learning. Europe already learned from the United States in the early years. U.S. researchers developed the idea of studying the dynamics of individual lives in the early 1970s when most Europeans were still preoccupied with holistic concepts of social structure and individual living conditions.

But even in Europe it took some time for the study of the life course and welfare-state research to meet each other (Allmendinger, Brückner, & Brückner, 1993; Falkingham & Hills, 1995; Leisering & Leibfried, 1999; Leisering & Walker, 1998; Mayer & Müller, 1986; Mayer & Schöpflin, 1989). One reason is that the far-reaching impact of the postwar welfare state on the lives of its citizens only became apparent after some decades of sustained growth of social legislation and bureaucracy. Scholarly attention to the life course is part of the switch from investigating the causes of the expansion of the welfare state to the analysis of its consequences (for the United States see Janowitz, 1976). Still, often only the isolated impact of single systems of social welfare comes into view.

The second reason for the growing interest in the relationship between state and life course is the renewed interest in cross-national comparison in the 1990s. In the study of one country, the institutional macro-constellation may be treated as constant and be taken for granted. When comparing across countries, however, the modeling of macro-constellations and hypotheses about the macro–micro link are needed (Mayer, 1997, discusses as an example the problem of explaining the different transition rates to nursing homes in European countries).

The impact of macro-factors on the life course, even within one country, is the third reason for bringing the analysis of political institutions to bear on the life course. In Meyer's view (1988: 49 f.) conventional analysis based on microdata cannot reveal the societal and cultural background of individual life courses. Meyer sees the life course as a social construction in an individualistic society which is enshrined in and produced by the core institutions of the society, especially education, the economy, law, and the state. American life course researchers obviously deal with contexts like peer groups and neighborhoods, but few authors emphasize secondary institutions and organizations as Meyer does. In his classical study "The children of the Great Depression", Elder went beyond earlier individualistic approaches by introducing the principle of "historical time and place" as structural influences on individual life courses (though this did not lead him to study the impact of social security regulations under the New Deal).

THE INTEREST OF GOVERNMENTS IN INDIVIDUAL LIVES

The modern state, especially in Europe, and the modern individual did not emerge in opposition to each other, as deemed by some individualistic thinkers, but their historical rise was closely intertwined. The 16th and 17th centuries witnessed the emergence of the territorial state. By demarcating their territories, these states discovered "their" populations. Population statistics and "political arithmetic" came to the fore. Thus began a history of growing interest of the state in individual persons (Thomas et al., 1987). The mercantilist state under absolutistic rulers developed an interest in its workforce. These rulers aimed to increase their populations (including the promotion of migration), to boost the economy and the ensuing revenue. The nation-state of the 19th and 20th centuries with its industrial economy and political democracy was interested in the quality, not only the quantity, of its workforce for economic as well as military purposes. In this context, the tripartitioning of the life course—childhood/youth, working age, old age—gradually evolved. Unproductive child labor was barred from the labor market and public education installed instead. The exclusion of old-age pensioners from employment served both the interest of employers in productive labor and of trade unions in keeping labor supply scarce. During this period individuals were transformed from objects of government into citizens who actively participated in social life on the basis of civil, political, and social rights (Marshall, 1964). The welfare state as the source of social rights became a major pillar of the legitimacy of governments—a path only hesitantly and partially followed by the United States in the 1930s and the 1960s. All in all, state social policy has been a major component of processes of nation building (or renewal of the national spirit), especially in Imperial Germany (Bismarck's social insurance 1883–1889), Britain (the "welfare state" of the late 1940s) and in the U.S. New Deal of the 1930s.

Though state traditions differ considerably between countries, some American sociologists have also emphasized that the institutional requisites of individualism extend beyond the economic market. Parsons identified the Educational Revolution, together with the Industrial Revolution and the Democratic Revolution, as the main sources of "institutionalized individualism" (Parsons & Platt, 1974, p. 1). Janowitz (1976) sees the welfare state as a stage in the development of liberal democracy, as an institution that promotes the Enlightenment's idea of the self-perfection of the individual through therapy and social treatment. Meyer (1986, 1988) takes this further by a temporal conception of the modern individual. In his view the individual is constituted as a "self " directed towards self-development. The "self" is a cultural project of personal growth and development, produced and disseminated by Western development agencies, teachers, and psychologists across the world.

The emergence of the self is related to structural needs of modernization. Modern society has economic, political, and social spheres—what sociologists call structural or "functional differentiation". Each sphere (or "system") has its own logic or functional rationality, for example, the logic of collective power in the case of the political sphere or the logic of profit-making in the economic sphere. The functional systems need persons to operate. To secure "inclusion" (Parsons), that is, the participation of individuals in the spheres, a separate symbolic entity distinct from the functional rationalities is needed, the self. The self and its developmental form, the life course, thus frame the participation of individuals in functional spheres. Mayer and Schöpflin (1989, p. 195) conceive of a mapping of the functional differentiation of society (of the spheres) onto the temporal differentiation of individual lives (the three standard phases of life), with the economy being mapped onto the middle phase. Levy (1996) allows for a more complex, multidimensional participation of individuals in key "interaction fields". Meyer (1988) sees the individual and the life course as cultural entities which are constructed by all core institutions of society. In this view, as in Janowitz's, the state promotes individualism just as the modern family and the labor market do.

STATE AND LIFE COURSE—HOW ARE THEY RELATED?

Basic norms and institutions of the welfare state, and associated expectations by the citizens, are linked to the life course. While both critics and advocates of the welfare state tend to interpret it in egalitarian terms as a form of vertical redistribution (from rich to poor), redistribution across the life course dominates in most welfare states. The aim is *security* rather than equality. The expectation of a secure life span widens the temporal frame of action for the citizens. Especially in social insurance states like Germany, security is paramount to equality as the key value. But even in the British welfare state with its strongly egalitarian self-image, intertemporal redistribution was already explicit in the early 1940s in the concept of a postwar welfare state developed by William Beveridge, the intellectual father of the British "welfare state" (Glennerster, 1995, 13 f.). Age groups—not the poor as such—were the first modern "welfare classes" in European welfare states, namely the children (first major prohibition of child work in Britain in 1833, in Prussia/Germany in 1842) and the elderly (Bismarckian old-age pensions in 1889).

In a theoretical interpretation, Kohli (1987) aims to show that welfare state and life course are linked in view of the "work society". Work (wage labor) alone cannot cover the entire life course, gaps remain due to periods of incapacity to work—these are filled by the welfare state. Filling the gaps is a moral, not only a technical issue, or, from the point of view of the individuals, not only a matter of rational calculation as depicted in economic theories of life-cycle saving. By filling the gaps the welfare state sustains the "*moral economy*" of the work society: only a retirement income—as a just reward for a life's toil—in addition to the wage received during employment, enables the moral justification and acceptance of work society. This argument is culture-specific. Kohli's interpretation links up with static, not explicitly life course related elements of welfare state theory: Neo-Marxists have ascribed to state social policy the function of securing and controlling "forms of existence outside the labor market" (Offe, 1984, p. 94). This is depicted as one of three modes by which social policy achieves a continuous "transformation of non-wage laborers into wage laborers", which is required for capitalism to operate. Similarly, Esping-Andersen (1990) defines the welfare state as a state that aims at "decommodification". Decommodification means enabling individuals to maintain a livelihood outside the labor market as a matter of right, thereby reducing the commodity character of their labor. Examples include entitlements to benefits at times of illness, unemployment, or old age. Especially in liberal welfare regimes like the USA with a low degree of decommodification, gaps in working lives remain.

Following Kohli we are led to the conclusion that the state completes the institution of the life course. Out of the major forces that shape the life course—family, work, social networks, state—the state is the only overarching agency that extends to the entire life course, including periods of non-work and lack of a family. The state may impinge on the life course at any point, "from cradle to grave". Still, only small groups like long-term welfare recipients or persons in residential care or in sheltered workshops are set on a lasting and exclusive welfare state trajectory. Welfare benefits mostly remain subsidiary; as a result, the political legitimacy of the welfare state at large, even in Europe, is weaker than the legitimacy of the market economy and the nuclear family.

The most basic reference of the welfare state to the life course can be seen in the individualized rights and services it provides. Kaufmann (2002) defines "social policy" as political measures with the explicit aim of influencing the life situation of individuals. Policies aiming to influence aggregate outcomes, like GNP or exports of goods, are not social policy. Measures directed to institutions, for instance, federal grants to schools, are social policy only if a desired outcome (e.g., better opportunities for school children in poor areas) is specified and can be measured on the level of individuals. Especially personal social services like medical treatment, care, counseling, and therapy impinge on individuals in a direct way—"people processing". They change the physical, psychological, and social competencies and capacities of individuals. This makes for a very immediate micro–macro link. The welfare state, like other institutions, changes the opportunity structure and the incentive structure for individuals, especially through cash benefits, but it also exerts a more direct influence.

Policies intended by political actors to change the structure of the life course may be termed "*life course policies*" (Leisering & Leibfried, 1999; see section four). Policies may impact on the life course in various degrees, ranging from merely influencing an aspect of the life course to regulating it or even constituting a pattern, such as the creation of old age by statutory old-age pensions in some welfare states. A special case is the immediate involvement of individuals with the state, through employment at government agencies, military service, or war (for an example see section six below). Mayer (1991) only accepts these cases as state-constituted life courses in a strict sense. The most direct and pervasive control of life courses by the state is found in authoritarian regimes, such as China (see "The children of the cultural revolution", Zhou & Hou, 1999). Some life course policies are "*tacit*" or "implicit" to a degree. However, in each case, a policy analysis is needed to uncover the tacit objectives—having actual life course outcomes is not enough for a policy to qualify as life course policy.

The distinction between "positive" and "*negative*" *life course policy* further elaborates the conceptual framework. A policy which does not aim to shape the life course by politico-administrative intervention (which would be "positive" life course policy) may still influence the life course, but in a "negative" way—by intentionally leaving the formation of the life course to non-state forces such as markets, private companies, private charity, and to the family. Negative policy is a powerful and frequently used tool. But again, not every non-policy is negative policy in this sense. An analysis of political actors and their strategies is required to uncover and specify the negative intention. A unique example of negative life course policy (combined with some positive elements) is the restriction of welfare receipt to a maximum of 5 years in a life time, enacted in the welfare reform of 1996 in the United States.

Life course patterns may not only be the outcome of current policies towards the life course but also of *politico-administrative structures*. These can be seen as the institutional legacy of earlier policies. This legacy includes the institutional structure of the implementation of policies, of providers of services, of the kind of public-private partnership, of regional and sectional segmentation, and so forth. Such factors are, for example, needed to explain the different transition rates to nursing homes in European countries, which cannot be fully explained by current policies, nor by general values prevalent in a country, nor by socio-demographic variables like the proportion of elderly in the population or female employment rates (as indicator of the availability of care givers; Mayer, 1997).

LIFE COURSE POLICIES IN THE WELFARE STATE

In the recent European research literature, the relationship between state and life course is addressed, but normally in a selective way, touching only on few aspects on both sides. In this section we propose a new model that pieces together the elements and adds new ones so as to reveal the overall logic of the relationship (cf., Leisering & Walker, 1998; Leisering & Leibfried, 1999 [German 1995]). The model identifies three core *fields* (sets of programs) of social policy and three *modes* of operation of the welfare state in shaping the life course. The two dimensions—fields and modes—cut across each other: each set of programs involves two or three modes of operation. The three core fields include education, old-age pensions, and systems of "risk management". Together these fields, which cover the bulk of the activity of the welfare state, make up the entire life course. The three modes of the welfare state include structuration/differentiation, integration, and normative modeling. In Figure 10-1 the three modes are depicted as three layers or "onion skins".

STRUCTURATION/DIFFERENTIATION.   As shown in Figure 10-1, education and old-age pensions contribute to the social definition of childhood, youth, and old age, thereby structuring or differentiating the life course with the three standard phases of youth, adulthood, and old age. In this way *life phases* and related *transitions* are created. The phases are associated with statuses and roles, such as "school children", "students" (in the institutionalized system of vocational training in Germany, also "apprentices"), and "old-age pensioners". These roles may define social identities and membership of a "welfare class". The temporal structuring of the life course is much more complex than Figure 10-1 shows. Using the method of sequence analysis, Han & Moen (1999) take a new look at retirement by analyzing it not just as a transition but as embedded in multidimensional trajectories that lead to retirement.

INTEGRATION.   Social policy systems also establish connections between the different phases and stages of life and hence integrate the life course. Education in youth enhances life chances in adulthood. Likewise, pensions allow adults in their working life to be certain about their retirement prospects. In this way *trajectories* or careers that extend across longer periods of life are supported. Systems of risk management such as unemployment insurance, accident insurance, health insurance/services, social assistance, and personal social services, like therapy and counseling, bridge life's discontinuities and transitions at whatever stage they occur. They "mend" the life course, thus producing continuity across the entire *life course*.

NORMATIVE MODELING.   There is a sometimes hidden or implicit social policy agenda geared to shaping the life course according to normative models relating to class, gender, and ethnicity. Schools and universities not only convey knowledge but also distinctive norms of

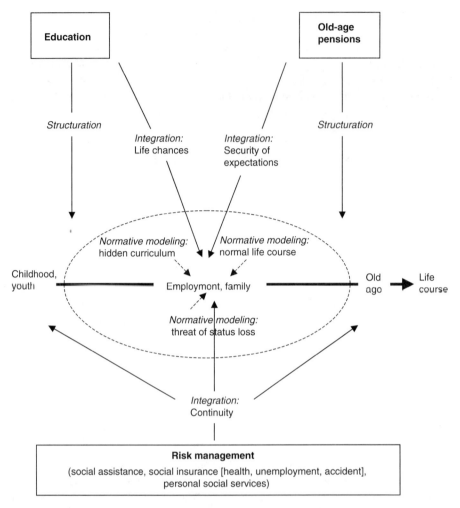

FIGURE 10-1. Life course policies in the welfare state—programs and modes of operation.
Source: Adapted from Leisering & Walker (1998, p. 10).

behavior, life style, and habits. This "hidden curriculum" in education, most pronounced in Germany and the United Kingdom, reinforces differences of class (in Germany by a tripartite high school system), gender, and ethnicity. Earnings-related old-age pensions put a premium on "normal life courses" based on a full employment history of the male breadwinner. Especially in Germany this produces a gendered life course split into a male and female normal biography (Allmendinger et al., 1993; Levy, 1977). For women, the tripartite model of the life course in the "work society"—preparing for work (education), working, retiring—is not equally applicable. The stigma attached to the least respectable tiers of risk management, social assistance, further underpins the normalcy of seeking one's welfare in the market.

The model shows that the life course is political. Since its introduction in the 19th century, state social policy has made a considerable contribution to shaping the modern life course. Social scientists have hitherto dealt with the key state influences—education, old-age pensions, risk management—only in isolation from one another. Education's directive function relative to the occupational system is emphasized by studies of mobility, which demonstrate that the life course is an "endogenous causal nexus" (Karl Ulrich Mayer). The cultural and socializing functions of the educational system are highlighted in John W. Meyer's conception of "the self" and "the life course" as cultural projects of modernity. The security-giving function of old-age insurance enables people to extend their plans and expectations to the entire life span, which in Martin Kohli's view is fundamental to the institutionalization of the life course. The various forms of the welfare state's risk management, by contrast, have only received some attention in biographical studies of marginal groups, with a focus on social work and agencies of social control. In the USA there is a large literature on the effects of welfare policy on poor families, though the quantitative longitudinal studies normally lack an explicit life course perspective (e.g., Bane & Ellwood 1994). Henly and Lyons (2000) analyze the heterogeneity of child care arrangements of low-income parents as a challenge for the new welfare policy since the reform of 1996. Our model suggests that risk management programs have a much wider significance for the study of the life course. All in all, the life course as formed by the state—its structure and its vulnerabilities—is only comprehensible if perceived as the outcome of the interaction of all three elements of life course policies.

The systems of risk management deserve close attention since this aspect of the welfare state has until recently been almost totally overlooked by students of the life course (for an exception see Hirschhorn, 1977, who, similar to Beck, 1992 [German 1986], emphasizes the function of social policy in mending the discontinuities of increasingly fluid life courses). The agencies of risk management react mainly to short-term circumstances that may affect individuals at various points in their lifetime. Although transitions and critical life events (or "status passages", Heinz, 1991) are key topics of life course research, they have not normally been linked to social policy (e.g., see George, 1993). The relevance of risk management for the life course has not been so easy to grasp as the relevance of educational or retirement systems. Why?

First, the middle stages of the life course have been merely seen as periods of working and family life, even though state interventions directed to social risks are especially important. Second, the variables and categories used in the conventional study of mobility—education, occupation, family status, social class, and socio-economic group—are too crude to embrace the discontinuities in the life course which are at stake in this context, like ill-health or unemployment. But discontinuity is a pervasive element of normal life. Third, Allmendinger and Hinz (1998, p. 64) maintain that "situational programs" like social assistance exhibit a "life course indifference" because, unlike "continuous programs" such as earnings-related pensions, their benefits do not reflect the previous life patterns of recipients. However, such programs do impinge on the subsequent life course and, through anticipation, change the structure of expectations of the individuals vis-à-vis the entire life span. Fourth, qualitative research that focuses on discontinuities and on deviant "careers" (Luckenbill & Best, 1981) tends to adopt a one-sided perspective in viewing such life courses as unilinear decline leading towards stigmatization and marginalization, for example in case of the homeless and the long-term unemployed. The total institution—the asylum, the psychiatric ward, or the sheltered workshop—exemplifies the extreme of a totally state-controlled life course. Going beyond the limitations of both mobility studies and research on deviant careers, we maintain that the management of risk is a basic form of life course policy. Though impinging situationally, systems of risk management shape the expectations of the citizens and thus secure the unity of the life course as a whole.

The modeling of the life course by state policy goes deeper than setting norms. The basic forms of everyday behavior and categories of knowledge are imbued by the operation of the welfare state. Individual behavior is increasingly shaped by law, money, and bureaucracies, individuals become clients and "protoprofessionals" (the latter term is explained below)—all these processes infiltrate into the primary worlds and informal settings of the citizens. Being old, being young, being ill, being disabled, or being poor—these social conditions assume a new meaning. They become a legal status, documented in certificates and ID cards, tied to eligibility to certain services, and subject to control by administrators and social professionals. Identities and roles are transformed or even created in the process: The elderly become "pensioners", the sick become "patients", and the poor become welfare recipients, or even, with stigma attached, "welfare mums". These processes of redefinition entail a narrowing of meaning of a social condition or life situation. As a rule, they imply a quantification and dichotomization of conditions, like old/not old (eligible to pensions or not) or "60% disabled". However, eligibility has become increasingly differentiated and flexible, for example allowing for various stages of early retirement.

The welfare state also implies new power relationships. People become clients of bureaucrats, social professionals, and experts such as doctors, psychologists, lawyers, and sociologists. Experts do not only provide services but redefine the identities and knowledge categories by which people perceive themselves and their situation. This may entail a "proto-professionalization" (de Swaan, 1988), that is, clients incorporate the professional categories in their self-perception. On the one hand, protoprofessionalization is a further intrusion by the welfare state into the life world of individuals. On the other hand, it may indicate the active client, patient, etc. who challenges the asymmetrical power structure of the client–expert relationship by active use of professional knowledge.

All this implies that new time structures are imposed on individual lives, concerning age norms, life phases, the duration of episodes, and trajectories. (1) *Age norms*: Childhood and youth are defined by various age norms, especially by the legal age of school entry (in countries with compulsory schooling), the minimum number of years of school attendance, the upper age limit for the prohibition of child work, and the age of majority. There are numerous other legal thresholds like the legal marriage age, the age of getting a driving license, or the age of being admitted to jury service. The impact of legal age norms on behavior varies (Mayer & Schöpflin, 1989, 198 f.). Behavior may follow norms only with delay—historically this has often been the case for compulsory entry to school—or, conversely, norms may only codify previous practices—as has often occurred in the case of the age of retirement fixed by old-age pensions. Social law becomes part of the institutionalization of the life course only if it becomes entrenched in the everyday culture and attitudes of the individuals. Old-age pensions, for example, only come to dominate the social definition of old age when pensions account for a major share of total income in old age, when they are widespread in the population, when there is a long period of retirement (longevity) and when they are rooted in a normative idea such as intergenerational solidarity. Events and transitions defined by social policy may thus become "life course markers" (see section 1). (2) *Life phases*: By structuring the life course by age, social policy largely turns into age-group policy: Socially defined age—rather than need—becomes a criterion for benefits and services. Conversely, age groups are defined by welfare law and administration. In this way dividing lines between age groups are created: Children, youth, the young-old, the very old—each group is subject to different definitions of social problems, to different institutions, and different social professionals. (3) *Duration*: The welfare state defines the duration of life episodes and transitions because eligibility to benefits and services is often limited in time, for example in the case of unemployment benefit and sick pay. (4) *Trajectories*: The division of domains between social programs and agencies gives rise to welfare careers: people "travel" between and within systems like unemployment benefit, food stamps, welfare, social work, psychiatric wards, and courts.

"LIFE COURSE REGIMES"—COMPARING
LIFE COURSES ACROSS NATIONS

There are many cross-national comparisons of particular welfare programs like old-age pensions or medical services, and some of these comparisons shed light on the life course impact of the programs. But the overall impact of the welfare state, of the whole structure of programs, agencies, and ideas, has received little attention: "so far there have ... been (no) systematic cross-national comparisons of the effects of differing welfare state regimes on life course outcomes" (Mayer, 2000, p. 273). Initial studies include Leisering & Leibfried (1999 [German 1995], ch. 2), Mayer (1997, 2001; elaborating a working paper of 1997 by Esping-Andersen, Mayer, & Myles), and Allmendinger and Hinz (1998). This section presents some concepts, methodological problems and hypotheses of this new branch of comparative research.

Comparing the relationship between state and life course across nations is a demanding task. Two methodological problems arise. First: Do policies (does the welfare state, do core institutions of society) matter at all? Or do variables like economic prosperity, demographic change, and cultural values explain why life course patterns differ between nations? The answer is suggested by the previous section. Given that government policies matter in one country, we can expect that they also make a difference between countries (though it is still possible that different institutions may lead to similar life course outcomes).

Second: Is there such a thing as a national "life course regime"? The term "life course regime"—like "labor market regime" or "gender regime"—implies that the life course in one country has some overall logic that reflects the institutional structure (including the structure of the welfare state) in that country. The existence of life course regimes can only be asserted with considerable qualification (for the following see Mayer, 1997). Both sides—life course as the dependent variable and welfare state as the independent variable—are too complex to make a uniform correspondence likely. We can hardly expect that the entire life course in one country, an overall logic, could be uniformly explained by the welfare state model prevalent in that country. The life course falls into different parts, like phases and transitions, each of which may require a different explanation. Equally, the welfare state falls into different parts—like education, social security, and labor market regulation—that often obey different logics and may be influenced by different actors and power relationships.

There are two approaches to the explanation of life course patterns by welfare state institutions: *social policy analysis* and *"political economy"*. Social policy analysis centers on the side of the welfare state (Leisering & Leibfried, 1999), political economy on the side of the life course with an emphasis on employment careers in the labor market (Mayer and the other authors). The two approaches correspond to different research communities: to welfare state research on the one hand which takes a closer look at the institutional design of welfare programs and draws on institutional and qualitative data; and, on the other hand, to mobility studies, labor market research, and labor economics. The latter approach, political economy, takes a more differentiated look at employment trajectories but refers to institutions only in more general terms as reflected in the (quantitative longitudinal) microdata used by these scholars.

The most basic though not very informative assertion to make is that extensive state regulation produces a more continuous and standardized life course, whereas in countries with a small scope of government intervention we can expect a more "fluid" life course. A more complex classification of welfare states than small/large has been proposed by Esping-Andersen (1990). He defined three "welfare regimes" or "worlds of welfare capitalism": the liberal regime, including the United States and Britain, with a low degree of decommodification (see the definition of decommodification in section three); the conservative regime with a medium degree of decommodification, mainly countries of the West European continent like Germany; and the social democratic regime of the Scandinavian countries with a high degree of decommodification. The three welfare regimes are at the center of recent comparative welfare state research. A seminal approach is to examine if and how the three welfare regimes give rise to, for example, distinct "labor market regimes", or if the attitudes of citizens towards their welfare state are related to the regime type. The question, as to whether welfare regimes produce distinct life course patterns, has only recently been tackled.

When asking which life course patterns are produced by the three welfare regimes we must keep in mind that we cannot expect a uniform correspondence. The three regimes may have to be grouped differently depending on which aspect of the life course is under consideration. Moreover, the regimes are heterogeneous, so countries belonging to one type, for example, the United States and Britain, may have different life courses. Furthermore, with regard to specific policy areas (which shape specific aspects and transitions in the life course), welfare states may have to be classified in ways that differ from the classification of overall welfare regimes. With regard to social assistance, for example, seven types of welfare states could be identified (Gough et al., 1997). In this respect, Germany, although a different welfare regime, is close to Britain as a "welfare state with integrated safety nets", which promotes a continuous life course; whereas the United States belongs to a different type, which offers little security and continuity. With regard to old-age pensions, two main types can be distinguished, the Beveridge tradition of flat rate benefits and the Bismarckian tradition of earnings-related, contribution-based benefits (Myles & Quadagno, 1997). Here again, the USA and Britain, though both liberal welfare regimes, fall into different types (Bismarck and Beveridge respectively), while Sweden has gradually shifted from Beveridge to Bismarck. Contrary to a widespread view, Western countries do not converge on a basic pension or Beveridge-style (flat-rate) model. Rather, there is a proliferation of earnings-related elements (Schmähl, 2000, p. 206), which are particularly life-course sensitive.

The *political economy approach* gives a differentiated view of the life course outcomes of the three welfare regimes with regard to working lives (Table 10-1). Roughly speaking, working lives in liberal welfare regimes are long and loosely structured, whereas working lives in conservative regimes are short and tightly structured. Social democratic welfare regimes also produce long working lives, but with less job mobility and more class mobility than in liberal regimes.

In the following we present at greater length basic findings from the *social policy approach*. Compared to the political economy approach depicted in Table 10-1, the social

TABLE 10-1. Life Courses in Three Welfare Regimes—The Temporal Structure of Working Lives

	Liberal welfare regime	Conservative welfare regime	Social democratic welfare regime
Stratification of educational system	Low [high]	High	[Low]
Standardization of vocational training	Low	[High]	[Low]
Labor market entry	Early	Late	Early
Job mobility	High	Low	Low [high]
Class mobility	[Low]	[Low]	[High]
Retirement	Variable	Early	Late

Source: Mayer (2001, 102, based on theoretical hypotheses); Allmendinger & Hinz (1998, 78, based on empirical data from Mayer's *Eurocareers* project for Britain, Germany, and Sweden).
[...]: from Allmendinger & Hinz.

policy approach yields a similar though more complex picture, based on the model outlined in section four (Figure 10-1). This model includes three fields of welfare policy (education, old-age pensions, systems of risk management) and three modes of shaping the life course (structuration, integration, normative modeling). Welfare states differ in both dimensions.

FIELDS/WELFARE PROGRAMS.   Welfare states differ with regard to the emphasis they put on each of the three fields. In the United States, public policy gives priority to education, whereas the German welfare state, for example, centers on social security, above all on a comprehensive scheme of old-age insurance (Heidenheimer, 1981). Risk management is stronger in the United Kindgom and in Germany than in the United States, where health insurance, unemployment benefit, and social assistance are weakly developed. In short, the U.S. model places a high emphasis on education, some emphasis on social security (old-age pensions), and least emphasis on risk management. Germany is strong on risk management, with the major exception of personal social services that would enable women to combine family and employment. All in all, redistribution is the core of the German welfare state, whereas the United States emphasizes social investment and, since the Clinton welfare reform of 1996 (Blank, 2002), activating policies, though with less support and more sanctions *(workfare)* than in Sweden. "Activation" means inducing people to help themselves rather than just paying benefits. Sweden manages to do both: the Swedish welfare state combines extensive redistribution with social investment and activation, especially active labor market policy. Activation has been an integral part of the Swedish model long before the discourse on new, activating social policies by the new social democrats in Western Europe started in the 1990s.

MODES OF LIFE COURSE POLICY.   The first mode, *structuration*, correlates with the degree of regulation. The life course in the United States is less structured than the life course in Western and Northern Europe. The mode of *integration* refers to the ways in which life phases are connected through social policies. There is a variety of patterns. Rather than only identifying high or low integration we can distinguish two dimensions of integration: a welfare program can be called *"life-course sensitive"* if benefits reflect previous life course patterns of the recipients. It is *"life-course relevant"* if it exerts an impact on the subsequent life of recipients. Programs can differ along both dimensions independently. Even programs designed to be not sensitive or not relevant to the life course may influence life courses in a "negative" way—they leave the formation of the life course to non-state forces such as markets and private charity. Such programs amount to "negative life course policy" as defined in Section Three.

   In the United States the connection between an individual's life course and the welfare state is generally loose or non-existent in both respects (for further explication see Leisering & Leibfried, 1999, pp. 48–51): The benefit systems put little weight on previous contributions—with the major exception of national social security pensions—and similarly contribute little towards the prospective formation of biographies. Welfare programs offer no more and often less than minimal support. They do not positively shape individual life courses. But the American system does have lasting effects on life courses, in a "negative" manner. The minimum benefits for welfare recipients are so designed as to give them a powerful incentive to return to work quickly, even at very low wages, or even illicitly. The Welfare Reform Act of 1996 has further restricted cash assistance while improving support for low-wage earners, such as child care subsidies and health insurance (Blank, 2002).

   In the original Swedish model as designed in the 1930s, only one side of the integrative linkage between welfare state and life course has been developed. Following the idea of equal provision for all citizens, benefits do not depend on a "normal" record of employment or tax-paying. However, as far as services are concerned, the Swedish welfare state lastingly affects the whole life course, by active labor market policy, by service jobs for women in the public sector, and by social services that enable the integration of paid work with motherhood. The state ensures that a working career is the norm in the lives of both sexes. Over the years, Swedish old-age pensions have become increasingly life course sensitive by an earnings-related layer that started in 1960.

In the German model, the life course is very closely bound up with social policy, in both directions, life course sensitive as well as life course relevant. Major benefits depend on individual contributions made during working life, with normal biographies being positively rewarded by social insurance. More than in many other welfare states, this is done in a gendered way—differences between male and female life courses are reinforced by social policy.

NORMATIVE MODELING. The three regimes differ in three dimensions that reflect (and affect) the basic normative order of society: work, gender, and (what Esping-Andersen, 1990, called the stratification dimension of welfare regimes) inequalities of welfare provisions. The different weight attached to each field of social policy in a welfare regime indicates the normative fabric of the regime. Both in the United States and in Sweden social policy and the life course center on *work*, though in different ways; while in Germany, even if most benefits are earnings-related, working life is curbed from all sides: people enter late, leave early, and women are discouraged from entering at all (for the temporal structure of working lives in the three countries see also Table 10-1 above). With regard to *gender*, Germany also stands out, with a gendered life course based on a male breadwinner model that is still influential even if declining. The patterns of *inequality in welfare provision* differ sharply (Esping-Andersen, 1990): in the United States there is a dualist structure of those who live on social assistance and other inferior welfare sources and those who can afford private provisions (for health, old age, etc.) in the market. In Germany social security is fragmented by occupation, related to corporatist interests, although this structure is receding. Sweden is characterized by egalitarian and universal services, though elements of earnings-related benefits have modified the original blueprint.

All in all, the U.S. American welfare state offers good opportunities but high risks for its citizens, adding up to a fluid and insecure life course. The key value is *equality of opportunity*. Risks in the life course tend to be seen as evidence of personal failure. The poor are often categorized as "deserving" and "undeserving". Sweden, by contrast, also offers good opportunities but with less risks attached—a comparatively egalitarian, secure life course. *Equality of outcomes* is the leading value. Germany also offers good opportunities and low risks, but both are unequally distributed with regard to gender and employment status. The key value is (segmented) *security*.

PROBLEMS AND DILEMMAS OF LIFE COURSE POLICIES

Life course policies face various problems and dilemmas: First, to what extent can government really influence and change life courses (effectiveness)? Second, do life course policies counteract basic values of a free society by unduly constraining lives? Third, do they even make people dependent on external aid, thus eroding personal autonomy and the capacity of self-help? Fourth, do they foster an "age-constrained" life course, thereby creating age-divisiveness and ageism?

EFFECTIVENESS. What potential of effectively changing lives do life course policies have— against strong economic forces like recession and mass unemployment and against the barriers of class, gender, and ethnicity? Life course policies would also have to fight against time: against the "cumulative stratification of the life course" (O'Rand, 1995), that is, the increasing entrenchment of inequality in the course of life. Or is education in the early years the only effective lever of life course policy? These are empirical questions. Answers will differ between fields of policy and between countries. Generally, social policies have been found to be reasonably effective. Schmidt (2001) has drawn together results from numerous empirical studies. Comparative welfare state research has shown, for example, that bigger welfare states have a better record of reducing inequality and poverty than those countries that spend less on social welfare. Even if low spenders concentrate their efforts on the poor ("targeting"), they score low in the fight against poverty (Korpi & Palme, 1998). The assumption that the welfare state undermines the individual sense of responsibility and inflates expectations, is not confirmed by most studies. However, social policy does not prevent or reduce crime and deviance (but see Uggen & Massoglia, this volume). The evidence that social policy undermines the potential for self-help and mutual help is mixed: some studies confirm this assertion, some do not.

It is also a question of the yardstick to be applied. Even if the overall structure of class remains largely unaltered, small differences and movements in the life course may matter for the individuals concerned. For example, receiving welfare during a period of personal crisis, say after divorce, may be significant for this person although it does not entail a change of class. The extension of maternity leave in Germany, to give another example, has changed the lives of mothers. Most of them claim it, so that "extended maternity leave has become an institution" (Bird, 2001). In his study of the children of the Great Depression, Elder identifies three avenues of "turning lives around" (1999, pp. 320–330), two of which are related to government action: education as provided by the GI Bill for veterans of World War II, marriage, and military service, the latter often acting as a bridge to the two former: "the GI Bill became a primary factor in the life opportunity that veterans from the California studies experienced." "Full-scale mobilization for war in the early 1940s broadened their [men and women] exposure to life opportunities … military service became our focus as a turning point because it frequently provided new options for marriage and advanced education" (1999, 322 f.). In this way, Elder challenges a deterministic concept of the life course and rather supports a view that allows for openings and turning points.

CONSTRAINTS. The infiltration of human lives by law, money, and social bureaucracies implies restrictions on individual action that may counteract the value of individuality basic to modern society. But the relationship between individuality and structure is more complex. Agency is a key element of the life course (Elder, 1999, 308 f.) but agency has to be conceived as "agency within structure" (Settersten, 1999, p. 253). Individuals are embedded in structures and institutions. Institutions can be and often are sources of agency by providing continuity and coherence of biographical orientations. Welfare programs, in particular, provide competencies, resources, opportunities, and individual rights that empower individuals outside and inside of the market and the family (Kaufmann, 2002). Institutions may also enable effective life planning.

This hints at a fundamental ambivalence of social policy. "Existential questions become institutionally repressed at the same time as new fields of opportunity are created for social activity and for personal development" (Giddens, 1991, 164 f.). Paradoxically, constraints on the life course by institutions and policies may widen the choice of individuals. Constraints and opportunities may arise at different points in the life time, for example, mandatory pension plans may prevent welfare dependency in old age. This ambivalence is not peculiar to social policy. In fact, it is characteristic of all major institutions of modern society, especially the economic market and large business corporations. The ambivalence is not a matter of state or private. Private hospitals and private pension plans also constrain individual lives.

DEPENDENCY. The notion that welfare programs, and social assistance in particular, make people "dependent" looms large in the U.S. debate on social policy and, since the 1990s, also in Europe, especially in Blairite Britain. The welfare state is deemed to create the problems it seeks to solve. Aid by state bureaucracies is seen as an inroad into the basic values of personal autonomy, self-direction, and individualism so deeply rooted in the Anglo-Saxon culture. The idea is that welfare programs not only stifle individual initiatives but positively destroy and undermine morality and the capacity for self-help.

Longitudinal studies of welfare careers both in the United States and Europe could not confirm these assertions (Bane & Ellwood, 1994; Leisering & Leibfried, 1999, ch. 6). Most new applicants for welfare leave after a limited period of time. Most of those who remain have a severe condition of a long-term nature. A comparison of welfare careers in the USA and Germany on the basis of panel data revealed that more generous benefits (in Germany), contrary to expectation, do not result in longer periods of receipt. Qualitative biographical research has further expanded these findings (for both see Leisering & Leibfried, 1999, chs. 5 and 6). Many welfare recipients, especially single mothers and divorced women, use welfare as a resource to reorient themselves in situations of personal crisis. These recipients often pursue wider biographical goals beyond welfare. Comparing employment careers in the USA and Germany on the basis of panel data, Gangl (2003) could show that the more generous German unemployment benefit system prolongs the duration of unemployment but, at the same time, raises post-unemployment job quality. The benefit system enables workers to maintain previously accumulated human capital through reemployment in jobs that are equivalent to earlier jobs with regard to earnings, occupation, and job duration. In this way the welfare state stabilizes employment careers.

Depending on the institutional design, welfare programs may weaken the capacity for self-help. But again, this is not peculiar to the welfare state. Markets and mass consumerism can equally erode self-control. Janowitz (1976, p. 108) generally spoke of a diffusion and "democratization" of hedonism and deviant behavior in the affluent society. He asserted that the welfare state may foster these changes in life styles but only as part of wider tendencies of our civilization. Dismantling the welfare state would not do away with the problem. Janowitz rather proposed institutional reforms to reduce the negative impacts of the welfare state.

AGE DIVISIVENESS. The life course is based on age grading. "Chronologization" (Kohli, 1986) is an element of the institutionalization of the life course. Life phases and age groups are defined in the process. Among North American scholars there is a tendency to criticize the current patterning of the life course as an "age-constrained life course" (Riley & Riley, 1994; Settersten, 1999, pp. 42–64). Social policy contributes to these constraints by a rigid partitioning of the life course (structuration). Entitlements and measures are often differentiated by life phase so that social policy largely turns into age-group policy. Age-group policy can be challenged on two accounts. First, it implies a social construction of identities that may give rise to age divisiveness and ageism. Second, age is seen as increasingly socially irrelevant. Age is not adequate as an indicator of need or as basis of entitlement. In the debate about "age or need?" (Neugarten, 1982) at least combinations of age with other criteria are considered. Critics of the age-constrained life course, above all Riley and Riley (1994), aim "to modify existing 'age-differentiated' structures and instead build 'age-integrated' structures, in which opportunities for roles and activities in education, work, and leisure are open to all people, regardless of age" (Settersten, 1999, p. 254). Key issues include work in old age and education and leisure in midlife.

The notion of an age-integrated life course raises normative questions. Answers vary between countries. Mandatory retirement is a case in point. In contrast to the United States, it is not unconstitutional in Germany. The majority of German workers is subject to mandatory retirement through collective labor agreements between employers and the trade unions.

What to American observers may appear as an undue infringement of basic rights, appears in a different light in the strong state tradition in Continental Europe. In this view giving up mandatory retirement would imply an undesirable depoliticization of the life course. The structure of age and life course would disappear from the political agenda. In a society that views the basic structure of the life course as a matter of collective deliberation and decision, this narrowing of the agenda would not be acceptable. Using T. H. Marshall's terminology of rights we could say that Americans view retirement as a matter of civil rights while Europeans view it as a matter of social and political rights.

But even concepts of a more age-integrated life course would not necessarily imply a reduction of the welfare state. To the contrary, a less structured life course is prone to produce new insecurities that may induce demands for new institutional frames such as income support, health services, and protective rights (cf. Settersten, 1999, pp. 53, 60). Moreover, extending education and leisure in midlife means to expand rather than curtail conventional policies.

PROSPECTS: DEPOLITICIZING THE
LIFE COURSE?

Life course policy has a history (for the following see the first tentative sketch by Mayer, 2001, pp. 92–97). The *traditional* life course (till 1900) was characterized by unstable and unpredictable life patterns and the absence of life course policy. In most countries "social policy" was not more than poor relief. The *industrial* life course (*c.* 1900–1955) was still almost exclusively shaped by family and work. The occurrence of poverty followed the life cycle, as depicted by Rowntree at the turn of the century. Welfare services beyond social assistance were little developed in many countries. The *"Fordist"*/welfare state life course (*c.* 1955–1973) saw the full emergence of the welfare state as part of the hybrid society called "democratic welfare capitalism" by T. H. Marshall. Fordism is characterized by a stable and standardized life course, based on the male breadwinner and the nuclear family, lifelong full employment, and income progression (Myles, 1990). The name "Fordist" stems from the structure of industrial employment in the auto sector. The *"Post-Fordist"* or post-industrial life course (since 1973) implies a destandardization with increasing discontinuities in family and working lives. This goes along with a restructuring of the welfare state, and new social problems like mass unemployment and social exclusion. The European equivalent to Post-Fordism is the debate on the "erosion of the normal biography", the rise of discontinuous biographies and "individualization" (Beck, 1992 [German 1986]; Shanahan, 2000; see also the U.S. debate on "disorderly lives").

What future for the life course and for life course policy? Are we facing a *deinstitutionalization* of the life course (Han & Moen, 1999; Kohli, 1986; Settersten, 1999, 254) and a concomitant demise of life course policy? Is the life course empirically verging towards deinstitutionalization or is this a vision propagated and propelled by vested interests, to support a more flexible work life in an age of globalization? This is an open debate. It leads back to the question about the role institutions should play in the formation of the life course. Life courses are less standardized than earlier (Shanahan, 2000). But destandardization is not the same as deinstitutionalization. Standardization refers to "the degree to which ... life patterns exhibit regularity, especially with regard to the timing of major life experiences", while institutionalization refers to the structuration of lives by social institutions and the state and its policies (Settersten, 1999, 253 f.). Destandardization, then, need not lead to deinstitutionalization.

To the contrary, destandardization may induce demands for novel institutionalization. Destandardized and more flexible life courses entail insecurities and vulnerabilities that create a demand for institutional support (see already Hirschhorn, 1977). Regarding the vision of an age-integrated life course, we have argued in the previous section that it does not imply the outright rejection of social policy but rather the creation of new policies. Social policy may strengthen the capacity of individuals to cope with the exigencies of a more flexible life. One could talk of the institutionalization of flexibility, pointing at re- rather than deinstitutionalization. This could be a new stage of the institutionalization of individualism. Examples include more differentiated routes to retirement. An empirical analysis of the increasing variability of retirement paths and its causes in the United States is given by Han & Moen (1999) and Moen (this volume). We can also expect that with the proliferation of a more flexible life course, the systems of risk management will become more important in enabling smooth transitions in life. By contrast, benefit systems like old-age pensions that are in effect for longer periods of life might be subject to downsizing and restructuring to allow for greater flexibility.

In political practice such reinstitutionalization is already underway. One focus is the concept of *activation* in the field of labor market policy, social assistance, and other areas like health promotion in the USA and all over West Europe. This indicates a shift from the old-style redistributive welfare state, that has dominated in some countries, to social services and investment in human capital designed to enable (activate) people to help themselves. New terms like "flexicurity"—combining security of social protection and flexibility in the labor market—and "employability" have entered the social policy debate. The concept of activation has partially been informed by longitudinal, life-course oriented studies. A second focus is a shift towards the *"enabling state"* (Gilbert & Gilbert, 1989)—a state that enables non-state agencies to provide services previously provided by the state itself. Again, this does not imply a dismantling of the welfare state per se but goes along with new regulatory tasks, bureaucracies, and powers for the state. Analyses of the outcomes of the current restructuring of the welfare state find security, the key aim of social policy, weakened (Bonoli, George, & Taylor-Gooby, 2000). Still there is a far-reaching consensus in the recent research literature that we are facing not the demise but rather "new politics of the welfare state" (Pierson, 2001). A blueprint of a "new welfare architecture for Europe", commissioned by the Belgian Presidency of the European Union (Esping-Andersen, 2002), is explicitly organized around the life course as reference for social policy.

To the extent that the life course would or should be deinstitutionalized and the welfare state retrenched, the life course would be *depoliticized*. Welfare state regulations and provisions differ from other (formal and informal) types of provision on two accounts: they are grounded in individual social rights (entitlements) to withstand the structural forces of markets and families; and they are the outcome of political deliberations about a good life and constantly require legitimization in the political process. Deinstitutionalization—if mainly defined as retrenchment rather than restructuring—would do away with both. The life course would become more a matter of civil rights and less of social and political rights. The balance between the three types of rights—and hence between the components of "democratic welfare capitalism"—would shift. This leads back to differences of state traditions between countries. If the citizens of a country want government to have only a moderate influence on their welfare, then a low degree of politicization seems adequate. The shape of the life course—how fluid it should be, which risks and opportunities it should provide, and for whom—is then considered to be beyond the scope of politics.

However, the boundaries of government intervention are not fixed but continually contested. Public concern for individual lives, voiced, for example, in local communities at times of distress and taken up by local associations and non-profit organizations, can feed into government action in various ways. Moreover, even in countries with less government intervention in individual lives, there is a wide range of what we called "tacit" and "negative" life course policies (see section three). Knowingly not interfering may also be an intentional life course policy. Therefore, life course policy keeps cropping up as a matter of political controversy. The life course remains a political issue.

ACKNOWLEDGMENTS: I thank the editors for helpful comments and encouragement. I also thank Walter Heinz and my former colleagues from the Special Research Program of the National Science Foundation on the life course at Bremen University, Germany, from which this chapter flows, for support and cooperation over many years.

REFERENCES

Allmendinger, J., Brückner, H., & Brückner, E. (1993). The production of gender disparities over the life course and their effects in old age—results from the West German Life History Study. In A. B. Atkinson & M. Rein (Eds.), *Age, work and social security* (pp. 188–223). New York: St Martins Press.

Allmendinger, J., & Hinz, T. (1998). Occupational careers under different welfare regimes: West Germany, Great Britain and Sweden. In L. Leisering & R. Walker (Eds.), *The dynamics of modern society. Poverty, policy and welfare* (pp. 63–84). Bristol: The Policy Press.

Bane, M. J., & Ellwood, D. T. (1994). *Welfare realities: From rhetoric to reform*. Cambridge, Mass.: Harvard University Press.

Beck, U. (1992). *Risk society. Towards a new modernity*. London/Newbury Park/ New Delhi: Sage Publications (German 1986).

Bird, K. (2001). Parental leave in Germany—An institution with two faces? In L. Leisering, R. Müller, & K. F. Schumann (Eds.), *Institutionen und Lebensläufe im Wandel* (pp. 55–87). Weinheim/München: Juventa.

Blank, R. M. (2002). Evaluating welfare reform in the United States. *Journal of Economic Literature, 40*, 1105–1166.

Bonoli, G., George, V., & Taylor-Gooby, P. (Eds.). (2000). *European welfare futures. Towards a theory of retrenchment*. Cambridge: Polity Press.

Brim, O. G., Jr., & Phillips, D. A. (1988). The life-span intervention cube. In E. M. Hetherington, R. M. Lerner, & M. Perlmutter (Eds.), *Child development in life-span perspective* (pp. 277–299). Hillsdale, New Jersey/Hove/ London: Lawrence Erlbaum Associates.

Dyson, K. (1980). *The state tradition in Western Europe*. Oxford: Robertson.

Elder, G. H., Jr. (1991). Lives and social change. In W. R. Heinz (Ed.), *Theoretical advances in life course research* (pp. 58–86). Weinheim: Deutscher Studien Verlag.

Elder, G. H., Jr. (1999). *Children of the Great Depression. Social change in life experience*. 25th Anniversary Edition. Boulder, Col./Oxford: Westview Press.

Esping-Andersen, G. (1990). *The three worlds of welfare capitalism*. Princeton, NJ: Princeton University Press.

Esping-Andersen, G., with Gallie, D., Hemerijck, A., & Myles, J. (2002). *Why we need a new welfare state*. Oxford: Oxford University Press.

Falkingham, J., & Hills, J. (Eds.) 1995. *The dynamic of welfare. The welfare state and the life cycle*. New York/London/Toronto: Harvester Wheatsheaf.

Gangl, M. (2003). *Unemployment dynamics in the United States and West Germany: Economic restructuring, institutions, and labor market processes*. Heidelberg, New York: Springer/Physica.

George, L. K. (1993). Sociological perspectives on life transitions. *Annual Review of Sociology, 19*, 353–373.

Giddens, A. (1991). *Modernity and self-identity*. Oxford: Polity Press.

Gilbert, N., & Gilbert, B. (1989). *The enabling state. Modern welfare capitalism in America*. New York/Oxford: Oxford University Press.

Girvetz, H. (1968). Welfare state. *International Encyclopedia of the Social Sciences, 16*, 512–521.

Glennerster, H. (1995). The life cycle: Public or private concern? In J. Falkingham & J. Hills (Eds.), *The dynamic of welfare. The welfare state and the life cycle* (pp. 6–20). New York/London/Toronto: Harvester Wheatsheaf.

Gough, I., Bradshaw, J., Ditch, J., Eardley, T., & Whiteford, P. (1997). Social assistance in OECD countries. *Journal of European Social Policy, 7*, 17–43.

Han, S.-K., & Moen, P. (1999). Clocking out: Temporal patterning of retirement. *American Journal of Sociology, 105*, 191–236.

Heidenheimer, A. J. (1981). Education and social security entitlements in Europe and America. In P. Flora & A. J. Heidenheimer (Eds.), *The development of welfare states in Europe and America* (pp. 269–306). New Brunswick, NJ: Transaction Books.

Heinz, W. R. (Ed.) (1991). *Theoretical advances in life course research*. Weinheim: Deutscher Studien Verlag.

Heinz, W. R., & Krüger, H. (2001). Life course: Innovations and challenges for social research. *Current Sociology, 49*, 29–45.

Henly, J. R., & Lyons, S. (2000). The negotiation of child care and employment demands among low-income parents. *Journal of Social Issues, 56*, 683–706.

Hirschhorn, L. (1977). Social policy and the life cycle: A developmental perspective. *Social Service Review, 51*, 434–450.

Janowitz, M. (1976). *Social control of the welfare state*. New York: Elsevier.

Kaufmann, F.-X. (2002). *Sozialpolitik und Sozialstaat. Soziologische Analysen*. Opladen: Leske + Budrich.

Korpi, W., & Palme, J. (2000). The paradox of redistribution and strategies of equality: Welfare state institutions, inequality, and poverty in Western countries. *American Sociological Review, 63*, 661–687.

Kohli, M. (1986). The world we forgot: An historical review of the life course. In V. W. Marshall (Ed.), *Later life: The social psychology of aging* (pp. 271–303). Beverly Hills: Sage.

Kohli, M. (1987). Retirement and the moral economy: An historical interpretation of the German case. *Journal of Aging Studies, 1*, 125–144.

Leisering, L., & Leibfried, S. (1999). *Time and poverty in Western welfare states. United Germany in perspective* (pb ed. 2001; German 1995). Cambridge, New York: Cambridge University Press.

Leisering, L., & Walker, R. (1998). The dynamics of modernity. In L. Leisering & R. Walker (Eds.), *The dynamics of modern society. Poverty, policy and welfare* (pp. 3–16). Bristol: Policy Press.

Levy, R. (1977). *Der Lebenslauf als Statusbiographie. Die weibliche Normalbiographie in makrosoziologischer Perspektive*. Stuttgart: Enke.

Levy, R. (1996). Toward a theory of life course institutionalization. In A. Weymann & W. R. Heinz (Eds.), *Society and biography. Interrelations between social structure, institutions and the life course* (pp. 83–108). Weinheim: Deutscher Studien Verlag.

Luckenbill, D. F., & Best, J. (1981). Careers in deviance and respectability: The analogy's limitations. *Social Problems, 29*, 197–206.

Marshall, T. H. (1964). Citizenship and social class. In T.H. Marshall, *Class, citizenship, and social development* (pp. 71–134). Chicago/London: University of Chicago Press.

Marshall, T. H. (1981). Value problems of welfare-capitalism (with Afterthought—The 'hyphenated society'). In T. H. Marshall, *The right to welfare and other essays* (pp. 104–136). London: Heinemann Educational Books.

Marshall, V. W., & Mueller, M. M. (2003). Life course concepts in North America. In W. R. Heinz & V. W. Marshall (Eds.), *The life course: Social dynamic of transitions, institutions and interrelations*. New York: Aldyne/de Gruyter.

Mayer, K. U. (1991). Life courses in the welfare state. In W. R. Heinz (Ed.), *Theoretical advances in life course research* (pp. 171–186). Weinheim: Deutscher Studien-Verlag.

Mayer, K. U. (1997). Notes on a comparative political economy of life courses. *Comparative Social Research, 16*, 203–226.

Mayer, K. U. (2000). Promises fulfilled? A review of 20 years of life course research. *European Journal of Sociology, 41*, 259–283.

Mayer, K. U. (2001). The paradox of global social change and national path dependencies: Life course patterns in advanced societies. In A. Woodward & M. Kohli (Eds.), *Inclusions and exclusions in European societies* (pp. 89–110). New York: Routledge.

Mayer, K. U., & Müller, W. (1986). The state and the structure of the life course. In A. B. Sørensen, F. E. Weinert, & L. R. Sherrod (Eds.), *Human development: Interdisciplinary perspectives* (pp. 217–245). Hillsdale, NJ/London: Erlbaum.

Mayer, K. U., & Schöpflin, U. (1989). The state and the life course. *Annual Review of Sociology, 15*, 187–209.

Meyer, J. W. (1986). The self and the life course: Institutionalization and its effects. In A. B. Sorensen, F. E. Weinert, & L. R. Sherrod (Eds.), *Human development and the life course: Multidisciplinary perspectives* (pp. 199–216). Hillsdale, NJ/London: Erlbaum.

Meyer, J. W. (1988). Levels of analysis: The life course as a cultural construction. In M. W. Riley (Ed.), *Social change and the life course, volume 1: Social structures & human lives* (pp. 49–62). Newbury Park/Beverly Hills/London/New Delhi: Sage.

Myles, J. (1990). States, labor markets and life cycles. In R. Friedland & A. F. Robertson (Eds.), *Beyond the marketplace: Rethinking economy and society* (pp. 271–300). New York: de Gruyter.

Myles, J., & Quadagno, J. (1997). Recent trends in public pension reform: A comparative view. In K. G. Banting & R. Boadway (Eds.), *Reform of retirement income policy: International and Canadian perspectives* (pp. 247–271). Ontario: Queen's University, Kingston.

Neugarten, B. L. (Ed.) (1982). *Age or need? Public policies for older people*. Beverly Hills/London/New Delhi: Sage.

Offe, C. (1984). *Contradictions of the welfare state*. London and others: Hutchinson.

O'Rand, A. M. (1995). The cumulative stratification of the life course. In R. H. Binstock, J. H. Schulz, L. George, V. W. Marshall, & G. C. Myers (Eds.), *Handbook of Aging and the Social Sciences* (4th ed., pp. 188–207). San Diego: Harcourt Brace & Company.

Parsons, T., & Platt, G. M. (1974). *The American university*. Cambridge, MA: Harvard University Press.

Pierson, P. (Ed.). (2001). *The new politics of the welfare state*. Oxford/New York: Oxford University Press.

Riley, M. W., & Riley, J. W., Jr. (1994). Structural lag: Past and future. In M. W. Riley, R. L. Kahn, & A. Foner (Eds.), *Age and structural lag: Society's failure to provide meaningful opportunities in work, family, and leisure* (pp. 15–36). New York: John Wiley & Sons.

Schmähl, W. (2000). Pay-as-you-go versus capital funding: Towards a more balanced view in pension policy. In G. Hughes & J. Stewart (Eds.), *Pensions in the European Union: Adapting to economic and social change* (pp. 195–207). Boston and others: Kluwer Academic Publishers.

Schmidt, M. G. (2001). The democratic welfare state. In H. F. Zacher (Ed.), *Pontificae Academiae Scientiarum Socialium Acta 6. Democracy. Reality and responsibility. The proceedings of the sixth plenary session of the Pontifical Academy of Social Sciences 23–26 February 2000* (pp. 257–276). Vatican City.

Settersten, R. A., Jr. (1999). *Lives in time and place: The problems and promises of developmental science*. Amityville/New York: Baywood Publishing Company.

Shanahan, M. J. (2000). Pathways to adulthood in changing societies: Variability and mechanisms in life course perspective. *Annual Review of Sociology, 26*, 667–692.

Swaan, A. de (1988). *In care of the state. Health care, education and welfare in Europe and the USA in the modern era*. Oxford/New York: Oxford University Press.

Thomas, G. M., Meyer, J. W., Ramirez, F. O., & Boli, J. (1987). *Institutional structure—Constituting state, society, and the individual*. Newbury Park and others: Sage.

Zhou, X., & Hou, L. (1999). Children of the Cultural Revolution: The state and the life course in the People's Republic of China. *American Sociological Review, 64*, 12–36.

B. Transitions

CHAPTER 11

The First-Grade Transition in Life Course Perspective

Doris R. Entwisle
Karl L. Alexander
Linda Steffel Olson

A life course perspective prompts a decided shift in how sociologists have traditionally approached issues of schooling and educational attainment. The core assumption of life course theory—that developmental processes and outcomes are shaped by the life trajectories children follow—has increasingly focused attention on cultural differences and socioeconomic variation in school outcomes and redirected attention to the *process* of schooling. Children, like adults, are socially organized in ways that have strong implications for their life experiences, including those in school. A life course perspective makes it natural to think about life transitions as turning points, and about the social basis of change and continuity through the successive phases of life (see McLeod and Almazan, this volume).

The beginning school transition is a timed life event critically important for children's future development because it marks the start of a life trajectory that encompasses both schooling and work careers. For example, how does delaying the first-grade transition (academic red shirting) affect children's subsequent progress in school? Children who are older when they start school will have higher test scores than their younger classmates and probably will be taller and heavier too. But the consequences of redshirting are not limited to what happens in first grade—they echo down through the years. These children on average will go through puberty earlier than their classmates. Throughout their school careers redshirting will change children's social

Doris R. Entwisle, Karl L. Alexander, and Linda Steffel Olson • Department of Sociology, Johns Hopkins University, Baltimore, Maryland 21218-2685.

Handbook of the Life Course, edited by Jeylan T. Mortimer and Michael J Shanahan. Kluwer Academic/Plenum Publishers, New York, 2003.

contexts in ways that could affect their academic growth. For example, teachers' and parents' expectations are often based on children's physical size, with taller children expected to be more competent (Brackbill & Nevill, 1981). Parents and teachers take actions in line with the perceived competence of children, such as providing the taller or bigger ones with more social responsibility than they would otherwise. By one critical action, delaying school entry, the child's social context is shifted significantly not only at that point but from that time forward.

This chapter begins by emphasizing the social embeddedness of the first-grade transition, and then summarizes evidence about the low achievement levels and difficulties of adjustment that disadvantaged children experience. It underscores the greater importance of time spent in school compared to chronological age in predicting children's progress over the transition. Connections between children's success in first grade and long-term outcomes like dropout and the likelihood of adult employment are emphasized. The chapter concludes with some policy suggestions about preschools and summer school for disadvantaged children. Throughout, the importance of trajectories and the overlap of developmental contexts (families, neighborhoods, and schools) are central themes.

We start by describing particulars of children's first grade experience.

THE SOCIAL EMBEDDEDNESS OF THE
FIRST-GRADE TRANSITION

The first-grade transition is profoundly social in nature. It signals the move from being a "home child" to being a "school child." This move is a big change, for one reason, because preschools and kindergartens are discretionary with caregivers directly answerable to parents. At the end of the preschool day parents often get a tally of the child's meals, bumps, naps, and problems. By contrast, first grade is not under parents' control in that way. Grade school is legally compulsory, the atmosphere is formal, and parents are not expected to make surprise visits. Teachers have authority over the child during the school day and jealously guard their prerogatives. Direct communications between teachers and parents are relatively infrequent and mostly in written form.

The first-grade transition is an especially bumpy ride for "at risk" children because the differences between home and school, for those brought up outside the middle-class mainstream, are dramatic. The conventions of the school—its achievement orientation, its expectation that children will stay on task and work independently, its tight time schedule, its use of network English, its insistence on punctuality, and its frequent evaluation of children—all can be daunting. Children are evaluated *with respect to their classmates* rather than with respect to their own prior standing as was true before they began first grade. Before they start formal schooling, children are evaluated mainly with respect to their own past performance— as bigger this year than last, for example. Failure thus becomes a real possibility in first grade. Moreover, in many classrooms where teachers and children do not share the same social or ethnic background, even classroom language can be ambiguous. When the teacher uses mitigating forms such as "I'd like you to do ..." she means "DO IT," but this meaning may not be inferred by a student whose sociolinguistic background differs from that of the teacher.

The Student Role

The formal student role that children assume when they start first grade is one that youth occupy for many years. Any doubt that children's earliest performance in this role matters is fast fading. From the Beginning School Study (BSS) in Baltimore,* which has followed nearly 800 children from age 6 (1982) to the present, we know that educational attainment and even job status in young adulthood can be predicted partly on the basis of first grade performance. BSS children who participated more often in class during first grade were more likely to go on to post-secondary education, even with family SES, standardized test scores, and many other factors controlled (Entwisle, Alexander, & Olson, in preparation). Even first-grade work habits mattered, because good work habits in first grade boosted the odds of employment in young adulthood, again after taking account of other key factors listed above.

In light of the foregoing, it is worrisome that elementary schools are organized to parallel so closely the social fault lines in the larger society. At the time of the first-grade transition, which coincides with a rapid spurt in cognitive growth, children tend to be surrounded by others who are more like themselves than the rest of society. The "common school" is in fact socially patterned. In relatively affluent neighborhoods, children starting school have higher test scores than children starting school in less affluent neighborhoods (Entwisle, Alexander, & Olson, 1997). The Baltimore study shows that children's marks, standardized test scores, and reading group assignments in first grade shadowed their social addresses (Entwisle et al., 1997; Entwisle & Alexander, 1993).

Marks

To be more precise, the BSS, which traced the school experience of a representative group of 6-year-old Baltimore children starting in 1982, found that in high-SES schools, children's first reading marks were a little above a C (2.15) (see Table 11-1). In low-SES schools, children's first reading marks averaged 1.64 (below a C) and in these schools almost no one received a mark higher than a C. In fact, in a school where 88% of students were on subsidy, all BSS students in that school received a failing mark in the first quarter of first grade. Such wide disparity in the marks first graders received has to be weighed in light of the fact that the children in the low-SES schools made gains on standardized tests in reading and math over first grade (September to June) just as large as the gains made by children in the high-SES schools (see Table 11-2). (See Entwisle and Alexander, 1992, 1994; Entwisle, Alexander, and Olson, 2000, 2001.) For example, during the school year (winter) students in the low-SES schools averaged a 41.3 point gain in reading CAT scores over the first 5 years of school, compared with a 37.9 point average gain for the students in the high-SES schools. A similar pattern exists in math CAT scores (see bottom, Table 11-2). This equivalence in achievement gains, however, was not reflected in the reading and math marks students received. Simply put, children were marked in terms of where they started school, not in terms of how much they gained over the school year (see Figure 11-1 and Table 11-2).

*This research is a prospective longitudinal study of children's academic and social development beginning in first grade and continuing through high school graduation and up to age 22/23. Data collection began in 1982 and is ongoing. In 1982 a two-stage random sample of youngsters beginning first grade in the Baltimore City Public Schools was selected for study. First, a sample of 20 schools, stratified by racial mix (6 predominantly African American, 6 White, 8 integrated) and by socioeconomic status (14 inner city or working class and 6 middle class) was selected. Second, within each school students were randomly sampled from every first-grade classroom by using kindergarten lists from the previous spring supplemented by class rosters after school began in the fall. Parents' permission was obtained for 97% of the children so chosen, resulting in a final sample of 790 youngsters beginning first grade for the first time in 1982. See Entwisle, Alexander, and Olson (1997) *Children, schools, and inequality*, for an overall presentation of the Beginning School Study (BSS) and for more information on the study design and procedures.

TABLE 11-1. **Ratings of Children's First-Grade Performance by Socioeconomic Status (SES) Level of School (Baltimore Beginning School Study)**

| | SES level of school, fall 1982 (% Meal subsidy)[a] | | | | |
| | Low SES[c] | | | High SES[c] | |
	Mean	SD	t-test	Mean	SD
Reading mark, Qtr 1	1.64	0.58	*	2.15	0.74
Reading mark, Qtr 4	1.94	0.73	*	2.65	0.95
Math mark, Qtr 1	1.99	0.75	*	2.52	0.85
Math mark, Qtr 4	2.26	0.86	*	2.88	0.90
Proportion retained, Year 1	0.23	0.42	*	0.12	0.31
Reading instruction level, Qtr 1[b]	1.93	0.51	*	2.21	0.80
Reading instruction level, Qtr 4[b]	3.69	1.12	*	4.29	0.96

[a] Percent of children on meal subsidy in each school used to define SES level of school. The 20 schools are divided into "low SES" (10 schools with highest meal subsidy rate) and "high SES" (10 schools with lowest meal subsidy rate).
[b] 1 = readiness; 2 = preprimer; 3 = primer; 4 = level 1; 5 = level 2; 6 = level 3.
[c] For low-SES schools, sample sizes range from 355–405; for high-SES schools, sample sizes range from 332–349.

TABLE 11-2. **Seasonal Test Score Gains in Reading and Math for Years 1 through 5 by Average Meal Subsidy of School[a] (Baltimore Beginning School Study)**

| | Winter gains | | | Summer gains | | |
	Low-SES Schools (n = 10)	t-test	High-SES Schools (n = 10)	Low-SES Schools (n = 10)	t-test	High-SES Schools (n = 10)
Reading						
Year 1	59.9		61.7	−7.3	*	12.0
Year 2	50.6	*	38.8	−5.5	*	8.7
Year 3	33.8		31.3	−0.5	*	11.4
Year 4	36.5		32.2	4.4		5.4
Year 5	25.5		25.7	0.4		−1.5
Average	41.3		37.9	−1.7		7.2
Math						
Year 1	50.4		47.1	−7.7	*	5.3
Year 2	43.6		41.6	−6.1	*	3.1
Year 3	35.2		36.9	1.0		−0.5
Year 4	32.0		36.3	5.6		4.0
Year 5	25.0		29.4	−0.4		3.0
Average	37.2		38.3	−1.5		3.0

*p 0.05.
[a] Percent of children on meal subsidy defines SES level of school.

Marks are an especially important kind of feedback because report cards are public and come out frequently. Classmates as well as family often see them. In Baltimore, even though standards and curricula were uniform throughout the school system, marks reflected minority group membership. Allowing for standardized test scores and family background, which

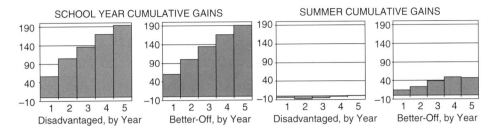

FIGURE 11-1. **Cumulative gains during the school year and summer.**
*Cumulative gains on California Achievement Test in reading over elementary school years and summers. Sample consists of Baltimore Public School students who entered first grade in 1982. Test "scale scores" are California Achievement Test Scores calibrated to measure growth over a student's 12-year school career.
Source: Doris Entwisle, Karl Alexander, and Linda Olson, *Children, Schools, and Inequality*, Table 3-1.

were measured *before the first marking period*, we find that African-American children got lower first-grade marks than whites did in both reading and math. The race difference in marks increased over the first-grade year from about one third of a standard deviation to about half a standard deviation (Entwisle & Alexander, 1988). These mark disparities associated with race emerged even though race differences in these children's scores on standardized tests at the beginning of first grade were small or negligible. (Such parity in beginning test scores is in agreement with other reports. See Ginsburg & Russell, 1981 and Tizard, Blatchford, Burke, Farquhar, & Plewis, 1988.) Social patterning in ratings of children's early academic performance is not surprising, but to have such comparisons for a randomly selected group of children right at the start of school is rare. The "invisible hand" of racial discrimination begins to sort individuals very early in life.

Test Scores

In beginning test scores, differences by race in the BSS sample, as just noted, are negligible but differences across SES levels are considerable—from a third to almost a full standard deviation depending on the specific comparison (Entwisle & Alexander, 1990). Preschool and kindergarten attendance were both strong predictors of higher test scores at the beginning of first grade. Just over half of BSS children (51.4%) attended some kind of out-of-home care prior to kindergarten. Those who did attend had significantly higher standardized test scores when they started first grade (with race, sex, and parents' educational attainment controlled, Table 11-3). For example, students with pre-kindergarten experience began first grade with CAT scores more than 5 points higher than those without pre-kindergarten.

BSS children who had *more* kindergarten (full day as compared to half day sessions) also had higher test scores (8 points verbal, 5 points math) when they started first grade, with race, sex, parents' educational attainment, and pre-kindergarten experience controlled, and these separate effects of pre-kindergarten and kindergarten are about equal in size (see Table 11-3). Both kinds of preschool also predicted lower absence rates over first grade and the children with fewer absences gained more on standardized tests of reading over first grade (see Entwisle, Alexander, Pallas, & Cadigan, 1987), so preschool and kindergarten attendance as well as out-of-school learning opportunities contribute to these SES differences in first-grade performance (Entwisle & Alexander, 1988). National data likewise show that fewer preschoolers

TABLE 11-3. The Influence of Preschool and Kindergarten on First-Grade Performance

Independent variables	Fall California Achievement Test		Absence, grade 1
	Verbal	Math	
Sex (1=Female)	2.276 (0.037)	−1.279 (−0.025)	1.620+ (0.069)
Race (1=African American)	−3.073 (−0.049)	−7.380* (−0.144)	0.562 (0.024)
Parent's educ. attain.	3.379* (0.279)	2.903* (0.291)	−0.464* (−0.102)
Prekindergarten	5.732* (0.093)	5.126* (0.101)	−1.787* (−0.077)
Amount of kindergarten	7.751* (0.137)	5.301* (0.114)	−2.800* (−0.131)

Standardized coefficients are in parentheses next to metric coefficients.
*p 0.05.
+p 0.10.

in families below the poverty line recognize all the letters of the alphabet compared to those in families above the poverty line (10% vs. 28%) (Nord, Lennon, Liu, & Chandin, 1999).

Seasonal Trends

Children in the Baltimore panel who were economically disadvantaged thus started school with initial achievement scores below those of classmates whose families were better off and got lower marks in first grade, but over that first school year (when school was in session from September to June) *those who were of relatively low SES gained just as much on standardized achievement tests as did those of higher SES* (see Entwisle et al., 1997). Still, and despite this parity in achievement gains when schools were in session, over the summer after first grade when they were *out of school*, children's gains were decidedly unequal. In summer when school closed, differences in achievement associated with family economic level were striking (see Figure 11-1 and right half of Table 11-2). Then the children from more advantaged homes moved smartly ahead while those from poorer homes did not gain or even regressed a little. These differences are particularly striking in the first 3 years of school. For example, in the summer after first grade, students in the low-SES schools *lost* an average seven points in their reading CAT score while students in high-SES schools gained 12 points.

The seasonal trends in children's reading and math scores over the first 5 years of school show that during winters, when children attended school, SES background made little or no difference in achievement gains. On average richer and poorer children gained the same amounts. In summer, however, children's SES backgrounds made a considerable difference—the more advantaged continued to gain but the less advantaged did not. These disparities in summer gains were cumulative—over the 5 summers low-SES students lost 8.5 points while the higher-SES groups gained 36 points, a total disparity of 44 points. Furthermore, the psychological capital of high-SES parents potentiated effects of SES (see Entwisle, Alexander, & Olson, 2001). As a consequence, when winter gains and summer gains are added together, children's gains on standardized tests over elementary school vary directly with their families' economic resources (see Entwisle et al., 1997). Those whose families had more resources started school with somewhat higher test scores, so relatively small differences among children of various SES levels existed from the start. Then, the longer children were in school, the wider the gap, because children progressed at different rates in summers when school was closed. Large seasonal differences in test score gains like those seen for Baltimore first-graders are found in other localities as well (Murnane, 1975 in New Haven and Heyns, 1978 in Atlanta).

Most research on schooling focuses on children at or above third grade (by then most children have rudimentary reading skills), even though by then the rapid spurt in children's cognitive growth between ages 4 and 8 has passed. Actually, the number of points children gain on standardized tests diminishes each year (Entwisle & Alexander, 1996; Schneider, 1980), so effects of social inequality on development appear largest in the primary grades. The deceleration in children's cognitive growth over middle childhood is not a new phenomenon (see 1916 data on speed of silent reading, or the 1944 Stanford Achievement Test scores in Stephens [1956]), but its implications for understanding the transition into elementary school have been overlooked. As one obvious corollary, the pay-offs for interventions in the earliest grades are likely to be greater than pay-offs from interventions in later years (Entwisle et al., 2000). As another corollary, even though yearly gains on test scores diminish over middle childhood, the variance across test scores inevitably grows larger with time. The power of first-grade scores to predict children's rankings relative to their peers therefore gets better and better the further they go in school.

So far, the emphasis has been on cognitive development. The next section takes up socioemotional issues, including teacher and parent influences.

SCHOOL ADJUSTMENT: THE STUDENT–SCHOOL FIT

Standardized achievement represents only one strand of development over the first-grade transition. Early "school adjustment" or socioemotional well-being is another strand. Poor children's challenges in first grade are not limited to academics and, as with test scores, socioeconomic status rather than race/ethnicity is the main divide (Entwisle et al., 1997). Compared to better-off children, lower-SES children in the Baltimore study were much more often identified in kindergarten as being at risk for serious academic problems, were absent more often in first grade, and received lower ratings on interest/participation and attention span/restlessness from first grade teachers.

In one school where only 11% of children were on meal subsidy, teachers rated pupils about one SD higher in interest/participation than did teachers in a school where 90% of children were on subsidy (see Entwisle et al., 1997). The rank-order correlation between a school's meal subsidy level and teachers' average interest/participation rating of their first-grade students is 0.71. Furthermore, in schools where a majority of children were on subsidy, some children were literally rated "off the scale" (i.e., they were rated at 3 SDs less than their school's mean on interest and participation). No student was rated off the scale in the more affluent schools.

SES patterns also characterize teachers' expectations. At the end of first grade, when teachers predicted their students' performance in second grade, teachers in the 10 high-SES schools expected their pupils to get more As and Bs than Cs (or below) in reading during the next year, whereas in the 10 low-SES schools teachers expected almost all children to get Cs or below.

But "adjustment" is a two-way street. Teachers' own social origins exercise a strong influence on how they react to the status attributes of their students. Other things equal, low-status and minority pupils experience their greatest difficulties in the classrooms of high-status teachers. Their teachers evaluate them as less mature and hold lower expectations for them, and more so than low-status teachers do. Not surprisingly, such children's gains on standardized tests and marks in first grade apparently are depressed by these indicators of pupil–teacher social distance and teacher disaffection (Alexander, Entwisle, & Thompson, 1987). High-status teachers experienced special difficulty with minority students irrespective of whether they themselves were African American or White. Social distance between teachers and first-grade students depends on teachers as well as students, and because it affects achievement, could generate some of the inequality in outcomes that emerges over the first-grade transition.

Parents' expectations for their children's performance were not nearly as stereotyped by SES as were teachers'. *Before any report cards were issued*, parents' expectations for children's first marks in reading, ascertained either shortly before or just after children began school in September 1982, show only a slight gradient by SES level of the school (average parent expectations in the high-SES schools were 2.74 in reading versus 2.59 in the low-SES schools, where $2 = C$ and $3 = B$). When children's performance does not match parents' expectations, however, which is bound to happen with poorer children and their parents because these children's marks are relatively low, the children soon change from attending to their parents' expectations to not being influenced by those expectations (Alexander, Entwisle, & Bedinger, 1994; Entwisle & Hayduk, 1981). Parents' expectations are a key support for children's schooling, but mainly for high-SES children (see Entwisle, Alexander, & Olson, 2001), in part because the mismatch produced by mark feedback in low-SES schools vitiates parents' expectations as a learning resource.

The social organization of the school and its institutional character also affect children's school progress. This facet of schooling is discussed next.

TIME SPENT IN SCHOOL VERSUS AGE: ADMINISTRATIVE PRACTICES

Age is the prepotent determinant of elementary school organization in the United States. Typically all children born within a designated 12-month period are placed in one grade-school cohort. In Baltimore, the Beginning School Study children were born during the calendar year 1976 so they began first grade in September 1982. Children who would turn six January 1, 1982 or after but before January 1, 1983 were enrolled in September, 1982. Those born January 1, 1977 or later had to wait to enroll until September 1983. This age rule determined that Baltimore children up to 6 years and 8 months of age began first grade with others as young as 5 years and 8 months.

Entrance age does *not*, however, predict children's cognitive growth in first grade (Alexander & Entwisle, 1988; Jones & Mandeville, 1990; Shepard & Smith, 1986). Or, put another way, children's growth on achievement tests in middle childhood is independent of their age over relatively long (1-year) time spans. When "young" Beginning School Study first-graders (those with birth dates in November–December 1976, one or two months before the cut-off) are compared with "old" first-graders (those with birth dates in January–February 1976, 11 or 12 months before the cut-off), average test scores of older children are higher than those of younger ones (Table 11-4), but the *gains* made over first grade by the "older" and "younger" Beginning School Study students are almost equivalent. The test scores of "young" first-graders at the end of the school year were lower than test scores of the "old" first-graders because they had lower test scores to start with. Yet children in both age groups *gained the same number of points* on standardized tests of achievement in reading and math over first grade, so age when children start first grade *does not* predict their ability to profit from schooling.

TABLE 11-4. Beginning California Achievement Test (CAT) Scores and First-Year Test Score Gains for "Young" and "Old" Beginning School Study (BSS) First-Graders[a]

	Young ($\bar{x}$ =69.5 months)	t-tests[b]	Old ($\bar{x}$ =79.5 months)
Beginning year 1 CAT score			
Reading	269	*	282
Math	277	*	301
Year 1 test score gains			
Reading	64.0		68.7
Math	54.0		49.4

*p 0.05.
[a]"Young" BSS first-graders are those with birthdays in November or December, 1982. "Old" is defined as those with birthdays in January or February, 1982.
[b]t-tests compare means of "young" and "old" BSS students.

Further direct evidence on the lack of a relationship between age and children's progress in school comes from a study of redshirting in the United States (Graue & DiPerna, 2000) and an Israeli study of fourth-, fifth-, and sixth-grade students in Jerusalem's state-controlled elementary schools. In the American study, students who had attained a minimum age of 7 when they began first grade were compared with others of typical (not early) age. By third grade scores on a statewide reading test for the redshirts who started at age 7 were almost identical to scores of students admitted around age 6. In other words, three years of school led to the same outcome, although the groups were one year apart in age.

In Israel, Cahan and Cohen (1989) compared the mean scores predicted for the youngest children in one grade with scores for the oldest children in the next lower grade. If age mattered, then the oldest child in grade 4, say, should have the same score as the youngest child in grade 5 because their ages are very close. Yet this kind of comparison showed a jump in scores between the *similarly aged* children in adjacent grades that unambiguously points to the amount of children's schooling rather than age as the key factor in explaining cognitive growth.

Evidence from natural experiments also suggests that *time spent in school* rather than age explains how much children know. Ceci (1991) estimates that children's IQ scores drop between 0.25 and 6 points per year when schools are shut down. He notes that when the public schools in Prince Edward County, Virginia closed between 1959 and 1964 to avoid integration, most African American children received no formal education. On average, their IQs dropped by about 6 points per year for every year they missed school, with children of all ages affected (Green, Hofman, Morse, Hayes, & Morgan, 1964). For another example, when World War II forced Holland's schools to close, the IQ scores of children whose schooling was delayed dropped by about 7 points (DeGroot, 1951).

Other facts are consistent with the importance of school attendance rather than children's age for their cognitive growth. The number of hours of schooling children receive correlates with their scores on verbal and math aptitude tests (Wiley & Harnischfeger, 1974), and the number of children's absences is inversely related to their test score gains (Alexander & Entwisle, 1988; Bond & Dykstra, 1967; Heyns, 1978; Karweit, 1973). Most persuasive, however, is that all children's achievement scores in the spring exceed their scores in the preceding fall, but some children's growth slows down or stops when school is closed for the summer. All children get three months older in summer but only those whose families can provide sufficient resources continue to make achievement gains over the summer (see Ceci, 1991; Entwisle & Alexander, 1992, 1994; Heyns, 1978).

Because of these rigid age rules, the first-grade transition is a period when biological and institutional time can be pitted against each other in order to separate effects of attending school from effects of cognitive maturation. This comparison makes clear that children's chronological age may not be the best or only criterion to use in organizing elementary schools. Since exposure to school rather than chronological age leads to cognitive growth, it may be highly worthwhile to start school as early as possible for children who come from homes where resources are in short supply (see Entwisle et al., 2000). Poor preschool children need to be where they can be surrounded by resources that are scarce in their homes. Impeccable evidence demonstrates that disadvantaged children make a smoother first-grade transition and derive significant long-lasting benefit from attending good preschools (see Barnett, 1995). Also mounting evidence indicates that family background probably matters more for cognitive development of preschool and younger children in general than it does for that of older children (Alwin & Thornton, 1984; Duncan, Yeung, Brooks-Gunn, & Smith, 1998; Marjoribanks, 1979).

Since the relationship between family economic background and cognitive growth begins so early (Alexander & Entwisle, 1996; Marjoribanks, 1979; Murnane, 1975), the dearth of good preschools for 3- and 4-year-olds is an important issue, unfortunately one beyond the scope of this chapter. Still, enrollments in pre-primary education vary by race-ethnicity and poverty status. In 1999, over twice as many 3-year-old children whose parents were high school dropouts were not enrolled in schools, compared to children with college-educated parents (29% vs. 60%) (U.S. Department of Education, 2000a). Preschool experience for disadvantaged or minority-group youngsters prior to kindergarten could be a major way to smooth the first-grade transition. A few extra test points conferred by attending a good preschool could be enough to protect economically disadvantaged youngsters against low placements in reading groups or even retention in the first couple of grades (see Entwisle, 1995).

Transitions are generally easier if they are not abrupt and if they can be rehearsed. Both reasons suggest that schooling prior to first grade will ease the first-grade transition. In poverty-stricken cities like Baltimore, many children fail first grade (17% in the BSS), but only a few studies address the transition issues that face children starting school (Barr & Dreeben, 1983; Entwisle & Hayduk, 1978, 1982; Entwisle et al., 1997; Reynolds, 1989, 1991, 1992). The variation in test scores by socioeconomic status when children start school could be considerably reduced by attending Headstart (Consortium, 1983) or full-day kindergarten (Entwisle et al., 1987), and no doubt by other means as well.

To this point children's elementary school experience, and especially the first-grade transition, has been examined from a number of vantage points. In what follows that experience is related to later schooling and even to events in the adult transition.

SCHOOLING TRAJECTORIES

The beginning school transition sets the stage for all that follows. Children's achievement trajectories are remarkably stable (see Alexander, Entwisle, & Dauber, 1994, 2002). BSS children with the highest scores on standardized tests in reading and math when they began first grade had the highest scores at grade 7. Weller, Schnittjer, and Tuten (1992) likewise report a correlation of 0.57 between a reading readiness test given at the start of first-grade and tenth-grade reading and math tests (see also Butler, Marsh, Sheppard, & Sheppard, 1985).

A number of studies show that the quality of children's performance at the end of third grade is a good indicator of future performance. In the standardization sample for the California Achievement Test (1979) battery, for example, third-grade reading scores in fall correlate highly (0.87) with scores the next spring. The parallel correlation for mathematics scores is 0.84. These correlations are close to the reliability of the test, so they are at a practical ceiling. Husén's (1969) large cross-national study showed that intelligence scores and teachers' ratings in third grade were strong predictors of children's long-term educational careers, and Kraus (1973), who followed children in New York City for more than 20 years, found that reading achievement scores were the best predictors of adult status.

The disparities in school achievement separating first-grade children from better-off as compared to disadvantaged homes becomes more marked the longer children are in school. In a school where more than 90% of students were on subsidy, only 47% of the children in the BSS who had started first grade in that school had reached fifth grade 5 years later—53% had either been retained or placed in special education. By contrast, in schools where 50% or less of the children were on subsidy, 77% of children in the BSS who had started first grade there were in fifth grade 5 years later. Over the first-grade transition these children effectively entered upon a track. Children of high SES had test scores a little higher as they began first grade than did children of lower SES, but for BSS children, initial CAT scores in reading and math in the *fall of first grade* correlate 0.41 and 0.55 with scores on higher levels of the same tests at the end of elementary school (grade 5) (see also Alexander & Entwisle, 1996; Kerckhoff, 1993). But the story does not end there. The noticeable but small gap at the start of first grade translated into separate tracks in middle school as well. Children who had the highest test scores at the end of elementary school took algebra and a foreign language in middle school and thus ended up with the needed prerequisites to move into a college preparatory program in high school, while students with lower scores at the end of elementary school did not take those prerequisites in middle school (Dauber, Alexander, & Entwisle, 1996). To be more specific, 62% of children who were placed in the lowest reading group in their first-grade classroom took low-level English in sixth grade. Likewise, 51% of children who had been retained in first grade were in low-level math in sixth grade. First-grade placement decisions set in motion consequent events and processes that greatly reduce the odds that these children would go to college.

First-grade marks also tended to define an achievement envelope for the ensuing years. For example, at the end of the first quarter in first grade a comparison of (a) the BSS students who had the *lowest* marks in reading and math, with (b) the BSS students with the next-to-lowest marks, and (c) the BSS students with the highest marks shows that these rankings are the same 7 years later (Alexander, Entwisle, & Dauber, 1993). The average marks of those who had the lowest marks in first grade were just under a C 7 years later, the average marks of those who were the next lowest after 7 years were just a little bit better (exactly C), and those who had been in the highest group in first grade came out on top again (more Bs than Cs).

The long-term persistence of early rankings means that inequities visible in first grade translate into deficits all along the line. Long before secondary school, social inequality governs schooling. Ironically, studies of social inequality in education have focused mainly on high school, when the optimum time for counteracting these inequities has long since passed.

In terms of policy, gaps in achievement scores and behavioral indicators at the beginning of first grade that reflect socioeconomic differences in family background and neighborhoods are key. To close those gaps requires a better understanding of what happens to middle-class children before they start school, as well as over summers in the primary grades. Some preliminary research implicates both parents' economic capital and their psychological capital (Entwisle et al., in press).

Two kinds of parental resources predict children's gains over the summer when school is closed. Economic capital is one, because it allows parents to purchase trips to cultural centers, games, books, computers, and the like. Although necessary, the presence of economic resources is not sufficient, though. Psychological capital is also necessary. For children to gain on achievement tests over the summer, parents' psychological resources are also essential. These resources are no doubt multiple, as indicated by high expectations for their children's achievement in both the short and long run. In our view, for compensatory programs to accomplish the desired result, they need somehow to embrace both components—economic, in terms of providing the materials and activities required to support children's cognitive growth *and* psychological, in terms of providing the kind of stimulating interaction with an invested adult or group of adults that engages children in pleasurable and profitable activities. One might say "there is no escalator up Parnassus."

Social stratification in the larger society determined the events and experiences of BSS children over the first-grade transition. The implications of this linkage are profound, because retention rates in first grade were higher than in any later grade, and repeating a grade or getting poor marks in first grade greatly increased the odds that students would later drop out (see Alexander et al., 1994, 2002; Ensminger & Slusarcick, 1992; Entwisle et al., 1997). One way to reduce effects of stratification, noted earlier, is for children to attend preschools and kindergarten (Barnett, 1995; Entwisle, Alexander, Cadigan, & Pallas, 1987; Lazar & Darlington, 1982). For example, in Baltimore attending full day rather than half day kindergarten by itself almost doubled children's chances of avoiding retention in first grade (with initial test scores and other key variables controlled). How does this happen? The mechanisms have yet to be clearly established but Woodhead (1988) makes the case that preschools groom children so they are easier to teach in first grade. An ethnographic study of how both suburban and inner city kindergarten teachers used time found that *all* teachers spent more time on procedural activities (lining up, transitions between activities, and the like) than on any other single activity, including cognitive activities (Berkeley, 1970). In short, preschool training changes the child's social context in first grade.

The qualities that pay off are effective use of time and talent, interest in the subject matter, a sufficient attention span and active participation in the classroom. Youngsters who are interested and involved in classroom activities, and who pay attention, spend more time on task and more of this is quality time (Brown & Saks, 1986; Karweit, 1983). As noted, such qualities lead to superior test score gains during the first year. But as important as positive adaptive behaviors are for test scores, they matter even more for teachers' marks. Behavior ratings have direct effects on teachers' marks in *every* year we studied (grades 1, 2, and 4), but the *first*-grade teacher's ratings have lagged effects on marks in the second and fourth grades as well.

LONG-TERM LINKS TO THE
ADULT TRANSITION

At the start of a new century we can lay out a series of studies based on the Baltimore BSS archive (Table 11-5) or on data collected from many other localities (Table 11-6) that show substantial long-term consequences of events or circumstances children experience over the first-grade transition.

TABLE 11-5. Long-Term Outcomes Related to the First-Grade Transition (Baltimore Beginning School Study)

Citation	Early school measure	Outcome
Entwisle, Alexander, Cadigan, & Pallas, 1987	Amount of kindergarten	First-grade absence Beginning CAT scores Beginning marks in reading, math
Unpublished		Retention in grade 1
Dauber, Alexander, & Entwisle, 1993	Beginning marks Grade 1 math CAT score	Retention in Yrs 1–4
Alexander, Entwisle, & Dauber, 1993	Teacher behavioral ratings in Grade 1	School performance in Yr 4: –reading and math marks –reading and math CAT scores
Alexander, Entwisle, & Dauber, 1994	Grade 1 retention	Academic self-image, Yr 8 student mark expectations, Yr 8 reading and math marks in grade 6 and 7 CAT reading and math, math scores in grade 6, 7
Pallas, Entwisle, Alexander, & Stluka, 1994	Grade 1 reading group assignment	Yr 4 CAT scores, reading marks, parent and teacher expectations
Alexander & Entwisle, 1996	Grade 1 reading groups Grade 1 tracking (reading groups, Special Education, retention)	Retention in elementary school Grade 6 course placements
Alexander, Entwisle, & Horsey, 1997	Grade 1 CAT reading and math scores; grade 1 reading and math marks; grade 1 retention	High school dropout
Unpublished	Grade 1 parent educ. expectation for student; Grade 1 marks in reading and math	Middle school placement in advanced course tracks
Unpublished	Work habits grade 1; Number of school transfers	Retention in Yr 1 Test scores in Yr 5 Educational attainment Idleness ages 18–23 Employment ages 18–23

The most recent follow-up of the BSS panel (age 22–23) reveals many connections between the first-grade transition and the level of educational attainment and/or labor market success they have achieved in early adulthood. At age 22–23 (5 years after "normal" gradua-tion), 67.8% of those who had been retained in first grade had dropped out of school. Of these a substantial number (25%), after dropping out had either returned and obtained a diploma or passed the GED. Even so, over four times as many first-grade retainees as never retained stu-dents (43% vs. 10%) failed to achieve high school certification by their mid-twenties (Alexander, Entwisle, & Kabbani, 1999).

For the BSS panel a number of first-grade indicators predict the more general level of educational attainment by age 22–23. With race, sex, family SES, grade one standardized

TABLE 11-6. Long-Term Effects of First-Grade Transition (Other Investigators' Research)

Study	Early schooling	Lasting effect
Fitzsimmons, Cheever, Leonard, & Macunovich, 1969 ($n = 270$)	Achievement test scores in reading and math, grades 1–3	Performance in high school
Pedersen, Faucher, & Eaton, 1978 ($n = 59$; urban disadvantaged)	Exceptional first-grade teacher	Achievement of high adult status Completion of at least 10 years of school
Pope, Lehrer, & Stevens, 1980 ($n = 545$)	Kindergarten achievement (Wide Range Achievement Test)	Reading achievement in grade 5 ($r = 0.50$)
Lazar & Darlington, 1982 ($n = 2008$)	Participation in Headstart preschool programs	Reading achievement (grade 3), Math achievement (grades 3–5) Lower rates of retention and Special Education
Richman, Stevenson, & Graham, 1982 ($n = 705$; United Kingdom)	Preschool attendance	Higher IQ-adjusted reading scores at age 8
Palmer, 1983 ($n = 240$)	One-to-one preschool instruction at ages 2–3 for 8 months	Higher reading and math achievement at grades 5 and 7; Lower rates of retention
Royce, Darlington, & Murray, 1983 ($n = 1104$)	Preschool attendance	Achievement in reading (grade 3) and math (grade 5) Lower rates of Special Education and retention High school graduation
Schweinhart & Weikart, 1983 ($n = 123$)	Preschool attendance (Perry Preschool)	Higher CAT scores at ages 7–14 Lower rates of Special Education placement and delinquent behavior
Meyer, 1984 ($n = 165$)	Kindergarten through grade 3 participation in Distar curriculum with increased allocation of time to basic skills	Higher-grade 9 CAT reading achievement Lower retention rates Higher rates of high school graduation, application and acceptance to college
Berrueta-Clement, Schweinhart, Barnett, Epstein, & Weikart, 1984 ($n = 123$)	High-quality preschool program (Perry Preschool)	Higher GPA in high school; Lower rates of Special Education; Positive outcomes at age 19: –high school graduation –postsecondary education –employed –lower rates of crime, delinquency –lower rates of pregnancy
Hess, Holloway, Dickson, & Price, 1984 ($n = 47$)	Maternal expectations for achievement in preschool	Grade 6 ITBS scores, vocabulary and math

(continued)

TABLE 11-6. (continued)

Study	Early schooling	Lasting effect
Butler, Marsh, Sheppard, & Sheppard, 1985 ($n = 286$)	Battery of tests in kindergarten Grade 1 reading achievement	Reading achievement tests in grade 6
Stevenson & Newman, 1986 ($n = 105$)	Pre-kindergarten cognitive measures	Grade 10 test scores in reading and math Grade 10 self-concept and expectancy for success in reading
Wadsworth, 1986 ($n = 1675$; U.K.)	Preschool attendance	Higher verbal skills at age 8
Entwisle & Hayduk, 1988 ($n = 654$)	Teacher's mark expectations in grades 1 and 2	English and math achievement tests 4–9 years later, current ability level controlled
Cairns, Cairns, & Neckerman, 1989 ($n = 475$)	Elementary school retention	High school dropout
Barrington & Hendericks, 1989 ($n = 214$)	Grade 3 ITBS achievement test scores	High school dropout
Morris, Ehren, & Lenz, 1991 ($n = 785$)	Grade 4 reading achievement scores	High school dropout
Simner & Barnes, 1991 ($n = 193$)	Grade 1 reading and math marks	High school dropout
Ensminger & Slusarcick, 1992 ($n = 917$)	Grade 1 math mark Grade 1 aggressive behavior (especially for males)	High school dropout
Weller, Schnittjer, & Tuten, 1992 ($n = 415$)	Metropolitan Reading Readiness, beginning of grade 1	CTBS reading and math scores, grade 10
Brooks-Gunn, Guo, & Furstenberg, 1993 ($n = 254$)	Pre-school attendance Pre-school cognitive ability	High school graduation Post-secondary education
Roderick, 1993 ($n = 757$)	Grade retention, K through grade 3	High school dropout
Reynolds, 1994 ($n = 1106$)	Follow-on intervention in grades 1–3 (school-based comprehensive service program providing instructional support and parental involvement)	ITBS reading and math, grade 5 Cumulative grade retention, grade 5
Schweinhart, Barnes, & Weikart, 1993	High-quality preschool program (Perry Preschool)	Positive outcomes at age 27: –lowest arrest rates –higher incomes –home ownership –more stable marriages
Ramey, Campbell, Burchinal, Skinner, Gardner, & Ramey, 2000	5 years of preschool support K through grade 2	Positive outcomes at age 15 Lower retention rate Less need for Special Education

Note: For full references not listed for this chapter see Entwisle, Alexander, and Olson, 1997.

scores in reading and math as well as retention taken into account, first-grade behavior ratings by teachers predict level of educational attainment (Entwisle et al., in preparation). The same set of variables also predicts whether panel members are employed at age 22–23, and the degree to which they have been unemployed. An impressive body of evidence from other sources (Table 11-6) likewise shows that performance in preschool, kindergarten and/or the primary grades predicts outcomes in high school and beyond.

The actual mechanisms that link the quality or character of early schooling to outcomes later in life remain to be determined and are far beyond the scope of this chapter. Still, a few words are in order. Consider first some statistical issues. First, the correlations between standardized test scores in first grade and scores on later tests increase with time because of the relentless increase in test score variance. At the end of grade 5 in the standardization sample for the California Achievement Test Form C Reading Comprehension, the standard deviation is much greater than it was at the beginning of grade 1 (68.4 vs. 43.5), as is also true for the BSS sample (73.9 vs. 41.0). Second, children's school experiences are more differentiated earlier than later. The Coleman Report (p. 293), which divides variance in achievement into between-school and between-family segments, finds the proportion of variance in Reading Comprehension between schools in grade 3 is 20.86% compared to 13.24% in grade 12; likewise in Math Achievement, 21.48% compared to 10.55%. At the very least, these figures suggest that between-school differences in elementary schools are relatively larger than between-school differences in high schools. Third, some early contextual influences have lasting effects probably because they translate into achievement levels (or perhaps personal characteristics like work habits) early in the game. BSS data show that the first-grade teachers' ratings, for example, have stronger effects on children's fourth-grade achievement than do the ratings of the fourth-grade teachers. Likewise, in an earlier study (Entwisle & Hayduk, 1988) the third-grade teachers' expectations predicted high school performance net of ability level (see also Hess, Holloway, Dickson, & Price, 1984; Stevenson & Newman, 1986). Clearly these kinds of questions are multiple, complex, and not likely to be resolved soon. Even so, the range of studies showing long-term sequelae of early school experiences suggest that the present day specification of schooling models is at best incomplete.

With the first-grade transition and its impact on the later life course having been laid out, we now turn to policy issues. While not a "policy study" in the sense that interventions or other changes were instituted as part of the BSS research, there are notwithstanding some key lessons to be drawn.

POLICY ISSUES

Most research on school transitions deals with the move from elementary to middle or junior high school (see Entwisle, 1990; Eccles, Midgley, & Adler, 1984), because adolescence is a time when students' developing sense of identity and self-worth occupy center stage. This research so far has examined mainly socioemotional or affective outcomes. Generally a decrease in self-image accompanies the junior high transition, but susceptibility to that decline depends on youths' personal characteristics (Simmons & Blyth, 1987), family characteristics (Rosenberg & Simmons, 1971), and the social-structural characteristics of the schools they attend, such as peer group patterns (Eccles et al., 1984).

In light of the remarkable pay-offs from research on the junior high transition, the dearth of research on the first-grade transition is surprising. Along with Reynolds (1992), who focused on disadvantaged African American youth, the BSS is one of the first studies to examine children's transition into full-time schooling in relation to students' long-term demographic and achievement trajectories. BSS data show convincingly that children's relative standing when they start first grade forecasts where they will be at much later points in their lives. School helped BSS children of various SES backgrounds gain the same amounts on achievement tests, as shown in Table 11-2, but those who started ahead tended to stay ahead. Those who started behind gained just as much when school was open as did their more fortunate classmates, but they stayed behind because they were behind to start with. The importance of where children cross the starting line for defining children's long-term life trajectories makes it imperative to focus more research on getting children up to speed in the preschool period, or as they make the first-grade transition (see Entwisle et al., 2000).

A major way to improve the school climate in poor neighborhoods would be to correct the mistaken public perception that elementary schools are falling down on the job. Elementary schools in Baltimore prompted just as much growth in achievement of children who were poor as in children who were better off. Schools appear to be doing a much better job of reaching disadvantaged children than they have been credited with. The success of schools in fostering development of young children irrespective of poverty backgrounds is hard to overrate.

A fascination with inequality in society is one mark of a sociologist. Along with it goes a fascination for how social inequality is perpetuated (Kerckhoff, 1993). The imagery is strong that a set of occupational slots at the top of the school ladder is ready for the new generation to move into. To us, the authors, this image of society as divided into a set of occupational pigeonholes seems to be upside down. High schools do reflect the stratification patterns in the larger society, but the critical sorting processes occur at the beginning rather than near the end of children's school careers. Elementary schools are already stratified according to the economic resources of neighborhoods, and neighborhood SES levels correlate with the kind and amount of early schooling children receive. This early sorting is a kind of "sponsoring", but not in terms of demands of the larger society (i.e., that certain slots must be filled by certain types of people). Rather, parents' choice of a neighborhood determines their choice of a school, and most of what defines a neighborhood are the economic differences that separate it from other neighborhoods.

Organizational theorists visualize the internal structure of schools as either vertical or horizontal because they assume that the school's needs determine its structure. This approach is rational for organizations such as banks or factories, but does not work for schools because the internal structure of schools, or of school systems, depends on the structure of the society in which they sit rather than on their own production goals. Elementary schools became common at the beginning of the 19th century, ostensibly because they fulfilled the need to prepare youth (mainly boys) to function as citizens in a participatory democracy. A *latent* purpose was that they occupied children's time in the winter months when farms lay dormant. Later in the 19th century, when a steady flow of immigrants led to an oversupply of labor, enrolling children in schools kept them from competing for jobs in factories (Bakan, 1974). Thus social forces largely unrelated to children's own needs dictated when schools became universal and the length and calendar of the school year.

To this day, organizational patterns of schools are driven by economic and social pressures. Parents try to maximize their own and their family's social status, which leads them to place their children on what they perceive to be the most effective paths to compete successfully in the labor markets of the 21st century. They struggle to send their children to Ivy League schools, or even to preschools that lead up to the Ivies, not so much because they are deeply committed to their children's intellectual development or because of what their children might learn, but because they believe that once school is over, adult success depends mainly on social capital. Also, they themselves draw prestige from the quality of the child's college or preparatory school. Schools as institutions serve to perpetuate the social status quo, but the engine that drives the overall social system is located mainly in the individual family, not in its schools.

Elementary schools tend to have socially homogeneous student bodies because the social status of neighborhoods determines the social status of students in elementary schools. This distribution does not serve children or society well (see Kahlenberg, 2001). As stated before, schools are less the problem than most people seem to believe. The distribution of resources across families and neighborhoods is the problem. Problems in families and neighborhoods cannot be solved only by tinkering with schools.

At the same time, the lack of good preschools for impoverished 3- and 4-year-olds is an important means by which social inequality undercuts schooling. At present, teenage parents or high school dropouts are the least likely to enroll their preschool children in center-based programs (U.S. Department of Education, 2000b). If disadvantaged children do not attend preschools prior to kindergarten, and they take less advantage of public kindergartens, relatively lower achievement of poor children in elementary school is the consequence. Kindergartens are widely available, so some key resources already are there, but kindergarten attendance is discretionary in most localities. Children must be encouraged and/or required to attend public full-day kindergartens, preferably in the same schools where they will start first grade. A few extra test points conferred by preschool and kindergarten attendance could be enough to protect many disadvantaged children from low placements or retention in the first few grades (see Entwisle, 1995). The boost children get from preschool and kindergarten eases the first-grade transition. A giant step toward educational equity would be to improve the skills of children whose backgrounds are problematic before they begin first grade.

The next logical stop after increasing poor children's attendance in full-day preschool is to develop summer school programs specifically for poor children that add on to preschool (Entwisle et al., 2000). Preschools can reduce the achievement gap when children start first grade, but during the summer we need to give poor children the extra resources that middle-class parents provide for their children.

What should these summer programs consist of? Summer activities related to reading top the list. Low-income children involved in Atlanta's summer schools tended to read more on their own than did students not attending (Heyns, 1978). Likewise, in Baltimore, first- and second-graders who went to the library more often in summer and who took out more books did better than other children, although those who went to the library had other advantages such as parents with higher expectations for their school performance.

Probably summer programs for disadvantaged children should feature activities that include a substantial amount of physical activity for both boys and girls, especially games like soccer, field hockey, or softball that require very little equipment but have complicated rule systems and require children to take multiple roles. Adult leaders need to be cast in the role of "coach" rather than teacher.

Program content is not the only concern, however. Perhaps most important, coaches need to encourage children to enjoy themselves: engagement is key to learning, and engagement can be difficult to achieve if summer programs are perceived as punitive or boring. Summer programs need careful planning, especially in terms of teachers who can establish strong attachments to students and parents. The programs need to be located near pupils' homes, so children can get to them easily and so parents can become involved. Changing the summer environment of young children in low-income families may require community intervention. No single approach is likely to close the academic gap between low- and high-income children, but summer programs bracketing first grade could help.

THE LARGER PICTURE

Families sort themselves by income into neighborhoods; then neighborhood schools tend to segregate students from different income levels. Because of the unequal distribution of resources across families (and neighborhoods), the engine that drives the schooling system is located mainly in the individual family. This inequity so far has not been reduced by tinkering with schools as they presently exist. The good news is that despite poverty and family disruption, young children's ability to learn *during the school year* seems little impaired by scarce family resources (Entwisle et al., 1997). Poor children fall behind in summer when schools are closed. In seeking to address the achievement gap between rich and poor, we should first recognize the efficacy of elementary schools in leveling the playing field. Most press coverage of American education dwells on its failures, especially its failures with respect to disadvantaged students. These negative perceptions undercut popular support for schools and public education. Missed in these perceptions is the extent to which schools make up for deficits in poor children's backgrounds. Lower-status children are assumed to be "slower" learners, less capable of absorbing the curriculum. The Beginning School Study shows, however, that the achievement deficit of poorer children builds up over summer vacations when schools are closed. Children can learn only if they have the necessary resources.

To make a difference in the lives of poor students, parents and communities must be involved in the schooling process. All parents, not just middle-class parents, need to be active collaborators in the education of their children. Preschool and summer programs, properly organized, could help to empower economically disadvantaged parents and their neighborhoods to become active supporters of children's academic endeavors. These parents need to know, for example, that such simple activities as reading aloud to their children can have big payoffs in supporting children's academic careers. Neighborhoods need playgrounds and coaches to encourage organized sports and craft activities in the summer. Workshops and other outreach efforts could help disadvantaged adults develop some of the psychological and social capital that is so important in undergirding their children's learning.

ACKNOWLEDGMENTS: Data collection for this research was supported by the W. T. Grant Foundation grant no. 83079682 and National Institute of Child Health and Development grant no. 1 R01 16302. The analysis was supported by National Science Foundation grant no. SES 8510535 and National Institute of Child Health and Development grants no. 1 R01 21044, 5 R01 23738, and 5 R01 23943. Preparation of this chapter was supported by W.T. Grant Foundation (Grant Number 9819298), the Spencer Foundation (B1517, 199800106) and the Office of Education and Improvement, U.S. Department of Education (R306F70128). We thank the children, parents, and teachers who gave us such splendid cooperation in all phases of this research.

REFERENCES

Alexander, K. L., & Entwisle, D. R. (1988). Achievement in the first two years of school: Patterns and processes [Serial No. 218]. *Monographs of the Society for Research in Child Development, 53*(2).

Alexander, K. L., & Entwisle, D. R. (1996). Educational tracking during the early years: First grade placements and middle school constraints. In A. C. Kerckhoff (Ed.), *Generating social stratification: Toward a new research agenda* (pp. 83–113). New York: Westview Press.

Alexander, K. L., Entwisle, D. R., & Bedinger, S. D. (1994). When expectations work: Race and socioeconomic differences in school performance. *Social Psychology Quarterly, 57*(4), 283–299.

Alexander, K. L., Entwisle, D. R., & Dauber, S. L. (1993). First grade classroom behavior: Its short- and long-term consequences for school performance. *Child Development, 64*(3), 801–814.

Alexander, K. L., Entwisle, D. R., & Dauber, S. L. (1994, 2002). *On the success of failure: A reassessment of the effects of retention in the primary grades.* Cambridge, MA: Cambridge University Press.

Alexander, K. L., Entwisle, D. R., & Kabbani, N. (1999, November 29–December 1). *Grade retention, social promotion and 'third way' alternatives.* Presented at the National Invitational Conference on Early Childhood Learning: Programs for a New Age. Alexandria, VA.

Alexander, K. L., Entwisle, D. R., & Thompson, M. S. (1987). School performance, status relations and the structure of sentiment: Bringing the teacher back in. *American Sociological Review, 52*(5), 665–682.

Alwin, D. F., & Thornton, A. (1984). Family origins and the schooling process: Early versus late influence of parental characteristics. *American Sociological Review, 49*(6), 784–802.

Bakan, D. (1974, Fall). Adolescence in America. *Daedalus, 100,* 979–995.

Barnett, W. S. (1995). Long-term effects of early childhood care and education on disadvantaged children's cognitive development and school success. *The future of children, 5*(3), 25–50.

Barr, R., & Dreeben, R. (1983). *How schools work.* Chicago: University of Chicago Press.

Berkeley, M. V. (1978). *Inside kindergarten: An observational study of kindergarten in three social settings.* Unpublished doctoral dissertation, Johns Hopkins University, Baltimore, Maryland.

Bond, G. L., & Dykstra, R. (1967). The cooperative research program in first grade reading instruction. *Reading Research Quarterly, 2*(4), 1–42.

Brackbill, Y., & Nevill, D. D. (1981). Parental expectations of achievement as affected by children's height. *Merrill-Palmer Quarterly, 27,* 429–441.

Brown, B. W., & Saks, D. H. (1986). Measuring the effects of instructional time on student learning: Evidence from the Beginning Teacher Evaluation Study. *American Journal of Education, 94*(4), 480–500.

Butler, S. R., Marsh, H. W., Sheppard, M. J., & Sheppard, J. L. (1985). Seven year longitudinal study of the early prediction of reading achievement. *Journal of Educational Psychology, 77*(3), 349–361.

Cahan, S., & Cohen, N. (1989). Age versus schooling effects on intelligence development. *Child Development, 60*(5), 1237–1249.

Ceci, S. J. (1991). How much does schooling influence general intelligence and its cognitive components? A reassessment of the evidence. *Developmental Psychology, 27*(5), 703–722.

Coleman, J. S., Campbell, E. Q., Hobson, C. J., McPartland, J., Mood, A., Weinfeld, F. D., & York, R. L. (1966). *Equality of educational opportunity.* Washington, DC: U.S. Government Printing Office.

Consortium for Longitudinal Studies. (1983). *As the twig is bent: Lasting effect of preschool programs.* Hillsdale, NJ: Lawrence Erlbaum Associates.

Dauber, S. L., Alexander, K. L., & Entwisle, D. R. (1996). Tracking and transitions through the middle grades: Channeling educational trajectories. *Sociology of Education, 69*(4), 290–307.

DeGroot, A. D. (1951). Short articles and notes: War and the intelligence of youth. *Journal of Abnormal and Social Psychology, 46,* 596–597.

Duncan, G. J., Yeung, W. J., Brooks-Gunn, J., & Smith, J. K. (1998). How much does childhood poverty affect the life chances of children? *American Sociological Review, 63*(3), 406–423.

Eccles, J. S., Midgley, C., & Adler, T. (1984). Grade-related changes in the school environment: Effects on achievement motivation. In J. G. Nicholls (Ed.), *The development of achievement motivation* (pp. 283–331). Greenwich, CT: JAI Press.

Ensminger, M. E., & Slusarcick, A. L. (1992, April). Paths to high school graduation or dropout: A longitudinal study of a first-grade cohort. *Sociology of Education, 65*(2), 95–113.

Entwisle, D. R. (1990). Schools and the adolescent. In S. S. Feldman & G. R. Elliott (Eds.), *At the threshold: The developing adolescent* (pp. 197–224). Cambridge, MA: Harvard University Press.

Entwisle, D. R. (1995). The role of schools in sustaining benefits of early childhood programs. *The Future of Children, 5*(3), 133–144.

Entwisle, D. R., & Alexander, K. L. (1988). Factors affecting achievement test scores and marks received by black and white first graders. *The Elementary School Journal, 88*(5), 449–471.

Entwisle, D. R., & Alexander, K. L. (1990). Beginning school math competence. *Child Development, 61*(2), 454–471.

Entwisle, D. R., & Alexander, K. L. (1992). Summer setback: Race, poverty, school composition, and mathematics achievement in the first two years of school. *American Sociological Review, 57*(1), 72–84.

Entwisle, D. R., & Alexander, K. L. (1993). Entry into schools: The beginning school transition and educational stratification in the United States. In *Annual Review of Sociology* (Vol. 19, pp. 401–423). Palo Alto, CA: Annual Reviews, Inc.

Entwisle, D. R., & Alexander, K. L. (1994). Winter setback: School racial composition and learning to read. *American Sociological Review, 59*(3), 446–460.

Entwisle, D. R., & Alexander, K. L. (1996). Family type and children's growth in reading and math over the primary grades. *Journal of Marriage and the Family, 58*(2), 341–355.

Entwisle, D. R., Alexander, K. L., Cadigan, D., & Pallas, A. M. (1987). Kindergarten experience: Cognitive effects or socialization? *American Educational Research Journal, 24*(3), 337–364.

Entwisle, D. R., Alexander, K. L., & Olson, L. S. (1997). *Children, schools and inequality.* Boulder, CO: Westview Press.

Entwisle, D. R., Alexander, K. L., & Olson, L. S. (2000). Summer learning and home environment. In R. D. Kahlenberg (Ed.), *A notion at risk: Preserving public education as an engine for social mobility* (pp. 9–30). New York: Century Foundation Press.

Entwisle, D. R., Alexander, K. L., & Olson, L. S. (2002). Teenage smoking and the adult transition. *Adolescent and Family Health, 2*(3).

Entwisle, D. R., Alexander, K. L., & Olson, L. S. (In preparation). *First grade predictors of education and employment status in young adulthood.*

Entwisle, D. R., Alexander, K. L., & Olson, L. S. (2001). *Socioeconomic status and children's achievement: A faucet analogy.* Paper presented at conference "After the bell: education solutions outside the school" presented by the Jerome Levy Economics Institute, Bard College and New York University Center for Advanced Social Science Research. Annandale-on-Hudson, NY.

Entwisle, D. R., Alexander, K. L., Pallas, A. M., & Cadigan, D. (1987). The emergent academic self-image of first graders: Its response to social structure. *Child Development, 58*(5), 1190–1206.

Entwisle, D. R., & Hayduk, L. A. (1978). *Too great expectations: The academic outlook of young children.* Baltimore: Johns Hopkins University Press.

Entwisle, D. R., & Hayduk, L. A. (1981). Academic expectations and the school attainment of young children. *Sociology of Education, 54*(1), 34–50.

Entwisle, D. R., & Hayduk, L. A. (1982). *Early schooling: Cognitive and affective outcomes.* Baltimore, MD: Hopkins Press.

Entwisle, D. R., & Hayduk, L. A. (1988). Lasting effects of elementary school. *Sociology of Education, 61*(3), 147–159.

Ginsburg, H. P., & Russell, R. L. (1981). Social class and racial influences on early mathematical thinking. *Monographs of the Society for Research in Child Development, 46*(6).

Graue, M. E., & DiPerna, J. (2000). Redshirting and early retention: Who gets the gift of time and what are its outcomes? *American Educational Research Journal, 37*(2), 509–534.

Green, R. L., Hofman, L. J., Morse, R. J., Hayes, M. E., & Morgan, R. F. (1964). *The educational status of children in a district without public schools* (Cooperative Research Project). Michigan State University: Bureau of Educational Research.

Hess, R. D., Holloway, S. D., Dickson, W. P., & Price, G. G. (1984). Maternal variables as predictors of children's school readiness and later achievement in vocabulary and mathematics in sixth grade. *Child Development, 55*(5), 1902–1912.

Heyns, B. (1978). *Summer learning and the effects of schooling.* New York: Academic Press.

Husén, T. (1969). *Talent, opportunity & career.* Stockholm: Almqvist & Wiksell.

Jones, M. M., & Mandeville, G. K. (1990). The effect of age at school entry on reading achievement scores among South Carolina students. *Remedial and Special Education, 11*(2), 56–62.

Kahlenberg, R. D. (2001). *All together now: Creating middle-class schools through public school choice.* Washington, DC: Brookings Institution Press.

Karweit, N. (1973). *Rainy days and Mondays: An analysis of factors related to absence from school* (Report No. 162). Baltimore, MD: Center for the Social Organization of Schools.

Karweit, N. L. (1983). *Time on task: A research review* (Report no. 332). Johns Hopkins University Center for Social Organization of Schools.

Kerckhoff, A. C. (1993). *Diverging pathways: Social structure and career deflections.* New York: Cambridge Press.

Kraus, P. E. (1973). *Yesterday's children.* New York: Wiley.

Lazar, I., & Darlington, R. (1982). Lasting effects of early education: A report from the Consortium for Longitudinal Studies. *Monographs of the Society for Research in Child Development, 47*(2–3), ix–139.

Marjoribanks, K. (1979). *Families and their learning environments.* London: Routledge.

Murnane, R. J. (1975). *The impact of school resources on the learning of inner city children.* Cambridge, MA: Ballinger.

Nord, C. W., Lennon, J., Liu, B., & Chandin, K. (1999). *Home living activities and signs of children's emerging literacy* (NCES 2000-026). Washington, DC: US Department of Education, National Center for Education Statistics.

Ramey, C. T., Campbell, F. A., Burchinal, M., Skinner, M. L., Gardner, D. M., and Ramey, S. L. (2000). Persistent effects of early childhood education on high-risk children and their mothers. *Applied Developmental Science, 4*(1), 2–14.

Reynolds, A. J. (1989). A structural model of first-grade outcomes for an urban, low socioeconomic status, minority population. *Journal of Educational Psychology, 81*, 594–603.

Reynolds, A. J. (1991). Early schooling of children at risk. *American Educational Research Journal, 28*, 393–422.

Reynolds, A. J. (1992). Grade retention and school adjustment: An explanatory analysis. *Educational Evaluation and Policy Analysis, 14*(2), 101–121.

Rosenberg, M., & Simmons, R. G. (1971). Black and White Self-Esteem: The Urban School Child. *Arnold M. and Caroline Rose Monograph Series.* Washington, DC: American Sociological Association.

Schneider, B. L. (1980). *Production analysis of gains in achievement.* Paper presented at the the American Educational Research Association Annual Meeting. Boston, MA.

Shepard, L. A., & Smith, M. L. (1986). Synthesis of research on school readiness and kindergarten retention. *Educational Leadership, 44*, 78–86.

Simmons, R. G., & Blyth, D. A. (1987). *Moving into adolescence: The impact of pubertal change and school context.* Hawthorn, NY: Aldine de Gruyter.

Stephens, J. M. (1956). *Educational psychology.* New York: Holt, Rinehart & Winston.

Stevenson, H. W., & Newman, R. S. (1986). Long-term prediction of achievement and attitudes in mathematics and reading. *Child Development, 57*, 646–659.

Tizard, B., Blatchford, P., Burke, J., Farquhar, C., & Plewis, I. (1988). *Young children at school in the inner city.* London: Erlbaum.

U.S. Department of Education. (2000a). *The condition of education, 2000* (NCES 2000-062). Washington, DC: U.S. Government Printing Office.

U.S. Department of Education. (2000b). *Digest of education statistics, 1999* (NCES 2000-031). Washington, DC: U.S. Department of Education, National Center for Education Statistics.

Weller, L. D., Schnittjer, C. J., & Tuten, B. A. (1992). Predicting achievement in grades three through ten using the Metropolitan Readiness Test. *Journal of Research in Childhood Education, 6*(2), 121–129.

Wiley, D. E., & Harnischfeger, A. (1974). *Explosion of a Myth: Quantity of Schooling and Exposure to Instruction, Major Educational Vehicles* (Report No. 8, Department of Education). Chicago: University of Chicago. Studies of Educative Process.

Woodhead, M. (1988). When psychology informs public policy: The case of early childhood intervention. *American Psychologist, 43*, 443–454.

CHAPTER 12

From Student to Worker

ALAN C. KERCKHOFF[†]

The transition from adolescence to adulthood in Western societies is marked by many changes. Young people leave school, enter the labor force, move out of the parental home, marry, and establish their own families of procreation. These changes are often interdependent; young people simultaneously follow "interlocking careers" (Elder & Rockwell, 1979). A change in one domain often affects the likelihood of a change in another domain. The focus of this chapter, however, is limited to the part of the adolescence-to-adulthood transition involving leaving school and entering the labor force.

Hogan and Astone (1986) correctly observe that modern societies use age-graded organizations such as schools to generate regularities in the life course. It is also true that the structural features of these organizations vary across Western societies. That variation affects the ways in which young people make the transition from being a student to being a worker. The structural arrangements set limits on the ways young people can make the transition from school to work, but the structural arrangements do not wholly determine the transition patterns we observe. The way the structures are *defined* and *responded to* by members of the societies also affect the transition patterns. For instance, structures may impinge on males and females in different ways. Both structures and norms must be taken into account in order to understand the different observed patterns of transition from school to work.

In this chapter, I use the educational systems of three major Western societies (Germany, Great Britain, and the United States) as the framework for the discussion, showing how both structural and normative features of the three educational systems affect the transition patterns followed by young people in those three countries. Although the primary focus is on the educational institutions, an important part of the societal variation is due to the different

[†]Deceased.

ALAN C. KERCKHOFF • Department of Sociology, Duke University, Durham, North Carolina 27708-0088.

Handbook of the Life Course, edited by Jeylan T. Mortimer and Michael J. Shanahan. Kluwer Academic/Plenum Publishers, New York, 2003.

ways schools are related to the organizations that employ students when they leave school. The transition process reflects the school–work relationship as much as it does the characteristics of the educational system.

A life course approach to understanding the transition from school to work must necessarily take into account the ages of the young people involved. Educational institutions are age-graded in all three of the societies considered. Age is a salient factor in the opportunities provided to young people both in school and in the labor force, and it is an important influence on the decisions they make during the period of transition.

STRUCTURAL VARIATIONS OF
EDUCATIONAL SYSTEMS

The structural features of the educational systems of Western societies are often discussed under three headings: stratification, standardization, and vocational specificity (Shavit & Müller, 1998). The educational systems of Germany, Great Britain, and the United States vary on all of these dimensions, and their differences provide a useful framework for understanding their different patterns of transition from school to work.

Stratification

In the analysis of educational systems, the term "stratification" is used to recognize that some systems clearly differentiate types of schools whose offerings can be viewed in terms of "higher" and "lower" levels of academic quality or demand (Allmendinger, 1989). Stratification is most often found at the secondary school level. Most European systems have historically distinguished between secondary schools that prepare students for university attendance and schools intended for those who will not participate in higher education (Archer, 1979). European systems have undergone considerable reorganization since World War II, but much stratification remains. The three educational systems considered here differ sharply in their degree of stratification.

Of the educational systems considered here, the German secondary schools are most clearly stratified (OECD, 1996). Students are separated at about age 10 into three kinds of secondary schools that differ greatly in their curricula. Transfers between the types of school are rare. The elite school, the *Gymnasium*, serves students from grade 5 to grade 13. Those who successfully complete the program obtain the *Abitur*, a certificate entitling the student to enter university-level education. The *Realschule* offers an enriched general curriculum in Grades 5 through 10. Successful students obtain a certificate that entitles them to continue their education in advanced vocational schools such as the *Fachoberschule*. The lowest level secondary school is the *Hauptschule* which provides a basic general education through grades 9 or 10. *Hauptschule* students have only very limited access to later vocational schooling. Both *Hauptschule* and *Realschule* graduates, however, may enter apprenticeships with both educational and work components.

The early separation of German secondary school students strongly influences the highest level of education they are likely to obtain. And their level and kind of educational attainment sets clear limits on the kinds of positions available to young people in the labor force.

The British secondary schools were almost as sharply stratified as those in Germany between World War II and the late 1960s. Students were separated at about age 11 into Grammar schools that had strong academic programs and Secondary Modern schools that had more limited general curricula. Grammar schools were designed to prepare students for university admission by passing A-level examinations. Students had to remain in school through the sixth form (about age 18) to prepare for A-levels. Secondary Modern schools seldom offered sixth-form courses; their students generally left school at about age 16. Besides these two types of state-supported secondary schools, Great Britain has historically had a small but highly visible Independent (private) school component. Private schools are not part of the German system.

State-supported Comprehensive schools were introduced in Great Britain in the late 1960s. They were designed to replace the Grammar and Secondary Modern schools by combining their programs and offering admission to all secondary school students. The transition to a fully comprehensive state-supported system is not complete, however. The great majority of British secondary school students attend Comprehensive schools, but Grammar schools and Secondary Modern schools still exist. The British system thus continues to be somewhat stratified. It is useful to differentiate among Comprehensive, Secondary Modern, and Elite schools, the latter category combining Grammar schools and Independent schools (Kerckhoff, Fogelman, Crook, & Reeder, 1996).

Compared with the German and British systems, American secondary schools are essentially unstratified. The comprehensive public high school is well established (Kaestle, 1983). About one tenth of American high school students attend private schools (NCES, 1998), but their programs are not as uniformly oriented toward preparation for university attendance as the British Independent schools' programs are. Local control of public education leads to variation in the quality of programs offered, but there is no standard institutional stratification of programs. Stratification occurs within American high schools through curricular tracks, but students in academic, general, and vocational tracks do not take highly differentiated curricula (Lucas, 1999; Vanfossen, Jones, & Spade, 1987). German schools are the most clearly stratified, and American secondary schools are the least stratified of the three systems.

Standardization

Standardization refers to the degree to which the organization and curricular offerings of schools are similar throughout the country. Local control of American schools leads to variation in the substance and quality of the programs they offer. There is greater standardization in both the German and the British schools, although it is due to different sources of influence in the two countries.

Local control of British elementary and secondary education has diminished significantly since the 1960s. Schools are even permitted to opt out of local control and seek direct national government funding. In addition, the Education Reform Act of 1988 introduced a "national curriculum" for all students of compulsory school age as well as a national assessment framework with "attainment targets" for students at several age levels (Gordon, Aldrich, & Dean, 1991). Standardization has thus been increased through the imposition of national control over the local education authorities.

A high level of standardization has been maintained in Germany for many decades. Elementary and secondary education is formally controlled by the individual states (*Länder*), but well-established cooperative mechanisms insure a high degree of similarity of organizational form and educational programs. In particular, the differentiation among the three stratified types of secondary schools is firmly established throughout the country. A high degree of standardization insures that stratified secondary education is uniformly experienced (Müller, Steinmann, & Ell, 1998).

Vocational Specificity

Countries' educational systems vary widely in the degree to which the credentials they award have specific vocational relevance, and the educational systems of Germany, Great Britain, and the United States cover the full range. Their differences are most apparent at the post-secondary level, but their secondary school programs provide the basis for the post-secondary differences.

The three types of German secondary schools set limits on the kinds of post-secondary programs available to students. Only *Gymnasium* students can qualify for university attendance and thereby prepare for high level professional, commercial, and financial occupations. *Realschule* and *Hauptschule* students only have access to vocational programs that prepare them for lower-level occupations.

The great majority of British students obtain General Certificates of Secondary Examinations (GCSEs), many of which have some substantive specialization potential employers may consider in choosing among recent school-leavers. Also, because much British occupation-specific schooling occurs after leaving secondary school, the GCSEs passed provide a basis for qualifying for entry into post-secondary programs.

American high schools have historically had curricular "tracks," some defined in vocational terms. As the differentiation among tracks declined (Lucas, 1999), tracks became less relevant to students' futures. More important is the degree to which students take high school courses expected of four-year college applicants because college attendance increases access to high-status occupations. Courses in mathematics, science, and foreign languages are most often expected of college applicants.

At about 15 or 16, German students begin to enter the so-called "dual system" of occupation-specific apprenticeships. Those who enter the dual system at such young ages are primarily *Realschule* and *Hauptschule* students. Some *Gymnasium* students, including some who will later obtain university degrees, enter the dual system at older ages. Dual-system students have contracts with employers for a combined program of classroom courses and work experience. The dual system covers a wide range of occupations, not just blue-collar occupations (OECD, 1996). The system is highly standardized through cooperation among state, employer, and labor organizations. Those who successfully complete apprenticeships obtain nationally recognized occupation-specific certification. The German system has also introduced specialized higher education vocational programs in polytechnics (*Fachhochschulen*).

Most British students obtain post-secondary vocational training on a part-time basis while employed. Employers often arrange for this training and may even require it as part of the employees' job requirements. Most courses are taken at employers' training centers or at state-supported Colleges of Further Education. The important feature of the British post-secondary vocational education is the extensive array of national vocational "qualifications" it certifies. These are awarded by such nationally recognized groups as The Business and Technician Education Council (BTEC), The City and Guilds of London Institute (CGLI), and The Royal Society of Arts (RSA), based on actual job performance assessments.

The organization of American post-secondary education is strikingly different from both the German and the British systems. Few American students leave school and enter the labor force with vocational credentials. Neither of the system's most commonly awarded credentials (a high school diploma and a college degree) has any specific occupational relevance. Most American post-secondary students enroll in four-year college programs having no specific vocational focus. American community colleges and vocational institutes offer courses leading to vocational certification, but only a relatively small proportion of American students enter such programs, and the certificates they award are not nationally standardized or recognized.

Overview of Educational Institutions

The German, British, and American educational institutional arrangements differ on all three of the dimensions discussed. The German system is by far the most stratified and standardized, and its educational credentials are much more occupation-specific than those of the other two systems. The great majority of German students emerge from the educational system with nationally standardized occupation-specific certification. The German system has rightly been said to have "the capacity to structure" the flow of its students from school into the labor force (Maurice, Sellier, & Silvestre, 1986).

The American system is at the other extreme on all three dimensions. It is not stratified or standardized, and it awards few credentials that have any specific vocational relevance. The system is organized around a common school philosophy that leads to an emphasis on very broad, general credentials. The American system has almost no "capacity to structure" the flow of its students into the labor force. Although vocational credentials are awarded by lower level post-secondary institutions, they are not nationally standardized, and the programs that award them are widely demeaned because they divert students from pursuing a four-year college education (Brint & Karabel, 1989).

The British system is between the German and American systems on all three dimensions. It is more stratified and standardized than the American system but much less so than the German. It awards many more nationally recognized vocational credentials at the post-secondary level than does the American system, but the overall certification pattern is less uniformly occupation-specific than in Germany.

SOCIETAL DEFINITIONS OF EDUCATION

The three countries' educational systems are organized in strikingly different ways, and the three organizational patterns are bound to shape the transition from school to work to different degrees. More than institutional structure is involved in creating the flow of students into the labor force, however. Equally important are the societies' different definitions of the role of education in people's lives.

Germans view the educational system as a mechanism for distributing successive cohorts into the labor force. This view has been maintained during a half century during which many other European systems have undergone important changes (Müller et al., 1998). The central purpose of education is to prepare students to take their place in the adult world of work (Maurice et al., 1986).

The American definition of education is quite different. The "common school" view of education sees it as a common good open to all citizens on an even basis (Soltow & Stevens, 1981). Students are urged to obtain as much education as they can, but there is little differentiation among "kinds" of education. Higher levels of education open up more labor force opportunities, but the comprehensive high school and the breadth of most college curricula insure that educational attainment has little direct effect on the distribution of American students in the labor force (Walters, 1984).

Before World War II the British system was highly stratified. It defined upper secondary schooling solely as a means of gaining access to a university education which provided the basis for an upper-status life style (Turner, 1960). Reforms since the War have redefined the system in two ways (Heath & Cheung, 1998). First, there has been increased recognition that all Britons need to have at least a basic secondary school education. This has led to the widespread introduction of Comprehensive schools. Second, there has been an increased emphasis on vocational education and vocationally specific credentials. This has led to the expansion of the post-secondary education alternatives through the polytechnics and the further education system.

The view of the role of education in people's lives is thus quite different in the three countries. The German view is directly relevant to preparation for the world of work. The American view is as a broad preparation for adult life. These perspectives have not changed appreciably in either country despite the economic and political changes during the past half century. The British system has changed much more, and the changes have reflected the emphases of both the German and American systems. Consistent with the German system, there has been an increased vocational emphasis, but consistent with the American system, there has been an increased emphasis on providing an adequate general education for all students.

THE ROLE OF EMPLOYERS IN THE
TRANSITION PROCESS

Differences in the educational systems are closely associated with differences in the ways employers participate in the transition process (Rosenbaum, Kariya, Settersten, & Maier, 1990). Although there are some modulating inputs from organized labor and the state, the German apprenticeship system is essentially controlled by the employers. Students may apply for many kinds of apprenticeships (Mortimer & Krüger, 2000), but the employers decide which apprenticeships will be available and which students are offered which opportunities. The employers also control the evaluation of apprentices and determine which ones will be certified as having successfully completed their training. The range of openings, the selection of trainees, and the certification of successful completion are all controlled by the employers (Culpepper & Finegold, 1999).

Employers have very little direct effect on the transition process in the United States. They neither define the nature of the educational programs students engage in nor do they provide certification of student skills. Local employers sometimes cooperate with community colleges in presenting vocational courses to students, but there is no nationally recognized system of certificates obtainable by students completing such courses. When American students enter their first full-time jobs, employers select among applicants; very few have formally certified job qualifications. Many selection errors are made, and young people often experience a period of unstable employment before finding a stable job (Rosenbaum et al., 1990).

British employers make important contributions to the process by which students move from school to work, but their role is less comprehensive than in Germany. Except for the small minority who attend university, most British students obtain either very general qualifications in secondary school (O-levels, A-levels, etc.) or post-secondary vocational qualifications. British employers participate in students' transition from school to work by providing vocational courses in their training centers or facilitating workers' attendance at colleges of further education. They also contribute to the transition process through participation in the industrial groups that provide the certification of nationally recognized occupation-specific qualifications. Certification of qualifications by these organizations motivates employers to help employees obtain them.

STUDENT CHOICE

The effects German and British employers have on students' transitions from school to work are similar to the extent that in both countries employers define criteria for certification of occupation-specific skills and control the evaluation process that certifies workers' qualifications on a national scale. German and British students have very different degrees of latitude in choosing how to relate to the certification process, however. While the German system now offers greater flexibility (Mortimer & Krüger, 2000), most German students enter an apprenticeship at the appropriate time of entry or they may risk losing the opportunity to do so. There is much more flexibility in the timing of British students' entry into post-secondary vocational courses.

Also, German students' entry into apprenticeships involves a long-term (three- or four-year) commitment on the part of the student and the employer. A student's failure to successfully complete an apprenticeship has serious implications for both parties. Compared to German apprenticeships, most British vocational courses are relatively short-term, and neither the worker nor the employer needs to make a major commitment. British workers can improve their qualifications in relatively small steps, and both the worker and the employer can easily reassess the merits of the course-taking.

American students face very different alternatives than either German or British students as they approach the transition from school to work. American students are strongly encouraged to obtain a high school diploma, and once they obtain it, they are strongly encouraged to go to college. They can "choose" to complete high school, and they can "choose" to enter college, but neither of these choices has much effect on the kinds of first jobs they are likely to enter. This lack of specific occupational relevance insures that many young American workers will be dissatisfied with their first jobs, and many employers will be dissatisfied with their young workers. This leads to many job changes during the early years in the labor force. It also leads many American workers to return to school in hopes of improving their job options.

The choices available to young people in the three countries reflect the nature of the educational credentials available to them before and after making the transition to the labor force and the points in the transition process at which choices are offered. British workers frequently improve their qualifications through part-time vocational courses after entering the labor force. American workers frequently leave their jobs and return to full-time schooling after entering the labor force. German workers are the least likely to return to school once they have completed their apprenticeships and have entered the labor force in jobs for which their apprenticeships prepared them.

STAGES IN THE TRANSITION PROCESS

The transition from school to work seldom consists of a single move from full-time school to full-time work. It more often involves several stages, but the pattern of those stages varies both between and within societies. I first discuss the different stages that are often involved in the transition and the ways these stages occur in Germany, Great Britain, and the United States. I then describe how students' experience with these stages shapes the transition from school to work in the three countries. In particular, the stages are experienced at different ages.

These age differences affect the life course patterns for the whole transition from adolescence to adulthood in the three countries.

School, Work, or Both?

Instead of a single move from full-time school to full-time work, two other patterns are more common. First, young people can move from full-time school to a simultaneous involvement in school and work. Second, young people may move back and forth between full-time school and full-time work. The frequency with which these two patterns are observed and the degree to which they are part of a society's institutional arrangements vary widely.

We see in the German apprenticeship system a highly institutionalized combination of working and going to school. The great majority of young Germans pass through a period during which they are essentially required to do both. That is the only way they can obtain the all-important occupation-specific credentials.

The British system of post-secondary vocational schooling also combines student and worker roles, but it is a looser linkage of the roles than in Germany, and young Britons have more latitude in choosing the degree and form of the combination. Yet, it is important to recognize that many highly regarded British vocational credentials are available only by combining work and school. British institutional arrangements specify the process by which these credentials can be obtained and normative pressures motivate young Britons to obtain them.*

Young Americans often combine going to school and working at the same time. This mix may be due to full-time students taking part-time jobs while still in school or to full-time workers taking courses during their non-working hours. The combination is not as institutionalized a part of the school-to-work transition as in either Germany or Great Britain, however. Most American students who work do so to obtain spending money rather than to initiate a career in the labor force, although early part-time work sometimes does improve later job opportunities (Mortimer & Johnson, 1998). Workers who take part-time courses are often motivated by a desire for a better job, but not all of those who take such courses obtain additional credentials or obtain better jobs (Grubb, 1993; Kerckhoff & Bell, 1998; Monk-Turner, 1990).

British and German adolescents are made very conscious of the strong institutionalized linkage between school and work early in their teens (Bynner & Roberts, 1991; Mortimer & Krüger, 2000), and they begin early to take the linkages into account. However, "in the United States, the pattern of employment is individualized and emergent, constructed by youths themselves in the relatively uncertain school-to-work context" (Mortimer & Krüger, 2000, p. 484).[†]

Another transition pattern can involve a combination of school and work. The individual can enter the labor force full-time, then leave the labor force and return to school full-time,

---

*It is interesting to note that, although large proportions of young people are led to combine work and school in both the German and British systems, those combinations are treated quite differently in most scholarly analyses. German apprentices are almost always classified as being in school, whereas young Britons who combine work and employer-sponsored training are classified as having left school. Thus, in comparative research about the school to work transition, Germans' "first jobs" are defined as those they obtain after completing an apprenticeship, whereas Britons' "first jobs" are defined as those they obtain when they leave full-time school (Shavit & Müller, 1998).

[†]It is not possible to take into account the part-time jobs of full-time American students or the occasional courses taken by full-time American workers in what follows because adequate national data do not exist on these joint activities or their effects on young people's careers. However, there are national data on part-time enrollments. For purposes of the discussion, I have assumed that those who are enrolled part-time are combining school and work.

and then return to the labor force. Americans use this method of mixing school and work over a period of time much more often than either Britons or Germans (Arum & Hout, 1998). Although such a pattern does not simultaneously "combine" school and work, it constitutes another way in which the transition from school to work can be other than a simple one-time change. My discussion of the patterns of transition from school to work in the three countries takes this largely American pattern into account to the extent possible, given the limited available data.

Another kind of deviation from a one-step transition from school to work needs to be acknowledged. Not everyone who leaves school actually enters the labor force, and of those who do, not everyone actually finds a job. Any comprehensive view of the transition from school to work needs to consider those exceptions. They are discussed briefly in a later section. In this section I focus on the schooling stages in the transition: full-time school, a combination of school and work, and the final departure from school. The discussion is thus concerned with leaving school rather than entering the labor force.

Age, Stage, and Leaving School

It is helpful to think about the departure from school as an overall population process, a process by which a youth cohort moves out of school and into adult roles. In any given country, there is a time when essentially all members of a cohort are in school, and there is a time when all have departed for good. It is informative to consider how old the cohort members are at those two points in time and to chart the overall flow of the members between the two points. Even in the same country, some members complete school at much younger ages than others, and in general, the more time spent in the role of full-time student, the older the individual is when leaving for good. However, some may spend more time than others in the transition stage that combines being a student and a worker, and that may affect the age at which they finally leave school for good.

In what follows I make estimates of the ages at which Germans, Britons, and Americans cease being students. To do this, I consider both the patterns of full-time schooling in the three countries and the patterns of involvement in a transition stage that combines school and work activities. I also estimate the effects of returns from the labor force to school. There are no wholly adequate data to make these estimates for cohorts in the three countries, so what follows is more speculative than ideal.

It is possible to specify the ages at which all young people in these three countries are in school, but it is not possible to exactly specify an age at which all members of a cohort in any of the three countries have completed school. Enrollments in graduate and professional schools, returns from the labor force to school, and enrollments in adult education courses all extend the ages of "students" beyond any age limit we might adopt.

Both Great Britain and the United States require school attendance to age 16 (although there is some variation among American states), but Germany requires attendance to age 18. We can assume that students are attending school up to those ages. To simplify the discussion, I will only chart young people's locations in the three countries up to age 28, even though small minorities are in school at that age in all three countries. Besides estimating the patterns of movement out of school by members of recent cohorts in the three countries, I suggest how the organizational and normative features of the three educational systems affect these patterns of movement.

Assuming that all 16-year-olds are in full-time school in all three countries, it is informative to ask where they are at various ages after that. Table 12-1 indicates, at two-year intervals,

TABLE 12-1. **Estimated Percentage Distributions of German, British, and American Cohorts in School Situations between 16 and 28 Years of Age**

Age	16	18	20	22	24	26	28
Germany							
Full-time School	100%	35%	17%	18%	20%	16%	9%
School & Work		49	51	16	6	2	1
Out of School		16	32	66	74	82	90
Great Britain							
Full-time School	100%	16%	13%	5%	2%	1%	1%
School & Work		21	11	8	3	2	1
Out of School		63	76	87	95	97	98
United States							
Full-time School	100%	42%	28%	20%	12%	9%	7%
School & Work		10	7	6	3	2	1
Out of School		48	65	74	85	89	92

the estimated proportions in each country that are in school full-time, in a status that combines school and work, or are completely out of school. The bases for these estimates are described in the Appendix. These proportions are estimates of the distributions of young people's locations in October of the year they were each age. As I explain later, such cross-sectional distributions do not tell the whole story, but they at least provide an overview of the flow of young people out of school.

Several country differences are immediately apparent:

1. Much larger proportions of both Britons and Americans are completely out of school at relatively early ages than are Germans.
2. Britons leave full-time school much earlier than do either Germans or Americans.
3. Germans most often combine school and work, and Americans least often combine school and work.
4. Although Americans are most likely to be in full-time school in their early twenties, Germans are most likely to be in full-time school in their late twenties.

These different distributions are clearly created by the organizational features of the three countries' educational systems. The central role of formal apprenticeships in the German educational system makes "school & work" the primary location of 18- and 20-year-old Germans. *Gymnasium* students and a few students in full-time vocational schools are in full-time school at 18, but by age 20 full-time students are almost all *Gymnasium* students. Yet, even at 20, only one third of the Germans have left school completely. Those Germans who enter higher education often do so relatively late by British and American standards, and they may remain in full-time school well into their twenties.

The definition of the British secondary school sixth form (between ages 16 and 18) as preparatory for university, together with highly restricted access to higher education, leads many Britons to leave full-time school before the age of 18. The great majority of these school-leavers get jobs, mostly full-time jobs. Because 16-year-old school-leavers have few job skills or vocational credentials, a sizeable proportion of those in beginning jobs engage in a combination of work and vocational training, usually with the assistance (and often the insistence) of their employers. This dual arrangement is concentrated in the early years, however. Higher education is also concentrated in the early post-secondary years. British university programs are for three years, so most university students leave full-time school by 22. Thus, most Britons are completely finished with school in their early twenties.

The strong emphasis on going to college in the United States keeps a large proportion of Americans in full-time school at 18 and 20. But that same emphasis means that young Americans have few other choices. The American choice tends to be "college or nothing." Thus, those who are not in full-time school are likely to be out of school. Only small proportions participate in programs that combine school and work, although many American students do take on part-time jobs on an ad hoc basis.

It is important to remember that the estimates in Table 12-1 are of the cohort members' locations in October of the year they were the indicated ages. They are cross-sectional snap shots of the distributions at particular points in time. As such, they cannot indicate the full process of change. Two important kinds of information are missing.

First, there is an implicit logic to Table 12-1 that the overall flow is from full-time school to a combination of school and work and then to being out of school. Overall, the flow of young people is like that in all three countries, although many Americans, especially, never enter a formally combined school and work status (though almost all work at least some time while attending secondary and post-secondary schools). However, there are "back flows" as well. Some who at one time combine school and work move back to full-time school. This happens most clearly in Germany among apprentices who earlier attended the *Gymnasium* and after their apprenticeships enter university as full-time students. Also, some who have left school completely return to school either full-time or in a combined school and work arrangement. Returns to full-time school are most common in the United States, whereas returns to a combined school and work arrangement are most common in Great Britain. Having left school, Germans do not seem to return to school as frequently as Britons or Americans, but some do return (Heinz, 1999).

Second, because Table 12-1 reports locations at two-year intervals, it cannot show changes that occur during those two-year intervals. Many post-secondary courses cover relatively brief periods. More than one change of location can occur in a two-year period. Someone can be out of school at two successive measurement points but return to school briefly to take a course between them. This is especially likely for Britons' combined school and work arrangements, but Americans can also take short-term vocational courses or return for a year of college between measurement points.*

Given the complex sets of locations available at each age, there are large numbers of possible pathways students can follow as they move out of the school system. Adequate data do not exist to chart these multiple pathways in the three countries, and it is apparent that Table 12-1 provides only a crude indication of what they would be.

Entering the Labor Force

Once young people have left school completely, it is expected that they will enter the labor force. The vast majority does so, although there are many patterns of entry. To some extent, the varied patterns of entry are a function of age and educational attainments at the time of entry, but they are also due to the state of the economy at that time. In general, older entrants and those with higher educational attainments have smoother transitions into the labor force.

---

*Table 12-1 suggests that, at most, 26% of the Americans and 13% of the Britons were in any kind of school situation between ages 22 and 28. (This is because 74% of the Americans and 87% of the Britons were out of school at 22.) Yet, more detailed analyses of the data from those two countries show that 33.3% of the Americans and 17.6% of the Britons took some kind of course between those ages (Kerckhoff et al., 2000).

The younger and more poorly educated are more likely to have difficulty finding a job. This is especially likely if the economy is weak and unemployment rates are high (Arum & Hout, 1998; Brauns et al., 1999).

There are some exceptions to the general association between level of educational attainment and ease of labor force entry, however. In Germany, for instance, students with high academic secondary school credentials (the *Abitur*) more often experience difficulty finding a job than those who have completed a lower level vocational program (Brauns et al., 1999). Certified vocational skills make it easier to find a job. This is why some *Gymnasium* students complete an apprenticeship before entering the university. The firm where they were apprenticed may wish to hire them because of their combined technical skills and higher education credentials. The apprenticeship certification serves as a safety net for those in the less structured university labor market.

The patterns of labor force entry also vary by gender in all three countries. Both men and women in all three countries seek employment when they leave school. Women seldom leave the labor force even when they marry, but they are very likely to leave when they become mothers. Yet, men's and women's different kinds and levels of educational attainment as well as their different opportunities in the labor force produce gender differences in labor force entry.

The German labor force entry pattern reflects women's more restricted choices of apprenticeships. Many more German women than men fail to obtain apprenticeships in any of their chosen fields; the women can only prepare for female stereotyped jobs (Mortimer & Krüger, 2000). Partly as a result of these restrictions, female labor force participation declines by age more rapidly in Germany than in either Great Britain or the United States (Arum & Hout, 1998; Brauns et al., 1999).

More British women than men leave school at 16, and more British men than women attend vocational post-secondary courses at training centers and colleges of further education (Kerckhoff, Bell, & Glennie, 2000). British men thus have better chances of employment soon after leaving full-time school, and they are more likely to be hired by employers that are willing to invest in their vocational schooling.

American men and women differ much less in educational attainment (Kerckhoff et al., 2000; NCES, 1998). American men drop out of high school somewhat more often, and American women are somewhat more likely to obtain a college degree, but the differences in educational attainment are quite small compared with the gender differences of Germans or Britons. So, Americans' early labor force experiences do not differ by gender as much as those of young Germans or Britons.

Young workers of both genders in all three countries are always at greater risk of unemployment than are older workers. In addition, changes in the economy impact more immediately on their employability. Young British and American workers are more at risk for periods of unemployment than are German workers, however, because young Germans more often have certified skills when they enter employment. Some of the sorting into kinds of jobs that occurs after labor force entry in Great Britain and the United States occurs in Germany at the time apprentices are recruited. If at all possible, employers will not offer apprenticeships leading to jobs that will be in short supply when the apprenticeships are completed.

THREE PATTERNS OF TRANSITION FROM SCHOOL TO WORK

The transition from school to work follows very different patterns in Germany, Great Britain, and the United States. Those patterns differ primarily as the result of the way the educational systems are organized in the three countries and the way they interface with the labor markets. We can think of them as "highly structured," "loosely structured," and "unstructured" patterns of transition.

The Highly Structured German Pattern

German secondary schools are highly stratified, programs at all levels are standardized, there are firm linkages between the organizational units at different levels, and most educational credentials are defined in highly specific occupational terms. Pathways through school and into the labor force are clearly outlined and differentiated. The German educational system has the "capacity to structure" the flow of young Germans into the labor force in the sense that Maurice et al. (1986) meant. By the time students exit the educational system, the great majority have a well-defined location to enter in the labor force.

The German educational system also has the "capacity to structure" the flow of students in another sense, however. Its highly structured channels, with firm linkages between stages, also structure the flow of students into the labor force according to age. Very few *Hauptschule* students remain in school much past age 18, and only *Gymnasium* students are likely to be in school past their mid-twenties. The age at which German students will enter the labor force can be predicted with some accuracy at the time they are separated into the three types of secondary schools. In fact, to the extent that leaving school and becoming a worker increases the likelihood of leaving the parental home, getting married, and becoming a parent, it can be said that the German educational system has a powerful influence on structuring the entire multi-dimensional transition from adolescence to adulthood.

The Loosely Structured British Pattern

British secondary schools have limited degrees of stratification, programs are only recently becoming standardized, organizational units at different levels are only loosely linked, and there is a mix of academic and vocational credentials. The only clearly outlined British educational pathway is the one that leads through the sixth form of secondary school to higher education. British secondary school students generally leave full-time school rather early (at 16 or 18) and enter the labor force. Very few enter any form of higher education.

If we assume that those who do leave at early ages are permanently "out of school," we miss a major part of the British transition process. Much of the sorting into the labor force occurs through vocational courses taken after they leave full-time school and obtain a full-time job. A wide range of important vocational qualifications can only be obtained through a combination of work and school after leaving full-time school. Those combinations are similar in many ways to the German apprenticeship arrangements in that they require an agreement between a worker and employer on a program of study. But they are much more individually negotiated in Great Britain than in Germany, and they depend much less on students' earlier accomplishments.

To the extent that there is a fit between vocational credentials and kinds of jobs, the British educational system does have the capacity to structure the flow of young people into the labor force. But it is a much more passive "capacity" than in the German case. Whereas the German system acts as an external force directing young people into particular niches in the labor force, the British system only provides the channels through which young people can move. The actual pathways followed are much more a function of ad hoc negotiations between young workers and employers.

The Unstructured American Pattern

American secondary schools are neither stratified nor standardized, there are no formal link-ages between the organizational units at different levels, and nearly all credentials are aca-demic rather than vocational. Equally important, in contrast to the wide array of credentials offered by the German and British systems, there are few nationally recognized American cre-dentials. The two most significant credentials (a high school diploma and a Bachelor's degree) are widely spaced; it takes four years or more of full-time study to obtain the higher level credential once the lower level credential has been obtained. Because of the personal, academic, and economic problems involved in completing a four-year program, only about half of the Americans who go to college actually obtain a Bachelor's degree (NCES, 1998). Educational credentials between a high school diploma and a Bachelor's degree are available, but they are neither widely respected nor frequently obtained.

Very few American students who enter the labor force can present a potential employer with any kind of skill certification. Being a high school dropout, a high school graduate, a col-lege dropout, or a college graduate affects the initial distribution of young Americans in the labor force, but only in a very general way. At each educational level, there is a wide range of jobs available, but there is almost no basis upon which to make a person-job match. The American educational system has almost no capacity to structure the flow of students into the labor force. The transition from school to work is less structured and orderly in the United States than in any other Western industrial country.

American students are urged to obtain as much education as possible, and the great majority at least obtains a high school diploma. The diploma, in turn, provides access to a college education, and a large proportion actually enters college. However, while more uni-versity degrees are obtained in the United States than in any other Western industrial country, even a university degree has little direct labor force relevance. Whatever their educational attainments, American students face a very ill-defined interface between school and the world of work. Thus, the transition from school to work is a journey that has less order and greater diversity in the United States than elsewhere.

Educational Systems and the Transition from School to Work

All three educational systems discussed here affect the transition process, but they do so in very different ways. The German system actively organizes and monitors the process from pre-adolescence on. It effectively guides students through pre-established channels and dis-tributes them into "appropriate" jobs. It is a very "hands on" system. The British system provides several levels of general secondary school credentials, restricts access to higher education, but offers many post-secondary opportunities to obtain specialized credentials. However, access to those post-secondary opportunities is much less restricted by earlier school experiences than in Germany, and it depends much more on individual negotiations between workers and employers.

The American system leaves young people completely on their own to find their way through the transition process. It does not actively select students to follow specific transition pathways. It does not even provide nationally recognized programs of study leading to voca-tionally meaningful credentials. Except at the college level, it does little to facilitate students' contacts with employers. It emphasizes the importance of the amount, not the kind, of edu-cation obtained, and it imposes few limitations on students' access to additional education.

Whatever the amount of education obtained, however, negotiations with potential employers depend more on general intellectual and personal qualities (being well-organized, dependable, persistent, polite, etc.) than on job-related skills (Dreeben, 1968). Americans take pride in the "openness" of our educational system. Everyone can succeed by working hard and staying involved. But the very "openness" of the American system leaves its students with few explicit goals to pursue and little guidance about how to reach them.

APPENDIX

The age distributions shown in Table 12-1 are based on less than wholly adequate data. I have access to good longitudinal data for Great Britain and the United States, but the German estimates are based on secondary sources. Thus, the data are least adequate for Germany. Even the British and American data are limited by the fact that data were collected at wider intervals than two years, so some interpolation is required. All three sets of estimates are based on data from the mid-1970s to the early 1990s. Some data for all three countries are available in OECD (1996) and in Shavit and Müller (1998). In addition, the following sources were the basis for the estimates.

Great Britain

The National Child Development Study (NCDS) followed a cohort from their births in 1958 until 1991, with data collected when they were 7, 11, 16, 23, and 33 years old. I have used that data set in several of my previous studies (Kerckhoff, 1990, 1993; Kerckhoff et al., 2000). Another particularly relevant publication based on that data set is Bynner & Fogelman (1993). Some of the publications that compare Great Britain and Germany (listed for Germany) were also useful. The NCDS is the primary British data source used here.

The United States

The basic data source for the American estimates is the sophomore cohort of the High School and Beyond study. The original sample members were sophomores in American high schools in 1980, and additional data were collected in 1982, 1986, and 1992. These data have also been used in some of my previous research: Kerckhoff and Bell, 1998; Kerckhoff and Glennie, 1999; Kerckhoff et al., 2000. These data are the primary basis for the American estimates in Table 12-1.

Germany

A number of informal and published accounts helped to generate the German data in Table 12-1. Most of these sources used the younger age groups in the German General Social Survey or the Socio-Economic Panel. None of the sources is wholly adequate for the task, but the most useful were: Brauns, Gangl, and Scherer, 1999; Brauns, Müller, and Steinmann, 1997; Büchtemann, Schupp, and Soloff, 1994; Heinz, 1999; Scherer, 1999.

REFERENCES

Allmendinger, J. (1989). Educational systems and labor market outcomes. *European Sociological Review,* *5*, 231–250.

Archer, M. (1979). *Social origins of educational systems.* Beverly Hills, CA: Sage.

Arum, R., & Hout, M. (1998). The early returns: The transition from school to work in the United States. In Y. Shavit & W. Müller (Eds.), *From school to work: A comparative study of educational qualifications and occupational destinations* (pp. 471–510). Oxford: Clarendon Press.

Brauns, H., Gangl, M., & Scherer, S. (1999). Education and unemployment: Patterns of labour market entry in France, the United Kingdom and West Germany. *Arbeitspapiere, Nr. 6—Mannheimer Zentrum für Europäische Sozialforschung.*

Brauns, H., Müller, W., & Steinmann, S. (1997). Educational expansion and returns to education: A comparative study on Germany, France, the UK, and Hungary. *Arbeitsbereich I, Nr. 23—Mannheimer Zentrum für Europäische Sozialforschung.*

Brint, S., & Karabel, J. (1989). *The diverted dream: Community colleges and the promise of educational opportunity in America, 1900–1995.* New York: Oxford University Press.

Büchtemann, C. F., Schupp, J., & Soloff, D. (1994). In J. Schwarze, F. Buttler, & G. G. Wagner (Eds.), Labour market dynamics in present day Germany (pp. 112–141). Boulder, CO: Westview Press.

Bynner, J., & Fogelman, K. (1993). Making the grade: Education and training experiences. In E. Ferri (Ed.), *Life at 33: The fifth follow-up of the National Child Development Study* (pp. 36–59). London: National Children's Bureau.

Bynner, J., & Roberts, K. (Eds.). (1991). *Youth and work: Transition to employment in England and Germany.* London: Anglo-German Foundation.

Culpepper, P. D., & Finegold, D. (Eds.). (1999). *The German skills machine.* Oxford: Berghahn Books.

Dreeben, R. (1968). *On what is learned in school.* Reading, MA: Addison-Wesley.

Elder, G. H., Jr., & Rockwell, R. C. (1979). The life course and human development: An ecological perspective. *International Journal of Behavioral Development, 2,* 1–22.

Gordon, P., Aldrich, R., & Dean, D. (1991). *Education and policy in England in the twentieth century.* London: Woburn Press.

Grubb, W. N. (1993). The varied economic returns to postsecondary education: New evidence from the class of 1972. *Journal of Human Resources, 28,* 365–382.

Heath, A., & Cheung, S. Y. (1998). Education and occupation in Britain. In Y. Shavit & W. Müller (Eds.), *From school to work: A comparative study of educational qualifications and occupational destinations* (pp. 71–101). Oxford: Clarendon Press.

Heinz, W. R. (1999). Job-entry patterns in a life-course perspective. In W. R. Heinz (Ed.), *From education to work: Cross-national perspectives* (pp. 214–231). New York: Cambridge.

Hogan, D. P., & Astone, N. M. (1986). The transition to adulthood. *Annual Review of Sociology, 12,* 109–130.

Kaestle, C. (1983). *Pillars of the republic: Common schools and American society, 1780–1960.* New York: Hill & Wang.

Kerckhoff, A. C. (1990). *Getting started: Transition to adulthood in Great Britain.* Boulder, CO: Westview.

Kerckhoff, A. C. (1993). *Diverging pathways: Social structure and career deflections.* New York: Cambridge.

Kerckhoff, A. C., & Bell, L. (1998). Hidden capital: Vocational credentials and attainment in the United States. *Sociology of Education, 71,* 152–174.

Kerckhoff, A. C., Bell, L., & Glennie, E. (2000). Comparative educational attainment trajectories in Great Britain and the United States. A paper presented to the International Sociological Association, Research Committee on Social Stratification, Libourne, France.

Kerckhoff, A. C., Fogelman, K., Crook, D., & Reeder, D. (1996). *Going comprehensive in England and Wales: A study of uneven change.* London: Woburn Press.

Kerckhoff, A. C., & Glennie, E. (1999). The Matthew effect in American education. *Research in Sociology of Education and Socialization, 12,* 35–66.

Lucas, L.R. (1999). *Tracking inequality: Stratification and mobility in American high schools.* New York: Teachers College Press.

Maurice, M., Sellier, F., & Silvestre, J.-J. (1986). *The social foundations of industrial power: A comparison of France and Germany.* Cambridge, MA: MIT Press.

Monk-Turner, E. (1990). The occupational achievements of community and four-year college entrants. *American Sociological Review, 55,* 719–725.

Mortimer, J. T., & Johnson, M. K. (1999). Adolescent part-time work and postsecondary transition pathways in the United States. In W. R. Heinz (Ed.), *From education to work: Cross-national perspectives* (pp. 111–148). New York: Cambridge.

Mortimer, J. T., & Krüger, H. (2000). Transition from school to work in the United States and Germany. In M. T. Hallinan (Ed.), *Handbook of the sociology of education*. New York: Plenum.

Müller, W., Steinmann, S., & Ell, R. (1998). Education and labour-market entry in Germany. In Y. Shavit & W. Müller (Eds.), *From school to work: A comparative study of educational qualifications and occupational destinations* (pp. 143–188). Oxford: Clarendon Press.

NCES. (1998). *The condition of education, 1998*. Washington, DC: National Center for Education Statistics.

OECD. (1996). *Education at a glance: OECD indicators*. Paris: Organization for Economic Co-operation and Development.

Rosenbaum, J. E., Kariya, T., Settersten, R., & Maier, T. (1990). Market and network theories of the transition from high school to work: Their application to industrialized societies. *Annual Review of Sociology, 16*, 263–299.

Scherer, S. (1999). Early career patterns: A comparison of Great Britain and West Germany. *Arbeitspapiere, Nr. 7—Mannheimer Zentrum für Europäische Sozialforschung*.

Shavit, Y., & Müller, W. (1998). *From school to work: A comparative study of educational qualifications and occupational destinations*. Oxford: Clarendon Press.

Soltow, L., & Stevens, E. (1981). *The rise of literacy and the common school in the United States*. Chicago: University of Chicago Press.

Turner, R. H. (1960). Sponsored and contest mobility and the school system. *American Sociological Review, 25*, 855–867.

Vanfossen, B., Jones, J., & Spade, J. (1987). Curriculum tracking and status maintenance. *Sociology of Education, 60*, 104–122.

Walters, P. (1984). Occupational and labor market effects of secondary and post-secondary school expansion in the United States. *American Sociological Review, 49*, 659–671.

CHAPTER 13

Midcourse

Navigating Retirement and a New Life Stage

PHYLLIS MOEN

Family scholars as well as scholars of occupations and organizations have long viewed retirement—that is, exiting one's primary career* occupation—as an important life marker. In the middle of the 20th century retirement became a common transition, particularly for men; it was part of their lockstep life course from education through employment to retirement. Reaching age 65 (or 62 for some), leaving the workforce, becoming eligible for Social Security and pensions, defining oneself as "retired"—all occurred simultaneously with exiting one's career occupation. However, today these are increasingly separate events, making the definition of "retirement" problematic. Most economists define retirement as the "final" exit from the labor force or, alternatively the time of pension receipt. Sociologists and psychologists also use these definitions, as well as various additional ones, including being over 60 or 65, exiting from one's primary career job (but not necessarily the workforce), or simply a self-definition, "being retired." But many scholars neglect to offer *any* definition, assuming that, like marriage or parenthood, this is a commonly understood, taken-for-granted, clearly demarcated status passage.

This chapter describes the usefulness of a life course approach to retirement as a *process that occurs over time*, a process embedded in a number of overlapping contexts, including the ecology of what is emerging as a new life stage, after traditional adulthood yet prior to the frailty

---

*Note that, due to the complexity of multiple careers and multiple retirements, I use the term "career job" or "primary career job" to characterize the job with the longest duration. In the 1950s and 1960s "career" meant one job or a related sequence; retirement meant one event. This was rarely true of women or minority men, and is less typical of all workers today.

PHYLLIS MOEN • Department of Sociology, University of Minnesota, Minneapolis, Minnesota 55455.

Handbook of the Life Course, edited by Jeylan T. Mortimer and Michael J. Shanahan. Kluwer Academic/Plenum Publishers, New York, 2003.

and dependency traditionally associated with growing old. The contemporary "blurred" retirement status passage, together with changes in lifestyle, longevity, and health, is spawning this new life stage, *midcourse* between the years of career building and old age. Accordingly, I term this emerging life stage *midcourse*, suggesting it spans the fifties, sixties, and even seventies. It is not the middle of adulthood so much as the period when many contemporary midlife adults begin contemplating and moving toward shifting gears. Retirement as an institutionalized transition was increasingly possible for women and minority men as jobs with pensions became accessible to them in the second half of the 20th century as Social Security benefits offered an alternative to employment. However, this new life phase may not be available to all segments of society. Many of those disadvantaged in earlier years continue to be at risk: shifts in pension and Social Security policies may render them unable to afford to retire "early." More vulnerable to unexpected layoffs and without financial assets or prospects, those in poor health, in physically demanding jobs, and without health insurance may view the midcourse years more as a cumulation of risk than a time of possibility. For the advantaged, the disadvantaged, and the vast numbers in between, the midcourse years are increasingly a time of uneven, unscripted transition.

The early years of the life course have been categorized by progressively finer delineations: infant, toddler, preschooler, kindergartner, child, youth, tween, teen, adolescent. Often these reflect organizational regimes associated with child care and educational entry and exit portals as much as developmental demarcations. However, middle and later adulthood has had but one official organizational, social, and biographical status passage, retirement from paid work and one less official and less recognized status passage for parents, the emptying of the nest as children move from home and toward adulthood. Some people do not retire, some never have children, some have children who never leave home, but I argue that the midcourse period is on the cusp of becoming a virtual if not actual life stage for three reasons: increasing longevity, the ambiguity around retirement timing and the expanding period of life after retirement, and the aging of the large baby boom cohort (born 1946–1964) who do not want their parents' version of either retirement or growing older.

For many Americans, the midcourse years are a progression of moving from planning* and talking about retirement possibilities to exiting one's primary career job, moving into unpaid volunteer work or a second or third (paid) career, caring for aging or infirm relatives, becoming eligible for Social Security and Medicare, developing concerns about one's health, and, finally, leaving the workforce altogether. All these changes occur in tandem with witnessing one's children grow up, marry or not, start families or not, become economically self-sufficient or not. Simultaneously, one's spouse, friends, and colleagues begin to think about and actually retire from their own career jobs, developing alternative lifestyles for the midcourse years. Like the midcourse years in which it is embedded, the retirement transition is no longer either "crisp" or lockstep; it unfolds at a wide variety of ages, in a multitude of sequences and durations. This extended process of moving to and through various retirement exits—along with declining morbidity, increasing longevity, progressively earlier retirement, and the aging of the baby boom cohort—means that defining all people over a certain age— be it 60, 62, or 65—as "seniors," "elders," "old," or "retirees" obscures more than it reveals.

Life course scholars (e.g., Han & Moen, 1999; Kim & Moen, 2001b) offer a view of retirement as a *process* that occurs over time, not a single event. A life course, *role context* approach (Moen, Fields, Quick & Hofmeister, 2000; Musick, Herzog, & House, 1999; Spitze, Logan,

---

*Scholars gauge "planning" many ways: the answer to a question "have you begun to plan…?" as well as an objective measure of financial savings or whether people have attended formal "retirement planning" sessions. Most people engage in financial planning; few think about planning for their lives (apart from economically) after retirement.

Joseph, & Lee, 1994) emphasizes the complexity of the midcourse years as they play out within individual, relational, and temporal biographies (and, in particular, historical, organizational, and situational contexts). As an institutionalized role exit from one's primary job, retirement is first and foremost an occupational career transition. However, family and life course scholars view it as a key family transition as well (and, in fact, now increasingly involving the career exits of both spouses), affecting the lifestyles, life chances, and life quality of both spouses. It is also a personal, biographical transition, taking form in the light of people's past biographies (such as the timing of their childbearing) (see Moen, Sweet, & Swisher, 2001) and their personal resources (health, income, and sense of personal control) (see Kim & Moen, 2002), while also shaping future identities and opportunities for growth, generativity, and social participation. From a larger, societal vantage point, retirement is both an institutionalized aspect of the life course as well as an example of *structural lag*, with existing policies and practices out of step with changing demographic, gender, and economic realities (Riley, Kahn, & Foner, 1994). A life course approach to retirement captures: (1) the complex dynamisms linking individual lives and social structures (including the shifting economic, political, and demographic environment affecting retirement planning and actions), as well as agency in planning and executing mid-course transitions; (2) the diverse impacts of retirement-related events and their timing (such as exiting one's career job or entry into postretirement community service or employment) on life chances and life quality; and (3) the social construction of this new, midcourse life stage in which individuals think about and execute the retirement status passage. One thing this chapter will make increasingly clear, retirement is no longer the passage to old age.

To develop a model of the midcourse years, along with the retirement transition and its impacts (see Figure 13-1), I consider four sets of contexts and contingencies (see also Elder, 1995, 1998a; Giele & Elder, 1998; Moen, 2003): (1) historical, (2) biographical, (3) relational, and (4) organizational and occupational. These contexts form the structure of this chapter. Throughout I touch upon various theoretical approaches to decision-making (tied to the life course notion of agency) around the retirement status passage. For illustrations, I draw on existing life course literature, including my own research.

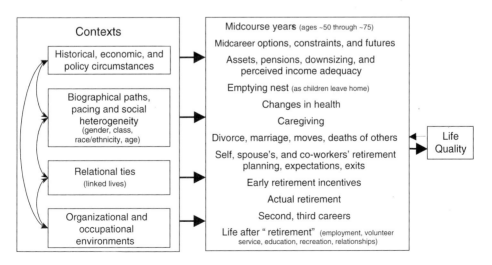

FIGURE 13-1. Midcourse as a series of choices and changes in context.

RETIREMENT AND MIDCOURSE IN
HISTORICAL AND POLICY CONTEXTS

A life course focus on retirement emphasizes the significance of the changing *historical context*; it underscores the ways various policy regimes routinize or problematize the social organization of lives (Han & Moen, 1999; Kim & Moen, 2001b; Moen, 1998, 2003; Quick & Moen, 1998; Settersten & Mayer, 1997). Retirement as a structural aspect of the life course is a relatively recent phenomenon, institutionalized in industrialized societies only in the 20th century (Costa, 1998; Graebner, 1980), but now embedded in established social and organizational policy and practices. In the middle of the 20th century, normative expectations, in conjunction with the institutionalization of income supports (in the form of Social Security payments and private pensions), set *retirement* apart from *unemployment* as a later life work exit (typically at 65 or 62) that can be planned for, anticipated, and positively defined. "Retirement" has typically meant later life withdrawal from the workforce, often in conjunction with public and/or employer-provided pension benefits. In fact, trends in government financial support in the later years of adulthood (Social Security, Supplemental Security Income (SSI), and Medicare) and employer-provided pensions have been key in shaping the later adult life course (Quadagno, 1988). Retirement may be a relatively recent social invention, but it has come to be a key individual, family, organizational, political, and cultural phenomenon. It is in fact now a fundamental dimension of life course organization, for most workers an almost universal status passage, still culturally defined as a passage *from* productive adulthood and *to* old age.

For contemporary workers and recent retirees, however, this institutionalized transition is very much in flux. My thesis is that the historical factors problematizing what has been a taken-for-granted component of occupational career paths and aging are precisely the conditions conducive to the development of the new *midcourse* life stage. Consider first recent economic changes. In the late 20th century, mergers, downsizing, and restructuring began destroying traditional lockstep career/retirement patterns, making both midcareer and retirement prospects and possibilities increasingly uncertain. These changes in the employer/employee contract (as a consequence of the growth of an information economy and globalization, as well as cycles of economic recession) mean that seniority is no longer accompanied by job security. Workers in their fifties and sixties typically command higher salaries than their younger colleagues; employers view many of them as costly and expendable. Growing numbers find themselves pushed into accepting early retirement incentive packages or else at risk of being laid off.

Second, the graying baby boom generation, now moving through their fifties, refuses to accept a lockstep march into old age. Many boomers (along with the retirees immediately preceding them) want to live productive, meaningful lives by engaging in work they like to do or that is useful—paid or unpaid—and typically part time and/or part year. Moreover, the sheer size of the aging baby boom cohort calls into question the long-term viability of federal programs around retirement (such as Social Security). That, in conjunction with the fact that employers in the United States are increasingly moving from "defined benefit" to "defined contribution" pension plans and the importance of maintaining employer-sponsored health insurance until eligibility for Medicare at age 65, makes the retirement transition increasingly problematic and ambiguous (see Ekerdt, DiViney, & Kosloski, 1996; Ekerdt, Hackney, Kosloski, & DiViney, 2001; Hardy & Shuey, 2000; Moen & Han, 2001a, 2001b; Mutchler, Burr, Massagli, & Pienta, 1999). Uncertainties about job and retirement security are contributing to the deinstitutionalization, individualization, and, eventually, reinstitutionalization of what I call the midcourse years, as older workers and retirees in their fifites, sixties, and seventies begin to take charge of their own retirement exits and life plans.

Third, the rising numbers of women in the workforce is another historical trend challenging taken-for-granted assumptions and underscoring the inadequacy of conventional policies and practices. Retirement and related income supports are based on what is now an outmoded, lockstep occupational career model built into existing workforce arrangements, meaning that women's (along with minority men's) more diverse and frequently more intermittent career paths tend to produce less income, benefits, and security compared to White middle-class and working-class men's more typical "orderly" careers (Han & Moen, 1999). Federal regulations presume wives will receive their husbands' Social Security benefits; however, when husbands die, benefits to survivors are often reduced. Because Social Security benefits are earnings sensitive (see Leisering, this volume) and because of other elements of Social Security structures, many single, divorced, and widowed women are at risk of poverty or near poverty in old age. And women are more likely to be single, divorced, or widowed in retirement than are men (Moen, 2001b). Moreover, the changing gender composition of the workforce means that many married couples must negotiate *two* retirements. The majority of both men and women workers have to take into account their spouses' career plans in the formulation of their own retirement preferences and expectations (Kim & Moen, 2001a, 2001b; Moen, Kim, & Hofmeister, 2001; Moen, Sweet et al., 2001).

Yet a fourth historical trend is the aging of the population, a worldwide phenomenon as (1) medical and lifestyle advances delay the onset of serious medical symptoms and promote longevity, (2) the large post World War II baby boom cohort (born 1946–1964) begins to turn 55, and (3) fertility rates remain at unprecedented lows. Growing numbers of older Americans (and, indeed, older individuals throughout the world) can expect to live longer and healthier lives than their parents or grandparents. Old age is increasingly defined by functional incapacities, rather than a particular birthday. Gerontologists have begun to separate the "young old" from the "old old," but the fact is most people in their fifties, sixties, and seventies (what I call *midcourse*) do not see themselves as any kind of "old."

As a consequence of these historical forces, growing numbers of workers "retire" from their career jobs only to take on employment in another job (often for their same employer) and/or participate in unpaid community work (Freedman, 1999; Moen & Fields, 2002; Moen et al., 2000; Quinn, 1999). Retirement—in terms of eligibility for a pension—can no longer be equated with a one-way, one-time final exit from the workforce or with the cessation of all productive activity. Neither is retirement occurring at any one set age. The proliferation of public and private retirement income programs has encouraged a worldwide trend toward progressively earlier retirement from career jobs (Delsen & Reday-Mulvey, 1996; Guillemard & Rein, 1993), as well as greater diversity and heterogeneity in the age, order, and experience of the retirement status passage (see Figure 13-2). This, I believe, is spawning the *midcourse* life stage, between the early occupational career years and the onset of severe health problems restricting independence in later adulthood. And it is this transition to dependency, not retirement, that is increasingly the new marker of old age.

To summarize, in the 1950s retirement was a one-way, one-time, irreversible exit made primarily by men, almost always at age 65. It was culturally defined as the gateway to old age. Today, both men and women retire at a wide range of ages, couples find they must now coordinate two retirements, and people can expect to live many healthy years as "retirees."* Women's retirement and the coordination of both spouses' retirement are now commonplace, but organizational and governmental policies and practices have not kept pace with the realities of a

---

*Especially those who retire in their early fifties. While there are also of course retirees who are in poor health, there is and will be more heterogeneity in the ages, health, assets, and experiences of the "retired" segment of the population.

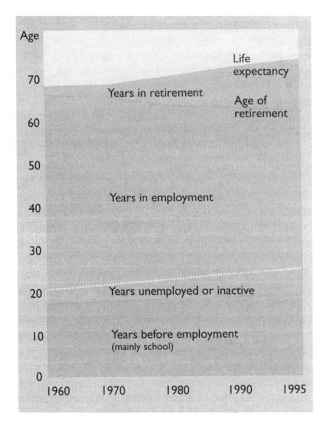

FIGURE 13-2. **Changes in the way men spend their time, 1960–1995.** This chart is based on an average from 15 countries: Australia, Canada, Denmark, Finland, France, Germany, Ireland, Italy, Japan, Norway, New Zealand, Spain, Sweden, United Kingdom, United States. This chart shows average life expectancies and labor force patterns as they existed in the year in question.
Source: Organization for Economics Co-operation and Development (1998).

changing—and aging—workforce and a growing, healthy, and vital "retired" force. The fact that policies remain geared to the middle of the 20th century not the realities of the 21st, is producing a structural lag affecting individual lives, but also the social organization of the life course (Riley et al., 1994). Many of today's 50, 60, and 70 year olds—and certainly tomorrow's—are unwilling to go quietly into their fathers' one-way, one-time, irreversible retirement exit and lifestyle.

    Midcourse, as a new life stage, captures the realities of population aging and other historical trends, as individuals come to spend more years in retirement but are also healthier, better educated, and more vital than retirees in the 1950s. This stage—roughly the fifties, sixties, and seventies—connotes the period in which individuals begin to think about, plan for, and actually disengage from their primary career occupations and the raising of children, launch second or third careers, develop new identities and new ways to be productively engaged, establish new patterns of relating to spouses, children, siblings, parents, friends, and leave some existing relationships and begin new ones. As in adolescence (Mortimer & Johnson, 1998; Shanahan 2000a, 2000b), people in the midcourse years are thinking about and enacting role shifts that are both products of their past and precursors of their future life course. Vanguard members of the current pre-baby boom cohort are in the process of constructing the midcourse life stage.

However, I believe members of the baby boom cohort, now moving to and through their fifties, will institutionalize it as part of the contemporary, taken-for-granted 21st century life course.

BIOGRAPHICAL CONTEXTS

As seen throughout this volume, the life course approach charts the chronologization of events, roles, and resources over the life span (Elder, 1978; Giele & Elder, 1998; Kohli, 1986; Moen, 1996, 2001a, 2001b; O'Rand & Henretta, 1999). Individuals leave old roles or enter new ones, such as "retiree," at particular points in their life biographies. The concept of *biographical pacing* builds on the life course emphasis of time and timing, as well as cultural prescriptions about the timing of parenthood, schooling, and retirement. With the exception of Han and Moen (1999; Moen & Han, 2001a, 2001b), there has been to date little research on biographical pacing (apart from age) as a predictor of retirement planning or expected retirement timing. And yet it makes intuitive sense that the pacing and structure of their occupational and family biographies should shape people's retirement plans and expectations.

Retirement at age 65 or sometimes age 62 (the ages of complete and partial Social Security eligibility) became the norm in the 1950s, producing the lockstep life course of education, employment, leisure (Riley et al., 1994). This is still seen as "normal" or "on time" retirement (Ekerdt, Kosloski, & DiViney, 2000; Ekerdt; Hackney, Kosloski, & DiViney, 2001; Han & Moen, 1999; Settersten & Hagestad, 1996a, 1996b), even though growing numbers are retiring "early," before age 62 or even before age 60. There are three broad theoretical explanations of the biographical timing of retirement transitions: allocation, socialization, and choice. How much control do individuals have related to their retirement timing or life after retirement? How many of their "choices" are products of socialization processes? What are the structural and normative mechanisms by which governments and businesses allocate individuals to retirement? Life course scholars focus on the *agentic* role of individuals in the shaping of their life biographies, but in the context of situational and structural constraints. Although most research on retirement assumes that individuals are active, purposive agents in planning their retirement, recall that in the 1950s retirement was a taken-for-granted workforce exit at age 65, with few options, few choices. Today, even though laws in the United States have eliminated mandatory retirement, allocation processes continue to operate, with workers "choosing" to retire in response to changes in incentives and disincentives in pensions (Fields & Mitchell, 1984; Hanks, 1990; Hayward & Hardy, 1985; Quinn & Burkhauser, 1990). And when early retirement suddenly becomes mandatory (in the face of buy-outs or incentive programs associated with employer restructuring), individuals are no longer in control of the timing of their own retirement.

Socialization processes remain important, but are less rigid given the growing individualization of this status passage. Sociologists hold that the institutionalized nature of the life course provides individuals at different life stages with "available lists of reasons, motives, and aspirations," such as expectations regarding retirement (Meyer, 1986, p. 205). However, such anticipatory socialization as an explanation for retirement timing makes more sense in periods of relative stability, rather than in the face of increasing uncertainty regarding retirement and the prospect of health and vitality for many years after retirement.

A Life Course Model

Those in the midcourse years engage in various adaptive strategies in assessing their current and future needs and options. The life course notion of *adaptive strategies* is part of a larger "cycles of control" model of decision-making (Elder, 1995; Moen & Wethington, 1992). As family and occupational environments change across the life course, workers experience corresponding shifts in both needs and resources (e.g., in time or money). Research evidence (see the review by Kim & Moen, 2001a) points to health and income adequacy as key predictors of whether midcourse individuals are planning to retire and when they expect to do so. Income and health permit people to take control of their midcourse years—actively planning their futures. However, the direction of effects is not obvious. For example, good health can either facilitate retirement from one's primary career job to do other things, or else enable workers to postpone retirement. Similarly, economic resources permit workers to retire early if they want to, but can also push people into retirement, since workers frequently face financial penalties if they continue to work beyond the normative retirement age of 65 (Quadagno & Quinn, 1997).

An important personal resource serving as a protective mechanism at all stages of the life course is a sense of *mastery* or personal control. Sociologist Leonard Pearlin defines mastery as "the extent to which people see themselves as being in control of the forces that importantly affect their lives" (Pearlin, Menaghan, Lieberman, & Mullan, 1981, p. 340; Pearlin & Schooler, 1978). One's sense of mastery both affects and is affected by life experiences. Psychologist Albert Bandura (1977, 1986) points to the importance of personal control in shaping behavior. How competent individuals feel affects what activities they take on and their persistence in them. One can expect, therefore, that a sense of mastery or personal control is an important resource facilitating active retirement planning, as well as a productive midcourse.

A life course model of retirement suggests two competing propositions. First, sufficient resources may permit workers to take control of their midcourse biographical development, using the resources at their disposal (in terms of personal control, health, adequate incomes) to envision and plan for a life after retirement and, consequently, expecting to retire early. Alternatively, such resources may delay retirement planning and timing as workers with such resources postpone retirement to enjoy and/or seek to expand their already advantaged occupational positions in the social hierarchy. Personal control or mastery is an important resource, one that directly affects the psychological well-being of those in the midcourse years whether retired or not. Research shows that personal control, as well as increases in it over time, is a key mechanism linking the actual transition to retirement with subsequent psychological well-being (Kim & Moen, 2001b).

Decision-making Theories

Another related but quite different strand of theoretical development about the ways biographies unfold comes from psychological theories of decision-making. Prospect theory was developed to explain decision-making under risky conditions (such as gambling behavior and insurance policies) (see Kahneman & Tversky, 1983; Thaler, 1980; Tversky & Kahneman, 1991). Decisions about retirement timing can also be seen as "risky" choices, made without advance knowledge of future conditions, particularly with regard to health and/or the risks of downsizing. Theorists adopting this viewpoint see decisions as made in the context of possible future outcomes, conceptualizing outcomes in terms of gains or losses relative to a given reference point, rather than as final assets. Those who are concerned with the loss of the income, status, and/or the purposeful activity their career jobs provide may envision the "risks" associated with retirement. Those who are concerned with job stress and overload, poor health, or with being laid off can envision the "gain" of retirement. One is a view of retirement to avoid the risk of a loss; the other is a view of retirement as the gaining of a less stressful lifestyle. Prospect theory holds that people tend to be more distressed at the prospect of a loss than pleased by a potential gain ("loss aversion"). Because losses are more salient than gains, perceived disadvantages of retirement will tend to seem more important than perceived advantages, which biases the decision in favor of *not* expecting to retire early. But then there is also the risk of retiring "too late" to enjoy it, when a stroke or cancer cuts short the healthy midcourse years. Those seeking to avoid the loss of vital retirement years may plan on and actually retire from their career jobs as early as possible.

From a "cycles of control" framework, the actual age of retirement may not matter as much for life quality as whether individuals retire when they expect to. Results from the Cornell Retirement and Well-Being Study indicate that men and women who retire at the age that they expected to are more likely to report that they are very satisfied with life in retirement (Quick & Moen, 1998, p. 55). After controlling for reasons for retirement, Quick and Moen found that, for women, "early" retirement (before age 60) is especially conducive to a positive assessment of the retirement years, whereas "late" retirement (after 65) is detrimental to women's retirement satisfaction. But women's early retirement seems to be beneficial for their subsequent life quality so long as it is not unexpected.

Unfortunately, no amount of planning can prepare one for an unanticipated layoff or a major illness. Research shows that people tend to retire earlier than they had planned (see Han & Moen, 1999). A sudden, unexpected retirement plays an important (and negative) role in subsequent retirement satisfaction (Floyd et al., 1992; Martin Matthews, & Brown, 1988; McGoldrick, 1989; Szinovacz, 1987, 1996). "Involuntary" retirees have the most negative retirement experience, whereas voluntary retirees (e.g., who retired to pursue their own interests) report high satisfaction with retirement (Floyd et al., 1992; Quick & Moen, 1998). Men and women who retire for family needs or health reasons are more likely to have preferred a later retirement, a preference that is negatively related to their retirement satisfaction (Szinovacz, 1987, 1996).

Prospect theory complements the life course emphasis on cycles of control and strategies of adaptation. Individuals make decisions that provide them with the greatest sense of control. These decisions are both shaped by and shape socialization and allocation processes (see also Shanahan, Hofer, & Miech, 2002). Many Americans are responding to demographic, policy, and economic changes by customizing their own retirement exits, frequently leaving a primary career job for other paid or unpaid work. This customizing process is contributing to the development of an emerging *midcourse* life stage, one in which people, arguably more than at any other stage, construct their own life course.

RELATIONAL CONTEXTS

Both the life course, role context perspective (Elder, 1998b; Giele & Elder, 1998; Moen, 2001b; Moen Dempster-McClain & Williams, 1989; Settersten, 1999; Spitze et al., 1994) and reference group theory (Merton, 1968; Williams, 1970) locate expectations and experiences in social–relational contexts. For example, colleagues and co-workers can serve as key reference points in workers' lives, as discussed in the next section and reference group theory is also relevant to understanding biographical pacing and the "meaning" of age. While one can expect older workers to be both more full of plans and more clear as to the timing of their (imminent) retirement, chronological age may actually be less consequential than life stage. For example, midcoursers in their fifties with preschool or elementary school children may be more similar to other, younger parents of young children in their putting off thinking about retirement than either their fellow midcoursers without children or those whose children are grown and gone.

Other networks of relations matter as well. The implicit relationship between family "careers" (Aldous, 1996) and occupational careers has a long history of exploration in the social sciences (e.g., Burkhauser & Duncan, 1989; Goode, 1960; Kanter, 1977; Modell, 1978; Rowntree, 1901). The dynamic interplay between work and family is exemplified in the transition to retirement, historically meaning withdrawal from career and employment, but simultaneously meaning as well changes in the family economy and changes in family relationships. The fact that existing studies produce mixed evidence regarding the links between retirement and wellbeing may be related to the failure to disentangle the multiple contexts and changes involved. In the remainder of this section I focus on family, both the marital ties and caregiving responsibilities of those in the midcourse years.

Marital Relations

An understanding of the midcourse years for married people requires information on the characteristics of (1) both spouses (including their biographical pacing, health, race/ethnicity, and gender), (2) features of their environments (his job, her job, their families, friends), and (3) information on the processes that shape both and bind the two over time (e.g., Bronfenbrenner, 1995).

The fact that many contemporary couples of midcourse age are having to navigate two retirements underscores the reality of retirement as both an occupational and family transition. Their retirement/employment circumstances illustrate the complexity of midcourse couples' conjoint retirements. Looking at the entire sample of 534 married respondents (men and women combined) ages 50–72 in the Cornell Retirement and Well-Being Study, about one in four are in couples where neither spouse has yet retired from their primary career jobs and even more are in situations where both are retired and out of the labor force. These husbands and wives can be seen as *homophilous* regarding their labor force attachment. In some couples both spouses are employed, but at different stages, such as a retiree who is working at a postretirement job married to someone who has not yet retired. Others represent a variety of arrangements: those who have not retired but with spouses who are not employed, those retired but (re)employed with spouses who are not working, those retired and no longer working but with a spouse still employed. The fact that almost one in five of the married retirees in this sample is currently engaged in paid work points to the growing blurredness of retirement.

One in three (33%) of the wives who have not yet retired in the *Cornell Retirement and Well-Being Study* has a husband who is no longer working for pay, and over one in four (29%) of the husbands who have not retired has a wife who is not employed.*

In the midcourse years, as in other life stages, couples engage in constructing and reconstructing gender (cf. Bem, 1999; Berk, 1985; Brines, 1994; Browne & England, 1997; Risman, 1998). For example, working wives in their fifties may enjoy their jobs and desire to postpone retirement, feeling they are just starting new lives once their children have left home. Yet their (typically older) husbands may be counting the months to their own retirement and expect their wives to retire at the same time they do. Research shows that women do in fact often coordinate their own retirement passages with those of their husbands, but men do not tend to time their retirement around that of their wives (Smith & Moen, 1998, in press; Moen et al., 2001a,b). An analysis by Blau (1998) of married couples (using data from the Retirement History Survey) show the strong proclivity of couples to schedule joint retirement transitions. Moreover, having

*Of these, only a few (5%) have wives who have never worked for pay.

one spouse not employed reduces the likelihood that the other re-enters the labor force. Blau (1998) point out that this has major policy implications; incentives affecting the retirement behavior of one spouse are likely to affect the behavior of the other spouse as well.

If an employed husband retires first, both he and his not-yet-retired wife are in a *status dissonant* role relative to traditional gender expectations, in that wives are employed and husbands are not. Wives may resent their husbands' free time in the face of their own employment obligations. This resentment may be exacerbated if retired husbands still expect their employed wives to perform much of the housework. Evidence indicates that wives' participation in the workforce is linked to negative marital quality when their husbands do not share equally in the domestic labor of the household (Piña & Bengtson, 1995). Both husbands and wives expect husbands to spend more time on domestic chores following the husbands' retirement, which may or may not come to pass (Dorfman, 1989, 1992; Vinick & Ekerdt, 1992).

If wives retire first, husbands still in their career jobs benefit from their wives performing most of the household responsibilities, reproducing the traditional gendered division of labor. Retirement can even increase women's role strain, for example, when employed husbands who had shared household labor with their working wives revert back to traditional housework expectations and arrangements once their wives retire from paid work. Evidence suggests that gender conformity, in terms of who is or is not employed, benefits men more than women, as does having at least one spouse not in the workforce.

Using panel data from two waves of the Cornell Retirement and Well-Being Study, Moen, Kim et al. (2001) examined the effects of work/retirement continuity and change on shifts in marital quality over a 2-year period.* For midcourse men (ages 50–75), retiring from one's primary career job is the strongest (negative) predictor of marital quality and is related to reductions in marital satisfaction and increases in marital conflict. Moreover, newly retired men and women whose spouses remain employed report higher marital conflict than those where both spouses are newly retired. This finding points to the stressfulness of the actual retirement transition. This study underscores the ways status similarity and gender conformity shape life quality in the midcourse years. Recently retired men and women whose spouses are still employed report the highest marital conflict, while recently retired men and women whose spouses are also retired report slightly lower levels of conflict in their marriages, but still more than those midcourse who have not yet retired and long-term (more than 2 years) retirees. Despite the short-term strains on the marital relationship that Moen, Kim et al. (2001) found around the transition into retirement, Pienta, Hayward, and Jenkins (2000) have shown the health benefits of marriage for those in their retirement years.

Caregiving

Caregiving relations also shape retirement timing and the dynamics of the paid work/care work relationship in the midcourse years. Spouses' poor health may cause employed wives to remain in the labor force, possibly for financial reasons (O'Rand, Henretta, & Krecker, 1992). And having to care for ailing relatives may become an impetus for retirement, especially for women (Moen, Robison, & Fields, 1994; Pavalko & Artis, 1997; Pavalko & Smith, 1999). A study (using data from the 1987–1988 National Survey of Families and Households) found that women in their mid-fifties and mid-sixties were more apt to be caregivers of an ill

---

*Their multiple regression models included age, education, income adequacy, and subjective health rating as well as retirement status and transitions.

or disabled household member if they were retired from the workforce rather than still employed (Hatch & Thompson, 1992). O'Rand et al. (1992) found that having an older female relative living with them increases the likelihood of wives' (but not husbands') retirement. Pavalko and Artis (1997) examined two waves (1984 and 1987) of data from the National Longitudinal Survey of Mature Women (ages 47–61 in 1984) to find that short-term caregiving increases women's likelihood of either reducing their work hours or leaving the workforce. Dentinger and Clarkberg (2002), drawing on data from the Cornell Retirement and Well-Being Study, report similar findings, with short-term caregiving resulting in an early retirement exit (although long-term caregiving reduces the likelihood of an early exit). Caregiving for an aged or infirm relative predicts women's earlier but men's later retirement (Dentinger & Clarkberg, 2002). Carr and Sheridan (1999) (drawing on panel data from 1975 and 1992/1993 from the Wisconsin Longitudinal Study) found that men (ages 35–53) who were informal caregivers (providing instrumental assistance) were more apt than those not providing care to leave their career jobs (an exit but not necessarily retirement). They did not find this to be the case for women in their study.

Other Relations

Social relations in terms of integration into the broader community in the midcourse years is also related to health, and in both directions (Pillemer, Moen, Wethington, & Glasgow, 2000). One important source of continuing integration is friends and neighbors, with older women having larger networks than men (Campbell & Lee, 1992; Wethington & Kavey, 2000). However, participation in the broader society matters as well. Two major forms of integration into meaningful social roles and relations are postretirement employment and unpaid community service, as discussed in the next section.

ORGANIZATIONAL, OCCUPATIONAL, AND OPPORTUNITY CONTEXTS

Weiss (1990) describes *relationships of community* that provide a sense of place and of membership in a valued collectivity; this sense of place in turn provides people with personal meaning and a feeling of self-worth. Workplaces furnish a community of friends and workmates, a sense of place and of social meaning. They also provide yardsticks in terms of (1) past experiences of downsizing and early retirement incentives, (2) customary or emerging norms as to planning and retirement timing, and (3) midcourse colleagues who serve as reference groups planning and/or making the transition to retirement.

Consider workers' organizational location, a bundle of norms and circumstances reflecting corporate and co-worker culture. Midcourse workers in organizations with a history of downsizing and restructuring (resulting in the push to take early retirement incentives) can be expected to take that into account in developing their own plans and expectations. Similarly, organizational customs and norms about retirement timing also influence the expectations of individual workers. Whether and when one's co-workers expect to retire can shape workers' own plans and expectations. Data on contemporary workers of all ages show that the average age of one's co-workers is related to retirement planning. Regardless of their own age, workers who are part of an older workforce are more likely to be planning for their own retirement (Moen, Sweet et al., 2001).

Occupational and organizational location also shape people's position in the broader opportunity structure, which in turn affects their range of strategies and options. Older men who are well educated and in professional jobs are the most likely to continue working (Hayward, Hardy, & Grady, 1990). A body of earlier research in the 1960s and 1970s found male blue-collar workers to be particularly eager to retire early, with those in higher status jobs more apt to want to keep their employment and retire later (Barfield, 1970; Boskin, 1977; Streib & Schneider, 1971).

Kahn (1994) points out that chronological age is a poor indicator of the abilities of individual workers. He describes the "goodness-of-fit" between the demands of the job and the abilities of the person who holds it, that is, the needs, goals, aspirations, and skills of workers on the one hand and the requirements and opportunities of the job on the other. The nature of this fit between individuals and their primary career jobs should affect whether or not workers begin planning their retirement and/or choose to retire early. It also affects whether employers view workers in their fifties, sixties, and seventies as valued resources or expendable (Kahn, 1994).

Scholars have demonstrated that demanding jobs with little autonomy or control are negatively related to health and wellbeing (e.g. Karasek & Theorell, 1990; Moen, 1989). Those in poor health in their midcourse years, as well as those in demanding jobs (which may take a toll on future health), are more likely to have plans for retirement to leave the labor force early and to retire unexpectedly (Anderson & Burkhauser, 1985; Chirikos & Nestel, 1989; Herzog, Kahn, Morgan, Jackson, & Antonucci, 1989; Mutchler et al., 1999; Quinn & Burkhauser, 1990; Stanford, Happersett, Morton, Molgaard, & Peddecord, 1991). Moreover, poor health is more likely to encourage those with demanding jobs to retire (Chirikos and Nestel 1989; Hayward, Grady, Hardy, and Sommers 1989) and even people in good health in long-hour, high-stress jobs may opt to retire as a way of preserving their health. The psychological impact of retirement appears to depend both on gender and on previous job stress, with men who leave high-stress jobs experiencing a reduction in distress symptoms and men who leave low-stress jobs reporting an increase in distress symptoms. There are fewer effects, in either direction, for women undergoing retirement (Wheaton, 1990). As Herzog, House, and Morgan (1991) found among older U.S. workers, being able to work one's preferred number of hours (rather than more or less) is positively related to physical health and life satisfaction and negatively related to depression, regardless of gender or occupational status. Those who stopped work and felt they had little or no choice report lower levels of health and wellbeing than both the voluntarily retired and those working the amount they would like. Another study (Gallo, Bradley, Siegel, & Kasl, 2000) found that late-life involuntary job loss through downsizing is related to declines in both physical functioning and mental health. While particular conditions of jobs at one point in time have been associated with health and well-being on the one hand or stress and illness on the other (Karasek & Theorell, 1990), a life course, role context approach suggests the importance of considering an individual's work *patterns* throughout adulthood. Moreover, the fact that most retirees in the Cornell Retirement and Well-Being Study say they retired "to do other things" (Moen et al., 2000) suggests that many midcoursers are retiring to move *to* something else, not simply *from* boring or demanding jobs.

The nature of jobs and career trajectories can have long-term health implications. Studies have shown that men retiring from high-status occupations and "orderly" career paths experience better health and greater longevity than those in manual occupations or those who have held a series of unrelated jobs (Moore & Hayward, 1990; Pavalko, Elder, & Clipp, 1993). Most of the research linking health with career patterns has focused on White men. Ethnic and racial minorities, as well as women generally and non-unionized workers low in socioeconomic status, are more disadvantaged in terms of their career paths, health, and retirement pensions, creating a cumulation of disadvantage in addition to their increased risk of retiring because of a disability (Shea, Miles, & Hayward, 1996). Whether the findings about the longevity and health benefits of orderly career paths and high-status jobs apply to majority and minority women as well as minority men is an important topic for future investigation. One recent study suggests that employment for women in their fifties and sixties may slow the onset of physical limitations (Pavalko & Smith, 1999).

The organization of career paths and retirement exits follows a breadwinner/homemaker template, most typical of middle-class and union member households in the middle of the 20th Century (Moen, 2001a). When White men—both white collar and blue collar—leave their jobs, they are exiting from a role that has typically dominated their adult years (Weiss, 1997). Women, on the other hand, commonly experience greater discontinuity, moving in and out of the labor force, in and out of part-time jobs in tandem with shifting family responsibilities (Clausen & Gillens, 1990; Moen, 1985; Quick & Moen, 2002; Rosenfeld, 1980; Sorensen, 1983). Quick and Moen (1998) found that individuals in their fifties and sixties who work longer throughout adulthood tend to be better prepared for retirement; midcoursers who take fewer year-long breaks and spend more years in the labor force are more likely to plan substantially for retirement. Those with a continuous employment history are more apt to be eligible for retirement incentive packages, which is also positively associated with retirement quality (Quick & Moen, 1998, p. 56).

Minority men and women from all race and ethnic backgrounds also tend to experience employment discontinuities, often being the last hired, the first fired. Consequently, most women and minority men come to the midcourse years without the same duration of employment or accumulation of work experience as White men (Han & Moen, 1999; Henretta & O'Rand, 1980). Gendered and racial/ethnic occupational segregation, along with less stable employment histories, means that midcourse women and minority men are less likely to be covered by a pension than are White men and those who do have pensions have incomes far lower than those of White men. Quick and Moen (1998) found that midcourse (mostly White) men in the Cornell Retirement and Well-Being Study were more likely than the women to have engaged in at least some planning.

Post-Retirement Employment

While employment provides a key source of generativity (Danigelis & McIntosh, 1993; MacDermid, Franz, & De Reus, 1998), postretirement employment is a key yet understudied aspect of employment history. "Bridge jobs" following retirement are often very different from the career jobs from which workers retired (Henretta, 1992; Kim & Feldman, 2000), but they may ease the potentially disruptive transition out of the labor force. It is important to examine both pre- and postretirement employment histories in order to understand the linkages between work, retirement, and health fully and to consider various forms of productive engagement following retirement.

Men are more likely than women to take on paid work after retirement from their primary "career" jobs (Han & Moen, 1999; Hardy, 1991; Herzog et al., 1989; Moen et al., 2000; Moen, Kim et al., 2001). In fact, the U.S. Census Bureau (2000) reports that 17.5% of men 65 and older are in the labor force, compared to only 9.4% of women. Occupational position and pathways shape individuals' positions in the broader opportunity structure, which in turn affect the range of strategies and options older persons have from which to construct their retirement transitions.

Volunteer Community Service

Another key form of generativity is formal community participation as a volunteer. While Herzog et al. (1989) found that older women were slightly more likely than older men to participate in volunteer work, other studies have reported little difference (e.g. Fischer, Mueller, & Cooper, 1991). A number of people have highlighted the value of unpaid community service for those in their retirement years (Freedman, 1999; Moen, 1998; Moen & Fields, 2002; Moen et al., 2000). A recent national survey found that 45% of retired women describe community service as playing an important role in retirement, compared to 35% of men (Peter D. Hart Research Associates, 1999).

Both paid and unpaid volunteer work after retirement have been linked to longevity, health, and psychological wellbeing (Moen, Dempster-McClain, & Williams, 1992; Moen & Fields, 2002; Moen et al., 1989, 2000; Musick et al., 1999; Young & Glasgow, 1998). This confirms the protective effects of role participation, but studies have shown that the *context* of that participation matters as well. For example, Musick et al. (1999) found that volunteering has a protective effect on mortality, but only for those with low levels of informal social interaction. And Moen and Fields (2002) show formal volunteering (for an organization or agency) in the midcourse years to be related to psychological well-being for those not working for pay.

CONCLUSIONS

Both popular culture and social science foster a view of retirement as a *state*, not a process. Scholars either study retired individuals as if they were independent of prior experiences or examine retirement trends as part of larger demographic, economic, social, political, and cultural environments. Retirement researchers also tend to accept the commonplace notion of individualism, too frequently ignoring the interdependence of husbands and wives, aging parents and adult children, adult parents and young children, employers and co-workers. Often investigators look for static "antecedents" of retirement timing or snapshot "consequences," not the dynamics of the retirement process as it develops over occupational and family careers and in particular historical, organizational, and social contexts.

A life course approach puts together individual lives and institutions, retirement and employment, husbands and wives, gender and age, as well as locating them in occupational, organizational, historical, and policy environments (e.g., Elder & O'Rand, 1995; Han & Moen, 1999; Moen & Han, 2001a, 2001b; Moen, Sweet, et al., 2001; Pavalko, 1997). In this chapter I have proposed that demographic, medical, economic, and lifestyle changes are producing a new, unscripted, stage of adulthood, *midcourse* between the career-building years and old age. As Shanahan (2000b) noted in describing the transition to adulthood, the midcourse years represent a demographically dense time in which many basic decisions about the life course are made. One fundamental transition during the midcourse years is the status passage out of one's primary career job and, eventually, out of the workforce altogether. Retirement as a dimension of social organization remains institutionalized by pension and Social Security policies, yet is in the process of being individuated, as people set about constructing their own "midcourse." For growing numbers of workers, retirement is no longer the culmination of a lockstep (male) career of continuous, full-time (or more) employment in one or two related occupations. Rather, occupational career paths, retirement transitions, and the emerging midcourse life stage are in flux, characterized by growing heterogeneity and blurred boundaries around each.

Most research shows that being retired per se has no deleterious effects on either physical or psychological health; most retirees say they are satisfied with their retirement and some even report better health (Atchley, 1976; Ekerdt, Bossé, & Locastro, 1983; Quick & Moen, 1998). The issue is not *whether* retirement influences health or vice versa, but the *pathways* to health and wellbeing in the postretirement years. Research evidence makes it clear that good health is an important prerequisite for the enjoyment of the retirement years, as is economic security (Szinovacz & Washo, 1992) and retirees in the 21st century as a group tend to be healthier, better educated, and more active compared to those in the middle of the 20th century.*

Part of the difficulty in assessing workers' (and couples') expectations, planning, and behavior related to retirement is that it constitutes both a positive and negative transition, is both voluntary and involuntary, and is being reconstructed by members of the baby boom generation and those immediately preceding them. In qualitative interviews from the Cornell Retirement and Well-Being Study, some workers in their fifties report literally counting the days until they can retire (much like military draftees used to mark off the days until their discharge). However, this is retirement from their *primary career jobs*. Many want to keep working, but not at their current (more than) full-time, full-year, demanding jobs. Others become defensive when queried about the timing of their retirement, claiming adamantly that they will "never" retire, that they will be carried off their career jobs in a coffin. What matters along with health and adequate financial circumstances—is whether individuals are retiring from constraining, boring, or hazardous jobs and whether they see themselves as moving *to* new opportunities and challenges or simply *from* their current employment.

A Research Agenda

Life course scholars can view the emerging midcourse years as a strategic research site for assessing the links between agency, structure, biography, and social change. Much of the theoretical and conceptual development around the transition to adulthood (e.g., Hogan, 1981; Modell, 1978; Mortimer & Johnson, 1998; Shanahan, 2000a, 2000b) may well prove fruitful in promoting an understanding of retirement and other midcourse transitions. Each of the links in Figure 13-1 provides opportunities for updating and refining theories and evidence about life before, during, and after the retirement transition. As shown in Figure 13-1, studying the midcourse years involves more than simply investigating an occupational status passage; it also involves family, lifestyle, social–relational, and identity transitions. Midcourse and the retirement transition embedded in it can offer occasions for the development of new identities and can foster the adoption of new roles and new lifestyles. Workers retire, not only because of poor health, but sometimes *because* of good health, wanting to do something else and/or recognizing the potentially damaging effects of their current highly demanding, high-stress jobs. In fact, retirees with excellent health are more likely to return to the workforce (Mutchler et al., 1999; Quinn, 1999).

How older workers differentially located in the social structure think about and respond to the risks and rewards of this unscripted life phase is a promising area of inquiry. Race and ethnicity are confounded with social class, gender, and career paths, leading to few clear-cut findings to date about retirement related to race and ethnicity. What matters is the fact that biographical pacing, resources, and employment experiences are a function of location in the

*Of course, there are people who experience poor health "pushing" them into retirement.

social structure—a combination of the effects of race/ethnicity, gender, class, occupation, and age—which has thus far provided a cumulation of advantage for many White, middle-class, and blue-collar union men and often a cumulation of disadvantage for those less favorably positioned in the social hierarchy. How midcourse develops for different subgroups of society remains to be investigated by life course scholars.

Life course scholars can capture retirement as a multi-stage process, involving preparation (planning), execution (actually exiting the career job), and constructing a postretirement lifestyle. How do midcoursers negotiate a series of strategic choices? How do these choices come to be embedded in the social organization of the life course, part of the developing organization of the new midcourse life stage? We know very little about this process, as it is emerging in the 21st century or about the social relations (family, coworkers) shaping it.

Another fruitful research agenda item is the life course itself as a socially constructed and reconstructed regime, produced and reproduced by market forces as well as state regulations. For example, as a social institution, retirement remains a key though outdated component of the social organization of the workforce, age hierarchies, aging, and the life course. As such, retirement is both a private passage and a public issue (e.g., Bury, 1995; Moen, 1996, 1998) and on both these dimensions remains very much in flux.

A Policy Agenda

People in the United States, individually and collectively, are uncertain and often divided as to what it means to be midcourse in a society where increasing numbers of people are in and beyond their sixth decade. Prevailing attitudes about growing older and about retirement are ambivalent and contradictory. This is a matter of pivotal importance in seeking to understand the absence of coherent political and private sector response to the demographic revolutions in this country. As yet, few organizations, communities, government agencies, or employers recognize the potential of the growing numbers of healthy, skilled, committed, energetic individuals in their fifties, sixties, and seventies who are in the midst of forging this new midcourse life stage. There is considerable ambiguity around the retirement transition (as growing numbers of retirees from primary career jobs move back into the workforce in part-time, contract, or temporary work, start their own businesses, or develop a "volunteer" career) and its timing. Existing structural arrangements, policies, norms, and practices provide few institutionalized opportunities for meaningful engagement after retirement (Riley et al., 1994). This suggests two key avenues for policy development: (1) support for individuals and families as they negotiate the midcourse years and (2) opportunities for productive engagement. Both suggest the need for new intermediary institutions specifically addressing this life phase.

To meet the needs of those in or entering the midcourse years, powerful forces for change must be mustered, leading to new social inventions (structural "leads" rather than lags) in the policy arena (such as the institutionalization of [1] phased exits from primary career jobs, [2] second or third careers, [3] social community participation, and [4] various bridges to "total retirement") that permit productive engagement for those seeking it (e.g., Freedman, 1999; Kim & Feldman, 2000; Moen, 1994; Pampel, 1998). Reforms in Social Security and pension policies, as well as health insurance availability and the reframing of cultural stereotypes, could help facilitate active, meaningful engagement throughout all adulthood. Only then will the United States—as well as other nations—provide the opportunities and challenges that can fully exploit the possibilities of life—and life quality—midcourse.

ACKNOWLEDGMENTS: This research was supported by grants from the Alfred P. Sloan Foundation (Sloan FDN #96-6-9, #99-6-23 and #2002-6-8, Phyllis Moen, principal investigator) and the National Institute on Aging (#P50AG11711–01, Karl Pillemer and Phyllis Moen, co-principal investigators). The author wishes to thank the editors for their helpful suggestions, as well as Sarah Jaenike Demo and Donna Dempster-McClain for their excellent technical assistance.

REFERENCES

Aldous, J. (1996). *Family careers: Rethinking the developmental perspective*. Thousand Oaks, CA: Sage.
Anderson, K. A., & Burkhauser, R. V. (1985). The retirement–health nexus: A new measure of an old puzzle. *The Journal of Human Resources, 20*, 315–330.
Atchley, R. (1976). *The sociology of retirement*. New York: Schenkman.
Bandura, A. (1986). *Social foundations of thought and action: A social cognitive theory*. Englewood Cliffs, NJ: Prentice-Hall.
Barfield, R. E. (1970). *The automobile worker and retirement*. Ann Arbor, MI: University of Michigan Institute for Social Research.
Bem, S. (1999). Gender, sexuality, and inequality: When many become one, who is the one and what happens to the others? In P. Moen, D. Dempster-McClain, & H. A. Walker (Eds.), *A nation divided: Diversity, inequality, and community in American society* (pp. 70–86). Ithaca, NY: Cornell University Press.
Berk, S. F. (1985). *The gender factory: The appointment of work in American households*. New York: Plenum Press.
Blau, D. M. (1998). Labor force dynamics of older married couples. *Journal of Labor Economics, 16*, 595–629.
Boskin, M. J. (1977). Social Security and retirement decisions. *Economic Inquiry, 15*, 1–25.
Brines, J. (1994). Economic dependency, gender, and the division of labor at home. *American Journal of Sociology, 100*, 652–688.
Bronfenbrenner, U. (1995). The bioecological model from a life course perspective: Reflections of a participant observer. In P. Moen, G. H. Elder, Jr., & K. Lüscher (Eds.), *Examining lives in context: Perspectives on the ecology of human development* (pp. 599–618). Washington, DC: American Psychological Association.
Browne, I., & England, P. (1997). Oppression from within and without in sociological theories: An application to gender. *Current Perspectives in Sociological Theory, 17*, 77–104.
Burkhauser, R. V., Couch, K. A., & Phillips, J. W. (1996). Who takes early Social Security benefits: The economic and health characteristics of early beneficiaries. *The Gerontologist, 36*, 789–799.
Burkhauser, R. V., & Duncan, G. J. (1989). Economic risks of gender roles: Income loss and life events over the life course. *Social Science Quarterly, 70*, 3–23.
Bury, M. (1995). Ageing, gender and sociological theory. In S. Arber & J. Ginn (Eds.), *Connecting gender and ageing: A sociological approach* (pp. 15–19). Buckingham, UK: Open University Press.
Campbell, K. E., & Lee, B. A. (1992). Sources of personal neighbor networks: Social integration, need, or time? *Social Forces, 70*, 1077–1100.
Carr, D., & Sheridan, J. (1999). *Family transitions at midlife: Do they trigger men's and women's career changes.* Paper presented at Population Association of America Annual Meeting, New York.
Chirikos, T. N., & Nestel, G. (1989). Occupation, impaired health, and the functional capacity of men to continue working. *Research on Aging, 11*, 174–205.
Clausen, J. A., & Gillens, M. I. (1990). Personality and labor force participation across the life course: A longitudinal study of women's careers. *Sociological Forum, 5*, 595–618.
Costa, D. (1998). *The evolution of retirement: An American economic history, 1880–1999*. Chicago: University of Chicago Press.
Danigelis, N. L., & McIntosh, B. R. (1993). Resources and the productive activity of elders: race and gender as contexts. *Journal of Gerontology: Social Sciences, 48*, S192–S203.
Delsen, L., & Reday-Mulvey, G. (1996). *Gradual retirement in the OECD countries: Macro and micro issues and policies*. Brookfield, VT: Dartmouth Publishing.
Dentinger, E., & Clarkberg, M. (2002). Informal caregiving and retirement timing among men and women: Gender and caregiving relationships in late midlife [Special issue]. *Journal of Family Issues, 23*(7), 857–859.
Dorfman, L. T. (1989). Retirement preparation and retirement satisfaction in the rural elderly. *Journal of Applied Gerontology, 8*, 432–450.

Dorfman, L. T. (1992). Couples in retirement: Division of household work. In M. Szinovacz, D. Ekerdt, & B. Vinick (Eds.), *Families and retirement* (pp. 159–173). Newbury Park, CA: Sage.

Ekerdt, D. J., Bossé, R., & Locastro, J. S. (1983). Claims that retirement improves health. *Journal of Gerontology, 38,* 231–236.

Ekerdt, D. J., DiViney, S., & Kosloski, K. (1996). Profiling plans for retirement. *Journal of Gerontology: Social Sciences, 51B,* S140–S149.

Ekerdt, D. J., Hackney, J., Kosloski, K., & DiViney, S. (2001). Eddies in the stream: The prevalence of uncertain plans for retirement. *Journal of Gerontology: Social Sciences, 56B,* S162–S170.

Elder, G. H., Jr. (1978). Family history and the life course. In T. K. Hareven (Ed.), *Transitions: The family and the life course in historical perspective* (pp. 17–64). New York: Academic Press.

Elder, G. H., Jr. (1998a). *Children of the Great Depression.* New York: HarperCollins.

Elder, G. H., Jr. (1998b). Life course theory and human development. *Sociological Analysis, 1*(2), 1–12.

Elder, G. H., Jr. (1995). The life course paradigm: Social change and individual development. In P. Moen, G. H. Elder, Jr., & K. Lüscher (Eds.), *Examining lives in context: perspectives on the ecology of human development* (pp. 101–139). Washington, DC: American Psychological Association.

Elder, G. H., Jr., & O'Rand, A. M. (1995). Adult lives in a changing society. In J. S. House, K. Cook, & G. Fine (Eds.), *Sociological perspectives on social psychology* (pp. 452–475). Needham Heights, MA: Allyn & Bacon.

Fields, G. S., & Mitchell, O. S. (1984). *Retirement, pensions, and Social Security.* Cambridge, MA: MIT Press.

Fischer, L. R., Mueller, D. P., & Cooper, P. W. (1991). Older volunteers: A discussion of the Minnesota senior study. *The Gerontologist, 31,* 183–194.

Floyd, F. J., Haynes, S. N., Doll, E. R., Winemiller, D., Lemsky, C., Burgy, T. M., Werle, M., & Heilman, N. (1992). Assessing retirement satisfaction and perceptions of retirement experiences. *Psychology and Aging, 7,* 609–621.

Freedman, M. (1999). *Prime time: How baby boomers will revolutionize retirement and transform America.* New York: Public Affairs.

George, L. K. (1993). Sociological perspectives on life transitions. *Annual Review of Sociology, 19,* 353–373.

Giele, J. Z., & Elder, G. H., Jr. (1998). *Methods of life course research: Qualitative and quantitative approaches.* Thousand Oaks, CA: Sage.

Goode, W. I. (1960). A theory of role strain. *American Sociological Review, 25,* 483–496.

Graebner, W. (1980). *A history of retirement.* New Haven, CT: Yale University Press.

Guillemard, A.-M., & Rein, M. (1993). Comparative patterns of retirement: Recent trends in developed societies. *Annual Review of Sociology, 19,* 469–503.

Hagestad, G. O., & Neugarten, B. L. (1984). Age and the life course. In R. Binstock & E. Shanas (Eds.), *Handbook of aging and the social sciences* (pp. 35–61). New York: Van Nostrand Reinhold.

Han, S.-K., & Moen, P. (1999). Clocking out: Temporal patterning of retirement. *American Journal of Sociology, 105,* 191–236.

Hanks, R. S. (1990). The impact of early retirement incentives on retirees and their families. *Journal of Family Issues, 11,* 424–437.

Hardy, M. A. (1991). Employment after retirement: Who gets back in? *Research on Aging, 13,* 267–288.

Hardy, M. A., & Shuey, K. (2000). Pension decisions in a changing economy: Gender, structure and choice. *Journal of Gerontology: Social Sciences, 55B,* S271–S277.

Hatch, L. R., & Thompson, A. (1992). Family responsibilities and women's retirement. In M. Szinovacz, D. Ekerdt, & B. Vinick (Eds.), *Families and retirement* (pp, 99–113). Newbury Park, CA: Sage.

Hayward, M. D., Grady, W. R., Hardy, M. A., & Sommers, D. (1989). Occupational influences in retirement, disability, and death. *Demography, 26,* 393–409.

Hayward, M. D., & Hardy, M. A. (1985). Early retirement processes among older men. *Research on Aging, 7,* 491–515.

Hayward, M. D., Hardy, M. A., & Grady, W. R. (1990). Work and retirement among a cohort of older men in the United States, 1966–83. *Demography, 27,* 337–356.

Hayward, M. D., & Liu, M.-C. (1992). Men and women in their retirement years: A demographic profile. In M. Szinovacz, D. J. Ekerdt, & B. H. Vinick (Eds.), *Families and retirement* (pp. 23–50). Newbury Park, CA: Sage.

Henretta, J. C. (1992). Uniformity and diversity: Life course institutionalization and late-life work exit. *Sociological Quarterly, 33,* 265–279.

Henretta, J. C., & O'Rand, A. M. (1980). Labor force participation of older married women. *Social Security Bulletin, 43,* 29–39.

Herzog, A. R., House, J. S., & Morgan, J. N. (1991). Relation of work and retirement to health and well-being in older age. *Psychology and Aging, 6,* 202–211.

Herzog, A. R., Kahn, R. L., Morgan, J. N., Jackson, J. S., & Antonucci, T. C. (1989). Age differences in productive activities. *Journal of Gerontology: Social Sciences, 44*, 129–138.

Hogan, D. (1981). *Transitions and social change.* New York: Academic Press.

Kahn, R. L. (1994). Opportunities, aspirations, and goodness of fit. In M. W. Riley, R. L. Kahn, & A. Foner (Eds.), *Age and structural lag* (pp. 37–56). New York: Wiley-Interscience.

Kahneman, D., & Tversky, A. (1983). Can irrationality be intelligently discussed. *Behavioral and Brain Sciences, 6*, 509–510.

Kanter, R. M. (1977). *Work and family in the United States: A critical review and agenda for research and policy.* New York: Russell Sage.

Karasek, R. A., & Theorell, T. (1990). *Healthy work: Stress, productivity, and the reconstruction of working life.* New York: Basic Books.

Kim, J., & Moen, P. (2001a). Moving into retirement: Preparation and transitions in late midlife. In M. Lachman (Ed.), *Handbook of midlife development* (pp. 498–527). New York: John Wiley & Sons.

Kim, J., & Moen, P. (2001b). Is retirement good or bad for subjective well-being? Retirement as a life course transition in time and in ecological context. *Current Directions in Psychological Science, 10*, 83–86.

Kim, J., & Moen, P. (2002). Retirement transitions, gender, and psychological well-being: A life-course, ecological model. *Journal of Gerontology: Psychological Sciences, 57B*, P212–P222.

Kim, S., & Feldman, D. C. (2000). Working in retirement: The antecedents of bridge employment and its consequences for quality of life in retirement. *Academy of Management Journal, 43*, 1195–1210.

Kohli, M. (1986). Social organization and subjective construction of the life course. In A. B. Sorensen, F. E. Weinert, & L. R. Sherrod (Eds.), *Human development and the life course: Multidisciplinary perspectives* (pp. 271–292). Hillsdale, NJ: Lawrence Erlbaum.

Kohli, M., Rein, M., Guillemard, A. M., & Van Gunsteren, H. (1991). *Time for retirement: Comparative studies of early exit from the labor force.* New York: Cambridge University Press.

MacDermid, S. M., Franz, C. E., & De Reus, L. A. (1998). Generativity: At the crossroads of social roles and personality. In D. P. McAdams & E. de St Aubin (Eds.), *Generativity and adult development: How and why we care for the next generation* (pp. 181–226). New York: American Psychological Association.

Martin Matthews, A., & Brown, K. H. (1988). Retirement as a critical life event: The differential experiences of men and women. *Research on Aging, 9*, 548–557.

McGoldrick, A. E. (1989). Stress, early retirement and health. In K. S. Markides & G. L. Cooper (Eds.), *Aging, stress and health* (pp. 91–118). New York: John Wiley and Sons.

Merton, R. K. (1968). *Social theory and social structure.* New York: The Free Press.

Meyer, J. W. (1986). The institutionalization of the life course and its effect on the self. In A. B. Sorenson, F. E. Weinert, & L. R. Sherrod (Eds.), *Human development and the life course: Multidisciplinary perspectives* (pp. 199–216). Hillsdale, NJ: Lawrence Erlbaum.

Modell, J. (1978). Patterns of consumption, acculturation, and family income strategies in late nineteenth-century America. In T. K. Hareven & M. Vinovski (Eds.), *Family and population in nineteenth-century America.* Princeton: Princeton University Press.

Moen, P. (1985). Continuities and discontinuities in women's labor force participation. In G. H. Elder, Jr. (Ed.), *Life course dynamics: 1960s to 1980s* (pp. 113–155). Ithaca, NY: Cornell University Press.

Moen, P. (1989). *Working parents: Transformations in gender roles and public policies in Sweden.* Madison, WI: University of Wisconsin Press.

Moen, P. (1994). Women, work and family: A sociological perspective on changing roles. In M. W. Riley, R. L. Kahn, & A. Foner (Eds.), *Age and structural lag: The mismatch between people's lives and opportunities in work, family, and leisure* (pp. 151–170). New York: John Wiley & Sons.

Moen, P. (1996). A life course perspective on retirement, gender, and well-being. *Journal of Occupational Health Psychology, 1*, 131–144.

Moen, P. (2001a). The career quandary. *Population Reference Bureau Reports on America, 2*(1), 1–15.

Moen, P. (2001b). The gendered life course. In L. George & R. H. Binstock (Eds.), *Handbook of aging and the social sciences* (5th ed. pp. 179–196). San Diego, CA: Academic Press, Inc.

Moen, P., Dempster-McClain, D., & Williams, R., Jr. (1989). Social integration and longevity: An event history analysis of women's roles and resilience. *American Sociological Review, 54*, 635–647.

Moen, P., Dempster-McClain, D., & Williams, R. M., Jr. (1992). Successful aging: A life course perspective on women's roles and health. *American Journal of Sociology, 97*, 1612–1638.

Moen, P., & Fields, V. (2002). Midcourse in the United States: Does unpaid community participation replace paid work? *Ageing International, 27*, 21–48.

Moen, P., Fields, V., Quick, H., & Hofmeister, H. (2000). A life course approach to retirement and social integration. In K. Pillemer, P. Moen, E. Wethington, & N. Glasgow (Eds.), *Social integration in the second half of life* (pp. 75–107). Baltimore, MD: The Johns Hopkins Press.

Moen, P., & Han, S.-K. (2001a). Gendered careers: A life course perspective. In R. Hertz & N. Marshall (Eds.), *Families and work: Today's realities and tomorrow's possibilities* (pp. 42–57). Berkeley, CA: University of California Press.

Moen, P., & Han, S.-K. (2001b). Reframing careers: Work, family, and gender. In V. Marshall, W. Heinz, H. Krueger, & A. Verma (Eds.), *Restructuring work and the life course* (pp. 424–445). Toronto: University of Toronto Press.

Moen, P., Kim, J. E., & Hofmeister, H. (2001). Couples' work/retirement transitions, gender, and marital quality. *Social Psychology Quarterly, 64*, 55–71.

Moen, P., Robison, J., & Fields, V. (1994). Women's work and caregiving roles: A life course approach. *Journal of Gerontology: Social Sciences, 49*, S176-S186.

Moen, P., Sweet, S., & Swisher, R. (2001). *Planning for retirement: American workers and the setting of career clocks*. Presented at the 17th World Congress of the International Association of Gerontology, Vancouver, BC.

Moen, P., & Wethington, E. (1992). The concept of family adaptive strategies. *Annual Review of Sociology, 18*, 233–251.

Moore, D. E., & Hayward, M. D. (1990). Occupational careers and mortality of elderly men. *Demography, 27*, 31–53.

Mortimer, J., & Johnson, M. K. (1998). New perspectives on adolescent work and the transition to adulthood. In R. Jessor (Ed.), *New perspectives on adolescent risk behavior* (pp. 425–496). New York: Cambridge University Press.

Musick, M. A., Herzog, A. R., & House, J. S. (1999). Volunteering and mortality among older adults: Findings from a national sample. *Journal of Gerontology: Social Sciences, 54B*, S173–S180.

Mutchler, J. E., Burr, J. A., Massagli, M. P., & Pienta, A. (1999). Work transitions and health in later life. *Journal of Gerontology: Social Sciences, 54B*, S252–S261.

Neugarten, B. L., Moore, J., & Lowe, J. C. (1965). Age norms, age constraints and adult socialization. *American Sociological Review, 54*, 635–647.

Organization for Economic Cooperation and Development. (1998). *Maintaining prosperity in an aging society*. Labour Force Statistics. Paris: OECD.

Palmore, E. B., Burchett, B. M., Filenbaum, G. G., George, L. K., & Wallman, L. M. (1985). *Retirement: Causes and consequences*. New York: Springer.

Pampel, F. C. (1998). *Aging, social inequality, and public policy*. Thousand Oaks, CA: Pine Forge.

Pavalko, E. K. (1997). Beyond trajectories: Multiple concepts for analyzing long-term process. In M. A. Hardy (Ed.), *Studying aging and social change: Conceptual and methodological issues* (pp. 129–147). Thousand Oaks, CA: Sage Press.

Pavalko, E. K., & Artis, J. E. (1997). Women's caregiving and paid work: Causal relationships in late mid-life. *Journal of Gerontology: Social Sciences, 52B*, S1–S10.

Pavalko, E. K., Elder, G. H. Jr., & Clipp, E. C. (1993). Work lives and longevity: Insights from a life course perspective. *Journal of Health and Social Behavior, 34*, 363–380.

Pavalko, E. K., & Smith, B. (1999). The rhythm of work: Health effects on women's work dynamics. *Social Forces, 77*, 1141–1162.

Pearlin, L. I., Menaghan, E., Lieberman, M. A., & Mullan, J. T. (1981). The stress process. *Journal of Health and Social Behavior, 22*, 337–356.

Pearlin, L. I., & Schooler, C. (1978). The structure of coping. *Journal of Health and Social Behavior, 19*, 2–21.

Peter D. Hart Research Associates (1999). Study #5486a, Milken Senior tack-on [On-line]. Available: http://www.mff.org/conf1999/newsroom/Seniors.pdf.

Pienta, A. M., Hayward, M. D., & Jenkins, K. R. (2000). Health consequences of marriage for the retirement years. *Journal of Family Issues, 21*, 559–586.

Piña, D. L., & Bengtson, V. L. (1995). Division of household labor and the well-being of retirement-aged wives. *The Gerontologist, 35*, 308–317.

Quadagno, J. (1988). Women's access to pensions and the structure of eligibility rules: Systems of production and reproduction. *Sociological Quarterly, 29*, 541–558.

Quadagno, J., & Quinn, J. F. (1997). Does Social Security discourage work? In E. Kingson & J. Schulz (Eds.), *Social Security in the 21st century* (pp. 127–146). New York: Oxford University Press.

Quick, H. E., & Moen, P. (1998). Gender, employment, and retirement quality: A life-course approach to the differential experiences of men and women. *Journal of Occupational Health Psychology, 3*, 44–64.

Quick, H. E., & Moen, P. (2002). *Careers in competition? An analysis of U.S. working couples' employment trajectories*. Unpublished manuscript.

Quinn, J. F. 1999. *Retirement patterns and bridge jobs in the 1990s* (Employee Benefit Research Institute Issue Brief No. 206). Washington, DC: Employee Benefit Research Institute.

Quinn, J. F., & Burkhauser, R. V. (1990). Work and retirement. In R. H. Binstock & L. K. George (Eds.), *Handbook of aging and the social sciences* (3rd ed., pp. 307–327). San Diego, CA, Academic Press.

Repetti, R. L., Matthews, K. A., & Waldron, I. (1989). Effects of paid employment on women's mental and physical health. *American Psychologist, 44*, 1394–1401.

Riley, M. W., Kahn, R. L., & Foner, A. (1994). *Age and structural lag: Society's failure to provide meaningful opportunities in work, family, and leisure*. New York: John Wiley.

Risman, B. J. (1998). *Gender vertigo: American families in transition*. New Haven, CT: Yale University Press.

Rosenfeld, R. A. (1980). Race and sex differences in career dynamics. *American Sociological Review, 45*, 583–609.

Rowntree, B. S. (1901). *Poverty: A study of town life*. London: Macmillan.

Settersten, R. A., Jr. (1999). *Lives in time and place: The problems and promises of developmental science*. Amityville, NY: Baywood.

Settersten, R. A. Jr. & Hagestad, G. O. (1996a). What's the latest? Cultural age deadlines for family transitions. *The Gerontologist, 36*, 178–188.

Settersten, R. A. Jr. & Hagestad, G. O. (1996b). What's the latest? II. Cultural age deadlines for family transitions. *The Gerontologist, 36*, 602–613.

Settersten, R. A., Jr. & Mayer, K. U. (1997). The measurement of age, age structuring, and the life course. *Annual Review of Sociology, 23*, 233–261.

Shanahan, M. J. (2000a). Adolescence. In E. Borgatta (Ed.), *Encyclopedia of sociology* (pp. 1–17). New York: Macmillan.

Shanahan, M. J. (2000b). Pathways to adulthood in changing societies: Variability and mechanisms in life course perspective. *Annual Review of Sociology, 26*, 667–692.

Shea, D. G., Miles, T., & Hayward, M. (1996). The health-wealth connection: Racial differences. *The Gerontologist, 36*, 342–349.

Smith, D. B., & Moen, P. (1998). Spouse's influence on the retirement decision: His, her, and their perceptions. *Journal of Marriage and the Family, 60*, 734–744.

Smith, D. B., & Moen, P. (in press). Retirement satisfaction for retirees and their spouses: Do gender and the retirement decision-making process matter? *Journal of Family Issues*.

Sorensen, A. (1983). Women's employment patterns after marriage. *Journal of Marriage and the Family, 45*, 311–321.

Spitze, G., Logan, J.R., Joseph, G., & Lee, E. J. (1994). Middle generation roles and the well-being of men and women. *Journal of Gerontology: Social Sciences, 49*, S107–S116.

Stanford, E. P., Happersett, C. J., Morton, D. J., Molgaard, C. A., & Peddecord, K. M. (1991). Early retirement and functional impairment from a multi-ethnic perspective. *Research on Aging, 13*, 5–38.

Streib, G. F., & Schneider, C. J. (1971). *Retirement in American society*. Ithaca, NY: Cornell University Press.

Szinovacz, M. (1987). Preferred retirement timing and retirement satisfaction in women. *International Journal of Aging and Human Development, 24*, 301–317.

Szinovacz, M. (1996). Couples' employment/retirement patterns and perceptions of marital quality. *Research on Aging, 18*, 243–268.

Szinovacz, M., & Washo, C. (1992). Gender differences in exposure to life events and adaptation to retirement. *Journal of Gerontology: Social Sciences, 47*, S191–S196.

Thaler, R. (1980). Toward a positive theory of consumer choice. *Journal of Economic Behavior & Organization, 1*, 39–60.

Tversky, A., & Kahneman, D. (1991). Loss aversion in riskless choice: A reference-dependent model. *Quarterly Journal of Economics, 106*, 1039–1061.

Vinick, B. H., & Ekerdt, D. J. (1992). Couples view retirement activities: Expectation versus experience. In M. Szinovacz, D. J. Ekerdt, & B. H. Vinick (Eds.), *Families and retirement* (pp. 129–144). Newbury Park, CA: Sage.

Weiss, R. (1990). Losses associated with mobility. In S. Fisher & C. L. Cooper (Eds.), *On the move: The psychology of change and transition* (pp. 3–12). Chichester, UK: John Wiley.

Weiss, R. (1997). Adaptation to retirement. In I. H. Gotlib & B. Wheaton (Eds.), *Stress and adversity over the life course* (pp. 232–248). New York: Cambridge University Press.

Wethington, E., & Kavey, A. (2000). Neighboring as a form of social integration and support. In K. Pillemer, P. Moen, N. Glasgow, & E. Wethington (Eds.), *Social integration in the second half of life* (pp. 190–210). Baltimore, MD: Johns Hopkins University Press.

Wheaton, B. (1990). Life transitions, role histories, and mental health. *American Sociological Review, 55,* 209–223.

Williams, R. M., Jr. (1970). *American society: A sociological interpretation.* New York: Knopf.

Young. F. W., & Glasgow, N. (1998). Voluntary social participation and health. *Research on Aging, 20,* 339–362.

C. Turning Point

CHAPTER 14

Desistance from Crime over the Life Course*

ROBERT J. SAMPSON

JOHN H. LAUB

There is no shortage of explanations in the field of criminology for the onset of criminal behavior, which is typically assumed to occur in childhood or early adolescence. What is not known with much certainty is why some offenders *stop* committing crimes when they do, while others continue over large portions of the life course. What accounts for stability and change in patterns of criminal offending over time? Unfortunately, the longitudinal studies needed to answer this central question are virtually non-existent. Most criminological research consists of cross-sectional "snapshots" or relatively short-term panel studies of offending. Long-term studies that follow the same individuals over time are as rare as they are difficult to carry out.

In this chapter we address these issues by examining a theoretical taxonomy of explanations for desistance from crime.[†] We organize our discussion by presenting and critiquing four conceptual accounts that have been prominently advanced to explain desistance from crime—maturation, development, rational choice, and social learning. We then present an integrated

*Portions of this chapter are taken from "Understanding Desistance from Crime" (*Crime and Justice*, 2001, Volume 28, pp. 1–69, edited by Michael Tonry. Chicago: University of Chicago Press).

[†]Although we seek to paint a fairly broad theoretical picture, our research base is considerably more detailed. For a traditional "review of the literature" on desistance from crime and other problem behavior, see our in-depth treatment in Laub and Sampson (2001).

ROBERT J. SAMPSON • Department of Sociology, Harvard University, Cambridge, Massachusetts 02138.
JOHN H. LAUB • University of Maryland, College Park, Maryland 20742-8235.

Handbook of the Life Course, edited by Jeylan T. Mortimer and Michael J. Shanahan. Kluwer Academic/Plenum Publishers, New York, 2003.

account based on the core principles of life course inquiry, building in large part from our previous research on crime across the life course (Sampson & Laub, 1993). We believe that a life course perspective offers the most compelling and unifying framework for understanding the processes underlying continuity (persistence) and change (desistance) in criminal behavior over the life span. Before addressing specific theoretical accounts, however, we must first confront the relevant facts about crime and key definitional issues surrounding the concept of desistance.

DEFINING THE PROBLEM

Drawing on the accumulation of criminological research to date, we believe there is consensus on several important findings relating to offending patterns over time. Any reasonable theory of desistance from crime must be able to accommodate the following facts.

1. The prevalence of crime declines with age, although there is more variability in the age distribution across offense types than is commonly believed (Steffensmeier, Allan, Harer, & Streifel, 1989). Typically, criminal offending begins in preadolescence, peaks sharply during adolescence, and rapidly declines in the transition to young adulthood.
2. The incidence of crime does not necessarily decline with age and may in fact increase with age for certain types of crime and subgroups of offenders (Blumstein, Cohen, Roth, & Visher, 1986; Farrington, 1986; but see Hirschi & Gottfredson, 1983).
3. There appears to be substantial continuity in offending from childhood to adolescence and from adolescence into adulthood, with the earlier the onset of criminal activity, the longer the criminal career (Blumstein et al., 1986; Robins, 1966; Wolfgang, Figlio, & Sellin, 1972).
4. Despite this continuity, there is a great deal of heterogeneity in criminal behavior over the life span. Cline (1980) argued that although there is "more constancy than change ... there is sufficient change in all the data to preclude simple conclusions concerning criminal career progressions" (p. 665). Cline (1980, pp. 669–670) concluded, rightfully we suggest, that there is far more heterogeneity in criminal behavior than previous work has suggested and that many juvenile offenders do not go on to become career offenders. Loeber and LeBlanc (1990) made a similar point: "Against the backdrop of continuity, studies also show large within-individual changes in offending" (p. 390).
5. Finally, the literature focusing directly on desistance from crime indicates that there are multiple pathways. Some of the most important elements in the desistance process appear to be attachment to a conventional person such as a spouse, stable employment, transformation of personal identity, and the aging process. Moreover, the predictors and processes of desistance do not seem to vary much by offender characteristics or type of crime (see Laub & Sampson [2001] for a complete review).

As Rutter (1988, p. 3) pointed out, a major unanswered question is whether the predictors of desistance are unique or simply the opposite of predictors leading to offending. One school of thought argues that the predictors of desistance are the reverse of risk factors predicting offending (Gottfredson & Hirschi, 1990; LeBlanc & Loeber, 1993, p. 247). On the other hand, Farrington (1992) contends that the onset of delinquency is due to changes in social influence from parents to peers and that desistance is due to changes in social influence from peers to spouses. The implication is that the predictors of desistance may be distinguished from the predictors of the onset of crime. There is evidence for this "desistance" position as found in Glueck and Glueck's (1943) research on criminal careers conducted in the 1930s and 1940s. Uggen and Piliavin (1998) refer to this idea as "asymmetrical causation."

In short, despite some promising leads and an accumulation of facts on age and crime, much remains to be discovered about the *processes* of desistance from criminal behavior across various stages of the life course. We maintain that to understand desistance from criminal behavior requires a theory of crime and the criminal "offender." Crime is typically defined as a violation of societal rules of behavior that are embodied in law. When officially recognized, such violations may evoke sanctions by the state. Deviance is typically defined as violations of social norms or generally accepted standards of society (i.e., institutionalized expectations). Even given these definitions, the operational definition of an "offender" remains ambiguous, as does the point at which persistent offending or desistance occurs. Therefore, before we begin our review of the explanations of desistance from crime, we need to take a closer look at the term itself.

IS DESISTANCE A MEANINGFUL TERM?

Defined as ceasing to do something, desistance from crime is commonly acknowledged in the research literature. Most offenders, after all, eventually stop offending. Yet there is relatively little conceptualization about crime cessation. As Maruna (2001) notes, "Desistance from crime is an unusual dependent variable for criminologists because it is not an event that happens, rather it is the sustained *absence* of a certain type of event (in this case, crime)" (p. 17). Compounding this lack of conceptual clarity is the confounding of desistance with aging. It is well known that crime declines with age in the aggregate population (Gottfredson & Hirschi, 1990). The decline of recidivism with age led Hoffman and Beck (1984, p. 621) to argue for the existence of an age-related "burnout" phenomenon. These authors found that rates of recidivism decline with increased age and that this relationship persists after controlling for other factors linked to recidivism (e.g., prior criminal record). Moreover, there is evidence that offenders' fear of doing time in prison becomes especially acute with age (see Shover, 1996).

Several additional questions remain unanswered. For example, can desistance occur after one act of crime? If so, are the processes of desistance from a single act of crime different from desistance after several acts of crime? Is there such a thing as "spontaneous remission" and, if so, can the term be precisely defined? Stall and Biernacki (1986) defined spontaneous remission as desistance that occurs absent of any external intervention. How can "genuine desistance" be distinguished from "false desistance"? How long a follow-up period is needed to establish desistance? Baskin and Sommers (1998) argue that a 2-year hiatus indicates "temporary cessation" and is a long enough period to consider the "processes that initiate and sustain desistance" (p. 143). Yet how does one distinguish "intermittency in offending" from "true desistance"? For instance, Elliott, Huizinga, and Menard (1989, p. 118) employ the term suspension because suspension implies either temporary or permanent cessation. Farrington (1986) stated that "even a five-year or ten-year crime-free period is no guarantee that offending has terminated" (p. 201). And in fact, Barnett, Blumstein, and Farrington (1989) found a small group of offenders who stopped offending and then restarted after a long period of time.

In a similar vein, if offending ceases, but problem behavior remains or increases, what does that say about desistance? Weitekamp and Kerner (1994) make the point that "Desistance of crime could quite contrary be considered as a process which may lead to other forms of socially deviant, unwanted or personally dreadful problems" (p. 448). Some offenders, even though they desist from criminal activity, continue to engage in a variety of acts that are considered "deviant" or the functional equivalents of crime (Gottfredson & Hirschi, 1990). For example, they may drink alcohol excessively, have children out of wedlock, "loaf" instead of work, gamble, and congregate in bars. Can these people accurately be called desisters? Perhaps from the narrow confines of the criminal justice system they are, but from a theoretical vantage point, they display traits that imply little change in their antisocial trajectory.

Conceptual Framework

Although answers to these questions are difficult, we believe that some ground rules are possible and in fact necessary before meaningful research can proceed. We believe it is first important to distinguish termination of offending from the concept of desistance. Termination is the point in time at which one stops criminal activity, whereas desistance is the causal process that supports the termination of offending. While it is difficult to ascertain when the process of desistance actually begins, it is apparent that it continues after the termination of offending. In our view, the process of desistance maintains the continued state of non-offending. Thus, both termination and the process of desistance need to be considered in understanding cessation from offending. By using different terms for these distinct phenomena, we separate termination (the outcome) from the dynamics underlying the process of desistance (the cause), which have been hopelessly confounded in the literature to date.

The termination of offending is characterized by the absence of continued offending (a non-event). Unlike, say, stopping smoking, where setting a specific quit date is so important, criminal offenders typically do not set a date to quit offending. The actual period of time necessary to establish that termination has occurred is a sticky issue, but one that is possible to overcome. For example, in the criminal career literature, the end of the criminal career is defined as the age at which the last crime is committed. Thus, it seems reasonable to specify the date of last crime as the point of termination of offending, recognizing that there are serious measurement problems in ascertaining if in fact a person has stopped committing crimes after a certain point.

Desistance, by contrast, evolves over time in a process. According to Vaughan (1986), "uncoupling" is the process of divorce and separation. The process of uncoupling occurs prior to, during, and after divorce. Like desistance, uncoupling is not abrupt, but a gradual transition out of an intimate relationship. Similar to quitting smoking or uncoupling (Fisher, Lichtenstein, Haire-Joshu, Morgan, & Rehberg, 1993; Vaughan, 1986), we would similarly argue that desistance is best viewed as a process rather than a discrete event. The process is a social transition that entails identity transformation, for example, from a smoker to a non-smoker, or from a married/coupled person, to a divorced/uncoupled person, or from an offender to a non-offender. Also, like quitting smoking or uncoupling, desistance is not an irreversible transition.

Because low rate offending is so common, especially during adolescence, we further argue that criminologists will not learn much more than is already known about the near ubiquity of delinquency during the teen years. Following this logic, it does not seem fruitful for criminologists to spend much time studying termination or desistance for low rate adolescent offenders (defined as involvement in a single event or a series of relatively isolated events in the teenage years). Furthermore, it follows that termination and desistance should be studied among those who reach some reasonable threshold of frequent and serious criminal offending. The precise details of measurement depend upon the data set and the research question under investigation. For example, we have argued for a focus on desistance from persistent and serious delinquency, operationalized in our own research using a delinquent group of 500 formerly incarcerated juveniles with lengthy and serious criminal records (Sampson & Laub, 1993).

Finally, whether or not one embraces the criminal career paradigm (Blumstein et al., 1986), good theories of crime ought to account for the onset, continuation, and desistance from criminal behavior across the life span. At the heart of this focus on persistence and desistance is a conceptualization of stability and change over the life course. Consider that desistance can occur when there is a change in criminal propensity or a change in opportunities to commit crime. Is desistance related to one or both of these domains? Defining criminality as the stable propensity to offend, Gottfredson and Hirschi (1990) argue that desistance occurs when there is a change in the opportunity to offend. In their view, criminality is stable over the life course and, thus, cannot account for desistance from crime. Like Gottfredson and Hirschi (1990), we maintain that crime changes over time (Sampson & Laub, 1993), but we also contend that opportunities for crime are ubiquitous (Sampson & Laub, 1995). However, so far we have been silent as to whether criminality (propensity) changes or remains stable over time, although we imply that traits like self-control can change over time as a consequence of changes in the quality or strength of social ties. Ultimately, the concern with propensity (assuming that such an entity exists) may not be an important issue in the study of crime over the life course. LeBlanc and Loeber (1998), for example, recognize that "manifestations of deviancy in the course of individuals' lives may change, while the underlying propensity for deviancy may remain stable" (p. 179). We believe the focus ought to be on the heterogeneity of criminal behavior over the life span and not some unobserved latent concept.*

EXPLANATIONS OF DESISTANCE FROM CRIME

There are two distinct models in the criminological literature that have been applied to the desistance phenomenon. One stems from the idea of *population heterogeneity*. This perspective argues that behavior over the life course is a reflection of differences that vary between persons (usually, but not necessarily, individual differences or "traits") and that are established early in life with consequent stability over time. For example, Nagin and Paternoster (2000) argue that "there may be differences between individuals in socialization, personality, or biological/constitutional attributes which makes crime more likely over time" (p. 119). Once identified, time-stable traits like self-control, temperament, and intelligence are posited to account for continuity in antisocial behavior—indeed, all behavior—over time.

A second process involves the idea of *state dependence*. According to this model, past behavior causally influences future events and these events can in turn affect current and future behavior. For example, getting arrested because of criminal behavior may weaken one's future employment prospects, which in turn leads to an increased risk for later crime. As Nagin and Paternoster (2000, p. 118) point out, "committing crimes has the two-pronged effect of both weakening restraints/inhibitions and strengthening incentives for additional criminal behavior."

---

*In our view, there is an implicit theory underlying the concept of propensity—the positing of fixed attributes that are related to crime yet never observed.

What is lacking in both these models, however, is a reasonable and persuasive explanation of change in behavior. Theories of change in behavior—in our case, desistance from crime—are less developed than theories of the onset and continuation in crime. As one can see from the models described above, the idea of change is problematic. For instance, if individuals share the same individual traits that increase their propensity to crime and these traits are stable over time, how can one explain differential desistance from criminal behavior? Similarly, if current criminal activity has a causal effect on subsequent criminality, as argued in the state dependence model, then how can one explain how criminals stop offending? In short, the population heterogeneity and state dependence models emphasize one side of the coin—continuity in offending—and do not provide much insight into the processes of change. Combining the processes of population heterogeneity and state dependence is a step in the right direction, but it too begs the issue of change. What is the process of change if persistent heterogeneity and state dependence are present? If the idea of state dependence is that "criminal behavior has a genuine causal effect on subsequent criminality by eroding constraints and strengthening incentives to crime" (Nagin & Paternoster, 2000, p. 117), it is not clear how "state dependence can also explain why there is change or cessation in offending over time" (Nagin & Paternoster, 2000, p. 127).* Ultimately, the only way for models of population heterogeneity and state dependence to provide an adequate explanation of continuity and change in criminal behavior is to adopt a typological approach or one that argues that different offenders have different causal pathways to crime and as a result different prospects for desistance. We return to this crucial point below.

FRAMEWORKS FOR UNDERSTANDING THE DESISTANCE PROCESS

To explain change in offending over time we turn to several conceptual accounts of desistance from crime. While there is overlap across these frameworks, we highlight what we see as the differing elements of emphasis within each framework. We make the case that the life course perspective is the most promising approach for advancing the state of knowledge regarding continuity (persistence in) and change (desistance) in crime *and* other problem behaviors.

Maturation and Aging Accounts of Desistance

The Gluecks developed the idea of maturation as the key factor in explaining desistance from crime. Their theory was that "the physical and mental changes which enter into the natural process of *maturation* offer a chief explanation of improvement of conduct with the passing of years" (Glueck & Glueck, 1974, p. 149). Desistance occurred with the passage of time, specifically, there was a "decline in recidivism during the late twenties and early thirties" (Glueck & Glueck, 1974, p. 175). Thus, for the Gluecks, desistance was normative and expected unless an offender had serious biological or environmental deficits. At the same time, the Gluecks argued that persistent recidivism could be explained by a lack of maturity;

---

*Extant theories employing the idea of state dependence predict, all else equal, that crime will generate more crime, thus, leading to continuity in offending over time. For example, labeling theory (Lemert, 1972), social learning theory (Akers, 1998), general strain theory (Agnew, 1992), interactional theory (Thornberry, 1987), and the theory of cumulative disadvantage (Sampson & Laub, 1997) all seem to predict escalating crime.

offenders who eventually desisted experienced delayed or belated maturation. Although perhaps tautological in nature, the Gluecks argued that the men under study "finally achieved enough integration and stability to make their intelligence and emotional–volitional equipment effective in convincing them that crime does not lead to satisfaction and in enhancing their capacity for self-control" (1974, p. 170).

The Gluecks believed that maturation was a complex concept and process. They wrote that maturation "embraces the development of a stage of physical, intellectual, and affective capacity and stability, and a sufficient degree of integration of all major constituents of temperament, personality and intelligence to be adequate to the demands and restrictions of life in organized society" (Glueck & Glueck, 1974, p. 170). The Gluecks were quite clear that desistance "cannot be attributed to external environmental transformations" (p. 173). The Gluecks called for more research into the "striking maturation" phenomenon from biological, psychological, and sociological perspectives, with the goal to "dissect maturation into its components" (p. 270). Interestingly, for the Gluecks age and maturation were not one and the same. It was the case that as age increased, recidivism declined. However, age alone was not enough to explain maturation. "It was not the achievement of any particular age, but rather the achievement of adequate maturation regardless of the chronological age at which it occurred that was the significant influence in the behavior change of our criminals" (Glueck & Glueck, 1945, p. 81). Nonetheless, the basic idea of this approach is that desistance is the result of offenders growing out of crime and settling down.

A variation of the Gluecks approach is found in Gottfredson and Hirschi's (1990) *A general theory of crime*. Like the Gluecks, Gottfredson and Hirschi (1990) argue that crime declines with age for all offenders (see also Hirschi & Gottfredson, 1983). Gottfredson and Hirschi contend that the age distribution of crime—including onset, frequency, and desistance—is, for all intents and purposes, "invariant" across time, space, and historical context and, therefore, cannot be explained by variables currently proposed in mainstream criminology (e.g., poverty, subculture). Gottfredson and Hirschi state, "This explanation suggests that maturational reform is just that, change in behavior that comes with maturation; it suggests that spontaneous desistance is just that, change in behavior that cannot be explained and change that occurs regardless of what else happens" (1990, p. 136).

A fundamental aspect of the Gottfredson and Hirschi (1990) account of desistance is the distinction between crime and criminality. According to Gottfredson and Hirschi crimes are short-term, circumscribed events that presuppose a set of conditions. In contrast, criminality refers to relatively stable differences across individuals in the propensity to commit crime. Gottfredson and Hirschi go on to argue that, while crime everywhere declines with age, criminality—differences in propensities, like self-control—remain relatively stable over the life course. They write, "Desistance theory asserts that crime declines with age because of factors associated with age that reduce or change the criminality of the actor. The age theory asserts that crime, independent of criminality, declines with age" (Gottfredson & Hirschi, 1990, p. 137). For Gottfredson and Hirschi criminality was impervious to institutional involvement and impact.

Unlike the Gluecks, Gottfredson and Hirschi do not invoke the process of maturation, but rather a direct effect of age on crime. Decreases in offending over time are "due to the inexorable aging of the organism" (Gottfredson & Hirschi, 1990, p. 141). From this theoretical perspective, it follows that criminal behavior is largely unaffected by life course events—marriage, employment, education, etc.—or any situational or institutional influences. The problem with maturational or "ontogenetic" accounts, well noted by Dannefer (1984), is that they do not really offer an explanation—things are thought to just "naturally" happen. The basic idea is that desistance "just happens" and that the age effect cannot be explained with the available terms and concepts.

Developmental Accounts of Desistance

A similar problem is seen in developmental accounts that are rooted in ontogenetic reasoning (Dannefer, 1984). One explanation is that identity changes account for reductions and cessation in crime (see Maruna, 2001; see also Gartner & Piliavin, 1988; Shover, 1996). Mulvey and LaRosa (1986) focus on the period from age 17 to 20, the period they call the time of "natural" recovery. They argue that desistance is the result of shifts in behavioral patterns that characterize adolescence, especially late adolescence (see Mulvey & Aber, [1988] for details on this developmental perspective). This process is similar to the one advanced by Shover (1996) in his study of behavioral shifts in response to aging among men involved in crime. Such accounts of desistance suggest two themes.

1. Desistance is normative (ontogenetic) and expected across the life span. Some "rough and tumble" toddlers will desist from antisocial behavior as they enter school, some adolescent delinquents will desist while in high school, and some older delinquents will desist as they make the transition to young adulthood, and so on.
2. Cognitive change is a precursor to behavioral change. What Maruna (2001) calls "identity deconstruction" is necessary to begin the long-term process of desistance.

A second developmental account of desistance is offered by Gove (1985). He argues that explanations of the cessation of various forms of crime and deviance must incorporate biological, psychological, and sociological variables. Like Hirschi and Gottfredson (1983), Gove (1985) maintains that sociological theories of crime are unable to explain the patterns of desistance revealed in the data. Gove (1985) reviewed six sociological theories of deviance, including labeling, conflict, differential association, control, anomie, and functional theory and concluded that "all of these theoretical perspectives either explicitly or implicitly suggest that deviant behavior is an amplifying process leading to further and more serious deviance" (p. 118). By contrast, changes in socially structured roles, psychological wellbeing, psychological maturation, and biological factors such as physical strength, physical energy, psychological drive, and the need for stimulation provide reasonable accounts of desistance from crime with age. Gove (1985) concludes that "biological and psychological factors appear to play a critical role in the termination of deviant behavior" (p. 136). The peak and decline in physical strength, energy, psychological drive, and the need for stimulation maps fairly well the peak and decline in deviant behavior.

A third and the most influential developmental account of persistence in and desistance from crime is offered by Moffitt (1993, 1994). Moffitt spells out two distinct categories of individuals, each possessing a unique natural history of antisocial behavior over the life course. From a desistance standpoint, what is important is that these two antisocial trajectories have unique etiologies that in part account for the differences in desistance. Life-course persistent offenders start early in childhood and persist in offending well into adulthood. For this small group of offenders, neuropsychological deficits in conjunction with disrupted attachment relationships and academic failure drive long-term antisocial behaviors. Simply put, life-course persistent offenders do not desist from crime. As Moffitt states, it is not the traits or the environment per se that account for continuity. Rather her theory of continuous antisocial behavior (and by definition, no desistance) "emphasizes the constant *process* of reciprocal interaction between personal traits and environmental reactions to them" (Moffitt, 1994, p. 28). Antisocial dispositions infiltrate into all domains of adolescence and adulthood and this "diminishes the likelihood of change" (Moffitt, 1994, p. 28).

Adolescence-limited offenders are involved in antisocial behavior only during adolescence. This large group of offenders has no history of antisocial behavior in childhood. The delinquency of the adolescence-limited group is situational and, as a result, virtually all of these offenders desist from criminal behavior over time. Adolescence-limited offenders seek to enjoy the spoils of adulthood (what Moffitt calls the maturity gap) and they mimic the antisocial styles of life-course persisters and, in turn, they are socially reinforced by the "negative consequences" of delinquent behavior (Moffitt, 1994, pp. 30–33). Adolescence-limited offenders desist from crime in response to changing contingencies and reinforcements. For the adolescence-limited group, desistance, like delinquency, is normative. Because adolescence-limiteds have no history of childhood antisocial behavior resulting from neuropsychological deficits, the forces of cumulative continuity are much weaker. Simultaneously, adolescence-limited offenders have more prosocial skills, more academic achievement, and stronger attachments than their life-course persistent counterparts, characteristics that facilitate desistance from crime.

In sum, Moffitt (1994) argues that "the age of desistance from criminal offending will be a function of age of onset of antisocial behavior, mastery of conventional prosocial skills, and the number and severity of "snares" encountered during the foray into delinquency. Snares are consequences of crime, such as incarceration or injury, that constrain conventional behavior" (p. 45). "Adolescence-limited delinquents can profit from opportunities for desistance, because they retain the option of successfully resuming a conventional lifestyle. Life-course-persistent delinquents may make transitions into marriage or work, but their injurious childhoods make it less likely that they can leave their past selves behind" (Moffitt, 1994, p. 45).

Rational Choice Accounts of Desistance

The main idea of the rational choice framework is that the decision to continue or give up crime is based on a conscious reappraisal of the costs and benefits of crime (see Clarke & Cornish, 1985; Cornish & Clarke, 1986; & Gartner & Piliavin, 1988). According to this perspective, persisters and desisters are seen as "reasoning decisionmakers" (Cornish & Clarke, 1986, p. 13). One important component of this decision is the increasing fear of punishment with aging, as discussed above (see also Cromwell, Olson, & Avary, 1991). However, as we have seen, aging is not necessarily tied to the decision to give up crime.

Some researchers have tried to understand the context of rational decisions to stop offending. For example, Cusson and Pinsonneault (1986) contend that the decision to give up crime is triggered by a "shock" of some sort (e.g., a shoot out during a crime) or "delayed deterrence" (e.g., increased fear of doing more time) or both. Cusson and Pinsonneault (1986, p. 78) found the decision to give up crime was "voluntary and autonomous." These findings are highly speculative, as conceded by the authors, since the study was based primarily on interviews with 17 ex-robbers in Canada. In a similar vein, Leibrich (1996) studied 37 men and women in New Zealand who were on probation and in the process of going straight. She found that shame was the primary factor in the desistance process in that it was the most commonly identified cost of offending. Three kinds of shame were reported: public humiliation, personal disgrace, and private remorse. As Leibrich (1996, p. 297) stated, "shame was the thing which most often dissuaded people from offending and the growth of self-respect was the thing which most often persuaded them to go straight." In another interesting study, Paternoster (1989) integrated deterrence and rational choice perspectives in an attempt to understand decisions to participate in and desist from delinquency (i.e., marijuana use, drinking liquor, petty theft, and vandalism). Drawing on data from 1,250 high school students surveyed at three points in time, Paternoster (1989) found that the decision to desist was not related to formal sanction threats (e.g., the perceived severity and certainty of punishment). Decisions to desist were instead related to changes in moral tolerance of the delinquent act. Those offenders who made a decision to stop offending began to have stronger moral reservations about the illegal acts in question. This finding held for all four delinquent offenses. It is noteworthy that changes in moral beliefs were associated with changes in peer delinquency and the degree of peer support for delinquency. Whether changes in moral beliefs and tolerance can be properly understood to support rational choice theory is questionable. What seems important to know is *why* individuals underwent changes in their moral reasoning.

Social Learning Accounts of Desistance

Social learning has been offered as an integrative framework to provide explanations of desistance from crime and other forms of problem behavior. In fact, Akers (1990) forcefully argued that social learning accounts incorporate all of the major elements of rational choice and deterrence frameworks, including moral reasoning. One of the strengths of the social learning approach is its application to all crime types as well as illicit drug use, alcohol abuse, and other problem behaviors (see Akers [1998], for an extensive review of the research literature).

In the social learning framework, the basic variables that explain initiation into crime are the same variables that account for cessation from crime. That is, for the most part, the account of desistance is the account of initiation in reverse. For example, differential association with non-criminal friends and significant others, less exposure to or opportunities to model or imitate criminal behavior, developing definitions and attitudes favorable to conformity and abiding by the law, and differential reinforcement (social and non-social) discouraging continued involvement in crime are all part of the desistance story. Imitation appears less important after onset while social and non-social reinforcements become more important (see Akers, 1998). As for onset and continuation, the most important factor in desistance is peer associations.

In perhaps the most important application of social learning theory to desistance, Warr (1993) argued that differential association accounts for the decline in crime with age. Using data from the first five waves of the National Youth Survey for respondents aged 11–21, he found that peer associations (e.g., exposure to delinquent peers, time spent with peers, and loyalty to peers) changed dramatically with age. With respect to desistance, declines in crime were linked with declines in peer associations. When peer variables were controlled, "the association between age and crime is substantially weakened and, for some offenses, disappears entirely" (Warr, 1993, p. 35). Along similar lines, Warr (1998) argued that changing peer relations account for the association between marital status and desistance from crime. Using longitudinal data, again from the National Youth Survey, he found that the transition to marriage is followed by "a dramatic decline in time spent with friends" and "reduced exposure to delinquent peers" (Warr, 1998, p. 183). Warr concludes that marriage is important because of its effect on peer influences, a finding consistent with social learning theory but also other perspectives. For example, marriage may lead to the greater social control of men (Sampson & Laub, 1993), there by explaining their desistance. To fully understand desistance we thus need to better understand mediating social processes.

A LIFE COURSE ACCOUNT OF DESISTANCE

We believe that a life course perspective offers the most compelling and unifying framework for understanding the processes underlying continuity (persistence) and change (desistance) in criminal behavior over the life span. According to Elder (1998), the life course perspective contains several principles: (1) a focus on the historical time and place that recognizes that lives are embedded and shaped by context, (2) the recognition that the developmental impact of life events is contingent on when they occur in a person's life, that is timing matters, (3) the acknowledgment of intergenerational transmission of social patterns—the notion of linked lives and interdependency, and (4) the view that human agency plays a key role in choice making and constructing one's life course. The major objective of the life course perspective is to link social history and social structure to the unfolding of human lives. A life course perspective thus looks to within-individual variations over time, regardless of whether one is interested in understanding persistence or desistance in crime.

Applying the life course framework to the study of desistance leads to a focus on continuity and change in criminal behavior over time, especially its embeddedness in historical and other contextual features of social life. We took such a position in our book, *Crime in the making: Pathways and turning points through life* (Sampson & Laub, 1993), where we developed and tested a theory of crime over the life course using a unique data archive—the *Unraveling juvenile delinquency* study and subsequent follow-ups conducted by Sheldon Glueck and Eleanor Glueck of the Harvard Law School. This study is considered to be one of the most influential in the history of criminological research. Gluecks' (1950) data were derived from a three-wave prospective study of juvenile and adult criminal behavior that originated with *Unraveling juvenile delinquency* (1950; see also Glueck and Glueck, (1968) *Delinquents and nondelinquents in perspective*). The research design involved a sample of 500 male delinquents ages 10–17 and 500 male non-delinquents ages 10–17 matched case-by-case on age, race/ethnicity, IQ, and low-income residence in Boston. Extensive data were collected on the 1,000 boys at three points in time—ages 14, 25, and 32. We reconstructed and analyzed the full longitudinal data set.

In the resulting *Crime in the making* (Sampson & Laub, 1993), we developed an age-graded theory of informal social control to explain childhood antisocial behavior, adolescent delinquency, and crime in adulthood. Our theory emphasized the importance of social ties and bonds to society at all ages across the life course. The organizing principle was that crime and deviance are more likely to occur when an individual's bond to society is weak or broken. We highlighted the role of informal social controls that emerge from the role reciprocities and structure of interpersonal bonds linking members of society to one another and to wider institutions such as work, family, school, and community. The first building block in our life course theory focused on the mediating role of informal family and school social bonds in explaining child and adolescent delinquency (Sampson & Laub, 1993, Chs 4 and 5). The second building block incorporated the role of continuity in childhood problem behavior that extends into adulthood across a variety of life's domains, such as crime, alcohol abuse, divorce, and unemployment (Sampson & Laub, 1993, Ch. 6). The third building block examined change in antisocial behavior over time. A fundamental theme of our age-graded theory of informal social control and crime is that, while individual traits and childhood experiences are important for understanding behavioral trajectories, experiences in adolescence and adulthood can redirect those trajectories in either a more positive or more negative manner. Our theory thus incorporates both stability and change in criminal behavior over the life course.

The logical question of interest then is what factors explain stability and change over the life course? In *Crime in the making* (Sampson & Laub, 1993), we examined the predictors of desistance and persistence in adult crime and violence and found that despite differences in early childhood experiences, adult social bonds to work and family had similar consequences for the life course trajectories of the 500 delinquents and 500 non-delinquent controls we studied. More precisely, job stability and marital attachment in adulthood were significantly related to changes in adult crime—the stronger the adult ties to work and family, the less crime and deviance among both delinquents and non-delinquent controls. We concluded that "turning points" related to work, marriage, and military service were crucial for understanding processes of continuity and change across the adult life course (see also Laub & Sampson, 1993; Sampson & Laub, 1993, 1996). A number of recent studies have confirmed the predictive power of social ties, such as marital bonds, for explaining desistance from crime (Farrington & West, 1995; Horney, Osgood, & Marshall, 1995; Warr, 1998).

CONCLUSION

The life course approach offers a number of advantages over the traditional accounts of desistance from crime noted above, even developmental perspectives.* Developmental accounts, from developmental psychology, focus on regular or law-like individual development over the life span. Implicit in developmental approaches are the notions of stages, progressions, growth, and evolution (Dannefer, 1984; Lewontin, 2000). The resulting emphasis is systematic pathways of development (change) over time, with the imagery being one of the execution of a program written at an earlier point in time. Although there are aspects of developmental approaches that rely on pure population heterogeneity models, some developmental theorists, such as Moffitt explicitly recognize the possibility of change. Still, change is usually explained by childhood characteristics and experiences—some people are simply more programmed early on for change than others. *In other words, desistance is possible only for those with the "right" characteristics that were previously determined.* Developmental models are thus ultimately forced to assume that there are "groups" or "types" of offenders (e.g., life course persisters) that display distinct and different causal pathways and probabilities of continuity and change, even if the manifestations of these pathways vary by age.

In contrast, life course approaches, while incorporating individual differences and notions of law-like development such as aging, emphasize variability and exogenous influences on the course of development over time that cannot be predicted by focusing solely on enduring individual traits (population heterogeneity models) or even past experiences (state dependence models). Flowing mainly from sociology and history, life course accounts embrace the notion that lives are often unpredictable and dynamic and that exogenously induced changes are ever present. Some changes in life course result from chance or random events, while other changes stem from macro-level "shocks" largely beyond the pale of individual choice (e.g., war, depression, natural disasters, revolutions, plant closings, industrial restructuring). Another important aspect of life course criminology is a focus on situations and time-varying social contexts that impede or facilitate criminal events.

---

*The life course perspective can also be distinguished from a criminal career perspective. We regard the life course perspective as broader in scope and driven by theoretical rather than policy concerns. In contrast, the criminal career model is largely atheoretical and more concerned with developing policy about "career criminals" than theory about "criminal careers."

At the end of the day, however, the fundamental difference from developmental (especially psychological) accounts is the theoretical commitment to the idea of social malleability across the life course and the focus on the constancy of change, including the dynamic processes that serve to reproduce stability socially (Dannefer, 1984). A life course focus recognizes emergent properties and rejects the metaphor of "unfolding" that is inextricably part of the developmental paradigm. To be more specific, like Lewontin (2000) we reject the idea of determinism and "ontogenetic" predictability from childhood factors. It follows that we must reject the pure version of the so-called "population heterogeneity" models. We argue that the traits that are at the heart of this perspective, whether derived from genetics or childhood experiences, do not sufficiently predict behavior over the long haul. In our view, the full life course matters, especially postchildhood, adolescence, and adult experiences.* We are also compelled to reject the pure version of "state dependence." Although state dependence models improve upon population heterogeneity models, they too do not sufficiently account for change—there are simply too many outcomes that cannot be explained by focusing on the past.

Although the life course perspective can be integrated with several criminological theories (e.g., social control, social learning, and rational choice), for both theoretical and empirical reasons noted above, we favor a modified version of social control theory. Because of its explicit focus on lives in social context, we believe that a life course perspective integrated with an age-graded theory of informal social control offers a means of understanding onset, continuation, *and* desistance from criminal behavior (see Sampson & Laub [1993] for background). We would thus argue for a focus on the structural sources of both continuity and change and their role in the processes of persistence in and desistance from crime. Drawing inspiration from the life course paradigm, the idea of "turning points" plays a central role in such accounts, especially when linked to the interaction of human agency, situations, and historical context.†

REFERENCES

Agnew, R. (1992). Foundation for a general strain theory of crime and delinquency. *Criminology, 30*, 47–87.

Akers, R. L. (1990). Rational choice, deterrence, and social learning in criminology: The path not taken. *Journal of Criminal Law and Criminology, 81*, 653–676.

Akers, R. L. (1998). *Social learning and social structure: A general theory of crime and deviance.* Boston, MA: Northeastern University Press.

Barnett, A., Blumstein, A., & Farrington, D. P. (1989). A prospective test of a criminal career model. *Criminology, 27*, 373–388.

Baskin, D. R., & Sommers, I. B. (1998). *Casualties of community disorder: Women's careers in violent crime.* Boulder, CO: Westview Press.

Blumstein, A., Cohen, J., Roth, J., & Visher, C. (Eds.) (1986). *Criminal careers and "career criminals".* Washington, DC: National Academy Press.

Clarke, R. V., & Cornish, D. B. (1985). Modeling offenders' decisions: A framework for research and policy. In M. Tonry & N. Morris (Eds.), *Crime and justice: An annual review of research* (Vol. 6, pp. 147–185). Chicago: University of Chicago Press.

*This view is consistent with recent research in the health area. For instance, Lamont et al. (2000) found that adult lifestyle and biological risk markers measured in adulthood explained more variance in cardiovascular disease risk than the direct and indirect contributions of early childhood experiences.

†We emphasize, however, that there remain critical unresolved issues and important data limitations that have hampered the progress of life course criminology. These issues are beyond the scope of the present paper. For a detailed discussion, see Laub and Sampson (2001).

Cline, H. F. (1980). Criminal behavior over the life span. In O. G. Brim & J. Kagan (Eds.), *Constancy and change in human development* (pp. 641–674). Cambridge, MA: Harvard University Press.

Cornish, D. B., & Clarke, R. V. (1986). *The reasoning criminal: Rational choice perspectives on offending*. New York: Springer-Verlag.

Cromwell, P. F., Olson, J. N., & Avary, D. W. (1991). *Breaking and entering: An ethnographic analysis of burglary*. Newbury Park, CA: Sage.

Cusson, M., & Pinsonneault, P. (1986). The decision to give up crime. In D. B. Cornish & R. V. Clarke (Eds.), *The reasoning criminal: Rational choice perspectives on offending* (pp. 72–82). New York: Springer-Verlag.

Dannefer, D. (1984). Adult development and social theory: A paradigmatic reappraisal. *American Sociological Review, 49*, 100–116.

Elder, G. H., Jr. (1998). The life course as developmental theory. *Child Development, 69*, 1–12.

Elliott, D. S., Huizinga, D., & Menard, S. (1989). *Multiple problem youth: Delinquency, substance use, and mental health problems*. New York: Springer-Verlag.

Farrington, D. P. (1986). Age and crime. In M. Tonry & N. Morris (Eds.), *Crime and justice: An annual review of research* (Vol. 7, pp. 189–250). Chicago: University of Chicago Press.

Farrington, D. P. (1992). Explaining the beginning, progress, and ending of antisocial behavior from birth to adulthood. In J. McCord (Ed.), *Facts, frameworks, and forecasts* (pp. 253–286). New Brunswick, NJ: Transaction Books.

Farrington, D. P., & West, D. J. (1995). The effects of marriage, separation, and children on offending by adult males. In Z. S. Blau & J. Hagan (Eds.), *Current perspectives on aging and the life cycle*: Vol. 4. *Delinquency and disrepute in the life course* (pp. 249–281). Greenwich, CT: JAI Press.

Fisher, E. B., Jr., Lichtenstein, E., Haire-Joshu, D., Morgan, G. D., & Rehberg, H. R. (1993). Methods, successes, and failures of smoking cessation programs. *Annual Review of Medicine, 44*, 481–513.

Gartner, R., & Piliavin, I. (1988). The aging offender and the aged offender. In P. B. Baltes, D. L. Featherman, & R. M. Lerner (Eds.), *Life-span development and behavior*, (Vol. 9, pp. 287–315). Hillside, NJ: Lawrence Erlbaum Associates.

Glueck, S., & Glueck, E. (1943). *Criminal careers in retrospect*. New York: The Commonwealth Fund.

Glueck, S., & Glueck, E. (1945). *After-conduct of discharged offenders*. London: Macmillan.

Glueck, S., & Glueck, E. (1950). *Unraveling juvenile delinquency*. New York: The Commonwealth Fund.

Glueck, S., & Glueck, E. (1968). *Delinquents and nondelinquents in perspective*. Cambridge, MA: Harvard University Press.

Glueck, S., & Glueck, E. (1974). *Of delinquency and crime*. Springfield, IL: Charles C. Thomas.

Gottfredson, M. R., & Hirschi, T. (1990). *A general theory of crime*. Stanford, CA: Stanford University Press.

Gove, W. R. (1985). The effect of age and gender on deviant behavior: A biopsychosocial perspective. In A. S. Rossi (Ed.), *Gender and the life course* (pp. 115–144). New York: Aldine.

Hirschi, T., & Gottfredson, M. R. (1983). Age and the explanation of crime. *American Journal of Sociology, 89*, 552–584.

Hoffman, P. B., & Beck, J. L. (1984). Burnout—age at release from prison and recidivism. *Journal of Criminal Justice, 12*, 617–623.

Horney, J., Osgood, D. W., & Marshall, I. H. (1995). Criminal careers in the short-term: Intra-individual variability in crime and its relation to local life circumstances. *American Sociological Review, 60*, 655–673.

Lamont, D., Parker, L., White, M., Unwin, N., Bennett, S. M. A., Cohen, M., Richardson, D., Dickinson, H. O., Adamson, A., Alberti, K. G. M. M., & Craft, A. W. (2000). Risk of cardiovascular disease measured by carotid intima-media thickness at age 49–51: Lifecourse study. *British Medical Journal, 320*, 273–278.

Laub, J. H., & Sampson, R. J. (1993). Turning points in the life course: Why change matters to the study of crime. *Criminology, 31*, 301–325.

Laub, J. H., & Sampson, R. J. (2001). Understanding desistance from crime. In M. Tonry (Ed.), *Crime and justice: A review of research* (Vol. 28, pp. 1–69). Chicago: University of Chicago Press.

LeBlanc, M., & Loeber, R. (1993). Precursors, causes, and the development of criminal offending. In D. F. Hay & A. Angold (Eds.), *Precursors and causes in development and psychopathology* (pp. 233–263). New York: John Wiley.

LeBlanc, M., & Loeber, R. (1998). Developmental criminology updated. In M. Tonry (Ed.), *Crime and justice: A review of research* (Vol. 23, pp. 115–198). Chicago: University of Chicago Press.

Leibrich, J. (1996). The role of shame in going straight: A study of former offenders. In B. Galaway & J. Hudson (Eds.), *Restorative justice: International perspectives* (pp. 283–302). Monsey, NY: Criminal Justice Press.

Lemert, E. (1972). *Human deviance, social problems and social control (2nd ed.)*. Englewood Cliffs, NJ: Prentice-Hall.

Lewontin, R. (2000). *The triple helix: Gene, organism, and environment*. Cambridge, MA: Harvard University Press.

Loeber, R., & LeBlanc, M. (1990). Toward a developmental criminology. In M. Tonry & N. Morris (Eds.), *Crime and justice: A review of research* (Vol. 12, pp. 375–473). Chicago: University of Chicago Press.

Maruna, S. (2001). *Making good: How ex-offenders reform and rebuild their lives.* Washington, DC: American Psychological Association Books.

Moffitt, T. E. (1993). Adolescent-limited and life-course-persistent antisocial behavior: A developmental taxonomy. *Psychological Review, 100*, 674–701.

Moffitt, T. E. (1994). Natural histories of delinquency. In E. G. M. Weitekamp & H.-J. Kerner (Eds.), *Cross-national longitudinal research on human development and criminal behavior* (pp. 3–61). Dordrecht, The Netherlands: Kluwer Academic.

Mulvey, E. P., & Aber, M. (1988). Growing out of delinquency: Development and desistance. In R. L. Jenkins & W. K. Brown (Eds.), *The abandonment of delinquent behavior* (pp. 99–116). New York: Praeger.

Mulvey, E. P., & LaRosa, J. F. (1986). Delinquency cessation and adolescent development: Preliminary data. *American Journal of Orthopsychiatry, 56*, 212–224.

Nagin, D., & Paternoster, R. (2000). Population heterogeneity and state dependence: State of the evidence and directions for future research. *Journal of Quantitative Criminology, 16*, 117–144.

Paternoster, R. (1989). Decisions to participate in and desist from four types of common delinquency: Deterrence and the rational choice perspective. *Law and Society Review, 23*, 7–40.

Robins, L. (1966). *Deviant children grown up.* Baltimore, MD: Williams Wilkins.

Rutter, M. (1988). Longitudinal data in the study of causal processes: Some uses and some pitfalls. In M. Rutter (Ed.), *Studies of psychosocial risk: The power of longitudinal data* (pp. 1–28). Cambridge: Cambridge University Press.

Sampson, R. J., & Laub, J. H. (1993). *Crime in the making: Pathways and turning points through life.* Cambridge, MA: Harvard University Press.

Sampson, R. J., & Laub, J. H. (1995). Understanding variability in lives through time: Contributions of life-course criminology. *Studies on Crime and Crime Prevention, 4*, 143–158.

Sampson, R. J., & Laub, J. H. (1996). Socioeconomic achievement in the life course of disadvantaged men: Military service as a turning point, circa 1940–1965. *American Sociological Review, 61*, 347–367.

Sampson, R. J., & Laub, J. H. (1997). A life-course theory of cumulative disadvantage and the stability of delinquency. In T. P. Thornberry (Ed.), *Developmental theories of crime and delinquency* (pp. 133–161). New Brunswick, NJ: Transaction.

Shover, N. (1996). *Great pretenders: Pursuits and careers of persistent thieves.* Boulder, CO: Westview Press.

Stall, R., & Biernacki, P. (1986). Spontaneous remission from the problematic use of substances: An inductive model derived from a comparative analysis of the alcohol, opiate, tobacco, and food/obesity literatures. *The International Journal of the Addictions, 21*, 1–23.

Steffensmeier, D. J., Allan, E. A., Harer, M. D., & Streifel, C. (1989). Age and the distribution of crime. *American Journal of Sociology, 94*, 803–831.

Thornberry, T. P. (1987). Toward an interactional theory of delinquency. *Criminology, 25*, 863–891.

Uggen, C., & Piliavin, I. (1998). Asymmetrical causation and criminal desistance. *Journal of Criminal Law and Criminology, 88*, 1399–1422.

Vaughan, D. (1986). *Uncoupling: Turning points in intimate relationships.* New York: Oxford University Press.

Warr, M. (1993). Age, peers, and delinquency. *Criminology, 31*, 17–40.

Warr, M. (1998). Life-course transitions and desistance from crime. *Criminology, 36*, 183–216.

Weitekamp, E. G. M., & Kerner, H.-J. (1994). Epilogue: Workshop and plenary discussions, and future directions. In E. G. M. Weitekamp & H.-J. Kerner (Eds.), *Cross-national longitudinal research on human development and criminal behavior* (pp. 439–449). Dordrecht, The Netherlands: Kluwer Academic.

Wolfgang, M., Figlio, R., & Sellin, T. (1972). *Delinquency in a birth cohort.* Chicago: University of Chicago Press.

CHAPTER 15

Desistance from Crime and Deviance as a Turning Point in the Life Course

CHRISTOPHER UGGEN

MICHAEL MASSOGLIA

The transition to adulthood has generally become more individualized in the past 50 years, with fewer young people attaining the classic markers of adult status in an orderly progression (Buchman, 1989; Rindfuss, Swicegood, & Rosenfeld, 1987). The average age of first marriage or age of entry into full-time employment has also increased dramatically in recent decades (Shanahan, 2000). Despite such changes, however, the notion that adults eventually "settle down" and desist from delinquent and deviant behaviors persists across shifting familial and economic arrangements. As they become fully fledged adults, people generally cease or at least moderate many forms of criminal behavior, substance use, and other antisocial activities. In this chapter, we summarize theory and research on desistance from crime and deviance and explore the extent to which such desistance constitutes a separate dimension of the multifaceted transition to adulthood.

As in other areas of life course research, the study of desistance is concerned with the socially embedded processes that foster discontinuity in life pathways. Desistance from

CHRISTOPHER UGGEN AND MICHAEL MASSOGLIA • Department of Sociology, University of Minnesota, Minneapolis, Minnesota 55455.

Handbook of the Life Course, edited by Jeylan T. Mortimer and Michael J. Shanahan. Kluwer Academic/Plenum Publishers, New York, 2003.

deviance is likely to influence and be influenced by transitions to marriage, full-time employment, and other markers (Sampson & Laub, 1993). Apart from its effects on other transitions,
however, we argue that desistance from deviant roles may *itself* constitute an important
dimension of the transition to adulthood. That is, "adult" status is less likely to be conferred
on those who continue to engage in forms of deviant behavior associated with the adolescent
period.

How can desistance from crime constitute a separate dimension of the transition to adulthood when most adults have no criminal history from which to desist? First, rates of official
criminal punishment are rising rapidly. Approximately 59 million Americans had a state criminal history record on file in 1999 (U.S. Department of Justice, Bureau of Justice Statistics,
2001a) and one study estimated that 28.5% of African American males will be incarcerated
in a state or federal penitentiary over their lifetime (Bonczar & Beck, 1997). More importantly for our purposes, however, a long line of self-report research has demonstrated that
almost every adolescent admits to some form of delinquency (e.g., see Gabor, 1994) and that
rates of both official and self-reported criminal behavior decline precipitously in adulthood.
According to the 2001 Monitoring the Future Study, for example, a majority of U.S. students
have taken illicit drugs (primarily marijuana) and participated in binge drinking by the time
they are seniors in high school (Johnston, O'Malley, & Bachman, 2002). The vast majority of
these young people will soon settle down by moderating their substance use, ceasing activities such as shoplifting and fighting altogether and simultaneously assuming adult work and
family roles. In this chapter, we discuss how desistance from crime is likely to be both a cause
and consequence of transiting other life course markers and becoming an adult.

We begin by presenting some descriptive statistics illustrating the life course position of
those officially defined as deviant—persons under correctional supervision. We then present
some self-reported data from the general population, showing how markers of adult attainment co-vary with some forms of deviant and criminal behavior. Next we discuss important
conceptual and methodological issues in defining and measuring desistance. After a brief
discussion of existing theories of desistance, we consider the problem of reintegration. In
particular, socioeconomic reintegration, familial reintegration, and civic reintegration operate
as organizing concepts for understanding the relationship between desistance and life course
transitions. Finally, we address cross-national or comparative work on desistance and the
potential for future interventions to inform policy debates and scientific knowledge about
desistance as a turning point in the life course.

DEVIANCE AND THE TIMING OF
ADULT TRANSITIONS

Deviance and Adult Transitions in the Prison Population

In part because of their involvement with the criminal justice system, prison inmates and former inmates are generally "off-time" with regard to important markers of the transition to
adulthood (Caspi, Elder, & Herbener, 1990). In taking stock of their circumstances, many
lament that they have not got farther in life, building careers, forming families, purchasing
houses, and taking on other adult roles (Shover, 1996; Uggen, Manza, & Behrens, 2002).
Both qualitative and quantitative research suggests that the relationship between deviant
behavior and normative role transitions is complex and reciprocal. For example, Sullivan's

(1989) *Getting paid*, an ethnographic study of youth work and crime in New York, showed how early delinquency may disrupt employment patterns, which in turn may engender further criminal behavior. This pattern of association has also been identified in a number of important quantitative studies. Analyzing a cohort of London boys born in the 1950s, Hagan (1993) finds that adolescent criminal "embeddedness," measured by delinquent activities, friends, and parental criminal convictions, delays the transition into full-time employment in young adulthood. Similarly, in a sample of American delinquent and non-delinquent boys born in the 1920s, Sampson and Laub (1993) report that early juvenile incarceration decreases later job stability, which, in turn, exacerbates adult criminal behavior. Thus, deviant activities and entry into adult occupational roles are likely to be reciprocally determined.

Many officially defined deviants are "off-time" because they have done time. State prison inmates represent the most extreme example of delayed entry into adult roles. Table 15-1 presents data from a large-scale nationally representative survey of state inmates conducted at approximately 5-year intervals since 1974. These repeated cross-sectional data show that the mean age of prison entry has risen steadily over this period, with prisoners now averaging over 30 years of age at admission. Despite their advancing age, however, few have attained the minimal markers of entry into adult status.

The classic markers for assessing socioeconomic transitions generally include school completion and entry into full-time employment. These data indicate that inmates have relatively low levels of educational attainment, with fewer than one third having achieved a high school diploma. Full-time employment levels have declined gradually since 1974, with a slim majority holding a full-time job prior to their most recent arrest in the 1997 survey. In contrast, over three fourths of males of comparable age in the general population held full-time jobs and 87% had attained a high school diploma or equivalency.

With regard to family markers, the percentage of married inmates has declined over time, from 24% in 1974 to 18% in 1997. The comparable figure in the general population is 53% for males in this age range. Despite low rates of marriage, most inmates are parents: 56% reported having one or more children in the most recent survey. Although trends such as declining rates of marriage and non-marital births mirror shifts in the larger society, the characteristics of the inmate population have remained relatively stable over the past 25 years. Compared to the non-institutionalized population, inmates have long been significantly off-time in terms of educational attainment and entry into full-time employment and marital unions.

What has changed, however, are the rate and absolute number of offenders entering prison and ex-offenders leaving prison. The state and federal prison population grew sixfold between 1974 and 1997 and now exceeds 1.4 million, with an additional 687,000 inmates currently held in local jails (U.S. Department of Justice, Bureau of Justice Statistics, 2000a). When parolees and probationers are added to these figures, the total number of persons under correctional supervision now exceeds 6.3 million (U.S. Department of Justice, Bureau of Justice Statistics, 2000a, 2000b). Although prison and jail inmates lag the farthest behind their contemporaries in the general population, members of other officially defined correctional populations are also likely to be off-time with regard to key adult life course transitions.

Deviance and Adult Transitions in the General Population

Of course, the incarcerated population represents the most extreme combination of socioeconomic disadvantage and high rates of criminal activity. Many people who commit crime

TABLE 15-1. Life Course Markers of Prison Inmates Prior to Incarceration, 1974–1997[a] and Comparable Data for Males Ages 25–34 in the General Population 1997[b,c]

Variables	State prison inmate population			General population
	1974	1986	1997	1997
Age at admission	26.5 (9.3)	27.6 (8.7)	32.5 (10.4)	
Current age	29.6 (10.0)	30.6 (9.0)	34.8 (10.0)	29.7
Education markers				
With HS Diploma/GED (%)	21.1	31.9	30.6	87.3
Mean years education	9.9 (2.5)	10.9 (2.7)	10.7 (2.5)	
Employment markers				
Full-time employed (%)	61.6	57.3	56.0	77.0
Part-time/Occasional (%)	7.3	11.6	12.5	12.1
Looking for work (%)	12.5	18.0	13.7	3.9
Not employed/Not looking (%)	18.5	13.0	17.8	7.0
Family markers				
Never married (%)	47.9	53.7	55.9	40.4
Currently married (%)	23.7	20.3	17.7	53.0
With children[e] (%)	60.2	60.4	56.0	66
Number of children	1.7 (2.0)	2.3 (1.7)	2.5 (1.9)	
Other characteristics				
Sex (% male)	96.7	95.6	93.7	100
Black, non-Hispanic (%)	49	45	47	12
White, non-Hispanic (%)	39	40	33	69
Hispanic (%)	10	13	17	14
Other (%)	2	3	3	5
Population				
Prisoners[d]	218,466	544,972	1,249,959	
Total supervision[d]		3,239,400	5,692,500	
Conviction offense				
Violent (%)	53	64	47	
Property (%)	33	22	22	
Drug (%)	10	9	21	
Other (%)	4	4	10	

Standard deviations for continuous variables in parentheses.
[a]Source: Uggen et al. (2000), adapted from U.S. Department of Justice's *Survey of Inmates in State and Federal Correctional Facilities.*
[b]General population data adapted from U.S. Census Bureau *Statistical Abstract* series and U.S. Bureau of Labor Statistics' *Current Population Reports* series.
[c]No general population estimates are available for male fertility in the United States. The 66% figure is taken from the 1991 National Child Development Study in England (Ferri, 1993).
[d]Prisoners includes inmates in state and federal correctional facilities. Total supervision includes prison inmates, parolees, probationers, and jail inmates.

escape detection and many who are arrested or convicted are never incarcerated. To what extent does deviant activity co-vary with adult life course transitions in the *general* population? Age-graded transition norms and cultural definitions of appropriate behavior appear to govern desistance patterns in the general population. If a person smokes marijuana or shoplifts at age 16, the behavior is more normative in both a statistical and a sociological sense than identical conduct at the age of 30 or 40.

Table 15-2 presents some descriptive data on adult deviance and life course markers taken from the Youth Development Study (YDS) (e.g., see Mortimer & Kirkpatrick Johnson,

TABLE 15-2. Deviant Behavior and Life Course Markers of Youth Development Study Respondents, Males and Females Aged 25–26 in 1999

Variables	Number of cases	Drunk driving	Shop-lifting	Simple assault
Males				
Education markers				
Less than associate's degree	133	40.2	7.5	25.6***
Attained associate's degree	182	39.6	4.4	13.3
Employment markers				
Not full-time employed	44	25.0**	11.4*	18.1
Full-time employed	270	42.4	4.8	18.6
Family markers				
Not married	206	49.9***	6.8*	23.4***
Married	109	28.4	2.7	8.3
No children	206	40.8	5.3	17.5
Children	108	38.9	6.5	20.4
Combined transitions				
Unmarried or not full-time	217	44.2**	6.9	22.6**
Married full-time workers	99	30.3	3.0	9.1
Females				
Education markers				
Less than associate's degree	157	28.9	5.7	15.3**
Attained associate's degree	264	28.0	3.4	3.8
Employment markers				
Not full-time employed	88	23.9	7.9	12.4
Full-time employed	335	29.6	3.3	6.8
Family markers				
Not married	271	33.2**	4.4	9.5
Married	152	19.7	4.0	5.3
No children	226	32.3**	2.6*	2.6**
Children	197	23.9	6.0	14.1
Combined transitions				
Unmarried or not full-time	307	31.3**	4.2	9.1
Married full-time workers	120	20.8	4.2	5.0

*Significant at 0.10 level, **significant at 0.05 level, ***significant at 0.01 level (two-tailed tests).

1999), a prospective longitudinal investigation of 1,000 young adults who had been students in St. Paul (Minnesota) public schools. In contrast to Table 15-1, Table 15-2 compares offenders and non-offenders based on self-reported questionnaire data, rather than official statistics. These data therefore allow us to test whether those who have attained a certain marker are more or less likely to commit certain deviant acts as adults. The YDS data on life course markers and deviant behaviors were collected in the eleventh wave of the study in 1999, when most participants were 25 or 26 years old. We consider three types of self-reported deviance: driving while intoxicated, shoplifting, and simple assault. In national arrest data, shoplifting and simple assault rates rise to a sharp peak in the mid to late teens, with most offenders desisting in late adolescence (U.S. Department of Justice, Federal Bureau of Investigation, 1999). Arrests for driving while intoxicated peak at age 21 and decline much more slowly throughout the twenties and thirties. In the YDS data, a small but non-trivial proportion of young adults reported engaging in each of these activities within the past year. Data for men and women are presented separately because the meaning of each transition and its relationship to adult offending is likely to differ by sex.

Overall, these data show some association between attaining adult markers and committing deviance in adulthood, though not always in the expected negative direction. Only a handful of respondents had yet to attain their high school diploma or general educational development equivalency in this highly educated sample. Among both males and females in the study, those who had attained at least an associate's degree were significantly less likely to engage in simple assault within the past year than those who had not attained a postsecondary degree. Men who were working full-time were significantly *more* likely to report drunk driving and marginally less likely to report shoplifting relative to the small number of men who were not employed full-time. The positive association between automobile ownership and employment may be partially responsible for the drunk driving results, while the negative association between economic need and employment is likely to explain the shoplifting results.

Married men were less deviant than unmarried men on all three outcomes, although rates of drunk driving, shoplifting, and simple assault were equivalent for men with and without children. Among females, in contrast, those with children were significantly less likely to report drunk driving, but more likely to report shoplifting and simple assault. When the transitions are examined in combination, those who have both married and entered full-time employment report less drunk driving and simple assault. The latter finding suggests a potentially intriguing interaction: full-time employment alone may increase drunk driving, whereas full-time employment conditioned by marriage appears to reduce it.

Taken together, the descriptive data from the inmate surveys and the young adults in the YDS suggest a complex relationship between criminal behavior, official punishment, and life course transitions. The prison data show that officially defined offenders are likely to lag behind their contemporaries in terms of education, employment, and marriage. Rates of childbearing appear to be high among this group, though reliable comparative data are unavailable for the general population in the United States (see note *c* of Table 15-1). Data from the general community sample of young adults in the YDS suggest that some common forms of deviance are less prevalent among those who have attained certain markers of adult status, particularly marriage. Yet, for males in particular, having a full-time job or a child does not diminish the likelihood of violent or substance-related offenses, such as simple assault and drunk driving.

These illustrative data show how offending is related to life course markers at a single point in time, but can only hint at how life course transitions may affect the process of desistance from crime. Whether desistance constitutes a separate dimension of the multifaceted transition to adulthood depends, in part, on the particular definitions of deviance and desistance under consideration. If only those who have been incarcerated in a penitentiary are considered at risk of desisting from crime, then the pool of eligible desisters is a relatively small proportion of the adult population. Alternatively, if behaviors such as disorderly conduct, petty theft, and marijuana use constitute deviance, then the pool of eligible desisters is correspondingly larger. The next section of this chapter reviews general definitions of desistance and an emerging understanding of desistance as a life course process rather than a fixed state.

GENERAL DEFINITIONS OF DESISTANCE

Because conceptual and operational definitions of desistance vary across existing studies, it is difficult to draw empirical generalizations from the growing literature on desistance from crime. In addition to considerations of theory and basic ontological assumptions, many definitions of desistance have been driven by the availability of data and empirical evidence. In every case, however, the relationship between age and crime is central. As Hirschi and Gottfredson (1983) noted most forcefully, individuals in most societies over most historical periods tend to commit less crime as they age, so distinguishing a process of desistance from simple aging can pose methodological and conceptual problems. Despite this difficulty, a substantial research literature has emerged to describe the life course transition of desistance from criminal behavior.

Perhaps the most influential and important study of crime over the life course, Sampson and Laub's (1993) *Crime in the making: Pathways and turning points through life*, defines "desisters" as those who had an official delinquent history as juveniles but no arrests as adults. To explain desistance, they look to turning points in the life course such as marriage or employment. Thus, while Sampson and Laub operationalized desistance as the presence or absence of an event (arrest), their conceptual model leaves room for life course processes that foster change over time. In the life history interviews included in *Crime in the making* and in subsequent work (Laub, Nagin, & Sampson, 1998), Laub, Sampson, and their colleagues have moved toward studying desistance as a process, with a focus on changing rates of offending.

Desistance as a Process

Our view of desistance as a separate dimension of the transition to adulthood is consistent with the idea that desistance is a process characterized by particular behavioral states or markers. We therefore conceptualize the process of desistance from crime as analogous to the gradual assumption of adult occupational and family roles. The state of desistance, in contrast, is analogous to discrete life course markers such as school completion. By this logic, the transition to adulthood may be viewed as a set of interrelated incremental processes that culminate in transiting these basic markers. Of course, reversals of transitional events may occur: those we classify as "desisters" may return to crime just as educational "completers" may return to school or those who have established an independent residence may return to live with parents.

More generally, criminologists have begun to consider desistance as the process leading to the cessation of criminal involvement, rather than as a discrete state of non-offending (see Sampson & Laub, this volume). Bushway, Piquero, Broidy, Cauffman, and Mazerolle (2001) follow Gottfredson and Hirschi (1990) in conceptualizing "criminality" as an individual propensity to offend. In contrast to Gottfredson and Hirschi's contention that criminality is a *stable* trait, however, Bushway et al. (2001) hold that this propensity varies with age. In choosing a dynamic rather than a static conception of desistance, Bushway et al. argue that statistical models of desistance should capture changes in the rate of offending rather than offending itself.

Dynamic models are consistent with Maruna's (2001) understanding of desistance, although that author emphasizes social relationships as well as individual behavior. Based on his intensive interviews with offenders, Maruna (2001) contends that the transition out of crime involves both a change in the way an individual interacts with society and an individual identity shift. Desistance is thus a social process that ultimately results in the cessation of criminal activity. Although Maruna (2001) is agnostic about whether researchers can actually identify people who are in the process of desisting, his working definition is based on a respondent's ability to avoid criminal activity for at least 1 year.

Shover (1996) adopts a similar approach to desistance in studying the careers of persistent thieves. Shover posits that a combination of individual social–psychological processes and the development of conventional social bonds strengthen offenders' resolve to abandon crime. Again, desistance is viewed as a process, defined as "voluntary termination of serious criminal participation" (Shover, 1996, p. 121), rather than a discrete event.

Shover's (1996) sophisticated understanding of desistance as a process illuminates some of the most vexing areas for further study of crime over the life course and highlight some of the basic dilemmas in studying the process of desistance. For example, should we count among the desisters those who cease drug use when they are incarcerated? What about those who never rise to the level of serious criminal involvement or offenders who had committed serious crimes in the past who continue to commit petty crimes? We next consider five distinctions that may help refine conceptions of desistance from crime and deviance in relation to other life course transitions.

IMPORTANT DISTINCTIONS

Desistance from What? Specific versus General Desistance

Criminologists have long noted that offenders tend to be versatile in their offending, rather than narrow specialists in a particular type of crime (Hindelang, 1981). Despite the generality of deviant behavior in the adolescent stage of the life course, the rate and causes of desistance are likely to differ across offense types. In fact, Piquero, Paternoster, Mazerolle, Brame, and Dean (1999) report some evidence of increasing offense specialization as offenders age. Some have suggested that the process of desistance among drug offenders or sex offenders may differ from more general desistance processes. In a small sample of sex offenders on probation, for example, Kruttschnitt, Uggen, and Shelton (2000) found few differences in the predictors of desistance from sex crimes versus other offense types, though age effects on desistance from sex crimes appeared to be significantly weaker than age effects on desistance from other types of crime. In a similar study of domestic violence offenders, Eckberg (2001) reports significant differences in the effects of age and probation supervision level on violent and non-violent arrests and on new domestic violence cases versus other violent arrests.

"Status offenses," or delinquent acts that would be legal if committed by adults, pose a paradox in life course research. In addition to the legal status of a particular behavior, age-graded transition norms and cultural definitions of appropriate behavior define what is normative and what is deviant at particular life cycle stages. In the contemporary United States, for example, alcohol use is generally considered illegal and deviant at age 10, illegal yet normative at age 18, and legal and normative at age 21 (McMorris & Uggen, 2000).

Desistance researchers are generally less concerned with status offenses than with more serious violations of the criminal code. In our view, however, the simple existence of status offenses—age-graded standards of deviant and conforming behavior—underscores how desistance is bound up with the multifaceted transition to adulthood. Once an individual reaches the legal drinking age, for example, claims to adult status may be undermined by binge drinking but not by moderate alcohol use. The desistance process involved in the cessation of binge drinking is therefore likely to differ from the desistance process involved in a culturally approved behavior such as moderate drinking. The latter activity is not considered deviant, in part, because it is consistent with other adult roles in the contemporary United States.

Recent scholarship offers the potential to link desistance from crime with analogous behaviors that are not illegal, such as alcohol use. Most studies find that even moderate drinking declines with age (Fillmore, Hartka, Johnstone, Leino, Motoyoshi, & Temple, 1991), although distinct trajectories of binge drinking have been identified as subjects pass from late adolescence to early adulthood (Schulenberg, O'Malley, Bachman, Wadsworth, & Johnston, 1995). In general, however, studies of desistance from substance use are quite consistent with studies of desistance from criminal behavior: the assumption of adult roles alters social interactions and belief patterns that produce a steady decline in legal and illegal substance use in young adulthood (Bachman, O'Malley, Schulenberg, Johnston, Bryant, & Merline, 2002). Although empirical research on desistance from analogous phenomena is rarely linked to desistance from criminal offending, it is likely that the same principles underlying desistance research on crime and substance use hold for a wide range of deviant role exits, such as homelessness, welfare receipt, eating disorders, certain sexual activities, and non-traditional careers (Uggen & Piliavin, 1998).

Offending Rates and Trajectories

Apart from the particular mix of activities in which they engage, offenders may also be distinguished by their rate of criminal activity and the onset and duration of their criminal careers (Nagin, Farrington, & Moffitt, 1995; Nagin & Land, 1993). In this line of research, desistance patterns help to identify distinctive trajectories when considered in combination with the age of onset and the frequency of offending. For example, members of a "late onset" group begin offending and desist later in life than other youth (D'Unger, Land, & McCall, 1998). Groups such as "high-rate chronics," "adolescent-limiteds," and "low-rate chronics" also tend to differ on characteristics such as truancy, peer popularity, and intelligence (Nagin & Land, 1993). Although age- or trajectory-specific determinants of desistance have yet to be consistently identified, it is likely that desistance patterns are a function of career length and intensity as well as characteristics such as age and offense mix.

Official Desistance versus Behavioral Desistance

When desistance is measured by contact with the criminal justice system rather than by individual self-reports, individuals generally appear to desist at an earlier age. This pattern is due in part to the differing legal standards for juveniles and adults. Therefore, part of the variation in arrest rates is a function of the age-graded penalties in the criminal code. Uggen and Kruttschnitt (1998) distinguish between official desistance, measured by arrest, and behavioral desistance, measured by self-reported offending. They attribute the greater gender differences in official desistance than behavioral desistance to criminal justice practitioners' sex-typed responses to the social positions of male and female offenders. For example, the effects of criminal history on behavioral desistance are virtually identical for men and women, but its effects on official desistance are significantly larger for women than for men.

Discrepancies between self-reported and official data may also undercut efforts to understand group differences in the desistance process, either through biases in enforcement or differential reporting. If police apply differential enforcement standards by race, geographic area, or historical period, then arrest-based desistance indicators are problematic if used to make comparisons across these groups, areas, or periods (e.g., see Elliott, 1995).

Unfortunately, self-reported offending data are subject to similar problems because systematic response biases may also vary across groups and with the shifting social acceptability of a behavior over place and time. If response biases are not uniform across different life course stages (and there is some evidence that this is the case [Geerken, 1994]), a distorted picture of offending trajectories and the desistance process is likely to emerge.

Levels and Thresholds—What Constitutes Desistance?

One practical problem in measuring desistance is the level or threshold of behavior that would constitute a new offense and remove individuals from a state of desistance. In research using official outcomes, the level of scrutiny varies with the form of correctional supervision. For example, a probationer in an intensive supervised probation (ISP) program has much greater opportunity to commit a technical violation than other probationers. A RAND study (Turner, Petersilia, & Piper-Deschenes, 1992) showed that ISP participants had more technical violations (primarily for drug use) relative to traditional probationers and parolees and are more likely to be returned to prison. In such cases, the putative desistance of the regular probation group may be a function of the lesser degree of scrutiny, rather than changing behavior patterns. More generally, Gottfredson, Mitchell-Herzfeld, and Flanagan (1982) find that whether inmates are considered successes or failures (whether they desist or fail to desist from crime) depends largely on the criteria used to assess desistance and recidivism.

Each of these practical distinctions in defining and measuring desistance—what sorts of crimes to consider, how to model desistance among different types of offenders, whether to examine official data or self-reported data, and the level of deviance necessary to trip a desistance switch—implies different research design considerations. Perhaps more importantly, such considerations must be driven by the particular theories or conceptual models thought to govern the desistance process.

LIFE COURSE THEORIES OF DESISTANCE
FROM CRIME

Various theories have been developed to explain the life course transition away from criminal behavior. In our view, the most compelling explanations provide a parsimonious explanation of the relationship between criminal behavior and the passage through various life course markers in the transition to adulthood.

Gottfredson and Hirschi's (1990) Propensity Theory

Gottfredson and Hirschi's (1990) theory of self-control emphasizes person-specific differences in the propensity to commit criminal behavior, but a direct effect of age on crime across all individuals. They argue that the age distribution of crime is invariant across a broad range of social conditions and cannot be accounted for by any variable or combination of variables currently available to criminologists. Since the age effect is constant and need not be explained, simple aging rather than entry into adult roles causes diminished offending in adulthood. In this model, life course events such as entry into marriage or full-time employment are spurious correlates of desistance rather than true causes.

Moffitt's (1993) Age-Graded Typology

In contrast to Gottfredson and Hirschi (1990), Moffitt (1993) proposes a developmental life course theory based on a typology of two distinct classes, adolescent-limited offenders and life course-persistent offenders. The two are characterized by different precursors to and rates of involvement in antisocial behavior. Whereas the life course-persistent group is characterized by a small number of early and persistent offenders who maintain involvement in crime throughout their lives, the adolescent-limited group is a much larger class with little history of childhood antisocial behavior and little likelihood of antisocial behavior in adulthood. Life course-persistent offenders develop both *cumulative* and *contemporary* disadvantages relative to their peers through a series of disrupted relationships, attachments, and academic failures. Over time, these disadvantages and their antisocial behavior afford them ever-narrowing options to desist from crime. In contrast, adolescent-limited offenders are not compromised by such disadvantages and have a greater repertoire of behavioral options available to them. They recognize the negative consequences of crime, as well as the diminishing rewards and increasing costs of crime as they age. Adolescent-limited offenders are thus well situated to desist from crime in response to changing life circumstances.

In our view, Moffitt's (1993) adolescent-limited group exemplifies the notion of desistance as part of the transition to adulthood. Life course-persistent offenders, in contrast, are likely to be much more severely off-time relative to their birth cohort with more tenuous claims to adult status.

Sampson and Laub's Age-Graded Informal Social Control Theory

Sampson and Laub's (1993) age-graded theory of informal social control is currently the dominant sociological theory in life course criminology. While acknowledging that crime is due in part to individual propensities, Sampson and Laub show that adult bonds to conventional institutions play a causal role in the desistance process. As people enter marriage and full-time employment, they form adult social bonds that hasten desistance from crime and deviance independent of the aging process. For Sampson and Laub, the life events themselves are less important than the informal social controls and social capital that generally accompany these events. As individuals gain social capital in interaction with conventional others, they are more responsive to informal social controls that engender desistance from deviant activities. Sampson and Laub thus emphasize good marriages or stable employment rather than family formation or employment markers in themselves.

Symbolic Interactionist Theories of Deviance over the Life Course

Matsueda and Heimer's (1997) symbolic interactionist life course theory offers a social–psychological explanation of desistance in the transition to adulthood. The interactionist model holds that one's self-concept as deviant or conforming is developed through role-taking processes and social interaction. To explain changes in offending with age, symbolic interactionists look to the different deviant and conforming roles that individuals are likely to take at each life course stage—the "socially recognized and meaningful categories of persons" it is possible to be at a particular age (Cohen, 1965, p. 12). The choice of roles in a given situation is the product of the relative salience of deviant or law-abiding identities, which, in turn, are functions of social relationships and role commitments.

Adult work and family roles are again critical in explaining desistance from crime. Commitment to work roles (as co-worker, supervisor, or employee) and family roles (as spouse or parent) is linked to desistance from deviant roles, although precocious or off-time events such as teenage pregnancy may solidify already marginalized identities. Symbolic interactionists thus explain the life course transition away from crime through the adoption of work and family roles, the changing identity that accompanies these new roles, and the stabilization of this identity through role commitments.

Hagan's Theory of Criminal Embeddedness

Hagan's (1991, 1993) model of crime and desistance over the life course is linked to stratification processes in the larger society. Hagan's (1993) theory of criminal embeddedness highlights the stratified and cumulative nature of criminal involvement and its relationship to life course transitions. For example, Hagan (1991) finds that identification with a subculture of delinquency reduces early adult occupational attainment for males from working-class origins, but not for males from non-working-class origins. For males from non-working-class backgrounds, identification with a "party subculture" that engages in substance abuse and minor delinquency actually has a net positive effect on attainment, once its effect on educational performance is removed. Hagan explains this finding by suggesting that the party subculture helps socialize adolescents to the activities and networks that drive later workplace advancement.

Hagan contends that early criminal involvement and associations with delinquent peers reduce the likelihood of later legitimate adult employment. Involvement in criminal behavior "embeds" youth within a different life course trajectory than youths not involved in crime. Young people who repeatedly engage in delinquent activity tend to associate with others who participate in illicit activity. This process isolates delinquents from those who might provide access to legitimate employment or educational success. These limited behavioral options have far-reaching implications across the life course, such as decreased levels of employment and status attainment, which help to explain why some individuals persist in criminal activities while others desist. While Sampson and Laub (1993) emphasize the malleability of early criminal trajectories, Hagan's model suggests that early delinquency is likely to have more sustained socioeconomic effects throughout the adult life course.

SOCIAL INTEGRATION AND
REINTEGRATION ACROSS THREE DOMAINS

Although theories of informal social control, symbolic interactionism, and criminal embeddedness emphasize different mechanisms connecting desistance with other life course transitions, we believe that they are all compatible with the notion of desistance from deviant activities as a facet of the transition to adulthood. Moreover, they each conceptualize desistance in terms of social integration or reintegration. People generally cease or moderate their criminal and deviant behavior as they become more integrated or reintegrated into other domains of social life, suggesting that desistance is a consequence of becoming an adult. In addition, desisting from adolescent deviant activities facilitates integration into work, family, and community life. In our view, desistance is thus both a cause and consequence of transiting the other markers of adulthood. What are the changing life circumstances that accompany and engender desistance from crime? We conceptualize integration as occurring across three primary domains: socioeconomic, familial, and civic (Uggen et al., 2002; Uggen, Thompson, & Manza, 2000).

Socioeconomic Reintegration

Socioeconomic reintegration refers to labor force participation and educational and occupational attainment. A large research literature suggests that job stability (e.g., Sampson & Laub, 1990, 1993) and job quality (e.g., Uggen, 1999) are tied to desistance from crime, although it is very difficult in such non-experimental studies to separate "job effects" from the processes of selection that guide persons into jobs of varying quality (Uggen & Staff, 2001). Experimental evidence suggests that the effect of publicly subsidized employment on crime may be age graded. One study found that offenders older than 26 were significantly more likely to desist from crime when provided a minimal work opportunity, but that younger offenders provided such jobs were no more likely to desist than a control group (Uggen, 2000). In general, subsidized job programs are less salient to youthful offenders and less successful among youth in the general population as well (Orr, Bloom, Bell, Doolittle, Lin, & Cave 1995), although the residential Job Corps program may provide an important exception (Mallar, Kerachsky, Thornton, & Long, 1982).

Among official correctional populations, the problem of reintegrating large numbers of criminal offenders into the labor force—and providing employers with needed workers in a tight labor market—is increasingly attracting policy attention. For example, some have argued that the conviction records of some misdemeanants and non-violent felons should be sealed in an effort to enhance the employability of these groups (Lueck, 2000). At the same time, a new wave of public and private ventures has emerged since the late 1990s to connect offenders and ex-offenders with employers (Buck, 2000). Although the employment opportunities of convicted felons are severely limited relative to those in the general population, even marginal employment fosters a sense of adult participation in society as a productive citizen (Uggen et al., 2002).

Familial Reintegration

Socioeconomic reintegration is intimately tied to the problem of reintegrating offenders into their families. The family of origin has long been considered among the most important factors in the etiology of juvenile delinquency (Hirschi, 1969). While the initial causes of crime and the causes of desistance are likely to differ (e.g., see Uggen & Piliavin, 1998), the family also plays a pivotal role in the desistance process. In the latter case, however, the assumption and management of the adult family roles of spouse and parent are most significant.

As detailed in Table 15-1, most prison inmates are unmarried fathers, though the number of mothers in prison has risen steadily in recent years. Although marriage in itself is not consistently related to desistance from crime, the quality of the marital union has been shown to affect the likelihood of desistance in both qualitative (Shover, 1996) and quantitative work (Laub et al., 1998). Again, however, it is difficult to disentangle marital quality from highly selective assortative mating processes.

The relation between childbearing and desistance may depend on the gender of the offender. One study found that female offenders with children are more likely to self-report desistance than those without children, as well as a significant gender difference in the effects of children on desistance (Uggen & Kruttschnitt, 1998). It remains unclear whether the effect of children is due to informal social controls, the fear of losing custody, or changes in self-concept that accompany the parent role (Uggen et al., 2002). The issue of familial reintegration is especially salient, however, in light of rising rates of incarceration and the effect of parental convictions on their children's criminality (Hagan, 1993). The U.S. Department of Justice, Bureau of Justice Statistics (2000b) estimates that the number of minor children with at least one parent in a state or federal prison rose from 1 million to 1.5 million between 1991 and 1999. Overall, about 2% of all children and more than 7% of African American children currently have an incarcerated parent. Many more have parents who are ex-prisoners or felons currently serving parole or probation sentences. While family reintegration offers important benefits for offenders, it is problematic from the perspective of children if their parents remain active in crime or substance use. Reintegration programs must therefore balance the rights and interests of parents, children, and society in aiding offenders to assume or resume their family roles.

Civic Reintegration

Although a large research literature has focused on work or marriage as potential turning points in the life course of criminal offenders, the subject of reintegration into community life and civic participation has received comparatively little attention. Civic reintegration represents a third domain in which increased social participation may alter patterns of desistance. Following Maruna's contention that desistance is only possible when ex-offenders "develop a coherent prosocial identity for themselves" (2001, p. 7), Uggen et al. (2002) suggest that the self-concept as a deviant or conforming citizen is the principal mechanism linking adult role transition and desistance. When criminologists refer to "citizens" they generally use the term in opposition to criminal offenders, placing criminals on one side of the street and law-abiding community residents on the other. Yet Uggen et al. find that felons think of *themselves* as citizens, assuming roles as taxpayers, homeowners, volunteers, and voters.

In both officially defined correctional populations and in the general population, civic participation in the form of volunteerism and membership in community groups is likely to co-vary with desistance patterns. Among correctional populations, a 1987 law in Israel permitted courts to commute short prison sentences for community service work (Nirel, Landau, Sebba, & Sagiv, 1997). After adjusting for the non-random selection into service work with a propensity score methodology, Nirel et al. (1997) report significantly lower odds of recidivism (and correspondingly higher odds of desistance) among service workers relative to offenders not assigned to service work. Although few studies of community service and desistance have been conducted within the general population, at least one investigation finds a robust negative relationship between volunteer work and arrest in late adolescence and young adulthood (Uggen & Janikula, 1999).

Civic engagement may also take the form of voting or other forms of political participation (Uggen & Manza, 2000). Citizenship roles may seem peripheral relative to socioeconomic and family roles, yet prisoners and other correctional populations are ultimately defined in terms of their legal relationship with the state and their separation from their fellow citizens. As part of the desistance process, prisoners and ex-prisoners often adopt a language of civic mindedness and make efforts to connect with the lives of their communities (Maruna, 2001; Uggen et al., 2002). As Ernest Thomas, an ex-offender who was disenfranchised because of a felony conviction stated, "They say I'm a citizen, but I'm not a citizen. A citizen has a right to vote" (Davis, 2001). If persons enmeshed in interdependent social relations are less likely to reoffend, as informal social control theories suggest, then civic reintegration merits further investigation in desistance research.

DESISTANCE AND THE LIFE COURSE IN COMPARATIVE PERSPECTIVE

Most of the desistance research cited in this chapter has been drawn from studies of the United States. The need for comparative analysis stems from potential U.S. exceptionalism with regard to the timing of life course transitions, deviant behavior, and punishment policies. Moreover, comparative analysis can help to determine how macro-level structures shape the desistance process. For example, the United States utilizes the penal system at rates far higher than other advanced Western societies (Mauer, 1999), with an incarceration rate that exceeds Germany's rate by a factor of seven and Japan's rate by a factor of 17. Although U.S. rates of criminal victimization have been relatively stable over the period, the number of state and federal prisoners has grown by over 700% in the past three decades, from 196,429 in 1970 to 1,381,892 in 2000 (U.S. Department of Justice, 1973, p. 350; U.S. Department of Justice, Bureau of Justice Statistics, 2001b, p. 1). This creates disproportionately large officially defined deviant populations in the United States. Yet the United States lacks well-defined institutional mechanisms for the socioeconomic, familial, and civic reintegration of juvenile and adult offenders (Braithwaite, 1989).

With regard to socioeconomic transitions, U.S. labor markets are comparatively stable when contrasted with the dramatic rise in U.S. imprisonment rates (Savelsberg, 1994; Western & Beckett, 1999). Despite this, young offenders have become so socially isolated and economically marginal that they are no longer considered productive by employers (Holzer, 2000). As the U.S. industrial mix has shifted in the postwar era, the demand for low-skill workers has fallen. Thus, a postindustrial skill mismatch may have rendered an increasingly large segment of potential desisters "unemployable" (and "unmarriageable" as well) even in tight labor markets. In contrast, the transition of youth into the labor market is much more orderly in countries such as Germany and in Japan, which may buffer potential skill mismatches and employer reluctance to hire criminal offenders (Harada, 1995; Krymkowski, 1991; Schumann, 1995). Unfortunately, there is little direct comparative evidence on socioeconomic reintegration of criminal offenders, in part because the proportion of the population affected is very small in other industrialized nations.

Culturally specific age-graded role expectations (Braithwaite, 1989) and distinctive institutional structures, such as those guiding the school-to-work transition, are likely to engender different desistance patterns in different societies. For example, Japan has lower rates of crime and a higher rate of juvenile offenses among total offenses than the United States, but an earlier average age of desistance (Harada, 1995). Perhaps the more rationalized school-to-work transition fosters early desistance just as it facilitates the integration of Japanese youth into adult society more generally (Rosenbaum, Kariya, Settersten, & Maier, 1990).

In sum, the United States appears to be exceptional for both the size of its officially defined deviant populations and the lack of institutional mechanisms for socioeconomic and civic reintegration at pivotal life course stages. Further comparative analysis is needed to qualify, extend, or refine generalizations based on the American case.

INTERVENTIONS

In addition to cross-national or comparative work, further study of social policy interventions is likely to inform knowledge of the relationship between life course transitions and desistance. In particular, the study of age-by-correctional treatment interactions can help determine whether the same set of causal factors are operative at different life course stages. For policy purposes, such research can identify those most amenable to a given program. For scientific purposes, such research can show how the transition out of crime is linked to other life course processes.

For example, research on socioeconomic reintegration suggests that older offenders who are given jobs are more likely to desist from crime than those of comparable age who were not provided such opportunities (Uggen, 2000), but that younger offenders may be less amenable to subsidized employment programs. With regard to familial or civic reintegration, a similar strategy could be undertaken by studying the effectiveness of randomized family support or community service interventions (e.g., see Nirel et al., 1997). In the general population, coupling self-reported offending data with analysis of social interventions such as the G.I. Bill (Sampson & Laub, 1996), changes in tax policy, or public assistance guidelines would help illuminate the desistance process among those outside the criminal justice system.

SUMMARY

Much of the extant literature on crime and desistance over the life course has been concerned with how the transition to adult roles affects criminal behavior (Sampson & Laub, 1990) or how criminal behavior affects the transition to adult roles (Hagan, 1991). Throughout this chapter we have explored a slightly different question: whether desistance from minor delinquency and crime itself constitutes a separate and important dimension of the multifaceted transition to adulthood.

We began by presenting some basic illustrative data to show how officially defined deviants are "off-time" with respect to the basic socioeconomic and familial markers of adult status. After cross-tabulating similar markers with three forms of common deviance among a general community sample of young adults, we noted that adult offending tends to co-vary with the occurrence of certain adult transitions. We then reviewed some of the practical design considerations involved in measuring desistance at different life course stages as well as existing theories of crime and desistance over the life course.

The relationship between desistance from crime and other adult role transitions has been difficult to determine with certainty. In most research settings, social scientists or correctional administrators cannot randomly assign life course transitions such as marriage or employment to gauge their effects on criminal behavior. Therefore, when these transitions occur it is virtually impossible to tell whether they are causes or correlates of changes in offending. Some suggest that the apparent effects of work or marriage are really due to pre-existing amenability to change, or "person effects" that drive people to select into these adult roles (Gottfredson & Hirschi, 1990). For example, those most likely to desist are also likely to self-select into higher quality jobs. In contrast, others have suggested that the role transitions actually cause desistance from crime. Today, an increasing body of empirical evidence suggests there is truth in both positions—that the amenability of offenders that leads them to select into these statuses is accentuated by interaction in these roles. As individuals develop adult socioeconomic, familial, and civic role commitments, the salience of their identities as law-abiding citizens rises and the salience of their identities as rule violators recedes. With this gradual shift during the transition to adulthood, the actions of rule violators begin to meet the expectations of the adult citizen role more consistently and they desist from crime.

Much of the empirical research on desistance from crime has been productively organized around the domains of work and family or problems of socioeconomic and familial reintegration. We suggest that consideration of a third domain, civic reintegration, may help to identify forms of community involvement and civic participation that engender desistance among both officially defined correctional populations and the much larger population of adolescents and young adults who engage in criminal and deviant behaviors (e.g., see Uggen et al., 2000).

Although we present some basic descriptive information showing the timing of life course markers and deviant behavior, we have yet to test the idea of desistance as a separate dimension of the transition to adulthood. To subject such ideas to empirical testing, we conclude on a programmatic note. In particular, we argue for greater attention to variations in desistance patterns across space and time and to the life course implications of social policy experiments and quasi-experiments that may hasten the desistance process.

ACKNOWLEDGMENTS: We thank Melissa Thompson for helpful suggestions and assistance with data analysis. We are also indebted to the editors for their especially constructive comments and advice.

REFERENCES

Bachman, J. G., O'Malley, P. M., Schulenberg, J. E., Johnston, L. D., Bryant, A. L., & Merline, A. C. (2002). *The decline of substance use in young adulthood: Changes in social activities, roles, and beliefs.* Mahwah, NJ: Lawrence Erlbaum Associates.

Bonczar, T. P., & Beck, A. J. (1997). *Lifetime likelihood of going to state or federal prison.* Washington, DC: U.S. Government Printing Office.

Braithwaite, J. (1989). *Crime, shame and reintegration.* Cambridge: Cambridge University Press.

Buchman, M. (1989). *The script of life in modern society: Entry into adulthood in a changing world.* Chicago: University of Chicago Press.

Buck, M. (2000). *Getting back to work: Employment programs for ex-offenders.* New York: Public/Private Ventures.

Bushway, S., Piquero, A., Broidy, L., Cauffman, E., & Mazerolle, P. (2001). An empirical framework for studying desistance as a process. *Criminology, 39,* 491–515.

Caspi, A., Elder, G., & Herbener, E. (1990). Childhood personality and the prediction of life-course patterns. In L. Robins and M. Rutter (Eds.), *Straight and devious pathways from childhood to adulthood* (pp. 13–35). Cambridge: Cambridge University Press.

Cohen, A. K. (1965). The sociology of the deviant act: Anomie theory and beyond. *American Sociological Review, 30,* 5–14.

Davis, P. (2001). Efforts under way in Florida to restore voting rights to ex-felons. National Public Radio's *All Things Considered,* 7 February 2001.

D'Unger, A., Land, K., & McCall, P. (1998). How many latent classes of delinquent/criminal careers? Results from mixed poisson regression analyses. *American Journal of Sociology, 103,* 1593–1630.

Eckberg, D. (2001). *Desistance from domestic assault: An application of event history analysis.* Unpublished doctoral dissertation, University of Minnesota.

Elliot, D. (1995). *Lies, damn lies and arrest statistics.* Sutherland Award Presentation, The American Society of Criminology Meetings. Boston, MA.

Ferri, E. (1993). *Life at 33: The fifth follow-up of the national child development study.* London: National Children's Bureau.

Fillmore, K., Hartka, E., Johnstone, B., Leino, V., Motoyoshi, M., & Temple, M. (1991). A meta-analysis of life course variation in drinking. *British Journal of Addiction, 86,* 1221–1268.

Gabor, T. (1994). *Everybody does it.* Toronto: University of Toronto Press.

Geerken, M. (1994). Rap sheets in criminological research. *Journal of Quantitative Criminology, 10,* 3–21.

Gottfredson, M., & Hirschi, T. (1990). *A general theory of crime.* Stanford, CA: Stanford University Press.

Gottfredson, M., Mitchell-Herzfeld, S., & Flanagan, T. (1982). Another look at the effectiveness of parole supervision. *Journal of Research in Crime and Delinquency, 19,* 277–298.

Hagan, J. (1991). Destiny and drift: Subcultural preferences, status attainments, and the risks and rewards of youth. *American Sociological Review, 56,* 567–582.

Hagan, J. (1993). The social embeddedness of crime and unemployment. *Criminology, 31,* 465–491.

Harada, Y. (1995). Adjustment to school, life course transitions, and changes in delinquent behavior in Japan. In Z. Blau and J. Hagan (Eds.), *Current perspectives on aging and the life cycle: Delinquency and disrepute in the life course* (pp. 35–60). Greenwich, NY: JAI Press.

Hindelang, M. (1981). Variations in sex–race–age-specific incidence rates of offending. *American Sociological Review, 46,* 461–474.

Hirschi, T. (1969). *Causes of delinquency.* Berkeley, CA: University of California Press.

Hirschi, T., & Gottfredson, M. (1983). Age and the explanation of crime. *American Journal of Sociology, 89,* 552–584.

Holzer, H. (2000). *Employers' attitudes toward hiring ex-offenders.* Paper presented at the Economic Policy Institute Conference, Alternative Crime Prevention Policies—Improving the Transition from Prison to Work, Washington, DC.

Johnston, L. D., O'Malley, P. M., & Bachman, J. G. (2002). *The Monitoring the Future national survey results on adolescent drug use: Overview of key findings, 2001* (NIH Publication No. 02-5105). Bethesda, MD: National Institute on Drug Abuse.

Kruttschnitt, C., Uggen, C., & Shelton, K. (2000). Predictors of desistance among sex offenders: The interaction of formal and informal social controls. *Justice Quarterly, 17,* 61–87.

Krymkowski, D. (1991). The process of status attainment among men in Poland, the U.S., and West Germany. *American Sociological Review, 56,* 46–59.

Laub, J., Nagin, D., & Sampson, R. (1998). Trajectories of change in criminal offending: Good marriages and the desistance process. *American Sociological Review, 63,* 225–238.

Lueck, T. (2000). Plan to seal some criminal records debated. *New York Times,* Section 8, Page 4, Column 4, October 20.

McMorris, B., & Uggen, C. (2000). Alcohol and employment in the transition to adulthood. *Journal of Health and Social Behavior, 41,* 276–294.

Mallar, C., Kerachsky, S., Thornton, C., & Long, D. (1982). *Evaluation of the economic impact of the job corps program: Third follow-up report.* Princeton, NJ: Mathematica Policy Research, Inc.

Maruna, S. (2001). *Making good: How ex-convicts reform and rebuild their lives.* Washington, DC: American Psychological Association.

Matsueda, R., & Heimer, K., (1997). A symbolic interactionist theory of role-transitions, role-commitments, and delinquency. In T. Thornberry (Ed.), *Developmental theories of crime and delinquency* (pp. 163–213). New Brunswick, NJ: Transaction Publishers.

Mauer, M. (1999). *Race to incarcerate.* New York: The New Press.

Moffitt, T. (1993). Adolescent-limited and life-course persistent antisocial behavior: A developmental taxonomy. *Psychological Review, 100,* 674–701.

Mortimer, J., & Kirkpatrick Johnson, M. (1999). Adolescent part-time work and post-secondary transition pathways: A longitudinal study of youth in St. Paul, Minnesota (U.S.). In W. Heinz (Ed.), *From education to work: Cross national perspectives* (pp. 111–148). New York: Cambridge University Press.

Nagin, D., & Land, K. (1993). Age, criminal careers, and population heterogeneity: Specification and estimation of a nonparametric, mixed poisson model. *Criminology, 31,* 327–362.

Nagin, D., Farrington, D., & Moffitt, T. (1995). Life-course trajectories of different types of offenders. *Criminology, 33,* 111–139.

Nirel, R., Landau, S. F., Sebba, S., & Sagiv, B. (1997). The effectiveness of service work: An analysis of recidivism. *Journal of Quantitative Criminology, 13,* 73–92.

Orr, L., Bloom, H., Bell, S., Doolittle, F., Lin, W., & Cave, G. (1995). *Does training for the disadvantaged work? Evidence from the national JTPA study.* Washington, DC: National Institute Press.

Piquero, A., Paternoster, R., Mazerolle, P., Brame, R., & Dean, C. W. (1999). Onset age and offense specialization. *Journal of Research in Crime and Delinquency, 36,* 275–299.

Rindfuss, R. R., Swicegood, C. G., & Rosenfeld, R. (1987). Disorder in the life course: How common and does it matter? *American Sociological Review, 52,* 785–801.

Rosenbaum, J., Kariya, T., Settersten, R., & Maier, T. (1990). Market and network theories of the transition from high school to work: Their application to industrialized societies. *Annual Review of Sociology, 16,* 263–299.

Sampson, R., & Laub, J. (1990). Crime and deviance over the life course: The salience of adult social bonds. *American Sociological Review, 55,* 609–627.

Sampson, R., & Laub, J. (1993). *Crime in the making: Pathways and turning points through life.* Cambridge, MA: Harvard University Press.

Sampson, R., & Laub, J. (1996). Socioeconomic achievement in the life course of disadvantaged men: Military service as a turning point, circa 1940–1965. *American Sociological Review, 61,* 347–367.

Savelsberg, J. (1994). Knowledge, domination, and criminal punishment. *American Journal of Sociology, 99,* 911–943.

Schulenberg, J., O'Malley, P., Bachman, J., Wadsworth, K., & Johnston, L. (1995). Getting drunk and growing up: Trajectories of frequent binge drinking during the transition to young adulthood. *Journal of Studies on Alcohol, 57,* 289–304.

Schumann, K. (1995). The deviant apprentice: The impact of the German dual system of vocational training on juvenile delinquency. In Z. Blau & J. Hagan (Eds.), *Current perspectives on aging and the life cycle: Delinquency and disrepute in the life course* (pp. 91–104). Greenwich, NY: JAI Press.

Shanahan, M. (2000). Pathways to adulthood in changing societies: Variability and mechanisms in life course perspective. *Annual Review of Sociology, 26,* 667–692.

Shover, N. (1996) *Great pretenders: Pursuits and careers of persistent thieves.* Boulder, CO: Westview Press.

Sullivan, M. (1989). *Getting paid.* Ithaca, NY: Cornell University Press.

Turner, S., Petersilia, J., & Piper-Deschenes, E. (1992) Evaluating intensive supervision probation/parole (ISP) for drug offenders. *Crime and Delinquency, 38,* 539–556.

Uggen, C. (1999). Ex-offenders and the conformist alternative: A job quality model of work and crime. *Social Problems, 46,* 127–151.

Uggen, C. (2000). Work as a turning point in the life course of criminals: A duration model of age, employment, and recidivism. *American Sociological Review, 65,* 529–546.

Uggen, C., & Janikula, J. (1999). Volunteerism and arrest in the transition to adulthood. *Social Forces, 78,* 331–362.

Uggen, C., & Kruttschnitt, C. (1998). Crime in the breaking: Gender differences in desistance. *Law & Society Review, 32,* 339–366.

Uggen, C., & Manza, J. (2000). *Political consequences of felon disfranchisement in the United States.* Paper presented at American Sociological Associations Meetings, Washington, DC.

Uggen, C., Manza, J., & Behrens, A. (2002). Stigma, role transition, and the civic reintegration of convicted felons. In S. Maruna & R. Immarigeon (Eds.), *After crime and punishment: Ex-offender reintegration and desistance from crime* (pp. 000–000). Albany, NY: SUNY Press.

Uggen, C., & Pilliavin, I. (1998). Asymmetrical causation and criminal desistance. *The Journal of Criminal Law & Criminology, 88,* 1399–1422.

Uggen, C., & Staff, J. (2001). Work as a turning point for criminal offenders. *Corrections Management Quarterly, 5,* 1–16.

Uggen, C., Thompson, M., & Manza, J. (2000). *Crime, class, and reintegration: The socioeconomic, familial, and civic lives of offenders.* Paper presented at American Society of Criminology Meetings, San Francisco.

U.S. Department of Justice. (1973). *Sourcebook of criminal justice statistics.* Washington, DC: U.S. Government Printing Office.

U.S. Department of Justice, Bureau of Justice Statistics. (2000a). *Prison and jail inmates at midyear 1999.* Washington, DC: U.S. Government Printing Office.

U.S. Department of Justice, Bureau of Justice Statistics. (2000b). *Correctional populations in the United States, 1997.* Washington, DC: U.S. Government Printing Office.

U.S. Department of Justice, Bureau of Justice Statistics. (2001a). *Use and management of criminal history record information: A comprehensive report.* Washington, DC: U.S. Government Printing Office.

U.S. Department of Justice, Bureau of Justice Statistics. (2001b). *Prisoners in 2000.* Washington, DC: U.S. Government Printing Office.

U.S. Department of Justice, Federal Bureau of Investigation. (1999). *Crime in the United States 1998.* Washington, DC: U.S. Government Printing Office.

Western, B., & Beckett, K. (1999). How unregulated is the U.S. labor market: The penal system as a labor market institution. *American Journal of Sociology, 104,* 1030–1060.

CHAPTER 16

Migration, Human Development, and the Life Course

Guillermina Jasso

INTRODUCTION

Every year and at every age humans move. They move from one house to another, from one school to another, from one job to another, from one state to another, and, in moves that rouse the notice of nation states, they move from one country to another. In moving, they are displaying the hallmarks of the human condition. Impelled by fundamental forces of survival and human development, keen to attain the ends for which they were made, they search for a better country, make plans for a new life, and move to undertake that new life.

All the processes associated with migration are rooted in time. They occur in particular historical eras and bear the imprints of those eras. They occur at different ages and bear the imprints of those ages. How difficult it was to migrate, how successful the migration, how permanent the move—all these depend jointly on the historical context and the migrant's age. Of course, many other factors shape the migration process, including, importantly, conditions and laws in both the origin and destination countries and including as well the migrant's enduring endowments and characteristics.

Migration always affects a person's future. Sometimes it affects a person's past as well, for the vision of immigration may shape a wide variety of decisions and behaviors, from a junior–high schooler's decision to learn another language to a marriageable young person's decision to date foreigners to a parent's decision to invest heavily in a particular child who may someday be the first pioneer into the new country.

GUILLERMINA JASSO • Department of Sociology, New York University, New York, New York 10003.
Handbook of the Life Course, edited by Jeylan T. Mortimer and Michael J. Shanahan. Kluwer Academic/Plenum Publishers, New York, 2003.

Migration is "planful" to use Clausen's (1991, p. 811) evocative word (see also Clausen [1993], Elder [1994, p. 6], and Elder, Johnson, & Crosnoe's chapter in this volume) and it links the migrant to a range of individuals in both origin and destination countries, linking not only individuals who know each other, as in the case of an immigrant and the employer or family member who sponsors the immigrant, but also individuals far removed from each other, such as the immigrant and the possibly many others in both origin and destination countries whose lives may improve or deteriorate as a result of the migration.

Migration thus exemplifies the four themes Elder (1994) highlights as emblematic of the life course perspective in social science: interplay between lives and historical time and place, linked lives, timing of lives, and human agency. It is no surprise that one of the classics in the study of the life course is also a classic in the study of migration—Thomas and Znaniecki's ([1918–1920] 1958) *The Polish Peasant in Europe and America.*

In this chapter, I provide an overview of migration analysis, highlighting aspects which embody elements central to the life course perspective and providing both theoretical and empirical illustration. The framework for migration analysis is general, as is the theoretical illustration, but many of the examples as well as the empirical illustration will pertain to immigration to the contemporary United States. The chapter is organized as follows. The overview of migration analysis is presented in the next section. Next, the third section examines migration from a life course perspective, in the spirit of Clausen (1991), Elder (1994), Mayer (1986), and Riley (1986). In the fourth section we assess data requirements for empirical migration analysis and provide a brief description of a new body of data designed to address migration questions, the New Immigrant Survey and its pilot, the New Immigrant Survey Pilot. To illustrate theoretical migration analysis, in the fifth section we report an analysis of the propensity to emigrate, based on two formal sociobehavioral theories, justice theory and status theory; this analysis shows both how two principal concepts from the life course perspective—cohort and context—operate to shape migration streams and also how sociobehavioral and social psychological theories can be used to illuminate demographic phenomena. To illustrate empirical migration analysis, in the sixth section we report a model of health changes pre- and post immigration and provide empirical estimates of the effects of culture and of exposure to the U.S. environment using data from the New Immigrant Survey Pilot. A brief note concludes the paper.

OVERVIEW OF MIGRATION ANALYSIS

Like all of sociological analysis, migration analysis consists of three kinds of activities—constructing theories, carrying out empirical work, and, even more basic, developing the framework that assembles the main elements which will be used in both theoretical and empirical analysis. Each of these three activities has distinctive goals and distinctive methods. Together they can be portrayed in the form of a triptych, as in Figure 16-1. As shown, the center panel of the triptych represents the framework for migration analysis. The left panel represents theoretical migration analysis and the right panel represents empirical migration analysis.

The framework collects the central questions of the field and the basic building-blocks for addressing them. The theoretical panel accommodates, via two subpanels, two kinds of theories: deductive theory, in which testable implications are deduced from postulates, and hierarchical theory, in which testable propositions are constructed by linking terms in the postulates with other terms. The empirical panel provides, via three subpanels, for three kinds of empirical work: testing the implications of deductive theories, testing the propositions

Theoretical Migration Analysis	Framework	Empirical Migration Analysis
Deductive **Postulates** **Predictions** ------------------ *Hierarchical* **Postulates** **Propositions**	Questions Actors Quantities Functions Distributions Matrices Contexts	Measure/ estimate terms/relations ------------------ **Test deduced** **predictions** ------------------ **Test** **propositions**

FIGURE 16-1. Migration analysis.

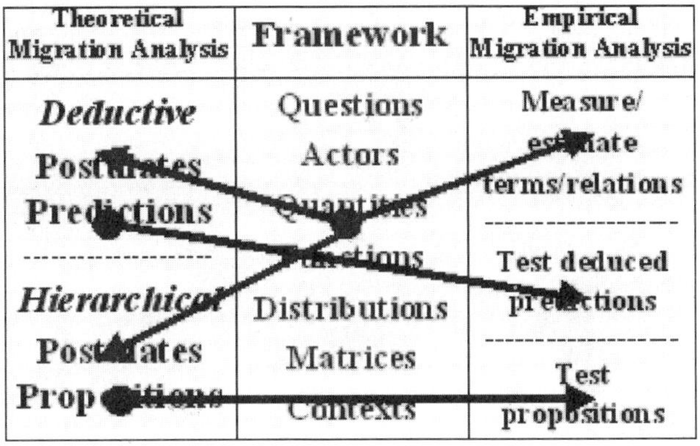

Theoretical Migration Analysis	Framework	Empirical Migration Analysis
Deductive **Postulates** **Predictions** ------------------ *Hierarchical* **Postulates** **Propositions**	Questions Actors Quantities Functions Distributions Matrices Contexts	Measure/ estimate terms/relations ------------------ **Test deduced** **predictions** ------------------ **Test** **propositions**

FIGURE 16-2. Links between the panels in the triptych of migration analysis.

constructed in hierarchical theories, and basic measurement and estimation of quantities and relations in the framework.*

The framework and the theoretical panel are linked because the theories address questions posed in the framework and because some of the building-blocks in the framework become the assumptions of theories (and others later appear among the predictions of theories). The theoretical panel and the empirical panel are of course linked, as two of the empirical subpanels test the predictions and propositions of theories. The empirical panel, however, is also linked directly to the framework, as an important undertaking is to measure the quantities identified in the framework and estimate the relations developed in the framework. To illustrate the interconnections among the three kinds of activities, we present the triptych of migration analysis in Figure 16-2, with arrows superimposed to link the panels.

*Comprehensive exposition of the tripartite structure of sociological analysis appears in Jasso (in press). The framework, which plays a central part in the tripartite structure, is rooted in Merton's ([1949, 1957] 1968) notion of "theoretical orientation," discussed by Elder, Johnson, and Crosnoe (this volume) and is in many ways similar to Berger and Zelditch's (1993) notion of "orienting strategy." The importance of the framework has recently been noted by Stryker (2001) and Wallerstein (2002). The theoretical analysis part of the tripartite structure is elaborated in Jasso (2001b).

Thus, the framework provides building-blocks which become the starting assumptions of theories and which also lead immediately to empirical work. The framework for migration analysis is sufficiently basic that we discuss some of its elements.

Elements from the Framework for Studying Migration: Four Central Questions

In the study of migration there are four central questions. These pertain to (1) migrants at entry, (2) the progress of migrants, (3) migrant children and the children of migrants, and (4) the impacts of migration. For example, questions about the characteristics of immigrants at entry and the forces of selectivity, such as whether there has been a decline in immigrant quality across cohorts (Barrett, 1996; Borjas, 1985; Cobb-Clark, 1993; Jasso, Rosenzweig, & Smith, 2000; Loaeza Tovar, Planck, Gómez Arnau, Martin, Lowell, & Meyers, 1997; Smith & Edmonston, 1997), exemplify the first central question. Similarly, questions about what happens to immigrants post immigration—discussed variously as assimilation, acculturation, adaptation, integration, incorporation, convergence, and so forth and encompassing broad domains from employment and earnings to health and fertility to language, religion, and identity—exemplify the second central question (Loaeza Tovar et al., 1997; Smith & Edmonston, 1997). All questions concerning immigrant children and the children of immigrants, including questions about their initial characteristics as well as their progress over time, obviously fall under the third central question (Committee on the Health and Safety Implications of Child Labor, Board on Children, Youth, and Families, National Research Council/Institute of Medicine, 1998; Hernandez & Charney, 1998; Portes & Rumbaut, 2001). Finally, questions about the impacts of immigration seek to assess impacts of various kinds on both individuals and societies at both origin and destination countries; examples include questions about remittances, the "brain drain," prices of consumer goods, and artistic excellence (Loaeza Tovar et al., 1997; Smith & Edmonston, 1997).

Of course, the four central questions are interrelated and many studies address more than one of them, for example studies comparing the skills of immigrants by their class of admission—the provision of U.S. immigration law which made them eligible for an immigrant visa—may both compare skills at entry and also compare skill trajectories over time (Duleep & Regets, 1996; Jasso & Rosenzweig, 1995; Jasso, Rosenzweig et al., 2000).*

Elements from the Framework for Studying Migration: Three Fundamental Actors

As even the foregoing abbreviated look at the four central questions suggests, there are three fundamental actors in the study of migration: the migrant, who is usually thought of as the chief protagonist; others at the place of origin; and others at the place of destination. All three kinds of actors make pertinent decisions, play parts in the migration processes, and

*To illustrate, a recent study addressed the question of whether immigrants screened for skills do better than immigrants admitted as the spouses of U.S. citizens and concluded that, while there is a substantial skill differential at entry, the skill differential narrows over time, with employment immigrants experiencing occupational downgrading and marital immigrants experiencing occupational upgrading—possibly the result of the screening process itself: While employers may screen for the short term, Americans marrying a foreigner may screen for the long term (Jasso & Rosenzweig, 1995).

experience migration impacts. Moreover, migration involves special relations between different kinds of actors. For example, consider the relation between migrant and others at origin—others may force or, alternatively, make possible the migration; and the migrant may, in turn, provide financial assistance and information, leading to the diffusion of ideas and practices from the migrant's destination. Similarly, consider the relation between a migrant and the others at the destination—migration may originate with or be made possible by the actions of others at the destination, who act as sponsors of desired workers or spouses; and more distant others at the destination may experience a variety of gains and losses as workers, consumers, owners of capital, taxpayers, artists, and biological beings with healthiness to develop and protect.

Elements from the Framework for Studying Migration: Quantities, Relations, and Models

Migration analysis encompasses the totality of immigrant and societal characteristics, and, thus, the quantities of interest span broad topical domains, including not only migration-centered phenomena—like emigration and naturalization—but also phenomena from the larger sociobehavioral world—like language acquisition, identity formation, skill prices and skill transferability, religion, and so on. In addition, the quantities of interest span varying levels of generality, from the characteristics of individual immigrants to the social, economic, and political characteristics of both origin and destination countries, including, importantly, their laws on exit and entry.

Reasoning about the central questions leads quickly to specification of relations between basic quantities and, thus, to basic overarching models that embed several relations.

For example, the first central question focuses on the selection of immigrants and their characteristics at entry—how a given individual becomes a migrant, moving from origin to destination. Understanding the selection of immigrants requires understanding the decision to migrate, in the context of social, economic, and political conditions in both origin and destination countries, including laws governing exit and entry. Models that have been advanced suggest that the underlying behavioral principle may be, as the Romans put it, "ubi bene, ibi patria"—where one is well-off, there is one's country. The prospective migrant compares his or her expected well-being in the two locales. Both the decision to migrate and the strategy for achieving migration are shaped by both the migrant's own characteristics and conditions in the origin and destination areas, together with the migrant's information about them. The basic models quickly become complicated when the migrant is modeled with a family; for example, not all family members may gain from migration, and, alternatively, an adult migrant's decision may be based on the expected well-being of his or her children.

Similarly, reasoning about the second central question not only suggests the continuing operation of both the migrant's characteristics and conditions in the origin and destination countries but also introduces a dynamic element. An important new conceptual tool is the trajectory; for example, the skill trajectory, earnings trajectory, health trajectory, language trajectory, religion trajectory, and so on.*

---

*Our notion of "trajectory" encompasses both sequences of states, as characterized by Elder, Johnson, and Crosnoe (this volume) and continuous increases or decreases in quantitative characteristics. For example, the religion trajectory may be a sequence of realizations of the categorical variable "religious preference," while the health trajectory may be a curve describing increases and decreases in the quantitative variable "healthiness."

Elements from the Framework for Studying Migration:
The Importance of U.S. Immigration Law

More persons would like to immigrate to the United States than current or foreseeable law permits*. Consider four indicators of the scarcity of a legal immigrant visa.

1. In January 1997, the most recent year for which the State Department released figures of the number of approved visa applicants waiting for numerically limited visas, the number on the waiting list was 3,622,897 (U.S. Department of State, *Visa Bulletin* VII, Number 73A, April 1997).
2. In March 2003, though there were no backlogs in any of the employment preference categories, the shortest waiting period in the family preference categories was 3.7 years (for adult unmarried sons and daughters of U.S. citizens from all countries except Mexico and the Philippines) and the longest waiting period was 21 years (for siblings of U.S. citizens from the Philippines).[†]
3. More than 8 million applications are received every year for the 50,000 immigrant visas awarded by lottery to natives of countries which have been underrepresented in recent U.S. immigration.[‡]
4. Several million foreign-born persons are in the United States illegally, the most recent official estimate being 7 million as of January 2000, with an estimated net annual increase of 350,000 per year.[¶]

In the face of high demand for immigrant visas, the United States allocates visas by means of a system that includes family reunification and employment criteria, as well as humanitarian and diversity concerns. In brief, the system of visa allocation in the period since 1921 may be characterized by three features. First, the United States restricts the number of immigrants (restricting since 1921 the number from the Eastern Hemisphere and since 1968 the number from the Western Hemisphere). Second, immediate relatives of adult U.S. citizens—defined as spouses, minor children, and parents—are exempt from numerical restriction.** Third,

---

*Following standard practice, we use the term "immigrant" synonymously with "legal immigrant" and "legal permanent resident alien." Legal immigrants have the right to reside permanently in the United States, to engage in most occupations, to sponsor the immigration of certain relatives, and, after completing a residency requirement, to become citizens of the United States. Besides legal immigrants, there is a large set of legal nonimmigrants who have temporary residence visas; legal temporary visas provide for legal residence for a temporary period and for a specific purpose. Examples of nonimmigrants include foreign students, tourists, and a variety of workers, including representatives of foreign news media, computer specialists, athletes, and entertainers. Additionally, there are individuals in the United States illegally who qualify for neither legal permanent residence nor legal temporary residence or who have violated the terms of a legal temporary visa. Both legal temporary residents and illegal migrants may be desirous of attaining legal permanent residence.

†Information is drawn from the *Visa Bulletin*, issued monthly by the U.S. State Department and available at http://travel.state.gov/visa_bulletin.html.

‡For example, in the DV-2002 program, for which the application period ran from 2 October 2000 to 1 November 2000, 13 million applications were received, of which 10 million were qualified entries (*Visa Bulletin*, Vol. VIII, Number 32, June 2001). Not surprisingly, in the DV-2003 program, which ran during October 2001, the number of entries dropped to 8.7 million, of which 6.2 million were qualified entries (http://travel.state.gov/DV-2003/results.html).

¶Estimates are drawn from the report issued in January 2003, available on the INS website (www.ins.usdoj.gov).

**A few other classes of individuals are also exempt from numerical restriction, some as a permanent feature of U.S. law (e.g., American Indians born in Canada and children born abroad to alien residents), others under temporary provisions (e.g., the special 3-year program in effect in 1992–1994 for spouses of aliens legalized under the Immigration Reform and Control Act of 1986). Additionally, special legislation has permitted refugees previously admitted with temporary documents to adjust to permanent resident status outside the numerical limitations.

numerically limited visas are allocated via two sets of preference categories, one for family-sponsored immigrants and the other for employment-based immigrants. Over the years, the United States has altered both the definition of immediate relatives of U.S. citizens (e.g. in 1952 extending to U.S. citizen women the right, already held by men, to sponsor the immigration of an alien spouse outside the numerical limitations) and the system for granting numerically limited visas (e.g., establishing a structure of preference categories in 1965 but not placing the Western Hemisphere under that structure until 1977 and subsequently revising the preference categories in the Immigration Act of 1990). Under current law, the number of visas available annually in the family preference categories is at least 226,000, but may be larger (though never larger than 480,000) depending on the previous year's volume of numerically unrestricted immigration; in the employment-based categories, the annual number of visas available is at least 140,000, but may be larger if there are unused family preference visas.*

Additionally, U.S. immigration law provides legal permanent resident visas on humanitarian and diversity grounds. On humanitarian grounds, persons admitted to the United States with refugee visas or given asylee status (both refugee and asylee visas are nonimmigrant temporary visas) may adjust to legal permanent residence after residing in the United States for 1 year. There is no ceiling on refugee adjustments to permanent residence and the number has ranged in recent years from a low of 39,495 in FY 1999 to 118,528 in FY 1996; in contrast, asylee adjustments are constrained to 10,000 per year. On diversity grounds, the United States grants 50,000 visas annually to nationals of countries from which the number of numerically limited immigrants is less than 50,000 in the preceding 5 years. Eligibility requirements include a high school degree or equivalent; or 2 years' work experience (within the preceding 5 years) in an occupation requiring 2 years of training; or experience; and selection is by lottery.[†]

Among family-based and employment-based immigrants, a key actor in the migration process is the visa sponsor (also known as the "petitioner")—the individual (or firm in the case of some employment-based immigrants) who, as relative or employer of the prospective immigrant, establishes the latter's eligibility for an immigrant visa.[‡] The visa sponsor initiates the paperwork. For all family-sponsored immigrants and for a subset of employment immigrants, the visa sponsor must also become the main support sponsor, assuming responsibility for the immigrant's support should the immigrant require assistance, and signing an affidavit of support contract.[¶] Note that the sponsorship feature of visa allocation engenders a wide range of behavioral possibilities.

To illustrate the behavioral implications of U.S. law, consider the interplay between marriage and migration. U.S. law grants U.S. citizens the right to marry almost anyone they choose and to reside in the United States with the chosen mate. As noted, immigrant spouses of U.S. citizens are granted visas outside the numerical limitations. Such immigrants constitute

---

*For a succinct description of U.S. visa allocation law, see the INS and State Department websites, in particular, the INS *Statistical Yearbook* and the State Department *Visa Bulletin*. For elaboration from a social science perspective, see Jasso, Rosenzweig et al. (2000).

[†]The number of persons admitted as refugees is set annually by the U.S. President in consultation with Congress; the ceiling has fluctuated in the range of 75,000 to 100,000. The diversity lottery program was begun in FY 1987 on a trial basis and made a part of U.S. immigration law under provisions of the Immigration Act of 1990. For further information on refugees, asylees, and diversity immigrants, see the INS and State Department websites.

[‡]A small number of family-sponsored and employment-based immigrants may self-petition. These include, in the case of family visas, spouses and children of deceased or abusive U.S. citizens and legal permanent residents and, in the case of employment visas, investors and individuals of great renown. For elaboration, see the requisite forms, forms I-130, I-140, I-360, and I-526, available on the INS website.

[¶]Additional "joint" sponsors may be brought in if the visa sponsor cannot fulfill the support requirement alone. For details, see the I-864 affidavit of support package of forms on the INS website.

approximately one third of all adult non-refugee legal immigrants admitted each year. Against this backdrop, there is a vigorous interplay of behavioral processes, namely a job market and a marriage market: the "smoke-gets-in-your-eyes" phenomenon, where the smoke is U.S. citizenship and U.S. citizens may appear more attractive as potential mates than they, perhaps, actually are. Accordingly, many new questions arise. How strong are the marriages between U.S. citizens and the immigrants they sponsor? What is the schooling disparity among spouses in these couples? How much scope do these marriages provide for the continuing human development of the two spouses? What kind of childrearing environment do these couples provide? How do schooling attainment and schooling disparity change over time?

As would be expected, qualifying for an immigrant visa is an overriding concern for prospective immigrants to the United States and visa allocation law is a critical component of the environment faced by prospective immigrants. U.S. immigration law selects immigrants and thereby shapes the characteristics of immigrant cohorts. This shaping is especially visible in two ways: (1) by comparing immigrants admitted in different years and (2) by comparing immigrants who entered in different classes of admission. Put differently, cohort and context exert a large influence on the characteristics of immigrants at entry and this influence continues over time, visible in the progress of immigrants, in their children, and in their impacts on both origin and destination countries.*

MIGRATION ANALYSIS FROM A LIFE COURSE PERSPECTIVE

The four themes in the life course perspective identified by Elder (1994)—interplay between lives and historical time and place, linked lives, timing of lives, and human agency—can be cross-classified with the four questions of migration analysis, providing a mutually enriching view.† Table 16-1 reports the cross-classification.

Consider, for example, the first question of migration analysis about the characteristics of immigrants at admission. Immigrant characteristics are importantly shaped by the social, economic, political, and legal context in both the origin and destination countries. Both origin country laws on emigration and U.S. immigration law shape each cohort. These are the factors examined by life course researchers under the rubric of "lives and historical time and place."

Immigrant cohorts are also characterized and shaped by the timing at which immigration occurs—the "timing of lives" element in the life course perspective—visible, among other things, in the immigrant's age and the time previously spent in the United States. Here, too, U.S. immigration law plays a part, as it notices age in the visa allocation process. For example, children of U.S. citizens must be under 21 (and unmarried) into order to qualify for numerically unlimited visas. Similarly, diversity visas require a certain level of education or occupational experience. In addition, legalization programs for illegal immigrants—such as the statutory program for individuals who have resided in the United States since 1972 and the special amnesty programs under the Immigration Reform and Control Act of 1986—notice time in the United States.

---

*The date of admission to permanent residence is an important milestone in an immigrant's biography. The new immigrant, who may be arriving from abroad at a U.S. port of entry (a "new arrival") or may be adjusting to permanent residence from a legal temporary visa in the United States (an "adjustment of status"), acquires a set of privileges, including that of sponsoring the immigration of certain kin. The passport is stamped to indicate admission to legal permanent residence, the "green card"—the paper evidence of legal permanent residence—is ordered, and the clock starts on the residency requirement for naturalization.

†The four themes constitute four of the five principles proposed by Elder, Johnson, and Crosnoe (this volume) as central to the life course framework. The missing principle is the foundational principle that human development is a lifelong process. Its effects are visible in every cell of Table 16-1.

TABLE 16-1. Interplay between the Four Questions of Migration Analysis and the Four Themes of the Lifecourse Perspective

Four questions of migration analysis	Four themes of the life course perspective			
	Lives and historical time/place	Timing of lives	Linked lives	Human agency
Migrants at entry	Cohort and context Laws on emigration in origin country Laws on immigration in United States	U.S. immigration laws notice age and duration in the United States	U.S. immigration laws notice kin and work relationships	Strategies and decisions for achieving immigration
Progress of migrants	U.S. laws on naturalization Other U.S. laws affect naturalization Origin country laws affect naturalization	U.S. naturalization laws notice age and duration in the United States	U.S. naturalization laws notice kin and work relationships Kin and work relationships also affect naturalization behavior	Decisions to acquire English and/or other skills, to remain in the United States, and to naturalize
Migrant children and children of migrants	U.S. laws on child immigration and adoption and on derivative citizenship	U.S. immigration and naturalization laws notice children's age and duration in the United States	U.S. immigration and naturalization laws notice kin and work relationships	Children may be "tied movers" or alternatively may be "engines of migration"
Impacts of migration	Impacts on origin and destination countries differ by historical period and by population characteristics	Impacts differ by age structure of emigrant and immigrant populations	Migrant's leaving affects those left behind Migrant's arriving affects natives of destination country	At both origin and destination, decisions are made and laws passed to affect future migration

Note: The four themes in the life course perspective are based on Elder (1994) and Elder, Johnson, and Crosnoe (this volume).

The life course perspective element "linked lives" has special resonance in migration analysis, for, as noted above, most immigrants (excepting refugees, diversity immigrants, and a small set of other groups) require a sponsor—a family member or employer who establishes the immigrant's eligibility for a visa. In the study of migration, the immigrant's life is inextricably linked to the life of the sponsor. Moreover, under the provisions of the Immigrant Reform and Responsibility Act of 1996, the sponsor assumes a contractual obligation for the support of the immigrant.

Finally, migration is quintessentially about human agency—individuals moving in search of a better life—thus giving new meaning to the "human agency" element of the life course perspective. At admission to legal permanent residence, human agency is visible in the strategies and decisions by which immigration was achieved.

As shown in Table 16-1, the other three central questions in the study of migration also have a natural correspondence with the four elements of the life course perspective. Note, in particular, how U.S. immigration law appears in many of the cells. Note also that in migration analysis many of the life course factors shaping behavior are laws, not merely customs. For example, the age-related stipulations in U.S. immigration law have the force of law; they are not "merely" social norms.

A close look at Table 16-1 suggests that each cell encompasses important questions for further research. The following are a few examples.

1. Naturalization and linked lives. The cell combining the linked lives theme with the question on the progress of migrants covers, inter alia, phenomena associated with naturalization. Besides the statutory effects of kin and work relationships on the decision and timing of naturalization—for example, immigrants admitted as the spouses of U.S. citizens have reduced residency requirements, and the residency requirement may be waived altogether for persons who have served honorably with the U.S. military—there are behavioral effects. Immigrants who gained permanent residence as spouses of U.S. citizens may decide not to naturalize in order to construct a diversified citizenship portfolio for the family (Jasso & Rosenzweig, 1990). There is also anecdotal evidence that immigrants who do not wish to sponsor the immigration of their kin decide not to naturalize.
2. Remittances and linked lives. The cell combining the linked lives theme with the question on the impacts of migration covers, inter alia, phenomena associated with impacts on the origin country, such as impacts of remittances. It has become an icon of Mexico–U.S. migration that entire villages in Mexico are sustained by remittances from villagers working in the United States. Estimates for 1995 provided by Loaeza Tovar et al. (1997) put the total remittances at between $2.5 and $3.9 billion.
3. Human agency and migrant children. The cell combining the human agency theme with the question on migrant children covers, inter alia, phenomena associated with children as "engines of migration." An important question concerns the magnitudes of the effects of aspirations for self and aspirations for one's children in an adult's decision to migrate. If, for example, migration is selective by offspring's gender, then children are operating as engines of migration (Jasso, 1997).

The foregoing examples show the vastness and richness of the research that can be undertaken under the Table 16-1 umbrella. Indeed, Table 16-1 provides the blueprint for a set of inquiries that could be presented at a conference and assembled as a book.*

*There would be sixteen studies each prototypical of one of the sixteen cells. The envisioned book would contain sixteen chapters plus introductory and concluding chapters. Of course, one quickly imagines a series of such books, each one devoted to a particular topic and organized by the cross-classification of the central questions in the study of that topic and Elder's (1994) four themes of the life course perspective.

DATA FOR MIGRATION ANALYSIS

The empirical study of migration presents formidable data challenges. To appreciate these, consider the following aspects of migration.

1. There may be important differences across entering cohorts of new legal immigrants—reflecting both changes in the United States and its immigration laws and also changes in countries around the world (including natural disasters and political upheavals).
2. Assimilation occurs over time.
3. Immigrants leave, and entering cohorts are thinned over time by non-random emigration.
4. Both migration and assimilation behaviors are shaped by individual and family characteristics and are responsive to conditions in both countries, including the legal environment faced by the migrant.

Table 16-1 underscores these features of migration and points naturally to the necessary data. For example, it shows vividly that addressing the first central question of migration—concerning immigrants at entry—requires information on cohort and context, age and duration, kin and employment relationships, and behavioral strategies, decisions, and outcomes. Together, these features dictate the data requirements.

In brief, the data should consist of probability samples drawn periodically from entering cohorts of immigrants of identifiable legal status—of identifiable legal status so that the context and the environment they face may be correctly characterized; of entering cohorts so that they can be examined before the non-random emigration begins; of multiple cohorts because conditions change in both origin and destination countries. The design should be longitudinal (not only to study assimilation but also to distinguish between effects associated with year of immigration and effects associated with length of time in the United States). Information should be obtained both from the sampled individual and from or about all other persons in the household and the (extended) family, including persons living abroad and new members added over time. Finally, the information collected should cover premigration experience and include complete retrospective and prospective histories of schooling, work, migration (including legal status), sponsorship, and health, and of linguistic, marital, and reproductive behaviors.

In principle, the earlier in the migration process the migrants enter the study the better. For example, one can envision a sampling design in which a random sample is drawn from among all first-time entrants to the United States. Such a set would include not only legal immigrants but also a variety of temporary "nonimmigrants" (students, diplomats, temporary workers, etc.). Following them over time, one would observe the process by which some among them decide to seek permanent residence in the United States, as well as the process by which some among them become illegal (by overstaying a temporary visa or by violating the terms of their visa, say, by accepting unauthorized employment). Unfortunately, the requisite sampling frame for such a study does not yet exist.*

The United States does maintain excellent records on all persons newly admitted to legal permanent residence. In its annual reports, the *Annual Report of the Immigration and Naturalization Service* (published in the years 1943–1978) and the *Statistical Yearbook of the Immigration and Naturalization Service* (published since 1979), the U.S. Immigration and

---

*However, complete enumeration of new holders of visas in certain nonimmigrant classes, such as those for students and temporary workers, may soon become possible, paving the way for feasible sampling designs.

Naturalization Service (INS) publishes tabulations describing the basic characteristics of each annual cohort of immigrants; the volumes for recent years are posted on the INS website.

We may distinguish between three levels of specificity in the data for studying legal immigrants.

Data with Level 1 Specificity

At level 1, data consist of published tabulations based on new immigrant cohorts. For example, the INS *Statistical Yearbooks* make it possible to track the total volume of immigration from year to year, as well as the volume by origin country and by class of admission. To illustrate, information posted on the INS website indicates that the total number of persons admitted to legal permanent residence in FY 2000 was 849,807; that of these, 48% were new arrivals and 52% were adjusting from a nonimmigrant visa; that 55% were female; and that the most popular state of intended residence was California, attracting almost 26%, followed by New York, attracting 12%.

Data with Level 2 Specificity

Suppose, however, that interest centers on more detailed information, such as the sex ratio among immigrants admitted as spouses of U.S. citizens. In such a case, it is necessary to go beyond published tabulations and obtain the complete microdata sets from the annual immigrant cohorts. These, which exemplify what we may call level 2 specificity, are available for sale by the National Technical Information Service (U.S. Department of Justice, 2001), suitably devoid of personal identifiers. With the public use microdata, many new kinds of analyses become possible, for example, analysis of the sex ratio of immigrants by country, class of admission, and age group and of intended residence by origin country and class of admission.

Data with Level 3 Specificity

The public use immigrant cohort data sets, however welcome they are for providing information on a complete set of each year's new legal immigrants, leave much to be desired. They have no information on schooling or on earnings; the information is organized by individuals and, thus, it is not possible to reconstitute family groupings; and so forth. The solution is obvious: use INS administrative records as a sampling frame, draw a random sample, and carry out interviews, not only soon after admission to legal permanent residence but also, in a panel design, periodically for many years. We may think of such data as exhibiting level 3 specificity—like level 1 data, level 3 data cover legal immigrants newly admitted to permanent residence; like level 2 data, level 3 data are microdata with observations on individuals; and, now, at level 3, the records-based data are augmented by information collected in personal interviews.

Many panels and workshops assembled in both the public and private sectors, for example, panels of the National Academy of Sciences, the National Institutes of Health, the Rockefeller Foundation, have contributed to the evolving vision of the required data. With contributions from many scholars, a new plan was formulated for collecting immigrant data that would enable research that substantially advances understanding of the social and economic characteristics of immigrants and the effects of immigration in the United States. This new plan—the New Immigrant Survey (NIS)—has a prospective–retrospective design in which large probability samples are drawn from new cohorts of legal permanent resident aliens, using the administrative records of the INS. Sampled immigrants will be interviewed immediately after admission to permanent resident status and re-interviewed periodically thereafter. Information will be collected on the sampled immigrants' spouses and family and household members, including their children, both the immigrant children they brought with them and the U.S. citizen children born to them in the United States.*

Because such a design had never been tried before, a pilot—the NIS-P—was carried out, with support from National Institutes of Health, the National Science Foundation, and the INS. The pilot survey both confirmed the soundness of the design, highlighted the importance of contacting sampled immigrants immediately after admission to permanent residence, and provided new information on immigrants never before available (e.g., on the schooling of new legal immigrants, on assortative mating in schooling, on religion).[†]

Remark on Illegal Migrants

As already noted, the magnitude of illegal migration is far from trivial. The INS estimates that, as of January 2000, there were approximately 7 million foreign-born persons in the United States illegally, with an estimated net annual increase of 350,000 per year (INS website). There is no sampling frame for illegal migrants and, thus, it is not possible to draw a representative sample for study. The NIS and the NIS-P, however, provide information on migration history, including illegal spells. Thus, the NIS-P indicates, among other things, that among the FY 1996 legal immigrants, approximately 25% had been in the United States illegally at some previous time. Immigrants with illegal experience differed from immigrants with no illegal experience along many dimensions—for example, they had on average 2 years less schooling than immigrants with no illegal experience (11 years vs. 13 years); they were more likely to have gained permanent residence as the spouse of a US citizen or permanent resident and less likely as a parent or employment-based immigrant; and, for equal time in the United States, they traveled less out of the country (Jasso, Massey, Rosenzweig, & Smith, 2000c). Additionally, sampled immigrants may have family members or co-residents who are illegal and information about them will also be obtained. Thus, it would appear that the NIS can shed some light on the illegal experience—albeit limited light, given that illegals who become legal or who are related to or reside with legal immigrants are not randomly drawn from among all illegals.

---

*The sample to be drawn consists of 10,000 adult immigrants (drawn from among both "principal" immigrants— those who qualify for an immigrant visa under U.S. law—and immigrants who obtained their visas as accompanying spouses of principal immigrants) and 1,000 children who are principal immigrants (and therefore would not be covered in the households of sampled adult immigrants). Information will be obtained about both the sampled immigrant and members of the immigrant's family and household. For further description of the New Immigrant Survey, see the NIS website (www.pop.upenn.edu/nis). When the baseline round of the NIS is completed (the baseline round will be in the field from mid-2003 to early 2004) and the data compiled, the data will be posted to the website in the form of public use microdata sets.

[†]Comprehensive exposition of the design of the NIS-P, together with information obtained in the pilot, may be found in the initial papers from the project (Jasso, Massey, Rosenzweig, & Smith, 2000a, 2000b, 2000c, 2003) and on the NIS website.

Remark on Comparison Samples

The NIS design focuses on immigrants. There are two natural comparison groups, natives in the United States and non-migrants in the origin countries (corresponding to the fundamental actors identified in the framework for migration analysis—others in the origin country and others in the destination country). To achieve comparability with these groups, the NIS adopted the principle of having all the questionnaire modules except those focusing specifically on the migration experience be identical to the questionnaire modules used in the major surveys in the United States and abroad. For example, question sequences on schooling, labor force participation and occupation, earnings and wealth, marital and fertility histories, health and religion, are identical to corresponding sequences in U.S. surveys such as the Panel Study of Income Dynamics, the National Longitudinal Surveys of Labor Market Experience, the U.S. Census, the Health and Retirement Study, and the General Social Surveys, and in surveys abroad, such as the International Social Survey Programme (covering 33 countries) and the International Social Justice Project (covering 13 countries). Additionally, the NIS design calls for obtaining information about the sampled immigrant's family members abroad, so that migration selectivity can be assessed both with respect to the origin country and with respect to the immediate family.

THEORETICAL ILLUSTRATION:
JUSTICE, STATUS, AND THE PROPENSITY TO EMIGRATE

The cross-classification of the four central questions of migration analysis and the four themes of the life course perspective (Table 16-1) highlights the impact of cohort and context for producing the characteristics of immigrants at entry. In this section we examine theoretically the part played by aspects of the origin country context. The work reported in this section is drawn from a larger project, the objective of which is to derive implications for migration phenomena from two theories of basic sociobehavioral processes—justice theory and status theory. Derivation of predictions from justice theory for migration was initiated in Jasso (1996). The current project extends that work by deriving predictions from status theory and by building a new joint model in which both justice and status are operating (Jasso, 2002b).

Preliminaries

THEORETICAL ANALYSIS.   It may be useful to discuss briefly the scientific tradition underlying this illustration. A good research portfolio will typically include both theoretical and empirical elements. A brief contrast between these two approaches will help set the stage for the theoretical work.

In empirical analysis, especially in inductive and exploratory empirical analysis, we begin by focusing on an outcome—a dependent variable—thinking about what produces it or generates, shapes it or influences it. These latter factors are the inputs, and much of empirical analysis is concerned with discovering the inputs and assessing their effects on the outcome. Symbolically, when we do empirical work we are obsessed with a Y and we seek to learn the identity of the Xs which produce it and, later, the effects of each X on Y.

In theoretical analysis we do something quite different. Rather than starting with an outcome, we start with an input—which may itself resemble an X-affects-Y relation—and focus on this input, investing it with the character of an assumption and asking what may be its effects or implications, that is, what outcomes it generates. The goal is to discover the outcomes it produces and, later, its effect on each outcome. The input's importance depends on the variety of outcomes it generates and the part it plays in generating them.

Often the assumption is an idea about human nature and it defies direct test. Thus, in order to assess its validity, we derive its implications and it is the implications that we test. This strategy, invented by Newton and often referred to as the hypothetico-deductive model, makes it possible to learn about human nature by learning about the implications of our assumptions.*

JUSTICE AND STATUS.   Justice theory and status theory are obvious candidates for the effort to derive predictions because of two features. First, they describe the operation of aspects of human behavior which seem to be basic and universal. Though justice and status may turn out not to be fundamental forces, but rather the outcomes of the working out of truly fundamental forces shaping human behavior—that is, though they may turn out to be processes of the middle range, to use Merton's ([1949, 1957] 1968) evocative language—nonetheless they are sufficiently basic that their reach extends through broad areas of behavior. Second, there has been sufficient progress in understanding the operation of both justice and status that well-axiomatized, mathematical theories are available. The assumptions of both justice theory and status theory have been made explicit and, thus, the task of deriving implications from them is made possible. Moreover, in both cases the assumptions have been given precise mathematical statement, and, thus, derivation of predictions is both simpler and richer, given the large set of mathematical tools available to carry out derivation.

Justice theory and status theory share another feature which makes them potentially rich sources of mechanisms influencing migration phenomena. They explicitly accommodate and distinguish between caring about cardinal things—like wealth—and caring about ordinal goods—like beauty, intelligence, bravery, athletic skill, and so on. Status theory, however, in its current axiomatization—the foundation of which is the status function proposed by Sørensen (1979), which incorporates Goode's (1978) convexity condition—notices only ranks, ignoring amounts of cardinal goods.

Of course, not all persons are covered by both theories. As is well known, some individuals are impervious to ideas of status—like St John of the Cross, who "saw only souls." Others seem untouched by justice concerns, never experiencing the all too familiar, "It's not fair."[†]

THREE WORLD-VIEWS.   Combining the ideas that individuals may care about justice or status and that as well they may care about material or non-material goods leads to a wide range of possible configurations, including three ideal-typical world-views—justice–materialistic, in which people care about justice and value material goods; justice–non-materialistic, in which people care about justice and value non-material goods; and status,

---

*Note that both the theoretical and the empirical approaches illuminate causation. Note also that when empirical work tests a theoretical prediction, the two approaches coalesce in a special way—the test indicating not only the effect of an X on a Y but as well the robustness and scope of the theory predicting the effect of X on Y. See Jasso (2002a) for further elaboration.

[†]Like the tone deaf or color blind who do not notice tone or color, the justice oblivious seem devoid of a sense of justice and the status oblivious of a sense of status.

in which people care about status (and it is irrelevant whether they value material or non-material goods). We will use these ideal–typical world-views to characterize not only individuals but also entire societies.

In general, there are two ways to ascertain a person's or society's world-view. First, words signal the valued good and whether justice or status concerns dominate. Second, justice theory and status theory generate many predictions, and these can be used to construct comprehensive portraits. To illustrate, status words signal status concerns, and justice words signal justice concerns. An individual who talks much of "equity" is likely to have a justice world-view, and a person who makes much of who salutes whom and how deep a bow should be is likely to have a status world-view. Similarly, words signal goods valuation. Persons and societies which emphasize quantitative amounts of cardinal things (such as income and wealth) are likely to be materialistic in outlook, while persons preoccupied with beauty or with horse bloodlines are likely to favor ordinal things. As for reasoning from theoretical predictions, consider the following. A country which welcomes immigrants must be a justice–materialistic society; in a justice–non-materialistic society, individuals are always closer to the neighbor above in a valued-good hierarchy than to the neighbor below, but the opposite holds in a status society; a husband and wife can be truly equal only in a justice–materialistic society, not in a justice–non-materialistic society or a status society; and monastic institutions increase the public welfare in justice–non-materialistic societies, but in justice–materialistic societies only mendicant institutions do so.* Current research is consolidating these ideas into a protocol for efficient classification of individuals and societies according to their world-view.

A MULTIFACTOR WORLD.   Probably, all sociologists would agree that behavioral and social phenomena have a multifactor etiology. For example, in the realm of theory, Parsons (1968) noted that Durkheim was a multifactor theorist, and empirically, multivariate methods are the staple of empirical tools. But everyone also recognizes the difficulties involved in modeling jointly two or more disparate processes and in testing their implications. Theoretically, the challenge is to build theories about the operation of single basic processes and then integrate them into a larger whole. Empirically, the multifactor view poses special challenges, for the operation of two factors may lead to opposite effects. It may at first appear that one prediction is rejected, but in fact it may be that one of the two effects is stronger than the other. For example, suppose that justice theory predicts that Y is an increasing function of X and status theory predicts that Y is a decreasing function of X. The empirical finding that Y is an increasing function of X does not constitute, in a multifactor world, evidence that status processes are not operating, but rather is consistent with the operation of both processes such that the effect of justice processes is stronger than or "dominates" the effect of status processes.

In this new multifactor world, the basic processes, previously unconnected, are now not only connected but, more than that, their fates are inextricably linked. There is a new sense that progress in understanding the operation of a basic process requires progress in understanding the operation of all basic processes. This is because basic processes may differ in the strength and direction of their effects across diverse phenomena, and assessing the effects of one basic process thus requires assessing the effects of the others.

TWO BASIC MECHANISMS.   In the migration application, one of the functions from justice analysis and one of the functions from status analysis will play central parts. These are the

---

*For references to the articles describing derivation of these predictions, see Jasso (2001a, 2001b).

justice evaluation function and the S1 status function. Both are mathematical functions, and both exhibit the who–what–whom form which may be especially fruitful in social science. Both are functions of an individual's personal quantitative characteristics, such as beauty, wealth, intelligence, athletic skill, and so on. Both functions were introduced over 20 years ago, and there is considerable knowledge about their properties and operation. Finally, both have been used as assumptions in theories, yielding a variety of testable implications for phenomena in disparate domains.

JUSTICE EVALUATION FUNCTION.   The justice evaluation represents the judgment that a rewardee (which may be self or other) is justly or unjustly rewarded and, if unjustly rewarded, whether underrewarded or overrewarded and to what degree. The justice evaluation is represented by the full real-number line, with zero representing the point of perfect justice, negative numbers representing degrees of unjust underreward and positive numbers representing degrees of unjust overreward. The justice evaluation function, proposed in Jasso (1978), specifies the justice evaluation as a function of the logarithm of the ratio of the actual to the just reward:

$$J = \theta \ln\left(\frac{A}{C}\right),$$
(1)

where J denotes the justice evaluation, A denotes the actual reward, and C denotes the just reward. The reward may be cardinal, like wealth, or ordinal, like beauty. The form in Equation (1) also includes the signature constant, denoted θ, which captures both the observer's framing of the reward as a good or a bad and the observer's expressiveness.

STATUS FUNCTION.   In the status framework, S1 status—hereafter simply status—represents the status that an individual accords to another or expects to receive from another. The status function, introduced by Sørensen (1979) and embodying properties held by Goode (1978) to be important in an individual-level status function, specifies status as the logarithm of the target's rank on a valued quantitative characteristic such as beauty, intelligence, or wealth:

$$S = \ln\left(\frac{1}{1 - r}\right),$$
(2)

where S denotes status and r denotes the relative rank (between zero and one) on the valued quantitative characteristic. In this axiomatization, status is represented by positive numbers.*

EXAMPLES OF PREDICTIONS.   The justice evaluation function and the status function have been used as assumptions in justice theories and status theories, respectively and have been shown to yield implications for a wide range of behavioral and social phenomena.
　　To illustrate, predictions of justice theory include (1) parents of two or more non-twin children will spend more of their toy budget at an annual gift-giving occasion rather than at the children's birthdays, (2) things change value as their owners move across social contexts, (3) in historical periods when wives predecease their husbands, mothers are mourned more than fathers, but in historical periods when husbands predecease their wives, fathers are mourned more than mothers, (4) conflict severity between the subgroups of a collectivity

*Comprehensive exposition of properties of the justice evaluation function appears in Jasso (1999) and of the status function in Jasso (2001c). The two functions are systematically contrasted in Jasso (2002a).

increases the greater the overall income inequality, and (5) veterans of wars fought on foreign soil are more vulnerable to post-traumatic stress syndrome than veterans of wars fought on home soil (Jasso, 2001a, 2001b).

Similarly, predictions of status theory include (1) status inequality is lower if the valued goods are negatively correlated, (2) in a two-subgroup society, the least advantaged from both subgroups gain status from discrimination, and the most advantaged from both subgroups lose status from discrimination, leading to cross-subgroup coalitions, (3) the status gap between two subgroups increases with the relative size of the disadvantaged subgroup, (4) when two subgroups are fighting for and against discrimination, it is more difficult to prevent defections in the bottom subgroup than in the top subgroup, and (5) opponents of discrimination are outnumbered (Jasso, 2001c).

Procedures

MODELING THE PROPENSITY TO EMIGRATE.   In both justice theory and status theory, it has long been thought that the distributions of the justice evaluation and of the status score, respectively, can be used to characterize fundamental aspects of a group or society. For example, in justice theory it is said that society is "a meeting of justice sentiments" and status theory views social interaction as structured by the participants' status.

Accordingly, among individuals with a justice world-view, we model the propensity to emigrate as a function of the justice score and among individuals with a status world-view as a function of the status score. At the societal level, the proportion at risk of emigrating will be related to the distribution of justice evaluations in a justice society and, in a status society, to the distribution of status scores.

But what kind of a function is the propensity to emigrate? How does it vary with the justice evaluation or with the status score? An important idea, going back at least as far as Aristotle (Book IV of the *Politics*) and receiving renewed impetus from Blau (1964, pp. 296–297), is that the middle class is the backbone of society—the "solid core" in Blau's (1964) words—the lower and upper classes being less integrated into the whole. Extending this idea to the realm of migration, we reason that the middle class is more attached to a country than either the lower or the upper classes and, therefore, less at risk of emigration.

On the basis of classical reasonings, together with Blau's (1964) analyses and informed as well by Simmel's ([1896–1917] 1950) examination of the stranger, Jasso (1996) proposed to model the propensity to emigrate using a discontinuous function which assumes the value zero in the middle region and positive values in the lower and upper regions. Accordingly, we partition both the justice evaluation continuum and the status continuum into three regions, with cutpoints at −1 and +1. The set of persons with a justice evaluation or a status score between −1 and +1 are designated the mainstream. We assume that individuals in the mainstream constitute the backbone of society, the "solid core" in Blau's (1964) words, and will have zero propensity to emigrate. Individuals with a justice evaluation or a status score either below −1 or above +1 will be somewhat disaffected and prone to wander, to use Simmel's ([1896–1917] 1950) word, to other collectivities.

We have restricted the active propensity to emigrate to two regions of the justice evaluation or status distribution, but the task still remains of specifying the function in those two regions. As in Jasso (1996), here we model the propensity to emigrate using the principal branches of the inverse secant function, denoted arcsec(x). The principal branch specification of the inverse secant function has several appealing features as an approximation to the propensity to emigrate. First, it is undefined for arguments between −1 and +1; thus, it represents well the notion that the mainstream does not have a propensity to emigrate. Second, its values in the lower region are higher than its values in the upper region, ranging between $\pi/2$ and π in the lower region and between zero and $\pi/2$ in the upper region; thus, the propensity to emigrate is greater among the poor than among the rich. Third, in each region the arcsecant function is an increasing function of the argument; thus, the propensity to emigrate is higher for the less poor than for the poorest and also higher for the richest than for the less rich.

ANALYZING THE PROPENSITY TO EMIGRATE.   What proportion of the population has a propensity to emigrate? And how does the proportion at risk of emigrating vary with economic inequality? Justice theory and status theory provide a set of techniques—known as the macromodel strategy—that can be used to address these questions.* The macromodel strategy begins with the distribution of a theoretically based quantity in a collectivity, for example, the justice evaluation distribution or the status distribution. Interest centers on parameters of that distribution and on a variety of other features, such as substantively pertinent subdistribution structures. For example, in justice theory, two kinds of subdistribution structures are studied: (1) the truncated subdistribution structure associated with splitting the collectivity into subgroups defined by the values of the justice evaluation at the cutpoints (e.g., the underrewarded, the justly rewarded, and the overrewarded) and (2) the censored subdistribution structure associated with splitting the collectivity into subgroups defined by a qualitative characteristic such as race, ethnicity, religion, gender, and the like.[†]

Our strategy is to investigate the distributions of J and S and of arcsec(J) and arcsec(S) using mathematically specified distributions to model the distributions of the valued goods. Accordingly, the method has three steps. First, select the modeling distributions for the valued goods and, using change of variable techniques, obtain the distributions of S and of the goods component of J that arise from each of the valued good distributions.[‡] Second, using techniques from the study of probability distributions, find the proportion with a J or S less than -1 and the proportion with a J or S greater than $+1$. Third, in the special case of a justice–materialistic society, obtain the first partial derivatives of the proportions at risk of emigrating with respect to inequality in the distributions of the valued cardinal goods.

Results

Following the procedures described above, Jasso (1996) found that a justice society can have both a bottom and a top; that is, the propensity to emigrate may be non-zero at one or both of the extreme regions. A justice–non-materialistic society, however, has only a bottom region with a propensity to emigrate; this region contains approximately 18% of the population. In justice–materialistic societies, whether the propensity to emigrate is positive in only the

---

*Currently there are four main techniques for deriving predictions from justice theory and status theory—the micromodel, macromodel, mesomodel, and matrixmodel strategies. For description of these techniques, see Jasso (2002a).

[†]Our use of the terms "censored" and "truncated" follows the usage in Moses (1968) and in Johnson and Kotz (1969, p. 27). In this usage, censoring refers to selection of the units by their ranks or percentage (or probability) points; truncation refers to selection of the units by values of the variate. For example, the group with incomes less than $20,000 forms a truncated subdistribution; the top 5% of the population forms a censored subdistribution.

[‡]Status and the justice evaluation about ordinal goods give rise to a particular distribution—the negative exponential in the justice–non-materialistic case and the positive exponential in the status case. In the justice–materialistic case, however, the justice evaluation distribution depends on the distributions of the actual reward and the just reward. Selection of modeling distributions for cardinal goods is attentive to several parameters, including the lower and upper bounds; the search for new modeling distributions utilizes standard sources such as Johnson and Kotz (1970a, 1970b) and Stuart and Ord (1987) and the little handbook by Evans, Hastings, and Peacock (2000). See Jasso (2002a) for further details.

TABLE 16-2. Who Migrates: Predicted Effects of Justice Theory and Status Theory, by Justice versus Status Society and Materialistic versus Non-materialistic Society

	Materialistic society	Non-materialistic society
Justice society	Persons with incomes <37% of the mean or >271% of the mean	Bottom 18%
Status society	Top 37%	Top 37%

TABLE 16-3. Predicted Effects of Overall Economic Inequality on Emigration, by Justice versus Status Society and Materialistic versus Non-materialistic Society

	Materialistic society	Non-materialistic society
Justice society	Increasing	None
Status society	None	None

bottom or only the top or in both bottom and top depends on the distributional shape of the valued cardinal good. In such societies, individuals with incomes less than 37% of the mean or higher than 271% of the mean will be at risk of emigrating. Similarly, the proportions in the bottom and top depend on the distributional shape of the valued cardinal good.

Jasso (1996) provides formulas and representative quantities for three distributional forms that can be used to model the distribution of cardinal goods, the lognormal, the Pareto, and the power function. In justice–materialistic societies, it is also possible to find the effect, on the proportion at risk of emigrating, of overall inequality in the distribution of the valued cardinal good. In the three distributional families analyzed, the total proportion at risk of emigrating, drawing from both the bottom and the top, is always an increasing function of inequality in the distribution of the valued cardinal good.

The macromodel strategy for deriving theoretical implications is now being used with status theory. Results obtained to date indicate that, in a status society which values a single good (whether cardinal or ordinal), the propensity to emigrate is positive only in a top region containing about 37% of the population. Moreover, because, as noted above, the status function, proposed by Sørensen (1979) and satisfying Goode's (1978) convexity condition, notices only ranks, the proportion at risk of emigrating from a status society is unrelated to inequality in the distribution of cardinal goods even if cardinal goods are valued.

Tables 16-2 and 16-3 summarize the results obtained to date.

As shown in Tables 16-2 and 16-3, these results thus suggest that emigration streams will look very different depending on whether the society is a justice–materialistic society, a justice–non-materialistic society, or a status society. Whether an origin country's emigration stream is dominated by individuals from the top or bottom of the society depends on whether its people value justice or status and whether they care about material or non-material goods.*

In this illustration, the first central question of migration analysis—What are the characteristics of immigrants at entry, and why?—is answered in part by important features of the

---

*Of course, a deeper analysis will also endogenize the processes by which justice or status concerns dominate and, similarly, cardinal or ordinal goods are valued. Jasso (1987) provides initial analyses of the problem of "choosing a good." As for caring for justice or status, Jasso (2002b) explores the possibility of a general set of rules, for example, stipulating that in conditions of poverty or hunger, justice concerns are always activated.

origin country context—exemplifying the first element in the life course perspective—including the distributional form of valued material goods. The link between the migration phenomenon of interest and the origin country context is provided by theories of two basic processes. The operation of justice processes and of status processes generates the link and makes salient the life course perspective. Thus, we are working in the top subpanel of the theoretical panel in the triptych of migration analysis (Figures 16-1 and 16-2), and that work lands us in the top left-hand corner of Table 16-1.

EMPIRICAL ILLUSTRATION:
MIGRATION, THE LIFE COURSE, AND HEALTH

Health is an important attribute which plays a part at all stages of the migration process and which, given that it unfolds over time, requires a life course perspective for its correct understanding. Looking at Table 16-1, it is evident that health permeates virtually every cell. In this section we address health aspects of the first two central questions of migration analysis—concerning immigrants at entry and the progress of immigrants. We develop a model of health and migration that incorporates health selectivity, stresses due to the process of applying for legal permanent residence, and the effects of U.S. exposure and we report preliminary estimates using data from the NIS-P.

Modeling Immigrant Health

Consider an adult residing in a foreign country and contemplating a permanent move to the United States. At the time of the migration decision—roughly when the first steps are taken to obtain legal permanent residence in the United States—he or she has a certain level of healthiness. The distribution of healthiness among all prospective immigrants to the United States around the world at this stage of the immigrant career is determined by selectivity forces, including U.S. immigration criteria. Of course, the intensity of self-selection on healthiness may vary; for example, refugees may be less self-selected on health than employment immigrants. The healthiness distribution may be a composite distribution, consisting of several distinct subdistributions corresponding to distinct migration flows.*

There follows a period of time during which the prospective migrant must wait for admission to legal permanent residence, carrying out whatever tasks are required in order to satisfy visa requirements (e.g., obtaining a medical examination, a police and military record, etc.).† This waiting period has two phases. The first phase, applicable only to prospective migrants who do not qualify for a numerically unlimited visa, involves waiting for the availability of a visa. Visa waiting times vary by both class of admission and origin country; for example, as discussed above, in March 2003, there was no delay for employment-based visas, but the delay for family-based visas ranged from 3.7 years in the family first category (unmarried sons and daughters of U.S. citizens) for natives of all countries except Mexico and the

---

*Jasso, Massey, Rosenzweig, & Smith (2002) explore health selectivity among immigrants, focusing on immigrant skills and country conditions. As will be seen, the model presented here focuses on health changes after the initial selection, and the empirical work controls for the initial selection.

†See the State Department and INS websites for comprehensive description of procedures for obtaining legal permanent residence. For example, the INS website includes a section describing all the pathways to legal permanent residence (www.ins.usdoj.gov/graphics/services/residency/index.htm).

Philippines, for whom such visas had a waiting period of 10 and 13 years, respectively, to 21 years in the family fourth category (siblings of U.S. citizens) for persons from the Philippines.*

The second phase of the waiting period consists of application processing. Of course, for prospective migrants who qualify for a numerically unlimited visa, this phase is co-terminous with the entire waiting period. The length of this phase varies with a number of administrative factors, including the number of personnel assigned to immigrant visa processing and whether changes in immigration law make necessary the design of new forms and/or retraining of personnel.

In some situations, all or some of the waiting period is spent in the United States. For example, persons with legal temporary nonimmigrant visas—as foreign students, say, or H-1B specialty workers—may be applying for legal permanent residence under family or employment provisions of the law. Some persons do not qualify for a legal permanent visa, under any provision of the law. They may enter the United States with a legal temporary visa and then lapse into illegality. Or they may enter the United States illegally (i.e., "without inspection").

We conceptualize overall healthiness as having two components, a permanent component, denoted h^p, and a transitory one, denoted h^t.[†] We assume that migrants make their initial migration decision based on the permanent component of their healthiness. The process of applying for permanent residence is highly stressful, however, and the transitory component declines in response to the immigration process stresses. Similarly, living in the United States illegally is highly stressful, and the transitory component declines.[‡]

The decline in the transitory component of health can be characterized by its magnitude, by the length of time during which the decline occurs, and by the shape of the decline (e.g., its steepness). These aspects of the decline may vary by migration stream. For example, the stresses may be greater for immigrants requiring an affidavit of support (all family immigrants and a subset of employment immigrants) than for other immigrants, and, therefore, the magnitude of the decline may be greater for these immigrants; and the stresses may be greater for illegals.

Among applicants for legal immigrant visas, permanent residence is eventually obtained. At that point the immigration process stresses end, and we may conjecture that observed healthiness—more precisely, the transitory component of health—begins an upward trajectory. The incline, like the decline, may be characterized by its magnitude, by the length of the recovery period, and by its shape. And, as with the decline, aspects of the recovery period may also vary by immigrant stream. Except for normal aging, one might imagine that following the recovery period the immigrant returns to the original level of observed healthiness, so that the magnitude of the decline would equal the magnitude of the incline, unless, of course, the

---

*For further details and monthly updates, see the *Visa Bulletin* at the State Department website.

[†]Following the standard model, pioneered by Grossman (1972), health is an important form of human capital and includes both a persistent time-invariant component and a time-varying component (Strauss & Thomas, 1998). The idea that many phenomena of interest have time-invariant and time-varying components plays a part in many social science models, see, for example, Jasso's (1985) analysis of frequency of sexual intercourse and England, Kilbourne, and Farkas' (1988) and Kilbourne, England, and Beron's (1994) analyses of race, gender, and wage dynamics.

[‡]For discussion of migration-related stresses, see Kasl and Berkman (1983) and Vega and Amaro (1994). Illustration of these stresses is plentiful. For example, the website for an immigration law firm begins with the following statement: "Immigrating to the United States is a complicated procedure that can cause tremendous stress for the individual wishing to immigrate. MacKenzie-Hughes, LLP is the area's premier immigration law firm, and we work hard to smooth the process and minimize the anxiety for our clients" (www.imm-usa.com). And the stresses may be even greater for illegal migrants, who must live partly in the shadows and face threats of deportation. Other stresses include the constraints on international travel, which may cause family hardships (U.S. Immigration and Naturalization Service, 1992).

stresses have been so severe or prolonged that the body's physiology is altered (Seeman, Singer, Rowe, Horwitz, & McEwen, 1997; Smith, 1999).*

This model raises several new empirical questions, including (1) whether the steepness of the decline and the steepness of the recovery are related, (2) whether the duration of the application process and the duration of the recovery period are related, and (3) whether, within the application and recovery periods, steepness and duration are related.

Additionally, there is another mechanism that must be incorporated into the model, and it involves the possibly deleterious effect of the U.S. environment. It has been conjectured that the combination of a possibly less healthy diet and environmental agents may induce a deterioration of the immigrant's health (Frisbie, Cho, & Hummer, 2001; Rumbaut & Weeks, 1996). Of course, an opposite conjecture is also plausible, given that (1) health-relevant conditions are more favorable in the United States than in many origin countries, (2) immigrants experience large gains in earnings, on average, after immigration,[†] and (3) immigrants, whose propensity to invest in themselves is visible in their migration behavior, are likely to invest in their health, taking advantage of their earnings gains and new opportunities in the United States.[‡]

Thus, the point at which inception of U.S. residence occurs—and thus exposure to the U.S. environment begins—marks the start of a possible new effect. The visible effect, if any, of U.S. exposure will differ depending on whether inception of U.S. residence occurs before admission to permanent residence or at admission to permanent residence, that is, during the decline associated with immigration process stresses or at its conclusion. If there is no U.S. exposure effect, both the immigration process decline and the postimmigration recovery are unaffected. However, when inception of U.S. residence occurs prior to admission to legal permanent residence, a positive effect of U.S. exposure would attenuate the immigration process decline, while a negative effect would exacerbate it. Moreover, a U.S. exposure effect would also alter the recovery incline, exaggerating it if positive, attenuating or even reversing it if negative.[¶]

There is a further complication. Adjusting to life in a new locale may pose new challenges and stresses, so that in the initial period of U.S. residence two distinct effects, of U.S. exposure and of adjustment to a new life, may be intertwined.

---

*For some categories of immigrants, the trajectory would be somewhat different. For example, refugees gain permanent admission when they are admitted with a (nonimmigrant temporary) refugee visa; arguably, for refugees, the stressful part of the application process ends with arrival in the United States. Refugees may, but need not, adjust to legal permanent residence; they are eligible to do so after 1 year. Asylees also may, but need not, adjust to legal permanent residence, and they are eligible to do so after 1 year; however, in contrast to refugees, there is an annual ceiling of 10,000 on their adjustment. We may surmise that the ceiling generates stress, and, thus, for asylees the immigration process stress would continue until admission to permanent residence. Similarly, among immigrants admitted as spouses of U.S. citizens, those married less than 2 years acquire only conditional permanent residence, and the immigration process stresses may continue for 2 more years until the conditionality restriction is removed. Immigrants admitted under the employment creation provisions of immigration law (i.e., as investors) also face conditionality restrictions for 2 years.

†Among immigrants in the nationally representative NIS-P who were employed in the United States at the time of the baseline round and who had worked abroad within the past 10 years, earnings gains, denominated in dollars based on estimates of the country-specific purchasing power of the currencies from the Penn International Comparisons Project, described in Summers and Heston (1991), were substantial—on average, $10,306 for men (a 68% increase) and $6,146 for women (a 62% increase).

‡For elaboration of the relationship between income and health, see Smith (1999).

¶Among illegals, a positive effect of U.S. exposure would attenuate the decline, while a negative effect of U.S. exposure would exacerbate the decline.

Empirical Framework

Empirical assessment of the immigrant health model we have sketched is quite demanding, requiring health measures at several carefully chosen points in time: (1) at or just before the start of the application process, (2) at inception of U.S. residence, (3) at admission to legal permanent residence, (4) at several points between the start of the application process and admission to legal permanent residence, and (5) at several points after inception of U.S. residence and after admission to permanent residence.

Further, measuring health is no simple matter. Here, the measure used is the subjective assessment of overall health widely used in U.S. data collection. This measure asks "In general, would you say your health is?" and provides five response categories: excellent, very good, good, fair, and poor.* Previous research suggests that subjective assessment of overall health accords well with objective measures (Wallace & Herzog, 1995; Ware & Donald, 1978). Nonetheless, it is possible that measured healthiness includes a new component—the immigrant's style of reporting, a style which may be understated or overstated. Moreover, the style of reporting, too, may have both a permanent component and a transitory component.

Thus, overall health, subjectively measured, may contain four distinct components: the two health components introduced earlier plus two style of reporting components, a permanent component of the style of reporting, denoted s^p, and a transitory component of the style of reporting, denoted s^t. The challenge is to isolate the four components or at least some of the four and assess their determinants and correlates.

Our main interest is in the effects of immigration process stresses and of exposure to the U.S. environment. Both these elements operate on the transitory component of health. Assessing these effects thus requires controlling for the three remaining components, the permanent health component h^p and the two style components s^p and s^t.

Applying fixed-effects techniques to longitudinal data would control for the two permanent components, h^p and s^p, but the transitory component of style would still remain entwined with the transitory component of health. A possible solution would be to find variables which operate on only the transitory style component, thus controlling for it.

In this illustration, I draw on a recent study which uses data from the NIS-P to obtain estimates of the effects of U.S. exposure on health (Jasso, Massey, Rosenzweig, & Smith, 2002). As discussed earlier, the NIS-P interviewed a probability sample of new legal immigrants admitted to permanent residence in 1996. Interviews were conducted at baseline, at 6 months, and at 12 months, with a randomly selected half also interviewed at 3 months (to gauge the effects of periodicity on attrition). The subjective evaluation of own health was measured at the 6-month and 12-month rounds. At the 6-month round, the average time since admission to legal permanent residence was 13–14 months; the 12-month interviews took place on average 9 months later.†

Because our data cover only the period after admission to permanent residence, they cannot be used to assess the health decline associated with the immigration process stresses. Accordingly, we focus on the effects of U.S. exposure.

---

*As noted, the subjective health assessment is a category scale. It thus constrains both the respondent and the analyst. In general, it is desirable to use a scale that maps as faithfully as possible the conceptual healthiness space in the respondent's head. The magnitude estimation techniques pioneered by Stevens (1975) would seem ideal, in particular, the technique called "number matching" in which the respondent uses the number system to describe the magnitude of interest. Number matching techniques are gaining currency in social research, for example, in factorial survey analysis.

†NIS-P data exemplify what we have called level 3 specificity.

We specify a fixed-effects model in which subjective health assessment is a function of the date of the interview; the coefficient of interview date thus represents the effect of U.S. exposure or, equivalently, the effect of the passage of time between the two interviews. Our goal is to obtain estimates of the effect of U.S. exposure on the transitory component of health. Because the health assessment still contains the transitory style component, we must find a way to control for it.

Respondents in the NIS-P were interviewed in English plus a total of 18 other languages. Among bilingual and bicultural persons, it is commonly thought that the same question can elicit different responses in different languages. For example, a person in excellent health may casually respond "excellent" to the health question in English, but in another language may understate health to avoid hubris or offending the interviewer. Thus, the language in which the interview was conducted may capture culture effects on the transitory component of the style of reporting. Accordingly, we include in the specification a term for whether the interview was conducted in English.*

To ensure that interview language does not operate as a proxy for English language skill, which could be associated with investments in health, given that an underlying investment propensity might generate both the propensity to invest in English language skill and the propensity to invest in health, we include in one of the specifications the full set of binary variables from two five-category measures of English language skill, a measure of understanding English and a measure of speaking English.†

The health assessment variable, as noted, is a five-category variable, coded with one indicating poor health and five indicating excellent health. There is no assurance, however, that respondents treat the five categories as a quantitative scale, and, thus, the scale may at best be ordinal. Accordingly, it would be useful to conduct all analyses twice, both in least-squares versions which treat the health variable as quantitative and in ordered-logit versions which treat it as ordinal. Thus, we set up a specification in which the dependent variable represents the change in healthiness—whether health improved, stayed the same, or deteriorated—and in which the explanatory variables include two binary variables for each of the language variables, one of these representing no change and the other representing, in the interview language variable, change from an interview language other than English to English, and, in the English skill variables, improvement in the English language skill. This specification simulates a fixed-effects specification.

Correct interpretation of the results hinges on the timing of the recovery from the immigration process stresses. The first observation point is at the 6-month round; respondents had on average been admitted to legal permanent residence 13–14 months earlier. If recovery from the immigration process stresses is complete by this date, then the time trend between the two rounds unambiguously indicates the effect of U.S. exposure. If, on the other hand, recovery is not complete, then this effect will reflect both the positive effect of recovery and the effect—in whatever direction—of U.S. exposure. Thus, a negative effect would indicate a negative U.S. exposure effect, the magnitude of which could range from the estimated effect, if recovery is complete, to a larger effect, if recovery is not complete and the estimated effect is the net of two opposing processes. A zero effect could indicate either that (1) the recovery is not complete and the

*For example, in a recent *New York Times* article, Riding (2002) quotes the French actress Rachida Brakni, whose first language was Arabic and who subsequently learned French and, more recently, English, as saying, "In English I have no inhibitions. I feel very free. It's a very good sensation."

†The two questions ask "How well would you say you understand English?" and "How well would you say you speak English?" The five response categories range from "Not well at all" to "Very well." These English language skill questions were asked at all rounds of the NIS-P.

recovery effect and a negative U.S. exposure effect exactly offset each other or (2) the recovery is complete and there is no U.S. exposure effect. Finally, a positive effect could indicate either (1) that the recovery is not complete and (a) the recovery effect is equal to or larger than a negative U.S. exposure effect, or (b) there is no U.S. exposure effect, or (c) both the recovery and U.S. exposure effects are positive, or (2) the recovery is complete and the U.S. exposure effect is positive.

Results

Table 16-4 reports the average subjective health assessment of the new legal immigrants at both the 6-month and 12-month rounds, as well as at the 6-month round for those immigrants also interviewed at the 12-month round. The averages are reported for all immigrants and also for selected subsets based on visa category, prior illegal experience, sex, continent of birth, and religion. As shown, the average health assessment rose across the period. Of course, this could reflect changes in the transitory component of style of reporting as well as changes in the transitory component of health. The figures also indicate that, while most subsets registered an increase in the health assessment, in some subsets the assessment declined. For example, while both men and women registered an increase, immigrants in two visa categories—spouse of a sibling of U.S. citizen and spouse of a diversity principal—registered a decrease.

Immigrant health differs by visa category. In general, the healthiest immigrants, according to the subjective assessment, are spouses of U.S. citizens and employment-based immigrants (both principals and spouses). The least healthy immigrants are refugees and those admitted as parents of U.S. citizens. These patterns reflect immigrant selectivity forces; for example, within immigrants not related by blood to U.S. citizens or residents, spouses of U.S. citizens and employment-based immigrant principals are "screened" by employers and U.S. citizen spouses (and employment-based spouses are in turn "screened" by the screened principal).*

Interestingly, immigrants with prior illegal experience are healthier than immigrants without such experience. Moreover, those former illegals who eluded detection by the INS are healthier than the ones known to the INS. We may speculate that migrants willing to endure the hardships of illegality must be healthier and that the skill necessary to avoid detection is correlated with health.

Table 16-4 also provides an indication of selective attrition. On average, the health assessment at the 6-month round is higher among those who were also interviewed at the 12-month round. Though the difference is tiny, this result suggests that the less healthy—and/or those who reported themselves as less healthy at the 6-month round—did not participate in the 12-month round.

When we compare reported health at the two rounds for individuals, we find that 49% registered no change in their health, while 29% reported greater healthiness at the 12-month round and 22% reported themselves to be less healthy at the 12-month round. Of course, as discussed above, the measure confounds four separate components of health. For a sharper view of health changes, we turn to the multivariate, fixed-effects estimates.

Table 16-5 reports the estimates of the fixed-effects specifications in which the health assessment is treated as quantitative (1 = poor health and 5 = excellent health). For a more accurate implementation of the model, the sample is restricted to immigrants without conditionality restrictions on their admission to permanent residence—thus, newlywed spouses of U.S. citizens are excluded, as are two respondents with conditional investor visas; additionally,

---

*See Jasso et al. (2002) for further discussion of selectivity and its links to visa category.

TABLE 16-4. Average Subjective Health Assessment at 6-month and 12-month Rounds, by Personal and Visa Characteristics: FY 1996 Immigrants Aged 18+ Years

Characteristic	6-month round		12-month round
	All	In 12-month round	
Sex			
Male	3.712	3.729	3.856
Female	3.598	3.606	3.671
Visa category			
Spouse of US citizen, > 2 years	3.864	3.871	3.935
Spouse of US citizen, < 2 years	4.112	4.102	4.181
Parent of US citizen	2.903	2.862	2.898
Sibling of US citizen, principal	3.538	3.538	3.538
Sibling of US citizen, spouse	3.75	3.684	3.632
Employment-based, principal	4.146	4.138	4.158
Employment-based, spouse	3.933	3.939	4.052
Refugee	2.778	2.793	3.073
Diversity, principal	3.6	3.536	3.536
Diversity, spouse	3.8	3.8	3.533
Spouse of permanent resident	3.2	3.203	3.541
Other	3.806	3.847	3.914
Illegal experience			
None	3.618	3.631	3.721
Eluded detection by INS	3.837	3.853	3.889
Known to INS	3.657	3.658	3.810
Continent of birth			
Africa	4.350	4.360	4.081
North America	3.683	3.678	3.808
South America	3.805	3.808	3.930
Asia	3.5	3.531	3.715
Europe	3.531	3.539	3.541
Oceania	4.75	4.75	4.5
Religious preference			
Catholic	3.676	3.676	3.775
Protestant	3.799	3.802	3.944
Muslim	3.971	3.971	3.867
Jewish	2.830	2.830	3.02
Buddhist	3.404	3.404	3.629
Hindu	4.186	4.186	3.833
Orthodox Christian	3.514	3.514	3.523
Other religion	3.268	3.268	3.493
No religion	3.409	3.409	3.578
All immigrants	3.747	3.755	3.842
Number of respondents	1028	969	973

Notes: Health assessment is a five-category rating with 1 = poor and 5 = excellent. Estimates are based on weighted data, to adjust for oversampling employment-based immigrants. Spouses of U.S. citizens are distinguished according to whether they have been married less than 2 years and, thus, have only conditional permanent residence.

TABLE 16-5. Fixed-effects Estimates of Subjective Health
Assessment: FY 1996 Immigrants Aged 25–59 Years

	Specification	
Variable	(1)	(2)
Interviewed in English	0.243	0.249
	(2.00)	(2.07)
Time between interviews	0.0000822	0.0000348
(days)	(0.44)	(0.19)
Understands English		
Not very well	—	− 0.0442
		(0.23)
Average	—	0.269
		(1.21)
Fairly well	—	0.461
		(1.89)
Very well	—	0.655
		(2.51)
Speaks English		
Not very well	—	− 0.122
		(0.80)
Average	—	− 0.0883
		(0.49)
Fairly well	—	0.0657
		(0.31)
Very well	—	0.0725
		(0.31)
R-squared	0.820	0.828
Number of respondents	631	630

Notes: Analysis excludes immigrants with conditional permanent residence
(mostly spouses of U.S. citizens who have been married less than 2 years).
Absolute values of t-ratio appear in parentheses beneath coefficients. English
language skill coefficients in the second specification are jointly significant at
the 0.007 level (F-ratio with 8 and 610 degrees of freedom = 2.65).

the sample is restricted to immigrants in the 25–59 age range. Two specifications are reported,
one with and one without the English-language skill variables. As discussed above, the interview language variable is included to capture cultural effects on the style of reporting, and the
English language skill variables are included so that the culture effect is not contaminated by
English language skill. As shown, the estimated effect of the time between interviews is positive but negligible in magnitude and not significant.

Assuming that the time coefficient captures the effects of U.S. exposure on the transitory
component of health, the results suggest that if recovery from the immigration process
stresses is complete by the time of the 6-month interview, then the effect of U.S. exposure is
non-negative. If recovery is not yet complete, then a negative effect of U.S. exposure cannot
be ruled out, as it could be offset or dominated by the positive recovery effect. Because by the
first observation point, more than 1 year has passed since admission to permanent residence,
we believe that these results indicate that the effect of U.S. exposure in the approximately
9 months between the two rounds is either zero or positive. Of course, the U.S. exposure
effect in this initial period of residence may contain a negative effect of the initial adjustment
to life in a new locale. If so, the effect of dietary and environmental aspects would be positive and offset by the negative adjustment effect.

This interpretation assumes that age is not a factor—in part because the period of time between interviews is small, in part because the analysis is confined to immigrants under age 60. Of course, if the time effect includes a negative aging effect, then the possibility of a negative U.S. exposure effect is even smaller.

Note that in the full NIS respondents will be followed indefinitely, so that at some point it will be possible to declare the recovery period as well as the initial adjustment period complete so that all subsequent time effects reflect the operation of only U.S. exposure—and age.

The effect of interview language is positive, as predicted, and unambiguously statistically significant. As discussed above, this effect is presumed to operate on the transitory component of the style of reporting. The fact that the coefficient remains almost exactly the same even when the English language variables are included increases our confidence that it is a pure culture effect, affecting style of reporting only and not healthiness.

Meanwhile, the English skill variables are jointly significant and the coefficients roughly consistent with a pattern in which, as widely conjectured, investments in health go hand in hand with investments in other forms of human capital.

Table 16-6 reports the results of the ordered-logit specifications in which all variables are expressed as changes over time. The U.S. exposure effect is negative but not significant, suggesting that the effect of U.S. exposure is negligible, although it may be positive and offset by a negative adjustment effect in the initial period of residence.

TABLE 16-6. **Ordered Logit Estimates of whether Health Improved, Stayed the Same, or Deteriorated: FY 1996 Immigrants Aged 25–59 Years**

	Specification	
Variable	(1)	(2)
Interview language		
No change	0.566	0.582
	(1.41)	(1.45)
Change from other language	0.876	0.947
to English	(1.71)	(1.83)
Time between interviews	−0.00129	−0.00140
(days)	(1.37)	(1.48)
Understands English		
No change	—	0.524
		(2.12)
Improvement	—	0.579
		(1.91)
Speaks English		
No change	—	0.291
		(1.21)
Improvement	—	0.350
		(1.18)
Cut 1	−0.968	−0.280
Cut 2	1.437	2.159
Number of respondents	625	625

Notes: Analysis excludes immigrants with conditional permanent residence (mostly spouses of U.S. citizens who have been married less than 2 years). Absolute values of z appear in parentheses beneath coefficients. English language skill coefficients in the second specification are jointly significant at the 0.0295 level (χ^2 with 4 degrees of freedom = 10.75).

The language variables behave in a similar way as in the specifications reported in Table 16-5. The interview language variables, though not significant, operate in the expected direction—using English as the interview language increases a positive health assessment. The English skill variables are jointly statistically significant and again suggest that investments in health are associated with investments in language skills.

Taken together, the results of both sets of analyses indicate that language use is implicated in the style of reporting healthiness, that improvements in English language skill are associated with improvements in observed healthiness, and that the effect of U.S. exposure per se is negligible. We cannot reject the hypothesis that the effect of U.S. exposure is zero.

The larger sample size of the full NIS will make possible many further analyses, such as estimation of fixed-effects models within subsets of the sample, defined by visa category, say, or sex. As discussed above, it is possible that the steepness of the recovery and the length of the recovery period may differ systematically by such characteristics as visa category or sex. Moreover, the effects of U.S. exposure may also differ systematically by visa or other characteristics. Additionally, information on migration history will enable pinpointing the date of inception of U.S. residence as well as controlling for previous time spent in the United States, so that the effects of U.S. exposure and adjustment to a new locale can be distinguished. Although the NIS samples immigrants just after admission to legal permanent residence, NIS data will enable preliminary assessment of the immigration process decline in healthiness in two ways: first, by asking for a self-report of healthiness at the time the immigration application process started and, second, because it may happen, fortuitously, that the spouses or household partners of some sampled immigrants, who themselves will also be interviewed, may be involved in the visa application process.

It is also useful to speculate about the conditions under which we would expect a negative time trend in the health of immigrants. In our model, the transitory component of health deteriorates during the visa application period and deteriorates among illegal migrants. If a sample includes persons who are not legal permanent residents, then it is eminently possible that their health is deteriorating over time. Attentiveness to visa status is thus important in understanding immigrant health.

In this illustration, the first two central questions in the study of migration are addressed empirically via a model of the immigrant health trajectory that begins with the initial decision to immigrate to the United States and continues through the visa application process, admission to legal permanent residence, and for over 1 year afterwards. We are working in the top subpanel of the empirical panel of the triptych of migration analysis (Figures 16-1 and 16-2), and that work spans the first two rows of Table 16-1, reflecting all four themes of the life course perspective.

CONCLUDING NOTE

In this chapter we provided an overview of migration analysis from the life course perspective, taking as our point of departure (1) the four central questions of migration analysis and (2) the four themes in the life course perspective identified by Elder (1994). Because migration unfolds over the life course, its analysis is naturally suited to the life course perspective. Migration analysis from the life course perspective provides a coherent framework for examining the parts played by cohort and context, age and duration, the myriad of interactions and relationships embodied and generated in the migration process, and the strategies and decisions of all the actors in the migration process.

We presented two illustrations of migration analysis from the life course perspective, a theoretical illustration and an empirical illustration.

In the theoretical illustration, we used justice and status theory, together with a proposition which goes back to the Greeks and which has recently been analyzed by Blau (1964), to derive predictions for the propensity to emigrate. This work distinguishes between three basic world-views—justice–materialistic, in which individuals and societies care about justice and value material goods, justice–non-materialistic, in which individuals and societies care about justice and value non-material goods, and status, in which individuals and societies care about status (and may care about either material or non-material goods). The predictions indicate that, while in justice–materialistic societies, emigration may be from the bottom or the top of social hierarchies, in justice–non-materialistic societies emigration is likely to be from the bottom and in status societies from the top. The precise configuration of emigration from the bottom and top in justice–materialistic societies depends on the shape of the income distribution and its overall inequality. Moreover, in justice–materialistic societies, the total proportion with a positive propensity to emigrate is an increasing function of the overall inequality in the income distribution.

In the empirical illustration, we developed a model of the immigrant health trajectory that distinguishes between (1) health at the initial selection into migration, (2) health deterioration during the (stressful) process of applying for immigration, (3) recovery and health improvement after admission to legal permanent residence, and (4) the possible effect (positive or negative) of exposure to the U.S. environment. We estimated the model using data from the NIS-P. Two sets of analyses yielded non-significant results of opposite sign and negligible magnitude for the effect of U.S. exposure. Thus, we cannot reject the hypothesis that U.S. exposure per se has no effect on observed health, although, concomitantly, investments in health made possible by higher income and health-enhancing opportunities in the United States may be producing improvements in health. Results also indicate a culture effect in the subjective evaluation of health, with immigrants interviewed in English providing more optimistic assessments, net of English language skill. Substantially sharper analyses will be possible with the data from the full NIS, the baseline round of which will go in the field in mid-2003.

Migration, like the life course perspective, is about human development. And human development is a lifelong concern. Migration analysis from the life course perspective may provide substantial positive synergies and illuminate human development in a new way.

ACKNOWLEDGMENT: Support for the New Immigrant Survey Pilot was generously provided by the National Institutes of Health under grant HD33843, with partial support from the National Science Foundation and the Immigration and Naturalization Service. I am grateful to colleagues at those institutions as well as to my fellow Principal Investigators, Douglas S. Massey, Mark R. Rosenzweig, and James P. Smith, for many stimulating discussions of immigration questions and research.

REFERENCES

Barrett, A. (1996). Did the decline continue? Comparing the labor-market quality of United States immigrants from the late 1970s and late 1980s. *Journal of Population Economics, 9*, 57–63.

Berger, J., & Zelditch, M., Jr. (1993). Orienting strategies and theory growth. In J. Berger and M. Zelditch, Jr. (Eds.), *Theoretical research programs: Studies in the growth of theory* (pp. 3–19, references 453–454). Stanford, CA: Stanford University Press.

Blau, P. M. (1964). *Exchange and power in social life*. New York: Wiley & Sons.

Borjas, G. J. (1985). Assimilation, changes in cohort quality, and the earnings of immigrants. *Journal of Labor Economics, 3*, 463–489.

Clausen, J. S. (1991). Adolescent competence and the shaping of the life course. *American Journal of Sociology, 96*, 805–842.

Clausen, John A. (1993). American Lives: Looking Back at the Children of the Great Depression. Berkeley: University of California Press.

Cobb-Clark, D. A. (1993). Immigrant selectivity and wages: The evidence for women. *American Economic Review, 83*, 986–993.

Committee on the Health and Safety Implications of Child Labor, Board on Children, Youth, and Families, National Research Council/Institute of Medicine. (1998). *Protecting youth at work: Health, safety, and development of working children and adolescents in the United States*. Washington, DC: National Academies Press.

Duleep, H. O., & Regets, M. C. (1996). Admission criteria and immigrant earnings profiles. *International Migration Review, 30*, 571–590.

Elder, G. H., Jr. (1994). Time, human agency, and social change: Perspectives on the life course. *Social Psychology Quarterly, 57*, 4–15.

England, P., Kilbourne, B. S., & Farkas, G. (1988). Explaining occupational sex segregation and wages: Findings from a model with fixed effects. *American Sociological Review, 53*, 544–558.

Evans, M., Hastings, N., & Peacock, B. (2000). *Statistical Distributions* (3rd ed.). New York: Wiley & Sons.

Frisbie, W. P., Cho, Y., & Hummer, R. (2001). Immigration and the health of Asian and Pacific Islander adults in the United States. *American Journal of Epidemiology, 153*, 372–380.

Goode, W. J. (1978). *The celebration of heroes: Prestige as a control system*. Berkeley, CA: University of California Press.

Grossman, M. (1972). On the concept of health capital and the demand for health. *Journal of Political Economy, 80*, 223–255.

Hernandez, D. J., & Charney, E. (Eds.) (1998). *From generation to generation: The health and well-being of children in immigrant families*. (Report of the National Research Council and the Institute of Medicine). Washington, DC: National Academy Press.

Jasso, G. (1978). On the justice of earnings: A new specification of the justice evaluation function. *American Journal of Sociology, 83*, 1398–1419.

Jasso, G. (1985). Marital coital frequency and the passage of time: estimating the separate effects of spouses' ages and marital duration, birth and marriage cohorts, and period influences. *American Sociological Review, 50*, 224–241.

Jasso, G. (1987). Choosing a good: Models based on the theory of the distributive-justice force. *Advances in Group Processes: Theory and Research, 4*, 67–108.

Jasso, G. (1996). Deriving implications of comparison theory for demographic phenomena: A first step in the analysis of migration. *The Sociological Quarterly, 37*, 19–57.

Jasso, G. (1997). Migration and the dynamics of family phenomena. In A. Booth, A. C. Crouter, & N. Landale (Eds.), *Immigration and the family: Research and policy on U.S. immigrants* (pp. 63–77). Mahwah, NJ: Lawrence Erlbaum.

Jasso, G. (1999). How much injustice is there in the world? Two new justice indexes. *American Sociological Review, 64*, 133–168.

Jasso, G. (2001a). Comparison theory. In J. H. Turner (Ed.), *Handbook of sociological theory* (pp. 669–698). New York: Kluwer Academic/Plenum Press.

Jasso, G. (2001b). Formal theory. In J. H. Turner (Ed.), *Handbook of sociological theory* (pp. 37–68). New York: Kluwer Academic/Plenum Press.

Jasso, G. (2001c). Studying status: An integrated framework. *American Sociological Review, 66*, 96–124.

Jasso, G. (2002a). Seven secrets for doing theory. In J. Berger and M. Zelditch, Jr. (Eds.), *New directions in contemporary sociological theory* (pp. 328–354). Boulder, CO: Rowman and Littlefield Press.

Jasso, G. (2002b). *Justice, status, and migration*. Presented at the Quadrennial Meeting of the International Sociological Association, Brisbane, Australia.

Jasso, G. (in press). The tripartite structure of social science analysis. *Sociological Theory*.

Jasso, G., Massey, D. S., Rosenzweig, M. R., & Smith, J. P. (2000a). Assortative mating among married new legal immigrants to the United States: Evidence from the New Immigrant Survey Pilot. *International Migration Review, 34*, 443–459.

Jasso, G., Massey, D. S., Rosenzweig, M. R., & Smith, J. P. (2000b). Family, schooling, religiosity, and mobility among new legal immigrants to the United States: Evidence from the new immigrant survey pilot. In L. F. Tomasi and M. G. Powers (Eds.), *Immigration today: Pastoral and research challenges* (pp. 52–81). Staten Island, NY: Center for Migration Studies.

Jasso, G., Massey, D. S., Rosenzweig, M. R., & Smith, J. P. (2000c). The New Immigrant Survey Pilot (NIS-P): Overview and new findings about U.S. legal immigrants at admission. *Demography, 37,* 127–138.

Jasso, G., Massey, D. S., Rosenzweig, M. R., & Smith, J. P. (2003). Exploring the religious preference of recent immigrants to the United States: Evidence from the New Immigrant Survey Pilot. In Y. Haddad, J. I. Smith, and J. L. Esposito (Eds.), *Religion and Immigration: Christian, Jewish, and Muslim Experiences in the United States.* Oxford, UK: Oxford University Press.

Jasso, G., Massey, D. S., Rosenzweig, M. R., & Smith, J. P. (2002). *Immigrant health—selectivity and acculturation.* Paper prepared for the National Academy of Sciences Conference on Racial and Ethnic Disparities in Health, Washington, DC.

Jasso, G., & Rosenzweig, M. R. (1990). *The new chosen people: Immigrants in the United States* (a volume in *The population of the United States in the 1980s: A census monograph series*). New York: Russell Sage.

Jasso, G., & Rosenzweig, M. R. (1995). Do immigrants screened for skills do better than family-reunification immigrants? *International Migration Review, 29,* 85–111. (Reprinted in K. F. Zimmerman (Ed.), *The Economics of Migration* Elgar Press, 2002.)

Jasso, G., Rosenzweig, M. R., & Smith, J. P. (2000). The changing skill of new immigrants to the United States: Recent trends and their determinants. In G. J. Borjas (Ed.), *Issues in the Economics of Immigration* (pp. 185–225). Chicago, IL: University of Chicago Press.

Johnson, N. L., & Kotz, S. (1969). *Distributions in statistics: Discrete distributions.* New York: Wiley.

Johnson, N. L., & Kotz, S. (1970a). *Distributions in statistics: Continuous univariate distributions—1.* Boston, MA: Houghton Mifflin.

Johnson, N. L., & Kotz, S. (1970b). *Distributions in statistics: Continuous univariate distributions—2.* Boston, MA: Houghton Mifflin.

Kasl, S. V., & Berkman, L. (1983). Health consequences of the experience of migration. *Annual Review of Public Health, 4,* 69–90.

Kilbourne, B. S., England, P., & Beron, K. (1994). Effects of individual, occupational, and individual characteristics on earnings: Interaction of race and gender. *Social Forces, 72,* 1149–1176.

Loaeza Tovar, E. M., Planck, C., Gómez Arnau, R., Martin, S., Lowell, B. L., & Meyers, D. W. (Eds.) (with contributions by Bean, F. D., Corona, R., Tuirán, R., Woodrow-Lafield, K., Bustamante, J., Jasso, G., Taylor, J. E., Trigueros, P., Escobar Latapí, A., Martin, P., Donato, K., Lopez Castro, G., Tienda, M., Verduzco, G., Greenwood, M., Unger, K., Alba, F., Weintraub, S., Fernández de Castro, R., García, M., & Griego) (1997). *Report of the Binational Study of Migration between Mexico and the United States.* Washington, DC: U.S. Commission on Immigration Reform (English): (Mexico, DF: Mexican Ministry of Foreign Affairs) (Spanish).

Mayer, Karl-Ulrich. (1986). Structural Constraints on the Life Course. *Human Development 29,* 163–170.

Merton, R. K. [1949, 1957] (1968). *Social theory and social structure.* New York: Free Press.

Moses, L. E. (1968). Statistical analysis: Truncation and censorship. In D. L. Sills (Ed.), *International encyclopedia of the social sciences* (Vol. 15, pp. 196–201). New York: Macmillan.

Parsons, T. (1968). Émile Durkheim. In D. L. Sills (Ed.), *International Encyclopedia of the Social Sciences* (Vol. 4, pp. 311–320). New York: Macmillan.

Portes, A., & Rumbaut, R. G. (2001). *Legacies: The story of the immigrant second generation.* Berkeley, CA: University of California Press.

Riding, A. (2002). Unlikely star captivates the French. *New York Times,* April 4.

Riley, Matilda White. (1986). The Dynamisms of Life Stages – Roles, People, and Age. *Human Development 29,* 150–156.

Rumbaut, R. G., & Weeks, J. (1996). Unraveling a public health enigma; Why do immigrants experience superior prenatal health outcomes? *Research in the Sociology of Health Care, 13B,* 337–391.

Seeman, T. E., Singer, B. H., Rowe, J. W., Horwitz, R. I., & McEwen, B. S. (1997). Price of adaptation—allostatic load and its health consequences. *Archives of Internal Medicine, 157,* 2259–2268.

Simmel, G. [1896–1917] (1950). *The sociology of Georg Simmel* (K. H. Wolff, Trans., Edited, Introduction). New York: Free Press.

Smith, J. P. (1999). Healthy bodies and thick wallets: The dual relation between health and economic status. *Journal of Economic Perspectives, 13,* 145–166.

Smith, J. P., & Edmonston, B. (Eds.) (1997). *The new Americans: Economic, demographic, and fiscal effects of immigration* (Report of the National Research Council). Washington, DC: National Academy Press.

Sørensen, A. B. (1979). A model and a metric for the analysis of the intragenerational status attainment process. *American Journal of Sociology, 85,* 361–384.

Stevens, S. S. (1975). In G. Stevens (Ed.), *Psychophysics: an introduction to its perceptual, neural, and social prospects.* New York: Wiley.

Strauss, J., & Thomas, D. (1998). Health, nutrition, and economic development. *Journal of Economic Literature, 36*, 766–817.

Stryker, S. (2001). Traditional symbolic interactionism, role theory, and structural symbolic interactionism: The road to identity theory. In J. H. Turner (Ed.), *Handbook of sociological theory* (pp. 211–231). New York: Kluwer Academic/Plenum Press.

Stuart, A., & Ord, J. K. (1987). *Kendall's advanced theory of statistics. Volume 1: Distribution theory* (5th ed.). New York: Oxford University Press.

Summers, R., & Heston, A. (1991). The Penn World Table (mark 5): An expanded set of international comparisons, 1950–1988. *Quarterly Journal of Economics, 106*, 327–368.

Thomas, W. I., & Znaniecki, F. [1918–1920] (1958). *The Polish peasant in Europe and America* (2 Vols.). New York: Dover.

U.S. Department of Justice. (2001). *Immigrants admitted into the United States as legal permanent residents, fiscal year 1972 through fiscal year 1998.* Springfield, VA: National Technical Information Service.

U.S. Immigration and Naturalization Service. (1943–1978). *Annual Report of the Immigration and Naturalization Service.* Washington, DC: U.S. Government Printing Office.

——. (1979–). *Statistical Yearbook of the Immigration and Naturalization Service.* Washington, DC: U.S. Government Printing Office.

U.S. Immigration and Naturalization Service. (1992). *Immigration Reform and Control Act: Report on the legalized alien population.* Washington, DC: U.S. Government Printing Office.

Vega, W., & Amaro, H. (1994). Latino outlook: Good health, uncertain prognosis. *Annual Review of Public Health, 15*, 39–67.

Wallace, R. B., & Herzog, R. (1995). Overview of the health measures in the Health and Retirement Study. *The Journal of Human Resources, 30*, S84–S107.

Wallerstein, I. (2002). The itinerary of world-systems analysis; Or, how to resist becoming a theory. In J. Berger & M. Zelditch, Jr. (Eds.), *New directions in contemporary sociological theory.* Boulder, CO: Rowman and Littlefield Press.

Ware, J., Davies-Avery, A., & Donald, C. (1978). *General health perceptions.* Santa Monica, CA: RAND.

PART V

LIFE COURSE
CONSTRUCTION

A. Agency

CHAPTER 17

Self-Agency and the Life Course

Viktor Gecas

The course of our lives is shaped by many forces and events, not the least of which by ourselves. For good and bad, we are to a large extent architects of our life course. Within the constraints imposed by biology, history, social structure, good and bad fortune, and other factors we may or may not be aware of, we try to control the direction of our lives by exerting our will, pursuing our goals, and affecting our circumstances. While we are indeed products of social and physical forces, we are also causal agents in the construction of our environments and ourselves.

At the core of human agency is the self. It is involved in most cognitive and affective processes, such as regulating perception, processing experience, memory, emotion, and motivation. The self as a source of agency is a prominent feature of most contemporary social psychological theories, especially symbolic interactionism. The view of the self as an active and creative agent in its environment—managing impressions, making decisions, negotiating, controlling, manipulating, deceiving, etc.—is, in Blumer's (1969) terms, one of the "root images" of symbolic interactionism, eloquently demonstrated in Goffman's (1959) insightful observations of impression management and self-presentation in everyday interactions. Emphasis on self-agency is also conspicuous within cognitive social psychology. Baumeister (1999) calls it the self's "executive function," involved in making choices, taking responsibility, initiating action, and exerting control over the environment. Snyder (1981) maintains that individuals play a very active part in choosing, influencing, and structuring the situations in their lives, in keeping with their self-conceptions as well as other attitudes and dispositions. Also, self-agency is central to Bandura's (1982, 2001) sociocognitive theory of self-efficacy, which views people as agentic, self-reflecting, self-regulating, creative, and proactive and not

Viktor Gecas • Departments of Sociology and Rural Sociology, Washington State University, Pullman, Washington 99164-4020.

Handbook of the Life Course, edited by Jeylan T. Mortimer and Michael J. Shanahan. Kluwer Academic/Plenum Publishers, New York, 2003.

simply reactive creatures shaped by external events. For Bandura and these other self-theorists, the self is at the heart of causal and agentic processes.

Reflexivity, the defining quality of the self for Mead (1934) and most self-theorists, is a major source of the self's agency. Reflexivity refers to the capacity of humans to be both subjects ("I") and objects ("me") to themselves, to reflect on themselves, and to act toward themselves as objects. Reflexivity enables a wide range of what Rosenberg (1988) calls self-objectification processes, such as self-evaluation, self-control, self-criticism, and self-motivation. These self-objectification processes are typically guided by one's self-concept, also a self-objectification consisting of role identities, values, morals, aspirations, and other elements of self-definition. Reflexivity, therefore, is the foundation for numerous, more specific manifestations of the self's agency.

Of the various specific manifestations and mechanisms of self-agency, none is more important than people's beliefs in their causative and agentic capabilities, that is, in their self-efficacy (Bandura, 1997). Self-efficacy is an aspect of the self-concept critically relevant to agency and motivation. It refers to the perception of oneself as a causal agent in one's environment, as having some control over one's circumstances, and being capable of carrying out actions to produce intended effects. Individuals with high self-efficacy think of themselves as competent, effective, and able. Those with low self-efficacy are more likely to see themselves as powerless, helpless, and fatalistic. A large body of evidence has accumulated on the beneficial consequences of self-efficacy for individual functioning and well-being (e.g., academic and occupational achievement, recovery from illness, general physical and mental health, life satisfaction). Much of this research is provided by Bandura and his colleagues (see Bandura, 1997, for a review).

Such beliefs are a major basis of action and inaction over the life course. Those with high self-efficacy, especially in such consequential domains as education, interpersonal relations, and occupational contexts, are more likely to be architects of their lives and to see themselves as such. Those with a low sense of personal efficacy are more likely to see their lives as products of forces and circumstances beyond their control. The life courses of both types of persons may correspond to their self-efficacy expectations, since there is a self-fulfilling prophecy element to such beliefs.

There is also a motivational component to self-efficacy. People are motivated to *experience* themselves as causal, efficacious agents. White's (1959) concept of "effectance motivation" emphasized the motivational aspect of self-efficacy. He conceptualized effectance motivation as intrinsic and pleasurable, typically expressed in such activities as play, exploration, and creativity. Baumeister (1999) states that "the nature of the self includes a strong desire for control and choice. The motive to control is as pervasive and as well established as the motivation for self-esteem. Moreover, the desire to achieve control is more beneficial and adaptive than the desire for esteem" (p. 12). A number of other theories, such as DeCharms (1979) theory of personal causation and Deci's (1979; Ryan & Deci, 2000) theory of self-determination (see Gecas, 1989, for a review), have stressed the experience of agency, control, and efficacy as powerful motivations in personal and interpersonal conduct.

The motivational significance of self-efficacy is underscored not only by the efforts people expend in developing and maintaining this self-motive, which may involve self-improvement as well as self-deception, but also in observations of what happens when self-efficacy is undermined or destroyed. Seligman's (1975) theory of "learned helplessness" deals with the chronic sense of inefficacy resulting from learning that one's actions have no effect on one's environment, leading to apathy and depression. Many aspects of modern societies can undermine self-efficacy, with negative consequences for individual wellbeing.

A major basis of Marx's critique of capitalism was that it undermined workers' sense of agency and efficacy by depriving workers of control over the products of their labor, thereby leaving them powerless and alienated. The inability to affect outcomes in other spheres of life, such as government, school, or even one's family, can lead to a sense of powerlessness and alienation as well. The amount of control one has is, of course, a matter of degree and is typically relative to specific domains. Sense of control, agency, and efficacy in one domain (e.g., the workplace) may or may not carry over into another domain, such as family. Nevertheless, people are motivated to feel efficacious in the important spheres of their lives.

Self-efficacy is an important self-motive both in its own right and in its relationship to other self-motives, especially self-esteem and self-authenticity (Gecas, 1991, 2001)—two other components of self-agency. Self-authenticity refers to the motivation to experience oneself as meaningful, real, and true to one's core values and standards. Much of authenticity involves the moral domain of self-conception (Taylor, 1989). Agency directed towards moral conduct involves self-sanctions as well as actions guided by moral standards and precepts (Bandura, 2001). Self-efficacy in the form of moral agency (i.e., the perception of one's ability to live up to one's values and moral standards) is relevant to this self-motive. With regard to the self-esteem motive, that is, the motivation to have a positive view of oneself, self-efficacy as reflected in efficacious action is an important source of self-esteem and is a more solid basis than favorable reflected appraisals for maintaining a positive self-image (Gecas & Schwalbe, 1983).

As a major aspect of the self's agency, self-efficacy is a key factor in life course construction. Actions are more likely to be initiated, goals and plans are more likely to be pursued, efforts to change oneself and one's circumstances are more likely to be undertaken by those with a strong sense of self-efficacy and personal agency. The vision of one's desired future self in the form of goals and aspirations (what Markus & Nurius [1986] call "possible selves" and Buhler & Massarik [1968] conceptualized as "the goal-directed life") is more likely to be actualized by those with high self-efficacy. One's life course is more likely to be viewed as one's own construction by those with high self-efficacy. Those with a low sense of personal efficacy are more likely to feel little control over the direction and course of their lives, to view their lives as products of external forces beyond their control.

Some empirical evidence for the long-term consequences of efficacy beliefs developed in childhood and adolescence for the course of adult lives is provided by Elder (1974) and Clausen (1993), both utilizing the same unique longitudinal data sets of the Berkeley and Oakland studies. Elder's (1974) influential study *Children of the Great Depression* demonstrated (among many other findings) how the experience of economic hardship by adolescent boys had beneficial consequences later in their lives. These boys were called upon and were able to contribute to their families' resources during the Great Depression, often when the father was out of work, thereby gaining confidence, self-efficacy, and higher status within the family. These agency-relevant qualities contributed to economic, educational, and even marital success in later life. By contrast, the younger cohort of boys (the Berkeley sample) were too young to be of much help to their families, while still suffering the privations of the Great Depression. Their self-efficacy and self-worth suffered as a result and had negative consequences later in their life course. Similarly, Clausen (1993) found that a cluster of personality characteristics which he called "planful competence" (in which self-confidence is a prominent component), measured during the adolescent years of the Oakland and Berkeley cohorts, had pronounced effects over the life course. Adolescents high in planful competence, through their actions and the choices they made, set their life courses on trajectories leading to greater economic and personal success later in life.

The consequences of planful competence during adolescence, however, are not uniformly positive or consequential, but rather are contingent on historical circumstance (Shanahan, Elder, & Meich, 1997; Shanahan, Hofer, & Miech, 2002). Drawing on the longitudinal data from the Stanford–Terman sample, Shanahan et al. (1997) found that planful competence of adolescents has little consequence for later life when historical circumstances substantially restrict occupational or educational choices. They found that, for men whose lives were severely disrupted by the Great Depression and World War II, high levels of planfulness did not matter for later life. By contrast, for men born a few years later (the younger cohort), these same historical events were less disrupting for their life course and the levels of planfulness of these men had significant consequences for their occupational attainment and marital stability.

One of the major principles of life course theory, as developed by Elder (1995, 1997), is the importance of human agency in life course construction: "Individuals construct their own life course through the choices and actions they take within the constraints and opportunities of history and social circumstances" (p. 961). However, people vary greatly in their sense of self-efficacy and control over the direction of their lives. And these beliefs regarding personal agency have important consequences for the direction and outcome of their lives. Self-efficacy is not the only aspect of human agency or even self-agency, but it is among the most important. In the pages that follow, I will discuss the processes and factors affecting the development of self-efficacy within significant contexts of interaction at key points in the life course. I will also consider how some of these processes and outcomes regarding self-efficacy vary by gender, race, class, and culture.

THE DEVELOPMENT OF SELF-EFFICACY

Self-efficacy, which encompasses the individual's beliefs about personal agency, causality, and competence, develops primarily out of the interactions between individual and environment. Specifically, it is the environment's *responsiveness* to the individual's actions that is critical to the development of self-efficacy, as well as the development of mind and self in general (Mead, 1934; Piaget, 1954). Among the earliest and most important lessons that the infant learns is that events are causally related (e.g., shaking a rattle produces a sound) and that the infant can produce that effect. Causing things to happen is the means by which the infant begins to understand causality and to exercise some control over its environment. The process begins very early in life, within the first few months. The developmental progression of the sense of personal agency goes from perceiving causal relations between events, to understanding causation through action, and finally to recognizing oneself as the agent of the action (Bandura, 1997, p. 164). The quality of the environment matters. Environments that are responsive to the infant's actions promote the development of causal agency, whereas those that are unresponsive to the infant's actions or where events occur independently of the infant's actions retard the development of personal agency. Watson's (1977) experiments with mobiles over infants' cribs supported this proposition. He found that mobiles that responded (i.e., made sounds and motions) to the infant's actions, such as touching or kicking, accelerated the development of agency (and other cognitive abilities) in infants, whereas the automatic (wind-up) mobiles did not. The intentional production of effects and the recognition that they produced it creates the initial, rudimentary sense of personal agency in infants, even before the emergence of "self" (which requires language and role taking). However, with the acquisition of language (around age 2), the development of personal agency becomes intertwined with the developing self and self-efficacy and the range of environmental processes affecting self-agency greatly increases.

Although efficacious actions continue to be the most important source of self-efficacy, beyond infancy other sources that depend more on symbolic interaction emerge as consequential. Bandura (1997) discusses three other sources of efficacy information: vicarious experience (i.e., seeing others successfully perform challenging or dangerous activities), verbal persuasion (i.e., information from others about one's abilities), and emotional arousal (i.e., inferences individuals make about their capabilities from their emotional states, such as fear). But the most effective source of efficacy information remains the individual's actions and their consequences. Not surprisingly, these processes overlap with the more general processes of self-concept formation: self-attribution, social comparison, and reflected appraisals, which are all relevant to the development of self-efficacy, but not equally so. Self-attribution refers to the process of making inferences about oneself from observing one's behavior and its consequences. As discussed above, inferences about one's efficacy and competence are often based on observations of one's performance. Such self-observations are the most important source of efficacy beliefs. It should be noted, however, that a person's self-efficacy corresponds only roughly to self-observations of performance or actions. Usually there is plenty of room for misinterpretation (especially if standards of evaluation are ambiguous) and the occurrence of rationalization, disclaimers, excuses, the "illusion of control," and other manifestations of bias and self-defense are not uncommon. Of course, distortions and illusions apply to most other aspects of self-concept as well. Self-motives are the main sources of distortion in the perception and processing of self-relevant information. People utilize various mechanisms in order to protect a positive self-image, self-efficacy, and self-authenticity.

The processes of social comparison and reflected appraisals also affect self-efficacy. Our judgment of how we compare to others on some ability or achievement factors into our sense of self-efficacy. Social comparison processes are pervasive in peer group interactions, as well as sibling relations. Reflected appraisals refer to our perceptions of how others, especially significant others, view and evaluate us. Evaluative feedback from significant others, such as parents, teachers, mentors, or friends, regarding our abilities and accomplishments can be expected to affect our self-efficacy, depending on the importance of the ability or accomplishment evaluated, the credibility of the source, and other qualifiers. Mechanisms of self-defense and distortion operate in muting the influence of reflected appraisals and social comparison processes, as they do in self-attributions, in affecting the development of self-efficacy. These defenses and distortions are another manifestation of the self's agency.

The quality of the individual–environment interaction, primarily with regard to the opportunities it provides for engaging in efficacious action (i.e., a stimulating, challenging, responsive environment and the freedom to engage it), is the major condition for the development and maintenance of self-efficacy throughout a person's life. Environments vary greatly with regard to the opportunities they provide for exercising agency and self-efficacy. Social environments are characterized by social structures of various power and role relationships, differential access to resources, degree of complexity, formality, and interdependence, among other things. Occupancy of different roles or positions within a social structure—as defined, for example, by gender, class, age—gives people access to different kinds and amounts of resources and therefore different possibilities for efficacious action (Sewell, 1992). In general, the higher one's position within a social structure or stratification system, the greater one's opportunities for efficacious action and the greater one's sense of self-efficacy (Gecas & Schwalbe, 1983). We should keep in mind, however, that the relationship between individual and environment is highly reciprocal and mutually constitutive.

Social structure is both a constraint on action and a product of action (Giddens, 1984). Even though environments (social and physical) set constraints and provide differential opportunities, individuals exercise their self-efficacy (at whatever level) to select, avoid, and manipulate their environments to their own advantage.

DEVELOPMENTAL CONTEXTS OF SELF-EFFICACY

Different periods of life are associated with certain developmental or socialization contexts that present the individual with challenges and competency demands. Family, peer groups, and school are especially important developmental contexts for children and adolescents. Workplace and family of procreation are important contexts for developing self-efficacy and exercising agency for most adults. For some adults there are other important developmental contexts as well, such as the military, prison, and other voluntary and involuntary or coercive institutions. These contexts vary considerably in structure, purpose, duration, and consequences for self-efficacy.

Family

Initially, the family is the most important context for developing self-efficacy. Agency and competencies in many aspects of life develop from the family experiences of children—learning language, motor skills, knowledge of the physical and social worlds, the rules and values of one's family and how to live by them. Of the first four stages of Erikson's (1959) developmental theory, which cover the first 12 years of life, three deal directly with agency-related issues and conflicts ("autonomy," "initiative," and "industry"), mostly played out in the family context.

Parents are the most significant aspect of the family environment for the child. The child's developing sense of agency and efficacy is facilitated by parents who encourage problem solving, experimentation, exploratory behavior, learning by doing, questioning, and, in short, a learning environment that is engaging, stimulating, and responsive to the child. The voluminous research on child socialization has consistently found that parental responsiveness, support, and encouragement, use of inductive control (i.e., control that relies more on reasoning than coercion), and high achievement demands are significantly related to the development of children's self-efficacy and a number of other positive socialization outcomes, such as achievement motivation, self-confidence, self-esteem, and moral development (for reviews, see Grolnick, Deci, & Ryan, 1997; Rollins & Thomas, 1979). In particular, the combination of parental support/encouragement with the use of inductive control is most conducive to the development of competent, efficacious children, who also perceive themselves as competent and efficacious. Parents affect children's self-efficacy in other ways as well. The feedback or reflected appraisals they give with regard to their child's mastery attempts can either build the child's efficacy and confidence in further mastery attempts or squelch them. High performance expectations and supportive encouragement to pursue them can increase the child's motivation and efforts. Parents also serve as role models for their children and children may learn to be efficacious (or inefficacious) by modeling their parents.

Parents are the first and in many ways the most important teachers for their children. Children learn a great deal from their parents through direct instruction, through selective reinforcement and observation, and through the continuous feedback parents give children on their behavior—socializing children to become competent and moral adults is a big part of the job description of parents. Parents are often judged in terms of their success in developing moral agency and instrumental competence in their children, qualities that are critical in shaping the life course. It should be noted, however, that influence in the parent–child relationship is highly reciprocal, with children having a substantial effect on their parents as well as the reverse. From early infancy, children are continually asserting themselves in ways that are pleasing or displeasing to parents. These self-assertions elicit parental responses which, in turn, may affect the child's behavior and disposition. The temperament of the child (e.g., some children are active, some passive, some more rebellious, others more accommodating), as well as that of the parent and a host of other factors set the stage for the continuing reciprocal influences in parent–child relations throughout the life course.

Family structure affects children's self-efficacy in a number of ways, although the nature and valence of effects is not always clear. Children in single-parent as compared with those in two-parent families may be considered at a disadvantage in developing self-efficacy because they have fewer social and economic resources available. On the other hand, they may be given greater responsibility for household tasks and perhaps for caring for younger siblings, thereby increasing their self-efficacy and sense of worth. The self-efficacy of older children is more likely to benefit and that of younger children to suffer from this family situation, but there are many qualifying and conditional factors involved. For example, helpfulness with household chores does not necessarily contribute to adolescents' sense of competence and efficacy. Call, Mortimer, and Shanahan (1995) found that it might even have the opposite effect if it is imposed on the adolescent. The positive benefits of helpfulness may only accrue if it is voluntarily undertaken.

Family size seems to have a negative effect on children's sense of control. Blake (1989) found that children from large families did more poorly on most indicators of academic and intellectual achievement. She explained these findings in terms of resource depletion, that is economic and social resources are less available for any one child in a large family compared with a small family. Rodin (1976) found children's sense of personal control to decrease with family size. She suggests that the increase in the density of living conditions associated with large families increases the probability that events will be more unpredictable and resources, including personal "space," more constrained. Furthermore, as family size and density increase, parental control tends to become more rigid and authoritarian (Elder & Bowerman, 1963), thereby restricting children's freedom and opportunities for efficacious action. Large families may also be restrictive for parents, with negative consequences for their self-efficacy (Duncan & Morgan, 1980).

Large families also mean a large number of siblings. Sibling interaction is almost as important as parent–child interaction in shaping the child's self-efficacy and other aspects of personality and self-concept. Children are more likely to aggress against, to resist control attempts of, to compete with, and to compare themselves with siblings than with parents. Social comparison processes are pervasive in sibling relations. Siblings close in age and same sexed are most likely to engage in rivalrous comparisons. The older sibling has an advantage in these comparisons. Younger siblings compensate by trying to develop skills in areas in which their older siblings do not excel. For example, if an older sibling is good at sports, the younger sibling may try to excel in academics or, if both want to be good students (perhaps because of parental pressure), they may focus on different subjects. Such adaptations by younger siblings, what Sulloway (1996) refers to as "niche picking," diminish or neutralize to some extent the potentially negative consequences for self-efficacy and self-esteem of social comparisons with an older sibling.

Position in the sibling stratification system is a major factor in family dynamics, affecting relations with siblings as well as parents. Even though the research on birth order is notoriously problematic (Schooler, 1972), there is enough basis for extracting a few observations about the consequences of ordinal position for the child's self-efficacy and related characteristics. Conventional wisdom claims that firstborns are rule enforcers and keepers of the faith, seeking self-efficacy and self-expression in the pursuit of conventional goals, while later borns are rebels, expressing their agency in activities that challenge conventions. There is some truth in this. Sulloway (1996) provides an interesting and wide-ranging historical analysis in support of his thesis that rebels are overrepresented among later borns and that establishmentarians are overrepresented among firstborns. He finds overwhelming support for this birth order effect in his analysis of 28 important scientific controversies over the last four centuries (as well as the French Revolution and the Protestant Reformation) and the birth orders of the major figures involved (but see Modell, 1997, for a critique).

Children differently located in the sibling order experience different patterns of interaction with parents and siblings. Firstborns receive more parental attention, are more likely to be given responsibility and control over younger siblings, and have higher expectations associated with their performance. The high parental support and control they receive, combined with high performance expectations, contributes to the greater tendency of firstborns to identify with parents, to internalize parental values, to be more achievement oriented, to do better in school, and to have high self-efficacy (Adams, 1972; Zajonc, 1976). Because younger children in the birth order are subject to more child-level interaction, especially in large families and are at a power disadvantage compared to firstborns, they tend to develop better role-taking skills, enabling them to adjust to the moods and dispositions of their older siblings better. These skills also enable smoother interactions with peers. But there are many factors that mitigate these relationships, such as family size, spacing between ordinal positions, sex composition of sibship, families' social class, and parents' education level. Since research on birth order rarely takes all of these factors into account, support for birth order effects is weak and inconsistent (see Blake, 1989; Zajonc, Markus, & Markus, 1979, for critical appraisals).

Peers

Next to family, the peer group is the most important context for the development of children's self-efficacy. In terms of structure and function, the peer group is a very different developmental context from family. Peer groups are relatively voluntary associations of individuals of more or less equal age and experience and are based essentially on friendship bonds (see Crosnoe [2000] for a review of theory and research on the developmental implications of children's friendships). These conditions are most conducive to social comparison processes. Bandura (1997, p. 173) observes that, because of similarities in age and experience, peers provide the most relevant points of reference for children's efficacy appraisals and verification. Consequently, children are especially sensitive to their relative standing among their peers with regard to competence, prestige, and popularity.

Children's peer groups are typically segregated by sex and differ in organizational patterns: girls' peer groups tend to be closely knit and egalitarian friendships, whereas boys' peer groups tend to be loosely knit, larger groups, with more pronounced status hierarchies (Kuttler, LaGreca, & Prinstein, 1999; Thorne, 1993). Maccoby (1998) observes that even young children segregate play activities by gender and punish attempts of their peers at cross-sex interaction. Sex segregation in children's peer groups and friendships create subcultures of opposition between boys and girls that exaggerate gender roles and norms (Adler & Adler, 1998; Crosnoe, 2000; Thorne, 1993). An important socialization consequence of intensive association with same-sex peers and involvement in sex-typed activities is that it strongly reinforces identification with one's sex. It also contributes to the development of stereotypical and negative attitudes towards the opposite sex. The development of gender identities and much of children's sexual socialization occur in the context of peer rather than family associations.

Peer interactions have a wide range of consequences for children's self-concept and self-efficacy (Adler & Adler, 1998; Eder, Evans, & Parker, 1995). In his field studies of pre-adolescent boys, Fine (1987) observed that friendship groups are especially appropriate contexts for the mastering of self-presentation and impression management skills, often in displays of exaggerated masculinity, since inept performances are usually ignored or corrected without severe loss of face. A wider latitude of behavior is allowed in peer groups and even encouraged, since friends, unlike parents, are not responsible for child-rearing.

Peers provide an alternate reference group for children, an alternate source of self-efficacy and identity, and a context for the exercise of independence from adult control. Often they provide "arenas of comfort" or safe havens where adolescents can relax and rejuvenate from the pressures and stresses of family and school (Call & Mortimer, 2001). Peers may also give rise to subcultures with values and behavior distinct from and in opposition to the culture of adults, such as the adolescent subcultures described by Coleman (1961) and in much of the literature on juvenile delinquency. The self-agency developed and fostered in peer groups may be directed toward constructive or to destructive ends and may serve the individual well or poorly later in the life course.

School

Even though they are very different in structure and function, there is an ecological relationship between peer groups and schools as developmental contexts for children. Schools provide favorable circumstances for the emergence of peer groups—the presence of large groups of children, divided into same-age groupings, and exposed to similar social circumstances. School is the first formal organization that children experience and it constitutes a large part of most children's lives. The primary mandate of schools is to educate children and to develop their cognitive skills. It is the setting where knowledge and thinking abilities are constantly tested, evaluated, and compared with other students and where children develop a sense of their intellectual efficacy (Bandura, 1993).

Many school activities have implications for the child's self-efficacy. One of the most important is evaluation of the student's academic performance and this evaluation is more public than evaluations by parents and peers. Success in academic performance is good for self-efficacy and self-esteem. But failure is not and public failure is worse. Schools in which students are evaluated against their classmates (i.e., grading on a curve), rather than against their previous performance or on the basis of cooperative activities, guarantee that some students will succeed and some will fail, thereby increasing self-efficacy for some and decreasing it for others. Performance evaluations may also result in the labeling of students by teachers and classmates as "smart," "dumb," "lazy," etc. Such labels affect the way others respond to the student and thereby influence the student's conception of self, including their self-efficacy, affecting their motivation and subsequent academic performance (Wilkins, 1976).

Of course students and others are not passive recipients of the pressures they experience. Some resist negative labels, some try to change them by working harder, some withdraw emotionally and intellectually, and some adopt strategies of rationalizing failure that enable them to maintain self-esteem but at the expense of academic performance (Covington & Beery, 1976). U.S. public schools, concerned with this problem, began to develop strategies to enhance children's self-esteem. By the mid-1980s, self-esteem enhancement became part of the curriculum in many public (especially elementary) schools. Grading and public evaluation of students were discouraged, negative feedback of any kind was also discouraged, and positive feedback and affirmations of self-worth were encouraged. In short, the demonstration of competence and mastery were no longer the primary basis for teachers' evaluative feedback. This focus on self-esteem enhancement resulted in more problems than it solved, by diverting schools from their main mission of enhancing children's substantive knowledge and increasing their cognitive skills. Furthermore, in a culture that is already highly individualistic, self-preoccupied, and inclined to "look out for number one," as Hewitt (1998) argues, the emphasis on self-esteem enhancement contributes to even more self-centeredness and self-preoccupation.

Although high self-esteem is generally a good quality to have, how it is obtained matters. Effective performance is a more solid and constructive basis of self-esteem than is reflected appraisals (Gecas & Schwalbe, 1983). Self-enhancement programs in public schools tended to emphasize the enhancement of self-esteem primarily through positive reflected appraisals and to diminish its association with competence and effective performance. Children may have felt good about themselves, but their school performance declined and public criticism of these school programs increased. By the early 1990s, this social experiment in self-esteem enhancement in public schools began to decline.

Education has a pervasive influence on self-efficacy, affecting one's overall sense of efficacy as well as developing specific skills and competencies. As individuals gain knowledge, either through formal instruction in schools or through independent study, they gain self-efficacy. Kohn and Schooler (1983) found education to be as important as occupational conditions (both are considered indicators of socioeconomic status and are strongly interrelated) for adults' intellectual flexibility and related personality variables. Mirowsky and Ross (1983) and others (Gurin, Gurin, & Morrison, 1978) have found that education increases the sense of mastery and personal control, which in turn increases the pursuit of higher educational and occupational goals. Grabowski, Call, and Mortimer (2001) found that domain-specific self-efficacy (i.e., economic self-efficacy) of high school students had a significant effect on their pursuit of postsecondary education.

Schools are also the settings for the development of skills and capabilities other than intellectual. Opportunities are available in most schools, especially at the high school level, for the development of athletic, social, artistic, musical, and other skills, providing children and adolescents with a wide range of self-efficacy possibilities. With the possible exception of children's early family experiences, no social context and stage of life is more focused on the development of efficacy and agency than are the school years. And some of the most important decisions (concerning career, life goals, interpersonal relations, and identity issues) that the person will make occur near the end of those years (Shanahan, 2000).

Work and Occupation

For most adults, work is the context of greatest relevance for the development and expression of self-efficacy and other aspects of agency and self-definition. Considering the amount of time men and women spend working and preparing for occupational roles, as well as the importance of work for personal identity and lifestyle, we would expect it to be consequential for self-efficacy and personal agency. But workplace and occupational conditions vary considerably with regard to factors affecting the development and expression of self-efficacy, such as the nature of the work involved, power relations, degree of structure, presence of co-workers, and degree to which the worker has autonomy and control over the conditions and the products of their labor. Work enhances self-efficacy when it is complex, challenging, and interesting and when the worker has a high degree of autonomy and responsibility (Mortimer & Lorence, 1995). The opposite conditions, for example, boring, routinized work in which the worker has very little autonomy and decision-making responsibility, depress self-efficacy and increase workers' alienation and dissatisfaction (a theme that Marxist scholars have emphasized in their critique of capitalism).

There is substantial research supporting these relationships between work environment and worker's self-efficacy and related aspects of psychological functioning. The most extensive empirical support is provided by Kohn and Schooler (1969, 1983) and their colleagues. In a series of studies spanning over three decades, Kohn examined how work conditions affect the values and psychological functioning of workers. He focused on several conditions of work that enable or inhibit self-direction: degree of supervision, degree of routinization, and the substantive complexity of work. These occupational conditions are highly related to social class, with occupations located in the upper end of the class structure characterized by work activities high in self-direction, while those in the lower classes are low in self-direction. Occupational conditions, then, are a major means by which social class impinges on people. The extensive research conducted by Kohn and Schooler and others (for reviews, see Kohn & Schooler, 1983; Miller, 1988; Schooler & Oats, 2001) has found that the greater the freedom experienced on the job and the more complex and challenging the work, the more likely is the worker to value self-direction, to be intellectually more flexible, and to have greater self-efficacy (as measured by indicators of self-confidence, powerlessness, and fatalism). Kohn and his colleagues have found these occupational conditions (especially work complexity) to have substantial psychological consequences not only for U.S. workers, but also for workers in socialist countries (Kohn & Slomczynski, 1990) and for women as well as men (Miller, Schooler, Kohn, & Miller, 1979). It should be noted that these relationships are not unidirectional but rather reciprocal, that is individuals try to choose work that is congruent with their dispositions (including their self-efficacy) and then to affect their work environments as much as possible. However, Kohn and Schooler (1973) maintain that this reciprocity is not equal: "In all cases (of their analysis of relative influence), job affects man more than man affects job" (p. 114). On the other hand, as workers' self-direction and efficacy increase, because of job conditions or other factors, their influence on their jobs also increases.

Other scholars have also found that work autonomy, flexibility, and complexity are conducive to the development of workers' self-efficacy. Mortimer and Lorence (1979) and Mortimer, Lorence, and Kumka (1986) found, in their panel study of college students, that work autonomy significantly affects self-perceived competence. Staples, Schwalbe, and Gecas (1984) found the degree of routinization and supervision at work to affect workers' occupational self-efficacy negatively. Gecas and Seff (1987) found these same occupational conditions to be related to general self-efficacy for a sample of employed men. Spenner and Otto (1985) found that work complexity had a significant effect on the sense of personal control for men and women. Schwalbe (1986) found that problem-solving demands at work were positively related to workers' intellectual flexibility and negatively related to "reification" (i.e., belief in external control). It is evident from this line of research that occupational conditions that enable efficacious action enhance the development of self-efficacy.

Income is also positively related to self-efficacy and personal control (Downey & Moen, 1987), especially when the income is earned rather than received from charity or welfare (Duncan & Morgan, 1980). Income provides resources that individuals use in exercising agency and increases their range of choices and options. Not surprisingly, disruptions in income and employment status—being laid off, downgraded, losing one's job because of injury, etc.— decrease individuals' sense of efficacy and increase powerlessness and associated psychological distress (Pearlin, Leibermann, Menaghan, & Mullan, 1981; Seff, Gecas, & Ray, 1992).

Other Developmental Influences: Race and Ethnicity

Evidence for the effects of race and ethnicity on self-efficacy and perceived control is sparse, but what there is suggests that racial and ethnic minorities have lower self-efficacy (Gurin et al., 1978; Mirowsky, Ross, & Van Willigen, 1996). Some of this effect is due to the association of race and ethnicity with social class, since racial and ethnic minorities disproportionately occupy the lower levels of the social class structure. Gurin et al. (1978) found African Americans to have a significantly lower sense of personal control than White Americans. However, they did not find any difference between the races in "control ideology," that is the belief in the degree to which people in general have control over their lives. This is somewhat surprising since control ideology, in the form of "system blame," has been suggested as a psychological defense used by the powerless to account for their subordinate status (Taylor & Walsh, 1979).

The lower self-efficacy of Blacks compared to Whites may be a function of economic disadvantage and racial discrimination and their consequences for power, control, and access to resources. Their lower sense of personal control may indeed be a realistic assessment of their circumstances. Interestingly, these conditions of economic disadvantage and racial discrimination do not seem to affect Black self-esteem in the same way. Studies have generally found little or no difference in the self-esteem of Blacks and Whites (Jackson & Lassiter, 2001; Rosenberg & Rosenberg, 1989). One explanation of these findings is that self-esteem is primarily dependent on one's interpersonal context (i.e., local contexts of interaction and frames of reference, namely friends, neighbors, and kin), whereas self-efficacy is more affected by social structural influences (Gecas & Schwalbe, 1983). Hughes and Demo (1989) provide empirical evidence for this observation in their study of the self-perceptions of Black Americans.

Culture may be more important than social structure in influencing ethnic differences in self-efficacy, although both sources play a part: social structure because of the disproportionate representation of ethnic minorities in the lower classes and culture because of the differential emphasis on agency beliefs in the cultures of ethnic minorities. Cultures and world views that emphasize fatalism and external control (divine or secular) are associated with lower self-efficacy. Much of the evidence for cultural influences on self-efficacy comes from comparisons of Hispanics and Anglos. Hispanics are found to have stronger beliefs in external control and weaker beliefs in personal agency than Anglos, even after the effects of social class are controlled (Madsen, 1973; Ross, Mirowsky, & Cockerham, 1983). Fatalism is not as prominent a feature in the cultures of ethnic minorities from Japan, Korea, and other Asian countries, where the emphasis on personal agency and efficacy (especially academic efficacy) is as great or greater than it is in mainstream U.S. culture.

GENDER DIFFERENCES IN SELF-EFFICACY

Research indicates that males and females differ in their sense of self-efficacy, with males being perceived (by self and others) as having a stronger sense of general self-efficacy and

personal control than females in our society. Several extensive reviews of the child development research on sex differences (Block, 1976, 1983; Maccoby & Jacklin, 1974) indicate that
boys are more active, impulsive, aggressive, engage in more exploratory and risk-taking
behavior, seek opportunities to exert control over their environments, and have more self-
confidence than do girls. Based on her extensive review of this research, Block (1983,
pp. 1339–1340) concludes that the self-concepts of males, in contrast to females, include
stronger beliefs in being able to control the external world. The self-descriptions of males are
more likely to include concepts of agency, power, control, and instrumentality—all reflections
of a self-concept in which efficacy and mastery are important components. In contrast,
females describe themselves as more generous, sensitive, nurturing, and considerate of others. The self-concepts of females emphasize interpersonal relations and communion and not
competition and mastery in the way that they relate to their environments.

These observations on general self-efficacy, while important, tend to gloss over sex differences on domain-specific self-efficacies, especially those based on actual abilities. Males tend to
do somewhat better at spacial and analytical tasks, whereas females are more efficacious in language and role-taking abilities (Maccoby & Jacklin, 1974). These domain-specific competencies
are reflected and exaggerated (because they are sex typed) in the self-conceptions of males and
females—there is a tendency for boys to overestimate their efficacy in mathematics and for girls
to underestimate theirs (Betz & Hackett, 1981; Hackett, 1985). These self-conceptions have
important consequences for academic and career decisions, with substantially more men than
women choosing careers in scientific and technical fields (Eccles & Hoffman, 1984).

Most of the research on sex differences in self-efficacy is done on children. But these
differences are also found in studies of adults (Gurin et al., 1978). They tend to vary, however,
by age and stage of family life course. The largest sex differences in the self-efficacy of men and
women (as indicated by male-instrumental and female-expressive self-perceptions) occur during the active parenting stage of the family. By contrast, postparental men and women are more
likely to identify cross-sex traits in their self-conceptions, making sex differences in self-
efficacy less evident with increasing age (Bengtson, Reedy, & Gordon, 1985).

Explanations of gender differences in self-efficacy are predominantly cultural and social
structural. Cultural explanations maintain that sex differences in self-efficacy reflect cultural
conceptions of "masculinity" and "femininity," with the former stressing agency, independence, and assertiveness and the latter emphasizing passivity, dependence, and sensitivity.
Through sex-role socialization, primarily in the family but also in schools and peer groups,
boys and girls acquire the sex-appropriate gender identities with their differential implications
for self-efficacy. While there has been substantial change in our culture over the last half century toward greater emphasis on equality between the sexes and de-emphasis of gender differences, the early socialization experiences of boys and girls still differ with regard to the
development of gender identities. For example, Eccles, Jacobs, and Harold (1990) found, in
their longitudinal studies of children and adolescents, that parents distort their perceptions of
their children in gender stereotypic activities such as mathematics and sports, that the child's
sex affects parents' causal attributions for their children's performance in sex-role stereotypic
activities (i.e., exaggerating the child's success in sex-stereotypic activities and diminishing it
in cross-sex activities), and that these parental biases influence the children's self-conceptions
and activity choices. Similarly, in his longitudinal study of parents' socialization values, Alwin
(1991) found that sex-based differentiation in parental values have not changed substantially,
despite the changes found over the past five decades or so of increasing parental preferences
for autonomy and decreasing emphasis on obedience in child-rearing (Alwin, 1988).

Gender stereotypic socialization is even more pronounced within children's same-sex
peer groups, as discussed above and structural explanations of children's play and games also

recognize these processes. Structural explanations of sex differences in self-efficacy emphasize power differences between men and women in society, women's more restricted occupational opportunities, division of household labor along sex-role lines, and the nature of women's jobs (Mirowsky & Ross, 1986). Lever (1978) provides one of the most interesting structural explanations, focusing on the nature and organization of children's play and games. Through careful observations of children's (fifth graders) playground activities Lever (1978) found that boys' and girls' games differed with regard to degree of complexity, role differentiation, player interdependence, number of players involved, explicitness of goals and rules, and team formation, with boys' games high and girls' games low on these dimensions of complexity (the typical boys' game was baseball and the typical girls' game was hopscotch). Lever (1978) suggests that boys' games further independence training, the development of organizational skills, and seeing things from the perspective of the team or group. By contrast, girls' games may enhance the development of socio-emotional skills, since they occur in smaller, more intimate groups. In Meadian terms, boys develop the ability to take the role of the *generalized other*, while girls develop greater competence in role taking *particular others* (Lever, 1978). These peer group activities, Lever (1978) speculates, better prepare boys for occupational roles and girls for domestic roles and occupational roles in which interpersonal skills predominate.

However, children's games have been undergoing considerable change over the past 20 years, for girls. With the increased emphasis on girls' participation in team sports (such as soccer, basketball, and baseball) and de-emphasis of sex role differences, the playground observations of girls' games that Lever (1978) observed in the 1970s are less apparent today. To the extent that the structure of girls and boys games is more similar now, the cognitive consequences may be more similar as well (see Maccoby [1998] for analyses and discussion of the differential socialization consequences of the structure of boys' and girls' play and games).

STABILITY AND CHANGE IN
SELF-EFFICACY OVER THE LIFE COURSE

There seems to be a curvilinear pattern of self-efficacy and sense of control over the life course, with efficacy increasing through childhood and early adulthood, reaching a plateau in middle age, and gradually declining after age 60 or so. But empirical support for this overall pattern is spotty and weak, since there are few longitudinal studies of self-efficacy over large segments of the life course (Gurin & Brim, 1984). The research evidence is strongest for the uphill slope of this pattern. McAdams (1989), in his follow-up of the Mississippi Freedom Summer participants, found political activism and efficacy to still be high for these men and women 20 years later and to have a major effect on the course of their lives.

The stability of self-efficacy and its effect on life course construction suggest that there is an element of self-fulfilling prophecy in operation. Mortimer et al. (1986) found a high level of stability in "self-competence" in their 10-year panel study of college men. Mortimer, Finch, and Kumka (1982) demonstrate how self-competence in the college years shaped the lives of these men in the areas of work and family and how this, in turn, had an independent effect on self-competence 10 years later. In addition, success or failure in education and early occupational experiences during adolescence effect self-efficacy, motivation, and levels of aspiration which have consequences in adulthood (Mortimer, Harley, & Aronson, 1999). Gecas & Mortimer (1987) suggest that efficacy beliefs give rise to spiraling patterns of increasing success or failure. Conceptions of self-efficacy formed early in life tend to become self-fulfilling prophecies, by either encouraging or discouraging persons from taking risks and undertaking new and challenging tasks. Subsequent success in new endeavors fosters an increasing sense of personal efficacy over time: subsequent failure has the opposite effect. This process of spiraling reciprocity is well illustrated in Clausen's (1993) analysis of the Berkeley longitudinal studies, mentioned above: "planful competence" in adolescence leads to the kinds of decisions these men and women made, especially during times of opportunity (Shanahan et al., 1997), affecting the quality of their family and work lives into the middle years. Elder's (1974) work as well has documented the long-term consequences of efficacy-relevant childhood experiences for the shaping of adult lives. In spite of fluctuations associated with role transitions, historical events, and successes and failures in various domains of self-agency, general self-efficacy may be one of the more stable aspects of personality over the life course, at least into middle age.

It seems reasonable to expect a gradual decline in self-efficacy and personal control in the later years of life, when physical and cognitive abilities decline, social networks contract, and occupational and family roles decrease in importance. But evidence for the downward slope of self-efficacy in the later years comes mostly from cross-sectional studies, which have a tendency to confound maturational with historical or cohort effects (Bengtson et al., 1985; Elder, 1997). There is reason to suspect that at least some of the difference in self-efficacy found in these non-longitudinal studies is due to cohort differences. The earlier cohorts (i.e., those born in the 1920s and 1930s) had less formal education and perhaps less benefit of other intellectual experiences (e.g., computer technologies) than persons born later, accounting for some of the differences in self-efficacy (Bandura, 1997; Schaie, 1995). This is not to say that self-efficacy does not decline in old age, but that the documented decline based on cross-sectional studies may be exaggerated.

Our conceptions of the elderly may also exaggerate the extent to which their abilities have declined. Riley, Kahn, and Foner (1994) argue that there is a "culture lag" in our conceptions of the elderly that is a carry-over of conceptions from an earlier time, when the elderly were indeed more feeble, infirm, and dependent than the majority of the elderly are in contemporary society. Greater affluence, technological changes, and modern medicine have increased longevity and the quality of life for the elderly in modern societies, and undoubtedly have enabled the maintenance of higher levels of self-efficacy than was possible for past generations of elderly.

When physical and mental capabilities do decline, as they inevitably do if one lives long enough, people minimize the negative consequences for self-efficacy in a number of ways. Gains in wisdom, knowledge, and expertise compensate for some of the physical declines (Baltes, 1987). People also engage in various "self-immunizing" processes (Brandtstädter & Greve, 1994) that protect and stabilize their self-concepts. These include advantageous social comparisons (e.g., comparing one's abilities with people the same age or older makes one's declining abilities less evident), selective reflected appraisals (e.g., paying more attention to evaluative feedback from one's peers than from younger folks), and selective attributions (e.g., attributing inefficacy in a particular domain to lack of interest, motivation, or to external circumstances), as well as selective memory, perception, and other defense mechanism we use to protect our sense of efficacy and self-worth (Fung, Abeles, & Carstensen, 1999). So, while physical and mental abilities decline with old age, the self-efficacy of old people may not show the same level of decline because of these compensatory processes, shifts in arenas of comparison, and other self-protective mechanisms.

CONCLUDING OBSERVATIONS

We all exercise agency in the construction of our lives through the choices we make and the courses of action we pursue. But agency can be constructive or misguided, have desirable or undesirable consequences, lead to self-fulfillment or regret. To say that we are architects of our lives is not to say that our lives turn out as we intended. The self as a reflexive phenomenon and a motivated system is a multidimensional source of human agency (see Gecas, 2001, for an elaboration). A major aspect of self-agency affecting life course construction is our sense of self-efficacy, that is our belief in our efficacy and personal control. The main theme of this paper is that self-efficacy is a positive and constructive force in the life course. Those with high self-efficacy are more effective in shaping their circumstances and their lives in the intended direction.

Beliefs about one's efficacy are among the earliest beliefs formed, developing out of the initial interactions between the individual and his or her environment and shaped by subsequent contexts of socialization across the life course. Environments that are complex, stimulating, challenging, and responsive are most conducive to the development and maintenance of self-efficacy at any stage of life. Exposure to such environments varies with one's position in systems of stratification (e.g., social class, race, gender, birth order), among other things. In general, those higher in a system of stratification have more power, autonomy, and greater access to resources, enabling efficacious action. Social struggles for racial and gender equality are not only struggles for resources and justice, but also for greater opportunity for self-determination.

While my discussion of self-efficacy is hopefully not a parochial view, I have been considering it largely within the framework of modern Western societies. U.S. society in particular, with its ethos of individualism and self-reliance, might be an especially favorable cultural context for the development of beliefs in personal control and efficacy. Mirowsky et al. (1996), in a study based on a representative national sample, found that over 90% of Americans think that they control their own lives. Self-efficacy might have somewhat different relevance and implications for life course construction in non-modern or non-Western societies. For example, self-efficacy may be less important in cultures or societies that are less individualistic and more collectivistic than ours, although Bandura (1997) argues strongly against this suggestion, maintaining that self-efficacy is important to the achievement of personal or collective goals irrespective of cultural orientation. Nevertheless, cultural orientations could affect the development and maintenance of self-efficacy by their emphasis on fatalism and de-emphasis of personal control ideology. Sastry and Ross (1998) found that respondents from Asian countries were significantly less likely to report that they had control over their lives than respondents from Western countries. Furthermore, responses to success and to failure, with implications for the development of self-efficacy, seem to differ for these cultures. Heine et al. (in press) found that the Japanese work harder when focusing on their shortcomings (e.g., in response to failure at a task), whereas North Americans work harder when focusing on their strengths (e.g., in response to successful performance), suggesting that the Japanese are motivated more by self-improvement and Americans by self-enhancement. In addition, cultural differences in attitudes toward the elderly may have implications for self-efficacy in this segment of the life course. Cultures in which the elderly are honored and revered and in which they maintain substantial authority may not show the pattern of decline in self-efficacy found among the elderly in Western cultures.

U.S. society and culture, along with most modern societies, have been undergoing major and rapid changes, giving rise to a number of new questions and concerns regarding self-agency and the life course. Will the emerging postmodern, high tech information society give us a greater sense of agency and efficacy or will it make us feel less in control of our lives, more powerless and vulnerable in the face of powerful and increasingly invasive bureaucracies? Which social groups (e.g., social classes, minority groups) are most affected by these major social changes and at what points in the life course? Considering the major cultural and social structural changes in modern societies regarding gender roles, is the gap between men and women narrowing with regard to general self-efficacy as well as domain-specific (especially, gender stereotypic) self-efficacy? How have changes in self-efficacy for girls and women affected their choices and decisions at key points in the life course? At a more fundamental level we might ask, is self-efficacy an unequivocal good? Throughout this chapter I have been arguing for the positive consequences of self-efficacy. But is there also a down side to self-efficacy? For example, what if self-efficacy is largely illusory, that is, not based on one's actual abilities or achievements? Illusion, of course, is a matter of degree and most aspects of self-concept are illusory to some extent. But when the gap between one's abilities and one's self-efficacy is great, is this "illusion of efficacy" functional for the individual? Taylor and Brown (1988) think so. I am not so sure. We could use more research on these issues.

ACKNOWLEDGMENTS: I wish to thank Michael Shanahan and Jeylan Mortimer for their helpful comments and suggestions on earlier drafts of this paper. Work on this paper was supported by Project 00963, Department of Rural Sociology, and the Agricultural Research Center, Washington State University

REFERENCES

Adams, B. (1972). Birth order: A critical review. *Sociometry, 35*, 411–439.

Adler, P. A., & Adler, P. (1998). *Peer power: Preadolescent culture and identity.* New Brunswick, NJ: Rutgers University Press.

Alwin, D. F. (1988). From obedience to autonomy: Changes in traits desired in children, 1924–1978. *Public Opinion Quarterly, 52*, 33–52.

Alwin, D. F. (1991). Changes in family roles and gender differences in parental socialization values. *Sociological Studies of Child Development, 4*, 201–224.

Baltes, P. B. (1987). Theoretical propositions of life-span developmental psychology: On the dynamics between growth and decline. *Developmental Psychology, 23*, 611–626.

Bandura, A. (1982). The self and mechanisms of agency. In J. Surs (Ed.), *Psychological perspectives on the self* (Vol. 1, pp. 3–40). Hillsdale, NJ: Lawrence Erlbaum.

Bandura, A. (1993). Perceived self-efficiency in cognitive development and functioning. *Educational Psychologist, 28*, 117–148.

Bandura. A. (1997). *Self-efficacy: The exercise of control.* New York: Freeman.

Bandura, A. (2001). Social cognitive theory: An agentic perspective. *Annual Review of Psychology, 52*, 1–26.

Baumeister, R. F. (1999). The nature and structure of the self: An overview. In R. F. Baumeister (Ed.), *The self in social psychology* (pp. 1–20). Philadelphia, PA: Psychology Press.

Bengston, V. L., Reedy, M. N., & Gordon, C. (1985). Aging and self-conceptions: Personality processes and social contexts. In J. E. Birren & K. W. Schaie (Eds.), *Handbook of the psychology of aging* (2nd ed., pp. 544–593). New York: Van Nostrand Reinhold.

Betz, N. E., & Hackett, G. (1981). The relationship of career-related self-efficacy expectations to perceived career options in college women and men. *Journal of Counseling Psychology, 28*, 399–410.

Blake, J. (1989). *Family size and achievement.* Berkeley, CA: University of California Press.

Block, J. H. (1976). Issues, problems, and pitfalls in assessing sex differences: A critical review of *The Psychology of Sex Differences. Merrill-Palmer Quarterly, 22*, 283–308.

Block, J. H. (1983). Differential premises arising from differential socialization of the sexes: Some conjectures. *Child Development, 54*, 1335–1354.

Blumer, H. (1969). *Symbolic interactionism: Perspective and method.* Englewood Cliffs, NJ: Prentice-Hall.

Brandtstädter, J., & Greve, W. (1994). The aging self: Stabilizing and protective processes. *Developmental Review, 14*, 52–80.

Buhler, C., & Massarik, F. (Eds.) (1968). *The course of human life: A study of goals in the humanistic perspective.* New York: Springer.

Call, K. T., & Mortimer, J. T. (2001). *Arenas of comfort in adolescence: A study of adjustment in context*. NJ: Lawrence Erlbaum.

Call, K. T., Mortimer, J. T., & Shanahan, M. J. (1995). Helpfulness and the development of competence in adolescence. *Child Development, 66*, 129–138.

Clausen, J. A. (1993). *American lives: Looking back at the children of the Great Depression*. New York: The Free Press.

Coleman, J. S. (1961). *The adolescent society*. New York: Free Press.

Covington, M. V., & Beery, R. G. (1976). *Self-worth and school learning*. New York: Holt, Rinehart, and Winston.

Crosnoe, R. (2000). Friendships in childhood and adolescence: The life course and new directions. *Social Psychology Quarterly, 63*, 377–391.

DeCharms, R. (1979). Personal causation and perceived control. In L. C. Perlmuter & R. A. Monty (Eds.), *Choice and perceived control* (pp. 29–41). Hillsdale, NJ: Erlbaum.

Deci, E. L. (1975). *Intrinsic motivation*. New York: Plenum.

Downy, G., & Moen, P. (1987). Personal efficacy, income, and family transitions: A longitudinal study of women heading households. *Journal of Health and Social Behavior, 28*, 320–333.

Duncan, G. J., & Morgan, J. N. (1980). The incidence and some consequence of major life events. In G. J. Duncan & J. N. Morgan (Eds.), *Five thousand American families: Patterns of economic progress* (Vol. 8, pp. 183–240). Ann Arbor, MI: Institute for Social Research.

Eccles, J. S., & Hoffman, L. W. (1984). Socialization and the maintenance of a sex-segregated labor market. In H. W. Stevenson & A. E. Siegel (Eds.), *Research in child development and social policy* (pp. 367–420). Chicago: University of Chicago Press.

Eccles, J. S., Jacobs, J. E., & Harold, R. D. (1990). Gender role stereotypes, expectancy effects, and parents' socialization of gender differences. *Journal of Social Issues, 46*, 183–201.

Eder, D., Evans, C., & Parker, S. (1995). *School talk: Gender and adolescent culture*. New Brunswick, NJ: Rutgers University Press.

Elder, G. H., Jr. (1974). *Children of the Great Depression*. Chicago: University of Chicago Press.

Elder, G. H., Jr. (1995). Life trajectories in changing societies. In A. Bandura (Ed.), *Self-efficacy in changing societies* (pp. 46–68). New York: Cambridge University Press.

Elder, G. H., Jr. (1997). The life course and human development. In R. M. Lerner (Ed.), *Handbook of child psychology, Vol. 1: Theoretical models of human development* (pp. 939–991). New York: Wiley.

Elder, G. H. Jr., & Bowerman, C. (1963). Family structure and childrearing patterns: The effects of family size and sex composition. *American Sociological Review, 28*, 891–905.

Erikson, E. H. (1959). *Identity and the life cycle*. New York: International University Press.

Fine, G. A. (1987). *With the boys: Little league baseball and preadolescent culture*. Chicago: University of Chicago Press.

Fung, H. H., Abeles, R. P., & Carstensen, L. L. (1999). Psychological control in later life. In J. Brandtstädter & R. M. Lerner (Eds.), *Action and self-development: Theory and research through the life span* (pp. 345–372). Thousand Oaks, CA: Sage.

Gecas, V. (1989). The social psychology of self-efficacy. *Annual Review of Sociology, 15*, 291–316.

Gecas, V. (1991). The self-concept as a basis for a theory of motivation. In J. A. Howard & P. L. Callero (Eds.), *The self-society dynamic: Cognition, emotion, and action* (pp. 171–188). New York: Cambridge University Press.

Gecas, V. (2001). The self as a social force. In T. J. Owens, S. Stryker, & N. Goodman (Eds.), *Extending self-esteem theory and research* (pp. 85–100). New York: Cambridge University Press.

Gecas, V., & Mortimer, J. T. (1987). Stability and change in the self-concept from adolescence to adulthood. In T. Honess & K. Yardley (Eds.), *Self and identity: Perspectives across the lifespan* (pp. 265–286). London: Routledge & Kegan Paul.

Gecas, V., & Schwalbe, M. L. (1983). Beyond the looking-glass self: Social structure and efficacy-based self-esteem. *Social Psychology Quarterly, 46*, 77–88.

Gecas, V., & Seff, M. A. (1987). *Social class, occupational conditions, and self-esteem*. Paper presented at the American Sociological Association Meetings, Chicago.

Giddens, A. (1984). *The constitution of society*. Berkeley, CA: University of California Press.

Goffman, E. (1959). *The presentation of self in everyday life*. Garden City, NJ: Doubldeay.

Grabowski, L. J. S., Call, K. T., & Mortimer, J. T. (2001). Global and economic self-efficacy in the educational attainment process. *Social Psychology Quarterly, 64*, 164–179.

Grolnick, W. S., Deci, E. L., & Ryan, R. M. (1997). Internalization within the family. In J. E. Grusec & L. Kuczynski (Eds.), *Parenting and children's internalization of values: A handbook of contemporary theory* (pp. 135–161). New York: Wiley.

Gurin, P., & Brim, O. G., Jr. (1984). Change in self in adulthood: The example of sense of control. In P. B. Baltes & O. G. Brim (Eds.), *Life-span development and behavior* (Vol. 6, pp. 281–334). New York: Academic Press.

Gurin, P., Gurin, G., & Morrison, B. M. (1978). Personal and ideological aspects of internal and external control. *Social Psychology, 41*, 275–296.

Hackett, G. (1985). The role of mathematics self-efficacy in the choice of math-related majors of college women and men: A path analysis. *Journal of Counseling Psychology, 32*, 47–56.

Heine, S. J., Kityama, S., Lehman, D. R., Takata, T., Ide, E., Leung, C., & Matsumoto, H. (2002). Divergent consequences of success and failure in Japan and North America: An investigation of self-improving motivations and malleable selves. *Journal of Personality and Social Psychology, 93*, 247–268.

Hewitt, J. P. (1998). *The myth of self-esteem*. New York: St Martin's Press.

Hughes, M., & Demo, D. H. (1989). Self-perceptions of Black Americans: Personal self-esteem, racial self-esteem, and personal efficacy. *American Journal of Sociology, 45*, 139–159.

Jackson, P. B., & Lassiter, S. P. (2001). Self-esteem and race. In T. J. Owens, S. Stryker, & N. Goodman (Eds.), *Extending self-esteem theory and research* (pp. 223–254). New York: Cambridge University Press.

Kohn, M. L., & Schooler, C. (1973). Occupational experience and psychological functioning: An assessment of reciprocal effects. *American Sociological Review, 38*, 97–118.

Kohn, M. L., & Schooler, C. (1983). *Work and personality: An inquiry into the impact of social stratification*. Norwood, NJ: Ablex.

Kohn, M., & Slomczynski, K. M. (1990). *Social structure and self-direction: A comparative analysis of the United States and Poland*. Oxford: Basil Blackwell.

Kuttler, A. F., LaGreca, A., & Prinstein, M. (1999). Friendship qualities and socio-emotional functioning of adolescents with close cross-sexed friendships. *Journal of Research on Adolescence, 9*, 339–366.

Lever, J. (1978). Sex differences in the complexity of children's play. *American Sociological Review, 43*, 471–482.

McAdams, D. (1989). The biographical consequences of activism. *American Sociological Review, 54*, 744–760.

Maccoby, E. E. (1998). *The two sexes: Growing up apart, coming together*. Cambridge, MA: Harvard University Press.

Maccoby, E. E., & Jacklin, C. N. (1974). *The psychology of sex differences*. Stanford, CA: Stanford University Press.

Madsen, W. (1973). *The Mexican-Americans of south Texas*. New York: Holt.

Markus, H., & Nurius, P. (1986). Possible selves: The interface between motivation and the self-concept. In K. Yardley & T. Honess (Eds.), *Self and identity: psychosocial perspectives* (pp. 213–232). New York: Wiley.

Mead, G. H. (1934). *Mind, self, and society*. Chicago: University of Chicago Press.

Miller, J. (1988). Jobs and work. In N. J. Smelser (Ed.), *Handbook of sociology* (pp. 327–359). Newbury Park, CA: Sage.

Miller, J., Schooler, C., Kohn, M., & Miller, K. (1979). Women and work: The psychological effects of occupational conditions. *American Journal of Sociology, 85*, pp. 66–94.

Mirowsky, J., & Ross, C. E. (1983). Paranoia and the structure of powerlessness. *American Sociological Review, 48*, 228–239.

Mirowsky, J., & Ross, C. E. (1986). Social patterns of distress. *Annual Review of Sociology, 12*, 23–45.

Mirowsky, J., Ross, C. E., & Van Willigen, M. (1996). Instrumentalism in the land of opportunity: Socioeconomic causes and emotional consequences. *Social Psychology Quarterly, 59*, 322–337.

Modell, J. (1997). Family niche and intellectual bent. (Review of F. Sulloway, *Born to Rebel*). *Science, 275*, 624–625.

Mortimer, J. T., Finch, M. D., & Kumka, D. (1982). Persistence and change in human development: The multidimensional self-concept. In P. B. Baltes & O. G. Brim, Jr. (Eds.), *Life-span development and behavior* (Vol. 4, pp. 263–312). New York: Academic Press.

Mortimer, J. T., Harley, C., & Aronson, P. J. (1999). How do prior experiences in the workplace set the stage for the transition to adulthood? In A. Booth, C. Crouter, & M. Shanahan (Eds.), *Transitions to adulthood in a changing economy* (pp. 131–159). Westport, CT: Greenwood.

Mortimer, J. T., & Lorence, J. (1979). Occupational experience and the self-concept: A longitudinal study. *Social Psychology Quarterly, 42*, 307–323.

Mortimer, J. T., & Lorence, J. (1995). Social psychology of work. In K. S. Cook, G. A. Fine, & J. S. House (Eds.), *Sociological perspectives on social psychology* (pp. 497–523). Boston, MA: Allyn & Bacon.

Mortimer, J. T., Lorence, J., & Kumka, D. S. (1986). *Work, family and personality: Transition to adulthood*. Norwood, NJ: Ablex.

Pearlin, L. I., Leibermann, M. A., Menaghan, E. G., & Mullan, J. T. (1981). The stress process. *Journal of Health and Social Behavior, 22*, 337–356.

Piaget, J. (1954). *The construction of reality in the child*. New York: Basic Books.

Riley, M. W., Kahn, R. L., & Foner, A. (Eds.) (1994). *Age and structural lag*. New York: Wiley.

Rodin, J. (1976). Density, perceived choice, and response to controllable and uncontrollable outcomes. *Journal of Experimental Social Psychology, 12,* 564–578.

Rollins, B. C., & Thomas, D. L. (1979). Parental support, power, and control techniques in the socialization of children. In W. R. Burr, R. Hill, F. I. Nye, & I. L. Reiss (Eds.), *Contemporary theories about the family* (Vol. 1, pp. 317–364). New York: Free Press.

Rosenberg, M. (1988). Self-objectification: Relevance for the species and society. *Sociological Forum, 3,* 548–565.

Rosenberg, M., & Rosenberg, F. R. (1989). Old myths die hard: The case of Black self-esteem. *Revue Internationale de Psychologie Sociale, 2,* 355–365.

Ross, C. E., Mirowsky, J., & Cockerham, W. C. (1983). Social class, Mexican culture and fatalism: Their effects on psychological distress. *American Journal of Community Psychology, 11,* 383–399.

Ryan, R. M., & Deci, E. L. (2000). Self-determination theory and the facilitation of intrinsic motivation, social development, and well-being. *American Psychologist, 55,* 68–78.

Sastry, J., & Ross, C. E. (1998). Asian ethnicity and the sense of personal control. *Social Psychology Quarterly, 61,* 101–120.

Schaie, K. W. (1995). *Intellectual development in adulthood: The Seattle longitudinal study.* New York: Cambridge University Press.

Schooler, C. (1972). Birth order effects: Not here, not now. *Psychological Bulletin, 78,* 161–175.

Schooler, C., & Oats, G. (2001). Self-esteem and work across the life course. In T. J. Owens, S. Stryker, & N. Goodman (Eds.), *Extending self-esteem theory and research* (pp. 177–197). New York: Cambridge University Press.

Schwalbe, M. L. (1986). *The psychosocial consequences of natural and alienated labor.* Albany, NY: State University New York Press.

Seff, M., Gecas, V., & Ray, M. P. (1992). Injury and depression: The mediating effects of self-concept. *Sociological Perspectives, 35,* 573–591.

Seligman, M. E. P. (1975). *Helplessness: On depression, development, and death.* San Francisco: Freeman.

Sewell, W. H., Jr. (1992). A theory of structure: Duality, agency, and transformation. *American Journal of Sociology, 98,* 1–29.

Shanahan, M. J. (2000). Pathways to adulthood in changing societies: Variability and mechanisms in life course perspective. *Annual Review of Sociology, 26,* 667–692.

Shanahan, M. J., Elder, G. H., Jr., & Meich, R. A. (1997). History and agency in men's lives: Pathways to achievement in cohort perspective. *Sociology of Education, 70,* 54–67.

Shanahan, M. J., Hofer, S. M., & Miech, R. A. (2002). Planful competence, aging, and the life course: Retrospect and prospect. In S. Zarit, L. Pearlin, & K. Warner Schaie (Eds.) *Societal impacts on personal control in the elderly* (pp. 198–211). New York: Springer.

Snyder, M. (1981). On the influence of individuals on situations. In N. Cantor & J. F. Kihlstrom (Eds.), *Personality, cognition, and social interaction* (pp. 309–329). Hillsdale, NJ: Lawrence Erlbaum.

Spenner, K. I., & Otto, L. B. (1985). Work and self-concept: Selection and socialization in the early career. In A. C. Kerckhoff (Ed.), *Research in sociology of education and socialization* (Vol. 5, pp. 197–238). Greenwich: JAI.

Staples, C., Schwalbe, M. L., & Gecas, V. (1984). Social class, occupational conditions, and efficacy-based self-esteem. *Sociological Perspectives, 27,* 85–109.

Sulloway, F. J. (1996). *Born to rebel: Birth order, family dynamics, and creative lives.* New York: Pantheon.

Taylor, C. (1989). *Sources of the self.* Cambridge, MA: Harvard University Press.

Taylor, M. C., & Walsh, E. J. (1979). Explanations of Black self-esteem: Some empirical tests. *Social Psychological Quarterly, 42,* 242–253.

Taylor, S. E., & Brown, J. D. (1988). Illusions and well-being: A social psychological perspective on mental health. *Psychological Bulletin, 103,* 193–210.

Thorne, B. (1993). *Gender play: Girls and boys in school.* Brunswick, NJ: Rutgers University Press.

Watson, J. S. (1977). Depression and the perception of control in early childhood. In J. G. Schulterbrandt & A. Raskin (Eds.), *Depression in childhood* (pp. 129–139). New York: Raven.

White, R. W. (1959). Motivation reconsidered: The concept of competence. *Psychological Review, 66,* 297–333.

Wilkins, W. E. (1976). The concept of self-fulfilling prophecy. *Sociology of Education, 49,* 175–183.

Zajonc, R. B. (1976). Family configuration and intelligence. *Science, 192,* 227–236.

Zajonc, R. B., Markus, H., & Markus, G. B. (1979). The birth order puzzle. *Journal of Personality and Social Psychology, 37,* 1325–1341.

B. *Connections between Early and
Subsequent Life Phases*

CHAPTER 18

Connections between Childhood and Adulthood

Jane D. McLeod
Elbert P. Almazan

The study of the relationship between childhood and adulthood is an inherently interdisciplinary project. Psychologists, psychiatrists, sociologists, and epidemiologists have all made central contributions to our understanding of the processes through which early material, experiential, and psychological endowments shape subsequent development. In areas as diverse as the childhood predictors of adult health, the long-term sequelae of childhood adversity, and life course continuities in antisocial behavior researchers have presented compelling evidence for childhood–adulthood links and have begun to elucidate the mechanisms responsible for them. These investigations draw on life course concepts such as transitions and trajectories and affirm their utility for understanding the long-term implications of early life experiences.

Childhood is defined differently by different researchers. We adopt a broad definition here, as the pre-adult years of life encompassing infancy through adolescence. That having been said, our review emphasizes research on the life course sequelae of experiences in the pre-adolescent years in order to avoid overlap with chapters covering the transition to adulthood (this volume) and to highlight theories concerned with continuity and change over the full life course.

Empirical evidence for the relationship between childhood and adulthood reveals far more complexity than a simple claim of life course continuities allows. The relationships between childhood experiences and adult outcomes are generally modest and vary significantly

JANE D. McLeod and Elbert P. Almazan • Department of Sociology, Indiana University, Bloomington, Indiana 47405

Handbook of the Life Course, edited by Jeylan T. Mortimer and Michael J. Shanahan. Kluwer Academic/Plenum Publishers, New York, 2003.

with the broader social and historical context (Elder, 1974; Werner, 1985), specific characteristics of the experience (e.g., Harris, Brown, & Bifulco, 1986), subsequent events (Rutter,
1989), and the child's physical and psychological capacities (Masten & Garmezy, 1985). By
implication, research concerned with the relationship between childhood and adulthood must
attend to discontinuities as well as continuities over the life course.

    Our review begins with a discussion of factors that contribute to these continuities and dis-
continuities, covering factors both internal and external to the individual. We then introduce
three broad classes of models for the analysis of continuity and change—linear, contingent, and
transactional. We describe how these models have been applied in research on childhood—adulthood links, focusing on studies of the childhood antecedents of adult disease and the effects of
childhood adversity on adult life. Our review highlights the strengths and limitations of these
models and concludes with a consideration of theoretical challenges for future research.

FORCES OF CONTINUITY AND CHANGE

The continuity and change we observe from childhood to adulthood depend on a complex
interplay of competing personal and environmental forces. Internal dispositions, environmental stability, and the cumulative nature of biological and cognitive development all work
toward creating continuity in feelings, behaviors, and attainments over the life course. At the
same time, physiological development, subsequent life events and transitions, and the individual assertion of choice create variation in developmental pathways.

Internal Dispositions

Several psychological traditions, in particular various forms of psychoanalytic theory, emphasize the formative nature of the first years of life. Although their specific accounts diverge,
these traditions share the assumption that early relationships with caregivers influence later
development through the internalization of psychological functions (e.g., emotion regulation)
or the development of enduring mental representations of those relationships (see Fonagy,
1999, for a review). For example, attachment theory (Ainsworth, Blehar, Waters, & Wall,
1978; Bowlby, 1969, 1973, 1980) proposes that children develop internal working models of
their relationships with primary caregivers (i.e., attachment relations) that serve as the foundation for later interpersonal relationships (Bretherton & Munholland, 1999). Early experiences of sensitive or insensitive care constitute an experiential basis for children's broader
representations concerning their caregivers' accessibility and responsiveness and their own
deservingness of care. These representations guide the relational choices that children make
throughout the life course, as well as their relationship expectations, self-appraisals, and
behaviors and, thereby, create continuity in experience (Hazan & Shaver, 1994; Thompson,
1999). Subsequent work in attachment theory has elaborated this general claim, giving more
emphasis to alternative processes through which early attachment relations influence later
development (e.g., through their effects on the developing brain and on affective and behavioral regulation; Weinfeld, Sroufe, Egeland, & Carlson, 1999) and to discontinuities in
attachment relations over the life course.

    Temperament also creates continuity over the life course (Caspi, 2000; Caspi & Silva,
1995). Temperament has been defined in a number of different ways, including as
constitutional (i.e., biologically based) differences in reactivity and self-regulation

(Rothbart & Derryberry, 1981), basic stable personality characteristics that are evident early in life (Buss & Plomin, 1975), and behavioral style (Thomas & Chess, 1977). However defined, temperament is thought to influence subsequent development primarily through its relationship with the nature and quality of interpersonal interactions (e.g., "difficult" children elicit more critical responses from their parents) which, in turn, define the child's risk of experiencing interpersonal stressors and the subsequent likelihood of negative sequelae. Temperament and personality also moderate the effects of other stressful circumstances on long-term development. For example, among a cohort of children from disadvantaged backgrounds (poverty, low maternal education, family disruption), those children who enjoyed success as adults were more likely than those who did not to have been described by their caregivers as active, cuddly, and good-natured at age 1—characteristics that were also correlated with later childhood autonomy, good peer relations, and an internal locus of control (Werner, 1989).

Finally, sociological theories of socialization attribute life course continuities to internalized societal norms, knowledge, behavioral tendencies, attitudes, and values (Bush & Simmons, 1981). Through interaction with their families, schools, and peers, children develop cognitive, emotional, and social skills and knowledge that they then apply in future social interactions. Socialization has been often invoked as an explanation for intergenerational continuities in behavior and attainment (Sewell & Hauser, 1980). For example, Kohn (1969) showed that working-class parents place high value on conformity to external authority among their children, whereas middle-class parents emphasize children's self-direction. These class differences in parental values perpetuate inequality across generations by preparing children to occupy similar class positions in adulthood. Other research on socialization evaluates the later-life outcomes of specific socialization experiences, such as parenting styles (e.g., Peterson & Rollins, 1987). For example, youth whose parents were nurturing and involved behave in warmer, more supportive ways towards romantic partners in early adulthood than do other youth and therefore enjoy better marital quality (Conger, Cui, Bryant, & Elder, 2000).*

Of course, socialization does not end in childhood and occurs within diverse contexts that may present conflicting opportunities and challenges (Bush & Simmons, 1981). Nevertheless, values, skills, and behaviors learned early in life are importantly linked to later life experiences through their associations with interpersonal interactions and the selection of environments.

The Stability of Environments

Continuity in social and interpersonal environments over the life course is sustained by two distinct types of processes: macro-level processes of stratification that impede major changes in location within social hierarchies and micro-level processes of environmental selection that support and reinforce pre-existing psychological and behavioral tendencies. These types of processes are usually studied independently, but they may interact in important ways. For example, the association between adolescent ambition and later achievements may reflect motivated selection of challenging environments by ambitious youth, but may also demonstrate the influence of structural constraints on motivation (Kerckhoff, 1995). Consistent with this possibility, Gamoran (1996) finds that the same socially structured experiences that allocate students into hierarchically differentiated positions within school tracking systems also

---

*More recent research on socialization emphasizes children's active creation of social environments and the importance of socialization in peer contexts (Corsaro & Eder, 1995).

foster orientations that are consistent with the students' eventual destinations. To the extent that the outcomes of development are jointly determined by persons and their environments, macro- and micro-level processes that encourage environmental stability create continuity over the life course.

With respect to stratification processes, there is strong consistency both in the status levels of parents and their children and in the status locations persons occupy within different social hierarchies (e.g., educational and occupational; Kerckhoff, 1995). The intergenerational consistency in status has been explained variously with reference to: (1) social psychological processes through which parental socioeconomic status influences parental encouragement and support of children's educational attainments (e.g., Haller & Portes, 1973; Sewell & Hauser, 1980), (2) structural features of the labor market, that concentrate power over occupational allocation and rewards in the hands of relatively few powerful owners and managers (e.g., Horan, 1978), (3) school-based ability groupings that privilege children from advantaged backgrounds (e.g., Bowles & Gintis, 1976; Entwistle & Hayduk, 1988), and (4) class-based access to social and cultural capital (Bourdieu, 1973; Coleman, 1990). There are also race and gender differences in the relationship between educational achievement and occupational attainment (e.g., Marini, 1989; Porter, 1974) that demonstrate a lack of openness in the occupational hierarchy for members of lower status groups. Whereas social mobility occurs both across and within generations, intergenerational continuity in status and status consistency imply that persons are likely to encounter similar educational, occupational, and class-related environments over the life course.

The stability of environments over the life course also reflects the motivated selection and creation of environments by individuals. Individuals show a preference for social situations that are compatible with their personalities and for affiliation with similar others (Allport, 1937; Alwin, Cohen, & Newcomb, 1991; Caspi & Herbener, 1990; Newcomb, 1961). Selective entry into compatible social environments, in turn, reinforces individual dispositions. While recognizing the importance of active environmental selection, Caspi, Bem, and Elder (1989) posit the existence of a complementary transactional process in which behaviors, expectations, and self-motives elicit reciprocal, sustaining responses in social interaction. In essence, individual predispositions create social environments that support them. (See Moffitt [1993] for an extended discussion of similar processes as they apply to life course continuities in antisocial behavior.)

Social psychologists emphasize the self as a motivational system in the selection of social and interpersonal environments. Theorists propose variously that individuals are motivated to maintain and enhance positive self-conceptions (Gecas, 1991; Gecas, this volume), to maintain consistency in the self (self-consistency or self-verification; McNulty & Swann, 1991; Swann, 1983), and to seek social relations that are consistent with their self-conceptions (Backman, 1988). Although some of these processes may operate at the cognitive and affective levels, each may also influence behavioral choices. For example, persons with negative self-views tend to select interaction partners who provide them with negative feedback or to behave in ways that elicit such feedback (see De La Ronde & Swann, 1993, for a review). Persons with negative self-views also set low goals and self-handicap to prevent damage to their self-concepts (Coopersmith, 1967; Tice, 1991). The interpersonal and achievement-related failures associated with these processes may further reinforce their low self-concepts, setting into motion self-reinforcing, negative trajectories of self-worth. Notably, such trajectories are not necessarily inevitable. Higgins (1996) and Kiecolt and Mabry (2000) articulate the ways in which perceived discrepancies between actual and ideal selves lead to deliberate efforts to change the self, some of which may prove self-enhancing.

Thus, self-motives may create both continuities and discontinuities in the self through the life course.

The Cumulative Nature of Development

Although we will not dwell on this point, the cumulative nature of biological and cognitive developmental achievements also promotes life course continuities. Early biological insults, such as prenatal alcohol exposure and poor maternal nutrition, limit future neurological and physiological potential (Stewart, 1983). The existence of critical stages of development remains controversial within research on cognitive capacities (Bates, 1999; Cynader & Frost, 1999; Nelson, 2000). Nevertheless, at least some researchers contend that there are specific stages during which children must develop cognitive and emotional capacities or they will lose the ability to achieve full developmental potential in the future (Gewirtz, 1969; Williams, 1972).

Transitions, Turning Points, and Human Agency

Stability in the life course is punctuated by physiological alterations, life transitions, and turning points that alter developmental and experiential trajectories (Clausen, 1993; Elder, 1997). Physiological alterations, such as the hormonal changes associated with puberty, create new physical and social selves that require adjustment and adaptation (Rutter, 1986b). Transitions involve age-graded movement into and out of major social roles and/or institutions, such as entering elementary school, gaining or losing a parent, or a parent's job loss. They can occur on- or off-time and be either expected or unexpected, although transitions that are off-time and unexpected have the most profound effects (Thoits, 1983). In contrast, turning points are defined as periods or points in time "in which a person has undergone a major transformation in views about the self, commitments to important relationships, or involvement in significant life roles" (Wethington, Cooper, & Holmes, 1997, p. 216). Turning points are often associated with major life events such as family formation or unemployment (see the chapters by Sampson and Laub and Uggen and Massoglia in this volume) but they may also result from self-realizations or reinterpretations of past events (Wethington et al., 1997).

Bodily alterations, transitions, and turning points have the potential to open up new opportunities, alter life goals, and create stress. Their influence on the life course depends on how individuals interpret and respond to them, as well as on the constraints that limit those responses (Elder, 1997; Rutter, 1989). Although constraints are often conceptualized as structurally based, people vary in their perceptions of the limitations imposed by similar structural contingencies and in their perceptions of their abilities to surmount them (Bandura, 1986). As a result, different persons faced with the same situation will assert different types and levels of effort to change it, creating diverse life pathways. Shanahan's (2000) notion of bounded strategic action captures this complex interplay between structure and agency in purposive action. Further elaboration of the concept would bring us closer to the type of theory of social action that House (1995) envisions and that a comprehensive account of life course continuities and discontinuities requires. Notably, any such account must allow for the possibility that people assert agency not only in response to transitions and turning points, but also in anticipation of them.

Empirical discontinuity between childhood and adulthood also occurs because of the multidetermined and differentiated nature of adult outcomes. There exist multiple pathways to specific outcomes such as adult depression or high socioeconomic attainment, each of which may be independent of the others. In complement, specific childhood experiences, such as parental divorce, have the potential to be linked to an array of adult outcomes. Most theories of life course continuities are insufficiently specific to predict which adult outcomes should be most strongly predicted by which childhood experiences and vice versa, implying a theoretical and empirical slippage that diminishes observed continuities.

THREE MODELS OF CONTINUITY AND CHANGE

These diverse forces of continuity and change have been incorporated into more general theoretical models that guide contemporary scholarship on childhood–adulthood links. The models can be classified into three broad categories: those that emphasize linear processes of development, those that focus on contingencies, and those that assign central importance to transactions between individuals and their environments. Although the distinctions among these categories blur in practice, they nevertheless provide a useful orienting framework.

Linear models posit the existence of stable physical, cognitive, or psychological competencies that the child carries through life and that place constraints on what the child can accomplish or on the choices the child makes in later life. These competencies are often seen as having their origins in childhood deprivations or traumas, such as prenatal exposure to toxins or childhood parental loss and thereby serve both as explanations for the effects of specific childhood circumstances on adult outcomes as well as precursors in their own right. The linear nature of the models does not necessarily imply simplistic conceptualization. For example, attachment theory's notion of internal working models, discussed above, constitutes a complex set of representational systems involving social expectations of caregivers, events, autobiographical narratives, and understandings of human beliefs and motivations. Moreover, studies that apply linear models often present detailed accounts of the causal mechanisms responsible for the links. What linear models share is the assumption that early experiences and competencies have continued influence over the life course regardless of subsequent events. Linear models are common in areas as diverse as the effects of early childhood poverty on later socioeconomic attainment (e.g., Duncan, Yeung, Brooks-Gunn, & Smith, 1998; Hill & Sandfort, 1995), the psychological sequelae of childhood parental divorce (e.g., McLeod, 1991), and the fetal origins of coronary heart disease (Barker, 1995).

In contrast, contingent models emphasize the potential for both continuity and discontinuity in development. Explicated most clearly by developmental psychopathologists (Rutter, 1986a), these models conceptualize early life events as the beginnings of chains of experience that extend out into the future. Each link in the chain represents alternative possible future paths, with the selection of paths being influenced by strengths and vulnerabilities associated with prior experiences, structural constraints, individual motivation, and luck. In essence, as children move through their lives, alternative pathways open and close in response to their previous experiences and actions. Contingent models of childhood–adulthood continuities acknowledge that children often take active steps to change their environments and that these active steps modify their risk of long-term deleterious outcomes. Turning points in development become central foci of analysis.

Finally, transactional models offer a more fully realized account of person–environment interaction than either linear or contingent models. Drawing on elements of both, they assert that continuities in development occur because of the effects of personal and behavioral predispositions on the selection and creation of proximal social environments and the evocation of interactional responses that validate or support those predispositions (Caspi et al., 1989; Hinde, 1992; Sameroff, 1983). In essence, they contend that stability in personal dispositions is not mediated simply by internal psychological processes, but that it depends as well on the nature of person–environment interactions. Transactional models take as their starting point the general claim that individuals and their environments are mutually determining (e.g., Buss, 1987; Plomin, 1986), but elaborate that claim by considering the specific motives and mechanisms by which that determination occurs. Given their emphasis on predispositions as motivating forces in those interactions, it is not surprising that transactional models have been applied most successfully to understanding continuities in personality, psychopathology, and behavior problems between childhood and adulthood. We believe that they have untapped potential in other areas of research, which we elaborate below. Because transactional models focus on micro-interactions, they give relatively little attention to structural constraints on development.

We illustrate key features of these broad classes of models through a review of research in two substantive areas: the childhood antecedents of adult disease and the effects of childhood adversity on adult life. In each area, we summarize important empirical findings, highlight the most influential theoretical orientations, and discuss critical disjunctions between the two.

CHILDHOOD ANTECEDENTS OF ADULT DISEASE

Research on the childhood antecedents of adult disease follows a linear model. Empirical studies have focused primarily on early (i.e., prenatal and infant) physical development and childhood socioeconomic status as they relate to adult disease and mortality. The indicators for physical development and socioeconomic status are often used interchangeably (e.g., low birthweight used as a proxy for low socioeconomic status), leading to substantial debate about the interpretation of any observed relationships. Complicating matters further, the processes presumed to underly those relationships are not measured explicitly making it difficult to choose among alternative interpretations.

Low birthweight, placenta size, and weight gain in the first year of life increase the risk of a variety of chronic diseases in adulthood, including coronary heart disease, diabetes, obstructive lung disease, and schizophrenia (Barker, 1992; Wahlbeck, Forsen, Osmond, Barker, & Eriksson, 2001; see Joseph & Kramer, 1996, for a review). Childhood height and leg length, among other anthropometric measurements, are also associated with adult mortality from diverse causes (Gunnell et al., 1998; Waaler, 1984). Certain specific childhood diseases also increase the risk of cause-specific adult mortality. For example, children who experience respiratory tract infections at young ages have higher rates of mortality from chronic obstructive lung disease in adulthood (Elo & Preston, 1992). Together, these studies suggest that adult health problems can be traced to early-life nutritional and developmental disadvantages.

These studies have spawned considerable debate about the primacy of physiological processes in the associations between childhood indicators and adult health. On one side of the debate, Barker (1990) contends that adult diseases are "programmed" by biological processes during the prenatal period and infancy. Initially, Barker focused on fetal under-nutrition during middle to late gestation as it relates to stunted fetal growth and, in turn, to risk factors for and the prevalence of coronary heart disease in adulthood. Barker et al. then extended the programming hypothesis to other fetal and infant deprivations and to other adult health outcomes (e.g., slow weight gain during the first year of life in association with adult risk of suicide) (Barker & Osmond, 1995). Throughout these studies, birthweight and weight gain are used as proxies for nutritional deprivations which are not measured directly. Whereas Barker et al. acknowledge that the environment may contribute to health later in life, they contend that its contribution is constrained by levels of susceptibility determined during fetal development (Barker, 1992, 1995).

On the other side of the debate, critics of the programming hypothesis assert that infant developmental indicators serve as markers for generally poor living conditions during childhood that have effects on later health through both contemporaneous and subsequent risks to health (Bartley, Power, Blane, Davey Smith, & Shipley, 1994; Gunnell et al., 1998; Power & Hertzman, 1997). For example, low birthweight and infant weight gain may represent a variety of nutritional and social disadvantages that influence adult health through their associations with specific childhood illnesses (e.g., respiratory tract infections) and/or subsequent life disadvantages (e.g., low socioeconomic status in adulthood).* Most of the studies that support the programming hypothesis are based on data collected over 50 years ago for other purposes, so they do not include measures of health and health behaviors over the life course that would allow them to address this alternative.[†]

Pursuant to the interest in early-life disadvantage, several studies have evaluated the later-life health implications of early socioeconomic differentials. The results are mixed but, overall, suggest that low socioeconomic status during childhood is related to risk factors for and the prevalence of adult disease (e.g., Gliksman et al., 1995; Kaplan & Salonen, 1990; Lynch, Kaplan, & Salonen, 1997; see Haste, 1990; Lynch et al., 1994 for exceptions), to adult mortality (Davey Smith, Hart, Blane, Gillis, & Hawthorne, 1997; Davey Smith, Hart, Blane, & Hole, 1998), and to self-rated health and physical symptoms in early adulthood (Power and Matthews 1997; Power, Matthews, & Manor, 1998). The effects of childhood socioeconomic status on adulthood appear to be specific rather than general (e.g., Davey Smith et al., 1998), implying that any comprehensive explanation for them must be able to account for the absence of relationships for some outcomes as well as their presence for others.

Identifying the mechanisms that account for these associations is complicated by the complex, interlocking nature of trajectories of health and socioeconomic status. Childhood deprivations may affect later health through their associations with contemporaneous risks (e.g., parental smoking, childhood infections) that themselves have long-term effects on health (Wadsworth, 1997). For example, *Helicobacter pylori* infection is more common among lower class children (Mendall et al., 1992) and is an important cause of adult stomach cancer (Forman et al., 1991). Alternatively, low socioeconomic status in childhood may be associated with subsequent health risks due to the enduring effects of poor health behaviors adopted early in life (e.g., poor diet; Power, Manor, & Fox, 1991), the subsequent risks of encountering unhealthy environments (e.g., persons from lower class backgrounds are more likely than others to be exposed to air pollution throughout their lives); Holland, Berney,

---

*Barker et al. controlled for childhood social class in their analyses and found that the relationships between infant health and adult disease were robust to that control. Critics doubt the validity of their measures of social class, however, because they do not correlate with birthweight as one might expect (Paneth & Susser, 1995).

†Much of the evidence for the childhood origins of adult disease derives from studies in England and Scotland in which child participants in surveys carried out in the first half of the 1900s were tracked toward the end of the century and their current health status and/or mortality assessed. Pointed critiques of these studies have appeared in the literature, which note the possible biasing effects of high rates of missing data, the inadequacy of measures of the presumed physiological mechanisms (e.g., early nutrition and diet), and the lack of direct measures of childhood socioeconomic status (Joseph & Kramer, 1996; Paneth & Susser, 1995).

Blane, Davey Smith, Gunnell, & Montgomery, 2000), and the stability of socioeconomic status over the life course (Elo & Preston, 1992; Lynch et al., 1994). Finally, early physical and mental health problems predict low socioeconomic attainment in later life net of controls for origin status (Conley & Bennett, 2000; Miech, Caspi, Moffitt, Wright, & Silva, 1999; Montgomery, Bartley, Cook, & Wadsworth, 1996).

The plausibility of these diverse pathways suggests that the full relevance of childhood socioeconomic circumstances for adult health can only be determined through a complete accounting of life course trajectories. Studies that estimate the effects of socioeconomic status during any specific life stage on health during the same (or a subsequent) life stage may misidentify the risks to health because they fail to consider prior and intervening experiences that explain and/or modify the observed associations. The duration of socioeconomic deprivation also appears to matter in the prediction of child cognitive and emotional health (Duncan, Brooks-Gunn, & Klebanov, 1994; McLeod & Shanahan, 1993, 1996) and, based on the limited evidence that exists, for adult health as well (Davey Smith et al., 1997).

Although there is consensus about the value of life course approaches to the study of socioeconomic differentials in health, the conceptual and empirical challenges of studying complete health and socioeconomic trajectories are substantial. Many prior studies have not even been able to control adult socioeconomic status (SES) when estimating the effects of childhood SES on adult health (Holland et al., 2000), let alone consider trajectories. Prospective, cohort studies hold promise for this type of inquiry. As the empirical inadequacies of existing cohort data sets reveal, however, it is not always possible to anticipate which variables might be of interest in future years and cohort studies confound the effects of aging with changes in historical time.

There are several key issues that beg attention in future research. First, we need more information about changes in socioeconomic conditions throughout the early life course and the effects of these changes as the child grows older (e.g., in prenatal, infancy, childhood, and adolescent stages). Barker's programming hypothesis implies that early childhood socioeconomic conditions have stronger effects on adult health than socioeconomic conditions in later childhood, but systematic evidence for or against this expectation is lacking. Power et al. (1998) found that the effects of social class at birth on adult health held through age 33, even in the presence of controls for current socioeconomic circumstances and were stronger than the effects of adolescent school achievement. Unfortunately, most studies do not have measures of socioeconomic status that span the life course. There may also be some diseases for which there is no socioeconomic differential during childhood or adolescence, but for which childhood and adolescent socioeconomic status predict adult health status through their associations with accumulated risk behaviors (Harley & Mortimer, 2000). Wadsworth (1997) suggests, for example, that, although there is little socioeconomic variation in respiratory function during adolescence, socioeconomic differentials in adolescent and parental smoking create the potential for lagged effects of adolescent socioeconomic status on adult respiratory health.

Second, the effects of childhood conditions on adult health are likely to depend on subsequent life experiences. To date, however, researchers in this area have not examined these contingencies systematically. Barker (1995) acknowledges that "we do not yet know whether socioeconomic influences that affect nutrition and infection in childhood (and thereby influence postnatal growth) can modify the effects of suboptimal growth in utero (p. 311)". Others suggest that poor nutrition in early life leads to adult diabetes only among persons whose life circumstances and nutrition improve in later life because those improvements tax the body's capacity to produce insulin (Hales et al., 1991). Even researchers who have been attentive to socioeconomic trajectories (e.g., Bartley et al., 1994) have not examined interactions between earlier and later socioeconomic circumstances when predicting adult health. Subsequent life stressors, such as parental divorce or residential changes, might also exacerbate childhood health disadvantages.

Finally, researchers who study the childhood antecedents of adult disease have shown little interest in the reciprocal relations between individuals and their environments. Because health problems are conceived as biological in origin, even when influenced by the social environment, researchers within this area conceptualize people as passive with respect to their environments: they may be affected by their environments, but their responses to those environments and the meanings they give to environmental circumstances are not objects of study. The lack of attention to person–environment interactions means that we do not yet know how people's efforts to cope with their physical and social environments over the life course reinforce and/or mitigate socioeconomic differentials in health.

THE EFFECTS OF CHILDHOOD ADVERSITY ON ADULT LIFE

Researchers from diverse disciplines have contributed to our understanding of how early experiences in a child's life influence adult attainments and well-being. Psychologists and psychiatrists tend to focus on the psychopathological outcomes of childhood separations and traumas, whereas demographers, economists, and sociologists have been more concerned with the economic or marital sequelae of parental divorce, living in female-headed households, or early economic disruptions. Nevertheless, there is substantial overlap in the concerns of these diverse groups of researchers, yielding a rich and varied body of empirical research from which to draw conclusions.

Adverse childhood events constrain future life options, but also create opportunities for development (Elder, 1999). The vast majority of empirical studies in this area emphasize the former over the latter. Children who lose their parents, who are separated from their parents for long periods of time (due, for example, to extended hospitalizations or out-of-home placements), and whose parents divorce experience a variety of physical and emotional problems in adulthood and fare less well than others in the marital and occupational markets—clear evidence for the deleterious effects of childhood adversity. This evidence does not obviate the need to consider the potential for positive outcomes resulting from these same experiences, however. Shanahan and Mortimer (1996) elaborate the social psychological mechanisms through which stressors can increase adaptive capacity and promote positive development including, for example, motives to maintain and enhance self-efficacy. Similarly, the steeling hypothesis suggests that encountering and successfully coping with stressors enhances psychological well-being (Masten & Garmezy, 1985; Rutter, 1985). Despite the clear relevance of these arguments for research on childhood adversities, the strength and nature of the relationships of childhood adversities to adult maladaptation, the circumstances under which they hold, and the specific mechanisms that account for them remain underanalyzed. To illustrate the strengths and limitations of existing research on adversity, we compare and contrast research on childhood parental divorce with research on other childhood losses. Studies in these areas draw on both linear and contingent models of development, affording an opportunity to discuss both types of models within the same general substantive area.

Research on the adult outcomes of childhood parental loss through divorce, death, or out-of-home placement (such as in a group home) has focused on three main sets of outcomes: psychological well-being, marital outcomes, and socioeconomic attainment. We review studies of parental divorce first, followed by studies of other parental losses, because the two sets of studies derive from different research traditions and employ different conceptual models.

Parental Divorce

Childhood parental divorce has a modest but significant association with psychological well-being in adulthood. The association holds across diverse indicators of well-being, including overall happiness (Amato, Loomis, & Booth, 1995; Glenn & Kramer, 1985), life satisfaction (Glenn & Kramer, 1985), behavior problems (Zill, Morrison, & Coiro, 1993), antisocial behavior (Pakiz, Reinherz, & Giaconia, 1997), depressive symptoms (McLeod, 1991), substance use (Kuh & Maclean, 1990; Wheaton, Roszell, & Hall, 1997), and major psychiatric-III-R disorders (Wheaton et al., 1997). Whereas the adults in several of these studies are only in their early twenties (e.g., Amato et al., 1995; Furstenberg & Teitler, 1994), other study samples included adults through at least their mid-fifties, implying that psychological effects of divorce persist and possibly even strengthen through the adult life course (Cherlin, Chase-Lansdale, & McRae, 1998).

The simple conclusion that parental divorce generates long-term psychological disadvantages belies the complexity of the relationship between childhood parental divorce and adult psychological well-being (Hetherington & Kelly, 2002). Studies disagree about whether divorces during preschool, elementary school, or later ages are more damaging (Chase-Lansdale, Cherlin, & Kiernan, 1995; Zill et al., 1993) and about whether boys or girls are most affected in the long-run (Glenn & Kramer, 1985; Rodgers, 1990). The effects of family conflict appear to be comparable to the effects of divorce (Amato & Booth, 1991), suggesting that parental divorce serves as a marker for a general period of upheaval and stress in children's lives. Interestingly, recent studies indicate that childhood parental divorce has weaker (or, in some cases, positive) effects on adult psychological well-being if the parents had experienced marked marital conflict or violence prior to the divorce (Kessler, Gillis-Light, Magee, Kendler, & Eaves, 1997; Amato et al., 1995).

The latter findings affirm the importance of seeing parental divorce as part of a matrix of related stressors that jointly determine the environments in which children live (Barber & Eccles, 1992; Furstenberg & Teitler, 1994). As stress researchers have noted, with the possible exception of parental death, childhood adversities cluster within families (Wheaton et al., 1997). Whereas the clustering of adverse experiences complicates analyses of the outcomes of specific events (Rutter, 1990), attempts to disaggregate the effects of clustered adversities may offer relatively little insight into processes of risk and resilience. The different clusters of events that children experience have different meanings that are lost when those events are studied in isolation.

The effects of childhood parental divorce on marital and economic outcomes are stronger and more consistent than its effects on psychological well-being. Data from two prospective, longitudinal, cohort studies in Britain indicate that boys and girls from divorced homes marry at earlier ages, have more premarital pregnancies, and are more likely to cohabit premaritally and get divorced themselves than other children (e.g., Kiernan & Cherlin, 1999; Kuh & Maclean, 1990; Wadsworth, 1979), even in the presence of controls for origin socio-economic status. U.S. studies observe similar patterns (e.g., Glenn & Kramer, 1987; Pope & Mueller, 1976; Thornton, 1991). Children from divorced homes also fare less well economically than children from stable, two-parent homes. They attain lower levels of education and are employed in lower status occupations as adults (e.g., Greenberg & Wolf, 1982; Kuh, Head, Hardy, & Wadsworth, 1997; McLanahan, 1985).

Psychologists and sociologists favor different explanations for the effects of childhood parental divorce on adult outcomes. Not surprisingly, psychologists offer intrapsychic arguments that posit the existence of psychological deficits that interfere with the establishment of stable, committed romantic relationships (Wallerstein & Blakeslee, 1989; Werner & Smith, 1992). In Wallerstein & Blakeslee's (1989) words, "as these young men and woman faced the developmental tasks of establishing love and intimacy, they most felt the lack of a template for a loving, enduring and moral relationship between a man and a women" (pp. 299–300). This anxiety about interpersonal relationships, in turn, leads to declines in psychological adjustment in early adulthood. Sociologists also contend that the marital and socioeconomic problems of children from divorced homes are implicated in their diminished well-being (e.g., Kuh & Maclean, 1990; McLeod, 1991). In contrast to psychologists, however, they see these problems as deriving from structured lack of access to economic resources, changes in parent–child relations, and disrupted socialization in divorced families rather than from disturbed psychological development per se (for reviews see Amato & Keith, 1991; Glenn & Kramer, 1987).

Despite their clear differences, all of these explanations share the implicit assumption that parental divorce affects children's long-term development because it creates early psychological, economic, or experiential disadvantages that follow the child through the life course. They emphasize continuity rather than change and linear progressions of experience rather than contingency. Yet existing research indicates that for all of the societal concern about the long-term effects of divorce, they are modest and, by implication, dependent on the specific nature of the divorce experience, including the level of predivorce parental conflict and subsequent changes in financial status and in parent–child relations.

Other Parental Losses

In contrast to research on parental divorce, the more general body of research on the psychological sequelae of parental losses and separations incorporates explicit consideration of subsequent life experiences that ameliorate or exacerbate their effects. Descriptive studies substantiate that maternal death and other parental separations (e.g., being reared in a group home) predict high rates of depressive and anxious disorders in adulthood (e.g., Brown, Harris, & Bifulco, 1986; Harris et al., 1986; Kessler et al., 1997; McLeod, 1991; Quinton & Rutter, 1988) and are related to problems in marital relationships, as a parent, and in more general social functioning (Harris, Brown, & Bifulco, 1990; Quinton & Rutter, 1988; Quinton, Rutter, & Liddle, 1984). In each case, the long-term effects appear to derive from the circumstances surrounding the loss rather than the loss itself, specifically the subsequent lack of adequate care for the child (Harris et al., 1986).

One pathway through which early adversities might be linked with problems in adult life is their contemporaneous effects on mental health problems and the independent persistence of those problems into adulthood (Rutter, 1981). Evidence for this pathway is mixed. Results from a national U.S. sample indicate that most of the effect of childhood adversity on adult psychiatric disorders can be explained by early-onset disorders; persons who experienced adverse childhood events were more likely to develop disorders at early ages (less than age 20), but were at no greater risk for developing disorders at later ages (Kessler et al., 1997). If that result is replicated, it implies that some of the observed associations between childhood adversities and adult marital and socioeconomic attainments may be attributable to early-onset disorders. However, at least two other studies disagree. Quinton and Rutter (1988) found that the association between institutional rearing and poor parenting and psychosocial problems in adulthood was independent of the presence of psychosocial problems during childhood. In addition, Cherlin et al. (1998) observed that childhood parental divorce led to increases in emotional problems through age 33 even among in the presence of controls for emotional problems during childhood. Transactional models (i.e., models that emphasize person–environment interactions) have not been integrated into research on parental losses, but might offer insight into the complex relations between losses, early mental health problems, subsequent life experiences, and adult adjustment.

Alternatively, childhood adversities might influence later adjustment because they alter sensitivities to later stressors or influence life options and choices (Rutter, 1981). For example, attachment theory predicts that children who lose a parent in early life (particularly the mother) have trouble coping adequately with the loss and develop a helpless–hopeless cognitive bias that leads to the development of deviant attachment patterns in subsequent relationships (e.g., ambivalence and anxiety). These deviant attachment patterns, in turn, increase vulnerability to later stressors (Bowlby, 1980). Developmental psychopathology (Rutter, 1986a) emphasizes the role of experiences leading to, surrounding, and following adversities in their associations with adult adjustment. Although distinct, both orientations acknowledge that early adversities are best conceptualized as part of a stream of life experiences rather than as isolated events.

Two programs of research that draw on these ideas point to the critical importance of considering turning points and trajectories in the life course following early childhood deprivations. In the first, Brown et al. (1986) and Harris et al. (1990) found that maternal losses were significantly and consistently associated with depression, particularly when followed by inadequate care. They traced the effects of childhood maternal losses on adult depression through two parallel causal pathways: one which links childhood helplessness following a maternal death to poor decision-making (as evidenced by premarital pregnancy and marriage to an unsupportive spouse) and the other of which links the premarital pregnancies and spousal choices to low social class in adulthood, high levels of stress, stress vulnerability, and, thereby, to depression. Key for our purposes here, they found that women who were able to overcome their early life disadvantages (including those brought about by premarital pregnancy) and successfully enter into happy, satisfying marriages were much less likely to become depressed as adults than women who were not.

Quinton, Rutter and their colleagues extend this causal pathway in their analysis of the contingencies that shape the future life course for girls who were reared in institutional settings in Great Britain (akin to group homes in the United States). Whereas on average those girls had high rates of poor parenting and psychosocial problems in adulthood, the link from institutional rearing to adult problems could be broken by marriage to a supportive spouse. Tracing the process further back in time, they observed that women with supportive and unsupportive spouses were distinguished primarily by their paths into marriage: the latter entered into marriage after having known their future spouses for relatively short amounts of time, often as the result of a premarital pregnancy, whereas the former tended to marry men whom they had known longer, without outside pressure. On the basis of these patterns, Quinton and Rutter (1988) concluded that disadvantaged girls who took a more active, planning stance towards their futures could create favorable pathways into adulthood.

The focus on turning points in these studies implies agency on the part of the individual that is lacking from many other studies of childhood events. Future research might expand this focus by examining the links between socially structured experiences and individual predispositions. Whereas planfulness and helplessness appear critical in the studies we described, the studies themselves offer little insight into their experiential origins, the predictors of their variations, and the structural contingencies that modify their developmental relevance. In Quinton and Rutter's (1988) study of girls raised in institutional settings, girls who were placed (apparently randomly) in better schools were more likely to be planful during the transition to adulthood, but children are not often distributed across social settings in a random manner. Shanahan and Elder's (2002) research on the differential effectiveness of planfulness for achievement following the Great Depression as compared to World War II draws our attention to the importance of historical circumstances in modifying the developmental relevance of individual predispositions.

More generally, we believe that studies of parental divorce and other parental losses would benefit from a more fully realized life course analysis that takes into account positive sequelae of childhood adversities as well as the broader social and historical context in which they occur. Elder's studies of children who grew up during the Great Depression testify to the potential of this approach. He found, for example, that girls from middle-class homes who experienced economic deprivation during the Great Depression developed family-centered values that remained with them throughout adult life. They were less able than their peers from non-deprived homes to acquire education beyond high school and they married at relatively early ages. In contrast, similarly situated boys enjoyed a certain freedom that allowed them to try out adult roles earlier in life, such as taking work outside the home and developed a keener motivation for adult success than their less deprived peers. Both boys and girls from middle-class deprived backgrounds were judged to be healthier and psychologically stronger in adulthood than their middle-class children from non-deprived homes. Moreover, economic deprivation made less difference to the subsequent life course of working-class youth who had less to lose but also less to gain from the experience. In subsequent analyses, Elder and Caspi (1990) and Elder, Downey, and Cross (1986) further elaborated the diverse pathways through which children of the Great Depression entered adult life, highlighting the importance of military experience and education for men and marriage, educational sacrifice, and childbearing for women. In similar fashion, studies of parental divorce could consider the opportunities created by divorce as well as the limitations it imposes and the changing historical contexts that shape the meaning of divorce for individual families.

SUMMARY AND CONCLUSIONS

Our review focused on two areas of research that illustrate alternative approaches to the association between childhood experience and adult life and that have corresponding strengths and weaknesses. Taking a linear approach, research on the childhood antecedents of adult health provides compelling evidence for the importance of early physical and social environments over the life course, but has not given adequate attention to subsequent life circumstances. Research on the psychological outcomes of childhood losses takes a much more contingent approach, but nevertheless fails to articulate the determinants of those contingencies, in particular, the balance of structure and agency and the role of environmental responses to individual behavior. Neither area of research has adequately considered reciprocal relations between persons and their environments (i.e., transactional models) as they shape subsequent life course trajectories.

Research on childhood–adulthood links is central to the broader project of life course research because of its potential to illuminate the relationship between structure and agency and the nature of psychological and social structures, how they are perceived, and how they influence behavioral choices. To date, however, this research has failed to achieve its full potential because of inadequacies in the conceptualization of meaning and structure. For example, despite the central relevance of subjective interpretation in theories of life stress (e.g., Brown & Harris, 1989), studies of the long-term outcomes of childhood experiences do not consider the meaning of childhood environments and experiences from the child's perspective. Kessler et al. (1997) note that parental divorce is associated with less adult psychopathology when it serves as the end-point in family conflict than when it occurs in the absence of such conflict, following Wheaton's (1990) discussion of the relevance of role histories for the psychological impact of life transitions. Brown et al. (1986) and Quinton and Rutter (1988) incorporate meaning into their interpretations of the links between childhood parental losses and adult well-being, but can only infer meaning from the relationships between the loss, psychological dispositions, and subsequent life choices. There are, of course, clear conceptual and empirical obstacles to incorporating meaning into these analyses, not the least of which is the complexity of assessing subjective meaning among children. Nevertheless, to the extent that childhood–adulthood relations result from selection into different life pathways, meaning must be central to any satisfying theory (Jessor, 1981).

Similarly, research on childhood–adulthood links has failed to develop a compelling conceptual model of the nature of social structural influences over the life course. Social structures shape children's exposures to risks and the resources they have available to cope with those risks, even before birth. What remains unclear is how best to conceptualize the nature of and changes in social structures with age (McLeod & Lively, in press). Theories of human development identify multiple, interactive contexts each of which has multiple dimensions (e.g., Bronfenbrenner, 1979). Those contexts can be further defined with respect to both their structural (e.g., marital status) and functional (e.g., parent–child relationships) aspects (Boyce et al., 1998) each of which is subject to change over time. The MacArthur Network on Psychopathology and Development (Boyce et al., 1998) asserts the need for more research on transactions between children and their environments and on the processes through which those environments translate into biological experiences.

Each of these insights has begun to infiltrate empirical research. Call and Mortimer (2001) demonstrate that experiences in one context can dampen or amplify experiences in another. Wu and Martinson (1993) present a compelling case for elaborating the dynamics of childhood context, further substantiated by research that evaluates the implications of duration of childhood statuses for adult health (e.g., Davey Smith et al., 1997). For all this progress, however, the broader structural underpinnings of social contexts and the relevance of those structures for shaping the form and effects of those contexts remain underspecified.

Underlying these comments is the need for researchers in this area, particularly sociologists, to make contingencies central rather than peripheral to their analyses. As we noted at the outset, the connections between childhood and adulthood are often small in magnitude, implying that discontinuities are the rule rather than the exception. Whereas developmental psychopathologists assume the relevance of both continuity and change, sociological studies of the life course implications of childhood experiences more often rely on linear models for theoretical and methodological guidance. By their very nature, such models do not yield information about how disadvantaged youth surmount early challenges.

More generally, research on childhood–adulthood links would benefit from explicit attention to life course principles. Whereas certain life course concepts such as transitions and trajectories permeate this research, other life course notions such as the age-graded nature of social roles, the centrality of human agency, and the historically contingent nature of development are much less evident. The life course perspective makes central processes that have been treated as peripheral in prior research (e.g., choice and action), opening new avenues of potentially fruitful investigation. Moreover, it serves as a natural bridge between sociological and psychological perspectives and between social structure and individual development. As such, it provides leverage with which to develop models of life course continuities that transcend disciplinary boundaries.

In sum, future progress in elucidating childhood–adulthood links will require a nuanced theory of social action that is sensitive to the changing nature of cognitive capacities, social structures, and environmental responsiveness with age (House, 1995; House & Mortimer, 1990). This theory can be built in part from analyses of the divergent paths through which children become adults and the joint relation of those paths to structure, meaning, and action. The most satisfying empirical studies of the links between childhood and adulthood move back and forth between individuals and their environments, focusing in on the outcomes of key transitions and turning points over the life course (e.g., the role of planfulness in specific life transitions). Studies that examine person–environment interactions during those periods would complement existing broad-based studies by elaborating the nature of constraints and responses to specific historical and personal conditions. The broader theoretical agenda that our comments suggest cannot be accomplished in any one study, but requires the collective efforts of numerous scholars across multiple disciplines.

ACKNOWLEDGMENTS: We are indebted to the editors for their thoughtful comments on an earlier draft. Mr. Almazan's work on this chapter was supported by the ASA Minority Fellowship Program (T32 MH15722).

REFERENCES

Ainsworth, M. D. S., Blehar, M. C., Waters, E., & Wall, S. (1978). *Patterns of attachment.* Hillsdale, NJ: Erlbaum.
Allport, G. (1937). *Personality: A psychological interpretation.* New York: Hold, Rinehart, & Winston.
Alwin, D. F., Cohen, R. L., & Newcomb, T. M. (1991). *Political attitudes over the life span: The Bennington women after fifty years.* Madison, WI: University of Wisconsin Press.
Amato P. R., & Booth, A. (1991). The consequences of parental divorce and marital unhappiness for adult well-being. *Social Forces, 69*, 895–914.
Amato, P. R., & Keith, B. (1991). Parental divorce and adult well-being: A meta-analysis. *Journal of Marriage and the Family, 53*, 43–58.
Amato, P. R., Loomis, L. S., & Booth, A. (1995). Parental divorce, marital conflict, and offspring well-being during early adulthood. *Social Forces, 73*, 895–915.
Backman, C. W. (1988). The self: A dialectical approach. *Advances in Experimental Social Psychology, 21*, 229–260.
Bandura, A. (1986). *Social foundations of thought and action: A social cognitive theory.* Englewood Cliffs, NJ: Prentice-Hall.
Barber, B. L., & Eccles, J. S. (1992). Long-term influence of divorce and single parenting on adolescent family and work related values, behaviors, and aspirations. *Psychological Bulletin, 111*, 108–126.
Barker, D. J. P. (1990). The fetal and infant origins of adult disease. *British Medical Journal, 301*, 1111.
Barker, D. J. P. (Ed.) (1992). *Fetal and infant origins of adult disease.* London: BMJ Publishing.
Barker, D. J. P. (1995). Fetal origins of coronary heart disease. *British Medical Journal, 311*, 171–174.
Barker, D. J. P., & Osmond, C. (1995). Low weight gain in infancy and suicide in adult life. *British Medical Journal, 311*, 1203.
Bartley, M., Power, C., Blane, D., Davey Smith, G., & Shipley, M. (1994). Birth weight and later socioeconomic disadvantage: Evidence from the 1958 British cohort study. *British Medical Journal, 309*, 1475–1479.
Bates, E. (1999). Plasticity, localization, and language development. In S. H. Broman & J. M. Fletcher (Eds.), *The changing nervous system: Neurobehavioral consequences of early brain disorders* (pp. 214–253). New York: Oxford University Press.
Bourdieu, P. (1973). Cultural reproduction and social reproduction. In R. Brown (Ed.), *Knowledge, education, and cultural change* (pp. 71–112). London: Tavistock.
Bowlby, J. (1969/1982). *Attachment and loss: Vol. 1. Attachment.* New York: Basic Books.
Bowlby, J. (1973). *Attachment and loss: Vol. 2. Separation: Anxiety and anger.* New York: Basic Books.

Bowlby, J. (1980). *Attachment and loss: Vol. 3. Loss: Sadness and depression.* New York: Basic Books.

Bowles, S., & Gintis, H. (1976). *Schooling the capitalist America: Educational reform and the contradictions of economic life.* New York: Basic Books.

Boyce, W. T., Frank, E., Jensen, P. S., Kessler, R. C., Nelson, C. A., Steinberg, L., & The MacArthur Foundation Research Network on Psychopathology and Development. (1998). Social context in developmental psychopathology: Recommendations for future research from the MacArthur Network on psychopathology and development. *Development and Psychopathology, 10*, 143–164.

Bretherton, I., & Munholland, K. A. (1999). Internal working models in attachment relationships: A construct revisited. In J. Cassidy & P. R. Shaver (Eds.), *Handbook of attachment: Theory, research, and clinical applications* (pp. 89–111). New York: Guilford Press.

Brofenbrenner, U. (1979). *The ecology of human development: Experiments by nature and design.* Cambridge, MA: Harvard University Press.

Brown, G. W., & Harris, T. O. (1989). *Life events and illness.* New York: Guilford Press.

Brown, G. W., Harris, T. O., & Bifulco, A. (1986). Long-term effects of early loss of a parent. In M. Rutter, C. E. Izard, & P. B. Read (Eds.), *Depression in young people: Developmental and clinical perspectives* (pp. 251–296). New York: Guilford Press.

Bush, D., & Simmons, R. (1981). Socialization processes over the life course. In M. Rosenberg & R. Turner (Eds.), *Social psychology: Sociological perspectives* (pp. 133–164). New York: Basic Books.

Buss, A. H., & Plomin, R. (1975). *A temperament theory of personality.* New York: Wiley-Interscience.

Buss, D. M. (1987). Selection, evocation, and manipulation. *Journal of Personality and Social Psychology, 53*, 1214–1221.

Call, K. T., & Mortimer, J. T. (2001). *Arenas of comfort in adolescence: A study of adjustment in context.* Mahwah, NJ: Lawrence Erlbaum.

Caspi, A. (2000). The child is the father of the man: Personality continuities from childhood to adulthood. *Journal of Personality and Social Psychology, 78*, 158–172.

Caspi, A., Bem, D. J., & Elder, G. H., Jr. (1989). Continuities and consequences of interactional styles across the life course. *Journal of Personality, 57*, 375–406.

Caspi, A., & Herbener, E. S. (1990). Continuity and change: Assortative marriage and the consistency of personality in adulthood. *Journal of Personality and Social Psychology, 58*, 250–258.

Caspi, A., & Silva, P. A. (1995). Temperamental qualities at age three predict personality traits in young adulthood: Longitudinal evidence from a birth cohort. *Child Development, 66*, 486–498.

Chase-Lansdale, P. L., Cherlin, A. J., & Kiernan, K. E. (1995). The long-term effects of parental divorce on the mental health of young adults: A developmental perspective. *Child Development, 66*, 1614–1634.

Cherlin, A. J., Chase-Lansdale, P. L., & McRae, C. (1998). Effects of parental divorce on mental health throughout the life course. *American Sociological Review, 63*, 239–249.

Clausen, J. A. (1993). *American lives: Looking back at the children of the great depression.* New York: Free Press.

Coleman, J. S. (1990). *Foundations of social theory.* Cambridge, MA: Harvard University Press.

Conger, R. D., Cui, M., Bryant, C. M., & Elder, G. H., Jr. (2000). Competence in early adult romantic relationships: A developmental perspective on family influences. *Journal of Personality and Social Psychology, 79*, 224–237.

Conley, D., & Bennett, N. G. (2000). Is biology destiny? Birth weight and life chances. *American Sociological Review, 65*, 458–467.

Coopersmith, S. (1967). *The antecedents of self-esteem.* San Francisco, CA: W. H. Freeman.

Corsaro, W. A., & Eder, D. (1995). Development and socialization of children and adolescents. In K. S. Cook, G. A. Fine, & J. S. House (Eds.), *Sociological perspectives on social psychology* (pp. 421–451). Needham Heights, MA: Allyn & Bacon.

Cynader, M. S., & Frost, B. J. (1999). Mechanisms of brain development: Neuronal sculpting by the physical and social environment. In D. P. Keating & C. Hertzman (Eds.), *Developmental health and the wealth of nations: Social, biological, and educational dynamics* (pp. 153–184). New York: Guilford Press.

Davey Smith, G., Hart, C., Blane, D., Gillis, D., & Hawthorne, V. (1997). Lifetime socioeconomic position and mortality: Prospective observational study. *British Medical Journal, 314*, 547–552.

Davey Smith, G., Hart, C., Blane, D., & Hole, D. (1998). Adverse socioeconomic conditions in childhood and cause specific adult mortality. *British Medical Journal, 316*, 1631–1635.

De La Ronde, C., & Swann, W. B., Jr. (1993). Caught in the crossfire: Positivity and self-verification strivings among people with low self-esteem. In R. F. Baumeister (ed.) *Self-esteem: The puzzle of low self-regard* (pp. 147–165). New York: Plenum Press.

Duncan, G. J., Brooks-Gunn, J., & Klebanov, P. K. (1994). Economic deprivation and early childhood development. *Child Development, 65*, 296–318.

Duncan, G. J., Yeung, W. J., Brooks-Gunn, J., & Smith, J. R. (1998). How much does childhood poverty affect the life chances of children? *American Sociological Review, 63*, 406–423.

Elder, G. H., Jr. (1974). *Children of the great depression: Social change in life experience*. Chicago: University of Chicago Press.

Elder, G. H., Jr. (1997). The life course and human development. In R. M. Lerner (Ed.), *Handbook of child psychology, volume 1: Theoretical models of human development* (pp. 939–991). New York: Wiley.

Elder, G. H., Jr. (1999). *Children of the Great Depression: Social change in life experience* (25th anniversary ed.). Boulder, CO: Westview.

Elder, G. H., Jr., & Caspi, A. (1990). Studying lives in a changing society: Sociological and personological explorations. In A. I. Rabin, R. A. Zucker, R. A. Emmons, & S. Frank (Eds.), *Studying persons and lives* (pp. 201–247). New York: Springer.

Elder, G. H., Jr., Downey, G., & Cross, C. E. (1986). Family ties and life chances. Hard times and hard choices in women's lives since the Great Depression. In N. Datan, A. L. Greene, and H. W. Reese (Eds.), *Life-span developmental psychology: International relations* (pp. 167–186). Hillsdale, NJ: Erlbaum.

Elo, I. T., & Preston, S. H. (1992). Effects of early-life conditions on adult mortality: A review. *Population Index, 58*, 186–212.

Entwistle, D. R., & Hayduk, L. A. (1988). Lasting effects of elementary school. *Sociology of Education, 61*, 147–159.

Fonagy, P. (1999). Psychoanalytic theory from the viewpoint of attachment theory and research. In J. Cassidy & P. R. Shaver (Eds.), *Handbook of attachment: Theory, research, and clinical applications* (pp. 595–624). New York: Guilford Press.

Forman, D., Newell, D. G., Fullerton, F., Yarnell, J. W. G., Stacey, A. R., Wald, N. et al. (1991). Association between infection with *Helicobacter pylori* and risk of gastric cancer: Evidence from a prospective investigation. *British Medical Journal, 302*, 1302–1305.

Furstenberg, F. F., & Teitler, J. O. (1994). Reconsidering the effects of marital disruption: What happens to children of divorce in early adulthood? *Journal of Family Issues, 15*, 173–190.

Gamoran, A. (1996). Educational stratification and individual careers. In A. C. Kerckhoff (ed.) *Generating social stratification: Toward a new research agenda* (pp. 59–74). Boulder, CO: Westview.

Gecas, V. (1991). The self-concept as a basis for motivation. In J. A. Howard & P. L. Callero (Eds.), *The self-society dynamic: Cognition, emotion and action* (pp. 171–188). Cambridge: Cambridge University Press.

Gewirtz, J. L. (1969). Mechanisms of social learning: Some roles of stimulation and behavior in early human development. In D. A. Goslin (Ed.), *Handbook of socialization theory and research* (pp. 57–212). Chicago, IL: Rand McNally.

Glenn, N. D., & Kramer, K. B. (1985). The psychological well-being of adult children of divorce. *Journal of Marriage and the Family, 47*, 905–912.

Glenn, N. D., & Kramer, K. B. (1987). The marriages and divorces of the children of divorce. *Journal of Marriage and the Family, 49*, 811–825.

Gliksman, M. D., Kawachi, I., Hunter, D., Colditz, G. A., Manson, J. E., Stampfer, M. J., Speizer, F. E., Willett, W. C., & Hennekens, C. H. (1995). Childhood socioeconomic status and risk of cardiovascular disease in middle aged US women: A prospective study. *Journal of Epidemiology and Community Health, 49*, 5–10.

Greenberg, D., & Wolf, D. (1982). The economic consequences of experiencing parental marital disruption. *Child and Youth Services Review, 4*, 141–162.

Gunnell, D., Davey Smith, G., Frankel, S., Nanchahal, K., Braddon, F. E. M., Pemberton, J., & Peters, T. J. (1998). Childhood leg length and adult mortality—follow up of the Carnegie survey of diet and growth in pre-war Britain. *Journal of Epidemiology and Community Health, 52*, 142–152.

Hales, C. N., Barker, D. J. P., Clark, P. M. S., Cox, L. J., Fall, C., Osmond, C., & Winter, P. (1991). Fetal and infant growth and impaired glucose tolerance at age 64. *British Medical Journal, 303*, 1019–1022.

Haller, A. O., & Portes, A. (1973). Status attainment processes. *Sociology of Education, 46*, 51–91.

Harley, C., & Mortimer, J. T. (2000). *Social status and mental health in young adulthood: The mediating role of the transition to adulthood*. Presented at the Biennial Meeting of the Society for Research on Adolescence, Chicago, IL.

Harris, T., Brown, G. W., & Bifulco, A. (1986). Loss of a parent in childhood and adult psychiatric disorder: The role of lack of adequate parental care. *Psychological Medicine, 16*, 641–659.

Harris, T. O., Brown, G. W., & Bifulco, A. (1990). Loss of a parent in childhood and adult psychiatric disorder: A tentative overall model. *Development and Psychopathology, 2*, 311–328.

Haste, H. (1990). Association between living conditions in childhood and myocardial infarction. *British Medical Journal, 300*, 512–513.

Hazan, C., & Shaver, P. R. (1994). Attachment as an organizational framework for research on close relationships. *Psychological Inquiry, 5*, 1–22.

Hetherington, E. M., & Kelly, J. (2002). *For better or for worse: Divorce reconsidered*. New York: W. W. Norton & Co.

Higgins, E. T. (1996). Ideals, oughts, and regulatory focus: Affect and motivation from distinct pains and pleasures. In P. M. Gollwitzer & J. A. Bargh (Eds.), *The psychology of action: Linking cognition and motivation in behavior* (pp. 91–114). New York: Guilford Press.

Hill, M. S., & Sandfort, J. R. (1995). Effects of childhood poverty on productivity later in life: Implications for public policy. *Children and Youth Service Review, 17,* 91–126.

Hinde, R. A. (1992). Developmental psychology in the context of other behavioral sciences. *Developmental Psychology, 28,* 1018–1029.

Holland, P., Berney, L., Blane, D., Davey Smith, G., Gunnell, D. J., & Montgomery, S. M. (2000). Life course accumulation of disadvantage: Childhood health and hazard exposure during adulthood. *Social Science and Medicine, 50,* 1285–1295.

Horan, P. M. (1978). Is status attainment research atheoretical? *American Sociololgical Review, 43,* 534–541.

House, J. S. (1995). Social structure and personality: Past, present, and future. In K. S. Cook, G. A. Fine, & J. S. House (Eds.), *Sociological perspectives on social psychology* (pp. 387–395). Needham Heights, MA: Allyn & Bacon.

House, J. S., & Mortimer, J. T. (1990). Social structure and the individual: Emerging themes and new directions. *Social Psychology Quarterly, 53,* 71–80.

Jessor, R. (1981). The perceived environment in psychological theory and research. In D. Magnusson (Ed.), *Toward a psychology of situations: An interactional perspective* (pp. 297–317). Hillsdale, NJ: Erlbaum.

Joseph, K. S., & Kramer, M. S. (1996). Review of the evidence on fetal and early childhood antecedents of adult chronic disease. *Epidemiological Review, 18,* 158–174.

Kaplan, G. A., & Salonen, J. T. (1990). Socioeconomic conditions in childhood and ischaemic heart disease during middle age. *British Medical Journal, 301,* 1121–1123.

Kerckhoff, A. C. (1995). Social stratification and mobility processes: Interaction between individuals and social structures. In K. S. Cook, G. A. Fine, & J. S. House (Eds.), *Sociological perspectives on social psychology* (pp. 476–496). Needham Heights, MA: Allyn & Bacon.

Kessler, R. C., Gillis-Light, J., Magee, W., Kendler, K. S., & Eaves, L. J. (1997). Childhood adversity and adult pathopsychology. In I. H. Gotlib & B. Wheaton (Eds.), *Stress and adversity over the life course: Trajectories and turning points* (pp. 29–49). New York: Cambridge University Press.

Kiecolt, K. J., & Mabry, J. B. (2000). Agency in young adulthood: Intentional self-change among college students. *Advances in Life Course Research, 5,* 181–205.

Kiernan, K. E., & Cherlin, A. J. (1999). Parental divorce and partnership dissolution in adulthood: Evidence from a British cohort study. *Population Studies, 53,* 39–48.

Kohn, M. L. (1969). *Class and conformity: A study in values.* Homewood, IL: Dorsey.

Kuh, D., Head, J., Hardy, R., & Wadsworth, M. (1997). The influence of education and family background on women's earnings in midlife: Evidence from a British national birth cohort study. *British Journal of Sociology of Education, 18,* 385–405.

Kuh, D., & Maclean, M. (1990). Women's childhood experience of parental separation and their subsequent health and socioeconomic status in adulthood. *Journal of Biosocial Science, 22,* 121–135.

Lynch, J. W., Kaplan, G. A., Cohen, R. D., Kauhanen, J., Wilson, T. W., Smith, N. L., & Salonen, J. T. (1994). Childhood and adult socioeconomic status as predictors of mortality in Finland. *Lancet, 343,* 524–527.

Lynch, J. W., Kaplan, G. A., & Salonen, J. T. (1997). Why do poor people behave poorly? Variation in adult health behaviors and psychosocial characteristics by stages of the socioeconomic lifecourse. *Social Science and Medicine, 44,* 809–819.

McLanahan, S. (1985). Family structure and the reproduction of poverty. *American Journal of Sociology, 90,* 873–901.

McLeod, J. D. (1991). Childhood parental loss and adult depression. *Journal of Health and Social Behavior, 32,* 205–220.

McLeod, J. D., & Lively, K. J. (in press). Social structure and personality. In J. DeLamater (Ed.) *Handbook of social psychology.*

McLeod, J. D., & Shanahan, M. J. (1993). Poverty, parenting, and children's mental health. *American Sociological Review, 58,* 351–366.

McLeod, J. D., & Shanahan, M. J. (1996). Trajectories of poverty and children's mental health. *Journal of Health and Social Behavior, 37,* 207–220.

McNulty, S. E., & Swann, W. B., Jr. (1991). Psychotherapy, self-concept change, and self-verification. In *The relational self: Theoretical convergences in psychoanalysis and social psychology* (pp. 213–237). New York: Guildford Press.

Marini, M. M. (1989). Sex differences in earnings in the United States. *Social Science Research, 9,* 307–361.

Masten, A. S., & Garmezy, M. (1985). Risk, vulnerability, and protective factors in developmental psychopathology. In B. B. Lahey & A. E. Kazdin (Eds.), *Advances in clinical child psychology* (Vol. 8, pp. 1–52). New York: Plenum.

Mendall, M. A., Goggin, P. M., Molineaux, N., Levy, J., Toosy, T., Strachan, D., & Northfield, T. C. (1992). Childhood living conditions and *Helicobacter pylori* serpositivity in adult life. *The Lancet, 339*, 896–897.

Miech, R. A., Caspi, A., Moffitt, T. E., Wright, B. R. E., & Silva, P. A. (1999). Low socioeconomic status and mental disorders: A longitudinal study of selection and causation during young adulthood. *American Journal of Sociology, 104*, 1096–1131.

Moffitt, T. E. (1993). Adolescence limited and life-course-persistent antisocial behavior: A developmental taxonomy. *Psychological Review, 100*, 674–701.

Montgomery, S. M., Bartley, M. J., Cook, D. G., & Wadsworth, M. E. J. (1996). Health and social precursors of unemployment in young men in Great Britain. *Journal of Epidemiology and Community Health, 50*, 415–422.

Nelson, C. A. (2000). Neural plasticity and human development: The role of early experience sculpting memory systems. *Developmental Science, 3*, 115–130.

Newcomb, T. M. (1961). *The acquaintance process*. New York: Holt, Rinehart, & Winston.

Pakiz, B., Reinherz, H. A., & Giaconia, R. M. (1997). Early risk factors for serious antisocial behavior at age 21: A longitudinal community study. *American Journal of Orthopsychiatry, 67*, 92–101.

Paneth, N., & Susser, M. (1995). Early origin of coronary heart disease ('the Barker hypothesis'). *British Medical Journal, 310*, 411–412.

Parker, J., & Asher, S. (1987). Peer relations and later personal adjustment: Are low-accepted children at risk? *Psychological Bulletin, 102*, 357–389.

Peterson, G., & Rollins, B. (1987). Parent–Child socialization. In M. Sussman & S. Steinmetz (Eds.), *Handbook of marriage and the family* (pp. 471–507). New York: Plenum.

Plomin, R. (1986). *Development, genetics, and psychology*. Hillsdale, NJ: Erlbaum.

Pope, H., & Mueller, C. W. (1976). The intergenerational transmission of marital instability: Comparisons by sex and race. *Journal of Social Issues, 32*, 49–66.

Porter, J. N. (1974). Race, socialization and mobility in educational and early occupational attainment. *American Sociological Review, 39*, 303–316.

Power, C., & Hertzman, C. (1997). Social and biological pathways linking early life and adult disease. *British Medical Bulletin, 53*, 210–221.

Power, C., & Matthews, S. (1997). Origins of health inequalities in a national population survey. *The Lancet, 350*, 1584–1589.

Power, C., Matthews, S., & Manor, O. (1998). Inequalities in self-rated health: explanations from different stages of life. *The Lancet, 351*, 1009–1014.

Power, C., Manor, O., & Fox, J. (1991). *Health and class: The early years*. London: Chapman & Hall.

Quinton, D., & Rutter, M. (1988). *Parenting breakdown: The making and breaking of inter-generational links*. Aldershot: Avebury.

Quinton, D., Rutter, M., & Liddle, C. (1984). Institutional rearing, parenting difficulties, and marital support. *Psychological Medicine, 14*, 107–124.

Rodgers, B. (1990). Adult affective disorder and early environment. *British Journal of Psychiatry, 157*, 539–550.

Rothbart, M. K., & Derryberry, D. (1981). Development of individual differences in temperament. In M. E. Lamb (Ed.), *Advances in developmental psychology* (Vol. 1, pp. 17–86). Hillsdale, NJ: Erlbaum.

Rutter, M. (1981). Stress, coping and development: Some issues and some questions. *Journal of Child Psychology and Psychiatry, 22*, 323–256.

Rutter, M. (1985). Resilience in the face of adversity: Protective factors and resistance to psychiatric disorder. *British Journal of Psychiatry, 147*, 598–611.

Rutter, M. L. (1986a). Child psychiatry: The interface between clinical and developmental research. *Psychological Medicine, 16*, 151–169.

Rutter, M. (1986b). The developmental psychopathy of depression: Issues and perspectives. In M. Rutter, C. E. Izard, & P. B. Read (Eds.), *Depression in young people: Developmental and clinical perspectives* (pp. 3–30). New York: Guilford Press.

Rutter, M. (1989). Pathways from childhood to adult life. *Journal of Child Psychology and Psychiatry, 30*, 23–51.

Rutter, M. (1990). Psychosocial resilience and protective mechanisms. In J. E. Rolf, A. S. Masten, D. Cicchetti, K. H. Neuchterlein, & S. Weintraub (Eds.), *Risk and protective factors in the development of psychopathology* (pp. 181–214). New York: Cambridge University Press.

Sameroff, A. J. (1983). Developmental systems: Contexts and evolution. In W. Kessen (Ed.), *History, theory, and methods* (4th ed., Vol. 1, pp. 237–294). New York: Wiley.

Sewell, W. H., & Hauser, R. M. (1980). The Wisconsin longitudinal study of social and psychological factors in aspirations and achievements. *Research in Sociology of Education and Socialization, 1*, 59–99.

Shanahan, M. J. (2000). Pathways to adulthood in changing societies: Variability and mechanisms in life course perspective. *Annual Review of Sociology, 26*, 667–692.

Shanahan, M. J., & Elder, G. H., Jr. (2002). History, agency, and the life course. In L. Crockett (Ed.), *Agency, motivation, and the life course* (pp. 145–186). Lincoln, NE: University of Nebraska Press.

Shanahan, M. J., & Mortimer, J. T. (1996). Understanding the positive consequences of psychosocial stressors. *Advances in Group Processes, 13*, 189–209.

Stewart, A. (1983). Severe perinatal hazards. In M. Rutter (Eds.), *Developmental neuropsychiatry* (pp. 15–31). New York: Guilford Press.

Swann, W. B., Jr. (1983). Self verification: Bringing social reality into harmony with the self. In J. Suls & A. G. Greenwald (Eds.), *Psychological perspectives on the self* (pp. 33–66). Hillsdale, NJ: Erlbaum.

Thoits, P. A. (1983). Dimensions of life events that influence psychological distress: An evaluation and synthesis of the literature. In H. B. Kaplan (Eds.), *Psychosocial stress: Trends in theory and research* (pp. 33–103). Orlando, FL: Academic Press.

Thomas, A., & Chess, S. (1977). *Temperament and development*. New York: Brunner/Mazel.

Thompson, R. A. (1999). Early attachment and later development. In J. Cassidy & P. R. Shaver (Eds.), *Handbook of attachment: Theory, research, and clinical applications* (pp. 265–286). New York: Guilford Press.

Thornton, A. (1991). Influence of the marital history of parents on the marital and cohabitational experiences of children. *American Journal of Sociology, 96*, 868–894.

Tice, D. M. (1991). Esteem protection or enhancement? Self-handicapping motives and attributions differ by trait self-esteem. *Journal of Personality and Social Psychology, 60*, 711–725.

Tweed, J. L., Schoenbach, V. J., George, L. K., & Blazer, D. G. (1989). The effects of childhood parental death and divorce on six-month history of anxiety disorders. *British Journal of Psychiatry, 154*, 823–828.

Waaler, H. T. (1984). Height, weight and mortality. *Acta Medica Scandinavica, 679* (Suppl.), 1–56.

Wadsworth, M. E. J. (1979). *Roots of delinquency: Infancy, adolescence and crime*. Oxford: Martin Robertson.

Wadsworth, M. E. J. (1997). Health inequalities in the life course perspective. *Social Science and Medicine, 44*, 859–869.

Wahlbeck, K., Forsen, T., Osmond, C., Barker, D. J., & Eriksson, J. G. (2001). Association of schizophrenia with low maternal body mass index, small size at birth, and thinness during childhood. *Archives of General Psychiatry, 58*, 48–52.

Wallerstein, J., & Blakeslee, S. (1989). *Second chances: Men, women and children a decade after divorce*. New York: Ticknor and Fields.

Weinfield, N. S., Sroufe, L. A., Egeland, B., & Carlson, E. A. (1999). The nature of individual differences in infant–caregiver attachment. In J. Cassidy & P. R. Shaver (Eds.), *Handbook of attachment: Theory, research, and clinical applications* (pp. 68–88). New York: Guilford Press.

Werner, E. E. (1985). Stress and protective factors in children's lives. In A. R. Nicol (Ed.), *Longitudinal studies in child psychology and psychiatry* (pp. 335–355). New York: Wiley and Sons.

Werner, E. E. (1989). High-risk children in young adulthood: A longitudinal study from birth to 32 years. *American Journal of Orthopsychiatry, 59*, 72–81.

Werner, E. E., & Smith, R. S. (1992). *Overcoming the odds: High risk children from birth to adulthood*. Ithaca, NY: Cornell University Press.

Wethington, E., Cooper, H., & Holmes, C. S. (1997). Turning points in midlife. In I. H. Gotlib & B. Wheaton (Eds.), *Stress and adversity over the life course: Trajectories and turning points* (pp. 215–231). New York: Cambridge University.

Wheaton, B. (1990). Life transitions, role histories, and mental health. *American Sociological Review, 55*, 209–223.

Wheaton, B., Roszell, P., & Hall, K. (1997). The impact of twenty childhood and adult traumatic stressors on the risk of psychiatric disorder. In I. H. Gotlib & B. Wheaton (Eds.), *Stress and adversity over the life course: Trajectories and turning points* (pp. 50–72). New York: Cambridge University.

Williams, T. R. (1972). *Introduction to socialization: Human culture transmitted*. St Louis: Mosby.

Wu, L. L., & Martinson, B. C. (1993). Family structure and the risk of a premarital birth. *American Sociological Review, 58*, 210–232.

Zill, N., Morrison, D. R., & Coiro, M. J. (1993). Long-term effects of parental divorce on parent–child relationships. Adjustment, and achievement in young adulthood. *Journal of Family Psychology, 7*, 91–103.

CHAPTER 19

How and Why the Understanding of Developmental Continuity and Discontinuity is Important

The Sample Case of Long-term Consequences of Adolescent Substance Use

JOHN E. SCHULENBERG

JENNIFER L. MAGGS

PATRICK M. O'MALLEY

> No story is a straight line. The geometry of human life is too imperfect and too complex, too distorted by the laughter of time and the bewildering intricacies of fate to admit the straight line into its system of laws. (Pat Conroy, 1995, p. 104)

In the complex array of distal and proximal causes of adulthood functioning, how prominent are the experiences and events of adolescence in general and adolescent substance use in particular? Indeed, what is the basis for expecting long-term consequences of any sort of behavior, characteristic, event, or social context across the life course? A typical way to address these fundamental questions is to invoke notions of developmental continuity or coherence across the life course and to focus, for example, on continuity of individual and

JOHN E. SCHULENBERG and PATRICK M. O'MALLEY • Institute for Social Research, University of Michigan, Ann Arbor, Michigan 48104-2321

JENNIFER L. MAGGS • Family Studies and Human Development, University of Arizona, Tucson, Arizona 85721

Handbook of the Life Course, edited by Jeylan T. Mortimer and Michael J. Shanahan. Kluwer Academic/Plenum Publishers, New York, 2003.

contextual characteristics over time or the formative influence of earlier experiences on later functioning and adjustment (see McLeod and Almazon, this volume). Thus, to the extent that we find long-term consequences of adolescent substance use (or of any characteristic, behavior, social context, or event), we can assume a certain amount of developmental continuity across the life course.

But there is more than just continuity to a developmental perspective, especially one founded on dynamic person–context interactions across the life course. Discontinuity is as fundamental to development as is continuity. Both, as we discuss in this chapter, are critically important for understanding the long-term consequences of adolescent behavior, including substance use. The roots of adulthood functioning do not always extend back to childhood or adolescence. An acknowledgement that the influence of earlier experiences may be mediated, erased, or even reversed by later experiences (cf., Bandura, 1982; Lewis, 1999) provides a more realistic basis for considering how adolescent behaviors, characteristics, events, and social contexts relate to adulthood functioning. In particular, the transition from adolescence to adulthood can engender considerable discontinuity in ongoing trajectories of health and well-being. Thus, for some young people heavily involved in substance use as adolescents, the experiences that constitute the transition to adulthood are sufficiently positive to counter the influence of earlier substance use; for others, difficulties with transition experiences serve as catalysts of earlier substance use difficulties. Failure to recognize these and a multitude of other diverging pathways might lead to inaccurate conclusions about the possible long-term consequences of adolescent substance use.

In this chapter, we consider issues related to developmental continuity and discontinuity as they relate to linkages across the life course in general and particularly to long-term consequences of adolescent substance use on health and psychosocial adjustment in adulthood. Clearly, the topic of substance use consequences is of central concern in the substance use etiology and prevention literature. Building on decades of research that has often revealed relatively small long-term effects and inconsistent findings, scholars increasingly recognize that more complex questions about moderated effects and developmental pathways need to be considered. One purpose of this chapter is to facilitate this direction in the substance use literature by elucidating developmental considerations. At the same time, our focus on substance use consequences provides an important substantive vantage point for illustrating developmental issues regarding continuity and discontinuity across the life course. Thus, our second purpose is to illustrate various ways to conceptualize linkages between adolescent characteristics, behaviors, and events and adulthood functioning and adjustment. We hope to offer some insights into how and why considerations of continuity and discontinuity are essential for understanding developmental effects across the life course.

In the first section, we set the stage by drawing principles and concepts from life course development scholarship (and developmental science in general), defining continuity and discontinuity, and briefly describing developmental transitions and tasks. In the second section, we start with a selective overview of the substance use consequences literature. Then, informed by broader developmental perspectives on substance use etiology during adolescence and young adulthood (e.g., Cicchetti, 1999; Schulenberg & Maggs, 2002; Schulenberg, Maggs, Steinman, & Zucker, 2001; Windle & Davies, 1999), we discuss three central themes concerning continuity and discontinuity and examine their implications for understanding the long-term consequences of adolescent substance use: (1) temporally and developmentally causal linkages as they relate to developmental transitions, (2) the meaning of a given set of behaviors in terms of developmental tasks, and (3) interindividual differences in intraindividual change and variability. In the final section, we offer a summary of the mechanisms and conditions of long-term consequences of substance use, discuss substantive and methodological challenges, and consider implications for theory and research on developmental linkages between adolescence and adulthood.

INDIVIDUAL DEVELOPMENT IN LIFE COURSE PERSPECTIVE: HOW AND WHY CONTINUITY AND DISCONTINUITY ARE IMPORTANT

There is not one unified, agreed-upon developmental theory and, indeed, developmental scientists often disagree about the very meaning of development. Such disagreement has many benefits for our science and, given the enormity and complexity of human development, it is unlikely we will have a unified, fully agreed-upon theory of development any time soon (for comprehensive efforts, see e.g., Cairns, Elder, & Costello, 1996; Ford & Lerner, 1992). Nonetheless, there has been growing consensus about the need to consider the dynamic interplay between active individuals and social contexts in our conceptualizations and studies of human development (Baltes, Lindenberger, & Stausinger, 1998; Bronfenbrenner & Morris, 1998; Cairns, 2000; Elder, 1998; Lerner, 1998). Furthermore, while the points of entry into the study of human development are typically different for life course and life span studies (e.g., social structure and roles vs intraindividual phenomena, respectively), reflecting their respective origins in sociology and psychology, the two converge more than they diverge on such key issues as dynamic person–context interactions, cultural and historical embeddedness, multidirectional change, and lifelong development (e.g., Settersten, 2003; Shanahan & Porfeli, 2002). Also, more generally, concern with these issues reflects a developmental science perspective (e.g., Cairns et al., 1996), a broad framework that emphasizes holistic considerations of developing individuals in changing contexts, and advocates that the study of development (human and otherwise) is best advanced by interdisciplinary efforts.

The perspective we offer in this chapter is consistent with the broad interdisciplinary developmental science framework that emphasizes multidimensional and multidirectional developmental change across the life course, characterized by successive and dynamic mutual selection and accommodation of individuals and their contexts (Baltes, 1987; Elder, 1998; Lerner, 1982; Sameroff, 1987). Humans are considered to play a strong active role in their own development and social and physical environments are viewed as also playing strong roles (Brandtstädter & Lerner, 1999; Caspi & Moffitt, 1993; Lerner, 1982; Scarr & McCartney, 1983). Through a process of niche selection, individuals select environments and activities from differing ranges of options based on personal characteristics, beliefs, interests, and competencies. Selected ecological niches then afford various opportunities (Nurmi, 1993; Plomin, Fulker, Corley, & DeFries, 1997; Scarr & McCartney, 1983). This progressive accommodation suggests the qualities of coherence and continuity that appear to describe much of human development. But consistent with an emphasis on dynamic person–context interactions and multidirectional change, development is not necessarily expected to exhibit a smooth and progressive function and early experiences may not always have strong or lasting effects (e.g., Cairns, 2000; Lewis, 1999; Loeber & Stouthamer-Loeber, 1998). Thus, both continuity and discontinuity are anticipated across the life course.

Our emphasis on the conditions and mechanisms of continuity and discontinuity is informed by essential themes that have emerged from life course scholarship, specifically the notion of trajectories across the life course and how various developmental transitions relate to those trajectories including how transitions can serve as turning points (Elder, 1998; Laub & Sampson, 1993; Rutter, 1996; Settersten, 2003). In addition, we draw heavily from broader life course developmental themes about interindividual (and inter- and intracohort) variation in life course trajectories and social role transitional experiences, the interplay of distal and proximal experiences and events, linked lives, and the cultural and historical embeddedness of the life course (Elder, 1998; Settersten, 2003; Shanahan, 2000).

Next, based on life course themes and more broadly a developmental science framework, we consider definitions of continuity and discontinuity and briefly discuss developmental transitions and tasks and their relation to continuity and discontinuity.

Continuity and Discontinuity in Development: Overview of Issues

Notions of developmental continuity and discontinuity are complex, in part because they involve systems-level considerations and also because of definitional ambiguity and complexity (e.g., Kagan, 1980; Rutter, 1989; Sameroff, 2000; Werner, 1957). They are slippery and amorphous concepts, but such qualities do not take away from their critical importance to the understanding of development. Continuity and discontinuity are often viewed as being distinct from or at least more general than stability and change. Stability typically pertains to the rankorder stability of interindividual differences over time. If the rank ordering of individuals along a specific dimension changes little over time, then individual differences are viewed as stable (regardless of mean level changes). Change typically pertains to mean level change over time, usually at the group or subgroup level (regardless of rank order stability). These distinctions are not always followed in the literature, of course, but they are generally accepted (e.g., Baltes, Reese, & Nesselroade, 1977; Lerner, 1986). In contrast, there is less agreement about or at least less systematic use of terms concerning the meaning of continuity and discontinuity. In particular, views of continuity and discontinuity range from concern with qualitative or structural-level change to a concern with the overall level of adaptation across the life course.

Traditionally, within organismically based developmental psychology, continuity and discontinuity have been viewed in terms of underlying structural or qualitative change (e.g., Piaget, 1970; Werner, 1957). That is, discontinuity can reflect both quantitative and qualitative change, but the main distinction relates to qualitative change; if the underlying structure changes, for example, the emergence of new structure, purpose, or meaning, then there is discontinuity (Lerner, 1986). Similarly, continuity and discontinuity may be considered as descriptive or as explanatory, which draws a distinction between manifest behaviors (descriptive) and underlying purposes, functions, and meanings (explanatory) (e.g., Lerner, 1986). But continuity and discontinuity may also be considered in terms of connections and causative linkages across periods in life (e.g., Lewis, 1999), which we term ontogenic continuity (reflecting strong developmentally distal effects) and ontogenic discontinuity (reflecting strong developmentally proximal effects). In this chapter, we are primarily concerned with descriptive and explanatory, along with ontogenic, continuity and discontinuity; more generally, we are interested in the continuity and discontinuity of overall functioning and adjustment across the life course.

DESCRIPTIVE AND EXPLANATORY CONTINUITY AND DISCONTINUITY. Descriptive continuity refers to the same behavior or characteristic over time and explanatory continuity refers to the same underlying purpose, function, or meaning of behaviors/characteristics over time. Table 19-1 illustrates these dimensions.

TABLE 19-1. **Descriptive and Explanatory Continuity and Discontinuity**

Explanatory	Descriptive	
	Continuity	Discontinuity
Continuity	Homotypic continuity	Heterotypic continuity
Discontinuity	Functional discontinuity	Complete discontinuity

Homotypic continuity refers to the presence of both descriptive and explanatory continuity (Caspi & Roberts, 1999; Kagan, 1969). For example, high school students attending academically selective and challenging high schools may study hard through high school and college, with the goal of pursuing competitive professional careers. Despite changes in context, significant continuity may be visible in both their academic behaviors and the underlying purpose. Another example would be a young person who continues occasionally to use marijuana primarily for the sensation of getting high; if both the drug use and the main motivation (i.e., sensation seeking) remain unchanged over time, this would reflect homotypic continuity.

Often, however, behaviors vary across time while the underlying purpose or meaning of those varying behaviors remains invariant. This is termed *heterotypic continuity* (Caspi & Roberts, 1999; Kagan, 1969). So, once the academically oriented young people complete their formal education, their focus shifts from studying hard to working hard, with their underlying strong success orientation remaining unchanged. Likewise, if the sensation-seeking young person shifts from marijuana use to skydiving to invoke the same sensation, this would reflect heterotypic continuity. In general, positive adaptation to life's tasks may be continuous across the life course, but many of the activities and behaviors associated with positive adaptation tend to be discontinuous (Masten & Curtis, 2000; Moffitt & Caspi, 2001; Rutter, 1996); thus, as we discuss in a later section, heterotypic continuity is especially useful in understanding how developmental tasks relate to substance use consequences.

Functional discontinuity, which can be considered the opposite of heterotypic continuity, occurs when the manifest behavior appears unchanged yet the underlying function or meaning of that behavior changes over time (i.e., descriptive continuity and explanatory discontinuity). For example, the sensation-seeking young person may continue to use marijuana but the primary reasons for using may shift, for example, from curiosity and rebellion to coping and affect regulation. Indeed, the reasons that one begins substance use (e.g., experimentation or social reasons) often are very different reasons for continued substance use (e.g., coping or self-medication reasons) reflecting functional discontinuity (e.g., National Institute on Alcohol Abuse and Alcoholism [NIAAA] 2000).

Shifts over time in both the manifest behaviors and underlying meanings/functions of those behaviors reflects *complete discontinuity*. The young person who uses drugs to cope with a high school that offers her or him no opportunities to succeed may no longer have such extreme coping problems once he or she leaves high school and thus may discontinue drug use.

ONTOGENIC CONTINUITY AND DISCONTINUITY. Development is a cumulative process and, thus, one's life history sets the stage for current cognitive, emotional, and social functioning. This does not mean that early experiences inevitably determine later functioning (Lewis, 2000). Indeed, from a developmental science perspective emphasizing plasticity and development across the life course, the effects of early experiences may be countered or reversed by later experiences. This tension between the effects of earlier (developmentally distal) and later

TABLE 19-2. Developmentally Distal and Proximal Effects (Ontogenic Continuity and Discontinuity)

Developmentally proximal effects (ontogenic discontinuity)	Developmentally distal effects (ontogenic continuity)	
	Yes	No
Yes	Independent distal and proximal effects or mediated effects of distal effects via proximal effects	Only proximal (e.g., transition-based) effects or proximal effects cancel or reverse distal effects
No	Only distal (e.g., childhood) effects	No developmental effects

(developmentally proximal) experiences reflects an emphasis on what we term ontogenic continuity and discontinuity (cf. Masten, 2001). Table 19-2 illustrates these dimensions.

Ontogenic continuity reflects a progressive and individual coherence perspective of development, where early experiences are strong contributors to future functioning and adjustment (cf. Caspi, 2000; Roberts, Caspi, & Moffitt, 2001). For example, within this perspective, events and experiences of childhood and adolescence are formative and become causes of future outcomes in adulthood. This perspective is the implied one underlying much of the literature that attempts to establish connections across different periods of the life course in general and the substance use consequences literature in particular. In contrast, a focus on more developmentally proximal influences (e.g., transition effects) reflects an ontogenic discontinuity perspective, whereby functioning and adjustment are assumed to be due more to recent and current experiences (Lewis, 1999). This general theme of indeterminacy in developmental course due to powerful proximal influences is consistent with Gergen's (1977) model of aleatory change, as well as the life course literature suggesting the power of developmental transitions in reversing the effects of earlier violence and delinquency (e.g., Laub & Sampson, 1993; Sampson and Laub, this volume; Uggen, 2000; Uggen and Massoglia, this volume).

As shown in Table 19-2, ontogenic continuity and discontinuity are not necessarily mutually exclusive. Distal and proximal influences are often intertwined: distal influences (e.g., ongoing parental unemployment during childhood) may structure proximal influences (e.g., limited financial resources, association with low achieving peers during late adolescence) and proximal influences may mediate the effects of distal influences (e.g., childhood events contribute to adulthood functioning via difficulties with the transition to adulthood). But proximal developmental influences in general and developmental transitions in particular may operate independently of distal influences or may even disrupt distal influences, thus setting the stage for discontinuity (see top right quadrant in Table 19-2). As we discuss in a later section, an emphasis on how developmentally distal and proximal effects interrelate is particularly, useful in understanding how developmental transitions relate to substance use consequences.

CONTINUITY AND DISCONTINUITY AS MORE THAN INDIVIDUALISTIC CHARACTERISTICS.
The understanding of consequences of behaviors at one point in time on outcomes at another point in time must be immersed in considerations of not just individual continuity and discontinuity, but also the continuity or discontinuity of surrounding social context along with considerations of the broader cultural context and historical time (Shanahan, Sulloway, & Hofer, 2000). For example, any distinction between ontogenic continuity and discontinuity might rest on the continuity of one's social context. Likewise, as discussed more later, the transition to adulthood is typically accompanied by shifting role expectations (Mortimer & Simmons,

1978), which in turn can reflect descriptive or explanatory discontinuity. Cultures vary regarding support for and expectations regarding continuity and discontinuity across the life course (Furstenberg, 2002; Shanahan, Mortimer, & Krueger, 2002) and the same holds true for varying historical periods marked by technological and political shifts. And linkages across the life course in terms of the impact of consequences of earlier behavior on later adjustment are likely to be influenced by the normativeness of the given behavior, which often shifts historically. Specifically, it is reasonable to ask whether the consequences of adolescent substance use vary in part as a function of substance use prevalence (which has shifted dramatically over the past few decades) (Johnston, O'Malley, & Bachman, 2002). For example, would the increasingly normative behavior serve to decrease the long-term consequences for the average adolescent substance user?

Finally, questions about continuity and discontinuity are ultimately methodologically bound (Lerner, 1986; Mortimer, Finch, & Kumka, 1982; Werner, 1957), introducing the notion of artifactual continuity and discontinuity. Depending on one's approach, one may find more or less continuity than is actually the case (McAdams, 1994); moreover, what is found for the general case in regard to continuity and discontinuity may have little to do with the given individuals when they are combined to make up the general case (Cairns, 2000).

Additional important questions pertain to the mechanisms of continuity and discontinuity across the life course. Many of these mechanisms exist in the dynamic interplay between developing individuals and their changing contexts; two of particular interest here include developmental transitions and developmental tasks.

Developmental Transitions and Tasks in Adolescence and Early Adulthood

Developmental transitions and tasks are related and sometimes even overlapping (e.g., the transition to marriage vs the task of selecting a mate). In general, transitions pertain more to the actual process of change and tasks relate more to accomplishments that contribute to and result from the changes (Elder, 1996; Schulenberg & Maggs, 2002). Both are of central concern when issues of continuity and discontinuity across the life course are considered.

The content and timing of developmental transitions and tasks, being historically and culturally embedded, are influenced greatly by social context (Bynner, 2000; Oerter, 1986). This chapter focuses on development within Western, pluralistic societies that are characterized by diverse, first world, postindustrialized economies. Our characterization of the ecological niches experienced by adolescents and young adults is based primarily on the United States and assumes a flexible educational system, significant individual freedom, and many opportunities for advancement, yet large income and social capital discrepancies and a limited social safety net. With the end of compulsory and fully publicly funded education after high school, U.S. adolescents are faced with many more choices and options, along with far less automatic institutional support. Divergence in life paths can be expected to increase as individual adolescents pursue or find themselves falling into a vast range of life situations, with diverse combinations and sequences of possible living arrangements, educational pursuits, jobs, romantic partnerships, parenting roles, and family relationships. While U.S. culture tolerates and often encourages some period of experimentation and "changing of mind" in the post-high school years (for single, non-parents attending college), the decisions, activities, accomplishments, and even "chance events" of these years can have lifelong salience (Bandura, 1982; Clausen, 1991; Maggs, Frome, Eccles, & Barber, 1997; Schulenberg, Maggs, & Hurrelmann, 1997).

DEVELOPMENTAL TRANSITIONS. Developmental transitions include major transformations in individuals, their contexts, and the relations between individuals and their contexts across the life course; transitions can and often do contribute in important ways to individual development (e.g., Bronfenbrenner, 1979; Graber & Brooks-Gunn, 1996; Schulenberg et al., 1997). Developmental transitions are often viewed globally as the connections between major life periods, such as the transition from childhood to adolescence. These global transitions usually include other identifiable (and less global) developmental transitions. In particular, there are internally based developmental transitions concerning physical, cognitive, emotional, and identity-related change and externally based developmental transitions concerning changes in social roles and contexts (Rutter, 1996). For example, the global transition from adolescence to adulthood includes a series of transitions involving perspective taking, emotional regulation, and identity, as well as transitions in social context (e.g., transitions into college, marriage, full-time employment).

Individuals can shape their own developmental transitions as they actively influence and are influenced by their contexts (Lerner, 1982; Scarr & McCartney, 1983). As mentioned earlier, the transition to adulthood is characterized by increasingly diverse options, opportunities, and constraints (Shanahan, 2000) and, thus, behavioral choices may influence transition outcomes to a greater extent than ever before. Developmental transitions are embedded in a sociocultural context and therefore may vary by gender, class, culture, and historical period. Culturally and biologically based age-related expectations or "scripts" shape these transitions by providing normative timetables and developmental deadlines, for example for employment and parenthood (Heckhausen, 1999; Neugarten, 1979). Developmental transitions can be normative or non-normative and can vary in timing, sequence, and importance depending on their prevalence within a given population and on personal goals and life situations (Baltes, 1987; Nurmi, 1997).

Issues of continuity and discontinuity are central to understanding the power of major developmental transitions on individuals' lives (Petersen, 1993; Rutter, 1996). At a global level, continuity in functioning tends to prevail during major transitions. Some developmentalists and personality psychologists have highlighted continuity in functioning, for example, because of ongoing person–context match across the transition (e.g., Davis & Millon, 1994) or because individuals rely on their intrinsic tendencies and behavioral repertoire in novel and ambiguous situations (e.g., Caspi, 2000). And when discontinuity in functioning is apparent during a major transition, it may simply reflect momentary disturbances (e.g., temporary identity difficulties during the transition to college), after which one's ongoing trajectory will resume. Likewise, change in functioning during a transition that appears to reflect discontinuity may represent the continuity of adaptation (Rutter, 1992; Zucker, 2000). But consistent with a dynamic person–context interaction perspective and particularly with the notion of ecological transitions (Bronfenbrenner, 1979), major developmental transitions can permanently alter one's ongoing trajectory of health and well-being (e.g., Schulenberg, Bryant, & O'Malley, in preparation). In a later section, we consider more specifically how developmental transitions contribute to continuity and discontinuity across the life course, focusing on implications for understanding long-term consequences of adolescent substance use.

DEVELOPMENTAL TASKS. Historically, developmental tasks have been defined as socially, psychologically, and biologically determined activities or projects that individuals are expected to accomplish at certain ages or stages of life (Havighurst, 1952). The content of such tasks originates in an interaction between species-typical biological capabilities and socially constructed norms and expectations (Neugarten & Datan, 1973; Oerter, 1986). While such conceptualizations allow for some variation in the content, timing, and salience of tasks by gender, social capital, culture, and historical period (Hogan & Astone, 1986; Marini, 1985), a narrow interpretation of the task construct may be too prescriptive for most contextually oriented life span conceptualizations of human development (e.g., Baltes et al., 1998; Brandtstädter & Lerner, 1999). We offer a descriptive rather than a prescriptive interpretation of the concept of developmental tasks, concentrating on the normative activities, goals, and focus of various periods in the life course. In this regard, "normative" refers to what many people within a given social context or ecological niche commonly do, rather than what they *should* do (see Settersten, this volume). Moreover, despite observed similarities in the activities and interests of individuals within given periods of life, it is also important to remember that individual development is also idiosyncratic and regulated by goals unique to each person (Brunstein, Schultheiss, & Maier, 1999; Cantor, 1994; Oerter, 1986).

Although the discussion of developmental tasks has become less common in developmental theory and empirical research, viewing behaviors as indicative of the pursuit of developmentally normative tasks provides an organizational structure and explanation for otherwise apparently unrelated actions within and across time. For example, the task of developing an occupational identity may give meaning to diverse behaviors, including changing college majors, trying various volunteer and paid job experiences, or leaving a romantic partner to pursue an educational or job opportunity. Developmental tasks also illuminate process links of social constraints and expectations with individual behavior; within the range of perceived possibilities and options individuals may internalize normative developmental timetables, endorse particular tasks, and use them to guide their behavior (e.g., Heckhausen, 1999; Nurmi, 1993).

Descriptions of the major developmental tasks of adolescence and early adulthood often focus either on domains of development (e.g., biological, interpersonal) or on the acquisition of abstract personal qualities (e.g., responsibility, personal values) (Erikson, 1968; Havighurst, 1952; Neugarten & Datan, 1973; Oerter, 1986; Schulenberg et al., 1997; Wadsworth & Ford, 1983). Common developmental tasks of adolescence include adapting to the changes of puberty, developing independent or interdependent relationships with parents, and deciding on and pursuing educational goals. Sociological definitions of adulthood focus on the attainment of social roles (typically those of spouse, parent, worker) (Hogan & Astone, 1986); more recent evidence indicates that young adults themselves define adulthood more intangibly (and often inconsistently) in terms of taking responsibility for one's actions and deciding on beliefs and values (Arnett, 2000, 2001; Shanahan, 2000). Although the specific tasks of adolescence are somewhat distinct from tasks of early adulthood (thus suggesting some discontinuity in behaviors and activities), the underlying purposes of general adaptation as well as of certain developmental tasks may nevertheless remain continuous (e.g., Masten & Curtis, 2000; Mortimer & Simmons, 1978). An adolescent who experiments with alcohol may be partly doing so in relation to affiliative developmental tasks associated with gaining independence from parents and bonding with peers; as a young adult, the young person may decrease alcohol use partly in connection with the affiliative developmental task of mate attraction/selection. While the behavior may be discontinuous over time, the functions of accomplishing the given developmental tasks reflect some continuity; clearly, as we discuss in a later section, developmental tasks and the continuities and discontinuities they engender promote understanding of substance use consequences.

Building on this general discussion of developmental continuity and discontinuity and how they relate to developmental transitions and tasks, we now turn to a more specific consideration of how these general concepts can help us to understand better the long-term consequences of adolescent substance use.

IMPLICATIONS OF DEVELOPMENTAL CONTINUITY AND DISCONTINUITY FOR UNDERSTANDING CONSEQUENCES OF ADOLESCENT SUBSTANCE USE

A better understanding of the long-term consequences of adolescent substance use is important not only for the health and well-being of young people, but also for theoretical reasons concerning linkages across the life course. The implications of "getting it wrong" in terms of coming to erroneous conclusions about the existence and mechanisms of long-term effects of substance use are sizeable. One way to address fundamental questions about long-term consequences is to focus on cause–effect relations: the adolescent behavior (e.g., substance use) is the cause, some aspect of adulthood functioning is the effect (directly or indirectly), and all that transpires in between represents a fairly passive intervening variable that connects the two. Much of the empirical literature has approached the subject of the consequences of adolescent substance use in essentially this way, although recent work has started to attend more to the "in between" time. This chapter is offered to help conceptualizations and empirical studies continue in the more recent direction by elucidating developmental concerns and insights. Substance use consequences include a broad range of outcomes ranging from neurochemical to community-level ones and include, for example, physical, psychological, social, economic, educational, and legal consequences (e.g., Kandel, Davies, Karus, & Yamaguchi, 1986; Newcomb & Bentler, 1988a, 1988b). Our focus is on substance use consequences on health and psychosocial adjustment in adulthood; our emphasis is conceptual and selective (rather than comprehensive), illustrating the various ways to conceptualize linkages between characteristics, behaviors, and events across adolescence and adulthood, as well as across the life course.

In 1978, Kandel pointed out that the determinants of adolescent drug use had been investigated far more than the consequences. A decade later, Newcomb and Bentler (1988a) stated "There has been little theory development regarding the impact of adolescent drug use on later life" (p. 25). To that point, there had been a scarcity of empirical studies testing theories about the impact of adolescent drug use on later outcomes and, indeed, an overarching problem of the substance use empirical literature has been that it is often atheoretical. Since then a number of longitudinal studies have examined the effects and sequelae of substance use in early to late adolescence on many aspects of adult functioning in young adulthood. The findings from the various studies have been mixed, in part because results differ somewhat for alcohol use versus the use of illicit drugs. In general, however, there has been more support for negative consequences than for positive consequences. One study that took an explicit life-course perspective found that use of alcohol and illicit drugs in early adolescence increased the risk of dropping out of school and making "precocious transitions" such as becoming pregnant or impregnating someone and premature independence from parents (Krohn, Lizotte, & Perez, 1997). Newcomb and Bentler (1988a, 1988b) found that marijuana use, use of illicit drugs other than marijuana, and heavy alcohol use (but not moderate alcohol use) had significant negative effects on aspects of young adult functioning, including family problems, health problems, psychosomatic complaints, relationship problems, emotional distress, and trouble with drugs/alcohol. Brook, Adams, Balka, and Johnson (2002), in a sample composed largely of African Americans and Puerto Ricans in New York city, reported that early adolescent marijuana use predicted significantly to less favorable education and occupation outcomes 5 years later. In a very different sample—adolescents in Colombia—Brook, Rosen, and Brook (2001) found that marijuana use in early adolescence predicted later anxiety and depressive symptoms.

Other studies (e.g., Brook, Richter, & Rubenshane, 2000; Brook, Richter, Whiteman, & Cohen, 1999; Brook, Whiteman, Finch, & Cohen 1996; Chassin, Pitts, & DeLucia 1999; Friedman, Granick, Bransfield, Kreisher, & Schwartz, 1996; Kandel et al., 1986; Newcomb, Scheier, & Bentler, 1993; Windle, 1999) have found that substance use (as measured by several substances including alcohol use, heavy drinking, marijuana, illicit drugs) in middle to late adolescence (ages 15–21) can be significantly although not always powerfully predictive of poor function-ing in young adulthood (usually ages 18–27). In these and other relevant studies, measures of adult functioning included poor occupational performance, unconventional adult roles, psychi-atric disorders, mental health, adult drug use, delinquency, autonomy, and competence.

In some studies, however, some unclear and ambiguous relationships of adolescent substance use and adulthood functioning were found. Chassin et al. (1999) found that while illicit drug use had a negative effect on young adult autonomy and competence, heavy alcohol use in young adulthood was either uncorrelated or positively correlated with higher levels of competence. Newcomb and Bentler (1988a) found that while there were several neg-ative consequences of drug and *heavy* alcohol use during adolescence, adolescent *moderate* alcohol use predicted reduced family problems, loneliness, and self-derogation in young adulthood.

One theme in most studies is that a primary mechanism of long-term substance use consequences is the continuity (or at least descriptive continuity) of substance use. Indeed, it does appear to be the case that substance use (especially the use of licit drugs) is relatively stable (in terms of rank order stability) from adolescence to adulthood (e.g., Bachman, Wadsworth, O'Malley, Johnston, & Schulenberg, 1997; Bachman, O'Malley, Schulenberg, Johnston, Bryant, & Merline, 2002; Galaif, Stein, Newcomb, & Bernstein, 2001; Kandel et al., 1986; Ullman & Newcomb, 1999).

The relative stability notwithstanding, it is clear that there are different patterns of sub-stance use trajectories during adolescence and the transition to adulthood (e.g., Bates & Labouvie, 1997; Muthén & Muthén, 2000; Schulenberg, Wadsworth, O'Malley, Bachman, & Johnston, 1996) and recent research has started to consider how these different trajectories relate to consequences (e.g., Hill, White, Chung, Hawkins, & Catalano, 2000; O'Malley & Schulenberg, 1997; Schulenberg & O'Malley, 1998). For example, Rehm and Fischer (1997) found that long-term "harm" is not linked to alcohol use per se but is associated with differ-ent patterns of consumption and Hill et al. (2000) found that distinct trajectories of binge drinking during adolescence significantly predicted both positive and negative outcomes in adulthood.

As mentioned at the beginning of this chapter, a developmental perspective on substance use etiology (e.g., Schulenberg & Maggs, 2002; Schulenberg et al., 2001; Windle & Davies, 1999) provides three foci that are central to our purpose here: (1) temporally and develop-mentally causal linkages as they relate to developmental transitions, (2) the meaning of a given set of behaviors in terms of developmental tasks, and (3) interindividual differences in intraindividual change and variability. Next, we discuss the implications of each of these foci for the understanding of long-term consequences of adolescent substance use.

Temporally and Developmentally Causal Linkages: A Focus on Developmental Transitions between Adolescence and Adulthood

The issue of causal linkages must be considered first in any attempt to understand how func-tioning in adolescence and in adulthood may be related and more specifically how substance use in the adolescent years may relate to adjustment/functioning in adulthood. In particular, in the case where evidence of cross-time prediction is obtained, one must ask to what extent such a relationship is due to adolescent characteristics, behaviors, or events *causing* adulthood functioning. Alternatively, the relationship could be due to selection ("third variable") influences or to a mutually reinforcing web of contemporaneous influences. In the case of selection, a more fundamental or temporally prior characteristic (e.g., academic orientation) (Newcomb, McCarthy, & Bentler, 1989) may contribute to both teenage substance use and adulthood functioning. In the case of concurrent influences, for example, the intertwined and related factors of teenage substance use, delinquency, and spending time with deviant friends may all combine to shape adulthood functioning. If the relationship appears to be causal (e.g., effects on adulthood functioning remain after controlling for potential third variable effects and effects contemporaneous with adolescent substance use), then what does the causal linkage look like? For example, the effects of adolescent substance use on adulthood occupational attainment appear to be mediated through educational attainment, at least for men (Schuster, O'Malley, Bachman, Johnston, & Schulenberg, 2001). This set of key issues is fairly well understood, or at least recognized, in the relevant substance use consequences literature (e.g., Brook & Brook, 1990; Newcomb & Bentler, 1988a).

Another set of key issues that appears to get less attention in the substance use consequences literature pertains to what happens in between adolescent substance use and adulthood functioning. Of course, few if any researchers would want to argue that this "in between" time is largely a passive medium through which individuals pass unscathed. However, by not attending to this interval, the implied assumption is that events and experiences during the interval period are not of central concern for understanding long-term consequences. From our perspective, the events and experiences during this interval in general and the various developmental transitions in particular can help explain continuities and discontinuities between adolescence and adulthood and, thus, help provide a better understanding of the conditions and mechanisms of substance use consequences. In particular, in drawing on the previous discussion of ontogenic continuity and discontinuity, we see the advantages of focusing on the relation between developmentally distal effects (e.g., potential effects of earlier substance use) and developmentally proximal effects (e.g., experiences of success and failure in negotiating the various transitions into adulthood).

How can developmental transitions help explain continuity and discontinuity? Schulenberg and Maggs (2002; see also Schulenberg et al., 2001) discuss five interrelated conceptual models concerning how developmental transitions relate to health risks in general and substance use in particular. These models have broad implications (see also Graber & Brooks-Gunn, 1996) for the study of development and, as we discuss in this section, they also have implications for understanding continuities and discontinuities in overall adjustment during developmental transitions. In the *overload model*, major or multiple transitions overwhelm one's coping capacity, resulting in decrements in health and well-being. In the *developmental match/mismatch model*, transitions serve to increase or decrease the match between the individual's developmental needs and contextual affordances, resulting in increases or decreases in health and well-being. In the *increased heterogeneity model*, developmental transitions exacerbate individual differences in ongoing well-being trajectories. In the *heightened vulnerability to chance events model*, the exploratory behavior engendered by major transitions can increase exposure and reactivity to positive and negative novel experiences. In the *transition catalyst/impediment model*, health risks (e.g., getting drunk with peers) can assist in or impede successfully negotiating various transitions and tasks. These five models are not mutually exclusive; given the multiplicity of developmental transitions as well as of health risks and opportunities, all five models are likely to operate across individuals in a given population and within individuals over time. While some of the models can be viewed as competing ones (especially the first three), they are more appropriately viewed as representing the diverse array of connections between developmental transitions and the course of well-being (see Schulenberg & Maggs, 2002; Schulenberg et al., 2001).

DEVELOPMENTAL TRANSITIONS AS CONDUITS OF CONTINUITY. Developmental transitions can contribute to or be associated with developmental continuity, such that adolescent behaviors and experiences (e.g., substance use) are likely to have more powerful effects on adulthood functioning, for better or worse. For example, major developmental transitions, such as from high school to college or from living with parents to living alone, oftentimes function more as proving grounds than as turning points (cf. Rutter, 1996). Consistent with the developmental match/mismatch model (Eccles, Lord, Roeser, Barber, & Hernandez Jozefowicz, 1997), if such transitions provide a progressive increase in developmentally appropriate challenges through which young people can experience competence, then it is likely that those who were doing well prior to the transition will continue to do well during and after the transition. Likewise, if a developmental transition serves to maintain a continued person–context mismatch or continued developmentally unstimulating opportunities, then the effects of previous difficulties on adult adjustment may be amplified. In this sense, developmental transitions (representing proximal effects) can serve to mediate the impact of earlier experiences (distal effects) on later adjustment.

Consistent with the increased heterogeneity model previously noted, challenging transitions can serve to magnify existing strengths and weaknesses, thus increasing interindividual differences in adjustment (i.e., the so-called "Matthew effect"); (Dannefer, 1987; Merton, 1968). Young people with a history of difficulties (perhaps with negotiating earlier transitions) may have trouble negotiating new transitions and, thus, fall further behind their well-functioning peers. Thus, those who do well during adolescence, academically and otherwise, continue to do well in negotiating the transition to postsecondary education; in contrast, those who were doing poorly during high school, academically or otherwise, might experience increased difficulties during the transition to postsecondary education (e.g., Compas, Wagner, Slavin, & Vannatta, 1986). To the extent that substance use was a reason for or a component of difficulties during high school, then it is likely that the transition will intensify effects of substance use. Those doing well already likely have more resources to deal with the stress of the multiple transitions and perhaps more resources to select those post-high school contexts that best match their needs, which will increase positive adjustment. Previous substance use for this group, if any, will likely have few long-term effects given the continued positive direction of all aspects of their lives.

DEVELOPMENTAL TRANSITIONS AS TURNING POINTS. Transitions can also contribute to/explain developmental discontinuity, such that the effects of adolescent behaviors and events on adulthood functioning are minimized or even countered. In this way, developmental transitions serve as turning points (Elder, 1998; Rutter, 1996), providing developmentally proximal effects that outweigh or overturn developmentally distal effects (i.e., high ontogenic discontinuity and low ontogenic continuity)—(see Table 19-2). Thus, consistent with the developmental match/mismatch model, if the transition from full-time school to full-time work results in a markedly better match between activities and challenges offered by the context and the young person's interests and life goals, then difficulties experienced during adolescence (e.g., use of illegal drugs to alleviate boredom and feelings of incompetence) may not have lasting effects. Likewise, if the given transition results in a markedly worse match, then the effects of positive experiences of (or lack of difficulties during) adolescence on adulthood functioning may be muted or reversed. To the extent that both of these cases are represented in longitudinal study samples, then the long-term consequences of adolescent substance use would be found to be limited. Similar findings would likely result when transitions overwhelm young people's coping capacities (the overload model) or contribute to the occurrence and effects of novel experiences (heightened vulnerability to chance events model).

SUBSTANCE USE AS A DETERRENT TO SUCCESSFUL DEVELOPMENTAL TRANSITIONS. Thus far we have considered transitions as conduits of continuity (thus intensifying adolescent effects) or as turning points (thus dampening or reversing adolescent effects). In both cases, the implications are that transitions can intensify or dampen the long-term consequences of adolescent substance use. But it is also important to view developmental transitions as being influenced by substance use and its short-term consequences. Thus, consistent with the transition catalyst/impediment model, adolescent substance use may contribute to a postponement of developmentally appropriate transitions. This has been recognized in the substance use consequences literature as the "amotivational syndrome" (Newcomb, 1987; Newcomb & Bentler, 1988a) in which substance use is thought to contribute to the avoidance of developmentally beneficial experiences related to identity formation. In addition, adolescent substance use may contribute to (or be associated with) an earlier entry into adulthood roles (premature adulthood) related to, for example, employment (Bachman, Safron, Syala, & Schulenberg, in press; Mortimer & Johnson, 1998; Newcomb & Bentler, 1988a). In such cases, difficulties with successfully negotiating developmental transitions into adulthood can be viewed as long-term consequences of adolescent substance use.

Meaning of Substance Use: A Focus on Developmental Tasks

At the population level, the adolescent years are characterized by an increased willingness to engage in behaviors considered by society to be risky, harmful, or even antisocial (Elliott, Huizinga, & Ageton, 1985; Johnston et al., 2002; Moffitt, 1993). For the majority of individuals, the likelihood of committing a delinquent act, engaging in substance use, or perpetrating some form of misbehavior is at its lifetime peak during, roughly, the decade following the start of high school. The high prevalence of some risk behaviors, such as alcohol use and sexual behavior, suggests that these behaviors are normative, at least in a statistical sense, for older adolescents and young adults. Such a statement does not suggest these activities should be considered ideal, only that they are common. For the majority of individuals, involvement with minor delinquency and with frequent or heavy substance use tends to subside with the acquisition of adult roles, particularly the roles of spouse, parent, and worker (Bachman et al., 1997; Gotham, Sher, & Wood, 1997). For an important minority of individuals, however, substance use during adolescence represents a sign or a potential cause of significant, ongoing problems. So, how can we know if someone will be in the "maturing out" group or in the ongoing problem group?

There are several ways to address this question. The frequency and/or intensity of substance use represent intrinsic risks for developing tolerance or addiction and increasing the probabilistic risk of serious injuries or other negative outcomes. Prior adjustment difficulties such as inadequate social skills, low academic performance, or psychopathology may represent a prior third cause of both the substance use and the negative "outcomes" or such prior difficulties may interact with substance use, making experimentation more risky for some than others (Maggs et al., 1997). And from a developmental perspective, it is essential to examine the meaning of substance use from the young person's perspective—specifically, to consider substance use in relation to developmental tasks (e.g., Schulenberg et al., 1997, 2001; Windle & Davies, 1999).

Despite the sizeable destructive aspects of substance use (e.g., Brook et al., 2002; Newcomb & Bentler, 1988a, 1988b; Kandel et al., 1986), there may also be some constructive aspects in terms of developmental tasks, particularly in regard to identity exploration and bonding with peers (e.g., Baumrind, 1987; Chassin, Presson & Sherman, 1989; Maggs, Almeida, & Galambos, 1995; Shedler & Block, 1990; Silbereisen & Noack, 1986). When substance use is limited in intensity and time, when it occurs in conjunction with otherwise healthy exploration and experimentation, and when rare but acute negative consequences are avoided, young people typically move safely into young adulthood where they take on new developmentally appropriate tasks such as occupational exploration and commitment and family formation. This represents heterotypic continuity, namely the combination of descriptive discontinuity and explanatory continuity, as the behavior changes but underlying purpose of adaptation remains. Specifically, during adolescence substance use may function at least in part to accomplish particular developmental tasks, thus reflecting age-normative (while not necessarily optimal) behavior; during early adulthood, substance use may cease but the underlying purpose of adaptation continues as new age-appropriate tasks are approached and accomplished. In such cases, the long-term consequences of adolescent substance use would likely be slight. In contrast, when substance use during adolescence is frequent, intense, and prolonged, when it reflects prior adjustment difficulties, or when it is used as a dominant coping strategy, then more serious acute and continuing difficulties and longer term consequences are likely to be extensive. And, of course, there is always a risk that substance use during adolescence (or at any other time) can have serious acute effects that may have enduring consequences.

Substance use that begins with the purpose of exploration and then escalates and becomes more a matter of coping style than of exploration represents functional discontinuity (i.e., behavior is continuous, purpose is discontinuous). This change in purpose illustrates the difficulties both of young people to regulate their experimental substance use and of researchers trying to study substance use in relation to developmental tasks. To the extent that substance use during adolescence moves beyond experimental use (e.g., in the service of various developmental tasks) and becomes more a strategy of coping, long-term negative consequences of substance use would be expected. Furthermore, as was true in regard to substance use deterring successful negotiation of developmental transitions, substance use also may deter the approach to and successful resolution of various developmental tasks. To the extent that success in resolving developmental tasks represents competence (Masten & Curtis, 2000), then some important consequences of substance use during adolescence may play out in terms of continued problems with developmental tasks.

Interindividual Differences in Intraindividual Variability and Change

Issues of intraindividual variability and change and interindividual differences in such variability and change have long been defining themes of life course studies, life span development, and perhaps most explicitly developmental science (e.g., Cairns et al., 1996; Settersten, 2003). Given the common themes of dynamic person–context interactions and multidirectional change, individual differences in processes and effects of linkages across the life course are expected. Implicit throughout much of this chapter is the notion that there are wide individual differences in the long-term consequences of adolescent substance use, partly as a function of differential experiences of continuity and discontinuity during the transition from adolescence to adulthood (Windle, 1988). Simply, what is found to be true in our research regarding the elusive normative case may not be true for many or most young people. Instead, it may be more meaningful to identify developmental types according to how constructs are found to co-vary over time within individuals (e.g., Cairns, Cairns, Rodkin, & Xie, 1998; Magnusson & Bergman, 1988; Nagin & Trembley, 2001; Schulenberg et al., 2001; Seidman, Chesir-Teran, Friedman, Yoshikawa, Allen, & Roberts, 1999).

Rapid developments in statistical modeling and software are significantly expanding the potential focus and scope of longitudinal analyses. Whereas repeated measures analyses of variance examine mean-level developmental trajectories within stable groups (e.g., male vs female), the newer generations of growth modeling procedures simultaneously estimate intraindividual time-based trajectories and test whether interindividual differences in the parameters of these trajectories are a function of time invariant and time-varying predictors (Muthén & Curran, 1997; Nezlek, 2001; Raudenbush, Bryk, Cheong, & Congdon, 2001). No longer are researchers forced by their selection of ANOVA versus regression-based approaches to focus only on mean-level group differences or on the stability of interindividual differences. By moving beyond the sole analysis of fixed between-person effects over a series of two-wave chunks of time, growth curve and variability models open up an exciting range of new questions that can now be addressed when adequate data are collected (Nesselroade & Ghisletta, 2000; Rose, Chassin, Presson, & Sherman, 2000; Stoolmiller, 1995). For example, in our use of some of the newer approaches to growth curve modeling, we have examined across-time linkages between susceptibility to peer pressure, peer alcohol use, and adolescent alcohol use (Schulenberg & Maggs, 2001) and have considered the long-term impact of trajectories of substance use during adolescence and young adulthood on mid-adult functioning (O'Malley & Schulenberg, 1997; Schulenberg & O'Malley, 1998).

Important questions about the correlates and consequences of adolescent substance use can be addressed using these new methods. For example, there are strong within- and across-time positive associations between the substance use of adolescents and that of their peers. In addition to examining whether association with deviant or substance-abusing peers in early adolescence predicts later heavy substance use, when developmental trajectories in substance use are plotted at the individual level across multiple occasions, between-person predictors of differential change patterns can be identified (Maggs & Schulenberg, 1998; Schulenberg & Maggs, 2001). Moreover, the extent to which fluctuations and changes across time in peer associations co-vary with substance use can be evaluated, asking whether adolescents engage in heavier use when they are in the company of heavier using peers. Trajectories can also be used as predictors of outcomes, for example, do adolescents who exhibit early and steep onset of substance use experience greater consequences than those who start later or increase more slowly? (For example, see O'Malley & Schulenberg, 1997.)

CONCLUSIONS AND IMPLICATIONS

Drawing from a developmental science framework in general and life course developmental scholarship in particular, we have argued that a better understanding of developmental continuity and discontinuity provides a more realistic and fruitful basis for examining linkages across the life course. Consistent with an organismic metamodel (Reese & Overton, 1970), developmental psychology has traditionally viewed continuity and discontinuity in terms of underlying structural/organizational change at the individual level (e.g., Werner, 1957). Consistent with a life course perspective, developmental continuity and discontinuity can be considered at the individual level, at the individual–context interaction level, and at the cultural/social level; clearly, developmental continuity and discontinuity are inextricably connected with constancy and change in one's social contexts (Lewis, 2001; Shanahan et al., 2000) and are directly and indirectly influenced by historic trends and events.

In this final section, we briefly consider the mechanisms and conditions of long-term consequences of substance use, substantive and methodological challenges, and implications for theory and research on developmental linkages between adolescence and adulthood.

The Conditions and Mechanisms of Long-term Consequences

In the substance use consequences literature, our hope is that the driving questions evolve from "are there long-term effects of adolescent substance use? and, if yes, what are they?" to "under what conditions do long-term effects occur?"

Powerful linkages across the life course are more likely to be found when there is strong continuity in functioning and adjustment, in one's primary social contexts, in the match between individual needs and contextual affordances, in the underlying goals of adaptation, and in the specific culture and historical period. In such cases, what happens early in life may have powerful connections (though not necessarily directly causal connections) to what happens later, for better and worse. In addition, with specific regard to substance use, it is likely that adolescent substance use will have long-term consequences for adult functioning under some or all of the following conditions: (1) substances are used as a major part of one's coping repertoire during adolescence, more than in service to various normative developmental tasks; (2) substance use contributes to life-altering accidents or other negative events (e.g., arrest), and (3) substance use is ongoing.

Thus, we argue that developmental continuity and discontinuity serve to structure and otherwise influence long-term consequences. In particular, continuity/discontinuity may function as moderators of consequences, where the greater the continuity, the stronger the anticipated consequences. Or, continuity/discontinuity may serve as intermediate steps in a causal chain, for example, substance use itself may contribute to continuity or discontinuity, which themselves are part of a web of outcomes.

Substantive and Methodological Challenges

Identification of continuity and discontinuity is often a subjective and imprecise undertaking. Likewise, metaphors and definitions of developmental transitions are often complex, conceptually rich, and very difficult to define operationally. As we have discussed, developmental transitions can operate as a source of potentially long-term discontinuity, a cause of temporary fluctuations or disturbances in adjustment, or a possible conduit of continuity in functioning. Furthermore, between-person differences in the content, timing, and sequence of transitional changes such as the completion of full-time education or the transition to parenthood are great. They may vary systematically (but often in unknown and complex ways) by gender, cohort, social class, ethnicity, country, and other social contextual moderators.

Despite recent improvements in software and statistical modeling capabilities, important methodological challenges remain in the quest to document and understand the extent to which human behavior influences subsequent health and development. This is no less true in the domain of adolescent substance use. Although anecdotal evidence of tragic and irrevocable effects of substance use abound, long-term consequences of adolescent substance use often elude scientific documentation. One key challenge is to distinguish temporary perturbations from long-term cumulative and systematic change. Adjustment difficulties during major life transitions may simply represent transitory states or behaviors or they may be the first signs of continuing maladjustment. A second challenge is the selection of optimal time intervals between data collections in order to best capture phenomena that occur with variable timing, rates, and sequences for different individuals. Developmentalists have traditionally emphasized the need for longitudinal data collection over long intervals but are increasingly recognizing the complementary value of intensive data collection over shorter intervals, known as measurement bursts (Nesselroade & Schmidt, McCollam, 2000). A third set of challenges has to do specifically with substance use: many grave negative consequences (e.g., death or spinal cord injury) are very low frequency events and as such are difficult to predict statistically, resulting in low percentage of variance accounted for at the population level; likewise, individuals who suffer significant negative effects are much more likely to be lost to attrition in long-term longitudinal follow-ups (e.g., Hedeker & Rose, 2000). Fourth, even with large samples followed longitudinally (Loeber & Farrington, 1997; Offord, 1997), researchers are faced with the perennial challenge of ruling out selection effects and third variable causes. Experimental designs, the hallmark of clean conclusions regarding causal linkages, are impossible or inappropriate for many questions regarding the consequences of potentially risky human behaviors such as substance use. Finally, drawing connections between earlier behaviors and events and later potential consequences will remain one of the fundamental challenges of our science; often such connections are circuitous and indirect (e.g., Rutter, 1996) and, just as often, the connections that apply to some individuals in some contexts do not apply to all (e.g., Cairns, 2000).

Extending the Sample Case

Our focus on the long-term consequences of adolescent substance use provides an important substantive vantage point for considering how developmental continuity and discontinuity relate to linkages across the life course. Obviously, much of what we have considered would apply equally well to other so-called adolescent problem behaviors. But it is also likely that the conditions and mechanisms of continuity and discontinuity operate in a similar fashion for indices of optimal development and across other major life transitions.

Nearly a half century ago, Werner (1957) concluded, "Development cannot be comprehended without the polar conceptualizations of continuity and discontinuity" (p. 137). We wish to conclude here with a similar thought: although conceptualizations of development have undergone radical changes regarding dynamic person–context interactions over the past four decades, the dialectics of continuity and discontinuity still represent the core of development.

ACKNOWLEDGMENTS: We gratefully acknowledge grant support from NIDA (DA 01411) and NIMH (MH59396), the assistance of Ginny Laetz and Tanya Hart, and the gracious and helpful comments of the editors.

REFERENCES

Arnett, J. J. (2000). Emerging adulthood: A theory of development from late teens through the twenties. *American Psychologist, 55*, 469–480.

Arnett, J. J. (2001). Conceptions of the transition to adulthood: Perspectives from adolescence through midlife. *Journal of Adult Development, 8*, 133–143.

Bachman, J. G., O'Malley, P. M., Schulenberg, J. E., Johnston, L. D., Bryant, A. L., & Merline, A. C. (2002). *The decline of substance use in young adulthood: Changes in social activities, roles, and beliefs.* Mahwah, NJ: Lawrence Erlbaum Associates.

Bachman, J. G., Safron, D. J., Syala, S. R., & Schulenberg, J. E. (in press). Wishing to work: New perspectives on how adolescents' part-time work intensity is linked to educational disengagement, drug use, and other problem behaviors. *International Journal of Behavioral Development.*

Bachman, J. G., Wadsworth, K. N., O'Malley, P. M., Johnston, L. D., & Schulenberg, J. (1997). *Smoking, drinking, and drug use in young adulthood: The impact of new freedoms and new responsibilities.* Mahwah, NJ: Lawrence Erlbaum Associates.

Baltes, P. B. (1987). Theoretical propositions of life-span developmental psychology: On the dynamics between growth and decline. *Developmental Psychology, 23*, 611–626.

Baltes, P. B., Lindenberger, U., & Stausinger, U. M. (1998). Life-span theory in developmental psychology. In R. M. Lerner (Ed.), *Handbook of child psychology: vol.1. Theoretical models of human development* (pp. 1029–1143). New York: Wiley.

Baltes, P. B., Reese, H. W., & Nesselroade, J. R. (1977). *Life-span developmental psychology: Introduction to research methods.* Mahwah, NJ: Lawrence Erlbaum Associates.

Bandura, A. (1982). The psychology of chance encounters and life paths. *American Psychologist, 37*, 747–755.

Bates, M. E., & Labouvie, E. W. (1997). Adolescent risk factors and the prediction of persistent alcohol and drug use into adulthood. *Alcoholism: Experimental and Clinical Research, 21*, 944–950.

Baumrind, D. (1987). A developmental perspective on adolescent risk taking in contemporary America. In C. E. Irwin (Ed.), *Adolescent social behavior and health* (Vol. 37, pp. 93–125). San Francisco: Jossey-Bass.

Brandtstädter, J. & Lerner, R. M. (Eds.) (1999). *Action and self-development: Theory and research through the life span.* Thousand Oaks, CA: Sage.

Bronfenbrenner, U. (1979). *The ecology of human development: Experiments by nature and design.* Cambridge, MA: Harvard University Press.

Bronfenbrenner, U., & Morris, P. A. (1998). The ecology of developmental process. In R. M. Lerner (Ed.), *Handbook of child psychology: Volume 1. Theoretical models of human development* (5th ed., pp. 993–1028). New York: Wiley & Sons.

Brook, J. S., Adams, R. E., Balka, E. B., & Johnson, E. (2002). Early adolescent marijuana use: Risks for the transition to young adulthood. *Psychological Medicine, 32*, 79–91.

Brook, D. W., & Brook, J. S. (1990). The etiology and consequences of adolescent drug use. In R. R. Watson (Ed.), *Drug and alcohol abuse prevention* (pp. 339–362). Clifton, NH: Humana Press.

Brook, J. S., Richter, L., & Rubenstone, E. (2000). Consequences of adolescent drug use on psychiatric disorders in early adulthood. *Annals of Medicine, 32*, 401–407.

Brook, J. S., Richter, L., Whiteman, M., & Cohen, P. (1999). Consequences of adolescent marijuana use: Incompatibility with the assumption of adult roles. *Genetic, Social, and General Psychology Monographs, 125*, 193–207.

Brook, J. S., Rosen, Z., & Brook, D. W. (2001). The effect of early marijuana use on later anxiety and depressive symptoms. *NYS Psychologist, 13*, 35–40.

Brook, J. S., Whiteman, M., Finch, S. J., & Cohen, P. (1996). Young adult drug use and delinquency: Childhood antecedents and adolescent mediators. *Journal of the American Academy of Child and Adolescent Psychiatry, 35*, 1584–1592.

Brunstein, J., Schultheiss, O. C., & Maier, G. W. (1999). The pursuit of personal goals: A motivational approach to well-being and life adjustment. In J. Brandtstädter & R. M. Lerner (Eds.), *Action & self-development: Theory and research through the life span* (pp. 169–196). Thousand Oaks, CA: Sage.

Bynner, J. (2000). Social change and the sequencing of developmental transitions. In L. J. Crockett & R. K. Silbereisen (Eds.), *Negotiating adolescence in times of social change* (pp. 89–103). New York: Cambridge University Press.

Cairns, R. B. (2000). Developmental science: Three audacious implications. In L. R. Bergman, R. B. Cairns, L.-G. Nilsson, & L. Nystedt (Eds.), *Developmental science and the holistic approach* (pp. 49–62). Mahwah, NJ: Lawrence Erlbaum Associates.

Cairns, R. B., Cairns, B. D., Rodkin, P., & Xie, H. (1998). New directions in developmental research: Models and methods. In R. Jessor (Ed.), *New perspectives on adolescent risk behavior* (pp. 13–40). New York: Cambridge University Press.

Cairns, R. B., G. H. Elder, Jr., & Costello, E. J. (Eds.) (1996). *Developmental science*. New York: Cambridge University Press.

Cantor, N. (1994). Life task problem solving: Situational affordances and personal needs. *Personality & Social Psychology Bulletin, 20*(3), 235–243.

Caspi, A. (2000). The child is father of the man: Personality continuities from childhood to adulthood. *Journal of Personality and Social Psychology, 78*, 158–172.

Caspi, A., & Moffitt, T. E. (1993). When do individual differences matter? A paradoxical theory of personality coherence. *Psychological Inquiry, 4*, 247–271.

Caspi, A., & Roberts, B. W. (1999). Personality change and continuity across the life course. In L. A. Pervin & O. P. John (Eds.), *Handbook of personality theory and research* (Vol. 2, pp. 300–326). New York: Guilford.

Caspi, A., Wright, B. R. E., Moffitt, T. E., & Silva, P. A. (1998). Early failure in the labor market: Childhood and adolescent predictors of unemployment in the transition to adulthood. *American Sociological Review, 63*(3), 424–451.

Chassin, L., Pitts, S. C., & DeLucia, C. (1999). The relation of adolescent substance use to young adult autonomy, positive activity involvement, and perceived competence [Special issue]. *Development and Psychopathology, 11*, 915–932.

Chassin, L., Presson, C. C., & Sherman, S. J. (1989). "Constructive" vs "destructive" deviance in adolescent health-related behaviors. *Journal of Youth & Adolescence, 18*, 245–262.

Cicchetti, D. (1999). A developmental psychopathology perspective on drug abuse. In M. D. Glantz & C. R. Hartel (Eds.), *Drug abuse: Origins and interventions* (pp. 97–117). Washington, DC: American Psychological Association.

Clausen, J. A. (1991). Adolescent competence and the shaping of the life course. *American Journal of Sociology 96*, 805–842.

Compas, B. E., Wagner, B. M., Slavin, L. A., & Vannatta, K. (1986). A prospective study of life events, social support, and psychological symptomatology during the transition from high school to college. *American Journal of Community Psychology, 14*, 241–257.

Conroy, P. (1995). *Beach music*. New York: Doubleday.

Dannefer, D. (1987). Aging as intracohort differentiation: Accentuation, the Matthew effect, and the life course. *Sociological Forum, 2*, 211–236.

Davis, R. D., & Millon, T. (1994). Personality change: Metatheories and alternatives. In T. F. Heatherton & J. L. Weinberger (Eds.), *Can personality change?* (pp. 85–119). Washington, DC: American Psychological Association.

Eccles, J. S., Lord, S. E., Roeser, R. W., Barber, B. L., & Hernandez Jozefowicz, D. M. (1997). The association of school transitions in early adolescence with developmental trajectories through high school. In J. Schulenberg, J. L. Maggs, & K. Hurrelmann (Eds.), *Health risks and developmental transitions during adolescence* (pp. 283–320). New York: Cambridge University Press.

Elder, G. H., Jr. (1996). Human lives in changing societies: Life course and developmental insights. In R. B. Cairns, G. H. Elder, Jr., & E. J. Costello (Eds.), *Developmental science* (pp. 31–62). New York, NY: Cambridge University Press.

Elder, G. H., Jr. (1998). The life course and human development. In W. Damon (Series Ed.) and R. M. Lerner (Vol. Ed.) *Handbook of child psychology: Vol. 1, Theoretical models of human development* (pp. 939–991). New York: Wiley.

Elliott, D. S., Huizinga, D., & Ageton, S. S. (1985). *Explaining delinquency and drug use*. Newbury Park, CA: Sage.

Erikson, E. H. (1968). *Identity, youth and crisis*. New York: Norton.

Ford, D. H., & Lerner, R. M. (1992). *Developmental systems theory: An integrative approach*. Newbury Park, CA: Sage.

Friedman, A. S., Granick, S., Bransfield, S., Kreisher, C., & Schwartz, A. (1996). The consequences of drug use/abuse for vocational career: A longitudinal study of a male urban African-American sample. *American Journal of Drug and Alcohol Abuse, 22*, 57–73.

Furstenberg, F. F., Jr. (Ed.) (2002). Early adulthood in cross-national perspective. *The annals of the American academy of political and social science*, Vol. 58. Thousand Oaks, CA: Sage.

Galaif, E. R., Stein, J. A., Newcomb, M. D., & Bernstein, D. P. (2001). Gender differences in the prediction of problem alcohol use in adulthood: Exploring the influence of family factors and childhood maltreatment [Special issue]. *Journal of Studies on Alcohol, 62*, 486–493.

Gergen, K. (1977). Stability, change, and chance in human development. In N. Datan & H. Reese (Eds.), *Life-span developmental psychology: Dialectical perspectives on experimental research* (pp. 136–158). New York: Academic Press.

Gotham, H. J., Sher, K. J., & Wood, P. K. (1997). Predicting stability and change in frequency of intoxication from the college years to beyond: Individual-difference and role transition variables. *Journal of Abnormal Psychology, 106,* 619–629.

Graber, J. A., & Brooks-Gunn, J. (1996). Transitions and turning points: Navigating the passage from childhood through adolescence. *Developmental Psychology, 32,* 768–776.

Havighurst, R. (1952). *Developmental tasks and education.* New York: McKay.

Heckhausen, J. (1999). *Developmental regulation in adulthood: Age-normative and sociostructural constraints as adaptive challenges.* New York: Cambridge University Press.

Hedeker, D., & Rose, J. S. (2000). The natural history of smoking: A patter-mixture random-effects regression model. In J. S. Rose, L. Chassin, C. C. Presson, & S. J. Sherman (Eds.), *Multivariate applications in substance use research: New methods for new questions* (pp. 79–112). Mahwah, NJ: Lawrence Erlbaum Associates.

Hill, K. G., White, H. R., Chung, I.-J., Hawkins, J. D., & Catalano, R. F. (2000). Early adult outcomes of adolescent binge drinking: Person- and variable-centered analyses of binge drinking trajectories. *Alcoholism: Clinical & Experimental Research, 24,* 892–901.

Hogan, D. P., & Astone, N. M. (1986). The transition to adulthood. *Annual Review of Sociology, 12,* 109–130.

Johnston, L. D., O'Malley, P. M., & Bachman, J. G. (2002). *National survey results on drug use from the Monitoring the Future study, 1975–2001. Volume I: Secondary school students. Volume II: College students and young adults* (NIH Publication No. 02-5106 & 02-5107). Bethesda, MD: National Institute on Drug Abuse.

Kagan, J. (1969). The three faces of continuity in human development. In D. A. Goslin (Ed.), *Handbook of socialization theory and research* (pp. 983–1002). Chicago: Rand McNally.

Kagan, J. (1980). Perspectives on continuity. In O. G. Brim, Jr. & J. Kagan (Eds.), *Constancy and change in human development* (pp. 26–74). Cambridge MA: Harvard University Press.

Kandel, D. B. (Ed.) (1978). *Longitudinal research on drug use: Empirical findings and methodological issues.* Washington: Hemisphere Pub. Corp.

Kandel, D. B., Davies, M., Karus, D., & Yamaguchi, K. (1986). The consequences in young adulthood of adolescent drug involvement: An overview. *Archives of General Psychiatry, 43,* 746–754.

Krohn, M. D., Lizotte, A. J., & Perez, C. M. (1997). The interrelationship between substance use and precocious transitions to adult statuses. *Journal of Health and Social Behavior, 38,* 87–103.

Laub, J. H., & Sampson, R. J. (1993). Turning points in the life course: Why change matters to the study of crime. *Criminology, 31,* 301–325.

Lerner, R. M. (1982). Children and adolescents as products of their own development. *Developmental Review, 2,* 342–370.

Lerner, R. M. (1986). *Concepts and theories of human development* (2nd ed.). New York: Random House.

Lerner, R. M. (Ed.) (1998). *Handbook of child psychology: Vol. 1. Theoretical models of human development.* New York: Wiley.

Lewis, M. (1999). Contextualism and the issue of continuity. *Infant Behavior & Development, 22,* 431–444.

Lewis, M. (2000). Contextualism and the issue of continuity. *Infant Behavior & Development, 22,* 431–444.

Lewis, M. (2001). Issues in the study of personality development. *Psychological Inquiry, 12,* 67–83.

Loeber, R., & Farrington, D. P. (1997). Strategies and yields of longitudinal studies on antisocial behavior. In D. M. Stoff, J. Breiling, & J. D. Maser (Eds.), *Handbook of antisocial behavior* (pp. 140–147). New York: Wiley.

Loeber, R., & Stouthamer-Loeber, M. (1998). Development of juvenile aggression and violence: Some common misconceptions and controversies. *American Psychologist, 53,* 242–259.

McAdams, D. P. (1994). Can personality change? Levels of stability and growth in personality across the life span. In T. F. Heatherton & J. L. Weinberger (Eds.), *Can personality change?* (pp. 299–313). Washington, DC: American Psychological Association.

Maggs, J. L., Almeida, D. M., & Galambos, N. L. (1995). Risky business: The paradoxical meaning of problem behavior for young adolescents, *Journal of Early Adolescence, 15,* 344–362.

Maggs, J. L., Frome, P. M., Eccles, J. S., & Barber, B. L. (1997). Psychological resources, adolescent risk behaviour and young adult adjustment: Is risk taking dangerous for some than others? *Journal of Adolescence, 20,* 103–119.

Maggs, J. L., & Schulenberg, J. (1998). Reasons to drink and not to drink: Altering trajectories of drinking through an alcohol misuse prevention program. *Applied Developmental Science, 2,* 48–60.

Magnusson, D., & Bergman, L. R. (1988). Individual and variable-based approaches to longitudinal research on early risk factors. In M. Rutter (Ed.), *Studies of psychosocial risk* (pp. 45–61). Cambridge: Cambridge University Press.

Marini, M. M. (1985). Determinants of the timing of adult role entry. *Social Science Research, 14*(4), 309–350.

Masten, A. S. (2001). Ordinary magic: Resilience processes in development. *American Psychologist, 56,* 227–238.

Masten, A. S., & Curtis, W. J. (2000). Integrating competence and psychopathology: Pathways toward a comprehensive science of adaptation in development. *Development and Psychopathology, 12*, 529–550.

Merton, R. (1968). The Matthew effect in science: The reward and communications systems of science. *Science,
199*, 55–63.

Moffitt, T. E. (1993). Adolescence-limited and life-course-persistent antisocial behavior: A developmental taxonomy.
Psychological Review, 100, 674–701.

Moffitt, T. E., & Caspi, A. (2001). Childhood predictors differentiate life-course persistent and adolescent-limited
antisocial pathways among males and females. *Development and Psychopathology, 13*, 355–375.

Mortimer, J. T., Finch, M. D., & Kumka, D. S. (1982). Persistence and change in development: The multidimensional self concept. In P. B. Baltes & O. G. Brim, Jr., (Eds.), *Life-span development and behavior*
(Vol. 4, pp. 263–313). New York: Academic.

Mortimer, J. T., & Johnson, M. K. (1998). New perspectives on adolescent work and the transition to adulthood. In
R. Jessor (Ed.), *New perspectives on adolescent risk behavior* (pp. 425–496). New York: Cambridge University
Press.

Mortimer, J. T., & Simmons, R. G. (1978). Adult socialization. *Annual Review of Sociology, 4*, 421–454.

Muthén, B. O., & Curran, P. J. (1997). General longitudinal modeling of individual differences in experimental
designs: A latent variable framework for analysis and power estimation. *Psychological Methods, 2*,
371–402.

Muthén, B. O., & Muthén, L. K. (2000). The development of heavy drinking and alcohol-related problems from ages
18 to 37 in a U.S. national sample. *Journal of Studies on Alcohol, 61*, 290–300.

Nagin, D. S., & Tremblay, R. E. (2001). Analyzing developmental trajectories of distinct but related behaviors:
A group-based method. *Psychological Methods, 6*, 18–34.

National Institute on Alcohol Abuse and Alcoholism. (2000). *Tenth special report to the U. S. Congress on alcohol
and health: Highlights from current research* (NIH Publication No. 00–1583) (pp. 28–53). Bethesda, MD:
Department of Health and Human Services.

Nesselroade, N. R., & Ghisletta, P. (2000). Beyond static concepts in modeling behavior. In L. R. Bergman, R. B.
Cairns, L. G. Nilsson, & L. Nystedt (Eds.), *Developmental science and the holistic approach* (pp. 121–135).
Mahwah, NJ: Lawrence Erlbaum Associates.

Nesselroade, J. R., & Schmidt McCollam, K. M. (2000). Putting the process in developmental processes.
International Journal of Behavioral Development, 24, 295–300.

Neugarten, B. L. (1979). Time, age, and the life cycle. *American Journal of Psychiatry, 136*, 887–894.

Neugarten, B. L., & Datan, N. (1973). Sociological perspectives on the life cycle. In P. B. Baltes & K. W. Schaie
(Eds.) *Life-span developmental psychology* (pp. 53–69). New York: Academic Press.

Newcomb, M. (1987). Consequences of teenage drug use: The transition from adolescence to young adulthood.
Drugs and Society, 1, 25–60.

Newcomb, M. D., & Bentler, P. M. (1988a). *Consequences of adolescent drug use: Impact on the lives of young
adults*. Newbury Park, CA: Sage.

Newcomb, M. D., & Bentler, P. M. (1988b). Impact of adolescent drug use and social support on problems of young
adults: A longitudinal study. *Journal of Abnormal Psychology, 97*, 64–75.

Newcomb, M. D., McCarthy, W. J., & Bentler, P. M. (1989). Cigarette smoking, academic lifestyle, and social impact
efficacy: An eight-year study from early adolescence to young adulthood. *Journal of Applied Social Psychology,
19*(3), 251–281.

Newcomb, M. D., Scheier, L. M., & Bentler, P. M. (1993). Effects of adolescent drug use on adult mental health:
A prospective study of a community sample. In G. A. Marlett, Gary R. Vanden Bes (Eds.) *Addictive behaviors:
Readings on etiology, prevention, and treatment* (pp. 169–211). Washington, DC: American Psychological
Association.

Nezlek, J. B. (2001). Multilevel random coefficient analyses of event- and interval-contingent data in social and
personality psychology research. *Personality and Social Psychology Bulletin, 27*, 771–785.

Nurmi, J. E. (1993). Adolescent development in an age-graded context: The role of personal beliefs, goals, and strategies in the tackling of developmental tasks and standards. *International Journal of Behavioral Development, 16*,
169–189.

Nurmi, J. E. (1997). Self-definition and mental health during adolescence and young adulthood. In J. Schulenberg,
J. L. Maggs, & K. Hurrelmann (Eds.), *Health risks and developmental transitions during adolescence*
(pp. 395–419). New York: Cambridge University Press.

Oerter, R. (1986). Developmental tasks through the life span: A new approach to an old concept. In P. B. Baltes,
D. L. Featherman, & R. M. Lerner (Eds.), *Life span development and behavior* (Vol. 7, pp. 233–271). Hillsdale,
NJ: Lawrence Erlbaum.

Offord, D. R. (1997). Bridging development, prevention, and policy. In D. M. Stoff, J. Breiling, & J. D. Maser (Eds.), *Handbook of antisocial behavior* (pp. 357–364). New York: Wiley.

O'Malley, P. M., & Schulenberg, J. (1997). *The individual trajectories of substance use: How alcohol and other drug use changes from adolescence through young adulthood.* Paper presented at the 1997 Biennial Meetings of the Society for Research in Child Development, Washington, DC.

Petersen, A. C. (1993). Creating adolescents: The role of context and process in developmental trajectories. *Journal of Research on Adolescence, 3*, 1–18.

Piaget, J. (1970). Piaget's theory. In P. H. Mussen (Ed.), *Carmichael's manual of child psychology* (Vol. 1 pp. 703–732). New York: Wiley.

Plomin, R., Fulker, D. W., Corley, R., & DeFries, J. C. (1997). Nature, nurture, and cognitive development from 1 to 16 years: A parent–offspring adoption study. *Psychological Science, 8*(6), 442–447.

Raudenbush, S., Bryk, A., Cheony, Y., & Congdon, R., Jr. (2001). *HLM 5: Hierarchical linear and nonlinear modeling.* Lincolnwood, IL: Scientific Software International, Inc.

Reese, H. W., & Overton, W. F. (1970). Models of development and theories of development. In L. R. Goulet, & P. B. Baltes (Eds.), *Life-span developmental psychology: Research and theory* (pp. 115–145). New York: Academic Press.

Rehm, J., & Fischer, B. (1997). Measuring harm: Implications for alcohol epidemiology. In *Alcohol: Minimising the harm: What works?* (pp. 248–261). London: Free Association Books Ltd.

Roberts, B. W., Caspi, A., & Moffitt, T. E. (2001). The kids are alright: Growth and stability in personality development from adolescence to adulthood. *Journal of Personality and Social Psychology, 81*, 670–683.

Rose, J. S., Chassin, L., Presson, C. C., & Sherman, S. J. (Eds.) (2000). *Multivariate applications in substance use research: New methods for new questions.* Mahwah, NJ: Lawrence Erlbaum.

Rutter, M. (1989). Isle of Wight revisited: Twenty-five years of child psychiatric epidemiology. *Journal of the American Academy of Child and Adolescent Psychiatry, 28*, 633–653.

Rutter, M. (1992). Adolescence as a transition period: Continuities and discontinuities in conduct disorder. *Journal of Adolescent Health, 13*, 451–460.

Rutter, M. (1996). Transitions and turning points in developmental psychopathology: As applied to the age span between childhood and mid-adulthood. *International Journal of Behavioral Development, 19*, 603–626.

Sameroff, A. J. (1987). The social context of development. In N. Eisenberg (Ed.), *Contemporary topics in developmental psychology* (pp. 273–291). New York: Wiley.

Sameroff, A. J. (2000). Developmental systems and psychopathology. *Development & Psychopathology, 12*, 297–312.

Scarr, S., & McCartney, K. (1983). How people make their own environments: A theory of genotype–environment effects. *Child Development, 54*, 424–435.

Schulenberg, J., Bryant, A. L., & O'Malley, P. M. (2002). *A National Panel Study on Thriving and Floundering during the Transition to Adulthood: How Success with Developmental Tasks Relates to Trajectories of Well-Being.* Paper presented at the Michigan Symposium on Development and Psychopathology: Continuity and Discontinuity during the Transition to Adulthood. University of Michigan, Ann Arbor, MI, June 2002.

Schulenberg, J., & Maggs, J. L. (2001). Moving targets: Modeling developmental trajectories of adolescent alcohol misuse, individual and peer risk factors, and intervention effects. *Applied Developmental Science, 5*, 237–253.

Schulenberg, J., & Maggs, J. L. (2002). A developmental perspective on alcohol use and heavy drinking during adolescence and the transition to young adulthood. *Journal of Studies on Alcohol, 1* (Suppl. 14), 54–70.

Schulenberg, J., Maggs, J. L., & Hurrelmann, K. (Eds.) (1997). *Health risks and developmental transitions during adolescence.* New York: Cambridge University Press.

Schulenberg, J., Maggs, J. L., Steinman, K., & Zucker, R. A. (2001). Development matters: Taking the long view on substance abuse etiology and intervention during adolescence. In P. M. Monti, S. M. Colby, & T. A. O'Leary (Eds.), *Adolescents, alcohol, and substance abuse: Reaching teens through brief intervention* (pp. 19–57). New York: Guilford Press.

Schulenberg, J., & O'Malley, P. M. (1998). *The consequences of substance use during young adulthood on subsequent parenting practices and attitudes: Latent growth models of alcohol and other drug use.* Paper presented at the 1998 Scientific Meeting of Research Society on Alcoholism, Hilton Head, SC.

Schulenberg, J., Wadsworth, K. N., O'Malley, P. M., Bachman, J. G., & Johnston, L. D. (1996). Adolescent risk factors for binge drinking during the transition to young adulthood: Variable- and pattern-centered approaches to change. *Developmental Psychology, 32*, 659–674.

Schuster, C., O'Malley, P. M., Bachman, J. G., Johnston, L. D., & Schulenberg, J. (2001). Adolescent marijuana use and adult occupational attainment: A longitudinal study from age 18 to 28. *Substance Use & Misuse, 36*, 997–1014.

Seidman, E., Chesir-Teran, D., Friedman, J. L., Yoshikawa, H., Allen, L., & Roberts, A. (1999). The risk and protective functions of perceived family and peer microsystems among urban adolescents in poverty. *American
Journal of Community Psychology, 27*, 211–237.

Settersten, R. A., Jr. (2003). *Invitation to the life course: Toward new understandings of later life*. Amityville, NY:
Baywood Publishing Co., Inc.

Shanahan, M. J. (2000). Pathways to adulthood in changing societies: Variability and mechanisms in life course
perspective. *Annual Review of Sociology, 26*, 667–692.

Shanahan, M. J., Mortimer, J. T., & Krueger, H. (2002). Adolescence and adult work in the twenty-first century
[Special Issue]. *Journal of Research on Adolescence, 12*(1), 99–120.

Shanahan, M. J., & Porfeli, E. (2002). Integrating the life course and life-span: Formulating research questions with
dual points of entry. *Journal of Vocational Behavior, 61*, 396–406.

Shanahan, M. J., Sulloway, F. J., & Hofer, S. M. (2000). Change and constancy in developmental contexts.
International Journal of Behavioral Development, 24, 421–427.

Shedler, J., & Block, J. (1990). Adolescent drug use and psychological health. *American Psychologist, 45*, 612–630.

Silbereisen, R. K., & Noack, P. (1986). On the consructive role of problem behavior in adolescence. In N. Bolger,
A. Caspi, G. Downey, & E. M. Moorehouse (Eds.), *Persons in context: Developmental processes* (pp. 152–180).
Cambridge, MA: Cambridge University.

Stoolmiller, M. (1995). Using latent growth curve models to study developmental processes. In J. M. Gottman (Ed.),
The analysis of change (pp. 105–138). Mahwah, NJ: Lawrence Erlbaum Associates, Inc.

Uggen, C. (2000). Work as a turning point in the life course of criminals: A duration model of age, employment, and
recidivism. *American Sociological Review, 67*, 529–546.

Ullman, J. B., & Newcomb, M. D. (1999). The transition from adolescent to adult: A time of change in general and
specific deviance. *Criminal Behavior & Mental Health, 9*, 74–90.

Wadsworth, M., & Ford, D. H. (1983). Assessment of personal goal hierarchies. *Journal of Counseling Psychology,
30*(4), 514–526.

Werner, H. (1957). The concept of development from a comparative and organismic point of view. In D. B. Harris
(Ed.), *The concept of development: An issue in the study of human behavior* (pp. 125–148). Minneapolis, MN:
University of Minnesota Press.

Windle, M. (1988). Critique: Are those adolescent to early adulthood drinking patterns so discontinuous? A response
to Temple and Fillmore. *International Journal of the Addictions, 23*(9), 907–912.

Windle, M. (1999). Alcohol use among adolescents. In *Developmental clinical psychology and psychiatry series*
(Vol. 42). Thousand Oaks, CA: Sage.

Windle, M., & Davies, P. T. (1999). Developmental theory and research. In K. E. Leonard & H. T. Blane (Eds.),
Psychological theories of drinking and alcoholism (2nd ed., pp. 164–202). New York: Guilford Press.

Zucker, R. A. (2000). Alcohol involvement over the life course. In National Institute on Alcohol Abuse and
Alcoholism, *Tenth special report to the U.S. Congress on alcohol and health* (pp. 25–53). Bethesda, MD:
Department of Health and Human Services.

CHAPTER 20

Adolescent Work and the Early Socioeconomic Career

Jeylan T. Mortimer
Jeremy Staff
Sabrina Oesterle

Though formulated well before the life course paradigm had been generally accepted, the sociological theory of status attainment is, in essence, a life course model of the socio-economic career. The central focus is on pathways of attainment. What do they look like? What are their precursors? What are the mechanisms through which they are produced? Elder's (1998) principles of life course study are well illustrated by this paradigm as well as by the research it has inspired. Studies of the process of stratification clearly demonstrate the connections between earlier and later life events, the consequences of linked lives, career trajectories marked by key transitions, and the importance of human agency. In this chapter, we investigate a relatively neglected set of issues surrounding the place of early work experience in the early socioeconomic career. We describe the diverse features of adolescent work careers, the characteristics of young people who select into them, and the consequences of these pathways for early postsecondary education and full-time work. We consider whether various strategies of investment in early work "pay off" as youth complete school and enter the full-time labor force.*

*This chapter synthesizes work that has been undertaken since the initiation of the Youth Development Study. For a more complete exposition of the central argument and relevant empirical evidence, see Mortimer (2003).

Jeylan T. Mortimer and Jeremy Staff • Department of Sociology, University of Minnesota, Minneapolis, Minnesota 55455
Sabrina Oesterle • University of North Carolina-Chapel Hill, North Carolina 27516

Handbook of the Life Course, edited by Jeylan T. Mortimer and Michael J. Shanahan. Kluwer Academic/Plenum Publishers, New York, 2003.

Investigators of status attainment have long recognized the significance of achievement in adolescence for subsequent educational and occupational attainments (Featherman, 1980). Blau and Duncan's (1967) seminal model of status attainment posited that the socioeconomic standing of the family of origin was a major determinant of a young person's educational attainment. Educational attainment, in turn, was a strong predictor of the prestige level of the first job after finishing school, the starting point of the ensuing occupational career. The status attainment model was subsequently extended by Sewell and Hauser (1975) and their colleagues to include key social psychological mediators, including family members' and other "significant others'" expectations for the adolescent and the adolescent's own aspirations and plans with respect to future educational and occupational attainments. Attitudes and achievement in high school foretell the highest level of schooling that is likely to be reached, which in turn establishes credentials for more or less prestigious, remunerative, and otherwise rewarding occupational positions. Because of its central importance to the attainment process, education has for several decades held center stage in empirical studies of stratification. Typical pathways of educational attainment from the first grade of elementary school have been charted (see Entwisle, Alexander, & Olson, this volume; Gamoran, 1996). Much empirical support has been generated for the model of status attainment; education is clearly a central mediator of the effects of the family of origin on the attainments of each succeeding generation (e.g., see Jencks, Crouse, & Mueser, 1983).

Blau and Duncan (1967) drew attention to the critical importance of the first job after leaving school; in their model, this position constituted the entry portal to more or less rewarding career trajectories. Educational attainment set important limits on the prestige level of the first job, which in turn established the potential for subsequent intragenerational occupational mobility. The status attainment model thus highlighted the first job *after* completing full-time schooling as the starting point to the lifelong occupational trajectory. This model of attainment conforms well to the reigning tripartite conceptualization of the life course: education as preparation for work, adult labor force participation, and retirement (Kohli, 1986).

Still, this portrayal of the transition from education to full-time work bore little resemblance to the reality of most youth's experience in North America and, increasingly, in other modern societies even at the time of its formulation. As a result, researchers in the United States soon recognized that the measurement of this first occupational milestone was not so easy. Even at a time when the early life course was less variable, young adults' frequent movements between full-time schooling and full-time work made it quite difficult to identify the first full-time job. Complex decision rules were formulated (Marini, 1987).

Further departing from this model, most U.S. youth have paid jobs during their teen years and have accumulated a considerable amount of work experience even prior to leaving high school. Those who go on to college continue to combine school and mostly part-time work as they pursue postsecondary studies (Choy, 2002). Status attainment researchers' lack of attention to this early work experience reflects their assumption that jobs held prior to completion of schooling are, for the most part, of relatively little importance for future attainments. As a result, investigators in this tradition have given little attention to the linkages between pathways of adolescent work experience and subsequent socioeconomic outcomes.

Instead, consistent with status attainment researchers' interest in educational attainment, studies of adolescent work experience have focused almost exclusively on its potentially detrimental impact on adolescents' success in school. Attention is directed to the effects of adolescent employment and, particularly, hours of work, on school grades (Marsh, 1991; Mortimer & Johnson, 1998b; Steinberg & Dornbusch, 1991; Steinberg, Fegley, & Dornbusch, 1993;

Warren, LePore, & Mare, 2000) and high school drop-out (D'Amico, 1984; McNeal, 1997; Marsh, 1991; Warren et al., 2000). Prominent developmental psychologists hold that work experience in adolescence poses major opportunity costs, distracting young people from school and other beneficial activities. In their view, adolescent employment should be discouraged (Greenberger & Steinberg, 1986; Steinberg & Cauffman, 1995). Those in public health and employment policy circles have worried about the risks of injury and exploitation of youth in the workforce. Reflecting these concerns, a report commissioned by the National Academy of Sciences was aptly titled *Protecting Youth at Work* (Panel on Child Labor, 1998).

Rather little attention has been given in academic or policy circles to the possibility that early jobs constitute a mechanism through which young people acquire knowledge about the labor force, form occupational values, learn how to behave appropriately in the workplace, and acquire skills that will facilitate their adaptation to work and enhance the likelihood of later success in this domain. The lack of attention to these possibilities is especially surprising in view of the fact that an exceedingly positive view of adolescent paid work is shared by most parents in the United States, as well as by some social scientists. Parents look upon their own past experience, as working teenagers, in a most favorable light (Aronson, Mortimer, Zierman, & Hacker, 1996; Phillips and Sandstrom, 1990). They also think that work experience will enable their adolescent children to acquire a sense of responsibility, to learn the importance of being on time, and to gain interpersonal skills that will assist them in workplace transactions with supervisors, co-workers, and customers. They especially believe that paid jobs during high school will help to make their children more self-reliant.

Sociologists have recognized the potential benefits of employment for subsequent achievement, but mainly in the context of economic hardship and distress. Most notably, Elder (1974) and Elder and Conger (2000) emphasize that Great Depression era teenagers' work experience, as well as that of contemporary rural youth in hard-pressed farm families, builds confidence, instills positive work values, and has other lasting benefits. In like vein, Newman (1999) describes early jobs, even menial fast-food work, as an escape from the disorder and violence of city streets in poor urban areas. For disadvantaged teenagers who grow up in the inner city, even these kinds of jobs serve as an entry to legitimate occupational career paths, otherwise closed off to poor minority youth. They are respected and gain a sense of self-respect as they contribute to their own living expenses and reduce the economic burdens of their families. Studies such as these have drawn attention to the positive role of teenage work under conditions of poverty and economic distress; they do not herald its benefits for the early socioeconomic careers of mainstream youth.

There is reason to believe, however, that work experience during adolescence could be generally advantageous in the contemporary U.S. context. In fact, economists have long recognized that human capital or individual productive capacity is gained through work experience (most clearly, but not exclusively, through explicit job training), as well as through formal education (Becker, 1993). Moreover, particular contemporary conditions may give young people who have had prior work experience a special advantage as they compete for jobs in the full-time, entry-level labor market.

First, in accord with the growing income differentials between college-educated and high school-educated workers in the United States, ever larger numbers of high school students are seeking postsecondary education. The strong emphasis on getting into college (Schneider & Stevenson, 1999) leaves little room for significant vocational guidance or other forms of occupational preparation in high school. Youth who wish to acquire knowledge about the world of work must seek information elsewhere. Though school-to-work programs have sought to remedy this problem by establishing closer connections between high schools and employers, internships, and other innovative programs, they do not reach the vast majority of U.S. youth.

Second, the degrees that are obtained by most school-leavers in the United States, high school diplomas, as well as both 2- and 4-year college degrees, signify general educational attainment, not occupationally-specific credentials. Most young people enter the labor force with no vocationally-relevant credentials that would signal to the employer (or to the job seeker) the kinds of jobs that would constitute a good match with their knowledge and skills (see Kerckhoff, this volume). In their absence, employers base their judgments about the capacity to do particular kinds of work on the highest degree the individual has obtained, a general indicator of intelligence, persistence, and other relevant traits, and, as most youth (and their parents) apparently understand, on prior work experience.

Third, there are few institutional supports that would smooth the transition from school to work. In fact, the school to work transition in the United States is the most loosely structured of all Western countries (Kerckhoff, 2002; and in this volume). Especially unlike Germany, Austria, and Denmark, with their apprentice systems or Japan, with its connections between schools and employers, young people in the United States move into the workplace without clear institutional bridges (Shanahan, Mortimer, & Krüger, 2002). While college graduates can make use of career placement services, most youth who enter the full-time labor force upon leaving high school must rely on their own resources, contacts, and initiative in finding jobs. Approximately two-thirds of recent cohorts of U.S. youth do not obtain 4-year college degrees (Kerckhoff, 2002).

Fourth, structural changes in the character of the labor force have increased the difficulty of becoming established in the world of work. Globalization has heightened economic competition and fostered non-standard employment relations that reduce the employer's commitment to the employee and thereby lessen the worker's security. These employment relations—such as temporary work, part-time employment, employment limited by contract, and outsourcing—are especially prevalent among young people (Kalleberg, Reskin, & Hudson, 2000; Kerckhoff, 2002).

In this contemporary context of prolonged general education and continuing structural changes in the labor force, and the absence of institutional bridges between these spheres, adolescent work experience may have become an important means of human capital acquisition for many young people. Work could, in fact, constitute an integral feature of the adolescent's "biographical action orientation" (Heinz, 1996, 1999, 2002). That is, activities and experiences come to have meaning in the context of long-term self-conceptions, goals, and aspirations for the future. Young people select among the immediate options before them in light of their perceived long-term consequences. Their choices, however, are importantly constrained by the institutional context. As Heinz (2002) observed,

> Transitions and status sequences in the life course are understood not only from the perspective of opportunity structures, career contingencies, and institutionalized rationality, but also in relation to self-initiated and enforced actions that influence the shape and direction of one's life course. (p. 226)

A strategy featuring early employment may be especially germane when resources for higher education appear to be limited. We might expect that adolescents who have restricted interest in or expectations for postsecondary schooling would seek greater work experience and perhaps particular kinds of jobs, so as to advantageously position themselves upon entry to the full-time labor market. But even more advantaged youth, whose parents have higher educational credentials themselves, or greater economic wherewithal to support their children's higher education, may seek employment for the longer-term, as well as the immediate advantages it can provide. Parents at higher socioeconomic levels show much enthusiasm for their adolescent children's employment, as do their less well-off counterparts (Phillips & Sandstrom, 1990). They especially want their children to develop the requisite independence and sense of responsibility that will serve them well as managers and professionals of the future (Kohn & Schooler, 1983). And parents believe that these traits will be inculcated through experience in part-time jobs.

Young people are urged by their teachers and parents to attend college, but some are limited by their socioeconomic backgrounds, their self-conceptions (e.g., their perceptions of themselves as having limited academic ability), and their prior degree of success in school. They can direct their efforts toward obtaining a 4-year degree or settle for lesser educational accomplishments. Unlike youth in other countries with more clearly specified and differentiated school-to-work mechanisms, they do not encounter clear pathways toward well-defined occupational objectives.

Thus, it is not the case, as has been observed with respect to the global transition to adulthood, that there are innumerable meaningful pathways from school to work (Shanahan, 2000). The number has been seriously constrained by the unique character of the educational system (see Kerckhoff, this volume). As Shanahan and Hood (1999) pointed out, agency is frequently bounded by societal forces, which engender a circumscribed set of pathways.

In this chapter, we examine how initial employment pathways, traversed during the teen years, reflect choices within the context of the U.S. educational system. We analyze data from a unique panel study of adolescents which allow us to address the phenomenon of adolescent employment and its consequences for the early socioeconomic career.

THE YOUTH DEVELOPMENT STUDY

For more than a decade, researchers at the University of Minnesota have been following a panel of adolescents as they move through high school, take up postsecondary schooling, and enter the full-time labor force. The Youth Development Study (YDS) is unique among longitudinal studies of the transition to adulthood in its focus on early work experience—its character during the years of high school, its influence on adolescent mental health, achievement, and behavioral adjustment, and its impacts on the timing and character of the transition to adulthood.

In the 1987–1988 school year, a panel of 1,010 randomly chosen adolescents, from students registered in the St Paul, Minnesota public school district, agreed to participate in the study; 1,000 of these completed first-wave questionnaires. The local character of this panel poses certain advantages (facilitating the logistics of the research and enhancing respondent commitment), as well as disadvantages. Of course, opportunities for employment differ across the United States; work patterns are different in rural areas and urban areas and teenagers in inner cities have especially limited opportunities for employment. But socioeconomic indicators for the city of St Paul and the nation as a whole, as documented by the 1990 Census, are for the most part comparable (see Mortimer, 2003). For example, per capital income nationally (in 1989) was $13,727 in St Paul; in the nation at large it was $14,420. Poverty was slightly more prevalent in St Paul: 12.4% of families fell below the poverty line, in comparison to 10% in the United States. However, the labor market in St Paul presented comparatively good employment opportunities, with relatively low unemployment (4.7% in 1990 vs. 5.5% in the United States) and a relatively high level of labor force participation

(63% vs. 60% in the country at large). As a result, employment conditions for youth in the Twin Cities metropolitan area were quite good during the period in which the YDS participants were attending high school (Fall of 1987 to Spring of 1991). In fact, among 16–19 year olds enrolled in school, 54.1% of youth in the Minneapolis–St Paul area were counted as employed in 1990; the corresponding figure for the nation at large was 37.6%. Given its vibrant economy and abundant opportunities for adolescent job seekers, St Paul might be considered a particularly opportune site for investigating adolescent employment and its attainment-related consequences.

The panel has been shown to well represent the St Paul community and its student body at the initiation of the study. Seventy-four percent of the panel self-identified as White, 10% African-American, 5% Hispanic, and 4% Asian (6% gave "mixed" responses). Among the parents, 11% had less than a high school degree, 39% were high school graduates, 28% had attended but not completed college, 9% had graduated from a 4-year college, and 11% had done graduate work or obtained professional degrees (Mortimer, Finch, Shanahan, & Ryu, 1992). Median household income fell in the range of $30,000–$39,000 in 1988. Though males and socioeconomically disadvantaged young people were more likely to leave the study, the social background of first-wave and twelfth-wave panel members and their work-related attitudes and plans (measured in the ninth grade), were quite similar.

The YDS panel has been surveyed annually from the ninth (1988) to the twelfth (1991) grades in high school, with excellent panel retention (93%) through this period. Yearly questionnaires, administered in school, included a large battery of items tapping experiences in work, occupationally-relevant attitudes, and plans for the future. To understand parental perspectives on teenage employment and to obtain accurate information about socioeconomic status and other family background characteristics, mothers and fathers were surveyed by mail in the first and fourth years of the study. Parents of 96% of the students responded in the first and 79% in the fourth year.

After the young people left high school, they were surveyed annually by mail. The questionnaires again addressed work experiences and orientations, and obtained detailed monthly records (via life history calendars, Freedman, Thornton, Camburn, Alwin, & Young-DeMarco, 1988) of residential arrangements, educational attendance, and both part- and full-time labor force participation. Seventy-six percent of the initial participants have been retained through the twelfth wave of the study, when most respondents were 26 and 27 years old.

We have supplemented annual surveys with qualitative interview studies to better understand the subjective transition to adulthood, how youth themselves perceive the opportunities and constraints that confront them. Interviewees have been selected based on their experiences with welfare dependency (Grabowski, 2001), divergent passages to adulthood featuring early parenthood, higher education, and work (Aronson, 1998), and distinctive patterns of occupational decision-making (Mortimer, Zimmer-Gembeck, Holmes, & Shanahan, 2002). This chapter draws on both the surveys and some illustrative qualitative data in addressing the place of adolescent work in the early socioeconomic career.

EARLY EMPLOYMENT PATHWAYS

Teenage Jobs and Hours of Work

Consistent with national studies (Panel on Child Labor, 1998), the vast majority of adolescents in the YDS held paid jobs. In fact, only 7% of YDS panelists reported no work experience during high school (while school was in session). But despite the prevalence of paid employment among teenagers, little attention has been directed to the kinds of jobs that young people actually do and the ways they change as youth acquire more work experience. This practice would be justified if, in fact, all teenage jobs were essentially the same, with little attainment-relevant variation or temporal change. But to the contrary, our study reveals considerable variability and distinct shifts over time. We examine early work pathways in several ways (for further detail, see Mortimer, 2003). First, we describe the changing distributions of job types as young people, in the aggregate, move through high school. Second, we assess the young people's increasing hours of work, as well as longer-term and more complex patterns of adolescent investment in employment. Third, we address trends in the quality of adolescent work experience.

We find evidence that adolescent work becomes more "adult-like" and therefore relevant for future socioeconomic attainment as young people progress through high school. Most adolescents start off doing informal work, mainly babysitting and yardwork in their own neighborhoods. After the ninth grade (for most, coinciding with their sixteenth birthday when they are no longer subject to most child labor restrictions), many take on restaurant jobs, particularly in the fast-food industry. Finally, in the latter years of high school, they fan out across a wider range of retail, service, clerical, and laboring jobs (see Mortimer, Finch, Dennehy, Lee, & Beebe, 1994, for these distributions). Viewed in the aggregate, adolescent paid work appears to have some career-like attributes, moving from the kinds of jobs that children and adolescents might otherwise do as unpaid chores in their own households; to stereotypically "teenage" work, often in fast-food outlets whose clientele includes other young people like themselves; to less age-segregated settings, with more opportunities to observe and to relate to older workers in more "adult-like" jobs.

Given the view of adolescent work as "opportunity cost," it is essential to also consider the number of hours young people spend working. Figure 20-1 describes the activity patterns of YDS youth during high school across multiple domains, including homework, extracurricular activities, domestic chores and caregiving, and volunteer work, as well as paid work (for those who participated in each activity). YDS adolescents who were employed during the ninth grade worked on average about 11 hr per week; their mean hours of work increased to more than 20 by the senior year of high school. Clearly, these adolescents spent considerable

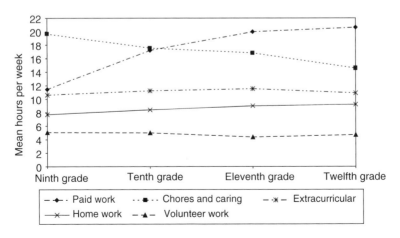

FIGURE 20-1. Average hours of activities in adolescence (1988–1991).

amounts of time working, as do their counterparts nationally (Panel on Child Labor, 1998). In the aggregate, as this activity increased, YDS youth spent less time doing chores in their homes (a trend especially notable for boys; not shown), but their involvement in homework, on average, remained relatively low and remarkably stable during the high school years. Commitment to extracurricular activities and volunteer work also remained quite stable during this period.

As we have seen, concerns about adolescent employment are largely based on the presumption that hours spent in paid jobs cannot be utilized in more developmentally beneficial activities, especially those connected to the school like studying, homework, special school projects, and extracurricular activities. The aggregate trends reported in Figure 20-1 do not speak directly to the notion of opportunity cost, since investigating such trade-offs requires assessment of individual-level patterns. Such analyses, reported elsewhere, provide substantial evidence that this "zero-sum" premise is fundamentally flawed (Mortimer, 2003; Osgood, 1999; Shanahan & Flaherty, 2001). Still, research on adolescent work continues to focus almost exclusively on this simple indicator of temporal investment: hours of employment per week.

A Typology of Investment in Work

Focus on hours of work at single times, or at successive occasions, ignores much of the potentially vocationally-relevant variation in adolescents' employment trajectories. Because adolescents move in and out of the labor force and change their work schedules to enable participation in other activities—in school and elsewhere—hours of employment at any single point in time is a rather poor indicator of longer term labor force involvement (Mortimer & Johnson, 1999). Even measurement of cumulative work hours, summed across years, does not do justice to the complexity of adolescent work patterns.

To obtain a more sensitive indicator, we distinguished two temporal dimensions of adolescent work, duration (in months) and intensity (hours per week) and created a typology of work investment based on their combination. The first dimension, duration, signifies the months of employment during the years of high school (not including the ninth grade, since most paid work at this time is informal). The second dimension, intensity, refers to the hours of work per week during the period of time the adolescent is employed. To construct the typology, both variables were initially dichotomized. Duration was divided at the mean, 18 months of employment (over the total 24 months of observation). Intensity was considered high or low, using the cut point of 20 hr per week (on average, during periods of employment). This amount of employment is widely thought to divide "acceptable" from "excessive" adolescent work (Panel on Child Labor, 1998). The resulting typology based on the cross-classification of these two dimensions is shown in Table 20-1, along with the distribution of the panel, by gender, in each cell.

Employed adolescents in the "most invested" (high duration–high intensity) and least invested "occasional" (low duration–low intensity) categories accrue the most and the least work experience, respectively, during high school. It is especially noteworthy, however, that the two groups in between, the "steady" (high duration–low intensity) and "sporadic" (low duration–high intensity) workers accumulate almost identical cumulative hours of work experience. Yet, these patterns of work were found to have quite different precursors and consequences, as we shall detail later in this chapter, indicating that the pattern of work investment deserves greater attention in studies of the socioeconomic consequences of adolescent employment.

TABLE 20-1. Patterns of Labor Force Participation by Gender

	Percentage distribution			Mean months of work		Mean hours of work	
	Total	Boys	Girls	Boys	Girls	Boys	Girls
Not working	7.0	9.9	4.6	0.0	0.0	0	0
Occasional: Low duration– Low intensity	23.7	23.2	24.1	9.8	11.7	578	650
Sporadic: Low duration– High intensity	18.4	23.2	14.3	10.4	11.8	1,216	1,376
Steady: High duration– Low intensity	24.9	18.2	30.6	22.0	22.0	1,263	1,328
Most invested: High duration– High intensity	26.0	25.6	26.4	21.9	22.2	2,678	2,587
Total	100.0	100.0	100.0				
n	887	406	481				

The Quality of Adolescent Work

Aside from the temporal investment in employment, adolescent work pathways are characterized by varying qualities of experience. Each year the respondents were asked about a variety of job dimensions, including their tasks, their intrinsic and extrinsic rewards, and the stressors to which they were exposed. Most adolescents described their jobs in quite favorable terms, as allowing them to use their skills and abilities, enabling them to help others, and to learn new things. They tended to perceive opportunities for advancement in their employing organizations and to feel that they could keep their jobs for as long as they wished (Mortimer et al., 1994). Importantly, the adolescents' jobs became more complex and required them to assume greater responsibility as they moved through high school. They received more training from their employers, they were more likely to be supervisors themselves, and their jobs came to have higher mean *Dictionary of Occupational Titles* complexity ratings.

Thus, we find substantial evidence that the character of adolescents' jobs changes and becomes more challenging as they mature, invest more time in work, and acquire greater work experience. Such would have to be the case if adolescent work is to be a continuing source of human capital acquisition.* Importantly, we find that investment in work and work quality are linked;[†] more intensive employment (including the "most invested" and "sporadic" patterns) is both more stressful and associated with more learning potential and opportunities for advancement. Adolescents who pursued "occasional" and "steady" work limited their hours of work while at the same time obtaining lower earnings, experiencing less stress, and gaining fewer experiences that are likely sources of human capital development (Mortimer, 2003).

---

*More subjective evaluations of their employment, however, such as assessments regarding learning opportunities, stressors, and relationships in the workplace, remain rather constant in the aggregate over time. These judgments may be responsive to shifting standards of evaluation, as well as change in objective work conditions.

[†]Unlike the continuous measures of duration and intensity drawn from retrospective work histories obtained annually, measures of the quality of work were only obtained for jobs held at the time of each survey administration. The quality of work through time was measured by averaging work quality scale scores at each observation (tenth, eleventh, and twelfth grades). As a result, they are based on one to three jobs.

These patterns suggest two general pathways of human capital acquisition during high school. Whereas both involve paid work, the pathway involving moderate work accommodates greater involvement in both the academic and extracurricular dimensions of school activities, as well as other components of adolescent life. Adolescents who pursue less-intensive employment (20 hr per week or less, on the average) can participate in "well-rounded" adolescent lifestyles, involving multifaceted time use patterns (Mortimer, 2003; Shanahan and Flaherty, 2001). Their work experience is less demanding and stressful than that of their more intensively-employed peers, but it is also less rewarding (intrinsically and extrinsically).

Adolescents who pursue the second pathway have heightened work investment. Their more "adultlike" work experience—characterized by longer hours, higher incomes and more occupational prestige, greater advancement possibilities, more stressors, but also and, quite importantly, greater learning opportunities—would appear to maximize their capacity for human capital acquisition through work.

In accord with this line of reasoning, the distinctive work experiences that were obtained by the more intensively employed adolescent workers were found to be associated with shifts in work attitudes that signify progress in vocational development. For example, learning opportunities at work enhance both intrinsic and extrinsic work values (Mortimer, Pimentel, Ryu, Nash, & Lee, 1996). Evaluations of the rewards that work has to offer are prominent bases of occupational choice and career decision-making.

Finally, there is evidence that even stressors on the job, a more prominent feature of the jobs of those youth who pursued highly intensive work patterns, can serve as beneficial preparation for adult employment. For those young people who experienced less stress in adolescent jobs, self-esteem and self-efficacy declined as they encountered similar conditions in their jobs 4 years after high school (Mortimer & Staff, 2002). The frequency of depressed mood states also rose as they experienced increasing adult job stressors. In contrast, those young people who had more stressful adolescent work experiences did not suffer these decrements in psychological functioning as their early adult job stress rose. There was some evidence that work stressors in adolescence contributed to coping skills in dealing with problems at work, which partially mediated these conditional effects.

Selection to Employment Pathways

It is quite apparent from our analyses that patterns of adolescent labor force activity do not occur randomly. Instead, they are related to the adolescents' social backgrounds and their early proclivities for the educational enterprise. Table 20-2 presents estimates from a multinomial logistic regression analysis predicting selection to the five patterns of labor force activity during adolescence (the "most invested" high duration–high intensity work pattern is the reference category). The table shows logistic regression coefficients and their standard errors. It also provides the exponents of the coefficients (odds ratios), indicating differences in the likelihood of being in each employment category, in comparison to the most highly invested reference category, as one moves across levels of the independent variables. The Wald test statistic indicates whether each independent variable has a statistically significant effect on the outcome (Long, 1997).

As shown in Table 20-2, adolescents in each of the work pattern categories came from higher socioeconomic backgrounds (as indicated by the highest educational degree of their mother or father) than those in the "most invested" reference category. At their first year of high school (ninth grade), those who were to become low-intensity workers (steady and occasional)

TABLE 20-2. Multinomial Logistic Regression: Selection to High School Work Investment Patterns

Background	Wald test	Not employed[a]		Occasional: low duration–low intensity[a]		Sporadic: low duration–high intensity[a]		Steady: high duration–low intensity[a]	
		b (S.E.)	exp(b)	b (S.E.)	exp(b)	b (S.E.)	exp(b)	b (S.E.)	exp(b)
Male (vs. female)	23.04***	0.666 (0.325)	1.95*	0.017 (0.209)	1.02	0.475 (0.226)	1.61*	−0.489 (0.212)	0.61*
White race (vs. non-White)	14.95**	−0.620 (0.396)	0.54	−0.329 (0.275)	0.72	−0.796 (0.277)	0.45**	0.227 (0.298)	1.25
Parental education	24.13***	0.386 (0.113)	1.47***	0.341 (0.080)	1.41***	0.295 (0.091)	1.34**	0.265 (0.080)	1.30***
Family income	4.16	−0.151 (0.085)	0.86	−0.053 (0.056)	0.95	−0.087 (0.060)	0.92	−0.054 (0.055)	0.95
Intact family (vs. non-intact)	13.66**	0.100 (0.379)	1.10	−0.256 (0.248)	0.77	0.581 (0.276)	1.79*	0.487 (0.264)	1.63
U.S. born (vs. foreign born)	12.19*	−0.077 (0.575)	0.93	0.140 (0.443)	1.15	2.068 (0.802)	7.91**	0.570 (0.489)	1.77
Peer orientation									
Time with friends	10.20*	−0.027 (0.065)	0.97	−0.025 (0.043)	0.97	−0.002 (0.047)	1.00	−0.123 (0.043)	0.88**
Problem behavior									
School misconduct	19.16***	−0.171 (0.091)	0.84	−0.063 (0.052)	0.94	0.110 (0.049)	1.12*	−0.084 (0.054)	0.92
Educational promise									
High promise (vs. low promise)	18.52***	0.160 (0.346)	1.17	0.724 (0.227)	2.06***	−0.055 (0.253)	0.95	0.664 (0.223)	1.94**
Intercept	14.25**	−1.153 (0.821)		−0.557 (0.598)		−3.03*** (0.943)		−0.625 (0.632)	
−2 log likelihood	−2252.5								
Number of cases	808								

[a]Reference category for high school work categories is most invested (high duration, high intensity).
***$p < 0.001$, **$p < 0.01$, *$p < 0.05$.

had higher "educational promise" than the most invested workers; that is they had experienced both more success in the school domain and were more optimistic about their future achievement in school. (Our indicator of "educational promise" was based on grade point average, the degree of intrinsic motivation toward school work, the sense of academic self-esteem, and educational plans in the ninth grade.)[*] Youth who followed a pattern of sporadic employment (low duration–high intensity) and the non-workers were similar to the most invested workers (the reference category) in their educational promise in the ninth grade. Those who were to become sporadically employed during high school may also have faced higher levels of employment discrimination, as they were disproportionately non-White. They also were found to have higher levels of school misconduct (as indicated by an index formed by two indicators: the frequency of getting into trouble at school and having to go to the principal in the ninth grade).

Indicating their distinctive orientations to work, the low-intensity adolescent workers were also found to be more likely to be saving their earnings to go to college (not shown); youth who opted for high-intensity jobs were especially likely to report that they sought their jobs to obtain work experience (see Mortimer, 2003).

The entire pattern of findings suggests that adolescents exercise agency in their decisions about employment—in their temporal investment in work and their selection into jobs of varying quality. Ninth graders whose aspirations, attitudes, and prior achievements indicated higher educational promise opted for less-intensive employment. Youth whose family background and orientation indicate greater resources and greater likelihood of being successful in college opt for patterns of lesser investment in employment. Those who are less advantaged at the outset, and whose psychological orientations indicate less interest in academic achievement, opt for greater human capital accumulation through work experience. The findings also indicate that adolescent work, particularly intensive work, has the potential to enhance vocational development and the capacity to successfully enact adult work.

We now consider whether work experiences in adolescence do in fact predict early adult activities that have pronounced relevance for socioeconomic attainment. Since the YDS panel members have now (at the time of the most recent data collection, in 2000) been out of high school for 9 years (since the spring of 1991), we can observe their initial investments in post-secondary education and movements into the full-time labor force, as well as longer-term trajectories of these experiences. We assess months of education and full-time work during the years after high school.

It should be noted that these variables have distinct meaning and importance at this phase of life. During this transitional period, the more advantaged young people invest in postsecondary education which yields future gains in occupational prestige and economic attainment. The payoff of their educational investment will not be evident for some years, as they become more or less successful in obtaining 4-year college degrees and other educational credentials. They forego full-time work in favor of part-time employment which is more compatible with higher education. It is for this reason that we chose to examine months in education and full-time work during the years immediately after high school, not "final" educational attainment or occupational prestige, which would be more appropriate indicators of socioeconomic attainment subsequently. Though months of education and full-time work are not "attainments" per se, they are strongly linked to them. For example, average months of education (during the years following high school) are linked to final degrees attained (F-value,

---

[*]Youth were coded 1 if they had scores above the median in ninth grade on each of these four variables, or were below the median on only one, and 0 if they scored below the median on two or more of the measures.

$p < 0.001$). Those who received MA degrees by age 26–27 (in 2000) obtained 7.6 months of postsecondary education on average per year, those who obtained BA degrees gained 6.3 months on average, those who obtained associates degrees went to school for 4.6 months, "some college" 3.5 months; etc. The correlation between average months of postsecondary education and occupational prestige (Stevens & Hoisington, 1987) at age 26–27 (2000) is 0.332 ($p < 0.001$). The correlation between log income and average months of full-time work is 0.330 ($p < 0.001$). The more highly educated youth have had relatively little time, however, to advance to higher paid positions; when most respondents are 26–27 there is relatively little association between income and average months of education (the correlation of log income is 0.125 [$p < 0.01$] with average months of schooling). We would expect that the income "payoff" for educational investment will become more pronounced as occupational careers unfold.

Months of Postsecondary Education

The patterns of work investment during high school are significantly linked to higher education. The "steady" work pattern, characterized by high-duration and low-intensity employment, was found to be conducive to obtaining more months of postsecondary education in the 4 years immediately after high school (Mortimer & Johnson, 1998a, 1998b). While many youth move in and out of education over an extended period (Pallas, this volume), higher education is especially likely to be obtained in the years immediately following high school. The distinctive proclivity for higher education among the prior "steady" workers was manifest even when a variety of relevant background characteristics and early indicators of educational interest and achievement were controlled. As is evident from Figure 20-2 (which displays unadjusted mean months of education each year), youth who worked at lower intensity during high school (steady and occasional workers, as well as non-workers) obtained more months of education thereafter than the higher intensity (sporadic and most invested) workers. This pattern persisted until 6 years following high school (up to 1997, when the respondents were about the

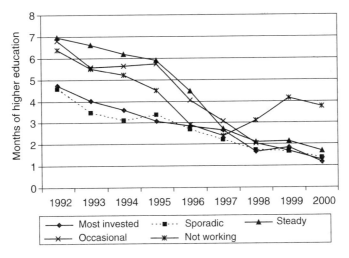

FIGURE 20-2. Months of higher education in young adulthood (1992–2000) by high school work investment (unadjusted means).

age of 23 and 24), when four of the groups converge. (The small group of non-workers during high school increases their educational investment after this point.)

We use growth curve analysis (see Halaby, this volume), a method well-suited to the analysis of panel data involving change over time. It uses a dynamic approach by modeling the starting point of individuals' trajectories, as well as their patterns of change. We are especially interested in the consequences of adolescent work patterns. That is, net of well-known precursors of attainment, do work patterns make a difference for early attainment-relevant activities? Do youth who limit their employment during high school have more postsecondary schooling than those who have the most invested work pattern, net of socioeconomic background and earlier measured educational promise? We examine the two outcomes described above: months of education and months of full-time employment after high school over the 9-year period 1992–2000. Each model predicts initial status in 1992 and a linear rate of change over the full period.

The first column of the upper panel of Table 20-3 provides estimates of the effects of early work careers (and other predictors) on the number of months of postsecondary education obtained initially in 1992 or the first year after high school. The first column in the lower panel presents the effects of the predictors on change in months of education each year over the period after high school. In these analyses, the work investment patterns are represented by dummy variables. As before, those who made the greatest investment in employment during high school (the "most invested" high-duration/high-intensity workers) constitute the reference category. Control variables in the analyses include social background characteristics and other variables that are likely to influence higher educational and other attainments—gender, race, nativity, the intact or non-intact character of the family of origin, parental education, family income, school misconduct, peer orientation (indicated by time spent with friends), and educational promise.

The results of this analysis yield further evidence that the pattern of adolescent work influences postsecondary educational investment. Looking first at initial status (top panel), it is not surprising to find that parental education, family income, and educational promise have significant positive effects on the number of months of schooling obtained during the first year after high school, 1992.* Foreign birth also confers an advantage. Early school misconduct reduces educational attendance during the year after high school. Controlling these influences, we still find that youth who pursued low-intensity employment during high school, the steady and occasional workers, initially obtain more months of postsecondary schooling (than the high-duration–high-intensity group). In contrast, those who pursued sporadic, low-duration/high-intensity employment and those who did not work at all are not significantly different from the most invested, high-duration/high-intensity workers in their educational investment right after high school.

As shown in Figure 20-2, the general trend is one of declining months of higher education as the youth progress beyond high school. The observed pattern of change, as well as the direction and magnitude of the estimates on change, is governed to some extent by initial status. For example, youth who are full-time students in 1992, attending school 9 or 10 months, start out near the ceiling of the yearly indicator (there are only 12 months during the year and most college programs involve summer vacations). As young people move out of school into the labor force, they show declines in yearly months of educational attendance. Thus, a negative effect on the estimated rate of change indicates a steeper slope of decline in annual

---

*Of the YDS panel, 24% indicated that they had no months of education, that is, they did not attend school in 1992. Fifty-seven percent reported no work involvement during that year. These persons were scored zero in the analysis.

TABLE 20-3. Growth Curve Analysis: The Effects of Early Work Patterns (1989–1991) on Months of Higher Education and Full-time Employment (1992–2000)

INITIAL STATUS (1992)	School		Full-time work	
Background variables	*Est.*	*(S.E.)*	*Est.*	*(S.E.)*
Male (vs. female)	−0.055	(0.28)	0.584*	(0.27)
White race (vs. non-White)	0.240	(0.36)	1.337***	(0.37)
U.S. born (vs. foreign born)	−1.882**	(0.60)	−0.779	(0.56)
Intact family (vs. non-intact)	0.354	(0.34)	0.141	(0.35)
Parental education	0.503***	(0.09)	−0.417***	(0.08)
Family income	0.189**	(0.07)	0.033	(0.07)
Time with friends	−0.111	(0.06)	0.128*	(0.06)
School misconduct	−0.293*	(0.14)	0.040	(0.13)
Educational promise	2.360***	(0.32)	−1.351***	(0.31)
Work Patterns (1989–1991)[a]				
Sporadic (low duration–high intensity)	−0.263	(0.42)	−0.296	(0.45)
Steady (high duration–low intensity)	1.468***	(0.39)	−1.635***	(0.39)
Occasional (low duration–low intensity)	0.969*	(0.40)	−1.541***	(0.41)
Not employed	−0.043	(0.51)	−1.395*	(0.56)
Intercept	3.698***	(0.83)	4.137***	(0.83)
RATE OF CHANGE (1992–2000)				
Background variables				
Male (vs. female)	−0.003	(0.05)	0.120*	(0.05)
White race (vs. non-White)	−0.083	(0.07)	−0.093	(0.07)
U.S. born (vs. foreign born)	0.238*	(0.11)	0.160	(0.12)
Intact family (vs. non-intact)	−0.034	(0.06)	−0.084	(0.06)
Parental education	−0.024	(0.02)	0.012	(0.02)
Family income	−0.019	(0.01)	0.025	(0.01)
Time with friends	0.006	(0.01)	−0.006	(0.01)
School misconduct	0.051	(0.03)	−0.056*	(0.03)
Educational promise	−0.244***	(0.06)	0.226***	(0.06)
Work Patterns (1989–1991)[a]				
Sporadic (low duration–high intensity)	0.034	(0.08)	−0.022	(0.09)
Steady (high duration–low intensity)	−0.207**	(0.07)	0.198*	(0.08)
Occasional (low duration–low intensity)	−0.157*	(0.07)	0.203*	(0.08)
Not employed	0.096	(0.11)	0.006	(0.13)
Intercept	−0.387*	(0.15)	0.473**	(0.17)
n	782		782	

[a]Reference category for high school work categories is most invested (high duration–high intensity).
***$p < 0.001$, **$p < 0.01$, *$p < 0.05$.

months of education, as one would expect for those whose starting points are high. As shown in Table 20-3 (lower panel), the low-intensity steady and occasional workers during high school experienced more rapid linear declines in annual months of school attendance over time (consistent with their high starting points). Youth who had higher educational promise also experienced more rapid declines. The native born manifested a less rapid rate of decline in months of education than the foreign born.*

*Although the results reported in Table 20-3 are based on a linear rate of change in months of schooling and full-time work in the period following high school, we also considered the possibility of non-linear growth. We found significant "deceleration" or a slowing in the growth process in the rate of change in full-time employment from 1992–2000. These results must be viewed with caution, however, as this non-linear effect is likely artifactual resulting from the "ceiling" by which growth in full-time work is limited to 12 months in a year. We did not find a significant non-linear rate of change in months of school. As more waves of data are collected, we will continue to explore possible non-linear change.

We thus find that the steady and occasional (low intensity) workers acquired more months of postsecondary education initially after leaving high school and manifest a relatively steep reduction in their educational investment over time. But is there an advantage in educational attainment for the low intensity workers? To examine this possibility, the analysis shown in Table 20-4 estimates the likelihood of obtaining a BA degree by the ninth year after high school (in 2000) based on early work histories. Using logistic regression analysis, we find the steady workers (high duration–low intensity) are more likely to receive a BA than their most invested peers (high duration–high intensity) even after controlling average months of schooling from 1992–2000, socioeconomic background, and prior educational promise, and other relevant variables. With the latter taken into account, the occasional (low duration–low intensity) pattern appears to confer no advantage.

We also found a significant interaction between educational promise and the steady (high duration–low intensity) work pattern on BA receipt by 2000 (analysis not shown). Figure 20-3 shows unadjusted mean differences in BA receipt by the work pattern groups, conditional on high and low promise. Youth who had lower educational promise upon entry to high school were markedly more likely than their similar low-potential counterparts to achieve BA degrees if they pursued the "steady" high-duration/low-intensity work pattern. Thus, while low-promise youth were in general more likely to select intensive work patterns, when they did take on the steady work pattern it was particularly beneficial for them.

TABLE 20-4. The Effects of Early Work Patterns (1989–1991) and Average Months of School (1992–2000) on Educational Attainment (BA degree, 2000)

	BA degree by 2000	
	b	(S.E.)
Average months of school (1992–2000)		
Average months of school	0.771***	(.076)
Work patterns (1989–1991)[a]		
Sporadic (low duration–high intensity)	−0.133	(.532)
Steady (high duration–low intensity)	0.954*	(.396)
Occasional (low duration–low intensity)	0.476	(.413)
Not employed	0.937	(.726)
Background variables		
Male (vs. female)	−0.204	(.276)
White race (vs. non-white)	0.198	(.403)
U.S. born (vs. foreign born)	−0.633	(.597)
Intact family (vs. non-intact)	0.095	(.361)
Parental education	0.419***	(.098)
Family income	−0.033	(.070)
Time with friends	−0.020	(.044)
School misconduct	−0.150	(.087)
Educational promise	1.545***	(.331)
Intercept	−6.461***	(.901)
Number of cases	665	

[a]Reference category for high school work categories is most invested (high duration–high intensity).
***$p < 0.001$, **$p < 0.01$, *$p < 0.05$.

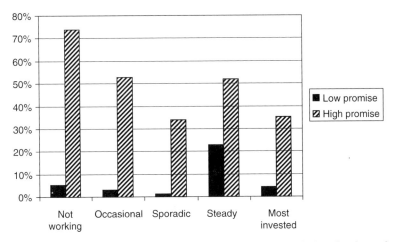

FIGURE 20-3. **BA degree receipt by high school work investment and educational promise.**

Full-time Employment

We now consider the starting point and trajectory of full-time work following high school. We find that the most invested and sporadic (higher intensity) workers during high school pursued more months of full-time employment than the other groups, until about 6 years after high school, in 1997 (Figure 20-4 shows unadjusted means).

Returning to the growth curve analyses (Table 20-3), males have more months of full-time employment than females and Whites more than non-Whites at the start. Early peer orientation also predicts more full-time work after high school. Parental education reduces investment in full-time employment immediately after high school, as does the young person's educational promise. The steady and occasional (low intensity) career patterns and the non-working pattern are associated with less early investment in full-time work. Finally, the increase in involvement in full-time employment in the years after high school is enhanced by the prior steady and occasional work patterns, as well as by being male and by educational promise. As one might expect, earlier school misconduct reduced growth in full-time employment.

These analyses indicate the trade-off between higher education and employment in the years after high school. That is, the lower intensity adolescent workers show greater propensity toward higher education initially, in the year immediately after high school and less propensity toward full-time work. The pattern is reversed thereafter, as they increase their full-time labor force involvement and diminish their investment in education (comparing columns 1 and 2 in Table 20-3). Many of the more intensively working adolescents also balance school and work after high school. However, high-intensity workers during high school start out working more months of the year than the occasional and steady workers and show less rapid increase in involvement in full-time employment, as they do not have as far to reach the maximum number of months on this variable.

It might be expected that youth who pursued distinct pathways of employment during high school, having accrued varying amounts of labor force experience, would be more or less "savvy" about finding jobs and would use distinct (and differentially productive) job search strategies. Attesting, however, to the unstructured transition from school to work in the U.S.

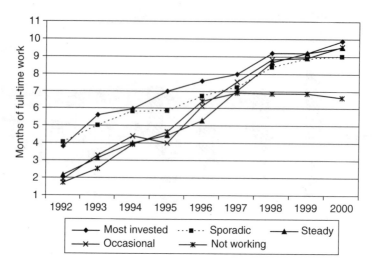

FIGURE 20-4. **Months of full-time employment in young adulthood (1992–2000) by high school work investment (unadjusted means).**

context, we find substantial use of "informal" networks and very little difference between the adolescent work pattern groups in their job-locating methods. All appear to take rather similar actions in seeking employment. Each year we asked about how the youth located their present jobs, providing somewhat different response options geared to their changing circumstances. (Fifteen potential ways of finding jobs were provided in 2000 and the respondents checked all that applied to them.) Taking the 2000 data (9 years after high school) as a case in point (patterns in other years were similar), we observe that youth use several direct modes of job acquisition. They locate jobs through friends (24%), parents (15%), other relatives (12%), neighbors (9%), and contacts at work (10%). They also inquire about job openings (13%) and answer advertisements (18%). Thus, most young adults appear to draw on their social networks and use their own initiative to situate themselves advantageously in their early forays into the labor force, irrespective of their work investment pattern during high school.

DATA FROM THE QUALITATIVE INTERVIEWS

Qualitative interviews provide a glimpse into young people's subjective understandings of how their early work might have influenced their future occupational attainments. Whereas status attainment researchers assess the level of educational and occupational aspirations and others have measured control orientations of various kinds (Bandura, 1997; Clausen, 1991; Grabowski, Call, & Mortimer, 2001; see Shanahan & Hood, 1999, for a review), these general constructs do not capture the specificity and nuances of how youth think about their futures. YDS interviews reveal young people's understandings about how their early employment contributed to their capacity to perform adult work and to the occupational decision-making process itself.

Our qualitative interviews show that young people in their mid-twenties (1999) give high marks to their early work experiences, just as their parents did when describing their own adolescent jobs (Aronson, Mortimer, Zierman, & Hacker, 1996). For example, the jobs they held as teenagers were seen as improving their interpersonal skills. The youth thought that their early jobs helped them to learn how to get along with other people in the workplace, to overcome shyness and insecurity in relating to adults, and to be assertive. As one respondent noted,

> ... the development I've had was from working because I remember being very shy when I first started. Like, I never wanted to talk to anybody and I was like, ah, I can't talk now, but after working, I think, it's more like you realize that, especially in the context of selling something to somebody, that everyone is just a person and they have the same needs ... So, I think that was one of the things that I took from it is kind of developing more interpersonal skills ... (female)

The youth appreciated many other advantages of employment that their parents also recognized: working during high school gave them greater confidence and made them more aware of labor force opportunities and the credentials that they would need to reach their career goals. The experience also enhanced their sense of responsibility and independence. We provide two illustrative quotes:

> I learned to work for what I want in life. I learned some responsibility. I had to be on time. I had to get it done before I went to school. I had to collect the money. (male)

> I think it helped me to develop a good work ethic like my parents hoped. (female)

Occupational decision-making sometimes involves an exploratory process of successive elimination, as individuals come to recognize that they are not suited for certain options (Mortimer et al., 2002). Some of our respondents learned through their high school jobs more about what they did not want to do later in life:

> It taught me I never wanted to work in an office again. Seriously. (female)

> It taught me I didn't want to work at a gas station for the rest of my life. (female)

> [High school jobs] narrowed it down and helped me figure out what I did not want to do. (male)

> Made me resolve never to have another food service job. I promised myself, I said, oh, God, I really got to do well in college, so I don't have to do this the rest of my life. (female)

Less frequently, teenagers acquired vocational skills through their early jobs, which developed later as careers. For example, one female interviewee obtained considerable human capital through her employment in a photography shop in high school, before going to photography school.

> It helped me learn a lot more about photography and printing on a basic level. I learned about overexposure and under-exposure. I learned what the different film speeds did. I learned a lot more about customer service. I learned how to work the printing machine. (female)

Space limitations preclude more ample illustration of youth's own thinking about their early employment experiences in relation to their subsequent work careers and attainments (for additional illustration, see Mortimer, 2003; Mortimer et al., 2002). Suffice it to say here that youthful agency is not only indicated by the selection to employment patterns (which showed the significant effect of educational promise) and their attainment-relevant consequences, as revealed by the multinomial logistic regression and the growth curve analyses. Young people themselves recognize that their early work experiences contributed to their career decision-making and their human capital development.

CONCLUSION

In an institutional environment characterized by an absence of clear bridges from school to work, adolescents in the United States make their way to adult full-time employment by constructing distinct combinations of secondary school and work experience. They do this in a variety of ways, depending on their socioeconomic and personal resources, especially their interest in and proclivity for education. Young people who are less likely in fact to be able to complete college, invest in more intensive work during high school. Many seek employment to gain job skills (along with a host of other reasons). Intensive employment is more adult like, both with respect to its temporal features, as well as its extrinsic rewards, advancement and learning opportunities, and stressors. In contrast, those young people who have greater resources early on—higher socioeconomic backgrounds and stronger educational engagement—also hold paid jobs while in high school, but their investment in employment is likely to be limited.

This research thus points to two general pathways for U.S. adolescents as they make the transition to adulthood. The first features employment in the naturally occurring labor market during high school that is often fairly continuous but limited in intensity, followed by prolonged postsecondary schooling and delayed entry to the full-time labor force. These youth appear to intentionally limit their early work involvement and thereby optimize their educational qualifications.

The second involves more intensive labor force participation during high school, more limited postsecondary schooling, and rapid acquisition of full-time employment. These youth develop human capital through high school work experience; this strategy pays off in terms of the rapid acquisition of full-time employment. Adolescents who do not work at all during high school are a small but especially interesting group, with particularly lengthy transitions from school to full-time labor force participation. More attention should be directed to selection processes surrounding the non-workers—the reasons why persons in this group forego employment during high school.

It is important to emphasize that high school work patterns are influenced by young people's social locations and prospects for the future—defined by gender, race, parental education, and early educational promise. But even when these and other relevant factors are controlled, teenage work patterns have independent influence on postsecondary educational investment and the acquisition of full-time work. These attainment pathways may be considered the consequences of agency—biographical accomplishments in the fullest sense of the term (Heinz, this volume; Heinz, 2002), resulting from long-term patterns of investment in schooling and work from adolescence onwards.

The findings of the YDS indicate that adolescent work experience is an integral part of the process of socioeconomic attainment among contemporary adolescents. The work pattern groups are found to have significant explanatory power in our growth curve models predicting initial (first year after high school) months of educational investment and full-time work. They also influence patterns of growth or change during subsequent years, taking into account the differences in initial starting points (and the many associated bases of heterogeneity) and even after a wide range of well-established predictors of attainment have been controlled. The work patterns also exert significant independent influence on receipt of the highly coveted BA degree.

The strategies of transition involving social background, educational engagement, and teenage work that we observe in the YDS panel must be understood within the contemporary institutional context. As we have noted in the introduction to this chapter, they take place in a context of expansion of higher education, "destandardization" of education and work sequences, rapid change in technology and occupational structures, and increasing fragility and transience of the employment contract. These environments represent new challenges and opportunities for contemporary youth as they make the transition to adulthood.

Our data suggest that young people are exercising agency in their rapidly changing environments, as they pursue distinct strategies of transition from school to work, linked to their personal resources and outlooks for the future. Youth who pursue different patterns of employment during high school seek jobs for different reasons and use their earnings in different ways (see Mortimer, 2003). The important role that educational promise plays in the analyses presented here is especially pertinent. High promise youth are more likely to pursue low-intensity employment during high school, which independently enhances their proclivity to obtain postsecondary education immediately after high school, while foregoing immediate full-time employment. Moreover, both high educational promise and low-intensity work patterns promote increases in full-time work during the 9 years following high school, while at the same time investment in postsecondary education diminishes.

Clearly, pathways through the life course are products of choice-making and institutional processes. The patterns of adolescent work investment we have identified, along with their subsequent attainment-relevant sequelae, are reflections of both social structure and individual agency as young people make the transition to adulthood. As we observed at the outset, low- and high-intensity employment patterns must be understood within the context of "bounded agency" (Shanahan & Hood, 1999). Our relatively undifferentiated educational system, which provides general credentials, presents the prospect of what Kerckhoff (2002) has called "college or nothing" and offers little in the way of occupationally-relevant credentials for young people who are less successful in the academic enterprise. Still, they can augment their human capital through work experience during high school. But even the more academically promising youth seek employment, albeit of limited intensity, so as to reach immediate economic goals as well as to acquire work experience. Through further qualitative and survey research, we plan to continue following this panel to monitor the continuing consequences of early work experiences for socioeconomic attainments as the youth become more established in their occupational careers, exhibit diverse patterns of intragenerational occupational mobility, and traverse other significant markers of adulthood.*

ACKNOWLEDGMENTS: This research is supported by grants from the National Institute of Mental Health, "Work Experience and Mental Health: A Panel Study of Youth" (MH 42843), and the National Institute of Child Health and Human Development (HD44138). The authors would like to thank Scott Eliason, Ross Macmillan, Michael Shanahan, and Christopher Uggen for very helpful comments on a prior draft of this chapter.

REFERENCES

Aronson, P. J. (1998, June). *Coming of age in the 1990s: Women's identities, life paths, and attitudes towards feminism*. Doctoral dissertation.

Aronson, P. J., Mortimer, J. T., Zierman, C., & Hacker, M. (1996). Generational differences in early work experiences and evaluations. In J. T. Mortimer & M. D. Finch (Eds.), *Adolescents, work, and family: An intergenerational developmental analysis*. (pp. 25–62) Newbury Park, CA: Sage.

---

*Furthermore, we will address the possibility that gender conditions the patterns described in this chapter; the linkages between early work experience and attainment-relevant experiences are likely to be different for males and females.

Bandura, A. (1997). *Self-efficacy: The exercise of control*. New York: Freeman.

Becker, G. S. (1993). *Human capital. A theoretical and empirical analysis, with special reference to education* (3rd ed.). Chicago: University of Chicago Press.

Blau, P., & Duncan, O. D. (1967). *The American occupational structure*. New York: John Wiley & Sons.

Choy, S. P. (2002). *Access and persistence: Findings from 10 years of longitudinal research on students*. Washington, DC: American Council on Education.

Clausen, J. S. (1991). Adolescent competence and the shaping of the life course. *American Journal of Sociology, 96*, 805–842.

D'Amico, R. J. (1984). Does employment during high school impair academic progress? *Sociology of Education, 57*, 152–164.

Elder, G. H., Jr. (1974). *Children of the Great Depression*. Chicago: University of Chicago Press.

Elder, G. H., Jr. (1998). The life course as developmental theory. *Child Development, 19*(1), 1–12.

Elder, G. H., Jr., & Conger, R. D. (2000). *Children of the land. Adversity and success in rural America*. Chicago: University of Chicago Press.

Featherman, D. L. (1980). Schooling and occupational careers: Constancy and change in worldly success. In O. G. Brim, Jr., & J. Kagan (Eds.), *Constancy and change in human development*. (pp. 675–738). Cambridge: Harvard University Press.

Freedman, D., Thornton, A., Camburn, D., Alwin, D., & Young-DeMarco, L. (1988). The life history calendar: A technique for collecting retrospective data. In C. C. Clogg (Ed.), *Sociological methodology* (Vol. 18, pp. 37–68). San Francisco, CA: Jossey-Bass.

Gamoran, A. (1996). Educational stratification and individual careers. In A. C. Kerckhoff (Ed.), *Generating social stratification: Toward a new research agenda*. (pp. 59–74). Boulder, CO: Westview Press.

Grabowski, L. S. (2001, June). Welfare participation and self-efficacy. Doctoral dissertation.

Grabowski, L. S., Call, K. T., & Mortimer, J. T. (2001). Global and economic self-efficacy in the attainment process. *Social Psychology Quarterly, 64*, 164–179.

Greenberger, E., & Steinberg, L. (1986). *When teenagers work: The psychological and social costs of adolescent employment*. New York: Basic Books.

Heinz, W. R. (1996). Status passages as micro–macro linkages in life course research. In A. Weymann & W. R. Heinz (Eds.), *Society and biography: Interrelationships between social structure, institutions and the life course*. (pp. 51–65). Weinheim, Germany: Deutscher Studien Verlag.

Heinz, W. R. (1999). Job-entry patterns in a life course perspective. In W. R. Heinz (Ed.), *From education to work: Cross-national perspectives*. (pp. 214–231). Cambridge: Cambridge University Press.

Heinz, W. R. (2002). Transition discontinuities and the biographical shaping of early work careers. *Journal of Vocational Behavior, 60*, 220–240.

Jencks, C., Crouse, J., & Mueser, P. (1983). The Wisconsin model of status attainment: A national replication with improved measures of ability and aspirations. *Sociology of Education, 56*, 3–19.

Kalleberg, A., Reskin, B. F., & Hudson, K. (2000). Bad jobs in America: Standard and nonstandard employment relations and job quality in the United States. *American Sociological Review, 65*, 256–278.

Kerckhoff, A. (2002). The transition from school to work. In J. T. Mortimer & R. Larson (Eds.), *The future of adolescent experience: Societal trends and the transition to adulthood*. (pp. 52–87). New York: Cambridge University Press.

Kohli, M. (1986). The world we forgot: A historical review of the life course. In V. W. Marshall (Ed.), *Later life: The social psychology of aging*. (pp. 271–303). Beverly Hills, CA: Sage.

Kohn, M. L., & Schooler, C. (1983). *Work and personality: An inquiry into the impact of social stratification*. Norwood, NJ: Ablex.

Long, J. S. (1997). *Regression models for categorical and limited dependent variables*. London: Sage.

McNeal, R. B., Jr. (1997). Are students being pulled out of high school? The effects of adolescent employment on dropping out. *Sociology of Education, 70*, 206–220.

Marini, M. M. (1987). Measuring the process of role change during the transition to adulthood. *Social Science Research, 16*, 1–38.

Marsh, H. E. (1991). Employment during high school: Character building or a subversion of academic goals?. *Sociology of Education, 64*, 172–189.

Mortimer, J. T. (2003). *Working and growing up in America*. Cambridge, MA: Harvard University Press.

Mortimer, J. T., Finch, M. D., Dennehy, K., Lee, C., & Beebe, T. (1994). Work experience in adolescence. *Journal of Vocational Education Research, 19*, 39–70.

Mortimer, J. T., Finch, M. D., Shanahan, M., & Ryu, S. (1992). Work experience, mental health and behavioral adjustment in adolescence. *Journal of Research on Adolescence, 2*, 25–57.

Mortimer, J. T., & Johnson, M. K. (1998a). New perspectives on adolescent work and the transition to adulthood. In R. Jessor (Ed.), *New perspectives on adolescent risk behavior.* (pp. 425–496). New York: Cambridge University Press.

Mortimer, J. T., & Johnson, M. K. (1998b). Adolescent part-time work and educational achievement. In K. Borman & B. Schneider (Eds.), *The adolescent years: Social influences and educational challenges.* (pp. 183–206). Chicago: National Society for the Study of Education.

Mortimer, J. T., & Johnson, M. K. (1999). Adolescent part-time work and post-secondary transition pathways: A longitudinal study of youth in St. Paul, Minnesota (U.S.). In W. R. Heinz (Ed.), *From education to work: Cross national perspectives.* (pp. 111–148). New York: Cambridge University Press.

Mortimer, J. T., Pimentel, E. E., Ryu, S., Nash, K., & Lee, C. (1996). Part-time work and occupational value formation in adolescence. *Social Forces, 74,* 1405–1418.

Mortimer, J. T., & Staff, J. (2002, August 22–25). *Stress-sensitization vs. stress inoculation: The impact of early work stressors on young adult mental health.* Paper presented at the Annual Meeting of the American Psychological Association, Chicago.

Mortimer, J. T., Zimmer-Gembeck, M., Holmes, M., & Shanahan, M. J. (2002). The process of occupational decision-making: Patterns during the transition to adulthood. *Journal of Vocational Behavior, 61,* 1–27.

Newman, K. S. (1999). *No shame in my game.* New York: Alfred A. Knopf, Inc., and The Russell Sage Foundation.

Osgood, D. W. (1999). Having the time of their lives: All work and no play? In A. Booth, A. C. Crouter, & M. J. Shanahan (Eds.), *Transitions to adulthood in a changing economy. No work, No family, No future?* (pp. 176–186). Westport, CT: Praeger.

Panel on Child Labor (Committee on the Health and Safety Implications of Child Labor, Board on Children, Youth, and Families, Commission on Behavioral and Social Sciences and Education, National Research Council, Institute of Medicine.) (1998). *Protecting youth at work: Health, safety, and development of working children and adolescents in the United States.* Washington, DC: National Academy Press.

Phillips, S., & Sandstrom, K. L. (1990). Parental attitudes towards youth work. *Youth and Society, 22,* 160–183.

Schneider, B., & Stevenson, D. (1999). *The ambitious generation.* New Haven, CT: Yale University Press.

Sewell, W., & Hauser, R. (1975). *Education, occupation and earnings: Achievement in the early career.* New York: Academic Press.

Shanahan, M. J. (2000). Pathways to Adulthood in changing societies: Variability and mechanisms in life course perspective. *Annual Review of Sociology, 26,* 667–692.

Shanahan, M. J., & Flaherty, B. P. (2001). Dynamic patterns of time use in adolescence. *Child Development, 72,* 385–401.

Shanahan, M. J., & Hood, K. E. (1999). Adolescents in changing social structures: Bounded agency in life course perspective. In R. K. Silbereisen & L. J. Crockett (Eds.), *Negotiating adolescence in times of social change: Cross national perspectives on developmental processes and social intervention.* (pp. 123–134). New York: Cambridge University Press.

Shanahan, M. J., Mortimer, J. T., & Krüger, H. (2002). Adolescence and adult work in the twenty-first century. *Journal of Research on Adolescence, 12,* 99–120.

Steinberg, L., & Cauffman, E. (1995). The impact of employment on adolescent development. *Annals of Child Development, 11,* 131–166.

Steinberg, L., & Dornbusch, S. M. (1991). Negative correlates of part-time employment during adolescence: Replication and elaboration. *Developmental Psychology, 27,* 304–313.

Steinberg, L., Fegley, S., & Dornbusch, S. M. (1993). Negative impact of part-time work on adolescent adjustment: Evidence from a longitudinal study. *Developmental Psychology, 29,* 171–180.

Stevens, G., & Hoisington, E. (1987). Occupational prestige and the 1980 U.S. labor force. *Social Science Research, 16,* 74–105.

Warren, J. R., LePore, P. C., & Mare, R. D. (2000). Employment during high school: Consequences for students' grades in academic courses. *American Educational Research Journal, 37,* 943–969.

PART VI

METHODS AND INTERDISCIPLINARY APPROACHES

A. Modes of Studying the Life Course

CHAPTER 21

Distinguishing Age, Period, and Cohort Effects

Norval D. Glenn

Assessing the effects of growing older has always been a central task of scholars and researchers in the academic specialties that focus on age-related phenomena. Although effects have rarely been attributed to chronological aging or the mere passage of time after birth, such age-related changes as the accumulation of experience, role changes, and biological maturation and decline have been thought to bring about changes in attitudes, values, behavior, affective states, cognitive ability, and relations with other people. A fairly typical hypothesis about attitudinal change and aging, for instance, is that accommodation and adaptation to existing social arrangements tend to make aging persons more conservative in the sense of being resistant to change (Glenn, 1974). An example of a hypothesis concerning aging and behavior is that declines in energy and risk-taking propensities associated with biological aging tend to diminish participation in conventional crime (Hirschi & Gottfredson, 1983).

In the early decades of the 20th century, most conclusions about the effects on humans of growing older were based on comparisons of persons of different ages at one point in time, in other words on cross-sectional data. Some scholars were aware of the hazards of this method of inferring age effects, but much of the academic literature and almost all of the journalistic and popular literature on aging neglected the fact that cross-sectional age differences in a variable may reflect the effects of being born at different times and having different formative experiences rather than or in addition to the effects of growing older. For instance, most current elderly people in the United States reached adulthood or late adolescence before television viewing became common and are likely to differ in many ways from younger people because they were not influenced by television while they were growing up. Any such

NORVAL D. GLENN • Department of Sociology, University of Texas, Austin, Texas 78712-1088

Handbook of the Life Course, edited by Jeylan T. Mortimer and Michael J. Shanahan. Kluwer Academic/Plenum Publishers, New York, 2003.

age differences caused by being born at different times are cohort effects rather than the effects of any aspect of aging.

By mid-century there was widespread awareness among students of aging that age and cohort effects were likely to be confounded in the differences by age (such as in attitudes, values, and personality) on which most conclusions about the effects of human aging had been based. It was acknowledged that even physiological differences among people of different ages could have resulted partly from variation in such early influences as those from the quality of prenatal care and the quality of nutrition during childhood. This awareness led to much advocacy of panel studies, which provide data on specific individuals at different points in time, and a good many such studies were conducted and started.

Some of the more enthusiastic proponents of panel studies during this period seem not to have realized that the data from those studies are, by themselves, not necessarily better than cross-sectional data for inferring the effects of aging, at least in dynamic modern societies. Persons in such societies grow older in changing rather than in stable social, cultural, and physical environments; therefore, changes in the persons' characteristics may be the result of shifts in the environment rather than or in addition to the effects of growing older. That is, they may be period effects. For instance, if there is a general political shift towards conservatism in a society as persons mature from young adulthood to middle age, any increase in conservative attitudes among those persons may result from the general societal change rather than from aging. Therefore, age and period effects are likely to be confounded in the data from panel studies. Of course, the same kind of confounding of effects is likely in aggregate-level data that indicate how people born during a particular period of time—those in a birth cohort—change as they grow older.

The third quarter of the 20th century was marked by substantial clarification of the conceptual and logical problems involved in studying age, period, and cohort effects, thanks to the work of such scholars as Baltes (1968), Riley (1973), Ryder (1965), and Schaie (1965). By the last quarter of the century, most gerontologists and students of the life course had at least an elementary understanding of what is now known as the age–period–cohort conundrum or of the confounding of age effects with either period or cohort effects in any kind of data in which chronological age is an independent variable.

The conundrum is best illustrated by the use of a standard cohort table, that is a table in which multiple sets of cross-sectional data relating age to a dependent variable are juxtaposed and in which the intervals between the periods for which there are data are equal in years to the range in each age category. For instance, if 10-year age categories are used, data gathered at 10-year intervals are presented, as in Table 21-1, in which the dependent variable is whether or not respondents to the 1974, 1984, and 1994 U.S General Social Surveys said that extramarital sex relations are "always wrong." In such a table, trends within cohorts can be traced by starting with any but the oldest age category in the left-hand column and reading diagonally down and to the right. For instance, according to the data in Table 21-1, in the birth cohort that was 20–29 years old in 1974, the percentage of "always wrong" responses went from 59.2% in 1974, to 63.9% in 1984, to 76.7% in 1994. This change could be an age effect, a period effect, or a combination of the two and age and period effects may be confounded in the trend shown in any cohort diagonal in a standard cohort table. Likewise, in Table 21-1 as in any standard cohort table, period and cohort effects may be confounded in each row, and age and cohort effects may be confounded in each column. If a person's value on any two of the three interrelated variables—age, period, and cohort—is known, then that person's value on the third variable is also known and he or she can be correctly placed in a cell of the standard cohort table.

TABLE 21-1. Percentage of Respondents to the 1974, 1984, and 1994 U.S. General Social Surveys Who Said that Extramarital Sex Relations are "Always Wrong" by Age

Age	1974		1984		1994	
	%	(n)	%	(n)	%	(n)
20–29	59.2	(392)	68.3	(384)	83.8	(346)
30–39	70.9	(291)	63.9	(304)	77.7	(462)
40–49	75.3	(270)	70.8	(241)	76.7	(411)
50–59	80.8	(278)	78.6	(181)	77.2	(272)
60–69	83.0	(194)	79.7	(166)	85.8	(165)

Note: The data are weighted by number of respondents in the household age 18 and older to increase representativeness.

The age–period–cohort conundrum is a special case of the "identification problem," which occurs whenever there are three or more independent variables that may affect a dependent variable and when each of those variables is a perfect linear function of the other ones (Blalock, 1967). For instance, if one knows a person's earnings this year and last year, the 1-year change in earnings can be computed from that information. In other words, the identification problem is the most extreme form of collinearity, because the multiple correlation of each variable with the others is unity. Once the other variables are statistically held constant, the variance of the remaining variable is zero. Therefore, one cannot simultaneously estimate the effects of all the independent variables by any straightforward method, such as by including them in continuous form as predictor variables in a regression equation. If one tries to do that, the computer program will not run.

The identification problem occurs frequently in social research, including when a difference between two variables is hypothesized to have an effect over and above the effects of the two defining variables. For instance, in research designed to study the effects of social mobility, the three interrelated independent variables are status of origin, status of destination, and the difference between those two variables. And in heterogamy effects research, the interrelated variables are husband's characteristics, wife's characteristics, and the difference between the spouses. It is in cohort analysis, however, that the identification problem has received the most attention.

STATISTICAL ATTEMPTS TO SEPARATE THE EFFECTS

The age–period–cohort conundrum was explicated with unprecedented clarity in an article by Mason, Mason, Winsborough, and Poole (1973), which at least in sociology arguably contributed more than any other publication to increased understanding of the logical problems involved in assessing effects in life course research. That article also raised hopes that the effects confounded in cohort data could be separated through statistical analysis and it introduced the method most widely used to try to do that. Variants of the method are still frequently used, one of the latest examples being in an article that appeared as this chapter was nearing completion (Robinson & Jackson, 2001).

That method, which I call the dummy variable method, is a way of simultaneously estimating the effects of age, period, and cohort by making simplifying assumptions—identifying restrictions—that allow estimation of a regression model in which age, period, and cohort are entered as sets of dummy variables. (In a variant of the method, one of the variables is entered in continuous form.) The method requires only that the effects of two categories (usually adjacent ones) of either age, period, or cohort be assumed to be equal (e.g., see Table 21-3). Of course, when a set of dummy variables is entered as independent variables in a regression, one of the variables must be omitted and the Mason et al. (1973) method requires only that one additional variable from one of the sets be dropped. This simple procedure allows the regression program to run and generates estimates of the effects on the dependent variable of the age, period, and cohort dummy variables. Of course, stronger identifying restrictions can be made and proponents of the method recommend additional assumptions if they seem justified on the basis of theory or what one already knows about the phenomena being studied. If one can be confident that either age, period, or cohort has no effect on the dependent variable, that variable can be omitted from the analysis and the age–period–cohort conundrum dissolves.

The dummy variable method has often been used as an all purpose solution to the identification problem in cohort analysis (though Mason et al. [1973] essentially say in a footnote that it cannot be used to separate linear effects) that is assumed to yield reasonable estimates as long as the assumptions on which identifying restrictions are based are not gross distortions of reality. The reasoning has been that the effects of adjacent narrowly defined age, period, or cohort categories are unlikely to be very different and that the error involved in assuming equal effects is only on the order of that involved in grouping the values of a continuous variable. It is acknowledged that it is important not to assume equality of effects for periods in which social change is known to have been unusually great or for cohorts of substantially different sizes because of changes in fertility. And it is considered wise to concentrate on the relatively stable middle years of adulthood in selecting adjacent age categories. Use of very rudimentary "side information" (information from outside the cohort data being analyzed) should, according to this point of view, assure that the estimates of effects will be about as nearly correct as the levels of sampling and measurement error allow.

Although other procedures to achieve a statistical separation of age, period, and cohort effects have not been widely used, a method that requires no use of "side information" was developed by Japanese scholar T. Nakamura and introduced to U.S. social scientists by Sasaki and Suzuki (1987). That method, based on Bayesian statistics, selects the simplest combination of age, period, and cohort effects that could account for a set of cohort data, as simplicity is operationally defined by the method. Stated differently, the method is based on the invariant simplifying assumption that "successive parameters change gradually…"(Sasaki & Suzuki, 1987, p. 1063). If the researcher does not use theory and side information to evaluate the reasonableness of the results yielded by this method, such terms as "mechanical" can accurately be applied to its use (Glenn, 1989).

That no mechanically applied statistical procedure can be relied upon to provide an even approximately accurate separation of age, period, and cohort effects is illustrated by the different combinations of effects that could account for the data in Table 21-2, which is a standard cohort table reporting hypothetical data. The simplest interpretation of the data is that they reflect pure linear age effects, whereby each additional 10 years of age produces a five-point increase in the dependent variable. For some dependent variables, this may be the only plausible interpretation, but as the alternative explanations at the bottom of Table 21-2 indicate, it is not the only logically possible one. Rather, there is an infinite number of combinations of age, period, and cohort effects that could produce the pattern of variation in the dependent variable shown in Table 21-2. When the pattern of variation is not as simple as that in Table 21-2, which is usually the case, the combination of effects producing the data must

TABLE 21-2. **Pattern of Data Showing Pure Age Effects, Offsetting Period and Cohort Effects, or a Combination of Age Effects and Offsetting Period and Cohort Effects**

	Year					
Age	1950	1960	1970	1980	1990	2000
20–29	50	50	50	50	50	50
30–39	55	55	55	55	55	55
40–49	60	60	60	60	60	60
50–59	65	65	65	65	65	65
60–69	70	70	70	70	70	70
70–79	75	75	75	75	75	75

Numbers in the cells are hypothetical values of a dependent variable.
Alternative explanations.
1. Each 10 years of aging produces a five-point increase in the dependent variable.
2. There is a five-point per 10 years positive period effect on the dependent variable and a five-point per 10 years negative cohort effect.
3. There is some combination of age and offsetting period and cohort effects on the dependent variable. An infinite number of combinations of such effects could produce the pattern of variation in the dependent variable shown in the table.

be somewhat complex. It should be obvious that no mechanically applied statistical analysis can reveal which of the many possible complex combinations of effects is the correct one.

However, the dummy variable method, unlike the one introduced by Sasaki and Suzuki (1987), is never applied in a completely mechanical fashion; the researcher must decide what identifying restriction or restrictions to make. The crucial question is does the judicious selection of an identifying restriction (or restrictions) assure the approximate correctness of the estimates of effects? If the assumptions on which identifying restrictions are based are approximately correct, must the estimates of effects also be nearly correct, given minimal levels of sampling and measurement error?

The answer to these questions is no. I base this conclusion largely on simulation experiments in which a set of effects is assumed, a data set is constructed reflecting those effects, and an attempt is made to reconstruct the effects through statistical estimation procedures (for explication and examples see Glenn, 2004, forthcoming). With such simulations, the researcher plays God, and thus he/she knows what the true effects are and the accuracy with which they are estimated through statistical model testing. A few simple examples of these experiments can demonstrate how inaccurate statistical estimates of age, period, and cohort effects can be even when the simplifying assumptions do not substantially distort reality.

In Table 21-3, I report estimates from four dummy variable age–period–cohort models applied to the data in Table 21-2. (I created an individual-level data set by constructing 10 cases for each cell in the table.) The equality-of-effects assumption is applied to two cohorts in the first model, to two periods in the second, and to two age categories in the third. These different identifying restrictions are about equally defensible; none can involve a very drastic distortion of reality. However, which restriction is used can make a very substantial difference in the estimated effects. The first two models select the one-variable interpretation of the data, while the third model selects the two-variable one. It is necessary to make equality assumptions within at least two of the sets of dummy variables in order to arrive at a three-variable solution, as illustrated by model 4. Obviously, one must know a priori whether a one-, two- or three-variable solution is the correct one in order to make the right identifying restriction or restrictions.

TABLE 21-3. Four Dummy Variable Age–Period–Cohort Models Estimating the
Effects Reflected in Table 21-2 (Unstandardized Regression Coefficients)

	Model			
Variable	1	2	3	4
Constant	50.0	50.0	25.0	28.7
Age				
20–29	*	*	0.0	*
30–39	5.0	5.0	0.0	*
40–49	10.0	10.0	*	3.6
50–59	15.0	15.0	*	6.1
60–69	20.0	20.0	0.0	8.6
70–79	25.0	25.0	0.0	11.4
Year				
1950	*	0.0	*	*
1960	0.0	0.0	5.0	*
1970	0.0	0.0	10.0	3.6
1980	0.0	*	15.0	6.1
1990	0.0	*	20.0	8.6
2000	0.0	0.0	25.0	11.4
Cohort (year of birth)				
1871–1880	0.0	0.0	50.0	25.0
1881–1890	0.0	0.0	45.0	23.9
1891–1900	0.0	0.0	40.0	21.5
1901–1910	0.0	0.0	35.0	19.1
1911–1920	0.0	0.0	30.0	16.8
1921–1930	0.0	0.0	25.0	14.0
1931–1940	0.0	0.0	20.0	11.8
1941–1950	0.0	0.0	15.0	9.1
1951–1960	*	0.0	10.0	6.5
1961–1970	*	0.0	5.0	3.9
1971–1980	0.0	*	*	*

*Reference category: value set at zero.

A careful reading of the article by Mason et al. (1973) would prevent one from applying
the dummy variable method to data in which all of the variation is perfectly linear, as it is in
Table 21-2. Buried in a footnote of the article is the following statement, which has been
ignored by most researchers who have used the method:

> These pure effects [the hypothetical effects used to illustrate the method] have deliberately been
> made nonlinear in form … We create our data in this way because perfectly linear pure effects are
> inherently ambiguous to interpret, and can be estimated equally well by the pure effect variable or
> by the two remaining variables in the cohort analysis … (Mason et al., 1973, p. 248).

It is true that non-linear effects of age, period, and cohort are not confounded with one
another in the way that linear effects are, which suggests that non-linear effects might be
accurately estimated through statistical model testing. However, it can be shown that the
dummy variable method can rarely if ever be relied on to do that.

Consider, for instance, the hypothetical data in Table 21-4, in which the consistent non-
linear pattern of variation in the dependent variable by age at the different periods is amenable
to only one plausible interpretation. It is hard to imagine how any combination of period and

TABLE 21-4. Pattern of Data Showing Non-linear Variation in a Dependent Variable That Can Reasonably Only Be Interpreted to Reflect Age Effects*

Age	Year					
	1950	1960	1970	1980	1990	2000
20–29	50	50	50	50	50	50
30–39	52	52	52	52	52	52
40–49	62	62	62	62	62	62
50–59	62	62	62	62	62	62
60–69	50	50	50	50	50	50
70–79	45	45	45	45	45	45

Numbers in the cells are hypothetical values of a dependent variable.
*Assuming no effects from differential mortality.

cohort effects could have created or substantially contributed to this pattern of variation, which must therefore reflect largely or entirely non-linear age effects (assuming that the dependent variable is not correlated with longevity). At any rate, in one's role of God in a simulation experiment, one can assume that only age effects are reflected in the table. I am able, therefore, to select simplifying assumptions for the first three dummy variable age–period–cohort models in Table 21-5 that I know to be precisely correct, and each of these models yields correct estimates of the effects. However, for model 4 I assume that the effects for the 20–29 and 30–39 age categories are equal, which is nearly but not quite correct. This small distortion of reality makes the estimates of effects grossly inaccurate, showing, for instance, substantial period and cohort effects even though there are no such effects. This finding reveals a very serious problem with the dummy variable method even when the effects are non-linear, because in real-world research being able to make a simplifying assumption known to be precisely correct is very unlikely.

There is an additional reason for being wary of statistical attempts to separate age, period, and cohort effects. The Sasaki and Suzuki (1987) method and all major variants of the dummy variable method are based on the assumption that the effects are additive, even though it is likely that age, period, and cohort interact in their effects on most dependent variables of interest to social scientists and psychologists. According to theory, supported by a great deal of empirical evidence, young adults tend to respond more to stimuli for change than do older adults, so that period effects generally vary by age and, thus, among cohorts of different ages (Alwin, Cohen, & Newcomb 1991; Glenn, 1980). For instance, when major changes in attitudes occur, the change tends to be greater at the younger than at the older adult ages. This differential change often creates age differences in attitudes, often leaving older persons more conservative than younger ones. However, when change is in a conservative direction, young people still tend to change more than older ones, sometimes leading to a decline in age differences in attitudes. This was the case, for instance, when attitudes concerning extramarital sex relations became more restrictive in the United States during the 1970s, 1980s, and 1990s. Figure 21-1 shows how the attitudes in four birth cohorts converged during that time and attitudes at the different age levels converged even more (not shown in the figure). The difference between persons in their twenties and those age 60 and older in the percentage who said extramarital relations are "always wrong" went from 26.5 points in 1972–1976 to 2.0 points in 1992–1996.

TABLE 21-5. Four Dummy Variable Age–Period–Cohort Models Estimating the Effects Reflected in Table 21-4 (Unstandardized Regression Coefficients)

Variable	Model			
	1	2	3	4
Constant	62.0	50.0	50.0	60.0
Age				
20–29	−12.0	*	*	*
30–39	−10.0	2.0	2.0	*
40–49	*	12.0	12.0	8.0
50–59	*	12.0	12.0	6.0
60–69	−12.0	0.0	0.0	−8.0
70–79	−17.0	−5.0	−5.0	−15.0
Year				
1950	*	*	*	*
1960	0.0	0.0	*	2.0
1970	0.0	0.0	0.0	4.0
1980	0.0	0.0	0.0	6.0
1990	0.0	0.0	0.0	8.0
2000	0.0	0.0	0.0	10.0
Cohort (year of birth)				
1871–1880	*	*	*	20.0
1881–1890	0.0	*	0.0	18.0
1891–1900	0.0	0.0	0.0	16.0
1901–1910	0.0	0.0	0.0	14.0
1911–1920	0.0	0.0	0.0	12.0
1921–1930	0.0	0.0	0.0	10.0
1931–1940	0.0	0.0	0.0	8.0
1941–1950	0.0	0.0	0.0	6.0
1951–1960	0.0	0.0	0.0	4.0
1961–1970	0.0	0.0	0.0	2.0
1971–1980	0.0	0.0	0.0	*

*Reference category: value set at zero.

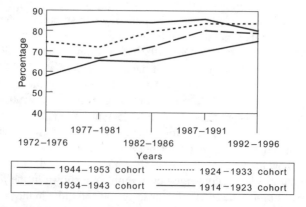

FIGURE 21-1. Percentage of persons in four birth cohorts who said that extramarital sex relations are "always wrong" by period, United States.

Source: The 1972 through 1996 U.S. General Social Surveys.

Furthermore, many kinds of age effects are likely to change through time and, thus, to vary among birth cohorts. Social expectations for behavior at various chronological ages have shifted considerably in recent decades, an example being an increased expectation for middle-aged and older people to be sexually active. Physiological aging has changed only moderately, but some aspects of social and psychological aging have changed more substantially.

If, as I argue, age–period–cohort interactions are ubiquitous, additive age–period–cohort statistical models would not be very useful and would often be misleading, even if they were not afflicted with other problems.

More than a quarter of a century ago, I called statistical attempts to separate age, period, and cohort effects "a futile quest" (Glenn, 1976). The quest continues, but it seems as futile now as it did then.

WALKING AROUND THE IDENTIFICATION PROBLEM: AGE–PERIOD–COHORT–CHARACTERISTIC (APCC) MODELS

A recent innovation in the study of some aspects of cohort effects is the introduction of APCC models (see O'Brien, 1989; 2000; O'Brien, Stockard, & Isaacson, 1999). These models do not include cohort but do include one or more "cohort characteristics," such as cohort size or some measure of family structure that varies by cohort. Whereas it is impossible to control age and period and let cohort vary, it is possible to control age and period and let the selected cohort characteristics vary. If the interest is only in estimating the effect of cohort size, for instance, such models should serve the purpose reasonably well. These models are not true age–period–cohort models, however and, if they are misconstrued to be such, they are likely to be misused and the results from testing them are likely to be misinterpreted.

It is unlikely that the cohort effects on any independent variable result only from the cohort characteristics included in the models, and any remaining cohort effects are confounded in the model estimates with age and period effects. Therefore, the estimates of age and period effects provided by the models are not meaningful. Even more troubling is the fact that, to the extent that cohort characteristics are linearly related to cohort, their effects also will be confounded with age and period effects. Fortunately, in recent U.S. data, the relationship of cohort size to date of birth (cohort) is largely non-linear, but some other cohort characteristics, including such family ones such as the proportion of babies born out of wedlock, bear a positive monotonic relationship to cohort. Although the relationships are not perfectly linear, they have strong linear components and, thus, age–period–cohort–characteristic models are unlikely to provide accurate estimates of the effects of these cohort characteristics.

The bottom line is that age–period–cohort–characteristic models can be useful in estimating the effects of cohort size and some other cohort characteristics, but they are in no sense a solution to the age–period–cohort conundrum.

INFORMAL MEANS OF DISTINGUISHING THE EFFECTS

The fact that one cannot rely on statistical model testing to separate age, period, and cohort effects accurately does not mean that one must give up on trying to distinguish the effects.

Once the quest to separate the effects with precision and absolute certainly is abandoned, reasonable judgments about the effects can usually be made. One needs only to draw on theory, common sense, and information about the dependent variable being studied from all available sources and then be appropriately tentative in the conclusions made.

There is no formula, no cookbook approach, for distinguishing the effects that will work well in all cases. On rare occasions, only an eyeballing of cross-tabular data is needed, as would be the case if one found variation in a dependent variable similar to that in Table 21-4. Similarly, there is only one plausible interpretation when there is a non-linear pattern of variation in the dependent variable among cohorts that is consistent across age categories and periods or if there is a nonlinear pattern of variation among periods that is consistent across age categories and cohorts.

Usually, making reasonable judgments about the effects is at least moderately more difficult. Consider, for instance, how the data in Table 21-1 should be interpreted. The cross-sectional data in the first column and the intracohort trend data in the cohort diagonals both suggest a positive age effect on disapproving of extramarital sex relations; of the eight 10-year intracohort changes shown, six are upward and the two downward changes are slight. However, the upward trend across the periods at ages 20–29 is evidence for rather strong period influences toward more restrictive attitudes; a change in attitudes and values among young adults usually results from period influences that impinge on persons at all ages, though often with less effect among the older ones. Therefore, the intracohort trends shown in the table could well be entirely period rather than age effects. And the positive relationship between age and restrictive attitudes shown in the first column could have resulted from earlier period influences toward permissive attitudes that affected younger persons more than older ones.

Of course, no serious cohort study of attitudes toward extramarital sex relations would be based only on the data in Table 21-1, especially since the question yielding the data has been asked on other General Social Surveys (see Figure 21-2), nor would the study stop with a simple examination of tabular data. However, given the basic evidence available, a definitive answer as to whether there has been any age effect on restrictive attitudes would elude even the most sophisticated study possible.

On the other hand, more nearly definitive evidence of age effects on attitudes toward premarital sex is possible; there is little indication of appreciable period influences on those attitudes, in either a restrictive or a permissive direction, during the time when the General Social Surveys have been conducted (see the data on young adults in Figure 21-2), and, thus, intracohort trends should reflect largely age effects (see the intracohort trend data in Figure 21-2). The youngest cohort represented in Figure 21-2 did experience an increase in restrictive attitudes ($p < 0.01$ on a two-tailed test), but attitudes in the older cohorts remained stable. The most reasonable conclusion to be drawn from these findings is that aging through the earliest stages of adulthood in this cohort increased restrictiveness but there was no age effect beyond that.

Often it is necessary to look at the data in a variety of ways and to bring in different kinds of "side information" in order to arrive at fairly confident conclusions about age, period, and cohort effects (for examples, see Abramson & Englehart, 1995; Alwin, 1991; Converse, 1976; Glenn, 1998; Robinson & Jackson, 2001, pp. 117–131). For instance, if one can identify a variable that almost certainly intervenes between either age, period, or cohort and the dependent variable, bringing it into the analysis will be useful. To illustrate, in the United States the percentage of persons who grew up in rural areas varies considerably by birth cohort; thus any variation by age in the dependent variable that is removed by controlling the size of the community of origin is probably a cohort rather than an age effect.

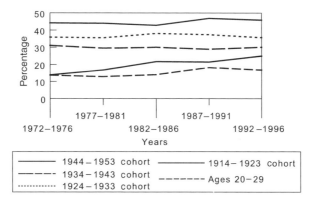

FIGURE 21-2. Percentage of persons in four birth cohorts and ages 20–29 who said that premarital sex relations are "always wrong," by period, United States.
Source: The 1972 through 1996 U.S. General Social Surveys.

Informal means of examining cohort data may not be satisfying to persons who have a high psychological need for certainty. However, accepting the fact that there is always some ambiguity in the evidence concerning age, period, and cohort effects is more scientific than dogmatically embracing statistical model estimates that are likely to be substantially in error.

CONCLUSIONS

Inferences about the effects of growing older are crucial to the study of aging and the life course and should be based on rigorous and systematic research, but a definitive separation of age effects from period and cohort effects through statistical model estimation is not possible. Belief that the effects can be separated statistically has led to much pseudo-rigorous research and almost certainly to many incorrect conclusions. If statistical model testing is used to estimate the effects, the credibility of the estimates should be evaluated by using theory, common sense, and various kinds of "side information." There is a danger that the model testing will create an illusion of rigor that will prevent the proper application of human judgment in the research process.

I therefore recommend that researchers usually skip the statistical model testing and proceed directly to more informal means of distinguishing age, period, and cohort effects. These methods are fallible, of course, but they are generally recognized as such and, hence, are less likely than formal model testing to lead to dogmatic, overly confident conclusions.

REFERENCES

Abramson, P. R., & Englehart, R. (1995). *Value change in global perspective*. Ann Arbor, MI: University of Michigan Press.

Alwin, D. F. (1991). Family of origin and cohort differences in verbal ability. *American Sociological Review, 56*, 625–638.

Alwin, D. F., Cohen, R. L., & Newcomb, T. M. (1991). *Political attitudes over the life span: The Bennington women after fifty years*. Madison, WI: University of Wisconsin Press.

Baltes, P. B. (1968). Longitudinal and cross-sectional sequences in the study of age and generation effects. *Human Development, 11*, 145–171.

Blalock, H. M., Jr. (1967). Status inconsistency, social mobility, status integration, and structural effects. *American Sociological Review, 32*, 790–801.

Converse, P. E. (1976). *The dynamics of party support: Cohort analyzing party identification*. Beverly Hills, CA: Sage.

Glenn, N. D. (1974). Aging and conservatism. *Annals of the American Academy of Social and Political Science, 175*, 176–186.

Glenn, N. D. (1976). Cohort analysts' futile quest: Statistical attempts to separate age, period, and cohort effects. *American Sociological Review, 41*, 900–905.

Glenn, N. D. (1980). Values, attitudes, and beliefs. In O. G. Brim, Jr. & J. Kagan (Eds.), *Constancy and change in human development*. (pp. 596–640). Cambridge, MA: Harvard University Press.

Glenn, N. D. (1989). A caution about mechanical solutions to the identification problem in cohort analysis: A comment on Sasaki and Suzuki. *American Journal of Sociology, 95*, 754–761.

Glenn, N. D. (1998). The course of marital success and failure in five American ten-year marriage cohorts. *Journal of Marriage and the Family, 60*, 569–576.

Glenn, N. D. (2004). *Cohort analysis* (2nd ed.). Thousand Oaks, CA: Sage Publications.

Hirschi, T., & Gottfredson, M. (1983). Age and the explanation of crime. *American Journal of Sociology, 89*, 552–584.

Mason, K. O., Mason, W. M., Winsborough, H. H., & Poole, W. K. (1973). Some methodological issues in the cohort analysis of archival data. *American Sociological Review, 38*, 242–258.

O'Brien, R. M. (1989). Relative cohort size and age-specific crime rates: An age–period–relative-cohort-size model. *Criminology, 27*, 57–78.

O'Brien, R. M. (2000). Age–period–cohort–characteristic models. *Social Science Research, 29*, 123–139.

O'Brien, R. M., Stockard, J., & Isaacson, L. (1999). The enduring effects of cohort characteristics on age-specific homicide rates, 1960–1995. *American Journal of Sociology, 104*, 1061–1095.

Riley, M. W. (1973). Aging and cohort succession: Interpretations and misinterpretations. *Public Opinion Quarterly, 37*, 35–49.

Robinson, R. V., & Jackson, E. F. (2001). Is trust in others declining in America? An age–period–cohort analysis. *Social Science Research, 30*, 117–145.

Ryder, N. B. (1965). The cohort as a concept in the study of social change. *American Sociological Review, 30*, 843–861.

Sasaki, M., & Şuzuki, T. (1987). Changes in religious commitment in the United States, Holland, and Japan. *American Journal of Sociology, 92*, 1055–1076.

Schaie, K. W. (1965). A general model for the study of developmental problems. *Psychological Bulletin, 64*, 92–107.

CHAPTER 22

Event History Models for Life Course Analysis

Lawrence L. Wu

The questions posed by life course researchers often differ in fundamental ways from those posed by sociologists, developmental psychologists, or economists (Elder, 1998; Mayer & Tuma, 1990). For example, life course researchers often focus analytic attention on transitions marking adolescence or early adulthood and the roles and statuses accompanying such transitions (Hogan & Astone, 1986; Modell, Furstenberg, & Hershberg, 1976; Shanahan, 2000). Prototypical questions along these lines include whether certain social groups experience a more rapid transition to adulthood or whether the timing of such transitions (or the duration spent in selected life course statuses) has changed for successive cohorts (Winsborough, 1980). As Mayer and Tuma (1990) note, work in this vein often implicitly conceives of social structure as arising out of individual experiences of varying duration, as opposed to alternative perspectives that see social structure in terms of collectivities of persons with particular fixed attributes (Blau, 1977), as generated from relational networks (and resulting "structural holes") among individual actors (White, Boorman, & Breiger, 1976) or from the aggregate behavior of rational actors (Becker, 1991).

Consider, for example, the linkage between early and later life course events, roles, and attitudes often posited by life course researchers (Elder, 1999).* Positing such linkages often generates a quite wide range of questions, which in turn carries important implications for the types of covariates and statistical models appropriate for life course research.

---

*This focus is not unique to the life course; indeed, precursors can be found in much work in the status attainment literature (see e.g., Blau & Duncan, 1967; Sewell & Hauser, 1975).

LAWRENCE L. WU • Department of Sociology, University of Wisconsin, Madison, Wisconsin 53706

Handbook of the Life Course, edited by Jeylan T. Mortimer and Michael J. Shanahan. Kluwer Academic/Plenum Publishers, New York, 2003.

Focusing on current and future trajectories of behavior has often led life course researchers to think more deeply about the various temporal and dynamic processes underlying past events, experiences, and the larger social forces shaping individual biographies and trajectories. One consequence of such a focus is that life course researchers have come to reject, by and large, the notion that the life course can be understood simply as a process of unilinear aging (Mayer & Tuma, 1990; Settersten & Mayer, 1997). Instead, life course researchers have increasingly emphasized the analytical importance of multiple dimensions of time, for example, age, duration in various statuses, and historical dimensions of time as measured by period or cohort.*

A related issue concerns interrelationships in the life course, two aspects of which are often stressed. One concerns the assertion, testable in principle, that domains such as work, marriage, childbearing, and emotional development, which are typically analyzed in isolation, in fact cannot be adequately understood without considering these domains as a unified whole. Another is the assertion, again testable in principle, concerning "linked" lives—that, for example, the events, behaviors, and outcomes experienced by one individual in a couple profoundly influences the course of events, behaviors, and outcomes experienced by a spouse.

In this chapter, I review methods relevant to life course research when event history data— that is, data on one or more discrete outcomes followed through time—are available. Several excellent monographs and textbooks (Allison, 1985; Blossfeld, Hamerle, & Mayer, 1989; Cox & Oakes, 1984; Fleming & Harrington, 1991; Hougaard, 2000; Lancaster, 1990; Tuma & Hannan, 1984; Yamaguchi, 1991) provide extensive coverage of relevant statistical models and issues. In this chapter, I provide a condensed summary of such issues, but also depart from these accounts by devoting attention to how existing models speak to (or, in some cases, do not speak to) the types of questions often posed by life course researchers.

CONCEPTUALIZING TRANSITIONS BETWEEN DISCRETE LIFE COURSE STATUSES

Event history analysis is well-suited to an analysis of life course transitions.[†] Indeed, the very concept of a transition is central both to research on the life course and to the conceptual and statistical modeling of event histories. For concreteness, consider Figure 22-1, which sketches two ways a researcher might conceptualize a particular life course transition for women—that of the transition to single motherhood. Panel A of Figure 22-1 presents a simple and highly stylized conceptualization of this process in which women can occupy two statuses of interest—that of being a single mother and that of not being a single mother. All women thus begin life at birth in the status labeled "1" (not a single mother), with some women subsequently transiting to the status labeled "2." Those who have become single mothers can exit this status as well, transiting back to the status labeled "1" and so forth.

---

*Another important line of life course research has emphasized the long historical view. The most influential work of this sort has emphasized the collective life trajectories of birth cohorts (Elder, 1999; Mayer, 1988). Other work in this vein has traced, for example, the increasing diversity of family and work experiences (Bumpass, 1990; Spain & Bianchi, 1996) and institutional influences on the increasing historical differentiation of individuals (Meyer, 1986). For an overview of statistical issues that arise in this line of research, see Glenn (this volume).
[†]For an alternative view, see Abbott and Tsay (2000) and the resulting commentary (Abbott, 2000; Levine, 2000; Wu, 2000).

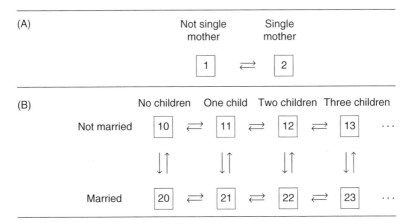

FIGURE 22-1. Two alternative "state spaces" for the transition into and out of single motherhood.

Panel B presents an alternative conceptualization of this process that cross-classifies a woman's marital status and number of children. Women begin life unmarried and with no children (status labeled "10"), and may then transit to subsequent statuses. (Child mortality is depicted in this panel by the leftward pointing arrows.) Note that there are now several possible transitions to single motherhood—the transition 10 → 11 consisting of a non-marital first birth and the transitions 21 → 11, 22 → 12, and 23 → 13 representing changes to not married statuses of married women.

Because panel B is an elaboration of panel A, the corresponding models are nested within one another, with the model in panel A equivalent to that in panel B when a variety of behavioral assumptions are imposed on the model in panel B. Equivalently, panel A can be said to "pool" across the various transitions in panel B, where, as in more standard contexts, such "pooling" assumptions can be tested empirically in ways that are formally equivalent to tests of pooling across race and ethnicity. Note that one could add further conceptual distinctions to the model in panel B—one could, for example, distinguish between the childbearing of women who are never married, divorced, or widowed, or between the childbearing of women in cohabiting and marital unions compared to the childbearing of single non-cohabiting women. Still, the point to be emphasized is the importance of considering alternative conceptualizations of the transitions of *theoretical* interest, even when not all such transitions are observed or available in the data at hand.

Another important notion is the pool of individuals at *risk* of a particular transition. In panel A, the risk set is straightforward—women at risk of a transition to single motherhood consist of those who are not single mothers, while those at risk of the other transition consist of single mothers—while in panel B, different risk sets of women are distinguished. Under either conceptualization of the process, however, it is clearly important to restrict the sample analyzed to those at risk of a particular transition, with departures from this rule of thumb undertaken only when the researcher has clear substantive or theoretical grounds to do so.

SINGLE TRANSITION FOR
A HOMOGENEOUS POPULATION

I now formalize ideas starting with the simple case of a single transition for a homogeneous population, for example, age-specific mortality in a population that is assumed to be behaviorally identical.* An important issue is that the event in question (mortality in this example) will often vary substantially with time (age in this example), with this pattern of time variation often exhibiting substantial nonlinearities. For example, age variation in mortality typically follows a so-called "bathtub" pattern, in which mortality is high at young and old ages, but low during the adolescent and adult years. Accounting for such patterns of time variation is of critical importance; in particular, estimation of other quantities of interest will, in general, be biased, sometimes substantially, if the underlying pattern of time variation is not accounted for adequately.

In modeling life course transitions, the quantity of fundamental interest is the so-called *hazard rate*. Equation (1) gives three equivalent definitions of this quantity:

$$r(t) = \lim_{\Delta t \downarrow 0} \frac{\Pr(T \leq t + \Delta t | T \geq t)}{\Delta t} = \frac{f(t)}{1 - F(t)} = \frac{f(t)}{S(t)} \tag{1}$$

where t denotes time (e.g., age), T denotes the random variable for the time of the event (age at death), and $f(t)$, $F(t)$, and $S(t) = 1 - F(t) = \Pr(T \geq t)$ denote the *density, cumulative distribution*, and so-called *survivor probability*, respectively.

The hazard rate provides the dependent variable of interest when modeling a single transition and is also a key building block for more complicated problems like that depicted in panels A and B of Figure 22-1. It is, however, not an immediately intuitive quantity. Some insight can be gained by considering its component parts. For example, note that the units for $f(t)$ and $S(t)$ are percent per unit time and percent, respectively; thus, the unit for $r(t)$ is "per unit time" as in "the age-specific first birth rate per month." Note also that because $f(t)$ and $S(t)$ are non-negative quantities, $r(t)$ is also a non-negative quantity that can assume any value between 0 and ∞. Finally note that, as is the case for a logistic regression model or for the probability p governing a coin flip, the outcome—the probability p, the log odds $\log(p/1 - p)$, or the hazard rate, $r(t)$—is not directly observed in the way a continuous outcome y_i is observed in a static linear regression model.

The quantity $\Pr(T \leq t + \Delta t | T \geq t)$ in Equation (1) gives the probability of having the event between time t and $t + \Delta t$, conditional on the event of interest not yet having occurred; hence, conditional on the population at risk, this quantity provides the probability that the event will occur between "now," as indexed by t, and some time in the future, as indexed by $t + \Delta t$. For events occuring in continuous time, it is desirable to define $\Pr(T \leq t + \Delta t | T \geq t)$ over all possible positive t; this is done via the limit in Equation (1), with the limit restricted to positive values of t so as to restrict intervals to those in the future. Combining these two parts—the limit and the conditional probability—yields the hazard rate, which is typically

---

*Within an event history context, homogeneity does not imply that individuals in such a population will experience the event of interest at the same time. As a rough analogy, consider a hypothetical population of coins in which the probability of heads is 0.5, where flipping 100 coins sampled from such a population will not yield 100 identical outcomes. A closer analogy is to radioactive material, in which individual atoms, even when chemically identical, will decay at different times. In the latter case, the *distribution* of event times can be shown to be exponential even though the event time for any given atom cannot be predicted.

interpreted as the "risk" of an event, where risk refers to the "instantaneous" conditional probability that the event of interest occurs at time t.

To see that the three alternative definitions in Equation (1) are equivalent, first consider the quantity $[\Pr(T < t + \Delta t|T \geq t)]/S(t)$, putting aside momentarily consideration of the limit and where for analytical convenience I assume an absolutely continuous $f(t)$. Recall from elementary probability theory that for $\Pr(B) > 0$ one can write

$$\Pr(A|B) = \frac{\Pr(A \text{ and } B)}{\Pr(B)}$$

Let $A = T < t + \Delta t$ and $B = T \geq t$, in which case

$$A \text{ and } B = \{T < t + \Delta t\} \text{ and } \{T \geq t\} = t \leq T < t + \Delta t$$

Then

$$\Pr(T < t + \Delta t|T \geq t) = \Pr(A|B)$$
$$= \frac{\Pr(A \text{ and } B)}{\Pr(B)}$$
$$= \frac{\Pr(t \leq T < t + \Delta t)}{\Pr(T \geq t)}$$
$$= \frac{\Pr(t \leq T < t + \Delta t)}{S(t)} \tag{2}$$

recalling that $S(t) = 1 - F(t) = \Pr(T \geq t)$.

Note that the limit in Equation (1) is absent from Equation (2). To reintroduce the limit, recall from elementary probability theory that for an absolutely continuous density $f(t)$, one can write

$$f(t) = \lim_{\Delta t \downarrow 0} \frac{\Pr(t \leq T < t + \Delta t)}{\Delta t}$$

Then applying the limit in Equation (1) to Equation (2) yields

$$\lim_{\Delta t \downarrow 0} \frac{\Pr(T < t + \Delta t|T \geq t)}{\Delta t} = \lim_{\Delta t \downarrow 0} \frac{\Pr(t \leq T < t + \Delta t)}{\Delta t S(t)}$$
$$= \frac{f(t)}{S(t)}$$

which establishes the equivalence between the alternative definitions in Equation (1).

A somewhat more intuitive quantity than $r(t)$ is the survivor probability $S(t)$; in population terms, this quantity for a single transition can be thought of as giving the proportion of the population that survives to time t without having experienced the event of interest. The hazard rate and survivor function are related according to

$$S(t) = \exp\left[-\int_0^t r(s)ds\right] = \exp[-H(t)] \tag{3}$$

where the so-called *integrated hazard* is given by

$$H(t) = \int_0^t r(s)ds \tag{4}$$

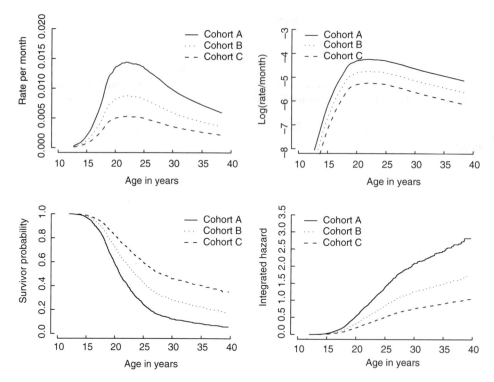

FIGURE 22-2. **Hypothetical examples of a proportional decline in the Hazard rate of first marriage for three successive birth cohorts. Implications for S(t), H(t), r(t), and log r(t).**

To gain further insight into the quantities $S(t)$, $H(t)$, $r(t)$, and $\log r(t)$, consider some hypothetical data on age at first marriage for three successive birth cohorts as presented in Figure 22-2. In this example, I constructed the curves for $r(t)$ from those for $\log r(t)$, with the three curves for $\log r(t)$ shifted vertically from one another by an additive constant:

$$\log r_A(t) = \log r_B(t) + c = \log r_C(t) + 2c$$

The two upper panels present graphs of $r(t)$ and $\log r(t)$ for these three cohorts, with the solid curves in both panels lying uniformly above the dotted and dashed curves and the dashed curve lying uniformly below the dotted curve. Exponentiating the above shows that the corresponding relationships for $r(t)$ take a multiplicative form, with

$$r_A(t) = r_B(t) \times \exp(c) = r_C(t) \times \exp(2c)$$

This is an example of the widely used *proportional hazard specification*, in which plots of $\log r(t)$ are parallel or in which the ratio of hazard rates is a constant that does not vary with t:

$$\frac{r_A(t)}{r_B(t)} = \exp(c), \quad \frac{r_A(t)}{r_C(t)} = \exp(2c), \quad \text{and} \quad \frac{r_B(t)}{r_C(t)} = \exp(c)$$

The quantities $\exp(c)$ and $\exp(2c)$ can be interpreted as relative risks. For example, in constructing Figure 22-2, I took $c = 0.5$; thus, for this hypothetical example, the age-specific "risk" of first marriage is $\exp(+0.5) = 1.65$ or 65% higher for the cohort A (solid curve), relative to that for cohort B (dotted curve), while the age-specific risk of first marriage for cohort C (dashed curve) is $\exp(-0.5) = 0.61$ or 39% lower relative to cohort B (dotted curve) and $\exp(-1.0) = 0.37$ or 63% lower relative to cohort A (solid curve).

The bottom two panels of Figure 22-2 plot the corresponding survival probabilities and integrated hazard functions. Note in particular the inverse relationship between $r(t)$ and $S(t)$, with higher rates corresponding to lower survival probabilities. Similarly, because the solid curve for $r(t)$ lies uniformly above the dotted curve for $r(t)$, it then follows that the solid curve for $S(t)$ will lie uniformly below the dotted curve for $S(t)$. In the context of age at first marriage, then, cohort A experiences uniformly higher age-specific rates of entry into first marriage than cohorts B or C (upper panels for $r(t)$ and log $r(t)$); likewise, the proportions remaining never-married (lower left-hand panel) are uniformly lower in cohort A than in cohorts B or C. Similarly, by age 40, 5.6, 17.4, and 34.6% of individuals in cohorts A, B, and C, respectively, remain single and never-married. Thus, if cohorts A, B, and C represented successive birth cohorts of women, these results would indicate both a delay in age at first marriage and a greater propensity to forgo entry into first marriage for successive birth cohorts of women.

The four panels of Figure 22-2 illustrate how graphical plots of $r(t)$, log $r(t)$, and $S(t)$ can convey useful information. For example, the two upper panels of Figure 22-2 reveal age-graded differences in first marriage. The quantity $S(t)$ similarly provides information on how the proportion of the population remaining single and never-married, that is surviving in the origin state, varies with age. Similar analyses can be conducted for successive birth cohorts, by race and ethnicity, or for cross-classifications by other characteristics.

Although the proportional hazard model is heavily used, many of the questions posed by life course researchers in fact imply violations of proportionality. For example, there has been considerable debate on whether the behavior of successive cohorts of women is best understood as a "retreat" from marriage (e.g., see Gilder, 1986; Popenoe, 1996) or whether observed behaviors instead reflect delayed but eventual entry from marriage (Oppenheimer, 1997). The important point is that a proportional specification carries strong assumptions concerning this question—if invoked for successive cohorts of women, it implies both delay and retreat. The difficulty is that, while retreat logically implies delay, delay need not logically imply retreat; hence, invoking proportionality in fact is equivalent to staking a strong a priori position on such an issue. Figure 22-3 presents a hypothetical example in which retreat—in the sense of increases in the proportions who never marry—need not follow from delayed marriage. In the two upper panels of Figure 22-3, the curves for $r(t)$ and log $r(t)$ are shifted horizontally, with the peak age at entry into first marriage occurring at ages 18, 20, and 22 for cohorts A, B, and C, respectively. The lower left-hand panel traces the consequences by age in the proportions who remain single and never-married. The differences in these proportions are large between 15 and 30 but narrow substantially at later ages. Under this hypothetical marriage regime, then, there is no change in the proportion of women who never marry across successive cohorts, despite marked delays in entry into marriage. Thus in Figure 22-3, delay does not imply retreat; in Figure 22-3, both delay and retreat occur.

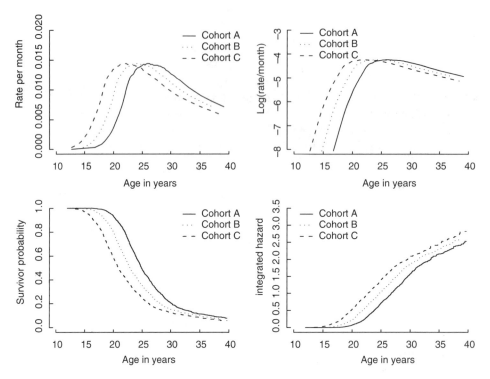

FIGURE 22-3. Hypothetical example of a "pure" delay in the hazard rate of first marriage for three successive birth cohorts. Implications for $S(t)$, $H(t)$, $r(t)$, and $\log r(t)$.

NONPARAMETRIC ANALYSES OF A SINGLE TRANSITION

As Figures 22-2 and 22-3 suggest, much can be learned from exploratory analyses that permit the visual inspection of quantities such as $S(t)$, $H(t)$, $r(t)$, and $\log r(t)$. Such analyses typically make heavy use of *nonparametric estimators* of quantities such as the survival probability (Kaplan & Meier, 1958), integrated hazard (Aalen, 1978; Nelson, 1972), and hazard rate (Cox & Oakes, 1984), where "nonparametric" refers to the lack of strong distributional assumptions concerning the distribution of event times, that is the shape of the hazard rate with respect to t.

As in the previous section, I begin by considering the case of a single transition in a homogeneous population. Let T_i denote the random variable for individual i's time at the event of interest. Not all individuals may experience the event by the time of last interview, in which case these individuals are then said to be *right censored*. As a result, representing data on the outcome requires a pair of variables, (t_i, δ_i), where t_i is the realization of the random variable T_i and $\delta_i = 1$ if the event is observed for individual i and 0 if the outcome for i is right-censored.

The Kaplan–Meier (1958) estimator of the survival probability, which can be shown to be the nonparametric maximum-likelihood estimator for this quantity, is given by

$$S_{\text{KM}}(t) = \prod_{R(s):s \leq t} \left[1 - \frac{d(s)}{\#R(s)} \right] \tag{5}$$

where the product is taken over all individuals at risk of the event at time t, $d(t)$ denotes the number of individuals with events at time t, $R(t)$ is the set of individuals at risk of the event at time t, and $\#R(t)$ denotes the number of individuals at risk at time t. The Nelson–Aalen estimator

(Aalen, 1978; Nelson, 1972), which can be shown to be the nonparametric maximum-likelihood estimator for the integrated hazard, is given by

$$H_{NA}(t) = \sum_{R(s):s \leq t} \frac{d(s)}{\#R(s)} \qquad (6)$$

For technical statistical reasons, no sensible nonparametric maximum-likelihood estimator of the hazard rate exists. Still, one can obtain a nonparametric estimator of the hazard rate that possesses good properties using the classic demographic life table or methods for nonparametric density estimation (e.g., see Allison, 1995; Cox & Oakes, 1984; Wu, 1989).

Figure 22-4 presents nonparametric estimates of the two most intuitive quantities $S(t)$ and $r(t)$ for age at first marriage for White and Black women in the 1980 Current Population

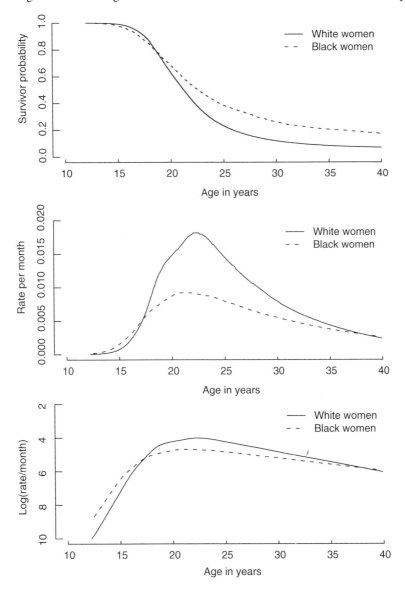

FIGURE 22-4. Non-parametric estimates of $S(t)$, $H(t)$, and $r(t)$, for White and Black women, 1980 Current Population Survey.

Survey (CPS). The upper panel, which presents Kaplan–Meier estimates of $S(t)$, shows that $S_{KM}(t)$ yields a monotonically declining step function, with values varying between 1 and 0. For these cohorts of women, the curves decline steeply between ages 20 and 40; roughly 64% of White women were never married by age 20, with about 7% never married by age 40. By contrast, about 69 and 17% of Black women were never married by ages 20 and 40, respectively. The middle panel of Figure 22-4, which presents smoothed nonparametric estimates of $r(t)$, shows that Black/White differences in the transition to first marriage are indeed most pronounced between ages 20 and 40. The lower panel, which presents smoothed nonparametric estimates of $r(t)$, shows that Black/White differences are not constant with age, but rather widen during early and middle adulthood, and then narrow at later ages. This panel makes clear that proportionality appears to be violated for White and Black patterns in age at first marriage; note also that Black/White first marriage rates do not appear to follow a pattern of "pure" delay such as that exhibited in Figure 22-3.

These examples also illustrate the prototypical steps in how one might conduct exploratory analyses of event history data. In particular, observed characteristics of individuals can be used in conjunction with the nonparametric methods outlined above, for example, by classifying individuals using observed values of a discrete covariate or by discretizing the values of a metric covariate, followed by visual inspection of graphical displays such as those in Figure 22-4, with such analyses providing, roughly speaking, an event history equivalent to exploratory methods using cross-tabulations or comparisons of group means.

PARAMETRIC MODELS FOR A SINGLE TRANSITION

To this point, our discussion has focused on a single transition for a homogeneous population; thus, we have proceeded by and large without consideration of right-hand side covariates. In this section, we consider how one might obtain estimates of the association of observed covariates with the hazard rate $r(t)$. To simplify matters, we continue to focus on a single transition.

The most common parametric specification for covariates is the so-called *proportional hazard* model given by

$$r[t|\mathbf{x}_i(t)] = q(t) \exp[\mathbf{b}\mathbf{x}_i(t)] \tag{7}$$

or

$$\log r[t|\mathbf{x}_i(t)] = \log q(t) + \mathbf{b}\mathbf{x}_i(t) \tag{8}$$

where i indexes individuals and $\mathbf{x}(t)$ denotes a vector of observed covariates, some of which may be time varying. A key assumption in Equations (7) and (8) is that time variation in $\log r(t)$ is captured by a single function, the so-called baseline hazard $\log q(t)$, with all additional heterogeneity across individuals captured by the additive effects of the covariates $\mathbf{x}_i(t)$.

The types of covariates allowed by Equations (7) and (8) span a remarkably wide range; indeed, one can include any aspect of an individual's history up to time t (Aalen, 1978; Tuma & Hannan, 1984). Thus, event history models let life course researchers examine an unusually rich set of covariates in ways that capture changes in the social and economic contexts of individuals that might influence the outcome of interest. One can, for example, investigate the effect of earlier life events, current social circumstances, cumulative experiences, and exposure to particular statuses, which allows researchers to contrast effects of past, current, and cumulative experience on current behavior (Wu & Martinson, 1993; Wu & Thomson, 2001). See also Wu (1996), who compared three alternative effects of income in an individual's family of origin—a simple measure of income at time t, permanent and transitory measures of income, and measures of income level and income change. One can also incorporate future predictions (e.g., projected income, marriage market opportunities, or characteristics of potential mates; e.g., see Dechter, 1992) when the predicted values of such covariates are obtained from models using current and past covariate information for a given individual. As Mayer and Tuma (1990) noted, this flexibility meshes well with a central presupposition of many life course researchers, which is that an individual's social context can vary considerably over time in ways rarely reflective of some stable social equilibrium. If so, then a central analytical task is to capture central features of this variation over time for individuals.

Several measurement issues arise when incorporating time-varying covariates into Equations (7) and (8). For example, if a time-varying covariate $x_i(t)$ is discrete and gathered as an event history, the analyst can determine the value of $x_i(t)$ at all observed times t during which person i is at risk. In other circumstances, the value of $x_i(t)$ may be difficult to determine at all possible times. Examples include covariates such as income, work hours, expenditures, depression scales, or attitudes that can vary from one moment to another but which will often be measured only sporadically. In such cases, a commonly invoked and analytically convenient assumption is that the value of such a covariate is constant between measurements.*

The popularity of proportional hazard models stems in part from practical and theoretical considerations. The asymptotic properties of these models are well understood under a variety of conditions (e.g., Cox & Oakes, 1984; Fleming & Harrington, 1991), including quite general conditions on the distribution of censoring times. Furthermore, under proportionality, covariates have linear effects on the logarithm of $r(t)$; hence, intuitions from ordinary and logistic regression carry over in a straightforward way to the proportional hazard model. Empirically, proportionality is often adequate in that estimated coefficients under proportionality are often similar to those when proportionality is relaxed; this can often hold when the observation period is short relative to the mechanisms that generate variation over time in the effect of a covariate.

Proportionality is nevertheless a strong assumption and violations can occur empirically. As noted above, Figure 22-4 provides an empirical example where proportionality appears suspect; indeed, visual displays like those in the lower panel of Figure 22-4 provide a useful exploratory way to check proportionality. Fortunately, the models in Equations (7) and (8) can be generalized to incorporate non-proportional effects of covariates; indeed, by appropriate definition of time-varying covariates, one can adopt standard software to estimate certain non-proportional models. Recall that when proportionality is violated, the effect of a covariate on the logarithm of the hazard rate will not be an additive constant, but rather will vary with t. Thus, one way to relax the proportionality assumption is to code a set of time-varying dummy variables that represent an exhaustive and mutually exclusive partition of the observation period. Interacting these dummy variables with a covariate x hypothesized to have a non-proportional effect then yields a specification that models the effect of x as a step function of time. Other approaches suggested in the literature include a log multiplicative specification (Xie, 1994), piecewise linear splines (Wu & Martinson, 1993), and a local likelihood approach that makes few assumptions about the form of time variation in covariate effects (Wu & Tuma, 1990).

---

*For alternative specifications relaxing this constancy assumption, see, for example, Tuma and Hannan (1984). Note also that the plausibility of such an assumption will depend not only on the number and frequency of measurements, but also on the temporal variation in the covariate relative to the frequency of measurements.

In practice, assumptions concerning the baseline hazard $q(t)$ are typically of greater concern than possible non-proportionalities in the effects of covariates; very roughly speaking, this often occurs when the baseline hazard accounts for a greater proportion of the observed variation in $r(t)$ than do the covariates $\mathbf{x}(t)$, as is often true in practice. A popular choice is a model due to Cox (1972), in which the baseline hazard $q(t)$ is allowed to be an unknown and unspecified function of time. Under this model, maximum likelihood estimation is not possible, but the method of partial likelihood (Cox, 1975) can be shown to yield consistent and asymptotically efficient estimates of the parameters $\mathbf{b}$ under quite general conditions, including mild assumptions concerning the distribution of censoring (Andersen & Gill, 1982).

While the Cox model yields estimates of the parameters $\mathbf{b}$ for the effects of covariates, it does not provide any direct estimate of the baseline hazard function $q(t)$. Knowledge of $q(t)$ is often unnecessary for a number of important analytical purposes, for example comparisons of control and treatment groups in medical trials evaluating the efficacy of a new drug or treatment in which the outcome is mortality from a specific form of cancer. However, many of the questions routinely posed by life course researchers require knowledge of $q(t)$; examples include comparisons across appropriately defined cohorts of individuals in the specific pace of childbearing, the timing of entry into marriage, or median time to divorce. Although estimates of $q(t)$ can be recovered in the Cox model, obtaining inferences about $q(t)$ under the Cox model is more difficult. As a result, it can be useful to consider parametric alternatives to the Cox model.

Various parameterizations for $q(t)$ have been proposed, including the exponential, Weibull, Gompertz, Makeham, log logistic, log Gaussian, Hernes, sickle, and Coale–McNeil models (Blossfeld et al., 1989; Tuma & Hannan, 1984; Wu, 1990). Sometimes theory provides grounds to motivate a particular choice, but more often practical considerations (e.g., software availability) underlie these choices. Unfortunately, estimated effects of covariates can sometimes vary considerably across different functional forms, complicating matters for the analyst.

One reason for this sensitivity is that the models vary markedly in their specification of time variation in the baseline hazard. For example, some models assume that the baseline hazard increases or decreases monotonically (e.g., the Weibull, Gompertz, and Makeham models), while other models assume a unimodal shape for the baseline hazard, with the rate rising and then declining (e.g., the log logistic, log Gaussian, Coale–McNeil, Hernes, and sickle models). In addition, some models yield a distribution of event times that integrates to unity, implying that all individuals will experience the event of interest if observed for a sufficiently long period of time (e.g., the exponential, Weibull, Makeham, log logistic, and log Gaussian models), while other models can, in some cases, yield a so-called defective distribution in which some individuals will never experience the event of interest, even if observed for an arbitrarily long time. Note that a defective distribution of event times is often substantively plausible; examples include marriage or sexual initiation in which some individuals, for example, those who have taken vows of celibacy or chastity, may never marry; parity-specific fertility, in which some individuals may never proceed to, say, a fifth birth; and residential moves, where some individuals may live all their lives in the residence in which they were born. Similarly, there are other instances in which a non-defective distribution of event times is desirable, with a classic example being human mortality.

As a result, many researchers use models that mimic the Cox model in the sense of providing a flexible functional form for the baseline hazard. One popular and easily implemented parametric alternative to the Cox model specifies the baseline hazard as a piecewise constant function, that is as a step function of t. More formally, consider P time intervals, $(0, \tau_1]$,

$(\tau_1, \tau_2], \ldots, (\tau_{P-2}, \tau_{P-1}], (\tau_{P-1}, \infty]$, where the τ_P are prespecified by the analyst; then let $q(t)$ be defined by a series of constants on these intervals, that is

$$q(t) = \begin{cases} \exp(\lambda_1), & t \in (0, \tau_1], \\ \exp(\lambda_2), & t \in (\tau_1, \tau_2], \\ \ldots \\ \exp(\lambda_P), & t \in (\tau_{P-1}, \infty] \end{cases} \tag{9}$$

Equivalently,

$$\log q(t) = \begin{cases} \lambda_1, & t \in (0, \tau_1], \\ \lambda_2, & t \in (\tau_1, \tau_2], \\ \ldots \\ \lambda_P, & t \in (\tau_{P-1}, \infty] \end{cases} \tag{10}$$

The resulting piecewise exponential model for the baseline hazard is easily implemented, for example, by defining P time-varying dummy variables corresponding to the P time intervals.*

A slight variant of the above lets log $r(t)$ vary linearly within intervals, with the linear segments splined to yield a continuous function:

$$\log q(t) = \begin{cases} \lambda_1 + \gamma_1 t, & t \in (0, \tau_1], \\ \lambda_2 + \gamma_2 t, & t \in (\tau_1, \tau_2], \\ \ldots \\ \lambda_P + \gamma_P t, & t \in (\tau_{P-1}, \infty] \end{cases} \tag{11}$$

subject to the $P - 1$ equality constraints

$$\lambda_1 + \gamma_1 \tau_1 = \lambda_2 + \gamma_2 \tau_1$$
$$\lambda_2 + \gamma_2 \tau_2 = \lambda_3 + \gamma_3 \tau_2 \tag{12}$$
$$\ldots$$
$$\lambda_{P-1} + \gamma_{P-1} \tau_{P-1} = \lambda_P + \gamma_P \tau_{P-1}$$

yielding the so-called splined piecewise Gompertz model for the baseline hazard.

Both the piecewise constant function in Equation (11) and the piecewise linear spline in Equation (12) provide very flexible specifications for log $q(t)$. Note, for example, that both can accommodate a variety of shapes for the baseline hazard, including monotonically increasing, monotonically decreasing, unimodal, or multimodal patterns of time variation. Note that, given P prespecified time intervals, the piecewise constant specification in Equation (11) uses P degrees of freedom, while the piecewise linear spline in Equation (12) uses $P + 1$ degrees of freedom.[†]

Table 22-1 presents estimates from three proportional hazard models for age at entry into first marriage using data on White women from the 1980 CPS. We contrast estimates from a

---

*Note that Equations (7) and (8) lack a time-invariant constant term—what would be the intercept in a linear regression. One can retain such a constant term by omitting one of the P intervals from estimation, in which case the estimates λ_p and $\exp(\lambda_p)$ provide contrasts with respect to the overall constant term.

[†]The piecewise linear spline uses $2P$ parameters but then invokes $P - 1$ equality constraints, thus requiring $2P - (P - 1) = P + 1$ free parameters.

Cox model, a piecewise constant, and piecewise linear spline model; for the latter two models, we have specified three time intervals, corresponding to ages 12 and 18, 18 and 25, and 25 and older. Note that these data provide large samples but relatively few covariates; hence, Table 22-1 reports estimates only for respondent's years of schooling completed by time of interview (discretized into 0–11, 13–15, and 16 or higher, with 12 years the omitted category) and year of birth (1930–1949 and 1950 or later, with 1929 or earlier the omitted category). Estimates agree closely across the three models, with estimates from the Cox and three-period linear spline model agreeing particularly closely. For the Cox and three-period linear spline models, White women with 11 or fewer years of schooling completed have a 28% ($\exp(0.25) = 1.28$) higher rate of first marriage than White women with 12 years of schooling, while White women with some college education have a 30% ($\exp(-0.35) = 0.70$) lower rate of first marriage than White women with 12 years of schooling.

Results from these models also show that the piecewise linear spline specification for $q(t)$ provides a substantially better fit to the data than the piecewise constant specification. Table 22-2 compares log likelihood values corresponding to four models for these data using a piecewise constant baseline with and without covariates and a piecewise linear spline baseline with and without covariates. The lower panel of Table 22-2 provides two sets of χ^2 comparisons that provide tests of adding the five covariates in Table 22-1 and for modeling log $r(t)$ using three constants versus three linear splines. Adding covariates yields a χ^2 increment in fit of around 4,300, while allowing log $r(t)$ to vary linearly yields a χ^2 increment in fit around 13,500. This is a typical result when analyzing life course data, with careful modeling of the baseline hazard often yielding much more substantial improvements in fit than the introduction of covariates. Intuitively, such large increments in fit are often observed because typical life course outcomes exhibit substantial within-individual time variation, with this time variation often greater than the variation observed across individuals. As a consequence, it is generally advisable to devote careful modeling attention to the form of time variation in $q(t)$ to ensure that conclusions about other parameters are not biased by incorrect or inappropriate assumptions about time dependence in $q(t)$.

TABLE 22-1. Comparison of Covariate Effects for Cox, Three-period Exponential, and Three-period Splined Gompertz Models: Age at First Marriage, White Women, 1980 Current Population Survey

	Cox	Three-period exponential	Three-period Gompertz
Years of schooling completed			
0–11	0.25***	0.18***	0.25***
	(0.01)	(0.01)	(0.01)
13–15	−0.35***	−0.35***	−0.35***
	(0.02)	(0.02)	(0.02)
16+	−0.71***	−0.68***	−0.70***
	(0.02)	(0.02)	(0.02)
Year of birth			
1930–1949	0.48***	0.54***	0.48***
	(0.01)	(0.01)	(0.01)
1950+	0.16***	0.16***	0.17***
	(0.01)	(0.01)	(0.01)

Note: Standard errors in parentheses. See text for additional details.
*p < 0.01, **p < 0.001, ***p < 0.0001 (two-tailed test).

TABLE 22-2. **Selected Comparisons of Model Fit for the Three-period Exponential and Three-period Splined Gompertz Models: Age at First Marriage, White Women, 1980 Current Population Survey**

Model	Model for baseline hazard	Covariates?	log £
Panel A: Model description and statistics			
1	Three-period constant	No	$-214,452.8$
2	Three-period constant	Yes	$-212,293.0$
3	Three-period linear spline	No	$-207,678.2$
4	Three-period linear spline	Yes	$-205,490.1$

Comparison	Test for	df	χ^2
Panel B: Model comparisons			
1 versus 2	Adding covariates	5	4,319.6
3 versus 4	Adding covariates	5	4,376.2
1 versus 3	Three-period constant versus linear spline	1	13,549.2
2 versus 4	Three-period constant versus linear spline	1	13,605.8

The proportional models in Equations (7)–(12) can be easily extended to accommodate multiple dimensions of time. Consider, for example, the transition between a first and second child as depicted in panel B of Figure 22-1. Empirically, the second birth rate varies less with the age of a woman than with the duration since first birth, yet age variation in the second birth typically cannot be ignored. Because of examples like this, analysts often have sound reasons to extend Equations (7)–(12) to multiple dimensions of time. Let t denote age and u the duration since a first birth; then a straightforward extension of the proportional hazard model in Equation (7) is

$$r[t, u|\mathbf{x}_i(t)] = q_1(t)q_2(u) \exp[\mathbf{b}\mathbf{x}_i(t)] \tag{13}$$

or, equivalently,

$$\log r[t, u|\mathbf{x}_i(t)] = \log q_1(t) + \log q_2(u) + \mathbf{b}\mathbf{x}_i(t) \tag{14}$$

Note that Equations (13) and (14) yield an age- and duration-specific model of second births under the assumption that the second birth rate is separable into two components, $q_1(t)$ and $q_2(u)$ (Lillard, 1993; Wu & Martinson, 1993). As for a single time dimension, one can use numerous parameterizations for $q_1(t)$ and $q_2(u)$, including those in Equations (10) or (11).

It has long been recognized that linear regression models can be unidentified when controlling for multiple dimensions of time, with the classic example being simultaneous linear terms for age, period, and cohort (Glenn, this volume). Although t and u will co-vary in strong ways for each individual in the sample, identification in Equations (13) and (14) is often possible because $q_1(t)$ and $q_2(u)$ are typically highly non-linear functions of t and u, with these non-linearities helping to identify model parameters. For example, Wu and Martinson (1993) presented models that control duration, age, period, and cohort; however, identification will in general become increasingly problematic as the number of time dimensions or parameters used to model the baseline functions increases. Given these issues, one sensible procedure is to identify, theoretically or empirically, those time dimensions which induce the greatest variation in the underlying hazard rate. One can then invest greater modeling effort for the "primary" time dimensions, for example using the specification in Equation (11) and less effort for "secondary" time dimensions, for example by using the specifications in Equations (10) or (11) coupled with relatively widely-spaced intervals.

A wide class of diagnostics for the above models can be obtained using so-called martingale residuals (e.g., see Fleming & Harrington, 1991, Chapter 4). Graphical displays of such residuals can be used to assess the influence of particular observations and to check assumptions concerning proportionality and the functional form of covariate effects (i.e., are effects linear in x or in log x) in ways analogous to diagnostic residual displays in linear regression.

MULTIPLE ORIGIN AND DESTINATION STATES

Thus far, we have formalized issues for a single transition, but the models discussed above generalize in straightforward ways to more complicated processes such as those depicted in panel B of Figure 22-1. To simplify details, let us return to a single homogeneous population but generalize the above to multiple origin and destination states. Let j and k index the origin and destination states, respectively; then let the transition rate $r_{jk}(t)$ be defined as

$$r_{jk}(t) = \lim_{\Delta t \downarrow 0} \frac{\Pr(T_{jk} \leq t + \Delta t \mid T_{jk} \geq t)}{\Delta t} = \frac{f_{jk}(t)}{1 - F_{jk}(t)} = \frac{f_{jk}(t)}{S_{jk}(t)} \qquad (15)$$

Thus, Equation (15) generalizes Equation (1) by representing each transition $j \rightarrow k$ by a unique transition rate $r_{jk}(t)$.

The generalization of the survivor probability to multiple origins and destinations involves some subtle but important shifts. Returning momentarily to the case of a single event, recall that the survivor probability has two equivalent interpretations: (1) as the probability of not yet having experienced the event of interest and (2) as the probability of remaining in the origin state. When multiple destination states exist, (1) and (2) will, in general, differ; in addition, the interpretation of (1) is complicated by an identifiability issue when so-called competing risks are present.

To make issues concrete, consider panel A of Figure 22-1, in which there is only one transition out of each origin status. In this case, matters reduce to the case for a single transition, conditional on status at origin. By contrast, in panel B of Figure 22-1, each origin state has multiple destination states, for example from the origin state 01, there are two possible transitions, $01 \rightarrow 11$ and $01 \rightarrow 20$, while from the origin state 21, there are three possible transitions, $21 \rightarrow 11$, $21 \rightarrow 20$, and $21 \rightarrow 22$. When individuals in an origin state are subject to multiple destination states, they are said to be subject to competing risks. When competing risks are present, it can be shown that the interpretation given in (1) is unaffected but that in (2) must be modified in ways detailed below.

To formalize these ideas, suppose that individuals observed in origin state j are subject to multiple destination states, indexed by $k = 1, \ldots, K_j$, where $K_j > 1$. Let $r_{jk}(t)$ denote the K_j transition rates corresponding to each of these transitions; then the probability of surviving to time t in state j, is given by

$$S_j(t) = \exp\left[-\int_0^t \sum_{k=1}^{K_j} r_{jk}(s)ds \right] = \exp\left[-\sum_{k=1}^{K_j} \int_0^t r_{jk}(s)ds \right] = \prod_{k=1}^{K_j} \exp\left[-\int_0^t r_{jk}(s)ds \right] \qquad (16)$$

Thus, the second interpretation of $S_j(t)$—the probability of surviving in origin state j—is identical to that for a single transition, except that $S_j(t)$ conditions on origin state j—that is, it refers to the survival to time t of those individuals who have not exited the origin state j by time t.

Now consider the probability in (1)—that of not having experienced the event of interest. When competing risks are present, there is not a single event but rather multiple events that must be considered when accounting for exits from an origin state j. Consider a classic example in which age-specific mortality in humans is classified by cause of death—for example, deaths due to (1) cardiovascular disease, (2) cancer, (3) homicides and other acts of violence, (4) accidents, and (5) a residual category for all other causes of death. Distinguishing between multiple types of events gives rise to additional complications; in particular, the interpretation of $S_{jk}(t)$ and $r_{jk}(t)$ will in general differ from more familiar quantities such as the proportion in the population observed to experience the event k conditional on origin state j.

To see this, consider two birth cohorts followed until death and suppose that cohort members are identical in all respects except that deaths due to cardiovascular disease have been eliminated in cohort A but not in cohort B. It then follows that, in cohort A, if one cause of death is eliminated, the proportion in A experiencing other causes of death will necessarily increase. Let p_k^A and p_k^B denote the proportion of deaths of type k that occur in cohorts A and B; then if cohorts A and B are identical save for $p_{A1} = 0$, it will nevertheless follow that $p_k^A \geq p_k^B$ for all remaining causes of death. The researcher only possessing estimates of p_k^A and p_k^B will observe that $p_{Ak} \geq p_{Bk}$ for $k \neq 1$ and, hence, might be tempted to conclude that mortality in A and B differ fundamentally, with mortality from causes other than cardiovascular disease systematically higher in cohort A than in B. Yet by construction, the two cohorts have identical mortality risks save for the elimination of deaths from cardiovascular disease in cohort A. This apparent paradox would be avoided were comparisons based on the quantities $r_k(t)$ or $S_k(t)$. Thus, sufficiently large samples would reveal that $r_1^A(t) = 0$ while $r_1^B(t) > 0$—mortality from cardiovascular disease is eliminated in cohort A but not B—but that mortality from other causes is otherwise identical, that is, that $r_k^A(t) = r_k^B(t)$ for $k \neq 1$.

Turning this example on its head makes it clear that, under competing risks, the $S_{jk}(t)$ cannot be interpreted as if they provided the proportions of those in origin state j who experience the event k, a statement that holds even when censoring is absent. Rather, the $S_{jk}(t)$ should be interpreted as giving the proportion in an origin state who would have experienced the kth transition were all other competing transitions to be eliminated. Note, moreover, that the plausibility of this interpretation rests heavily on this independence assumption.* Violations of this assumption would include situations in which, say, those who are observed to die of one chronic condition—for example, cardiovascular disease—differ systematically in other ways that lead them to have higher (or lower) risk of another chronic condition. A difficulty is that the independence assumption under competing risks has been shown to be non-identifiable in the sense that one cannot obtain formal tests of this assumption (Tsiatis, 1975).[†]

---

*When covariates are included in the model, this assumption becomes one of conditional independence, that is, the competing risks are assumed to be independent conditional on the covariates $\mathbf{x}(t)$. This assumption is similar to the so-called "irrelevance of alternatives" in a multinomial logistic regression. It is possible to state conditions that are slightly weaker than full independence for the competing risk model; however, such conditions carry little practical import (see Cox & Oakes, 1984, for details).

[†]Consider the promotion of assistant professors in an academic department. If some junior faculty depart in anticipation of non-promotion, then simply distinguishing between two sorts of events (promotion vs. departure) will not correct the upward bias in estimates of tenure rates. Allison (1995) suggest a simple procedure to assess the sensitivity of estimates to such a possibility. Consider two situations, one in which all departing junior faculty would have in fact been fired at a time ϵ after they are observed to have departed and another in which all departing junior faculty would have been promoted had they remained. Estimates under these two behavioral extremes can be used to construct Manski-type bounds for the usual naive estimate (Manski 1995).

PARAMETRIC MODELS FOR MULTIPLE TRANSITIONS

Construction of parametric models for the $r_{jk}(t)$ in Equation (15) is straightforward, with the underlying issues similar to those for modeling a single transition. For example, a proportional hazard specification incorporating covariates will be given by

$$r_{jk}[t|\mathbf{x}_{jk}(t)] = q_{jk}(t) \exp[\mathbf{b}_{jk}\mathbf{x}_{jk}(t)] \tag{17}$$

where $q_{jk}(t)$ denotes the baseline for the transition from state j to k and $\mathbf{x}_{jk}(t)$ denotes a vector of (possibly time-varying) covariates. The jk subscript on $\mathbf{x}$ emphasizes that one can specify different covariates across transitions and that the effects themselves will differ across transitions. In practice, however, researchers often employ the same set of covariates across the multiple transitions to aid the substantive interpretation of the coefficients $\mathbf{b}_{jk}$.

One can estimate Equation (17) using a suitable generalization of the Cox model to multiple origin and destination states. Under this specification, the $q_{jk}(t)$ are assumed to be arbitrary unspecified functions of t that vary in arbitrary but unspecified ways across transitions. If the Cox model is not used, then Equation (17) will require parameterizing the $q_{jk}(t)$. Guidance for these parameterizations can be obtained from suitable generalizations to the nonparametric methods discussed above. The resulting patterns can then be used to select a particular parameterization of the $q_{jk}(t)$, with the underlying issues essentially identical to those for a single transition. Multiple dimensions of time can also be handled in ways similar to those discussed for a single transition.

Estimation of Equation (17) will, in general, yield a very large number of parameter estimates—there will, in general, be coefficients for each covariate and transition pair. For substantive and interpretive parsimony, one may wish to determine if the effect of a covariate is similar across selected transitions—for example, for the transitions depicted in panel B of Figure 22-1, if income effects are similar for third and higher-order marital births. Such hypotheses can be evaluated using log likelihood ratio or BIC (Bayesian Information Criterion) tests (Raftery, 1995; Schwarz, 1978) under equality constraints on the appropriate parameters across transitions. Suitable extensions of this same idea can be used to determine if one can "pool" across transitions, for example, if, in Figure 22-1, model fit is not substantially degraded under the more parsimonious model in panel A relative to the more complex model in panel B.

UNOBSERVED HETEROGENEITY

As noted at the outset of this chapter, life course theorists often assert that one must approach the life course holistically—that domains such as work, marriage, childbearing, and emotional development, typically analyzed in isolation, cannot be understood adequately without considering these domains as one unified whole. The models considered to this point help sharpen this idea. Take, for example, panel B of Figure 22-1, which depicts transitions in two domains—marriage and childbearing. One can show that the application of the nonparametric estimator in Equation (5) to these transitions will reproduce the distribution of individuals, both across the multiple statuses and over time. Extensions of these methods to incorporate covariates—the Cox model or the models in Equations (9)–(12)—will likewise also reproduce the across-state and across-time distribution of individuals when proportionality holds. This implies, then, that the importance of this assertion lies not at the level of aggregate distributions, but rather at the level at which individual behaviors are modeled.

One approach formalizing this idea lets events in one life course domain affect transition rates in another domain. The models considered thus far accomodate this type of dependence by letting the researcher condition on any aspect of an individual's past history—including the individual's trajectory or past history in another life domain—when modeling $r_{ijk}(t)$. Thus, measures constructed from a person's trajectory of work and labor force experience up to time t can be used as right-hand side covariates in modeling risks at time t of transitions in the realms of fertility, marriage, divorce, retirement, and so forth. Another possibility, often raised by economists, is that an individual's decisions about work, fertility, and marriage reflect an attempt to maximize utility across these joint spheres. If all relevant decision inputs are observed, then one can condition on suitable measures of these inputs, in which case no new issues arise. However, when some relevant inputs are unobserved, a number of subtle issues arise in ways that are substantially more troublesome in a hazard regression context than in a static linear regression.*

Recall that a standard result for linear regression is that, if an unobservable z is uncorrelated with a covariate x of interest, then the OLS (ordinary least squares) estimate of the effect of x will be unbiased although not optimally efficient. No analogous result holds in the hazard regression context; in particular, even if an unobservable z is initially uncorrelated with a covariate x, in general, as time passes, x and z will not remain uncorrelated. This gives rise to a number of difficulties and subtleties. One difficulty, first noted by Sheps and Menken (1973), is that unobserved heterogeneity can play havoc with attempts to make inferences about time or age dependence. A classic example is to consider a population which, when observed initially, is comprised of equal numbers of individuals from two groups, A and B. Suppose that in both groups, mortality is governed by a constant (exponential) hazard rate, with $r_A > r_B$ and suppose further that the analyst is ignorant of the existence of the two subgroups. Sheps and Menken (1973) observed that, in this situation, the analyst will observe a monotonically declining rate with age, despite the fact that, by assumption, mortality does not vary with age in either group. This is an example of unobserved "frailty": because members in A are frailer than those in B, they will die more quickly. As a consequence, the composition of the sample population will shift over time, moving from equal numbers of individuals from A and B to a population more heavily weighted towards those from B. Thus, what the analyst observes (technically, a distribution consisting of a mixture of the underlying r_A and r_B) will be mortality that is initially close to r_A but which will over time decline to r_B, as the sample composition of the population is increasingly selected against individuals from group A. See, for example, Trussell and Richards (1985) and Vaupel and Yashin (1985), with the latter providing informative examples showing how unobserved heterogeneity may affect conclusions about time variation in $r(t)$.

A second issue concerns potential biases in estimated covariate effects, an issue emphasized in a series of influential papers by Heckman and Singer (1982, 1984, 1985). In reanalyses of unemployment data of Kiefer and Neumann (1981) employing a Weibull specification for duration dependence, they found that covariate estimates fluctuated markedly depending on whether the unobservable z was assumed to be normal, log normal, or gamma distributed.[†] Their results, coupled with a series of Monte Carlo studies, led them to advocate an alternative approach to modeling unobserved heterogeneity using a discrete mixing distribution with

---

*A fixed-effects strategy, often used to analyze panel data on metric outcomes (e.g., see Halaby, this volume), was shown by Chamberlain (1985) to yield inconsistent estimates in an event history context; hence, researchers have concentrated attention on random effects models.

[†]Heckman and Singer (1982) motivated their use of a Weibull distribution on search theoretical grounds. In subsequent work (Heckman & Singer, 1985), they proposed an alternative Box–Cox-type parameterization for time dependence that has as special cases the exponential, Weibull, and Gompertz models.

finite points of support. One difficulty with this approach is that, while it proceeds nonpara-metrically with respect to the distribution of the unobservables, it nevertheless requires strong parametric assumptions concerning the distribution of event times (Trussell & Richards, 1985). Yet another possibility would be to proceed with reasonably flexible specifications for both the distribution of the unobservables (e.g., using a discrete mixing distribution) and of the event times (e.g., using the piecewise constant or spline specifications in Equations (10) or (11)). For theoretical results concerning such an approach, see Elbers and Ridder (1982) and Heckman and Singer (1984).

Another approach to handling unobserved heterogeneity is due to Lillard and colleagues (e.g., see Lillard, 1993; Lillard, Brien, & Waite, 1995; Lillard & Waite, 1993; Upchurch, Lillard, & Panis, 2001). It has long been recognized that when multiple transitions are observed for a sample of individuals, this added information might permit identification of additional distributional aspects of the unobservables. Lillard and colleagues built upon this insight to estimate models akin to simultaneous equation models for metric outcomes in which unobservables may be correlated across transitions. Consider extending the proportional specification in Equation (17) for multiple origin and destination states by adding an error term e_{jk}, where e_{jk} is assumed to capture unobserved heterogeneity specific to the transition from origin state j to destination state k:

$$\log r_{jk}[t|\mathbf{x}_{jk}(t)] = \log q_{jk}(t) + \mathbf{b}_{jk}\mathbf{x}_{jk}(t) + e_{jk} \tag{18}$$

Let $m = 1, \ldots, M$ index the full set of transitions $j \rightarrow k$ and let the e_{jk} be assumed normally distributed with mean 0 and covariance matrix

$$\text{cov}(e_m, e_p) = \begin{pmatrix} \sigma_1^2 & \sigma_{12} & \cdots & \sigma_{1M} \\ \sigma_{21} & \sigma_2^2 & \cdots & \sigma_{2M} \\ \vdots & \vdots & \vdots & \vdots \\ \sigma_{M1} & \sigma_{M2} & \cdots & \sigma_M^2 \end{pmatrix} \tag{19}$$

with the unobservables for two transitions, m and m', correlated according to

$$\rho_{mm'} = \frac{\sigma_{mm'}}{\sigma_m \sigma_{m'}} \tag{20}$$

Thus, the models in Equations (18)–(20) link different life course domains using observed *and* unobserved attributes of individuals and by allowing the effects of such unobservables to be correlated across life domains. Lillard, Brien, and Waite (1995) used such a modeling strategy to address whether the observed higher rate of divorce among those who have cohabited prior to marriage is an artifact of unobservables that differentially select couples into cohabitation. Thus, an unusual strength of these models is that they let researchers address endogenous selection. Nevertheless, it can be difficult to achieve identification of the many parameters in the variance–covariance matrix in Equation (19), with identification achieved in most empirical work to date by imposing exclusion restrictions or by exploiting data on repeated events. Alternatively, one might achieve identification structurally via instrumental variables (e.g., see Duncan, 1975), although finding adequate instruments can be difficult in practice.

It is nevertheless important to emphasize that all models for unobserved heterogeneity proposed to date assume that what is unobserved does not vary with time and can be proxied by a one-dimensional correction term. Often, these assumptions are plausible; this is especially true for economic models of behavior, where it is commonly assumed that behavior is determined by a parsimonious set of influences, including those not observed by the researcher. Moreover, in many economic models of behavior, individuals are assumed to act rationally, optimizing over the life span; under these assumptions, characteristics such as permanent income and long-term horizons play an important role. By contrast, a recurrent theme among many life course researchers, particularly those drawn from sociology and demography, concerns the relatively fluid nature of the social circumstances of individuals. If so, then extant models for unobserved heterogeneity address only one aspect of is unobserved—those unobserved characteristics of individuals that are fixed and unchanging—but not other aspects of what may be unobserved—unobserved characteristics of individuals that may be more fluid in nature.

COUPLED PROCESSES

To this point, the models I have considered focus on a single individual's life course transitions, but as noted earlier, life course theorists have often posited linkages across the life courses of multiple individuals, for example, that the events, behaviors, and outcomes for one member of a married couple might have profound effects on the events, behaviors, and outcomes for the person's spouse or partner. If such events, behaviors, or outcomes for both members of the couple are observed, if such covariates for a spouse or partner are exogenous to the outcome of the other, and if, conditional on these covariates, the processes for members of the couple can be assumed independent, then the problem reduces to the usual one of modeling effects of covariates on a transition of interest, with the set of covariates now expanded to include observed characteristics of a spouse or partner.

What is usually deemed implausible is the assumption of conditional independence; said another way, we often suspect that the set of observed covariates do not exhaust the set of what we would wish to observe theoretically and, in particular, that certain key characteristics for a couple are unobserved. A classic example concerns the problem of modeling the mortality of married couples, where the assumption of conditional independence is suspect if researchers do not observe aspects of diet or health-related behaviors that might affect both members of the couple, cumulative but unobserved health insults that are reflective of a couple's physical or social environment, or mate selection on unobserved characteristics that would tend to make couples more similar on health outcomes than two randomly chosen individuals in the population.

The specifications in Equations (18)–(20) can, in principle, be adapted to cover some, but not all, of these cases. Suppose, for example, that some unobserved characteristic of couples generates a positive correlation between their mortality experience relative to two individuals drawn at random from the same population. Concretely, let T_1 and T_2 denote the mortality of husbands and wives, respectively; then a model analogous to Equations (18)–(20) for the mortality for couple i can be written as

$$\log r_{i1}[t|\mathbf{x}_{i1}(t)] = \log q_1(t) + \mathbf{b}_1 \mathbf{x}_{i1}(t) + e_{i1}$$
$$\log r_{i2}[t|\mathbf{x}_{i2}(t)] = \log q_2(t) + \mathbf{b}_2 \mathbf{x}_{i2}(t) + e_{i2}$$

$$(21)$$

with $\mathbf{x}_{i1}(t)$, $\mathbf{x}_{i2}(t)$, e_{i1}, and e_{i2} denoting observed covariates and unobserved components for the husband and wife in couple i and where

$$\rho = \frac{\sigma_{12}}{\sigma_1^2 \sigma_2^2}$$

gives the correlation between members of a couple in age-specific mortality risks. As before, this model incorporates strong behavioral assumptions, in particular that the unobservables e_{i1} and e_{i2} do not vary over time; note, in particular, that such an assumption would not cover the case in which mortality is affected by cumulative health insults as shared by a couple. In addition, identification of the model parameters in Equation (21) can be difficult when the data available to the researcher do not contain instruments that would, for example, plausibly affect the mortality of husbands, but not wives. An alternative approach is to model the *joint* distribution, $f(t_1, t_2)$, for the two event times, which yields so-called bivariate survivor models. In practice, this approach also has proven difficult to implement, in part because researchers often have little guidance for specifying the parametric form of the resulting two-dimensional baseline hazard function $q(t_1, t_2)$. Mare and Palloni (1988), Mare (1994), and Poetter (2000) provide empirical examples and comprehensive discussions of these and other issues.*

CONCLUSION

Good methods often help sharpen theory—the translation of theoretical ideas stated verbally into testable propositions linked to data very often provides greater theoretical insight, for example, by revealing conceptual ambiguities or gaps in a theoretical formulation. In this chapter, I have reviewed some examples that typify how the interplay between life course theory and event history methods might yield such analytical insights. Examples include consideration of the populations deemed to be at "risk" of particular life course transitions; careful specification of the states and transitions between states characterizing a problem, not excluding those transitions of theoretical importance even if they may be difficult to observe empirically; how one might operationalize notions of age grading in the timing of various adult transitions, including extensions to other temporal dimensions—not just age—that might plausibly govern such transitions; how one might distinguish, conceptually and theoretically, notions such as marital "retreat" versus "delay" for successive birth cohorts; and what might be meant by an assertion about linkages across domains in the life course for a given individual and similarly what might be meant by an assertion that couple processes are linked.

   Another theme running throughout this chapter concerns the implicit trade-offs between nonparametric, semi-parametric, and parametric methods. In my own work, I have found it useful to begin with exploratory analyses via nonparametric techniques. Because nonparametric methods make few parametric assumptions, they can often provide important indications for how one might formulate more parametric models, especially when choosing among different models for the baseline hazard. I have also found it useful to use, where possible, flexible parametric models, for example, those utilizing piecewise linear splines in the place of a simple linear (or other parametric) specification. Such techniques can be used to model nonlinear effects of covariates or non-proportional effects of covariates; piecewise linear splines also yield quite flexible models for the baseline hazard. Note also that such models can be used to obtain tests of standard assumptions, for example, assumptions concerning linearity or proportionality in the effect of a covariate.

   The ability to relax such assumptions has led to increased interest in nonparametric and semi-parametric methods in the statistical and econometric literatures (e.g., see Härdle, 1990; Hastie & Tibshirani, 1990, 1993). Thus, when sufficiently large sample sizes are available to the researcher, it is often possible to devise methods that rely more heavily on information

---

*For a brief discussion of software to estimate these and other models, see the Appendix.

contained within the available data, for example, using this information to guide the choice of an appropriate functional form (e.g., as opposed to linearity or proportionality). Conversely, important insights follow from those models in which it is not possible to relax maintained assumptions even when arbitrarily large samples are available. In such circumstances, parameter estimates are obtained both from the observed data *and* from assumptions that cannot, even in principle, be tested (Manski, 1995). It is worth noting that, to date, while the classic work of Heckman and Singer (1982, 1985) on models for unobserved heterogeneity provides a semi-parametric framework for uncorrelated unobservables, researchers have not yet devised nonparametric or semi-parametric alternatives to the multiple transition models with correlated unobservables such as those in Equations (18)–(20).

The intersection of these issues—of how formal methods may clarify theoretical ideas and how nonparametric techniques can shed light on model identification—provides insight into a central assertion in the life course: that one cannot understand seemingly disparate life course domains in isolation or that the life courses of spouses or partners exert mutual influences on one another. For example, consider life course transitions defined by cross-classifying an individual's social statuses across two or more life course domains, as in Figure 22-1, which depicts the transitions of women through a cross-classification of fertility and marital statuses. It can be shown that standard nonparametric methods will reproduce the observed distribution across persons and across time through these multiple transitions and statuses. This result implies that the notion of linked life course domains must lie at some deeper level than the distribution of individuals across statuses over time.

What might constitute a "deeper" notion of linked lives? One possibility is that the researcher directly observes all relevant aspects of that which is hypothesized to drive such linkages across life course domains. If so, one can proceed in the usual way by incorporating these data as standard covariates in a hazard regression. However, researchers usually worry that one or more key factors driving such linkages are in fact unobserved. If so, then such unobservables can induce correlations across the life course transitions observed for individuals. The models outlined in Equations (18)–(20), which were developed to address precisely this problem, are thus of great intrinsic substantive interest to life course, since they would in principle allow researchers to address linkages and to obtain point estimates of the correlation between transitions for a sample of individuals or for the transitions observed for members of a couple paired. But, as noted above, it has been difficult to date to devise obvious nonparametric or semi-parametric alternatives to such models; hence, it remains unclear the degree to which parameter estimates from such models are identified solely or in part from such untestable model assumptions. Such statistical difficulties may, in turn, be reflective not just of technical issues but may be revealing of gaps in theoretical accounts, for example, ambiguities or incompleteness by life course theorists in specifying the range of theoretical and behavioral mechanisms that might generate behavioral linkages across different parts of the life course or across individuals in a couple.

APPENDIX: SOFTWARE

It is important to emphasize that, because software for event history models continues to evolve rapidly, any survey of available software will become dated rapidly. This being said, several readily available software packages (e.g., SAS, SPSS, Stata, S, S-Plus, and R) have modules that permit estimation of most basic models, including nonparametric estimation of the survivor, integrated hazard, and (sometimes) hazard functions, and estimation of the Cox model. Many of these packages also have provisions that permit the user to define time-varying covariates; in such cases, these models can be used to obtain estimates of the piecewise constant baseline model in Equations (9) and (10) by the appropriate coding of time-varying dummy variables representing the appropriate time intervals.

Some of these packages also permit the estimation of models with multiple origin and destination states. When this is not possible, one can obtain estimates for standard models (i.e., those that assume conditional independence in the transitions to the multiple destination states) using a two-step procedure: first, by separating the problem into each origin state and, second, for each origin state, estimating parameters for a given destination state k by treating as censored those transitions to the other destination states.* Allison (1995) provides a useful and comprehensive survey of hazard estimation using SAS.

There are also several packages that have been developed for estimation of less standardized event history models. An incomplete list of such packages includes aML (Lillard & Panis, 2000), CTM (Yi, Honoré, & Walker, 1987), RATE (Tuma, 1979), and TDA (Blossfeld et al., 1989), and a variety of supplemental libraries developed for S, S-Plus, and R (see e.g., Loader, 1999). Most (but not all) of these specialized packages also permit estimation of basic models, but they otherwise differ considerably in the model coverage; hence, it is difficult to identify any one package as providing superior coverage relative to another. For example, aML and RATE permit estimation of the piecewise linear spline for the baseline hazard function; provisions for piecewise linear splines in these packages also permit estimation of non-linear and non-proportional covariate effects. TDA provides an extensive array of more parametric baseline hazard functions such as the Gompertz, Weibull, log logistic, log Gaussian, and sickle models. Local likelihood models (Wu & Tuma, 1990) are most easily estimated using supplemental libraries available in S, S-Plus, and R (Loader, 2000). CTM and aML have the most comprehensive routines for estimating models for unobserved heterogeneity, with CTM permitting estimation of the models discussed by Heckman and Singer (1985) and aML the models discussed by Lillard (1993).

ACKNOWLEDGMENT: Research funding from the National Institute of Child Health and Human Development (HD 29550) and research facilities provided under HD 05876 to the Center for Demography and Ecology, are gratefully acknowledged.

REFERENCES

Aalen, O. O. (1978). Nonparametric inference for a family of counting processes. *Annals of Statistics, 6*(4), 701–726.
Abbott, A. (2000). Reply to Levine and Wu. *Sociological Methods and Research, 29*(1), 65–76.
Abbott, A., & Tsay, A. (2000). Sequence analysis and optimal matching methods in sociology: review and prospect. *Sociological Methods and Research, 29*(1), 3–33.
Allison, P. D. (1985). *Event history analysis: regression for longitudinal event data.* Beverly Hills, CA: Sage.
Allison, P. D. (1995). *Survival analysis using the SAS® system: A practical guide.* Cary, NC: SAS Institute.
Andersen, P. K., & Gill, R. D. (1982). Cox's regression model for counting processes: a large sample study. *Annals of Statistics, 10*(4), 1100–1120.
Becker, G. S. (1991). *A treatise on the family* (Enlarged ed.) Cambridge, MA: Harvard University Press.

*This follows because maximum likelihood estimation for the expression in Equation (15) can be shown to be separable by origin; intuitively, this follows because the origin state j determines the set of individuals at risk of the destination states k. Note that such an estimation strategy cannot be used for models that weaken the conditional independence assumption, for example, for those models in which terms for unobserved heterogeneity affect the transitions to the multiple destination states.

Blau, P. M. (1977). *Inequality and heterogeneity: A primitive theory of social structure.* New York: Free Press.

Blau, P. M., & Duncan, O. D. (1967). *The American occupational structure.* New York: Wiley.

Blossfeld, H.-P., Hamerle, A., & Mayer, K. U. (1989). *Event history analysis.* Hillsdale, NJ: Erlbaum.

Bumpass, L. L. (1990). What's happening to the family: interaction between demographic and institutional change. *Demography, 27*(4), 483–498.

Chamberlain, G. (1985). Heterogeneity, omitted variable bias, and duration dependence. In J. J. Heckman & B. Singer (Eds.), *Longitudinal analysis of labor market data* (pp. 3–38). Cambridge: Cambridge University Press.

Cox, D. R. (1972). Regression models and life tables [with discussion]. *Journal of the Royal Statistical Society, B34*(2), 187–220.

Cox, D. R. (1975). Partial likelihood. *Biometrika, 62*(2), 269–276.

Cox, D. R., & Oakes, D. (1984). *Analysis of survival data.* London: Chapman & Hall.

Dechter, A. R. (1992). The effect of women's economic independence on union dissolution. (Working Paper No. 92–28) Center for Demography and Ecology, University of Wisconsin-Madison, Madison, WI.

Duncan, O. D. (1975). *Introduction to structural equation models.* New York: Academic Press.

Elbers, C., & Ridder, G. (1982). True and spurious duration dependence: The identifiability of the proportional hazard model. *Review of Economic Studies, 49*(3), 403–410.

Elder, G. H., Jr. (1998). The life course as developmental theory. *Child Development, 69*(1), 1–12.

Elder, G. H., Jr. (1999). *Children of the Great Depression: Social change in life experience* (25th anniversary ed.). Boulder, CO: Westview.

Fleming, T. R., & Harrington, D. P. (1991). *Counting processes and survival analysis.* New York: Wiley.

Gilder, G. F. (1986). *Men and marriage.* Gretna, LA: Pelican.

Härdle, W. (1990). *Applied nonparametric regression.* Cambridge: Cambridge University Press.

Hastie, T., & Tibshirani, R. (1993). Varying-coefficient models [with discussion]. *Journal of the Royal Statistical Society, B55*(4), 757–796.

Hastie, T., & Tibshirani, R. (1990). *Generalized additive models.* London: Chapman & Hall.

Heckman, J. J., & Singer, B. (1982). The identification problem in econometric models for duration data. In W. Hildenbrand (Ed.), *Advances in econometrics* (pp. 39–77). Cambridge: Cambridge University Press.

Heckman, J. J., & Singer, B. (1984). A method for minimizing the impact of distributional assumptions in econometric models for duration data. *Econometrica, 52*(2), 271–320.

Heckman, J. J., & Singer, B. (1985). Social science duration analysis. In J. J. Heckman & B. Singer (Eds.), *Longitudinal analysis of labor market data* (pp. 39–110). Cambridge: Cambridge University Press.

Hogan, D. P., & Astone, N. M. (1986). The transition to adulthood. *Annual Review of Sociology, 12*, 109–130.

Hougaard, P. (2000). *Analysis of multivariate survival data.* New York: Springer-Verlag.

Kaplan, E. L., & Meier, P. (1958). Nonparametric estimation from incomplete observations. *Journal of the American Statistical Association, 53*(282), 437–481.

Kiefer, N. M., & Neumann, G. R. (1981). Individual effects in a nonlinear model: Explicit treatment of heterogeneity in the empirical job-search model. *Econometrica, 49*(4), 965–979.

Lancaster, T. (1990). *The econometric analysis of transition data.* Cambridge: Cambridge University Press.

Levine, J. (2000). But what have you done for us lately? Commentary on Abbott and Tsay. *Sociological Methods and Research, 29*(1), 34–40.

Lillard, L. (1993). Simultaneous equations for hazards: Marriage duration and fertility timing. *Journal of Econometrics, 56*(1/2), 189–217.

Lillard, L. A., Brien, M. J., & Waite, L. J. (1995). Premarital cohabitation and subsequent marital dissolution: A matter of self-selection? *Demography, 32*(3), 437–457.

Lillard, L. A., & Waite, L. J. (1993). A joint model of childbearing and marital disruption. *Demography, 30*(4), 653–681.

Loader, Clive. (1999). *Local Regression and Likelihood.* New York: Springer.

Manski, C. F. (1995). *Identification problems in the social sciences.* Cambridge, MA: Harvard University Press.

Mare, R. D. (1994). Discrete-time bivariate hazards with unobserved heterogeneity: An indirect contingency table approach. *Sociological Methodology, 24*, 341–383.

Mare, R. D., & Palloni, A. (1988). Couple models for socioeconomic effects on mortality among older persons (CDE Working Paper No. 88–07). Center for Demography and Ecology, University of Wisconsin-Madison.

Mayer, K. U. (1988). German survivors of World War II: The impact on the life course of the collective experience of birth cohorts. In M. W. Riley (Ed.), *Social structures and human lives* (Vol. 1, pp. 229–246). Newbury Park, CA: Sage.

Mayer, K. U., & Tuma, N. B. (1990). Life course research and event history analysis: An overview. In K. U. Mayer & N. B. Tuma (Eds.), *Event history analysis in life course studies* (pp. 1–20). Madison, WI: University of Wisconsin Press.

Meyer, J. W. (1986). The self and the life course: Institutionalization and its effects. In A. B. Sørensen, F. E. Weinert, & L. R. Sherrod (Eds.), *Human development and the life course: Multidisciplinary perspectives* (pp. 199–216). Hillsdale, NJ: Erlbaum Associates.

Modell, J., Furstenberg, F., & Hershberg, T. (1976). Social change and transitions to adulthood in historical perspective. *Journal of Family History, 1*(1), 7–32.

Nelson, W. (1972). Theory and applications of hazard plotting for censored failure data. *Technometrics, 14*(4), 945–966.

Oppenheimer, V. K. (1997). Women's employment and the gain to marriage: the specialization and trading model. *Annual Review of Sociology, 23,* 481–453.

Poetter, U. (2000). A multivariate Buckley–James estimator. In T. Kollo, E.-M. Tiit, & M. Srivastava (Eds.), *Multivariate statistics: New trends in probability and statistics* (Vol. 5). Utrecht: VSP.

Popenoe, D. (1996). *Life without father.* New York: Free Press.

Raftery, A. E. (1995). Bayesian model selection in social research. In P. V. Marsden (Ed.), *Sociological methodology 1995* (pp. 111–165). Cambridge, MA: Blackwell.

Schwarz, G. (1978). Estimating the dimension of a model. *Annals of Statistics, 6*(2), 461–464.

Settersten, R. A., Jr., & Mayer, K. U. (1997). The measurement of age, age structuring, and the life course. *Annual Review of Sociology, 23,* 233–261.

Sewell, W. H., & Hauser, R. M. (1975). *Education, occupation, and earnings: Education in the early career.* New York: Academic Press.

Shanahan, M. J. (2000). Pathways to adulthood in changing societies: Variability and mechanisms in life course perspective. *Annual Review of Sociology, 26,* 667–692.

Sheps, M. C., & Menken, J. A. (1973). *Mathematical models of conception and birth.* Chicago: University of Chicago Press.

Spain, D., & Bianchi, S. M. (1996). *Balancing act: Motherhood, marriage, and employment among American women.* New York: Russell Sage.

Trussell, J., & Richards, T. (1985). Correcting for unmeasured heterogeneity in Hazard models using the Heckman–Singer procedure. In N. B. Tuma (Ed.), *Sociological methodology 1985* (pp. 242–276). San Francisco: Jossey-Bass.

Tsiatis, A. (1975). A nonidentifiability aspect of the problem of competing risks. *Proceedings of the National Academy of Sciences, 72*(1), 20–22.

Tuma, N. B. (1979). *Invoking RATE* (2nd ed.). Menlo Park: SRI International.

Tuma, N. B., & Hannan, M. T. (1984). *Social dynamics: Models and methods.* Orlando, FL: Academic Press.

Upchurch, D. M., Lillard, L. A., & Panis, C. W. A. (2001). The impact of nonmarital childbearing on subsequent marital formation and dissolution. In L. L. Wu & B. Wolfe (Eds.), *Out of wedlock: Causes and consequences of nonmarital fertility* (pp. 344–380). New York: Russell Sage Foundation.

Vaupel, J. W., & Yashin, A. I. (1985). Heterogeneity's ruses: Some surprising effects of selection on population dynamics. *American Statistician, 39*(3), 176–185.

White, H. C., Boorman, S. A., & Breiger, R. L. (1976). Social structure from multiple networks. I. Blockmodels of roles and positions. *American Journal of Sociology, 81*(4), 730–780.

Winsborough, H. H. (1980). A demographic approach to the life cycle. In K. W. Back (Ed.), *Life course: Integrative theories and exemplary populations* (pp. 65–75). Boulder, CO: Westview.

Wu, L. L. (1989). Issues in smoothing empirical hazards. In C. C. Clogg (Ed.), *Sociological methodology 1989* (pp. 127–159). Washington, DC: American Sociological Association.

Wu, L. L. (1990). Simple graphical goodness-of-fit tests for Hazard rate models. In K. U. Mayer & N. B. Tuma (Eds.), *Event History Analyses in Life Course Research* (pp. 184–199). Madison, WI: University of Wisconsin Press.

Wu, L. L. (1996). Effects of family instability, income, and income instability on the risk of a premarital birth. *American Sociological Review, 61*(3), 386–406.

Wu, L. L. (2000). Some comments on 'Sequence Analysis and Optimal Matching Methods in Sociology: Review and Prospect'. *Sociological Methods and Research, 29*(1), 41–64.

Wu, L. L., & Martinson, B. C. (1993). Family structure and the risk of a premarital birth. *American Sociological Review, 58*(2), 210–232.

Wu, L. L., & Thomson, E. (2001). Racial differences in family change and early sexual initiation. *Journal of Marriage and the Family, 63*(3), 682–696.

Wu, L. L., & Tuma, N. B. (1990). Local Hazard models. In C. C. Clogg (Ed.), *Sociological methodology 1990* (pp. 141–180). Washington, DC: American Sociological Association.

Xie, Y. (1994). Log-multiplicative models for discrete-time discrete-covariate event-history data. In P. V. Marsden (Ed.), *Sociological methodology 1994* (pp. 301–340). Washington, DC: American Sociological Association.

Yamaguchi, K. (1991). *Event history analysis.* Newbury Park, CA: Sage.

Yi, K.-M., Honoré, B. & Walker, J. (1987). *CTM: A program for the estimation and testing of continuous time multi-state multi-spell models.* Chicago: NORC/ERC and University of Chicago.

CHAPTER 23

Panel Models for the Analysis of Change and Growth in Life Course Studies

CHARLES N. HALABY

INTRODUCTION

Panel data figure prominently in research on the many aspects of the life course. The longitudinal structure of panel data, with the properties of many units (individuals, families, etc.) measured on several occasions spread over time, is ideal for observational studies of life course processes. Panel data have proven useful for research on subjects as fundamental as the causes and consequences of marital stability and dissolution (Biblarz & Raftery 1993; Thornton, Axinn, & Teachman, 1995), the social psychological development and well-being of children and adults (Booth & Amato, 1991; Chase-Lansdale, Cherlin & Kiernan, 1995; Moen, Robison, & Dempster-McClain, 1995; Nagin & Tremblay, 1999), and the evolution of conventional (Diprete & McManus, 1996) and deviant careers (Land & Nagin, 1996; Sampson & Laub, 1992), as well as for research on the issues surrounding the timing of all these processes and related transitions. There is now widespread agreement that panel data and the analytical advances they make possible are essential for rigorously addressing the types of questions that drive and are central to many life course studies.

Two classes of questions encompass many lines of empirical research and hold a privileged place in life course studies. One class, rooted in the traditional scientific interest in causal processes, focuses on assessing how events or changes in one area of social life may

CHARLES N. HALABY • Department of Sociology, University of Wisconsin, Madison, Wisconsin 53706

Handbook of the Life Course, edited by Jeylan T. Mortimer and Michael J. Shanahan. Kluwer Academic/Plenum Publishers, New York, 2003.

bring about other significant changes along key dimensions of the life course. For example, Budig and England (2001) investigate the effect that children have on mothers' wages over a 12-year period of their career; similarly, McManus and DiPrete (2001) assess the impact of divorce and separation on the financial welfare of men. A second class of questions center not on estimating the effects of changes, but on describing how the trajectories that development and growth trace over time vary systematically across groups defined by different characteristics or by exposure to different "treatments" or life course experiences. For example, the Life Course Studies program at the Carolina Population Center explains that the The National Longitudinal Study of Adolescent Health "investigates key potential influences that shape trajectories of resilience and vulnerability from adolescence to young adulthood, with attention to potential sources of variation—such as gender, social contexts, race/ethnicity, and siblings."* These kinds of questions have moved to the forefront of life course studies and are also well-suited to panel analysis. At the same time, the distinction drawn here between classes of research is not sharp in theory or practice. Both types of analyses are joined, for example, in Cherlin, Chase-Lansdale, and McCrea's (1998) study of the effect of parental divorce on the mental health of children and on the role of social background in shaping the trajectory of mental health development during youth and early adulthood.

This paper reviews the core models and methods commonly used for assessing causal effects and charting trajectories of development and growth in panel data on the life course. This review is neither even-handed nor symmetrical. On the contrary, the purpose is to show how issues underlying the use of panel data to estimate causal effects extend to and illuminate the methods and limitations that accompany efforts to identify the forces that shape trajectories of development or growth. In the social sciences, panel models for estimating causal effects from observational data grow largely out of an econometric tradition, while models for tracing variation in development or growth trajectories grow out of a medical and biological research tradition that only recently has found application in life course studies. Because these divergent origins continue to separate applications of the two types of models, the way that econometric principles of causal analysis apply to growth modeling is not always explicitly acknowledged. I have found that the key principles motivating and governing the use of panel data for estimating causal effects are typically glossed over or lost entirely in treatments of the growth models used for investigating developmental trajectories. Consequently, important continuities that run through the formulation and testing of both types of models are obscured. Models aimed at estimating causal effects and charting growth trajectories rely ultimately on a common set of statistical principles. The goal of this review is to clarify these principles while acknowledging areas of uniqueness.

The substantive scope of this review is limited in a number of respects.[†] First, only panel models for metric response variables, not discrete or limited dependent variables, are considered. Second, since panel analyses for both causal effects and growth trajectories typically involve fitting only static models, this review does not consider models involving either "system" (i.e., lagged dependent variables) or "error" (serially correlated time-varying disturbances) dynamics. Third, only parametric models are discussed, since such models are

---

*This quote comes from the World Wide Web site http://www.cpc.unc.edu/projects/lifecourse/adhealth.html.
[†]The technical scope of this review is limited to applications in which the number of units (N) is large, the number of occasions (T) is small, and the data are balanced insofar as the number and spacing of observation occasions is the same for all units. For extensions to incomplete panels, including discussions of selection bias due to attrition or other sources of nonrandomly missing data, see Baltagi (1995, Chapters 9 and 10.5), Hsaio (1986, Chapter 8), and Wooldridge (1995).

most fully developed and most broadly applicable given available software. Accessible treatments of panel analysis that cast a broader net and include the many important subjects not covered here are available elsewhere.*

This chapter is organized into two main sections. The first section specifies the essential advantages that accompany even the simplest panel designs and identifies the main statistical principles that apply to the analysis of panel data. The second section uses the principles discussed in the first section to shed light on the issues that accompany the formulation and testing of growth models.

PANEL MODELS

Panel designs join the strengths of two fundamental observation schemes for making causal inferences about behavior (Holland, 1986). One observational protocol, typified by the static group comparison (Campbell & Stanley, 1963, p. 12), exposes different units to different values of a causal variable and compares their responses at a single point in time.[†] An advantage of this design is temporal homogeneity: confounding changes that might accompany the passage of time are ruled out as alternative causes. A disadvantage is that the units compared are different and, hence, heterogeneous with respect to unobserved properties that may confound the attribution of effect to the causal variable of interest. For this kind of design, "unit heterogeneity" is highly problematic, but temporal "instability" less so.

A second design involves the opposite observation scheme: at two different times the same unit is exposed to different values of the causal variable and the responses are compared. Because the unit is the same over time, many unobserved properties remain stable and, hence, are ruled out as explanations of change in the response variable. This design minimizes the threat of unit heterogeneity: one expects more similarity in the same unit observed at different times than in different units observed at the same time. A disadvantage is temporal instability: over time changes in unobserved extraneous variables are alternative explanations for change in the response variable.

Panel studies join these two designs and thereby achieve a measure of protection against the primary threats to causal inference in observational studies.[‡] By observing many units at the same time on several different occasions, panel studies can effectively deal with the threats of unit heterogeneity and temporal instability. Unit homogeneity over time can be exploited to deal with the unobserved between-unit heterogeneity that is potentially a confounding factor in cross-sectional designs. Similarly, the temporal stability that comes with observing different units at the same time can be exploited to deal with the temporal instability in unobserved extraneous causes that may threaten inferences from longitudinal data.

---

*Standard econometric treatments of panel data include Baltaggi (1995), Hsaio (1986), and Maddalla (1986). For growth models as well as more general accounts of multilevel modeling, see Bryk and Raudenbush (1992), Goldstein (1995), Snijders and Bosker (1999). Treatments with a more biomedical emphasis include Diggle, Liang, and Zeger (1994) and Lindsey (1999).

†Randomly assigning values of the causal variable to units transforms the static group comparison into the classical experimental protocol known as the "posttest-only" control group design (Campbell & Stanley, 1963, p. 25). Randomization is the best method for dealing with unobserved unit heterogeneity, but is typically not available to life course researchers. Hence, the necessity for the methods discussed in this paper.

‡Another advantage of panel data that is not discussed here is the gain in efficiency: observing each of N units T times is usually more efficient (i.e., less error variation) than observing each of $(N \times T)$ units once.

Random Effects, Fixed Effects, and Unobserved Heterogeneity

To see the inference problems that panel data address, it pays to begin with a cross-sectional design. Suppose the aim is to estimate the effect of parental conflict on the mental health of children. Assume that data are available on many children $i = 1,2, ..., N$ at a single point in time t. Let y_{it} be the mental health of the ith child at time t and let x_{it} be a metric measure of the degree of parental conflict. Then the equation for the mental health of the ith child at time t can be written as

$$y_{it} = \alpha + \gamma x_{it} + \theta_i + e_{it} \tag{1}$$

where α is an intercept, γ is the parameter for the effect of parental conflict (x), and e_{it} is a transitory disturbance that represents unobserved time-varying causes of mental health that are independent of x, are serially uncorrelated, have mean zero, and constant variance over all units. The term θ_i ($\Sigma\theta_i = 0$), which represents an effect that is assumed to be uncorrelated with the transitory disturbances e_{it}, can be viewed either as a summary measure of unobserved, time-invariant, child-specific causes of mental health or simply as the unobserved permanent component of the ith child's mental health. The key point is that θ_i represents forces that shape mental health, but are possibly unknown to and certainly unmeasured by the researcher. The claim that θ_i represent time-invariant determinants of mental health (y_{it}) not only means that these are stable properties, but also that their effect on mental health is stable over time. Left open for now is the relationship of θ_i to the causal variable of primary interest, parental conflict.

A cross-section equation like Equation (1) is commonly fitted by least-squares estimation. Given our assumptions, the least-squares estimator $\hat{\gamma}_{LS}$ of the effect of parental conflict (x) on mental health (y) has expectation

$$E(\hat{\gamma}_{LS}) = \gamma + \lambda_{\theta x} \tag{2}$$

where $\lambda_{\theta x}$ is the parameter from an auxiliary regression of θ_i on x_{it}. The least-squares estimator captures two quantities: the effect γ of parental conflict on children's mental health and the expected mean difference $\lambda_{\theta x}$ in the permanent unobserved component of mental health θ_i for persons one unit apart on the metric measure of the causal variable, parental conflict.* The quality of the least-squares estimator $\hat{\gamma}_{LS}$ depends on this last term, which represents "unobserved heterogeneity bias."

The way one treats the connection between person-specific effects like θ_i and the observed causal variable(s) has important implications for the kind and quality of estimators that are employed. There are two alternative approaches. One approach is to assume that the unobserved person-specific causes θ_i are mean independent of the causal variable. This would be plausible if, for example, values of the causal variable were randomly assigned to units. It then would be sensible to treat the θ_i as "random effects", which, like e_{it}, are uncorrelated with the causal variable, have mean zero, and constant variance. Under this assumption, Equation (1) is a random effects model with composite random disturbance $u_{it} = \theta_i + e_{it}$. This implies $\lambda_{\theta x} = 0$, so that the unobserved person effects would not be a source of heterogeneity bias and the least-squares estimator $\hat{\gamma}_{LS}$ would be appropriate.

*The best way to look at this term is to simply view it an indicator of an association between the unobservable causes given by θ_i and the causal variable of interest as given by x.

An alternative approach is called for if the unobserved person effects are correlated with the causal variable, for then $\lambda_{\theta x} \neq 0$ and the least-squares estimator employed under a random effects assumption would suffer from unobserved heterogeneity bias. For the case of assessing the effect of parental conflict on children's mental health, an alternative approach is certainly advisable: it is not plausible to think of parental conflict as if it were randomly assigned to children and therefore independent of all unobservable child-specific forces that shape mental health. For example, θ_i may include a child's persistent exposure to parental alcoholism or abusive child-rearing practices, forces that one would expect to be associated with the level of parental conflict. In this case, avoiding bias in the estimate of the causal parameter γ necessarily means taking account of the relationship between θ_i and parental conflict. To this end, θ_i may be treated not as a random variable, but as "fixed effects," as person-specific constants that shift the mean of mental health and that need to be dealt with in estimating γ. In this case, Equation (1) is a fixed-effects model.

Under a fixed-effects model, there are two approaches to adjusting the least-squares estimator to account for the correlation of θ_i with the causal variable. The first is the conventional cross-sectional solution, which amounts to measuring time-invariant person variables that are summarized by θ_i and that will control for the correlation when entered into Equation (1). For example, if θ_i is determined, except possibly for a random error, by

$$\theta_i = \Sigma \phi_k w_{ik} \tag{3}$$

where the w_k are $k = 1, \ldots, K$ measured variables (e.g., exposure to parental alcoholism, abusive child-rearing practices, etc.), then substitution into Equation (1) gives

$$y_{it} = \alpha + \gamma x_{it} + \Sigma \phi_k w_{ik} + e_{it} \tag{4}$$

which will render the least-squares estimator $\hat{\gamma}_{LS}$ unbiased by regression adjusting for the correlation of x with the w_k. Controlling for the measured covariates w_k is intended to validate the random effects assumption, thereby rendering the least-squares estimator unbiased. This solution is problematic, however, because it relies on the untestable assumption that the w_k exhaust the variation in θ_i that is associated with x_{it}. With cross-sectional data, then, the random effects assumption is required at some point if the least-squares estimator is to be unbiased.

Now suppose that observations on mental health (y) and parental conflict (x) at a second point in time become available. An equation for each time point $t = 1,2$ can be written as

$$y_{i1} = \alpha + \gamma x_{i1} + \theta_i + e_{i1} \tag{5}$$
$$y_{i2} = \alpha + \gamma x_{i2} + \theta_i + e_{i2} \tag{6}$$

where a period difference in intercepts has been suppressed. If θ_i and x_{it} are correlated, estimation of the pooled equations again yields the biased estimator $\hat{\gamma}_{LS}$ with expectation $(\gamma + \lambda_{\theta x})$. Averaging these equations over time yields the so-called "between" regression of $\bar{y}_i$ on $\bar{x}_i$.

$$\bar{y}_i = \alpha + \gamma \bar{x}_i + \theta_i + \bar{e}_i. \tag{7}$$

Least-squares estimation of this equation yields the "between" estimator $\hat{\gamma}_b$ of γ. The expectation of this estimator is

$$E(\hat{\gamma}_b) = \gamma + \lambda_{\theta \bar{x}_i}. \tag{8}$$

so it too is biased by the relationship of θ_i to the over time mean of the causal variable $\bar{x}_i$. This result will prove useful in understanding the models and methods discussed later. For now it shows that the bias in the least-squares estimator of the pooled regression of Equations (5) and (6) can be traced to between-unit variation in $\bar{x}_i$, since Equation (7) averages across all within-unit over time variation in x_{it}.*

All this suggests that an effective means of dealing with heterogeneity bias would be to exploit the within-unit over time variation that panel data make available. To this end, transform x and y to deviations from their unit-specific over time means (i.e., time-demean the data) by subtracting Equation (7) from Equations (5) and (6). The resulting model is

$$(y_{i1} - \bar{y}_{i.}) = \gamma(x_{i1} - \bar{x}_{i.}) + (e_{i1} - \bar{e}_{i.}) \tag{9}$$
$$(y_{i2} - \bar{y}_{i.}) = \gamma(x_{i2} - \bar{x}_{i.}) + (e_{i2} - \bar{e}_{i.}) \tag{10}$$

where the θ_i that were the source of bias in the least-squares estimator have been eliminated. Applying least squares to the pooled equations yields the unbiased and consistent *fixed effects* or *within* estimator $\hat{\gamma}_{FE}$ and yields standard errors and tests statistics that are valid.[†]

An alternative approach to exploiting within-person variation is to estimate by least squares a model in first differences. Subtracting the time 1 from the time 2 equation yields

$$(y_{i2} - y_{i1}) = \gamma(x_{i2} - x_{i1}) + (e_{i2} - e_{i1}) \tag{11}$$

where again the person effects have been eliminated. The first-differenced estimator $\hat{\gamma}_{FD}$ is unbiased and consistent and the least-squares standard errors and test statistics are all valid.[‡] For the two-period case, the first-differenced estimator and fixed-effects estimator are identical ($\hat{\gamma}_{FE} = \hat{\gamma}_{FD}$) and so too are their standard errors and test statistics.

Another "within" estimator that is equivalent to the fixed-effects and first differenced estimators for the two-period case and has a particularly simple form occurs when x is an indicator variable scored 1 for exposure to some event between time 1 and time 2 and 0 otherwise.[¶] For example, if x indicates not the level of parental conflict but the occurrence of divorce (see Cherlin et al., 1998; McManus & Diprete, 2001), applying least squares to

$$y_{i2} - y_{i1} = \alpha + \gamma x_i + (e_{i2} - e_{i1}) \tag{12}$$

yields the so-called *difference-in-differences* estimator of the effect γ on children's mental health:

$$\hat{\gamma}_{dd} = (\bar{y}_{2|x=1} - \bar{y}_{1|x=1}) - (\bar{y}_{2|x=0} - \bar{y}_{1|x=0}) \tag{13}$$

*The correlation between $\bar{x}_{i.}$ and θ_i completely accounts for the correlation between x_{it} and θ_i; controlling for $\bar{x}_{i.}$ renders $\lambda_{\theta x} = 0$. Equivalently, heterogeneity bias cannot be traced to within-unit over time variation in x_{it} around its mean $\bar{x}_{i.}$, since the person effects θ_i are orthogonal to $(x_{it} - \bar{x}_{i.})$.

[†]This supposes that the residual degrees of freedom correctly account for the estimation of N unit means $\bar{y}_{i.}$. Standard least-squares routines will yield degrees of freedom equal to $NT - k$ rather than the correct $(NT - k - N)$, where k is the number of regression coefficients. In this case, the reported standard errors must be multiplied by the square root of $(NT - k)/(NT - k - N)$.

[‡]The residual degrees of freedom are automatically adjusted because N observations are lost by the differencing procedure.

[¶]An excellent treatment of panel methods for estimating the effect of events is Allison (1994).

which is the difference in the over time mean change in children's mental health between the group that experienced parental divorce ($x = 1$) and the group that did not ($x = 0$). This estimator is unbiased and the least-squares standard errors and test statistics are all valid. Estimators based on within-unit over time variation are unbiased and consistent because they eliminate possible heterogeneity bias caused by unobserved individual effects. Denoting all these estimators as $\hat{\gamma}_w$ we have

$$E(\hat{\gamma}_w) = \gamma \tag{14}$$

in contrast to the between-unit estimator $\hat{\gamma}_b$

$$E(\hat{\gamma}_b) = \gamma + \lambda_{\theta\bar{x}} \tag{15}$$

This suggests that the difference between these two types of estimators $(\hat{\gamma}_w - \hat{\gamma}_b)$ gives evidence of a correlation between the explanatory variable and the person effects, that is, evidence of heterogeneity bias. This result hinges on the fact that the within estimators are unbiased and consistent whether or not person effects are correlated with the causal variable, whereas the between estimator is only unbiased and consistent if the correlation is zero.

Extensions and Specification Tests

The analysis above generalizes to more than two periods and regression adjustment for additional measured covariates. Consider a model of the form

$$y_{it} = \alpha + \sum_{t=2}^{T} \delta_t + \sum_k \beta_k w_{kit} + \sum_p \phi_p z_{ip} + \gamma x_{it} + \theta_i + e_{it} \tag{16}$$

for $i = 1, \ldots, N$ and $t = 1, \ldots, T$. This model includes $(T - 1)$ terms δ_t for time-specific effects, a term θ_i ($\Sigma\theta_i = 0$) for person effects, and a transitory disturbance e_{it} that obeys the earlier assumptions. The causal variable of interest is x_{it}, which may be metric or categorical and has an effect on y given by γ. Two distinct sets of explanatory variables are entered as controls: the w_{kit} ($k = 1,\ldots, K$ variables), which vary over time and across units and the z_{pi} ($p = 1,\ldots, P$ variables), which vary only between units because they represent time-invariant characteristics (e.g., gender, social origins).

Including measured time-invariant variables like z_p may account for the correlation between θ_i and the explanatory variables. If the unobserved θ_i are assumed to be uncorrelated with the observed regressors, nothing is gained in terms of bias control by distinguishing "within" and "between" unit variation in the estimation of the parameters. An unbiased and consistent estimator of γ (and the other parameters) can be obtained by treating the θ_i as random effects and applying least squares to the pooled panels of NT observations. There is, however, a gain in efficiency, as well as valid standard errors and test statistics, to be realized by taking account of the positive serial correlation in the errors of Equation (16) that is induced by the fact that $u_{it} = \theta_i + e_{it}$ and $u_{is} = \theta_i + e_{is}$, $s \neq t$ both contain the common θ_i. Hence, a better estimation procedure would be generalized least squares (henceforth, GLS), which would yield a consistent and efficient random effects estimator of the parameters, as well as valid standard errors and test statistics. Denote the GLS random effects estimator of γ as $\hat{\gamma}_{GLS}$.

Most statistical software for GLS estimation assumes that the unobserved person effects are uncorrelated with the explanatory variables. If this assumption is false, the GLS estimator is biased and inconsistent. Hence, the person effects should be treated as fixed and the longitudinal structure of the data exploited by using the same methods identified for the two-period case. First differencing Equation (16) gives

$$(y_{it} - y_{it-1}) = \alpha + \sum_{3}^{T}\delta_t + \sum_{k}\beta_k(w_{kit} - w_{kit-1}) + \gamma(x_{it} - x_{it-1}) + (e_{it} - e_{it-1}) \quad (17)$$

where one term for period effects is lost. Applying least squares to the pooled data yields the unbiased and consistent first-differenced estimator of the parameters. Alternatively, applying the fixed-effects transformation (i.e., time-demean the data) to Equation (16) yields

$$(y_{it} - \bar{y}_i) = \alpha + \sum_{t=2}^{T}\delta_t + \sum_{k}\beta_k(w_{kit} - \bar{w}_{ki}) + \gamma(x_{it} - \bar{x}_i) + (e_{it} - \bar{e}_i) \quad (18)$$

which can be estimated by least squares. Denote the fixed-effects estimator of γ as $\hat{\gamma}_{FE}$.

The fixed-effects estimator and the first-differenced estimator are unbiased and consistent, although for $T > 2$ they are not the same. The standard errors and test statistics that accompany the fixed-effects estimator are valid if the idiosyncratic transitory errors e_{it} are constant variance and serially uncorrelated; this holds as well for the first-differenced estimator if the disturbances $(e_{i2} - e_{i1})$ in the *transformed* equation are constant variance and serially uncorrelated. Under these assumptions, these estimators are fully efficient for a fixed effects model. The efficiency of both estimators depends directly on the over time variation in the explanatory variables. For example, the standard error of $\hat{\gamma}_{FE}$ depends on the independent variation in x_{it} about its time mean $\bar{x}_i$, since one cannot get precise estimates of the effect of a change in x if not much change actually occurred. For causes that change slowly, longer intervals between time periods may yield more efficient estimators, although this must be weighed against the increase in error variation from extraneous, unmeasured transitory causes. For example, if past research suggests that levels of hostility and conflict in a household are relatively stable over time, efficient estimation of their effect on children's mental health would call for longer intervals between panels.

The fixed effect estimator deserves special attention because it is more commonly used in applied work. A key issue concerns its performance compared to the GLS estimator if θ_i is uncorrelated with the explanatory variables. The fixed effects estimator is still unbiased and consistent, although less efficient than using GLS to estimate a random effects model. Yet when N is large and there is plenty of time variation in the explanatory variables, not much may be lost by using fixed-effects estimation when GLS estimation of a random effects model is best. However, if the random effects assumption is wrong, the GLS estimator is biased and inconsistent, while fixed-effects estimation is unbiased and efficient. This kind of trade off clearly favors the fixed-effects estimator, which is why Allison (1994; see also Nickell, 1981, p. 1418), for example, was led to conclude that "the [fixed-effect] estimator is nearly always preferable [to the GLS random effects estimator] for estimating effects ... with nonexperimental data" (p. 181).

The choice of model and estimators need not be made blindly. As indicated for the two-period case with a single explanatory variable, the difference $(\hat{\gamma}_w - \hat{\gamma}_b)$ between the "between" and "within" estimators is evidence of heterogeneity bias, so that large values of this statistic would lead to rejection of the hypothesis that the person-specific effects are uncorrelated with the regressors. This same principle carries over to the contrast $(\hat{\gamma}_{FE} - \hat{\gamma}_{GLS})$ between the GLS and fixed-effects estimator (Arellano, 1993; Baltagi, 1995; Hausman, 1978; Peracchi, 2001, p. 406). In models with several explanatory variables, the magnitude of the difference between the GLS estimates and the fixed-effect estimates is an indication of the heterogeneity bias induced in the GLS random effects estimator when the person effects are correlated with the explanatory variables. A statistic that summarizes the differences between the two sets of estimates is the basis for the most important specification test in panel data applications: the Hausman (1978) χ^2 test of the hypothesis that the person effects and the explanatory variables are uncorrelated. A small value of the Hausman (1978) χ^2 statistic fails to reject the null hypothesis and favors GLS estimation of a random effects model; a large value favors fixed-effects estimation of a fixed-effects model. If efficiency is not problematic (e.g., N is large and intervals between periods are long), it is conceivable that one might forgo the random effects model straight away in favor of fixed-effects estimation.* But there is little to recommend using GLS random effects estimation without a Hausman test for correlated person effects.

A comparison of Equations (16) and (18) (or 17) shows that one consequence of applying the fixed-effects (or first-difference) transformation is that measured time-invariant explanatory variables like z_p are swept away along with the individual effects, so that the parameters ϕ_p cannot be estimated.[†] This occurs because the effects of observed time-invariant explanatory variables cannot be separately identified from the effects of the unobserved time-invariant θ_i. Is the inability to identify parameters like ϕ_p a disadvantage of within estimators? Perhaps, but the disadvantage is only compelling if a fixed effects model is not warranted in the first place. Otherwise, the loss of time-invariant explanatory variables can hardly be construed as a serious cost, especially if research interest is largely confined to assessing how *changes* in explanatory variables bring about *changes* in a response variable. Indeed, to view the loss of information about the parameters of time-invariant explanatory variables as a serious disadvantage of within estimators is to misconstrue the principal purpose of panel data. Researchers who choose GLS estimation of random effects models solely for the efficiency gains that might come with exploiting between-unit variation and who ignore unobserved heterogeneity bias might as well settle for cross-section data and avoid the extra cost of collecting panel data. As Wooldridge (2000) correctly note, "In most applications, the only reason for collecting panel data is to allow for the unobserved effects $[\theta_i]$ to be correlated with the explanatory variables" (p. 421). Allison (1994) expresses similar sentiments on this issue.

Measured time-invariant explanatory variables are irrelevant for fixed effects estimation, but nevertheless figure prominently in the Hausman specification test for correlated person effects and, hence, in the evidence favoring a fixed or random effects model. Although the Hausman test is based only on estimates of the parameters of time-varying explanatory variables, time-invariant explanatory variables help determine the outcome of the test through their effect on the GLS estimator and its variance. Hence, important measured time-invariant explanatory variables must always be included in the random effects model estimated by GLS. Failure to do so will usually have a huge impact on the Hausman statistic, as it should, since it is sensitive to the omission of all time-invariant correlated effects, whether observed (but omitted) or strictly unobserved.

As an illustration that also shows the power of the test, Table 23-1 gives the results of fitting earnings equations to 1980–1987 data from the National Longitudinal Survey of Youth

---

*Even if fixed effects estimation is the default approach, a Hausman test may be informative about omitted causes of the response variable and the sources of heterogeneity bias.
[†] This conclusion will be qualified when growth models are discussed.

TABLE 23-1. **Generalized Least-squares and Fixed-effect Parameter Estimates and Hausman Test Statistics for Short and Long Versions of Earnings Equations; Full-time Employed Males, 1980–1987 ($N = 544$ and $T = 8$).**

Independent variables	Short model			Long model		
	Fixed-effect estimates	GLS random effect estimates	Difference	Fixed-effect estimates	GLS random effect estimates	Difference
Constant	1.33 (58.85)	1.28 (48.92)			0.486 (4.75)	
Year						
1981	0.113 (5.24)	0.109 (5.04)	0.003	0.113 (5.24)	0.110 (5.11)	0.002
1982	0.165 (7.62)	0.158 (7.26)	0.007	0.165 (7.62)	0.161 (7.40)	0.005
1983	0.208 (9.46)	0.199 (9.01)	0.009	0.208 (9.46)	0.202 (9.18)	0.006
1984	0.273 (12.26)	0.261 (11.67)	0.013	0.273 (12.26)	0.265 (11.92)	0.008
1985	0.323 (14.40)	0.311 (13.86)	0.012	0.323 (14.40)	0.316 (14.10)	0.008
1986	0.382 (16.83)	0.369 (16.26)	0.013	0.382 (16.83)	0.373 (16.54)	0.009
1987	0.441 (19.23)	0.425 (18.56)	0.017	0.441 (19.23)	0.430 (18.87)	0.011
Schooling (years)	—	—		—	0.071 (8.21)	—
Black (= 1)	—	—		—	−0.122 (2.63)	—
Married (= 1)	0.057 (3.08)	0.079 (4.71)	−0.023	0.057 (3.08)	0.077 (4.57)	−0.020
Occupational status (SEI/10)	0.012 (2.19)	0.024 (4.74)	−0.012	0.012 (2.19)	0.016 (3.17)	−0.004
Union (= 1)	0.086 (4.42)	0.116 (6.37)	−0.030	0.086 (4.42)	0.118 (6.53)	−0.032
Hausman χ^2			81 ($p < 0.0000$)			37.14 ($p < 0.0001$)

Note: Appearing in parentheses below the coefficients are the *t*-ratios.

Sample hereafter, NLSY.* The data are annual observations for $N = 545$ full-time working males who completed their schooling by 1980. The left-hand panel gives the GLS estimates, the fixed effect estimates, and the difference between these estimates for a model that includes only time-varying explanatory variables (year, occupational socioeconomic status, union membership, and marital status).[†] As the "difference" column shows, the GLS estimates of the coefficients of socioeconomic status, union membership, and marital status are considerably (i.e., 35–200%)

*These data were previously analyzed by Vella and Verbeek (1998). They are discussed by Wooldridge (2000) and available for downloading at http://ideas.uqam.ca/ideas/data/bocbocins.html.
[†]All the models and tests of this section were carried out using the *xtreg* command in Stata 7. This command will fit the between-, fixed-, and random-effects models and compute the relevant Hausman test.

larger than their fixed-effect counterparts. The largest difference is for socioeconomic status, with the GLS estimate twice the fixed effect estimate. The Hausman statistic is $\chi^2 = 81$ ($p < 0.0000$), so the null hypothesis is rejected in favor of the conclusion that important correlated individual effects have been omitted from the model. The right-hand panel of Table 23-1 gives the results when years of schooling and race, two time-invariant variables, are added to the random effects specification. The Hausman χ^2 statistic has fallen dramatically to $\chi^2 = 37$, a drop due largely to the decrease in the difference between the GLS and fixed-effects estimates of the coefficient of socioeconomic status, the one time-varying regressor that is most strongly related to schooling and race. Still, the Hausman statistic remains large enough to recommend fixed effects estimation.

The loss of information about the role of time-invariant explanatory variables in the process of change over time is hardly complete under fixed-effect estimation. Time-invariant explanatory variables may affect the rate of change in the response variable and may condition the effect of time-varying explanatory variables on the response variable; both types of inter-actions are estimable in a fixed-effects framework. Time-invariant variables with time-varying parameters are easily handled because neither the fixed effects nor first difference transformation eliminates them. For example, including interactions of parental schooling with a linear term for age in a fixed-effects model of child development would identify differences in the effect of parental schooling as children aged, even though the actual baseline effect of parental schooling on the level of child development could not be identified. Similarly, including in a model for marital satisfaction a term for the interaction of race with a time-varying explana-tory variable like economic welfare would identify race differences in the effect of changes in economic welfare, even though race differences in marital satisfaction would not be identified.

To illustrate, Table 23-2 gives the results of GLS and fixed-effect estimation of an earnings model that includes terms for race, schooling, and the interaction of each of these with a linear term for year.* A couple of points are noteworthy. First, adding the time-varying interaction terms has virtually no effect on the Hausman test, which changes from 36.64 (not shown) to 37.23. Second, the "difference" column shows that the two estimators yield virtually identical coefficients for the interaction terms. These coefficients indicate that the rate of change in wage is about 1.8% less for Blacks than for others and that each year of schooling increases the rate of change in wage by 0.36%. Finally, the equations of Table 23-2 are, in effect, growth models, although I have not formulated them from within the usual statistical framework for analyzing variation in growth trajectories. I now turn to a discussion of that framework.

GROWTH MODELS

Background and Fundamentals

Growth modeling is a specialized application of panel data methods that has gained some currency in life course research. Cherlin et al. (1998) used growth models to describe the relationship between divorce and mental health for a cohort of children and McLeod and Shanahan (1996) used growth models to describe the relationship between poverty and

---

*Because all men remained in the labor force and in the sample throughout the 8-year period, the year-to-year change in labor force experience is constant and equal to the year-to-year change in period. For the fixed effects model, this means that the linear period effect is perfectly collinear with the linear effect for labor force experience, so that both variables yield exactly the same estimates and other statistics.

TABLE 23-2. Generalized Least-squares and Fixed-effect Parameter Estimates of Race and Schooling Differences in the Rate of Change in Earnings; Full-time Employed Males, 1980–1987 (N = 544 and T = 8)

Independent variables	Fixed-effect estimates	GLS random effect estimates	Difference
Constant	1.36 (69.06)	0.65 (5.65)	
Year	0.019 (1.16)	0.018 (1.14)	0.000
Year × Black	−0.019 (2.53)	−0.018 (2.51)	−0.000
Year × Schooling	0.004 (2.73)	0.004 (2.64)	0.000
Schooling (years)	—	0.058 (5.93)	—
Black (= 1)	—	−0.058 (1.10)	—
Married (= 1)	0.053 (2.89)	0.073 (4.39)	−0.020
Occupational status (SEI/10)	0.012 (2.27)	0.016 (3.23)	−0.004
Union (= 1)	0.088 (4.53)	0.119 (6.63)	−0.031
Hausman χ^2			37.23 ($p < 0.0000$)

Note: Appearing in parentheses below the coefficients are the t-ratios.

mental health for a birth cohort observed on three occasions. Although new additions to the sociological literature, growth models have a long history in the biological and medical sciences, where they have been used to analyze how the parameters governing growth trajectories generated by developmental or aging processes may vary between populations defined by different treatments or characteristics. The early history of growth modeling involved the application of standard multivariate analysis of variance methods to balanced data. But the modeling technology used in sociological applications is tied more directly to the development of methods for analyzing growth processes when data are unbalanced by variation across units in the timing or spacing of measurements. For example, the NLSY wage data used above would be unbalanced if not all men appeared in the sample every year or if not all men worked every year. Methods for unbalanced panels were consolidated by Laird and Ware's (1982) exposition of what they termed "two-stage" random-effects regression models, but what now fall under the rubric of mulitlevel (Goldstein, 1995) or hierarchical models (Bryk and Raudenbush, 1992).* The hierarchical linear model approach to growth modeling that is elaborated below and which I favor for its close connection to econometric panel models can

*An alternative approach to developmental or growth trajectories in given by Nagin (1999).

be cast in terms of covariance structure analysis and developed in parallel fashion (McArdle & Epstein, 1987; Willett & Sayer, 1994).*

Growth modeling typically involves a somewhat different emphasis from and some extensions beyond the panel models discussed above. Rather than emphasizing the use of within-unit over time variation to avoid bias in the estimation of parameters governing the effect of changes in explanatory variables on changes in the mean of a response variable, growth modeling attends mainly to describing and quantifying between-unit variation in the time trajectory of a response variable. Such between-unit variation in patterns of change is conceptualized in terms of variation in the mean of the response variable and variation in its rate of change over time.

The first "stage" or "level" of a growth model is an equation for the measurements on a response variable y_{it} that is observed for the ith unit over a temporally ordered set of measurement occasions $t = 1, 2, \ldots, m.$[†] The argument of a growth model, the dimension with respect to which "growth" in y_{it} is assessed, is not always obvious or natural, but must meet certain mild restrictions. In the general model

$$y_{it} = f(T_{it}) + e_{it} \qquad (19)$$

the main restrictions on T are that it be measured on a metric scale and that it be monotonically non-decreasing and sometimes increasing over measurement occasions. Laird and Ware (1982, p. 972) model growth in children's pulmonary capacity as a function of height, so T_{it} is the height of the ith child at the tth measurement occasion. In life course applications, T is typically the date or time of observation or the age of the unit. In cohort studies like Cherlin et al. (1998) and McLeod and Shanahan (1996), the distinction between observation date and age is eclipsed because the two are perfectly collinear. Since data structures in which T_{it} is fixed across units at each measurement occasion are quite common, assume that T is either the time of observation or age in a cohort.

A general form for Equation (19) is

$$y_{it} = \delta_t + e_{it} \qquad (20)$$

where δ_t ($t = 1, \ldots, m$) are unrestricted time effects and e_{it} are time-varying disturbances that are assumed to be normal with mean zero and constant variance σ_e^2. Simple assumptions about disturbances are the rule when there are few time points or occasions per unit. Simple is also the rule when choosing one function $f(T_{it})$ that can serve as the trajectory for all units and that imposes a smooth structure on the time path of y_{it}. To be sure, neither simple nor smooth is necessary: Snijders and Bosker (1999) explore many elaborate and very flexible growth functions $f(T_{it})$ that researchers might find useful. In practice, linear models or models that are linear in some transformation of T are most common (Cherlin et al., 1998; McLeod & Shanahan, 1995), with quadratic functions also receiving attention (Bryk & Raudenbush, 1992; Horney et al., 1995).

The "level 1" specification for a linear growth model can be written as[‡]

$$y_{it} = \beta_{0i} + \beta_{1i} T_{it} + e_{it} \qquad (21)$$

---

*Each approach has its advantages. Hierarchical linear modeling is better for handling unbalanced data, while covariance structure analysis allows a more flexible treatment of the error covariance structure (Willett & Sayer, 1994, p. 368).

[†]Growth modeling can easily handle unbalanced data, but to maintain continuity and minimize notation, I again assume the data are balanced, so that $m_i = m$ and the timing of occasions is constant over units.

[‡]Throughout I adhere loosely to the conventional notation of hierarchical models (e.g., Snijders & Bosker, 1999).

where β_{0i} is an individual-specific time-invariant intercept and β_{1i} is an individual-specific time-invariant slope parameter for the rate of change in y_{it}. As the model stands, the parameter β_{0i} gives the mean of y_{it} for the ith unit when $T = 0$. When $T = 0$ is not substantively meaningful, centering T around a sensible reference point is a common procedure. Hence, the level 1 equation might be written as

$$y_{it} = \beta_{0i} + \beta_{1i}(T_{it} - T_0) + e_{it} \tag{22}$$

where T_0 is a useful reference point, perhaps the value of T at the start of the observation period. Centering gives the intercept a meaningful interpretation, for now β_{0i} is the level of the response variable for the ith unit at time (or age) $T_{it} = T_0$. Cherlin et al. (1998) observe a cohort of children beginning at age 7 and so used the age-centering transformation $(T_{it} - 7)$ in order to interpret β_{0i} as the level of a child's mental health at the start of the study. Since centering aids interpretation, but otherwise leaves the fundamental statistical properties of the growth model unchanged, assume that T is centered appropriately so that $T_{i1} = 0$ means that β_{0i} gives the "baseline" value of y at the start of the observation period.

In addition to a level 1 equation for the measurements y_{it}, growth models consist of a set of level 2 regressions for explaining between-unit variation in the level 1 parameters β_{0i} and β_{1i}. Although the goal is to identify the contribution of measured conditions to between-unit variation in these parameters, the simplest model omits explanatory variables in order to assess the overall amount of variation. One possible starting point for a stage-2 model is

$$\beta_{0i} = \gamma_{00} + u_{0i} \tag{23}$$

$$\beta_{1i} = \gamma_{10} \tag{24}$$

where u_{0i} is a random person effect that has mean zero, variance τ_0^2, and is independent of the time-varying level 1 disturbance e_{it}. For the time being, I have specified the slope parameter β_{1i} for the rate of change in y as just γ_{10}; there is no random person-specific slope effect.

The connection of this formulation to earlier models becomes apparent when the two levels are combined by substitution to form the full model:

$$y_{it} = \gamma_{00} + \gamma_{10}T_{it} + u_{0i} + e_{it} \tag{25}$$

which is exactly like the models considered earlier with one explanatory variable T, a random time-varying disturbance e_{it}, and a time-invariant person effect u_{0i}. The intercept giving the mean of y_{it} at baseline is $(\gamma_{00} + u_{0i})$, with γ_{00} giving the "fixed" component that applies to all persons and u_{0i} giving the part that applies only to the ith person. The error component u_{0i} is then just an alternative expression of the person effects (i.e., θ_i) that in earlier models were the source of unobserved heterogeneity. In most applications, u_{0i} is assumed to be random and independent of T without much discussion. In cohort studies in which T is age, this assumption is automatically met: the person-specific effect is by design uncorrelated with T_{it}, since the latter does not vary between units. The same is true if T_{it} tracks the occasion of measurement in a balanced design. Hence, under the assumptions set down above, heterogeneity bias in the estimator of the parameter γ_{10} for the rate of change in y_{it} is not an issue: The fixed effects and GLS random effects estimator of γ_{10} are identical, so a Hausman test would yield $\chi^2 = 0$.

A natural extension of the level 2 model of Equations (23) and (24) is

$$\beta_{0i} = \gamma_{00} + u_{0i} \tag{26}$$

$$\beta_{1i} = \gamma_{10} + u_{1i} \qquad (27)$$

where now a random person-specific effect u_{1i} has been added to the equation for the slope β_{1i}. Like u_{0i}, u_{1i} is assumed to have mean zero, variance τ_1^2, and to be independent of e_{ij}; it is also customary to allow for a covariance between the person effects, say, τ_{01}. Joining this level 2 model to the level 1 model of Equation (21) yields

$$y_{it} = \gamma_{00} + \gamma_{10}T_{ij} + u_{0i} + u_{1i}T_{it} + e_{it} \qquad (28)$$

The new feature of this model is the term $u_{1i}T_{ij}$, where u_{1i} appears as a random coefficient of the time variable.* The rate of change in y_{it} is now ($\gamma_{10} + u_{1i}$), with γ_{10} giving the mean ($E(\beta_{1i}) = \gamma_{10}$) or "fixed" component that applies to all units and u_{1i} giving the random part that applies only to the ith unit. This random slope effect is a source of unobserved heterogeneity that was not present in the panel models previously considered; it is the one fundamental innovation that renders the typical growth model statistically distinctive from earlier models. This random component of the rate of change in y_{it} varies across units, but for each unit is constant over time, just like the person effects u_{0i} for the mean level of y_{it}.[†]

The model of Equation (28) is a linear random effects growth model. The mean trend line of the response variable across all units is

$$E(y_{it}) = \gamma_{00} + \gamma_{10}T_{it} \qquad (29)$$

with variation around this mean in person-specific trend lines. Variation in the level of y_{i1} at baseline (i.e., $T = 0$) is generated by u_{0i} and measured by the level 2 variance τ_0^2 and variation in the slope is generated by u_{1i} and measured by the level 2 variance τ_1^2. All the panel models considered earlier had assumed, in effect, that $u_{1i} = 0$ for all units and hence $\tau_1^2 = 0$.

A major part of the attraction of random effects growth models is the capacity to assess the unexplained level 1 and level 2 variation. As Snijders and Bosker (1999) observe for hierarchical modeling more generally, "[The] partitioning of unexplained variability over the various levels is the essence of hierarchical random effects models" (p. 48). Given the special emphasis on the level 2 variation captured by τ_0^2 and τ_1^2, growth modeling generally calls for formal tests on these variance parameters. The null hypothesis that all units share a common intercept (i.e., $\beta_{01} = \beta_{02} = \ldots = \beta_{0n} = \gamma_{00}$) implies $u_{01} = u_{02} = \ldots = u_{0n} = 0$, which can be formulated as a test of $\tau_0^2 = 0$. Similarly, a test of the hypothesis of a common underlying rate of change (i.e., $\beta_{11} = \ldots = \beta_{1n} = \gamma_{10}$) and no person-specific random slope effects amounts to a test of $\tau_1^2 = 0$. Failure to reject the joint null $\tau_0^2 = \tau_1^2 = 0$ would lead one to constrain the u_{0i} and u_{1i} to zero, yielding a model with no random effects at all. Alternatively, rejecting the null would invite single parameter tests of each separate variance component. Judging from extant empirical applications, models with no explanatory level 2 variables yield estimated intercept variances that are almost always statistically significant, with $\tau_0^2 = 0$ easily rejected. In contrast, point estimates of τ_1^2 are usually considerably smaller than their intercept counterparts and less often statistically significant. For the NLSY wage data, fitting the model of Equation (28) yields the estimates (SEs) $\hat{\gamma}_{00} = 1.43$ (0.014) and $\hat{\gamma}_{10} = 0.063$ (0.003) for the baseline mean and slope, respectively

---

*This new terms renders the disturbance variance dependent on T and, hence, heteroscedastic.
[†]If the variable coefficient u_{1i} is correlated with T_{it}, the usual GLS estimator of the mean rate parameter γ_{10} will be biased and inconsistent. But our design assumptions imply that T_{it} does not vary between units and, hence, cannot be correlated with u_{1i}.

and $\hat{\tau}_0^2 = 0.168$ and $\hat{\tau}_1^2 = 0.003$ for the variance parameters. A likelihood ratio test of the null hypothesis $\tau_0^2 = \tau_1^2 = 0$ yields highly significant $\chi^2 = 2156$ and each individual variance estimate is highly significant in its own right. Hence, both the baseline mean of wages and the rate of growth in wages from 1980–1987 vary across workers.

The models considered to this point are all "unconditional": no explanatory variables have been introduced to account for the components of variation in y_{it}. Time-varying and time-invariant explanatory variables enter growth models in formally distinct ways. Time-varying explanatory variables are entered at level 1 (with slopes then fixed at level 2) (see Bryk & Raudenbush, 1992, p. 151), since this part of the model speaks to variation in y_{it} over time. In analogous fashion, time-invariant explanatory variables are accommodated at level 2, since this part of the model addresses between-unit variation in *time-invariant* intercepts and slopes. I begin with time-varying explanatory variables in order to underscore the connection between growth models and other panel models.

Time-Varying Explanatory Variables

Let x_{it} be a time-varying explanatory variable like economic welfare that is believed to affect the time path of a response variable y_{it} like marital satisfaction. The level 1 model then may be expanded as follows:

$$y_{it} = \beta_{0i} + \beta_{1i}T_{it} + \beta_{xi}x_{it} + e_{it} \tag{30}$$

with the coefficient β_{xi} specified as fixed rather than random at the second level:

$$\beta_{0i} = \gamma_{00} + u_{0i} \tag{31}$$

$$\beta_{1i} = \gamma_{10} + u_{1i} \tag{32}$$

$$\beta_{xi} = \gamma_x \tag{33}$$

A preliminary model of exactly this form is specified by Horney et al. (1995) in their study of the evolution of criminal careers, with x_{it} representing changing employment and personal circumstances that affect the propensity to offend. The combined model is

$$y_{it} = \gamma_{00} + \gamma_{1,0}T_{it} + \gamma_x x_{it} + u_{0i} + u_{1i}T_{it} + e_{it} \tag{34}$$

where interest generally centers on estimating γ_x as well as $\sigma_{0|x}^2$ and $\sigma_{1|x}^2$, which indicate the variation remaining to be explained by the introduction of variables at level 2. Introducing time-varying explanatory variables may account not just for level-1 variation in y_{it}, but also between-person variation in intercepts and slopes, so that all three conditional variance components, $\sigma_{e|x}^2, \sigma_{0|x}^2, \sigma_{1|x}^2$ are smaller than their unconditional counterparts in the "empty" model with only T. For example, adding socioeconomic status, marital status, and union membership to a linear wage growth model yields variance estimates $\hat{\sigma}_{e|x}^2 = 0.1063$ (vs. $\hat{\sigma}_e^2 = 0.1066$), $\hat{\sigma}_{0|x}^2 = 0.1544$ (vs. $\hat{\sigma}_0^2 = 0.1685$), and $\hat{\sigma}_{1|x}^2 = 0.0031$ (vs. $\hat{\sigma}_1^2 = 0.0032$), all smaller than their unconditional counterparts in an "empty" model.*

---

*The parameter estimates given here are the only ones reported for the fitted models. The rest of the parameter estimates are available upon request.

For the model of Equation (34), the GLS (or maximum likelihood) random effects esti-mator of γ_x, the parameter for the effect of changes in x_{it} on changes in y_{it}, will be biased and inconsistent if x_{it} is correlated with the unobserved random person effects u_{0i} and u_{1i}.* In order to highlight the connection between estimation in a growth modeling context and in the context considered earlier, a less general formulation is useful. As Bryk and Raudenbush (1992) advise, fitting models for mean effects is a prudent first step toward fitting models with random or non-random slopes. In that spirit, continue to let Equation (30) be the level 1 model and specify the level 2 model as

$$\beta_{0i} = \gamma_{00} + u_{0i} \tag{35}$$

$$\beta_{1i} = \gamma_{10} \tag{36}$$

$$\beta_{xi} = \gamma_x \tag{37}$$

Substitution yields the combined model

$$y_{it} = \gamma_{00} + \gamma_{1,0}T_{it} + \gamma_x x_{it} + u_{0i} + e_{it} \tag{38}$$

which is exactly like the typical panel model with unobserved individual effects. In a growth modelling framework, dealing with correlated individual effects that might bias the estima-tion of γ_x is mainly a matter of controlling for between-unit variation in x_{it} by explicitly mod-eling the dependence of the unobserved random intercept effect on $\bar{x}_{i\cdot}$.[†] Hence, the random effect u_{0i} can be written in terms of the auxiliary regression:

$$u_{0i} = \gamma_{0x}\bar{x}_{i\cdot} + v_{0i} \tag{39}$$

where v_{0i} is a residual that is uncorrelated by construction with $\bar{x}_{i\cdot}$. Upon substitution into Equation (38), the full combined model becomes

$$y_{it} = \gamma_{00} + \gamma_{10}T_{it} + \gamma_x x_{it} + \gamma_{0x}\bar{x}_{i\cdot} + v_{0i} + e_{it} \tag{40}$$

Introducing $\bar{x}_{i\cdot}$ to the intercept equation will account for the correlation of x_{it} with u_{0i}, the orig-inal source of unobserved hetergeneity bias.

The growth model of Equation (40) blurs the distinction between random and fixed effect models: it is a random effects model that yields the same estimators of key parameters as a fixed effects model. Generalized least-squares (or maximum likelihood) estimation of this random effects model will yield a consistent estimator of γ_x (and γ_{10}) even if x_{it} is corre-lated with the original person effect u_{0i}. In fact, GLS estimation yields exactly the same parameter estimates, standard errors and test statistics as least-squares applied to

$$(y_{it} - \bar{y}_{i\cdot}) = \gamma_{10}(T_{it} - \bar{T}_i) + \gamma_x(x_{it} - \bar{x}_{i\cdot}) + (e_{it} - \bar{e}_{i\cdot}) \tag{41}$$

---

*HLM5, a Windows program that I highly recommend and which I used to fit the wage growth equations, estimates the level 2 parameters (i.e., γ_{00}, γ_{10}, etc.) by generalized least-squares and the variance parameters by maximum likelihood. Except for those with random slope effects, all the growth models of this section could be fit with identical results using the *xtreg* command in Stata7.

[†]This method was first introduced in the econometrics literature by Mundlak (1978). This method is typically used, for example, to control for "contextual" effects in multilevel models of student outcomes observed across many schools (Bryk & Raudenbush, 1992, p. 71). In those applications x_{it} might be a measure of the socioeconomic status of the tth student in the ith school with $\bar{x}_{i\cdot}$ the mean socioeconomic status of all students in the ith school.

Hence, controlling for $\bar{x}_{i.}$ in Equation (40) has the same effect as the mean-deviation transformation (Baltagi, 1995, p. 117): it eliminates the correlation of x_{it} with the source of unobserved heterogeneity u_{0i}.*

Generalized least-squares estimation of the random effects model

$$y_{it} = \gamma_{00} + \gamma_{10}T_{it} + \gamma_x(x_{it} - \bar{x}_{i.}) + (\gamma_{0\bar{x}} + \gamma_x)\bar{x}_{i.} + v_{0i} + e_{it} \tag{42}$$

also yields the within estimator of the parameters. This model is statistically equivalent to the model of Equation (40): the point estimates of all the parameters are identical, as are the estimates of the variances (σ_e^2 and τ_0^2) and standard errors.[†] To be sure, the estimated coefficient of $\bar{x}_{i.}$ will usually differ between the two models, since it represents different parameters. In Equation (42), the parameter $(\gamma_{0\bar{x}} + \gamma_x)$ can be shown to be the coefficient of $\bar{x}_{it}$ from the "between" regression of $\bar{y}_{i.}$ on $\bar{x}_{i.}$ and $T_{i.}$. In contrast, $\gamma_{0\bar{x}}$, the coefficient of $\bar{x}_{it}$ in Equation (40), is the *difference* in the between and within estimators of γ_x. Hence, $\gamma_{0\bar{x}}$ reflects the extent to which x_{it} is correlated with the unobserved person effect u_{0i} (see Equation [39]), so that fitting Equation (40) yields a specification test. The estimated coefficient $\hat{\gamma}_{0\bar{x}}$ is an indication of the heterogeneity bias in the standard GLS random effects estimator of γ_x if $\bar{x}_{i.}$ were omitted from Equation (40). Indeed, squaring the ratio of $\hat{\gamma}_{0\bar{x}}$ to its standard error essentially yields a Hausman χ^2 test of correlated individual effects (Arrelano, 1993; Baltagi, 1995, p. 69; Hausman, 1978, p. 1263).[‡] If $\gamma_{0\bar{x}} = 0$ cannot be rejected, then $u_{0i} = v_{0i}$ and the model becomes

$$y_{it} = \gamma_{00} + \gamma_{10}T_{it} + \gamma_x x_{it} + u_{0i} + e_{it} \tag{43}$$

for which GLS random effects estimation will yield consistent and efficient estimators. If $\gamma_{0\bar{x}} = 0$ is rejected, then random effects estimation of Equation (40) (or 42) will yield the unbiased and consistent within estimator of γ_x.

The results of fitting Equations (38) and (40) to the NLSY wage data are given in columns 1 (standard GLS) and 2 (GLS fixed effect) of Table 23.3. The estimates for socioeconomic status, marital status, and union membership are virtually identical to those given earlier (Table 23.2).[¶] Before we saw that the difference between these estimates indicated that the time-varying explanatory variables are correlated with the person effects, making GLS estimates biased. This same result is indicated in column 2 by the coefficients of the time means (i.e., $\bar{x}_{i.}$, here called "heterogeneity terms") for the explanatory variables. As before, these coefficients, which are all significant, indicate that the GLS estimator overstates the effects of changes in socioeconomic status, marital status, and union membership on changes in hourly wage. Occupational socioeconomic status is most strongly correlated with omitted time-invariant person effects, as found earlier. The hypothesis that all three coefficients for heterogeneity bias are zero is easily rejected (Wald $\chi^2 = 71$), as is the hypothesis that the intercept variance $\tau_0^2 = 0$ ($\chi^2 = 1600$).

---

*The estimator of γ_x obtained by including $\bar{x}_{i.}$ as a regressor also has another interpretation: it is the instrumental variables estimator that results when $(x_{it} - \bar{x}_{i.})$ is used as an instrument for x_{it} in the least-squares regression of y_{it} on T_{it} and x_{it}.

[†]These equivalencies also hold when a random slope effect u_{1i} is included; they do not hold when the coefficient of x_{it} is itself random.

[‡]Relevant here is the omitted variable interpretation of the Hausman test (Maddalla 2000 p. 498). In particular, if $\bar{x}_{i.}$ in Equation (40) is replaced by the residuals from the regression of x_{it} on $(x_{it} - \bar{x}_{i.})$, the parameter estimates and standard errors would be exactly identical. Since the coefficient of the residuals indicates heterogeneity bias, so too does the coefficient of $\bar{x}_{i.}$, since they are the same.

[¶]The very slight difference is totally due to the different time functions.

TABLE 23-3. **Wage Models; Full-time Employed Males, 1980–1987 ($N = 544$ and $T = 8$)**

	Models						
Independent variables	1	2	3	4	5	6	7
Constant	1.31	0.904	0.907	0.985	0.702	0.702	0.539
	(55)	(17)	17)	(15)	(5.8)	(5.4)	(4.2)
Year	0.057	0.059	0.059	0.036	0.019	0.019	0.033
	(22)	(22.7)	(17)	(3.2)	(1.2)	(0.9)	(1.5)
Level 1 effects							
Occupational status	0.024	0.012	0.008	0.006			0.006
	(4.8)	(2.3)	(1.4)	(1.1)			(1.1)
Married (= 1)	0.081	0.059	0.059	0.058			0.057
	(4.8)	(3.2)	(3.1)	(3.0)			(3.0)
Union (= 1)	0.116	0.086	0.084	0.086			0.087
	(6.4)	(4.4)	(4.3)	(4.5)			(4.5)
Level 2 effects (intercept)							
Black (= 1)					−0.062	−0.062	−0.051
					(1.1)	(1.0)	(0.9)
Schooling (years)					−0.062	0.062	0.051
					(6.2)	(5.6)	(4.2)
Level 2 effects (slope)							
Black (= 1)					−0.019	−0.019	−0.017
					(2.6)	(1.9)	(1.7)
Schooling					0.003	0.004	0.001
					(2.9)	(2.1)	(0.4)
Heterogeneity terms (intercept)							
Occupational status (SEI/10)		0.103	0.106	0.073			0.031
		(7.0)	(7.2)	(4.2)			(1.6)
Union (= 1)		0.264	0.268	0.299			0.268
		(5.1)	(5.2)	(4.9)			(4.3)
Married (= 1)		0.140	0.142	0.198			0.182
		(3.2)	(3.2)	(3.8)			(3.5)
χ^2		71	75	49			33
Heterogeneity terms (slope)							
Occupational status (SEI/10)				0.010			0.009
				(3.6)			(2.8)
Union (= 1)				−0.010			−0.008
				(1.0)			(0.8)
Married (= 1)				−0.016			−0.019
				(1.9)			(2.2)
χ^2				22			17
Variance components							
τ^2_0	0.123	0.109	0.143	0.141	0.117	0.157	0.134
	(1695)	(1600)	(871)	(878)	(1710)	(972)	(830)
τ^2_1			0.003	0.003		0.003	0.003
			(183)	(165)		(180)	(162)
σ^2_e	0.125	0.125	0.106	0.106	0.125	0.107	0.106
Deviance $-2\log(L)$	4496	4428	4245	4224	4484	4304	4186

Note: Appearing in parentheses below the coefficients and variance components are the *t*-ratios and χ^2 statistics, respectively.

The next logical direction in which the level 2 model might be revised is given by

$$\beta_{0i} = \gamma_{00} + \gamma_{0x}\bar{x}_{i.} + v_{0i} \tag{44}$$

$$\beta_{1i} = \gamma_{10} + u_{1i} \tag{45}$$

$$\beta_{xi} = \gamma_{x} \tag{46}$$

where the rate of change is now subject to the random person effect u_{1i}. The full combined model is

$$y_{it} = \gamma_{00} + \gamma_{10}T_{it} + \gamma_{x}x_{it} + \gamma_{0x}\bar{x}_{i.} + u_{1i}T_{it} + v_{0i} + e_{it} \tag{47}$$

which is the final form of the models fit by Horney et al. (1995) in their study of criminal careers. GLS random effects estimation will yield a consistent estimator of γ_x if either $\tau_1^2 = 0$ or, failing that, x_{it} is uncorrelated with the individual time-invariant person slope effects u_{1i}. One signal of the latter problem would be a sharp difference between the fixed effects estimates of γ_x and the estimates when a random slope effect is added to the model. The results of fitting this model to the NLSY data are given in column 3 of Table 23.3. The hypothesis $\tau_1^2 = 0$ is easily rejected $\tau_1^2 = 0.003$, $\chi^2 = 183$, $p < 0.0001$), so there remains significant variation in wage growth rates even after taking account of within and between variation in occupational status, marital status, and union membership. Virtually all the coefficients unchanged from their previous values, with one exception: the coefficient of occupational status drops sharply to 0.008 from 0.012. This suggests correlated unobservable random slope effects, especially for occupational status.

One way to assess whether estimates of γ_x reflect unobservable slope effects is to model the correlation between u_{1i} and the explanatory variables. Hence, suppose that unobservable slope effects are related to the means of the explanatory variables as follows:

$$u_{1i} = \gamma_{1x}\bar{x}_i + v_{1i} \tag{48}$$

The level 2 regressions for the intercept β_{0i} and slope β_{1i} of the growth function then become

$$\beta_{0i} = \gamma_{00} + \gamma_{0x}\bar{x}_{i.} + v_{0i} \tag{49}$$

$$\beta_{1i} = \gamma_{10} + \gamma_{1x}\bar{x}_{i.} + v_{1i} \tag{50}$$

The full combined model is then

$$y_{it} = \gamma_{00} + \gamma_{10}T_{it} + \gamma_{x}x_{it} + \gamma_{0x}\bar{x}_{i.} + \gamma_{1x}\bar{x}_{i.}T_{it} + v_{0i} + v_{1i}T_{it} + e_{it} \tag{51}$$

where we see that introducing $\bar{x}_{it}$ to the slope equation yields an "interaction" term $\gamma_{1x}\bar{x}_{i.}T_{it}$ in the full model. The rate of growth in y_{it} is now $(\gamma_{10} + \gamma_{1x}\bar{x}_{i.} + v_{1i})$; γ_{1x} gives the expected difference in the rate of growth for persons who are one unit apart on the mean of the explanatory variable $\bar{x}_{i.}$. A χ^2 test of $\gamma_{1x} = 0$ can be used to check for an association between the explanatory variables and the rate of change in the response variable. Applied to the NLSY wage data, this test yields $\chi^2 = 22$ (see column 4 in Table 23-3), which is significant ($p < 0.001$). Judging by the t-statistics, the wage trajectory varies most with mean occupational status, which appears to be associated with a heightened rate of wage growth. The coefficients for union membership and marital status indicate that both are associated with a slower rate of wage growth, though only the latter is marginally significant. These results indicate that the GLS estimates of the γ_x parameters of the model of Equation (47) are biased by correlated slope effects, especially with respect to occupational status. Hence, comparing the estimates of the γ_x parameters in column 4 and column 3 shows that controlling for correlated slope effects has a proportionately larger impact on the coefficient of occupational status, which drops to 0.006 from 0.008, than on the coefficients of either marital status or union membership, which barely change. On the whole, this final model gives reliable evidence that changes in union membership and marital status, but probably not occupational status, yield changes in mean hourly wage. Note that the slope variance $\tau_1^2 = 0.003$ (Table 23-3, model 4) remains highly significant $\chi^2 = 165$), so that neither between nor within variation in this set of explanatory variables does much to account for individual differences in wage trajectories.

Time-Invariant Explanatory Variables

The principal reason behind including time-varying covariates in growth models is the same as in other contexts: to estimate the effect of changes in the explanatory variables on changes over time in the mean of the response variable.* Yet most applications of growth modeling omit time-varying covariates altogether: instead the focus is on describing between-unit variation in the parameters governing growth by expanding the level 2 model for the intercept and slope to include time-invariant properties of the units. This describes the Cherlin et al. (1998) study of the effect of divorce on children's mental health. Their growth models include no time-varying covariates at all in the level 1 regression; time-invariant properties are introduced to the level 2 intercept and slope equations. Similarly, McLeod and Shanahan's (1996) models for childhood depression and antisocial behavior are formulated exclusively in terms of time-invariant explanatory variables that appear in the level 2 equations. Such models follow the same principles already discussed for time-varying explanatory variables, though with limitations.

The typical level 2 equations for a model with time-invariant explanatory variables are

$$\beta_{0i} = \gamma_{00} + \gamma_{0z}z_i + u_{0i} \tag{52}$$

$$\beta_{1i} = \gamma_{10} + \gamma_{1z}z_i + u_{1i} \tag{53}$$

where z_i is a metric or categorical variable believed to influence both the baseline level of the response variable and its rate of growth.[†‡] Combining this level 2 model with a linear level 1 model for trend (ignoring time-varying explanatory variables) yields the full equation for y_{it}:

$$y_{it} = \gamma_{00} + \gamma_{1,0}T_{it} + \gamma_{0z}z_i + \gamma_{1z}z_iT_{it} + u_{0i} + u_{1i}T_{it} + e_{it} \tag{54}$$

---

*Our aim in including $\bar{x}_i$ in the level 2 regressions discussed above was largely a matter of controlling unobserved heterogeneity bias that threatened the estimation of γ_x; it was not a matter of "explaining" between-unit variation in the intercept and slope of the growth path.

†The analogy to contextual effects in research on schools or neighborhoods is again relevant. Hence, z_i might indicate for the ith school whether it is public or private or the proportion of teachers with advanced degrees; it would be student invariant, since it would take on the same value for all students in the ith school.

‡The same variables are usually included in both level 2 equations (e.g., Cherlin et al., 1998). At the very least, explanatory variables appearing in the slope equation would also appear in the intercept equation, the principal being the usual one of only including interactions after main effects have been accounted for.

The interpretations of the intercept and slope parameters governing the differences associated with z_i are identical to those discussed above for the case of the over time mean $\bar{x}_{i.}$.*

The time invariance of z_i has rather different implications for the estimation of the mean parameter γ_{0z} and rate parameter γ_{1z}. Because z_i is time invariant, the formulation used to deal with unobserved heterogeneity in the case of a time-varying explanatory variables is not available: there is no difference between z_i and its mean over time, no within-variation in z_i, so the parameter γ_{0z} for the effect of z_i on the mean of y_{it} cannot be distinguished from the person-specific effects u_{0i} with which z_i is perfectly correlated. This is not to say that an estimate $\hat{\gamma}_{0z}$ cannot be produced, but only that its relationship to the true parameter is clouded by unobserved heterogeneity. Hence, the GLS random effects estimator, $\hat{\gamma}_{0z}$ say, will be a function of the true parameter γ_{0z} and a parameter λu_{0iz}, say, for the correlation of z with the unobserved individual effects. There is no way within a random effects framework to identify these two parameters short of assuming that z_i is uncorrelated with u_{0i}.† Since such an assumption may be too strong with observational data, consistent estimation of γ_{0z} for the effect of z_i on the mean of y_{it} at baseline is problematic. Yet this is not of great consequence for most growth modeling applications: most researchers are not very interested in the effect of explanatory variables on the baseline mean of the response variable. Indeed, estimating such effects is mainly a cross-sectional exercise for which panel data are largely irrelevant.

In most growth modeling, the parameter of theoretical interest is γ_{1z} for the interaction of z_i and T_{it}, since this shows how the rate of change or trajectory of the response variable varies with z_i. For some models, this parameter can be consistently estimated without threat of heterogeneity bias, as in the model of Table 23.2. For example, when the slope equation is specified as non-random ($\tau_1^2 = 0$), the combined model becomes

$$y_{it} = \gamma_{00} + \gamma_{1,0}T_{it} + \gamma_{0z}z_i + \gamma_{1z}z_iT_{it} + u_{0i} + e_{it} \tag{55}$$

Although the term z_iT_{it} varies between-units as well as overtime, the "main effect" term for z_i partials out the between-variation and controls for unobserved heterogeneity generated by u_{0i}. The upshot is that GLS random effects estimation of Equation (55) yields the within estimator of the key parameter γ_{1z} and exactly the same standard errors and test statistics as fixed effects estimation.‡

Column 5 of Table 23.3 gives the fitted model (Equation [55]) showing the effects of race and schooling on the wage growth trajectory for the NLSY data. The estimated slope parameters indicate that Black wages grew at an annual rate of 1.9% less than that of others and that each year of schooling increased the rate of growth in wages by about 0.3% (equivalently, the annual rate of return to schooling increased by 0.3% over this 8-year period). Column 6 gives the estimates of Equation (54), where the random slope effect u_{1i} is included so that τ_1^2 is no longer fixed at zero. The point estimates are strikingly similar to their fixed effect counterparts in column 5, although the t-statistics are smaller because the fixed effect estimator understates the true standard errors when, as is the case here, $\tau_1^2 > 0$.

---

*The intercept is ($\gamma_{00} + \gamma_{0z}z_i + u_{0i}$), with γ_{0z} capturing the mean difference in the response variable at baseline for persons one unit apart on (or in different categories of) the z metric; the rate of change in y_{it} is ($\gamma_{10} + \gamma_{1z}z_i + u_{1i}$), with γ_{1z} capturing differences in the rate of change in y_{it} for different values of z. To the extent that z_i is a source of between-unit variation, the expectation is $\tau_{0|z}^2 < \tau_0^2$ and $\tau_{1|z}^2 < \tau_1^2$. Again, a likelihood ratio test of $\tau_{0|z}^2 = \tau_{1|z}^2 = 0$ would be appropriate.
†Instrumental variable estimation would be an appropriate alternative (Hausman & Taylor, 1981).
‡Note the parallel to the case of time-varying explanatory variables: just as consistent estimation of γ_x, the parameter for the effect of changes in x_{it} on changes in the response variable y_{it}, calls for controlling $\bar{x}_{i.}$, so too consistent estimation of γ_{1z}, the parameter for between-group variation in growth trajectories, calls for controlling z_i.

The GLS estimates of the γ_{1z} parameters for race and schooling differences in the rate of wage growth are consistent if both variables are uncorrelated with the unobserved random slope effect u_{1i}. In general, the prospects for obtaining consistent estimators of γ_{1z} parameters are less bleak than those for the γ_{0z} parameters: the existence of time-invariant, person-specific random *slope* effects is not nearly as theoretically or empirically compelling, especially over long periods, as person-specific random intercept effects. Hence, assuming that time-invariant covariates are uncorrelated with individual slope effects like u_{1i} is weaker than assuming they are uncorrelated with baseline effects like u_{0i}. There is also likely to be considerably less heterogeneity to begin with in random slope effects than in random intercept effects, so bias induced by the former in estimates of γ_{1z} parameters is likely to be much less than that induced by the latter in estimates of γ_{0i} parameters.*

Most applications of growth modeling focus on time invariant explanatory variables and exclude time-varying explanatory variables altogether. This practice might be justified by an interest in estimating reduced-form models for the "total effects" of time-invariant background variables, although such justification is rarely expressed. In any event, there is no reason why the two types of explanatory variables cannot be mixed just as in any panel analysis. Indeed, omitting relevant level 1 time-varying explanatory variables can impact estimates of the γ_{1z} rate parameters. As an illustration, column 7 of Table 23.3 gives a fitted model that joins the model of column 4 for the effects of changes in the time-varying explanatory variables on changes in wages, to the model of column 6 for the effects of time-invariant variables on the wage trajectory. The estimates of the level 1 γ_x parameters for occupational status, marital status, and union membership are virtually identical to their previous values; similarly, the estimates of the γ_{0z} parameters for the intercept effects of race and schooling are hardly changed. The estimates of the level 2 γ_{1z} slope parameters for race and schooling have diminished, especially that for schooling, which now appears to have no net association with wage growth when the time-varying explanatory variables are controlled.

CONCLUSION

The purpose of this review has been to give an integrated account of the considerations and methods that underlie the use of panel data in life course studies aimed at (1) the estimation of the effect of a change in an explanatory variable on the change in a response variable and (2) the analysis of variation in growth trajectories. Issues of bias and consistency due to unobserved heterogeneity have been a central theme because in static models they take priority over and are separable from questions of efficiency and the estimation of random components of variation. Methods for dealing with complex error structures, including those characterized by heterogeneity over time or serial correlation have not been discussed here, but are available for growth models as for more standard panel models (Bryk & Raudenbush, 1992; Goldstein, 1995; Wooldridge, 2000, Chs 12 and 13). Yet such methods assume less practical significance with the arrival of routine procedures for the robust estimation of standard errors. In contrast, the effect of unobserved heterogeneity on estimators is a persistent and core issue in the treatment of models that extend beyond those examined here and, hence, forms something of an organizing principle for those who wish to explore other applications of panel analysis to life course phenomena. For example, guarding against unobserved heterogeneity,

---

*As observed earlier, in observational studies τ_1^2 typically constitutes a much smaller fraction of the total variation in the response variable than does τ_0^2.

along with the attendant issues of fixed as compared to random effects, is at the heart of questions pertaining to the estimation of panel models for limited dependent variables (Maddalla, 1986) and for dynamic social processes (Nickell, 1981).

The effort to deal with unobserved heterogeneity has not always been at the forefront of the concerns motivating the choice of statistical methods by life course researchers. The irony in this is that life course research is uniquely positioned to take advantage of the simple procedures outlined here, since the use of longitudinal data is in a real sense constitutive of the mission of life course studies. Yet life course researchers have only recently begun to exploit the power of panel methods for illuminating the social and psychological changes that accompany the transitions that mark the stages of the life course and that drive the evolution of developmental trajectories. As the study of the life course matures, research increasingly will move away from the ad hoc application of regression methods that fail to exploit the potential of longitudinal data and toward the more systematic and theoretically grounded approaches to panel data that the methods reviewed in this chapter make possible.

REFERENCES

Allison, P. (1994). Using panel data to estimate the effects of events. *Sociological Methods and Research, 23,* 174–199.

Angrist, J. D. (1995). The economic returns to schooling in the West Bank and Gaza Strip. *The American Economic Review, 85,* 1065–1087.

Angrist, J. D., & Newey, K. N. (1991) Over-identification tests in earnings functions with fixed effects. *Journal of Business and Statistics, 9,* 317–324.

Arellano, M. (1993). On the testing of correlated effects in panel data. *Journal of Econometrics,* 87–97.

Ashenfelter, O., & Krueger, A. (1994). Estimates of the economic return to schooling from a new sample of twins. *The American Economic Review, 84,* 1157–1173.

Baltagi, B. H. (1995). *Econometric analysis of panel data.* Chichester: John Wiley & Sons.

Barnett, R. C., Raudenbush, S. W., Brennan, R. T., Pleck, J., & Marshall, N. (1995). Change in job and marital experiences and change in psychological distress: a longitudinal study of dual-earner couples. *Journal of Personality and Social Psychology, 69,* 839–850.

Biblarz, T. J., & Raftery, A. E. (1993) The effects of family disruption on social mobility. *American Sociological Review, 58,* 97–109.

Blau, D. M. (1999). The effects of child care characteristics on child development. *Journal of Human Resources, 34,* 786–822.

Booth, A., & Amato, P. (1991). Divorce and psychological stress. *Journal of Health and Social Behavior, 32,* 396–407.

Bryk, A. S., & Raudenbush, S. W. (1992). *Hierarchical linear models.* Newbury Park, CA: Sage.

Budig, M. J., & England, P. (2001). The wage penalty for motherhood. *American Sociological Review, 66,* 204–225.

Campbell, D. T., & Stanley, J. C. (1963). *Experimental and quasi-experimental designs for research.* Chicago: Rand McNally.

Chase-Lansdale, P. L., Cherlin, A., & Kiernan, K. (1995). The long-term effects of parental divorce on the mental health of young adults: A developmental perspective. *Child Development, 66,* 1614–1634.

Cherlin, A. J., Chase-Lansdale, P. L., & McRae, C. (1998). Effects of parental divorce on mental health throughout the life course. *American Sociological Review, 63,* 239–249.

Diggle, P. J., Liang, K.-Y., & Zeger, S. L. (1994). *Analysis of longitudinal data.* Oxford: Clarendon Press.

Goldstein, H. (1995). *Multilevel statistical models.* London: Edward Arnold.

Hausman, J. A. (1978). Specification tests in econometrics. *Econometrica, 46,* 1251–1272.

Hausman, J. A., & Taylor, W. E. (1981). Panel data and unobservable individual effects. *Econometrica, 49,* 1377–1398.

Holland, P. (1986). Statistics and causal inference. *Journal of the American Statistical Association, 81,* 945–960.

Horney, J., Osgood, D. W., & Marshall, I. H. (1995). Criminal careers in the short-term: intra-individual variability in crime and its relation to local life circumstance. *American Sociological Review, 60,* 655–673.

Hsaio, C. (1986). *Analysis of panel data.* New York: Cambridge University Press.

Johnson, D. R. (1995). Alternative methods for the quantitative analysis of panel data in family research. *Journal of Marriage and the Family, 57*, 1065–1086.

Karney, B. R., & Bradbury, T. N. (1995). Assessing longitudinal change in marriage: An introduction to the analysis of growth curves. *Journal of Marriage and the Family, 57*, 1091–1108.

Kreft, I. G., de Leeuw, J., & Aiken, L. S. (1995). The effect of different forms of centering in hierarchical linear models. *Multivariate Behavioral Research, 30*, 1–21.

Laird, N. M., & Ware, J. H. (1982). Random-effects models for longitudinal data. *Biometrics, 38*, 963–974.

Land, K., & Nagin, D. (1996). Micro-models of criminal careers: a synthesis of the criminal careers and life course approaches via semiparametric mixed poisson models with empirical applications. *Journal of Quantitative Criminology, 12*, 163–191.

Little, T. D., Schnabel, K. U., & Baumert, J. (Eds), (2000). *Modeling longitudinal and multilevel data*. Mahweh, NJ: Lawrence Erlbaum.

McArdle, J. J., & Epstein, D. (1987). Latent growth curves within developmental structural equation models. *Child Development, 58*, 110–133.

McLeod, J. D., & Shanahan, M. J. (1996). Trajectories of poverty and children's mental health. *Journal of Health and Social Behavior, 37*, 207–220.

McManus, P. A., & DiPrete, T. A. (2001). Losers and winners: The financial consequences of separation and divorce for men. *American Sociological Review, 66*, 246–268.

Maddalla, G. S. (1986). Limited dependent variable models using panel data. *Journal of Human Resources, 22*, 307–338.

Maddalla, G. S. (1988). *Introduction to econometrics*. New York: Macmillan.

Moen, P., Robison, J., & Dempster-McClain, D. (1995). Caregiving and women's well-being: A life course approach. *Journal of Health and Social Behavior, 36*, 259–273.

Mundlak, Y. (1978). On the pooling of time series and cross section data. *Econometrica, 46*, 69–85.

Muthen, B. (1997). Latent variable modeling with longitudinal and multilevel data. In A. Raftery (Ed.), *Sociological methodology* (pp. 453–480). Boston, MA: Blackwell.

Nagin, D. (1999). Analyzing developmental trajectories: a semiparametric, group-based approach. *Psychological Methods, 4*, 139–157.

Nagin, D., & Tremblay, R. E. (1999). Trajectories of boys' physical aggression, opposition, and hyperactivity on the path to physically violent and nonviolent juvenile delinquency. *Child Development, 70*, 1181–1196.

Nickell, S. (1981). Biases in dynamic models with fixed effects. *Econometrica, 49*, 1417–1426.

Peracchi, F. (2001). *Econometrics*. Chichester: John Wiley & Sons.

Sampson, R., & Laub, J. H. (1992). Crime and deviance in the life course. *Annual Review of Sociology, 18*, 63–84.

Snijders, T., & Bosker, R. (1999). *Multilevel analysis: An introduction to basic and advanced multilevel modeling*. London: Sage.

Thornton, A., Axinn, W. G., & Teachman, J. D. (1995). The influence of school enrollment and accumulation on cohabitation and marriage in early adulthood. *American Sociological Review, 60*, 762–774.

Waldfogel, J. (1997). The effects of children on women's wages. *American Sociological Review, 62*, 209–217.

Willett, J. B., & Sayer, A. G. (1994). Using covariance structure analysis to detect correlates and predictors of individual change over time. *Psychological Bulletin, 116*, 363–381.

Willett, J. B., Singer, J. D., & Martin, N. C. (1998). The design and analysis of longitudinal studies of development and psychopathology in context: Statistical models and methodological recommendations. *Development and Psychopathology, 10*, 395–426.

Wooldridge, J. M. (1995). Selection corrections for panel data models under conditional mean independence assumptions. *Journal of Econometrics, 68*, 115–132.

Wooldridge, J. M. (2000). *Introductory econometrics: A modern approach*. South-Western College Publishing.

CHAPTER 24

Characterizing the Life Course as Role Configurations and Pathways

A Latent Structure Approach

ROSS MACMILLAN

SCOTT R. ELIASON

The life course is a multi-faceted phenomenon. It involves a complex interplay among psychological orientations and behaviors; past experiences and future actions; age and cohort influences; network, historical, and institutional contexts that provide an environment of opportunities and constraints; and the interconnections among social roles that change over time in that environment. All of these coalesce to set the stage for life chances and personal wellbeing throughout one's life. The life course itself constitutes a social institution, cutting pathways through time and creating a gravity of sorts, varyingly attracting individual lives into role configurations conforming to age-graded norms. Research on the life course and the development of accompanying theories thus grapples with a wide array of issues, have numerous foci, and draw upon a number of disciplines in order to understand the social context of human lives over time (Elder, 1994).

George (*this volume*) argues that life course research involves two rather distinct avenues of inquiry. One focuses on the life course *itself*. This work examines the shape and structure of

ROSS MACMILLAN • Department of Sociology, University of Minnesota, Minneapolis, Minnesota 55455
SCOTT R. ELIASON • Department of Sociology, University of Minnesota, Minneapolis, Minnesota 55455

Handbook of the Life Course, edited by Jeylan T. Mortimer and Michael J. Shanahan. Kluwer Academic/Plenum Publishers, New York, 2003.

the life course, its historical emergence, its structural and cultural underpinnings, and the impact of historical events on the life course. The core of this work is variation in the life course and an examination of the social characteristics and conditions that generate diversity. A second body of research incorporates life course principles into a variety of substantive areas. Questions of stability and change, timing and order, the occurrence and sequencing of social roles, social relations, and social experiences are all important aspects of research in fields like stratification, social psychology, and social movements (Hagan, 2001; Warren, Hauser, & Sheridan, 2002; Wheaton, 1990). They are also central to research on a wide array of topics like work, family, health, and involvement in crime and deviance (Conger & Elder, 1994; Han & Moen, 1999; Sampson & Laub, 1993).

In both areas of inquiry, however, it is somewhat ironic that the life course as a *multifaceted phenomenon* is seldom precisely operationalized and measured. This is especially so if one adheres to Elder's (1985) characterization of the life course as the age-graded movement through social institutions or if one conceptualizes the life course as the interlocked trajectories, or pathways, of social roles over time. This phenomenon, as a whole, has seldom been the object of inquiry. Instead, researchers most often identify some specific aspect of the life course (e.g., the transition from school to work or the timing of first birth), operationalize its dimensions such that it is amenable to inquiry using traditional statistical techniques (e.g., linear and logit regressions or event history models), and then assess the implications of the empirical results. Such work ultimately dissects the life course into various components and focuses attention solely on these components. Although useful to a degree in our efforts to understand individual components of the life course, this approach necessarily limits attention to the specific (out-of-context) aspects of the life course. This, in turn, limits our efforts to understand the life course as a biographical, multi-faceted phenomenon and to understand the consequences for life chances in a multiplex of domains.

In this chapter we elaborate existing theory and introduce a statistical approach consistent with understanding the life course as probabilistically interlocked trajectories, or pathways, of social roles over time. Specifically, we draw upon Elder's (1985) conceptualization of the life course as the interdependent trajectories of social roles over time and propose a two-tiered latent class model derived from this conceptual understanding. This framework allows us to identify *configurations of social roles* over time and *life paths* that link these role configurations over the life course.

Below, we discuss the theoretical foundation and statistical mechanics of this approach, and demonstrate its utility for modeling the life course. We further provide an empirical example, focusing on the extended pathway from mid-adolescence to mid-adulthood in a national sample of Americans. We then discuss the applications of this framework for a wide range of life course issues. Finally, we conclude with some comments on the potential of this approach to address key theoretical and empirical issues in both life course research and the social sciences in general.

CONCEPTUALIZING THE LIFE COURSE—TRAJECTORIES AND TRANSITIONS

Elder (1985, p. 30) characterizes the life course as a "multidimensional concept of interdependent careers or trajectories—work life, marriage, and parenthood." A key aspect of the life course is thus the age-structured movement into, through, and out of social institutions, and the age-structured configuration of roles an individual takes on. Individual experience and agency interact with the broader social and cultural context to shape the occurrence, timing, and order by which individuals move through different institutional contexts and assume configurations of social roles.

Two concepts, *trajectories* and *transitions*, are considered central descriptors of the life course (Elder, 1985). Trajectories most often refer to long-term involvement in or connection to social institutions and corresponding roles. Conceptually similar to notions of "careers," trajectories can be charted by linking institutionally defined roles or "states" over time and are often characterized by specific events with a definable sequence, duration, and order. Institutionally defined role trajectories, in essence, indicate the degree to, and the way in, which someone is embedded in a particular institutional context over time.

The companion concept, transitions, typically refers to specific events that move an individual into or out of various institutional contexts and corresponding role configurations. We identify the transition to marriage by the event of actually "getting married." Transitions out of school can involve the dropping out of high school, graduating, or, as of late, simply quitting higher education. Transitions into work involve the acquisition of full-time, full-year work.

Each of these indicates movement from one set of roles to another, or a change in an individual's socially and/or institutionally defined role configurations. These transitions may be thought of as embedded in trajectories that give them specific form and meaning. They help to define trajectories by indicating when a particular trajectory began or ended and indicate duration, how long a particular trajectory has lasted. Information on the timing of such transitions in individual lives allows social scientists to consider the degree to which trajectories and transitions correspond or deviate from social expectations and whether this is consequential for life chances (Hogan, 1978; Marini, 1984; Rindfuss, Swicegood, & Rosenfeld, 1987).

Trajectories and transitions provide a useful conceptual apparatus to help us understand and describe the totality of the life course. They indicate stability or change over time in a given social role. Yet, they also provide tools for mapping out broader life course dynamics. Seldom can we describe the totality of the life courses by a single set of trajectories and transitions alone. Instead, an individual's life course involves the *interplay among multiple trajectories and transitions*, and the variable ways in which these interconnected trajectories unfold in concert over time (Elder, 1985, p. 32).

Life course trajectories are interdependent phenomena, with each trajectory in part influenced by the shape of other trajectories. Marriage, for example, may follow from the completion of school and movement into full-time work due to the stabilizing of socioeconomic resources (Hogan, 1978; Neugarten, Moore, & Lowe, 1965). Likewise, occurrences within one trajectory may also influence occurrences within another trajectory. Problems in higher education, for example, may lead to greater commitment to work or vice versa. Problems in higher education may also lead to an earlier than anticipated marriage, which then influences the onset of parenthood (Schneider & Stevenson, 1999).

Understanding the life course as such a dynamic phenomenon thus requires attention to an unfolding, multidimensional process that transcends individual trajectories or even pairs of trajectories. It requires attention to the simultaneous interlocking of various trajectories over time and how this, rather than the individual trajectories, characterizes the life course.

METHODOLOGICAL CHALLENGES

Standard methodological and statistical approaches cannot easily accommodate such theoretical issues. Several problems arise. Most generally, identification or designation of cause and effect becomes problematic. In much traditional research, causes and effects are clearly delineated, or at least they are articulated as aspects of an endogenous system in which initial effects become later causes. The notion of interlocked trajectories suggests that separating causes from effects may not be so easy.

First, the interlocking or conjoining of trajectories may not be the result of causal relations among variables in the traditional sense. Instead, they may reflect a process that is largely responsive to broader social or cultural conditions and/or norms. Elder (1998) notes in his classic study that the impact of the Great Depression was diverse: it simultaneously affected various life course trajectories. The economic downturn influenced who was working, when people moved into work, the timing of marriage, and consequently the timing of parenthood. More recently, scholars of the transition to adulthood suggest that a changing economy has altered school to work transitions, causing increased overlap and lengthening the time taken to move into full time work (Shanahan, 2000). Such structural change has further consequences for the occurrence and timing of marriage and parenthood (Oppenheimer & Lewin, 1999). A focus on causal relations, in the traditional counterfactual sense, may hide the life course as a biography, shifting inquiry away from the whole and towards individual parts as though these were independent processes.

Issues of cause and effect are further complicated by the emphasis on agency in life course research (Elder, 1994). In any context, agency can involve orientations towards the past, the present, and the future (Emirbayer & Mische, 1998). It can involve the effects of past experiences on current behaviors. It can involve the rational calculation and assessment of current situations and circumstances. It can involve a projection into the future that then serves to orient present activities. Interlocked trajectories that define the life course may thus involve the effects of the past on the future but also the anticipated future on the present. Hence, anticipated effects may produce what is often considered (by the researcher) to be the cause of that effect, a phenomenon that Marini and Singer (1984) refer to as "reverse causation." Individual propensities may also lead one to be more past oriented, more present oriented, or more future oriented. Such orientations may structure the overall interlocking of an individual's trajectories over time. In the context of multiple, interconnected orientations, explicit designations of cause and effect in the life course may ultimately bear little resemblance to the reality of decision-making and choice in the life course.

Life course inquiry of the type that we have highlighted also suggests the necessity of defining an object of study based on the simultaneous interplay among multiple factors over time. This type of formulation is difficult to reconcile with traditional scale-based approaches to measurement that focus on the attenuation of measurement error through the use of multiple, substitutable items, such as LISREL-like measurement models.

Though not impossible, an examination of the life course as a whole is not well accomodated with statistical models that require a researcher to clearly delineate independent and dependent variables, exogenous and endogenous variables, causes and effects. These include traditional regression models, path analysis and structural equation models, and even models that are designed for modeling temporally dynamic processes, such as the usual growth curve models and traditional event history models. Hence, researchers relying on many of the traditional statistical techniques typically have few tools to examine the life course as a phenomenon involving multiple trajectories or pathways.

As a final concern, it is not straightforward how one effectively examines *heterogeneity* in life courses with many popular statistical techniques. A key issue in life course theory is the degree to which life courses vary across individuals, across social groups, across various contexts, and across historical time, and then the degree to which this variation is consequential for the human experience (Elder, 1994). In the face of this, contemporary research has adopted two approaches. One approach has been the transformation of components of the life course into measurable variables. Examining the interlocked trajectories of education and marriage, for example, is studied by examining the association between educational attainment (i.e., number of years completed, highest degree) and age at first child (Marini, 1978). Heterogeneity is then measured by the variation in specific variables. With few exceptions, this branch of research is forced to examine one particular type of interlock. Within this framework, heterogeneity is by definition restricted to that which can be detected through that one particular type.

A second approach examines the order and timing of social roles. In this case, researchers are confronted with literally thousands of combinations indicating movement into and out of roles over time (Hogan, 1978; Marini, 1984; Rindfuss et al., 1987). Heterogeneity here is extreme, even when stringent and often unrealistic restrictions are placed on the data (see discussions in Hogan, 1978; Rindfuss et al., 1987). While there appears to be more promise in the latter approach, there is still the problem of how one would identify meaningful variation, conceptually or empirically. Such work recognizes the importance of heterogeneity in life courses but has not developed a means of organizing such information to delineate the actual structure(s) of the life course and how these vary across groups, contexts, and time periods. In the end, the explicit focus on heterogeneity in the structure of the life course that is a centerpiece of contemporary theory has little visibility in contemporary research.

To be sure, we are not arguing here that traditional approaches are not useful in understanding various aspects of the life course. They have been the cornerstone of contemporary life course research, and much about the life course has been learned over the past 30 or so years in this endeavor. We do however note that their conceptual origins and key statistical features are not particularly consistent with key features of contemporary life course theory. The conceptualization of the life course as a multi-dimensional process, the potential interchange of (hypothesized) cause and effect, contingency and interaction in social roles over time, the simultaneity and reversibility of social roles over time, and the resulting heterogeneity that all of these in concert introduce into the structure and process of human lives make for an empirical phenomenon that is less than conducive to examination with many traditional statistical approaches. Against this backdrop, we propose in the following section a two-stage latent class model that allows us to examine the life course as a whole, to identify *configurations of social roles* over time and *life paths* that link these role configurations over the life course.

EXTENDING THE BASIC FOUNDATION—ROLE CONFIGURATIONS, LIFE PATHS, AND THE LATENT CLASS MODEL

Before elaborating the latent class model as a tool for understanding the life course as a whole, we first make explicit the conceptual foundation underlying this approach. Our theoretical foundation rests firmly on the trajectory and transition concepts described earlier. Yet, it focuses the lens more tightly on the life course as age-graded sets of role configurations and pathways through the changing nexus of these role configurations over the course of individual lives.

More precisely, we view individuals as being probabilistically distributed across various role configurations and life paths, partly insofar as others view and treat individuals differently in different interactions and insofar as individuals view themselves differently across those different interactions. To see this more concretely, let $i(t)$ for any one individual be a vector denoting the observed role configurations at age t. For example, $i(t)$ could be a vector of 1's and 0's denoting the presence or absence, respectively, of some combination of roles for individual i at age t. More generally, $i(t)$ denotes a multidimensional matrix or cross-classification of a set of observed variables defining various states of some social roles at age t. In our example below, we focus on the presence or absence of schooling, work, family, and parental roles.

Next, let $m(t)$ denote the latent role configuration underlying the observed role configuration $i(t)$ at age t. Heuristically, $m(t)$, under a good fitting model (to be discussed below), can be thought of as the minimal intrinsic set of unobserved role configurations giving rise to the observed role configurations in $i(t)$. Finally let j denote the age-graded life path characterized by the probabilistic transitions through the latent and observed role configurations.

With this theoretical framework, the life course is fully characterized by a set of joint probabilities, denoted here as $\pi_{i(1) \ldots i(T)m(1) \ldots m(T)j}$, describing an individual's chances, from ages $t = 1, \ldots, T$, of experiencing transitions through specified observed role configurations $i(1) \ldots i(T)$, latent role configurations $m(1) \ldots m(T)$, and latent life path j. Moreover, individuals observed in a specific role configuration at age t, as given by the vector $i(t)$, may be characterized by the probability of "being on" or "coming from" a specific (latent) life path, $\pi_{i(t)|j}$, or probabilistically "spread across" the diverse $j = 1, \ldots, J$ (latent) life paths.

These conditional probabilities are useful tools both in the description of the interconnectedness of life chances across "role domains" over various life paths in a specific society and historical era (e.g., how do types of schooling, work, marital, and parental roles interrelate over time in the predominant life path in a specific society). They also contribute to the prediction of subsequent role transitions for individuals (e.g., to dropping out of school or to unemployment). Moreover, researchers may assess the impact of the probability distributions of "being on" or "coming from" specific life paths on subsequent outcomes of interest (e.g., criminal or delinquent behavior, or various health-related episodes). Insofar that these probabilities accurately characterize varying life chances and life paths in a society, assessing the impact of these conditional probabilities on subsequent outcomes in individuals' lives constitutes no less than assessing the impact of the "life course" on such outcomes.

We describe these probabilities here, beginning with the standard latent class assumptions (see discussion in Clogg, 1995) linking the joint probability $\pi_{i(1) \ldots i(T)m(1) \ldots m(T)j}$ to the product of conditional probabilities of the observed role configurations given the latent role configurations and life paths. Using the above notation, the standard conditional independence assumption allows us to equate

$$\pi_{i(1) \ldots i(T)m(1) \ldots m(T)j} = \pi_{i(1)|m(1) \ldots m(T)j} \cdots \pi_{i(T)|m(1) \ldots m(T)j}\pi_{m(1) \ldots m(T)j} \tag{1}$$

Standard (full information) techniques to estimate the relevant probabilities and latent class model parameters in this case dictate that we obtain the entire transition matrix for the observed role configurations over the T ages. This presents one of the most daunting empirical issues confronting any attempt to understand the life course in this manner due to exceedingly sparse data in the cross-classification of observed role configurations over time. Consider, for example, a relatively coarse coding scheme in which we have four role variables—a dichotomy for schooling (in school or out of school), a trichotomy for work (full time employed, part time employed, not employed), trichotomy for marital status (never married, married, separated/divorced/widowed), and a dichotomy for having or not having children. At any one age, their cross-classification gives $2 \times 3 \times 3 \times 2 = 36$ cells. Now consider the transition matrix cross-classifying this role configuration matrix across five time periods/ages.

This cross-classification forming the observed transition matrix has over 60 million cells ($36^5 = 60,466,176$). To obtain an average of five cases per cell, so that one may reasonably assume that the large sample properties hold for the standard estimators of parameters for most models of contingency tables (e.g., loglinear, logit, and related models), a sample size of over 300 million ($5 \times 36^5 = 5 \times 60,466,176 = 302,330,880$) is necessary. Clearly, there is no sample currently known to the social science community that can reasonably be used in this context. Nor is it likely that a data set of this size will exist in the near future.

To solve this problem we consider some additional assumptions, to supplement those of the standard latent class model, that effectively restrict the observed role configurations and latent life paths to interact only through the latent role configurations. This appears as a reasonable restriction given that the latent role configurations under a good fitting latent class model contain all of the sample information regarding the association among the observed role configurations (Clogg, 1995). That is to say, the latent role configurations are sufficient, from a statistical and informational standpoint, to understand the associations among the observed role configurations. These additional assumptions, which we elaborate in Appendix A, that lead to this restriction allow for a two-stage estimation of the probabilities in Equation (1), alleviating the need to construct the entire observed role configuration transition matrix. Thus, by allowing for a reasonable restriction, we are thus able to solve an otherwise intractable problem.

Incorporating the assumptions from Appendix A into Equation 1, we obtain

$$\pi_{i(1)\,\dots\,i(T)m(1)\,\dots\,m(T)j} = \pi_{i(1)|m(1)} \cdots \pi_{i(T)|m(T)}\pi_{m(1)|j} \cdots \pi_{m(T)|j}\pi_j \tag{2}$$

$$= [\pi_{i(1)_1|m(1)} \cdots \pi_{i(1)_k|m(1)}] \cdots [\pi_{i(T)_1|m(T)} \cdots \pi_{i(T)_k|m(T)}]\pi_{m(1)|j} \cdots \pi_{m(T)|j}\pi_j$$

Equation (2) reveals the core set of probabilities to be obtained in the estimation and calculation of the latent life path probabilities and the conditional probabilities discussed above. Equation (2) also reveals the separability of the probabilities that allows for the two-stage estimation procedure. As each set of $[\pi_{i(t)_1|m(t)} \cdots \pi_{i(t)_k|m(t)}]$ can be separated from one another, as well as from the $\pi_{m(1)|j} \cdots \pi_{m(T)|j}\pi_j$, estimation of the model parameters may be broken down into two steps. First, we obtain maximum likelihood estimates for each set of $\lfloor\pi_{i(t)_1|m(t)} \cdots \pi_{i(t)_k|m(t)}\rfloor$ parameters by constructing the observed role configuration cross-classification at each age t and estimating the usual latent class model on each cross-classification. At this stage, full maximum likelihood estimates for each set of parameters $\lfloor\pi_{i(t)1|m(t)} \cdots \pi_{i(t)k|m(t)}\rfloor$ are obtained. With sufficient sample sizes, the estimates, say $\lfloor\hat{\pi}_{i(t)_1|m(t)} \cdots \hat{\pi}_{i(t)_k|m(t)}\rfloor$, will have the usual properties associated with maximum likelihood estimators—they will be consistent, asymptotically unbiased, and efficient.

To obtain estimates for the set of $\pi_{m(1)|j} \cdots \pi_{m(T)|j}\pi_j$ parameters, the second stage uses multiple random draws from a uniform distribution for each sample case to distribute a case across each of the $m(t)$ latent classes based on the estimated conditional probabilities $\hat{\pi}_{m(t)|i(t)}$ obtained at the first stage. We then estimate the usual latent class model on the realizations of the latent transition table obtained from that distribution of cases. (See Clogg, 1995 for discussion related to using multiple random draws on some distribution as a method for assigning cases to latent classes.)

Given the assumptions discussed in Appendix A and described above, as the multiple random draws tend toward infinity, estimates for the $\pi_{m(1)|j} \cdots \pi_{m(T)|j}\pi_j$ at the second stage using typical ML algorithms will upon convergence be *conditional* maximum likelihood estimators, conditional on the estimates obtained at the first stage. These conditional ML estimators will be consistent, asymptotically unbiased, and efficient in the local likelihood

area defined by the (global) ML estimates obtained in the first stage. These conditional estimators are more desirable, in that their asymptotic properties are more likely to hold and they
will have less sampling variability, than their full maximum likelihood counterparts obtained
from the complete, but considerably sparse, transition matrix of the full set of observed role
configurations.

Estimation of this two-stage latent class model yields a number of parameters that have
substantive importance in modeling the life course. At the outset, goodness-of-fit may be
assessed separately for the latent role configuration models at each age t and the latent life
path models. Statistics for the independence (one class) model assess whether there are
significant associations between roles in the context of latent role configurations or between
role configurations over time in the case of latent life paths. Goodness-of-fit statistics also
provide guidance on the number of classes that are necessary to characterize the latent
structure of role configurations at each age t and of life paths. These indicate the extent of
heterogeneity in role configurations at a given point in time or life paths over time.

As with all latent class models, conditional probabilities of manifest variables given
latent classes may be obtained. These define the nature of the different classes of latent role
configurations and/or latent life paths. For the former, these describe the conditional probability of each of the various roles given a particular latent class of role configurations. For the
latter, these describe the conditional probability of a particular latent role configuration given
a particular class of latent life path.

Latent class probabilities are useful in substantively interpreting the nature of the life
course. These indicate the probabilistic distribution of cases across the latent classes or the
likelihood that any random individual would be characterized by a given latent class. Some
classes may have high probabilities; others may have low probabilities. Latent class probabilities indicate the expected distribution of cases across role configurations or life paths.
Thus, they indicate typical and atypical patterning of roles or pathways between roles over the
life course.

Similarly, latent life path probabilities indicate the degree to which a specific life path is
prominent in a society. Aside from using the goodness-of-fit statistics to assess the number of
latent life paths in a society, these probabilities indicate the propensity for individuals in
a society to adhere to a specific type of life path, as characterized by the interrelated role
configuration pathways. Importantly, these probabilities help to answer the questions of
whether a given path is normative (in a modal sense), whether there is a modal/normative path
at all (a modal/normative path would not exist if all paths were about as equally likely to occur
in the population), and whether there are rare non-normative or what may be considered
deviant pathways.

Finally, another quantity of interest is the probability of observing a specific role, say k,
at some age t given latent life path j. This probability, denoted here as $\pi_{i(t)_k|j}$, may be calcu-
lated from the basic model probabilities found in Equation (2),

$$\pi_{i(t)_k|j} = \sum_{m(t)} \pi_{i(t)_k|m(t)} \pi_{m(t)|j} \qquad (3)$$

Calculating the probabilities in Equation (3) for each role and each latent life path, and
combining these over time either graphically or in tabular form, produces over-time changes
in the probabilities of each role within given life paths. These show the temporal unfolding of
multiple roles and the explicit conjoining of trajectories of different social roles that characterize a specific latent life path in a specific society at a specific historical era. Furthermore,

examination of expected probabilities provides evidence of the probability of occurrence, probabilistic order, and probabilistic timing of various social roles over time. Variation in such probabilities across life paths indicates heterogeneity in life paths. Thus, they directly demonstrate the variable nature of the life course and reveal the temporal process by which lives unfold over time.

MODELING THE LIFE COURSE: AN
EMPIRICAL EXAMPLE

To provide an example of the usefulness of our approach, we use data from the National Longitudinal Survey of Youth, 1979 (NLSY79). These data were collected from a nationally representative sample of 12,686 young men and women who were 14 to 22 years old when they were first surveyed in 1979. Individuals were surveyed annually through 1994 and then on a biennial basis. A key strength of the NLSY79 data is its excellent sample retention. Retention rates for those considered eligible for interview have remained close to 90%, including the specific period in which we study (U.S. Department of Labor, 2000). The longitudinal structure of the data allows us to model the life course over an extended period of time.

In keeping with Elder's (1985) definition of the life course as the age-graded movement through social institutions over time, we focus on education, work, marriage, and parenthood. These constitute the major institutions in Western societies; alone and in concert they are seen as the key markers in the transition to adulthood (Booth, Crouter & Shanahan, 1999; Shanahan, 2000). We define school involvement simply as whether respondents reported being *in school* at the time of the interview. We define work as either being *unemployed*, being employed *part-time* (less than 35 hours per week), and being employed *full-time* (35 hours or more per week). We differentiate marital status in terms of being *single* (never married), being *married*, or being *separated, divorced, or widowed* at the time of each interview. Finally, we define parenthood in terms of whether each respondent had ever *had children* at any point prior to each interview.

While more complex operationalizations are possible, these are well-suited to our interest in modeling interlocked pathways of social roles over time. For all of these states, we examine their joint occurrence at discrete four-year intervals. With this strategy, we assess the degree to which each role is achieved by a specific age. (We also examine whether roles appear and disappear within each time interval as a check against our delineation of the interconnected paths that make up the modern life course.) Specific choice of interval should be made on both theoretical and empirical grounds. Our interest in broadly mapping the life course over an extended period of time and the inherent limitations of sparseness in large N-way tables requires a broad time span while maintaining a reasonable number of time points. With the NLSY79 data, a 4-year interval allows us to effectively model the life course over 16 years, from late adolescence to mid-adulthood. This time period characterizes almost the entire longitudinal series of these data. Researchers with other objectives would choose either shorter or longer time frames. We discuss this issue further in a later section of this chapter.

Our analytic sample consists of respondents who were 15 or 16 years of age during the 1980 data collection. With this group, we can examine movement from adolescence through adulthood. We increase our sample size and statistical power by focusing on two adjacent birth cohorts. This increases our ability to consider greater heterogeneity in the structure of the life course. At the same time, these cohorts are closely related in historical time and are thus unlikely to have experienced unique cohort or period effects that could also impact upon the structure of the life course (Alwin *this volume*; Elder 1998; Glenn *this volume*). As our analysis is largely for descriptive purposes, we do not differentiate by gender, race, or class, although each of these may structure the life course in important ways. Our sample consists of 2,152 respondents.

Latent Role Configuration Results

We begin by examining goodness of fit statistics for the first stage analysis of latent role configurations. Table 24-1 shows five panels and includes the likelihood ratio chi-square statistic (L^2), degrees of freedom (*df*), the index of dissimilarity (D), and Raftery's (1995) Bayesian Information Criterion (BIC). Each panel corresponds to a specific age, beginning with ages 15 and 16 (the 1980 wave of data collection) and concluding with ages 31–32 (the 1996 wave of data collection). In each panel, four models are compared. This includes a null (one-class) model, a two-class model, a three-class model, and a four-class model. These models indicate the number of classes of latent role configurations that effectively character- ize the sample at each age. As these models are not hierarchical, model selection is based on overall goodness of fit.

The one-class null model, if it were to fit the data well, would indicate that the observed social roles were independent of one another. Deviations away from a good fit, for this null model, indicate the degree to which the various social roles have significant associations among themselves. At no stage of the life course does the null model even approach a good fit. In each case, the ratio of L^2 to degrees of freedom is over ten indicating very poor fit. Hence, the important life course principle that social roles cohere in significant ways over the life span is borne out in these data.

TABLE 24-1. **Goodness of Fit Statistics for Latent Role Configurations**

Ages	Latent classes	L^2	df	D	BIC
15–16	I	444.59	35	—	—
	II	**50.33**	**23**	**0.0180**	**−126.17**
	III	37.08	18	0.0150	−101.05
	IV	13.45	15	0.0030	−101.67
19–20	I	1033.09	35	—	—
	II	281.79	23	0.1200	105.28
	III	**26.56**	**16**	**0.0280**	**−96.22**
	IV	11.50	9	0.0110	−57.56
23–24	I	443.47	35	—	—
	II	**83.39**	**22**	**0.0600**	**−82.44**
	III	67.40	15	0.0420	245.66
	IV	38.18	9	0.0340	−29.66
27–28	I	421.84	35	—	—
	II	**69.46**	**22**	**0.0610**	**−96.37**
	III	41.58	16	0.0280	−79.02
	IV	30.11	10	0.0220	−45.27
31–32	I	352.36	35	—	—
	II	91.99	22	0.0610	−73.83
	III	**28.09**	**15**	**0.0240**	**−84.98**
	IV	13.58	9	0.0180	−54.26

Beyond this starting point, the number of classes that effectively summarize the interconnections between social roles varies by stage of the life cycle. During adolescence, a two-class model provides a good fit to the data. This model has a L^2 to degrees of freedom ratio that is just over two, an index of dissimilarity of 0.018, and the lowest BIC value of -126.172. The more complex three- and four-class models provide only minimal improvement in fit when compared to the two-class model.

In late adolescence (ages 19–20), a three-class model effectively summarizes the associations between school, work, marriage, and parenthood. This model has a L^2 to degrees of freedom of less than two, an index of dissimilarity of 0.028 and a BIC of -96.223. At ages 23–24, we opt for a two-class model on the grounds that the L^2 to degrees of freedom ratio is less than four, the index of dissimilarity is less than 0.10 (0.060), and this model has the lowest BIC (-82.436). The more complex three- and four-class models do not improve on the L^2 to degrees of freedom ratio, show some small improvement in the index of dissimilarity, yet show poorer fit on the BIC statistic. During the late 20s, a two-class model again effectively summarizes the association between roles. This model has a L^2 to degrees of freedom ratio that is just over three, an index of dissimilarity of 0.061 and a BIC of -96.365. More complex models show minimal improvement in the L^2 to degrees of freedom ratio, some marginal improvement in the index of dissimilarity, yet generally smaller BIC statistics. There is clear support for a three-class model in the early 30s ($L^2/df = 1.87$, $\Delta = 0.024$, BIC $= -84.976$). At this age, the four-class model does not improve fit along any dimension.

Substantively, the number of classes in the preferred models indicates variation in latent role configurations at each age. Understanding the qualitative aspects of these latent role configurations requires examination of the conditional and latent class probabilities. These are shown in Table 24-2. Beginning in adolescence (ages 15–16), there are two distinct latent role configurations. In the first, individuals have a very high probability of being in school (0.9746), high probabilities of not working (0.6213) or if working, working part-time (0.3467) rather than full time (0.0320). They have virtually no probability of marriage (0.0014) or post-marriage roles of being separated, divorced, or widowed (0.0000), and a very low probability of having children (0.0117). This role configuration has a very high likelihood (0.8908) suggesting that 89% of the sampled population can be characterized by this role configuration. Substantively, this role configuration indicates the primacy of the student role, the secondary prevalence of the part-time work role, and very little adoption of familial roles.

In contrast, the second latent role configuration indicates respondents with comparatively low probabilities of being in school (0.1261) and a moderate probability of being employed full-time (0.3050). There is a higher but still relatively low probability of being married (0.1629), and a moderate probability of having children (0.2156). This latent role configuration has a latent class probability of 0.1092 indicating that just over 10% of the sampled population would conform to this pattern of social roles. The apparently early exit from school, combined with elevated risk of early entry into full-time work, marriage, and parenthood at such an early age may suggest that this latent role configuration captures "precocious" transitions (Newcomb & Bentler, 1988) that some suggest are associated with increased involvement in deviance and diminished life chances in later life. At the same time, this group lacks significant probabilities in *any* of the social roles and hence appears "roleless" and adrift from the major institutions in society. Studies of straight and deviant pathways through life (Robins & Rutter, 1990) might focus on the later patterning of social roles that would appear to stem from this early, somewhat deviant configuration.

There is more variability in latent role configurations in later adolescence (ages 19–20) as indicated by the best fitting three-class model. The first class describes individuals who

TABLE 24-2. Conditional Probabilities for Latent Role Configurations

Latent class	Ages 15–16		Ages 19–20			Ages 23–24		Ages 27–28		Ages 31–32		
	I	II	I	II	III	I	II	I	II	I	II	III
Role												
School												
No	0.0254	0.8739	0.1615	0.9257	0.9696	0.9071	0.9593	0.9148	0.9620	0.9177	0.9597	0.9446
Yes	0.9746	0.1261	0.8385	0.0743	0.0304	0.0929	0.0407	0.0852	0.0380	0.0823	0.0403	0.0554
Work												
None	0.6213	0.6378	0.5011	0.3209	0.5662	0.1749	0.3618	0.1754	0.3508	0.2039	0.4042	0.0228
Part-time	0.3467	0.0571	0.4510	0.0739	0.1063	0.0702	0.0936	0.0680	0.0666	0.1642	0.1744	0.1174
Full-time	0.0320	0.3050	0.0480	0.6051	0.3275	0.7550	0.5445	0.7567	0.5826	0.6319	0.4214	0.8598
Marital Status												
Single	0.9886	0.8243	0.9894	0.8356	0.4692	0.6448	0.2701	0.5669	0.1930	0.7280	0.2283	0.0004
Married	0.0014	0.1629	0.0106	0.1468	0.4480	0.3041	0.5620	0.3570	0.6245	0.1775	0.5910	0.8152
Other	0.0000	0.0128	0.0000	0.0176	0.0828	0.0511	0.1679	0.0761	0.1826	0.0945	0.1806	0.1844
Children												
No	0.9883	0.7844	0.9648	0.9962	0.1419	0.9808	0.0359	0.9789	0.0021	0.9619	0.0249	0.1970
Yes	0.0117	0.2156	0.0352	0.0038	0.8581	0.0192	0.9641	0.0211	0.9979	0.0381	0.9751	0.8030
Latent Class Probabilities	0.8908	0.1092	0.2800	0.4513	0.2687	0.5163	0.4837	0.3688	0.6312	0.1990	0.4967	0.3044

maintain high involvement in education (0.8385). This is coupled with little adoption of full-time work (0.0480), moderate involvement in part-time work (0.4510), and a likelihood of not being employed in any capacity that is quite large (0.5011). At the same time, the probability of any family role is very low (0.0106 and 0.0352 for marriage and parenthood, respectively). This suggests a life stage characterized by extended involvement in education, likely higher education, limited involvement in work, and the absence of family formation. This role configuration characterizes just over a quarter (0.280) of the sampled population.

A second role configuration involves comparatively little involvement in school (0.0743) and a much greater likelihood of full time work (0.6051). This is coupled with a low likelihood of marriage (0.1468) and a very low likelihood of parenthood (0.0038). This pattern of roles has the highest probability of occurrence (0.4513). Just over 45% of the sampled population could be characterized by this role configuration. The third class has the lowest likelihood of being in school (0.0304), bifurcated involvement in work (a likelihood of 0.5662 of not working and a likelihood of 0.3275 of working full-time), moderate likelihood of marriage (0.4480), and a high probability of having children (0.8581). The likelihood of this role configuration is similar to that of the first latent class (0.2687) with just over a quarter of the sampled population being characterized by this pattern of roles.

At ages 23–24, variability is lower. Two latent role configurations effectively characterize the latent structure of the life course. The first role configuration involves a low probability of school (0.0929), a high likelihood of full-time work (0.7550), yet only a moderate probability of marriage (0.3041) and a very low probability of parenthood (0.0192). This role configuration can be seen to characterize just over half (0.5163) of the sampled population.

The second latent class has an even lower likelihood of being in school (0.0380), a lower likelihood of full-time work (0.5445) and greater likelihood of not working at all (0.3618). It also has a greater likelihood of marriage (0.562), marital disruption (0.1679), and an almost certainty of having children (0.9641). This patterning of roles has a probability of 0.4837 and characterizes individuals whose life course involves a greater primacy of family, rather than work, roles.

During the late 20s, the similarity of the first class with the first latent role configuration 4 years earlier is remarkable. This class has a low probability of being in school (0.0852), an almost identical likelihood of full-time work (0.7567), a small increase in the likelihood of marriage (0.3570), yet an almost identical likelihood of parenthood (0.0211). However, the likelihood of this role configuration is markedly lower. The probability of this patterning is 0.3688 (as opposed to 0.5163), suggesting that just over one third of the sampled population would be characterized by this role configuration.

The second latent class at ages 27 and 28 is also remarkably similar to that observed 4 years earlier. Compared to the other latent class at this age, this second class has a comparatively lower likelihood of being in school (0.0380), lower likelihood of full-time work (0.5826) yet greater likelihood of not working (0.3508). This is coupled with a high probability of marriage (0.6245) or the post marriage roles of being separated, divorced, or widowed (0.1826), and an almost certainty of having children (0.9979). This latent role configuration is likely to characterize almost two thirds of the sampled population (0.6312). While latent role configurations may change little between the early and late 20's, the distributions across roles configurations and thus the modal character of social roles changes significantly.

Variability in role configurations increases in the early 30's. This point in the life course requires three latent classes to adequately characterize social roles. The first class has a low probability of involvement in school (0.0823), a moderate to large probability of full-time work (0.6319), yet still little probability of marriage (0.1775) or parenthood (0.0381).

Comparatively, this latent role configuration is infrequent. Only 20% (0.1990) of the sampled population are likely to have this pattern of roles in their early 30's.

The second class has even less likelihood of schooling (0.0403) and less likelihood of full-time work (0.4214). The probability of part-time work is similar, yet the likelihood of not working at all is almost double (0.4042). Such differences are, however, minor compared to those with respect to family roles. The likelihood of marriage is over three times greater (0.5910) and the likelihood of having been married is almost twice as great (0.1806). Even more dramatic, this class has an extremely high probability of having children (0.9751), substantially greater than that of either marriage or full-time work. Interestingly, this role configuration is likely to characterize almost half (0.4967) of the sampled population at this age. Family roles appear to be the defining dimension of this latent class.

The final aspect of the latent structure of social roles in the early 30s involves an equally low probability of being in school (0.0554), yet much greater likelihood of full-time work (0.8598) and virtually no likelihood of not working (0.0228). This is coupled with a high probability of being married (0.8152) or having been married (0.1844) and a high likelihood of having children (0.803). In concert, this role configuration characterizes the joint managing of work and family and characterizes almost one third of the sampled population (0.3044).

Before considering latent life paths and the derivative interlocking of role pathways over time, it is worth noting two things. First, this analysis considers the simultaneous or joint occurrence of multiple social roles at given points in the life cycle. This is significant as much research has been premised on the notion of a primary or dominant role (see discussions in Hogan, 1978 and Rindfuss et al., 1987). Our analysis suggests that it is difficult to identify a priori a primary or dominant role without explicit consideration of other roles. At various ages, latent role configurations indicate equal probabilities of different roles. In this respect, our approach is consistent with understanding phenomena in terms of the conjoint occurrence or non-occurrence of multiple roles in time.

Second, role variability over the life cycle is significant. As indicated by the number of latent classes, role configurations are more complex immediately following adolescence and during the early 30s. One explanation for this may be that a "normative" life course (Neugarten et al., 1965) provides options, choices and role conflicts at discrete ages. In the case of late adolescence, individuals in the late 20th century were faced with the discrete choice between continued education or entry into the labor force or family roles. These opportunities produce variability in role configurations given individuals who opt for different roles and thus made specific transitions from one role into another. This variability effectively disappears during the mid-to late 20s as most respondents have finished their schooling (most higher education degrees would be completed by ages 23 or 24 or at least be in some form of terminal phase). Role choices and role variability at this stage of the life course are thus constrained to work and family with little change in latent structure through the mid-to late 20s.

Increased variability in the early 30s suggests a somewhat different process. It suggests the variable ways in which individuals both adopt and *manage* multiple, jointly occurring roles. For one group, work and family remain detached; individuals have high likelihood of full-time work but low likelihood of any family role. This is distinct from a second group that shows significant involvement in family roles, yet comparatively less involvement in full-time work. Both these groups differ from a third group that combines full-time work, marriage, and parenthood. Thus, variation emerges not so much through discrete life course options but more through the strategies and practices by which individuals manage the overlap of existing roles. The identification of this variation and its meaning suggests the importance of greater systematic inquiry into this period of the life course, mid-life.

Latent Life Path Results

The identification of latent role configurations at successive stages provides the empirical backdrop for illumination of the dynamic structure of the life course. This is accomplished through the second stage latent class analysis that links latent role configurations over time. Inspection of goodness of fit statistics (see Table 24-3) indicates that the null model provides a very poor fit to the data (L^2 = 2978.08, 71 df). Latent role configurations thus have significant associations over time. The likelihood of a latent role configuration at one point of the life cycle is associated with a significantly greater or lower likelihood of having particular role configurations at other points in the life course. At the same time, there is very strong support for a three-class model, indicating three distinct "paths" through the school, work, marriage, and parenthood. This is demonstrated by a low ratio of the likelihood chi-square statistics to degrees of freedom (less than 1), an index of dissimilarity of 0.0402, and the lowest BIC of −330.3654. This model clearly provides a better fit to the data than a two-class model and a four-class model does not substantially improve on model fit.

The conditional probabilities associated with these latent life paths are shown in Table 24-4. Conditional probabilities within latent life paths indicate transition from and to latent role configurations. If latent role configurations were identical at each age, these conditional probabilities would indicate the specific likelihood of the transition or movement

TABLE 24-3. **Goodness of Fit Statistics for Latent Life Paths**

Latent classes	L2	df	D	BIC
I	2978.08	71	—	—
II	396.06	56	0.1388	−33.69
III	**37.99**	**49**	**0.0402**	**−330.37**
IV	30.33	41	0.0319	−284.31

TABLE 24-4. **Conditional Probabilities for Latent Life Paths**

Ages	Latent role configuration	Latent life path		
		I	II	III
15–16	I	0.9562	0.9325	0.7796
	II	0.0438	0.0675	0.2204
19–20	I	0.4348	0.3738	0.0129
	II	0.5290	0.5781	0.2666
	III	0.0362	0.0482	0.7205
23–24	I	0.9896	0.5350	0.0064
	II	0.0104	0.4650	0.9936
27–28	I	0.9971	0.0275	0.0116
	II	0.0029	0.9725	0.9884
31–32	I	0.5378	0.0077	0.0132
	II	0.1950	0.6342	0.7050
	III	0.2672	0.3580	0.2818
Latent class probabilities		0.3446	0.3262	0.3291

from and to stationary role configurations. Here, however, interpretation of these probabilities is complicated by the variable content of the latent role configurations at each age. For example, latent life path I indicates individuals who have a very high likelihood of being in latent role configuration I during adolescence (0.9562). This is followed by a high likelihood of transitioning to either latent role configuration I (0.4348) or latent role configuration II (0.5290) in late adolescence but an extremely low likelihood of transitioning to latent role configuration III (0.0362). In both the mid- and the late 20s, such individuals are very likely to have latent role configuration I (0.9896 and 0.9971) but are very unlikely to have latent role configuration II (0.0104 and 0.0029). In the early 30s, these individuals become more diversified across latent role configurations. They have the greatest likelihood of having latent role configuration I (0.5378), but also moderate probabilities of having latent role configuration II (0.1950) or latent role configuration III (0.2672). Other latent life paths indicate different patterns of latent role configurations over time and all are approximately equal in likelihood.

To render these conditional probabilities more meaningful we calculate expected role probabilities given (or within) each latent life path. As described earlier in Equation (3), these are calculated by multiplying the conditional probability of a latent role configuration within a latent life path (Table 24-4) by the conditional probability of a particular role within a latent role configuration (Table 24-2) and then summing over latent role configurations at each age. These conditional probabilities are then graphed at each age in order to describe the variable structure of the life course as indicated by the latent life paths. This is shown in Figure 24-1.

Latent life path I begins with very high involvement in school in adolescence that extends into adulthood (0.94 to 0.4). This is likely indicative of movement into higher education. The effective transition out of school between the ages of 19–20 and 23–24 (0.09) is accompanied by movement out of part-time work (from 0.24 to 0.07) and significant movement into full-time work (from 0.35 to 0.75). In many respects, this pattern describes classic conceptions of the school-to-work transition: the rapid acquisition of work following the completion of full-time schooling. Family roles in this life path effectively "lag" those of work. The probability of marriage is virtually zero in adolescence, shows only a small increase in the late teens and early 20s (from 0.01 to 0.10), but then increases steadily through the 20s and early 30s (from 0.1 to 0.3 to 0.35 to 0.4). Importantly, the likelihood of marriage occurs at a much lower rate than that of work indicating that individuals are effectively moving into full-time work *before* they move into marriage. Equally important, the probability of parenthood lags that of full-time work and marriage. The likelihood of having children is effectively zero up until ages 27–28 and then increases sharply through the early 30s (from less than 0.05 to 0.41). Life path I characterizes individuals who have children *after* moving into full-time work and getting married. This life path characterizes about one third of the sampled population, and has a structure similar to classic notions of the normative (Neugarten et al. 1965) or orderly (Hogan 1978) life course.

Latent life path II also involves high (0.92) involvement in school during adolescence that extends through the early 20s (0.36). This is coupled with steady movement out of part-time work (from 0.33 to 0.22 to 0.08) and steady movement into full-time work (from 0.05 to 0.38 to 0.66) by ages 23–24. This pattern of transitions is accompanied by the acquisition of family roles, particularly parenthood, during the early 20s. The probability of parenthood is very low (less than 0.10) up until ages 19–20, but then increases sharply through the mid-to late 20s. By ages 27–28, the likelihood of having children is almost 1.0. The likelihood of marriage follows a similar trajectory, but at a lower rate (from 0.2 at ages 23–24 to 0.60 at ages 27–28). Both rates appear to plateau between the late 20s and early 30s. It is further significant that the probability of parenthood passes that of full-time work as the latter plateaus

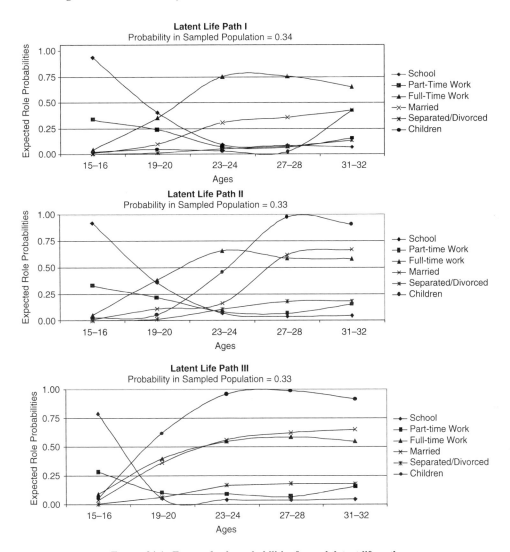

FIGURE 24-1. Expected role probabilities for each latent life path.

or even declines at a level below that observed for latent life path I. The likelihood of marital disruption increases steadily during the 20s and remains at a moderate level (0.20) through the early 30s. This life path characterizes the classic "work–family" linkage and the ensuing adjustment and accommodation of the multiple, overlapping involvement in work and family. It can be seen to typify about one third of the sampled population.

The final latent life path is distinct along all dimensions. Individuals characterized by this life path have comparatively less involvement in school in adolescence (0.78) and rapidly move out of school. By ages 19–20, their probability of being in school is extremely low (less than 0.05), indicating very little involvement in higher education. Movement out of school is much quicker when compared to the education trajectories of the other life paths. Importantly, the rapid movement out of school is accompanied by a rapid onset of parenthood. Between ages 15–16 and ages 23–24, the probability of parenthood increases from 0.06 to 0.96. In relation to other life paths, parenthood comes much earlier in the life course for this life path. The likelihood of full-time work and marriage appear to trend with parenthood, although at much lower levels. The likelihood of marriage increases from mid-adolescence to ages 19–20 (from 0.04 to 0.36), before plateauing (0.6) in the mid-20s and early 30s. Marriage thus appears much earlier in this life path. The likelihood of full-time work shows a similar trajectory, but has levels that are considerably lower (approximately 0.55 through the 20s and early 30s) than those observed in the other life paths. Finally, the likelihood of marital disruption increases steadily in this life path. This life path appears to characterize those individuals who make the transition to adulthood largely in the context of parenthood not necessarily accompanied by either marriage or full-time work. As with the other two latent life paths, this life path characterizes about one third of the sampled population.

Generally, the latent life paths as shown in Figure 24-1 provide an over-time snapshot of the interplay of probabilistic pathways of social roles that characterize the life course.* They simultaneously describe the timing of social roles, their probabilistic ordering, and the general diversity that exists in the structure of the life course. Importantly with respect to that diversity, for our nationally representative sample there appears to be no true normative life path in the modal sense. That is, each latent life path is characteristic of about one third of the sampled population, indicating maximal diversity probabilistically across these three latent life paths. Moreover, the general fact that there is considerable, yet probabilistically structured, variability in pathways through life indicates an opportunity to integrate holistic, multifaceted depictions of the life course within existing theoretical and empirical work.

FURTHER APPLICATIONS

Our example illuminates the potential of a two stage latent class approach, to delineate the interplay of pathways, the probabilistic timing and order of social roles, and heterogeneity in the life course. Yet, this example has only scratched the surface of the utility of such models to key theoretical questions in life course research. In this section, we discuss further applications for the latent class model of role configurations and life paths in studying the life course.

At the outset, a latent role configuration and life path approach could be used to examine other periods of the life course. Our example showcases the method by considering a broad slice of the life course. Nonetheless, this approach is equally useful in considering specific, shorter segments of the life course. These could include particularly pivotal stages such as the transition to adulthood (Booth, Crouter & Shanahan, 1999), the much understudied period of mid-life where work, marital, and parenting roles undergo considerable fluctuation (Gerson, 1985), or the later years characterized by movement out of work (Han & Moen, 1999). At the other extreme, such models could examine even broader periods of the life course such as those considered in Clausen's (1991) seminal work.

Our example is also quite specific. It examines the movement into and out of key social roles, notably involvement in school, work, marriage, and parenthood. The probabilistic role configured life path theoretical foundation and accompanying two-stage latent class

---

*Note that the probability of full-time work appears to decline in the last time period in all latent life paths. This is very likely a result of changes to the CPS module in the NLS that were designed to mirror methodological changes in the CPS instrument that were implemented in 1994. Methodological assessments of CPS data indicate that the new instrument increased the likelihood of the classification of "part-time" work (Polivka & Miller, 1994). Consistent with this interpretation, trajectories of part-time work in our analysis show a concomitant increase in probability in the last time period, suggesting that some reclassification from full-time worker to part-time worker did occur.

empirical methods we advance in this chapter are sufficiently flexible that one could consider social roles in greater detail, focusing on such issues as types of work, qualitative dimensions of marriage, and various dimensions of parenting and how these change over time. One could also consider the life course at different levels. This may involve examining the intersection of psychological orientations at various ages and how they unfold in consort with entry into and exit out of social roles.

For example, Gerson (1985) showcases the importance of human agency in life course studies by demonstrating the variable ways in which "orientations" towards work and family both shape and are shaped by experiences within social roles. For some, orientations may produce role transitions, like the case of family orientations inducing parenthood rather than continued education or full-time work after high school. For others, experiences in social roles may change orientations which, in turn, may induce subsequent changes in social roles. Those who leave the labor force to become full-time parents, or vice versa, often manifest the influence of role experience on orientations. In the context of the latent life path model, one might include "orientations" as the subjective counterpart of objectively observed role configurations at different points in time, thus accounting for heterogeneity in orientation-role linkages. For some in the study population, orientations may lead roles and role transitions, for yet others orientations may lag roles and role transitions. Results from this type of orientation-role analysis have the potential to reveal important connections and complexities among agency and social roles in the life course. Moreover, such research would nicely augment existing work that links social psychology and life course studies (George, 1996) to understand the role of human agency in the shaping of lives over time (Elder, 1994).

At what may be considered the opposite extreme, the intersection of individual life courses and the institutional configurations and contexts within which life courses play out may be fruitfully researched from within a latent life path framework. This may involve the examination of unfolding lives over time in concert with dynamic institutional contexts. Recall that, from a latent life path perspective, individuals may be viewed as probabilistically distributed across various role configurations and life paths. Social institutions, on the other hand, may be characterized by configurations of rules and, over the life of some social institution, the different pathways through various rule configurations over time. Analysis of this role/rule nexus from a latent life path perspective, as detailed in Eliason, Macmillan, and Stryker (2002), should serve to bring in to focus those aspects of the life course that are strongly shaped by society's social institutions, as well as those aspects of social institutions shaped by the life course.

Extending investigation of the life course could also involve inquiry into the social and psychological determinants of latent life paths. Our method generates a latent "variable" indicative of an unfolding process. This latent variable could be studied as an outcome of personal and social characteristics in childhood and adulthood using conventional analytic approaches. Through latent class assignment of individual respondents, researchers could model the probability of one latent life path relative to another using conventional binary or multinomial regression approaches (Long, 1997). At the same time, conditional probabilities of latent class assignment given combinations on observed characteristics could be used to construct ratio level measures that would be suitable for conventional OLS regression. Several extensions of this sort seem particularly promising. Clausen (1991), for example, argues that "planful competence" in adolescence sets the stage for a more successful adult life, including greater career success, greater marital stability, and personality resemblance through late adulthood. Consistent with this, we would encourage inquiry into the effect of planful competence and other important psychological constructs (i.e., self-esteem, locus of control, self-efficacy, gender role orientations) on the likelihood of particular life paths. Likewise, we would encourage research on social and behavioral determinants. Through the notions of "linked lives" (Elder, 1994), considerable research documents the role that others play in shaping life fortunes. Notions of "cumulative continuity" further suggest that early behaviors, both normative and deviant, can have profound effects on the structure of the life course (Caspi, Elder, & Herbener, 1990; Hagan, 1991; Sampson & Laub, 1993). A consideration of such factors in the context of multiple, interlocked pathways of social roles would enhance our understanding of the precursors of the variable ways in which individuals move into and through social institutions over the life course.

Implicit in both a life course perspective and the latent life path approach described in this chapter is the idea that the specific ways in which lives unfold over time is consequential for life chances. Elder's (1998) classic work on children of the Great Depression, for example, demonstrates how the timing of social roles was shaped by both personal and historical circumstances and how these were ultimately consequential for personal development. Likewise, research on "disorder" in the life course (Featherman & Carter, 1976; Hogan, 1978; Rindfuss et al., 1987) suggests that disorderly lives influence such things as income attainment, education, marital stability and the likelihood of parenthood. Against this backdrop, we see two roles for a latent life path perspective.

First, latent life paths can be seen as determinants of the qualitative aspects of social roles (i.e., occupational status, income attainment, marital satisfaction, child-rearing practices) or can be used as a determinant of psychological well-being and general life satisfaction (George, 1999). A latent life path approach could even be broadened to examine the intergenerational consequences of parental life courses for children's life courses, children's attainments, and children's well-being. Second, latent life paths could be seen as linking functions between social origins and destinations. The longitudinal links between early familial states and later life chances has occupied a central position in life course research. This approach informs studies of status attainment (Duncan, Featherman, & Duncan, 1972; Sewell & Hauser, 1974), marriage and divorce (Johnson & Booth, 1998), psychological well-being (Elder, George, & Shanahan, 1996), and crime and deviance (Sampson & Laub, 1993). Yet, researchers have seldom, if ever, studied explicit pathways through life as a mechanism that links origins and destinations. Likely due to methodological limitations, research has instead focused on specific variables (i.e., education in status attainment) or one or two role trajectories (i.e., the overlap of work and family roles). A consideration of life paths that indicate the interlocking of multiple role trajectories, their timing and order, would augment existing work by highlighting further contingencies in intergenerational and developmental processes.

The central aspect of most, if not all, previous applications is that they identify a priori one or more life courses or paths, and then proceed to examine their origins and consequences. Yet, a latent class approach is also amenable to direct comparison of latent structures across groups. This is done most easily by comparing models in which conditional probabilities are not constrained in any way with models in which some or all conditional probabilities are constrained to be equal. By doing so the analyst may directly and precisely examine any across-group differences in the (latent) structure of role configurations and/or life paths. Perhaps an obvious starting point for this type of research would be the assessment of latent role configurations and life paths across race, class, and/or gender, and the intersections among these. Explicit comparisons of life course structures across social groups would provide an important starting point for inquiry into the complex interplay of agency, structure, and culture in the shaping of life paths.

Elaborating further, latent life paths, their origins, and their consequences can be examined in light of broad historical contexts. Life course research explicitly attempts to account for "lives in historical times" by understanding human development as a product of historical context and the opportunities and constraints that it provides (Elder, 1994). One line of research focuses on the implications of broad historical circumstances, including the post-war economic boom (Blau & Duncan 1967; Modell 1989) and more recently the slow down in the American economy during the 1980s and early 1990s (Conger & Elder 1994; Furstenberg et al., 1999). Other research considers the developmental consequences of specific historical events, including the Great Depression (Elder, 1998), World War II (Elder, 1987; Sampson & Laub, 1996), and more recently, the Vietnam War (Hagan, 2001). Modell (1999) has recently called for greater consideration of history in the study of the life course, while Glenn (*this volume*) notes the continued importance of age, period, and cohort for social scientific inquiry.

In light of this, a further application of our approach would consider the effects of historical circumstances on latent role configurations and life paths. This might involve several dimensions. First, an examination of latent role configurations and life paths across birth cohorts would serve to identify variation in the structure of the life course over time. Such work would augment existing inquiry into historical shifts in the order and timing of life course experiences (Hogan, 1978; Modell, Furstenberg, & Hershberg, 1976). Second, research could consider the implications of significant historical events on life paths. This would involve consideration of adjacent cohorts for whom the timing of birth or particular role exits differentially expose them to historical events (Elder, 1998). In addition to revisiting classic questions like the impact of the Great Depression or World War II, researchers could address contemporary questions such as the life course implications of the recessions of the 1980s and early 1990s. Third, research should consider the contextualizing effect of historical conditions, the degree to which they interact with personal and social attributes and behaviors to determine specific life paths and the degree to which life paths interact with history to shape their consequences. Such research would build upon the recent work of Shanahan and colleagues and their inquiry into historical contingencies in expressions and consequences of human agency (Shanahan, Elder, & Miech, 1997; Shanahan, Miech, & Elder 1998).

In addition to historical considerations, life course inquiry is increasingly situated within the context of globalization and involves cross-national research. The GLOBALIFE project at the University of Bielefeld, for example, seeks to study the influence of global processes in OECD societies on the transition to adulthood, changes in career mobility and forms of employment and unemployment, the development of gender-specific patterns in work-family linkages, and the transition from employment to retirement (http://alia.soziologie.uni-bielefeld.de/~globalife/summary.htm). Other research compares the transition to adulthood under different national contexts, highlighting the impact of institutional structures on life course fortunes (Heinz, 1991). An application of our approach could examine the overall structure of the life course or specific segments across nations. Such research would assess whether the structure of the life course was substantively consistent, whether it was consistent along some dimensions but not others, or whether the overall structure bears little similarity across institutional and national contexts. This work would be not only useful in describing cross-national variation in the life course but would also set the stage for research into the structural, cultural, and institutional features of nations that shape the modern life course. (See also our related comments above on linking the life course to institutional contexts over time.)

Finally, further research should consider the implications of specific life events, their timing and their order, for both the overall unfolding of the life course and its implications. This issue has been a central feature of traditional life course inquiry. Greenberger and Steinberg (1986), for example, argue that early movement into full-time (or at least high-intensity) work leads to a host of psychological and behavioral problems. Similarly, Furstenberg and colleagues

(1987) have devoted considerable attention to adolescent parenthood and its consequences for personal and social well-being. Using our approach, researchers could "fix" particular states at particular ages to consider the specific ways in which life paths unfold thereafter. In the context of the key research traditions indicated, this could involve specifying a life path to contain child-bearing or full-time work in adolescence. One could further consider similarity and difference in the consequence of having a particular life course experience, such as early transition into full-time work or adolescent parenthood, across different social groups. As such work echoes broader concerns about the race, gender, and class contexts of human development, research in this vein would further illuminate the structural context of the life course.

CONCLUSIONS

Our purpose in this chapter is 2-fold. First, we highlight the need for further inquiry into the life course. For reasons that appear to center around the difficulty that many traditional empirical methods have in addressing the theoretical sophistication developed to understand the life course, the life course as a *multidimensional, dynamic* process has seldom been studied. The challenge this level of theoretical sophistication has posed for traditional empirical methods has had important consequences for life course research and our ability to examine the richness of the life course. In one respect, much of the empirical research that rests on traditional empirical techniques has had a difficult time addressing key questions arising from developments in life course theory. In part because of these difficulties, empirical research over the past couple of decades has not lived up to its promise, falling short of generating that rich and reliable body of knowledge on both precursors and consequences of the variable structure of the life course. By focusing more on the oft out-of-context individual components of the life course, and less so on the nexus of roles and pathways that make up the life course as an institutional whole, our cumulative understanding of the life course, its origins, and its consequences suffers. This need not be the case.

Hence, a second objective of this chapter was to propose a perspective and method for effectively modeling the life course *as an institutional whole*, to provide an illustration of its utility, and to elaborate its applicability to key questions arising from theories of the life course. Our formulation of a two-stage latent class approach is derived directly from, and thus consistent with, key concepts and theories buttressing our understanding of the life course. Specifically, the empirical model we present expands on the ideas of trajectories and transitions, conceptualizing the life course as probabilistically distributed life paths through age-graded role configurations. By comparing contemporary life course theory, contemporary research, and the approach offered in this chapter, we hope to indicate the important advantages of this approach for extending our knowledge of the life course.

It is important to also point out that we do not think our approach answers all life course questions. Its utility stems from its ability to capture and represent a multidimensional, time varying process. Hence, it shifts attention from explicit causes and effects between or among components of the life course to viewing the life course as a complex whole. Yet, it also has limitations. These include limitations on the volume of information it can handle (i.e., number of variables and number of periods), problems in modeling "turning points" due to a focus on summarizing a holistic time bound process, and traditional problems of unobserved heterogeneity that characterize most statistical approaches.

As a final comment, our approach may offer a means of synthesizing current research on the life course. George (*this volume*) differentiates life course research as studies of the life course and studies that apply life course concepts (i.e., order, timing, linked lives) in other substantive areas of inquiry. She predicts that the former, while interesting, will not play a large role in the future of life course research. Such work, she argues, paints too broad a picture of life course contours and diversity, is not useful for fine grained analysis, is ill-suited to hypothesis testing and causal inference, and is often not generalizable. Instead, she suggests that the future of life course research will rest on the use of life course concepts in other areas of research. In many respects we agree with her critique. Yet, we see it as a challenge that motivates our work on the utility of latent class techniques for modeling the modern life course, and the accompanying probabilistically based theoretical view of the life course. From our perspective, neither informal, non-systematic studies of the life course nor the incorporation of specific, decontextualized elements of the life course into other areas of research yield a particularly strong life course social science. We hope that this chapter provides both a theoretical and empirical foundation for bridging these avenues of inquiry such that it incorporates the best of both areas and ultimately lives up to the important theoretical ideas of the architects of a life course perspective (Elder, 1994; Modell, 1989; Thomas & Znaniecki, 1927).

APPENDIX A. STATISTICAL ASSUMPTIONS UNDERLYING THE LATENT LIFE PATH MODEL

The two-stage estimation of the latent life path model described in the text requires the following additional statistical assumptions. See the text for a more substantive description of these assumptions.

Assumption 1. The observed role configurations at age t are conditionally independent of the observed role configurations at age t', given the joint distribution of the latent role configurations and latent life path over $t = 1, \ldots, T$; That is, $i(t) \otimes i(t') \mid [m(t), j]$.

Assumption 1 states that the latent structure contains all of the information about the relationship in the transition table involving the observed role configurations. This is the typical conditional independence assumption for latent class models, but restated in the current context.

Assumption 2. The observed variables making up the cross-classification of observed role configurations at age t are conditionally independent given the latent role configuration at age t; $i(t)_k \otimes i(t)_{k'} \mid m(t)$ where k and k' index observed component variables k and k' of $i(t)$.

Assumption 2 states that the latent role configuration at age t contains all of the information about the relationship in the cross-classification of observed role configurations at age t. This too is very similar to the standard conditional independence assumption. However, in this case the assumption is specific to a subset containing only the information on role configurations at age t.

Assumption 3. The latent role configuration at age t, $m(t)$, is conditionally independent of the latent role configuration at age t', $m(t')$, given the latent life path j; $m(t) \otimes m(t') \mid j$.

Assumption 3 states that the latent life path contains all of the information about the relationship in the latent transition table. Again, this is similar to the standard conditional independence assumption. Here, however, this assumption is specific to the conditional independence relation among the latent role configurations (as given in the corresponding [latent] transition table) given the latent life path.

Assumption 4. Conditional independence of (a) the joint distribution of latent role configuration at age t' and the latent life path and (b) the observed role configuration at age t given the latent role configuration at age t; $[m(t'), j] \otimes i(t) \mid m(t)$.

Assumption 4 states that the relationship between a latent role configuration at age t' and the latent life path is not influenced directly by the observed role configuration at age t, conditional on the latent role configuration at age t. This assumption is noticeably different from the standard conditional independence assumption. Essentially, this assumption restricts the observed role configuration at one point in time from having a direct impact on the relationship between the latent life path and the latent role configuration at some other point in time. We hasten to point out that this relationship at t' can indeed be influenced by the *latent* role configuration at t. And it is through this latent mechanism that the observed role configuration at t may then *indirectly* influence the relationship between a latent role configuration at age t' and the latent life path.

REFERENCES

Blau, P., & Duncan, O. D. (1967). *The American occupational structure.* New York: Wiley.

Booth, A., Crouter, D., & Shanahan, M. (1999). *Transitions to adulthood in a changing economy: No work, no family, no future?* Westport, CT: Praeger.

Caspi, A., Elder, G., & Herbener, E. (1990). Childhood personality and the prediction of life-course patterns. In L. Robins & M. Rutter (Eds.), *Straight and devious pathways from childhood to adulthood* (pp. 13–35). New York: Cambridge University Press.

Clausen, J. (1991). Adolescent competence and the shaping of the life course. *American Journal of Sociology, 96,* 805–842.

Clogg, C. (1995). Latent Class Models. In G. Arminger, C. Clogg, & M. Sobel (Eds.), *Handbook of statistical modeling for the social and behavioral sciences* (pp. 311–359), New York: Plenum Press.

Conger, R., & Elder, G. H., Jr. (1994). *Families in troubled times: Adapting to change in rural America.* New York: Aldine de Gruyter.

Duncan, O. D., Featherman, D., & Duncan, B. (1972). *Socioeconomic background and achievement.* New York: Seminar Press.

Elder, G. H. (1985). *Life course dynamics: Trajectories and transitions, 1968–1980.* Ithaca, NY: Cornell University Press.

Elder, G. H. (1987). War mobilization and the life course: A cohort of World War II veterans. *Sociological Forum, 2,* 449–472.

Elder, G. H. (1994). Time, human agency, and social change: Perspectives on the life course. *Social Psychology Quarterly, 57,* 4–15.

Elder, G. H. (1998). *Children of the Great Depression.* Boulder, CD: Westview Press.

Elder, G. H., George, L., & Shanahan, M. (1996). Psychosocial stress over the life course. In H. Kaplan (Ed.), *Psychosocial stress: Perspectives on structure, theory, life course, and methods* (pp. 247–292). Orlando, FL: Academic Press.

Eliason, S. R., Macmillan, R., & Stryker, R. (2002). *Life histories in context: A comparative framework for analyzing the reciprocal shaping of social institutions and the life course.* Paper presented at the annual meetings of the Society for the Advancement of Socioeconomics (SASE), Minneapolis, June 27–30.

Emirbayer, M., & Mische, A. (1998). What is agency? *American Journal of Sociology, 103,* 962–1023.

Featherman, D., & Carter, M. (1976). Discontinuities in schooling and the socioeconomic life cycle. In W. Sewell, R. Hauser, & D. Featherman (Eds.), *Schooling and achievement in American society* (pp. 133–160). New York: Academic Press.

Furstenberg, F., Brooks-Gunn, J., & Morgan, S. (1987). *Adolescent mothers in later life.* New York: Cambridge University Press.

Furstenberg, F. et al. (1999). *Managing to make it*. Chicago: University of Chicago Press.

George, L. (1996). Missing links: The case for a social psychology of the life course. *The Gerontologist, 36*, 236–245.

George, L. K. (1999). Life course perspectives on mental health. In C. Aneshensel & J. Phelan (Eds.), *Handbook of the Sociology of Mental Health* (pp. 565–584). San Diego: Academic Press.

Gerson, K. (1985). *Hard choices: How women decide about work, career, and motherhood*. Berkeley: University of California Press.

Greenberger, E., & L. Steinberg. (1986). *When teenagers work: The psychological and social costs of adolescent employment*. New York: Basic Books.

Hagan, J. (1991). Destiny and drift: Subcultural preferences, status attainments, and the risks and rewards of youth. *American Sociological Review, 56*, 567–582.

Hagan, J. (2001). *Northern passage*. Cambridge: Harvard University Press.

Han, S., & Moen, P. (1999). Clocking out: Temporal patterning of retirement. *American Journal of Sociology*, 105, 191–236.

Heinz, W. (1991). *The life course and social change: Comparative perspectives*. Weinheim: Deutscher Studien Verlag.

Hogan, D. P. (1978). The variable order of events in the life course. *American Sociological Review, 43*, 573–586.

Johnson, D., & Booth, A. (1998). Marital quality: A product of the dyadic environment or individual factors? *Social Forces, 76*, 883–904.

Long, J. S. (1997). Regression models for cagtegoriat and limited dependent variables. Sage.

Marini, M. (1978). The transition to adulthood: Sex differences in educational attainment and age at marriage. *American Sociological Review, 43*, 483–507.

Marini, M. (1984). The order of events in the transition to adulthood. *Sociology of Education, 57*, 63–84.

Marini, M., & Singer, B. (1984). Causality in the social sciences. *Sociological Methodology*, 18, 347–409.

Modell, J. (1989). *Into one's own: From youth to adulthood in the United States, 1920–1975*. Berkeley: University of California Press.

Modell, J. (1999) When history is omitted. In A. Booth, A. Crouter, & M. Shanahan (Eds.), *Transitions to adulthood in a changing economy: No work, no family, no future?* Westport, CT: Praeger.

Modell, J., Furstenberg, F., & Hershberg, T. (1976). Social change and transitions to adulthood in historical perspective. *Journal of Family History, 1*, 7–32.

Neugarten, B., Moore, J., & Lowe, J. (1965). Age norms, age constraints, and adult socialization. *American Journal of Sociology, 70*, 710–717.

Newcomb, M., & Bentler, P. (1988). *Consequences of adolescent drug use: Impact on the lives of young adults*. Newbury Park: Sage.

Oppenheimer, V., & Lewin, A. (1999). Career development and marriage formation in a period of rising enequality: Who is at risk? What are their prospects? In A. Booth, D. Crouter, & M. Shanahan. (Eds.), *Transitions to adulthood in a changing economy : No work, no family, no future?* (pp. 189–225). Westport, CT: Praeger.

Polivka, A., & Miller, S. (1994). The CPS after the redesign: Refocusing the economic lens. A paper prepared for the *CRIW Labor Statistics Measurement Issues Conference*, Washington, D.C., December 15–16.

Raftery, A. (1995). Bayesian model selection in social research. *Sociological Methodology, 25*, 111–163.

Rindfuss, R., Swicegood, G., & Rosenfeld, R. (1987). Disorder in the life course: How common and does it matter? *American Sociological Review, 52*, 785–801.

Robins, L., & Rutler, M. (1990). Straight and devious pathways from childhood to adulthood. New York: Cambridge University Press.

Sampson, R., & Laub, J. (1993). *Crime in the making: Pathways and turning points through life*. Cambridge: Harvard University Press.

Sampson, R., & Laub L. (1996). Socioeconomic achievement in the life course of disadvantaged men: Military service as a turning point, circa 1940–1965. *American Sociological Review, 61*, 347–367.

Schneider, B., & Stevenson, D. (1999). *The ambitious generation: America's teenagers, motivated but directionless*. New Haven: Yale University Press.

Sewell, W., & Hauser, R. (1974). Education, occupation, and earnings: Achievement in the early career. New York: Academic Press.

Shanahan, M. (2000). Pathways to adulthood in changing societies: Variability and mechanisms in life course perspective. *Annual Review of Sociology, 26*, 667–692.

Shanahan, M., Elder, G., & Miech, R. (1997). History and agency in men's lives: Pathways to achievement in cohort perspective. *Sociology of Education, 70*, 54–67.

Shanahan, M., Miech, R., & Elder, G. (1998). Changing pathways to attainment in men's lives, historical patterns of school, work, and social class. *Social Forces, 77*, 231–256.

Thomas, W., & Znaniecki, F. (1927). *The Polish peasant in Europe and America*. New York: A A. Knopf.

U.S. Department of Labor. (2000). *The national longitudinal surveys handbook 2000*. Washington, D.C.: U.S. Department of Labor, Bureau of Labor Statistics.

Warren, J., Hauser, R., & Sheridan, J. (2002). Occupational stratification across the life course: Evidence from the Wisconsin longitudinal study. *American Sociological Review*.

Wheaton, B. (1990). Life transitions, role histories, and mental health. *American Sociological Review, 55*, 209–223.

CHAPTER 25

Linking Life Course and Life Story

Social Change and the Narrative Study of Lives over Time

BERTRAM J. COHLER

ANDREW HOSTETLER

Human development is embedded in the life course and historical time. Consequently its proper study challenges us to take all life stages into account through the generations, from infancy to the grandparents of old age. (Glen Elder, 1998, p. 9).

INTRODUCTION

The emergence of a life course perspective in the study of human development has provided a means for addressing the interplay of lived experience and socio-historical context, and the intertwining of subjective and shared meanings that shape lives over developmental and historical time. Grounded in the pioneering work of social theorist Karl Mannheim (1928), the life course approach may be contrasted both with life-cycle perspectives, which have tended to focus on relatively invariant, age-graded stages or phases, and with life-span perspectives,

BERTRAM J. COHLER AND ANDREW HOSTETLER • Committee on Human Development, University of Chicago, Chicago, Illinois, 60637

Handbook of the Life Course, edited by Jeylan T. Mortimer and Michael J. Shanahan. Kluwer Academic/Plenum Publishers, New York, 2003.

which have typically not acknowledged the far-ranging impact of "generation units" spanning some number of contiguous birth-years (Mannheim, 1928) or cohort-generational factors (Elder, 1995, 1997; Kertzer, 1983; Troll, 1970). The life course perspective maintains that developmental pathways reflect the distinctive social and historical changes experienced by members of particular generations and cannot be understood apart from this social and historical context (Dannefer, 1984; Denzin, 1989; Elder, 1995, Settersten, 1999).

Unfortunately, although the life course perspective offers conceptual tools for understanding the collective impact of historical change, there has been relatively less study of either inter-cohort or intra-cohort variation in the ways in which socio-historical circumstances are related to particular lives (Elder & O'Rand, 1995). As George (1996), Rosenfeld (1999), and Settersten (1999) have observed, members of a given cohort react in diverse and often unpredictable ways to social and historical circumstances. For example, the timing of transitions into and out of expectable roles—early, late, or on-time—can influence the ways in which those roles are experienced and can alter the timing of other expectable role entrances and exits. Similarly, individuals react differently to collective misfortune. Further, subgroups of individuals may hold many of the basic values and commitments of their generation-cohort, and yet have a somewhat different outlook relative to their larger cohort. Rosenfeld (1999) referred to such groups as "identity cohorts."

Study of the life story provides the theoretical and methodological complement to life course study and is necessary for understanding the course of individual lives. Accompanying the shift from a static to a dynamic approach to the study of lives is an increasing interest in the individual life story, which emerges in the interstices of socio-historical conditions and individual life-circumstances. Systematic study has illustrated the ways in which accounts of both the personal and collective past are rewritten over time (Barclay, 1996; Bruner & Feldman, 1996; Schiff & Cohler, 2001; Singer & Salovey, 1993). From earliest childhood to oldest age, we continue to tell stories of our lived experience in order to create and maintain a sense of coherence, integrity and/or identity (Baerger & McAdams, 1999; Bruner, 1987, 1990; Crites, 1971; Gergen, 1980; Gergen & Gergen, 1997; Linde, 1993; McAdams, 2001; Ochs & Capps, 1996, 2001; Ricoeur, 1977; Schutz & Luckmann, 1973, 1989). Individuals construct meanings from the stream of daily experience, integrating both positive and negative chance events and expectable role transitions (Pearlin 1980; Pearlin & Lieberman, 1979) into a narrative which itself changes across the course of life as a consequence of social and historical circumstances. Even narrative genres and the conventions for telling life stories at particular points in the life course are subject to social change (Elder & Caspi, 1990; Plummer, 1995a; Tonkin, 1992).

This chapter explores the significance of the life story method, incorporated into a broader life course perspective, as a means for understanding the structure and meaning of adult lives. While cohort or generation represents the more general level at which culturally and historically embedded "plots" of the life course are enacted, intra-cohort variation and idiosyncratic life-events give shape to the "differential developmental trajectories" (Savin-Williams, 2001) that make each life story unique. The present chapter focuses on one such differential trajectory, highlighting issues of intimacy among self-identified, single (i.e., without a primary relationship) gay men. Gay and lesbian lives have been among those most affected by the dramatic social transformations of the past half century, and the meanings and experience of intimacy between members of the same-sex have been particularly subject to change (Loughery, 1998). From this example emerge important insights regarding the relationship between socio-historical context and lived experience.

STUDYING SOCIAL CHANGE: THE
EMERGENCE OF A LIFE COURSE
PERSPECTIVE

In general, the human sciences have been much more successful in explaining the functions of social norms and institutions than in understanding the impact of historical change upon lived experience. Over the past three decades, however, several related factors have conspired to move issues of social change to the center of social-scientific study. The first factor concerns the rapid changes that gripped American society from the mid-1960s through the mid-1970s. The emergence of the Civil Rights Movement, Anti-Vietnam War protests, and a major transformation in values relating to gender and sexuality contributed to an unprecedented level of social change in this tumultuous decade, creating a sense of urgency and underscoring the general importance of understanding such change (Gitlin, 1987; Tipton, 1982). One effect of anti-war protests, in particular, was to raise difficult questions regarding constancy and change in values across generations within families and within the larger society (Smith & Haan, 1969; McAdam, 1989). These social upheavals also inspired a new brand of critical social theory, including the important work of Foucault (1973, 1976), which challenged the assumptions of more traditional approaches to the study of social life.

A second contributing factor was the publication of findings from major longitudinal studies (Kagan & Moss, 1962; Jones, Bayley, & MacFarlane, 1971), initiated many decades earlier, which collectively questioned the degree of stability in lives over long periods of time. For example, the work of Brim and Kagan and Kagan challenged the widely accepted notion that the course of development is regular and predictable. Perhaps even more influential was Elder's (1974/1998) integration and reformulation of findings from the several studies at the Institute of Human Development at The University of California, Berkeley. His restudy of two groups of research participants born nearly a decade apart transformed the general approach to birth cohorts from a problem of method (Baltes, Cornelius, & Nesselroade, 1979; Schaie, 1995) to a substantive recognition that social and historical changes, taking place at a particular point in the life course of a particular generation, govern the manner in which members of that generation make sense of a presently remembered past, experienced present and anticipated future.

Extending Troll's (1970) review of the several uses of the term "generation" in studies of the family, Kertzer's (1982, 1983) critique of the concept of generation in the social sciences addressed the confusion in using this term. It has referred to any succession through time, including both ranked descent within the family and also generation unit (Mannheim, 1928). The latter usage failed to recognize that not all those born within some particular span of birth years necessarily share a similar outlook. Kertzer notes that such factors as social stratification and cultural background may lead to somewhat different perspectives on particular historical events among members of a generation unit. However, the quote from Mannheim which he provides (1982, p. 28) clearly presages what Settersten (1999) has portrayed as intra-cohort variation.

Particularly relevant for the present discussion, Mannheim's (1928) concept of generation unit does recognize variation in meanings held by some members of the generation unit, such as sexual minority men. However, in other respects these men may share certain meanings of particular historical events with the rest of their generation-cohort. Kertzer (1982) also maintains that the concept of generational unit doesn't allow for the possibility that lives and outlooks may be altered by subsequent historical events. Mannheim (1928), however, recognizes that members of a generation unit or cohort may change their outlook on life as a result of sub-sequent historical and social change taking place across the course of adult life. The meaning of these social changes may be conditioned by historical events that take place at a particular age for members of a generation, typically events during young adulthood. Events occurring during young adulthood may be particularly salient for the formation of identity, including sexual identity (McAdams, 2001; Schuman, Belli, & Bischoping, 1997).

Referring to Elder's approach in formulating the concept of generation-cohort, Kertzer (1983, p. 143) has noted the application of the term generation to individuals living at partic-ular historical periods (and spanning some birth years) in order to facilitate an understanding of the effects of social change on lived experience. The term generation is used in a similar manner in the present chapter. Introducing the concept of "generational cohorts," Elder (1974/1998, 1995, 1996, 1997) has demonstrated that persons of approximately the same age respond similarly to socio-historical change. Elder further distinguishes between *period effects*, or the shared reaction to socio-historical events of everyone encountering them, and *cohort effects*, which reflect the differential impact and interpretation of events depending on membership in a particular generation-cohort and the point in the life course when the events are experienced.

Elder and Caspi (1990) have suggested that there is a range of events likely to have an impact upon individual lives, linking persons to historical context and creating some shared consciousness or collective mentality (Esler, 1984). However, certain events and time periods may be particularly significant for subsequent experience and development. For example, Schuman and his colleagues (Schuman Belli & Bischoping, 1997; Schuman, Rieger, & Gaidys, 1994; Schuman & Scott, 1989) have presented evidence for a "reminiscence bump," wherein historical events occurring in late adolescence and young adulthood remain highly salient in the subsequent personal accounts or narratives of members of a particular genera-tion-cohort. Although everyone presently living constructs meaning out of the stream of his-torical experience, different generation-cohorts—which experience these events at different points in the life course—may do so in distinctive ways. Another significant contribution of the concept of generational-cohort, then, is that it sensitizes us to the importance of place in the life course for understanding the differential impact of social change.

However, as Ortega Y Gasset (1922), Mannheim (1928), and others (Berger, 1960; Braungart & Braungart, 1986; Knoke, 1984; Rosow, 1978) have observed, the definition of a generation is a complex issue. For example, questions remain regarding the range of adjacent birth-year groups that comprise a generation. Questioning the intellectual justification for using a particular span of years to distinguish between generations, Rosow (1978) has pointed out that it is unlikely that a single year would make a difference in terms of outlook on self and social life. Further, a series of rapid and/or cataclysmic historical events, such as charac-terized the period between 1965 and 1975, can compress generations, reducing the range of birth years comprising a generation. Settersten (1999) has drawn attention to the intra-cohort differences that are inevitably glossed over in discussions of generation. He suggests that as advantages and disadvantages accumulate over the course of life, intra-cohort variability becomes ever greater. However, there is some agreement that adjacent birth cohorts over a period of roughly 15 to 30 years experience events more or less in common and therefore con-stitute a generation, distinguished at least somewhat by its fresh or innovative solutions to the problems of social life (Esler, 1984; Kertzer, 1882, 1983; Mannheim, 1928; Rosow, 1978).

Tied to the recognition that development is much less predictable than formerly presumed was the discovery that much of the appearance of order within lives over time was largely a consequence of method of study. For instance, Gergen (1977, 1994) and Gergen and

Gergen (1997) have posed the dilemma of an "aleotoric" account of human development which suggests that lives are founded on unpredictable events that are subsequently reordered so as to render an account of a life story which is experienced as coherent over time. Schafer (1980, 1981) suggested that, even within clinical psychoanalysis, what had been assumed to be a faithful reconstruction of a life history, was actually a collaboration between analyst and analysand that served to transform the latter's fragmented narrative (Freud, 1909) into a coherent sense of self. Similarly, the emergence of the concept of Post-Traumatic Stress Disorder (PTSD) (Shay, 1994; Sturken, 1997), and its more general extension to memories of childhood trauma (and particularly sexual abuse), raised important questions about the validity of "repressed" memories. Indeed, research has demonstrated that memories can be induced by suggestion and then integrated into a coherent history (Fivush, Gray, & Fromhoff, 1987; Halbwachs, 1950, 1980; Loftus, 1993, Loftus & Ketcham, 1994; Schachter, 1995; Singer & Salovey, 1993).

In general, shared understandings of the past are reshaped over time as a consequence of social and historical change (Halbwachs, 1950; Olick & Robbins, 1998; Schwartz, 1982, 1993, 2000). Hence, the effort to understand the shared elements of self-consciousness and/or common identities of a generation is greatly facilitated by the comparative study of the life stories of members of different generations (Denzin, 1989, 1997; Dunne, 1995; Plummer, 1995a). Moreover, realizing that each life story is unique, narrative study can illuminate the space between shared understandings and subjective experience. Indeed, in an intellectual climate characterized by post-modern skepticism and the demise of grand social narratives, the life story has emerged as perhaps the exemplary form of contemporary social inquiry.

THE LIFE STORY METHOD IN THE SOCIAL SCIENCES

In his review and analysis of the life story approach in the behavioral sciences, Handel (2000) defined the life story as the currently available autobiography reflecting present interpretations of self, others, and relationships and events, which both explains the past and guides future action and intent. McAdams (2001) portrays the development of the ability to construct a complete life story across the years of adolescence. He also shows that we revise our life stories across the course of life in order to maintain a sense of narrative coherence. Moreover, such social factors as gender and social status influence any telling of a life story.

The first-person account, personal narrative or life story is shaped by a complex interplay of distal and proximal social forces, told or written in the context of a particular time and place, and mediated through the relationship between teller/writer and listener/reader. The life story is successively told and retold across the course of life, into oldest age, always with a focus on maintaining narrative coherence (Ricoeur, 1977). Underlying this search for narrative coherence is the presumption that we need to realize order in our lives and are unable to live with uncertainty, ambiguity or radical discontinuity. At the same time, understandings of what constitutes ambiguity or discontinuity may vary across cultures. Moreover, factors such as education may somewhat increase tolerance for ambiguity (Ochs & Capps, 1996, 2001). Nevertheless, within the constraints imposed by culture, we strive over a lifetime to maintain a coherent life story. A life story that is disorganized or rigidly maintained, even in the context of social and historical change, poses problems for adjustment (Ricouer, 1977; Schafer, 1980, 1981).

Behavioral science study has long relied on life story accounts as evidence, from the traditional research interview (Mishler, 1986) to self-life writing, including memoir and autobiography (Bruner, 1987, 1990, 1993; Bruner and Weisser (1991); Plummer (2001).

Following Bakhtin (1981) and others (Briggs & Bauman, 1992; Schely-Newman, 1999), Smith (2001) observed that stories told to another, in the context of life story interviews (Atkinson, 2002) or oral histories (Tonkin, 1992), represent a genre that is relatively distinct from self-life writing (Cohler, in preparation). Plummer (1995b) further distinguishes between the total life story, which attempts to grasp the whole of a life and/or the essence of the person, and the more focused topical life story that is organized around one or more specific events or issues over the course of life.

Notable contributions grounded in study of personal accounts include: Thomas and Znaniecki's (1918) collection of letters and diaries from Eastern European immigrants to America, and the critique of this work (Blumer, 1946); Dollard's (1935) systematic study of personal narratives; Allport's (1965) publication of letters from his college roommate's mother; Franz (1995), Susanne and Lloyd Rudolph's (2000) presentation of the diary of the 19th century Indian nobleman, Amar Singh, and Stewart, Franz, and Layton's (1988) careful analysis of the writings of Vera Brittain, an Oxford educated feminist scholar; Berman's (1994) discussion of the work of the author May Sarton and other notable women authors; Clausen's (1993) detailed review of the lives of six men and women over the period of more than half a century, and Handel's (2000) report on the life of an urban working-class man. Among the important collections of narrative research are those edited by McAdams and Ochberg (1988) and Rosenwald and Ochberg (1992), and the six volumes in the series edited by Lieblich and Josselson.

In general, narrative study has been guided by methodological and epistemological assumptions quite different from the hypothetical-deductive perspective that has characterized so much of social and behavioral research (Mishler, 1990). Lieblich, Tuval-Mashiach, & Zilber, (1998) identified four distinct approaches to the study of life story narratives. The *holistic-content* approach is grounded in a close textual reading and focuses on salient themes in the life story as a whole. This approach is represented by the case-study or detailed life history, and examples include Lieblich's (1993) account of a young woman's experiences immigrating from Russia to Israel, Cole's (1997) conversations with a troubled civil rights leader, and the above-mentioned work of Berman (1994) and Handel (2000). This is contrasted with a *categorical-content* or "content analysis" approach, which focuses on tagging text and assigning codes to specific content largely irrespective of place in the account. Franz (1995) and Stewart, Franz, & Layton (1988) employ this method in their study of Vera Brittain. This second approach is facilitated by the application of computer programs such as the General Inquirer (Stone, 1966), which codes text into categories based on an internally stored dictionary, or The Ethnograph (Qualis Research Associates, 1999) or NVIVO (Richards, 2002), which provide ready access to particular codes or summaries of codes either within or across life stories.

A third, *holistic-form* method focuses on the structure rather than the content of an account, for instance charting the high and low points in a life story (Back & Bourque, 1970; Chiraboga, 1978; deVries, Blando, Southard, & Bubeck, 2001; Freedman, Thornton, Camburn, Alwin, & Young-DeMarco,1988; Runyan, 1980; Whitbourne & Dannefer, 1985–1986) or graphically representing the distance between events and/or relationships described in first-person accounts, as subjectively understood by the storyteller and using a particular metric (Josselson, 1996a). Finally, Lieblich et al. (1998) identify the *categorical-form* or "discourse analysis" approach, which focuses on the structure of narrative discourse as contained within the interview transcript and which is most characteristic of the linguistic study of personal accounts (Mishler, 1999; Schely-Newman, 1999; Schiffrin, 2000).

Regardless of the particular approach adopted, much of narrative study has proceeded according to what Mishler (1990) has termed an inquiry-guided perspective, which highlights the means by which individuals maintain a sense of continuity over time, construct identities, and manage tensions in personal and social life. Inquiry-guided research (Mishler, 1990) is grounded in the close study of evidence as the only appropriate basis for theory, with particular attention to the relationship between author and informant or text. Concerning the veracity and general epistemological status of self-reports, Mishler (1990) has suggested that "trustworthiness" rather than truth must be the fundamental requirement for validation in the social sciences. Given the likelihood of disagreement over the meanings of social life, this perspective allows for a range of possibilities with respect to acceptable evidence and interpretive techniques within a given field of inquiry. This approach to validation assumes that change over time—in what counts as evidence and what constitutes a "good story"—is inevitable, despite the fact that life stories themselves tend to reflect narratives of continuity. Issues of statistical representativeness are not of paramount concern. For example, Bertaux (1981) has observed that life stories become somewhat repetitive in content after a certain number has been collected, suggesting that saturation has been reached and that sufficient evidence has been obtained to address the particular research question.

Consistent with Mishler's (1990) approach, several other scholars have drawn attention to the reflexive dimension of life story research, suggesting that any account must be understood in terms of the full context of its writing or telling, including time, place and the interpretations made by the listener or reader (Iser, 1978; Kaminsky, 1992). Contemporary study of the life story recognizes that teller and listener are intertwined as a part of a shared activity, co-constructing meaning as a result of their collaboration (Fontana & Frey, 2000; Myerhoff and Ruby, 1982/1992; Ochs & Capps, 2001; Plummer, 1995b; Smith 2001; Tedlock, 2000). Following Bakhtin (1981), Josselson (1996b), and Kaminsky (1992) have both emphasized the plurality of voices that enter into an account, including but not necessarily limited to tellers and listeners. In keeping with reader response theory in literary criticism, which acknowledges that interpretation is not necessarily dictated by authorial intent (Denzin, 1997; Iser, 1978), the post-modern, post-realist social scientist is understood to be an active participant in the research process, a competent interpreter of social life who is reflexively aware of his or her own world view (Geertz, 1973, 1974) and place in the social world, including membership in a particular generation (Mannheim, 1928; Ortega y Gasset, 1921–1922). As Plummer (1995b) has observed, "No life story is simply that: a story. Instead it is built out of a series of social domains surrounding the life story-teller, the psychologist who is collecting the story, and the interaction between them (p. 56)."

Further, the life story changes over time with each successive telling or writing, as a function of both aging and social change, indicating the need for longitudinal study. For example, Novick (1999) and Schiff & Cohler (2001) have documented shifts in the narratives of Holocaust survivors, noting important differences between those accounts collected in the wake of the Eichmann trial and those collected several decades later by Steven Spielberg following release of the film, "Schindler's List." Subsequent tellings of collective narratives reflect prior accounts, of course, as well as the confluence of individual-developmental, and socio-historical change (Schiff & Cohler, 2001; Schiff, Noy, & Cohler, 2001). Similarly, the stories of a particular generation-cohort are shaped and reshaped by the shared understandings of both previous and successive generation-cohorts. From a life course perspective, there is little value in assigning causal primacy to either personal life-circumstances or socio-cultural context in the structuring and restructuring of life stories. Plummer (1995a) has suggested a bi-directional causal relationship in which personal stories can also provide a foundation for collective movements and social change, as appears to have been the case with respect to the both the "coming out" stories of gays and lesbians and the survival stories of victims of sexual abuse. Hence, context, lived-experience and life story are all intertwined in the meaning-making projects of individuals and generation-cohorts (Cohler, in preparation; Schiff & Cohler, 2001).

As an interpretive method, it has been somewhat difficult to integrate narrative study with quantitative social science inquiry, although several researchers have achieved some promising results in this direction. Baerger and McAdams (1999), for example, showed that it is possible to code life story narratives with satisfactory inter-rater reliability on an index of coherence (based on social and temporal orientation of the action, explicit goals and intentions, etc.). Interestingly, this index of coherence was negatively associated with depression scores and moderately positively associated with measures of happiness and of life-satisfaction.

The categorical-content approach to the study of life stories is generally compatible with quantitative analysis. Examples include the work of McAdams and colleagues on generativity (McAdams & de St. Aubin, 1992; McAdams, Hart & Maruna, 1998), and analytical treatments of the life story of Vera Brittain (Franz, 1995; Patterson & Stewart, 1990; Stewart, Franz, & Layton, 1989; Stewart & Vandewater, 1998). Among other things, statistically reliable coding categories enable researchers to study changes within personal accounts such as diaries, fictional writing, or repeated interviews. In the case of Vera Brittain's diary, for instance, a categorical-content analysis revealed a shift from an early-adulthood focus on identity concerns to a mid-life preoccupation with issues of intimacy and generativity, consistent with Erikson's (1982) model of psychosocial development. However, Mishler (1990) has questioned the level of standardization of this coding procedure, and he concludes that such efforts at quantification tend to be somewhat arbitrary and context bound, and hence less generalizable than investigators typically claim.

The holistic-form approach also lends itself to quantitative analysis, since estimates regarding high and low points in the life story can be studied both within persons over time and across groups. The important contributions of an ipsative, idiographic, or morphogenic analysis of holistic-form or life-chart methods have been reviewed by Allport (1965). It is somewhat more difficult to reconcile quantitative perspectives with the holistic-content or categorical-form perspectives, which focus on the integrity of the story as a narrative totality, and which highlight the relationship between listener and teller (Kaminsky, 1992; Tedlock, 2000; Tonkin, 1992) and the manner in which the life story is told.

We applaud the efforts of narrative researchers to formalize the life history method, and while we attempted to be systematic in our own research, we are careful not to sacrifice the integrity and the singularity of the individual life history. With this goal in mind, we attempt in the final section of this chapter to achieve a more thorough integration of the life course perspective and the life story method. Employing an example from the study of lesbian and gay lives, including a narrative illustration from our own research, we explore the intersections of social change and individual subjectivity.

LINKING LIFE STORY AND LIFE COURSE:
AN EXAMPLE FROM THE STUDY OF GAY
AND LESBIAN LIVES

As we have suggested, the comparative, cohort-generational study of life stories highlights the impact of a changing social context on the shape and course of individual lives. Not only do socio-historical events impact lives in specific and tangible ways, but shared, cohort-and period-specific social understandings and interpretive frameworks also establish the definitional boundaries of roles, relationships, identities, and hence subjective experience. Graff (1995) beautifully illustrates this perspective in a study of adult memoirs of childhood written between the eighteenth and early twentieth centuries, narratives that reflect the increasing subjective salience of categories of social class, ethnicity, and gender in American society.

Moreover, the impact of events cannot be understood apart from their social framing. For example, Elder and his colleagues (Elder, 1987; Elder & Clipp, 1989; Elder, Shanahan & Clipp, 1994) found military service during World War II to be a particularly meaningful and, in retrospect, "peak" experience for many returning veterans. On a structural level, service in the war delayed such expectable transitions as marriage and the completion of formal education, and it provided material support in the form of the G.I. Bill and a booming post-War economy, facilitating a comfortable middle-class life-style. On a symbolic level, participation in the "Good War" provided an enduring sense of pride and source of positive identity. This contrasts sharply with the experience of Vietnam veterans, who were generally younger, and who received an ambivalent and sometimes hostile reception when they returned home from an international conflict increasingly unpopular with the American public. Developmental outcomes for these men in the Vietnam cohort included high rates of homelessness, substance abuse and mental illness, raising important questions about the relationship between social context and psychological well-being.

The study of gay and lesbian lives is particularly well-suited to a comparative life history approach for two primary reasons. First, the social transformations of the 20th century had particularly dramatic effects on the lives of lesbians and gay men. Indeed, in some respects gay history is 20th-century history writ small: from rural isolation to the social realignments associated with processes of industrialization and urbanization; from wartime persecution, imprisonment and torture in the Nazi work camps to the post-war emergence of vibrant gay urban enclaves (Bérubé, 1990); from the heady, indulgent days of "free love" and Gay Liberation to the unimaginable devastation, renewed social stigmatization, and, ultimately, the cultural and political rebirth that followed in the wake of the AIDS pandemic.

Second, the life story has been an indispensable tool in the formation of gay and lesbian communities and lifeways, giving a common, shared voice to a previously unarticulated sense of individual difference and leading to a proliferation of structured opportunities for communal telling and listening. At the same time, the gay "coming out" story has been an exemplar of late-modern narratives, encapsulating themes of "suffering, surviving and surpassing" (Plummer, 1995a, p. 15).

Recent research and theory have highlighted the importance of studying "gay" and "lesbian" lives within the context of shared, cohort-specific understandings of sexual identities and lifeways (Boxer & Cohler, 1989; Cohler, in preparation; Cohler & Galatzer-Levy, 2000; Herdt & Boxer, 1996; Hostetler & Herdt, 1998). To this end, several life story collections have illustrated important cross-generational differences in the narrative self-understandings of gays and lesbians (Parks, 1999; Rosenfeld, 1999; Stein, 1997; Sadownick, 1997). However, with the exception of Sadownick's (1997) report on archival material, this research has relied on present-time accounts, obscuring the impact of developmental and age-related factors on the narration of past events. Indeed, the longitudinal study of life story telling within a given generation is necessary to more thoroughly comprehend the dynamics of change, and to distinguish between cohort- and developmentally based differences.

Nevertheless, given the sheer magnitude of the social shift in understandings of homosexuality, even cross-sectional study can reveal the boundaries of gay intergenerational difference. Following a series of more gradual shifts in the social organization of sexuality during the first half of the 20th century (Chauncey, 1994; D'Emilio & Freedman, 1997), gay and lesbian life exploded into public consciousness following the advent of the Gay Rights movement in the late 1960s and early 1970s (D'Emilio, 1998; Kaiser, 1997). Inspired by and modeled on the Civil Rights movement, Gay Liberation was ignited in the aftermath of patron resistance to a June, 1969 police raid on the New York gay bar, The Stonewall Inn (Duberman, 1993). This spontaneous protest and the overzealous police response led to a series of riots over the course of several days, inspiring further community activism among a new "gay" generation (although Murray [1992, 1996] and others have argued that the direct influence of the Stonewall Riots has been greatly exaggerated). An anniversary parade and celebration one year later drew a crowd of several thousand men and women to Central Park and became the forerunner of the annual gay pride parades held in many major cities across the United States each year over the last weekend in June.

Although the Gay Rights movement, most potently symbolized by the Stonewall Riots, forever altered the shape of gay and lesbian life, its impact was largely cohort-specific. Not only are different generations defined by different historical moments, but they also react in somewhat distinct ways to the same historical events. This is no less true of individuals who express a same-gender preference (Cohler, in preparation). Herdt & Boxer (1996) identified four distinct historical cohorts of American homosexual men and women, defined by the eras in which they came of age: World War I, World War II, Gay Liberation, and the AIDS epidemic. Although homosexual members of so-called "Generation X" coming to adulthood in the 1990s and the "baby boom" generation both experienced the events associated with Gay Liberation, these events had quite different implications for the lives—and the life stories—of the two cohorts. Further, many of those who were in the generation of the "pre baby boomers,"already in midlife at the time of the Stonewall riots, men and women who were more likely to see themselves as "homosexual" than as "gay" or "lesbian," had long-since accommodated their lives to the social stigma they believed was inevitably attached to their sexual orientation (Rosenfeld, 1999). These men and women avoided social opprobrium, for instance, by selecting careers that involved minimal supervision or interaction with coworkers, such as accounting or library science, and which therefore allowed them to "fly below the radar."

By contrast, those men and women who first came of age in the era of the Gay Rights movement were much more likely to view their homosexuality as a centrally defining aspect of their identities, an essentially "ethnic" form of difference that entitled them to demand civil rights and social respect (Parks, 1999; Rosenfeld, 1999; Sadownick, 1997). While a more confrontational style led to increased civil rights for sexual minorities, it also engendered greater social conflict within the workplace and the larger community and to more overt explicit experiences of discrimination. This is also the generation hit hardest by AIDS. The tragic and untimely deaths of far too many members of this generation would give birth to a new generation defined by its "safer sex" practices and its "queer" politics and ethos.

The self-understandings of different generations of gay men and women, and hence the kinds of stories they tell, not surprisingly bear the imprint of these repeated social transformations. As Kenneth Plummer (1995a) has argued, the gay "coming out" narrative is a genre highly specific to the late-modern, Western, capitalist context. And reflecting broader cultural themes of childhood developmental determinism, contemporary gay and lesbian life stories typically begin with memories of a nameless and strongly felt sense of childhood difference. But it is perhaps changing narratives of same-sex intimate and sexual expression that most profoundly communicate the impact of social change on the organization of the life story.

Summarizing the life stories of 23 lesbians, Parks (1999) finds marked generational differences in the experience of desire and intimacy. The 11 women who were middle-aged at the time of the Stonewall Riots reported feeling isolated and alone during their youth and young adulthood, experiencing a pervasive sense of stigma. Delayed in the realization of lesbian identities, their life stories are organized around themes of silenced desire. The narratives of twelve women who were young adults at the time of Stonewall reflect an increased sense of personal freedom and sociality. These women self-identified as lesbian at a much earlier age, which facilitated a more timely transition into intimate relationships. In comparing women from this same generation to a group of lesbians who entered early adulthood in the 1990s, Stein (1997) reports that the narratives of the younger women are less explicitly organized around themes of political activism, having come of age in a decade characterized by the increasing privatization of experience (Putnam, 2000). This younger generation of women appears more willing to accept contradiction, inconsistency and ambiguity in their sexual identity stories, moving with greater ease between same and opposite gender partnership. Against the backdrop of the "lesbian baby boom" (Patterson, 1995), many of these young women are also making the transition in greater numbers into parenthood in the context of lesbian partnership.

LIFE COURSE, SOCIAL CHANGE, AND THE
STUDY OF SAME-GENDER INTIMACY

Narratives of gay male desire and intimate expression similarly reflect these historical shifts in the meaning and structure of gay life. Employing archival data, Sadownick (1997) contrasts the narratives of homoerotically inclined men from two generations, men who came of age during the post-war era and men who entered young adulthood in the 1970s. The older generation, many of whom returned from war-time service to seaboard cities, offer stories centered around discrete public sexual experiences and nervous visits to bars in a context of periodic police shakedowns and congressional crusades against homosexuality. These men often found themselves playing the role of sexual detective, decoding little signs and bits of evidence to determine which men were potential sexual partners. These furtive explorations of desire contributed to a disconnect between their experiences of sexuality and intimacy (reinforced by gay male sexual culture, this tendency is something against which many gay men of succeeding generations have continued to struggle [Sullivan, 1998]).

Despite the substantial achievements of the Gay Liberation movement, including the declassification of homosexuality as a mental disorder, the Stonewall generation faced their own particular challenges. As Sadownick (1997, p. 107) reports, many of these men arrived at midlife experiencing a sense of guilt, having outlived many of their contemporaries and believing that their own sexual indulgences in the era of "free love" contributed to spread of AIDS. Twenty years into the epidemic, young gay men's narratives of intimacy and sexuality express a range of themes, from "survivor guilt," to reckless abandon and apathy bolstered by the false belief that current drug therapies have effectively ended AIDS, to the super-charged experience of unprotected sex and "semen exchange" in the context of committed relationships (Odets, 1995).

Today, gay dating, romance, and sexual experimentation occur against a backdrop in which long-term partnership is an increasingly expectable feature of the gay life course (Hostetler & Cohler, 1997; Hostetler & Herdt, 1998). Same-sex marriage and domestic partnership have risen to the top of the gay and lesbian political agenda, despite continuing debate within the community regarding the desirability of "heteronormative" relationship models, and an outspoken group of gay neo-liberals/neo-conservatives is publicly encouraging gay men to give up their sexual adventures and embrace the domestic bliss of committed partnership (Baer, 1981; Eskridge, 1996; Kirk & Madsen, 1993; Rotello, 1997; Sullivan, 1995, 1997).

Dating services, chat lines and online chat rooms, personal ads, and "how to" articles in glossy national gay magazines have emerged to assist gay men in the search for "Mr. Right." At the same time, somewhere in the vicinity of 50% of all gay men report that they are currently single (i.e., without a primary same-sex relationship) (Bell, & Weinberg, 1978; Harry, 1984; Herdt, Beeler, & Rawls, 1997; Kurdek, 1995). Although the increasing emphasis on long-term, committed relationships would suggest that it is becoming more difficult to be gay and single, single gay men are not necessarily reacting to these emergent norms in a straightforward or predictable manner: some bemoan their single status, while others appear to have adapted quite well. Not surprisingly, their responses are often filtered through a cohort-specific outlook.

Tied to a larger, ongoing narrative study of aging and adult development among gays and lesbians, one of the authors (Hostetler, 2001) has been investigating psychological well-being among middle-aged and older single gay men (i.e., without a primary same-sex partner), with particular attention to the ways in which single status is integrated, or not, into the larger life story. As part of this study, 94 men (35 and over) completed a structured interview, and 20 of these men were selected to participate in a follow up life history interview, with an eye toward representing the diversity of the larger sample. Whereas the focus of the structured interview was on identifying statistical relationships (and more specifically on variables that predict psychological well-being among this population), the life history interviews were employed to (preliminarily) identify narrative themes associated with being more or less satisfied with one's single status, and with one's life in general.

Although informed by Bertaux's (1981) concept of saturation, the primary goal of the qualitative analysis was not to establish additional statistical relationships (i.e., between outcome variables of well-being and particular narratives), but rather to examine through "thick analysis" (Geertz, 1973) the ways in which this particular group of men integrate their single status into their life histories. Among the topics of interest were the ways in which these narrative understandings reflect membership in a particular age-cohort. All interviews were conducted in person, either in participants' homes, at a Chicago-area lesbian and gay community center or, in one case, at a café. The interviews ranged in length from 1 hr and 20 min to almost $3\frac{1}{2}$; hr. Each interview was audio-recorded and later transcribed.

Our general approach to life history interviewing and narrative analysis is a hybrid of the approaches described above. We begin our interviews with a life history exercise (Cohler, Hostetler & Boxer, 1998; Hostetler & Cohler, 1997) adapted from Back and Bourque (1970), Runyan (1980), and Whitbourne and Dannefer (1985–1986). This exercise allows participants to think about and organize their life experience in ways that most make sense to them. Participants begin by working with the interviewer to place four or five specific life-events or general time periods, viewed by the former as personally important, on a chart that horizontally registers chronological order and vertically gauges relative mood or morale from low to high (despite the chronological scale, events are elicited in no particular order). They are then asked to fill in other important events/periods, and to discuss these different events/periods in greater detail.

Although this type of interviewing lends itself to an *holistic-form* analysis, our preferred method of analysis combines Lieblich, Tuval-Masiach, and Zilber's (1998) *holistic-content* and *categorical-content* approaches, discussed above. Accordingly, the life history exercise is used primarily as a means of orienting the discussion, and is followed by a series of questions covering a broad array of loosely structured topics, giving participants the opportunity to highlight what they see as most important in understanding their lives. These general topics include: experience of being gay, "coming out," relationships with family and friends, work and professional life, involvement in the community, including the LGBT community, religious background and involvement, ethnic/racial background and identity, experience of discrimination and harassment, feelings about aging, and feelings and attitudes about being single.

The first phase in our data analysis approximated the *holistic-content* approach. We were also guided in this phase by Mishler's (1990) inquiry-guided perspective and Strauss and Corbin's (1990) open coding methodology. We tried to approach each life history interview as if it were a single case study, and not part of larger study, analyzing it on its own terms. However, given our interest in issues of intimacy, we did focus our analysis on some of the following broad thematic areas: satisfaction with single status, overall life satisfaction and morale, perceived social support, relationship history, past and present life goals regarding partnership, and racial and age-related variations in the experience of and attitudes toward being single. One of the authors (Hostetler) was particularly interested in the meaning of being "single by choice," and how this relates to overall well-being. In the second phase we employed a content analysis approach. We looked for common themes in the men's understandings of their single status, and the interviews were then coded with the application of In-Vivo, a qualitative analysis software program (which also allowed us to explore the relationships between different themes and scores on quantitative measures from the structured interviews).

The analysis revealed seven primary themes in the men's understandings of their single status, five of which I discuss here; these themes sometimes overlapped and were not mutually exclusive. The "personal past" and "collective past" themes appeared, respectively, in 11 and 5 of the 20 life histories, and involved the attribution of one's single status to particular developmental/ biographical or historical circumstances (e.g., coming out late in life, the lack of available role models for relationships). Interestingly, while 9 of the 12 white men provided a developmental accounting for their single status, only 2 of the 8 men of color did so, suggesting the hypothesis that the predilection for developmental or ontological explanation may be primarily an artifact of the Anglo-American cultural tradition.

Another theme, "learning from experience," occurred in 7 of the 20 life histories. The men in this category, who were among the most content with their single status, considered themselves to be on a temporary or even permanent relationship hiatus as a result of past experiences (both positive and negative). Although the distribution of this theme was relatively even across age groups, there nevertheless appeared to be a (rather intuitive) age-related dimension. More precisely, the younger men (i.e., under 45) tended to see their single status as temporary, and their narratives express a sense of choice in terms that are more easily recognizable. They are currently "taking a break" from intimate relationships, for one reason or another, but fully expect to freely choose partnership in the future. Unlike their older counterparts, they believe the odds are still in their favor (with an apparently direct relationship between perceived choice and perceived likelihood of finding future partnership, confirmed by the quantitative data).

Another set of themes offer a different perspective on the meaning of being single by choice. The specter of the "loner" looms large in considerations of long-term singlehood, and we might expect the "true" loners to be the most well adjusted to their single status. But although many of the men in my sample possessed characteristics that might qualify them as loners, it was unclear in many cases whether I was dealing with an enduring personality trait or a life-pattern acquired as a result of many years spent alone. Hence, I distinguished between two groups of men, which I label the "loners" and the "aloners." The "loners" (9 out of 20) believe that their single status at least partially reflects a long-standing dispositional or temperamental characteristic, which they trace throughout their adult lives if not back to childhood (and which may or may not be tied to a developmental narrative). These men may see themselves as "too independent," as "control freaks," or they may even be self-defined loners.

The "aloners" (9 out of 20) also fear that they may be temperamentally unsuited for long-term relationships, but, in addition, they report an increasing pattern of social isolation with age that extends beyond the romantic and sexual realms. Hence, it is difficult to determine—perhaps for them as well as for me—which came first, the experience of social isolation or the posited personality trait. Compared to the "aloners," the "loners" perceive a relatively high degree of personal control over their intimate lives. For the "aloners," being single by choice seems to mean understanding and accepting the limits of their capabilities, taking control by recognizing that they do not have the power to alter the course of their intimate lives.

Although the small sample and the cross-sectional nature of data prevent me from making any general statements about age- and cohort-related differences, many of the narratives nevertheless appear to reflect the individual's membership in a particular cohort and how this has impacted his experience of being gay and single. Indeed, five of the twenty men explicitly attributed their single status, or at least situated their experience of being single, within the context of particular sociohistorical circumstances. Their narratives illustrate the intersection of idiosyncratic life events and historical circumstances, combining several of the themes discussed above, and they each have a keen sense of historical consciousness.

For example, although Martin and Bennett have very similar narrative profiles in terms of the themes employed, their life histories nevertheless reveal a divergence of worldviews, and their experience of singlehood appears to have been shaped by the era in which they came of age. Martin is a 46-year-old white lawyer who lives alone in a high-rise apartment on the Chicago River. A self-described "party boy" in his youth, Martin has become a bit more socially isolated in recent years, both for reasons of his own choosing and those out of his control. He is somewhat of a workaholic, and he has made a conscious effort to distance himself from his working-class roots (although he is still close to his family). At the same time, he wishes he had more friends with whom he could "just hang out." Martin's life has been complicated by a long history of depression and serious health problems, most notably kidney disease and an eventual transplant. Given an uncertain lifespan and a generally negative outlook, he adopted a "live for the moment" attitude with respect to both his career and his personal life, and he never really planned for the future:

> I never expected to live much more past 25 … I decided at 28 that it looked like I would be around for awhile, so I might as well do something.

The arrival of the AIDS epidemic in the early 1980s only served to intensify his conviction that he would die young:

> I think there was an overwhelming sense that we'll all be dead soon … One friend of mine used to say, 'Pass the donuts, we're all going to die anyway.'

His present-time orientation extended to his experience of relationships, and he claims he never expected nor strongly desired a long-term relationship with another man. Indeed, he appears to have had only one serious relationship, which lasted for approximately 2 years in the late 1970s. But it was not only the sense of an uncertain future, heightened by the cohort-defining AIDS pandemic, that shaped his expectations regarding partnership; Martin "came out" and came of age during the era of Gay Liberation, at which time the idea of "mimicking" heterosexual monogamy was anathema to many gay men and women:

> [Same-sex partnership] was inconceivable at that time, the '70s … That was the era where 30 seemed incredibly old. I can't tell you how old 30 seemed … I never ever conceived of having a husband or whatever. When I was 22 or 25, that part of the community that I hung out with, long-term relationships were just not part of it. The '70s were for the most part when we all started coming out. A whole lot of that was 'fuck you' towards the straight community. …I'm having a much better time than you could hope to have.

Although he says he is currently more open to having a relationship than in the past, he isn't actively looking nor does he expect to find one. He says he only wants a relationship if he can hold onto all the things he enjoys about being single, and he suspects he has become too independent and too self-centered to make one work. Indeed, he recently came to the conclusion that somewhere along the line he more or less implicitly decided to be single:

> I've come to the realization that I'm single because that's what I wanted ... Over the years there were a lot of choices I made that sort of insured that I wound up single. Lots of choices.

Remaining single does not mean that he is alone or lonely. He remains engaged in his work, retains close ties to certain family members, travels frequently, and socializes on a regular basis with his group of seven or so close friends. Despite his apparent disinterest in caring for the next generation as a parent or mentor, he appears to be reasonably content. Although he wouldn't mind having more people to "hang out with," he claims that he has "never been more satisfied." He never expected to live as long as he has, and he is surprised and grateful to still be here. And for the first time in his life he is experiencing a "feeling of completeness, wholeness," which, he says, comes from within.

Bennett is a 77-year-old white, retired social worker who has lived alone for many years in a large apartment in the heart of one of Chicago's most exclusive neighborhoods. Neither Martin nor Bennett could accurately be described as loners, but both men have nevertheless become more isolated as they have aged (hence the classification as "aloners"). Bennet is a Chicago native whose childhood unfolded against the backdrop of the Great Depression. He served in the military during the World War II, at which time he had his first sexual experience with another man. Upon returning from the war, Bennett experimented with several jobs before settling into his career as a social worker.

Bennett's gay life has been very secretive for the most part, and the few relationships he has had with men have been very circumspect. He came of age in the era of the "closet homosexual" (Herdt & Boxer, 1996), and he never expected or desired to lead an openly gay life. Given this cohort-specific outlook, the very idea of a long-term same-sex relationship strikes him as somewhat absurd:

> Gay relationships] never had any appeal. Certainly now I know a lot of gay couples, but I don't think I will now throw rocks at the partnership bit, but to me it is too new for me to be identified with ... I think there should be spouse insurance, partner insurance, whatever you want to call it. That's ok, but I suppose for the marriage thing I'm just too old fashioned.

He claims he always "dated girls," but these relationships were non-sexual. Two additional factors shaped his experience of intimacy. Like many of his contemporaries he had an affinity for married men, who were commonly viewed as more desirable than overtly homosexual men (Chauncey, 1994), albeit less obtainable. He reports that he had three "love affairs" with other men, all of whom were married. These relationships were primarily sexual, and included a 10-year, on-again, off-again affair with a man in England. Although many of his gay friends were also married, he claims he never wanted this for himself. He attributes this conviction to his parents' bad marriage—a final factor contributing to his view of relationships:

> They stayed married their entire lives. It was a Victorian marriage. They weren't good friends and...they had almost nothing in common...We could never figure out why they got married

He sums up his feelings about intimacy and relationships in the following way:

> I didn't want to go into the sunset holding anybody's hand, OK...It's been pretty consistent because the person I was in love with is almost invariable married. I really never have had any desire to get married because my parents made marriage look boring. I've lived alone too long. I couldn't stand it.

Like Martin, he claims to be "perfectly happy" with his present life. He continues to indulge a lifelong passion for travel, and has a particular fondness for London, and he remains quite involved with charitable work. However, in recent years he mourned the death of his closest friend, and his social network continues to shrink. And there remains the slightest hint of regret in his voice, perhaps expressing a sense of what could have been. This is most apparent in his evocation, on more than one occasion, of the "walking into the sunset" image, as in the following exchange at the completion of the interview:

Q: Obviously you're not waiting for Mr. Right?
A: Not unless somebody rises from the dead...
Q: By which you mean somebody who you know from your past?
A: Yes. And there could be no relationship that could touch those, straight or gay ... I mean I suppose we could hold hands like Brandon Scott and Cary Grant and go quietly into the sunset. No.

The purpose of these two very attenuated life stories is not to examine the reasons or "causes" for the chronic single status of these men, nor is the primary goal to prove that singles can be happy and well adjusted. Rather, the point of this very specific example is to demonstrate the broader value of the life story method for exploring the interplay between individual subjectivity, diverse developmental trajectories and sociohistorical circumstances. Both of these men make sense of their experience as single gay men through a complex interpretive framework that weaves together idiosyncratic live events, particular self-perceptions and shared and largely cohort-specific understandings of a constantly changing social world. The "success" of a life story can be judged, at least in part, by the extent to which the story-teller accomplishes this integration. The success of the life story researcher can be recognized in his or her good faith effort to represent this sometimes fragile, and always dynamic meaning-making process.

CONCLUSION

The emergence of a life course perspective represents both a methodological and substantive advance in the study of lives, highlighting the ways in which a seemingly natural life course is shaped and reshaped by social and historical forces. Men and women of roughly the same age constitute a convoy of consociates (Plath, 1980) traveling across the course of life, negotiating social change together, and co-constructing meanings from the stream of lived experience. These meanings are reflected in both told and written accounts (Mannheim, 1928; Ortega Y Gasset, 1921–1922), and thus study of the life story provides an important theoretical and methodological complement to the life course perspective.

The life story method highlights the often-ignored problem of intra-cohort variation, and offers a means by which to explore the interplay of sociohistorical context, individual subjectivity and lived experience from childhood to oldest age (Holstein & Gubrium, 2000). The life history interview and such forms of self-life writing, as memoirs, diaries, letters, and autobiographies, become important tools in the effort to understand how life-phases and life-transitions are fashioned into a coherent account of a presently remembered past, experienced present, and anticipated future to provide a continuing sense of personal integrity. Analysis of life history data can proceed along several different paths, but is typically informed by an inquiry-guided perspective (Mishler, 1990), which focuses on the means by which individuals maintain a sense of personal coherence and continuity over time. Finally, the comparative, inter-cohort study of life history narratives can illuminate the impact of social change on the shape, course and epistemological framework of different "lifeways." In sum, the life story represents an exemplary method for studying the ways in which history and life course shape subjectivity.

REFERENCES

Allport, G. W. (1942). *The use of personal documents in psychological science*. New York: Social Science Research Council.

Allport, G. W. (1965). *Letters from Jenny*. New York: Harcourt, Brace, and World.

Atkinson, R. (2002). The Life story interview. In J. F. Gubrium and J. A. Holstein (Eds.). *Handbook of interview research: Context and method*. (pp. 121–140) Thousand Oaks, CA: Sage Publications.

Back, K., & Bourque, L. (1970). Life graphs: Aging and cohort effects, *Journal of Gerontology, 25*, 249–255.

Baerger, D. M., & McAdams, D. P. (1999). Life story coherence and its relation to psychological well being, *Narrative Inquiry, 9*, 69–96.

Bakhtin, M. M. (1981). *The dialogic imagination*. (Trans. C. Emerson and M. Holquist). Austin, Texas: The University of Texas Press.

Baltes, P., Cornelius, S. & Nesselroade, J. (1979). Cohort effects in developmental psychology. In J. R. Nesselroade & P. B. Baltes (Eds.), *Longitudinal research in the study of behavior and development* (pp. 61–87). New York: Academic Press.

Barclay, C. (1996). Autobiographical remembering: Narrative constraints on objectified selves. In D. Rubin (Ed.). *Remembering our past: Studies in autobiogrpahical memory*. New York: Cambridge University Press.

Bawer, R. (1981). *A place at the table: The gay individual in American society*. New York: Poseidon Press.

Bell, A., & Weinberg, M. (1978). *Homosexualities: A study of diversity among men and women*. New York: Simon & Schuster.

Bengtson, V., & Black, K. D. (1973). Intergenerational relations and continuities in socialization. In P. B. Baltes and K. W. Schaie (Eds.), *Life span developmental psychology: Personality and socialization* (pp. 207–234). New York: Academic Press.

Bengtson, V., Furlong, M., & Laufer, R. (1974). Time, aging, and the continuity of social structure: Themes and issues in generational analysis. *Journal of Social Issues, 30*, 1–30.

Berger, B. (1960). How long is a generation?, *British Journal of Sociology, 11*, 10–23.

Berman, H. (1994). *Interpreting the aging self: Personal journals of later life*. New York: Springer Publishing Company.

Bertaux, D. (1981). From the life-history approach to the transformation of sociological practice. In D. Bertaux (Ed.). *Biography and Society: The Life History Approach in the Social Sciences*. Newbury Park, CA: Sage Publications, 28–46.

Bérubé, A. (1990). *Coming out under fire: The history of gay men and women in World War Two*. New York: Free Press.

Blos, P. (1980). The life cycle as indicated by the nature of the transference in the psychoanalysis of adolescents. *International Journal of Psychoanalysis, 61(2)*, 145–151.

Blumer, H. (1946). *Critiques of Research in the social sciences: I. An appraisal of Thomas and Znaniecki's "The Polish peasant in Europe and America"*. New York: Social Science Research Council.

Boxer, A., & Cohler, B. (1989). The life course of gay and lesbian youth: An immodest proposal for the study of lives. In G. Herdt (Ed.). *Gay and lesbian youth*. (pp. 315–355) New York: Harrington Park Press.

Braungart, R. G., & Braungart, M. M. (1986). Life-course and generational politics, *Annual Review of Sociology, 12*, 205–231.

Briggs, C., & Bauman, R. (1992). Genre, intertextuality, and social power, *Journal of linguistic Anthropology, 2*, 131–172.

Brim, O. G., Jr., Kagan, J. (1980). *Constancy and change in human development*. Cambridge, MA: Harvard University Press.

Bruner, J. (1987). Life as narrative, *Social Research, 54*, 11–32.

Bruner, J. (1990). *Acts of Meaning*. Cambridge, MA: Harvard University Press.

Bruner, J. (1993). The autobiographical process. In. R, Folkenflik (Ed.). *The culture of autobiography: Constructions of self-representation* (pp. 8–56). Stanford, CA: Stanford University Press.

Bruner, J., & Feldman, C. F. (1996). Group narrative as a cultural context of autobiography. In D. C. Rubin (Ed.), *Remembering our past: Studies in autobiographical memory*. (pp. 291–317). New York: Cambridge University Press.

Bruner, J., & Weisser, S. (1991). The invention of self: Autobiography and its forms. In. D. R. Olson and N. Torrance (Eds.). *Literacy and orality* (pp. 129–148). New York: Cambridge University Press.

Chauncey, G. (1994). *Gay New York: Gender, urban culture, and the making of the gay male world, 1890–1940*. New York: Basic Books.

Chiriboga, D. (1978). Evaluated time: A life-course perspective, *Journal of Gerontology, 33*, 388–393.

Clausen, J. (1993). *American lives: Looking back at the children of the Great Depression*. New York: Free Press.

Cohler, B. (in preparation). Writing desire, reading desire: History, generation and life writing among men loving other men, Manuscript in Preparation.

Cohler, B., & Galatzer-Levy, R. (2000). *The course of gay and lesbian lives: Social and psychoanalytic perspectives.* Chicago: The University of Chicago Press.

Cohler, B., Hostetler, A., & Boxer, A. (1998). Generativity, social context, and lived experience: Narratives of gay men in middle adulthood. In D. McAdams and E. de St Aubin (Eds.), *Generativity and adult development: Psychosocial perspectives on caring and contributing to the next generation.* (pp. 265–309). Washington, DC: American Psychological Association.

Cole, T. R. (1997). *No color is my kind; The life of Eldrewey Stearns and the integration of Houston.* Austin, TX: University of Texas Press.

Crites, S. (1971). The narrative quality of experience, *Journal of the American Academy of Religion, 49,* 291–311.

Dannefer, D. (1984). Adult development and social theory: A paradigmatic reappraisal. *American Sociological Review, 49,* 100–116.

D'Emilio, J. (1983/1998). *Sexual politics, sexual communities: The making of a homosexual minority in the United States, 1940–1970* (2nd ed.). Chicago: University of Chicago Press.

D'Emilio, J., & Freedman, E. B. (1997). *Intimate matters; A history of sexuality in America* (2nd ed.). Chicago: The University of Chicago Press.

Denzin, N. (1989). *Interpretive biography.* Thousand Oaks, CA: Sage.

Denzin, N. (1997). *Interpretive ethnography: Ethnographic perspectives for the 21st century.* Thousand Oaks, CA: Sage.

de Vries., B., Blando, J., Southard, P., & Bubeck, C. (2001). The times of our lives. In G. Kenyon, P. Clark, and B. de Vries (Eds), *Narrative gerontology: Theory, research, and practice* (pp. 137–158). New York: Springer.

Dollard, J. (1935). *Criteria for the life history: With analysis of six notable documents.* New Haven, CT: Yale University Press.

Duberman, M. (1993). *Stonewall.* New York: Penguin Books.

Dunne, J. (1995). Beyond sovereignty and deconstruction: The storied self, *Philosophy and Social Criticism, 21,* 137–157.

Eichorn, D., Clausen, J., Haan, N., Honzik, M., & Mussen, P. (1981). *Present and Past in Middle Life.* New York: Academic Press.

Elder, G. H., Jr. (1974/1998). *Children of the Great Depression: Social change in life experience.* Boulder, Colo.: Westview Press/Harper Collins.

Elder, G. H., Jr. (1987). War mobilization and the life course: A cohort of World War II veterans. *Sociological Focus 2,* 449–472.

Elder, G. H., Jr. (1995). The life-course paradigm: Social change and individual development. In P. Moen, G. H. Elder Jr., & Kurt Lüscher (Eds.), *Examining lives in context: Perspectives on the ecology of human development* (pp. 101–139). Washington, DC: American Psychological Association.

Elder, G. H., Jr. (1996). Human lives in changing societies: Life course and developmental insights. In *Developmental science: Multiple perspectives,* ed. R. Cairns, G. H. Elder Jr., & E. Costello. (pp. 31–62). New York: Cambridge University Press.

Elder, G. H., Jr. (1997). The life-course and human development. In R. M. Lerner (Ed.), (general editor W. Damon). *Handbook of child psychology,* vol. 1, *Theory,* New York: Wiley, 939–991.

Elder, G. H., Jr. (1998). The life course as developmental theory, *Child Development, 69,* 1–12.

Elder, G. H., Jr., & A. Caspi. (1988). Human development and social change: An emerging perspective on the life course. In N. Bolger, A. Caspi, G. Downey, & M. Moorehouse (Eds.), *Persons in context: Developmental processes,* (pp. 77–113). New York: Cambridge University Press.

Elder, G. H., Jr., & A. Caspi. (1990). Studying lives in a changing society: Sociological and personological explorations. In A. I. Rabin, R. A. Zucker, R. A. Emmons, & S. Frank *Studying persona and lives,* (pp. 201–247). New York: Springer.

Elder, G. H., Jr. & Clipp, E. (1989). Combat experience and emotional health: Impairment and resilience in later life. *Journal of Personality, 57*(2), 311–341.

Elder, G. H., Jr., & O'Rand, A. M. (1995). Adult lives in a changing society. In K. S. Cook, G. A. Fine, & J. S. House (Eds.), *Sociological Perspectives on Social Psychology.* (pp. 452–475). Boston, Allyn and Bacon.

Elder, G. H. Jr., M. Shanahan, & E. Clipp. (1994). When war comes to men's lives: Life course patterns in family, work, and health. *Psychology of Aging, 9,* 5–16.

Erikson, E. H. (1982). *The life-cycle completed: A review.* New York: Norton.

Esler, A. (1984). "The truest community": Social generations as collective mentalities, *Journal of Political and Military Sociology, 49,* 112.

Eskridge, W. (1996). *The case for same sex marriage: From sexual liberty to civilized commitment.* New York: The Free Press.

Fivush, R., Gray, J., & Fromhoff, F. (1987). Two-year olds talk about the past, *Cognitive Psychology* (Ablex), *2,* 393–409.

Fontana, A., & Frey, J. H. (2000). The interview: From structured questions to negotiated text. In N. K. Denzin and Y. S. Lincoln (Eds.). *Handbook of qualitative research* (2nd ed) (pp. 645–672). Thousand Oaks, CA: Sage.

Foucault, M. (1973). *The order of things: An archeology of the human sciences.* (Trans. E. Gallimard). New York: Random House/Vintage Books.

Flacks, R. (1971). *Youth and social change.* Chicago: Markham.

Franz, C. (1995). A quantitative case study of longitudinal changes in identity, intimacy, and generativity, *Journal of Personality, 63,* 27–46.

Freedman, D., Thornton, A., Camburn, D., Alwin, D., & Young-DeMarco, L. (1988). The life history calendar: A technique for collecting retrospective data, *Sociological Methodology, 18,* 37–68.

Freud, S. (1909/1955). Notes upon a case of obsessional neurosis. In J. Strachey (Ed. and Trans.). *The standard edition of the complete psychological works of Sigmund Freud* (Vol. 10, pp. 158–250). London: Hogarth Press.

Geertz, C. (1973). Thick description: Toward an interpretive theory of culture. In C. Geertz, *The Interpretation of Cultures* (pp. 3–30). New York: Basic Books.

Geertz, C. (1974/1983). 'From the native's point of view:' On the nature of anthropological understanding. In C. Geertz. *Local Knowledge: Further Essays In Interpretive Anthropology* (pp. 55–72). New York: Basic Books.

George, L. (1996). Missing links: The case for a social psychology of the life course, *The Gerontologist, 36,* 248–255.

Gergen, K. (1977). Stability, change and chance in understanding human development. In N. Datan and H. Reese (Eds.). *Life-Span Developmental Psychology: Dialectical Perspectives on Experimental Research* (pp. 32–65). New York: Academic Press.

Gergen, K. J. (1980). The emerging crisis in life-span developmental theory. In P. Baltes & O. G. Brim, Jr. (Eds.). *Life-Span Development and Behavior.* (Vol. 3). (pp. 31–63). New York: Academic Press.

Gergen, K. (1994). *Realities and relationships: Sounding in social construction.* Cambridge, MA: Harvard University Press.

Gergen, K. J., & Gergen, M. (1997). Narratives of the self. In L. P. Hinchman and S. K. Hinchman (Eds.), *Memory, identity, and community.* (pp. 161–184). Albany, NY: State University of New York Press.

Gitlin, T. (1987). *The sixties: Years of hope, days of rage.* New York: Bantam Books.

Graff, J. J. (1995). *Conflicting paths: Growing up in America.* Cambridge, MA: Harvard University Pres.

Gottschalk, L., Kluckhohn, C., & Angell, R. (1942). *The use of personal documents in history, anthropology, and sociology.* New York: Social Science Research Council.

Halbwachs, M. (1950/1980). *Collective memory.* New York: Harper & Row.

Handel, G. (2000). *Making a life in Yorkville: Experience and meaning in the life-course narrative of an urban working-class man.* Westport, CT: Greenwood Press.

Harry, J., & W. DeVall. (1978). *The social organization of gay males.* New York: Praeger.

Harry, J. (1984). *Gay couples.* New York: Praeger.

Herdt, G., J. Beeler, & T. Rawls. (1997). Life course diversity among older lesbians and gay men. *Journal of Lesbian, Gay and Bisexual Identity, 2,* 231–247. (Special issue: Coming of age: Gays, lesbians, and bisexuals in the second half of life, ed. G. Herdt, A. Hostetler, & B. Cohler.)

Herdt, G., & A. Boxer. (1996). *Children of horizons.* (2d ed.). Boston: Beacon Press.

Herek, G. (1996). Heterosexism and homophobia. In R. Cabaj and T. S. Stein (Eds.), *Textbook of homosexuality and mental health,* (pp. 101–113). Washington, DC: American Psychiatric Press.

Holstein, J. A., & Gubrium, J. F. (2000). *Constructing the life course* (2nd ed.). Dix Hills, NY, General Hall.

Hostetler, A. (2001). Single gay men: Psychological well-being, agency, and cultural models of adult development, Unpublished Dissertation, The Committee on Human Development, The University of Chicago.

Hostetler, A., & Cohler, B. (1997). Partnership, singlehood and the lesbian and gay life course: A research agenda, *Journal of gay, lesbian, and bisexual identity, 2,* 199–230.

Hostetler, A., & Herdt, G. H. (1998). Culture, sexual lifeways and developmental subjectivities: Rethinking taxonomies, *Social Research, 65,* 249–290.

Iser, W. (1978). *The Act of reading: A Theory of Aesthetic Response.* Baltimore, MD: The Johns Hopkins University Press.

Jones, M., Bayley, N., & MacFarlane, J. (1971). *The course of human development.* Waltham, MA: Xerox College.

Josselson, R (1996a). *The space between us: Exploring the dimensions of human relationships.* Thousand Oaks, CA: Sage.

Josselson, R. (1996b). *Revising herself: The story of women's identity from college to midlife.* New York: Oxford University Press.

Kagan, J., & Moss, H. (1962). *From birth to maturity.* New York: John Wiley.

Kagan, J. (1998). *Three seductive ideas.* Cambridge, MA: Harvard University Press.

Kaiser, C. (1997). *The gay metropolis, 1940–1996*. Boston, MA: Houghton-Mifflin.

Kaminsky, M. (1992). Introduction. In B. Myerhoff, *Remembered lives: The work of ritual, storytelling and growing older*. (Ed. M. Kaminsky) (pp. 307–340). Ann Arbor, MI: The University of Michigan Press.

Kertzer, D. I. (1982). Generation and age in cross-cultural perspective. In M. W. Riley, R. P. Abeles and M. S. Teitelbaum (Eds.). *Aging from birth to death, Volume 2: Sociotemporal perspectives*. (pp. 27–50). Boulder, CO: The Westview Press.

Kertzer, D. I. (1983). Generation as a social problem, *Annual Review of Sociology, 9*, 125–149.

Kirk, M., & Madsen, H. (1989). *After the ball: How America will conquer its fear and hatred of gays in the '90s*. New York: Plume Books.

Knoke, D. (1984). Conceptual and measurement aspects in the study of political generations, *Journal of Political and Military Sociology, 12*, 191–201.

Kurdek, L. (1995). Lesbian and gay couples. In A. R. D'Augelli & C. Patterson (Eds.), *Lesbian, gay, and bisexual identities over the life span*, (pp. 243–261) New York: Oxford University Press.

Lieblich, A. (1993). Looking at change: Natasha, 21: New immigrant from Russia to Israel, *Narrative Study of Lives, 1*, 92–179.

Lieblich, A., Truval-Mashiach, R., & Zilber, T. (1998). *Narrative research: reading, analysis and interpretation*. Thousand Oaks, CA: Sage Publications.

Linde, C. (1993). *Life stories: The creation of coherence*. New York: Oxford University Press.

Loftus, E. (1993). The reality of repressed memories, *American Psychologist, 48*, 518–537.

Loftus, E., & Ketcham, K. (1994). *The myth of repressed memory: False memories and allegations of sexual abuse*. New York: St. Martin's Press.

Loughery, J. (1998). *The other side of silence: Men's lives and gay identities: A twentieth century history*. New York: Henry Holt/Owl Books.

Mannheim, K. (1928/1993). The problem of generations. In K. H. Wolff (Ed.), *From Karl Mannheim* (2nd expanded ed). (pp. 351–398). New Brunswick, NJ: Transactions Books.

McAdam, D. (1989). The biographical consequences of activism, *American Sociological Review, 54*, 744–760.

McAdams, D. (1990). Unity and purpose in human lives: The emergence of identity as a life story. In A. I. Rabin, R. A. Zucker, R. A. Emmons, & S. Frank (Eds.), *Studying persons and lives*. New York: Springer, 148–200.

McAdams, D. (2001). The psychology of life stories, *Review of General Psychology, 5*, 100–122.

McAdams, D., & de St. Aubin, E. (1992). A theory of generativity and its assessment through self-report, behavioral acts, and narrative themes in autobiography, *Journal of Personality and Social Pschololgy, 62*, 1003–1015.

McAdams, D., Hart, H. M., & Maruna, S. (1998). The anatomy of generativity. In D. McAdams & Ed de St. Aubin (Eds.). *Generativity and adult development: How and why we care for the next generation*. (pp. 7–43). Washington, DC: American Psychological Association.

Myerhoff, B., & Ruby, J. (1982/1992). A crack in the mirror. In B. Myerhoff & M. Kaminsky (Eds.), *Remembered lives: The work of ritual, storytelling and growing older* (pp. 307–340). Ann Arbor, MI: The University of Michigan Press.

Mishler, E. (1986). *Research interviewing: Context and narrative*. Cambridge, MA: Harvard University Press.

Mishler, E. (1990). Validation: The social construction of knowledge—A brief for inquiry-guided research. *Harvard Educational Review 60*, 415–442.

Mishler, E. (1999). *Storylines: Craftartists' narratives of identity*. Cambridge, MA: Harvard University Press.

Murphy, L. B. (1962). *The widening world of childhood, paths toward mastery*. New York: Basic Books.

Murray, S. O. (1992). Components of gay communities in San Francisco. In G. H. Herdt (Ed.). *Gay culture in America: Essays from the field*. (pp. 107–146). Boston: Beacon Press.

Murray, S. O. (1996). *American gay*. Chicago: The University of Chicago Press.

Novick, P. (1999). *The Holocaust in American life*. Boston: Houghton-Mifflin.

Ochs, E., Capps, L. (1996). Narrating the self, *Annual Review of Anthropology, 25*, 19–43.

Ochs, E., Capps, L. (2001). *Living narrative: Creating lives in everyday storytelling*. Cambridge, MA: Harvard University Press.

Odets, W. (1995). *In the shadow of the epidemic: Being HIV-negative in the age of AIDS*. Durham, N.C.: Duke University Press.

Olick, J. K., & Robbins, J. (1998). Social memory studies: from collective memory to the historical sociology of mnemonic practices, *Annual Review of Sociology, 24*, 105–140.

Ortega y Gasset, J. (1921–1922/1961). *The modern theme*. New York: Harper Torchbooks.

Parks, C. (1999). Lesbian identity development: An examination of differences across generations, *American Journal of Orthopsychiatry, 69*, 347–361.

Patterson, C. (1995). Lesbian mothers, gay fathers, and their children. In A. R. D'Augelli and C. Patterson (Eds.). *Lesbian, gay, and bisexual identities over the life span* (pp. 262–292). New York: Oxford University Press.

Pearlin, L. (1980). Life strains and psychological distress among adults. In E. Erikson and N. Smelser (Eds.), *Themes of Work and Love in Adulthood.* (pp. 174–192). Cambridge, MA: Harvard University Press.

Pearlin, L., & Lieberman, M. (1979). Social Sources of emotional distress. In R. Simmons (Ed.), *Research in Community and Mental Health*, Vol. I (pp. 217–248). Greenwich, Conn.: JAI Press.

Plath, D. (1980). Contours of consocation: Lessons from a Japanese narrative. In P. B. Baltes & O. G. Brim, Jr. (Eds.), *Life-Span Development and Behavior, Volume 3.* (pp. 287–305) New York: Academic Press.

Plummer, K. (1995a). *Telling sexual stories: Power, change, and social worlds.* New York: Routledge.

Plummer, K. (1995b). Life story research. In J. A. Smith, R. Harré, & L Van Langenhove (Eds.), *Rethinking methods in psychology* (pp. 50–63). Thousand Oaks, CA: Sage.

Plummer, K. (2001). *Documents of life 2: An invitation to a critical humanism.* Thousands Oaks, CA: Sage Publications.

Putnam, R. D. (2000). *Bowling alone: The collapse and revival of American community.* New York: Simon & Schuster.

Qualis Research Associates (1999). *The Ethnograph.* (Version 5.1). Thousand Oaks, CA: Sage Publications/ Scalar.

Richards, L., & Qualitative Solutions and Research. (1999). *Using NVIVO in Qualitative Research.* (Version 1.1). Thousand Oaks, CA: Sage/scalar.

Richards, L., & Qualitative Solutions and Research. (2002). *Using NVIVO in Qualitative Research.* (Version 2.0). Thousand Oaks, CA: Sage Publications/Scalar.

Ricoeur, P. (1977). The question of proof in Freud's psychoanalytic writings, *Journal of the American Psychoanalytic Association, 25*, 835–872.

Rosenfeld, D. (1999). Identity work among lesbian and gay elderly, *Journal of Aging Studies, 13*, 121–144.

Rosenwald, G. C., & Ochberg, R. L. (1992) (Eds). *Storied lives: The cultural politics of self-understanding.* New Haven, CT: Yale University Press.

Rotello, G. (1997). *Sexual ecology: AIDS and the destiny of gay men.* New York: Dutton.

Rosow, I. (1978). What is a cohort and why? *Human Development, 21*, 65–75.

Rudolph, S., & Rudolph, I. with M. S. Kanota (1999). *Reversing the gaze: Amar Singh's diary, a colonial subject's narrative of imperial India.* New Delhi, India: Oxford University Press.

Runyan, W. M. (1980). The life satisfaction chart: Perceptions of the course of subjective experience, *International Journal of Aging and Human Development, 11*, 45–64.

Sadownick, D. (1997), *Sex between men: An intimate history of the sex lives of gay men postwar to the present.* San Francisco: Harper.

Sampson, R., & Lau, J. (1996). The military as a turning point in the lives of disadvantaged men. *American Sociological Review 61*, 347–367.

Sandler, A. M. (1978). Psychoanalysis in later life: problems in the psychoanalysis of an aging narcissistic patient, *Journal of Geriatric Psychiatry, 11*, 5–36.

Savin-Williams, R. (2001). *Mom, dad, I'm gay: How families negotiate coming out.* Washington, DC: The American Psychological Association.

Schachter, D. (Ed.). (1995). *Memory distortion: How minds, brains, and societies reconstruct the past.* Cambridge, MA: Harvard University Press.

Schaie, K. W. (1995). *Intellectual development in adulthood: The Seattle Longitudinal Study.* New York: Cambridge University Press.

Schafer, R. (1980). Narration in the psychoanalytic dialogue. *Critical Inquiry, 7*, 29–53.

Schafer, R. (1981). *Narrative actions in psychoanalysis.* Heinz Werner Lecture Series, vol. 14. Worcester, Mass: Clark University Press.

Schafer, R. (1982). The relevance of the "here-and-now" transference interpretation to the reconstruction of early development. *International Journal of Psychoanalysis 63*, 77–82.

Schafer, R. (1992). *Retelling a life: Narration and dialogue in psychoanalysis.* New York: Basic Books.

Schely-Newman, E. (1999). "I hear from people who read Torah:" Reported speech, genres, and gender relations in personal narrative, *Narrative Inquiry, 9*, 49–69.

Schuman, H., R. Belli, & and K. Bischoping. (1997). J. W. Pennebaker, D. Paez, and B. Rimé. (Eds.), The generational basis of historical knowledge. *In Collective memory of political events: Social psychological perspectives*, (pp. 47–78). Mahwah, N. J.: Lawrence Erlbaum Associates.

Schuman, H., Rieger, C., & Gaidys, V. (1994). Collective memories in the United States and Lithuania. In N. Schwartz & S. Sudman (Eds.), *Autobiogrpahical memory and the validity of retrospective reports* (pp. 313–333). New York: Springer-Verlag.

Schuman, H., & J. Scott. (1989). Generations and collective memory. *American Sociological Review 54*, 359–381.

Schutz, A. & Luckmann, T. (1973). *The structures of the life-world*. Evanston, IL: Northwestern University Press.

Schutz, A., & Luckmann, T. (1989). *The structures of the life world: Volume II*. Evanston, IL: Northwestern University Press.

Schwartz, B. (1982). The social forces of commeration: A study in collective memory, *Social Forces, 61*, 374–402.

Schiff, B., & Cohler, B. (2001). Telling survival backward: Holocaust survivors narrate the past. In G. Kenyon, P. Clark, & B. de Vries (Eds.), *Narrative gerontology: Theory, research, and practice* (pp. 113–136). New York: Springer Publishing Company.

Schiff, B., Noy, C., & Cohler, B. (2001). Collected stories of in the life narratives of Holocaust survivors, *Narrative Inquiry, 11*, 159–194.

Schiffrin, D. (1994). *Approaches to discourse*. Cambridge, MA: Blackwell.

Schiffrin, D. (2000). Mother-daughter discourse in a Holocaust oral history: "Because the you admit that you're guilty," *Narrative Inquiry, 10*, 1–44.

Schwartz, B. (1987). *George Washington: The making of an American symbol*. New York: The Free Press.

Schwartz, B. (2000). *Abraham Lincoln and the Forge of the National Memory*. Chicago: The University of Chicago Press.

Settersten, R. A., Jr. (1999). *Lives in time and place: The problems and promises of developmental science*. Amityville, NY: Baywood.

Shay, J. (1994). *Achilles in Vietnam: Combat trauma and the undoing of character*. New York: Atheneum.

Singer, J. A., & Salovey, P. (1993). *The remembered self: Emotion and memory in personality*. New York: The Free Press.

Smith, B. (2001). Genre and Life-History. The Committee on Human Development, The University of Chicago.

Stein, A. (1997). *Sex and sensibility: Stories of a lesbian generation*. Berkeley, CA: The University of California Press.

Stewart, A. J., Franz, C., & Layton, L. (1988). The changing self: Using personal documents to study lives, *Journal of Personality, 56*, 41–74.

Stewart, A. J., & Vandewater, E. A. (1998). The course of generativity. In D. McAdams & Ed de St. Aubin (Eds.), *Generativity and adult development: How and why we care for the next generation.* (pp. 75–100). Washington, DC: American Psychological Association.

Stone, P. J., Dunphy, D., Smith, M. S., Ogilvie, D. M. & Associates (1966). *The general inquirer: A computer approach to content analysis*.

Strauss, A., Corbin, J. (1990). *Basic of qualitative research*. Thousand Oaks, CA: Sage.

Sturken, M. (1997). *Tangled memories: The Vietnam war, the AIDS epidemic and the politics of remembering*. Berkeley, CA: The University of California Press.

Sullivan, A. (1995). *Virtually normal: An argument about homosexuality*. New York: Knopf.

Sullivan, A. (1997). (Ed.) *Same sex marriage: Pro and con*. New York: Vintage Books.

Sullivan, A. (1998). *Love undetectable: Notes on friendship, sex, and survival*. New York: Knopf.

Tedlock, B. (2000).Ethnography and ethnographic representation. In. N. K. Denzin and Y. S. Lincoln (Eds.), *Handbook of qualitative research* (Second Edition). Thousand Oaks, CA: Sage Publications, 455–486.

Tipton, S. (1982). *Getting saved from the sixties: Moral meaning in conversion and social change*. Berkeley: University of California Press.

Thomas, W. I., & Znaniecki, F. (1918–1920/1974). *The Polish peasant in Europe and America*. New York: Octagon Books.

Tonkin, E. (1992). *Narrating our pasts: The social construction of oral history*. New York: Cambridge University Press.

Troll, L. E. (1970). Issues in the study of generations, *Aging and Human Development, 1*, 199–218.

Whisman, V. (1996). *Queer by choice: Lesbians, gay men, and the politics of identity*. New York: Routledge.

Whitbourne, S. K., & Dannefer, W. (1985–1986). The "life drawing" as a measure of time perspective in adulthood, *International Journal of Aging and Human Development, 22*, 147–155.

White, R. W. (1959). Motivation reconsidered: The concept of competence, *Psychological Review, 66*, 297–333.

B. Interdisciplinary Collaborations

CHAPTER 26

Personality Trait Development in Adulthood

BRENT W. ROBERTS

RICHARD W. ROBINS

KALI H. TRZESNIEWSKI

AVSHALOM CASPI

In the middle part of the 20th century, a healthy dialogue existed between sociology and personality psychology. Leading scholars in sociology actively discussed the relationship between social structure and personality (Neugarten, 1968; Parsons, 1942), and between organizations and personality (Inkeles & Levinson, 1963). In turn, many personality psychologists studied similar phenomena (e.g., Sanford, 1956; Sarbin, 1964). However, over the past several decades the dialogue died out. One reason for the decreased interaction was that personality psychology turned inward as it examined fundamental issues that defined the field, including the scientific viability of core concepts such as stable personality traits (Block, 1968; Mischel, 1968).

Starting in the 1980s, personality psychology began a profound renaissance and has not only answered these basic questions but has become a diverse and intellectually stimulating

BRENT W. ROBERTS • Department of Psychology, University of Illinois at Urbana-Champaign, Champaign, Illinois 61820   RICHARD W. ROBINS • University of California, Davis, California 95616   KALI H. TRZESNIEWSKI • University of California, Davis, California 95616   AVSHALOM CASPI • Social, Genetic, and Developmental Psychiatry, Research Centre, London SE5 8AF, United Kingdom

Handbook of the Life Course, edited by Jeylan T. Mortimer and Michael J. Shanahan. Kluwer Academic/Plenum Publishers, New York, 2003.

field that encompasses a wide array of topics such as behavior genetics, temperament, motivation, evolutionary psychology, defense mechanisms, emotion, stress and coping, the neural
bases of individual differences, and personal narratives (see Pervin & John, 1999). Moreover,
the importance of personality traits is no longer in question as research has documented
numerous psychological, social, and health-related effects. For example, we now know that
childhood temperament not only predicts adult personality (Caspi & Silva, 1995), but it also
shapes an individual's accomplishments in work and marriage (Caspi, Elder & Bem, 1987;
1988). Furthermore, personality traits generalize across many different cultures (McCrae &
Costa, 1997), and also predict a wide range of outcomes including job performance, status, and
satisfaction (Judge, Higgins, Thoreson, & Barrick, 1999), relationship satisfaction (Robins,
Caspi, & Moffitt, 2000), divorce (Cramer, 1993), delinquency (Miller & Lynam, 2001),
personality disorders (Widiger, Verheul, & van den Brink, 1999), self-esteem (Robins, Tracy,
Trzesniewski, Gosling, & Potter, 2002), health (Friedman, 2000), and even longevity
(Friedman, Tucker, Tomlinson-Keasey, Schwartz, Wingard & Criqui, 1993).

Since the 1980s numerous longitudinal studies of personality also have been published,
providing enough evidence to move personality researchers toward consensus about the
degree to which personality traits change over the life course. The emerging story, based on
an accumulating body of empirical research, is that personality traits show remarkable levels
of continuity given the vast array of experiences that impinge upon a lived life. At the same
time, research also reveals that personality traits show important and systematic changes that
are meaningfully connected to particular life experiences and contexts.

In this chapter, we will review research on continuity and change in personality traits
across the life course. The first section of the chapter describes the debate about whether personality traits can change, and then summarizes longitudinal research on the degree of continuity (i.e., rank-order stability) in personality traits from childhood to old age. The second
section summarizes mean-level changes in personality traits from childhood to old age. The
third section addresses why personality traits change, and reviews findings from longitudinal
studies that have investigated the impact of life experiences on personality change.

RANK-ORDER STABILITY OF PERSONALITY
TRAITS FROM CHILDHOOD TO OLD AGE

We first consider the degree to which there is continuity in personality from childhood
through adulthood. Continuity can be measured using many different statistical indices, but
most often it is indexed by the correlation between personality scores across two points in
time (i.e., test–retest correlations). These differential, or rank–order, stability estimates reflect
the degree to which the relative ordering of individuals on a given trait is maintained over time.
Rank-order stability is influenced by maturational or experiential factors that differentially
affect people, as well as by measurement error.

Two contradictory predictions have been proposed about the rank–order stability of personality traits. The *classical trait perspective* argues that personality traits in adulthood are biologically based "temperaments" that are not susceptible to the influence of the environment and
thus do not change over time (McCrae et al., 2000). From this "essentialist" perspective, we
would expect the test–retest correlations to be high, even in young adulthood. In contrast, the
contextual perspective emphasizes the importance of life changes and role transitions in personality development and suggests that personality should be fluid, prone to change, and yield
low test–retest correlation coefficients, particularly during young adulthood (Lewis, 1999).

Existing longitudinal studies do not support either of these extreme positions. The findings of a recent meta-analysis of the rank–order stability of personality confirmed five major conclusions (Roberts & DelVecchio, 2000): Test–retest correlations over time (a) are moderate in magnitude, even from childhood to early adulthood. Furthermore, rank–order stability (b) increased as the age of the subjects increased. Test–retest correlations (unadjusted for measurement error) increased from 0.41 in childhood to 0.55 at age 30, and then reached a plateau around 0.70 between ages 50 and 70 (see Figure 26-1). Rank-order stability (c) decreased as the time interval between observations increased, (d) did not vary markedly from trait to trait, and (e) did not vary markedly from method to method (i.e., self-reports, observer ratings, and projective tests), or by gender.

Several conclusions can be drawn from this meta-analysis. First, the magnitude of rank–order consistency, although not as high as the essentialists would claim, is still remarkably high. The only psychological constructs more consistent than personality traits are measures of cognitive ability (Conley, 1984). Second, the level of continuity in childhood and adolescence is much higher than originally expected (cf. Lewis, 1999, 2001), especially after age 3. Although childhood character is by no means fate, there are striking continuities that point to the importance of childhood temperament and the effects of cumulative continuity from childhood through adulthood (Caspi, 2000). Even more impressive is the fact that the level of consistency increases in a relatively linear fashion through adolescence and young adulthood. Young adulthood has been described as demographically dense, such that people make more life-changing decisions (to marry, one's career, children, etc.) during this period than at any other time in the life course (Arnett, 2000; Rindfuss, 1991). Yet, despite these dramatic demographic shifts, personality differences remain remarkably consistent. Third, personality continuity in adulthood peaks later than expected. According to one prominent perspective, personality traits are essentially fixed and unchanging after age 30 (McCrae & Costa, 1994). However, the meta-analytic findings show that rank–order stability peaks some

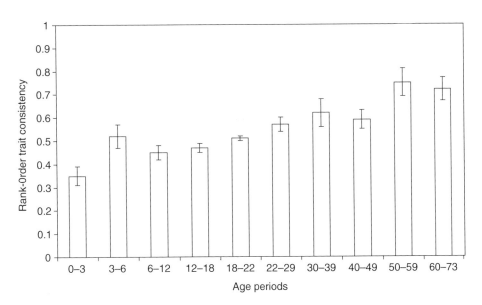

FIGURE 26-1. **Population estimates of mean consistency across age categories with 95% confidence level estimates.**

time after age 50, but at a level well below unity. Thus, personality traits continue to change throughout adulthood, but only modestly after age 50. Finally, the levels of consistency found in this meta-analysis replicated smaller studies dating back to 1941 (Conley, 1984; Crook, 1943; Schuerger, Zarrella, & Hotz, 1989). Apparently, there have been few if any cohort shifts in the level of rank-order stability in personality traits over the past 60 years.

MEAN-LEVEL CHANGES IN PERSONALITY TRAITS ACROSS THE LIFE COURSE

In the previous section we showed that personality traits show moderate levels of continuity across the lifespan when continuity is defined by rank-order stability. We next turn to mean-level changes in personality. Mean-level change refers to changes in the average trait level of a population. This type of change is thought to result from maturational or historical processes shared by a population (e.g., Helson & Moane, 1987; Roberts & Helson, 1997), and is typically assessed by mean-level differences in specific traits over time, which indicate whether the sample as a whole is increasing or decreasing on a trait. Mean-level stability is theoretically and statistically distinct from rank–order stability. For example, a population could increase substantially on a trait but the rank ordering of individuals would be maintained if everyone increased by the same amount. Similarly, the rank ordering of individuals could change substantially over time but without any aggregate increases or decreases (e.g., if the number of people who decreased offset the number of people who increased).

We will organize our review of mean-level changes in personality traits using the Big Five taxonomy of traits (Goldberg, 1993; John & Srivastava, 1999). The Big Five taxonomy is one of the most significant developments in the field of personality psychology in the last few decades. Many personality researchers now believe that the majority of personality traits can be categorized into five broad superordinate categories: extraversion, agreeableness, conscientiousness, neuroticism (or its opposite emotional stability), and openness to experience. One of the primary advantages of the Big Five framework is its ability to organize previous research findings on the development of personality traits into a manageable number of conceptually coherent domains. So, rather than review the voluminous literature on mean-level change for all possible traits, we can examine the evidence within these five broad domains.*

Studies can be further differentiated into cross-sectional studies of age differences and longitudinal studies of age-related changes. We will review both types of studies in an effort to determine whether there are consistencies across these two approaches to studying personality stability. Cross-sectional studies are often criticized for confounding the effects of age and cohort. That is, the differences found across age groups can be attributed to the culture or climate that an individual was born into and lived through, which is unique to each cohort. Longitudinal studies also are susceptible to cohort effects, but provide a much more direct test of actual change in personality over time. The combination of both types of information affords the most robust test of whether personality traits demonstrate coherent patterns of change with age (Schaie, 1965).

After reviewing the mean-level changes in personality traits demonstrated in each Big Five domain, we will address whether the aggregate pattern of change is consistent with

---

*Space limitations preclude citing all the relevant articles reporting mean-level changes in personality traits. A comprehensive listing of empirical reports on the topic of personality continuity and change can be obtained from the first author at broberts@s.psych.uiuc.edu

previous descriptions of the mature personality (Allport, 1961). That is, we will pose the question of whether people become more psychologically mature with age.

Mean-Level Changes in Extraversion

Extraversion refers to individual differences in the propensity to be sociable, active, assertive, and to experience positive affect (John & Srivastava, 1999). Interestingly, extraversion does not demonstrate a clear pattern of mean-level change unless one partitions the domain into two constituent elements: Social dominance and social vitality (Helson & Kwan, 2000). Social dominance reflects traits such as dominance, independence, and self-confidence, especially in social contexts. Social vitality corresponds more closely to traits such as sociability, positive affect, gregariousness, and energy level. In many studies, measures described as extraversion reflect more strongly the dimension of social vitality. If one organizes the cross-sectional and longitudinal literature around these two categories then the patterns of development are clear. People increase in measures of social dominance and decrease in measures of social vitality with age.

Cross-sectional aging studies conform closely to this hypothesis. Helson and Kwan (2000) reported a consistent pattern of negative correlations with age across measures of social vitality in six different samples drawn from three different countries. In addition, Goldberg, Sweeney, Merenda, and Hughes (1998) showed that assertiveness was positively correlated with age, while sociability was negatively correlated with age. McCrae et al. (1999) also found decreases in their measure of extraversion which corresponds closely to social vitality. The differentiation between social dominance and social vitality is bolstered by cross-sectional studies of positive affect, which tend to show either no increases or decreases in positive affect with age (see Mroczek & Kolarz, 1998).

Longitudinal studies tracking traits from the domain of extraversion further support the argument that people increase in social dominance and decrease in social vitality during young adulthood. For example, Roberts, Caspi, and Moffitt (2001) reported substantial increases on social potency in a birth cohort followed from ages 18 to 26. In contrast, other studies show declines or no change in extraversion measures that tap social vitality in young adulthood. Viken, Rose, Kaprio, and Koskenvuo (1994) found decreases in extraversion in young adulthood for both male and female twins, and Carmichael and McGue (1994) reported decreases in the EPQ extraversion scale from late adolescence to early adulthood in both women and men. Taken as a whole the evidence points to increases in social dominance and decreases in social vitality in young adulthood.

Longitudinal studies drawn from middle age demonstrate more support for partitioning extraversion into social dominance and social vitality. Four studies have reported increases in traits related to social dominance in the transition from young adulthood to middle age (Cartwright & Wink 1994; Helson & Moane, 1987; Helson & Wink, 1992; Stevens & Truss, 1985). The pattern of development for social vitality in midlife is less clear. Haan, Millsap, and Hartka (1986) reported increases in outgoingness for both men and women between the ages of 30 and 40. In contrast, data from the University of North Carolina Alumni Heart Study showed that three facets of extraversion did not change between the ages of 41 and 50, whereas warmth, activity, and excitement seeking decreased (Costa, Herbst, McCrae, & Siegler, 2000). Although the findings are somewhat inconsistent, the preponderance of evidence points to increases in social dominance and decreases in social vitality in midlife.

Only a few studies have examined change in extraversion-related traits in old age and these have focused exclusively on social vitality. Field and Millsap (1991) found that men and women decreased in measures of social vitality from ages 69 to 83. In addition, Leon, Gillum, Gillum, and Gouze (1979) found increases in the social-introversion scale of the MMPI in a sample of men from ages 62 to 77, and Pedersen and Reynolds (1998) reported no changes in extraversion in several thousand twins between the ages of 50 and 71. Based on these studies it appears that social vitality decreases in old age, though there is a need for more longitudinal personality studies on this period of the life course.

Taken as a whole, the longitudinal research to date indicates that the differentiation of extraversion into social dominance and social vitality helps to clarify developmental patterns, especially in the period between ages 30 and 60. A clear trend for increases in social dominance can be found through midlife. In addition, decreases in measures of social vitality appear to occur into old age.

Mean-Level Change in Agreeableness

Agreeableness refers to traits that reflect individual differences in the propensity to be altruistic, trusting, modest, and warm (John & Srivastava, 1999). Several cross-sectional studies have demonstrated increases in agreeableness across adulthood. Costa and McCrae (1986) found that a sample of adults between the ages of 35 and 85 scored higher on agreeableness than a college sample. Likewise, Johnson et al. (1983) reported that older people scored higher on agreeableness traits such as kind, warm, and pleasant, and lower on interpersonal abrasiveness (e.g., rude, foolish) than younger people. Most impressively, McCrae and colleagues (1999) showed that scores on the NEO–FFI agreeableness scale increased with age across five out of six cultures.

Longitudinal studies focusing on the transition from adolescence to young adulthood have demonstrated similar findings. Robins, Fraley, Roberts, and Trzesniewski (2001) found that college students increased in agreeableness from ages 18 to 21. Stein, Newcomb, and Bentler, (1986) reported large increases in the traits of congeniality and generosity from adolescence to young adulthood, and McGue, Bacon, and Lykken (1993) reported decreases in aggression from ages 20 to 30.

In middle age, Wink and Helson (1987) found that men showed a significant increase in affiliation between the ages of 27 and 52. Similarly, Haan et al. (1986) reported that both men and women increased in warmth from ages 40 to 54. Dudek and Hall (1991) found a relatively large increase in nurturance from age 40 to 70 in a sample of male architects. Field and Millsap (1991) showed that agreeableness increased for a sample of "old–old" individuals (80 to 90 years old). Although several studies have found little or no change in traits related to agreeableness (e.g., Costa et al., 2000; Stevens & Truss, 1985), the preponderance of evidence points to increases in traits related to agreeableness across the life course.

Mean-Level Change in Conscientiousness

Conscientiousness, which reflects the propensity to be self-controlled, task- and goal-directed, planful, and rule-following (John & Srivastava, 1999), shows changes much like agreeableness. Numerous cross-sectional studies have shown that older people score higher on multiple measures of conscientiousness. Johnson et al. (1983) found a positive correlation between age and traits such as industriousness in samples drawn from Caucasian, Chinese, and Japanese ancestry. McCrae et al. (1999) showed positive correlations between age and all facets of conscientiousness. Goldberg et al. (1998) found a positive relationship between age and both conscientiousness and restraint. Helson and Kwan (2000) reported almost uniformly positive correlations between age and measures of norm orientation (e.g., responsibility, socialization, self-control) in samples drawn from Great Britain, Baltimore, China, and Detroit.

The findings from longitudinal studies correspond almost perfectly to the cross-sectional data. Stein et al. (1986) reported increases in measures of orderliness, law abidance, and diligence from adolescence to young adulthood. McGue et al. (1993) followed a group of twins for 10 years and showed that they increased on measures of achievement, control, and constraint from ages 20 to 30. Roberts et al. (2001) reported increases in self-control and achievement from ages 18 to 26. Robins et al. (2001) found moderately large increases in conscientiousness from ages 18 to 21 (see also, Haan et al., 1986; Helson & Moane, 1987; Stevens & Truss, 1985).

Conscientiousness appears to either plateau or continue to increase in middle and old age. Costa et al. (2000) reported little or no change in measures of conscientiousness from ages 41 to 50. Likewise, Haan et al. (1986) reported no changes in observer ratings of dependability between ages 30 and 54. In contrast, self-report data drawn from the same sample showed increases in measures of socialization, self-control, and achievement via conformance from ages 33 to 75 (Helson & Kwan, 2000). Also, Helson and Wink (1992) found that women increased on measures of self-control, responsibility, and norm-orientation from ages 43 to 52. Similarly, Cartwright and Wink (1994) found increases in measures of self-control, responsibility, and achievement-via-conformance in a longitudinal study of female doctors from ages 31 to 46. The two studies that have examined changes in conscientiousness beyond middle age provide some evidence that conscientiousness-related traits continue to increase even up to age 75 (Dudek & Hall, 1991; Nilsson & Persson, 1984).

Although there appears to be strong evidence that conscientiousness increases across the life course, there is some contradictory evidence centered mostly in middle age (Cartwright & Wink, 1994; Helson & Moane, 1987). Nonetheless, it appears that the increase in conscientiousness is one of the most robust patterns in personality development, especially in young adulthood.

Mean-Level Changes in Emotional Stability

Emotional stability or its converse, neuroticism, contrasts even-temperedness with the experience of anxiety, worry, anger, and depression (John & Srivastava, 1999). Cross-sectional studies of neuroticism show that there may be slight decreases with age. Johnson et al. (1983) reported a small negative correlation between age and internal discomfort, a dimension marked by traits such as emotional, nervous, and worrying. McCrae et al. (1999) reported a negative relationship between age and neuroticism across six cultures, but the effect was small on average and less consistent than their findings for the other Big Five categories. Goldberg et al. (1998) reported small positive relationships between age and emotional stability and calmness. Carstensen, Pasupathi, Mayr, and Nesselroade (2000) reported that negative emotions declined in frequency up until age 60 and then showed a slight increase after age 60 (see also Costa & McCrae, 1986). Robins, Trzesniewski, Tracy, Gosling, and Potter (2002) examined age differences in self-esteem, which is strongly related to emotional stability (Robins et al., 2002); they found a gradual increase in self-esteem from young adulthood through late midlife, but a decline among individuals aged 70 to 90.

Findings from longitudinal studies are generally consistent with cross-sectional studies. McGue et al. (1993) found decreases in stress reaction and alienation in young adulthood.

Roberts et al. (2001) reported decreases in alienation, but not stress reaction from ages 18 to 26. Robins et al. (2001) reported significant drops in Neuroticism from ages 18 to 21. Viken, Rose, Kaprio, and Koskenvuo (1994) found decreases in Neuroticism in young adulthood. Likewise, Baltes and Nesselroade (1972) found decreases in a measure of guilt proneness and apprehensiveness in college students over a one-year period. Other studies have shown that the transition from adolescence to young adulthood is characterized by increasing self-acceptance (Stein et al., 1986) and decreasing negative emotionality (Carmichael & McGue, 1994; Watson & Walker, 1996). Several studies have found no change in measures of anxiety and well-being during this period (e.g., Roberts & Chapman, 2000). It seems that in young adulthood, people either decrease in neuroticism or do not change at all. There is no evidence for an increase in neuroticism.

The patterns of change on measures of neuroticism in middle age are quite consistent with the patterns found in young adulthood. People either decrease or do not change. For example, Charles, Reynolds, and Gatz (2001) reported decreases in negative affect from adolescence through age 60 in a cross-sequential longitudinal study and no change thereafter. In addition, Costa and McCrae (2000) reported decreases in neuroticism from ages 41 to 50. Several studies have found no changes in measures of neuroticism or its counterpart emotional stability (Costa & McCrae, 1988, 1998; Dudek and Hall, 1991). Studies focusing on old age also have found no change on measures of neuroticism or emotional stability (Field & Millsap, 1991; Nilsson & Persson, 1984; Pedersen & Reynolds, 1998). In contrast, Leon, et al. (1979) reported significant increases in several clinical scales drawn from the MMPI between the ages of 62 and 77 in a longitudinal study of men.

In summary, most studies show either decreases or little change in measures of neuroticism. If these studies were aggregated using meta-analytic procedures, we suspect that we would find that neuroticism decreased at a slow rate with age. Or conversely, we would find that emotional stability increased slowly with age.

Mean-Level Changes in Openness to Experience

Openness to experience refers to individual differences in the propensity to be original, complex, creative, and open to new ideas (John & Srivastava, 1999). Aging studies show either no relationship between openness to experience and age or decreases with age. For example, Goldberg et al. (1998) reported that the correlation between intellect (e.g., openness) and age was zero. Likewise, Helson and Kwan (2000) reported average correlations around zero between CPI measures of complexity and age in samples drawn from five different countries. In contrast, Costa & McCrae (1986) reported small, but statistically significant decreases in openness to experience in samples ranging in age from 35 to 84. Similarly, McCrae et al. (1999) found a negative relationship between openness and age in samples drawn from six different cultures.

Longitudinal studies show a more complex pattern of change in traits related to openness to experience across the life course. Studies based on adolescent and college-aged samples show increases in openness to experience. Baltes and Nesselroade (1972) reported significant increases on the 16PF scale of intelligence in longitudinal studies of college students. Robins et al. (2001) also found increases in the NEO–FFI measure of openness in a 4-year longitudinal study of college students. Unfortunately, the evidence for increases in openness during this age period is confounded by the fact that all of these studies tracked personality change in college students who are ostensibly being socialized to be more open to experience (Sanford, 1956).

Beyond the college years, the evidence is equivocal for mean-level changes in openness to experience with an equal number of studies demonstrating increases, decreases, or no change. For example, women from the Mills Longitudinal Study demonstrated increases in psychological mindedness from ages 21 to 27 (see also Helson and Kwan, 2000). McGue et al. (1993) reported increases on the MPQ Absorption scale in a sample of twins from ages 20 to 30. The Absorption scale measures the tendency to be emotionally responsive to sights and sounds, and to become absorbed in imaginative images and recollections. In contrast, other studies reported no changes in measures of openness to experience over similar age periods (Cartwright & Wink, 1994; Stevens & Truss, 1985). Several studies have even shown decreases in measures of openness to experience in middle and old age (Costa et al., 2000; Field & Millsap, 1991).

With the exception of the longitudinal studies of college students, the picture that emerges is mixed. However, overall, it appears that openness to experience increases in young adulthood and then plateaus thereafter.

Interpreting the Patterns of Mean-Level Change across the Life Course

We have summarized the findings from previous cross-sectional and longitudinal research on personality development in Table 26-1. This table shows that the patterns of personality change replicate across cross-sectional and longitudinal studies. The patterns also appear quite clear. People become more socially dominant, especially in young adulthood. They become more agreeable and conscientious through midlife and into old age. In addition, people show decreases in neuroticism across all age periods, small increases in openness to experience in the early stages of young adulthood and little change thereafter.

Although the patterns of change gleaned from previous research are intrinsically interesting, they beg the question of whether there is a more compelling or evaluative interpretation of the pattern. Specifically, one can ask whether the changes demonstrated across the Big Five conform to what we would expect from definitions of psychological maturity. What is psychological maturity? Maturity entails change in the direction of a desirable endpoint that once reached means a person is closer to being fully developed. This makes maturity an endpoint

TABLE 26-1.   **Personality Change across the Life Course: A Tabular Summary of Evidence from Cross-sectional and Longitudinal Studies of Mean-Level Personality Change**

Personality trait domain	Cross-sectional studies of different age groups	Longitudinal studies of people followed over time		
	Ages 18 to 80	Young adulthood (20–40)	Middle age (40–60)	Midlife to old age (over 60)
Extraversion:				
Social dominance	+	+	+	?
Social vitality	−	−	−	−
Agreeableness	+	+	+	+
Conscientiousness	+	+	+	+
Neuroticism	−	−	−	0
Openness to Experience	−	+	0	0

Note: "+" signifies developmental increase, "−" signifies developmental decrease, "0" signifies no change, and "?" signifies that more research is needed.

with trait-like features, and the study of maturity intrinsically the study of the development of traits. Two distinct definitions of maturity prevail in the developmental literature (see Helson & Wink, 1987; Roberts et al., 2001). The first definition equates maturity with self-actualization and personal growth. For example, Maslow (1954) described the self-actualized individual as creative, concerned with the ultimate nature of reality, and as having the capacity to appreciate art. Similarly, Rogers (1961) described personal growth as the process of becoming less defensive and rigid and more creative and open to feelings. Interestingly, these defining characteristics of self-actualization and personal growth fall unambiguously into the Big Five domain of Openness to Experience.

The second definition of maturity is more functional in nature. Hogan and Roberts (in press) argue that maturity is characterized by those qualities that serve to facilitate functioning in society—mature people are more liked, respected, and admired in their communities, social groups, and interpersonal relationships. This definition is quite similar to Allport's (1961) characterization of the mature person as happy, showing fewer traces of neurotic and abnormal tendencies, and having the capacity for warm and compassionate relationships. From this perspective, maturity is marked by higher levels of emotional stability, conscientiousness, and agreeableness. The interpretation of this definition as functional is bolstered by research demonstrating that people who score higher on these three traits tend to achieve more success in their careers (Judge et al., 1999), perform better on the job according to their supervisors and peers (Tett, Jackson, & Rothstein, 1991), do more for their organizations than their peers (Hogan, Rybicki, Motowidlo, & Borman, 1998), have more stable marriages (Cramer, 1993; Kelly & Conley, 1987), belong to more social organizations in the community (MacDonald, 2000), take fewer health risks (Caspi et al., 1997), and live longer (Friedman et al., 1993).

Assuming that maturity is a state that one achieves with time and experience, one would expect mean-level increases on traits related to maturity. For example, if the humanistic definition of psychological maturity were correct, one would assume a trend for people to increase in measures of openness to experience across the life course. However, the data do not provide strong support for a humanistic interpretation of psychological maturity. After college, people do not grow increasingly open to experience with age (not according to our review of the literature). Future research might profit from differentiating among the facets of openness. For example, it may be that wisdom increases with age (Baltes & Staudinger, 2000), but traits such as creativity and openness to feelings and ideas may decrease. In contrast, it appears that people do become more functionally mature. With age, people become warmer, more considerate, self-controlled, responsible, and emotionally stable.

The implications of the pattern of mean-level changes in personality traits are quite profound. First, it shows that the direction of change in personality traits over the first 40 years of adulthood is quite positive. Once people emerge from adolescence, they become warmer, more responsible, and more emotionally stable as they progress through young adulthood and enter middle age. Second, gains in these traits related to functional maturity might promote even more positive social outcomes than implied by the cross-sectional findings described above.

Finally, these findings show that personality traits, long thought to be immutable, not only change, but also continue to develop later in the life course than most theorists suggested. It appears that development does not end with the advent of adulthood.

WHY DO PERSONALITY TRAITS CHANGE?

If individuals do become more mature with age, then the most relevant question is why? Interestingly, answers to this question tend to fall into two categories described as "ontogenetic" and "sociogenic" (Aldwin & Levinson, 1994), which are analogous to the essentialist and contextualist positions described earlier. From an ontogenetic perspective, personality develops out of properties intrinsic to the organism, which has been interpreted as meaning that genes guide people to develop in a specific fashion across the life course (McCrae et al, 2000). This is, of course, an overly simplistic position as genes are manifest in contexts and interact with contexts to produce, change, and maintain personality (see Shanahan and Hofer, *this volume*).

In contrast, the sociogenic perspective assumes that the social structure is, in part, responsible for personality development. Specifically, change in personality is thought to result from the way a person interfaces with society through their ongoing participation in social roles (Aldwin & Levinson, 1994; Caspi & Roberts, 1999). For example, individuals are assumed to change their personality as they learn the norms associated with their work roles (Sarbin, 1964). Individuals also may change their personality traits based on feedback they receive in their social roles from peers, which is one of the essential ideas of symbolic interactionism (Stryker & Statham, 1985).

There is now a growing body of research demonstrating nontrivial relationships between changes in personality traits and sociogenic factors. For example, Elder (1969) found a distinct pattern of personality change from junior high school to the early 30s in men whose occupational achievements were greater than their fathers. Compared to men who achieved the same or less than their fathers, upwardly mobile men became more dependable and responsible, independent, and motivated for success. They also became less self-defeating, less susceptible to withdrawal when frustrated, and less likely to lack personal meaning in their life. Bachman and O'Malley (1977) found a small relation between occupational attainment and increases in self-esteem in a 10-year period following high school. Similarly, Mortimer and Lorence (1979) reported increases in competence for men who experienced more occupational autonomy in the 10-year period following graduation from college. Clausen and Gilens (1990) reported that women who had high labor force participation increased in self-confidence from adolescence to midlife. Finally, Roberts (1997) showed that women's participation and success in the paid labor force were associated with increases in measures of conscientiousness (responsibility, norm-orientation) and extraversion (dominance, independence). Furthermore, Roberts and Chapman (2000) showed that work satisfaction was associated with decreases in measures of neuroticism.

Moving beyond the domain of work, Helson and Picano (1990) tracked personality change from ages 20 to 43 in women who occupied either traditional or neo- or non-traditional role configurations. They found that women in a traditional role configuration (e.g., homemaker) demonstrated fewer positive developmental gains in personality traits when compared to women who occupied neo-traditional (e.g., some involvement in the paid labor force) or non-traditional (e.g., working full time for whole career) role configurations. Roberts and Chapman (2000) tested the association between changes in measures of neuroticism and marital experiences. They found that women who reported more marital tensions and lower marital satisfaction showed increases in measures of neuroticism and decreases in measures of dispositional well-being from ages 21 to 52. Roberts, Helson, and Klohnen (2002) reported that divorce was associated with a slower rate of increase in dominance when the divorce was experienced in young adulthood.

Consistent with these findings, Robins, Caspi, and Moffitt (2002) found that relationship experiences during young adulthood could serve as a catalyst for personality change. Young adults in dissatisfying and abusive relationship became more anxious, angry, and alienated over time. In contrast, young adults who remained in a stable relationship during their 20s became more cautious and restrained in their thoughts, feelings, and behaviors. This finding provides a plausible causal account for a particular intraindividual developmental pathway.

Impulse control tends to increase in young adulthood, but the reason for this change is not fully understood (Roberts et al., 2001). Robins et al.'s findings suggest that settling down in an intimate relationship may be a contributory cause. It may be that the norms, expectations, and sex-role stereotypes associated with intimate relationships create an environmental press for a more controlled, cautious, and traditional approach to life. Likewise, the finding that individuals in unhappy relationships tend to become more hostile, anxious, and alienated over time dovetails with recent research on depression. Negative relationship experiences—including dissatisfaction (Whisman & Bruce, 1999) and dissolution (Monroe, Rohde, Seeley, & Lewinsohn, 1999)—increase the risk of depression. However, the mediating mechanism remains to be understood. Repeated acts of aggression, recurrent negative emotional states, and other aversive experiences that chronically occur in maladaptive intimate relationships may increase an individual's disposition toward negative emotionality, which is a risk factor for depression (Krueger, 1999).

One additional sociogenic factor, historical context, has been long identified as a critical influence on personality development (Stewart & Sokel, 1989). Different historical periods bring different opportunities, values, and social roles that are thought to influence the person-alities of individuals living through those times (Baltes & Nesselroade, 1972; Twenge, 2001). Elder's (1979) study of the Great Depression is a classic example of how pervasive deprivation had differential developmental influences on the personality development of younger versus older children. More recent research has demonstrated the influence of modern historical phe-nomena. For example, Agronick and Duncan (1998) investigated the personality changes asso-ciated with the perceived importance of the women's movement of the 1960s and 1970s. Women who felt that the women's movement was important showed increases in social poise and self-assurance and decreases in several measures of norm-adherence. Roberts and Helson (1997) explored the antecedents and consequences of changes in culture or climate that occurred in the United States between 1950 and 1985, described as the "culture of narcissism." They found that changes in cultural climate were associated with increases in narcissism and decreases in social responsibility (e.g., decreasing psychological maturity).

These studies demonstrate that changes in personality traits are associated with experi-ences in careers, marriage, and the culture at large. Several aspects of these studies are worth highlighting. It seems apparent that certain life experiences are associated with increases in traits related to the functional definition of maturity. People who achieve more in work and remain in stable relationships become more conscientious (Elder, 1969; Roberts, 1997; Robins, Caspi, & Moffitt, in press). In addition, people who have satisfying jobs and mar-riages tend to increase in emotional stability (Roberts & Chapman, 2000; Robins, Caspi, & Moffitt, 2002). It should also be noted that life experiences could counteract the develop-mental trends toward functional maturity. The culture of narcissism in the United States dur-ing the 1960s, 1970s, and 1980s, was associated with decreases in norm adherence—a facet of conscientiousness (Roberts & Helson, 1997). Although the increases associated with func-tional maturity may be considered normative in that most people will demonstrate increases in agreeableness, conscientiousness, and emotional stability, these countervailing forces lend caution to the notion that maturity is inevitable. Some people, and some populations at cer-tain times in history, may not demonstrate a clear pattern of increasing maturity.

One problematic aspect of most research exploring the relationship between social struc-tures and personality development is the assumption that environments only affect change in personality. We describe this perspective as the "exposure" model of personality development in which it is often assumed that mere exposure to the social structure, role, or context will facil-itate change in personality. Exposure models underestimate the complexity of the relationship between personality and social structure in two ways. First, they ignore the fact that personality and social structure are often reciprocally related (Kohn & Schooler, 1978, 1982; Schooler, Mulatu, & Oates, 1999). For example, as these classic studies have shown, people who possess more ideational flexibility enter and maintain jobs that are more intellectually challenging, which in turn promotes increases ideational flexibility even in old age. Roberts, Caspi, and Moffitt (2002) have recast this as the principle of corresponsiveness. They have proposed that the most likely effect of life experience on personality development is to deepen the characteristics that lead people to those experiences in the first place (Roberts & Caspi, 2003). Thus, individuals drawn to stimulating work because of their own intellectual complexity will become more intellectually complex because of their experiences. The principle of corresponsiveness is important as it highlights the fact that individuals will have their own unique developmental trajectory based in part on their own personality. It also highlights the fact that people are not rudderless ships buffeted by the whims of the social context. Rather, the type of change they demonstrate will often grow out of their individuality and will therefore be somewhat predictable.

The second way in which exposure models are flawed is that they overlook the fact that social contexts may facilitate the more ubiquitous psychological phenomenon of adulthood: consistency. We believe that this more common effect of social context arises from people's attempts to build a personal niche that fits with their values, goals, and personality traits. At its broadest level the personal niche is built around primary social roles found in one's marriage, career, family, and community (e.g., religious, volunteer, and leisure time roles). To the extent that people can build a niche that fits with their psychological profile, then psychological adjustment should be facilitated, as should growth in the direction of the expectations of the social roles selected. In addition, because this niche should successfully reinforce a person's already existing dispositions, there should be less need for change and thus greater levels of consistency (see Roberts & Caspi, in press).

In our most recent research we tested these ideas by examining the relationship between a person's fit with their school environment and their personality development over a 4-year period (Roberts & Robins, in press). Consistent with our expectations, students who fit better with the school environment were more satisfied with school and better adjusted. Also as expected, we found that individuals who fit better with their school environment changed less than others. Finally, although they changed less than others we found that people who fit with the environment tended to change in the direction of the values of the school environment. As this was a highly regarded research university with a competitive and achievement oriented culture, the climate was pulling for students to become more competitive and better able to handle the stress of high achievement standards. Thus, those who fit better with the school environment grew to be more competitive, which was reflected in becoming less agreeable, and also more emotionally stable as they adapted to the demands of the university culture. This is one of the first studies to identify and test an environmental mechanism that is simultaneously associated with both change and continuity in personality over time.

Finally, the fact that change in personality traits is associated with life experiences has important ramifications for how one conceptualizes the field of personality psychology and personality development in particular. If personality changes are due to normative life experiences, then there is the possibility that people can be changed given the right intervention or context. From a theoretical perspective, we must ask why personality would remain an open system that is characterized by both consistency and change? What factors contribute to increasing consistency? What adaptive function, if any, does malleability serve in old age? Answering these questions entails a stark revision of our modal conceptualization of traits that is intrinsically more dynamic (e.g., Pervin, 1994). Rather than simply assuming that traits are consistent because they are traits, we need to understand the processes that account for continuity and change in personality (Whitbourne, 2001).

CONCLUSION

In closing we would like to make a modest proposal to rekindle the dialogue between sociology and personality psychology. It is clear from our perspective that a complete understanding of personality development cannot happen without explicit attention to sociological ideas and findings. Research on personality development would benefit greatly from the perspectives brought to bear by life-course sociology. In turn, we think that personality psychology today can provide sociologists with a much more conceptually elegant model of psychological functioning than was possible 60 years ago. We hope the invitation is accepted.

REFERENCES

Agronick, G. S., & Duncan, L. E. (1998). Personality and social change: Individual differences, life path, and importance attributed to the women's movement. *Journal of Personality and Social Psychology, 74*, 1545–1555.
Aldwin, C. M., & Levenson, M. R. (1994). Aging and personality assessment. In M. P. Lawton, J. A. Teresi (Eds.), *Annual review of gerontology and geriatrics: Focus on assessment* (pp. 182–209). New York: Springer Publishing.
Allport, G. W. (1961). *Pattern and growth in personality.* New York, NY: Holt, Rinehart, & Winston.
Arnett, J. J. (2000). Emerging adulthood: A theory of development from the late teens through the twenties. *American Psychologist, 55*, 469–480.
Bachman, J. G., & O'Malley, P. M. (1977). Self-esteem in young men: A longitudinal analysis of the impact of educational and occupational attainment. *Journal of Personality and Social Psychology, 35*, 365–380.
Baltes, P. B., & Nesselroade, J. R. (1972). Cultural change and adolescent personality development: An application of longitudinal sequences. *Developmental Psychology, 7*, 244–256.
Baltes, P. B., & Staudinger, U. M. (2000). Wisdom: A metaheuristic (pragmatic) to orchestrate mind and virtue toward excellence. *American Psychologist, 55*, 122–136.
Block, J. (1968). Some reasons for the apparent inconsistency of personality. *Psychological Bulletin, 70*, 210–212.
Carmichael, C. M., & McGue, M. (1994). A longitudinal family study of personality change and stability. *Journal of Personality, 62*, 1–20.
Carstensen, L. L., Pasupathi, M., Mayr, U., Nesselroade, J. R. (2000). Emotional experience in everyday life across the adult life span. *Journal of Personality and Social Psychology, 79*, 644–655.
Cartwright, L. K., & Wink, P. (1994). Personality change in women physicians from medical student years to mid-40s. *Psychology of Women Quarterly, 18*, 291–308.
Caspi, A. (2000). The child is father of the man: Personality continuities from childhood to adulthood. *Journal of Personality and Social Psychology, 78*, 158–172.
Caspi, A., Begg, D., Dickson, N., Harrington, H., Langley, J., Moffitt, T. E., & Silva, P. A. (1997). Personality differences predict health-risk behaviors in young adulthood: Evidence from a longitudinal study. *Journal of Personality and Social Psychology, 73*, 1052–1063.
Caspi, A., Elder, G. H., & Bem, D. J. (1987). Moving against the world: Life-course patterns of explosive children. *Developmental Psychology, 23*, 308–313.
Caspi, A., Elder, G. H., & Bem, D. J. (1988). Moving away from the world: Life-course patterns of shy children. *Developmental Psychology, 24*, 824–831.
Caspi, A., & Roberts, B. W. (1999). Personality change and continuity across the life course. In L. A. Pervin & O. P. John, *Handbook of personality theory and research* (pp. 300–326). New York: Guilford Press.
Caspi, A., & Silva, P. A. (1995). Temperamental qualities at age three predict personality traits in young adulthood: Longitudinal evidence from a birth cohort. *Child Development, 66*, 486–498.
Charles, S. T., Reynolds, C. A., Gatz, M. (2001). Age-related differences and change in positive and negative affect over 23 years. *Journal of Personality & Social Psychology, 80*, 136–151.

Clausen, J. A., & Gilens, M. (1990). Personality and labor force participation across the life course: A longitudinal study of women's careers. *Sociological Forum, 5*, 595–618.

Conley, J. J. (1984). The hierarchy of consistency: A review and model of longitudinal findings on adult individual differences in intelligence, personality, and self-opinion. *Personality and Individual Differences, 5*, 11–26.

Costa, P. T. Jr., Herbst, J. H., McCrae, R. R., & Siegler, I. C. (2000). Personality at midlife: Stability, intrinsic maturation, and response to life events. *Assessment, 7*, 365–378.

Costa, P. T., & McCrae, R. R. (1986). Cross-sectional studies of personality in a national sample: I. Development and validation of survey measures. *Psychology & Aging, 1*, 140–143.

Costa, P. T., & McCrae, R. R. (1988). Personality in adulthood: A six-year longitudinal study of self-reports and spouse ratings on the NEO Personality Inventory. *Journal of Personality and Social Psychology, 54*, 853–863.

Costa, P. T., McCrae, R. R., & Arenberg, D. (1980). Enduring dispositions in adult males. *Journal of Personality and Social Psychology, 38*, 793–800.

Cramer, D. (1993). Personality and marital dissolution. *Personality and Individual Differences, 14*, 605–607.

Crook, M. N. (1943). A retest with the Thurstone Personality Schedule after six and one-half years. *Journal of General Psychology, 28*, 111–120.

Dudek, S. Z., & Hall, W. B. (1991). Personality consistency: Eminent architects 25 years later. *Creativity Research Journal, 4*, 213–231.

Elder, G. H. (1969). Occupational mobility, life patterns, and personality. *Journal of Health and Social Behavior, 10*, 308–323.

Elder, G. H., Jr. (1979). Historical change in life patterns and personality. In P. B. Baltes & O. G. Brim, Jr. (Eds.), *Life-span development and behavior.* (Vol. 2, pp. 117–159). New York: Academic Press.

Field, D., & Millsap, R. E. (1991). Personality in advanced old age: Continuity or change? *Journals of Gerontology, 46*, 299–308.

Friedman, H. S. (2000). Long-term relations of personality and health: Dynamism, mechanisms, tropisms. *Journal of Personality, 68*, 1089–1107.

Friedman, H. S., Tucker, J. S., Tomlinson-Keasey, C., Schwartz, J. E., Wingard, D. L., & Criqui, M. H. (1993). Does childhood personality predict longevity. *Journal of Personality and Social Psychology, 65*, 176–185.

Goldberg, L. R. (1993). The structure of phenotypic personality traits. *American Psychologist, 48*, 26–34.

Goldberg, L. R., Sweeney, D., Merenda, P. F., & Hughes, J. E. Jr. (1998). Demographic variables and personality: The effects of gender, age, education, and ethnic/racial status on self-descriptions of personality attributes. *Personality & Individual Differences, 24*, 393–403.

Haan, N., Millsap, R., & Hartka, E. (1986). As time goes by: Change and stability in personality over fifty years. *Psychology and Aging, 1*, 220–232.

Helson, R., & Kwan, V. S. Y. (2000). Personality development in adulthood: The broad picture and processes in one longitudinal sample. In S. Hampson (Ed.), *Advances in personality psychology* (Vol. 1; pp. 77–106). London: Routledge.

Helson, R., & Moane, G. (1987). Personality change in women from college to midlife. *Journal of Personality and Social Psychology, 53*, 176–186.

Helson, R., & Picano, J. (1990). Is the traditional role bad for women? *Journal of Personality and Social Psychology, 59*, 311–320.

Helson, R., & Wink, P. (1987). Two conceptions of maturity examined in the findings of a longitudinal study. *Journal of Personality and Social Psychology, 53*, 531–541.

Helson, R., & Wink, P. (1992). Personality change in women from the early 40s to the early 50s. *Psychology and Aging, 7*, 46–55.

Hogan, J., Rybicki, S. L., Motowidlo, S. J., & Borman, W. C. (1998). Relations between contextual performance, personality, and occupational advancement. *Human Performance, 11*, 189–207.

Hogan, R., & Roberts, B. W. (in press). A socioanalytic model of maturity. *Journal of Career Assessment.*

Inkeles, A., & Levinson, D. J. (1963). The personal system and the sociocultural system in large-scale organizations. *Sociometry, 26*, 217–229.

John, O. P., & Srivastava, S. (1999). The Big Five trait taxonomy; History, measurement, and theoretical perspectives. In L. A. Pervin & O. P. John, *Handbook of Personality Theory and Research* (Vol. 2, pp. 102–138). New York: Guilford Press.

Johnson, R. C., Nagoshi, C. T., Ahern, F. M., Wilson, J. R., McClearn, G. E., & Vandenberg, S. G. (1983). Age and cohort effects on personality factor scores across sexes and racial/ethnic groups. *Personality and Individual Differences, 6*, 709–713.

Judge, T. A., Higgins, C. A., Thoreson, C. J., & Barrick, M. R. (1999). The Big Five personality traits, general mental ability, and career success across the life span. *Personnel Psychology, 52*, 621–652.

Kelly, E., & Conley, J. (1987). Personality and compatibility: A prospective analysis of marital stability and marital satisfaction. *Journal of Personality and Social Psychology, 52*, 27–40.

Kohn, M. L., & Schooler, C. (1978). The reciprocal effects of the substantive complexity of work and intellectual flexibility: A longitudinal assessment. *American Journal of Sociology, 84*, 24–52.

Kohn, M. L., & Schooler, C. (1982). Job conditions and personality: A longitudinal assessment of their reciprocal effects. *American Journal of Sociology, 87*, 1257–1286.

Krueger, R. F. (1999). Personality traits in late adolescence predict mental disorders in early adulthood: A prospective-epidemiological study. *Journal of Personality, 67*, 39–65.

Leon, G. R., Gillum, B., Gillum, R., & Gouze, M. (1979). Personality stability and change over a 30 year period— Middle age to old age. *Journal of Consulting and Clinical Psychology, 47*, 517–524.

Lewis, M. (1999). On the development of personality. In L. A. Pervin, & O. P. John (Eds.), *Handbook of personality theory and research* (pp. 327–346). New York: Guilford Press.

Lewis, M. (2001). Issues in the study of personality development. *Psychological Inquiry, 12*, 67–83.

McCrae, R. R., & Costa, P. T. (1994). The stability of personality: Observation and evaluations. *Current Directions in Psychological Science, 3*, 173–175.

McCrae, R. R., & Costa, P. T., Jr. (1997). Personality trait structure as a human universal. *American Psychologist, 52*, 509–516.

McCrae, R. R., Costa, P. T., Jr., Pedroso de Lima, M., Simoes, A., Ostendorf, F., Angleitner, A., Marusic, I., Bratko, D., Caprara, G. V., Barmbaranelli, C., Chae, J-H., & Piedmont, R. L. (1999). Age differences in personality across the adult life span: Parallels in five cultures. *Developmental Psychology, 35*, 466–477.

McCrae, R. R., Costa, P. T. Jr., Ostendorf, F., Angleitner, A., Hrebickova, M., Avia, M. D., Sanz, J., Sanchez-Bernardos, M. L., Kusdil, M. E., Woodfield, R., Saunders, P. R., & Smith, P. B. (2000). Nature over nurture: Temperament, personality, and life span development. *Journal of Personality and Social Psychology, 78*, 173–186.

MacDonald, D. A. (2000). Spirituality: Description, measurement, and relation to the Five-Factor Model of personality. *Journal of Personality, 68*, 153–197.

McGue, M., Bacon, S., & Lykken, D. T. (1993). Personality stability and change in early adulthood: A behavioral genetic analysis. *Developmental Psychology, 29*, 96–109.

Maslow, A. H. (1954). *Motivation and personality*. New York, NY: Harper.

Miller, J. D., & Lynam, D. (2001). Structural models of personality and their relation to antisocial behavior: A meta-analytic review. *Criminology, 39*, 765–798.

Mischel, W. (1968). *Personality and assessment*. New York: Wiley.

Monroe, S. M., Rohde, P., Seeley, J. R., & Lewinsohn, P. M. (1999). Life events and depression in adolescence: Relationship loss as a prospective risk factor for first onset of major depressive disorder. *Journal of Abnormal Psychology, 108*, 606–614.

Mortimer, J. T., & Lorence, J. (1979). Occupational experience and the self-concept—A longitudinal study. *Social Psychology Quarterly, 42*, 307–323.

Mroczek, D. K., & Kolarz, C. M. (1998). The effect of age on positive and negative affect: A developmental perspective on happiness. *Journal of Personality and Social Psychology, 75*, 1333–1349.

Neugarten, B. L. (1968). Age norms, age constraints, and adult socialization. In B. L. Neugarten (Ed.), *Middle age and aging: A reader in social psychology*. Chicago, IL: University of Chicago Press.

Nilsson, L. V., & Persson, B. (1984). Personality changes in the aged. *Acta Psychiatrica Scandanavica, 69*, 182–189.

Parsons, T. (1942). Age and sex in the social structure of the United States. *American Sociological Review, 7*, 604–616.

Pedersen, N. L., Reynolds, C. A. (1998). Stability and change in adult personality: Genetic and environmental components. *European Journal of Personality, 12*, 365–386.

Pervin, L. A. (1994). A critical analysis of current trait theory. *Psychological Inquiry, 5*, 103–113.

Pervin, L. A., & John, O. P. (1999). *Handbook of personality: Theory and research (2nd edition)*. New York, NY: The Guilford Press.

Rindfuss R. R. (1991). The young-adult years—Diversity, structural-change, and fertility. *Demography, 28*, 493–512.

Roberts, B. W. (1997). Plaster or plasticity: Are work experiences associated with personality change in women? *Journal of Personality, 65*, 205–232.

Roberts, B. W., & Caspi, A. (2003). The cumulative continuity model of personality development: Striking a balance between continuity and change in personality traits across the life course. U. Staudinger & U. Lindenberger (Eds.), *Understanding human development: Lifespan psychology in exchange with other disciplines* (pp. 183–214). Dordrecht, NL: Kluwer Academic.

Roberts, B. W., Caspi, A., & Moffitt, T. (2001). The kids are alright: Growth and stability in personality development from adolescence to adulthood. *Journal of Personality and Social Psychology 81*, 670–683.

Roberts, B. W., Caspi, A., & Moffitt, T. (2002). *Work Experiences and Personality Development in Young Adulthood.* Unpublished manuscript. The University of Illinois, Urbana-Champaign.

Roberts, B. W., & Chapman, C. (2000). Change in dispositional well-being and its relation to role quality: A 30-year longitudinal study. *Journal of Research in Personality, 34,* 26–41.

Roberts, B. W., & DelVecchio, W. F. (2000). The rank–order consistency of personality from childhood to old age: A quantitative review of longitudinal studies. *Psychological Bulletin, 126,* 3–25.

Roberts, B. W., & Helson, R. (1997). Changes in culture, changes in personality: The influence of individualism in a longitudinal study of women. *Journal of Personality and Social Psychology, 72,* 641–651.

Roberts, B. W., Helson, R., & Klohnen, E. C. (2002). Personality development and growth in women across 30 years: Three perspectives. *Journal of Personality, 70,* 79–102.

Roberts, B. W., & Robins, R. W. (in press). A longitudinal study of person-environment fit and personality development. *Journal of Personality.*

Robins, R. W., Caspi, A., & Moffitt, T. (2000). Two personalities, one relationship: Both partners' personality traits shape the quality of their relationship. *Journal of Personality and Social Psychology, 79,* 251–259.

Robins, R. W., Caspi, A., & Moffitt, T. (2002). It's not just who you're with, it's who you are: Personality and relationship experiences across multiple relationships. *Journal of Personality, 70,* 925–964.

Robins, R. W., Fraley, R. C., Roberts, B. W., & Trzesniewski. K. (2001). A longitudinal study of personality change in young adulthood. *Journal of Personality, 69,* 617–640.

Robins, R. W., Tracy, J. L., Trzesniewski, K. H., Gosling, S. D., & Potter, J. (2002). Personality correlates of self-esteem. *Journal of Research in Personality, 35,* 463–482.

Robins, R. W., Trzesniewski, K. H., Tracy, J. L., Gosling, S. D., & Potter, J. (2002). Global self-esteem across the lifespan. *Psychology and Aging, 17,* 423–434.

Rogers, C. R. (1961). *On becoming a person.* Boston, MA: Houghton Mifflin.

Sanford, N. (1956). Personality development during the college years. *Journal of Social Issues, 12,* 3–70.

Sarbin, T. R. (1964). Role theoretical interpretation of psychological change. In P. Worchel & D. Byrne (Eds.), *Personality change* (pp. 176–219). New York: John Wiley.

Schaie, K. W. (1965). A general model for the study of developmental problems. *Psychological Bulletin, 64,* 92–107.

Schooler, C., Mulatu, M. S., & Oates, G. (1999). The continuing effects of substantively complex work on the intellectual functioning of older workers. *Psychology and Aging, 14,* 483–506.

Schuerger, J. M, Zarrella, K. L., & Hotz, A. S. (1989). Factors that influence the temporal stability of personality by questionnaire. *Journal of Personality and Social Psychology, 56,* 777–783.

Stein, J. A., Newcomb, M. D., & Bentler, P. M. (1986). Stability and change in personality: A longitudinal study from early adolescence to young adulthood. *Journal of Research in Personality, 20,* 276–291.

Stevens, D. P., & Truss, C. V. (1985). Stability and change in adult personality over 12 and 20 years. *Developmental Psychology, 21,* 568–584.

Stewart, A. J., & Healy, J. M. (1989). Linking individual development and social changes. *American Psychologist, 44,* 30–42.

Stryker, S., & Statham, A. (1985). Symbolic interaction role theory. In G. Lindzey & E. Aronson (Eds.), *Handbook of social psychology.* (pp. 311–378). Hillsdale, NJ: Erlbaum.

Tett, R. P., Jackson, D. N., & Rothstein, M. (1991). Personality measures as predictors of job performance: A meta-analytic review. *Personnel Psychology, 44,* 703–742.

Twenge, J. M. (2001). Changes in women's assertiveness in response to status and roles: A cross-temporal meta-analysis, 1931–1993. *Journal of Personality and Social Psychology, 81,* 133–145.

Viken, R. J., Rose, R. J., Kaprio, J., & Koskenvuo, M. (1994). A developmental genetic analysis of adult personality: Extraversion and neuroticism from 18 to 59 years of age. *Journal of Personality and Social Psychology, 66,* 722–730.

Watson, D., & Walker, L. M. (1996). The long-term stability and predictive validity of trait measures of affect. *Journal of Personality and Social Psychology, 70,* 567–577.

Whisman, M. A., & Bruce, M. L. (1999). Marital dissatisfaction and incidence of major depressive episode in a community sample. *Journal of Abnormal Psychology, 108,* 674–678.

Whitbourne, S. K. (2001). Stability and change in adult personality: Contributions of process-oriented perspectives. *Psychological Inquiry, 12,* 101–103.

Widiger, T. A., Verheul, R., & van den Brink, W. (1999). Personality and psychopathology. In L. A. Pervin & O. P. John (Eds.), *Handbook of personality psychology: Theory and research* (2nd ed., pp. 347–366).

Wink, P., & Helson, R. (1993). Personality change in women and their partners. *Journal of Personality and Social Psychology, 65,* 597–606.

CHAPTER 27

Biological Models of Behavior and the Life Course

MICHAEL J. SHANAHAN

SCOTT M. HOFER

LILLY SHANAHAN

Many topics of interest to life course sociology are linked in significant ways to biological processes. These topics include, for example, trajectories of physical and mental health, the stress process, patterns of aggression and deviance, sexual behavior, fertility, parenting, and manifold dimensions of aging and mortality. Many other topics are also likely to be linked to biological processes, albeit less conspicuously, including educational and occupational careers, patterns of close interpersonal relationships both within and beyond the family, and one's involvement and status in organizations. With few notable exceptions, relatively little interest has been expressed in these possibilities to date. Yet as George (*this volume*) notes, the future of the life course will hopefully be characterized by its intellectual exchanges with other subfields. Given their many plausible links to the life course, biological models of behavior are excellent candidates for interdisciplinary research.

In this chapter we explore connections between life course sociology and contemporary biological approaches to human behavior. We focus on three such approaches: life-history theory, behavioral genetics, and behavioral endocrinology. Because all three subfields are vibrant, large areas of inquiry, our scope is necessarily limited: for each area, we provide a brief introduction

MICHAEL J. SHANAHAN • Department of Sociology, University of North Carolina, Chapel Hill, North Carolina 27599-3210

SCOTT M. HOFER AND LILLY SHANAHAN • Pennsylvania State University, University Park, Pennsylvania 16802-6504

Handbook of the Life Course, edited by Jeylan T. Mortimer and Michael J. Shanahan. Kluwer Academic/Plenum Publishers, New York, 2003.

to the biological principles that inform the perspective, an overview of characteristic themes and analytic strategies, and points of connection with the life course paradigm. That is, we do not consider specific areas of investigation in detail but rather explore possible links between these biological models and the life course at a thematic level. Moreover, because of the paucity of prior exchanges between biology and life course studies, our overview is largely conceptual in nature. Given space limitations, we focus on micro dimensions of the life course, with special attention to how social and biological forces jointly shape transitions between roles, and patterns of continuity and discontinuity that extend across the phases of life. We begin with several observations about both the appropriateness and the hazards of linking biology and sociology.

BIOLOGICAL AND SOCIAL FORCES: CAUTIONARY TALES AND PROMISE

The links between biology and sociology have not always been harmonious. The cases of Herbert Spencer (Peel, 1971) and his American champion Lester Ward (Scott, 1976) are instructive. A key proposition of Spencer's Synthetic Philosophy was that society and its institutions would become progressively complex, reflecting a universal, evolutionary process toward greater differentiation. This proposition predated the publication of *The origin of species* (1859) and was unfortunately at odds with Darwin's emphasis on natural selection as the primary mechanism of evolution. According to Darwin and his early followers, natural selection meant that organisms adapt to their ecological settings and this adaptation may or may not lead to a more complex organism. That is, evolution by natural selection was not viewed as inherently "progressive," but rather as adaptive to the prevailing conditions. Spencer was thus forced to reject natural selection as the predominant force of evolution in order to salvage his belief in the ever-increasing differentiation of society.

Lester Ward extolled the virtues of Spencer's vision and promoted sociology as a science that could hasten this progressive differentiation through social interventions. For Ward, the efficacy of these interventions hinged on Lamarckian inheritance, which held that characteristics acquired by one generation during their lifetime could be transmitted to their offspring. Thus, successful interventions in one generation would have lasting effects down the familial lineage. With the re-discovery and widespread appreciation of Mendel's Laws—which described basic rules of the heredity of innate, not acquired, characteristics—Ward believed that either Mendel was wrong or sociology and its interventions would hardly be worth the effort. In the final analysis, he chose his brand of sociology over his understanding of Mendel.

These case studies would be interesting footnotes to the history of the behavioral sciences except that many sociologists continue to resist the integration of biology with sociology, fearing that biological models run contrary to cherished values about the malleability of people and the importance of progress (not unlike both Spencer's and Ward's suspicions about natural selection) or that an appreciation of biology could lead to a simple-minded reductionism that views biological forces as necessary and sufficient conditions for behavior (not unlike Ward's fear of Mendelian genetics). Yet such reactions are both unwarranted and counter-productive. Contemporary biological theories of human behavior are not inherently laden with social values nor are they reductionistic. Rather, biological models of behavior have undergone nothing short of a paradigm shift in the last few decades, leading to the wide-spread assumption that "nature and nurture" interact in complex ways and indeed are often inseparable.

Such a view is consistent with propositions of systems theory (Ford & Lerner, 1992), several of which are especially relevant to a discussion of biology and the life course. First, human behavior is the product of multiple levels of analysis, including, for example, levels characteristically associated with sociology, psychology, biology, and anthropology. By extension, there is no *a priori* reason to believe that any one level will have special explanatory value. For example, genes do not simply cause behavior (Gottlieb, 1996) and, at the same time, behavior is not purely the result of social forces. Second, all levels of analysis are characterized by plasticity, which refers to the range of behavioral possibilities (Lerner, 1984). Thus, each person's behaviors represent one set of possibilities from among a finite range of possibilities; similarly, every social order represents one form of organization out of a range of possible social orders. Third, although each level is likely to operate according to its own laws, the levels interact to produce behavior (Cairns, McGuire et al., 1993). That is, systems theory assumes that many factors at multiple levels interact to form sets of "correlated constraints" that include the behaviors of interest and their covariates. These behaviors and their covariates represent organized systems, and ongoing reciprocal interactions among their levels explain continuity and provide a map of opportunities for change.

When viewed jointly, these principles define a central theme of life history theory, behavioral genetics, and behavioral endocrinology, and consequently of our chapter: *Social and biological forces interact in complex and dynamic ways to define ranges of likely behaviors*. By itself, this theme acknowledges the importance of context and its interplay with biology. Yet our review suggests a second overarching theme that links biological models of behavior to the life course more directly: *Behavior reflects a lifetime of reciprocal exchanges between person (including biological make-up) and context*. This theme acknowledges that behavior cannot be fully understood without reference to prior experience and indeed each of the three biological models that we consider promotes concepts consistent with this view.

Although biological models of behavior and life course sociology are thus thematically well-suited for interdisciplinary collaborations, care must nevertheless be exercised in avoiding the "the twin dangers of destructive cynicism and gullible expectations" (Rutter, 2002, p. 1). Gullible expectations are understandable given the excitement that currently surrounds developments in the biological sciences. In truth, however, once behavior is viewed as a product of long-standing interactions between biology and social context, the causal field becomes exceedingly complex. Quick progress is thus highly unlikely, as has already been demonstrated in the study of psychopathology (Rutter, 2002). Indeed, some scientists familiar with newly emerging insights from biology have tended toward a skeptical view that emphasizes the intractable contingency that characterizes how biological and social forces jointly produce behaviors. Whether such skepticism is warranted, however, can only be resolved through empirical study that accurately and dynamically assesses both biological and social features of the developing person and changing context. This phase of empirical research is only just beginning, and the purpose of our chapter is to consider, in very broad terms, the ways in which life course sociologists can contribute to these research efforts, and the ways in which biological models of behavior might inform life course research.

LIFE HISTORY THEORY AND THE
LIFE COURSE

Although several Darwinian approaches to behavior are often recognized,* life-history theory is most closely connected with life course sociology because of their mutual interest in transitions and connections among the phases of life (Charnov, 1993; Hill & Kaplan, 1999; Stearns, 1992). Life history theory applies principles of evolution to biological features of the life course that have demographic consequences (Stearns, 1992). For example, in his path-setting research, Cole (1954) observed that patterns of sexual maturation and reproduction in the lives of people have, when viewed in the aggregate, consequences for the size of the population. An understanding of the dynamics of a population thus depends on an understanding of how factors that relate to reproduction and survival actually occur in the lives of individual people.

These factors, or life-history traits, include, for example, patterns of growth, age of maturity, number and spacing of offspring, parental investments, mortality schedules, and length of life (Hill & Kaplan, 1999). Clearly, many of these concerns are linked to topics of interest to life course sociologists, including the pubertal transition, features of the family cycle (e.g., the transition to parenthood), and morbidity and mortality. Although life-history theory draws on evolutionary principles broadly, it characteristically emphasizes how natural selection favors specific constellations of these traits as they optimize survival and reproduction in a given time and place. We briefly review relevant principles of Darwinian evolution and then apply these principles to life history theory and research.

The Life History Perspective

Evolution by natural selection holds that there is variation in one or more characteristics in every generation, that heritable similarities exist between parents and their offspring, that some organisms are better suited to survive and reproduce in a particular environment than others, and that the proportion of these better-adapted individuals in the population will increase through time.[†] These central ideas are actually part of five theories that comprise the evolutionary synthesis of "variational evolution" (Mayr, 1982). One of these central ideas, natural selection, has special relevance for life-history theory.

The theory of natural selection provides a mechanism by which evolution occurs. Selection refers to differential survival and reproduction based on traits. Many biologists believe that selection works directly on the phenotype, which refers to the totality of all

---

*Evolutionary psychology tends to focus on naturally selected psychological mechanisms that ultimately promote survival and reproduction; these mechanisms include, most prominently, aspects of emotions, cognition, and motivation. Sociobiology focuses on fitness-enhancing mechanisms that are associated with social psychology, family and kin relations, and group behavior (Nielsen, 1994). Life history theory represents a subfield of behavioral ecology, an anthropological approach concerned with the material circumstances of ecologies and the adaptive responses that they evoke (Winterhalder & Alden Smith, 2000). A closely related anthropological approach, dual inheritance theory, emphasizes the interrelated evolution of genes and culture (Durham, 1990, 1992). While all of these perspectives are relevant to life course sociology in varying degrees—for example, for studies of educational and income trajectories inspired by evolutionary theories of kin investment, see Case et al., 2001 and Anderson, 2000—we focus on life history theory, which shares with life course sociology a central interest in the interconnectedness of life's phases.

[†]For a basic introduction to evolutionary theory, see Mayr (2001); for a specialized treatment, see Futuyma (1998). This summary is based on Futuyma & Mayr (1982) and necessarily glosses over many nuances in evolutionary biology.

observable features of an organism, including behavior. The response to selection refers to changes in the population across generations; these responses may include changes in phenotypes (i.e., the products of genes, including behaviors), genotypes (the genes of an organism), or both. Natural selection favors individuals who are "fit" or "adapted," although in many cases the opposite (i.e., the elimination of the "unfit") may be a more accurate characterization. Thus, adaptive traits "promote fitness," which means that they are positively associated with survival and especially with reproduction.

What is actually selected? According to life-history theory, natural selection determines the balance in trade-offs, which occurs when change in one trait is associated with change in another trait. Life-history recognizes over 45 such trade-offs (Stearns, 1992), including, for example, quantity versus quality of off-spring: as the quantity of off-spring increases, their "quality" (referring to, for example, the likelihood of successful maturation) decreases. Basically, natural selection will favor the right mix of quantity and quality so that reproductive fitness is optimized in a given setting. Thus, the biological life course may be viewed as a complex set of evolved trade-offs surrounding growth, maintenance of the self, and reproduction. In fact, many of the trade-offs link the early and later parts of the life course as one finds, for example, in the trade-off between age of sexual maturity and longevity: as age of sexual maturity decreases, longevity decreases. All of the trade-offs form a relatively cohesive set that describes how the phases of life are coordinated for a species. Thus, one focal point of life history research is the comparison of trade-offs across species (e.g., Charnov, 1993).

Some Darwinians maintain that behaviors were selected for their fitness through the late Miocene and Pleistocene, when humans are thought to have lived as nomadic hunter-gatherers in small groups on dry, cool savannas or perhaps in grassy woodlands. For these scholars, evolution favored features of human life—including body plan, metabolic processes, behaviors, and cognition and emotion—that optimized survival and reproduction to this "environment of evolutionary adaptedness." Life history research generally rejects this notion for several reasons (see Foley, 1995; Irons, 1998). Most importantly, the vast expanse during which humans evolved was characterized by substantial variability in environments both locally and globally (Potts, 1998).

Based on this variability in contexts, life history theory holds that natural selection has favored variability in behavior within a species. Accordingly, *natural selection in humans has produced mechanisms (not finished traits) by which features of context evoke a circumscribed range of adaptive behaviors* from a larger set of behavioral possibilities (Hill & Hurtado, 1996). Based on this supposition, a second focal point of life history research is how the specifics of context, life-history traits, and survival and reproduction are interrelated within a species.

Life History Research: Analytic Strategies and Themes

An example of the first focal point, which addresses between-species differences, comes from studies of the origins of menopause, which is believed to be virtually unique to humans. These studies typically focus on the possible functions of menopause when viewed in the context of other life-history traits. Several hypotheses now attempt to explain menopause in this way. Williams (1957) originally formulated the "grandmother hypothesis," which states that as women age, their evolved "strategy" to pass their genes to subsequent generations shifts from their own reproduction to the care of their children and grandchildren (for a related hypothesis, see Scott Peccei, 2001). That is, at a certain point in life, their reproductive fitness was optimized if they stopped having children and nurtured their children's children. Williams's hypothesis has been tested in hunter-gatherer societies by measuring the nutritional contributions of grandmothers to their offspring. The evidence is inconclusive at present, however, due to methodological and modeling problems (Blurton Jones, 1999; Hill & Hurtado, 1996). In any event, this line of research illustrates how life history research characteristically posits interactions between the social context—in this case, mode of subsistence and provisioning roles—and biology to explain features of the life course.

Of greater relevance to life course sociology are studies that reflect the second focal point, addressing how life-history traits "work" in specific contexts. This is a question based on the premise that evolution has selected variability and that contexts evoke responses from a range of possibilities. An example of this mode of inquiry concerns reproductive strategies. According to one prominent line of thinking, humans have evolved such that the first 5–7 years of life shape their subsequent pair-bonding and child-rearing behavior (Draper & Harpending, 1982). Specifically, children from families with marital discord, high stress, and inadequate resources are subject to harsh and inconsistent parenting; consequently, they develop an insecure attachment and opportunistic interpersonal orientation, leading to early puberty, early sexual activity, unstable pair bonds, and low levels of parental investment (Belsky, Steinberg et al., 1991). That is, in contexts marked by uncertainty, earlier reproduction is favored. At the other end of the continuum, children from homes characterized by spousal harmony and adequate resources receive responsive, positive parenting, and then develop a secure attachment, leading to later puberty, later sexual activity, long-term bonding, and high levels of parental investment.

Empirical research does not support all of this model's predictions, although there is considerable evidence that a range of stressors in the family are negatively associated with age of menarche (e.g., Moffitt, Caspi et al., 1992; Kim & Smith, 1998; Ellis & Graber, 2000, who also test a "step-father presence" hypothesis). In reviewing research related to this model, Surbey (1998) suggests that contextual cues associated with parental investment and the stability of the context affect the timing of menarche. These cues encompass a wide range of factors that bear on access to resources and environmental stressors, possibly including the presence of biological parents, the quality of the parent–child relationship, socioeconomic status, family size, birth order, and environmental stressors.

Taken together, these lines of research suggest that cohesive patterns of puberty, sexual behavior, and parental investment represent fitness-enhancing responses to earlier contextual cues in the family. Critics note that empirical support for the model is spotty, and some of its predictions run contrary to expectations derived from behavioral endocrinology (e.g., Susman et al., 1989). Nevertheless, the model illustrates an area of research that has been informed by principles of life-history theory, interweaving social roles, family dynamics, context, and biological features of the life course. Other lines of research address issues surrounding multiple aspects of the family cycle (including fertility and parenting), health and well-being, and longevity (see Hill & Kaplan, 1999, for a concise overview).

Integrating the Life History and Life Course Paradigms

Life history theory and the life course share common ground in that life phases and social roles are often intimately tied to biological events or trends. Further, both perspectives share the view that behavior reflects life-long interactions between persons and their contexts.

We can identify three advantages to an awareness of life history research by life course sociologists. First, with its emphasis on natural selection, life history theory alerts life course sociologists that human lives have evolved and thus behaviors may reflect selection pressures. That is, life course sociology should begin to entertain the possibility that behaviors can enhance fitness in response to contextual cues. Second, evolutionary theory can, in principle, serve as a broad framework that integrates diverse findings and leads to the generation of new hypotheses and explanations. Hence, evolutionary theory has the potential to provide an over-arching "distal frame" for mid-range research. Life-history research is certainly a lively field of emerging hypotheses that reflect biology-context interactions, and it would be unfortunate if sociologists remain oblivious or uninterested in these developments. Third, life history research often draws on cross-cultural comparisons, which greatly expand the variability to be explained in human lives. Unfortunately, by restricting its attention to contemporary Western societies, life course sociology has ignored significant variability in contexts, behaviors, and the allocation of roles with age (Dannefer, *this volume*).

At the same time, attempts to integrate life history and life course research should proceed with caution. The enhancement of reproductive fitness is a distinguishing feature of all evolutionary explanations based on natural selection, although fitness is in fact rarely measured, perhaps because it is notoriously difficult to define and assess (Beatty, 1992). The problem takes several different forms. For Darwinian theories that posit an environment of evolutionary adaptedness in the Pleistocene epoch, reproductive fitness is probably impossible to measure (e.g., Belsky et al., 1991, p. 649). At the other end of the historical spectrum, for applications of life-history theory to societies that have experienced the demographic transition (involving high levels of contraception), new ways of thinking about fitness are undoubtedly necessary (e.g., Perusse, 1993 and accompanying commentary). Whatever the society being studied, if an enhancement in reproductive fitness has not been empirically addressed in some fashion, then, strictly speaking, a Darwinian theory has not been directly tested. In fact, predictions derived from evolutionary theory but not concerned with fitness are often tested. These predictions can often be derived, however, from other theories that carry fewer assumptions (e.g., Maccoby, 1991 for alternatives to Belsky et al., 1991).

Furthermore, mechanisms not related to natural selection can account for phylogenetic change (Mayr, 1983). Darwinians often assume that behavior has evolved to optimize reproductive fitness, but many behaviors may not be the products of natural selection or, in the alternative, they may be selected but highly imperfect optimizations. Most constraints on selection and optimization reflect the fact that selection acts on holisms, not on a single, atomistic trait. In the context of this holism, selection is a compromise between advantages associated with different organs, portions of the life cycle, and environments. For example, a gene or genes may be naturally selected because of their beneficial effects early in the life course, although they have negative effects in the later course (i.e., antagonistic pleiotropy, which some scholars believe explains menopause, see Scott Peccei, 2001). Furthermore, a specific selected response to an environmental challenge is likely to limit future possibilities for change (i.e., a developmental constraint). Or the selection of one feature may bring with it a whole suite of non-adaptive features (i.e., a hitch-hiking effect). These and other possibilities caution against the simplistic notion that life-history traits have been selected to optimize fitness; more likely, they reflect highly complex combinations of several distinct processes occurring over millions of years (e.g., Vrba, 1990).

These criticisms are not meant to suggest that evolutionary theories of behavior are untestable. In some cases, theories are testable in crucial respects—including claims about reproductive fitness—according to conventions of the behavioral sciences (e.g., Blurton Jones, 1993;

Borgerhoff Mulder, 2000; Hill & Hurtado, 1996; Kaplan et al., 2000). Such tests typically involve the development of mathematical models that suggest optimizations with respect to, for example, age of sexual maturity and longevity, or quantity-quality trade-offs in offspring investment (Hill & Kaplan, 1999). On the other hand, the distinctly Darwinian elements of a theory may be untestable in any sense whatever. In this case, however, selection and optimization could be an "untestable core" that nevertheless leads to unique testable propositions—in much the same way that many nascent theories in the natural sciences have done (e.g., the theory of natural selection before Mendelian genetics). To some scholars, this untestable core is an unnecessary extrapolation; to others, it provides distal mechanisms that, combined with empirical evidence of more proximal processes, offers a holistic explanation.

In the final analysis, the utility of life history theory to the study of lives is an empirical question that is being answered slowly through the development of precise models and the collection of appropriate data. In evaluating evolutionary research, sociologists need to be cautious about what parts of a theory can and cannot be tested, and indeed what claims have and have not been tested (Kacelnik & Krebs, 1997). Ultimately, however, the question is not *whether* evolution has shaped behavior, but *how* (Betzig, 1988). Many subfields are seeking to answer this question and, in the least, life course sociologists should be aware of these developments.

BEHAVIORAL GENETICS AND THE LIFE COURSE

Life-history theory typically does not consider genetic information. In some instances, life history research focuses on variability in behaviors between species (e.g., the timing of puberty and life-span across species of primates), in which case the explanation does not concern genetic variability within species. In other instances, the focal point is variability in behaviors within a species (e.g., the timing of puberty in humans); in these cases, the central inquiry nevertheless remains focused on how context predictably canalizes (or contrains) observed behaviors.

In contrast, behavioral genetics focuses on the association between variation in genotypes (i.e., genetic make-up) and phenotypes (i.e., products of genes, including behaviors) within a population, and the mechanisms that account for these associations. The complex behaviors that are of interest to behavioral genetics can arise from two or more genes working together, from different contexts that evoke different phenotypes from the same genome, and from complex interactions among multiple genes and environments. We begin by sketching basic principles of genetics that are especially relevant to the study of behavior,* and then consider analytic strategies and connections with the life course.

Basic Principles of Genetics and Behavior

The nucleus of the cell contains chromosomes, structures that house the DNA molecule and that become visible to the optical microscope during cell division. The gene is the fundamental unit of heredity, consisting of a length of DNA at a particular chromosomal location (or locus). Genes code for proteins (specific sequences of 20 different amino acids) and these

*For an excellent introduction to behavioral genetics, see Plomin et al., (2000) and Falconer & Mackay (1996).

proteins in turn perform a wide array of functions, operating as enzymes, regulators of other processes, chemical messengers, and as structural components within the cell. (Proteomics, one aspect of the study of genetics, includes the identification and description of proteins and their role in biological systems.) Genes can take on different forms, known as "alleles," which may lead to variations in phenotypes. Behavioral genetics therefore focuses on those genes that exhibit allelic differences within populations.

The link between genes and behaviors is mediated by chains of biological processes that are almost certainly complex and currently not well understood. Nevertheless, much can be learned about associations between genes and phenotypes without a detailed understanding of all of the mechanisms that link them. In a relatively simple case, differences in continuously distributed traits (e.g., height) could arise from a few or many genes, each having an additive (and probably small) effect on the phenotype. Alternatively, dominance occurs when a particular allele exhibits a stronger effect than expected by an additive model.

These connections are likely to be intricate, however, because of complications surrounding genetic expression, which refers to the mechanisms by which specific genotypes are associated with specific phenotypes. One class of mechanisms involves interactions among genes, which occur when a gene's effect is contingent on other genes in non-linear ways. For example, multifactorial phenotypes likely result from the interactions among many genes (McClearn et al., 2001). Even if the complexities of genes themselves were understood, a second class of mechanisms precludes a simple mapping of genotypes onto phenotypes, as acknowledged by the norm of reaction, which refers to the unpredictable nature of phenotypes associated with the same genotype expressed across different contexts (Gottlieb, 1995, 1998).

Thus, genotypes and all levels of the system are likely to interact in nonlinear ways that preclude simple links between genotypes and phenotypes across different environments. Cattell (1963, 1965) was perhaps the first to describe systematically the interactions and correlations that reflect this complex interplay among genotypes, environments, and phenotypes. A gene-environment interaction (G × E) refers to the differential responses of organisms (genotypes) to particular settings, whereas a gene-environment correlation refers to the contextual features that are associated with the genetic predisposition of the individual. Penetrance refers to the probability of expressing a phenotype given a particular genotype. Incomplete penetrance is thought to reflect stochastic processes or interactions such as Cattell identified that are related to differing genetic and environmental backgrounds.

Cattell's approach was simplified to a smaller set of three types of correlations and interactions (Plomin et al., 1977) that are widely referenced today. The passive correlation refers to situations in which children inherit their parents' genes and grow up in settings that have been substantially shaped by those same genetic influences from the parents. In these situations, settings tend not be correlated or less correlated with the child's behaviors once the genotype has been controlled. The reactive correlation refers to situations in which the setting "reacts" to the child in ways consonant with his or her genotype. For example, parents may be more affectionate to children who exhibit warmth. Once again, when the genetic proportions of variance in the children are accounted for (genetic influences on parent and offspring warmth), the parents' degree of affection with the child may not be directly associated with the child's behavior. The active correlation refers to the person actively selecting and molding settings that are congruent with his or her genetic endowment. For example, a person with a genotype favoring high fluid reasoning ability may chose work that is substantively complex, which tends to provide further opportunities for enhanced intellectual functioning. (For extended examples of these correlations as applied to the transition to adulthood, see Plomin et al., 1977; Shanahan et al., 2000). Empirical evidence for particular gene-environment correlations and interactions, however, is sparse and so these modes of action are presently hypothetical.

Behavioral Genetics: Analytic Strategies and Themes

These complex links between genotypes and phenotypes have been studied from two vantage points that depend on whether or not the genotype has been directly measured. These two approaches yield different insights about links between genotypes and phenotypes. The decomposition of variance approach is used when the genotype has not been measured; this approach focuses on phenotypic associations across groups that vary in degrees of genetic relatedness. Models typically focus on estimating proportions of variance associated with genetic and environmental influences. Because this approach is correlational, results describe populations, not individuals. In contrast, studies involving the measured genotype permit statements about individual development, particularly if interactions with measured environments are considered. We briefly introduce each approach, review its strengths and weaknesses, and note connections with life course sociology.

DECOMPOSITION OF VARIANCE. A population approach seeks to partition variance in behavior according to aggregate genetic and environmental influences, and their interactions. A major focal point of this line of research is heritability (h^2), an estimate of genetic variance associated with phenotypic variance, expressed as the proportion of the total phenotypic variance in a population. *Quantitative genetic analysis* involves the analysis of genetically related individuals to understand total phenotypic variance (P) in a population in terms of heritable (G) and environmental (E) sources of variance, most simply:

$$V_P = V_G + V_E \tag{1}$$

A more complete representation of the decomposition of total reliable phenotypic variance contains additional terms, shown in the variance equation below. With certain samples and designs, genetic variance (V_G) can be decomposed into additive (A), dominance (D), and epistatic (I) sources which represent gene–gene interactions (McClearn, 2001). Environmental variance (V_E) can be separated into common or shared (C) and nonshared (E) components. Additionally, covariance and interaction among these genetic and environmental sources may be included (shown respectively as two simple additional components in the Equation (2), 2Cov_{GE} and V_{GXE}:

$$V_P = V_A + V_D + V_I + V_C + V_E + 2\text{Cov}_{GE} + V_{GXE} \tag{2}$$

All sources of phenotypic variance cannot be accounted for simultaneously in most genetically informative designs (i.e., twin, parent–offspring) and the additional role that time (i.e., development, aging) has on the system of influences must also be considered. Some family designs, however, are more powerful than others for evaluating particular effects (e.g., adoption designs for evaluating common environmental influences) and longitudinal genetic studies permit some understanding of the interactive effects of genes and environment over time. The basic twin design relies on the fact that monozygotic (MZ) twins share 100% of their segregating genes while dizygotic twins (DZ) share 50%, on average. If genetic factors are important for the variability in a trait, the correlation among MZ twins must be higher than among dizygotic twins as seen in comparison of their intraclass correlations. A simple estimate of heritability in twin samples is given as twice the difference between the MZ and

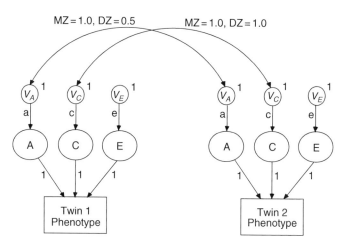

FIGURE 27-1. The expected correlations among twins.

DZ intraclass correlations [$h^2 = 2(r_{MZ} - r_{DZ})$]. To the extent that shared environment (c^2) is important for a trait, both MZ and DZ intraclass correlations will be positive and higher than expected given the genetic components of variance in the model ($c^2 = r_{MZ} - h^2$).

Maximum likelihood estimation is often used to obtain parameter estimates (e.g., abstract variances of additive genetic, shared and nonshared environment) by maximizing model estimates that make the observed and expected covariances (correlations) among twin pairs as similar as possible. The expected correlations, shown in Figure 27-1, are fixed and based on the expectations for genetic relatedness among twins (A; $r_{MZ} = 1.0$, $r_{DZ} = 0.50$), shared or common environment (C; $r = 1.0$ for both MZ and DZ twins), and nonshared environment (E; $r = 0.0$, path not shown). The paths from A, C, and E are fixed to 1.0 to identify these as variance components. Models such as this one, based on known expectations of genetic relatedness, are easily expanded to extended pedigrees including parents, siblings, half-siblings, and other designs such as adoption studies where siblings are reared apart (Neale & Cardon 1992).

This model and its many variants (e.g., extending into longitudinal models) yield information about the proportion of variance in a behavior that is attributable to genetic variance in a population and to environmental influences that make individuals more similar (C) or more different (E). For the many decades during which the available data did not include direct measurement of the genotype, this approach to the genotype–phenotype link proved immensely popular. Numerous elegant expansions on this basic model have been developed, including models for assortative (nonrandom) mating (Heath, 1985), sex-limitation (differential sex effects), cultural transmission (Eaves, Fulker, & Heath, 1989), and longitudinal models (Eaves, Hewitt, Meyer, & Neale, 1990) including the phenotypic simplex (Boomsa, 1987) and latent growth curve models (McArdle, 1990).

At the same time, weaknesses to this general modeling strategy are widely understood and acknowledged. Three major concerns are worth noting here. First, however it is calculated, heritability is an estimate of the proportion of genetic variance in a population. As with any correlation, a large number of underlying patterns among the genetic and environmental influences can produce an estimate of heritability in a population at a particular time. Care must be exercised in avoiding the ecological fallacy: a heritability estimate does not warrant statements about the genotype–phenotype link at the level of the individual because it says nothing about genetic expression (Gottlieb, 1995). Second, consistent with the mechanisms of genetic expression discussed earlier, a simple additive model for heritability may be unlikely for many complex phenotypes (McClearn & Vogler, 2001). Third, h^2 has some unusual properties that, if viewed uncritically, can be misleading. For example, low estimates of heritability do not necessarily imply that genes have less influence on particular phenotypes than higher estimates; it may be that these traits have undergone strong evolutionary selection (i.e., there is little genetic variability) but are nevertheless under a high degree of genetic control (Turkheimer, 1998). On the other hand, highly heritable phenotypes (such as height) do not imply that context is unimportant as secular trends in height vividly illustrate: Height is highly heritable, but it has increased substantially in the West through the 20th century because of improvements in nutrition and other factors.

The analysis of related individuals also leads to models of the Mendelian transmission of major gene effects. For example, in an Icelandic study of breast cancer, segregation analysis was used to evaluate the genetic influence on the age of onset of breast cancer (Baffoe-Bonnie, 2000). Segregation analysis draws on pedigrees (related individuals) to estimate the underlying Mendelian inheritance patterns (e.g., allelic frequency, penetrance) most likely to account for familial transmission of the outcome. In this case, a codominance model was found to fit the pedigree data best; such a model implies that the effects of the allelic variants (homozygous, heterozygous) are not additive but exhibit nonlinear risks in terms of age of onset and cumulative risk. The estimated age of onset for high-risk homozygotes, heterozygotes, and low-risk homozygotes was 51.8, 64.0, and 76.3 years, respectively, with the corresponding cumulative risk of breast cancer by age 60 estimated at 32.2%, 16.4%, and 5.0% for these same groups.

ANALYSIS OF THE MEASURED GENOTYPE. A second approach to the genotype–phenotype link has emerged from the increasingly likely situation in which the genotype has been measured directly (i.e., not inferred through degrees of relatedness to other people in the sample). The fundamental aim is to identify regions of the chromosome that contribute to the variation in quantitative traits, where quantitative traits are complex, multifactorial phenotypes. This approach relies on genetic markers, known as quantitative trait loci (QTL), which are markers of regions of a chromosome that contain multiple genes. The analysis of QTL can be performed in experimental populations (McClearn, 1999) or in naturally segregating populations. The availability of increasingly dense maps of the human genome permits detection of genes with weak effects, thus increasing the potential for identifying multiple genetic factors that can influence complex phenotypes.

In it simplest form, the association between particular genetic markers and quantitative traits take the form of regression analysis (or analysis of variance) where phenotypic values are regressed onto the coded values for allelic variants of particular genes or quantitative trait loci (QTL; segregating regions of a chromosome that contain one or multiple genes). Essentially, the analysis focuses on mean differences across classes of the measured genotype where all individuals having a particular allele would be considered to be of the same class (identical by descent or state). The proportion of phenotypic variance accounted for by a particular genetic locus (QTL) would be indicated by the R^2 value.*

---

*In many cases, the analytic strategy is often much more elaborate than a regression model. For example, genetic association analysis is one approach to map measured genotype on quantitative traits but this method is sensitive to population stratification (subgroups having different frequencies of alleles). Alternatively, linkage analysis (Ott, 1999) makes use of extended pedigree information to overcome these problems. Once a QTL is localized, higher resolution mapping of the QTL segment is usually performed in order to identify the precise location of the chromosome that is related to the quantitative phenotype.

There are numerous challenges to the identification of particular genes for complex outcomes and these are problems that are under intensive study. For example, analyses are typically based on hundreds of genetic markers and this increases the problem of Type I error. Indeed, many QTL-based efforts to understand behavior have been characterized by a lack of replication across studies (e.g., studies of schizophrenia). Further complications include phenocopy (having phenotype but not genotype), incomplete penetrance (having the same genotype but not phenotype), and polygenic traits (heterogeneous genotypes resulting in same phenotype). However, the potential of discovery using both quantitative and molecular genetic approaches is high. In particular, interactive models of measured genotypes, phenotypes, and context will permit unique and valuable contributions for the study of persons in context.

Integrating Behavioral Genetics and the Life Course

Virtually all research on the life course has proceeded without considering the influence of genes on behavior; at the same time, behavioral genetics has proceeded without regard to the sophisticated models of social context that often characterize life course research. Yet, many lines of research have now established that genotypes do not produce behaviors in a simple way (Gottlieb, 1995, 1998). Instead, phenotypes are likely to reflect the cumulative history of the individual's genotype, phenotype, and context. Indeed, there is widespread appreciation among behavioral geneticists that the links between genotypes and phenotypes are often heavily conditioned by social location and personal experiences. One of the forefronts of behavioral genetics—exploring gene–context interactions over many years in the development of behaviors—connects directly to life course interests in long-term continuity and discontinuity. More specifically, however, we can identify a set of problems that provide strategic points of integration between behavioral genetics and the life course.

First, whether the genotype is measured or not, life course sociologists have much to offer in the measurement of contexts, particularly as they capture the richness of prior experience. The direct measurement of dynamic contextual influences within genetically informative designs is crucial for understanding developmental sequences, pathways, transitions, and outcomes across the life course. For example, life course demographers continue to learn about the quality of data that results from various measurement strategies for assessing families and households over time (Brynin & Smith, 1995; Duncan, 1985); similarly, life course researchers have been at the forefront of efforts to measure neighborhoods and communities, family interactions, the workplace, and schools, as well as contextual influences that result from multiple domains (e.g., connections between work-school). The last several decades of life course research have been marked by increasing interest in how these contexts are structured when viewed longitudinally and such a focus is clearly relevant to the description of gene-environment correlations and interactions in development.

These correlations and interactions reflect the person as influenced by context, the context as influenced by person, and the interplay of both. In a life course framework, with its emphasis on dynamic views of context and individual agency, these possibilities become particularly interesting. The active correlation implies that there are periods of development where individuals actively select their environments. Perhaps these periods may be found in transitions between life phases or age-graded social settings. The transition to adulthood may be one such period, raising the issue of how individual differences in genotype, context, and phenotype interact over a period of transition and change. Additionally, an emphasis on the life course would focus on how adverse, immediate, or novel environmental changes might produce a reorganizing of individual differences, making genetically related individuals more similar if the events were shared and less similar if events differed across individuals. Such questions could be asked with respect to dramatic social changes, but also to comparatively normative transitions (e.g., the transitions from junior high school, to parenthood, and into retirement).

Second, life course sociologists interested in the description of populations can contribute to the study of how different contexts affect heritability. A growing body of research is focusing on the proportion of variance in a phenotype that is associated with genetic, shared environment, and nonshared environment across different populations defined by age or by social settings. Some researchers have hypothesized that heritability will increase with age, reflecting the increasing capacity of the person to select and mold his or her context, which in turn strengthens the active correlation. Studies of aging and heritability estimates typically compare the relative similarity of twins (by way of variance decomposition models) across subgroups defined by age.

Based on this strategy, research on cognitive functioning across the life-span indicates that the heritability of cognitive capabilities is relatively high and stable and may increase with age (Pedersen, 1996; McClearn & Vogler, 2001). However, the preponderance of evidence for age-related changes in the proportions of genetic and environmental influences has been obtained from cross-sectional designs. A limitation of these designs, particularly pertinent to twin studies that require the sampling of intact twin pairs across a wide age range, is nonrandom selection/survival processes leading to age-related population heterogeneity on outcomes of interest. In any event, the age-graded nature of heritability, and the processes that explain observed patterns, represent a strategic point of integration with life course sociology.

Similarly, a growing number of studies have shown that estimates of heritability are sensitive to context (Rose, 2001; Rowe et al., 1999). As Scarr (1974) explains, h^2 is a population average that does not necessarily apply to differences within and between subpopulations. Indeed, sociological theories often emphasize differential exposure to environmental conditions (e.g., stressors) across groups in a population, suggesting that the amount of variance in the phenotype accounted for by heritability will not infrequently vary across subgroups within a broadly defined population. Many, but certainly not all, studies in this area focus on how extreme circumstances can alter heritability, the assumption being that the normal range of settings provides many functionally equivalent opportunities to develop (Scarr, 1992). Further, most studies work from the assumption that strong settings increase the effect of the shared environment (c^2).

Several prominent hypotheses are being investigated along these lines. For example, Scarr (1974) argues that social disadvantages during prenatal and postnatal development can substantially lower the observed IQ among economically and socially marginalized groups, thereby reducing the genotype–phenotype correlation. Another hypothesis, proposed by Bronfenbrenner and Ceci's (1994) bioecological model, maintains that as proximal processes—defined as enduring forms of interaction that characterize a person's immediate setting—become progressively complex and strong, genetic potential is actualized, thereby increasing h^2 and the person's level of functioning. As they explain, "only those genetic predispositions of the individual can find realization for which the necessary *opportunity structures* exist, or are provided..." (p. 575, authors' emphasis). An additional hypothesis is that the regulatory power of values and norms can alter h^2, consistent with theories of social control. For example, Rose and his colleague show that the heritability of alcohol use is much higher in urban than in rural areas of Finland, because the latter setting is characterized by greater residential stability and increased community monitoring (Dick et al., 2001).

These and related hypotheses can be explored with cohort studies. For example, consistent with the social control hypothesis, Dunne et al. (1997) report that birth cohort moderated the heritability of age of first intercourse in an Australian sample. Specifically, h^2 accounted for 32% and 0% of the variance in age of first intercourse for women and men born between 1922 and 1952, respectively, but 49% and 72% of the variance for women and men born between 1952 and 1965, respectively. The authors suggest that earlier born cohorts were constrained by the higher levels of social control, when compared with the content and force of social controls encountered by youth in later born cohorts.

Third, also in the context of heritability studies, life course sociologists could contribute to the discussion of shared and nonshared environmental influences. Shared environmental influences are nongenetic environmental factors that make family members more similar and may have either transient or long-term effects. Nonshared environmental influences are those influences that are not shared and make family members less alike. Variance decomposition models currently assign weights to these sources of influence by setting the parameters at 1 and 0, depending on whether a twin, for example, is separated at birth or not. As Turkheimer (2000) notes, however, nonshared sources of variance may often result from common environmental influences that make siblings different. These common environmental differences may be related to sibling interaction or differential parental treatment, or the differential effects of processes and events within the family (e.g., marital discord). Surprisingly little research has investigated the details of family life as they relate to the shared–nonshared distinction.

Despite these opportunities, efforts to integrate behavioral genetics and the life course should be cognizant of several caveats. We have already observed that genes do not lead in simple ways to behavior. In fact, given the complexity of gene–gene and gene–context interactions, statements about "the effect" of a gene or genes may well make little sense (McClearn et al., 2001). That is, *the behavioral range associated with a genotype is contingent on the co-presence of other genes and the conditioning effects of context, both of which play out in developmentally complex ways in individuals.* For example, in a study of the lifespan of *drosophila melanogaster* (the fruit-fly), genotype was significantly related to longevity but these effects were highly interactive with sex and environmental influences (Vieira et al., 2000).

Beyond this caution about the complexity of genetic expression, however, is a caveat that is not sufficiently acknowledged by behavioral scientists. Most models of behavior actually focus on the interaction of the phenotype with the environment (Turkheimer & Waldron, 2000). This *developmental phenotypic focus* is a more tractable approach (than a focus that includes genes) for sufficiently understanding development since environmental influences have effects on the phenotype directly. Such a strategy is particularly defensible if genes are a distal causal mechanism and their effects are largely or fully mediated by more proximal, measurable phenomena. For example, Kardia, Haviland, Ferrell, & Sing (1999) examined the link between apolipoprotein E genotypes (apoE) and coronary artery calcification (CAC). Their study concluded that apoE was not associated with CAC after the prediction of CAC was made by a fairly small set of observed risk factors. That is, beyond several readily measurable, phenotypic risk factors, apoE had no significant explanatory value. Similarly, in their study of the development of delinquency and criminality, Sampson and Laub (1993) observe that "there is little, if any, need to introduce biological models of heredity if the direct effect of parental criminality on delinquency is null and instead is mediated by … family functioning."

Thus, knowledge of the genotype may be necessary for a full explanation of a behavior (such as CAC), but not necessary for its prediction.

In the final analysis, genes and context undoubtedly are correlated and undoubtedly interact to produce behaviors. However complex these processes may be can only be resolved through the empirical study of genotypes, phenotypes, and contexts over time. The life course is especially well-suited to contribute to these efforts with its interest in the conceptualization and measurement of dynamic contexts, and with its thematic emphasis on the long-term processes by which people and their contexts are reciprocally interrelated.

BEHAVIORAL ENDOCRINOLOGY AND THE
LIFE COURSE

Behavioral endocrinology focuses on the reciprocal links among hormones of the endocrine system, behavior, and context. The basic connections between these processes and evolution and genetics are straightforward. First, hormones have been subject to the forces of evolution (although, perhaps in most cases, the functions of hormones have changed through the millennia, but not their chemical structure). By extension, hormones probably contribute to reproductive fitness. Second, basal hormone levels are heritable and many hormonal effects directly or indirectly modify gene expression in the target cell. Efforts to link the endocrine system with behavior, however, rarely focus on evolutionary or genetic issues. Rather, behavioral endocrinology focuses on the presence, structure, and function of hormones and how they reciprocally interact with behavior and the individual's context.

Principles of Endocrinology

Hormones are chemical messengers that are produced, stored, and released by glands of the endocrine system.[*] Endocrine glands are located in different regions of the body and are characterized, in part, by their secretion of hormones directly into the blood stream, which is often triggered by a change in the concentration of a substance in the body. In turn, these secreted hormones can travel to specific binding sites (hormone receptors) located on the membrane of or within specific cells throughout the body. The hormone receptors then "translate" the message, initiating biochemical reactions that lead to altered functioning of the cell (e.g., via hormone-influenced DNA-synthesis). Because of the "lock and key" arrangement between specific hormones and their receptors (i.e., the hormone functions as a "key," opening the receptor-"lock" to influence metabolic processes of the cell), even very low concentrations of hormones in the bloodstream may be capable of regulating cellular functions.

In addition to the endocrine system, the study of hormones is also tied to the central nervous system via the neuroendocrine system. These two systems jointly regulate and coordinate bodily functions, such as metabolism or sexual reproduction, and adapt the body to changing short-term and long-term challenges, such as stress. The two systems are closely linked at the hypothalamic-pituitary interface, which is the decisive control center between hormonal and neural regulatory processes. Specifically, the hypothalamus, as a brain structure, and the pituitary gland, as part of the endocrine system, are organizers of the hypothalamic-pituitary axis that controls much of the endocrine system. The endocrine and the nervous

---

[*]This summary is based on Bierbaumer and Schmidt (1996), Nelson (2000), and Ojeda and Griffin (2000).

systems are also linked via the enervation of most endocrine glands, and the direct effects of hormones on the central nervous system.

Four classes of hormones are typically recognized. These four classes and their origins and functions are shown in Table 27-1. The table greatly simplifies the origins of hormones, which often involve, for example, complex cycles with other hormones produced by a variety of endocrine glands. The table also simplifies the functions of the listed hormones; in many cases, hormones perform a surprisingly wide array of known functions with the possibility of unknown functions as well. Despite these simplifications, however, Table 27-1 shows that the endocrine system is comprised of numerous glands located throughout the body. Further, hormones affect a wide range of biological processes, some of which, even at first inspection, are likely to correlate with behaviors associated with, for example, reproduction, reactions to stress, and physical and mental health.

Hormones are involved in maintaining homeostasis, which refers broadly to a biochemical balance among many subsystems. Levels of hormones are regulated in several ways. First, hormones are involved in feedback cycles (i.e., most commonly negative, but also possibly positive, or multiple hormone feedback cycles), in much the same way that a thermostat maintains temperature at a set level. For example, following a stressful event, levels of the corticotropin-releasing hormone (CRH) increase, which, in turn, leads to an increase in adrenocorticotrophin (ACTH). Cortisol is then released which, among other things, mobilizes nutrients, modifies the immune response, and regulates glucose concentrations in the blood. When large quantities of cortisol are set free, a negative feedback system causes a reduced output of ACTH and CRH, which, in turn, inhibits the release of cortisol. Second, hormones may also increase or decrease the number of their own receptors—which are continuously generated in response to the internal milieu (up- and down-regulation, respectively)—or regulate the receptors of other hormones (a permissive effect).

Because of these potentially intricate cycles and the interplay among numerous biological subsystems, hormones are often secreted in temporally complex ways. Nevertheless, most hormone secretion shows a high degree of temporal organization. Specifically, secretion of hormone levels is often a pulsatile/episodic rather than a continuous process. Hormones are produced in small amounts, and then released in bursts (or pulsatile secretions) that may be as frequent as every 5–10 min. Other temporal rhythms have also been observed.

Not surprisingly, the measurement of hormones in the study of human behavior is difficult owing to their complex biochemistry, their temporal patterns of secretion, the reactivity of some hormones (e.g., cortisol) to collection procedures, and to ethical and scientific issues surrounding the invasiveness of procedures. In fact, a surprisingly large number of studies do not directly measure hormones (e.g., testosterone or estradiol), relying instead on proxies such as whether a person is taking a medication (e.g., estrogen replacement, or a contraceptive), or whether a person belongs to a group characterized by specific hormone levels (e.g., post-menopausal women, pre- and post menarchal women, or a woman in a certain phase of the menstrual cycle). Direct measures of hormones can be obtained, however, by sampling blood (plasma), urine, or saliva. Increasingly reliable and valid measurement protocols for key hormones in behavioral studies are rapidly emerging (Granger, Schwartz et al., 1999), greatly facilitating the collection of accurate hormone data for social science research.

Analytic Themes and Life Course Research

BEHAVIORAL EFFECTS OF HORMONES. Two sets of distinctions are often observed among behavioral endocrinologists. The first set concerns the nature of behavioral effects.

TABLE 27-1. Classes and Types of Hormones, Their Primary Origins, and General Functions (Simplified; see also Nelson, 2000)

Class and types (with examples)	Primary origins	General functions of example hormones
1. Steroid hormones		
a. Progestins (e.g., progesterone)	adrenal glands	pregnancy
b. Corticoids (e.g., cortisol)	adrenal glands	body functions
c. Androgens (e.g., testosterone)	gonads	reproduction, secondary sex characters, metabolism
d. Estrogens (e.g., estradiol)	gonads	reproduction, secondary sex characters, metabolism
2. Protein/polypeptide hormones		
a. Hypothalamic (e.g., dopamine)	hypothalamus	neurotransmitter
b. Anterior pituitary (e.g., gonadotropins)	pituitary	reproduction
c. Posterior pituitary (e.g., oxytocin)	pituitary	reproduction, suckling reflex
d. Thyroid (e.g., thyroxine)	thyroid	metabolism, growth/differentiation
e. Parathyroid (e.g., parathyroid hormone)	parathyroid	calcuim metabolism
f. Gut (secretin)	duodenal mucosa	digestive
g. Pancreatic (insulin)	pancreas	glucose regulation
h. Adrenal Medullary (enkephalins)	adrenal medulla	adaptation to stress
3. Monoamine hormones		
a. Adrenal Medullary (e.g., epinephrine)	adrenal medulla	circulatory and metabolic systems
b. Pineal Gland (e.g., melatonin)	pineal gland	puberty onset
4. Lipid-based hormones		
a. Prostaglandins (e.g., E group)	throughout body	reproduction

In the perinatal life-stages (immediately before and shortly after birth), hormones have organizational effects, which refer to direct effects of hormones on the architecture of the brain, body and the distribution of hormone receptors (Buchanan et al., 1992). These organizational effects can in turn expand or limit the range of possible developmental pathways through childhood and into adulthood. In later stages of life, hormones have activational effects, which refer to the initiation of specific behaviors through their contemporaneous influence on neural-based and peripheral processes (Buchanan et al., 1992; Susman, 1997). Activational effects are also considered indirect effects, whereas organizational effects have a direct impact on brain development. Among other things, activational effects can be dependent on earlier organizational effects of hormones on the development of brain structures.

For example, Udry (2000) investigated the long-term consequences of fetal exposure to androgens (masculinizing hormones) during the second trimester, a sensitive period in neurological development. In adulthood, testosterone is thought to be associated with sex dimorphic behaviors (i.e., any behaviors that are differentially distributed in a population based on sex) through its action "on genes in the central nervous system that control the production of neurotransmitters" (p. 444). Udry hypothesized that the effects of post pubertal testosterone (an activational effect) on the sex-typical behaviors of women would be contingent on prenatal masculinization of the brain (an organizational effect). Consistent with this expectation, results showed that as fetal exposure to androgens in the second trimester increased, the effects of adult testosterone (assessed some 30 years later) decreased.

A particularly important class of organizational effects may reflect how experience alters thresholds or sensitivity to subsequent events (Susman, 1993). For example, the kindling model was developed to explain why initial episodes of depression are often linked to stressful events, whereas subsequent depressive episodes are comparatively spontaneous. Similarly, Susman (1993) reports that adolescents have a "trait" of reactivity to potential stressors only under conditions of maximum novelty. This suggests a complex interplay between earlier (possibly organizational) experiences and later reactions to contextual cues. As she concludes, these biological findings underscore the importance of knowing the person's experiential history.

HORMONES, CONTEXT, AND BEHAVIOR OVER TIME. A second set of distinctions refers to how hormones and behaviors interrelate over time (Susman, 1997). The basal model (Mazur & Booth, 1998) holds that changes in individual hormone levels lead to changes in behavior. An alternative model holds that behavior causes hormone change. Although these models are now recognized as over-simplifications (Susman, 1997), a great deal of research in behavioral endocrinology is consistent with one or the other of these views, albeit often implicitly. Research in this tradition is typically characterized by relatively limited time frames involving cross-sectional designs or assessments extending across a few hours or days (Mazur & Michalek, 1998). Given historical difficulties in the measurement of hormones and the need for research in non-naturalistic settings, these limitations are understandable.

Nevertheless, these models can have implications for life course phenomena in several important respects. First, cross-sectional studies that collect retrospective life-history data can link life course patterns to hormone data, although they rely on the assumption that the hormone in question is quite stable across the events being studied. For example, Booth and Dabbs (1993) examine the connection between testosterone and marital adversity in a sample of former serviceman. Drawing on a cross-sectional design, they find that testosterone is significantly related to marital adversity, reflecting whether the man ever divorced or separated, had extramarital sex, or had been abusive. The relationship can perhaps be accounted for in part by testosterone's negative effects on socioeconomic attainment and positive effects on the likelihood of unemployment, trouble with the law, and problems with alcoholism.

Second, long-term stability in a link between a behavior and a hormone could produce an accumulation effect. An excellent example concerns the stress response, which is characterized by the activation of the hypothalamus, which triggers the pituitary gland to secrete adrenocorticoid hormone (ACTH), which in turn triggers the secretion of glucocorticoids (e.g., cortisol) by the adrenal glands. This process supports the fast mobilization of the body's energy resources, which may be necessary to neutralize the stressor. If glucocorticoids remain at high basal levels for long periods of time, however, the chances of chronic disease greatly increase, including damage to the nervous system, suppression of the immune and reproductive systems, hypertension, and ulcers. Drawing on this biological model of the stress reaction, Sapolsky, (1992, 2000; Sapolsky, Alberts et al., 1997) has studied the effects of social position on hypercortisolism in baboons, the underlying assumption being that behaviors associated with social position predict hormones (specifically, cortisol). In one study, he examined the effects of "reversal interactions," which refer to interactions indicative of a loss of social status. Sapolsky and his colleagues (1997) report that as reversal interactions with the nearest lower ranking males increase, basal cortisol levels also increase. Although the link between social status and cortisol has not been studied extensively in humans (Decker, 2000), animal models suggest that specific dynamic patterns of social status and basal cortisol could lead to impaired health.

Third, even models of limited duration can inform life course studies of transitions. The biological stress model could certainly apply to some life course transitions, but other hormone models may also be relevant, especially in the family cycle (Booth et al., 2000). For example, animal models suggest that men whose partners are expecting a child may experience changes in hormone levels. Consistent with these models, research shows that the father's testosterone peaks immediately after the birth of his child, and then quickly decreases in the postnatal period; such a pattern is consistent with a protective posture at birth, followed by nurturing, paternal behaviors (Storey et al., 2000). At the same time, prolactin—a hormone associated with parental behaviors in many animals—increases from the early to the late prenatal periods and is high among men who are especially responsive to the cries of infants (Booth et al., 2000).

Research is increasingly focusing on conceptual models that move beyond unidirectional links between hormones and behavior. Thus, the reciprocal model (Mazur & Booth, 1998) holds that the relationship between hormones and behavior is reciprocal (i.e., bidirectionally influencing each other). For example, Udry (1988) found that, among adolescent boys, androgens have a positive indirect effect on sexual behavior through church attendance: androgens decreased church attendance, which normally decreases sexual behavior. An alternative model, however, supports a different (although not mutually exclusive) causal chain: androgens increase sexual behavior, which in turn decreases church attendance. Bi-directional influence, suggested by this model, is also nicely illustrated by a possible feedback loop between assertiveness and individual testosterone levels (Mazur, 1985). Specifically, in puberty, increasing levels of testosterone lead to assertiveness, which, in turn, leads to increasing levels of testosterone.

The most relevant model for life course sociology includes contexts in addition to the reciprocal relationship between hormones and behaviors. This model is consistent with a biosocial modeling strategy, which encourages the merger of sociological and biological models of a given behavior. Udry (1988) demonstrated the potential for this approach with his studies of androgens and social control theory. The generic model posited that androgens affect problem/sexual behaviors both directly and indirectly through pubertal development and social controls. For example, he showed that among adolescent boys with high levels of unbound testosterone, as the number of siblings increased (i.e., a form of social control), problem behaviors decreased (Udry, 1990). Similarly, for adolescent girls who are involved in sports and live with their biological fathers (again, forms of social control), the link between testosterone and sexual behavior becomes insignificant (Udry, 1988).

The interactive nature of hormones, context, and behaviors is likewise illustrated by Booth's studies of social integration and testosterone. For example, social integration may modify the association between delinquency and testosterone in young male adults. Specifically, young male adolescents who are socially integrated are less likely to be delinquent than young male adults who are not socially integrated (Booth & Osgood, 1993). In another study, Booth and his colleagues (1999) examine a curvilinear (u-shaped) relationship between testosterone and depression among men. They report that marriage and employment "cause the testosterone-depression link to recede to the point where men with above-average testosterone are no more likely to be depressed than men with average levels of testosterone" (p. 137). The authors explain that marriage and employment—as critical sources of social integration—serve as protective factors among high testosterone men.

In her overview of research on context, hormones, and sex dimorphic behaviors, Berenbaum (1998) observes parallels between gene–context correlations and interactions and the influence of hormones. Thus, people with differing levels of hormones may be exposed to different contexts because they chose them and/or because they were allocated to them (hormone–context correlations). For example, Booth and his colleagues (2000) review studies suggesting that testosterone is negatively related to success in school, occupational status, employment status, and marital status and positively associated with divorce and marital conflict. The developmental processes giving rise to these associations are not well understood, but they suggest that testosterone may be linked to the selection and allocation of these roles and career characteristics.

Further, people with different levels of hormones may respond differently to the same context (a hormone–context interaction)—a point illustrated in our discussion of reactivity. This is well illustrated by Udry's (2000) study of fetal exposure to androgens in the second trimester (discussed earlier). He reports that the effects of maternal encouragement of daughters (ages 5 to 15) to be feminine are contingent on androgen exposure during the mother's second trimester. Specifically, maternal encouragement had no effect on daughters exposed to the highest levels of androgens; conversely, encouragement had the maximum effect on daughters exposed to the lowest levels of androgens. As Udry explains, for women with high exposure to androgens, "no matter how much encouragement the mother provides it has little effect, and the daughter remains more masculine than average" (p. 450).

Integrating Behavioral Endocrinology and the Life Course

Developments in behavioral endocrinology have paved the way for collaborations with life course sociologists. First, behavioral endocrinologists recognize that hormones alone typically have modest explanatory value (Susman, 1997); rather, they interact with context in temporally complex ways to explain behavior. Second, although the designs of many earlier studies of hormones and behavior are cross-sectional or of limited duration, *sophisticated conceptual models often call for studies extending across the phases of life. As the preceding section documents, long-term processes include alterations in sensitivity to contexts, long-term sequences of organizational and activational effects involving complex chains of hormones, contexts, and behaviors, and the effects of accumulation processes.* Third, the science of hormones and their interactions with other biological subsystems (e.g., the immune system) continues to progress rapidly, offering much insight into the biological substrates that interact with context. Finally, emerging technologies are making the measurement of hormones in behavioral studies more efficient, reliable, and valid.

One point of integration seems especially promising: as with behavioral genetics, life course sociologists have much to offer in the assessment of contexts, particularly from a longitudinal perspective. Behavioral human endocrinology has paid little attention to such central concepts as careers (but see Booth et al., 1999), manifold aspects of social position in a hierarchy, pathways, or the social embeddedness of transitions. Understandably, much effort has been devoted to measuring hormones and assessing their basic associations with gross behaviors. Building on these foundations, research is now turning to increasingly sophisticated models of context (Susman, 1997).

At the same time, several caveats should be observed. First, hormones do not cause behaviors in a simple one-to-one coordinate fashion, but rather are expressed in ongoing reciprocal interactions that are significantly modified by context. Second, measurement protocols differ in their reliability and validity and can thus greatly affect observed associations between hormones and behavior (Shirtcliff et al., 2000; Shirtcliff et al., 2001). Third, both hormones and behaviors typically function in highly correlated "webs" of other hormones and behaviors. That is, the likelihood of some degree of spuriousness in observed relationships is quite high. For example, although many studies of reproductive behavior have focused on a few androgens, other classes of hormones need to be considered (Campbell & Udry, 1994). Similarly, a singular focus on a personality trait, intelligence, marital status, or aggression neglects, for example, the many covariates of these factors. Furthermore, because of the complexities involved with assessing biological and social systems through time and with modeling their dynamic interplay, observed associations among hormones, behaviors, and contexts are often not expected to be large in magnitude.

Despite these and related challenges, however, the thematic links between behavioral endocrinology and the life course paradigm are clear and represent excellent opportunities for interdisciplinary research.

CONCLUDING COMMENT: LINKING BIOLOGY AND THE LIFE COURSE

Biological models of behavior and the life course both emphasize interactions between person and context, as well as the importance of studying the development of behaviors across the phases of life. According to life history theory, evolution has produced mechanisms that promote or inhibit specific behaviors depending on cues from the organism's setting. Further, contextual cues influence sets of traits that are highly intercorrelated and that characterize growth and maturation, reproduction, and senescence. For example, if evolutionary forces have influenced the timing of puberty, we would expect that the timing of menarche and spermarche would be sensitive to contextual cues and would be "coordinated" with aspects of growth, reproduction, and aging across the entire life of the species. That is, the timing of puberty could not be understood without reference to setting or to other biological transitions in the life course.

Likewise, the field of behavioral genetics holds that genes do not produce finished traits, but rather interact with environments to constrain or enhance the range of possible behaviors. These interactions begin in the womb and cross the many decades of life. Each new data collection effort thus steps into an ongoing, personal history of passive, reactive, and active gene–environment correlations and interactions. Only through an appreciation of these life-long transactions can the analyst begin to understand the sources of continuity and possibilities for discontinuity in the present and future. Similarly, sophisticated conceptual models in behavioral endocrinology acknowledge the importance of context and its ongoing reciprocal interactions with behavior and hormones. These interactions may encompass sensitive periods, complex causal chains of organizational and activational effects, alterations in thresholds of reactivity, and processes of accumulation—all of which are also likely to encompass many decades of life. Behaviors observed in adulthood may originate in significant ways in the womb.

Both behavioral endocrinology and genetics recognize this fact and provide conceptual and empirical tools for the study of such long-term phenomena. These concepts acknowledge that people are "subjected" to environments as a matter of their lineage, that people evoke reactions through their own behaviors (including being selected for positions within organizations), and that people actively select and modify their settings. Yet these perspectives have yet to develop sophisticated models of social context. These dynamic interactions—and the accurate conceptualization and measurement of contexts that they require—define the central point of integration between biological and life course models of behavior.

Given these conceptual affinities, biological models and life course sociology are well suited as frameworks for interdisciplinary collaborations. Our review makes clear that life course sociologists have much work to do in acquainting themselves with recent developments in biological models of behavior. Yet such an acknowledgement is only half of the story. Biologists and biological oriented behavioral scientists have much to do in acquainting themselves with good models of social context and their attendant processes. Biological studies of behavior without reference to context are simplistic. But, equally true, life course studies of development must begin to incorporate biological insights. At this stage, the integration of biology and the study of the life course is in its infancy: a world of possibility awaits it and its future can only be suggested in broad terms.

ACKNOWLEDGMENT: The authors wish to acknowledge the helpful suggestions of Alan Booth, Glen H. Elder, Jr., Gilbert Gottlieb, Michael Grant, Kathryn E. Hood, Richard A. Miech, Jeylan T. Mortimer, Elizabeth J. Susman, and Richard Udry. The paper was largely completed while the first author was a professor of Human Development and Family Studies at the Pennsylvania State University.

REFERENCES

Anderson, K. G. (2000). The life-histories of American step-fathers in evolutionary perspective. *Human Nature, 11*, 307–333.

Baffoe-Bonnie, A. B., Beaty, T. H., Bailey-Wilson, J. E., Kiemeney, L. A. L. M., Sigvaldason, H., Olafsdottir, G., Tryggvadottir, L., & Tulinius, H. (2000). Genetic epidemiology of breast cancer: Segregation analysis of 389 Icelandic pedigrees. *Genetic Epidemiology, 18*, 81–94.

Beatty, J. (1992). Fitness: theoretical contexts. in E. F. Keller & E. A. Lloyd (Eds.), *Keywords in evolutionary biology.* (pp. 115–119). Cambridge, MA, Harvard University Press.

Belsky, J., Steinberg, L. & Draper, P. (1991). Childhood experience, interpersonal development, and reproductive strategy: an evolutionary theory of socialization. *Child Development, 62*, 647–670.

Berenbaum, S. A. (1998). How hormones affect behavioral and neural development: Introduction to the special issue on "Gonadal Hormones and Sex Differences in Behavior". *Developmental Neuropsychology, 14*, 175–196.

Betzig, L. (1988). Mating and parenting in Darwinian perspective. In L. Betzig, M. Borgerhoff Mulder, & P. W. Turke (Eds.), *Human reproductive behavior: A Darwinian perspective.* (pp. 3–20). Cambridge: Cambridge University Press.

Bierbaumer, N. & Schmidt, R. F. (1996). *Biologische Psychologie [Biological Psychology].* Berlin: Springer.

Blurton Jones, N. (1993). The lives of hunter-gather children: effects of parental behavior and parental reproductive strategy. In M. E. Pereira and L. A. Fairbanks (Eds.), *Juvenile primates: life history, development, and behavior* (pp. 309–338). New York, Oxford.

Blurton Jones, N. (1999). Some current ideas about the evolution of human life history. In P. C. Lee (Ed.) *Comparative primate socioecology*. (pp. 140–166). Cambridge, Cambridge University Press.

Boomsa, D. I., & Molenaar, P. C. M. (1987). The genetic analysis of repeated measures. *Behavior Genetics, 17*, 111–123.

Booth, A., Carver, K. et al. (2000). Biosocial perspectives on the family. *Journal of Marriage and the Family, 62*, 1018–1034.

Booth, A., & Dabbs, J. M., (1993). Testosterone and men's marriage. *Social Forces, 72*, 463–477.

Booth, A., D. Johnson, R., & Granger, D. (1999). Testosterone and men's depression: The role of social behavior. *Journal of Health and Social Behavior, 40*, 130–140.

Booth, A., & D. W. Osgood (1993). The influence on testosterone on deviance in adulthood: Assessing and explaining the relationship. *Crimonology, 31*, 93–117.

Borgerhoff Mulder, M. (2000). Optimizing offspring: The quanity-quality trade-off in agropastoral Kipsigis. *Evolution and Human Behavior, 21*, 391–410.

Bronfenbrenner, U., & Ceci, S. J. (1994). Nature-nurture reconceptualized in developmental perspective: A bioecological model. *Psychological Review, 101*(4), 568–586.

Brynin, M., & R. Smith (1995). Mapping the household. *Journal of Economic and Social Measurement, 21*, 127–144.

Buchanan, C. M., Eccles, J. S., & Becker, J. B. (1992). Are adolescents the victims of raging hormones: Evidence for activational effects of hormones on moods and behavior at adolescence. *Psychological Bulletin, 111*, 62–107.

Cairns, R. B., McGuire, A. M., & Ganepy, J.-L. (1993). Developmental behavior genetics: Fusion, correlated constraints, and timing. In D. F. Hay and A. Angold (Eds.), *Precursors and causes in development and psychopathology*. (pp. 87–122). New York: John Wiley.

Campbell, B. C., & Udry, R. J. (1994). Human reproductive ecology: Interactions of environment, fertility, and behavior. In K. L. Campbell & J. W. Wood (Eds.), *Annals of the New York Academy of Sciences* (pp. 117–127). New York: New York Academy of Sciences, *709*.

Case, A., Lin, I.-F., & McLanahan, S. (2001). Educational attainment of siblings in stepfamilies. *Evolution and Human Behavior, 22*, 269–289.

Cattell, R. B. (1963). The interaction of hereditary and environmental influences. *British Journal of Statistical Psychology, 16* 191–210.

Cattell, R. B. (1965). Methodological and conceptual advances in evaluating hereditary and environmental influences and their interaction. In S. G. Vandenberg (Ed.), *Methods and goals in human behavior genetics* (pp. 95–139). New York: Academic Press.

Charnov, E. L. (1993). *Life history invariants: some explorations of symmetry in evolutionary ecology.* Oxford: Oxford University Press.

Cole, L. (1954). The population consequences of life history phenomena. *Quarterly Review of Biology, 29*, 103–137.

Decker, S. A. (2000). Salivary cortisol and social status among men. *Hormones and Behavior, 38*, 29–38.

Dick, D. M., Rose, R. R., Viken, R. J., Kaprio, J., & Koskenvuo, M. (2001). Exploring gene-environment interaction: Socioregional moderation of alcohol use. *Journal of Abnormal Psychology, 110*(4), 625–632.

Draper, P., & Harpending, H. (1982). Father absence and reproductive strategy: an evolutionary perspective. *Journal of Anthropological Research, 38*, 255–273.

Duncan, G. J. (1985). A framework for tracking family relationships over time. *Journal of Economic and Social Measurement, 13*, 237–243.

Dunne, M. P., Martin, N. G., Statham, D. J., Slutske, W. S., Dinwiddie, S. H., Bucholz, K. K., Madden, D. A. F., & Heath, A. C. (1997). Genetic and environmental contributions to variance in age at first sexual intercourse. *Psychological Science, 8*, 211–216.

Durham, W. H. (1990). Advances in evolutionary culture theory. *Annual Review of Anthropology, 19*, 187–210.

Durham, W. H. (1992). Applications of evolutionary culture theory. *Annual Review of Anthropology, 21*, 331–355.

Eaves, L., Fulker, D. W., & Heath, A. C. (1989). The effects of social homogamy and cultural inheritance on the covariances of twins and their parents. *Behavior Genetics, 19*, 113–122.

Eaves, L., Hewitt, J. K., Meyer, J., & Neale, M. (1990). Approaches to the quantitative genetic modeling of development and age-related changes. In M. E. Hahn, J. K. Hewitt, N. D. Henderson, & R. Benno (Eds.), *Developmental behavior genetics: Neural, biometrical, and evolutionary approaches* (pp. 266–280). New York: Oxford University Press.

Ellis, B. J., & Graber, J. (2000). Psychosocial antecedents of variation in girls' pubertal timing: maternal depression, stepfather presence, and marital and family stress. *Child Development, 71*, 485–501.

Falconer, D. S., & Mackay, T. F. C. (1996). *Introduction to quantitative genetics.* Harlow, England: Addison, Wesley, Longman.

Finkel, D., Pedersen, N. L., Plomin, R., & McClearn, G. E. (1998). Longitudinal and cross-sectional twin data on cognitive abilities in adulthood: The Swedish Adoption/Twin Study of Aging. *Developmental Psychology, 34*, 1400–1413.

Foley, R. (1995). The adaptive legacy of human evolution: a search for the environment of evolutionary adaptedness. *Evolutionary Anthropology, 4*, 194–203.

Ford, D. H., & Lerner, R. M. (1992). *Developmental systems theory: an integrative approach*. Newbury Park, CA: Sage.

Futuyama, D. J. (1998). *Evolutionary biology*. Sunderland, MA: Sinauer Associates.

Gladue, B. A., Boehler, M., & McCaul, K. (1989). Hormonal response to competition among human males. *Aggressive Behavior, 15*, 409–422.

Gottlieb, G. (1995). Some conceptual deficiencies in "Developmental Behavior Genetics". *Human Development, 38*, 131–141.

Gottlieb, G. (1996). Developmental psychobiological theory. In R. B. Cairns, G. H. J. Elder, & E. J. Costello (Eds.), *Developmental science* (pp. 63–77). New York: Cambridge University Press.

Gottlieb, G. (1998). Normally occurring environmental and behavioral influences on gene activity: from central dogma to probabilistic epigenesis. *Psychological Review, 105*, 792–802.

Granger, D. A., Schwartz, E. B., Booth, A., & Areatz, M. (1999). Salivary testosterone determination in studies of child health and development. *Hormones and Behavior, 35*, 18–27.

Heath, A. C., & Eaves, L. J. (1985). Resolving the effects of phenotype and social background on mate selection. *Behavior Genetics, 15*, 15–30.

Hill, K., & A. M. Hurtado (1996). *Ache life history: The ecology and demography of a foraging people*. New York: Aldine De Gruyter.

Hill, K., & H. Kaplan (1999). Life history traits in humans: Theory and empirical studies. *Annual Review of Anthropology, 28*, 397–430.

Irons, W. (1998). Adaptively relevant environments versus the environment of evolutionary adaptedness. *Evolutionary Anthropology, 6*, 194–204.

Kacelnik, A., & Krebs J. R. (1997). Yanomamo dreams and starling payloads: the logic of optimality. In L. Betzig (Ed.). *Human nature: a critical reader*. (pp. 21–35). New York, Oxford University Press.

Kaplan, H., Hill, K., Lancaster, J. & Hurtado, M. (2000). A theory of human life history evolution: diet, intelligence, and longevity. *Evolutionary Anthropology, 9*, 156–185.

Kardia, S. L. R., Haviland, M. B., Ferrell, R. E., & Sing, C. F. (1999). The relationship between risk factor levels and presence of coronary artery calcification is dependent on apolipoprotein E genotype. *Arteriosclerosis, Thrombosis, and Vascular Biology, 19*, 427–435.

Kim, K. and P. K. Smith (1998). Retrospective survey of parental marital relations and child reproductive behavior. *International Journal of Behavioral Development, 22*, 729–751.

Lerner, R. M. (1984). *On the nature of human plasticity*. Cambridge: Cambridge University Press.

Maccoby, E. (1991). Different reproductive strategies in males and females. *Child Development, 62*, 676–681.

Mayr, E. (1982). *The growth of biological thought: diversity, evolution, and inheritance*. Cambridge, MA: Belknap Press.

Mayr, E. (1983). How to carry out the adaptationist program. *American Naturalist, 121*, 324–334.

Mayr, E. (2001). *What evolution is*. New York: Basic Books.

Mazur, A. (1985). A biosocial model of status in face-to-face primate groups. *Social Forces, 64*, 377–402.

Mazur, A. & Booth, A. (1998). Testosterone and Dominance in Men. *Behavioral and Brain Sciences, 21*, 353–363.

Mazur, A., Booth, A., & Dabbs, J. (1992). Testosterone and chess competition. *Social Psychology Quarterly, 55*(1), 70–77.

Mazur, A., & Michalek, J. (1998). Marriage, divorce, and male testosterone. *Social Forces, 77*, 315–330.

McArdle, J. J., & Goldsmith, H. H. (1990). Alternative common-factor models for multivariate biometric analyses. *Behavior Genetics, 20*, 569–608.

McClearn, G. E., & Hofer, S. M. (1999). Genes as gerontological variables: Genetically heterogeneous stocks and complex systems. *Neurobiology of Aging, 20*, 147–156.

McClearn, G. E., & Vogler, G. P. (2001). The genetics of behavioral aging. In J. E. Birren & K. W. Schaie (Eds.), *Handbook of the psychology of aging* (pp. 109–131). San Diego: Academic Press.

McClearn, G. E., Vogler, G. P., & Hofer, S. M. (2001). Environment–gene and gene–gene interactions. In E. J. Masoro, & Austad, S. N. (Eds.), *The biology of aging* (pp. 423–444). San Diego: Academic Press.

Moffitt, T. E., Caspi, A., Bekky, J., & Silva, P. (1992). Childhood experience and the onset of menarche: a test of a sociobiological model. *Child Development, 63*, 47–58.

Nelson, R. J. (2000). *An introduction to behavioral endocrinology*. Sunderland, MA: Sinauer Associates.

Nielsen, F. (1994). Sociobiology and sociology. *Annual Review of Sociology, 20*, 267–303.

Ojeda, S. R., & Griffin, J. E., (2000). Organization of the endocrine system. In S. R. Ojeda (Ed.), *Textbook of endocrine physiology*. Oxford: Oxford University Press.

Ott, J. (1999). *Analysis of human genetic linkage*. Baltimore: Johns Hopkins University Press.

Pedersen, N. (1996). Gerontological behavioral genetics. In J. E. Birren & K. W. Schaie. (Eds.), *Handbook of the psychology of aging*. (pp. 59–77). San Diego: Academic Press.

Peel, J. D. Y. (1971). *Herbert Spencer: The evolution of a sociologist*. New York: Basic Books.

Perusse, D. (1993). Cultural and reproductive success in industrial societies: testing the relationship at the proximate and ultimate levels. *Behavioral and Brain Sciences, 16*, 267–322.

Plomin, R., Defries, J., & Loehlin, J. (1977). Genotype-environment interaction and correlation in the analysis of human development. *Psychological Bulletin, 84*, 309–322.

Plomin, R., DeFries, J., McClearn, & McGuffin (2000). *Behavioral genetics*. New York: W. H. Freeman.

Potts, R. (1998). Variability selection in hominid evolution. *Evolutionary Anthropology, 7*, 81–96.

Rose, R. R., Dick, D. M., Viken, R. J., & Kaprio, J. (2001). Gene-environment interaction: Regional residency moderates longitudinal influences on alcohol use. *Alcoholism: Clinical and Experimental Research, 25*, 637–643.

Rowe, D. C., Jacobsen, K. C., & Van der Dord, E. (1999). Genetic and environmental influences on vocabulary IQ: Parental education level as moderator. *Child Development, 70*(5), 1151–1162.

Rutter, M. (2002). Nature, nurture, and development: From evangilism through science toward policy and practice. *Child Development, 73*(1), 1–21.

Sampson, R. J. & Laub, J. H. (1993). *Crime in the Making: Pathways and turning points through life*. Cambridge, MA: Harvarrd University Press.

Sapolsky, R. M. (1992). Cortisol concentrations and the social significance of rank instability among wild baboons. *Psychoneuroendocrinology, 17*(701–709).

Sapolsky, R. M. (2000). Stress hormones: Good and bad. *Neurobiology of Disease, 7*, 540–542.

Sapolsky, R. M., Alberts, C., & Altmann, J. (1997). Hypercortisolism associated with social subordinance or isolation among wild baboons. *Archives of General Psychiatry, 54*, 1137–1142.

Scarr, S. (1992). Developmental theories for the 1990s: Development and individual differences. *Child Development, 63*, 1–19.

Scott, C. H. (1976). *Lester Frank Ward*. Boston: Twayne Publishers.

Scott Peccei, J. (2001). Menopause: adaptation or epiphenomenon? *Evolutionary Anthropology, 10*, 43–57.

Shanahan, M., Sulloway, F., & Hofer, S. M. (2000). Change and constancy in developmental contexts. *International Journal of Behavioral Development, 24*, 421–427.

Shirtcliff, E. A., G. D. A., Granger, M., Schwartz, E., Curran, M., Booth, A., & Overman, W. H. (2000). Assessing estradiol in biobehavioral studies using saliva and blood spots: Simple radioimmunoassay protocols, reliability, and comparative validity. *Hormones and Behavior, 38*, 137–147.

Shirtcliff, E. A., Reavis, R., Overman, W. H., & Granger, D. A. (2001). Measurement of gonadal hormones in dried blood spots versus serum: Verification of menstrual cycle phase. *Hormones and Behavior, 39*, 258–266.

Stearns, S. C. (1992). *The evolution of life histories*. Oxford: Oxford University Press.

Storey, A. E., Walsh, C. J., Quinton, R. L., & Wynne-Edwards, K. E. (2000). Hormonal correlates of paternal responsiveness in new and expectant fathers. *Evolution and Behavior, 21*, 79–95.

Surbey, M. K. (1998). Parent and offspring strategies in the transition at adolescence. *Human Nature, 9*, 67–94.

Susman, E. J. (1993). Psychological, contextual, and psychobiological interactions: A developmental perspective on conduct disorder. *Development and Psychopathology, 5*, 181–189.

Susman, E. J. (1997). Modeling developmental compexity in adolescence: Hormones and behavior in context. *Journal of Research on Adolescence, 7*, 283–306.

Turkheimer, E. W. (1998). Heritability and biological explanation. *Psychological Review, 105*, 782–791.

Turkheimer, E. W. (2000). Nonshared environment: A theoretical, methodological, and quantitative review. *Psychological Bulletin, 126*, 78–108.

Udry, J. R. (1988). Biological predispositions and social control in adolescent sexual behavior. *American Sociological Review, 53*, 709–722.

Udry, J. R. (1990). Biosocial models of adolescent problem behaviors. *Social Biology, 37*, 1–10.

Udry, J. R. (2000). Biological limits of gender construction. *American Journal of Sociology, 65*, 443–457.

Vieira, C., Pasyukova, E. G., Zeng, Z.-B., Hackett, J. B., Lyman, R. F., & Mackay, T. F. C. (2000). Genotype-environment interaction for quantitative trait loci affecting life span in drosophila melanogaster. *Genetics, 154*, 213–227.

Vrba, E. S. (1990). Life history in relation to life's hierarchy. In C. J. DeRousseau (Ed.), *Primate life history and evolution* (pp. 37–46). New York, Wiley-Liss.

Williams, G. (1957). Pleiotropy, natural selection, and the evolution of senescence. *Evolution, 11*, 398–411.

Winterhalder, B. & Alden Smith, E. (2000). Analyzing adaptive strategies: human behavioral ecology at twenty-five. *Evolutionary Anthropology, 9*, 51–72.

CHAPTER 28

Socioeconomic Status and Health over the Life Course

Capital as a Unifying Concept

JENNIFER R. FRYTAK

CAROLYN R. HARLEY

MICHAEL D. FINCH

On average, individuals of lower socioeconomic status (SES)—based on education, income, or occupation—have worse health than their higher SES counterparts (Adler, Boyce, Chesney, Folkman, & Syme, 1993; Antonovsky, 1967; Feinstein, 1993; Feldman, Makuc, Kleinman, & Cornoni-Huntley, 1989; House, Kessler, & Herzog, 1990; Kitagawa & Hauser, 1973; Marmot, Shipley, & Rose, 1984; Pappas, Queen, Hadden, & Fisher, 1993; Preston & Taubman, 1994; Townsend & Davidson, 1982). This relationship is best depicted as a gradient in health with a fairly linear trend in better health associated with increasing levels of SES, rather than a threshold effect. Furthermore, this relationship is stratified by age; lower SES individuals begin to experience health problems shortly after adolescence, while higher SES individuals experience little health decline until around retirement age (House et al., 1990, 1994). This life course patterning of SES and health is intriguing since it suggests substantial variation in the ability of each group to sustain good health over the life course.

JENNIFER R. FRYTAK AND CAROLYN R. HARLEY • Economic Outcomes Research, Ingenix Pharmaceutical Services, Eden Prairie, Minnesota 55344   MICHAEL D. FINCH • Center for Health Care Policy and Evaluation, United Health Group, Minnetonka, Minnesota 55343
Handbook of the Life Course, edited by Jeylan T. Mortimer and Michael J. Shanahan. Kluwer Academic/Plenum Publishers, New York, 2003.

To date, the mechanisms underlying this SES stratification of health are not well understood, much less their pattern across the life course. However, it has become clear that we need to expand our understanding of health and how to sustain health beyond the narrow disease-focused medical model. Evidence suggests that health is strongly influenced by an individual's resources and lifestyle choices over the life course—more so than access to medical care (Adler et al., 1993; Marmot & McDowall, 1986; McGinnis and Foege, 1993; McKeown, 1976; McKinlay, McKinlay, & Beaglehole, 1989; Pincus, Esther, DeWalt, & Callahan, 1998). Adopting a more expansive model of health that includes non-medical determinants of health may allow us to seek less proximate and more influential causes of poor health and consequently a better understanding of SES differentials in health. In addition, we may increase our awareness of the dynamics among an individual's or family's basic resources that are the building blocks for good health, which, in turn, may allow us to more effectively implement preventive health strategies at critical points in the life course.

This chapter focuses on social capital, a potential non-medical determinant of health that has been receiving considerable interest in the literature of late. The driving force behind this chapter is a single question: Does the timing and distribution of capital derived from social relationships help explain the SES stratification of health over the life course? First, we review the evidence for the SES stratification of health over the life course. Then, the concept of social capital and its potential to affect the life course patterning of SES stratification and health is explored. Next, we present the results of two studies, each conducted at a pivotal point in the life course, that empirically examine the association between social capital and health. We conclude with a discussion of future directions for this line of inquiry.

EVIDENCE FOR THE SOCIAL STRATIFICATION OF HEALTH OVER THE LIFE COURSE

Substantial efforts have been undertaken to understand the non-medical determinants of population health. These support the notion that social structure is at least among the determinants of population health and likely a major one (Adler, Marmot, McEwen, & Stewart, 1999; Bunker, Gomby, & Kehrer, 1989; Evans, Barer, & Marmor, 1994). One well-established finding is the existence, and persistence, of an inverse gradient between socioeconomic status (SES) and poor health (Adler et al., 1993; Antonovsky, 1967; Feinstein, 1993; Feldman et al., 1989; House et al., 1990; Kitagawa & Hauser, 1973; Marmot et al., 1984; Pappas et al., 1993; Preston & Taubman, 1994; Townsend & Davidson, 1982). Socioeconomic inequality in life expectancy and mortality has been found in a broad range of studies since the late 1800s (Antonovsky, 1967) and differentials in health status by SES seem to be widening rather than narrowing over time (Feldman et al., 1989; Marmot & McDowall, 1986; Pappas et al., 1993). The relationship has been shown to exist for a variety of physical and mental health outcomes, as well as for self-reported health (Bartley & Plewis 1997; Hemingway, Nicholson, Stafford, Roberts, & Marmot, 1997; House et al., 1990; Kinney & Finch, 1998; Kitigawa & Hauser, 1978; Koskinen & Martelin, 1994; Lichtenstein, Harris, Pedersen, & McClearn, 1992; Marmot et al., 1991; Marmot et al., 1984; North et al., 1993) and it is apparent across the entire SES hierarchy (Adelstein 1980; Hemingway et al., 1997; Marmot et al., 1991; Marmot et al., 1984; North et al., 1993; Pappas et al., 1993).

Since 1985, published studies of SES and health have increased more than 5-fold (Adler & Ostrove, 1999). While early work in this area suffered from numerous limitations (i.e., social selection, social classification changes, and numerator and denominator biases) that raised questions about the validity of the research, research conducted since the mid-1980s has addressed these methodological issues (Feldman et al., 1989; Fox, Goldblatt, & Jones, 1985; House et al., 1990; House et al., 1994; Marmot, 1991; Marmot & McDowall, 1986; Marmot et al., 1984; Pamuk, 1985). This research also suggests that over the life course SES has a greater impact on health than the reverse, i.e., health status affecting SES through social drift or social selection (Bartley & Plewis, 1997; Fox et al., 1985; Haan, Kaplan, & Syme, 1989; Wilkinson, 1986; Beckett, 2000). This relationship seems to become more complicated, however, at ages over 65 when individuals are simultaneously exiting the workforce and facing declining health (Smith, 1998; Smith & Kington, 1997).

A stream of research by House and colleagues (1990, 1994) in the early 1990's found that inequalities in health status by SES varied systematically over the life course. This research had the effect of integrating the concept of the life course into research on SES and health—a perspective largely absent from the early literature on SES and health.

Using a composite measure of education and income for SES, House et al. (1990; 1994) demonstrated differences by socioeconomic status in a number of health outcomes, including a number of chronic conditions, limitations of daily activities, and functional status. Their analyses were conducted using 1986 data from the National Health Insurance Survey and the Americans' Changing Lives survey. Cross-sectional differences in health status between upper and lower socioeconomic groups were shaped like a football across age groups, with small differences in health status at young adult ages (25–34) that widened through the middle adult years (35–64), reaching their widest point in the 55–64 age range (i.e., the near old) and then converging again in later life (65+). Figure 28-1 provides a stylized representation of the cross-sectional SES/health association described by House et al. (1990).

House and colleagues (1994) concluded that differential exposure to, and differential impact of, psychosocial risk factors, including social support, risky health behaviors, and mastery, were responsible for the inverse gradient in poor health over the life course.

Other evidence from the SES and health literature shows a pattern of SES divergence in health trajectories in young adulthood (Power, Matthews, & Manor, 1998; West, 1997) and SES convergence in health trajectories by SES in old age (Antonovsky, 1967; Feldman et al., 1989; House et al., 1990; 1994; Kitagawa and Hauser, 1973). While there is strong evidence linking infant mortality and post-natal health status to socioeconomic status (Singh & Yu, 1996), the association between socioeconomic status and health is less striking during adolescence. West (1997), in his extensive review of the literature, found that during adolescence

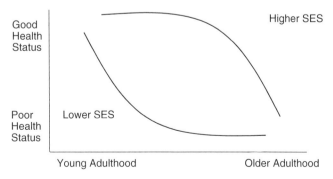

FIGURE 28-1. The socioeconomic status stratification of health over the life course.

there is relative equality in health across socioeconomic status, except for severe chronic illness where a gradient is evident. West (1997) notes that the inverse gradient in health emerges in later youth and early adulthood, when class influences take on more importance in individual lives. Similarly, Power et al. (1998), using data from the 1958 British birth cohort, found no association between parental social class and health during adolescence, but by age 23 years, a significant inverse gradient in poor health was found for both men and women. The gradient was again strongly evident 10 years later, when study participants were 33 years of age. Other research suggests that the inverse gradient in health in adolescence may still exist but may manifest in disease-specific measures such as cancer (Nelson, 1992) or depressed mood (Call & Nonnemaker, 1999), rather than in overall or general health.

Most research discovers wider health differentials in middle age and a lessening of differentials at older ages (Antonovsky, 1967; Feldman et al., 1989; House et al., 1990, 1994; Kitagawa and Hauser, 1973). Only a few studies have not documented convergence. Ross and Wu (1996) did not find convergence of health differentials by educational status at increasing ages using measures of general health, well-being, and physical functioning. Recently, a 29-year follow-up of a study of health by employment grade in Britain found the inverse gradient in health persisted well into old age for study survivors (Breeze et al., 2001). Selective mortality has been given as an explanation for the possible convergence in the inverse gradient in health, but recent empirical research disputes this explanation (Beckett, 2000).

MECHANISMS PRODUCING THE SOCIAL STRATIFICATION OF HEALTH OVER THE LIFE COURSE

The challenge faced by today's researchers is to understand the underlying mechanisms responsible for this inverse gradient of SES and poor health over the life course. Recent research has focused on potential intervening mechanisms in the relationship between SES and health, such as the physical and social environment, health behaviors, central nervous system and endocrine response, exposure to noxious substances, and psychological influences (Adler et al., 1999; Bunker et al., 1989; Evans et al., 1994). A victim of its own success—the research highlights so many promising mechanisms that it is difficult to assimilate all the potential pathways into a coherent policy or research agenda to address health disparities by SES. Moreover different disciplines of social scientists emphasize different causes and mechanisms underlying these differentials (Adler et al., 1999; Bunker et al., 1989; Evans et al., 1994; House et al. 1990, 1994; Smith, 1998; Smith & Kington, 1997).

After examining these many disciplinary-based attempts to understand the SES gradient in health, we propose the concept of capital as a potential unifying concept for the health disparities literature, which elucidates the role of social status and its empirical surrogate, SES, in the production of health. By focusing on capital, we have attempted to take a fundamental cause rather than a proximate cause approach (Link & Phelan, 1995) to understanding the inverse gradient in health over the life course. By *fundamental*, we mean "… the health effects of causes of this sort cannot be eliminated by addressing the mechanisms that appear to link them to disease," namely, the more proximal risk factors and intervening variables. Fundamental causes, which are inherently linked to social conditions, represent economic and social resources upon which individuals can draw to minimize or avoid risk for disease or illness. These resources are available over time and in different situations, so that even as proximal risk factors change over time, those with access to resources can continue to avoid the pitfalls of these health risks. This, in part, explains the persistence of the socioeconomic gradient in health over the life course, as those higher in social status continue to have access to money, prestige, knowledge, and other resources despite changes in the environment, which exacerbate existing, and/or give rise to new, illness and disease.

Capital refers to resources used to produce other goods or attain other outcomes, in this case, health. We posit that the differential distribution of these resources across social class results in the observed life course patterning of SES and health. Social structure has been defined as the "persisting and bounded patterns of behavior and interaction among people or positions and dynamically to the tangible or material forces that tend to maintain such patterns (e.g., physical, biological, or social resources and power deriving therefrom)" (House, 1995, p. 390). In our model, different forms of capital are the resources that produce and maintain social structure. We explore three types of capital—financial, human, and social (Coleman, 1990; Becker, 1993, 1996), but we are particularly interested in social capital.

Conceptually, financial capital refers to income and other assets which individuals own that affect future income and consumption (Becker, 1993). Vis-à-vis health, financial capital allows an individual to purchase health-promoting goods. Human capital refers to activities such as education and on-the-job training that increase resources within the individual that influence future income and consumption (Becker, 1993). Human capital, often considered to be synonymous with education, is a mechanism that increases or decreases one's efficiency in producing health—either by allowing one to benefit more from a given unit of health investment or by helping the individual select a better mix of health inputs—for instance, avoiding risky health behaviors. Link and Phalen (1995) consider human capital to be a *fundamental cause*—an integral part of the individual's social context that influences how he or she faces current and future risks to health. Social capital refers to capital generated from the structure of personal relationships (Becker, 1996; Coleman, 1990). Portes (1998) notes "the consensus is growing in the literature that social capital stands for the ability of actors to secure benefits by virtue of membership in social networks or other social structures" (p. 6).*

Social capital may prove to be a critical addition as it integrates both the economic and sociological domains. In theory, social relationships can generate social capital through multiple mechanisms: creation of obligations and expectations; providing information or information potential; establishing norms and effective sanctions; and vesting authority in a leader or creating social organizations to further a goal (Coleman, 1990). In turn, social capital may enhance health through various mechanisms: by creating a sense of belonging through reciprocal social relationships; by facilitating health promoting behaviors through the establishment of norms; by facilitating the sharing of (as opposed to the acquisition of) health-relevant information; by fostering positive cognitive orientations such as self-efficacy and hopefulness; by accessing financial and medical resources; or by generating other types of capital that directly facilitate health.

As is evident from the description of social capital, the conceptualization of social capital is made more difficult because of its broad and encompassing nature. Social capital theory draws heavily from the literature on social support, social ties, and networks. Yet, social capital is distinguished from these concepts since social capital has both relational and material aspects (Hawe & Shiell, 2000). Overall, social ties and networks might best be thought of as indicators of social capital and social support may best be described as a manifestation or product of one's social capital.

---

*Interestingly, some economists consider social capital to be a subset of human capital rather than an independent form of capital (Becker, 1996).

Empirically, early work found an association between social capital and the inverse gradient in health. At the societal level, both Kawachi, Kennedy, Lochner, & Prothrow-Stith (1997) and Wilkinson (1996) argue that growing income inequality in developed nations leads to disinvestment in social capital resulting in differential health outcomes by social strata. However, Mellor and Milyo (2001) make a compelling counter case against a strong association between income inequality, per se, and population health. A second stream of research focuses on individual level measures of social capital and related concepts such as social support, social ties, and networks. This literature reports a strong link between social networks and health outcomes at the individual level (Berkman & Syme, 1979; Falk, Hanson, Isacsson, & Ostergren, 1992; Kawachi et al., 1996; Lin, Simeone, Ensel, & Kup, 1979). But Veenstra, in a study of individual components of social capital, found few significant associations between the measures of social capital and health (Veenstra, 2000). Taken together, these studies demonstrate that the influence of social capital on health shows promise as an area of research, but also bring into sharper focus the need for stronger theoretical models and the struggle for conceptual clarity in the measurement of social capital.

SOCIAL CAPITAL AND HEALTH AMONG LATE ADOLESCENTS AND NEAR-OLD ADULTS

We believe that modeling the impacts of financial, human, and, in particular, social capital will provide a more complete understanding of the mechanisms through which social structure affects health. By focusing on capital rather than SES, we propose that it is the pattern of differential investment in, and spending of capital over the life course, that is responsible for the life course patterning of the inverse gradient in health. We contend that individuals of lower SES have spent down these types of capital, especially social capital, earlier in life or never acquired them in large amounts in comparison to their upper SES counterparts. To lay the foundation for our position, we explore the dynamics of capital at two pivotal points on the SES health gradient—late adolescence and early adulthood, the age when the inverse gradient in health begins to appear, and at retirement, where it begins to converge.

Adolescence is a critical time for capital development, since individuals are generally gaining more capital than they depreciate. Social capital is thought to be important in two respects: (1) promoting the development of human capital, and (2) influencing lifestyle choices and promoting a sense of belonging and acceptance. Numerous studies have shown that social capital in adolescence influences future educational and occupational achievement (Coleman, 1988; Hagan, Macmillan, & Wheaton, 1996; Hutchison & McNall, 1995; McNall, Hutchison, & Mortimer, 1997; Smith, Beaulieu, & Seraphine, 1995; Teachman, Paasch, & Carver, 1997). Adolescents' social networks influence important decisions involving higher education (Coleman, 1988; Teachman et al., 1997) and work. While the accumulation of human capital can be seen as a life-long process, most college education is obtained by the early 20s, following high school (Barbett & Korb, 1997). Educational attainment during adolescence and young adulthood sets the foundation for an individual's adult socioeconomic status, independent of his or her family of origin. Furthermore, social ties affect life style choices, such as the adoption of risky health behaviors (Bailey & Ennett, 1993; Ennett & Bauman, 1991, 1994).

Young adults also make enduring choices regarding their social networks. During the ages of 19–24, individuals develop social networks of close and casual friends while still maintaining ties with parents; coworkers and spouses are entering the networks as well (Burt, 1995). Although social capital is a function of social relationships, Becker (1996) proposes that a critical choice under the control of the individual is selecting what social networks to belong to and which social relationships to establish.

In older adults, individuals are generally depleting capital at a faster rate than they can reinvest in capital. Social networks are shrinking as older adults retire from the work force and parents, other friends, and even spouses pass away (Burt, 1995). Financial resources become more fixed as employment-related income is phased out. Human capital is not easily expanded as most higher education is completed during early adulthood and older adults are withdrawing from the full-time workforce rather than retraining (Schulz, 1995). Yet, in the face of declining health, both physically and mentally, older adults draw upon the different types of capital available to them to address these needs.

Social capital is a critical resource at older ages since it may substitute for human capital. As older adults experience cognitive and physical decline, their capacity for making informed decisions regarding their personal welfare, and implementing such decisions, declines. An individual may rely less on personal knowledge with regard to health questions and activities, and more on social networks for advice and instrumental help (Kane, Kane, & Ladd, 1998). In 1991, 9% of adults aged 65–69 reported needing assistance with everyday activities, and by the age of 85 years or older, 50% were in need of assistance (Bureau of the Census, 1995). Further, social capital and the relationships that express it take on a different tenor as relational transactions become less reciprocal in nature (Call, Finch, Huck, & Kane, 1999).

Several academic traditions have coined terms such as cumulative disadvantage (Shea, Miles, & Hayward, 1996) or cumulative adversity (Turner & Lloyd, 1995) to describe increasing vulnerability over the life course. Lower SES individuals exhibit cumulative disadvantage in wealth over the life course. Cumulative adversity refers to the accumulation of lifetime trauma, the experience of high levels of acute and chronic stress, and psychological disorder (Turner & Lloyd, 1995) that make it difficult for an individual to build resources. Both of these terms suggest that lower SES individuals are unable to effectively create and maintain capital. Conversely, an argument can be made that upper SES individuals experience cumulative advantage over the life course. For example, successfully coping with stressors may increase an individual's resistance and ability to cope with future stressors (Elder, 1974; Shanahan & Mortimer, 1996). Higher levels of family social capital promote higher levels of educational attainment, which in turn, foster the attainment of financial resources. Further, high levels of initial financial resources make it easier to build up additional financial resources over the life course, i.e., nothing increases an investment like time, given the power of compound interest.

Given these patterns of advantage and disadvantage over the life course, capital accumulation may assume a different character in lower versus upper SES individuals, with upper SES individuals being more strategic/proactive and lower SES individuals more reactive. Overall, lower SES individuals endure more noxious physical, social, and occupational environments than upper SES individuals over their lifetimes (Baum, Garofalo, & Yali, 1999; Brown, 1995; Dohrenwend & Dohrenwend, 1970; McLeod & Kessler, 1990; National Institute for Occupational Safety and Health, 2000; Nelson, 1992; Smith, Hart, Blane, & Hole, 1998; Stronks, Mheen, Van de Looman, & Mackenbach, 1998; Wallace & Wallace, 1998). Yet, they have fewer personal resources for coping with these harsher physical and social environments (Kessler & Cleary, 1980; McLeod & Kessler, 1990; Singer & Ryff, 1995).

Moreover, the social capital one develops over the life course is largely a function of these environments. Early in life, higher SES individuals derive their social capital typically from social networks that can help generate opportunities for growth and accumulation of other types of capital. For example, parents of higher SES have high expectations for educational and occupational achievement for their children. They also provide a model for how to succeed in these areas as well as numerous social contacts, and a value system that emphasizes self-direction (Kohn, 1969). It is much easier to be strategic when one has better resources, from a variety of sources, stemming from an early age. For lower SES individuals, the situation is reversed with social networks weaker in opportunity, fewer successful role models, and a value system that emphasizes conformity.

Thus, by virtue of their social location, social ties in adolescence and early adulthood are likely to be more promotive of human capital accumulation, as well as health, for higher SES youth than for youth from lower SES backgrounds. Close and communicative relationships with parents act as vehicles for the transmission of attitudes and values in high SES families that promote educational achievement. Similarly, friendships are likely to be formed with individuals of similar social class background, reinforcing the value of educational achievement. Moreover, family and friends at higher SES levels are likely to be better informed about health, and healthier themselves, providing more accurate guidance and better role models for healthy life styles. Thus, deficits in social capital contribute to the intergenerational stability in attainment (Anderson, 1980; Camburn, 1990; Lin, Vaughn, & Ensel, 1981), and may also generate intergenerational stability in health.

The convergence of the inverse gradient in health in older adults likely results from human and social capital decline in upper SES individuals at older ages, coupled with biological aging. At the point in the life course when SES and health differences begin to converge, upper SES individuals have accumulated greater stocks of all three types of capital as well as greater opportunity to invest in capital over the life course. However, social capital is depleted when social networks begin to shrink as individuals move through later life transitions, including retirement from the work force and widowhood. Similarly, even the benefits of high levels of human capital may begin to deteriorate as individuals experience cognitive decline. The aging process is a very effective equalizer at the end of the life course. We suggest this depletion of social and human capital is neither as apparent nor as strongly related to declines in health as among lower SES individuals, since individuals of lower SES have spent down these types of capital earlier in life or have never acquired large amounts of these types of capital.

AN EMPIRICAL TEST: CAPITAL AND HEALTH IN THE EARLY AND LATER LIFE COURSE

In the remainder of this chapter, we describe two preliminary studies that examine the impacts of social capital on health at two points in the life course. Since both analyses draw on secondary data sources, and since they both encompass only limited phases of the life course, they are not optimal for addressing the hypotheses regarding the dynamic relations of SES, social capital, and health as people move from adolescence through old age. They do, however, indicate significant associations between distinct forms of capital and health, and indicate how these relationships may differ across socioeconomic strata.

Both studies build on House's work and take a resource-based approach to understanding socioeconomic disparities in health over the life course. One study investigates the relationship between capital and health in adolescence and early adulthood—the time when the inverse gradient in health begins to appear. The other investigates the relationship between capital and health in near-old adults—the time when the inverse gradient in health is widest and begins to converge. Understanding the underlying mechanisms for the inverse gradient in health in these age groups is critical since the potential for preventable morbidity and mortality is high. In both age groups, we are interested in (1) understanding the effect of

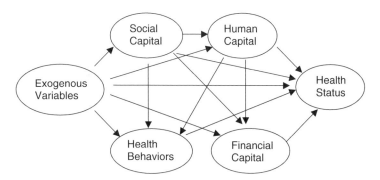

FIGURE 28-2. Conceptual model.

capital—social, human, and financial—on health status; and (2) whether the effects of capital, especially social capital, on health differ by SES.

Figure 28-2 presents a conceptual model of the interrelations of social, human and financial capital, health behaviors, and health status. Exogenous variables, including indicators of SES, are posited as having direct effects on all the subsequent variables in the model. Social capital influences health directly as well as indirectly, through its effects on human capital, financial capital and health behaviors. Human capital is posited as having a direct effect on health status, as well as indirect effects through health behaviors and financial capital. Financial capital is important because it provides the wherewithal to acquire health care services, especially when health is already threatened.

In neither of the two studies do we attempt to estimate the entire conceptual model. Instead, we focus on key relationships, estimated separately in high and low SES subgroups. In the adolescent study, we examine the associations between social capital and health, and between social capital and human capital development. It is hypothesized that access to social capital reduces the psychological burden and negative biological implications of relative deprivation, while also serving as a source of practical support and information. The relationship between social capital and educational attainment may help explain the emergence of an inverse gradient in health in young adulthood, when most individuals have accumulated a significant portion of their formal education, a key feature of human capital. The adolescent study considers the impact of social capital during high school on educational attainment by examining this relationship both 4 years and 7 years after high school. The latter is 3 years after a typical 4-year college degree would be completed. As we have noted, social capital would likely be more advantageous to high SES youth in both respects, for human capital acquisition as well as for health, largely because of the more valuable information and potential linkages that could be activated by their networks.

In near-old adults, we believe that financial resources will be more productive in maintaining health for lower SES individuals than upper SES individuals at this point in the life course. Financial capital allows them to make an investment in health care or other services to slow the rate of depreciation once health has deteriorated. Given their lack of basic financial resources and poorer health, a return on each unit of financial capital expended to produce health will be greater in lower SES individuals than in upper SES individuals. In the upper SES group, social and human capital will likely be more important to promoting health since material needs have already been met. The upper SES group will rely on human and social capital to achieve allocative efficiency in their health inputs as well as to more effectively access resources to maintain their health.

Following House, both studies measured SES as follows: (1) *lower*, where education is between 0 and 11 years, *and* annual income is less than $20,000; (2) *lower middle*, where education is 0–11 years, *or* income is less than $20,000, *but not both*; (3) *upper-middle*, where education is 12–15 years *and* income is greater than or equal to $20,000; and (4) *upper*, including educational attainment of college or greater (16 or more years of education) *and* annual income is greater than or equal to $20,000. In the near-old adult study, the income categories were adjusted for inflation.

In both studies, the primary outcome of interest is self-rated health status, which has been shown to be a strong indicator of observed clinical health (Gold, Franks, & Erickson, 1996; Jenkinson, Wright, & Coulter, 1994). In near-old adults, self-rated health was captured at both time periods by the question—Would you say your health is excellent, very good, good, fair, or poor? In adolescents, self-rated health was measured 4 years after high school by asking respondents to indicate their agreement with the statement, "My health is excellent," by choosing from 1 = "strongly disagree" to 4 = "strongly agree." The health status measure 3 years later is a similar self-reported health variable, with five categories from 1 = "poor" to 5 = "excellent", in response to "In general, would you say your health is ..."

In each study, we estimate the effects of social capital, human capital, and financial capital on self-reported health. In the adolescent study, social capital is conceptualized as a multifaceted construct, including family, work, and community domains, that influences human capital acquisition as well as health. The study of near-old adults utilizes a measure of social capital based on relationships in the family and neighborhood. In both sets of analyses, the samples are divided by socio-economic status to investigate whether social capital, and other forms of capital, have different consequences in these contexts.

SOCIAL CAPITAL AND HEALTH IN ADOLESCENCE

The data for the first analysis come from the Youth Development Study (YDS), a prospective longitudinal study of a community sample of adolescents and their parents. An initial panel of 1,000 adolescents, chosen randomly from students registered in the St. Paul, Minnesota public school district, was surveyed annually from the ninth to the twelfth grades in high school and periodically after graduation. The following time points are noteworthy: Time 1 (1988)—the start of the study during the first year of high school, Time 2 (1991)—the senior year of high school, Time 3 (1995)—4 years following the senior year of high school, and Time 4 (1998)—3 years later, when most subjects are between 24 and 25 years of age. Almost 76% of the original participants were retained through the 1998 survey. These time periods reflect the key phases of human capital development during the transition from adolescence to adulthood, capturing high school, the period following high school generally associated with post-secondary education, and the time at which most young adults have transitioned into full-time work. The fourth time period also captures the critical period when the differentiation in health status becomes increasingly evident in other research (House et al., 1990).

Social capital is measured at time 1, time 2, and time 3. Given that different types of social networks may produce social capital in adolescence, three domains—the family, work, and community—are considered. The quality of relationships and opportunity for social support in theses arenas indicate the social capital that is potentially available through social ties. Family social capital captures the quality of the relationship between the child and the parents. Work social capital reflects the character of relationships with supervisors and friends in the workplace. Community social capital reflects engagement in, and commitment to, the community: the value placed on citizenship involvement, participation in volunteer activities

TABLE 28A-1. Domains of Social Capital

Domain: Family	Lambda weights
How close do you feel to him/her (father/mother)?	1.00
When you are faced with personal concerns and decisions, do you talk them over with him/her?	1.06
How often does he/she talk over important decisions that he has to make with you?	0.93
How often does he/she listen to your side of an argument?	0.90
Overall social capital estimated each year	1.00
Domain: Work	
How close do you fell to your supervisor?	1.00
How often is your supervisor willing to listen to your problems and help find solutions?	1.02
How close do you feel to your best friend at work?	0.86
Overall social capital estimated each year	0.39
Domain: Community	
How important do you think the following thing will be to you when you are an adult: participation as a citizen in my community?	1.00
Count of years of volunteer work between time periods	0.81
Count of years of participation in extracurricular activities between time periods (Times 1 & 2)	1.07
When things get rough, do you have a friend (or friends) who you can really talk to, someone you can turn to for support and understanding? (Time 3)	0.46
Overall social capital estimated each year	0.70

during high school, participation in extracurricular activities (Times 1 and 2 only), and friend support (Time 3 only). All survey items are shown in Table 28A-1.

While these indicators are rather disparate, their underlying common feature is hypothesized to be social capital. Whereas most prior research has focused on each domain separately (family, school, or community), social capital is theorized as a general resource. As a result, the preferred strategy is to use a more general construct. Therefore, a measurement model was estimated to assess the association of each theorized domain of social capital and the overall social capital construct.* These associations were utilized as weights in estimating a global measure of social capital.

Human capital, measured at three time periods, is operationalized by the attainment of formal education at Time 3 and Time 4, including high school graduation, technical college, some college, a 4-year degree, and other advanced degrees (Coleman, 1988; Grossman, 1972). Work complexity, which is associated with intellectual flexibility as well as a constellation of psychological orientations that may be promotive of health (such as self-confidence), is also included in the analysis as a predictor of health (Kohn & Schooler, 1993).

Earnings and health insurance status are the two measures of *financial capital*. The measure of earnings is the reported hourly wage multiplied by the number of hours the individual worked per week. Health insurance status is treated as financial capital because it serves as an financial resource for accessing medical care services.

Measures of cigarette and alcohol use are also available. The background variables are *parental socioeconomic status*, *race*, and *gender*. Socioeconomic status is incorporated as

*See Appendix.

TABLE 28-1. Regression of 1998 Health Status on
T3 (1995) Social, Human, and Financial Capital, by
Socioeconomic Status, Youth Development Study

	High SES	Low SES
White	0.032	0.070
Male	0.015	0.009
Social capital – T3	0.176***	−0.073
Human capital – T3	0.029	0.040
Work complexity – T3	−0.081	−0.064
Earnings – T3	0.020	0.180
Health insuance – T3	0.001	−0.022
Smoking – T3	−0.051	−0.176*
Drinking – T3	0.013	−0.024
Health status – T3	0.398***	0.394***
R square	0.219	0.213
F	13.080***	4.212***

$*p < 0.05, **p < 0.01, ***p < 0.001.$

a composite measure of parental education and family income in the first year of data collection when all subjects were freshmen in high school, and was based on the House et al. (1990) measure. In the analyses, the middle-upper and upper SES categories were combined to constitute the high SES group (N = 477); the middle-lower and lower categories composed the lower SES group (N = 167).

Results. Table 28-1 presents the multivariate linear regression estimates (standardized) of the lagged effects of social, human, and financial capital measured at Time 3 (1995) on self-rated health status at Time 4 (1998), when most respondents were 24 and 25 years old, for the high and low SES groups. Because of the advantage associated with being White and male in American society, race and gender are controlled. The frequency of smoking and alcohol use, prominent health risk behaviors, are also included. Finally, because health status in 1995 is taken into account, the capital coefficients predict change in health over the 3-year period.

In the high SES group, social capital is found to have a significant positive effect on health. In contrast, social capital has no significant effect on health in the low SES group. In the latter, only smoking is found to significantly diminish health. It is noteworthy that health status 3 years earlier registers a strong and positive effect in both groups, indicating substantial stability in health over this period of early adulthood.

Contrary to our expectations, neither human capital (as indicated by educational attainment and work complexity) nor financial capital (earnings and health insurance) promote self-reported health in either group. Similarly, the demographic indicators of advantage (gender and race), and the health behaviors have no significant effects. It may be that too little time has elapsed for the health-relevant processes associated with these variables to be reflected in health.

Although the human capital indicators manifested no significant effect on self-reported health in these analyses, educational attainment has been found to have a robust association with health in later years. It is therefore instructive to observe whether it is responsive to early social capital. Table 28-2 shows the effects of social capital at Time 2 (1991), the senior year of high school, on educational attainment at Time 3 (1995), 4 years after high school, and Time 4 (1998), 7 years after high school, for the high and low SES groups. Again, race and gender, known correlates of educational attainment, are controlled. Consistent with our conceptual

TABLE 28-2. Regression of 1995 and 1998 Educational Attainment on Time 2 (1991) Social Capital, by Socioeconomic Status, Youth Development Study

	High SES		Low SES	
	1995	1998	1995	1998
White	0.003	−0.024	−0.024	−0.078
Male	−0.002	−0.024	0.074	0.115
Social capital – T2	0.127**	0.212*	0.069	0.122
R square	0.016	0.047	0.009	0.027
F	2.590	7.786***	0.476	1.497

$*p < 0.05, **p < 0.01, ***p < 0.001.$

model (Figure 28-2), social capital during high school has a significant positive association with educational attainment in the high SES group at both times 3 and 4. The effect is somewhat stronger in the latter period, which allows 3 more years for the accumulation of educational credentials. In the low SES group, social capital is not significantly associated with educational attainment at either time. Gender and race also appear to confer no advantage (or disadvantage) in either group.

From the adolescent study, there are indications that social capital has a positive effect on health in early adulthood among higher SES youth. We do not find evidence that social capital promotes health in lower SES youth beyond high school. Differences in the action, quality, or quantity of social capital between lower and higher social status youth may be relevant to the divergence of SES and health at this time in the life course. Moreover, by promoting human capital development among higher SES youth, social capital may also play an important indirect role in the SES stratification of health in future years. Interestingly, for lower SES youth, there was no association between educational attainment and social capital.

Differences in the role of social capital between lower and higher social status young adults may represent differences in the normative developmental progress of these social classes, as well as inequality in the productive capacity of their networks. As higher SES youth are more likely to maintain their reliance on family longer, and are more likely to move immediately into other strong social networks established by formal structures, such as college, lower SES youth may be more likely to develop social ties independent of their families of origin and the structure of school. Lower SES youth may be moving away from certain established social ties earlier than their higher SES counterparts, thus diminishing their potential to obtain social capital through these traditional structures.

Social Capital and Health in Near-Old Adults

In the second study, the first two waves of the longitudinal Health and Retirement Study (HRS, Juster & Suzman, 1995) were used to examine the relationship between SES and health in the near old. All adults aged 51–61 (1931–1941 birth cohort) who resided in households in the contiguous United States were the Wave 1 (1992) target population. Wave 2 data were collected in 1994. In 1992, 12,652 individuals (7,608 households) were interviewed with a response rate of 82%. In 1994, 11,596 individuals were interviewed with a response

TABLE 28-3. Standardized Effects of Capital on Self-rated Health Status for High and Low Socioeconomic Status Groups, Health and Retirement Study

	High SES			Low SES		
	Financial	Human	Social	Financial	Human	Social
Direct effect contemporaneous self-rated health	NS	0.37**	0.15**	0.16**	0.39**	NS
Indirect effect contemporaneous self-rated health	NS	NS	NS	NS	0.05**	0.03**
Direct effect change in self-rated health	NS	NS	NS	0.06**	0.15**	NS
Indirect effect change in self-rated health	NS	0.21**	0.15**	0.11**	0.31**	0.04**
RMSEA		0.059			0.068	

** $p < 0.01$, NS = nonsignificant.

rate of 89%. All age-eligible respondents (ages 51–61 at baseline) from the first two waves were included in the analytic sample.*

Social capital was measured as network-based resources that respondents utilize to secure health inputs or information, directly or indirectly. Individuals are thought to draw upon their social networks and relationships but the composition of the resources may vary (Boisjoly, Duncan, & Hofferth, 1995; Coleman, 1988; Hofferth, Boisjoly, & Duncan, 1999). We used an additive index of social capital indicators in the areas of family and neighborhood. They include the number of years married, whether the respondents enjoy the time spent with spouse or partner, spend free time doing activities with spouse/partner, have children living within 10 miles, have good friends in the neighborhood, know neighbors by name, and frequently visit neighbors.

Human capital was operationalized as number of grades completed in school (0–17 or more), self-rated ability to think quickly, and a word recall test. Financial capital was measured as annual household income. We also controlled smoking, drinking, obesity, exercise, exposure to health hazards on the job, age, race, and gender.

Latent variable structural equation modeling was used to examine the relative effects of the different types of capital on health status and change in health in low and high SES subgroups, defined in the same manner as in the first study.†

Results. The results of this analysis are shown in Table 28-3.‡ We find that even after holding constant health behaviors and the demographic variables, capital works differently in protecting health status for the lower ($n = 3140$) and upper SES groups ($n = 1269$). In the low SES group, the only effect of social capital on contemporaneous self-rated health was indirect, operating largely through risk factors. The risk factors in the model included alcohol use, smoking, exercise, obesity, and exposure to work hazards. However, both human capital and financial capital have significant positive direct effects on contemporaneous self-rated health, with human capital having more than twice the effect of financial capital (beta = 0.39, beta = 0.16 respectively). Human capital also has a significant indirect effect on heath.

For the high SES group, human (beta = 0.37) and social (beta = 0.15) capital, but not financial capital, have significant positive direct effects on contemporaneous self-rated health. Similar to the low SES group, human capital has the strongest effect on health. No indirect

*Appropriate sampling weights to correct for design effects were used in all analyses to assure correct standard errors.
†The model was initially developed in the full sample and then estimated separately in the low and high SES subgroups. In addition, the structural equivalence of the social capital and human capital measurement models was tested in the SES subgroups and confirmed.
‡All the coefficients presented in the table are standardized to allow comparison across the different types of capital.

effects of capital on self-reported health were evident in the high SES group. As in the younger panel, it is apparent that social capital has a stronger effect on health in the high SES group. (The social capital direct effect on contemporaneous health was significantly different between the low and high SES groups [$p < 0.01$], whereas the human and financial capital direct effects were not.)

With respect to change in health in the low SES group, both financial and human capital were positively and directly related to change in self-rated health (beta = 0.06, beta = 0.15 respectively) from wave 1 to wave 2. Social capital had no significant direct effect on this outcome. All types of capital were indirectly related to Wave 2 self-rated change in health (beta = 0.11, beta = 0.31, beta = 0.04).

In the high SES group, human and social capital (beta = 0.21 and beta = 0.15, respectively) both had indirect effects on change in self-reported health. It is apparent that social capital has a stronger indirect effect on health change in the higher than in the lower SES group. In contrast, financial capital is more important for change in perceived health in the lower SES group, both directly and indirectly. (The social capital indirect effect on change in the health coefficient was significantly different between the low and high SES groups [$p < 0.01$], as were both the financial capital direct and indirect effects.) The human capital direct and indirect effects on change in health were not significantly different between the SES groups.

Several other significant ($p < 0.05$) results (not shown) point to how social capital indirectly influences health. In near-old adults, social capital reduced the likelihood that individuals engaged in risky health behaviors in both the high and low SES groups. In the high SES group, increasing social capital was inversely related to the use of alcohol (beta = -0.23) and cigarettes (beta = -0.30) and positively related to vigorous exercise (beta = 0.17). In the low SES group, increasing social capital was related to a decrease in the use of alcohol (beta = -0.12), cigarettes (beta = -0.25) and exposure to work hazards (beta = -0.12), but was also related to an increase in obesity (beta = 0.07). Interestingly, in both the high SES and low SES groups, being white had an independent positive relationship with social capital (beta = 0.09, beta = 0.26, respectively).

In summary, differences in the action, quality or quantity of social capital between lower and higher social status near-old adults help explain the inverse SES gradient in health at this time in the life course. Social capital is a more effective resource for self-reported health status in the upper SES group, where it influenced contemporaneous health directly, and change in health indirectly. Social capital, largely a function of marital relations, reduced engagement in risky health behaviors. Financial capital was found to have stronger direct and indirect effects in the lower SES group on change in health. However, in both groups of the near-old, human capital had the strongest protective effect on health.

CONCLUSIONS

The results from the two studies raise interesting questions. With respect to self-rated health, social capital seems to work differently across socioeconomic groups at these two pivotal points in the life course. Interestingly, as found in both studies, the effects of social capital on health were larger for higher SES individuals than for lower SES individuals. This finding suggests social capital may play an important role in explaining the inverse gradient in health. Furthermore, while social capital appears to provide health-enhancing benefits directly, it may also have critical indirect effects on health that may vary at different stages of the life course.

For example, in adolescence, social capital has a significant effect on the accumulation of human capital—especially for upper SES youth. This process may serve to produce good health in the future, as evident by the substantial effect of human capital on health status, and change in health, among near-old adults. Moreover, in near-old adults, social capital significantly decreased participation in risky health behaviors for both lower and upper SES individuals at a point in the life course when such behaviors had significant negative effects on self-rated health.

In both studies, the use of secondary data limited our ability to fully explore and capture the concept of social capital. First, our measures of social capital may be too narrow, failing to address the full scope of this phenomenon. This points to a need to consider other domains of social capital and individual measures of social capital that which may better reflect different life contexts and stages of development. For example, extended familial relationships (e.g., with grandparents, siblings, etc.) could be sources of social capital in adolescence. In near old-adults, we were unable to capture such domains as coworkers and friends outside of the neighborhood. Moreover, our measures tapped the presence of relationships suggesting the potential for social capital rather than the specific uses of social capital to promote health.

Second, a more effective way to assess the influence of social capital may be a more explicit analysis of social networks. Since social capital emerges from relationships, our operationalization of social capital would benefit from an analytic strategy that focused on "detecting emergent social phenomena that have no existence at the level of the individual actor" (Knoke & Kuklinski, 1982, p. 10).

Granovetter (1973) showed the strength of weak ties in achieving goals, in this case getting a job. With respect to social ties and health, the emphasis has been on strong ties (House, Landis, & Umberson, 1988). However, an important function of weak ties is linking different groups or networks together; without these linkages, an individual may be isolated from important information or ideas (Ritzer, 1996). Social networks are only as good as the resources embedded in the relationship—if little material or supportive resources are available in the network, an individual's social capital will not be very productive. An argument can be made that higher SES individuals will have more diverse and productive networks with respect to promoting health compared to low SES individuals. Furstenberg et al.'s work (Furstenberg, Cook, Eccles, Elder, & Sameroff, 1999) suggests that at least for lower SES families with adolescents, access to social capital through a wide variety of domains is of greater importance than strong social capital in only one or a few domains.

Overall, we hypothesized that the pattern of divergence and convergence of the inverse gradient in health status over the life course could be explained by a failure to accumulate social and other types of capital in young adulthood and the erosion of social and the other two types of capital in late adulthood.

With respect to social capital, the primary focus of this chapter, we found it to be a significant predictor of self-reported health status at both points in the life course. Individuals were worse off if they did not have social capital, but social capital seemed to be more productive with respect to health among higher SES individuals. Moreover, social capital worked differently in high and low SES groups. Lastly, different types of capital appeared to be more important for health at different points in the life course. In adolescence, social capital seemed to be more important than the other types of capital, whereas, for near-old adults, human capital was the type of capital that was most productive of health. As hypothesized, financial capital was more important in protecting the health of near-old adults of lower socioeconomic status than for their more advantaged counterparts.

In the end, we have shown that not only is the concept of capital useful in explaining differences in health status over the life course, but the individual forms of capital—human, financial, and social—each appear to have independent effects on the production and mainte-nance of health. More research is needed to determine how the interaction of the different types of capital over the life course, and the differential timing of capital accumulation, contribute to the inverse gradient in health.* Another interesting question is whether it is the level of capital or change in capital that is more important to an individual's health status at different points in the life course. Sociological theory suggests that changes in capital may be as important as the level of resources (Elder & O'Rand, 1995; Mortimer, Finch, & Kumka, 1982).

Understanding the dynamics of the different types of capital over the life course and how they substitute and complement each other should lead to a more fruitful and fundamental understanding of the inverse gradient in health. Such an understanding is paramount as we seek to design and more effectively target policy interventions to reduce SES disparities in health.

APPENDIX—MEASURING SOCIAL CAPITAL
IN THE YOUTH DEVELOPMENT STUDY

A series of items, assessing the domains of family, peers, and community, were used to meas-ure social capital each year in the adolescent study (see Table 28A-1). The construction of the social capital construct proceeded in two stages. In the first stage, a series of confirmatory fac-tor analyses estimated the relations between the family, school, and work constructs and their respective indicators. After inspecting single-year models, and establishing adequate fit, both unconstrained and constrained models across years were estimated. In the latter, correspon-ding lambdas, coefficients expressing the relations between constructs and indicators, were constrained to be equal across time, with the exception of one parameter. Because commu-nity social capital incorporates a new variable in the third measurement year and excludes a variable used in the prior 2 years of measurement, this third lambda in the community capi-tal construct in the third year was freely estimated (not constrained to equal the correspon-ding lambdas estimated in the prior two time periods). Correlated error terms of similar measures across time were also included. Since the constrained model across years did not represent a significantly poorer fit than the freely estimated model (Hayduk, 1988), lambda coefficients from the constrained model were used as item response weights to calculate indices of family, work, and community social capital each year.

In the second stage of the analysis, these three indices of social capital—in family, work, and community—became indicators in "second-order" analyses used to calculate overall social capital each year. Similar constrained models were estimated across years, demon-strating that the measurement structure of overall social capital was not changing over time. Similarly, using multiple groups comparison procedures, the models were tested for differ-ences by gender. Since no statistically significant group differences in measurement structure were found, the final model was estimated for all subjects. The lambda coefficients were again used as weights in calculating overall social capital scores for each year. The resulting scores became the independent variables in the regression models displayed in the text.

Measures and their lambda weights are given in Table 28A-1.

---

*We observed a social gradient in adolescent mental health, but in our analyses of near old adults, we were unable to show convergence in the SES gradient in health. The upper SES near old adults were not at a point where they were rapidly depleting their capital resources or even their health. The rate of resource and health depreciation in this group was slower than expected. We still hypothesize that convergence is caused by decreasing levels of capi-tal in the high SES group but at this point this group was still reaping the benefits of their higher levels of capital.

REFERENCES

Adelstein, A. M. (1980). Life-style in occupational cancer. *Journal of Toxicology and Environmental Health, 6*, 953–962.

Adler, N. E., Marmot, M., McEwen, B. S., & Stewart, J. (Eds.). (1999). *Socioeconomic status and health in industrialized nations: Social, psychological, and biological pathways* (Vol. 896). New York: New York Academy of Sciences.

Adler, N. E., Boyce, W. T., Chesney, M. A., Folkman, S., & Syme, S. L. (1993). Socioeconomic inequalities in health. No easy solution. *JAMA, 269*(24), 3140–3145.

Adler, N. E., & Ostrove, J. M. (1999). Socioeconomic status and health: What we know and what we don't. [Review] [48 refs]. *Annals of the New York Academy of Sciences, 896*, 3–15.

Anderson, K. L. (1980). Educational goals of male and female adolescents: The Effects of parental characteristics and attitudes. *Youth and Society, 12*(2), 173–188.

Antonovsky, A. (1967). Social class, life expectancy and overall mortality. *Milbank Memorial Fund Quarterly, 45*(2), 31–73.

Bailey, S. L., & Ennett, S. T. (1993). Potential mediators, moderators, or independent effects in relationship between parent's former and current cigarette use and their children's cigarette use. *Addictive Behaviors, 18*(6), 601–621.

Barbett, S. F., & Korb, R. A. (1997). *Enrollment in higher education: Fall 1995*. Washington, DC: U.S. Department of Education.

Bartley, M., & Plewis, I. (1997). Does health-selective mobility account for socioeconomic differences in health? Evidence from England and Wales, 1971 to 1991. *Journal of Health & Social Behavior, 38*(4), 376–386.

Baum, A., Garofalo, J. P., & Yali, A. M. (1999). Socioeconomic status and chronic stress: Does stress account for SES effects on health? In N. Adler, M. Marmot, B. McEwen, & J. Stewart (Eds.), *Socioeconomic status and health in industrial nations: Social, psychological, and biological pathways* (pp. 131–144). New York: The New York Academy of Sciences.

Becker, G. S. (1993). *Human capital: A theoretical and empirical analysis with special reference to education* (3rd ed.). Chicago: The University of Chicago Press.

Becker, G. S. (1996). *Accounting for tastes*. Cambridge, MA: Harvard University Press.

Beckett, M. (2000). Converging health inequalities in later life: An artifact of mortality selection? *Journal of Health and Social Behavior, 41*(March), 106–119.

Berkman, L. F., & Syme, S. L. (1979). Social networks, host resistance, and mortality: A nine-year follow-up study of Alameda County residents. *American Journal of Epidemiology, 109*(2), 186–204.

Boisjoly, J., Duncan, G. J., & Hofferth, S. (1995). Access to social capital. *Journal of Family Issues, 16*(5), 609–631.

Breeze, E., Fletcher, A. E., Leon, D. A., Marmot, M. G., Clarke, R. J., & Shipley, M. J. (2001). Do socioeconomic disadvantages persist into old age? Self-reported morbidity in a 29-year follow-up of the Whitehall study. *American Journal of Public Health, 91*(2), 277–283.

Brown, P. (1995). Race, class, and environmental health: A review and systematization of the literature. *Environmental Research, 69*(1), 15–30.

Bunker, J. P., Gomby, D. S., & Kehrer, B. H. (Eds. 1989). *Pathways to health: The role of social factors*. Menlo Park, CA: The Henry J. Kaiser Foundation.

Bureau of the Census. (1995). Statistical brief: Sixty-five plus in the United States (SB/95–8). Washington, DC: United States Department of Commerce.

Burt, C. W. 1995. Injury-related visits to hospital emergency departments: United States, 1992. *Advanced Data*, Number 261 edition. Hyattsville, MD: National Center for Health Statistics.

Call, K. T., Finch, M. D., Huck, S., & Kane, R. (1999). Caregiver burden from a social exchange perspective: Caring for older people following hospital discharge. *Journal of Marriage and the Family, 61*, 688–699.

Call, K., & Nonnemaker, J. (1999). Socioeconomic disparities in adolescent health: Contributing factors. In N. Adler, M. Marmot, B. McEwen, & J. Stewart (Eds.), *Socioeconomic status and health in industrial nations: Social, psychological, and biological pathways*. (pp. 352–355). New York: The New York Academy of Sciences.

Camburn, E. (1990). College completion among students from high schools located in large metropolitan areas. *American Journal of Education, 98*(4), 551–569.

Coleman, J. S. (1988). Social capital in the creation of human capital. *American Journal of Sociology, 94*(Suppl.), S95–S210.

Coleman, J. S. (1990). *Foundations of social theory*. Cambridge: The Belknap Press of Harvard University Press.

Dohrenwend, B. S., & Dohrenwend, B. P. (1970). Class and race as status-related sources of stress. In S. Levine & N. A. Scotch (Eds.), *Social stress* (pp. 111–140). Chicago: Aldine.

Elder, G. H., Jr. (1974). *Children of the Great Depression: Social change in life experience*. Chicago: University of Chicago Press.

Elder, G. H., Jr., & O'Rand, A. M. (1995). Adult lives in a changing society. In K. S. Cook, G. A. Fine, & J. S. House (Eds.), *Sociological perspectives on social psychology* (pp. 452–475). Needham Heights, MA: Allyn & Bacon.

Ennett, S. T., & Bauman, K. E. (1991). Mediators in the relationship between parental and peer characteristics and beer drinking by early adolescents. *Journal of Applied Social Psychology, 21*(20), 1699–1711.

Ennett, S. T., & Bauman, K. E. (1994). Variability in cigarette smoking within and between adolescent friendship cliques. *Addictive Behaviors, 19*(3), 295–305.

Evans, R. G., Barer, M. L., & Marmor, T. R. (Eds.). (1994). *Why are some people healthy and others not? The determinants of health of populations.* New York: Aldine De Gruyter.

Falk, A., Hanson, B. S., Isacsson, S.-O., & Ostergren, P.-O. (1992). Job strain and mortality in elderly men: Social network, support, and influence as buffers. *American Journal of Public Health, 82*(8), 1136–1139.

Feinstein, J. S. (1993). The relationship between socioeconomic status and health: A review of the literature. [Review] [74 refs]. *Milbank Quarterly, 71*(2), 279–322.

Feldman, J. J., Makuc, D. M., Kleinman, J. C., & Cornoni-Huntley, J. (1989). National trends in educational differentials in mortality. *American Journal of Epidemiology, 129*(5), 919–933.

Fox, A. J., Goldblatt, P. O., & Jones, D. R. (1985). Social class mortality differentials: Artefact, selection or life circumstances? *Journal of Epidemiology & Community Health, 39*(1), 1–8.

Furstenberg, F. F., Cook, T. D., Eccles, J., Elder, G. H., Jr., & Sameroff, A. (1999). *Managing to make it: Urban families and adolescent success.* Chicago: University of Chicago Press.

Gold, M., Franks, P., & Erickson, P. (1996). Assessing the health of the nation: The predictive validity of a preference-based measure and self-rated health. *Medical Care, 34*(2), 163–177.

Granovetter, M. (1973). The strength of weak ties. *American Journal of Sociology, 78*, 1360–1380.

Grossman, M. (1972). *The demand for health: A theoretical and empirical investigation.* New York: National Bureau of Economic Research.

Haan, M. N., Kaplan, G. A., & Syme, S. L. (1989). Socioeconomic status and health: Old observations and new thoughts. In J. P. Bunker, D. S. Gomby, & B. H. Kehrer (Eds.). *Pathways to health: The role of social factors* (pp. 76–138). Menlo Park, CA: The Henry J. Kaiser Family Foundation.

Hagan, J., MacMillan, R., & Wheaton, B. (1996). New kid in town: Social capital and the life course effects of family migration on children. *American Sociological Review, 61*, 368–385.

Hawe, P., & Shiell, A. (2000). Social capital and health promotion: A review. *Social Science and Medicine, 51*, 871–885.

Hayduk, L. A. (1988). *Structural equation modeling with LISREL: Essentials and advances.* Baltimore, MA: Johns Hopkins University Press.

Hemingway, H., Nicholson, A., Stafford, M., Roberts, R., & Marmot, M. (1997). The Impact of socioeconomic status on health functioning as assessed by the SF-36 questionnaire: The Whitehall II study. *American Journal of Public Health, 87*(9), 1484–1490.

Hofferth, S. L., Boisjoly, J., & Duncan, G. J. (1999). The development of social capital. *Rationality and Society, 11*(1), 79–110.

House, J. S., Landis, K. R., & Umberson, D. (1988). Social relationships and health. *Science, 241*(4865), 540–545.

House, J. S. (1995). Introduction: Social structure and personality: Past, present, and future. In K. S. Cook, G. A. Fine, & J. S. House (Eds.). *Sociological perspectives on social psychology.* (pp. 387–395). Needham Heights, MA: Allyn & Bacon.

House, J. S., Kessler, R. C., & Herzog, A. R. (1990). Age, socioeconomic status, and health. *Milbank Quarterly, 68*(3), 383–411.

House, J. S., Lepkowski, J. M., Kinney, A. M., Mero, R. P., Kessler, R. C., & Herzog, A. R. (1994). The social stratification of aging and health. *Journal of Health & Social Behavior, 35*(3), 213–234.

Hutchison, R., & McNall, M. (1995). Neighborhood, culture, and capital: Early marriage and educational outcomes in the Hmong community. Presented at the Annual Meeting of the American Sociological Association.

Jenkinson, C., Wright, L, & Coulter, A. (1994). Criterion validity and reliability of the SF-36 in a population sample. *Quality of Life Research, 3*(1), 7–12.

Juster, F. T., & Suzman, R. (1995). An overview of the health and retirement Study. *The Journal of Human Resources, 30* (Supplement Special Issue: The Health and Retirement Study—Data Quality and Early Results), S7–S56.

Kane, R. A., Kane, R. L., & Ladd, R. C. (1998). *The heart of long-term care.* New York: Oxford University Press.

Kawachi, I., Colditz, G. A., Ascherio, A., Rimm, E. B., Giovannucci, E., Stampfer, M. J., & Willett, W. C. (1996). A prospective study of social networks in relation to total mortality and cardiovascular disease in men in the USA. *Journal of Epidemiology and Community Health, 50*, 245–251.

Kawachi, I., Kennedy, P. B., Lochner, K., & Prothrow-Stith, D. (1997). Social capital, income inequality, and mortality. *American Journal of Public Health, 87*(9), 1491–1498.

Kessler, R. C., & Cleary, P. D. (1980). Social class and psychological distress. *The American Sociological Review, 45*, 463–478.

Kinney, A. M., & Finch, M. D. (1998). *Continuing research in the social stratification of aging and health: Is access to health care an explanatory factor?* Paper Presented at the Minnesota Health Services Research Conference.

Kitagawa, E. M., & Hauser, P. M. (1973). *Differential mortality in the United States: A study in socioeconomic epidemiology.* Cambridge, MA: Harvard University Press.

Knoke, D., & Kuklinski, J. H. (1982). *Network analysis* (Vol. Series Number 07-028). Beverly Hills: Sage.

Kohn, M. L., & Schooler, C. (1983). *Work and personality: An inquiry into the impact of social stratification.* Norwood, NJ: Ablex.

Koskinen, S., & Martelin, T. (1994). Why are socioeconomic mortality differences smaller among women than among men? *Social Science and Medicine, 38*(10), 1385–1396.

Lichtenstein, P., Harris, J. R., Pedersen, N. L., & McClearn, G. E. (1992). Socioeconomic status and physical health, how are they related? An empirical study based on twins reared apart and twins reared together. *Social Science and Medicine, 36*(4), 441–450.

Lin, N., Simeone, R. S., Ensel, W. N., & Kup, W. (1979). Social support, stressful life events, and illness: A model and an empirical test. *Journal of Health and Social Behavior, 20*, 108–119.

Lin, N., Vaughn, J. C., & Ensel, W. N. (1981). Social resources and occupational status attainment. *Social Forces, 59*(4), 1163–1181.

Link, B. G., & Phelan, J. (1995). Social conditions as fundamental causes of disease. [Review] [90 refs]. *Journal of Health & Social Behavior, Spec No*, 80–94.

Marmot, M. G., Shipley, M. J., & Rose, G. (1984). Inequalities in death—specific explanations of a general pattern? *Lancet, 1*(8384), 1003–1006.

Marmot, M. G., & McDowall, M. E. (1986). Mortality decline and widening social inequalities [published erratum appears *in Lancet* 1987 Feb 14;1(8529):394]. *Lancet, 2*(8501), 274–276.

Marmot. (1991). Health inequalities among British civil servants: The Whitehall II study.

Marmot, M. G., Smith, G. D., Stansfeld, S., Patel, C., North, F., Head, J., White, I., Brunner, E., & Feeney, A. (1991). Health inequalities among British civil servants: The Whitehall II study. *The Lancet, 337*, 1387–1393.

McGinnis, J. M., & Foege, W. H. (1993). Actual causes of death in the United States. *JAMA, 270*, 2207–2212.

McKeown, T. (1976). *The role of medicine.* London: Nuffield Provincial Hospitals Trust.

McKinlay, J. B., McKinlay, S. M., & Beaglehole, R. (1989). A review of the evidence concerning the impact of medical measures on recent mortality and morbidity in the United States. [Review] [74 refs]. *International Journal of Health Services, 19*(2), 181–208.

McLeod, J. D., & Kessler, R. C. (1990). Socioeconomic status differences in vulnerability to undesireable life events. *Journal of Health and Social Behavior, 31*, 162–172.

McNall, M., Hutchison, R., & Mortimer, J. T. (1997) (unpublished). Social capital and educational outcomes of Hmong adolescents.

Mellor, J. M., & Milyo, J. (2001). Reexamining the evidence of an ecological association between income inequality and health. *Journal of Health, Politics, Policy and Law, 26*(3), 487–522.

Mortimer, J. T., Finch, M. D., & Kumka, D. (1982). Persistence and change in development: The multidimensional self-concept. In P. B. Baltes & O. G. Brim, Jr. (Eds.). *Life-span development and behavior.* New York: Academic Press.

National Institute for Occupational Safety and Health. (2000). *Worker health chartbook, 2000 (DHHS Publication Number 2000-127).* Washington, DC: Department of Health and Human Services.

Nelson, M. D. (1992). Socioeconomic status and childhood mortality in North Carolina. *American Journal of Public Health, 82*(8), 131–133.

North, F., Syme, S. L., Feeney, A., Head, J., Shipley, M. J., & Marmot, M. G. (1993). Explaining socioeconomic differences in sickness absence: The Whitehall II study. *British Medical Journal, 306*, 361–366.

Pamuk, E. R. (1985). Social class inequality in mortality from 1921 to 1972 in England and Wales. *Population Studies, 39*, 17–31.

Pappas, G., Queen, S., Hadden, W., & Fisher, G. (1993). The increasing disparity in mortality between socioeconomic groups in the United States, 1960 and 1986 [published erratum appears in *N Engl J Med* 1993 Oct 7;329(15):1139] [see comments]. *New England Journal of Medicine, 329*(2), 103–109.

Pincus, T., Esther, R., Dewalt, D. A., & Callahan, L. F. (1998). Social conditions and self-management are more powerful determinants of health than access to care. *Annals of Internal Medicine, 129*, 406–411.

Portes, A. (1998). Social capital: Its origins and applications in modern sociology. *Annual Review of Sociology, 24*, 1–24.

Power, C., Matthews, S., & Manor, O. (1998). Inequalities in self-rated health: Explanations from different stages of life. *The Lancet, 351*, 1009–1014.

Preston, S. H., & Taubman, P. (1994). Socioeconomic differences in adult mortality and health status. In L. G. Martin & S. H. Preston (Eds.). *Demography of aging.* Washington, DC: National Academy Press.

Ritzer, G. (1996). *Sociological theory* (4th ed.). New York: McGraw-Hill.

Ross, C. E., & Wu, C. L. (1996). Education, age, and the cumulative advantage in health. *Journal of Health & Social Behavior, 37*(1), 104–120.

Schulz, J. H. (1995). *The Economics of Aging* (6th ed.). Westport, CT: Auburn House.

Shanahan, M. J., & Mortimer, J. T. (1996). Understanding the positive consequences of psychosocial stressors. In B. Markovsky, M. J. Lovaglia, & R. Simon (Eds.). *Advances in Group Processes* (Vol. 13, pp. 189–209). Greenwich, CT: JAI Press, Inc.

Shea, D. G., Miles, T., & Hayward, M. (1996). The health-wealth connection: Racial differences. *Gerontologist, 36*(3), 342–349.

Singer, B., & Ryff, C. D. (1995). Social ordering/health linkages: Pathways and allostasis. Unpublished Manuscript.

Singh, G. K., & Yu, S. M. (1996). U. S. childhood mortality, 1950 through 1993: Trends and socioeconomic differentials. *American Journal of Public Health, 86*(4), 505–512.

Smith, J. (1998). Socioeconomic status and health. *AEA Papers and Proceedings, 88*(2), 192–196.

Smith, M. H., Beaulieu, L. J., & Seraphine, A. (1995). Social capital, place of residence, and college attendance. *Rural Sociology, 60*(3), 363–380.

Smith, G. D., Hart, C., Blane, D., & Hole, D. (1998). Adverse socioeconomic conditions in childhood and cause specific adult mortality: Prospective observational study. *British Medical Journal, 316*(7145), 1631–1635.

Smith, J. P., & Kington, R. (1997). Demographic and economic correlates of health in old age. *Demography, 34*(1), 159–170.

Stronks, K., Mheen, H. Van de, Looman, C. W. N., & Mackenbach, J. P. (1998). The importance of psychosocial stressors for socio-economic inequalities in perceived health. *Social Science and Medicine, 46*(4–5), 611–623.

Teachman, J. D., Paasch, K., & Carver, K. (1997). Social capital and the generation of human capital. *Social Forces, 75*(4), 1343–1359.

Townsend, P., & Davidson, N. (Eds.). (1982). *Inequalities in health: the Black report.* Harmondsworth, UK: Penguin.

Turner, R. J., & Lloyd, D. A. (1995). Lifetime traumas and mental health: The significance of cumulative adversity. *Journal of Health and Social Behavior, 36*, 360–376.

Veenstra, G. (2000). Social capital, SES and health: An individual-level analysis. *Social Science and Medicine, 50*(5), 619–629.

Wallace, D., & Wallace, R. (1998). Scales of geography, time, and population: The study of violence as a public health problem. *American Journal of Public Health, 88*(12), 1853–1858.

West, P. (1997). Health inequalities in the early years: Is there equalisation in youth? *Social Science and Medicine, 44*(6), 833–858.

Wilkinson, R. G. (Ed.). (1986). *Class and health: Research and longitudinal data.* New York: Tavistock.

PART VII

THE FUTURE OF THE LIFE COURSE

CHAPTER 29

Toward a Global Geography of the Life Course

Challenges of Late Modernity for Life Course Theory

DALE DANNEFER

INTRODUCTION

From the beginning, social change has been a central theme of work in the life course tradition (Cain, 1964; Elder, 1974, 1975; Elder & Crosnoe, *this volume*; Giele & Elder, 1998). In the present historical moment, we are confronted with processes of social transformation and knowledge transformation that are likely to change the enterprise of life course studies itself. In this chapter, I sketch some dimensions of the present situation that may impel such change. This task necessarily assumes a reasonably clear statement of how one conceptualizes "the life course" as an area of study. As this volume powerfully attests, the life course area encompasses a richly diverse and sometimes incommensurate set of questions, methods and principles. Clearly, it is a term that embodies multiple intellectual perspectives.

To provide an organizing framework, I employ the basic conceptual distinction between "life course as *phenomenon*" and "life course as *theory*", recently introduced into the literature (Dannefer & Uhlenberg, 1999; Hagestad & Dannefer, 2001). From one set of perspectives, life course refers to a *construct, a phenomenon to be described and explained*. Such is the

DALE DANNEFER • Margaret Warner Graduate School of Education and Human Development, University of Rochester, Rochester, New York 14627

Handbook of the Life Course, edited by Jeylan T. Mortimer and Michael J. Shanahan. Kluwer Academic/Plenum Publishers, New York, 2003.

perspective, for example, that informs work describing life course patterns at the macro-level and charting the aggregate stability and change of these patterns and associated factors over time. From another perspective, the life course refers to an *explanatory theory* which proposes to use earlier life course experiences as a *means of accounting for subsequent life outcomes*. Such work generally entails the tracing of individual change over time, exploring the degree to which later life outcomes can be predicted or interpreted from events or conditions experienced by the individual at a younger age.

In both of these domains—*phenomenon* and *theory*, the life course perspective faces challenges from recent and current social–structural, political, and technological developments. The developments in question are closely related to substantial changes of the structures of 20th century modernity, and the new conditions of what is variously called "postmodernism" (Harvey, 1989), late modernity (Giddens, 1994), or the "risk society" (Beck & Beck-Gernsheim, 1996). Whatever term one prefers, these developments reflect "time–space distentiation" (Giddens, 1991), evidenced by new modes of relation between technology and information, such as the deployment of widely accessible, instantaneous technologies of global communication, or the near-instantaneous processing of the routine transactions of large financial institutions by semi-skilled workers in third world countries. Such developments both enable and reflect the growth of trans-national corporations (Soros, 2002). Beyond the level of everyday human activities and institutional practices, concomitant changes have involved the weakening of national political boundaries and systems (Castells, 2000; Reich, 1992), and of traditional regimes of social mobility, including the one-life/one-career imperative (Dannefer, 2000; Riley & Riley, 1994), and thus, possibly, a concomitant erosion of the institutionalized life course (Kohli, 1986). Above all, this constellation of changes represents a new global interdependence (Castells, 2000) which is transforming, enriching, and challenging the knowledge base and problematics of the human sciences. Fueled by possibilities of low-cost and near-instantaneous global communication, new modes of social organization, exchange, and social interaction are emerging more rapidly than they can be studied—from web-based businesses and educational programs that have a worldwide market, to the use of a worldwide labor pool to market as well as manufacture products, to on-line sex, to new efficiencies in extortion and other criminal enterprises (Castells, 2001, pp. 5–6; Stiglitz, 2002). These broad trends amplify further the globalization of communication and production processes in the latter half of the 20th century. The debates surrounding the details of these broad changes (captured in such terminological alternatives as "postmodernism", "poststructuralism", or "late modernity") entail numerous controversies that lie well beyond the scope of this chapter. I use the term "late modernity" to refer to the constellation of forces that has produced a recognizably distinct historical period, even while many of the ideal-typical features of modernity remain robust and provide substantial continuity in the lives of both individuals and institutions (see Furlong & Cartmel, 1997; Giddens, 1994; Hagestad & Dannefer, 2001).

In this chapter, I sketch some dimensions of how these changes may affect the study of the life course, both as "phenomenon" and as "explanation." I argue that these developments are likely to pose major challenges to the current state of knowledge concerning the life course. Simultaneously, the same developments generate new questions, and provide opportunities for broader testing of generalizations and assumptions in the existing literature. I conclude by suggesting how the greater awareness of and access to cross-cultural data, and trends of social change emerging in both "less developed" and late modern societies over recent decades, may simultaneously offer research opportunities that transcend what is possible within a single society, and compel the attention of researchers to less familiar patterns of biography and relationship. We can, in short, now envision the need for a "global geography" of the life course.

THE LIFE COURSE AS *CONSTRUCT*

The structure and organization of biographical experience has comprised one of the central questions of life course research. To this end, a major theme in the literature on the modern life course has been to assert its relatively orderly and age-graded role structure. This theme has relied heavily on demographic and other traditions of research that provide descriptions of the life trajectories of large segments of a population (e.g., Henretta, 1992; Meyer, 1986; Modell, Furstenberg & Strong, 1978). Over much of the 20th century, these patterns became increasingly standardized in the familiar form that has come to be called the "three boxes of life"—of education, work and retirement (Riley & Riley, 1994). It is also seen in "personal life", in increasingly stable and prolonged family roles (e.g., Hagestad, 1988; Uhlenberg, 1978; Uhlenberg and Mueller, *this volume*.) As it has been increasingly defined by the crystallization of age grading in education, in the workplace and in the establishment of retirement, the life course itself has become a social institution (Kohli & Meyer 1986).

Some scholars have emphasized the role of individual choice in producing, paradoxically, uniform age-graded patterns (e.g., Hogan, 1981; Modell, 1989; cf. Dannefer, 1984). Others have pointed to the role of the state in shaping individual lives (e.g., Kohli, 1999; Meyer, 1986) and individual life chances (Crystal & Waehrer, 1996; Dannefer, 1988; 2000; O'Rand & Henretta, 1999) through the construction of the age-graded and stratified institutions of schooling, work careers and retirement (Phillipson, 1998; Riley, Johnson, & Foner, 1972; Rosenbaum, 1983). Despite these differences in interpretation, few have taken issue with the empirical reality of the life course as characterized by the "three boxes" as an empirically modal pattern generally characterizing modern societies through the 20th century and indeed, with the idea of the life course itself a social institution of modernity (Kohli, 1986)— an individual-level product of the combined effects of various age-graded institutions of childcare, schooling, work, retirement, and health care.

Cross-Societal Variations in the Shape and Degree of Life Course Institutionalization

Viewed in global perspective, it is clear that this "typical" life course pattern is not at all typical for much of the human population. Quite different patterns are found in the "Majority World"—the poorer and less developed countries where most of the people inhabiting the earth live (Ellwood & Crump, 1999). If the life course area is to encompass the full range of human diversity and human possibility, these diverse patterns cannot be ignored. Many "alternative" life course configurations are also strongly institutionalized. Such established patterns can be observed in spite of the high population turnover of countries that have not undergone the demographic transition—witnessing powerfully to the fact that the life course is indeed a social institution that transcends, and yet encases, the biographies of individuals. In some cases, such patterns are well entrenched, and are clearly older than the "three boxes" of the "modern" life course with which the term institutionalization has often been equated.

As an example, in some areas of Pakistan, India, and several other countries, the individual life course has, for substantial segments of the population, been shaped by intergenerational patterns of familial bondage and child labor. Families routinely "bind over" their children to employers as a means of income. Often, it is reported that this practice is sustained as laborers seek to repay large and sometimes insurmountable debts in an ongoing, squirrelcage-like cycle that has for many families persisted for multiple generations, and from which old age is no escape. Bondage is one specific mechanism through which individuals are drafted into the labor force as children. Overall, there are an estimated 250 million children between the ages of 5 and 15 on the planet who work, about half of them full time (ILO, 1998; see also Reddy, 1995; Weiner, 1991). A substantial number of these are actually working under conditions of slavery or prostitution (Seabrook, 1996; 2000; U.S. Congress, 1994a).

With such planetary diversity more fully and unavoidably in view, the conventional preoccupations of life course studies risk appearing myopic. The magnitude and robustness of such realities challenge the life course perspective to approach its subject matter at a level of generality that can be applicable across societies, and to countenance an array of life course patterns and sequences that look quite different from the "mainstream" life course, but that are nonetheless institutionalized in the social systems that have produced them.

This challenge poses a particular problem for the study of the life course due to the unavoidable scope of its subject matter which is, at the most general level, the *human* life course (not just the Western European or Japanese or North American experience) and the elaboration of general principles to account for the interplay of structures and lives (Riley & Foner, 2001; Riley & Riley, 1994) in whatever societal context they are located, however different from our own. It must be acknowledged that it is a tall order, to take seriously the task of the opening up of the problem of developing a general, global depiction and analysis of the life course. Yet to the extent that life course studies seeks to characterize the life course as a human (and not merely a modern and mainstream) phenomenon, it is a question that cannot readily be avoided.

But beyond the recognition of global diversity, serious attention to the underlying structural dynamics that produce such variant life course patterns across societies, and especially between rich and poor societies, cannot ignore the fact that these variegated life course patterns have long been *interdependent*. This interdependence takes many forms. Trans-national immigration is one long-recognized source of new interpersonal interdependencies, complicated by changes in lifestyle and new modes of relationship (e.g., Thomas & Znaniecki, 1918) that remains highly relevant in contemporary contexts (e.g., Phillipson, Bernard, Phillips, & Ogg, 2001).

More generally, mechanisms that create "linked lives" transnationally and transculturally impact large segments of the human population in ways that more directly shape life chances, the structure of opportunity and the meanings of work and career, of producer and consumer. For example, the lifestyles of affluent moderns depend on cheap raw materials and labor (including commonly practiced child labor)—in South America, the Caribbean, Asia and elsewhere (Lee & Brady, 1988; Lemoine, 1985; U.S. Congress, 1994a, 1994b). With globalization, these longstanding forms of linkage are expanded and further intensified.

The constellation of processes referred to as globalization cannot be seen as a generalized "first cause" of poverty, poor health, or inhumane work conditions. Indeed, many observers regard globalization as holding the promise of upgrading the material and perhaps cultural resources for all of humanity. Nevertheless, experts representing a range of theoretical and philosophical perspectives agree that the policies and institutional structures required to bring the promise of globalization have yet to be developed, and that powerful economic and political forces oppose their development (Soros, 2002; Stiglitz, 2002; Micklethwait & Wooldrich, 2000; Taylor, 2002). Again, a detailed consideration of these issues is well beyond the scope of this chapter. My purpose here is simply to outline some aspects of the life course and issues that shape the life course for large populations of individuals, whose neglect by life course studies can no longer be justified.

In sum, globalization confronts life course studies with what has always been true, but has been long overlooked: That the relationships and connections that shape life chances and lives through time always are centrally shaped by dimensions of power between individuals, and between individuals and the institutions that organize their lives. The inherent individual-level focus of the subject matter of the life course, combined with the strong influence of the traditional functionalism on many early strands of life course theorizing (e.g., Clausen, 1972) makes the lack of attention to social–structural dynamics understandable. As with other aspects of the study of aging, studies of the life course have suffered from "microfication" (Hagestad & Dannefer, 2001). The role of these structural dynamics can, however, no longer be ignored. They inevitably confront life-course studies with complex issues of the asymmetry of power and resources (Dannefer, 1999; Stiglitz, 2002) and of "inclusion and exclusion" (Woodward & Kohli, 2001) within and beyond national boundaries. I return to this general issue in the concluding section. The next task, however, is to acknowledge alternative life course configurations "closer to home".

Subcultural Variation in Life Course Patterns within Late Modern Societies

The theme of alternative, "nonstandard" life course patterns does not require travel to remote societies. They are also robustly institutionalized in minority subcultures within late modern societies. For example, in the United States structurally disadvantaged or privileged subpopulations have their own distinct patterns. The "lives of the rich and famous" often have not conformed very well to the standard, institutionalized life course, nor do those who belong to numerous subcultural minorities. Overall, the life course literature has largely ignored these alternative life course patterns. The work of Linda Burton and associates (e.g, 1996) comprises an important exception to this generalization; her careful research on disadvantaged minority families has documented well-institutionalized patterns of temporally compressed generations, and of generation-skipping patterns of functional parenthood.

Although not studied in detail from a life course perspective, we know that the social systems of urban street gangs in the United States throughout the 20th century also include a life course sequence institutionalized within the gang microculture. The sequence consists of temporally compressed but nonetheless objectively recognized stages of career development and something of a "normative life course" of gang membership, which includes an expectation of not surviving to age 30 (see, e.g., Bing 1991; for a detailed discussion in life course context, see Dannefer, 2002). "Homeboys" and "Tiny Gangsters" graduate, typically in their late teens, to the mainstream "adult" status of "Original Gangster"; older O.G.'s, in their 30s, have been called "Veteranos" or "Double O.G.'s".

In short, within as well as beyond late modern societies, the human life course includes many well-established patterns that bear little resemblance to the "three boxes of life" spanning the better part of a century, that we have come to think of as "normal" and even "natural" (Dannefer, 1999; Morss, 1996). Under such alternative configurations, thirtysomethings may be grandparents (Burton, 1996); elders are workers, parents mortgage their children (ILO, 1998) and children themselves are laborers and parents, prostitutes and soldiers, criminals and explorers (e.g., Bing, 1991; Kett, 1977; Seabrook, 2000). Some children become independent at a remarkably young age, while others lose their lives at an early age. Few studies have illuminated the life course patterns, norms, and expectations prevailing in such contrasting subcultures and circumstances.

To summarize, a global approach to the life course is confronted, initially, with a lack of knowledge about the diverse array of biographical experiences and concomitant life course patterns—the *global geography* of the life course. More than is usually the case with geography, however, such a task will inevitably encounter variation in the degree of stability of the life course itself at any given point in time, and varying rates of change in biographical patterning over time. In a time of extraordinarily rapid technical, organizational and social change, the life course in late modern societies is no exception.

Deinstitutionalization of the "Standard Life Course"?

In addition to the relatively straightforward matter of recognizing the global dimensions of the intellectual questions confronting the life course area, some have contended that the modern "standard life course" itself is now in a process of deinstitutionalization, in both private and public spheres. Whether or not this is seen as a manifestation of the general social deconstruction of modernity's "grand narrative" envisioned by postmodernism, it clearly reflects a powerful set of economic and technological changes that have had multidimensional impacts on individual lives.

In the private sphere, a life course pattern that included a sustained period of time in a single marriage and survival to grandparenthood increased until the mid-20th century, and then began to reverse (Shanahan, 2000; Uhlenberg, 1978). In recent decades, the events of cohabitation, childbearing and marriage have become "disordered." For example, cohabitation before first marriage has become the modal pattern for women (Bumpass & Lu, 1999), and the proportion of births to unmarried women has increased dramatically—more than 8-fold for white women from 1960 to 1992 (from 2% to 17%), and during the same time period nearly 3-fold for African-American women, increasing to nearly 70% in 1992 (Smith, Morgan, & Koropeckyj-Cox, 1996). In the public sphere, the traditional pattern of a single career and an orderly "three box" progression from school to work to retirement has also been dramatically eroded. Education is increasingly extended throughout the life course, and public K-12 education is encountering competition with the vigorous industries of home schooling and private schools. Corporations are no longer seen as staid, hierarchical entities within which career ladders durable enough to last a lifetime of work are enclaved, but as subject to recombinant activities of contraction, transnational merger, and relocation. As a result, the content and career-plan of jobs is often so precarious that the idea of advancing within a career is uncertain and, perhaps, implausible. "Lifelong learning" and innumerable announcements of the need to plan for "multiple careers", and multiple employers, have replaced the "one-career one-life imperative" (Sarason, 1977) in the rhetoric of employers and career counselors, and promises to erode the "three boxes" of the life course (Riley, Kahn & Foner, 1994).

At least in the United States, it is also contended that the pathways are also diversifying beyond midlife—as cross-pressures keep some employees working longer while early retirement options proliferate for others (e.g,. Henretta, 1992, 2001), and a steady stream of retirees re-enters the work force (O'Rand & Henretta, 1999; see also Moen, *this volume*). Thus, an increasingly diverse array of life-course configurations exists, and no single pattern can legitimately be proclaimed as "normative" in any meaningful sense, either statistically or culturally.

Some contend that the arguments for deinstitutionalization in the public sphere are overblown since—despite some variations between and within societies—the "three boxes" still represent a modal pattern across late modernity. Kohli (e.g., 1994) has contended that the rhetoric of deinstitutionalization has far outpaced the reality, and that the institutionalized life course remains robust, especially in the strong welfare states of Western Europe but also in Japan, other Asian societies, and North America. It may be that deinstitutionalization is progressing more rapidly in the United States, where school-to-work transition processes and labor market dynamics are both more fluid, unions are weaker, and both legal protections and norms of corporate obligation leave workers less secure. To the extent that this is true, it may be hypothesized that generalizations and projections that have been predicated on the institutionalized life course (concerning such matters as patterned role transitions, residential mobility and projected pension benefits) may become less powerful.

THE LIFE COURSE AS A *STRATEGY OF EXPLANATION*

As an explanatory strategy, life-course analysis seeks to understand the conditions under which events occurring early in the life course shape its direction in ways that can be observed decades later. Such analyses have produced valuable and often fascinating accounts of the long-term consequences of childhood deprivation (Elder, 1998), and the complex ways in which social-structural factors interact with exceptional or disruptive circumstances. It has been a highly fruitful strategy for demonstrating that diverse life outcomes can be ordered by relating them to differential constellations of early experience (see McLeod, *this volume*). Such analyses—which seek to understand the effects of a major disruptive event (e.g, the Vietnam War or the Great Depression) on people's lives—are generally predicated on an assumption of *general social orderliness throughout the time period in question, apart from that focal event.*

Modernity and the Efficacy of Life Course Theory

Although modernity has typically been characterized as a mode of social organization in which *change* is "normal", the development of modern societies has actually relied heavily upon the presupposition of a great deal of fundamental *stability* in basic institutional forms and in cultural, political, and economic conditions. This sustained period of relative political, cultural, and economic stability has both supported and benefited from the expansion of science, including the social and behavioral sciences. It has also provided an institutional matrix in which individuals have been able to lead comparatively orderly and predictable lives, and has thus provided a platform upon which the use of the life course as an explanatory strategy has been efficacious.

Thus, the "life course as explanation" has relied not merely upon the instititutionalized life course, but upon the predictability of life routines and the possibility of life planning that have been made possible by an array of key characteristics of modernity, including bureaucratic control, economic stability and growth, and general cultural stability and continuity. These conditions provide a firm foundation of social order upon which the disruptions of events such as a major war seem remarkable, and could be traced over a protracted period of time, without undue further disruption.

Although some recent analyses within the life course tradition have begun to look at conditions at intervening time periods, the overarching heuristic focus of the life course as an explanatory strategy has been upon the early-event/late-life connection—as a later life outcome is interpreted as importantly shaped by an earlier experience, event or circumstance. Such analyses typically have proceeded without considering the potential causal significance of socioenvironmental conditions or events occurring after the focal early-life event, thus implicitly assuming the irrelevance of such subsequent events for understanding subsequent outcomes. For purposes of empirical understanding and prediction, these subsequent social conditions and processes are thus rendered invisible (Dannefer & Uhlenberg, 1999). This assumption would seem easiest to justify and maintain when general social conditions are stable and orderly, allowing the effects of the early event to work themselves out on a placid historical landscape.

Thus, the general social conditions of modernity appear to have served especially well the research objective of finding empirical associations and causal speculations connecting early events and later-life circumstances. Clearly, they are conditions under which life-course research has produced a wealth of interesting findings and interpretations concerning, for example, the long-term effects upon coping skills and resilience of early experiences. Thus, a broad structure of social stability has provided the largely invisible and unremarked canvas upon which most of the lives studied from the life-course perspective are played out.

Life Course Explanation, Diversity, and Deinstitutionalization

Whether one uses the terminology of postmodernism or late modernity, few would disagree with the proposition that the character of the institutions of modernity entered a period of deep change in the last quadrant of the 20th century. The "standard" or "normal" life course sequences idealized through much of the twentieth century—the "three boxes of life" Riley, Kahn, & Foner, 1994) or more specifically, of "school-work-marriage" (Hogan, 1981), or of "marriage-cohabitation-childbearing" (Bachrach, Hindin, & Thomson, 2000) have for many people been rendered either unrealistic or undesirable, as has the "one-career imperative" (Sarason, 1977). Rather than being encouraged to develop loyalties in an anticipated context of lifelong employment situation, the cohorts of workers now young are being cautioned to expect to have multiple sites of employers and multiple careers over the course of their working lives.

Yet given the taken-for-grantedness of the broad conditions of institutional stability characterizing most of the 20th century, there has been little occasion to ask the question of *whether the apparent effects of earlier experience should be expected to have an impact of equal magnitude under these "late modern" conditions of institutional deconstruction.* To the extent that careers and family structures become disrupted and diversified, and to the extent that the deconstruction of families and corporate institutions as stable, enduring institutional entities expands, it may be questioned whether the rather robust connections often observed between say, the effects of the interaction of military service and childhood deprivation upon midlife accomplishments can be replicated. To the extent that observed T1–T2 life course connections rely upon conditions of institutional predictability and certainty, these connections may weaken or disappear if the institutional matrix is eroded. If late modernity is accurately characterized by greater variability and inequality across individuals, and by quicker pace, less predictability, and more career-switching or relational disruption within the experience of many individuals, how will this affect the explanatory potential of life course theory?

A Natural Experiment? Social Change and the Explanatory Potential of Life Course Theory

Interestingly, Caspi & Moffitt (1993) have proposed that these conditions of social turbulence and deconstruction are of special heuristic value. They contend that such conditions offer the strongest and clearest tests of whether robust intrapersonal developmental effects occur under times of social instability and rapid change, since such conditions afford the opportunity to disentangle those continuities of personal life that are strong enough to survive the collapse of social constraints and social support from continuities that are sustained only by the stability and normative and structural constraints of a densely institutionalized social environment. Under precisely such conditions of disruption or upheaval, not only is the self-directed "power" of the individual actor maximized, but the power of the institutionalized social forces to shape and order individual lives and experience is minimized (Dannefer, 1993).

Thus, the deinstitutionalizing forces of late modernity offer both danger and opportunity to life course studies. The *danger* is that without the support of a stable and predictable institutional matrix that became increasingly established in modern Western societies in the second half of the 20th century, the kinds of long-term correlations between early events and life course outcomes that have been so extensively observed and reported may fail to materialize in future cohorts. On the other hand, the *opportunity* is that if such connections do continue to be found with the same levels of robustness, it would provide impressive evidence that these internalized life experiences depend upon socioenvironmental forces less than some might expect. In other words, with deinstitutionalization would come the opportunity to test two very general and fundamentally competing hypotheses concerning the forces underlying the strong and intriguing long-term outcomes so frequently reported in the life course literature. The "social-structural" hypothesis would predict that the patterns of continuity would evaporate along with the structures of modernity, signaling that one could not properly understand those outcomes in the first place, without recognizing the role of the institutional platform in providing key "necessary conditions." Were such an outcome to eventuate, advocates of the social–structural view would properly point out that T2 outcomes that have been attributed to early experience in the life course literature have overlooked the essential importance of the enduring stability of social institutions as another set of vitally important contributing factors.

On the other hand, a strong version of the "selection" hypothesis would predict that the kinds of long-term associations reported in the life-course literature would be affected but little by even dramatically disruptive social changes and the permanent increase in levels of social unpredictability to which some attribute late modernity. In the event of such a finding, advocates of the selection hypothesis would have more grounds for disputing the claims and arguments coming from advocates of the social-structural hypotheses.

Thus, something of a "natural experiment" to identify forces underlying life-course connections may be facilitated by the changing conditions that we currently face, and will increasingly face. Whatever the outcome of such a natural experiment, undertaking it can only have the promise of strengthening the enterprise of life course studies, by applying it to an expanded range of social arrangements and populations, and by providing a more rigorous test that specifies the range of social conditions under which individual characteristics in later life can be associated with critical early experiences.

CONCLUSION: LIFE COURSE, GLOBALIZATION, AND SOCIAL THEORY

The end result of these challenges, if recognized and confronted directly, can only be good news for the study of the life course, both as phenomenon or construct to be explicated, and as explanation. I conclude with a comment on each of these.

First, as construct: Cross-cultural work that examines variations in the degree of orderliness in the structure of the life course, whether as institution or improvisation, can only mean that we gain in developing an understanding of the life course that is (1) global, encompassing a fuller range of human diversity and variation, and (2) more fully understood and specified in terms of the conditions associated with its various forms. A global geography would provide the foundation for a fuller and more rigorous test of the "institutionalization" hypothesis as a way of accounting for an age-graded sequence of social roles. At the same time, taking seriously the factors underlying the range of life-course diversity visible on the global landscape will ultimately require that we address modes of relationship among individuals that have heretofore received scant attention from life course scholars. For example, among the factors contributing to the differential shape of the life course in different societal contexts are transnational flows of capital, of labor market opportunities and consumer behavior. Millions of workers (many of them young people and even children) may be made better by the resultant access to jobs, while at the same time their life chances remain dramatically different than the late modern citizenry to whom their lives are connected. Under such conditions, the concept of "linked lives" (Elder, 1998) acquires a new and perplexing significance (Dannefer, 2002). Yet such dramatic power and resource differences are not reducible to a simple "inclusion/exclusion" formula of petrified advantage and disadvantage (Woodward & Kohli, 2001). By applying life course questions and principles to such global interconnections, the life course perspective may contribute to the larger discourses of theory and policy that are addressing such issues. As implied earlier, this task will necessarily require a new level of recognition and attention to the asymmetries of power and other structural variables in organizing aspects of the life course (Dannefer, 1999; Hagestad & Dannefer, 2001; Stiglitz, 2002).

With respect to "life course as explanation", we currently have little knowledge about the extent to which the effects of early life course experiences and developments upon later-life outcomes that have been consistently reported in studies of lives in 20th century modernity (Block & Haan, 1984; Clausen, 1993; Elder, 1999) will hold under different cultural circumstances, or in times of institutional or economic turbulence. A systematic examination of how these life course effects play out within lives under a variety of different social and cultural conditions would enable a more rigorous test of the power of life course explanations, and would constitute a significant step toward a field of life course studies that is globally applicable and relevant.

At the same time, the development of a global geography should be of great interest to those interested in an integrated theoretical understanding of social and psychosocial processes. It would enable us to identify the conditions under which individual-level processes set in motion early in the life course are efficacious, and the conditions under which various configurations of the life course roles and trajectories are likely to be found.

Whether one focuses on the life course as phenomenon to be explained or a set of explanatory principles that can increase our understanding of other outcomes, a globally grounded approach holds the promise of enriching the field of life course studies with fresh questions and new ways of testing the applicable scope of its current knowledge base, and also has the potential to expand the relevance of the life course for other areas of theory, and of policy and practice as well.

ACKNOWLEDGMENT: The author wishes to thank Elaine Dannefer, Jeylan Mortimer, Michael Shanahan and Peter Uhlenberg for valuable critical comments on an earlier version of this chapter.

REFERENCES

Bachrach, C. B., Hindin, M. J., & Thomson, E. (2000). The changing shape of the ties that bind: An overview and synthesis. In L. J. Waite, C. Bachrach, M. Hindin, E. Thomson, & A. Thornton (Eds.), *The ties that bind: Perspectives on marriage and cohabitation*. (pp. 3–17). New York: Aldine de Gruyter.

Beck, U., & Beck-Gernsheim, E. (1996). Individualization and 'precarious freedoms'. Perspectives and controversies of a subject-orientated sociology. In P. Heelas, S. Lasch, & P. Morris (Eds.), *Detraditionalization: Critical reflections of authority and identity*. Oxford: Blackwell Publishers.

Bing, L. (1991). *Do or die*. New York: Harper.

Block, J., & Haan, N. (1984). *Lives through time*. Hillsdale, NJ: Lawrence Erlbaum.

Bumpass, L., & Lu, H. (1999). *Trends in cohabitation and implications for children's family contexts in the U.S. Working Paper 98-15*. Madison: University of Wisconsin, Center for Demography and Ecology.

Burton, L. (1996). Age norms, the timing of family role transitions, and intergenerational caregiving among aging African-American women. *The Gerontologist, 36*(2), 199–208.

Cain, L. D. (1964). Life course and social structure. In R. E. L. Faris (Ed.), *Handbook of modern sociology*. Chicago: Rand, McNally.

Caspi, A., & Moffitt, T. E. (1993). When do individual differences matter? A paradoxical theory of personality coherence. *Psychological Inquiry 4*, 247–271.

Castells, M. (2000). *The network society*, (2nd edn). Malden, MA: Blackwell.

Castells, M. (2001). *The internet galaxy*. New York: Oxford.

Clausen, J. (1995). *American lives: Looking back at the children of the Great Depression*. New York: Free Press.

Crystal, S., & Waehrer, K. (1996). Late life economic inequality in longitudinal perspective. *Journal of Gerontology, Social Sciences, 51B*, S307–S318.

Dannefer, D. (1987). Aging as intracohort differentiation: Accentuation, the Matthew Effect, and the life course. *Sociological Forum, 2*, 211–236.

Dannefer, D. (1988). Differential aging and the stratified life course: Conceptual and methodological issues. In G. L. Maddox & M. P. Lawton (Eds.), *Annual Review of Gerontology, 8* (pp. 3–36). New York: Springer Publishing Co.

Dannefer, D. (1993). When does society matter for individual differences? Implications of a counterpart paradox. *Psychological Inquiry, 4*, 281–284.

Dannefer, D. (1999). Freedom isn't free: Power, alienation and the consequences of action. In J. Brandstadter & R. M. Lerner (Eds.), *Action and self-development: Theory and research through the life span*. Thousand Oaks, CA: Sage.

Dannefer, D. (2000). Paradox of opportunity: Education, work and age integration in the United States and Germany. *The Gerontologist, 40*, 282–286.

Dannefer, D. (2002). Whose life course is it, anyway? In R. Settersten (Ed.), *Invitation to the life course*. Amityville, NY: Baywood.

Dannefer, D., & Uhlenberg, P. (1999). Paths of the life course: A typology. In V. L. Bengtson & K. W. Schaie (Eds.), *Handbook of theories of aging: In honor of Jim Birren*. New York: Springer.

Elder, G. H., Jr. (1974). *Children of the Great Depression: Social change in life experience*. Chicago: University of Chicago Press.

Elder, G. H., Jr. (1975). Age differentiation and the life course. *Annual review of sociology, 1*, 165–190. Palo Alto, CA: Annual Reviews.

Elder, G. H. Jr. (1998). The life course and human development. In R. M. Lerner (Ed.), *Handbook of child psychology, Vol 1. Theoretical models for human development*. (pp. 939–991). New York: John Wiley & Sons.

Elder, G. H., Jr., & Liker, J. (1982). Hard times in women's lives: Historical differences across 40 years. *American Journal of Sociology, 58*, 241–269.

Ellwood, W., & Crump, A. (Eds.) (1999). *A to Z of world development*. Oxford: Oxfam Publishing.

Esping-Anderson, G. (1997). Welfare states at the end of the century: The impact of labour market, family and demographic change. In Hennesy & M. Peersen (Eds.), *Family, market and community: Equity and efficiency in social policy*. Paris: OECD, Social Policy Studies no. 21.

Estes, C. L. (1979). *The aging enterprise*. San Francisco: Jossey-Bass.

Foner, N. (1993). When the contract fails: Care for the elderly in nonindustrial cultures. In V. L. Bengtson & W. A. Achenbaum (Eds.), *The changing contract across generations*. New York: Aldine De Gruyter.

Fry, C. L. (1992) Changing age structures and the mediating effects of culture. In W. J. A. van den Hevel, R. Illsley, A. Jamiesen, & C. P. M. Knipscheer (Eds.), *Opportunities and challenges in an aging society*. Amsterdam: Royal Academy of Sciences.

Furlong, A., & Cartmel, F. (1997). *Young people and social change: Individualization and risk in late modernity.* Buckingham, UK: Open University Press. California Press.

Giddens, A. (1991). *Modernity and self-identity,* Palo Alto, CA: Stanford University Press.

Giddens, A. (1994). Living in a post-traditional society. In U. Beck, S. Lash, & A. Giddens (Eds.), *Reflexive modernization* (pp. 56–109). Palo Alto, CA: Stanford University Press.

Giele, J. Z., & Elder, G. H., Jr. (1998). *Methods of life course research: Qualitative and quantitative approaches.* Thousand Oaks, CA: Sage.

Hagestad, G. O. (1998). Towards a society for all ages: New thinking, new language, new conversations. *Bulletin on Aging, 2/3,* 7–13.

Hagestad, G. O., & Dannefer, D. (2001). Concepts and theories of aging: Beyond microfication in social science approaches. In R. Binstock & L. George (Eds.), *Handbook of aging and the social sciences* (2nd edn). New York: Academic.

Hagestad, G. O., & Neugarten, B. (1985). Age and the life course. In E. Shanas & R. Binstock (Eds.), *Handbook of aging and the social sciences* (2nd edn). New York: Van Nostrand Reinhold.

Harvey, D. (1989). *The condition of postmodernity.* Malden, MA: Blackwell.

Henretta, J. C. (1992). Uniformity and diversity: Life course institutionalization and late-life work exit. *The Sociological Quarterly, 33,* 265–279.

Henretta, J. C. (2001). Work and retirement. In R. Binstock & L. George (Eds.), *Handbook of aging and the social sciences* (2nd edn). New York: Academic.

Hogan, D. (1981). *Transitions and social change: The early lives of American men.* New York: Academic.

International Labor Organization. (1999). *Child labor: Targeting the intolerable.* International Labour Conference, 86th Session, 1998. Report VI, Part 1.

Kett, J. (1977). *Rites of passage: Adolescence in America, 1790–1920.* New York: Basic.

Kohli, M. (1999.) Private and public transfers between generations: Linking the family and the state. *European Societies, 1,* 81–104.

Kohli, M., & Rein, M. (1991). The changing balance of work and retirement. In M. Kohli, M. Rein, A.-M. Guillemard, & H. van Gunsteren (Eds.), *Time for Retirement.* New York: Cambridge.

Kohli, M., & Meyer, J. W. (1986). Social structure and the social construction of life stages. *Human Development, 29,* 145–149.

Kotlowitz, A. (1992). *There are no children here.* New York: Anchor.

Lemoine, M. (1985). *Bitter sugar: Slaves today in the Caribbean.* Chicago: Banner.

Mayer, K. U., & Muller, W. (1986). The state and the structure of the life course. In A. B. Sorensen, F. E. Weinert, & L. R. Sherrod (Eds.), *Human development and the life course: Multidisciplinary perspectives.* Hillsdale, NJ: Lawrence Erlbaum.

Meyer, J. W. (1986). The Self and the Life Course: Institutionalization and its Effects. In A. B. Sorensen, F. E. Weinert, & L. R. Sherrod (Eds.), *Human development and the life course: Multidisciplinary perspectives.* (pp. 209–221). Hillsdale, NJ: Laurence Erlbaum.

McDevitt, T. M., Adlakha, A., Fowler, T. B., & Harris-Bourne, V. (1996). *Trends in adolescent fertility and contraceptive use in the developing world,* IPC/95-1. Washington, DC: U.S. Bureau of the Census.

Micklethwait, J., & Wooldridge, A. (2000). *A future perfect: The challenge and hidden promise of globalization.* New York: Random House.

Modell, J., Furstenberg, F., & Strong, D. (1978). The timing of marriage in the transition to adulthood: Continuity and change. *American Journal of Sociology, 84,* 120–150.

Morss, J. (1996). *Growing critical: Alternatives to developmental psychology.* New York: Routledge.

Myles, J. (1989). *Old age in the welfare state.* Lawrence: University Press of Kansas.

O'Rand, A. M. (1996). The precious and the precocious: Understanding cumulative disadvantage and cumulative advantage over the life course. *The Gerontologist, 36,* 230–238.

O'Rand, A. M., & Henretta, J. C. (1999). *Age and inequality: Diverse pathways through later life.* Boulder, CO: Westview Press.

Phillipson, C., Bernard, M., Phillips, J., & Ogg, J. (2001). *The family and community life of older people: Social support and social networks in three urban areas.* London: Routledge.

Postman, N. (1994). *The disappearance of childhood.* New York: Vintage.

Preston, S. (1984). Children and the elderly in the U.S. *Scientific American, 251,* 44–49.

Reddy, Y. R. H. (1995). *Bonded labour sytem in India.* New Delhi: Deep & Deep.

Riley, M. W., & Foner, A. (2001). Sociology of age. In N. Smelser & P. B. Baltes (Eds.), *International encyclopedia of behavioral and social sciences,* Vol. 1 (pp. 275–278). London: Elsevier.

Riley, M. W., Johnson, M. E., & Foner, A. (1972). *Aging and society, Vol. III: A sociology of age stratification.* New York: Russell Sage.

Riley M. W., Kahn, R., & Foner, A. (1994). *Age and structural lag: Society's failure to provide meaningful opportunities in work, family and leisure*. New York: Wiley-Interscience.

Riley, M. W., Riley, J., & Foner, A. (1999). The aging and society paradigm. In V. L. Bengtson & K. W. Schaie (Eds.), *Handbook of theories of aging: In honor of Jim Birren*. New York: Springer.

Sarason, S. B. (1977). *Work, aging and social change: Professionals and the one life—one career imperative*. New York: Free Press.

Seabrook, J. (1996). *In the cities of the South: Scenes from a developing world*. London: Verso Press.

Seabrook, J. (2000). *No hiding place: Child sex tourism and the role of extraterritorial legislation*. Amsterdam: ECPAT Europe Law Enforcement Group.

Shanahan, M. J. (2000). Pathways to adulthood in changing societies: Variability and mechanisms in life course perspective. *Annual review of sociology, 26*, 667–692. Palo Alto, CA: Annual Reviews.

Shanahan, M. J., Elder, G. H., Jr., & Miech, R. A. (1997) History and Agency in Men's Lives: Pathways to Achievement in Cohort Perspective. *Sociology of Education, 70*(1), 54–67.

Shanahan, M. J., Sulloway, F. J., & Hofer, S. M. (2000). Change and constancy in developmental contexts. *International Journal of Behavioral Development, 24*, 421–427.

Smith, H. L., Morgan, S. P., & Koropeckyj-Cox, T. (1996). A Decomposition of trends in the nonmarital fertility ratios of blacks and whites in the United States, 1960–1992. *Demography*.

Soros, G. (2001). *On globalization*. New York: Public Affairs/Perseus.

Stiglitz, J. E. (2002). *Globalization and its discontents*. New York: Norton.

Taylor, T. (2002). The truth about globalization. *The public interest, 147*(Spring), 21–25.

Thomas, W. I., & Znaniecki, F. (1918). *The Polish peasant in Europe and America*. Chicago: University of Chicago Press.

Uhlenberg, P. (1978). Changing configurations of the life course. In T. K. Hareven (Ed.), *Transitions: The family and the life course in historical perspective* (pp. 65–87). New York: Academic.

United States Congress. (1994a.) *By the sweat and toil of children: A report to the Committees on Appropriations, Volume I: The use of child labor in American imports*. Washington, D.C: The Bureau.

United States Congress. (1994b.) *By the sweat and toil of children: A report to the Committees on Appropriations, Volume II: The use of child labor in U.S. agricultural imports and forced and bonded child labor*. Washington, DC: The Bureau.

Weiner, M. (1991). *The child and the state in India—child labor and education policy in comparative perspective*. Princeton: Princeton University Press.

Winn, M. (1984). *Children without childhood: Growing up too fast in a world of sex and Drugs*. New York: Viking Penguin.

Woodward, A., & Kohli, M. (2001). European societies: Inclusions/exclusions? In A. Woodward & M. Kohli (Eds.), *Inclusions and exclusions in European societies*. (pp. 1–17). London: Routledge.

CHAPTER 30

Reflections on the Future of the Life Course

Frank Furstenberg

The notion that the life course is both biologically based and also socially and culturally constructed can be traced back to a number of theoretical traditions in sociology and psychology in the early part of the last century (Mannheim, 1944; Thomas, 1937), while efforts to develop a theory of the life course began several decades later with the writings of C. Wright Mills (1959), Norman Ryder (1965), and Riley, Johnson, and Foner (1972) in sociology and Bernice Neugarten (1968) in psychology. These ideas were promoted and advanced by a variety of researchers in the 1970s and 1980s among them Glen Elder (1974, 1975), Tamara Hareven (1978), Modell, Furstenberg, and Hershberg (1976; 1989), Karl Ulrich Mayer (1991), Hagestad and Neugarten (1985), Walter Heinz (1996), and many others. With new methods and longitudinal data sets, life course research came of age in the last several decades and is now an established theoretical perspective in sociology and developmental psychology as is attested to in this volume.

The aim of this chapter is to speculate about the future of the life course and at the same time imagine what new developments might emerge in life course theory and research. This is a tall order in part because these two objectives are not inevitably linked together. I will begin with the first task of thinking about future trends in the social organization of the life course, which will lead me to make some observations about needed advances in theory and research.

FRANK FURSTENBERG • Department of Sociology, University of Pennsylvania, Philadelphia, Pennsylvania 19104-6299

Handbook of the Life Course, edited by Jeylan T. Mortimer and Michael J. Shanahan. Kluwer Academic/Plenum Publishers, New York, 2003.

CONSIDERING THE PAST, APPROACHING
THE FUTURE

This volume is not the place to review how the life course has changed or how the social and cultural construction of its form has been altered by economics, demography, history, and technology. Others have addressed these large issues in this volume and elsewhere in other publications (Buchmann, 1989; Heinz, 1996; Settersten, 1999; Weyman, 1996). It is probably sufficient to say that theories of the life course generally assume that cultures construct the life course differently, and that these cultural conceptions are in turn affected by historical, economic, and institutional forces. These dynamic models of ideal life course scenarios affect the distribution of actual life course patterns in ways that regulate, at least to some degree, the pace and process of human development in any given society. But it is also the case that contingencies created by historical circumstances, economic realities, and social constraints mean that individuals, separately and collectively, depart from accepted timetables, which ultimately alter cultural conceptions.

This rather abstract preamble cries out for an illustration. Consider the ways that childhood—a stage of life itself—that has not always been highly differentiated is being changed in developing societies as economic demands make the work of children less valuable and require increased educational investment in human capital (Coleman, 1988; Zelizer, 1985). Or in advanced societies, youth as a stage of life is being elongated and elaborated for much the same reasons: young people cannot become highly committed to work until they complete their education and training, which increasingly extends well into their third decade of life (Arnett, 2000; Brown, Larson, & Saraswathi, 2000; Furstenberg, 2000, 2002; Larson, 2002). Thus, life course scripts, as C. Wright Mills (1959) recognized many years ago, are a lens for observing the intersection of personal biography and history. And, Mills shrewdly observed that individual difficulty in conforming to social expectations relating to marriage, work, and parenthood often represent unresolved cultural contradictions; contradictions resulting from the clash between norms about the life course and the exigencies of everyday life that prevent people from behaving as they think that they should or even as they might desire. We see this today in America in many inner-city neighborhoods where men and women would like to marry but do not have the cultural and economic resources to manage matrimony (Edin, 2000; Furstenberg, 2001; Waller, 2002; Wilson, 1996).

To imagine a future life course involves, then, thinking both about how expectations might change—resulting in new social expectations about life scripts—and also foreseeing how constraints on behavior might create widespread violations of current norms that would shift cultural models of how lives ought to be organized. Quite an impossible task, but that is the nature of most futurological writings. I have approached this particular exercise in futurology by imagining how the life course might change along lines of four of the main pillars of sociological analysis: gender; race and ethnicity; social class; and age.

GENDER DIFFERENCES IN THE
LIFE COURSE

Mounting evidence suggests that gender differences in the organization of the life course have been diminishing for the past several decades in most Western nations (Bianchi & Spain, 1986; Mason & Jensen, 1995). Schooling, home leaving, independent living, marriage timing, and the age at first birth appear to be converging across gender in ways that make men and women's life courses more similar than they were at the beginning or the middle of the last century (Fussell & Furstenberg, 2002). At the same time, women's lower economic standing, due in part to their higher probability of living outside of marriage and their greater longevity, persists and may be widening. Will these sources of difference override the general pattern of convergence that we are seeing in the population at large?

The answer, I suspect, is that we may see two simultaneous trends regarding gender in the next several decades. Overall, gender differences may continue to decline in the United States in the timing of transitions, but we may also see that the divergence will continue to occur in particular subgroups. Here is how it could work: Among children of privilege and those in the middle-class, gender differences could diminish in the structuring of the life course. Girls and boys, men and women will operate on a more equal footing in the opportunities for health, schooling, work, and family life they are afforded. This is not to say that gender disparities will disappear, but they will follow the trend of the late 20th century and diminish over time.

To be specific, we might expect to see that girls will converge with boys in school achievement during high school and college; the two sexes will gain greater parity in the workplace, and age differentials in marriage and the timing of first birth will continue to decline within the top third or perhaps even the top half of the population. Women with means may opt out of the labor force during part of their childbearing years, but they will make up the time lost by a later age of retirement than men.

These general trends toward greater parity between men and women may be more complex when we examine the situation of lower-income Americans, especially disadvantaged minorities. Relative to boys, girls are gaining ground faster in education—or boys may actually be losing ground while girls are holding their own in school achievement, employment, and earnings. Among African-Americans and Puerto Ricans, the situation of low-income men has been steadily deteriorating while there is some evidence that women are holding their own (Hauser, Brown, & Prosser 1997; Mare, 1995). As a consequence, men and women are finding it more difficult to form lasting partnerships. Power relationships between men and women, always a delicate issue at the bottom of the social order, have been complicated by the relative decline in economic and perhaps social status of men. I do not foresee this trend abating in the near future unless less-educated and low-income men adopt middle-class ideals about gender equality. The problems of the declining fortunes of lower-income males undermine the family formation patterns at the bottom of the social structure, fostering high rates of non-marital childbearing and family instability (Cherlin, 1992). Tensions between men and women, that I have elsewhere referred to as the "culture of gender distrust," will persist unless we devise programs to incorporate less advantaged males more successfully in schools and the labor market (Furstenberg, 1995; 2001).

ETHNICITY AND RACE

The huge increase in ethnic diversity resulting from immigration and higher rates of fertility among native born African-Americans and second-generation immigrants in the latter decades of the last century will surely continue into this century though the pace of diversification may slow down as immigration is more tightly controlled. Nonetheless, America has reclaimed its heritage as a nation of immigrants: several states now have or are approaching levels at which a majority of children are born to first- or second-generation immigrants or native-born minorities (Portes & Rumbaut, 2001). If the composition of these newer cohorts is changing, can we expect to see more variation in the life course than was the case in the past century?

If historical precedence holds true, it is more likely that immigrants will quickly become "Americanized," that is adopt the prevailing patterns of the dominant population. Certainly, there is some evidence that over time second and third generations of many ethnic groups become more and more like those whose families have been living in the United States for many generations (Harris, 1999). This does not mean that variation will not be evident among ethnic and racial groups but rather that it will gradually diminish with acculturation to American institutions. This has certainly been the case in educational attainment, the timing of marriage and parenthood, fertility levels, and the like. Even if this is generally the case, we might expect to see certain groups lose their ethnic distinctiveness sooner than others, depending on such conditions as access to opportunity and discrimination as well as the strength of ethnic cultures.

I am prepared to make a bold prediction, perhaps even reckless by historical standards: racial barriers, an ugly hallmark of American society, will gradually disappear during the course of this century. Blacks, long held back by explicit discrimination, have been relegated to a lower-caste position in the United States along with Native Americans. Both legal changes in the second-half of the 20th century and greater access to educational opportunities are gradually eroding the longstanding pattern of racism.

Racial segregation in marriage, schooling, employment, and labor market patterns, and housing all contributed to the maintenance of a sharp dichotomy between black and white Americans (Farley, 1995; Massey & Denton, 1993). I foresee changes occurring in each of these areas, albeit at a different pace. Inter-marriage has been rising and is likely to continue to do so, and, confounding the racial classification of families, white parents are adopting a greater number of black children. Segregated schooling and housing continue to undermine opportunities for Blacks, but the tipping points establishing white flight in schools or neighborhoods that set off hyper-segregation may be not quite as low as in the past. In any case, Americans may be becoming more tolerant of inter-racial proximity in part because shades of color are becoming more prominent.

If this scenario sounds overly optimistic, I should add that I do not expect the changes to occur in dramatic fashion but foresee instead a gradual erosion of racism much as what took place among the Irish or Jews, groups once considered separate racial categories. The conversion of racial distinctions to ethnic differences would represent an enormous contribution to what William J. Wilson (1996) once referred to as the "declining significance of race." In part, Wilson expected that racial barriers would increasingly become class differences in much the same way that I described the complex interactions between gender and social class above.

We know relatively little about the varying life course patterns of foreign and native-born Americans today. As I will note in the next section, this is a topic ripe for future research. In any case, we can be quite confident that interest will grow in the next decades. Certainly, scholars are not going to be satisfied to work with simple classifications of White, Black, and Hispanic. Already, we can see that self-definitions are more complex than publicly imposed classifications in vital records or census data (Zuberi, 2001).

SOCIAL CLASS

Countless studies have shown that the most powerful determinant of life course patterns is not gender or race/ethnicity but social class (Farley, 1995). Interestingly, however, social class is a less salient topic in social science research than it was a half century ago even though there is strong evidence that inequality has grown. Americans understand that wealth or the lack of it affects opportunities, but rich and poor believe that they are in the middle class, and, with some notable exceptions, class differences are almost regarded as distinctions that are politically incorrect. We speak of inequality but not class position as if economic differences were a continuous variable. In fact, the literature accumulated a generation ago, suggests rather sharp and qualitative differences across the social spectrum owing to the strong inter-correlation of education, employment, income, and life style. As I have argued elsewhere, class position permeates the life course from birth to death (Furstenberg, 2001). Since its effect generally accumulates over time, it is strongly implicated in health, education and employment, leisure, and, especially, family life.

Contrary to my prediction that the significance of gender, race, and ethnicity will diminish in decades to come, current evidence suggests that class differences that are now relatively invisible may become more prominent in structuring the life course in the 21st century—unless, of course, policies to counteract this trend are put in place. Since the 1970s, inequality in American society has been growing. The economic stagnation of the 1970s and 1980s affected the bottom two-thirds adversely, especially those with low education and skills. The college educated saw increases in income while the rest of the population barely held their own or declined (Levy, 1988). In the 1990s, the more disadvantaged part of the population experienced real gains in the booming economy, but so did the very wealthy (Mishel, Bernstein, & Schmitt, 2001). The economic disparity between the top and the bottom quintiles is huge and is likely to grow in the first decade of the 21st century.

The unequal flow of economic resources in returns to education and skills is not offset by redistribution policies as occur in most other Western nations. In practical terms, this means that the State does very little to counterbalance the effects of the market economy on individuals and families. If families cannot afford pre-school programs, health insurance, after-school activities, tutoring, counseling, and other amenities purchased by affluent families, then children must suffer the consequences. In addition, families with means can provide more cultural capital—knowledge about how the system works, interpersonal skills, and symbolic resources that foster social mobility—and social capital in the form of connections, sponsorship, and normative support. The boundaries of social class may actually be tightening as children may be growing up in more class-segregated communities and schools now than a generation or two ago.

In fact, this hypothesis of the impact of growing inequality on social class distinctions has not been subjected to empirical examination. But if it is true, we might expect to discover large class differences in both expectations and behavior in the social timetables of growing up and growing older. Also, we might anticipate much less predictable or orderly careers in the negotiation of age-graded transitions such as schooling and entrance to the labor force, marriage and childbearing, and retirement. I would expect to see greater variability in life course patterns and transitions among children and youth in the bottom two-thirds of the population than among the affluent. A recent paper by Ellwood and Jencks (2001) on patterns of marriage and family formation shows that the declines in marriage, marital stability, and non-marital childbearing almost exclusively occur among the less educated two-thirds of the population. These findings provide some support for my predictions, but this area of class-related change is ripe for more research.

As we suggested above, social class crosscuts distinctions in gender, race, and ethnicity. The largest differences in life course patterns are likely to occur in marginalized groups that also lack economic resources. Consequently, we are likely to see the greatest variability among African-American or Puerto-Rican lower-class males and the least among non-Hispanic White males and females (Kmec and Furstenberg, in press). In other words, sociological analysis of life-course patterns by social class must also take account of how class intersects with gender, race and ethnicity.

AGE

As Matilda Riley and her colleagues (1972) were among the first to theorize, age is a source of stratification in every society. Age groups benefit or lose out in the distribution of resources because of political and cultural attitudes (resulting in public policy), historical circumstances, and demographic conditions that affect growth and attrition. Over the past half century, we have seen vast changes take place in the economic position of the elderly resulting from changes in social security, voting patterns, educational attainment, and increases in life expectancy because of health care and medical technology. At the same time, fertility has sharply declined, reducing the number of families with children and the time that adults spend in households with children. At a macro-level, the burden placed on the relatively small number of working adults has been growing as benefits to the elderly have increased along with the proportion of their share in the population (Preston, 1984). Children and young adults have probably lost out in the competition for economic resources. This competition for resources is most acute in Western European nations with very low rates of fertility (Sgritta, 1994). But all nations with a high proportion of elderly are likely to face a dilemma in how to share public expenditures between dependent children and dependent elderly.

The generational competition for resources has consequences for the timing of life course transitions because children are making greater demands on their parents for support as the age of attaining economic independence is becoming later in all societies with advanced economies (Furstenberg, 2002). The growing burden on parents may be a factor in declining fertility as parents do not wish to take on the private costs of childbearing for more than one or two children (if any at all). And, as indicated above, fertility declines further reduce the public's willingness to share the costs of childbearing (Fussell, 2002). This pattern is likely to be most evident in societies, like the United States and Italy, that spend relatively little public funds on children and which expect parents to assume the major share. If I am correct, the relatively high rate of fertility in the United States because of the contribution of immigrants and low-income families may not continue indefinitely. Our relatively early age of marriage and childbearing has contributed to the high level of fertility. As marriage drops off and non-marital childbearing becomes more costly for mothers and fathers, we may expect to see a declining rate of non-marital childbearing. (This does not mean that the ratio of non-marital to marital fertility will also drop; it will only do so if non-marital births decline faster than marital births.)

The response of many parents will be to devote a greater share of their resources to a lower number of children because children have become of more symbolic and emotional than material value to their parents. Parents with high levels of education are becoming ever more discriminating in their parental strategies aimed at producing "thoroughbred" offspring. The tendency in the United States to regard parenting responsibilities as sacred is likely to increase as parents attempt to build human, cultural, and social capital both inside and outside the family. Parents are likely to delay childbearing until they have more means to consume on children; and, when they have children, they will spend more and more on them in response to what they perceive to be other parents' consumption patterns. Thus, children are becoming the ultimate consumer good, contributing to greater inequality as wealthy parents have much more to spend than those with limited means. Moreover, wealthy parents have been more successful at controlling family size than poorer parents. A smaller number of children are, as a consequence, receiving a high proportion of the total dollars spent on children. Time-use studies suggest that these same children are probably receiving a greater share of time as well as money (Bianchi, 2000). This suggests that the difference in the skills of well-off children as compared to poor children might grow over time.

One correlate of this prediction is that the age of economic dependency of children may lengthen because children require more investment in their third decade of life owing to the extension of education. The period of youth or semi-autonomy, common in the 19th century, is reappearing as the transition to adulthood spans the 20s and even early 30s (Furstenberg, 2001).

At the other end of life, greater longevity may result in far more differentiation of what is currently "old age." Pressures to support children in early adulthood may keep some parents in the labor force longer. The early ages of retirement, now common in Western European countries, may give way to greater demands on younger seniors to remain in the labor market if pensions decline and responsibilities to children continue. In any case, the increasing health differentials between individuals in their late 60s and early 70s and those in the late 80s and early 90s are likely to lead to distinctions among the elderly. Just as we invented terms like adolescents or the teen years, so too could I imagine that we will devise terms to distinguish the young, middle, and older seniors (see Moen, *this volume*). Is it far-fetched to believe that cohort solidarity might develop among these sub-groups of elderly based on shared experiences in the past or life-style patterns in the present?

NEW METHODS IN THE STUDY OF THE LIFE COURSE

The stock of empirical knowledge about the life course grew tremendously in the second half of the 20th century, providing a goldmine of information for social historians accustomed to fragmentary materials and demographic data. Social surveys, longitudinal studies, and quali-tative accounts of growing up will provide a rich archive of data for future historians and social scientists with an historical bent. One of the likely advances now being pioneered in both historical and contemporary research is record linkage across data sets, using census and survey information with public records such as vital statistics or employment data. As more data are computerized and software in record linkage advances, the possibilities will grow for combining data sets and sources to build longitudinal records or augment longitudinal stud-ies with public record information. The problems of doing so are likely to result not from technological but ethical concerns.

Similarly, there is a strong movement for linking qualitative and quantitative data. Once a choice in data collection approaches, more and more researchers are being trained, so to speak, to work with both hands. I see this pattern continuing with the greatest methodologi-cal breakthroughs coming when researchers can crosswalk between intensive qualitative interviews and survey data that contains information on parallel issues. As yet, we have not invented ways of analyzing these sources of data using similar techniques. I am confident that breakthroughs will occur in the next couple of decades that will allow researchers to over-come this methodological obstacle. If I am correct, we will certainly see more attention to the ways that objective changes in life circumstances or anticipated and unanticipated transitions or turning points may alter subjective states and personal identities. The possibilities of exam-ining developmental changes in parallel with sociological and demographic shifts in situation and context will be much enhanced if we are able to capitalize on the strengths of qualitative and quantitative data in the same study.

It is remarkable how little cross-national research currently exists on the life course con-sidering the widespread interest in this perspective across the developed and developing world (Larson, 2002; Raffaelli & Larson, 1999). Economic and technological forces producing more global communication and commerce have not yet resulted in many truly collaborative cross-national studies on the life course. There is a growing tendency to replicate similar study instruments in different countries, but truly comparative data collection designs are rare. This will surely come, but real advances require international institutes of research with international funding. Collaboration across government offices often results in parallel studies that do not produce truly comparative research.

On the horizon are new technologies for studying life course events. The advent of the web, cell phones, and beepers has produced clever small-scale studies that do not always require traditional modes of data collection. However, these methods are potentially as intrusive as interviews even if they sometimes bypass some of the limitations of data collected through interview techniques. No doubt, researchers will devise means of gathering data with technologies that are more playful or, at least, less burdensome or evocative of self-consciousness. The rapidly developing surveillance industry is likely to produce new and, no doubt, controversial techniques for collecting unobtrusive information on individuals and families.

Bio-medical and biological developments will also offer new modes of inquiry for life course researchers. Formidable ethical problems must be overcome to make full use of potential genetic and hormonal determinants and consequences of life course patterns or intergenerational links. Yet, social scientists, sociologists in particular, who have long resisted studying the biological bases of social systems may be beginning to appreciate that nature versus nurture is no longer a tenable formulation. It would be surprising not to see advances in understanding how biology is implicated in the unfolding of life course patterns.

CONCLUSION

In the early 1980s, my colleague Andrew Cherlin and I published a paper entitled "The American Family in the Year 2000" (Cherlin & Furstenberg, 1983). Looking back on this exercise, some of our speculations turned out to be correct and very few were really wrong. What was dismaying, however, is how much we missed altogether because of our limited ability to foresee important changes like technological developments that allowed for novel developments in work and family. We were far better at predicting the continuities than the discontinuities in demographic trends. In other words, we could extrapolate reasonably well based on current trends, but we had little success in making creative leaps that involved the possibility of the unexpected.

There is no reason to believe that I have been any more adept in this chapter at imagining changes in the life course much beyond what is already visible on the horizon. What I am most confident of is that a half century from now—long after this book is being read by more than a few curiosity seekers—scholars will still be considering the forces that structure and organize the life course, and trying to speculate about changes that are likely to occur in the coming decades.

REFERENCES

Arnett, James. (2000). Emerging adulthood: A theory of development from the late teens through the twenties. *American Psychologist, 55*, 469–480.

Bianchi, Suzanne M. (2000). Maternal employment and time with children: Dramatic change or surprising continuity? *Demography, 374*(4), 401–414.

Bianchi, Suzanne M., & Spain, Daphne. (1986). *American women in transition.* New York: Russell Sage Foundation.

Brown, B. Bradford, Larson, Reed, & Saraswathi, T. S. (2002). *The world's youth: Adolescence in eight regions of the globe.* New York: Cambridge University Press.

Buchmann, Marlis. (1989). *The script of life in modern society.* Chicago: University of Chicago Press.

Cherlin, Andrew J. (1992). *Marriage, divorce, remarriage.* (Rev. and enlarged ed.) Cambridge, Mass.: Harvard University Press.

Cherlin, Andrew J. & Furstenberg, Frank F. (1983). The American family in the year 2000. *The Futurist* June, 237–241.

Coleman, James. (1988). Social capital in the creation of human capital. *American Journal of Sociology, 94* (Suppl. 95), S95–S120.

Edin, Kathryn. (2000). What do low-income single mothers say about marriage? *Social Problems, 47*(1), 112–133.

Elder, Glen H., Jr. (1974). *Children of the great depression.* Chicago: University of Chicago Press.

Elder, Glen H., Jr. (1975). Age differentiation and the life course. *Annual Review of Sociology, 1,* 165–190.

Elwood, David T., & Jencks, Christopher. (2001). *The growing differences in family structure: What do we know? Where do we look for answers?* Paper prepared for The New Inequality Program supported by the Russell Sage Foundation.

Farley, Reynolds. (Ed) (1995). *State of the Union: America in the 1990s. Volume one: Economic trends.* New York: Russell Sage Foundation.

Furstenberg, Frank F. (Ed.) (2002). Early adulthood in cross-national perspectives. *The Annals, 580.*

Furstenberg, Frank F. (2001). The fading dream: Prospects for marriage in the inner city. In Elijah Anderson and Douglas S. Massey (Eds.), *Problem of the century: Racial stratification in the United States.* (pp. 224–246). New York: Russell Sage Foundation.

Furstenberg, Frank F. (2000). The sociology of adolescence and youth in the 1990s. *Journal of Marriage and the Family, 62*(4), 896–910.

Furstenberg, Frank F. (1995). Fathering in the inner city: Paternal participation and public policy. In William Marsiglio (Ed.), *Fatherhood: Contemporary theory, research, and social policy* (pp. 119–147). Thousand Oaks, CA: Sage.

Fussell, Elizabeth. (2002). The transition to adulthood in aging societies. *The Annals 580,* 16–39.

Fussell, Elizabeth & Furstenberg, Frank F. (2002). Race, nativity, and gender differences in the timing of transition to adulthood during the 20th century. In Frank F. Furstenberg, Ruben G. Rumbaut, & Richard A. Settersten, Jr. (Eds.), *On the frontier of adulthood: Theory, research, and public policy.*

Hagestad, Gunhild and Bernice Neugarten. (1985). Age and the life course. In E. Shanas & R. Binstock (Eds.), *Handbook of aging and the social sciences,* 2nd ed. (pp. 36–61). New York: Von Nostrand and Reinold.

Hareven, Tamara K. (Ed.) (1978). *Transitions: The family and life course in historical perspective.* New York: Academic Press.

Harris, Kathleen Mullan. (1999). The health status and risk behaviors of adolescents in Immigrant families. In Donald J. Hernandez (Ed.), *Children of immigrants: Health, adjustment, and public assistance.* Washington, DC: National Academy of Sciences Press.

Hauser, Robert M., Brett V. Brown, & William R. Prosser. (Eds.) (1997). *Indicators of children's well-being.* New York: Russell Sage Foundation.

Heinz, Walter R. (1996). Status passages as micro-macro linkages in life course research. In Ansgar Weymann & Walter R. Heinz (Eds.), *Society and biography: Inter-relationships between social structure, institutions, and the life course.* (pp. 51–65). Weinheim: Deutscher Studien Verlag.

Kmec, Julie, and Frank F. Furstenberg. (in press). Racial and gender differences in the transition to adulthood: A follow-up study of the Philadelphia youth. In Richard Settersten & T. J. Owens (Eds.), *New perspectives in the life course, vol. 7: Socialization.* United Kingdom: Elsevier.

Larson, Reed. (2002). Globalization, societal change, and new technologies: What they mean for the future of adolescence. *Journal of Research on Adolescence, 12*(1), 1–30.

Levy, Frank. (1988). *Dollars and dreams: The changing American income distribution.* New York: Norton.

Mannheim, Karl. (1944). *Man and society in an age of reconstruction: Studies in modern social structure.* New York: Harcourt, Brace.

Mare, Robert D. (1995). Changes in educational attainment and school enrollment. In Reynolds Farley (Ed.), *State of the Union: America in the 1990s.* (pp. 155–213). New York: Russell Sage Foundation.

Mason, Karen Oppenheim, and An-Magritt Jensen. (1995). *Gender and family change in industrialized countries.* Oxford: Clarendon Press.

Massey, Douglas S. and Nancy A. Denton. (1993). *American apartheid: Segregation and the making of the underclass.* Cambridge, MA: Harvard University Press.

Mayer, Karl Ulrich. (1991). Life courses in the welfare state. In Walter R. Heinz (Ed.), *Theoretical advances in life course research.* (pp. 171–186). Weinheim: Deutscher Studien Verlag.

Mills, C. Wright. (1959). *The sociological imagination.* New York: Oxford University Press.

Mishel, Lawrence, Jared Bernstien, and John Schmitt. (2001). *The state of working America, 2000–2001.* Ithaca: Cornell University Press.

Modell, John. (1989). *Into one's own: From youth to adulthood in the United States, 1920–1975.* Berkeley: University of California Press.

Modell, John, Frank F. Furstenberg, and Theodore Hershberg. (1976). Social change and transition to adulthood in historical perspective. *Journal of Family History, 1*(1), 7–32.

Neugarten, Bernice. (1968). *Middle age and aging: A reader in social psychology.* Chicago: University of Chicago Press.

Portes, Alejandro and Ruben G. Rumbaut. (2001). *Legacies: The story of the immigrant second generation.* New York: Russell Sage Foundation.

Preston, Samuel. (1984). Children and the elderly: Divergent paths for America's dependents. *Demography, 21*(4), 435–457.

Raffaelli, Marcela and Reed Larson. (1999). *Homeless and working youth around the world: Exploring developmental issues.* San Francisco: Jossey-Bass.

Riley, Matilda, Marilyn Johnson, & Anne Foner. (1972). *Aging and society: A sociology of age stratification* (Vol. 3). New York: Russell Sage Foundation.

Ryder, Norman. (1965). The cohort as a concept in the study of social change. *American Sociological Review, 30,* 843–861.

Settersten, Richard. A., Jr. (1999). *Lives in time and place: The problems and promises of developmental science.* Amityville, NY: Baywood.

Sgritta, Giovanni B. (1994). The generational division of welfare: Equity and conflict. In J. Qvortrup et al. (Eds.), *Childhood matters: Social theory, practice and politics.* (pp. 335–362). Aldershot: Avebury.

Thomas, William Isaac. (1937). *Primitive behavior, an introduction to the social sciences.* New York: McGraw-Hill Book.

Waller, Maureen. (2002). *My baby's father: Unmarried parents and paternal responsibility.* Ithaca, NY: Cornell University Press.

Weymann, Ansgar. (1996). Interrelating society and biography: Discourse, markets and the welfare state's life course policy. In Ansgar Weymann & Walter R. Heinz (Eds.), *Society and biography: Interrelationships between social structure, institutions, and the life course.* (pp. 241–258). Weinheim: Deutscher Studien Verlag.

Wilson, William J. (1996). *When work disappears: The world of the new urban poor.* New York: Knopf.

Zelizer, Viviana. (1985). *Pricing the priceless child: The changing social value of children.* New York: Basic Books.

Zuberi, Tukufu. (2001). *Thicker than blood: How racial statistics lie.* Minneapolis: University of Minnesota Press.

CHAPTER 31

Life Course Research

Achievements and Potential

LINDA K. GEORGE

Recognizable life course research emerged in the social and behavioral sciences in the first half of the 20th century, although it was uncommon (Buhler, 1935; Thomas & Znaniecki, 1927). It is only since the mid-1970s, however, that the term "life course" began to be used frequently and scholars began to describe their studies as life course research (e.g., Elder, 1974; Hogan, 1978). Indeed, it was not until the 1980s, that consensus began to emerge about the differences between life course and related terms, especially life cycle (e.g., O'Rand & Krecker, 1990). Since then, the volume, quality, and sophistication of life course research has increased dramatically.

I have suggested previously that life course sociology is not a core of the discipline like broad areas such as social psychology and social stratification are, nor is it the equivalent of more middle-range theories such as the stress process and political economy (George, 1996,1999). Those, and other core components of sociological inquiry are characterized by bounded foci of interest, well articulated and elaborated theoretical foundations, and extensive research traditions. In contrast, the life course seems to me to be a set of perspectives that focus on time, timing, and long-term patterns of stability and change. There are certainly basic principles that characterize life course perspectives, but there is not an integrated theory of the life course; nor, I would argue, should there be one.

The purpose of this chapter is to convey my view of the future of life course research. It is divided into five sections. The first is a brief review of core life course principles—principles that I will argue are critical to the social and behavioral sciences, yet do not comprise an integrated theory. The second section provides my view of the two major forms of life course

LINDA K. GEORGE • Duke University, Durham, North Carolina 27708

Handbook of the Life Course, edited by Jeylan T. Mortimer and Michael J. Shanahan. Kluwer Academic/Plenum Publishers, New York, 2003.

research in the field to date, as well as my prognostications of their likely futures. In the third and fourth sections, I examine two overarching issues in the social and behavioral sciences— social causation and social selection—and the ways that life course principles have contributed to recent advances in our understanding of these issues and have the potential for further contributions. The final section is intended to combine the issues covered previously into a coherent depiction of the current achievements and probable future of life course research.

KEY LIFE COURSE PRINCIPLES

Elder and colleagues suggest that four major components or axioms underlie life course perspectives (Elder, George, & Shanahan, 1996). The first is a focus on time and timing. A key element of temporality is long-term patterns of stability and change, often conceptualized as trajectories. This life course principle also encompasses issues of duration and duration dependence, sequences of transitions, and timing of transitions. Second, life course perspectives focus on the intersection of social context and personal biography. Social context is appropriately examined at a variety of levels, ranging from the immediate social environment to the broad influences of history and culture. In this sense, life course perspectives are attentive to macro-micro linkages—a core issue in the discipline that is frequently ignored empirically. Third, life course perspectives explicitly involve investigation of linked lives, recognizing the importance of social relationships in all areas of life. Finally, life course perspectives emphasize the importance of human agency. For example, although both are seldom examined in the same study, life course research can focus on either the ways that social and historical contexts shape individual lives or on the ways that human agency modifies the life course and social structures more broadly. Similarly, with regard to linked lives, life course research includes investigations of both the effects of social relationships on individual lives and the effects of human agency on the structure and dynamics of those relationships. These are important principles that, until recently, did not receive the attention they deserve in sociological inquiry. Nonetheless, they do not comprise an integrated, stand-alone theoretical framework.

LIFE COURSE RESEARCH: TWO
PRIMARY FORMS

To date life course research has taken two primary forms. Both are legitimate and have yielded useful knowledge. Nonetheless, I predict that only one of these research traditions will flourish in the future. One research tradition—the smaller in terms of the sheer volume of studies—focuses on the life course itself. This fascinating body of research has focused on four primary issues. One emphasis has been describing the contours of the life course, both currently and across time and place (e.g., Hogan, 1981; Modell, 1989). A second focus has been the historical emergence of the life course as a recognizable pattern with accompanying norms, as well as the social conditions that fostered the emergence of the modern life course (Anderson, 1985; Mayer & Schoepflin, 1989). A third theme of research in this tradition has been the multiple ways that historical events or conditions alter the life course (e.g., Clausen, 1995; Mayer, 1988). A corollary issue in this research has been identification of the conditions under which historical effects persist across the life course or are of bounded duration. A final focus in this research tradition has been examination of heterogeneity in the life course and the social characteristics and conditions that generate that diversity (e.g., gender, race) (e.g., Gee, 1986; Hogan, 1985).

Research on these topics has generated a wealth of knowledge about the life course itself. Many of the studies cited above are now classics in life course research and, in some cases, in the discipline more broadly. As a whole, this research has described the emergence of the modern life course, its basic contours, and the ways that the life course varies across historical time, place, and social location. As important as these contributions are, I do not expect this type of inquiry to play a large role in future life course research. Basic knowledge of the life course was necessary for capturing the attention of a wide range of scholars and stimulating a temporal thought style previously uncommon in the social and behavioral sciences.

But research in this tradition also is limited in a number of ways. It tends to paint a very broad picture of life course contours and diversity, but is not as useful for more fine-grained understanding of specific outcomes of interest. Consequently, for many research questions, this type of investigation is ill-suited to hypothesis testing and causal inference. Generalizability of results is problematic as well. Much of the research in this tradition can be viewed as case studies of specific social contexts (e.g., the Great Depression, World War II), leaving open the question of whether the findings apply to similar historical conditions and to other circumstances (e.g., to what extent are the effects of combat on mental health similar to or different from other kinds of trauma?).

The second body of life course research focuses less on the life course itself as the outcome of interest. Instead, existing theories and substantively focused research are enriched by incorporating one or more of the central life course principles. Thus, studies in a variety of substantive areas—for example, stratification (e.g., Hardy & Hazelrigg, 1999; Mirowsky & Ross, 1999), work and retirement (e.g., Flippen & Tienda, 2000; Mortimer & Johnson, 1998; Mutchler, Burr, Pienta, & Massagli, 1997), and health (e.g., Landerman, George, & Blazer, 1991; Moen, Dempster-McClain, & Williams, 1989)—have explored issues of timing in greater depth and/or over longer periods. Similarly, although relatively few studies explicitly incorporate measures of exposure to historical events, interpretation of findings now often include discussion of the extent to which the results reflect macro-level social and historical conditions. And, a focus on linked lives and the opportunities and constraints posed by social relationships now is frequently found in research topics that previously paid little attention to them—for example, couple-based patterns of retirement (Henretta, O'Rand, & Chan, 1993; O'Rand, Henretta, & Krecker, 1992; Moen, *this volume*), and the influence of significant others on the decision to seek medical care (Bisconti & Bergeman, 1999; Edwardson, Dean, & Brauer, 1995).

This integration of life course principles with other sociological theories and research traditions will be, I believe, the dominant form of life course research in the future. Although we can already observe the impact that life course perspectives have had on a variety of research problems, these represent only the proverbial tip of the iceberg. There are literally hundreds of research topics for which no one has yet considered long-term patterns of change and stability; the effects of macro-level social, cultural, and historical contexts; and/or the significance of linked lives. Thus, I view the future of life course research as an integration of life course principles with the total range of theoretical and substantive themes of social and behavioral research.

SOCIAL CAUSATION AND
SOCIAL SELECTION

At a fundamental level, much, arguably most, research in the social and behavioral sciences focuses on issues of social selection and social causation. Traditionally, the terms "social selection" and "social causation" have been used rather narrowly and were typically posed as competing hypotheses about the relationships between social factors and outcomes of interest. This has been a dominant issue in the sociology of health and illness, for example, where scholars have debated and attempted to determine whether low socioeconomic status is a cause or consequence of illness (Johnson, Cohen, Dohrenwend, Link, & Brook, 1999; Reynolds & Ross, 1998), whether employment benefits health or whether healthier people are selected into the labor force (Pugliesi, 1995; Ross and Mirowsky, 1995; Waldron, Herold, Dunn, & Staum, 1982), and whether poor-quality social relationships are a risk factor for depression or, alternatively, whether depressed persons are unable to develop and/or sustain high-quality relationships (Holahan & Moos, 1991; Johnson, 1991). Recently it has been increasingly recognized that these may be competing hypotheses, but they are not mutually exclusive—that is both may operate to varying degrees.

In the research areas in which I work, investigators are theoretically aligned on the side of social causation—that is, there are strong theoretical expectations that social factors are causes of the outcomes of interest. My sense is that this is generally true of other social and behavioral research topics as well. Consequently, social selection is seen as a methodological nuisance (ultimately resulting from our inability to randomly assign individuals to the social characteristics of interest). We know that it is necessary to eliminate if possible or, more likely, adjust for or estimate the effects of selection in order to have confidence in our estimates of social causation. One outcome of this approach to social selection has been an emphasis on handling selection statistically (e.g., using the Heckman procedure [1979] to first estimate selection and then, in a second analytic step, estimate social causation with selection effects statistically controlled).

Serious attention to life course perspectives calls into question this view of social selection and how to appropriately handle it analytically. From a life course perspective, social selection is not a methodological nuisance. Rather, it is the heart of life course research, which is intended to delineate the long-term pathways associated with outcomes of interest. Moreover, life course perspectives call into question the distinction between social selection and social causation. Consider the example of employment and health. From a traditional social causation perspective, Investigator A hypothesizes that employment has positive effects on health, either protecting it or fostering improvements in it. Factors that lead some people to be employed and others to not be employed are the selection concern. The investigator is not concerned with the processes that lead to employment, only that those processes do not account for the association between employment and health. Meanwhile, Investigator B is interested in the determinants of employment among women (there is too little variability in employment among men to support such an investigation). This investigator knows that, among women, marital status is significantly related to employment—but selection effects are a potential problem for this investigator as well. Selection processes operate to increase the likelihood of some women being married and others being unmarried. A confident conclusion that marital status has a causal effect on employment status for women requires that selection effects associated with marital status be estimated and, if possible, ruled out. Thus, the independent variable for Investigator A (employment status) is the dependent variable for Investigator B—and both investigators must worry about selection effects.

From a life course perspective, the distinctions between social selection and social causation are much less important. An investigator can have an outcome of interest (e.g., health, employment status) and wish to identify the social factors associated with that outcome. But the distinction between selection and causation is relatively moot. The focus is on the long-term processes and pathways that result in the outcome of interest, not categorizing those processes and pathways as selection or causation.

Many investigators who address social selection and social causation from the traditional perspective apparently fail to understand that they are attempting to eliminate the life course from their inquiries. Using statistical procedures to estimate a coefficient that represents selection essentially means that the investigator is bundling the study participants' pasts into a neat little package that is ignored substantively and interpretatively. This is one of the ways in which social and behavioral research tends to be a historical—it ignores not only social history, but also personal history.

As life course perspectives are increasingly integrated into the broad spectrum of theories that undergird social and behavioral research, I believe that traditional notions of social selection and social causation will fade, to be replaced with an emphasis on processes and pathways. Important components of such inquiry will be identification of the conditions under which social location earlier in the life course does and does not have long-term effects and the processes that permit some individuals to overcome or compensate for conditions early in life that typically are associated with poorer outcomes (e.g., what permits some, but not most, individuals whose childhoods and adolescences were characterized by persistent poverty to achieve high levels of socioeconomic status in adulthood?).

THE PERSISTING PROBLEM OF HETEROGENEITY

Life course research would certainly be simpler if there was an "expectable life course," in which a majority, or even a significant minority, of individuals follow a modal pattern of transitions and trajectories. Such is clearly not the case. Evidence regarding the timing of significant life course transitions demonstrates the absence of an empirical timetable that can be used as a template of the expectable life course (Hogan, 1981; Watkins, Menken, & Bongaarts, 1987). Evidence regarding long-term sequences or trajectories of such transitions yields the same picture of extreme heterogeneity and empirical chaos (Hogan, 1981; Marini, 1984). A study by Rindfuss, Swicegood, and Rosenfeld (1987) illustrates this point dramatically. Using data from the National Longitudinal Survey of the High School Class of 1972, the authors coded participants' sequences of five roles—work, education, homemaking, military, and other—for 8 years after high school graduation. They report that 1100 sequences were needed to describe the experiences of the 6700 men in the sample; the corresponding number of sequences for the 7000 women was 1800. Consequently, a key challenge of life course research is to simultaneously do justice to long-term patterns of change and stability and to the heterogeneity of those patterns.

As is obvious from discussion thus far, the concept of trajectory is a staple of life course research. Trajectories are simply long-term patterns of change and stability; a corollary assumption is that trajectories are unlikely to conform to simple monotonic, linear, or even curvilinear forms. Thus, it is important that the statistical techniques used to identify life course trajectories are relatively free of constraints on the forms that trajectories can take. Statistical techniques that meet this requirement are relatively new in the social and behavioral sciences, but their availability has increased the volume and sophistication of life course research.

Currently, latent growth curve analysis (LGCA, see McArdle & Anderson, 1990; Meredith & Tisak, 1990), also known as hierarchical linear modeling (HLM, see Bryk & Roundenbush, 1992), is the most common technique used to delineate trajectories and to examine the predictors/correlates of trajectories (see Halaby, *this volume*). LGCA is ideally suited for analyzing three or more waves of panel data. LGCA uses a two-stage modeling process that can be used to answer a number of generic research questions. In the first stage, univariate growth curves (or trajectories) are constructed and within-subject error is estimated for each time point. Depending on the research question, univariate growth curves can be generated for time-varying predictors, as well as the outcome of interest. In the second stage, an average intercept (starting point) and slope (rate of change) are generated. With appropriate modeling, both linear and non-linear trajectories can be estimated. Another modeling option allows specification of correlated errors. Finally, both intercepts and slopes can be correlated with other fixed or time-varying variables. LGCA can be performed using standard structural equation modeling programs (e.g., Joreskog & Sorbom, 1993).

Two examples may help to illustrate how LGCA contributes to life course research. Ge and colleagues determined the extent to which trajectories of stressful life events predicted trajectories of depressive symptoms in a sample of adolescents who participated in four annual interviews (Ge, Lorenz, Conger, Elder, & Simons, 1994). Separate analyses were conducted for boys and girls. Univariate growth curves indicated that depressive symptoms typically remain stable or decrease slightly during adolescence. For girls, however, depressive symptoms tend to increase over time. Life events tended to increase over time for both boys and girls. Multivariate analysis indicated that, as expected, growth in stressful life events was associated with growth in depressive symptoms—but only for girls.

Using the same data set, Wickrama, Lorenz, and Conger (1997) used LGCA to examine the effects of parental support on symptoms of physical illness among a sample of adolescents who participated in five annual interviews. Two measures of parental support were available: one based on adolescents' self-reports, the other based on observational ratings of parent–adolescent interaction. In the first stage of analysis, univariate growth curves were estimated for the three major variables of interest. Both measures of parental support showed patterns of decline over time; in contrast, symptoms of physical illness generally increased over time. In the second stage, the two measures of parental support and a set of control variables were used to predict rate of growth in physical symptoms. As expected, trajectories characterized by declines in parental support over time significantly predicted greater growth of physical symptoms. As these studies illustrate, LGCA, unlike other statistical techniques, can be used to predict growth in a dependent variable of interest. It also is possible, given appropriate data, to determine the extent to which growth in an independent variable predicts growth in the dependent variable.

Although LGCA can make important contributions to life course research, it has limitations. First, although LGCA captures the direction and amount of change over time, it is not well suited to analysis of more complex patterns of change, for example discontinuity in rates of change across observational periods. Second, ultimately, LGCA is based on a single aggregate trajectory that best fits the sample as a whole. Certainly multivariate modeling can be used to explain variability around the aggregate trajectory. Nonetheless, it does not permit identification of the prevalence of trajectories taking specific forms, nor of the independent variables that predict distinctive trajectories.

Some scholars argue that a single trajectory cannot do justice to sample heterogeneity and instead recommend a disaggregated approach to trajectory construction (Dannefer & Uhlenberg,

1999; Manusson & Bergman, 1990). Using this approach, a set of mutually exclusive (but not necessarily exhaustive) trajectories are identified. Using date from the Terman men, for example, Clipp and colleagues identified five distinctive trajectories of health across 40 years: stable good health, stable poor health, improving health, declining health, and fluctuating health (Clipp, Pavalko, & Elder, 1992). The also identified specific demographic and social profiles associated with the various trajectories. In this way, they were able to examine multiple distinctive trajectories that varied widely in meaning. In this study, disaggregated trajectories formed the dependent variable. They also can be used as independent variables.

Barrett (2000), for example, examined the effects of marital status and marital history on mental health outcomes. She pointed out that current marital status leaves unmeasured heterogeneity with regard to marital history for everyone but the never married. She studied four trajectories among the currently married (one marriage, marriage-divorce-marriage, marriage-widowhood-marriage, and marriage-divorce-marriage-divorce-marriage); three trajectories among the currently widowed (married-widowed, married-widowed-married-widowed, and married-divorced-married-widowed); and two trajectories among the currently divorced (married-divorced and married-divorced-married-divorced). Results indicated that marital history matters—that there are significant differences in mental health among persons in the same current marital status, but whose marital histories differ. She also demonstrated that duration in a given marital state explained additional variance.

Although the use of disaggregated trajectories yields important information about distinctive patterns of change, it also has limitations. First, it is very time-consuming to develop and apply the decision rules that are used to form the typology of trajectories. Second, this method of trajectory construction increases the risk of arbitrary classifications and/or using trial-and-error to identify a set of trajectories that relate to other variables as hypothesized. Finally, of course, even a typology of trajectories does not completely take heterogeneity into account. Nonetheless, I would argue that it achieves a better balance between modeling temporal patterns and heterogeneity in those patterns than can be achieved with LGCA.

I believe that methods of exploiting longitudinal data measured at multiple times over an extended period of time will be one of the most active areas of life course research in the near future. Through those efforts, we will become better informed about the foundational assumptions and advantages/disadvantages of both aggregated and disaggregated approaches to analysis of trajectories. Hopefully both methods will prove viable, permitting investigators to match their analytic strategies to the research questions that they investigate.

FINAL THOUGHTS

In this chapter, I have briefly described the core principles of life course perspectives, the primary forms life course research has taken to date, and two issues that are challenges not only to life course research, but also the social and behavioral sciences more broadly: (a) social causation and social selection and (b) persisting problems of doing justice to heterogeneity. Although it is appropriate to examine these issues separately for purposes of organization, they are part of a greater whole.

It is unlikely that the emergence of life course principles and research is a random event. Instead, I would argue that life course research emerged when it did in response to the persistence of issues that have been inadequately handled in social and behavioral research and as a method of confronting those issues in conceptually and empirically grounded ways. The time had come when large numbers of scholars agreed that it is unacceptable to study the present in ever-increasing detail, in the absence of knowledge about the past, both personal and societal. The time had come when many scholars agreed that we must not only pay lip service to macro–micro links, but also identify the nature of those links. The time had come when investigators acknowledged the invalidity of studying isolated domains of experience as if they could be separated from other dimensions of people's lives. The time had come when researchers acknowledged that strict, positivistic determinism is often untenable.

Life course principles emerged as potential answers to those problems: examine time, timing, and their effects; recognize and measure the effects of personal biography and social history on human lives; recognize linked lives and the opportunities and constraints they represent; give human agency its due and reframe research questions in terms of pathways, trajectories, and patterns rather than causal chains. These are not issues relevant only to studies of child and adult development. They are relevant to most, arguably all, areas of social and behavioral research.

And, thus, my prediction is that the future of life course research will consist primarily of an integration of life course principles and analytic strategies into a broad range of theories and substantive topics in the social and behavioral sciences. As this happens, life course research will become increasingly less distinctive. And that will be a marker of its success rather than its failure. Indeed, the most successful outcome that I can imagine for life course scholarship is that it is incorporated into the major paradigms of the social and behavioral sciences—when, in fact, life course principles have become taken-for-granted assumptions of the research enterprise in general.

REFERENCES

Anderson, M. (1985). The emergence of the modern life cycle in Britain. *Social History, 10,* 69–87.

Barrett, A. E. (2000). Marital trajectories and mental health. *Journal of Health and Social Behavior, 41,* 451–464.

Bisconti, T. L., & Bergeman, C. S. (1999). Perceived social control as a mediator of the relationships among social support, psychological well-being, and perceived health. *The Gerontologist, 39,* 94–103.

Bryk, A. S., & Roundenbush, S. W. (1992). *Hierarchical linear models: Applications and data analysis methods.* Beverly Hills, CA: Sage.

Buhler, C. (1935). The curve of life as studied in biographies. *Journal of Applied Psychology, 19,* 405–409.

Clausen, J. (1995). *American lives: Looking back at the children of the Great Depression.* New York: Free Press.

Clipp, E. C., Pavalko, E. K., & Elder, G. H., Jr. (1992). Trajectories of health: In concept and empirical pattern. *Behavior, Health, and Aging, 2,* 159–177.

Dannefer, D., & Uhlenberg, P. (1999). Paths of the life course: A typology. In V. L. Bengtson & K. W. Schaie (Eds.), *Handbook of theories of aging.* (pp. 306–326). New York: Springer.

Edwardson, S. R., Dean, K. J., & Brauer, D. J. (1995). Symptom consultation in lay networks in an elderly population. *Journal of Aging and Health, 7,* 402–416.

Elder, G. H., Jr. (1974). *Children of the Great Depression.* Chicago: University of Chicago Press.

Elder, G. H., Jr., George, L. K., & Shanahan, M. J. (1996). Psychosocial stress over the life course. In H. B. Kaplan (Ed.), *Psychosocial stress: Perspectives on structure, theory, life course, and methods* (pp. 247–292). Orlando, FL: Academic Press.

Flippen, C., & Tienda, M. (2000). Pathways to retirement: Patterns of labor force participation and labor market exit among the pre-retirement population by race, Hispanic origin, and sex. *Journal of Gerontology: Social Sciences, 55B,* S14–S27.

Ge, X., Lorenz, F. O., Conger, R. D., Elder, G. H., Jr., & Simons R. L. (1994). Trajectories of stressful life events and depressive symptoms during adolescence. *Developmental Psychology, 30,* 467–483.

Gee, E. M. (1986). The life course of Canadian women: A historical and demographic analysis. *Social Indicators Research, 18,* 263–283.

George, L. K. (1996). Missing links: The case for a social psychology of the life course. *The Gerontologist, 36,* 236–245.

George, L. K. (1999). Life course perspectives on mental health. In C. S. Aneshensel & J. C. Phelan (Eds.), *Handbook of the sociology of mental health* (pp. 565–584). San Diego: Academic Press.

Hardy, M. A., & Hazelrigg, L. (1999). Fueling the politics of old age: On economic hardship across the life course. *American Sociological Review, 64*, 570–576.

Heckman, J. J. (1979). Sample selection as a specification error. *Econometrica, 47*, 155–161.

Henretta, J. C., O'Rand, A. M., & Chan, C. (1993). Joint role investments and synchronization of retirement: A sequential approach to couples' retirement timing. *Social Forces, 71*, 981–1000.

Hogan, D. P. (1978). The variable order of events in the life course. *American Sociological Review, 43*, 573–586.

Hogan, D. P. (1981). *Transitions and social change: The early lives of American men.* New York: Academic Press.

Hogan, D. P. (1985). The demography of life span transitions: Temporal and gender comparisons. In A. S. Rossi (Ed.), *Gender and the life course.* (pp. 65–78). Englewood Cliffs, NJ: Prentice Hall.

Holahan, C. J., & Moos, R. H. (1991). Life stressors, personal and social resources, and depression: A 4-year structural model. *Journal of Abnormal Psychology, 100*, 31–38.

Johnson, J. G., Cohen, P., Dohrenwend, B. P., Link, B. G., & Brook, J. S. (1999). A longitudinal investigation of social causation and social selection processes involved in the association between socioeconomic status and psychiatric disorders. *Journal of Abnormal Psychology, 108*, 490–499.

Johnson, T. P. (1991). Mental health, social relationships, and social selection: A longitudinal analysis. *Journal of Health and Social Behavior, 32*, 406–423.

Joreskog, K., & Sorbom, D. (1993). *LISREL 8: User's Reference Guide.* Chicago: Scientific Software International.

Landerman, R., George, L. K., & Blazer, D. G. (1991). Adult vulnerability for psychiatric disorders: Interactive effects of negative childhood experiences and recent stress. *Journal of Nervous and Mental Disease, 179*, 656–663.

Magnusson, D., & Bergman, R. (1990). A pattern approach to the study of pathways from childhood to adulthood. In L. N. Robins & M. Rutter (Eds.), *Straight and devious pathways from childhood to adulthood.* (pp. 101–115). Cambridge, UK: Cambridge University Press.

Marini, M. M. (1984). Age and sequencing norms in the transition to adulthood. *Social Forces, 63*, 229–244.

Mayer, K. U. (1988). German survivors of World War II: The impact on the life course of the collective experience of birth cohorts. In M. W. Riley (Ed.), *Social structures and human lives.* (pp. 229–246). Newbury Park, CA: Sage.

Mayer, K. U., & Schoepflin, U. (1989). The state and the life course. *Annual Review of Sociology, 15*, 187–209.

McArdle, J. J., & Anderson, E. (1990). Latent variable growth models for research on aging. In J. E. Birren & K. W. Schaie (Eds.), *Handbook of the psychology of aging.* (3rd ed.) (pp. 21–44). San Diego: Academic Press.

Meredith, W., & Tisak, J. (1990). Latent curve analysis. *Psychometrica, 55*, 107–122.

Mirowsky, J., & Ross, C. E. (1999). Economic hardship across the life course. *American Sociological Review, 64*, 17–31.

Modell, J. (1989). *Into one's own: From youth to adulthood in the United States, 1920–1975.* Berkeley: University of California Press.

Moen, P., Dempster-McClain, D., & Williams, R. M., Jr. (1989). Social integration and longevity: An event history analysis of women's roles and resilience. *American Sociological Review, 54*, 635–647.

Mortimer, J. T., & Johnson, M. K. (1998). New perspectives on adolescent work and the transition to adulthood. In R. Jessor (Ed.), *New perspectives on adolescent risk behavior.* (pp. 425–496). New York: Cambridge.

Mutchler, J. E., Burr, J. A., Pienta, A. M., & Massagli, M. P. (1997). Pathways to labor force exit: Work transitions and work instability. *Journal of Gerontology: Social Sciences, 52B*, S4–S12.

O'Rand, A. M., Henretta, J. C., & Krecker, M. L. (1992). Family pathways to retirement. In M. Szinovacz, D. J. Ekerdt, B. H. Vinick (Eds.), *Families and retirement* (pp. 81–98). Newbury Park, CA: Sage.

O'Rand, A. M., & Krecker, M. L. (1990). Concepts of the "life cycle": Their history, meanings, and uses in the social sciences. *Annual Review of Sociology, 16*, 241–263.

Pugliesi, K. (1995). Work and well-being: Gender differences in the psychological consequences of employment. *Journal of Health and Social Behavior, 36*, 57–71.

Reynolds, J. R., & Ross, C. E. (1998). Social stratification and health: Education's benefit beyond economic status and social origins. *Social Problems, 45*, 221–247.

Rindfuss, R. R., Swicegood, G. G., & Rosenfeld, R. A. (1987). Disorder in the life course: How common and does it matter? *American Sociological Review, 52*, 785–801.

Ross, C. E., & Mirowsky, J. (1995). Does employment affect health? *Journal of Health and Social Behavior, 36*, 230–243.

Thomas, W. I., & Znanecki, F. (1927). *The Polish Peasant in Europe and America.* Chicago: University of Chicago Press.

Waldron, I., Herold, J., Dunn, D., & Staum, R. (1982). Reciprocal effects of health and labor force participation among women: Evidence from two longitudinal studies. *Journal of Occupational Medicine, 24*, 126–132.

Watkins, S. C., Menken, J. A., & Bongaarts, J. (1987). Demographic foundations of family change. *American Sociological Review, 52*, 346–358.

Wickrama, K. A. S., Lorenz, F. O., & Conger, R. D. (1997). Parental support and adolescent physical health status. *Journal of Health and Social Behavior, 38*, 149–163.

CHAPTER 32

Success and Challenge in Demographic Studies of the Life Course

FRANCES K. GOLDSCHEIDER

INTRODUCTION

Beginning in the early 1970s social science research was transformed by new subfields in sociology, anthropology, developmental psychology, social history, and demography that emphasized the scientific study of personal lives. This refocus revolutionized demographic studies by enabling researchers to go beyond the *description* of populations and aggregate population groups to the *behavioral modeling* of the individual decisions and actions that constitute population dynamics.

Although this shift to understanding population dynamics through the study of individual lives can be described in a number of ways and from a variety of disciplinary perspectives, demography typically has characterized its studies as using a "life course" perspective. In this essay we outline some of the most impressive strides made in demography as a result of its paradigmatic shift to the life course perspective, and note missed opportunities.

We return to original conceptions of the life course to identify the ways in which the life course perspective challenges demography to continue to improve. Our particular emphasis is

DENNIS P. HOGAN AND FRANCES K. GOLDSCHEIDER • Department of Sociology, Brown University, Providence, Rhode Island 02912

Handbook of the Life Course, edited by Jeylan T. Mortimer and Michael J. Shanahan. Kluwer Academic/Plenum Publishers, New York, 2003.

681

on the importance of collecting complete and valid event histories, agency in life course decisions, and a better assessment of the context in which behaviors of individuals occur. We argue that by returning to the original conception of the life course perspective, as a few studies are now beginning to do, demography will make dramatic progress.

ORGANIZATION OF DEMOGRAPHY

The organization and structure of demography as a discipline was especially conducive to a rapid paradigmatic shift to the life course perspective for three reasons. First, demographers working singly or in small teams found it increasingly difficult to collect their own data from a nationally representative sample of the population in the United States. The need for specialized expertise in the complex and changing methodologies for sample and survey design, was associated with escalating costs of data collection. Since the 1970s, demography has relied heavily on *secondary data files* representative *of well-defined and geographically bounded populations.* These studies served multiple purposes, with a design that was driven by the broad community of researchers (by means of national advisory panels). Once the life course perspective was adopted by a few leading demographers on these advisory panels, it quickly became the standard by which major national surveys was judged. Thus, the data necessary to life course research were quickly available to all demographers.

Second, demographers depend on large research grants to fund their research teams. Reviewers of proposals, especially those submitted to the National Institutes of Health, expect demographic studies to use the latest methodologies, data, and statistical models. To maintain their research funding, demographers needed to adopt the research questions, data, and methodologies of the life course perspective. The study of individual demographic behaviors quickly became the norm in journals as well. (This is particularly important in demography where most publication is done through peer-reviewed journals.)

Third, demographers are motivated by their eagerness to develop and adopt new research methodologies. In contrast to many other disciplines, demography is inclined to accept and modify, rather than to debate and reject, innovations in research. Thus, demography as a discipline was receptive to the life course perspective, firmly establishing the study of individual lives as the preferred approach for demographic research.

DEMOGRAPHY AND THE LIFE COURSE
PERSPECTIVE

The "life course perspective" as used in demography was developed first and most fully in the work of Glen Elder (1975, 1978). The lives of ordinary persons became the prism for understanding the social impact of historic change by allowing scholars to examine the influence of social structures, culture, and personal environments on demographic behaviors. New research designs coupled with innovative strategies of data collection and statistical models appropriate to this new focus were developed (Cherlin, Kiernan, & Chase-Lansdale, 1995; Conger & Elder, 1994; Kertzer & Hogan, 1989).

Labor economists were important actors in this transition, using theories of the family from Becker (1991) to develop and test economic models of individual marriage and fertility behaviors. Economists also introduced the tools of econometrics to demography. As a result, demography made great advances *in behavioral modeling* during the 1980s and 1990s. While economists do not usually describe their work as guided by the life course perspective, they explain current individual demographic behaviors as a result of rational choices made to optimize lifetime economic rewards. This "economics of the family" approach accords well with the life course perspective as adopted in other parts of demography.

The intellectual revolution associated with the life course perspective offered the potential to forge new interdisciplinary collaborations among cultural anthropologists, life-span developmentalists, social historians, sociologists, and demographers. These disciplines share many research questions, and have often focused on the community context of the populations they study. The only substantial interdisciplinary collaboration that has developed is between labor economists and demographers. The potential for other interdisciplinary linkages, however, remained largely unrealized in demography until the 1990s. Based on the gains made by collaboration with economists, we believe that this reluctance to form other interdisciplinary linkages has had serious opportunity costs.

DATA COLLECTION

Many early surveys of individual demographic behaviors continued to rely on the measurement of behaviors at only a single point in time (the date of survey) or at a few points in time. From the 1980s onward major demographic surveys, done under government contract to highly professional survey organizations, have collected longitudinal data intended to capture the dynamics of peoples' lives. This was done retrospectively through the collection of event histories (e.g., the National Survey of Family Growth-V and the Demographic Health Surveys).

The development in the late 1980s of the life history calendar method to collect retrospective data on individual demographic behaviors offered an opening for demographers to improve the quality of retrospective life histories (Freedman et al., 1988). With this method, the recall and accuracy of life history information was improved by *simultaneously* collecting information on several life domains (such as education, work, cohabitation, marriage, fertility, and residence). The life history calendar identified discrepancies in the timing of events when one life domain is compared to another. The study of demographic behaviors worldwide would have benefited from the life history calendar method. Unfortunately, most demographic surveys still do not collect complete life histories using a life history calendar methodology.

An improvement over retrospective methods of collecting life histories involved *longitudinal* survey designs in which individuals are tracked from one survey wave to the next. These studies initially were developed to record changes of status for designated life domains (e.g., the National Longitudinal Study of Youth and the National Educational Longitudinal Study). This innovation in the portrayal of individual lives has made it possible to identify causes of adolescent fertility in the United States, the relationship of contraceptive use to fertility in developing nations, and husband/wife decision-making as it influences fertility, reproductive health, and child health behaviors.

Since the introduction of the life course perspective, demography has begun to rely heavily on prospective study designs (in which data are collected on life events that occur between survey waves). But many of these longitudinal surveys in demography initially did not collect complete information about the period of life before the initial interview (a situation demographers call left censoring). The lack of complete life histories hindered research on such key concepts as life turning points and biography.

Some studies have used a combination of the retrospective and prospective approaches. For example, the Panel Study of Income Dynamics began collecting panel data on marriage and fertility events between yearly interviews. Later, as the value of complete life histories came to be appreciated, the PSID collected retrospective lifetime data to capture behaviors before the panel began. Prospective panels in the PSID and some other studies have continued for much longer than was initially anticipated. As a result, demography now has available excellent life history data representing decades of life experience. This will permit a much fuller investigation of individual demographic behaviors, understood in the context of the entire life course.

Major demographic surveys tried to collect psychological data at the time of the survey waves. But these demographic studies almost always used abbreviated psychological instruments of uncertain scale reliability and validity. Demographers typically have not appreciated the magnitude of inaccuracies (bias and/or random noise) its abbreviated instruments might introduce in the research of other disciplines. The result was that many demographers analyzed psychological dimensions of the life course without benefit of collaboration with psychologists, and most psychologists steered clear of demographic surveys. The cost to demography was considerable, leading as it did to a failure to incorporate ideas of agency and biography.

HISTORICAL DEMOGRAPHY

We have thus far discussed demographic analyses of contemporary life events. But a large branch of demography has always been concerned with broader questions about how the forces of history have affected demographic behaviors, and how this impact might be accentuated for particular cohorts. This seemingly left a substantial portion of the demographic community stranded without a link to the life course perspective that had become the professional standard.

Demographers innovated by developing new sources of data that allowed them to use the life course perspective in historical research. Beginning first with the production of public use micro samples for each census as it was conducted (beginning in 1960) the Census Bureau provided a powerful tool that permitted individual level analysis of demographic behaviors. Demographers at the University of Wisconsin went one step further by going back to the manuscript census files for 1940 and 1950 to produce individual level data files.

The tremendous value of this new approach to the analysis of census data remained unappreciated, both because of the lack of data for long historical periods and because of incompatibilities among the censuses. Steven Ruggles (2002) and his associates at the University of Minnesota were among the first to recognize the potential value of enhanced census public use micro samples. These demographers went back to all existing census manuscript archives to cover much of U.S. population history from 1850 to the present). In addition, they have, in their preparation of the census files, provided data in a standardized format that facilitates intercensal comparisons (Ruggles, 2002). Examples of the research uses of these data are Ruggles (1993) and Hogan and Goldscheider (2001).

These census files (most based on at least a 1% sample of the national population) provide data on very large numbers of individuals. It is these data that allow demographers to examine the demographic behaviors of individuals in key population subgroups (race and ethnic minorities, immigrants, the very old), as well as over large periods of history.

While lacking information on individuals over time, successive censuses have provided data on individual persons in households that can be used to track the aggregate behaviors of carefully defined birth cohorts over time, and to interpret individual demographic behaviors in a given census year. The work of Steven Ruggles and his colleagues to produce census public use micro samples has greatly enhanced the potential for demographic study of social change using a life course perspective.

PERSONAL ENVIRONMENTS

Demography made tremendous strides in the representation of personal environments. An important innovation was the effort to better measure the *geographic* environments in which demographic behaviors occur. This involved matching individual respondents' records to information about the characteristics of geographic locales in which they live. Information on the local community of residence typically was provided by censuses, vital registers, or other administrative records for officially designated geographic units (such as block, tract, city, or county) to which individual respondents could be assigned. This methodology was adopted during the 1990s by the National Longitudinal Study of Youth (1979 cohort), the Panel Study of Income Dynamics, and NSFG-V.

Such information has made it possible for demographers to more fully investigate the influence of places on individual behaviors, a great step forward in life course studies in demography. But, despite its many values, this methodology did not fully capture personal environments as defined by a life course perspective, in so far as the local environment was *geographically* rather than *socially* defined. This difference was especially important in light of the influences of human agency and biography on life histories and perceived social environments.

Demographers have generally matched community data to individuals only for the *time of interview*, not to all places of residence over the life course (which would require residential histories). In fact, demographers still lack a working definition of neighborhood (Furstenberg & Hughes, 1997). Methods for collecting micro-community data over time were an important step towards collecting information on actual social environments of individuals (Axinn, Barber, & Ghimire, 1997).

An important development in demographic survey research has been the effort to capture individual environments through the relationships of individuals with social institutions, peer groups, and non-coresidential family. This approach may have been pioneered by the National Center for Education Statistics in its 1972 panel study of a school-based sample of students, which included information from students and schools; and its 1980 High School and Beyond study, which gathered data from students, parents, and schools.

By the 1990s population based demographic surveys on adolescents gathered personal environmental data about the family (from parent interviews), the school (from teachers and administrators), and sometimes the peer group (reported by self and peers), as well as information about economic and other social structural conditions in the geographically defined community. Examples of this comprehensive approach include the Early Childhood Longitudinal Study-Kindergarten Cohort, the 1997 Panel of the National Longitudinal Study of Youth, and the National Longitudinal Study of Adolescent Health.

SELECTIVITY

In another innovation, demographers recognized that residents in a given geographic area were selective of persons with particular sociodemographic characteristics since they included only persons who were locally born or moved to the area, and have stayed. Demographers also became cognizant of the potential error in inferring causal relation of individual behaviors from the characteristics of places (Firebaugh, 1978). The availability of individual person data from the censuses has largely eliminated the need for ecological correlation methods. Recent developments in Geographic Information Systems will enable demographers to portray the *community of each individual* in geographic terms, but without the use of arbitrary political boundaries.

Until recently, even when the necessary data were collected, demographers remained inattentive to the effects of personal environments on individual behaviors. These concerns about population selectivity and representativeness had the unfortunate consequence of leading demographers to question the value of all *community-based* studies. This happened even though community studies were proving an excellent vehicle for developmental, sociological, anthropological and historical studies of the life course (Elder, 1974, Conger & Elder, 1994, and Kertzer & Hogan, 1989).

In its efforts to define many characteristics of the local (geographic) environment, demography instead relied on the geographic distribution of persons selected in random national samples to identify neighborhoods in which particular environmental variables or combinations of variables might be found. Covariance models were used to show that demographic behaviors are affected largely by individual characteristics, with features of the community environment playing a minor role. Demographers failed to recognize that the *communities themselves were holistic environments* experienced and interpreted by individuals, based on their life course experiences.

Two studies that began in the 1990s—the Fragile Families and Child Wellbeing Study (directed by Sara McLanahan, 2002), and the Welfare, Children & Families: Three City Study (directed by Andrew Cherlin, 2002)—have returned to community study methodologies as an appropriate method of demographic research. The Three City study takes place in Boston, Chicago, and San Antonio to better understand the effects of welfare reform on the well-being of children and families and to follow these families as welfare reform evolves. The three cities chosen differ greatly in their economic and social characteristics, and in their welfare policies: Boston is a white city with a black minority (including many immigrants from the Caribbean) that is typical of a rustbelt economy, with Massachusetts policies on welfare reform being more flexible and more generous; Chicago is a former rustbelt economy that has gone through substantial economic renewal, with large numbers of blacks, Mexican Americans, and Puerto Ricans, in a state that has relatively stringent welfare reform policies; San Antonio is an economically bustling city typical of many Southern and Western cities, with large numbers of Mexican Americans (and undocumented persons), with welfare policies that are irrelevant to those who are not legal residents of the United States, and more inflexible and less generous than in the other three cities. The Three City Study thus selected particular cities for study, justifying their selection by the need to test specific hypotheses about welfare reform and families.

Greg Duncan has advocated a different approach that emphasizes the importance of sampling even when designating a set of areas for study. The Fragile Families Study in fact uses 18 different cities. The Fragile Families Study is designed as a prospective cohort study in each city, beginning with a sample of unmarried women selected at childbirth.

These scientifically rigorous, community-based, controlled comparison studies have also recaptured the interdisciplinary collaboration expected in life course studies. The longitudinal design of these studies will enable investigators to consider demographic behaviors during a time of dramatic changes in welfare and employment policies. We believe that these studies have set a new standard of excellence for demographic research, a standard by which future demographic work will be judged.

HISTORICAL CHANGE

Demographic studies have shown the potential for using information on individuals in a particular community to understand how historical changes have affected individual demographic behavior (see Kertzer & Hogan, 1989). Communities were selected on the basis of ideal types that would allow the testing of hypotheses. They do not produce coverage equivalent to nationally representative sample surveys. Clearly both national surveys and community studies offer valuable methodologies for the study of individual demographic behaviors.

Community studies have often relied on the long, painstaking retrieval of archival data on individuals matched to information (from legal documents, church records, tax information, newspaper/reported accounts) about social structure and change (Elder, Pavalko, & Clipp, 1993). Studies with this design proved useful for assessing the impact of broad historical changes on individual lives (Kertzer & Hogan, 1989).

But archival data on individuals in a community during a period of rapid social change have often lacked the longitudinal depth needed to assess the impact of social change in the early life course on the later life. In this kind of situation the archive can be used to identify persons who should be further studied. The study subjects were then located and interviewed (Elder, 1974).

The Wisconsin Longitudinal Study (directed by Robert Hauser, [2002]) is an example. The WLS began as a cross-sectional study of Wisconsin high school students in 1957. In the 1960s and 1970s the original archive was used to identify persons for longitudinal follow-up. The earliest follow-ups took the form of a panel study which recorded current statuses and statuses at particular ages. By the 1980s the WLS used each new survey wave to collect and update comprehensive retrospective life histories. Information from administrative records and places of residence at each point in the life course was collected to better define the social environment. Psychological and health information was collected at the baseline study and again during interviews as the respondents approached mid-life.

Imaginative foresight by the WLS investigators prompted the collection of information on health, savings, and later life aspirations for men and women in early midlife. Most recently, life course information was obtained as the cohort neared later middle age. The researchers hope to build on this first-rate research base by continuing interviews with this cohort as its members reach old age. The Wisconsin Longitudinal Study is unique in that it will allow the study of aging over the *full adult life course*, with data to measure agency and biographical change. This study, firmly rooted in the life course approach, provides a life-long perspective on aging that other longitudinal studies of aging (such as the Health and Retirement Study, which started when its respondents were at later mid-life) cannot.

METHODS

New methodologies (e.g., discrete time and continuous time approaches to the study of life histories) and statistical techniques (e.g., multinomial logistic regression, multistate increment decrement life tables) became popular tools to uncover the complexities of individual lives. Latent structure and grade of membership models were developed to enable investigators to empirically determine typical life pathways. All of these methods used dichotomous or categorical variables (measures of states and transitions) that have been the mainstay of demographic studies of the life course.

Research showed that the traditional demographic approach of matching behaviors in a population to the population at risk did not always work. An important example involved the estimation of the effect of women's wages on fertility. Traditional demographic methods would have first drawn the population for which such a decision could be made (i.e., the female labor force population doing paid work) and estimated the relationship. Demography's recognition of sequential decision making over the life course led to new conceptualizations and statistical models of the life course.

To accurately portray the effects of income on fertility behavior, for example, demographers developed a two-step model (Heckman, 1979). In its first step this involved the calculation of the expected wages of women who decide not to enter the labor force. In the second step, information from the first step is used to adjust for this joint "expected income/labor force entry" decision. Most demographers now recognize that sequential decision making is the essence of the life course perspective.

BIOGRAPHY

Longitudinal research on adolescents becoming adults indicated how adolescent values and aspirations for education, work, and marriage influence life plans and later demographic behaviors (Hogan & Astone, 1986; Hogan, 1985). This led researchers to more closely examine opportunities and constraints in the personal environment (family, community, culture, or social structures) that map alternative life pathways among which an individual can choose (i.e., constrained decision making). For an outstanding overview and insightful analysis of "bounded strategic action" as it applies to research on the transition to adulthood, see Shanahan (2000). As developed in Shanahan (2000) the concept of bounded strategic reaction provides a way to describe the dynamic interplay between person and context.

As noted above latent structure models and grade of membership models offer promising avenues for the successful analysis of these very complex relationships, especially when decisions at one point in the life are conditioned on anticipated future actions (Shanahan, 2000). Hogan, Sandefur, & Wells (2002) have successfully used this approach to study differences in the pathways to adult roles, for children with disabilities compared to other children, with differences noted by sex.

Changes in personal environments (associated with war and peace, depression and prosperity, expanded college opportunities, or the expansion of job opportunities and the acceptability of women's work) were recognized as factors that might alter the life course of individuals, as cohorts responded to period changes in age-appropriate ways. This innovation has led demographers, using ideas from the life course perspective, to examine continuity and change in life pathways for a variety of demographic events (fertility, welfare dependence, work, and disability).

In its demographic formulation, attention to changing lives leads to an examination of current behaviors in relation to the prior life history (e.g., Goldscheider & Speare, 1987 on migration; Cherlin et al., 1995 on cohabitation and marriage). Demographers have eschewed behavioral models based on developmental trajectories and theories of ontogenetic change. This led to empirically driven research that documented the extremely varied sequences of transitions that occur in a population, but lost analytic power by its failure to recognize general patterns and historical variations in transition sequences. With the emerging interest in genetic and biological factors in human behavior, demographers will need to reconsider this stance. This may take the form of collecting biological data for persons with different degrees of shared genetics and direct assays of biological tissues.

CHANGE

A fundamental problem in the study of lives is unraveling impacts of aging, cohort change, and historical events on individuals. Because most recent demographic surveys were age-restricted (e.g., to those in the childbearing years or entering adulthood), they were unsuitable for the examination of the effects of major social changes on individual lives, while those with a broader age range often have too few cases at given life course stages (e.g., the PSID). Even though demography has seldom collected data suitable for intercohort comparisons, demographers have recognized that cataclysmic historical changes and major dimensions of identity (such as ethnicity, religion, and language) were key elements in structural inequality. Some studies collected data for many different cohorts, while others attempted to disentangle the age-period-cohort puzzle with data from repeated cross-sections (see Glenn, *this volume*).

The common demographic practice has been to use arbitrary 5-year cohorts (ending in digits 4 and 9), 5-year age groups (which has its roots in demographic analysis of aggregate census data), and 5-year periods to operationalize these aspects of time rather than socially defined cohorts, age groups, and periods. This practice resulted in the development of many ingenious strategies to solve the statistical identification problem associated with any two variables (from age, period, and cohort) being sufficient to determine the third. We believe that these efforts tended to yield rather limited understandings of the impact of historical changes experienced by cohorts over their life course.

Demographers have not been especially attentive to the ways in which individuals understand and interpret their own life histories (i.e., the concept of biography). This has limited demographers in their studies to research on individual transitions and linked transitions during segments of the life course, rather than to the *meaning* of transitions over the life course (which is essential to understanding agency).

One recent development suggests that a group of life course researchers can be brought together to provide institutional direction for further improvement in certain areas of demographic research. The MacArthur Foundation Network on Transitions to Adulthood (2002), chaired by Frank Furstenberg, studies, from a developmental perspective, the period of the life course from ages 16 to 24. It examines the multiple transitions of young adulthood—leaving home, entering or leaving school, finding employment, marriage, cohabitation, childbearing—and the variety of combinations and sequences in which they occur. The network explores how development in one area relates to the others, and how societal institutions may facilitate the transition from adolescence to adulthood.

The economic theory of families and fertility linked past and current demographic behaviors by comparing the expected lifetime benefits and costs of demographic behaviors to rational actors, as well as their likely permanent income. More recently, the Fragile Families and Child Wellbeing Study and the Welfare, Children & Families: Three City Study have been especially innovative in their use of ethnographic methods and carefully designed situations of interpersonal interaction to interpret and understand individual lives.

CONCLUSIONS

We have argued that the life course perspective revolutionized demography. It did so by focusing attention away from the behaviors of aggregate populations to the consideration of the demographic behaviors of individuals. This paradigmatic change has led demography to remarkable improvements in study design, data collection, and methods of analysis.

Demography did not so readily adopt the full panoply of ideas and methodologies envisioned by the life course perspective. This has resulted in missed opportunities, which we believe were incurred at considerable cost to demography as a discipline. In this essay the challenges to demography over the next decade have been identified by returning to some basic tenets of the life course perspective. The challenges for demography are to collect complete and accurate life histories, attend to agency and biography, and improve the measurement of social environments in which individual lives unfold. If this is done, we believe that demography will improve its intellectual rigor, be better able to identify causal relationships, and increase its capacity to make convincing public policy recommendations. Very recent innovations in the demographic study of individual behaviors suggest that demography, as a discipline, will rise to the challenge.

REFERENCES

Axinn, W., Barber, J., & Ghimire, D. (1997). The neighborhood history calendar: A data collection method designed for dynamic multilevel modeling. *Annual Review of Sociology, 27,* 355–392.

Becker, G. (1991). *A treatise on the family (enlarged ed.).* Cambridge: Harvard University Press.

Cherlin, Andrew. (2002). http://www.jhu.edu/~welfare/

Cherlin, A., Kiernan, K., & Chase-Lansdale, P. (1995). Parental divorce in childhood and demographic outcomes in young adulthood. *Demography, 32,* 299–318.

Conger, R. D., & Elder, G. H., Jr. (1994). *Families in troubled times: Adapting to change in rural America.* New York: Aldine de Gruyter.

Elder, G. H., Jr. (1974). *Children of the great depression: Social change in life experience.* Chicago: University of Chicago Press.

Elder, G. H., Jr. (1975). Age differentiation and the life course. *Annual Review of Sociology, 1,* 165–190.

Elder, G. H., Jr. (1978). Approaches to social change and the family. *American Journal of Sociology, 84,* S1–S38.

Elder, G. H., Jr., Pavalko, E. K., & Clipp, E. C. (1993). *Working with archival data: Studying lives.* Newbury Park, CA: Sage.

Firebaugh, G. (1978). A Rule for inferring individual-level relationships from aggregate data. *American Sociological Review, 43,* 557–572.

Freedman, D., Thornton, A., Camburn, D., Alwin, D., Young-DeMarco, L. *et al.* (1988). The life history calendar: A technique for collecting retrospective data. *Sociological Methodology, 18,* 37–68.

Furstenburg, F. F., Jr., & Hughes, M. E. (1997). The influences of neighborhoods on children's development: A theoretical perspective and a research agenda. In R. M. Hauser, B. V. Brown, & W. Prosser (Eds.), *Indicators of children's well-being.* (pp. 346–371). New York: Russell Sage Foundation.

Goldscheider, F., & Speare, A., Jr. (1987). Effects of marital status change on residential mobility. *Journal of Marriage and the Family, 49,* 455–464.

Hauser, R. M. (2002). http://dpls.dacc.wisc.edu/WLS/

Heckman, J. (1979). Sample selection bias as a specification error. *Econometrica, 47,* 153–167.

Hogan, D. P. (1985). Parental influences on the timing of early life transitions. In Z. S. Blau (Ed.), *Current perspectives on aging and the life cycle, Volume 1.* (pp. 1–59). Greenwich, CT: JAI Press.

Hogan, D. P., & Astone, N. M. (1986). The transition to adulthood. *Annual Review of Sociology, 12,* 109–130.

Hogan, D. P., & Goldscheider, F. (2001). Men's flight from children in the U.S.: A historical perspective. In S. L. Hofferth & T. J. Owens (Eds.), *Advances in life course research, 6. Children at the millenium: Where have we come from, where are we going.* (pp. 193–229). London: Elsevier Science.

Hogan, D. P., Sandefur, G., & Wells, T. (2002). The transition to adulthood among young persons with special needs. Paper presented at the August 2000 meeting of the American Sociological Association, Washington, DC.

Kertzer, D. I., & Hogan, D. P. (1989). *Family, political economy, and demographic change: The transformation of life in Casalecchio, Italy, 1861–1921*. Madison: University of Wisconsin Press.

The MacArthur Foundation Network on Transitions to Adulthood (2002). http://macfound.org/research/

McLanahan, Sara. (2002). http://crcw.princeton.edu/fragilefamilies

Ruggles, Steven. (2002). http://www.ipums.umn.edu

Ruggles, Steven. (1993). Historical demography from the census: Applications of the American census microdata files. In D. S. Reher & R. Schofield (Eds.), *Old and new methods in historical demography*. (pp. 383–393). New York: Oxford University Press.

Shanahan, M. J. (2000). Pathways to adulthood: Variability and mechanisms in life course perspective. *Annual Review of Sociology, 26*, 667–692.

CHAPTER 33

The Future of the Life Course

Late Modernity and Life Course Risks

Angela M. O'Rand

The future of the life course in the United States over the next several decades, and in some other late-modern societies, is best considered in the light of major demographic and institutional changes. The life course—when defined as interdependent sequences of age-related social roles across life domains (family, education, work, health, leisure)—is a product of the linkages among state (welfare), market and familial (gender) institutions and demographic behaviors across the life span. When these linkages are tightly coupled and universally salient in a population their coherence and normative strength lead to a more highly institutionalized, age-graded life course. Alternatively, when these linkages are loosely coupled, variability (de-institutionalization) in the life course increases: the relationship of age to role transitions weakens and the synchronization of roles across life domains becomes less standardized.

Scholars do not agree on the extent of the de-institutionalization of the life course at this time. Some argue that structural lags in the responses of social institutions to demographic shifts are slowing the process of de-institutionalization—and slowing the progress in the re-institutionalization of the life course to fit the conditions of late-modern life. In this vein, Matilda White Riley (1998) argues that dominant institutions influencing work and family lives lag behind the real changes in lives, including extended life expectancies, declines in disability at younger adult ages, and variability in family and work transitions extending from youth through old age. Others argue that structural forces such as globalization and the service economy are acting in concert with demographic trends (especially declines in fertility) to erode traditional institutions of industrial societies and, in turn, to de-institutionalize the life course. Gosta

Angela M. O'Rand • Department of Sociology, Duke University, Durham, North Carolina 27708-0088

Handbook of the Life Course, edited by Jeylan T. Mortimer and Michael J. Shanahan. Kluwer Academic/Plenum Publishers, New York, 2003.

Esping-Andersen (1999) represents the second view in his argument that de-institutionalization follows from interdependent changes in welfare state, labor market, and family structures, respectively, in the forms of (1) declines in the public management of social risks, (2) diminished benefits of market participation, and (3) weakened reliance of individuals on family. He argues that these institutional changes stem from exogenous forces, especially economic globalization trends increasing unemployment levels and earnings inequality and fertility declines.

Following the second argument, this essay will consider the individualization of risk and variability in the life course. The concept of "life course risk" and its relevance for the future of the life course will be central. The concept of "risk" originated in the assessment of large technical systems (such as weaponry and nuclear power) and their individual and environmental impacts at different levels of effectiveness or failure. The concept of risk has since spread to the medical, social and behavioral sciences (Lupton, 1999), where attributes of individuals or populations are rated as "risks" in their negative impacts on well-being. Risk now frames the logic of policy debates over aging, income maintenance and health care. The idea of life course risk was founded on social insurance formulations, which sought institutionalized solutions (the public or private pooling of risks) to individual risks (such as illiteracy, job loss, income loss, and disability). Institutionalized solutions produced public education, social retirement, and national health systems, with variable universal or categorical features across advanced societies.

Today, with the retrenchment of public welfare programs and the expansion of private individualized insurance plans, individualized solutions are sought for institutional risks. The revisions of welfare institutions in the areas of education, health care and income maintenance—institutions that have framed the life course from childhood to old age—propose new instruments in the forms of vouchers, managed care options, and individual retirement and health accounts to protect institutions from the risks of earnings losses, insolvency, and bankruptcy by placing more responsibility on individuals as parents of school-age children, workers, and family heads. Some might argue that this is no more than *the individualization of risk against a baseline of public (or collective) risk*. Vouchers are given as entitlements to a basic education; managed care options are provided as workplace assurances of basic health care for those who cannot afford it otherwise; and individual retirement accounts are possible in addition to social security, to which every worker is entitled. Nonetheless, this shift exerts a centrifugal force on the life course towards individualization.

HAZARDS AND RISKS IN THE LIFE COURSE

In an earlier paper (see O'Rand, 2000a), I define *risk* as the probability or relative uncertainty of an anticipated outcome (either a positive opportunity or negative hazard)—denoting a likelihood function based on limited information. I argue further that the irony of risk in modern society is twofold. First, many old risks to the life course that dominated the first half of the twentieth century have largely disappeared. *Old risks* were based on an absence of information about and control over life-course hazards. The uninformed or unprotected exposure to objectively defined life-course *hazards** such as illiteracy, life-threatening diseases, job loss, or old age poverty comprised the old risks. Institutional responses to old risks reduced levels of premature death and disability and extended active life expectancy at accelerating

---

*Fox (1999: 12) draws from the British Medical Association the distinction between "hazard," as a set of circumstances that may cause harmful consequences, and "risk," as the likelihood of its doing so. He argues further that there are three positions on the relationship between hazard and risk—that (1) risks map directly onto underlying hazards, (2) hazards are natural but risks are cultural, and (3) risk perceptions fabricate hazards. This paper implicitly adopts elements of the second and third definitions.

rates up to the present time (Manton & Stallard, 1996; Willmoth, 1998). Similarly, working-life hazards such as involuntary transitions from work or health interruptions that threaten income maintenance also appeared to decline (on average) as market and state institutions were developed and coordinated to respond to these disruptions—albeit with episodic down-turns and dislocations in this trend resulting from business cycles and with uneven impact on subgroups of the working population. Public and private pensions "normalized" the retire-ment transition and reduced the hazard of extreme poverty in old age through social policies (e.g., Medicaid, Supplemental Security Income) developed over the 1960s and 1970s that recognized the inevitable vulnerability of segments of the aging population to poverty.

Meanwhile, *new risks* involve the presence of relatively more information about life course hazards available to institutions and individuals, but information presented in the forms of *probabilities or likelihoods of individual outcomes*. Inherited, environmental and lifestyle risks are calculated to differentiate risk pools in the population and to increase the responsibilities of individuals to monitor and choose among (often opaque) alternatives to protect against or alleviate these risks. Individuals are confronted with more decision-making vis-à-vis life course transitions from choosing schools for their children to selecting from among health insurance options and investing in equities or bonds. Consequently, variability in the timing of school, work, family, health, and retirement transitions is increasing with the seeming de-institutionalization of the life course.

Second, I have argued that in the presence of relative ignorance, old life course hazards were considered from a societal perspective to be exogenous factors, that is to be external shocks to which individuals and their families were randomly and, therefore, equally at risk. This conception of risk facilitated a political rationale (a "governmentality," following Foucault and others) oriented towards collective policies and public solutions. However, in the modern presence of greater information, hazards are considered to be more endogenous and risks more individual. Accordingly, individuals' relative access to and understanding and use of information regarding hazards to health or wealth bear directly on their own outcomes. This conception of risk induces more individualized policies and private solutions. It redis-tributes normal and exceptional life course risks from collective social insurance to individ-ual financial capacity and prerogative (O'Rand, 2000a).

Three global exigencies are associated with the individualization of risk. The first is pop-ulation aging, now referred to widely as "global aging." Population aging is most advanced in Western democracies, with the United States catching up to European levels with the aging Baby Boom. Population aging has also accelerated in the less-developed countries (Martin & Kinsella, 1994). Three general social policy alternatives are being considered in the face of an aging population (Uhlenberg, 1992): (1) intervention in the demographic process to change the age structure itself through such policies as pro-natalism, high and selective immigration of the young, and the age-specific rationing of health care; (2) the increase of the productivity—or alternatively the decrease in the dependence of—the older population through alternative benefit cutting proposals directed to raising the retirement age, changing benefit formulas, and making benefits fully taxable within the income tax code; and (3) the shift of the locus of responsibility for protecting the life course across the life-span away from public or collective-private bases and towards the individual and the family.

The privatization of welfare institutions is another global trend. The aging of the popu-lation is challenging existing pay-as-you-go welfare redistribution policies in liberal, conser-vative, and social democratic states alike. Even the strongest public welfare regimes have moved to greater privatization at the millennium, including Germany and Sweden (Sunden, 2000). Population aging legitimizes arguments regarding *political risk*. The fiscal legitimation for welfare reform has been couched in the language of prospective future public hazards (e.g., who can support the retired Baby Boom?). The publicly run defined-benefit pension arguably incurs such a risk. Since current workers cannot effectively contract with and bind future cohorts of taxpayers to support them in old age, they are more willing than before to accept a privatized system (Geanakoplos, Mitchell, & Zeldes, 1998).

Yet, nearly every scenario of privatization uncovers extra individual risks from such a system. A recent analysis of the extent of risks that the hypothetical pensions of U.S. workers during the past century would have obtained if they had accumulated individual retirement accounts is presented by Gary Burtless (2000). He tracks hypothetical workers for a century beginning with the first worker who enters the labor force in 1871 and retires in 1910 and ending with the last worker who enters the labor force in 1960 and retires in 2000. He assumes workers have identical careers, contribute fixed percentages of their wages to investment accounts, and convert their balances to level annuity streams. He also assumes that workers differ in their exposure to stock market returns, bond interest rates, and price inflation given *the differing start and end dates of their respective careers*. He finds financial risks to be quite large with an average of pre-retirement peak earnings replacements at 52%, within a range from 20% to 110%. Workers who follow identical investment strategies but retire a few years apart can receive dramatically unequal pensions. Meanwhile, all private annuity pension recipients are rarely protected against inflation. The risks are borne by individuals and cannot be spread over a broader population of contributors and beneficiaries.

The third global transformation pertains to the "new economy" that is reorganizing the employment relationship and reconfiguring the roles of market and state institutions in the provision of social insurance. The employment relationship that dominated the U.S. labor market through the middle of the century was maintained by institutions supporting long-term employer–employee relationships in advantaged sectors characterized by unionization and/or internal labor markets. These institutions included employee benefits with collectively based protections of workers and their families against life-course risks (hospitalization, job loss) and "promises" of future promotional and earnings trajectories. These institutions have become economic risks that constrain economic gains in a more competitive market. Consequently, employers are retreating from long-term commitments to employees and actively cooperating in the individualization of benefit structures.

In short, population aging, the revision of welfare policies, and the reorganization of the employment contract are moving in the direction of greater individualization and privatization—that is towards greater individual responsibility and towards market-centered *as opposed to* state-centered policies for what can be referred to as *"normal" life transitions* in education, work, family and health; and for more unevenly encountered ("random" or group-specific) *life course risks* such as ill health or disability, unemployment, and family disruption which vary across subgroups of the population. As such, the increased privatization of social policy is requiring the individual to assume new risk-taking roles and responsibilities in matters of wealth and health. This increases individual autonomy and choice. However, as Esping-Andersen (1999) argues, increased privatization also introduces new high-risk groups and underclasses.

INDIVIDUALIZATION OF PENSIONS, INCREASED INEQUALITY, AND THE END OF RETIREMENT?

The complexity of pension structures is increasing as different kinds of pensions are made available across the labor market. Defined benefit (DB) pensions, which once covered half of the labor force, particularly that portion in major industrial labor markets (manufacturing, high-end services, finance, and communications), are being replaced by new defined contribution (DC) plans (Ippolito & Thompson, 2000). DB plans are pensions whose monthly benefits at retirement are clearly defined in advance by formulae based on age, years of service, and peak salary levels. DC plans are retirement accounts accumulated from investments by workers (sometimes matched by employers) in a mix of equity, bond or money market funds that accumulate balances over time but do not promise a specific benefit level at retirement; lump sums or annuity streams are usually worker options upon retiring. More rapidly expanding employment sectors in low-end services and retail sectors appear to be far more likely to offer defined contribution (DC) plans as primary. In addition, many of these new plans are used as supplementary investments by workers already covered by (DB) plans. As such, workers in rapidly expanding service and new high-skill manufacturing sectors and those newly covered in the past decade are highly likely to have access to DC plans only, while other workers with longer-term attachments to the workforce have more access to DB and mixed DB/DC plans. The DC plans, of course, are individual retirement accounts of the sort simulated by Burtless's (2000) analysis summarized above.

The expansion of DC plans has positive implications for workers' retirement savings to the extent that they are portable (can be retained when workers change jobs), tax-sheltered, and can be transferred as wealth to others during and after the worker's lifetime (after taxes are paid). This flexibility recommends these accounts widely to workers at all wage levels. However, an overriding implication of the mix of DB and DC is their stratifying effects on retirement income. Choice and chance increase wealth dispersion. Private pensions have always contributed to aged income inequality. DB plans have been associated with closed employment regimes that historically excluded women and lower status workers via occupational segregation and coverage/participation rules. Access to the new investments in DC plans, either as supplementary or as primary retirement accounts, has only changed the mechanism of inequality. Increases in aged (as well as non-aged) income inequality are apparent in the United States and other advanced economies (Smeeding, 1997).

Two important correlates of these trends have been a growing education gap in pension coverage and new gender "gaps" in pension coverage. Even and Macpherson (2000) recently reported trends from the Current Population Surveys between 1979 and 1993. They report that the gap in pension coverage between workers with less than 12 years of education and those with more than 16 years of education nearly tripled among men and more than quadrupled among women. Moreover, while women's pension coverage rates have risen due to increased labor force attachment and growth in earnings, men's have declined with the decline of unionism and the contraction of employment in large manufacturing enterprises.

These inequalities are evident in time-series studies of pension saving inequality over the past two decades. O'Rand (2001) reports on the growing inequality of retirement income from employment-based pensions among men and women aged 50–64 reported in matched files of the Current Population Surveys between 1976 and 1995. The results reveal the overwhelming importance of within-group inequality (using Theil coefficients of income dispersion) over the period that remains relatively stable for the total population, but not for women. Men's average dispersion in employer-provided retirement pension income decreases over the period from 0.321 in 1976 to 0.281 in 1995, while women's increases from 0.377 to 0.478 over the period, reaching a level that is 36% higher than men's. Moreover, men's declines in inequality are relatively steady. Women's, on the other hand, follow a "roller-coaster" pattern that is arguably associated with sectoral shifts and the uneven introduction and spread of new pensions in the worker population over the last 15 years or so. Inequality rises among women between 1976 and 1980 before the introduction of 401k plans (a type of DC plan most widely available today), then vacillates over the 1980s and 1990s ending in 1996 at a level that is 27% higher than at the beginning of the observation period.

If we consider further that this inequality represents the pension-covered population only, then factoring in the incomes of non-pension covered retirees increases the inequality that much more and finds groups with the highest levels of inequality (especially women) the most at risk of the hazard of poverty (Smeeding, 1997; O'Rand & Henretta, 1999).

Finally, recent reversals in the trend towards early retirement, increases in the variability in the age at retirement, and rising post-retirement re-entry into employment among men and women portend the de-institutionalization of retirement (Quinn, 1997). These trends in the United States have preceded legislative changes in age-eligibility for Social Security and earnings limits in retirement. They reflect the weakening of age-based institutional life-course schedules and the increase in individualization stemming from increased active life expectancy in the population, extensive variability in lifetime transitions patterns, and economic inequality. They do not signal the end of retirement, but the reconfiguration of the life course.

What People Don't Know about Their Pensions

Survey researchers' faith in respondents' accounts of their pension plan rules and their account levels are being challenged by findings from recent efforts to link respondents' testimonies to their employers' records (Mitchell, 1988; Gustman & Steinmeier, 1999; Luchak & Gunderson, 2000). An analysis we reported recently using the employer match data linked to the 1989 National Longitudinal Survey of Mature Women (NLS–MW) illustrates the problem (O'Rand, 2000b). We examined the extent of agreement between a subsample of NLS respondents and their employers on the type of their primary pension plan based on their own employment in 1989. Among respondents, one in five did not know her type of pension plan. If the "Don't Knows" are excluded, respondents agree about 55% of the time with their employers (a figure only slightly above Gustman and Steinmeier's finding in 1992 among Health and Retirement Study (HRS) respondents; Gustman & Steinmeier, 1999). If "Don't Knows" are included, the agreement falls to 45%. The incongruence suggests high levels of misunderstanding about plan type, with significant over-estimation of DB coverage by workers and underestimation of mixed and DC only plan coverage.

Whether younger cohorts, and particularly those with increased experience with privatized retirement accounts, will be more informed and attentive to their savings accounts in the future is a matter of considerable speculation. Recent research suggests two things in this direction: (1) that in the absence of strong structural incentives for deferring income and investing for the future, individuals will under-invest or save the lower their capacities (earnings levels) (Employee Benefits Research Institute, 1993; Gordon, Mitchell, & Twinney, 1997); and (2) that even individuals who do invest are generally risk-averse and place greater value on what they expect to lose than on what they expect to gain (Bajtelsmit & VanDerhei, 1997; O'Rand, 2000a). Nevertheless, the financial risks incurred by even those most well-informed still pose obstacles to retirement saving in cyclical and volatile economies (Burtless, 2000).

These observations do not address the issue of the efficacy of privatization of social security. Rather they provide us with another aspect of individualization—the variability introduced by choice and propensity in savings and investment. This variability influences the scheduling of the work career and the timing of retirement. The 1990s brought considerable volatility in the stock market with large gains early in the period and substantial losses later in the period. We are only just beginning to identify how retirement patterns were influenced by these market factors, especially among defined contribution plan participants. Some delays in retirement were probably due to the insecurities introduced by the market. Some early retirements may have results from extraordinary gains.

THE RAPID RETREAT FROM HEALTH INSURANCE COVERAGE AND THOSE LEFT BEHIND

Employers are abandoning other long-term contracts including health insurance coverage. Farber and Levy (1998) report that the percent of private sector workers covered by employer's health insurance declined from 92% to 64.5% between 1979 and 1997. The decline was more dramatic for workers without a high school education, whose coverage fell from 67% to under 50% over the same period. As in the case of pension coverage, private sources of collective insurance for health and income loss risks have been withdrawn from lower-class workers. When we examine health insurance coverage trends among retirees the decline is even more readily apparent. The U.S. Department of Labor's (1995) findings from the 1988 and 1994 Current Population Surveys reveal declines in retiree health insurance coverage at *and* following retirement.

Rising health care costs are the primary contributors to the general decline in coverage as well as to the decline in coverage of the retired population where costs are the highest. Employers are reducing their risks by withdrawing from the system. Similarly, physicians are leaving the system to avoid administrative burdens and to achieve greater independence in risk assessment. Accordingly, the managed care system has become highly differentiated as a cost–graded system of uneven health-care delivery. A consequence of this system is that the lack of health care coverage stemming from assessments of financial risk for employers and governments augments individual hazards for disability and high-cost emergency care. Along these lines, a recent study of an epidemiological catchment area in North Carolina found the odds of developing disability to be between one third and one half times higher among those without private health insurance who were unimpaired at baseline. Even among low-income persons, after controlling for other baseline characteristics, health insurance coverage has significant net effects on the risk for subsequent disability (Landerman et al., 1998).

CONCLUSIONS

The foregoing discussion has examined trends in pension and health insurance provision that demonstrate the movement away from collective protections against hazards associated with income loss and health decline or disability and towards individualization. Employers have been abandoning old long-term liabilities in the private sector in response to perceived market risks. Public agendas for state policies advocate the expansion of individualized and privatized protections as part of the Social Security/Medicare system in response to perceived political risks. Both trends reflect the new "prudentialism"—a convergence of trends to cautiously manage the affairs of the market and the state by displacing life course risks to individuals and their families and pre-empting future system-level crises. These shifts also signal new autonomy and flexibility for workers, who can bridge employers with retirement savings and health plan support structures in ways that could not be managed in older systems.

Whatever the advantages or the risks of the new system, the most general outcome will be increased individualization of the life course. Individual or family-based choices in schooling, retirement saving, and health coverage produce greater heterogeneity in the aging population. This heterogeneity will be reflected in changes in the scheduling of lives and in the dispersion of outcomes. The scheduling of lives is already changing. Delayed completion of education and delayed and interrupted retirement are growing in prevalence, along with longer-term patterns of delayed marriage and fertility and increased job mobility. The dispersion of outcomes like educational attainment, retirement wealth, and level of health care utilization are producing well-documented educational "gaps," growing earnings and wealth inequalities, and health disparities. The trade-offs of individualization are between individual choice and individual vulnerability.

The future of the life course rests on the changing linkages among state, market and familial institutions. These linkages will not disappear, but transform over the current transition to an aging world. The discourse of change will be conducted in the language of risk in which individual and collective interests will be weighed in a new calculus. From our vantage point at the turn of the century, we can expect the life course to be longer and, for many, healthier, temporally more complex in its education, work and family transition sequences, and increasingly unequal in its fortunes.

REFERENCES

Bajtelsmit, V. L., & VanDerhei, J. L. (1997). Risk aversion and pension investment choices. In M. S. Gordon, O. S. Mitchell, & M. M. Twinney (Eds.), *Positioning pensions for the twenty first century*. (pp. 45–66). Philadelphia: University of Pennsylvania Pension Research Council.

Burtless, G. (2000). Social security privatization and financial market risk. *Working Paper No. 10*. Washington, DC: Brookings Institution Center on Social and Economic Dynamics.

Employee Benefits Research Institute (EBRI). (1993). *Public Attitudes on Investment Preferences*. Washington, DC: EBRI.

Esping-Andersen, G. (1999). *Social foundation of postindustrial economies*. New York: Oxford University Press.

Even, W. E., & Macpherson, D. A. (2000). The changing distribution of pension coverage. *Industrial Relations, 39*, 199–227.

Farber, H., & Levy, H. (1998). Recent trends in employer-sponsored health insurance coverage: are bad jobs getting worse. *NBER Working Paper No. 6709*. Cambridge, MA: National Bureau of Economic Research.

Fox, N. J. (1999). Postmodern reflection on 'risk,' 'hazards,' and life choices. In D. Lupton (Ed.), *Risk and sociocultural theory: New directions and perspectives*. (pp. 14–33). Cambridge: Cambridge University Press.

Geanakoplos, J., Mitchell, O. S., & Zeldes, S. P. (1998). Would a privatized social security system really pay a higher rate of return? *NBER Working Paper No. 2266*. Cambridge, MA: National Bureau of Economic Research.

Gordon, M. S., Mitchell, O. S., & Twinney, M. M. (Eds.). (1997). *Positioning pensions for the twenty-first century*. Philadelphia: University of Pennsylvania Pension Research Council.

Gustman, A. L., & Steinmeier, T. L. (1999). What people don't know about their pensions and social security: An analysis using linked data from the health and retirement study. *NBER Working Paper No. 7368*. Cambridge, MA: National Bureau of Economic Research.

Ippolito, R. A., & Thompson, J. W. (2000). The survival rate of defined benefit plans, 1987–1995. *Industrial Relations, 39*, 228–245.

Kane, R. L. (1999). Caution: Health care is hazardous to the aging self. In K. W. Schaie & J. Hendricks (Eds.), *The evolution of the aging self: The societal impact on the aging self*. (pp. 225–249). New York: Springer.

Landerman, L. R. et al. (1998). Private health insurance coverage and disability among older Americans. *Journal of Gerontology–Social Sciences, 53B*, S258–S266.

Luchak, A. A., & Gunderson, M. (2000). What do employees know about their pension plan? *Industrial Relations, 39*, 646–670.

Lupton, D. (Ed.). (1999). *Risk and sociocultural theory: New directions and perspectives*. Cambridge: Cambridge University Press.

Manton, K. G., & Stallard, E. (1996). Longevity in the United States: Age and sex-specific evidence on life span limits from mortality patterns, 1960–1990. *Journal of Gerontology—Biological Sciences, 51A*, B362–B375.

Martin, L. G., & Kevin, L. (1994). Research on the demography of aging in developing countries. In L. G. Martin & S. H. Preston (Eds.), *Demography of aging.* (pp. 356–404). Washington, DC: National Academy Press.

Mitchell, O. S. (1988). Workers' knowledge of pension provisions. *Journal of Labor Economics, 6*, 28–39.

O'Rand, A. M. (2000a). Risk, rationality and modernity: Social policy and the aging self. In K. W. Schaie & J. Hendricks (Eds.), *The evolution of the aging self: The societal impact on the aging self.* (pp. 225–249). New York: Springer.

O'Rand, A. M. (2000b). Life course risks and inequality. Presented in the Presidential Symposium on "Aging, Social Policy and Risk: Lessons Not Yet Learned," Gerontological Society of America, Washington, DC, November 2000.

O'Rand, A. M. (2001). Perpetuating women's disadvantage: Trends in US private pensions, 1976–1995. In J. Ginn, D. Street & S. Arber (Eds.), *Women, work and pensions: International issues and prospects.* (pp. 230–256). Buckingham, U.K.: Open University Press.

O'Rand, A. M., & Henretta, J. C. (1999). *Age and inequality: Diverse pathways through later life.* Boulder, CO: Westview.

Quinn, J. F. (1997). Retirement trends and patterns in the 1990s: The end of an era? *Public Policy and Aging Report, 8*, 10–15.

Riley, M. W. (1998). The hidden age revolution: emergent integration of all ages. *Policy Brief 12/1998.* Syracuse, NY: Syracuse University/Center for Policy Research.

Smeeding, T. M. (1997). Financial poverty in developed countries: The evidence from LIS. *Luxembourg Income Study, Working Paper No. 155.* Syracuse, NY: Syracuse University/Center for Policy Research.

Sunden, A. (2000). How will Sweden's new pension system work? *Issue in Brief (March, No. 3).* Chestnut Hill, MA: Boston College, Center for Retirement Research.

Uhlenberg, P. (1992). Population aging and social policy. *Annual Review of Sociology, 18*, 449–474.

U.S. Department of Labor. (1995) Retirement benefits of American workers: New findings from the September 1994 Current Population Survey. Washington, DC: USGPO.

Wilmoth, J. R. (1998). The future of human longevity: A demographer's perspective. *Science, 280*, 395–397.

CHAPTER 34

Future of the Life Course

ANSGAR WEYMANN

INTRODUCTION

The life course and life course policy have become a focus of attention and inquiry as a consequence of occidental modernization. Modern society is characterized by high degrees of complexity, differentiation, and functional specialization, resulting in individualized lives, as well as by the continuing rationalization of societal institutions. Individuals became liberated and at the same time disconnected from religion, tradition, and local communities—from everyday life-worlds. Highly specialized institutions tailored to all segments and situations in the life course, from cradle to grave, have replaced Gemeinschaft (community) with Gesellschaft (society).

Life course policy can lay the foundations for rational life conduct and help stabilize expectations, transitions, and trajectories in the course of life by designing and implementing institutional support. The main fields of life course policy are education and training, health, and old age provisions, social assistance and welfare, work and employment. Life course policy, for historical reasons, is bound to the modern nation-state. Nationally distinctive paths of life course policy have developed over centuries of modernization as a response by the nation-state to the challenge of modern life. But what will happen to national life course policy under the impact of globalization? Will the nation-state disappear in the course of globalization, and in the wake of this process will a powerless state lose the capacity for effective life course policy? Or will we observe the emergence of supra- and transnational life course regimes as an innovative response to the challenges of globalization—as in the case of the European Union? Either way, life course policy should become a focus of inquiry for life course researchers in a global world.

ANSGAR WEYMANN • University of Bremen Graduate School of Social Sciences, D-28359 Bremen, Germany

Handbook of the Life Course, edited by Jeylan T. Mortimer and Michael J. Shanahan. Kluwer Academic/Plenum Publishers, New York, 2003.

The first section of this chapter sketches the basic features of "the life course in modern society" as they have developed over centuries of Western modernization: individualization and temporalization; differentiation and mobilization; and the pluralization and erosion of life worlds. The second section describes "life-course policy as a response by the nation-state" to these particular conditions of modern life. With the establishment of the nation-state and of welfare state entitlements, individual lives were influenced by life course policy in profound and enduring ways. The nation-state has now reached its zenith, however, and globalization is under-way – and it may weaken the nation-state's capacity for life course policy. The concluding discussion of "globalization as a challenge for life course policy" reflects upon the impact of globalization on national life-course policy, focusing on the countries of the European Union.

THE LIFE COURSE IN MODERN SOCIETY

Individualization and the Multi-temporalization of Life

The first basic feature of life in modern society is the individualization and differentiation of time. Rousseau's well-known tract "Emile, Or About Education" describes Emile's personality development as a succession of transitions, sequences, and trajectories and he expounds on appropriate methods of education to enable a child to find his (not her) position in life and society. By the age of 20 a young adult should be the successful creation of his educator. Here we find the origins of our professional systems of socialization and education, conceived on the basis of an individual life course that is meticulously arranged passage by passage from birth to marriage. "You cannot imagine how Emile, at twenty, can possibly be docile? ... It took me fifteen years of careful preparation to secure that hold. ... I let him have, it is true, the appearance of independence, but never was he more subjected to me, for he is because he wants to be" (Rousseau, 1963, p. 672).

Time appeared in Rousseau as individual life time. Durkheim perceived time sociologi-cally as societal time. As a consequence of migration and urbanization, he observed, the sol-idarity among equals living together in a community was replaced by the interdependencies among non-equals living apart, based on the societal division of labor. The influence of the elderly on the maintenance of traditions and the behavior of the young broke down. The life course had become institutionalized through the formation of homogeneous age groups and by passages from age group to age group.

In a modern society, families are less able to prepare their offspring for the cultural demands of society, nor can they enduringly provide them with the means of subsistence or secure them desired occupational and social status. It is true, youth in modern society have unparalleled access to wealth and to opportunities to develop their potential. But this access is no longer the product of inherited privilege, inherited office, and private education. Families have lost this traditional gatekeeping power to allocate lifelong status and position. Instead, life courses are functionally or dysfunctionally integrated through organized socialization of the individual and the market allocation of labor power. Full membership in society is attained pro-gressively in the course of a long-range trajectory from younger to older age-strata.

Cohorts and generations render especially clear the importance of the social differentiation of modern societies according to time. Generations are age-groups bound together in the his-torical stream of societal events by their shared embeddedness in the specific economic and power relations of their time. This common historical fate tends to cultivate generation-specific conventions of behavior, feeling and thought. The consequence is that in societies characterized by rapid social change, different generations inhabit different life-worlds (see Alwin & McCammon, *this volume*).

Concepts such as transitions, sequences, trajectories, age-groups, age-strata, generations, and cohorts signify the differentiation of individual and social time and the increasingly complex relations between society and the life course in the process of modernization. Incongruities and clashes exist between temporal planning in individual lives, on the one hand, and the manifold normative time schedules of groups, institutions, society, and culture on the other. A profound need for life course policy thus arises as a means of guiding individualized lives through institutional settings ranging from educational curricula to pension plans in a world undergoing permanent social change.

Social Differentiation and Mobilization of Human Resources

Differentiation of society, coupled with the economic mobilization of human resources, is a second factor stimulating a demand for life-course policy. The process of modernization has differentiated social structure, leading from social relationships with comprehensive bonding claims to specialized and manifold relationships, from collectivism to individualization, from particular value orientations to universal norms, from ascribed to achieved status. Also characteristic of modern society are the decoupling of offices and bureaucracy from kinship systems; the general establishment of the market, property and a money economy; and the building of nation-states.

The historical rise of a small group of leading Western democratic industrial states was followed by the modernization of hitherto underdeveloped societies. In this increasingly competitive international environment, the more advanced societies have undertaken isolated and concerted efforts to retain their forerunner status (Boyer, 1996; Boyer & Drache, 1996; Crouch & Streeck, 1997, pp. 1–18; Kindleberger, 1996; Olson, 1982; Parsons, 1971). A key to maintaining a high societal standard of living is the capacity to continue to innovate, which after an initial "take-off" period leads consistently to new products and new leading industries, as well as to alternating leading nations (Rostow, 1960). To no small extent, technological progress is the motor of these innovations (Castells, 2001). Technological innovation goes hand in hand with a restructuring of the labor force within occupations, branches, sectors, and regions. This permanent process of innovation and human resource mobilization is Janus-faced. It can be seen as a powerful engine of progress, but also as a permanent source of long-term economic cycles and as an important source of disequilibria and inequality. Modernization goes hand-in-hand with the expansion of education, science, and the media, the rationalization and secularization of culture, linguistic assimilation and intensified national and international communication, and ever greater political participation. Modernization is also linked to a general and fundamental social mobility and personal flexibility among ever more population groups. Gradually, all previously unaffected individuals and collectivities are drawn into these processes.

This universal and omnipresent human experience again stimulates the demand for a life course policy which lays the foundations for rational life conduct and helps stabilize expectations, transitions, and trajectories in a world in flux.

The Pluralization and Erosion of Life Worlds

A third characteristic of life in modern society stimulating a need for life-course policy is the pluralization and erosion of life worlds. Rooted in religion and tradition, the foundations of life-world communities eroded over the course of centuries of modernization. Ever more rarely in modern societies can traditionally accustomed, proven and agreed-upon status quo conditions in any realm of social life be considered durable. The life worlds of traditional communities were "colonized", as Habermas put it, by the subsystems of modern society. These subsystems, such as justice, the market, politics, science, and education, became decoupled and autonomous from the life world context. As the medieval social order declined, religion and tradition, nobility and clergy gradually lost the power and authority to exert control over these rising fields of modern social activity. (An example of this conflict was the famous Galileo Galilei trial.) In the modern era, the power relations between life worlds and the main new social subsystems—economy, justice, the state and science—are reversed (cf. Mann, 1986, 1993). These subsystems subjugate the remaining everyday life worlds of communitarian association (e.g., tribal, feudal and religious communities as well as traditional family life and gender relations) to their specific rationality and procedures. Modern life is not shaped by primordial or perennial culture, but by a reflexive culture, by discursive procedures of norm-giving and norm legitimization. Life in modern society requires a high degree of individual self-regulation and self-guidance—risky human endeavors, foreign to life conduct in traditional communities (Habermas, 1981).

The most prominent response to colonization and pluralization in life course policy is communitarianism (e.g., Walzer, 1983). In opposition to the liberalism dominant in contemporary American and European society, communitarianism seeks to renew the grounding of societies in value communities. The value community of contemporary Western society is composed of Jewish, Christian, Greek, and Roman elements, of the Renaissance and Humanism, but also of Marxist and positivist utopias of progress. Individual freedom also numbers among Western community-bound values: indeed, only societies in the value community of the West hold freedom to be the highest value. Social contract theory—the notion of contracting among free individuals—is thus predicated on a communitarian value consensus.

This response raises fundamental questions: Are political communities integrated through markets, law, and constitution or through ethical understandings? Is it sufficient to reconcile the diversity of ethical communities of citizens through shared citizenship? Is citizenship based on cultural integration? Does the separation of citizen and human being suffice to establish a truce in pluralist societies? Communitarianism accuses liberalism of revering an individualism no longer founded on a societal consensus concerning the good. Society consists ever more of persons without history, destinations, and social ties.

Society no longer provides a universal canopy of meaning for individual life. For it is not market and contractual relationships that bond human beings, but lively communities of meaning. Life course policy can serve as a substitute for the lost universal horizon of life by supplying institutional, legal and fiscal arrangements that structure and support transitions, sequences and trajectories in the conduct of individualized lives (see Leisering, *this volume*).

The Impact of Modernization on the Life Course

Centuries of modernization have shaped the modern life course in a particular way: Life-time has been individualized and a multi-tiered, loosely integrated time structure of institutional affiliations has been established; social differentiation and the mobilization of human resources have required ever more groups in the global population to manifest general and fundamental flexibility in the conduct of their lives; and traditional, basically religious life worlds have experienced pluralization and erosion, followed by the decay of a sacred canopy of a universal meaning of life.

In the majority of the classics in the social sciences (e.g., the works of Machiavelli, Hobbes, Smith, Marx, Durkheim, Simmel, Tönnies, or Weber), modernization's impact has been seen as ambivalent: as having brought progress in many fields but at the same time crisis and anomie. On the one hand, modern society has vastly improved opportunity structures by offering many new options for the conduct of life; on the other hand, modern life is characterized by a high risk of individual failure which cannot be blamed on external forces.

Before the end of the 19th century, there was scant empirical research on the interrelations among occidental modernization, institutional change and the life course—two famous exceptions being Durkheim's (1966) study of suicide and Marx/Engel's study of the British working class (Engels, 1993). The first profound longitudinal analysis of the impact of modernization on the life course based on biographical data sets was carried out by the Chicago School of Sociology in the 1920s and 1930s. One prominent study of life courses under conditions of rapid modernization was William Thomas and Florian Znaniecki's (1918–1920/1984) *The Polish Peasant in Europe and America*. In this volume, the authors analyzed letters dating from the beginning of the 20th century exchanged between young Polish emigrants to the United States and their parents who remained in Poland, in addition to autobiographical material (Weymann, 1996).

Following these individuals' emigration, new life course experiences of Chicago's rapid social, economic, and cultural progress succeeded their previous experiences of Poland's economic, social, and cultural stagnation. The immigrants had left behind dangers arising from nature and stagnation, but upon their arrival in Chicago they now had to face new risks of life in a society in permanent flux. While the dangers of nature and stagnation in an agrarian society promote passivity and a habit of fatalism as the adequate mode of life course conduct, the freedom of modern urban society demands active long term life course planning, well-informed foresight and rational decision-making in which the chances and risks of various life course alternatives are weighed.

The findings of the Polish Peasant study are well in line with Max Weber's concept of the occidental rationalization of life, and with Norbert Elias' account of the process of civilization. In *The Protestant Ethic*, Weber (1920), holds that Western rationalization of society (with an efficient economy, administration, science and educational system) is strongly associated with the necessity of rational, well-planned ("ascetic") conduct of life. And Elias (1980) argues that the expansion of ever more complex interdependencies in the process of modernization forced individuals to develop civilized habits of life in order to successfully interact within the emerging large networks ("figurations") of commerce, power, and communication.

Certainly, life in modern society is less dangerous than it was in pre-modern times, but at the same time it is an individualized life at risk. Institutions and norms change much faster than heretofore and present a large variety of alternatives. The future is no longer similar to the past and the present. This creates a high individual risk of failure, that is, of not meeting expectations and requirements. The Polish immigrants learned that modern society requires predominately individualized, competitive behavior. Whereas the life course in Poland was shaped by communitarian, homogenous norms, values and rules of solidarity, the immigrants subsequently perceived the limited support of their families, relatives, and local communities. A new economy of life emerges: time is money and human capital must be accumulated. This new economy of life time undermines the traditional norms of solidarity.

Thomas and Znaniecki analyze the impact of modernization on the life course of these immigrants. The reader encounters descriptions of individualized life times and poorly integrated spheres of social time, for example, among generations and nations. There has been a fundamental social differentiation of life from agrarian to a highly developed industrial society.

The loss of religion and of traditional norms and values impacts the meaning of life and life conduct. Thomas and Znanieki deal extensively and in detail with the disorganization of life, which entails demoralization, economic dependency, the breaking of conjugal relations, delinquency, murder, vagabondage and sexual immorality (of girls). Their analysis corroborates Durkheim's well-known argument in his study on suicide, namely "anomia" characterizes differentiated and individualized modern society—anomia meaning the loss of "nomoi", that is communal rules and norms.

Chicago School sociologists launched many empirical studies in this field, on vagabondage (Anderson, 1923), organized crime (Landesco, 1929), youth delinquency (Shaw & Moore, 1931; Thrasher, 1927); vice (Cressey, 1932), segregation and the ghetto (Wirth, 1928). These phenomena were understood as a consequence of weak social coherence and of normative disorientation in life conduct.

Chicago School studies combine the analysis of social structure, institutions and the life course to promote understanding of the impact of modernization on the life course, biographical norms and values. In the wake of this tradition of life course research emerged the pathbreaking studies of Glen Elder (1999 [1974]) on the impact of economic depression and war on generations and biographies, and of Anselm Strauss (1991) on negotiated order in institutions, nations and international relations. According to Strauss, negotiated order is achieved by discursive procedures of norm giving and taking, and results in a preliminary, risky self-regulation and self-guidance in a reflexive world. This thesis accords well with Habermas's theory of social action in modern "discourse" society above.

LIFE COURSE POLICY AS A RESPONSE OF
THE NATION-STATE

In the course of centuries of occidental modernization, Gemeinschaft (community) has been replaced with Gesellschaft (society). One of the best definitions can be found in Tönnies (1979, p. 34). "The theory of society constructs a circle of human beings who, as in a community, live and reside peacefully side by side, but instead of being fundamentally connected are fundamentally divided; whereas in a community they remain connected despite all divisions, in a society they remain divided despite all ties." Community is for Tönnies the natural way of life. In society, on the other hand, a human being enters alien terrain. Society is an artifact. There, each is in a state of tension relative to all others, whereby the respective realms of activity and power interests are clearly separated from one another. In contrast to community, in society no one will perform a service without receiving a compensation considered to be of equal value. Exchange and contract—not communitarianism—are the essential elements of society.

In modern society, the individual life course is no longer conditioned by shared everyday life and traditional value-communities, but by personal interest—that is, utilitarian principles. Since people are free and (nearly) equal in their physical and mental abilities and conceive of themselves as equals, they compete for their share of coveted scarce objects, particularly for property, power, and pleasure. The state of modern society is thus the struggle of all against all. Political thinkers such as Machiavelli, Hobbes, and Karl Marx—with Italian Renaissance states, Cromwell's Britain and 19th-century class struggles in mind, respectively—conceived of this omnipresent competition as a permanent state of civil war; while social scientists such as Adam Smith, Schumpeter, Hayek, or Coleman (1990) viewed competition in liberal society as a great source of innovation and prosperity. In societies of the Western type, high labor productivity, a high employment rate, strong inputs of capital and science and the accumulating utilization of capital produce more wealth than necessary for subsistence. Additionally, free trade in expansive markets creates opportunities for specialization in areas of comparative advantage. Despite an extremely unequal distribution of wealth, this is the only society in the history of humankind which has enduringly generated grand surpluses.

However, liberté and egalité (plus productivité) do not foster fraternité, as a revised formulation of the famous slogan of the French revolution would have it. In small communities, it is not difficult to reconcile the striving for individual gain with the need for reliable cooperation. In larger ones, on the other hand, the tendency to sacrifice fair cooperation for even minor individual gains is strong (North, 1990; Olson, 1982). Whereas communities impose life course arrangements on their members according to religious rules and cultural norms of tradition, in modern society life course policy becomes a necessary means to provide institutional support for the conduct of individualized lives. Institutional arrangements and entitlements to education, to family support, to health insurance and old age provision are key elements of life course policy in modern society—shaping, supporting or enabling transitions, sequences, and trajectories in the course of life. Life course policy lays the foundations for rational life conduct and helps stabilize expectations, transitions and trajectories—in nationally specific ways (Esping-Anderson, 1990).

The life course policy of the contemporary nation state is shaped by the market and constitutional liberalism (Vanberg, 1999, p. 234) of civil society, on the one hand, and by a country's welfare state regime, on the other.

The state is a machine of community ends which is confronted by manifold, economizing individual ends. It can deprive privately economizing individuals of the fruits of their economic performance only up to the point where they stop investing their utmost energies (Schumpeter, 1918). This rationale presupposes that modern human kind has been transformed into homines oeconomici: a type of person who privileges the pursuit of profit and remunerated labor, who creates specialized, distinct economic institutions and perpetually strives for cost minimization (Polanyi, 1995). The universal competition in modern society points to the first condition prerequisite to peaceful and prosperous exchange and coexistence: agreement on a *contrat social*. Civil and political rights constitute the primary and essential foundation of life course policy in liberal, non-communitarian society.

With the supplementary establishment of the welfare state, individuals and population groups became linked in new, far-reaching networks that are deeply rooted and enduring. Only in the context of the secure institutional framework provided by the welfare state can the majority of the population undertake long-term life planning. The status of citizenship, however, harbors a conflict between its constitutive civil (freedom and liberty), political (political participation) and social rights (entitlements to welfare and social security) (cf., Marshall, 1992a, 1992b). Social rights limit the economic freedom of actors and reduce the influence of the market and its relative prices. Furthermore, the granting of social rights to an individual or group can mean inclusion in the form of access to certain privileges for the beneficiary, but at the same time exclusion for all others. Examples are tax regimes that offer selective entitlements to economic sectors, branches, professions and regions, and welfare regulations that target carefully defined groups.

In sum, society's members are bonded together in two principal ways: as market subjects (*bourgeois*) through antagonistic cooperation within the institutional framework of the marketplace; and as citizens (*citoyens*) through contract, law and constitution, and the welfare state. Modern nation states have established a legal framework for conflict resolution and a constitution (with the exception of Britain) that grants civil and political rights. Further, they have developed a welfare regime that provides minimal or adequate benefits and entitlements. This legal, fiscal and institutional framing and support of life through life course policy profoundly enhances the rationality and reliability of individual life course choices.

Life course policy, however, was and still remains a national endeavor. Ongoing processes of globalization are challenging the life course regime of the nation-state to which we are accustomed.

GLOBALIZATION AS A CHALLENGE FOR LIFE COURSE POLICY

In "Consequences of modernity" Anthony Giddens (1990) designates modernization as a project of Western civilization, and globalization as its youngest offspring. Globalization creates new risks of unparalleled dimensions and tends to undermine trust, confidence, and expectations in the course of history and individual life. This thesis corresponds with the argumentation of Pierre Bourdieu (1993) in "La misere du monde" ("The weight of the world: social suffering in contemporary society"), a collection of life course interviews.

Life course policy provides public goods in the fields of family support, education, health care, work, social assistance, and old age provision. In an era of globalization, can these ends still be sufficiently attained by national governments following their own particular pathways—or is inter- or supranational life course policy the better solution?

Globalization and the Nation-State

The nation itself is a product of modernization, a contingent configuration whose elements are an industrial-capitalist economy, a military, a bureaucratic administration and a (democratic) state. The nation state is a response to the decay of the pre-modern, hierarchic poly-ethnic type of religious and feudal society (Smith, 1998). Will the nation-state disappear with the dawn of globalization? Will this in turn lead to the destruction of the welfare state and citizenship? Will national life course regimes of education, public health, old age provision, and social assistance vanish?

The answer depends on how we understand globalization. The most radical and most simple idea is that all (advanced) industrial countries will converge toward common methods of production and economic life as a consequence of best practice, free trade, and free capital mobility (Crouch & Streeck, 1997). More sophisticated research shows a strong persistence of national pathways. National (or regional) co-location of multinational corporations, public goods like education, infrastructure, research and development, law, constitution, and tacit knowledge of language, culture and norms are strong forces contributing to a reduction in the transaction costs of conducting international activities (Berger & Dore, 1996).

Diagnoses of the powerlessness of governments in the face of transnational capital, the obsolescence of the nation-state as an organizing principle, the collapse of the welfare state, the death of industrial policy and the end of national diversity are exaggerated. What matters is the transformative capacity of modern states, the ability to adapt to external shocks and pressures (Boyer & Drache, 1996; Hollingsworth & Boyer, 1997; Weiss, 1998).

The Multi-tiered Pattern of European Life Course Policy

Are international regimes the better solution, serving as a more effective buffer against the impact of the global economy (Krasner, 1983; Sally, 1998)? The history of life course policy in European countries may suggest a preliminary answer.

In a comparative study, Abram de Swaan (1988) has investigated the development of what he terms "state care" in the realms of health, education, and welfare over centuries of modernization in England, France, Germany, Holland (and in part the United States). Beginning with measures against vagabondage, the care of the state grew to include social assistance and welfare, education and a national curriculum, public health and health care, health and retirement insurance, old age provision and family assistance. The driving force behind this process was that individuals, peasant families, villages, local governments, religious and worldly authorities alike had been overwhelmed by the looming problems of industrialization and the free market. Increasingly, poverty, starvation, epidemics, mass migration, violence, and anomie were overburdening the coping capacity of pre-modern individual and corporate actors. Only a new collective actor, the caring state, could deal effectively with the problems of modern society. The care of the state was in the interest of the suffering population, and at the same time the birth of the nation-state became an attractive instrument for the ascendant new elite—entrepreneurs, social movements, political parties, administrators, scientists, and intellectuals.

In Europe today, step-by-step, the European Union is becoming the dominant instrument for dealing with the challenge of a global economy. The mobility of goods, services and capital was of course followed by the mobility of people, and this has created a need for European life course policy. The EU converts globalization (partly) into an internal process of supranational institution building.

In the field of social policy, Stephan Leibfried and Paul Pierson (1995) have argued that the European Union is a response to shared problems, a spillover from the common market of goods, services, and capital. Social policy, originally a nation-state domain, is affected by the EU in many fields, including health insurance, safety regulations, employment and industrial policies, maternity laws, long-term care, education and vocational training, family assistance, immigration rules, provision for disability, poverty and old age, etc. "The process of European integration has eroded both the sovereignty (by which we mean legal authority) and autonomy (by which we mean de facto capacity) of member states in the realm of social policy" (Leibfried & Pierson, 1995, p. 44). Social policy as a central means of life course policy is being shaped more and more by supra-national institutions of the EU, for example, the European Parliament, the European Commission and the European Court of Justice. Benefit access, portability, and consumption have become issues of supranational life course policy.

Another field of European life course policy is education, especially vocational training, retraining and higher education. Examinations and certificates are now mutually acknowledged across states, regulations and restrictions have been imposed on fees, tuition, scholarships, and grants, exchange programs for students and scholars have been established (Barblan, Reichert, Schotte-Kmoch, & Teichler, 2000), and comparative studies of standards and effectiveness have been launched (Goedebuure, Kaiser, Maassen, Meek, Vught, & Weert, 1994; cf., Deutsches PISA–Konsortium, 2001). Governance and regulations converge. "These common trends arise not only from the policies of the European Commission … but also … from the common structural problems which most states in the EU face …" (Green, Wolf, & Leney, 1999). The development of European policies will have an impact on the traditional national diversity of relationships between the state and education (Henkel & Little, 1999). The educational life course regime is tending toward a new model of mixed governance: supranational EU, market and local community are gaining influence at the expense of the nation-state (Braun & Merrien, 1999).

Empirical life course research has begun to observe the impact of institutions and curricula on educational and professional careers—will transitions and trajectories be homogenized across EU or OECD nations? (Breen & Jonsson, 2000; Shavit & Blossfeld, 1993;

Shavit & Müller, 1998; on the impact of science, see Schofer, Ramirez, & Meyer, 2000). "What then are the reasons for the apparent international variations in the association between educational qualifications and occupational destinations?" (Shavit & Müller, 1998, p. 2). Shavit and Müller attribute such variations primarily to differences in the degree of stratification and standardization in national systems of education. The authors hold these two variables, together with whether a "dual system" of vocational training exists and whether a "qualificational" or "organizational" employment market predominates, responsible for the observed heterogeneity of the transitions and trajectories among the 13 nations studied. National differences of this kind could well become another focus of international life course policy of the European Union.

OUTLOOK

Globalization penetrates the contemporary world via worldwide markets of capital, labor, information, and commerce, and impacts individual lives everywhere. One consequence of globalization is the destruction of the kind of rigid social control native to traditional communities, thus liberating individuals by increasing their personal autonomy in the construction of their life course. On the other hand, the destruction of life worlds can be frightening due to the loss of values and norms, tradition and rituals, local solidarity, and communitarian support. The response to this experience can be alienation, disorientation, resentment, and a new inclination toward politically active fundamentalism. Fundamentalism amalgamates the utopia of a perfect world with the re-invention of the roots of an ideal moral life, whereby the latter is contrasted with the perceived decline and weakness of the Western hegemonic model (Huntington, 1996; Eisenstadt, 2000). Fundamentalism can be based on religion, but need not be, as evidenced by Marxist fundamentalism in the 19th and 20th century. In any case, fundamentalism is a resentful response to the perceived burden of life under conditions of modernization and globalization.

Since the 19th century, the modern Western nation-state has managed to cope successfully with the challenge of modernization by establishing life course policy in many realms of life. As discussed above, the state created manifold institutions that cushion individuals' transitions, sequences and trajectories from cradle to grave, minimizing their risk of failure in conducting their lives. The question is whether national life course policy can cope equally successfully with the consequences of globalization, modernization's latest offspring. Here again, increasing prosperity and liberty in certain realms are juxtaposed with the loss of solidarity in others, and gains in individualization go hand-in-hand with losses of orientation and with anomie.

Definitely, globalization is a challenge for the individual life course as well as for the type of national life course policy upon which we are accustomed to relying since the 19th century. Can future life course policy rest on inter- and supranational regimes—such as the European Union—and structure transitions, sequences, and trajectories the way national institutions do? This will only happen if the transaction costs of leaving national pathways behind are perceived as being less than the financial, legal, human-capital, and cultural gains expected from developing inter- and supranational life course regimes.

The relevance of globalization for so many fields of the life course makes national and international life course policy a very interesting field of life course analysis and research. Such research requires an internationally comparative and longitudinal perspective and, as outlined above, interdisciplinary cooperation among researchers from Sociology, Political Science, and Economics.

REFERENCES

Anderson, N. (1923). *The hobo*. Chicago/London: University of Chicago Press (reprint 1975).

Barblan, A., Reichert, S., Schotte-Kmoch, M., & Teichler, U. (2000). *Implementing European policies in higher education institutions*. Kassel, Germany: University of Kassel Press.

Berger, S., & Dore, R. (1996). National Diversity and Global Capitalism. Ithaca, NY: Cornell University Press.

Bourdieu, P. (1993). *La misere du monde*. Paris: Edition du Seuil (English: *The weight of the world: Social suffering in contemporary society*. Oxford: Polity Press).

Boyer, R. (1996). The convergence hypothesis revisited: Globalization but still the century of nations. In R. Boyer & D. Drache. (Eds.), *States against markets. The limits of globalization* (pp. 29–59). London: Routledge.

Boyer, R., & Drache, D. (Eds.) (1996). *States against markets. The limits of globalization*. London: Routledge.

Braun, D., & Merrien, F.-X. (1999). *Towards a new model of governance for universities?* London/Philadelphia: Jessica Kingsley.

Breen, R., & Jonsson, J. O. (2000). Analysing educational careers: Multinomial transition model. *American Sociological Review, 65*, 754–772.

Castells, M. (2001). *The rise of the network society*. Oxford/Malden, MA: Blackwell.

Coleman, J. (1990). *Foundations of social theory*. Cambridge, MA/London: The Belknap Press of Harvard University Press.

Cressey, P. G. (1932). *The taxi-dance hall*. Chicago/London: Chicago University Press (reprint 1968, New York: Greenwood Press).

Crouch, C., & Streeck, W. (1997). *Political economy of modern capitalism*. London/Thousand Oaks, CA/New Delhi: Sage.

Deutsches PISA-Konsortium (2001). *PISA 2000. Basiskompetenzen von Schülerinnen und Schülern im internationalen Vergleich*. Opladen: Leske + Budrich.

Durkheim, E. (1966). *Suicide: A study in sociology*. New York: Free Press.

Eisenstadt, S. N. (2000). *Die Vielfalt der Moderne*. Weilerswist: Velbrück Wissenschaft.

Elder, G. H., Jr., (1999). *Children of the Great Depression*. Boulder, CO/Oxford: Westview Press (1st ed. 1974, Chicago: University of Chicago Press).

Elias, N. (1980). Über den Prozeß der Zivilisation (7th ed.; 2 volumes). Frankfurt: Suhrkamp. (English: (2000). *The civilizing process: Sociogenetic and psychogenetic investigations*. Oxford: Blackwell.)

Engels, F. (1993). *The condition of the working class in England*. Oxford: Oxford University Press.

Esping-Andersen, G. (1990). *Three world of welfare capitalism*. Princeton: Princeton University Press.

Giddens, A. (1990). *The Consequences of Modernity*. Oxford: Polity Press/Basil Blackwell.

Goedebuure, L., Kaiser, F., Maassen, P., Meek, L., Vught, F. van, & Weert, E. de (1994). *Higher education policy. An international comparative perspective*. Oxford/New York/Seoul/Tokyo: Pergamon Press.

Green, A., Wolf, A., & Leney, T. (1999). *Convergence and divergence in European education and training systems*. London: University of London.

Habermas, J. (1981). *Theorie des kommunikativen Handelns*. Frankfurt: Suhrkamp.

Henkel, M., & Little, B. (1999). *Changing relationships between higher education and the state*. London/Philadelphia: Jessica Kingsley.

Hollingsworth, R. J., & Boyer, R. (1997). *Contemporary capitalism. The embeddedness of institutions*. Cambridge/New York: Cambridge University Press.

Huntington, S. P. (1996). *The clash of civilizations*. New York: Simon & Schuster.

Kindleberger, C. P. (1996). *World economic primacy: 1500–1990*. New York/Oxford: Oxford University Press.

Krasner, S. D. (1983). *International regimes*. Ithaca, NY/London: Cornell University Press.

Landesco, J. (1929). *Organized crime in Chicago*. Chicago/London: University of Chicago Press (reprint 1968).

Leibfried, S., & Pierson, P. (1995). *European social policy. Between fragmentation and integration*. Washington, DC: Brookings Institute.

Mann, M. (1986; 1993): *The Sources of social power*. (2 Volumes). Cambridge: Cambridge University Press.

Marshall, Th. H. (1992a). *Bürgerrechte und soziale Klassen*. Frankfurt/New York: Campus.

Marshall, T. H. (1992b). *Citizenship and social class*. London/Concord, MA: Pluto Press.

North, D. C. (1990). *Institutions, institutional change and economic performance*. Cambridge: Cambridge University Press.

Olson, M. (1982). *The rise and decline of nations: Economic growth, stagflation and social rigidies*. New Haven/London: Yale University Press.

Parsons, T. (1971). *The system of modern societies*. Englewood Cliffs, NJ: Prentice Hall.

Polanyi, K. (1995). *The great transformation*. Frankfurt: Suhrkamp.

Rousseau, J.-J. (1963). Emile oder Über die Erziehung. Stuttgart: Reclam. (English: *Emile: Or, on education.* New York: Basic Books.)

Rostow, W. W. (1960). *The stages of economic growth.* Cambridge: Cambridge University Press.

Sally, R. (1998). *Classical liberalism and international economic order. Studies in theory and intellectual history.* London/New York: Routledge.

Schofer, E., Ramirez, F. O., & Meyer, J. W. (2000). The effects of science on national economic development, 1970 to 1990. *American Sociological Review, 65,* 688–887.

Schumpeter, J. A. (1918). Die Krise des Steuerstaates. *Zeitfragen aus dem Gebiet der Soziologie, 4,* 3–75. Graz und Leipzig: Leuschner & Lubensky.

Shaw, C. R., & Moore, M. E. (1931). *The natural history of a delinquent career.* Chicago/ London: University of Chicago Press (reprint 1968, New York: Greenwood Press).

Shavit, Y., & Blossfeld, H.-P. (1993). *Persistent inequality. Changing educational attainment in thirteen countries.* Boulder, CO/San Francisco/Oxford: Westview Press.

Shavit, Y., & Müller, W. (1998). *From school to work. A comparative study of educational qualifications and occupational destinations.* Oxford: Clarendon Press.

Smith, A. D. (1998). *Nationalism and modernism. A critical survey of recent theories of nations and nationalism.* London/New York: Routledge.

Strauss, A. (1991). *Creating sociological awareness.* New Brunswick, NJ/London: Transaction.

Swaan, A. de (1988). *In care of the state. Health care, education and welfare in Europe and the USA in the modern era.* New York: Oxford University Press.

Thomas, W. I., & Znaniecki, F. (1918–1920). *The Polish peasant in Europe and America.* Boston: Richard G. Badger/ The Gorham Press (Abridged reprint, Eli Zaretsky (Ed.). (1984). Urbana/Chicago: University of Illinois Press).

Thrasher, F. M. (1927). *The gang.* Chicago/London: University of Chicago Press (reprint 1963).

Tönnies, F. (1979). Gemeinschaft und Gesellschaft. Darmstadt: Wissenschaftliche Buchgesellschaft. (English: Harris, J. (Ed.), *Community and civil society.* Cambridge/New York: Cambridge University Press.)

Vanberg, V. V. (1999). Markets and regulations. On the contrast between free-market liberalism and constitutional liberalisms. *Constitutional Political Economy, 10,* 219–243.

Walzer, M. (1983). *Spheres of justice. A defense of pluralism and equality.* New York: Basic Books.

Weber, M. (1920; 7th ed., 1978). Die protestantische Ethik und der Geist des Kapitalismus. In M. Weber. Gesammelte Aufsätze zur Religionssoziologie (17–206). Tübingen: J. C. B. Mohr (Paul Siebeck). (English: 2001). *The Protestant ethic and the spirit of capitalism.* London/New York: Routledge.

Weiss, L. (1998). *The myth of the powerless state.* Ithaca, NY: Cornell University Press.

Weymann, A. (1996). Modernization, generational relations and the economy of life time. *International Journal of Sociology and Social Policy, 16,* 37–57.

Wirth, L. (1928). *The ghetto.* Chicago/London: University of Chicago Press.

Index